Operas in English

Stacey Robinson as Casey in the December 1990 Juilliard Opera Center production of William Schuman's *The Mighty Casey* (see p. 391). Photograph by Beth Bergman. Copyright © Beth Bergman 1998. Used by permission.

Operas in English

A DICTIONARY

Margaret Ross Griffel

Adrienne Fried Block, Advisory Editor

GREENWOOD PRESS
Westport, Connecticut • London

Library of Congress Cataloging-in-Publication Data

Griffel, Margaret Ross.
    Operas in English : a dictionary / Margaret Ross Griffel.
      p.   cm.
    Includes bibliographical references and indexes.
    ISBN 0–313–25310–2 (alk. paper)
    1. Opera—Dictionaries.   I. Title.
  ML102.O6G74   1999
  782.1′03—dc21   97–11063

British Library Cataloguing in Publication Data is available.

Library of Congress Catalog Card Number: 97–11063
ISBN: 0–313–25310–2

First published in 1999

Greenwood Press, 88 Post Road West, Westport, CT 06881
An imprint of Greenwood Publishing Group, Inc.
www.greenwood.com

Printed in the United States of America

The paper used in this book complies with the
Permanent Paper Standard issued by the National
Information Standards Organization (Z39.48–1984).

10 9 8 7 6 5 4 3 2 1

Contents

For My Mother, Anny Ross

and

My Husband, Michael

Preface

Although many opera dictionaries and encyclopedias are available, very few are devoted exclusively to operas in a single language. The present volume, a companion to my earlier *Operas in German: A Dictionary* (Greenwood, 1990), addresses itself wholly to operas written specifically to an English text, whether the text comes from a source originally in English or from an English translation. The main body of this book provides entries on the operas themselves, rather than musical terms, characters, composers, performers, and other personages; in this way each of the 3,500 entries can be given a more thorough treatment.

Almost all the composers represented in this volume were born or did the majority of their work in English-speaking countries. There are a few exceptions, however, such as Carl Maria von Weber, whose *Oberon* was composed specifically for Covent Garden and to an original *English* text by James R. Planché. Certain works by other non-English-speaking composers are also included because they were written to dual texts: an example is Hans Werner Henze's *Die englische Katze/The English Cat*. Kurt Weill, who was born in Dessau but died in New York, wrote his first operas in German but his later ones in English; the English versions of *Die Dreigroschenoper* (as *The Threepenny Opera*) and *Silbersee* (*Silverlake*) are included since they were given to new English texts. So, too, were the translation-arrangements by composers such as Henry Rowley Bishop of works by Mozart, Auber, Gounod, and others. For obvious reasons the present volume does not include works that were written by English composers but to non-English texts and were meant to be performed in another language, such as Michael Balfe's Italian works, but it does list operas such as Ethel Smyth's *Der Wald/The Forest*, performed in German (1902, Berlin) and English (1902, London), and Gian Carlo Menotti's *Amelia al Ballo/Amelia Goes to the Ball* (1937, Philadelphia, in English), which has customarily been performed in the composer's English version.

The opera titles are listed alphabetically by letter (excluding articles, which are placed at the end). Each entry includes alternative titles, if any, in parentheses; a full, descriptive title, for example, "ballad opera"; the number of acts; the composer's name; the librettist's name, the original language of the libretto, and the original source of the text, with the source title in italics; the date, place, and cast of the first performance (the date of composition is included if it occurred substantially earlier than the premiere date); similar information for the first U.S. (including colonial) and British (i.e., in England, Scotland, or Wales) performances, if applicable; a brief plot summary; the main characters (names and vocal ranges, where known); some of the especially noteworthy numbers cited by name; additional information, where appropriate, including comments on special musical problems, techniques, or other significant aspects; and other settings of the text, including non-English ones, and/or other operas involving the same story or characters (cross references are indicated by asterisks). Entries also include such information as first and critical editions of the score and libretto; a bibliography, ranging from scholarly studies to more informal journal articles and reviews; a discography; and information on video recordings.

Choosing which entries to include and which to omit proved difficult and frustrating, and some of my decisions could have gone either way (space limitations aside). Any work with the designation "opera" is listed, but the vast array of stage works that fall too far afield is not: pantomimes, incidental music, and almost all oratorios (such works are covered admirably by Roger Fiske in his *English Theatre Music of the Eighteenth Century* [1986]). Musicals and operettas, which are detailed at great length in other studies, are, with few exceptions, omitted in the present book; the major exceptions are Gilbert and Sullivan's works, which, for most laypersons and also many musical cognoscenti, are considered operas anyway (they were called comic operas by their creators). Also covered are some opera-like works of the twentieth century that bridge the popular and classical genres and have often been mounted by opera houses and performed by opera singers—the seminal *Show Boat* and *West Side Story*, and, for its obvious nod to the world of opera, *Rent*. Ultimately, I have tried to include all works for which there is any information, ranging from primary and secondary sources (including, especially, accounts in newspapers and journals), to program books for performances I have attended (including premieres or near premieres of works such as *Mourning Becomes Electra* and *Carrie Nation*). For those works that I have omitted, I apologize in advance to their creators and fans.

Following the A–Z section are four appendixes, a selective bibliography, and two indexes. The first appendix lists composers, their places and years of birth and death, and their operas included in the text as entries. The second appendix contains the names of librettists and follows a similar format. The third is an appendix of authors whose works inspired or were adapted for the librettos of the operas included in the dictionary and the sources used by the librettists. The fourth is a chronological listing of the entries in the A–Z section. It provides the date of first performance of each entry (with date of composition, if the performance came significantly later, or just the date of composition, if the work remained unperformed), the city of the premiere, the short title of the opera, and the composer.

The bibliography is intended to help the reader obtain more detailed information on the subjects touched upon in this work. Classified sections include other dictionaries and encyclopedias, performance studies, collections of plot summaries, general bibliographies on operas, sources on locales where opera premieres took place, works on the history of operas in English, and selective bibliographies on individual opera composers, librettists, producers, directors, and designers.

The first index gives the main characters listed in each opera entry; the second index includes names of singers, conductors (excluding composers conducting their own work), producers, composers (of other English settings), directors, choreographers, and arrangers. The book includes entries on operas composed or given their premieres through December 1997, with a number of updates through 1998 concerning performance information and death dates for composers, librettists, and authors listed in the appendixes. Operas receiving their premieres in 1998 are included in the chronology but not in the A–Z section or in the other appendixes.

As with my *Operas in German*, I was inspired to write such a dictionary back in the 1960s, beginning with research conducted for my Ph.D. dissertation, "'Turkish' Opera from Mozart to Cornelius" (1975, Columbia University), which included a chapter on "Turkish" opera in England, as well as my personal acquaintance with opera composers on the Columbia faculty (Douglas Moore, Otto Luening, and Jack Beeson), and on the faculty of Hunter College of the City University of New York (Louise Talma and Myron Fink).

The primary sources I examined are located in libraries in London, New York, Washington, D.C., and Cambridge, Massachusetts. My work as a cataloger for G. Schirmer and Associated Music (1978–1988) also gave me access to primary source materials, ranging from the operas of contemporary composers such as Samuel Barber, Anthony Davis, John Eaton, Gian Carlo Menotti, Charles Strouse, and Virgil Thomson, to the music of English composers represented by Faber and Faber, especially Benjamin Britten. As the music production editor at Garland Publishing (1988–1996), I worked with the facsimiles for the series *Nineteenth-Century American Musical Theater*, edited by Deane Root, and with facsimiles of English-texted works by J. C. Bach and his contemporaries for the series *The Works of J. C. Bach*, edited by Ernest Warburton.

Acknowledgments

For their suggestions and access to the various sources, I wish to thank in particular the following: in London, the staffs of the British Museum and the Royal College of Music; in New York, Jane Gottlieb, at the Lila Acheson Wallace Library, the Juilliard School; Elliott Kaback, at the Jacqueline Grennan Wexler Library, Hunter College; Natalie Sonevytsky, at the Wollman Library, Barnard College; the staff of Butler Library and Elizabeth Davis and her staff, at the Gabe M. Wiener Music & Arts Library, Columbia University; and the staff of the Library of the Performing Arts, Lincoln Center Branch of the New York Public Library; in Washington, D.C., the staff of the Library of Congress; and, in Cambridge, Massachusetts, Barbara Wolff, at the Houghton Library, Harvard University.

I would also like to thank the editors at the Greenwood Publishing Group: Adrienne Fried Block, the advisory editor; Marilyn Brownstein, for agreeing to publish this dictionary; Alicia Merritt, for seeing it through to completion; and Jason Azze and Karen D. Treat, for preparing it for publication.

My thanks go, lastly, to my family: my husband, L. Michael Griffel, Ph.D., for his unbounded patience, suggestions, editorial proofing of the manuscript, and far-ranging expertise; my son, David S. Griffel, for his help with the appendixes and indexes; my mother, Anny Ross, for her support and loving interest; my sister, Marilyn Ross Cahn, M.D., for her unflagging encouragement; and my late father, Karl F. Ross, for teaching me that no project undertaken was ever too difficult.

Abbreviations

GENERAL ABBREVIATIONS

A	alto	LCCN	Library of Congress catalog number
ABC	American Broadcasting Corporation	lyr	lyric
AMS	American Musicological Society	mezzo	mezzo-soprano
		Mlle.	Mademoiselle
arr.	arranged	Mme.	Madame
assoc.	association	ms	manuscript
B	bass	NBC	National Broadcasting Corporation
bar	baritone		
BBC	British Broadcasting Corporation	n.d.	no date
		NET	National Educational Television
ca.	circa		
CBC	Canadian Broadcasting Corporation	n.p.	no place, no publisher
		NYPL	New York Public Library
CBS	Columbia Broadcasting System	orch.	orchestrated, orchestration, orchestra
col	coloratura	orig.	original
comp.	composer, composed, compiler	perf.	performed
		pno	piano
cond.	conductor, conducted	possib.	possibly
diss.	dissertation	prob.	probably
ed.	editor, edited, edition	pseud.	pseudonym
Fr	French	repr.	reprinted, reprint
fs	full score	rev.	revised
Ger	German	RTE	Radio Telefis Eireann
hpchd	harpsichord	S, sop	soprano
I.S.A.M.	Institute for Studies in American Music	Sp	Spanish
		ss	study score
It	Italian	sym.	symphony
kbds	keyboards	T, ten	tenor
Lat	Latin	transl.	translated
LC	Library of Congress	vs	vocal score

BIBLIOGRAPHIC ABBREVIATIONS

AM — *American Music*

Biddlecombe/ *EO* — George Biddlecombe. *English Opera from 1834 to 1864 with Particular Reference to the Works of Michael Balfe*. New York and London: Garland, 1994.

Bordman/ *AMT* — Gerald Bordman. *American Musical Theatre*. 2d ed. New York: Oxford University Press, 1992.

Bordman/*AO*   Gerald Bordman. *American Operetta: From H.M.S. Pinafore to Sweeney Todd.* New York: Oxford University Press, 1981.

C/*MS*   Milton Cross and Karl Kohrs. *More Stories of the Great Operas.* Garden City, N.Y.: Doubleday, 1971.

Clarke/*HW*   F. R. C. Clarke. *Healey Willan: Life and Music.* Toronto: University of Toronto Press, 1983.

COH   *Cambridge Opera Handbooks.* Cambridge, London, and New York: Cambridge University Press.

Eaton/*OP* I   Quaintance Eaton. *Opera Production. A Handbook.* Minneapolis: University of Minnesota Press, 1961. Repr. New York: Da Capo, 1974.

Eaton/*OP* II   Quaintance Eaton. *Opera Production II. A Handbook.* Minneapolis: University of Minnesota Press, 1974.

ENO   English National Opera

ENOG   *English National Opera Guides.* Edited by Nicholas John. London: Calder; New York: Riverrun Press.

Fiske/*ETM*   Roger Fiske. *English Theatre Music in the Eighteenth Century.* Oxford: Oxford University Press, 1973. 2d ed. Oxford and New York: Oxford University Press, 1986.

Gänzl/*BBM*   Kurt Gänzl. *Gänzl's Book of the Broadway Musical.* New York: Schirmer Books, 1995.

Gordon/*MM*   Eric A. Gordon. *Mark the Music. The Life and Work of Marc Blitzstein.* New York: St. Martin's Press, 1989.

HiFi   *Hi Fidelity*

HiFi/MA   *Hi Fidelity/Musical America*

Hipsher/*AO*   Edward Ellsworth Hipsher. *American Opera and Its Composers.* Philadelphia: Theodore Presser, [1934]. Repr. ed. New York: Da Capo, 1978.

Jacobs/*AS*   Arthur Jacobs. *Arthur Sullivan. A Victorian Musician.* 2d ed. Aldershot: Scolar Press, 1992.

JAMS   *Journal of the American Musicological Society*

K/*KOB*   *The Definitive Kobbé's Opera Book.* Edited, revised, and updated by the Earl of Harewood. New York: G. P. Putnam's Sons, 1987.

K/*NKOB*   *The New Kobbé's Opera Book.* Edited by the Earl of Harewood and Antony Peattie. New York: G. P. Putnam's Sons, 1997.

Kemp/*Tippett*   Ian Kemp. *Tippett: The Composer and His Music.* London: Eulenburg, New York: Da Capo, 1984.

Kornick/*RAO*   Rebecca Hodell Kornick. *Recent American Opera: A Production Guide.* New York: Columbia University Press, 1991.

Larpent   Dougald MacMillan, comp. *Catalogue of the Larpent Plays in the Huntington Library.* San Marino, Calif., 1939.

MA   *Musical America*

ML   *Music and Letters*

MO   *Musical Opinion*

MQ   *The Musical Quarterly*

MR   *The Music Review*

MT   *The Musical Times*

NAMT   *Nineteenth-Century American Musical Theater.* Edited by Deane L. Root. 16 vols. New York: Garland, 1994.

NY   *The New Yorker*

NYT   *The New York Times*

OJ   *Opera Journal*

ON   *Opera News*

OQ   *Opera Quarterly*

Porter/*WAD*   Susan L. Porter. *With an Air Debonair. Musical Theatre in America 1785–1815.* Washington, D.C., and London: Smithsonian Institution Press, 1991.

PRMA   *Proceedings of the Royal Musical Association*

Root/*APSM*   Deane L. Root. *American Popular Stage Music, 1860–1880.* Ann Arbor, Mich.: UMI Research Press, 1989.

Rubsamen/*BO*   Walter Rubsamen, ed. *The Ballad Opera: A Collection of 171 Original Texts of Musical Plays Printed in Photo-Facsimile.* 29 vols. New York: Garland, 1974.

SIMG   *Sammelbände der Internationalen Musik-Gesellschaft*

Smith/*MCM*   Catherine Parsons Smith. *Mary Carr Moore, American Composer.* Ann Arbor: University of Michigan Press, 1987.

Sonneck/*SIMG*   O. G. Sonneck, "Early American Operas," *SIMG* VI (1904–5), 428–95.

Stedman/*GBS*   Jane W. Stedman. *Gilbert before Sullivan.* Chicago: Chicago University Press, 1967.

Stedman/*WSG*   Jane W. Stedman. *W. S. Gilbert. A Classic Victorian and His Theatre.* Oxford: Oxford University Press, 1996.

Summers/*OOA*   W. Franklin Summers. *Operas in One Act. A Production Guide.* Latham, Md. and London: Scarecrow Press, 1997.

TLS   *Times Literary Supplement* (London)

Traubner/*O*   Richard Traubner. *Operetta. A Theatrical History.* New York and Oxford: Oxford University Press, 1983.

Virga/*AO*   Patricia H. Virga. *The American Opera to 1790.* Studies in Musicology, no. 61. Ann Arbor, Mich.: UMI Research Press, 1982.

Waters/*VH*   Edward N. Waters. *Victor Herbert: A Life in Music.* New York: Macmillan, 1955.

A Brief History of English Opera

The following brief history of English opera is meant to "set the stage" for the dictionary entries that follow. This history is divided into the seven English-speaking regions covered by the dictionary: England (whose composers penned the greatest number of operas in English before the twentieth century), Scotland, Wales, Ireland, Canada, Australia, New Zealand, South Africa, and the United States. For further information, the reader is referred to the detailed historical studies listed in the Bibliography section, as well as in many of the bibliographical citations in the entries; the Chronology (Appendix 4); and the Composers (Appendix 1).

ENGLAND

The beginnings of English opera lie in the genre of the Jacobean masque, a type of operatic stage entertainment that had its origins in the French ballet de cour. The masque, which consisted of poetry, music, singing, dancing, and acting, often concerned mythological subjects and emphasized the element of spectacle, with particular attention to elaborate costumes and scenery. The playwright Ben Jonson (1572–1637) was an important force in the development of the genre, and his output included the *Masque of Blackness* (1605), *The Hue and Cry after Cupid* (1608), *The Masque of Queens* (1609), and *Lovers Made Men* (1617), the last set to music by Nicholas Lanier (1588–1666). Among the later masques were *The Triumph of Peace* (1634), with text by James Shirley (1596–1666) and music by William Lawes (d. 1645), Simon Ives (1600–1662), and Davis Mell (1604–1662); *Britannia triumphans* (1638), with words by William Davenant (1606–1668) and music by William Lawes; and *Cupid and Death* (1653), with text by Shirley and music by Matthew Locke (ca. 1621–1677) and Christopher Gibbons (1615–1676).

The first "English" opera, that is, a work composed to a libretto with an English text and in an identifiably "English" style, comes from the middle of the seventeenth century. *The Siege of Rhodes* (1656, London) by William Davenant has long been cited as the first English opera, although it was preceded by *Ariadne Deserted by Theseus and Found . . .* (libr. pub. 1654) of Richard Flecknoe (d. ca. 1676), who described the work as "a dramatick piece a[da]pted for recitative musick." Flecknoe wrote both the music and the text; he also created the masque-like *The Marriage of Oceanus and Brittania* (libr. pub. 1659), described as "an allegoricall fiction"—the music of both Flecknoe works is lost, and there is no record of any performance of either.

English opera flourished in the seventeenth century, as epitomized by *Venus and Adonis* (ca. 1683), composed by John Blow (1649–1708). Henry Purcell (1659–1695) represented the apogee of the genre, with his *Dido and Aeneas* (1689, London), but English opera lost its preeminence upon Purcell's early death and the mounting competition from Italian opera, which gained ground at the end of the century. English opera did not recover fully until the twentieth century, when its numbers and popularity rivaled those of operas in other languages.

The scheduled performance of John Eccles's *Semele* in 1707 was scrapped in favor of John Pepusch's Italianate pastiche *Thomyris* (April 12, 1707, London). Even the successful George Frideric Handel (1685–1759) enjoyed his main operatic triumphs in England with his Italian operas and then his English-texted oratorios (after stage works were banned), beginning in the 1730s. His only English stage works are the masque *Acis and Galatea* (1718, Cannons), which received its first public performance in 1731 in London; his setting of *Semele* as a masque (1744, London); the semi-opera *Alceste* (comp. 1749, not performed); and the "musical drama" *Hercules* (1745, London, concert); no Handel opera was mounted on a stage between 1754 and 1920![1] The decline in the popularity of Handel's operas has been attributed to pressures brought on by rival opera companies and the growing popularity of ballad opera.

Thomas Arne (1710–1778), along with Henry Carey (1687–1743) and John Frederick Lampe (ca. 1703–1751), created a company in 1732 to perform English operas "after the Italian manner." Their first production was Lampe's *Amelia* (1732, London), with a text by Carey, followed by their unauthorized performance of Handel's masque *Acis and Galatea* on May 28, 1732, which Handel countered with his own rival performance on June 21. Following the split of the partners, Lampe achieved success with burlesque works, especially *The Dragon of Wantley* (1737, London), which parodied Italian operas, particularly those by Handel. Arne formed his own company, which produced *Teraminta* (1732, London) by John Christopher Smith (1712–1795) and Arne's own first opera, *Rosamond* (1733, London). He also composed several masques, among them *Comus* (1738, London) and *Alfred* (1740, London), the latter of which is famous today only for its "Rule Britannia," and a number of pastiches, including the extremely successful *Love in a Village* (1762, London). *Artaxerxes* (1762, London), which used the oft-set text by Pietro Metastasio (1698–1782), represented Arne's attempt to compose English opera "after the Italian manner." His son Michael Arne (ca. 1740–1786) was most successful with the dramatic *Cymon* (1767, London), whose text was written by the actor/theater manager David Garrick (1717–1779).

In the eighteenth century the true "English" style could be found in hundreds of ballad operas, which consisted of spoken dialogue that alternated with newly texted, preexistent melodies, such as ballads, folk tunes, or pieces by contemporary composers. The genre began with the famed *Beggar's Opera* (1728, London), to a text by John Gay (1685–1732), which helped seal Handel's operatic fate. It satirized politics and the excesses of Italian opera and its performers, in particular, the Italian works of Handel. *Polly*, "an Opera, being the second part of the Beggar's Opera" (composed and printed in 1729), was not mounted until 1777, because of interference from Walpole, another of Gay's targets. Gay also wrote the text for *Achilles* (1733, London), a comic treatment of the Greek hero. *Penelope* (1728, London), with a text by Thomas Cooke (1703–1756) and John Mottley (1692–1750), made the title character into the owner of a London alehouse.

Another famous ballad opera of the time was *The Devil to Pay* (1731, London), with a text by Charles Coffey (d. 1745) and Mottley. In it, the wife of the local lord switches places with the spouse of the cobbler, and the highborn lady is subjected to the cobbler's bullying, while his real wife is treated royally by the lord. *The Poor Soldier* (1783, London), itself a revision of the earlier comic opera *The Shamrock* (1777, Dublin), was written by William Shield (1748–1829). The prolific Shield also specialized in borrowing music from famous works by his European contemporaries, a practice common in English opera beginning after 1762 and described best as a "pastiche," one in which the vocal scores listed the name of the composer or song and one that, in the case of Italian works being given at the King's Theatre, "was thought [to be] educational . . . playhouse audiences should be able to hear such music in proportions they were willing to tolerate."[2] Such works include *Richard, Coeur de Lion* (1786, London), after Grétry's work (1784, Paris), and *Nina* (1786, Paris), after Dalayrac's *Nina* (1786, Paris). Shield's contemporary Charles Dibdin (1745–1814), in addition to *The Padlock*, mentioned earlier, was the composer of the comic *Love in the City* (1767, London), which contained music by, among others, Jommelli and Pergolesi, and *Lionel and Clarissa* (1768, London), a partial pastiche.

Like their French, German, and Italian counterparts, English librettists and composers also echoed the fascination with "exotic" subjects and locales. This interest can be found as far back as the seventeenth century (spurred by the constant threat of a Turkish invasion of Europe, which ended with the failed siege of Vienna in 1683). An early example is *The Siege of Rhodes*, which concerned the emperor Soliman, who was portrayed as a magnanimous leader, much like the Sultan in Mozart's 1782 *Die Entführung aus dem Serail*. In the eighteenth century this fascination could be found in a type of opera called "Turkish opera" because of its emphasis on settings in the Ottoman Empire and the use of pseudo-Turkish music, for example, unusual harmonies, drinking songs, marches, and, especially, instruments associated with the Turks, namely, the triangle, cymbals, and timpani. One eighteenth-century librettist who was particularly attracted to this genre was Isaac Bickerstaffe (1735–1812), who provided exotic comedies for various English composers. Among his texts was *The Captive* (1769, London), with music by Dibdin and several other composers; it is similar in story to *Die Entführung*, which it predates by thirteen years. Bickerstaffe's *The Sultan* (1775, London) was also set to music by Dibdin. Another "Turkish" work by Dibdin (words and most of the music) was *The Seraglio* (1776, London), in which the ruler Abdallah shows himself to be a "generous Turk" by releasing his European captives.

This trend continues in quite spectacular fashion in *The Siege of Belgrade* (1791, London), by Stephen Storace (1762–1796); its story concerns attempts to free the European girl Katherine from Turkish captivity. The work is complete with musical exoticism in the overture, which, in fact, is partially based on Mozart's rondo *alla turca* from the Sonata in A Major, K. 331 (1778). This fascination with exotic music and locales continued in the nineteenth century, especially in two works by Henry Rowley Bishop (1786–1855), his *Haroun Alraschid* (1813, London) and *The Fall of Algiers* (1825, London). The first has as its title character the famous ruler of the *1001 Nights*, while the second offers a plot composed of elements from *Die Entführung* and Rossini's *L'Italiana in Algeri* (1813). Musical exoticism is most evident in its three finales. Storace, whose first two operas were set to Italian librettos by Lorenzo Da Ponte, also wrote the pastiche *The Haunted Tower* (1789, London), set in the time of William the Conqueror, and the partially adapted rescue opera *The Pirates* (1792, London), both with texts by James Cobb (1756–1818). The success of these operas ensured Storace's position as one of the leading theater composers of the time in England.

The creations of composers such as Bishop, the Irish-born Michael Balfe (1808-1870) and Vincent Wallace (1812–1865), and the German-born Julius Benedict (1804–1885) were quite popular. In addition to the previously-mentioned "exotic" works, Bishop was known for his many partial and complete arrangements of famous operas, including *The Libertine* (1817, London), after *Don Giovanni* (1787, Prague), and *The Barber of Seville*

(1818, London), after *Il barbiere di Siviglia* (1816, Rome). Michael Balfe, who also wrote works in Italian, achieved his greatest success with *The Bohemian Girl* (1843, London), which involved the familiar tale of a noble child kidnapped and raised by gypsies (or, elsewhere, by pirates); its most famous number is the ballad "I Dreamt That I Dwelt in Marble Halls." He also supported the project to establish an English national opera by the Pyne-Harrison Company, formed in 1856. Vincent Wallace was most successful with his *Maritana* (1845, London), about a street singer who marries a nobleman; it contains elements of French and Italian opera; and his grandiose *Lurline* (1860, London), originally planned for Paris in 1848, is recalled today for having a scene at the bottom of the Rhine, predating Richard Wagner's *Das Rheingold* (1869) by nine years. Julius Benedict is most remembered for his grand romantic opera *The Lily of Killarney* (see below); he also wrote works in the style of the ballad opera, such as *The Brides of Venice* (1844, London).

In addition to Bishop, other English composers continued to turn the English stages into microcosms of the European operatic scene, since their pastiches and translations or adaptations of successful German, French, and Italian works, as well as their translated arrangements, often appeared soon after the premieres. Works by Mozart and Rossini were popular in the early decades of the century, while Gounod, Verdi, and even Wagner were represented toward midcentury. Another treatment of successful European works was the parody. Among the favorite targets was Weber's *Der Freischütz* (1821, Berlin): an 1824 travesty was described as "a new muse-sick-all and see-nick performance from the new German uproar"; and Meyerbeer's *Robert le diable* (1831, Paris) was parodied by *Robert the Devil, or, The Nun, the Dun, and the Son of a Gun,* by "Kettenus," with a text by William S. Gilbert (1868, London). Donizetti's *L'elisir d'amore* (1832, Milan) was Gilbert's target in *Dulcamara, or, The Little Duck and the Great Quack* (1866, London).

The results of the collaboration between William S. Gilbert (1836–1911) and Arthur S. Sullivan (1842–1900) were the thirteen works that are called operettas nowadays but were described by their creators as operas (and known as the "Savoy operas" because the London Savoy Theatre was the site of their premieres). Beginning with *Thespis,* which they described as "an entirely original grotesque opera," many of these were immensely popular in the second half of the nineteenth century and have remained so to the present day. Their music and text often parodied serious opera; their targets, in addition to the music of other composers, were often unmarried ladies of a certain age, the civil service, and the nobility; and the situations portrayed were patently ridiculous, as in *The Pirates of Penzance* (1879), in which Frederick, because of his nurse's misunderstanding, has been apprenticed to a group of pirates instead of pilots. Examples of the targets of Gilbert and Sullivan also include the constraints imposed by social stratification, in *H.M.S. Pinafore* (1878); aestheticism, in *Patience* (1881); the women's rights movement, in *Princess Ida* (1884); and the British rage for exotica, in *The Mikado,* set in Japan (1885).

Gilbert and Sullivan each worked with other partners before and after their collaboration. Sullivan composed several serious operas, such as *Ivanhoe* (1891), and Gilbert wrote various other librettos, for example, *Ages Ago* (1869), to music by Frederic Clay (1838–1889). In the twentieth century the operetta was taken a step further, into the genre of musical comedy. Its most successful proponents included the prolific Lionel Monckton (1861–1924); Sidney Jones (1861–1946), whose *The Geisha* (1896, London) continued the English interest in exotica inspired by *The Mikado*; Ivan Caryll (1861–1921), who numbered among his creations adaptations of French works for performance on English stages and the light opera *The Duchess of Dantzic* (1903, London); Howard

Talbot (1865–1928), whose sizable output included *The Chinese Honeymoon* (1899, London); and the playwright, actor, and composer Noël Coward (1899–1973), among whose works was the "operette" *Bitter-Sweet* (1929, London).

The operas of composers such as Ethel Smyth (1858–1944) and Frederick Delius (1862–1934) and the early works of Gustav Holst (1874–1934) reflected Germanic, particularly Wagnerian, influence at the end of the nineteenth century and beginning of the twentieth century. Smyth's *The Forest/Der Wald* (1902) was, in fact, first given in Berlin. A new direction toward a more native English style, however, could be found in Holst's works beginning with *Sāvitri* (1908) and those of Ralph Vaughan Williams (1872–1958), with his *Hugh the Drover* (1924, London) and *Sir John in Love* (1929, London) as prime examples. Arthur Benjamin (1893–1960), born in Australia, wrote all of his operas for the English stage; among his output are *The Devil Take Her* (1931, London), *A Tale of Two Cities* (1953, BBC), a setting of Dickens, and *Tartuffe* (1964, London), after Molière.

The zenith of modern English opera can be found in the output of William Walton (1902–1983), Lennox Berkeley (1903–1989), Michael Tippett (1905–1998), and Benjamin Britten (1913–1976). One type of opera that interested Britten and was especially popular in the twentieth century was opera for, and/or featuring, children (an interest evidenced by his 1946 *Young Person's Guide to the Orchestra*); two examples by Britten are *Paul Bunyan* (1941, New York) and *Let's Make an Opera/The Little Sweep* (1949, Aldeburgh). Other composers who have written works for children include Peter Maxwell Davies (b. 1934), with *The Two Fiddlers* (1978, Kirkwall) and *Cinderella* (1980, Kirkwall); Australian-born Malcolm Williamson (b. 1931), with *The Happy Prince* (1965); Richard Rodney Bennett (b. 1936), with *All the King's Men* (1969, London); and Scottish-born Thea Musgrave (b. 1928), with *Marko the Miser* (1963, Farnham, Surrey). Scottish-born Oliver Knudsen (b. 1952) has written two operas on children's stories, his fantasy opera, with a libretto cowritten with the children's author Maurice Sendak, *Where the Wild Things Are* (1980, Brussels, incomplete; 1982, London, complete version), and, also with Sendak, *Higglety Pigglety Pop!* (1984, Glyndebourne).

Walton's most famous opera is *Troilus and Cressida* (1954), after Shakespeare's play; his *The Bear* (1964, Aldeburgh) is also set to a literary work; it is one of many operas based on the play by Anton Chekhov (see later). Michael Tippett's impressive operatic output, for which he wrote his own librettos, includes *A Midsummer Marriage* (1955, London), which deals with the trials of a couple; *King Priam* (1962, Coventry) takes its subject matter from the Trojan War; and *The Knot Garden* (1970, London) views a troubled marriage that is saved in the end. Britten's greatest fame lies with his masterful adult operas, particularly *Peter Grimes* (1945, London), his most enduring opera, which presents the problems of an individual's fighting against the prevailing society; *Billy Budd* (1951, London), with its all-male cast, which sets the Herman Melville story; and *A Midsummer Night's Dream* (1960, Aldeburgh), based on the Shakespeare play, which features a countertenor in the role of Oberon. Other Britten works inspired by literature set librettos by Myfanwy Piper (1911–1997): *The Turn of the Screw* (1954, Venice) and *Owen Wingrave* (1971, London, BBC), after stories by Henry James, and *Death in Venice* (1973, Aldeburgh), after Thomas Mann's novella; Piper also wrote the texts for three works by Alun Hoddinott (see below).

Among the next generation is Harrison Birtwistle (b. 1934), who emphasizes the extra-operatic links in his works, which include *Punch and Judy* (1968, Aldeburgh), *Gawain* (1991, London), based on a fourteenth-century legend, and *The Second Mrs.*

Kong (1994, Aldeburgh), inspired by the King Kong movies. Richard Rodney Bennett (b. 1936) made quite a sensation with *The Mines of Sulphur* (1965, London), a twelve-tone work, whose plot, set in the eighteenth century, includes a play-within-a-play. His serial writing, tinged with tonality, is continued in *A Penny for a Song* (1967, London) and *Victory* (1970, London), inspired by Joseph Conrad's novel. Several operas of the prolific Stephen Oliver (1950–1992) are based on literary works, such as *The Duchess of Malfi* (1971, Oxford) and *Timon of Athens* (1991, London).

SCOTLAND

Edinburgh has been the center of operatic activity in Scotland. The first English opera to be given there, as in other English-speaking countries, was a ballad opera, specifically, *The Gentle Shepherd* (1729) by Allan Ramsay (1686–1758). Although stage works were subsequently banned, *The Dragon of Wantley* (1737) by John Frederick Lampe (1703–1751) was able to get a hearing. Italian-born Domenico Corri (1746–1825) presented *The Wives Revenged* in 1778. Performances of German and Italian works were very popular in the nineteenth century. Some native composers were active, however, including Hamish MacCunn (1868–1916), who wrote music on Scottish subjects, as in *Jeanie Deans* (1894, Edinburgh) and *Diarmid* (1897, London).

Donald Tovey (1875–1940), known primarily for his work in musicology, chose a mythological subject for his one opera, *The Bride of Dionysus*, on which he began to work in 1907 but which received its premiere in 1929 (Edinburgh). Three major Scottish composers of the present are Iain Hamilton (b. 1922), Thea Musgrave (b. 1928), and Judith Weir (b. 1954). Hamilton has favored Greek and Roman subjects for his opera plots, as in *Agamemnon* (worked on between 1967 and 1989 but not performed), *The Royal Hunt of the Sun* (1977, London), based on a play by Peter Shaffer; *Pharsalia* (1969, London); and *The Catiline Conspiracy* (1974, Stirling). He is also inspired by nineteenth-century literature, as in *Anna Karenina* (1981, London), after Tolstoy.

Musgrave chose a Scottish locale for her first opera, *The Abbot of Drimock* (1958, London); a Scottish mining disaster for *The Decision* (1967, London), a work that uses serial techniques; and a subject from Scottish history for her grand opera *Mary, Queen of Scots* (1977, Edinburgh). Musgrave's *Harriet, the Woman Called Moses* (1985, Norfolk, Virginia) examines the life of the escaped slave Harriet Tubman, who became a staunch abolitionist and "conductor" on the Underground Railroad before the American Civil War. Operas by Weir include *A Night at the Chinese Opera* (1987, Kent), which is partially based on a Chinese tale and uses the rituals of stylized Chinese opera in its second act, and *The Vanishing Bridegroom* (1990, Cheltenham), with a libretto after three Scottish folktales. *Blond Eckbert* (1994, Santa Fe) has a libretto based on a story by Ludwig Tieck.

WALES

Opera in Wales (in Cardiff, specifically) was confined mostly to performances by visiting companies until the middle of the twentieth century. The Welsh National Opera Company failed in 1890, and the Cardiff Grand Opera Society lasted only from 1924 to 1934. The new Welsh National Opera was launched in 1946 and commissioned several Welsh composers to write operas. Among them were Arwel Hughes (1909–1988), Alun Hoddinott (b. 1929), and John Metcalf (b. 1946). Hughes's *Menna* is based on a Welsh legend (1966, Cardiff).

Hoddinott has had his works performed on Welsh and English stages; they include *The Beach of Falesá* (1974, Cardiff), after a tale by Robert Louis Stevenson, and (as in the case of Britten) three works to librettos by Myfanwy Piper (1912–1997) based on literary works: the children's opera *What the Old Man Does Is Always Right* (1977, Fishguard Festival, Wales), after Hans Christian Andersen, *The Rajah's Diamond* (1979, London), after Robert Louis Stevenson, and *The Trumpet Major* (1981, Manchester), after Thomas Hardy. Metcalf has written two works for the Cardiff Opera, *The Crossing* (1984, Cardiff) and *Tornrak* (1990, Cardiff). His other operas include *The Journey* (1980, Cheltenham) and *Kafka's Chimp* (1996, Banff, Alberta).

IRELAND

The first English opera to reach Ireland was Daniel Purcell's *The Island Princess* (1705, Dublin), followed by *The Beggar's Opera*, which was performed in 1728 in Dublin shortly after its London premiere. Ballad opera continued to be popular on Dublin stages, and Thomas Arne lived there at two different times in his life; his *Comus* (1741, London) was popular in Dublin for forty years. Satire was favored by Thomas Roseingrave (1688–1766), whose *Phaedra* was staged in Dublin (1753), and by the composer/librettist Kane O'Hara (ca. 1711–1782), with his burlesque *Midas* (1762, Dublin). The famous opera *The Duenna* by Thomas Linley Sr. (1732–1795) and Jr. (1756–1778), with a text by Richard Brinsley Sheridan (1751–1816), reached the Dublin stage in 1777.

The end of the Irish parliament, brought about by the 1800 Act of Union, resulted, among other things, in causing many Irish composers to move to London. Among them were Thomas Cooke (1782–1848), whose Dublin premieres included *The Five Lovers* (1806) and *The First Attempt* (1807); and William Rooke (1794–1847), whose most famous work, *Amilie*, was written in 1818 but first given in 1837 in London. Michael Balfe (1808–1870) enjoyed great success with *The Bohemian Girl* (1843, London), among other works, but his attempt to establish English opera at the Lyceum Theatre in London with *Keolanthe* (1841) failed. Another Irish composer who succeeded in London was Vincent Wallace (1812–1865); his *Maritana* (1845, London) and *Lurline* (1860, London) were well received. Julius Benedict chose an Irish subject for his well-known opera *The Lily of Killarney* (1862, London), making it the first opera to use Irish characters and settings. Charles Stanford (1852–1924), born in Dublin, was successful with *Shamus O'Brien* (1896, London). Another native son, Victor Herbert (1859–1924), achieved immortality in the United States with his operettas and also wrote operas.

Subsequent Irish composers chose not only Irish subjects for their operas but Gaelic texts as well. O'Brien Butler (1862–1916) set the first such work, *Muirgheís* (1903, Dublin); Robert O'Dwyer (1862–1949) composed *Eithne*, which appeared in Dublin in 1910. This trend continued with the creation of an Irish State, as evidenced by Éamonn O'Gallchobhair (1906–1978), with his *Nocturne sa Chearnóig* (1942, not perf.) and *Traghadh na Taóide* (1950, Dublin). Several successful Irish composers concentrated again on English texts; among them were Gerard Victory (1921–1995), whose output, aside from his works in Gaelic, includes *Chatterton* (1971, concert, ORTF, Paris) and *Eloise and Abelard* (1972, RTE television, Dublin), and Archibald Potter (1918–1980), with *Patrick* (1965, RTE). Gerald Barry (b. 1952) is another contemporary Irish composer who has continued this trend; his output includes *The Intelligence Park* (1990, London).

CANADA

The first English operas available to the Canadian public were ballad operas, specifically, Charles Dibdin's *The Padlock* (1786, Quebec City) and the Linleys' *The Duenna* (1790, Halifax). The first "Canadian" opera that has survived is to a French, not English, text: *Colas et Colinette* (1790, Montreal) by Louis Joseph Quesnel (1786–1849), an after-piece that followed Molière's *Le médecin malgré lui*. The diet of comic operas continued until 1830, mixed in with Italian and French works. *The Devil's Bridge* by Charles E. Horn (1786–1849) and Stephen Storace's *No Song, No Supper* reached Toronto in 1825.

Although touring companies and prominent singers brought European opera to many Canadian stages in the nineteenth century, native creations were rare. Specifically, among the English-texted works were creations by Oscar Ferdinand Telgmann (ca. 1855–1946), such as *Leo, the Royal Cadet* (1889, Kingston, Ont.). Calixa Lavalée (1842–1891), known today for having written "O Canada," the national anthem, specialized in light operas, such as *The Widow* (1882, Springfield, Mass.). *Torquil* (1900, Toronto) by Charles Harriss (1862–1929) is another English-texted work.

In the twentieth century, many more Canadian composers added to the operatic repertory, beginning in the 1940s with the works (in French) of Eugène Lapierre (1899–1970) and Healey Willan (1880–1968). Willan's output includes *The Order of Good Cheer* (1928, Quebec), as well as *Deirdre* (1946, CBC radio). This trend was continued in the 1950s by Barbara Pentland (b. 1912), with her chamber opera *The Lake* (1954, Vancouver), and John Beckwith (b. 1927), with his chamber opera *Night Blooming Cereus* (1959, CBC radio). Beckwith also composed *The Shivaree* (1982, Toronto), a chamber opera, and *Crazy to Kill* (1989, Guelph, Ont.), a "detective opera." Composers active in the 1960s and 1970s included Murray Adaskin (b. 1902), with *Grant, Warden of the Plains* (1967, Winnipeg), Harry Somers (b. 1925), with his major opera, *Louis Riel* (1967, Toronto), and the U.S.-born Kelsey Jones (b. 1922), with the chamber opera *Sam Slick* (1967, Halifax). A composer whose works have spanned several decades and genres is Charles Wilson (b. 1931); his works range from a church opera, *The Summoning of Everyman* (1973, Halifax), and the traditional three-act *Heloise and Abelard* (1973, Toronto), to the multimedia *Phrases from Orpheus* (1971, Guelph) and the children's opera *The Selfish Giant* (1973, Toronto), set to a text by Oscar Wilde. The career of R. Murray Schafer (b. 1933) has also spanned several decades and styles. His works feature elements of musical theater, especially his *Patria* cycle, begun in 1974 and projected to include twelve parts, and *Loving/Toi* (1978, Toronto), in which one character speaks English and the other French, thereby representing the two official languages of Canada.

AUSTRALIA

The earliest performances of English operas in Australia involved ballad works. William Shield's *The Poor Soldier* (1783, see earlier) appeared in Sydney in 1796, and ballad works remained popular well into the nineteenth century. As in England, adaptations of European works were well received, including Bishop's 1819 version of Mozart's *Marriage of Figaro* (1833, Sydney). This was followed by *The Currency Lass* in Sydney (1844), a musical play to a text by Irish-born Edward Geoghegan (b. ca. 1812). *Don John of Austria* by English-born Isaac Nathan (1790–1864) has the distinction of being the first opera composed and performed in full in Australia (1847, Sydney); it was preceded by Nathan's 1843 work, *Merry Freaks in Troubled Times* (which received a partial performance that year in Sydney), again using the model of English opera. Nathan's earlier works were first performed in England; they included *Sweethearts and Wives* (1823, London) and *The Alcaide* (1824, London).

A new tack was taken by George W. K. Marshall-Hall (1862–1915), under the influence of Nietzsche and Wagner, but his efforts, which included *Harold* (1888, London) and *Alcestis* (1898, Melbourne), proved unsuccessful. English-born Fritz Hart

(1874–1949) composed eighteen works in Australia, although the bulk of them remained unperformed; they include *Malvolio* (1919, Melbourne, first act), after Shakespeare's *Twelfth Night*, and *The Woman Who Laughed at Faery* (1929, Melbourne). Australian-born Alfred Hill (1870–1960) was a cofounder of the Australian Opera League and wrote several operas himself, including the comic *The Rajah of Shivapore* (1917, Sydney) and *Auster* (1922, Sydney, concert; 1933, Sydney, staged). Before and following World War II, Arthur Benjamin (1893–1960) and Malcolm Williamson (b. 1931) wrote for the London stage (see earlier). Benjamin's operatic output included *The Devil Take Her* (1931, London) and *A Tale of Two Cities* (1953, BBC; 1957, London). Williamson's output includes *Our Man in Havana* (1963, London) and *The Violins of Saint-Jacques* (1966, London), as well as several operas for children. Peggy Glanville-Hicks (1912–1990) moved to the United States, where she composed most of her operas, among them *The Transposed Heads* (1954, Louisville, Ky.), to a story by Thomas Mann, and *The Glittering Gate* (1959, New York).

Several European refugees contributed to the operatic stage, among them Felix Werder (b. Berlin, 1922), whose output includes *The Affair* (1974, Sydney), and George Dreyfus (b. Wuppertal, 1929), with *Garni Sands* (1972, Sydney) and *The Gilt-Edged Kid* (1976, Melbourne). Born in China of Russian parents, Larry Sitsky (b. Tientsin, 1934) has among his creations *The Fall of the House of Usher* (1974, Sydney) and the children's opera *Three Scenes from Aboriginal Life* (1991, Canberra). Peter Sculthorpe (b. Tasmania, 1929) has found inspiration for his works in non-European sources, including the plotless *Rites of Passage* (1974, Sydney), which draws part of its text from Australian aboriginal poems and whose performance created a short-lived sensation, and his television opera *Quiros* (1982, ABC). Richard Meale (b. Sydney, 1932) renounced modernist music in 1980 and created accessible and popular operas such as *Voss* (1986, Adelaide) and *Mer de Glace* (1991, Sydney). The younger generation includes Barry Conyngham (b. Sydney, 1944), with operas such as *Fly* (1984, Melbourne) and the puppet opera *Bennelong* (1988, Groningen, Neth.); and Anne Boyd (b. Sydney, 1946), who has focused primarily on children's operas, such as *The Little Mermaid* (1986, Sydney).

NEW ZEALAND

The first operas to be heard in New Zealand were performed in 1864 by William Lyster's company, which originated in Melbourne and featured French and Italian operas. This was followed by the Pollard Opera Company, which flourished between 1881 and 1910 and concentrated on comic works. Alfred Hill's *Tapu*, about an Australian politician who is captured by the Maori, was first given by the Pollard Company in Wellington in 1903.

The New Zealand Opera Company was started in 1954 in Wellington. Modern New Zealand-born composers and their operas include Gillian Whitehead (b. 1941), with *Tristan and Iseult* (1978, Auckland) and *Pirate Moon* (1986, Auckland), and Ross Harris (b. 1945), with *Waituhi* (1984, Christchurch), about young Maori who leave their village homes for the city.

SOUTH AFRICA

The first operas to be given in South Africa were presented in Cape Town in the early nineteenth century and included works by composers such as Dibdin and Storace. Touring companies visited throughout the century. The University of Cape Town Opera Company was formed in 1929. It was run by Scottish-born Erik Chisholm (1904–

1965) from 1951 to 1965. Among his operas receiving their premieres there were *Dark Sonnet* (1952) and *The Pardoner's Tale* (1961). Native-born John Joubert (b. Cape Town, 1927) has among his works *In the Drought* (1956, Johannesburg) and *Silas Marner* (1961, Cape Town). The political and social problems of South Africa have been echoed in works created outside the country, such as Kurt Weill's *Lost in the Stars* (1949, see below) and Priti Paintal's *Biko* (1992, Birmingham).

UNITED STATES

As in other areas controlled by Britain, the first operatic offerings that reached the stages of the American colonies were mainly ballad operas; *Flora* was performed in 1735 in Charleston and *The Beggar's Opera* in 1750 in New York. The balance of the repertory was taken up by Italian opera, which was presented by various touring companies. *The Disappointment* (1767), to a text by Andrew Barton (prob. pseud. of Thomas Forrest, 1747–1825), has the distinction of being the first native American opera, but it was not performed, and its music was lost (its score was reconstructed in 1976 by Samuel Adler). Written by English-born Benjamin Carr (1768–1831), *The Archers* (1796, New York), a treatment of the William Tell story, is the first native work whose music has survived.

One popular type of musical theater was the melodrama. Among the early examples is the *Voice of Nature* (1802, London; 1803, New York), to a text by William Dunlap (1766–1839), who translated and adapted a biblical play by L. C. Caignez. Henry Rowley Bishop's (1786–1855) *The Aethiop* (1812, London), was presented in a version by Rayner Taylor (1747–1825) in 1814 in Philadelphia, with an orchestration by John Bray (1782–1822), composer of *The Indian Princess* (1808, Philadelphia). Following the trend in England, operatic adaptations of successful European works, especially those in Italian, were extremely popular on American stages in the nineteenth century; several of them were by Charles Edward Horn, who lived in the United States from 1827 to 1849. During his stay in this country Horn arranged Mozart's *Le nozze di Figaro* as *The Marriage of Figaro* (1828, New York) and Rossini's *La cenerentola* as *Cinderella* (1832, New York). His version of *Cenerentola* followed Michael Rophino Lacy's (1795–1867) adaptation performed in New York the previous year. Two English works, Arnold's *Children in the Wood* (1793) and Kelly's *Blue Beard* (1798), were also very successful. *Children in the Wood* was first mounted in 1794 in Philadelphia, under the direction of Benjamin Carr, and *Blue Beard* received its first American performance in 1799, also in Philadelphia.

Toward midcentury the issue of slavery was addressed in plays, the most famous of them being *Uncle Tom's Cabin* of Harriet Beecher Stowe; it was set to music by George Howard (1830–1876) and first performed in Troy, New York, in 1852. After the Civil War the issue was dealt with musically in two works described as "the earliest musical plays in history to treat the theme of American slavery from the perspective of the slave himself,"[3] *Out of Bondage* (1876, Lynn, Mass.), to a text by Joseph Bradford (1843–1886); and *Peculiar Sam* (1879, Boston), to a text by Pauline Hopkins (1859–1930). Both works were modeled on the format of ballad operas and were performed by the Hyers Sisters Comic Opera Company, joined by Sam Lucas.

The Native American experience intrigued several composers in the early twentieth century. Sympathetic portrayals were offered by Charles Cadman (1881–1946) in *Shanewis* (1918, New York); Mary Moore (1873–1957) in *The Flaming Arrow* (1922, San Francisco); and William Hanson (b. 1887) in *Sun Dance* (1913 Vernal, Utah).

Attempts to develop a genuine "American" operatic style were to be found in the works of George Frederick Bristow (1825–1898) and John Knowles Paine (1839–1906).

Bristow's *Rip Van Winkle* (1855, New York) was set to a typically American tale, while Paine's *Azara* (concert, 1903, Boston) had the Crusades as its setting; Paine's incidental music for *Oedipus tyrannus* and *The Birds* (1881 and 1901, Cambridge, Mass.) proved much more successful, as an American opera was not performed at the Metropolitan Opera until 1910 (*The Pipe of Desire* of Frederick Converse [1871–1940], first given in Boston in 1906). The efforts of Silas Gamaliel Pratt (1846–1916) to drum up support for native American opera failed, as did his own work, *Zenobia* (1883, New York), set in the third century and concerning historical characters. In fact, German works were added to the mix at the end of the nineteenth century, and attempts at purely "American" works were not encouraged, with American composers going to Europe for training, a practice that continued well into the twentieth century (Fontainebleau in France, e.g., was the stopping place for such composers as Leonard Bernstein and Aaron Copland). Black Patti's Troubadours, a touring vaudeville company, featured a "musical farce/operatic kaleidoscope" that contained arias and staged opera scenes starring the classically trained Sissieretta Jones (1868–1933), called "Black Patti" after Adelina Patti. She toured with the troupe between 1896 and 1915.

A national American style was developed in the lighter vein of operetta, with the works of Dublin-born Victor Herbert (1859–1924), like *Naughty Marietta* (1910, Syracuse); Rudolf Friml (1879–1972, born in Prague), such as *Rose-Marie* (1924, New York); and Hungarian-born Sigmund Romberg (1887–1951), like *The Student Prince* (1924, New York). The operettas of Reginald De [de] Koven (1859–1920) often had English themes, for example, *Robin Hood* and *The Highwayman* (1891 and 1897, both New York).

The operetta developed into the American musical comedy (musical), as epitomized by Jerome Kern (1885–1945); his *Show Boat* (1927, New York), with a libretto by Oscar Hammerstein II (1895–1960), is considered by many to be a masterpiece. Richard Traubner called it "the greatest of all American operettas," Gerald Bordman described it as "one of the masterpieces of our lyric stage,"[4] and it has been given on many operatic stages. It was the first major musical work to treat black-white relations and predated George Gershwin's (1898–1937) *Porgy and Bess* by eight years; *Show Boat* was also the first musical incorporated into the repertory of a major opera company (1954, New York City Opera).

The musical thrived with composer-librettist Cole Porter (1881–1964), whose output included *Kiss Me, Kate* (1948, New York), built on Shakespeare's *The Taming of the Shrew*. The genre flourished under, among others, Richard Rodgers (1902–1979), who first teamed up with Lorenz Hart (1895–1943) and then with Oscar Hammerstein II; and Frederick Loewe (1901–1988), working with Alan Jay Lerner (1918–1986). Opera companies have added some of their works to their repertories, especially the Rodgers-Hammerstein *Oklahoma* and *Carousel* (1943 and 1945; both New York); and the Lerner-Loewe *Brigadoon*, *My Fair Lady*, and *Camelot* (1947, 1956, 1960, all New York).

Gershwin's seminal American opera, *Porgy and Bess* (1935, Boston), was first presented as a musical because its subject matter and black cast were not deemed appropriate for the operatic stage. The earlier *Abyssinia* (1906, New York), a musical by Will Marion Cook (1869–1944), with African-American characters, failed to draw the hoped-for white audiences and closed after a handful of performances. A similar fate had befallen Cook's *In Dahomey* (1903, New York), which fared better in its British run. The later *Cabin in the Sky* (1940, New York) by Russian-born Vernon Duke (1903–1969) did much better and ran for twenty weeks. Scott Joplin (1868–1917), the master of ragtime, wrote two operas that went largely unnoticed by white audiences. His ragtime opera *A Guest of Honor* (1903, St. Louis) was performed sporadically (the music is lost), and *Treemonisha*, whose piano score Joplin had published at his own expense, received only a concert performance in 1915 (New York; it was not revived again until 1972, in Atlanta).

The genre of the musical was continued with great success by Leonard Bernstein (1918–1990). He gained fame with such operas as *Trouble in Tahiti* (1952, Waltham, Mass.) and *Candide* (1956, 1982; see below) and notoriety with his theater piece *Mass* (1971, Washington, D.C.), but his greatest triumphs came with the musicals *Wonderful Town* (1953, New York) and *West Side Story* (1957, Washington, D.C.), which, as with many other musicals of midcentury, chose American locations for their story lines.

Among the group of European-born composers seeking refuge in the United States with the ascent of the Nazis were several who became known for their stage works. Russian-born Louis Gruenberg (1884–1964) made a deep impression with *The Emperor Jones* (1933, New York); his subject matter has its parallels in native-born William Grant Still's *Troubled Island* (comp. 1941; perf. 1949, New York), which has as its main character the Haitian dictator Dessalines. Dessalines's predecessor, Toussaint L'Ouverture, is the subject of *Toussaint* (1977, London) by British-born David Blake (b. 1936). Still (1895–1978) also composed *A Bayou Legend* (comp. 1940; perf. 1981, PBS).

Other émigré composers of the same period included Kurt Weill (1900–1950), whose famed *Dreigroschenoper* hit its stride in English as *The Threepenny Opera* only in Marc Blitzstein's 1954 version (New York); the English version of *Silbersee* (1933), produced as *Silverlake* (1980, New York), was less successful. Works that Weill created originally for the American stage include his musical play *Lady in the Dark* (1940, New York) and the vaudeville *Love Life* (1948, New York) and the operas *Street Scene* (1947, New York), *Down in the Valley* (1948, Bloomington, Ind.), and *Lost in the Stars* (1949, New York), set to Alan Paton's searing novel *Cry the Beloved Country*, a tale of blacks and whites caught in a tragedy brought on by the apartheid in South Africa. The one full-length opera of Igor Stravinsky (1882–1971), his neoclassical *The Rake's Progress* (1951, Venice), was inspired by an eighteenth-century print by Hogarth at the Chicago Institute; its libretto was by W. H. Auden (1907–1973) and Chester Kallman (1921–1975). They also wrote the librettos for Britten's *Paul Bunyan* and two English-texted operas by Hans Werner Henze (b. 1926), *Elegy for Young Lovers* (Schwetzingen, 1961) and *The Bassarids* (1966, Salzburg), after *The Bacchae* of Euripides. *The Alcestiad* (1962, Frankfurt) of Louise Talma (1906–1996) is another setting of a Euripides play.

European-trained American composers who made notable contributions to opera beginning in the 1930s included Douglas Moore (1893–1969), Virgil Thomson (1896–1989), Aaron Copland (1900–1990), and Marc Blitzstein (1905–1964). Moore's fame rests on his works on American subjects, such as *The Devil and Daniel Webster* (1939, New York) and *The Ballad of Baby Doe* (1956, Central City, Colo.). Virgil Thomson's output includes *Four Saints in Three Acts* (1934, Hartford), with a libretto by Gertrude Stein (1874–1946), and *Lord Byron* (1972, New York), based on episodes from the famed poet's life. Marc Blitzstein gained attention with *The Cradle Will Rock*, considered controversial because of its pro-union stance (1937, New York), and his highly successful *Regina* (1949, New York), based on the play by Lillian Hellman and still performed occasionally. His unfinished *Idiots First*, after Bernard Malamud, was completed in 1973 by Leonard Lehrman (b. 1949) and paired with the latter's *Karla* as *Tales of Malamud* (1976, Bloomington, Ind.). George Antheil (1900–1959) employed jazz in his satirical opera *Transatlantic*, given first in German (1930, Frankfurt). Elie Siegmeister (1909–1991) used elements of jazz in *Angel Levine* (1985, New York), based on another tale by Malamud, about a poor Jewish tailor and a black Jewish angel.

Other contemporaries included Samuel Barber (1910–1981), Italian-born Gian Carlo Menotti (b. 1911), and Bernstein. Barber's most successful work was *Vanessa* (to a text by Menotti; 1958, New York); his *Antony and Cleopatra*, which opened the new Metropolitan Opera House in New York in 1966 with a star-studded cast, failed to stay in the repertory, even in its revised version (1975, New York).

Menotti, whose works have often been undervalued by critics, achieved considerable success with his earlier opera scores, especially with the powerful and moving *The Consul* (1950, Philadelphia), which depicted the callousness of bureaucrats and the despair of the victims of political oppression, and with the verismo-style *The Saint of Bleecker Street* (New York, 1954), which presented a slice of life in New York's Little Italy. The tragic *The Medium* (1946, New York) and the children's opera *Amahl and the Night Visitors* (see below) continue to be popular and are revived on a regular basis. Leonard Bernstein, whose main theatrical fame rests on *West Side Story*, has among his "real" operas *Trouble in Tahiti* (see above) and the occasionally revived *Candide* (1982, New York; a revision of the operetta version, 1956, New York). *A Quiet Place* (1983, Houston), a sequel to *Trouble in Tahiti*, is rarely revived.

Many U.S. operas of the last several decades have librettos inspired by or based on literary or religious works and, occasionally, on historical events or characters. The two operas of Roger Sessions (1896–1985) are *The Trial of Lucullus* (1947, Berkeley), after Bertolt Brecht, and the historically inspired *Montezuma* (1963, Berlin). Among the works of Ezra Laderman (b. 1924) are the biblical *Sarah* (1959, CBS television) and *And David Wept* (1971, CBS television) and *Shadows among Us* (1979, Philadelphia), about survivors of World War II at a refugee camp. *The Final Ingredient* (1965, ABC television) by David Amram (b. 1930) tells the fact-inspired tale of concentration camp inmates willing to risk all to find the necessary ingredients to celebrate the Jewish Passover. Norman Dello Joio (1913–1996) focused on Joan of Arc in *The Triumph of Joan* (1950, Bronxville, N.Y.), revised as *The Trial at Rouen* (1956, NBC television), and further as *The Triumph of St. Joan* (1959, New York).

The operas of Ned Rorem (b. 1923) are composed mostly to preexistent texts; they include *A Childhood Miracle* (1955, New York), after Nathaniel Hawthorne; *Miss Julie* (1965, New York), after August Strindberg; and *Fables* (1971, New York), after Jean de La Fontaine. The output of Hugo Weisgall (1912–1997) includes *The Tenor* (1952, Baltimore), after Frank Wedekind's *Der Kammersänger*; *The Stronger* (1952, Lutherville, Md./Westport, Conn.), after Strindberg's play; and *Six Characters in Search of an Author* (1959, New York), after Luigi Pirandello's play.

Robert Ward (b. 1917) has also looked to literary sources for his texts; *The Crucible* (1961, New York) is based on Arthur Miller's barely disguised protest against the hysteria of McCarthyism, and *Abelard and Eloise* (1982, Charlotte, N.C.) is inspired by the medieval lovers. The operas of Meyer Kupferman (b. 1926) includes several that use classical texts, among them his opera-monodrama *Antigonae* (1973, Lenox, Mass.) and *Prometheus* (1978, New York), to a German-English libretto using texts from Goethe.

Jack Beeson (b. 1921) employs American subjects for many of his operas; his most famous works are *Lizzie Borden* (1965, New York), based on the notorious murder trial of the title character in Fall River, Massachusetts, in 1892, and *My Heart's in the High-*

lands (1970, NET television), on a play by William Saroyan. *Dr. Heidegger's Fountain of Youth* (1978, New York) is based on a story by Hawthorne. The output of Lukas Foss (b. 1922) includes *The Jumping Frog of Calaveras County* (1950, Bloomington, Ind.), based on a tale by Mark Twain. Carlisle Floyd (b. 1926) has set a number of works to literary sources. His *Wuthering Heights* (1958, Santa Fe) has a text inspired by the novel of Emily Brontë, while *Of Mice and Men* (1970, Seattle) stems from the novel by John Steinbeck; his most enduring work, *Susannah* (1955, Tallahassee, Fla.), transfers a story from the Apocrypha to a town in the Tennessee mountains. Lee Hoiby's (b. 1926) *The Scarf* (1958, Spoleto, Italy) is after Anton Chekhov; *Natalia Petrovna* (1964, New York), after Turgenev; and *The Tempest* (1986, Indianola, Iowa), after Shakespeare's play.

Dominick Argento's (b. 1927) *The Boor* (1957, Rochester) bases its libretto on the Chekhov comedy; other settings of the same play include those by Mark Bucci (1949, New York); Myron Fink (1955, St. Louis); Lawrence Moss (b. 1927), as *The Brute* (1961); and Ulysses Kay (1968, Lexington, Ky.). Argento's later output includes *Christopher Sly* (1963, Minneapolis), after a scene in Shakespeare's *The Taming of the Shrew*, *Miss Havisham's Fire* (1979, New York), after Dickens's *Great Expectations*, and *The Aspern Papers* (1988, Dallas), after Henry James. Ulysses Kay (1917–1995) has also penned *The Capitoline Venus* (1971, Urbana, Ill.), after Mark Twain, and *Frederick Douglass* (1991, Newark, N.J.), a treatment of the great nineteenth-century African-American orator. Myron Fink (b. 1928) has also composed *Jeremiah* (1962, Binghamton, N.Y.) and the biblically inspired *Judith and Holofernes* (1978, Purchase, N.Y.). Among the works of Mark Bucci (b. 1924) are *Tale for a Deaf Ear* (1957, Lenox, Mass.), after Elizabeth Enright, and *The Hero* (1965, New York television), after Frank Gilroy's *Far Rockaway*.

As in England and elsewhere, the realm of children's opera has had its adherents among U.S.-based composers. Among Menotti's considerable output are several works written expressly for children, including his most famous, *Amahl and the Night Visitors*, which first appeared on television (1951, NBC); *Help, Help, the Globolinks!* (1968, Hamburg), which includes some electronically generated music; and *The Boy Who Grew Too Fast* (1982, Wilmington, Del.). Aaron Copland's first opera was *The Second Hurricane* (1937, New York), composed for performance by high school students. Of the six operas by Julia Smith (1911–1989), four are for children; they include *Cockcrow* (1954, Austin), which uses Anglo-American folk music, and *Daisy* (1973, Miami), which concerns the founder of the Girl Scouts of America. The operas of Martin Kalmanoff (b. 1920) include several about famous people, for example, *Young Thomas Edison* (1963, New York), *Christopher Columbus* (1976, New York), and *Alexander Graham Bell* (1977, New York). The extensive output of Seymour Barab (b. 1921) includes several works for children, among them *Little Red Riding Hood* (1962, New York) and *The Toy Shop* (1978, New York). Among Gunther Schuller's (b. 1925) three operas is the children's opera *The Fisherman and His Wife* (1970, Boston), after a Grimm fairy tale.

Other contemporary composers have continued the practice of writing operas to librettos based on literary works. The grand opera *Heracles* (1972, Bloomington, Ind.) by John Eaton (b. 1935) is based on works by Sophocles and Seneca; *Myshkin* (1973, PBS television), on Dostoyevsky; *The Cry of Clytaemnestra* (1980, Bloomington, Ind.), on Aeschylus; and *The Tempest* (1985, Santa Fe), on Shakespeare. The output of Conrad Susa (b. 1935) includes *The Love of Don Perlimplin* (1984, Purchase, N.Y.), after Federico García Lorca; and *Dangerous Liaisons* (1994, San Francisco), after Pierre Choderlos de Laclos. The interest in setting operas to classical works of literature is also seen in the output of Thomas Pasatieri (b. 1945). Among his many settings are *The Seagull* (1974, Houston), after Chekhov; *Washington Square* (1976, Detroit), after Henry James; and *Three Sisters* (comp. 1979; perf. 1986, Columbus, Ohio), again after Chekhov. The most famous work of Stephen Paulus (b. 1949) is *The Postman Always Rings Twice* (1982, St. Louis), with a libretto after the James M. Cain novel about a conniving pair of lovers.

The one opera of John Corigliano (b. 1938), *The Ghosts of Versailles* (1991, New York), is inspired by Beaumarchais's *La mère coupable*; it is constructed on a grand scale; its characters include not only Figaro, Count Almaviva, Susanna, and Cherubino (who are shown twenty years after the action in *Il barbiere di Siviglia*) but also the exotic Egyptian singer Samira, whose role is perhaps a nod to Baba the Turk in Igor Stravinsky's *The Rake's Progress*. The two major operas of John Harbison (b. 1938) use librettos based on literary works: *A Winter's Tale* (1979, San Francisco), on the Shakespeare play, and *A Full Moon in March* (1979, Cambridge, Mass.), after William Butler Yeats.

Mixed-media and music-theater pieces have a number of contemporary adherents. Michael Sahl (b. 1934) and Eric Salzman (b. 1933) have combined to write the music and text for a number of such works; they include *Stauf,* "an American Faust" ("Faust" spelled virtually backwards; 1976, New York), in which the title character is a nuclear physicist, and the buffa-like *Civilization & Its Discontents* (1977, New York), a "bedroom opera" that focuses on characters who frequent the singles bar scene; it features set pieces. Their *The Conjuror* (1975, New York) is labeled a "pop opera." Gunther Schuller describes his first opera, *The Visitation* (1966, Hamburg), as "third stream"; with a text inspired by Kafka, it mixes elements of classical opera and jazz. The later operas of Robert Ashley (b. 1930) have been composed for performance on the stage or on television; they include *Music with Roots in the Aether* (1976, Paris), *The Lessons* (1981, New York), and *Atalanta Strategy* (1985, Montreal).

The more famous works of Philip Glass (b. 1937) are written in a minimalist style, and he often favors multimedia pieces; his *Einstein on the Beach* (1976, Avignon) and *the CIVIL warS, Act V: The Rome Section* (1984, Rome) were written in collaboration with the designer/playwright/director Robert Wilson (b. 1941). Glass has continued to focus on important historical figures. His "portrait trilogy" includes *Satyagraha* (1980, Amsterdam), which concerns the life of Gandhi; *Akhnaten* (1983, Stuttgart), which looks at the ancient Egyptian king; and *The Voyage* (1992, New York), with Christopher Columbus and exploration as its themes. The works of William Bolcom (b. 1938) meld popular, jazz, classical, and Americana elements; they include the cabaret-style *Dynamite Tonite* (1963, New York), *Casino Paradise* (1990, Philadelphia), for singing actors, and the more traditional *McTeague* (1992, Chicago), whose title character is sung by a heldentenor. The works of Stanley Silverman (b. 1938) include music theater, for example, his *Columbine String Quartet Tonight!* (1981, Lenox, Mass.), and the opera *Madame Adare* (1980, New York). Laurie Anderson (b. 1947) has added to the body of multimedia works with her *United States: Parts I–IV* (1992, Brooklyn, N.Y.), which covers such themes as love and politics.

Operas about historical events and figures are also significant in the output of other U.S. composers. John Adams's (b. 1947) minimalist *Nixon in China* (1987, Houston) focuses on the president's visit there in 1972 and his meeting with Mao. The life and death of Malcolm X are treated in *X* (1986, Philadelphia), the first opera of Anthony Davis (b. 1951); Davis has continued his interest in the African-American experience with *Amistad* (1997, Chicago), about the slave ship of the same name that was the site in 1839 of a revolt of African slaves, bound for the United States, against the Spanish crew. The incestuous tale of *Emmeline* (1996, Santa Fe) by Tobias Picker (b. 1954), set in a Massachusetts mill town in 1841, is also based on a true story.

The gay presence in the United States is echoed in the musically eclectic opera *Harvey Milk* (1995, New York) by Stewart Wallace. It concerns the life and death of Milk, a gay city supervisor in San Francisco, who was murdered in 1978, along with the mayor, because of his sexual orientation and lifestyle.

Satire is another avenue traveled by current U.S. composers, the most "notorious" being "P. D. Q. Bach" (Peter Schickele, b. 1935). Bach-Schickele has gained much fame with his good-natured comedic parodies, often filled with topical humor, which include his takeoffs on Mozart, *The Stoned Guest* (1967, New York) and *The Abduction of Figaro* (1984, Minneapolis), and on Philip Glass, *Prelude to Einstein on the Fritz* (1989, New York).

The lines between the popular and classical genres, evident in works such as *Show Boat* and *West Side Story*, continue to be obscured. More recent examples include the "musical thriller" *Sweeney Todd* (1979, New York) by Stephen Sondheim (b. 1930). Another freshly minted "Broadway" work (its run began in Greenwich Village) uses a story taken directly from opera, namely, Jonathan Larson's (1961–1996) highly successful *Rent* (1996, New York). Its plot (the pathos of which increased when Larson died just before its opening) is an updating of *La bohème*, and the work was described by Clive Barnes as "Puccini meets the E.[ast] Village."[5]

Where operas in English will go from here is anybody's guess. The lines of demarcation between opera, theater, and multimedia are becoming increasingly blurred in all of opera, as composers seek to widen their audiences. This phenomenon is not new, however; in fact, it is as old as English opera itself, bringing the genre full circle. After all, the masque of the seventeenth century, which was also a combination of various elements, very few of them really operatic, evolved into English opera. In the 1720s, the ballad opera, a genre more akin to today's musicals, arose in opposition to the "foreign" and "elevated" Italian opera, which had virtually owned the operatic stage in England until that time. Today's composers, in addition to using texts based on traditional literature and drama, continue to express their concerns over social, political, and lifestyle issues, reflecting thereby the diverse, multicultural society of the United States and other English-speaking countries at the end of the twentieth century.

NOTES

1. Roger Fiske, *English Theatre Music in the Eighteenth Century*, 2d ed. (New York and Oxford: Oxford University Press, 1986), 275.

2. Ibid., 274–75. Fiske makes a careful distinction between ballad operas per se and the frequent practice, after 1762, of composers' borrowing music for their works; the resultant works have sometimes been described, incorrectly, as ballad operas.

3. Eileen Southern, *African American Theater*, NAMT, vol. 9 (New York: Garland, 1994), xiii.

4. Richard Traubner, *Operetta, A Theatrical History* (New York and Oxford: Oxford University Press, 1983), 393; Gerald Bordman, *American Musical Theatre. A Chronicle*, 2d ed. (New York and Oxford: Oxford University Press, 1992), 434.

5. *New York Post* (Feb. 14, 1996), 40.

Operas in English,
A–Z

A

Abbot of Drimock, The, comic chamber opera in one act by Thea Musgrave; libretto (Eng) by Maurice Lindsay, after John Mackay Wilson's *Tales of the Borders*. First performance (concert) June 22, 1958, London, Park Lane Opera Group, with Jill Nott-Bower, Constance Mullay, Margaret Fraser, David Hartley, Duncan Robertson, Donald Francke, and John Davies; conducted by Myer Fredman. First stage performance December 19, 1962, London, Morley College, National School of Opera, with David Palmer (the Abbot), Ann Dowdall, Johanna Peters, and Benjamin Luxon; conducted by Lawrence Leonard.

The Abbot of Drimock, helped by a witch, Geills, persuades the rich residents of the neighborhood who are near death to include him in their wills. The deceased local laird Sir William, whose wife, Bess, has secretly borne Maggie, fathered by the Abbot, has left his fortune to Maggie (whose mother does not approve of her marriage plans) and to the lepers of Edinburgh. Bess and the Abbot cover up Sir William's death and devise a plan to prevent Maggie's marriage and get the inheritance. They are thwarted when Geills, angered by the Abbot's subterfuge, helps Maggie.

Although the work is set in Scotland, the *Musical Opinion* reviewer of the 1958 performance detected the obviously strong resemblance to the plot of Puccini's *Gianni Schicchi* (1918, New York).

BIBLIOGRAPHY: H. S. R., "The Abbot of Drimock," *MO* LXXXI (Aug. 1958), 697 [on 1958 premiere]; Edmund Tracy, "London Diary," *MT* CIV (Feb. 1963), 118 [on stage premiere].

Abduction of Figaro, The, "opera" in three acts by "P. D. Q. Bach" (Peter Schickele); libretto (Eng) by the composer. First performance April 24, 1984, Minneapolis, Orpheum Theatre, with Marilyn Brustadt, Lisbeth Lloyd, Dana Krueger, Michael Burt, LeRoy Lehr, Bruce Edwin Ford, Jack Walsh, Will Roy, and John Ferrante; conducted by the composer.

The plot of this satire is a mishmash of several Mozart operatic stories (*Don Giovanni, Die Entführung aus dem Serail, Così fan tutte, Le nozze di Figaro, Die Zauberflöte*) and topical references (including those to Roseanne Rosannadanna, a character created by comedienne Gilda Radner on the television show *Saturday Night Live* in the 1970s, and the Organization of Petroleum Exporting Countries [OPEC, the oil cartel]). Set in the palace of Count Alma Mater, it opens with Figaro lying on his deathbed, with his wife, Susanna Susannadanna, caring for him. Other characters include Susanna's servant Peccadillo, who falls in love with Blondie; Al Donfonso, an old philosopher; Donald "Don" Giovanni, a wandering nobleman; Schlepporello, his servant; and Donna Donna, his jilted girlfriend. Enter the pirate Captain Kadd, who kidnaps Figaro, along with his bed. As Figaro's friends try to rescue him, they land at the palace of Pasha Shaboom and his servant Opec. Everything is resolved with the help of Papa and Mama Geno. Kadd finds his lost treasure, which turns out to be the Maltese Falcon, no doubt a nod to the famed 1941 movie.

Major roles: Blondie (sop), Donna Donna (sop), Pecadillo (ten); Donald Giovanni (bar), Captain Kadd (bass-bar), Schlepporello (bar), Al Donfonso (bar), Susanna Susannadanna (mezzo), and Figaro (speaking).

BIBLIOGRAPHY: Gary D. Lipton, "Prince of Pandemonium," *ON* XLVIII (Apr. 14, 1984), 35–36 [on premiere]; John Rockwell, "Opera: Peter Schickele's 'Abduction of Figaro,'" *NYT* (Apr. 30, 1984), C, 13.

VIDEO: L. Lehr, D. Krueger, B. Ford, M. Brustadt, L. Lloyd, M. Burt, J. Walsh, W. Roy, J. Ferrante, M. Montel, L. Hayden, J. Beatty, R. Roberts, K. Lavine, S. Schmidt; cond. P. Schickele, Minnesota Opera, Chorus, and "Corpse" de Ballet, live performance, Orpheum Theater, Minneapolis (1984), Video Arts International 69027.

Abelard and Heloise, music drama in three acts by Robert Ward; libretto (Eng) by Jan Hartman. First performance February 19, 1982, Charlotte, North Carolina, Owens Auditorium, with Nancy Shade (Heloise), Jerold Norman (Abelard), and Vern Sutton (Fulbert); conducted by Richard Marshall; directed by Rhoda Levine.

The story is told in flashbacks, with Peter the Venerable and Thibault bringing Abelard's body back to Paraclete for burial. Abelard is a popular and handsome teacher in Paris. He comes into conflict with Bernard, who warns him that his teaching borders on heresy. Heloise, the brilliant young niece of Fulbert, becomes Abelard's pupil and then his lover. When she becomes pregnant, she goes off to Brittany to have the child and then becomes a nun. Her uncle vows revenge on Abelard and hires two thugs, who attack and castrate him.

The former lovers meet again years later, and although Heloise still yearns for Abelard, he reminds her of her sacred vows. When Bernard manipulates a court to convict Abelard of heresy, Abelard refuses to accept the verdict and vows to take his case to the Pope.

In the opera's final scene Heloise appears for Abelard's burial. As she recalls their relationship, she sees him in a vision. The opera ends with the requiem service about to start.

Major roles: Peter the Venerable (bass); Thibault, protégé of Abelard (bass-bar); Heloise, niece of Fulbert, pupil of Abelard (sop); Abelard, cleric, scholar, and poet/philosopher (ten); Fulbert, a canon of Notre Dame, Heloise's uncle (ten); and Bernard, Abbot of Clairvaux (ten).

Among the settings of the story are E. Maconchy's dramatic cantata *Heloise and Abelard* (comp. 1978) and G. Victory's *Eloise and Abelard** (1973, Dublin).

SCORE: vs (New York: Highgate Press, Galaxy Music Corp., 1988).

BIBLIOGRAPHY: Harold F. Farwell, "Charlotte," *ON* XLVII (Sept. 1982), 46 [on premiere]; J. M. Shertzer, "Charlotte," *HiFi/MA* XXXII (June 1982), 20–21 [on premiere].

Abigail Adams, opera in two acts and an epilogue by Richard Owen; libretto (Eng) by the composer, after letters of Abigail, John, and John Quincy Adams. First performance January 14, 1987 (concert), New York, Lyric Opera, Lincoln Center, Bruno Walter Auditorium, with Lynn Owen (Abigail) and Rickey Owen (Johnny). First stage performance March 1987, New York, Harkness Center, New York Lyric Opera Company.

The action, based on various letters, centers on Abigail Adams. It covers events in the lives of the Adams family from 1762, includes the courtship of John Adams and Abigail, and finishes in 1845, when John Quincy Adams is nearing the end of his life.

Major roles: Abigail Adams (sop), John Adams (ten), John Quincy Adams (bar), and Johnny (boy sop).

For a detailed description, see Kornick/*RAO*, 216–18.

SCORE: vs, holograph (Mar. 1987, NYPL, signed photocopy).

Abou Hassan, opera by Thomas S. Cooke, an adaptation of Weber's *Abu Hassan* (1811, Munich; libretto (Eng) by William Dimond, after F. K. Hiemer's text. First performance April 4, 1825, London, Drury Lane Theatre.

The story is set in Baghdad and concerns the poor Abou Hassan and his wife, Fatime, who are trying to fend off their many creditors, especially the lecherous Omar, who is also after Fatime. The pair devise a scheme to collect money by going separately to the Caliph and his consort and telling them that Hassan and Fatime have died, thereby making the rulers give the "widower" and "widow" funeral presents. The deception is, of course, uncovered, but the generous Caliph forgives the indigent pair for their subterfuge.

SCORE: extracts (London, ca. 1825).

Abroad and at Home, comic opera in three acts by William Shield; libretto (Eng) by Joseph George Holman. First performance November 19, 1796, London, Covent Garden. First U.S. performance November 10, 1797, New York, John Street Theatre.

The plot concerns two old men, guardians of the young Miss Hartley. Each has a son and schemes to get the young woman to marry his offspring.

The work includes "Ah Divinité," from Gluck's *Alceste* (1767), which had been sung at the King's Theatre on April 30, 1795, by Brigitta Banti. Shield's opera was first called *The King's Bench, or, Abroad or at Home*, but the title was changed when the lord chamberlain objected.

For a more detailed description of the music, see Fiske/*ETM,* 556–57.

SCORE: vs (London: Longman and Broderip, n.d.).

LIBRETTO: English (London: J. G. Holman, 1796).

Abyssinia, musical comedy in three acts by Will Marion Cook and Bert Williams; libretto (Eng) by J. A. Shipp; lyrics by Alex Rogers. First performance February 20, 1906, New York, Majestic Theatre, with George Walker (Rastus Johnson) and Bert Williams (Jasmine Jenkins).

Rastus Johnson wins $15,000 in a lottery and uses the money to visit the home of his ancestors, Abyssinia, accompanied by his friend Jasmine Jenkins. The pair invariably run into trouble through their ignorance of native customs.

Despite the hopes of its producers, the work failed to draw white audiences, and it closed after thirty-one performances.

Achilles, ballad opera in three acts; libretto (Eng) by John Gay. First performance February 10, 1733, London, Theatre Royal, Covent Garden, with James Quin (Lycomedes), Thomas Salway (Achilles), Mr. Chapman (Ulysses), and Miss Narsa (Deidamia).

The plot centers on Achilles, who has been left on Scyros disguised as a girl, "Pyrrha," in order to escape fighting in the Trojan War. The King tries to seduce "Pyrrha," who in turn seduces the King's daughter, Deidamia. "Pyrrha" is unmasked by Ulysses, who has tricked him with a suit of armor. Achilles weds Deidamia and goes to Troy.

Gay's last work, which was unsuccessful, was performed shortly after his death. It also contains music by John Pepusch and Corelli.

For a detailed description of the music, see Fiske/*ETM,* 113–14.

The story is similar to that of A. Caldara's *Achille in Sciro* (1736, Vienna), D. Sarro's *Achille in Sciro* (1737, Naples), and G. F. Handel's *Deidamia* (1741, London). *Achilles in Petticoats** is a parody.

LIBRETTO: English, with unaccompanied melodies (London: J. Watts, 1733); repr. Rubsamen/*BO,* vol. 8 (1974).

Achilles in Petticoats, opera in two acts by Thomas A. Arne; libretto (Eng) by George Colman Sr., after John Gay. First performance December 16, 1773, London, Covent Garden.

The plot is a parody of Gay's *Achilles.** None of the original music is included in this version.

SCORE: condensed score (London: Welcker, [1774]).

LIBRETTO: English (London: W. Strahan, 1774).

Acis and Galatea, "all-sung" masque by John Eccles; libretto (Eng) by Peter Anthony Motteux. First performance May? 1701, London, Lincoln's Inn Fields Theatre, together with Motteux's *The Mad Lover,* with incidental music by Eccles.

The story of the two lovers Acis and Galatea is provided with a happy ending. Acis does not get crushed under a rock tossed by the giant Polyphemus but lives and marries Galatea.

See following entries for other settings.

LIBRETTOS: English, with music (London: R. Parker and H. Newman, 1701); repr. ed. introd. Lucyle Hook, Augustan Reprint Society, no. 208 (Los Angeles: William Andrews Clark Memorial Library, University of California, 1981).

Acis and Galatea, "English pastoral opera" in three acts by George Frideric Handel; libretto (Eng) by John Gay and others, after Ovid's *Metamorphoses,* XIII, 750–897. First performance, as masque, summer 1718, Cannons (see the Rogers article). First public performance, as pastoral, March 26, 1731, London, Lincoln's Inn Theatre, with Philip Rochetti, Elizabeth Wright (Mrs. Michael Arne), and Richard Leveridge. First complete performance, as pastoral (unauthorized, by the company of Lampe, Carey, and Arne), May 28, 1732, London, Little Theatre in the Haymarket); production by the composer, as serenata, June 10, 1732, London, Haymarket. First U.S. performance (concert) February 14, 1839, New York, Lyceum Building. First U.S. performance (stage) November 21, 1842, New York, Park Theater. The many revivals include one in Aldeburgh on June 15, 1966.

Galatea is unhappy because Acis, her beloved, is away. He returns, pursued by the giant Polyphemus, another admirer of Galatea. The giant crushes Acis under a rock, and Acis is transformed into a spring.

Major roles: Galatea (sop); Acis (ten); and Polyphemus, a giant (bass).

The work borrows practices from the rival Italian opera such as the pairing of recitative and da capo arias. Its numbers include the charming chorus "Happy We." Mozart was among its many revisers (ca. 1788).

Other operatic settings of the story include L. Vittori, *La Galatea* (Rome, 1639); M.-A. Charpentier, *Acis et Galatée* (1678, Paris); J.-B. Lully, *Acis et Galatée* (1686, Paris); J. Eccles (1701, London, see preceding entry); "serenata da camera" *Aci e*

Polifemo (1708); A. L. Carrión, zarzuela *Accis y Galatea* (1708, Madrid); G. H. Stölzel, *Acis und Galathea* (1715, Prague); J. G. Schürer, *La Galatea* (1746, Dresden); J. C. da Silva, *La Galatea* (1779, Lisbon); F. J. Haydn, *Acide* (1762, Eisenstadt); F. Bianchi (1792); J. G. Naumann, *Aci e Galatea* (1801); J. L. Hatton (1844); V. Massé, *Galatée* (1852, Paris); and Zarbo (1992).

SCORES: fs, in *W. A. Mozart, Neue Ausgabe* X/28/1, ed. Andreas Holschneider (Kassel: Bärenreiter, 1973); vs (London: I. Walsh [1743], [1750?]).

LIBRETTO: English (London: J. Watts, 1732).

BIBLIOGRAPHY: Emilie Dahnk-Baroffio, "Zu Aci e Galatea," *Göttinger Händeltage* 1966, 41ff.; Winton Dean, "Masque into Opera," *MT* CVIII (1967), 605ff.; Patrick Rogers, "Dating *Acis and Galatea*," *MT* CXIV (1973), 792; Stanley Sadie, "Aldeburgh . . .'Acis and Galatea,'" *Opera* XVII (Autumn 1966), 35–38; Jon Solomon, "Polyphemus's Whistle in Handel's 'Acis and Galatea,'" *ML* LXIV (1983), 37–43.

DISCOGRAPHY: J. Gomez, R. Tear, P. Langridge, B. Luxon, St. Martin-in-the-Fields; cond. N. Marriner, Argo ZRG–886/7 (2); N. Burrowes, R. Johnson, M. Hill, W. White, English Baroque Soloists; cond. J. E. Gardiner, DG Archiv 2708–038 (2); both rev. John W. Freeman, "Records," *ON* XLIII (Mar. 31, 1979), 40.

Acres of Sky, folk drama in two acts by Arthur Kreutz; libretto (Eng) by Zoë Lund Schiller, after the play by Charles Morrow Wilson (1930). First performance November 16, 1951, Fayetteville, Arkansas, University of Arkansas, Fine Arts Center. First New York performance May 7, 1952, Columbia University, Brander Matthews Theatre, with Milton Cardey (the Traveller), Frances Lehnerts (Omy Caldwell), Stephanie Turash (Nan Caldwell), and Lorenzo Herrara (Hal Gunter); conducted by Otto Luening.

The action is set on a farm in Arkansas. The Caldwell family has gathered to hear the reading of the will of the father. Among the characters are the mother, the son, the daughter, and the Traveller, who narrates and takes part in some of the goings-on.

BIBLIOGRAPHY: James Hinton Jr., "Kreutz Ballad Opera Produced at Columbia," *MA* LXXII (May 1952), 20; Howard Taubman, "Columbia Offers New Ballad Opera," *NYT* (May 8, 1952), 35.

Actors al fresco, burletta by Thomas S. Cooke, Jonathan Blewitt, and Charles Edward Horn; libretto (Eng) by W. T. Montcrieff. First performance 1823, London, Vauxhall Gardens. Revived as a vaudeville, June 9, 1827, London, Vauxhall Gardens.

LIBRETTO: English (London, ca. 1827).

Actor's Revenge, An, opera in a prologue, two acts, and an epilogue by Minoru Miki; libretto (Eng) by James Kirkup, after the story *Yukinojo Henge* by Otokichi Mikami. First performance October 5, 1979, London, English Music Theatre Company; directed by Colin Graham. First U.S. performance June 12, 1981, St. Louis, with Cynthia Clarey (Lady Namiji), Manuel Alum (Yukinojo, mimed), Mallory Walker (Yukinojo, sung), Stephen Alexus Williams, Richard Croft, and Gordon Holleman, directed by Colin Graham.

The setting is eighteenth-century Japan. In this "Kabuki" opera, Yukinojo, a famed actor, takes revenge on Lord Dobe, the corrupt magistrate who was responsible for the deaths of the actor's parents. Treated also is the love that develops between the actor and Lady Namiji, the daughter of the magistrate; she becomes another casualty of Yukinojo's quest for revenge. The story is told in flashbacks, as Yukinojo, living in a Buddhist monastery, remembers his past.

Major roles: Yukinojo (ten), Lord Dobe (bass), and Lady Namiji (sop).
LIBRETTO: English (London: Faber, 1979).
BIBLIOGRAPHY: Donal Henahan, "Opera: 'An Actor's Revenge,' by Miki," *NYT* (June 13, 1981), 15 [on U.S. premiere]; Nicholas Kenyon, "Musical Events," *NY* (June 29, 1981), 71–72 [on U.S. premiere]; Frank Peters, "St. Louis Opera Theatre: West Meets East: 'An Actor's Revenge' Unites Kabuki and Opera," *MA* XXXI (Oct. 1981), 21–22 [on U.S. premiere].

Adelaide, or, The Royal William, nautical burletta in one act by Henry Rowley Bishop; libretto (Eng) by Edward Fitzball. First performance July 23, 1830, London, Vauxhall Gardens.

Admirable Bashville, The, chamber opera in one act by Wallace Berry; libretto (Eng), after George Bernard Shaw. Composed 1954.

Adopted Child, The, musical drama in two acts by Thomas Attwood; libretto (Eng) by Samuel Birch. First performance May 1, 1795, London, Drury Lane Theatre, with Miss Leake, Master Thomas Walsh, and Thomas Sedgwick. First U.S. performance May 23, 1796, New York, John Street Theatre.

The plot centers on a young boy who is adopted by a ferryman and his wife. The youngster owns a mysterious trunk that is not to be opened until after Sir Edmond of Milford Castle has died. It turns out that the boy is in reality the rightful heir to the Milford fortune and estate, and the good-hearted ferryman first foils a plot to kidnap the child and then helps him regain his rightful title.

Roles: Bertrand, Le Sage, Record, Michael, Spruce, Flint, Clara, Lucy, Jannetta, and Nell.
SCORE: vs (London: Longman & Broderip, [1795?]).
LIBRETTOS: English (London: C. Dilly, 1795; New York: Samuel French & Son, [n.d.]; London: Longman, Hurst, Rees, and Orme, 1809; Boston: John West, 1798).

Adventure of Don Quixote, An, opera in two acts by George Alexander Macfarren; libretto (Eng) by George Macfarren Sr., after Cervantes's *Don Quixote*. First performance February 3, 1846, London, Drury Lane Theatre, with Mr. Weiss (Don Quixote), Mr. Stretton (Sancho Panza), Mr. D. W. King (Camacho), Mr. S. Jones (Rovedos), Mr. Hodges (Juan), Mr. Birt (Pedrillo), Mr. Heath (Lopez), Mr. Priorson (vicar), Mr. Allen (Basilius), and Miss Rainforth (Quiteria); conducted by Mr. R. Hughes; directed by Mr. W. West.

In this episode from Cervantes' work, the poor student Basilius manages, through the help of Don Quixote, to outfox the rich Camacho and marry Basilius's intended, Quiteria.

Major roles: Basilius (ten), a poor student; Quiteria; and Don Quixote.
For a description of the music, see Biddlecombe/*EO*, 153–54.
The numbers include Basilius's "Hear Me, Great Heav'n," which concludes the second act and Quiteria's "Ah, Why Do We Love."
An earlier setting of the story is F. Mendelssohn's *Die Hochzeit des Camacho* (1827, Berlin).
Also known as *Don Quixote* (see later for other settings).
LIBRETTO: English (London: Chappell, 1846).

Aesop, the Fabulous Fabulist, children's opera in one act by Martin Kalmanoff; libretto (Eng) by the composer. First performance August 1969, Camp Pemiqewasset, New Hampshire.

Aesop's Fables, rock opera by William Russo; libretto (Eng) by Jon Swan. First performance August 17, 1972, New York.

Aesop's Fables, children's opera by Gregg Smith; libretto (Eng). First performance April 11, 1985, De Kalb, Illinois.

Aesop's Fables, opera in one act by David Ahlstrom; libretto (Eng) by the composer. First performance April 1986, San Francisco.

Aethiop, The, or, The Child of the Desert, "grand romantick drama" in three acts by Henry Rowley Bishop; libretto (Eng) by William Dimond. First performance October 6, 1812, London, Covent Garden. Revised as *Haroun al Raschid** (1813, London).

The opera, with its exotic locale and Haroun al Raschid as its main character, was performed on April 5, 1813, in New York, with new music (no longer extant) by James Perossier.

See also R. Taylor's version (1812); S. Mercadante's *Aminta ed Agira* (1823) contains the role of Haroun al Raschid; also Weber's *Abu Hassan* (1811, adapted by T. S. Cooke as *Abou Hassan,** 1825); and G. Meyerbeer's *Wirth und Gast* (1813, Vienna).
SCORES: ms fs (1812, British Museum, Add. MS. 36941); ms fs, *Haroun Alraschid*, four airs: "Go, Mystical Flow'r," "Farewell, Farewell, the Golden Day," "Who Thrids [sic] the Gloom," "Now Fill the Air" (1813, British Library, Add. MS. 36963).
LIBRETTOS: English (London, 1812; New York: D. Longworth, 1813).

Aethiop [Ethiop], The, or, The Child of the Desert, opera in three acts by Rayner Taylor, after Bishop. A new production of Bishop's work was set for the fall season at the Chestnut Street Theatre, Philadelphia. "Mr. R. Taylor" was billed as composer of original "music and accompaniments." Because of the War of 1812, the premiere was postponed until New Year's Day, 1814.

Haroun Al-Raschid, the ruler of Baghdad, gains access to a group trying to seize his throne by disguising himself as a conjurer (the Aethiop) and pacifying the rebels. A comic aside concerns Zoe, the beautiful wife of a Greek liquor salesman, who is saved from lecherous clients of her husband when their wives appear.
SCORES: vs (Philadelphia: George E. Blake, [1813]); repr. ed. (as *The Ethiop*) by Martha Furman Schleifer, *American Opera and Music for the Stage*, vol. 5 ([Boston]: G. K. Hall, 1990); orchestral restoration of 1813 version by Victor Fell Yellin, *NAMT*, vol. 2 (1994).
LIBRETTO: English (New York: D. Longworth, 1813); repr. ed. *NAMT*, vol. 2 (1994).
DISCOGRAPHY: J. Otten, J. Porrello, R. Anderson, J. M. Ousley, M. Best, S. Belling, D. Vanderline, the Federal Music Society; cond. J. Baldon, New World Records NWR 232 (1 LP); rev. Peter G. Davis, "A Landmark Series of American Music Recordings," *NYT* (Jan. 14, 1976).

Affair, The, opera in one act by Felix Werder; libretto (Eng) by Leonard Radic. Composed 1969. First performance March 14, 1974, Sydney, Australia, Opera House.

Suspecting her husband, Sir Reginald, of having an affair with Olivia Tomas, Lady Celia concocts an elaborate plan to catch him in the act. She convinces her husband and Olivia to take part in the performance of an opera, whose plot is really a dramatization of Sir Reginald's life. When the character played by Olivia "shoots" the one played by Sir Reginald, he falls dead. His assistant, Gregory Jones, had switched the dummy bullets for live ones in order to get rid of his superior.

Major roles: Lady Celia (sop); Sir Reginald, Australian High Commissioner (ten); Olivia Tomas, wife of the South American ambassador (mezzo); and Gregory Jones, Second Secretary (bar).

This expressionist work employs traditional forms such as the aria only to emphasize the irony of the situation.

Afrancesado, The, or, Secrecy and Truth, opera by George Alexander Lee; libretto (Eng) by Thomas Serle. First performance October 19, 1837, London, Covent Garden.

Africa Is Calling Me, "modern-day black opera" by Bob Reid; libretto (Eng). First performance (excerpts) November 1976, New York, Jazzmania.
BIBLIOGRAPHY: Robert Palmer, "Bob Reid Plays Selections of 'Africa Is Calling Me,'" *NYT* (Nov. 23, 1976), 41.

African Heartbeat, opera in one act by Joseph Marais; libretto (Eng). First performance August 28, 1953, Idyllwild, California, Idyllwild School of Music.

African Kraal, The, opera in one act by Harry Lawrence Freeman; libretto (Eng) by the composer. First performance June 30, 1903, Chicago; conducted by the composer. Revised 1934.

Africanus Blue Beard, "musical Ethiopian burlesque" in one scene by Alfred B. Sedgwick; libretto (Eng) by Frank Dumont. First performance September 11, 1874, Gloucester, Massachusetts, with J. T. Gulick (Blue Beard), Lew Benedict (Gripanck), Frank Dumont and Thomas B. Dixon (Beppo/Greppo), Frank Kent (Fatima), and D. H. Smith (Mafairy).

In this treatment of the Bluebeard story, the wife-killer Blue Beard is eventually defeated by Beppo and Greppo when he tries to kill Fatima, their sister.

Major roles: Blue Beard, a model husband; Gripanck, his attendant; Beppo and Greppo, Fatima's brothers; Fatima, Blue Beard's "latest"; and Mafairy, a mother-in-law.

The musical numbers include Blue Beard's "Kind Friends, Let Me Now Introduce" (no. 3) and "Where Is That Key?" (no. 6) and Fatima's "Oh, Blue Beard!" (no. 4).
SCORE: vs (New York: De Witt, 1876); repr. ed. Michael Meckna, *NAMT*, vol. 7 (1994); with text and music.

Africanus Instructus, musical play by Stanley Silverman; libretto (Eng) by Richard Foreman. First performance January 14, 1986, New York.
LIBRETTO: English, in Richard Foreman, *Love & Science: Selected Music-Theatre Texts* (New York: Theatre Communications Group, 1991).

After the Wedding, opera in one act by Michael Head; libretto (Eng) by Nancy Bush. First performance 1972, London, Royal Academy of Music.

Agamemnon, opera in one act by Havergal Brian; libretto (Eng) by the composer, based on a translation (1906, with some additions) by John Stuart Blackie of Aeschylus' play. Composed 1957. First performance January 28, 1971, London, St. John's, with soloists of the Opera dei Giovanni.

The opera treats the story of Agamemnon's sacrifice of Iphigenia, the prediction of disaster by Cassandra, and Agamemnon's murder by his wife, Clytemnestra, and Aegisthus, her lover.
BIBLIOGRAPHY: Hugo Cole, "Music in London," *MT* CXII (1971), 257 [on premiere].

Agamemnon (The Agamemnon of Aeschylus), or, The Wages of Sin, opera in one act by Felix Werder; libretto (Eng) by the composer, after Aeschylus, in a translation by Gilbert Murray. First performance (concert) 1967, ABC. First stage performance, as *Agamemnon,* June 1, 1977, Melbourne, Australia, Grant Street Theatre.

The plot concerns King Agamemnon of Mycenae, who ignores the warnings of his lover, Cassandra, that his wife, Clytemnestra, and her lover, Aegisthus, plan to kill him. The king returns home and is murdered by the pair.

Major roles: King Agamemnon (bass); Cassandra (sop); Clytemnestra (sop); and Aegisthus (counterten).

The serial work is through-composed.

DISCOGRAPHY: Lyra SSM 007 (1 LP, ca. 1977).

Agamemnon, dramatic narrative in two acts by Iain Hamilton; libretto (Eng) by the composer, after Philip Vellacott's translation of Aeschylus' *Agamemnon.* Composed 1967–1969, 1987, 1989. Not performed.

The chorus tells the story of what follows from Agamemnon's sacrifice of his daughter Iphigenia. After Troy falls, the victorious Agamemnon brings back Cassandra as his prize. He ignores her prophecy of doom and is killed by Clytemnestra and her lover, Aegisthus.

Major roles: Clytemnestra (sop), Agamemnon (bass), Cassandra (sop), and Aegisthus (ten).

For a detailed description, see Eaton/*OP* II, 22–23.

Agamemnon, opera in two acts by Richard Morris; libretto (Eng) by Anthony Holden. First performance November 25, 1969, Oxford, Playhouse, Oxford University Opera Club.

LIBRETTO: English, transl. and ed. after Aeschylus (London: Cambridge University Press, 1969).

BIBLIOGRAPHY: G. Widdicombe, "Oxford," *MT* CXI (Jan. 1970), 71 [on premiere].

Ages Ago, a Ghost Story, musical legend in one act by Frederic Clay; libretto (Eng) by William S. Gilbert. First performance November 26, 1869, London, Gallery of Illustration, with Fanny Holland (Rosa), Thomas German Reed (Sir Ebenezer Tare), Priscilla Reed (Mistress MacMotherly), and Arthur Cecil (Columbus Hebblethwaite). First U.S. performance March 31, 1880, New York, Bijou Theater. Revivals include June 6, 1988, London, King's College, Morley Opera; conducted by Stuart Hutchinson.

In this tale of transformed identities, the characters become their ancestors for one night. Sir Ebenezer Tare, who has risen from lowly beginnings to become an alderman, takes possession of the haunted Castle Cockaleekie. The penniless Columbus Hebblethwaite, in love with Rosa, Sir Ebenezer's niece, is able to find proof that he owns the castle, when the ancestral portraits come to life and offer him assistance. Sir Ebenezer is allowed to retain control over the castle only after he agrees to let Hebblethwaite wed Rosa. Sir Ebenezer finds romance with his Scottish housekeeper, Mrs. MacMotherly.

For a detailed description, see Stedman/*GBS,* 26–30; Stedman/*WSG,* 74–76.

Gilbert used the story as a basis for his text for Sullivan's *Ruddigore.**

Roles: Sir Ebenezer Tare, later, Lord Carnaby Poppytop; Rosa, his niece, later Lady Maud; Mistress MacMotherly, later, Dame Cherry Maybud; Mr. Columbus Hebblethwaite, later, Sir Cecil Blount; and Steward, later, Brown.

SCORE: ms vs (n.p., [187-?], LCCN: 84-128682); vs (London: Boosey & Co., n.d.).

LIBRETTO: English, with the names of the original and borrowed airs to be sung (New York: n.p., 1875; London: J. Williams, New York: E. Schuberth, 1895).

TEXT AND MUSIC: Stedman/*GBS*, 81–106.

BIBLIOGRAPHY: Dilys Hartog, review, *Opera* XXXIX (Aug. 1988), 1010–11 [on revival]; Arthur Jacobs, "Cradled among the Reeds: Two Victorian Operettas," *MT* CXXIX (May 1988), 234–35.

Agincourt, dramatic scene for male voices by Rutland Boughton; libretto (Eng) by the composer, after Shakespeare's *Henry V* (1599). First performance August 26, 1924, Glastonbury.

SCORE: vs (London: Joseph Williams, 1926).

Agnes Sorel, opera by Mary A'Beckett; libretto (Eng) by Gilbert A. A'Beckett. First performance December 14, 1835, London, St. James's Theatre.

Set in the fifteenth century, the story concerns the influential mistress of Charles VII of France.

Also set by A. Gyrowetz (1806, Vienna).

Agreeable Surprise, The, comic opera in two acts by Samuel Arnold; libretto (Eng) by John O'Keeffe. First performance September 4, 1781, London, Little Theatre in the Haymarket, with John Edwin (Lingo), Mrs. Wells (Cowslip), and Mrs. Webb (Mrs. Cheshire). First U.S. performance January 27, 1787, Philadelphia, Southwark Theatre.

Sir Felix Friendly and Compton have made an agreement to raise each other's children. The children, now young adults, have fallen in love, but they are unaware of their backgrounds, Eugene thinking he is the son of the poor Compton and Laura believing she is an orphan and has been raised by Sir Felix, who has become wealthy. Eugene falls into the clutches of the older Mrs. Cheshire, who wants to marry him herself, but she is thwarted, and the young lovers are presented with the "agreeable surprise" when they are told their real identities. A side story involves Lingo, Sir Felix's butler, and the dumb farm girl Cowslip, whom he loves.

For a detailed description of the music, see Fiske/*ETM 2,* 438–39.

SCORE: vs (London: Harrison & Co., [1798?]).

LIBRETTO: English (London: J. Bland, [1781]; New York: D. Longworth, 1811).

Ahmad al Ramel, or, The Pilgrim of Love, grand opera by Charles Edward Horn; libretto (Eng) by H. J. Finn, after Washington Irving's *Alhambra* (1832). First performance October 12, 1840, New York, National Theatre.

Akhnaten, opera in three acts by Philip Glass; libretto (Eng, ancient Egyptian, Akkadian, biblical Hebrew) by the composer, Shalom Goldman, Robert Israel, and Richard Riddell. First performance March 24, 1984, Stuttgart, Stuttgart Opera, with Milagro Vargas (Nefertiti), Paul Esswood (Akhnaten), and Melinda Liebermann (Queen Tye); conducted by Dennis Russell Davies. First U.S. performance October 12, 1984, Houston, State Theater, with Marta Senn (Nefertiti), Christopher Robson (Akhnaten), and Marie Angel (Queen Tye); conducted by John DeMain. First British performance June

17, 1985, London, Coliseum, with Sally Burgess (Nefertiti), Christopher Robson (Akhnaten), and Marie Angel (Queen Tye).

The setting is 1875 B.C. The story concerns the life of the Egyptian pharaoh Akhnaten and his love for his wife Nefertiti. He builds a city to honor his new god, Aten. But his failure to father a male heir and his ignoring the suffering of his people lead to his defeat and fall at the hands of the triumvirate of the High Priest of Amon, Nefertiti's father, Aye, and the general Horemhab.

For a detailed plot synopsis see K/KOB, 1356–58; K/NKOB, 256–58.

Major roles: Akhnaten, King of Egypt (counterten); Nefertiti, his wife (alto); Queen Tye, his mother (sop); Horemhab, general and future pharaoh (bar); Aye, Nefertiti's father (bass); and High Priest of Amon (ten).

Musical highlights include Akhnaten and Nefertiti's love duet, sung to an Egyptian text, and Akhnaten's monologue, in English. The role of the title character is written for a countertenor, as is Oberon in Britten's *Midsummer Night's Dream.**

This is the third of Glass's series of "portrait" operas; the others are *Einstein on the Beach** (1976) and *Satyagraha** (1980).

SCORE: vs. (New York: Dunvagen, 1983 [1992]).

LIBRETTO: English (New York: Dunvagen Music; Bryn Mawr, Pa.: Presser, 1984).

BIBLIOGRAPHY: William Albright, "Houston," *ON* XLIX (Jan. 5, 1985), 39 [on U.S. premiere]; Robert Anderson, "London Diary," *MT* CXXVI (1985), 474–75 [on British premiere]; Paul John Frandsen, "Philip Glass's Akhnaten," *MQ* LXXVII (1993): 241–67; Andrew Porter, "Musical Events," *NY* LX (Nov. 19, 1984), 174, 177–78 [on U.S. premiere]; Mark Swed, "Editor's Note to Philip Glass's Akhnaten," *MQ* LXXVII (1993), 236–40.

DISCOGRAPHY: M. Vargas, M. Liebermann, P. Esswood, M. Holzapfel, T. Hannula, C. Hauptmann, Stuttgart State Opera; cond. D. R. Davies, CBS M3–42457 (3 LPs), M3T–42457 (3 tapes), M2K–42457 (2 CDs), rev. John W. Freeman, "Recordings," *ON* LII (Mar. 26, 1988), 42.

Aladdin, or, The Magic Lamp, "fairy opera" in three acts by Henry Rowley Bishop; libretto (Eng) by George Soane, after the *Thousand and One Nights*. First performance April 29, 1826, London, Drury Lane Theatre, with Mr. Horn and Miss Stephens. First U.S. performance November 12, 1830, Philadelphia.

The story is based on the tale of Aladdin and his magic lamp.

Commissioned by Robert Elliston, the assistant manager of the Drury Lane Theatre, the opera was mounted in an attempt to draw attention away from Weber's *Oberon*, which had received its premiere on April 12 at Covent Garden. The ploy failed, and the opera disappeared from the repertory after a handful of performances.

The work contains spoken dialogue and a hunting chorus.

Other theater pieces on the subject include W. Shield's pantomime (1788, London); Condell and Ware's pantomime *Aladdin, or, The Wonderful Lamp* (1813, London); A. Gyrowetz's *Aladin, oder, Die Wunderlampe* (1819, Vienna); N. Isouard's *Aladin, ou, La lampe merveilleuse* (1822, Paris); C. F. E. Hornemann's *Aladdin* (1888, Copenhagen); and N. Rota's *Aladino e la lampada magica* (1968, Naples).

SCORE: fs ms (British Library, Add. MS. 36957, 36958).

LIBRETTOS: English (London: Longman et al., 1826; New York: Murden, 1826).

Albatross, The, chamber opera in two acts by Diana Burrell; libretto (Eng) by the composer, after Susan Hill's short story. Composed 1987. First performance July 10,

1997, London, Spitafields Market Opera, Trinity Opera Group; conducted by Anne Manson; directed by Stephen Langridge.

Albergo Empedocle, opera by Paul Barker; libretto (Eng) by Nicholas Till, after E. M. Forster. First performance June 14, 1990, London, International Opera Festival.

On a trip through Europe Harold realizes, with help from his friend Tommy, that he and his fiancée, Mildred, are ill matched.

BIBLIOGRAPHY: Matthew Rye, review, *MT* CXXXI (Sept. 1990), 496–97 [on premiere].

Albert and Adelaide, or, The Victim of Constancy, musical drama (pastiche) in three acts by Thomas Attwood and Daniel Steibelt; libretto (Eng) by Samuel Birch, after Marsollier and Boutet de Monvel. First performance December 11, 1798, London.

The work uses music by Cherubini.

Albert Herring, comic opera in three acts by Benjamin Britten; libretto (Eng) by Eric Crozier, after the short story *Le rosier de Madonne Husson* (1828) by de Maupassant. First performance June 20, 1947, Glyndebourne, with Joan Cross (Lady Billows), Peter Pears (Albert), Frederick Sharp (Sid), Nancy Evans (Nancy), and Betsy de la Porte (Mrs. Herring); conducted by the composer; produced by Frederick Ashton. First U.S. performance August 8, 1949, Lenox, Massachusetts, Tanglewood, Theater Concert Hall.

The story concerns a small English town that tries to elect a May Queen. Failing to find a suitable candidate to satisfy the imperious Lady Billows, the officials choose Albert as its May King. Albert, raised strictly by his mother, is teased by his friend Sid and Sid's girlfriend, Nancy, for obeying her so completely. He reluctantly accepts his title but uses his prize money to get drunk, egged on by Sid and Nancy and imagining that Nancy is interested in him. He disappears, and when he returns, asserting a new independence, the townspeople and his mother are chagrined, but his friends are delighted.

For a detailed description, see Eaton/*OP* I, 17–18; K/*NKOB*, 107–10.

Major roles: Albert Herring, an employee of the greengrocer (ten); Lady Billows (sop); Florence Pike, her housekeeper (alto); Miss Wordsworth, head teacher (sop); Sid (bar); Nancy (mezzo); and Mrs. Herring, Albert's mother (mezzo).

For a detailed plot synopsis and musical analysis, see K/*KOB*, 1174–80.

This comic ensemble work employs a chamber orchestra. Its one extended solo is Albert's scena in act 2, scene 2, linked by the atmospheric orchestral night music to the preceding scene.

SCORE: vs (London, New York: Boosey & Hawkes, [1948]).

LIBRETTO: English (London: Boosey & Hawkes, [1947]).

BIBLIOGRAPHY: E. Stein, "Form in Opera: 'Albert Herring' Examined," *Tempo*, no. 5 (1947), 4–8; Andrew Porter, "Musical Events," *NY* LIV (July 3, 1978), 76–78 [on 1976 St. Louis production]; Eric W. White, *Benjamin Britten* (Berkeley: University of California Press, 1983), 155–60.

DISCOGRAPHY: S. Fisher, A. Cantelo, S. Rex, P. Pears, J. Noble, O. Brannigan, English Chamber Orch.; cond. B. Britten, London 421849-421850 (1964, Aldeburgh, 2 CDs).

VIDEO: Johnson, Rigby, Graham-Hall, Opie, Glyndebourne Festival Chorus, London Philharmonic Orch.; cond. B. Haitink, Castle VHS CV12051.

Alberto Albertini, or, The Robber King, dramatic romance by John Bray; libretto (Eng) by William Dunlap. First performance January 25, 1811, New York.

Albion and Albanius, opera in a prologue, three acts, and an epilogue by Louis Grabu; libretto (Eng) by John Dryden. First performance June 3, 1685, London, Dorset Gardens.

The opera, a tribute to the House of Stuart, has Albion symbolize Charles II, the reigning monarch, and Albanius as the King's brother, James, the Duke of York.

For a detailed discussion of the work, see Eric Walter White, *A History of English Opera* (London: Faber, 1983), 105–8.

SCORE: vs (London: Author, 1687).

LIBRETTO: English (London: J. Tonson, 1685).

Alcaid, The, or, The Secrets of Office, comic opera in three acts by Isaac Nathan; libretto (Eng) by James Kenney. First performance August 10, 1824, London, Haymarket Theatre, with Mr. Farren (Don Christopher Toxado), Madame Vestris (Felix), Mr. Hucke (Andreas de Caravajal), Mr. Liston (Pedrosa), Mr. Williams (Gregorio), Mr. Latham (Juan), Mr. Harley (Jabez), Mrs. Garrick (Donna Francisca), Miss Paton (Rosabel), Mrs. Glover (Theresina), Mrs. Gibbs (Margaretta), and Mrs. C. Jones (Giannetta).

The work is set in Spain.

LIBRETTO: English (London: T. Dolby, [1824]; London: John Cumberland, [1827?]).

Alceste, semi-opera in five acts by George Frideric Handel; libretto (Eng) by Tobias Smollett, after Euripides' tragedy *Alkestis* (438 B.C.). Composed 1749. Not performed.

When King Admetus becomes gravely ill, his wife, Alceste, offers to sacrifice her life in place of his, to satisfy the demands of Apollo. Hercules learns of her fate and intervenes to save her.

For a description, see Fiske/*ETM*, 200, who discusses why it was not performed.

The work ends with a gavotte. It was not performed, perhaps because John Rich, manager of Covent Garden, where it was to be played, thought Handel had not made it serious enough. Its music was used for the oratorio *The Choice of Hercules* (1751, London).

SCORES: ms autograph (British Museum, MS. Add. 30310); fs, ed. F. W. Chrysander, *G. F. Händels Werke*, vol. 46 (Leipzig, 18??; repr. Ridgewood, N.J.: Gregg Press, 1965).

DISCOGRAPHY: E. Kirkby, J. Nelson, Academy of Ancient Music; cond. C. Hogwood, L'Oiseau-Lyre 421 479-2 (1989, 1 CD).

Alcestiad, The, opera in three acts by Louise Talma; libretto (Eng) by Thornton Wilder, after his play *A Life in the Sun* (1955), based on Euripides' tragedy *Alkestis* (438 B.C.). First performance, in a German version by Herbert Herlischka, March 1, 1962, Frankfurt, Städtische Bühnen, as *Die Alkestiade*, with Inge Borkh (Alcestis), Richard Holm (Apollo), and Ernst Gutstein (Admetus); conducted by Wolfgang Rennert; directed by Harry Buckwitz.

The story concerns the legend of Alcestis, wife of Admetus. Her devotion to Apollo frees her from Hades with the help of Hercules.

The music includes the use of serial technique for motivic ideas. Its premiere was the first time an important work by an American woman composer was presented by a leading European opera house.

SCORE: vs, holograph (Yale University, 1958).

BIBLIOGRAPHY: Paul Moor, "Louise Talma's 'The Alcestiad' in Premiere at Frankfurt Opera," *NYT* (Mar. 2, 1962), 25; R. Steyer, "Frankfurt," *Opera* LXII (June 1962), 399–401 [on premiere].

Alcestis, opera in three acts by George Marshall-Hall; libretto (Eng) by the composer, after Euripides. First performance June 22, 1898, Melbourne, Town Hall.

Other operas on the subject include J.-B. Lully's *Alceste* (1674, Paris); C. W. Gluck's *Alceste* (1767, Vienna); and E. Wellesz's *Alkestis* (1924, Mannheim).

Alchemist, The, opera in three scenes by Cyril Scott; libretto (Eng) by the composer, after Ben Jonson (1612). First performance May 28, 1925, Essen (in a German translation by Helmut Andreae), as *Der Alchimist*; conducted by Felix Wolfe.

The story, set during the plague, concerns a servant who, left in charge of his master's house, uses the abode, with the help of a fake alchemist, to fleece a group of victims.

Major roles: the wise man (bar); the young maid (sop); the young man (ten); the ghost (bass-bar); and the fool (buffo ten).

Also set by Handel (incidental music) for Ben Jonson's play (1710, London); musical by Scott Eyerly and William Holab, as *The Confidence Game* (1986, New York). SCORE: vs (Mainz: B. Schott's Söhne, 1924).

Alchemist of Trenton, The, opera in one act by Dennis Busch; libretto (Eng) by the composer. Composed 1982.

For soprano, two tenors, bass, and instrumental ensemble.

SCORE: ms vs, holograph ([1982], photocopy, NYPL).

Alchymist, The, romantic opera in three acts by Henry Rowley Bishop, an adaptation, with music expanded and arranged, of Spohr's work *Der Alchymist* (1830, Kassel); libretto (Eng) translated by Thomas Haynes Bayly and Edward Fitzball (the songs), after Karl Pfeiffer's text, itself based on Washington Irving's story *The Student of Salamanca*. First performance March 20, 1832, London, Drury Lane Theatre.

A student wishes to marry the daughter of the alchemist, but the father will not allow the wedding to take place until he discovers the philosopher's stone. The young couple, aided by the lovers' servants, scare the father into agreeing to the marriage. When he finds out that he was the victim of a hoax, the father tries to go back on his promise, but the threat to reveal that he had been dealing in alchemy makes him honor his pledge.

Alfred (the Great), opera in three acts by Thomas Augustine Arne; libretto (Eng) by James Thomson and David Mallett. First performance August 1, 1740, London, Drury Lane Theatre. Revived in an expanded, all-sung version March 20, 1745, under the title *Alfred the Great*, May 12, 1753, London, Covent Garden. First U.S. performance January 1757, Philadelphia, College Hall (concert), as *The Redemption of the Danish Invasion by Alfred the Great*.

The story, set in the ninth century, opens with the Saxon king asleep under a tree; he is found by Corin, a shepherd, and his wife, Emma, who give him shelter from the Danes, not realizing who their guest is. Alfred is reunited with Eltruda, his wife, and Edward, their son. He leads his forces to triumph over the Danes.

For a description of the various versions, see Fiske/*ETM*, 224–29.

The work includes an overture in the Italian style, the royal trio "Let Not Those Who Love Complain," Eltruda's air "Gracious Heav'n, O Hear Me," and Emma's air "Safe beneath This Lowly Dwelling." It ends with the ode "When Britain First at Heav'n's Command," with each stanza closing with the famous choral refrain "Rule Britannia, Britannia rule the waves, Britons never will be slaves."

One of several operas on the monarch. Others include those by S. Mayr, *Alfredo il grande* (1818, Rome); G. Donizetti, *Alfredo il grande* (1823, Venice); J. M. Wolfram (1826); W. Reuling (1840); J. Schmidt, *Alfred der Grosse* (1830, Berlin); G. Rodwell's Christmas pantomime *Harlequin Alfred the Great!, or, The Magic Banjo, and the Mystic Raven!* (1850, London); J. Raff, *König Alfred* (Weimar, 1851); Stainford, *Alfred, King of Wessex* (1864); Bechtel (1880); and N. C. Gatty, *King Alfred and the Cakes** (1930, London).
SCORES: fs, ed. Alexander Scott, *Musica Britannica*, vol. 47 (London: Stainer and Bell [Galaxy], 1981); vs (London: Harrison & Co., ca. 1785).
LIBRETTOS: English (London, 1753; London: Harrison, 1781).
BIBLIOGRAPHY: Alexander Scott, "Arne's *Alfred*," *ML* LV (1974), 385–97.
DISCOGRAPHY: D. Montague, N. Sears, C. Pierard, M. Padmore, S. Wallace, R. Horton, Orch. of the Age of Enlightenment; cond. N. Kraemer, BBC Music Magazine (1995, London).

Algerian, The, "comedy opera" in three acts by Reginald De Koven; libretto (Eng) by Glen MacDonough. First performance October 26, 1893, Philadelphia, Garden Theatre, with Marie Tempest (Celeste) and Julius Steger (Col. La Grange).
    The setting is exotic Algiers, and the plot involves the poor Prince of Montenegro, who attracts tourists to his kingdom by inviting them to enjoy his harem, in reality composed of chorus members of an opera company. One such tourist is Col. La Grange, whose love for a "harem" member is derailed when Celeste, Countess of Monvel, who is in love with La Grange herself, reveals the deception.
SCORE: vs (New York: G. Schirmer, 1893).

Algerine Slaves, The. See **The Strangers at Home**.

Algonah, opera in three acts by Stephen Storace, with additional music by Michael Kelly; libretto (Eng) by James Cobb. First performance April 30, 1802, London, Drury Lane. This was an adaptation of Storace's *The Cherokee** (1794, London).
LIBRETTO: English (London: R. Lay, n.d.).

Alice, opera in one act by William Osborne; libretto (Eng), after Lewis Carroll. First performance March 19, 1985, Jerusalem.
BIBLIOGRAPHY: review, *Opera* XXXVI (July 1985), 811–12.

Alice, rock opera in two acts by Tom Waits; libretto (Eng) by Paul Schmidt, after Lewis Carroll's *Alice in Wonderland* (1865); songs by Waits and Kathleen Brennan. First performance December 19, 1992, Hamburg, Thalia Theater; with Stefan Kurt (Charles Dodgson/White Rabbit/White Knight) and Annette Paulmann (Alice); directed by Robert Wilson. First U.S. performance 1995, Brooklyn, New York, Brooklyn Academy of Music, with the same cast.
    The work focuses on imaginary letters that Lewis Carroll (here called by his real name, Charles Dodgson) writes to young Alice Liddell, his inspiration for the title character of *Alice in Wonderland*. The author destroys the missives after penning them. It opens with Dodgson trying to photograph the young Alice, after which she runs from him and falls into Wonderland. It ends with Alice as an old woman, singing the sorrowful "I Remember You with Leaves in Your Hair."

Part one of Robert Wilson's rock opera trilogy, which includes *The Black Rider**
(1990, Hamburg) and *Time Rocker** (1997, Paris).
BIBLIOGRAPHY: Robert Brustein, "Alice in Wilsonland," *New Republic* CCXIII (Nov. 6,
1995), 30–31 [on U.S. premiere].

Alice in Wonderland, dream play for children in two acts by Walter Slaughter; libretto
(Eng) by Henry Savile Clarke, after Lewis Carroll's *Alice's Adventures in Wonderland.*
Composed 1906.
SCORE: vs (London: Ascherberg, Hopwood & Crew; New York: Chappell-Harms, 1906).

Alice in Wonderland, opera in six or eight scenes by Robert Chauls; libretto (Eng) by
the composer, after Lewis Carroll. First performance January 16, 1976, Van Nuys,
California, Valley Opera; May 21, 1985, New York, Triplex Theater, Broque Opera,
with Darynn Zimmer (Alice); conducted by Robert Kopelson.
    The libretto sticks closely to the Carroll original and includes the important charac-
ters Alice meets on her adventures, such as the White Rabbit, the Cheshire Cat, the
Queen of Hearts, and the Mad Hatter.
    Major roles: Alice (sop); the Queen of Hearts (mezzo); the Cheshire Cat (ten/mezzo),
the Gryphon (bass); the Mock Turtle (ten); and the Duchess (bar).
    For a detailed description, see Kornick/*RAO*, 73–74.
SCORES: vs (Melville, N.Y.: Belwin-Mills, 1981, 1974); vs (New York: G. Schirmer; Milwaukee: H. Leonard, 1981).
BIBLIOGRAPHY: Tim Page, "Broque Opera Offers a 45-Minute 'Alice,'" *NYT* (May 23,
1985), C, 25 [on New York premiere].

Alice in Wonderland, opera in one act by Margaret Meachem; libretto (Eng) by the
composer, after Lewis Carroll. Composed 1982.
SCORE: ms score (NYPL, 1982).

Alice in Wonderland, opera for children by Wilfred Josephs; libretto (Eng) by the
composer, after Lewis Carroll. Composed 1985-1988.
    A "colorful interpretation" of the Lewis Carroll classic.
    The one-hour work has a cast of twenty-two characters and chorus and is scored for
chamber orchestra.
    Josephs also wrote *Through the Looking Glass.**

Alice in Wonderland. See **Final Alice.**

Alice Meets the Mock Turtle, opera by Susan Bingham; libretto (Eng), after Lewis
Carroll. First performance March 28, 1988, New York, After Dinner Opera.

Alissa, fantasy opera in one act by Raffaello de Banfield; libretto (Eng) by Richard
Miller. First performance May 15, 1965, Geneva, Grand Théâtre.
SCORE: vs, English-Italian (Milan: Ricordi, 1965).

Alkestis, opera in two acts by Rutland Boughton; libretto (Eng) by Gilbert Murray,
after Euripides' tragedy (438 B.C.). First performance August 26, 1922, Glastonbury,
with Astra Desmond (Alkestis), Steuart Wilson (Admetus), Clive Carey (Herakles),
Kathleen Davis (the handmaid), Frederick Woodhouse (Thanatos), and Arthur Clark
(chorus leader).

A telling of the story of Alkestis, who is prepared to sacrifice herself for her husband, Admetus, and how she is saved from Thanatos, the messenger of death, by Herakles (Hercules).

Among the highlights are the choruses "Oh, a House That Loves a Stranger" and "I Have Sojourned in the Muses' Land," both in act 2.

BIBLIOGRAPHY: A. J. Shelton, "Glastonbury Festival: Rutland Boughton's *Alkestis*," *MT* LXIII (Oct. 1, 1922), 719–20.

Allah. See **Zululand**.

All at Sea, ballad opera in three acts by Geoffrey Shaw; libretto (Eng) by Margaret Delamere and Sebastian Shaw. First performance May 12, 1952, London, Royal College of Music.

All Cats Turn Gray—When the Sun Goes Down, "jazz opera" by Herbert Six; libretto (Eng) by Dan Jaffe. First performance May 21, 1971, New York, Henry Street Settlement Playhouse, Opera Workshop, with Jimmy Owens (trumpet) and Julius Watkins (French horn).

The work contains a series of set pieces that feature two black gravediggers who confront several white groups, including beatniks and civic representatives.

Ostensibly dedicated to the memory of jazz saxophonist Charlie Parker, the opera's only musical tribute to him is in the overture.

BIBLIOGRAPHY: John S. Wilson, "Opera Explores Racial Questions," *NYT* (May 23, 1971), 58 [on premiere].

All Fool's Day, fantasy in one act by Clive Carey; libretto (Eng) by T. M. Baretti. First performance August 29, 1921, Glastonbury, England.

All in a Garden Fair, romantic opera in one act by Gerard Tonning; libretto (Eng) by Mrs. H. W. Powell. First performance November 1, 1913, Seattle, Moore Theater; conducted by the composer.

The love story is set during the summer in the early nineteenth century at the seashore villa of Mr. Hobart.

All the King's Men, opera for young people by Richard Rodney Bennett; libretto (Eng) by Beverley Cross. First performance March 28, 1969, Coventry, England, Coventry Schools Music Festival.

The story concerns King Charles I and the battle between the Royalists and the Roundheads. A certain Dr. Chillingworth has suggested three ways the King's troops can take the town of Gloucester, which is being defended by Colonel Massey and his troops. After the first two methods fail, Chillingworth suggests that the Royalists create a type of siege engine as used by the Romans. The citizens of the city, however, find out about the device, christened Humpty-Dumpty, and before it can be used to bridge the river, the defenders widen the breach, so that the device falls into the river, and "all the King's horses and all the King's men" are unable to rescue it. The King and his forces withdraw, unaware that Colonel Massey is down to his last three barrels of powder.

Major roles: King Charles I; Queen Henrietta Maria; Dr. Chillingworth; and Colonel Massey.

SCORE: vs (London: Universal Edition, 1968).

All the Tea in China, opera in one act by Stephen Oliver; libretto (Eng) by W. Harvey. First performance October 1969, Oxford, Clarendon Press Institute.

Almena, opera in three acts by Michael Arne and Jonathan Battishill; libretto (Eng) by Richard Rolt. First performance November 2, 1764, London, Drury Lane Theatre, with Joseph Vernon (Mohammed), Mr. Giustinelli (Mirza), Mr. Champness (Abudah), Clementina Cermonini (Aspatia), Elizabeth Wright (Almena), and Mrs. Vincent (Zara).

Mohammed, who has usurped the Persian throne after killing the Sultan, is in love with Aspatia, the ruler's widow, who is also desired by Abudah, a Persian nobleman. Mirza, a young prince and nephew of the late Sultan, loves Almena, Abudah's daughter, but Mirza is pursued by Zara, sister of the villainous Mohammed. Despite all these complications, the opera ends happily.

The part of Mirza was scored for a castrato.

For a detailed description, see Fiske/*ETM*, 312–13.

SCORE: vs (London: author, n.d.).

LIBRETTO: English (London: T. Becket, P. A. de Hondt, 1764).

Amahl and the Night Visitors, opera in one act by Gian Carlo Menotti; libretto (Eng) by the composer, inspired by Hieronymous Bosch's painting *Adoration of the Magi.* First performance December 24, 1951, New York, NBC television, with Chet Allen (Amahl), Rosemary Kuhlmann (the mother), Andrew McKinley (Kaspar), David Aiken (Melchior), Leon Lishner (Balthazar), and Francis Monachino (the page); conducted by Thomas Schippers. First stage performance February 21, 1952, Indiana University; conducted by Ernst Hoffman.

The story revolves around Amahl, a crippled shepherd boy, who lives with his poor mother. When she complains about their poverty, he comforts her in the duet "Don't Cry, Mother Dear." The Three Kings arrive on their way to Bethlehem, singing "Have You Seen a Child?" They are given shelter for the night. After the mother sees their treasure, she sings bitterly, "All That Gold." While the others are asleep, she tries to take a bit of it for herself and Amahl, but she is caught by the page. The monarchs forgive her, and Amahl offers his crutch as a present to the Christ child. He is healed for his generosity and is allowed to join the Kings on their journey to Bethlehem.

For detailed descriptions, see Eaton/*OP* I, 163–64; K/*KOB*, 1351–53; K/*NKOB*, 461–62.

Major roles: Amahl (boy sop), his mother (mezzo), King Kaspar (ten), King Melchior (bar), and King Balthazar (bass).

This was the first television opera, and it is often revived at Christmastime.

Among the other highlights are the Introduction, March, and Shepherds' Dance and Shepherds' Chorus.

SCORES: vs, fs (Eng) (New York: G. Schirmer, 1951).

LIBRETTO: English (New York: G. Schirmer, 1951).

BIBLIOGRAPHY: Quaintance Eaton, "New Menotti TV Opera Has Premiere on Christmas Eve," *MA* LXXII (Jan. 1, 1952), 3, 10.

DISCOGRAPHY: C. Allen, R. Kuhlmann, A. McKinley, D. Aiken, L. Lishner, NBC telecast orch. and chorus; cond. T. Schippers, RCA LM 1701 (1951 cast, 1 LP), reissued as RCA VIC 1512 (1 LP); K. Yagjian, Patrick, Cross, McCollum, Patterson; cond. H. Grossman, RCA LSC 2762 (1963 NBC cast, 1 LP).

VIDEO: T. Stratas, R. Sapolsky, Metropolitan Opera; cond. Cobos, AMA01V 1 VHS.

Amarantha, opera in two acts by Roger Ames; libretto (Eng), after Wilbur D. Steele's short story *How Beautiful with Shoes*, which he turned into a play with Anthony Brown (1935). First performance July 19, 1980, New London, Connecticut.

The setting is mountain country in the South. Amarantha Doggett is supposed to marry the crass Ruby Herter. Upon hearing her name, Humble Jewett, a murderous escapee from an asylum who is also a former teacher of literature, kidnaps her and takes her into the woods. She submits to his lovemaking, which stops abruptly when he learns that her name is really Mary, making him think that she is the mother of Jesus. Jewett is recaptured by the authorities, and Amarantha, now free and with new feelings, rejects her fiance's attentions.

Amazing Adventure of Alvin Allegretto, The, children's opera in one act by Bruce Adolphe; libretto (Eng) by Sarah Schlesinger. First performance January 27, 1995, New York, John Jay Theater, with Gregory Dolbashian (Alvin), Judith Engel, Adam Klein, Gregory Sheppard, and Laureen Vigil; conducted by Mel Marvin. Performed with the composer's *Marita and Her Heart's Desire.**

Alvin, a rebellious teenager in the town of Harmony, decides to go against the town's residents, all of whom sing, and talk instead. His actions create a scandal, of course, but he is saved at the end from being sent off to the Silence Academy for treatment when he sings.

The score contains citations from Mozart's *Don Giovanni.*
BIBLIOGRAPHY: Edward Rothstein, "Young Rebel with a Cause: He Doesn't Want to Sing," *NYT* (Jan. 31, 1995), C, 14 [on premiere].

Amber Witch, The, opera in four acts by Vincent Wallace; libretto (Eng) by Henry F. Chorley, after Wilhelm Meinhold's novel *Maria Schweidler, Die Bernsteinhexe*, translated by Lady Duff Gordon (1844). First performance February 28, 1861, London, Her Majesty's Theatre, with Euphrosyne Parepa (Mary), Miss Huddart (Elsie), Mr. Swift (Rudiger), and Charles Santley (the Commandant); conducted by Charles Hallé.

The setting is Pomerania. Mary, a young woman who collects amber, is accused of witchcraft, the community being roused by Elsie, servant to the Commandant, whose attentions Mary has rebuffed. Mary is saved from being burned at the stake by Count Rudiger, her beloved.
SCORE: vs (New York: William Hall, 1861).
LIBRETTO: English (London: Cramer, Beale, & Chappell, [1861]).
BIBLIOGRAPHY: Biddlecombe/*EO*, 136–37 (which lists Helen Lemmens-Sherrington in the role of Mary and Sims Reeves as Rudiger).

Ameer, The, comic opera in three acts by Victor Herbert; libretto (Eng) by Frederic Ranken and Kirke La Shelle. First performance October 9, 1899, Scranton, Pennsylvania, with Frank Daniels (Iffe Khan), Helen Redmond (Constance), George Devoll (Ralph Winston); repeated December 4, 1899, New York, Wallack's Theatre, with the same cast.

Iffe Khan, the ameer of Afghanistan, is searching for a wealthy wife in order to have the money to pay the annual tribute demanded by the British. He decides to marry Constance, an American girl; she, however, is in love with Ralph Winston, captain of the militia. The Westerners foil the ameer's plan, but he is consoled when he finds a rich native girl to wed instead.

For a detailed description, see Waters/*VH*, 161–62.
SCORE: vs (New York: M. Witmark, 1899).

Amelia, "a new English opera . . . after the Italian manner" by John Frederick Lampe; libretto (Eng) by Henry Carey. First performance March 13, 1732, London, Little Theatre in the Haymarket.

After the faithful Amelia's Hungarian husband, Prince Casimir, falls into the hands of the Turks, Amelia, disguised as a Turk, goes to save him. She is accompanied by a friend, Rodolpho, who aids in the rescue, but Casimir, once freed, believes that the two are having an affair and sentences them to death. Just as the sentences are to be carried out, Casimir has a change of heart.

For a detailed description, see Fiske/*ETM*, 133–34.

LIBRETTO: English (London: J. Watts, 1732).

Amelia, afterpiece in two acts by Charles Dibdin et al.; libretto (Eng) a revision of Richard Cumberland's text for *The Summer's Tale.** First performance December 14, 1771, London, Drury Lane Theatre.

Another version, with music by Piccinni and others, was published in 1768.

LIBRETTO: English (London: T. Becket, 1771).

Amelia Goes to the Ball, buffo opera in one act by Gian Carlo Menotti; libretto (It) by the composer, as *Amelia al ballo*. First performance, in an English translation by George Meade, April 1, 1937, Philadelphia, Curtis Institute, with Margaret Daum (Amelia), Conrad Mayo (the husband), William Martin (the lover), and Leonard Treash (the chief of police); conducted by Fritz Reiner.

In this satire, the flighty Amelia, getting ready for a ball, is interrupted by her husband, who has discovered that she has a lover. Determined to go to the ball anyway, she hits her husband over the head with a vase and tells the police chief, whom she has called, that the assailant was her lover. She then leaves for the ball, accompanied by the policeman.

Major roles: Amelia (sop); the husband (bar); the lover (ten); and the chief of police (bass).

For detailed plot synopses, see K/*KOB*, 1341–43; K/*NKOB*, 455–56; Eaton/*OP* I, 164–65.

SCORE: vs, Italian-English (Milan: Ricordi, 1938, 1952).

America (Amerika), tragicomedy in three acts by Ellis B. Kohs; libretto (Eng and Ger) by the composer, after Edwin Muir's translation of Kafka's novel (1927) and the dramatization by Max Brod. First performance May 19, 1970, Los Angeles (concert), Western Opera Theater.

The plot centers on Karl Rossmann, a native of Prague, who is sent to America to escape the scandal caused by his affair with a maid. In this country he is seduced by Clara, the daughter of Pollunder, a friend of Karl's uncle, Senator Edward Jacob. After running into two tramps, Robinson and Delamarche, Karl gets a good job at a hotel and falls in love with Therese, the secretary of the Hotel Manageress. He is unjustly fired, after machinations by Robinson, and is forced to leave his beloved Therese. He meets her again when he goes to work for a theater company, but the two are forced to part once more.

For a detailed description, see Eaton/*OP* II, 24–25.

Major roles: Karl Rossmann (ten), Robinson (ten), Delamarche (bar), Pollunder (bar), Senator Jacob (bass), Clara (sop); Therese (sop), and Hotel Manageress (mezzo).

Also set by R. Haubenstock-Ramati, as *Amerika* (1966, Berlin).

America, I Love You, comic opera in three acts by David Ahlstrom; libretto (Eng), after poems by E. E. Cummings. First performance January 6, 1981, New Orleans, Opera America; June 25, 1983, San Francisco.
SCORE: War Suite (nos. 9–12, act 1), ms score, holograph (1965, excerpts, signed photocopy, NYPL; 1980, photocopy, NYPL).
LIBRETTO: English, typescript (1980, photocopy, NYPL).

Americana, or, A New Tale of the Genii, "being an allegorical mask in five acts"; anonymous libretto (Eng). First performance February 9, 1798, Charleston, City Theatre.
    The patriotic work, dedicated to Thomas Jefferson, opens in the "Allegany Mountains" and contains among its characters Typhon, Hybla, Elutheria, and Americana.
LIBRETTO: English (Baltimore: W. Pechin, 1802).

Americana, or, A New Tale of the Genii, opera in four acts by Neely Bruce; libretto (Eng) by Tony Connor, after the masque of the same name (see previous entry). First performance April 1980, Middletown, Connecticut, Wesleyan University. Revived (concert) October 1985, New York, Symphony Space, Orchestra of New England, soloists from Wesleyan College; conducted by James Sinclair.
    In this allegory, Typhon, the spirit of tyranny, and Fastodio, the spirit of pride, oppose Elutheria, the spirit of liberty, and Americana, her protectress, who is aided by thirteen genii (representing the states). The figures of George Washington, Thomas Jefferson, and Benjamin Franklin also appear.
    The score includes snatches of battle symphonies and Handel operas, and elements of bluegrass and disco music.
BIBLIOGRAPHY: Jack Hiemenz, review, *HiFi/MA* XXXV (Oct. 1985), 21 [on revival].

American in London, An, musical entertainment by Benjamin Carr; libretto (Eng). First performance March 28, 1798, Philadelphia, New (Chestnut Street) Theatre.

American Romance. See **The Flapper.**

Americans, The, comic opera in three acts by Matthew King and John Braham; libretto (Eng) by Samuel J. Arnold. First performance April 27, 1811, London, Drury Lane Theatre.
    The work includes "The Death of Nelson."

American Triptych, An, three one-act operas by Stephen Douglas Burton; libretto (Eng) by the composer. Composed 1975:
    Maggie, after Stephen Crane;
    Dr. Heidegger's Experiment, after Nathaniel Hawthorne; and
    Benito Cereno, after Herman Melville.
First performance July 29, 1989, Alexandria, Virginia.

American Volunteer, The, opera in four acts by Felix Vinatieri; libretto (Eng) by the composer. Composed 1891, for 1893 Columbian World's Fair, Chicago. One act performed March 4, 1961, Yankton, South Dakota, Yankton College; conducted by Latien Weed.
    The story, a version of the Faust legend, has a soldier from Washington's army sell his soul to the devil to save himself from being disgraced. The soldier spends a century in hell but then awakens and leads a successful rebellion there.
    The composer, a graduate of the Naples Conservatory, was the bandmaster of General George Custer but did not accompany him on his doomed stand at Little Big Horn.

BIBLIOGRAPHY: James Boeringer, "Custer's Bandmaster's Opera," *NYT* (Mar. 26, 1961), II, 13.

Amiable Beast, The, opera in one act by George Welner; libretto (Eng) by the composer. First performance July 25, 1961, New York, Central Park Mall.

Amilie, or, The Love Test, "grand romantic opera" in three acts by William Michael Rooke (O'Rourke); libretto (Eng) by John Thomas Haines. Composed 1818. First performance December 2, 1837, London, Covent Garden. First U.S. performance October 15, 1838, New York, Park Theatre, with Jane Shirreff (Amilie).
    The heroine's actions, unknown to her, cause problems with her beloved, the Count.
LIBRETTO: English (Baltimore: J. Robinson, [1839?]).

Amintas, afterpiece, pastiche, an adaptation of George Rush's *The Royal Shepherd** (1764, London), with additional music by Samuel Arnold, Pietro Guglielmi, and Thomas C. Carter; libretto (Eng) by Ferdinando Tenducci, after Richard Rolt's text, an adaptation of Metastasio's *Il re pastore.* First performance December 15, 1769, London, Covent Garden.
LIBRETTO: English (London: T. Lowndes, 1769).

Amistad, opera in two acts by Anthony Davis; libretto (Eng) by Thulani Davis. Composed 1996. First performance November 29, 1997, Chicago, Lyric Opera, with Mark Doss (Cinque), Florence Quivar (Goddess of the Waters), and Thomas Young (the Trickster); conducted by Dennis Russell Davies; directed by George C. Wolfe.
    The setting is at sea in 1839 near the coast of Long Island. The slave ship *Amistad,* which has been used by Spanish slave traders to smuggle slaves illegally through Cuba, is discovered adrift. The African slaves aboard it have revolted against the Spanish crew, killing all but two members. The U.S. Navy jails the Africans and releases their hostages.
    The fate of the Africans is debated by the courts for almost three years, with Spain wishing to recover its "property" and a group of abolitionists suing for the Africans' freedom. John Quincy Adams argues their case before the Supreme Court, which the former president wins, and the navy is ordered to return the Africans to their home continent. Remaining behind is the omnipotent Trickster God, who has joined the slaves, led by Cinque.
    The work is scored for soloists and a largely male chorus, African percussion ensemble, and saxophone quartet.
    The same story was set as a movie, directed by Steven Spielberg (1997).
BIBLIOGRAPHY: Justin Davidson, "Slave Ship," *ON* (Oct. 1997), 38; Paul Griffiths, "Captives Who Confront Presidents and Gods," *NYT* (Dec. 1, 1997), E, 1, 7 [on premiere].

Amoroso, King of Little Britain, "serio-comick bombastick operatick interlude" (burlesque) in one act by Thomas S. Cooke; libretto (Eng) by James R. Planché. First performance April 21, 1818, London, Drury Lane Theatre.
LIBRETTO: English (London: R. White, 1818).

Amorous Judge, The, comic opera by Eric Gross; libretto (Eng) by Len McGlashan, after Heinrich Kleist's *Der zerbrochene Krug* (1811). First performance April 2, 1965, Sydney, Australia, with Alan Light (Adam).

Adam, a village judge, gets into trouble when he becomes the focus of a suit brought by a woman whose jug he had broken while trying to escape from an unsuccessful romantic tryst.

Other settings include *Der zerbrochene Krug* by F. Geissler (1971, Leipzig).

SCORE: ms vs, holograph (National Library of Australia, 1964).

Amphitryon 4, comic opera in three acts by Harold Blumenfeld; libretto (Eng) by the composer, after Molière's *Amphitryon* (1668). Composed 1962.

A treatment of the Amphitryon legend, in which, in order to get his way with Amphitryon's wife, Alcmene, Jupiter takes on the appearance of her husband. When the real husband appears, trouble results.

Other settings include Grétry's opera (1786, Versailles); R. Kunad's musical comedy (1984, East Berlin); and operas by R. Oboussier (1951, East Berlin and Dresden) and H. Hermann. Dibdin's *Jupiter and Alcmena** (1781, London) is a setting of the legend after Dryden's text.

SCORE: ms, orchestral excerpts (1962, photocopy, Belwin-Mills, N.Y.).

Amy Robsart, opera in three acts by Isadore de Lara; libretto (Fr) by Paul Milliet, after Augustus Harris's original English text, based on Scott's *Kenilworth* (1821). First performance July 20, 1893, London, Covent Garden, in French. First English performance May 14, 1920, London, Grand Croydon.

A setting of the Scott tale, in which Robert Dudley, Earl of Leicester, ignores and then kills his wife, Amy Robsart, in order to become consort to Queen Elizabeth I.

Another setting of the story is B. O. Klein's *Kenilworth* (1895, Hamburg).

LIBRETTO: French (Milliet's version—Paris: Choudens, 1894).

Anachronism, The, opera in one act by Arnold Franchetti; libretto (Eng) by E. R. Mills. First performance March 4, 1956, Hartford, Connecticut, Hartt College of Music.

Ancient Britons, The, opera in one act by Thomas German Reed; libretto (Eng) by Gilbert A. A'Beckett. First performance January 25, 1875, London, St. George's Hall.

And David Wept, opera in eleven sections by Ezra Laderman; libretto (Eng) by Joe Darion. First performance April 10, 1971, New York, CBS television. First stage performance May 31, 1980, New York, 92nd Street Y, with Howard Bender (David), Annie Lynn Bornstein (Bathsheba), and Kenneth Bell (Uriah); conducted by Amy Kaiser.

The story focuses on the tale of David and Bathsheba and emphasizes the character of Uriah the Hittite, Bathsheba's wronged husband. The tale is told through a mix of song and spoken recitation.

SCORE: vs (New York: Oxford University Press, 1971).

BIBLIOGRAPHY: Nicholas Kenyon, "Musical Events," *NY* LVI (June 16, 1980), 98–100 [on stage premiere]; Herbert Kupferberg, "New York," *MA* (1981), 23–24.

And the Walls Came Tumbling Down, opera in one act by Willard Roosevelt; libretto (Eng) by Lofton Mitchell. First performance March 16, 1976, New York, Alice Tully Hall, with Max Bertrandt, Christopher Dean, Ruth Elmore, Keith Hawkins, and Betty Lane; conducted by Thomas Scherman.

The setting is New Amsterdam, 1664. A black preacher, Joshua, attempts to convince his community of free blacks to help the Dutch against the invading British. When the British are victorious, Hermann, fearing that he will become a slave once again, declares Joshua to be a traitor. On his way to his execution Joshua voices words of hope to Mary, his wife, and his other supporters.

For a description, see Kornick/*RAO*, 259–60.

Major roles: Joshua (bass), Mary (alto), and Hermann (bar).

BIBLIOGRAPHY: Robert Sherman, review, *NYT* (Mar. 18, 1976), 51 [on premiere].

Angel Face, opera in one act by Roger Ames; libretto (Eng) by Laura Harrington. First performance 1988, St. Paul, Minnesota.

Angelina, musical farce in two acts by Henry Rowley Bishop and Gesualdo (?) Lanza; libretto (Eng) by M. Goldsmith. First performance August 30, 1804, London, Theatre Royal.

Angel Levine, opera in one act by Elie Siegmeister; libretto (Eng) by Edward Mabley, after Bernard Malamud's story. First performance October 5, 1985, New York, 92nd Street Y, Kaufmann Auditorium, with Richard Frisch (Nathan Manischevitz), John Freeman-McDaniels (Angel Levine), and Molly Stark (Fanny Manischevitz); conducted by Amy Kaiser. Revival set for May 25, 1999, New York, Center for Contemporary Opera.

A down-on-his luck Jewish tailor, Nathan Manischevitz, sends away a black visitor, Alexander Levine, who claims to be a Jewish angel on probation. Overhearing the man's story, Nathan's dying wife, Fanny, convinces her husband to locate their potential savior. Nathan finds Levine in a Harlem nightclub and, enduring derision from the patrons, finally convinces Levine to help Fanny. When Nathan return home, he sees that Fanny is cured. A black feather floats from the sky, indicating that Levine has earned his wings.

The work contains elements of Hebrew chant, jazz, and gospel.

SCORE: vs (New York: Carl Fischer, 1985).

BIBLIOGRAPHY: Will Crutchfield, review, *NYT* (Oct. 7, 1985), C, 18 [on premiere].

Angelo, chamber opera in two acts by Alan Ridout; libretto (Eng) by J. Platt, after Quentin Blake (1970). First performance 1971, Canterbury.

Angelus, The, opera in a prologue and four acts by Edward Naylor; libretto (Eng) by Wilfrid Thornely. First performance January 27, 1909, London, Covent Garden.

Also opera by C. Gide (1834, Paris).

SCORE: vs (London: J. Ricordi, 1908).

Angle of Repose, opera by Andrew Imbrie; libretto (Eng) by Oakley Hall, after Wallace Stegner's novel. First performance November 6, 1976, San Francisco, San Francisco Opera, with Chester Ludgin (Lyman Ward) and Susanne Marsee (Shelly).

The story, told in flashbacks, focuses on three generations of Californians, from the opening of the West to the present. Lyman Ward, a historian, is suffering from a crippling disease. His wife, unable to deal with his condition, deserts him. After studying the history of his grandparents' lives in order to recount their tale, he finds that, because of their lack of understanding the importance of forgiveness, their existence was a series of unhappiness, betrayal, guilt, and tragic death. Determined not to end up like his grandparents, Lyman, first having refused to make amends with his repentant wife, accepts her return, an event welcomed by their daughter, Shelly, who has terminated an unsuccessful relationship and come to her father for support.

Major roles: Lyman Ward (bar) and Shelly (sop).

BIBLIOGRAPHY: review, "Imbrie's 'Angle' Has Debut on Coast," *NYT* (Nov. 9, 1976), 28.

Anna Karenina, opera in three acts by Iain Hamilton; libretto (Eng) by the composer, after Tolstoy's novel (1876). First performance May 7, 1981, London, Coliseum, with Lois McDonall (Anna), Geoffrey Pogson (Vronsky), and Geoffrey Chard (Karenin); conducted by Howard Williams. First U.S. performance March 1983, Los Angeles.

The opera treats the tragic tale of the ill-fated love between Anna and Vronsky, thwarted by Anna's husband and society. In the end, having lost any rights to her son and unable to obtain a divorce from Vronsky, she throws herself under a train.

For a detailed plot description, see K*INKOB*, 293–94.

Major roles: Anna (sop), Vronsky (ten), and Karenin (bar).

The story was also set by J. Hubay, as *Karenina Anna* (1923, Budapest); and I. Robbiani, as *Anna Karenina* (1924, Rome).

SCORE: vs (Bryn Mawr, Pa.: Presser, 1979).

BIBLIOGRAPHY: Noel Goodwin, "Hamilton's 'Anna Karenina,'" *Opera* (May 1981), 457–62; Edward Greenfield, "Iain Hamilton's 'Anna Karenina,'" *MA* XXXI (Oct. 1981), 28–29, 39 [on premiere]; Iain Hamilton, "Anna Karenina: An Operatic Vision," *MT* CXXII (1981), 295–97; Nicholas Kenyon, "Musical Events," *NY* (June 1, 1981), 126–28 [on premiere]; Andrew Porter, "Musical Events," *NY* LIX (Apr. 4, 1983), 92–96 [on U.S. premiere]; *ON* (June 1983), 42 [on U.S. premiere].

Anna Marguerita's Will, monodrama in one act by Robert Starer; libretto (Eng) by Gail Godwin. First performance February 6, 1981, New York, Workshop Theater.

Anne Boleyn, chamber opera in one act by Jeremy Beck; libretto (Eng) by the composer. First performance (concert) January 27, 1984, New York, Mannes College of Music. First stage performance June 27, 1985, New York, Golden Fleece.

The work covers the demise of King Henry VIII's ill-fated wife.

SCORE: vs, ms holography (1983, photocopy, NYPL).

Annette, adaptation by Charles Edward Horn of Rossini's *La gazza ladra* (1817, Milan). First performance July 6, 1822, Dublin, Theatre Royal.

Annette and Lubin, comic opera in one act by Charles Dibdin; libretto (Eng) by the composer, an adaptation of the text for Blaise's *Annette et Lubin* (1762, Paris) by Charles and Marie Favart and J. B. Lourdet de Santerre, after a story in Marmontel's *Contes moraux*. First performance October 2, 1778, London, Covent Garden, with Mrs. Farrell (Lubin).

Two cousins, Annette and Lubin, live quietly in a cabin on the banks of the Seine, unaware that the law does not permit them to live together without being married, and they cannot marry since they are related. When they are informed that they are violating the law, they get a special dispensation, with the help of the lord of the manor, to wed.

LIBRETTO: English (London: G. Kearsly, 1778).

Anniversary, The, unfinished opera in two acts by Ned Rorem; libretto (Eng) by Jascha Kessler. Composed ca. 1961.

Rorem's work of the same name for voice and piano, with words by Herbert Kubly, was written in 1946.

SCORE: ms, holograph, 1946 (for voice and piano, photocopy, NYPL).

Antigonae, opera-monodrama in one act by Meyer Kupferman; libretto (Eng) after Hölderlin's translation of Sophocles. First performance 1973, Stockbridge, Massachusetts, Lenox Art Center.

Antigone, radio opera in four scenes by John Joubert; libretto (Eng) by Rachel Trickett, after Sophocles. First performance July 21, 1954, London, BBC.

The plot concerns the tragedy of Oedipus' daughter Antigone, who defies the order of King Creon of Thebes by performing the burial rites for her brother Polyneices, who has been dishonored. The King sentences her to be buried alive, ignoring the pleas of his son Haemon, Antigone's husband. Rather than live without her, Haemon chooses to die with his wife. The blind prophet Tiresias informs the king of his fateful error and, grief-stricken, Creon hurries to the cave to prevent the deaths of the two; his efforts, however, are in vain.

The work has six singing parts, speaker, and chorus.

Antiquary, The, musical play in three acts by Henry Rowley Bishop; libretto (Eng) by Isaac Pocock and Daniel Terry, after Scott's novel of the same name (1816). First performance January 25, 1820, London, Covent Garden.

The work is set at the time of George III. Major Neville, a young officer, is in love with Isabella, the daughter of Sir Arthur Wardour, but her father forbids the union since Neville is thought to be illegitimate. He changes his name to Lovel and follows his beloved to Scotland, where he becomes friendly with the talkative antiquary Jonathan Oldbuck, a neighbor of Wardour. After saving Sir Arthur and his daughter from death and from the schemes of the dishonest Dousterwivel, Lovel turns out to be the son and heir of the earl of Glenallan. The story ends happily for the young lovers.

LIBRETTO: English (London: William Stockdale, 1820).

Antonio, lyrical opera by Silas Pratt; libretto (Eng). Composed 1870–1871. First performance (excerpts) 1874, Chicago, Farwell Hall.

Revised as *Lucille** (1887).

Antony and Cleopatra, opera in three acts by Louis Gruenberg; libretto (Eng) by the composer, after Shakespeare's play. Composed 1955. Revised 1958, 1961.

SCORE: ms fs, vs, holograph (1958, photocopies, NYPL).

Antony and Cleopatra, opera in three acts by Samuel Barber; libretto (Eng) by Franco Zeffirelli, after Shakespeare. First performance September 1, 1966, New York, Metropolitan Opera, with Leontyne Price (Cleopatra), Jess Thomas (Octavius Caesar), Justino Díaz (Antony), Rosalind Elias (Charmian), Mary Ellen Pracht (Octavia), and Ezio Flagello (Enobarbus); conducted by Thomas Schippers. Revised (shortened) version performed February 6, 1975, New York, Juilliard American Opera Center, with Ronald Hedlund (Antony), Esther Hinds (Cleopatra), Joseph McKee (Enobarbus), and Faith Esham (Charmian); conducted by James Conlon. First British performance (concert) March 27, 1982, London, Logan Hall, Abbey Opera.

Taking place in the Roman Empire from 41 to 31 B.C., the story revolves around Antony and Cleopatra and their famous love affair. Antony, who has fallen in love with the Egyptian queen, is forced to return to Rome and wed Octavia, sister of the Roman ruler Octavius Caesar. Antony flees back to Cleopatra, whereupon Octavius attacks the forces of Antony and Cleopatra. When the lovers' troops are defeated, Antony kills himself, expiring in Cleopatra's arms, and Cleopatra dies from the bite of a poisonous asp to escape Octavius' vengeance.

For a detailed description, see Eaton/*OP* II, 29–30; K/*NKOB*, 20–21.

Major roles: Antony, a Roman general (bar); Cleopatra, Queen of Egypt (sop); Octavius (ten); Charmian, Cleopatra's attendant (mezzo); and Enobarbus, a friend of Antony (bass).

The opera was commissioned specifically for the opening of the new Metropolitan Opera House in 1966 at Lincoln Center, and its leading roles were performed by American singers. The premiere was attended by numerous dignitaries, including Lady Bird Johnson, then the First Lady. Despite all the hoopla and high hopes for the work, production problems on opening night, including bulky sets and costumes and poor acoustics, detracted from its effectiveness. These difficulties, combined with lukewarm reviews, contributed to its removal from the repertory. Typical was Harold Schonberg's opening-night comments: "Almost everything about the evening, artistically speaking, failed in total impact. . . . The production was a hybrid . . . [and] Mr. Barber's score also is something of a hybrid—neither fully traditional nor fully modern" (*NYT* [Sept. 17, 1966]), 16).

After the work's poor reception it was revised by Barber and Gian Carlo Menotti, resulting in a substantially streamlined version, both musically and textually, which concentrates more on the title characters and has the beautiful love duet "Oh Take, Oh Take Those Lips Away." This version, first performed in 1975, was it was treated more kindly. Two other numbers from the opera, for soprano and orchestra, are occasionally performed in concert: "Give Me Some Music" and "The Death of Cleopatra." They are known as Two Scenes, Op. 40.

Among the numerous settings of the story of Antony and Cleopatra are those by J. Mattheson (1704, Hamburg); K. H. Graun (1742, Berlin); M. Morales (1891, Mexico City); A. Enna (1894, Copenhagen); J. Massenet (1914, Monte Carlo); H. K. Hadley (1920, New York); G. F. Malipiero (1938, Florence); and L. Gruenberg (1950; see previous entry).

SCORES: vs (New York: G. Schirmer, 1966); vs rev. version (New York: G. Schirmer, 1976).
BIBLIOGRAPHY: John Freeman and William Mayer, "The Met's Double Christening," *Music Journal* (Oct. 1966), 23–25; Barbara B. Heyman, "The Second Time Around," *ON* LVI (Dec. 7, 1991), 56–57; Irving Kolodin, "Barber's 'Antony,' after Zeffirelli," *Saturday Review* (Oct. 1, 1966), 35–36 [on premiere]; Robert Jacobson, "New York," *ON* XXXIX (Apr. 5, 1975), 36–37 [on rev. version].
DISCOGRAPHY: E. Hinds, J. Wells, Westminster Choir, Spoleto Festival Orch.; cond. C. Badea, New World NW 322/4 (3 LPs); rev. John W. Freeman, "Records," *ON* XLIX (Nov. 1984), 64; available on 2 CDs as 322/24–2.

Apache Dance, opera in one act by Joseph Fennimore; libretto (Eng) by the composer, after James Purdy. First performance January 4, 1975, New York, Lincoln Center.

Apollo and Daphne, masque by John Pepusch; libretto (Eng) by John Hughes. First performance January 12, 1716, London, Drury Lane Theatre, with Margherita de L'Epine (Apollo).

Other English settings include the pantomime by Henry Carey and Richard Jones (1725, London); John Galliard (pantomime, 1726, London); Lewis Theobald, librettist (entertainment, 1726, London); Nicolo Pasquali (masque, 1749, London); and James Hook (opera, 1773; see next entry).
SCORE: ms (London: Royal College of Music).
LIBRETTO: English (London: Jacob Tonson, 1716).

Apollo and Daphne, serenata by James Hook; libretto (Eng) by John Hughes. First performance September 27, 1773, London, Marylebone Gardens.

Apollo and Persephone, comic opera in one act by Gerald Cockshott; libretto (Eng) by the composer. First performance October 14, 1954, Intimate Opera Company, Kirkwall, Scotland. First U.S. performance February 22, 1956, New York, Finch College Auditorium, After Dinner Opera Company.

The young Persephone, daughter of the goddess Demeter, is pursued by Pluto. She is saved by Apollo, who, dressed as a shepherd, convinces Pluto that Persephone is not worth the effort. Apollo woos Persephone himself and convinces her to marry him.

For a detailed description, see Eaton/*OP* II, 247–48.

Major roles: Persephone (sop), Apollo (ten), Pluto (bass-bar), and Demeter (alto).
SCORE: vs (New York: Broude, 1969).
BIBLIOGRAPHY: Harold Schonberg, "Three One-Act Operas," *NYT* (Feb. 23, 1956), 33 [on U.S. premiere].

Apollonia, melodrama in two acts by Robert Starer; libretto (Eng) by Gail Godwin. First performance May 22, 1979, St. Paul, Minnesota, Minnesota Opera Workshop. Revived May 3, 1990, Brooklyn, New York, Brooklyn College Opera Theater.

Mindful of having caused the death of a young man who played her lover in a performance, Apollonia assists Mrs. Everett, the type of woman Apollonia once hoped to become. She also helps Marius, an opera singer who has lost his desire to sing. When he regains his ambition and begins to sing again, he separates from Apollonia, who has become his lover, saying he must achieve his success on his own. Driven to the point of suicide, Apollonia changes her mind and realizes that she must live for herself.

Major roles: Apollonia (sop) and Marius (bar).
For a detailed description, see Kornick/*RAO*, 296–97.

Apology of Bony Anderson, The, opera in one act by Barry Conyngham; libretto (Eng) by Murray Copland. First performance September 1, 1978, Melbourne, Australia, University of Melbourne. Revised as *Bony Anderson*, June 30, 1979, Sydney.

Roles: Bony (bar), convict (ten), judge (ten), and lady (mezzo).
The work is scored for chamber ensemble.

Apparition, The, "musical dramatic romance" in two acts by William Reeve; libretto (Eng) by James C. Cross, after Ann Ward Radcliffe's novel *The Sicilian Romance, or, The Apparition of the Cliffs*. First performance September 3, 1794, London, Little Theatre.
SCORE: vs (London: Preston & Son, 1794).
LIBRETTO: English (London: J. Barker, 1794).

Appointment, The, television opera by Wilfred Josephs; libretto (Eng) by Bernard Kops. First performance 1968, BBC.

April Day, all-sung burletta in three acts by Samuel Arnold; libretto (Eng) by Kane O'Hara. First performance August 22, 1777, London, Little Theatre in the Haymarket.
LIBRETTO: English (London: T. Cadell, 1778).

Arabesque, opera in one act by Robert Marek; libretto (Eng) by Wayne Knutson. First performance April 14, 1967, Vermillion, South Dakota, University of South Dakota.

The work is written for soprano, mezzo, three baritones, and speaking part.

Arcadia, or, The Shepherd and the Shepherdess, opera by John Harroway; libretto (Eng) by Edward Blanchard. First performance April 19, 1841, London, Grecian Theatre.

Arcadia, or, The Shepherd's Wedding, all-sung dramatic pastoral in one act by John Stanley; libretto (Eng) by Robert Lloyd. First performance October 26, 1761, London, Covent Garden. Revived 1986, London, BBC broadcast.

Composed for the wedding of George III to Queen Charlotte.

The king was represented by the character of the shepherd Thyrsis, a nonsinging role.

LIBRETTO: English (London: J. and R. Tonson, 1761).

Arcadian Nuptials, The, all-sung masque by Thomas Augustine Arne. First performance January 20, 1764, London, Covent Garden, with Miss Hallam.

The piece was written for the marriage of Princess Augusta and the Prince of Brunswick.

SCORE: English, in *A Favourite Collection of Songs* (London: J. Walsh, 1764); repr. (Wyton, Huntingdon, Cambs., England: King's Music, [1989?]).

Arcadian Pastoral, The, pastoral opera in five acts by William Beckford; libretto (Eng) by Lady Craven. First performance April 13, 1782, London, Queensbury House, with Giusto Ferdinando Tenducci, Venanzio Rauzzini, and Gasparo Pacchierotti.

For a description of the performance, see Fiske/*ETM*, 439–40.

Revived as *The Descent of Belinda*, February 13, 1955, London, BBC.

Archers, The, or, The Mountaineers of Switzerland, opera in three acts by Benjamin Carr; anonymous libretto (Eng) after *Helvetic Liberty, or, The Lass of the Lakes*, "an opera in three acts by a Kentish bowman," inspired by Schiller's *Wilhelm Tell* (1804). First performance April 18, 1796, New York, John Street Theatre, with Mrs. Hodgkinson (Cecily), Mr. Hallam (Conrad), Mr. Hodgkinson (Tell), Mrs. Melmoth (Tell's wife), Miss Harding (their young son), Mr. Hallam Jr. (Werner Staffach), Mr. Johnson (Walter Furst), Mr. Tyler (Arnold Melchthal), Miss Broadhurst (Rhodolpha), Mr. Cleveland (Gesler), Mr. Jefferson (Gesler's lieutenant), and Mr. King (Leopold).

A treatment of the William Tell legend, this ballad opera is set in Altdorf. Cecily is a basket seller in love with the street vendor Conrad. When the Austrian army needs more soldiers, an Austrian lieutenant looks for young Swiss men to be pressed into military service, and among his victims is Conrad. William Tell, meanwhile, plans to resist. Various leaders of the Swiss Archers, Werner Staffach, Walter Furst, and Arnold Melchthal, also plan ways to combat the impressment. Tell, after instructing the citizenry to fight, is arrested and faces execution by order of the wicked Gesler. The tyrant is about to have the execution carried out when learns that the Austrian ruler, Leopold, has died. Gesler offers to spare Tell's life on one condition, that the archer shoot an apple off his young son's head. Gesler nonetheless reneges on his promise and takes Tell away by boat across the lake. A storm comes up and buffets the vessel, allowing Tell to escape, after he has shot Gesler. Tell then leads the Swiss against the Austrian army, and the lovers Rhodolpha, daughter of Furst, and Melchthal sing of their admiration for the Swiss hero.

For a detailed description, see Sonneck/*SIMG*, 465–73.

The work contains among its airs "Why, Huntress, Why?" It is the first American opera from which music survives (two numbers).

Other settings of this story include Grétry's *Guillaume Tell* (1791, Paris); and Rossini's opera, with the same title (1829, Paris).

LIBRETTO: as *Helvetic Liberty*, English (London: L. Wayland, 1792).

Architect, The, chamber opera by David McIntyre; libretto (Eng) by Tom Cone. First performance June 11, 1994, Vancouver, Vancouver Opera, Playhouse Theatre, with Gloria Parker (Sandra), Valdine Anderson (Madeline), John Fanning (Julian), and André Clouthier (Even); conducted by Leslie Uyeda; produced by Kelly Robinson.

In this symbolic tale the architect of the title is the successful Sandra, whose stable life with Julian, her lover, and Madeline, his sister and her best friend, is thrown into confusion after she meets Even, a scavenger, while she walks on the beach. After their encounter she tries to renounce her corporate life, which results in the efforts of Julian and his sister to destroy Even, whom they see as a threat to their well-being.

BIBLIOGRAPHY: F. B. St. Clair, "Vancouver," *ON* LIX (Dec. 10, 1994), 54–55 [on premiere].

archy and mehitabel, "a back-alley opera" in two acts by George Kleinsinger; libretto (Eng) by Joe Darion and Mel Brooks, after the comic strip by Don Marquis. First performance (concert) December 6, 1954, New York, Town Hall, Little Orchestra Society, with Jonathan Anderson (archy), Mignon Dunn (mehitabel), Richard Sharretts (bill), the Four Heathertones—Bix Brent, Marianne McCormick, Nancy Swain Overtone, and Jean Swain (alley cats); conducted by Thomas Scherman. First stage performance April 13, 1957, New York, Broadway Theatre, as *Shinbone Alley*, with Eartha Kitt (mehitabel) and Eddie Bracken (archy).

The story comes from a comic strip with a talkative cockroach, archy, who types but is unable to produce capital letters, and a cat, mehitabel, as its main characters.

BIBLIOGRAPHY: Howard Taubman, "Opera: archy and mehitabel," *NYT* (Dec. 7, 1954), 45 [on premiere].

DISCOGRAPHY: C. Channing, E. Bracken, D. Wayne; cond. G. Kleinsinger, Columbia OL 4963 (1955) (1 LP, mono).

Arden Must Die, opera in two acts by Alexander Goehr; libretto (Ger) by Erich Fried, after an anonymous sixteenth-century play, *Arden of Faversham*; English version by Geoffrey Skelton. First performance, in German, as *Arden muss sterben*, March 5, 1967, Hamburg, Staatsoper, with Toni Blankenheim (Arden), Kerstin Meyer (Alice Faversham), and Manfred Schenk (Black Will); conducted by Charles Mackerras. First British performance April 17, 1974, London, Sadler's Wells; conducted by Meredith Davies.

The opera is set around Faversham and London in the sixteenth century and concerns Arden, a rich entrepreneur, whose dealings have filled many people with the desire to kill him. The third attempt on his life is made by Shakebag and Black Will, employed by Arden's wife, and the two landowners Greene and Reede, whose fortunes were ruined by Arden. The plotters succeed but are caught by the police.

Major roles: Arden, a rich businessman (bass); Alice Faversham, Arden's wife (mezzo); Shakebag (ten) and Black Will (bass), both employees of Alice; Greene, a landowner (bar); and Reede, a landowner (bass).

SCORE: vs English-German (London: Schott and New York: Associated Music Publishers, 1967).
BIBLIOGRAPHY: Christopher Shaw, "'Arden Must Die,'" *Tempo* CX (Sept. 1974), 42–43 [on British premiere]; John Warrack, "Goehr's New Opera," *Opera* XVIII (1967), 369–71.

Argonauts, The, "California tetralogy" by Quinto Maganini, composed ca. 1937. The work concerns the California gold rush and consists of:
I. *Prologue*; 1850, at Sutter's mill.
   Major roles: Singing Sue (sop), Sacramento Sadie (mezzo), Loran (ten), Plem (bass-bar), Larry (ten), Kentucky Jack (bar), Tennessee (bar), Tennessee's partner (ten), and Maria (sop).
II. *Tennessee's Partner*, in two acts; 1854; first performance May 28, 1942, New York, WOR radio.
   Major roles: the judge (bass-bar); the stranger (ten); Tennessee (bar); Dungaree Jack (ten); Bill, the sheriff (bass); Folinsbee (bar); and Tennessee's partner (ten).
III. *The Discovery at Dead Horse Gulch*; 1856.
   Major roles: Larry, a prospector (ten); and Kentucky Jack, a prospector (bass).
IV. *Christmas at Angels*; interior of the Blazing Star, Christmas Eve, 1855.
   Major roles: Pedro (bar), Singing Sue (sop), Plem (bass-bar), Sacramento Sadie (mezzo), Loran (ten), and Maria (sop).
SCORE: vs (New York: Edition Musicus, 1937).

Aria da Capo, opera by Burdette Fore; libretto (Eng), after Edna St. Millay's play. First performance May 19, 1951, Stockton, California, College of the Pacific.

Aria da Capo, opera in one act by Cardon Burnham; libretto (Eng), after Millay. First performance April 17, 1955, New Orleans, Tulane University.

Aria da Capo, chamber opera in one act by Allan Blank; libretto (Eng), after Millay. Composed 1958–1960.
   The anti-war plot focuses on the deadly rivalry between Corydon and Thyrsis.
   Roles: Columbine (sop), Pierrot (ten), Thyrsis (ten), Corydon (bar), and Cothurnus (bass).

Aria da Capo, opera in one act by Robert Baksa; libretto (Eng) by the composer, after Millay. First performance February 6, 1968, New York. Revived May 11, 1981, Philadelphia, Academy of Vocal Arts.
   As in Richard Strauss's *Ariadne*, serious and comic works clash in this tale about performers. The work opens with Pierrot and Columbine preparing to present a comedy. They are interrupted by the Stage Director, who insists that his pastoral tragedy, which features the shepherds Corydon and Thyrsis, take place also. The shepherds begin to quarrel and end up killing each other. Pierrot and Columbine then resume their comedy.
   For a detailed description, see Summers/*OOA*, 23–24.
   Major roles: Columbine (sop), Pierrot (ten), Corydon (ten), Thyrsis (bar), and Stage Director (bass).
   Also set by John Bilotta (not perf.).

Ariadne Abandoned by Theseus in the Isle of Naxos, melodrama by Victor Pelissier; libretto (Eng) after J. J. C. Brandes's setting for Benda's *Ariadne auf Naxos* (1775, Gotha). First performance April 26, 1797, New York.

Ariadne, having helped Theseus escape from the Minotaur's lair on Crete, falls in love with Theseus. She takes refuge with him on Naxos, but Theseus feels that he must return to his home in Greece and leaves the sleeping Ariadne. When she learns that Theseus has abandoned her and that her only redemption can be through death, she climbs a cliff and, struck by lightning, falls to her death.

Ariadne Deserted by Theseus and Found and Courted by Bacchus, "a dramatick piece a[da]pted for recitative musick"; music and libretto (Eng) by Richard Flecknoe. Although the libretto was published in 1654, there is no known performance.

This work, which was all sung, seems to be the first English opera, supplanting the claim of William Davenant's *Siege of Rhodes** (1656) for that honor.

The music itself is lost. The subject was a popular one (see following list).

The many settings of the Ariadne story include C. Monteverdi's *Arianna* (1608, Mantua); *Adriane* by J. S. Kusser (1692, Brunswick); *Ariane, ou, Le mariage de Bacchus* by R. Cambert and L. Grabu (1674, London); *Ariadne* by J. G. Conradi (1691, Hamburg); R. Keiser's arrangement, as *Die betrogene und nachmals vergötterte Ariadne* (1722, Hamburg); *Arianna in Nasso* by N. Porpora (1733, London) and Leo (1729), and by G. F. Handel, as *Arianna in Creta* (1734, London); G. Benda's duodrama *Ariadne auf Naxos* (1775, Gotha); J. Massenet's *Ariane* (1906, Paris); R. Strauss's *Ariadne auf Naxos* (1912, Stuttgart; 2d version 1916, Vienna); D. Tovey's *The Bride of Dionysus** (1929, Edinburgh); B. Martinů's *Ariadne* (1961, Gelsenkirchen, to a French text); and A. Goehr, as *Arianna* (1995, London, to Rinuccini's Italian text).
LIBRETTO: English (London: n.p., [1654]).

Armo[u]rer, The, comic opera by Captain Warner; libretto (Eng) by Richard Cumberland. First performance April 4, 1793, London, Covent Garden.
LIBRETTO: English, songs and choruses (London: Printed for C. Dilly, 1793).

Armor of Life, The, lyric opera in one act by Kenneth Newbern; libretto (Eng). First performance February 26, 1957, New York, Carl Fischer Hall.

Armourer of Nantes, The, "grand romantic opera" in three acts by Michael Balfe; libretto (Eng) by John Vipon Bridgeman, after Hugo's *Marie Tudor* (1833). First performance February 12, 1863, London, Covent Garden, with Louisa Pyne (Marie), W. Harrison (Raoul), and Charles Santley (Fabio).

The story takes place in late fifteenth-century Nantes, unlike the Hugo original. It concerns the poor Raoul, an armorer, who loves Marie, whom he has raised since she was an infant. Her happiness is threatened by the evil Fabio Fabiani, who plots to ruin her reputation and thereby cover up her noble heritage.

For a detailed description, see Biddlecombe/*EO*, 32–33.
SCORE: ms fs, mostly autograph (1863, British Library, Add. MS. 29363, 29364).
LIBRETTO: English (London: [Royal English Opera, 1863]).

Arrangement, The, television opera in one act by Carl Davis; libretto (Eng) by Leo Lehman. First performance May 30, 1965, London, BBC television.
BIBLIOGRAPHY: A. Blyth, review, *Opera* XVI (July 1965), 539 [on premiere].

Arrived at Portsmouth, operatic drama in two acts by William Shield; libretto (Eng) by William Pearce. First performance October 30, 1794, London, Covent Garden. Performed in one act January 13, 1796, London.

According to the libretto, the story bears a slight resemblance to the history of Howe's victory of June 1, 1794.

LIBRETTO: English (London: T. N. Longman, 1794).

Arsinoe, Queen of Cyprus, opera in three acts by Thomas Clayton; libretto (Eng) by P. A. Motteux, after the Italian libretto by T. Stanzani, set by P. Franceschini (1676, Bologna). First performance January 16, 1705, London, Drury Lane Theatre.

As the work opens, Arsinoe, the Queen, asleep in a garden, is saved from assassination by one of her generals, Ormondo. He again prevents her from being killed by Dorisbe, his former lover. Through trickery Arsinoe is made to believe that Ormondo, with whom she has fallen in love, has betrayed her, and she throws him into prison. When Ormondo talks in his sleep, Dorisbe, who had gained entrance into his cell, discovers that he not only is innocent of any betrayal but is really Pelops, son of the Athenian king. When he refuses to give her his love, she tries to kill herself. She survives, and Ormondo and Arsinoe are reunited.

For a detailed account, see Fiske/*ETM*, 32–33.

Major roles: Arsinoe (sop), Ormondo (counterten), and Dorisbe (sop).

This was the first all-sung English opera in the Italian style and was reviled in the decades that followed its premiere by people such as Burney because of its Italianate nature.

SCORE: vs (London: I. Walsh, 1706).

Artaxerxes, serious opera in three acts by Thomas Augustine Arne; libretto (Eng) by the composer, after P. Metastasio. First performance February 2, 1762, London, Covent Garden, with Charlotte Brent (Mandane), Miss Thomas (Semira), Giusto Ferdinando Tenducci (Arbace), Nicolo Peretti (Artaxerxes), John Beard (Artabanes), and George Mattocks (Rimenes). Revised version by Henry Rowley Bishop, September 23, 1813, London, Covent Garden. First U.S. performance January 31, 1828 (with new orchestrations by Charles E. Horn), New York. Revived March 14, 1962, London, St. Pancreas Town Hall, with Heather Harper (Arbace), Barbara Holt (Mandane), John Stoddart (Artabanes), and Johanna Peters (Artaxerxes); conducted by Charles Farncombe.

The story involves Arbace, son of Artabanes; Arbace has been sent into exile for falling in love with Mandane, daughter of King Serse and sister of Artaxerxes. Serse is then killed by Artabanes, but Arbace is accused of the crime. Artaxerxes becomes the new king; he is in love with Semira, Arbace's sister. Arbace saves Artaxerxes from Artabanes's machinations, and Artaxerxes then exiles Artabanes, marries Semira, and allows Arbace to wed Mandane.

Arne's highly popular work was the only serious English opera of its time that was successful. It is a blend of Italian and English elements, with recitative instead of spoken dialogue. Two noteworthy arias are "The Soldier Tir'd" and "Fly Soft Ideas," both sung by Mandane.

For a detailed musical description, see Fiske/*ETM*, 305–13.

Major roles: Artaxerxes (alto), Artabanes (ten), Arbace (sop), Rimenes (ten), Mandane (sop), and Semira (sop).

The first setting of the Metastasio text was by L. Vinci (1730, Rome); the many other settings include those by J. A. Hasse (1730, Venice); Gluck (1741, Milan); C. H. Graun (1743, Berlin); D. Terradellas (1744, Venice); G. Scarlatti (1747, Lucca); N. Jommelli (1749, Rome); B. Galuppi (1749, Vienna); J. C. Bach (1761, Turin); N. Piccinni (1762, Rome); A. Sacchini (1768, Rome); G. Paisiello (1771, Modena); D. Cimarosa (1784, Turin); P. Anfossi (1788, Rome); N. A. Zingarelli (1789, Trieste); G. Andreozzi (1789, Livorno); and N. Isouard (1794, Florence).

SCORE: ms fs, autograph, rev. by Bishop (1831, British Museum, MS. Add. 33308, 33309); vs (London: Harrison & Co., 178-?, 1797?; Huntingdon, Cambs: King's Music, [1987?]).
LIBRETTO: English (London: J. & R. Tonson, 1761; repr. ed., introd. William Gillis [Los Angeles: University of California, 1963]).
BIBLIOGRAPHY: Charles Farncombe, "Arne and 'Artaxerxes,'" *Opera* XIII (1962), 159–61 [the same issue has a review by Julian Herbage, 333–34, on the 1962 revival].
DISCOGRAPHY: C. Bott, C. Robson, P. Spence, I. Partridge, R. Edgar-Wilson, Parley of Instruments; cond. R. Goodman, Hyperion CDA 67051/2.

Artifice, The, comic opera in three acts by Michael Arne, libretto (Eng) by William Augustus Miles. First performance April 14, 1780, London, Drury Lane Theatre.
LIBRETTO: English (London: T. Cadell, 1780).

Ashoka's Dream, opera by Peter Lieberson; libretto (Eng) by Douglas Penick. First performance July 26, 1997, Santa Fe, Santa Fe Opera, with Kurt Ollmann (Ashoka), Greer Grimsley (prime minister), and Lorraine Hunt (Triraksha); conducted by Richard Bradshaw; directed by Stephen Wadsworth.

This work is about the third-century B.C. Indian warrior king Ashoka Maurya and his attempts to unify India. Ashoka is transformed from a hostile, isolated young warrior to an enlightened ruler after he follows the advice of his exiled first wife, Lakshmi. The unscrupulous second wife, Triraksha, tries to ensure that her son will become the next ruler by blinding Lakshmi's son, but Ashoka exiles her and designates his now blind son as his heir.
BIBLIOGRAPHY: Patrick J. Smith, "Santa Fe," *ON* LXII (Nov. 1997), 59–60 [on premiere].

Aspern Papers, The, opera in two acts by Philip Hagemann; libretto (Eng) by the composer, after Henry James's novella (1888). First performance December 4, 1980, Bloomington, Indiana. Also November 19, 1988, Evanston, Illinois, Northwestern University.

The plot concentrates on the relationship of Miss Tina and Henry Jonson, a critic.
For a description, see Kornick/*RAO*, 131–32.
Major roles: Henry Jonson (bar) and Miss Tina (sop).
SCORE: vs (New York: American Music Center, 1988).

Aspern Papers, The, opera in two acts by Dominick Argento; libretto (Eng) by the composer, after James. First performance November 19, 1988, Dallas, Music Hall, Dallas Opera, with Elisabeth Söderström (Juliana), Frederica von Stade (Tina), Richard Stilwell (the Lodger), Neil Rosenshein (Aspern), Eric Halfvarson (Barelli), and Katherine Ciesinski (Sonia); conducted by Nicola Rescigno. Revived February, 2, 1990, Washington, D.C., Washington Opera, with Pamela South (Juliana), Katherine Ciesinski (Tina), Robert Orth (the Lodger), David Kuebler (Aspern), Eric Halfvarson (Barelli), and Susan Graham (Sonia); conducted by Philip Brunelle.

The plot concerns the Lodger, biographer of a dead composer, Aspern, who takes a room at the Italian villa of Juliana Bordereau, a former opera singer and onetime mistress of Aspern. The Lodger is searching for the composer's missing score of an opera based on the Medea legend, a score that Juliana has hidden.

In an attempt to unearth the music the Lodger befriends the singer's lonely niece, Tina. When he fails in his quest, he leaves her, and the opera closes with the niece's tearing off each page of the elusive score and hurling the music into the fireplace. Throughout the unfolding of the plot, the scenes switch between 1895, the present time, and 1835, when Juliana had her affair with Aspern.

Musically, the work is written in a conservative style (the brief section of twelve-tone music being the exception); its highlights include a sextet of the various lovers.

Story also set by S. Sciarrino, as *Aspern* (1978, Florence).

BIBLIOGRAPHY: Charles Jahant, "Washington, D.C.," *ON* LIV (Apr. 14, 1990), 50 [on 1990 revival]; James Helme Sutcliffe, "The Argento Papers," *ON* (Nov. 1988), 14–16, 18; Patsy Swank, "In Review," *ON* LIII (Feb. 18, 1989), 38 [on premiere].

SCORE: vs (New York: Boosey & Hawkes, 1991).

LIBRETTO: English (New York: Boosey & Hawkes, 1988?).

Asses' Ears, opera for children in three scenes by Hugo Cole; libretto (Eng) by the composer. First performance December 12, 1950, London, Wimbledon, Rokeby School.

As punishment for refusing the decision of Timolus that Apollo, the god of music, plays the pipes better than King Midas and Pan, Midas is forced to grow asses' ears. Midas hides his new appendages under his crown until he has to go to the barber, who reveals the secret to everyone.

SCORE: vs (London: Novello, [1953]).

Atalanta (Acts of God), multimedia/television opera in three anecdotes by Robert Ashley; libretto (Eng) by the composer. First performance November 1982, Paris. First U.S. performance January 5, 1983, New York, Marymount Manhattan Theater.

The "plot" concerns the enactment of a bank holdup, with references to the Judgment of Paris and the myth of Atalanta, specifically, the race with the golden apples and Aphrodite's curse to turn the lovers into leopards. Atalanta becomes the Odalisque and is courted by three suitors who represent the three original apples: Max Ernst, the painter; Willard Reynolds, a shaman storyteller; and Bud Powell, a concert pianist.

Revised as part of a trilogy:

Requirements of Desire M (1989)

Wuh . . . Mountain Country Courtship (1991)

Odalisque B with Leopards (1988).

BIBLIOGRAPHY: Dominic Gill, "'Atalanta,'" *Opera* XXXVIII (June 1987), 692–93; John Rockwell, "Opera: Uptown Foray in 'Lovely Music' Unit," *NYT* (Jan. 7, 1983), C, 18 [on U.S. premiere].

DISCOGRAPHY: R. Ashley, T. Buckner, J. Humbert, C. Tato, "B." G. Tyranny (kbds), P. Shorr (electronics), Lovely VR–3301 (1985, Rome, 3 LPs, reissued as 2 CDs); rev. John Rockwell, "Myth Inspires Operas 250 Years Apart," *NYT* (Oct. 27, 1985), II, 21, 33.

Atalanta Strategy, multiprojector program for stage and broadcast media by Robert Ashley and Lawrence Brickman; libretto (Eng). First performance 1985, Montreal.

A revision of the music of the preceding entry, including the anecdotal material of the second episode, "Willard," about a character born in the mountains of Tennessee.

VIDEO: R. Vance, W. Dafoe, R. Ashley, Lovely Music (1984, New York).

Athalia, grand opera in a prologue and three acts by Harry Lawrence Freeman; libretto (Eng) by the composer. Composed 1916. First performance 1923, New York.

Athaliah, opera in two acts by Hugo Weisgall; libretto (Eng) by Richard Franko Goldman, after Racine's play *Athalie* (1691). First performance (concert) February 17, 1964, New York, Philharmonic Hall, Little Orchestra Society, with Shirley Verrett (Athaliah), Irene Jordan (Yehosheba), and John Reardon (Yehoyada); conducted by Thomas Scherman; directed by Edwin Levy.

The story, set in biblical times, concerns Athaliah, the murderous daughter of Ahab and Jezebel and widow of Jehoram. After her son is killed, she accedes to the throne by murdering all the princes of the house of David, but one, Joash, has been hidden and raised by Yehosheba, his aunt and wife of Yehoyada, the high priest. Athaliah is killed after Yehoyada proclaims Joash the true king.

Weisgall, in talking about his dissonant, partially twelve-tone work, said that he was aiming for a number opera "that would make extensive use of the chorus . . . . a 'frontal' work—one in which the singers simply turn to the audience and sing; an opera in which plot considerations would be of secondary importance" (see Bibliography).

Other settings of the Racine work include J. A. Peter Schulz's music for the play (1814, Munich); and J. N. Poissl's *Athalia* (1814, Munich).

SCORE: vs, choral excerpts (Bryn Mawr, Pa.: Theodore Presser, 1977).

BIBLIOGRAPHY: H. Wiley Hitchcock, "Current Chronicle. New York," *MQ* L (1964), 233–36 [on premiere]; Harold C. Schonberg, "Opera: World Premiere of 'Athaliah,'" *NYT* (Feb. 18, 1964), 28; Hugo Weisgall, "Birth of 'Athalia,' a New Opera," *NYT* (Feb. 16, 1964), II, 11.

Atlas, "an opera in three parts," music, choreography, and direction by Meredith Monk. First performance February 22, 1991, Houston, Wortham Center Cullen Theater, with Meredith Monk (Alexandra Daniels, aged twenty-five to forty), Robert Een and Chen Shi-Zheng (fellow travelers), and Ching Gonzalez and Allison Easter (guides); conducted by Wayne Hankin.

Taking as its inspiration the life of Alexandra David-Neel, an explorer, the story follows the attempts of Alexandra Daniels and several friends to find adventure and nirvana. They undergo life-threatening situations in the tropics, the Arctic, a desert, and a forest and find, ultimately, that the adventures lie within themselves. The work contains no sung text, with a sprinkling of spoken text interjected, and the singers are supported by repetitive instrumental accompaniment.

BIBLIOGRAPHY: Simi Horowitz, "Meredith Monk," *Opera Monthly* V (July 1, 1992), 17; Donna Perlmutter, "Houston," *ON* LV (June 1991), 46–47 [on premiere]; John Rockwell, "Opera: A Woman's Spiritual Journey in 'Atlas,'" *NYT* (June 10, 1991), C, 11, 16 [on Philadelphia performance]; Robert Weaver, "Spiritual Discovery," *ON* LV (Feb. 16, 1991), 8–11. DISCOGRAPHY: Chen Shi-Zhen, A. Easter, R. Een, C. Gonzalez, M. Monk; cond. W. Hankin, ECM Records (1992, 2 LPs).

At Last I've Found You, comic opera in one act by Seymour Barab; libretto (Eng) by the composer, after the short story by Evelyn E. Smith. First performance 1984, Charlotte, South Carolina, Charlotte Opera Association.

When two aliens from a distant galaxy come to earth, they are met by two government agents interested in discovering the secrets of intergalactic space flight. The agents are too successful. The knowledge drives them insane.
SCORE: vs, ms holograph (1984?, photocopy, NYPL).

Aton, the Ankh, and the Word, opera by Halim El-Dabh; libretto (Eng) by the composer. First performance December 1972, Washington, D.C., Hawthorne School.
Part of the trilogy *Ptahmose and the Magic Spell*, which includes *The Osiris Ritual** and *The Twelve Hours Trip.**

Atonement of Pan, The, music drama by Henry Hadley; libretto (Eng) by Joseph Redding. First performance August 10, 1912, San Francisco, Bohemian Club.
SCORE: vs of prologue, holograph copy (NYPL, [1912]).
LIBRETTO: English (San Francisco: Taylor, Nash, & Taylor, 1912).

At the Boar's Head, opera in one act by Gustav Holst; libretto (Eng) by the composer, after Shakespeare's *Henry IV* (1598). First performance April 3, 1925, Manchester, with Constance Willis (Doll Tearsheet), Tudor Davies (Prince Hal), Miss Treweek (Dame Quickly), and Norman Allin (Falstaff); conducted by Malcolm Sargent. First U.S. performance February 16, 1935, New York, MacDowell Club. Revivals include November 5, 1964; May 11, 1982, Liverpool (concert); May 17, 1982, London, with John Tomlinson (Falstaff), Philip Langridge (Prince Hal), Elise Ross (Mistress Quickly), and Felicity Palmer (Doll Tearsheet); conducted by David Atherton.
When Falstaff arrives at the Boar's Head Inn, he encounters Bardolph and Pistol, who are drinking. He also learns that Prince Hal and Poins have tricked him. The pair follow Falstaff in disguise to see his pursuit of Doll Tearsheet. Prince Hal is called back to Westminster, and Doll informs Falstaff through Bardolph that she still wants to see him.
For a detailed plot description, see K/*NKOB*, 368–69.
Major roles: Falstaff (bass); Bardolph (bar); Pistol (bar); Poins (bass); Prince Hal (ten); and Doll Tearsheet (sop).
The work is founded on thirty-eight old English melodies and three by the composer.
BIBLIOGRAPHY: Imogen Holst, "'At the Boar's Head,'" *MT* CXXIII (1982), 321–22; Ernest Newman, "'At the Boar's Head,'" *MT* LXVI (May 1, 1925), 413–14 [on premiere].

Audience, opera in one act by Royce Dembo; libretto (Eng) by Glen Miller. First performance May 7, 1982, New York, Soho Repertory.
Defying her husband, Martha takes voice lessons from Arthur Romanoff. When she starts to sing with her teacher, her husband tries to get her to stop by threatening to leave. He eventually relents, and the work ends with a trio of the three.
For a detailed description, see Summers/*OOA*, 93–94.
Roles: Martha (sop); Raymond, her husband (bar); and Arthur Romanoff, a voice teacher (bar).
SCORE: vs, holograph (photocopy, NYPL).

Audition, The, opera in one act by Alfred Goodman; libretto (Eng) by Elliot Arluck. First performance July 27, 1954, Athens, Ohio, Ohio University, Ewing Auditorium.
Roles: Walter Harmond, an actor (ten); Mrs. Crane, his landlady (high alto); Sidney Hodkins, a theater agent (bar); Mr. Westerly, the director (bass-bar); Rosalind Ross, a young actress (col sop); and Peter Wembly, a policeman (ten).

Audition, The, opera in one act by Martin Kalmanoff; libretto (Eng) by the composer and Sigmund Spaeth, with sections by Illica and Giacosa. First performance August 21, 1968, Pittsburgh.

The story involves eight applicants who are trying for a position in an opera workshop. For their auditions the singers must each perform a heretofore undiscovered piece of a famous composer. Unable to decide who is best and believing they are all very good, the opera director takes them all into the company.

The composers whose "lost" works are represented in this opera include Handel, Wagner, Puccini, Debussy, and Richard Strauss.

For a detailed description, see Summers/*OOA*, 163–64.

Roles: Dawn Aurora (sop), Melisande Jardin (mezzo), Veronica (sop), Maria Callas Epstein (alto), Renata Tebaldi O'Rourke (sop), Hedy Ingeborg (sop), Gisella Iceberg (sop), Birgit Blumberg (sop), Carmen Carmen (sop), and the director (nonsinging).

Auld Robin Gray, afterpiece in two acts, a partial pastiche by Samuel Arnold; libretto (Eng) by the composer. First performance July 29, 1794, London, Little Theatre in the Haymarket, with Charles Kemble (Jemmy), Miss Leake (Jenny), and Richard Suett (Robin Gray). First U.S. performance May 4, 1795, Philadelphia, New (Chestnut Street) Theatre, with "new music" by Alexander Reinagle.

In the story Jenny, believing that her beloved, Jemmy, a sailor, has been lost at sea, marries the kindly older Robin Gray, whom she does not love, in order to have enough money for her parents. To the dismay of all, Jemmy, quite alive, returns at the end.

Also set by Jonathan Blewitt (see next entry).
SCORE: vs (London: Preston & Son, 18??).
LIBRETTO: English (London: Geo. Goulding, 1794).

Auld Robin Gray, operetta in three acts by Jonathan Blewitt; libretto (Eng) by George Macfarren. First performance May 17, 1828, Surrey.

The work was composed by Blewitt, not George Alexander Lee, according to Biddlecombe/*EO*, 75.
LIBRETTO: English (London: S. G. Fairbrother, 1828).

Auster, romantic opera in three acts by Alfred Hill; libretto (Eng), after Emily Congeau's poem *Princess Mona*. First performance (concert, abridged), August 31, 1922, Sydney, Australia. First full stage performance March 1935, Melbourne, Australia, Royal Grand Opera Company, with Isolde Hill (Auster); conducted by the composer.

Author's Farce, The, ballad opera; libretto (Eng) by Henry Fielding. First performance March 30, 1730, London, Little Theatre in the Haymarket, with Mr. Jones (speaker/Bookweight/Dr. Orator), Mr. Mullart (Luckless), and Mrs. Mullart (Mrs. Moneywood/Goddess of Nonsense).

The author of the title, Luckless, is attempting to mount a puppet play, *The Pleasures of the Town*. Fielding uses the work to mock theater managers and the pieces they consider worthy of performance.
LIBRETTOS: English (London: J. Roberts, 1730; 3d ed., London: J. Watts, 1750); repr. ed., Charles B. Woods (1730) (Lincoln: University of Nebraska Press, 1965); repr. ed. (1750) Rubsamen/*BO*, vol. 5, *Satire, Burlesque, Protest, and Ridicule*, I (1974).

Avalon, music drama in two acts by Rutland Boughton; libretto (Eng) by the composer. Composed 1944–1945. Not performed.

Part five of Boughton's Arthurian cycle, which also includes *The Birth of Arthur** (1909), *The Round Table** (1916), *The Lily Maid** (1934), and *Galahad** (comp. 1944, not perf.).

Avon, opera in three acts by Ingelis Gundry; libretto (Eng) by the composer. First performance April 11, 1949, London, Scala Theatre.
BIBLIOGRAPHY: review, *MT* XC (May 1949), 318 [on premiere].

Azara, opera in three acts by John Knowles Paine; libretto (Eng) by the composer, after *Aucassin et Nicolette* (thirteenth cent.). Composed 1883–1898. First performance (concert) May 7, 1903, Boston, Symphony Hall.

The work is set in Provence during the early Crusades.

The lead was written to be sung by Emma Eames, but Paine could not get the Metropolitan Opera to perform the work, which contains Wagnerian elements in its orchestration, significant use of chromaticism, semi-leitmotifs, and continuous musical structure, albeit with distinct "numbers."

Major roles: Rainulf, King of Provence (bass); Gontran, his son (ten); Azara, ward of Aymar (sop); Aymar, a count, vassal of Rainulf (bar); Odo, a count, royal page (mezzo); Malek, Saracen chief (bar); Garsie, shepherdess (alto); and huntsman (ten).
SCORE: vs, German-English (Leipzig, New York: Breitkopf und Härtel, 1901).

Azora, the Daughter of Montezuma, opera in three acts by Henry Hadley; libretto (Eng) by David Stevens. First performance December 26, 1917, Chicago, The Auditorium, with Anna Fitziu (Azora), Cyrena Van Gordon (Papantzin), Forrest Lamont (Xalca), Arthur Middleton (Ramatzin), Frank Preisch (Canek), and James Goddard (Montezuma); conducted by the composer.

The work is set in 1519 in Mexico. In the story, Xalca, a Tlascalan prince, is in love with Azora, who is the daughter of Montezuma, who has conquered the prince's people. The high priest Canek, Azora's betrothed, warns Xalca to abandon his love for Azora. Her father chastises her for her attachment but is interrupted by the news that the Spanish forces are approaching.

Even though Xalca has been victorious in battle, Montezuma rejects his request for Azora's hand in marriage and plans to have the lovers offered as sacrifices instead. Canek is about to perform the sacrifice of Azora, who has rejected her father's pardon if she were to marry Canek, when the ceremony is interrupted by the appearance of Cortez and his soldiers. Azora is thus saved, and Canek falls senseless. The opera ends with sounds of the *Gloria in Excelsis Deo.*

For a detailed description, see Hipsher/*AO*, 231–33.

Major roles: Azora, daughter of Montezuma; Papantzin, Montezuma's sister; Xalca, Tlascalan prince; Ramatzin, general in Montezuma's army; Canek, high priest; and Montezuma.
SCORE: vs (New York and Boston: G. Schirmer, 1917).
LIBRETTO: English (New York: G. Schirmer, [1917]).

B

Baa Baa Black Sheep, "jungle tale" by Michael Berkeley; libretto (Eng) by David Malouf, after Kipling. First performance July 3, 1993, Cheltenham, England, Cheltenham Festival, with Henry Newman (the Captain), Fiona Kimm (Auntirosa), Malcolm Lawrence (Punch Mowgli), William Dazeley (Mowgli as a young man), Ann Taylor-Morley (Judy), and Eileen Hulse (the Mother); conducted by Paul Daniel; produced by Jonathan Moore.

In the story the young Kipling, returned to England from India by his family, escapes into the animal world of the *Jungle Book* to cope with the harshness of his environment, as epitomized by the fearsome Auntirosa.

The score includes a part for gamelan.

LIBRETTO: English (London: Chatto & Winds, 1993).

BIBLIOGRAPHY: Kenneth Loveland, "Cheltenham," *MO* (Oct. 1993), 325 [on premiere].

Babar the Elephant, children's opera in one act by Nicolai Berezowsky; libretto (Eng) by Dorothy Hartzell Heyward; lyrics by Judith Randal. First performance (semi-concert) February 21, 1953, New York, Hunter College, Assembly Hall, Little Orchestra Society, with William Diehl (Babar), Edith Gordon (Celeste), Ruth Kobart (the old lady), and Max Leavitt (narrator/ringmaster); conducted by Thomas Scherman.

The musical numbers include Celeste's aria "A Heart That Is Mortal."

SCORE: vs (New York: C. Fischer, 1953).

BIBLIOGRAPHY: R. P., "Youngsters Hear Opera Premiere," *NYT* (Feb. 22, 1953), 64.

Baby Doe, opera in two acts by Max DiJulio; libretto (Eng) by the composer, after Caroline Bancroft's historical account *Silver Queen* (1950). First performance May 24, 1952, Denver, Loretto Heights College.

The opera appeared just before Douglas Moore's *Ballad of Baby Doe,** another treatment of the subject.

Bacchae, The/Bakxai, opera in one act by John Buller; libretto (Eng-Greek) by the composer, after Euripides. First performance May 5, 1992, London, English National Opera, with Thomas Randle (Dionysius) and Sarah Walker (Agave).

Dionysius, son of Zeus and Semele, returns in the guise of a mortal to Thebes, where he was born. He punishes Semele's sisters for denying his divinity. They retreat to Mount Cythera. Pentheus, King of Thebes, attempts to destroy Dionysius but is in turn killed by the sisters, now Bacchae, when he watches them at their rites.

Major roles: Dionysius (ten); Pentheus (ten); Shadow of Euripides (speaking).

English is used in the prologue only. See *The Bassardids* for another setting of the story.

BIBLIOGRAPHY: Patrick J. Smith, "London," *ON* LVII (Aug. 1992), 46 [on premiere].

Bad Boys in School, opera in one act by Jan Meyerowitz; libretto (Eng) by the composer, after the play *Die schlimmen Buben in der Schule* by Nestroy (1847). First performance August 17, 1953, Lenox, Massachusetts, Tanglewood Music Festival. Performed May 21, 1955, New York, Hunter College Playhouse, Hunter College Opera Association, with Jeffrey Wolfe (Dr. McGillicuddy), Marvin Snow (the instructor), Robert Scheuer

(Raymond), Oscar Schlegel (Mr. Brixcowicz), Lucille Field (Mrs. Brixcowicz), Elaine Bonazzi (Willibald Smiley), and Martina Arroyo (Bertha); conducted by François Jaroschy.

Major roles: Dr. McGillicuddy, superintendent emeritus (ten); the inspector (bass-bar); Adrian Hodgepodge, the instructor (bar); Raymond, a supervisor (bar); and Mr. Brixcowicz and Mrs. Smiley, parents (bar, mezzo); a number of the roles of young male students are sung by women.

BIBLIOGRAPHY: Howard Taubman, "Opera: Trio at Hunter," *NYT* (May 21, 1955), 10 [on New York premiere]; review, *MA* LXXV (June 1955), 32.

Bad Times, opera in one act by Stephen Oliver; libretto (Eng) by the composer. First performance June 24, 1975, London, Eltham Palace.

Balcony, The, opera in two acts by Robert DiDomenica; libretto (Eng) by the composer, after Jean Genet's play (1956). First performance May 9, 1975, Boston. Also June 14, 1990, Boston, Opera Company of Boston, with Mignon Dunn (Irma) and Susan Larson (Carmen); conducted by Sarah Caldwell.

The work is set in a bordello, with Irma as the madam and Carmen as her favorite employee. The music of each of the nine scenes employs a basic tone row.

SCORE: vs (Newton Centre, Mass.: Margun Music, 1985).

BIBLIOGRAPHY: James E. Oestreich, review, *NYT* (June 17, 1990), I, 51.

Bald Prima Donna, The, satiric opera in one act by Martin Kalmanoff; libretto (Eng) by Donald Watson, after Ionesco's "antiplay" *La cantatrice chauve* (1948). First performance February 15, 1963, New York, Community Opera.

The story makes fun of middle-class values, with the characters spouting nonsense. Mr. and Mrs. Smith invite Mr. and Mrs. Martin for dinner, which never takes place, a fireman arrives and tells mindless stories, and the maid recites nonsensical lines. After a blackout, the piece begins again but with the players reversing their lines.

For a detailed description, see Eaton/*OP* II, 249.

Major roles: Mrs. Smith (sop), Mary, the maid (sop), Mrs. Martin (alto), Mr. Smith (ten); Mr. Martin (bass-bar); and the fireman (bass).

Also set by Robert Gross (1962, Los Angeles).

BIBLIOGRAPHY: Ellis Renard, "The Operas of Martin Kalmanoff," *OJ* VII (1974), 17.

Ballad of Baby Doe, The, opera in two acts by Douglas Moore; libretto (Eng) by John Latouche. First performance July 7, 1956, Central City, Colorado, Opera House, with Dolores Wilson (Baby Doe), Martha Lipton (Augusta), Walter Cassel (Horace Tabor), and Lawrence Davidson (William Jennings Bryan); conducted by Emerson Buckley; directed by Hanya Holm and Edwin Levy; designed by Donald Oenslager. Revised version April 3, 1958, New York, City Opera, with Beverly Sills (Baby Doe).

The story is based on real characters in American history, including William Jennings Bryan. It takes place during Colorado's mining boom and concerns the wealthy Horace Tabor, mayor of Leadville, who falls in love with the much younger Elizabeth ("Baby") Doe. Baby Doe and Tabor divorce their spouses and marry, but they are faced thereafter by social scorn from the leading families of the town and are ruined financially when the silver standard, supported by Bryan, collapses. Tabor dies a broken man, having lost everything, and Baby Doe struggles on, keeping her pledge to her husband not to sell the Matchless Mine. Descending into poverty and delusion, she freezes to death in the bitter cold.

For detailed descriptions, see C/*MS*, 39–50; Eaton/*OP* I, 27–28.

Major roles: Baby (Elizabeth) Doe (sop); Horace Tabor, mayor of Leadville (bar); and Augusta, Horace's first wife (mezzo).

The score contains a number of American folk-music nuances, especially from pieces of the 1890s. The opera is a tour de force for its title character, a role that propelled Beverly Sills to fame. It is Douglas Moore's most successful and popular stage work.

Among the highlights is Baby Doe's electric "Willow Song" in act 1, which first attracts Tabor's attention, and the concluding chorus, "So Fleet the Works of Man."

Another setting of the Baby Doe story, M. DiJulio's *Baby Doe*,* appeared just before the Moore version (May 24, 1956, Denver).

SCORE: vs (New York: Chappell Music Co., 1958).

BIBLIOGRAPHY: Paul Jackson, "Gold Standard in Central City," *ON* XXI (Nov. 5, 1956), 12–13 [on premiere]; David McKee, "You've Come a Long Way, Baby Doe," *ON* LXI (Jan. 11, 1997), 26–27, 43, 51.

Ballad of Kitty the Barkeep, The, "cabaret" opera in one act by Dai-Keong Lee; libretto (Eng) by the composer and Robert Healey. Composed 1979.

Based on the composer's *Speakeasy** (1957, New York).

Ballad of the Bremen Band, The, children's opera in one act by Dennis Arlan; libretto (Eng) by James Billings, after *The Brementown Musicians* by the Brothers Grimm. First performance June 25, 1977, Katonah, New York, Caramoor Festival.

Four animals, Dobbin, a donkey, Herefred, a dog, Melissa Mew, a cat, and Sir Reginald, a rooster, have run away from their owners and desire to go to Bremen to join its renowned band. They discover, however, that the town's instruments have been stolen by a group of thieves, whom they come upon when searching for a place to spend the night. After tricking the thieves, the animals go to Bremen, the instruments in tow, and are rewarded by being named the official Band of Bremen by the grateful mayor.

Major roles: Claude Hopper (bar), Bruno Broast (high bar), Claudia Hopper (mezzo), mayor of Bremen (bar), Molly Mistress (mezzo), and Dobbin, Herefred, Melissa Mew, and Sir Reginald (children or adults).

For a detailed description, see Kornick/*RAO*, 32–34.

Another setting is A. Balkin's *The Musicians of Bremen** (1972).

SCORE: vs (Clifton, N.J.: European-American Musical Corp., 1977).

Balseros, opera by Robert Ashley; libretto (Eng) by Maria Irena Fornes. First performance May 16, 1997, Miami Beach, Colony Theatre, with Joan La Barbara, Jacqueline Humbert, Sam Ashley, Thomas Buckner, Demetra Adams, Christina Clark, Amy Van Roekel, Emmanuel Cadet, David Dillard, Nattacha Aador, and Mario Salas-Lanz; conducted by the composer; directed by Michael Montel.

The work focuses on the often fatal attempts of Cubans to flee the island by boat and obtain sanctuary in the United States. It consists of four parts: preparations for departure, setting sail, experiences at sea, and arrival. The text is based on the testimony of boat people who survived the treacherous journey.

BIBLIOGRAPHY: Pamela Gordon, "Impressionistic 'Balseros,'" *USA Today* (May 27, 1997), D, 5 [on premiere]; Tim Page, "Miami Beach," *ON* (Aug. 1997), 37–38 [on premiere].

Bandanna, opera in two acts and a prologue by Daron Hagen; libretto (Eng) by Paul Muldoon. Composed 1997. First performance scheduled for February 25, 1999, Austin, University of Texas.

Residents of a Mexican border town clash about the problem of illegal immigrants.

Bandit, The, tragic opera in one act by Val Patacchi; libretto (Eng) by William Ashbrook. Fist performance April 7, 1958, Columbia, Missouri, Stephens College.

Banditti, The, or, Love's Labyrinth, partial pastiche in two acts by Samuel Arnold; libretto (Eng) by John O'Keeffe. First performance November 28, 1781, London; enlarged into three acts as *The Castle of Andalusia** (1782, London). First U.S. performance April 21, 1788, New York.
LIBRETTO: English (London: T. Cadell, 1781).

Bang!, opera for young people by John Rutter; libretto (Eng) by David Grant. Composed 1976.
SCORE: vs (London: Oxford University Press, [1976]).

Bannian Day, afterpiece in two acts by Samuel Arnold; libretto (Eng) by George Brewer, after John Cross's *The Apparition,** set by William Reeve (1794, London). First performance June 11, 1796, London, Little Theatre in the Haymarket, with John Johnstone and Richard Suett.
The story is concerned with naval life.
LIBRETTO: English (London: T. N. Longman, 1796).

Bantry Bay, opera in one act by William Reeve; libretto (Eng) by G. N. Reynolds. First performance February 18, 1797, London, Covent Garden.
SCORE: vs (London: Preston & Son, [1797]).

Barbara Allen, opera in one act by David Broekman; libretto (Eng) by Edward Eager, after Allan Ramsay's ballad (1724). First performance (concert) December 27, 1954, New York, 92nd Street Y, "Y" Symphonic Workshop, Kaufmann Auditorium, with Shannon Bolin (Barbara Allen), Robert Goss (Jemmy Grove), Jean Handzlik (Hannah), Geraldine Beitzel (Lucy), and Philip Coolidge (narrator); conducted by Maurice Levine.
The folk song "Barbara Allen" is used to tie the various scene changes together.
BIBLIOGRAPHY: Harold Schonberg, review, *NYT* (Dec. 27, 1954), 20 [on premiere].

Barber of New York, The, opera in one act by Ashley Vernon; libretto (Eng) by Greta Hartwig. First performance May 26, 1953, New York, Hunter College, Playhouse, with Carlos Sherman (Jacob Vredenburgh), Petra Garrial (Sally), and Paul Lester (Captain Crozier); conducted by Siegfried Landau; produced by Sally Smith.
The setting is colonial New York. A barber, Jacob Vredenburgh, heads the Sons of Liberty, who oppose British rule. Young Sally is in love with Jeff, a carpenter and member of the group. Jeff is tricked by Captain Crozier into signing a contract to work for the British. But when Crozier comes in for a shave, the barber gets Crozier to destroy the contract and refuses to finish shaving him, tossing him out into the street, to be laughed at by the neighbors.
For a description, see Summers/*OOA*, 299–300.
Major roles: Jacob Vredenburgh (bass); Captain John Crozier (bar); Jeff, a carpenter (ten); Sally, a dressmaker (sop); and Miss Pritt, Sally's aunt (alto).
The music includes musical quotes from Richard Strauss, Arthur S. Sullivan, and Gershwin.
SCORE: vs (Bryn Mawr, Pa.: Mercury Music Corp., 1948).
BIBLIOGRAPHY: R. P., "Workshop Offers Opera by Vernon," *NYT* (May 27, 1953), 27.

Barber of Seville, The, comic opera in three acts, a partial adaptation by Henry Rowley Bishop (with a new overture and other new pieces) of Rossini's *Il barbiere di*

Siviglia (1816, Rome); libretto (Eng) translated by John Fawcett and Daniel Terry from Sterbini's text, after Beaumarchais's *Le barbier de Séville* (1775). First performance March 13, 1818, London, Covent Garden. First U.S. performance May 3, 1819, New York, Park Theatre.

The work includes the duet "Oh! Maiden Fair," after Paisiello's version (1782, St. Petersburg).

SCORE: ms fs, overture, additional music (British Library, Add. MS. 36950).
LIBRETTO: English (London: E. Macleish, 1818).

Barbers of Bassora, The, comic opera in two acts by John Hullah; libretto (Eng) by John M. Morton. First performance November 11, 1837, London.

The story is one of the later treatments of the "Oriental" tale of Sadak, along the lines of Weber's *Abu Hassan* (1811, Munich); G. Meyerbeer's *Wirth und Gast* (1813, Stuttgart); E. Loder's *Nourjahad** (1834); C. Packer's *Sadak and Kalasra** (1835, London); and P. Cornelius's *Der Barbier von Bagdad* (1858, Weimar).

See Biddlecombe/*EO*, 46, for a description.
LIBRETTO: English (London: Chapman and Hall, [1837?]).

Bargain, The, opera in one act by Philip M. Slates; libretto (Eng) by the composer. First performance July 26, 1956, Athens, Ohio, Ohio University.

Barnstable, or, Someone in the Attic, opera in one act by Francis Burt; libretto (Eng) by James Saunders, after his radio play of the same name. First performance November 30, 1969, Kassel, Staatsoper, in German, in a translation by Hilde Spiel.

The story, set in an English country house, concerns the mischief that a ghost creates for the house's inhabitants.
SCORE: vs, German (Kassel: Bärenreiter, 1982, 1969).

Baron Kinkverkankotsdorsprakingatchdern, afterpiece by Samuel Arnold; libretto (Eng) by Miles Peter Andrews, after Lady Craven's *A Tale for Christmas* (1779). First performance July 9, 1781, London, Little Theatre in the Haymarket.
LIBRETTO: English (London: T. Cadell, 1781).

Barrier, The (Mulatto), music drama in two acts by Jan Meyerowitz; libretto (Eng) by Langston Hughes, after his play *Mulatto* (1935). First performance January 18, 1950, New York, Columbia University, Brander Matthews Theatre, with Robert Goss (Bert), Muriel Rahn (Cora Lewis), and Paul Elmer (Colonel Norwood); conducted by Willard Rhodes; directed by Felix Brentano; designed by H. A. Condell.

The story focuses on the travails of Bert, a young mulatto, who is the son of Colonel Thomas Norwood, a Georgia plantation owner, and Cora Lewis, his housekeeper. Although the boy has been educated in the North, he is not allowed to be part of white society in his own community and clashes endlessly with his father. Bert chokes his father to death during an argument and, pursued by a lynch mob, shoots himself.

For a detailed description, see Eaton/*OP* I, 32–33.

Major roles: Bert (bar), Cora Lewis (sop), and Colonel Thomas Norwood (bar).

Among the score's few instances of passages drawing on specifically black music is Cora's spiritual-like prayer in the first act.
SCORE: ms vs ([1949]; LCCN: 84-196246).
BIBLIOGRAPHY: Cecil Smith, "Columbia University Stages Musical Drama by Meyerowitz," *MA* LII (Feb. 1950), 244 [on premiere]; Howard Taubman, "'The Barrier' Given by Columbia Opera," *NYT* (Jan. 19, 1950), 34 [on premiere].

Bartleby, opera in two acts by William Flanagan; libretto (Eng) by James Hinton Jr., after Melville's story *Bartleby the Scrivener* (1835). First performance January 24, 1961, New York, Town Hall, Composers of Today, with Morton Shames (Bartleby); conducted by Robert Mandel. Revived May 5, 1981, New York, Bel Canto Opera; conducted by Mara Waldman.

See next entry for the story.

SCORE: ms vs ([1968], NYPL).

BIBLIOGRAPHY: Peter G. Davis, review, *NYT* (May 7, 1981, C, 20 [on New York revival]; R. P., review, *NYT* (May 11, 1954), 25 [on premiere].

Bartleby, opera in a prologue and two acts by Walter Aschaffenburg; libretto (Eng) by Jay Leyda, after Melville's story. First performance November 12, 1964, Oberlin, Ohio.

The lawyer is the narrator of the story. He, his clerks, Trodden and Nippers, and the office boy, Ginger, are baffled by the behavior of Bartleby, the newly hired scrivener. First he "prefers" not to do his work. When he is fired, he "prefers" not to leave until he is taken to prison. Finally, despite the efforts of the lawyer to save him, Bartleby dies of starvation, having "preferred" not to eat.

For a detailed description, see Eaton/*OP* II, 37.

Major roles: the lawyer (bar), Bartleby (ten), Trodden (bass), Nippers (ten), and Ginger (sop).

The story was also set by M. Niehaus (1967, Cologne and Berlin).

SCORE: vs (Bryn Mawr, Pa.: Theodore Presser, 1964).

BIBLIOGRAPHY: Walter Aschaffenburg, "Random Notes on Bartleby," *OJ* II/3 (1969), 5–10.

Bartolo, opera by G. William Bugg, after Mozart's *Nozze di Figaro* and Rossini's *Barbiere di Siviglia*. First performance September 13, 1986, Birmingham, Alabama, Stamford University Workshop.

Basket Maker, The, afterpiece in two acts by Samuel Arnold; libretto (Eng) by John O'Keeffe. First performance September 4, 1790, London, Little Theatre in the Haymarket.

LIBRETTO: English (London: T. Woodfall, 1798).

Bassarids, The, opera seria with an intermezzo in one act by Hans Werner Henze; libretto (Eng) by W. H. Auden and Chester Kallman, after *The Bacchae* of Euripides. First performance (in a German translation by Maria Basse-Sporleder) as *Die Bassariden*, August 6, 1966, Salzburg, with Ingeborg Hallstein (Autonoe), Kerstin Meyer (Agave), Vera Little (Beroe), Loren Driscoll (Dionysus), Helmut Melchert (Tiresias), Kostas Paskalis (Pentheus), and William Dooley (the captain; conducted by Christoph von Dohnányi. First U.S. performance (in English) August 7, 1968, Santa Fe, Santa Fe Opera, with Joan Caplan (Beroe), Regina Sarfaty (Agave), Evelyn Mandac (Autonoe), Loren Driscoll (Dionysus), Charles Bressler (Tiresias), John Reardon (Pentheus), Thomas Jamerson (the captain), and Peter Harrower (Cadmus); conducted by the composer; designed by Rouben Ter-Arutunian. First British performance (concert, in English) September 22, 1968, London, BBC, with Sarfaty (Agave) and Alexander Young (Dionysus); conducted by Edward Downes. First British stage performance October 10, 1974 (in English), London, Coliseum, with Josephine Barstow (Autonoe), Katherine Pring (Agave), Dennis Wicks (Cadmus), Gregory Dempsey (Dionysus), Norman Welsby (Pentheus), and Tom McDonnell (the captain); conducted by the composer.

Pentheus is the new king of Thebes. He decrees that Semele, whose tomb is revered by the Bassarids, who are devotees of her son, Dionysus (Bacchus), was really loved by a mortal, not by Zeus, so that Dionysus is not a god. Cadmus, Pentheus's grandfather and Semele's father, tries to advise him to reverse the decree. Nonetheless, Pentheus ignores his warnings and those of Beroe, his old nurse, and sends the captain of the guards to arrest members of the Bassarid cult. The captain returns with a group that includes the seer Tiresias, a disguised Dionysus, Agave, Pentheus's mother, and Autonoe, her sister. During an earthquake the prisoners escape. Pentheus is convinced by Dionysus to go to Mount Cythaeron dressed as a woman, in order to observe the Bassarids at their rites. When Pentheus is discovered, he pleads in vain with Agave, one of the group, to save him. She returns to Thebes with his severed head, whereupon she is made to realize what has happened. Dionysus appears and orders the city to be burned to the ground, in revenge for the disgrace done to his own mother.

For detailed descriptions, see K/*KOB*, 926–31; K/*NKOB*, 348–52; Eaton/*OP* II, 38–39.

Major roles: Dionysus (ten); Pentheus, King of Thebes (bar); Cadmus, his grandfather (bass); Tiresias, a blind seer (ten); captain of the guards (bar); Agave, daughter of Cadmus and mother of Pentheus (mezzo); Autonoe, her sister (high sop); and Beroe, an old slave (mezzo).

The opera, whose style may be described as neoclassic, is set in the form of a symphony, in four movements, each of which represents a change of mood. The first movement concerns the ascent of Pentheus; the second, the dismay of Cadmus; the third, the hunting down of the Bassarids by Pentheus's guards; an intermezzo, in which Agave and Autonoe laugh at Pentheus's behavior; and the fourth, the death of the king and the burning of Thebes.

Also set by E. Wellesz, as *Die Bakchantinnen* (1931, Vienna); G. Ghedini, as *Le baccanti* (1948, Milan); and W. Harper, as *The Bacchae* (1998, Cambridge, Mass.). See also *The Bacchae* and *Semele*.

SCORE: vs, German-English (Mainz: B. Schott's Söhne; New York: Associated Music Publishers, 1966).

LIBRETTO: German-English (Mainz: B. Schott's Söhne; New York: Schott Music, 1966.

BIBLIOGRAPHY: Terry Apter, "'Tristan' and 'The Bassarids,'" *Tempo* CXII (Mar. 1975), 27–30 [on British stage premiere]; Alan Blyth, "Henze's New Opera," *Opera* XVII (1966), 608-10; Paul Griffiths, "The Bassarids: Hans Werner Henze Talks to Paul Griffiths," *MT* CXV (1974), 831–32; Everett Helm, "Austria," *MQ* LIII (1967), 408–15 [on premiere]; Frank Merkling, "Santa Fe," *ON* XXXIII (Sept. 21, 1968), 20-21 [on U.S. premiere]; Andrew Porter, "Salzburg. Henze's 'Bassarids,'" *MT* CXII (1966), 886-87; Harold Rosenthal, "Salzburg. The Bassarids. Aug. 26," *Opera* XVII (Autumn 1966), 50–54; Harold C. Schonberg, "Opera: Henze at Santa Fe," *NYT* (Aug. 11, 1968), 75 [on U.S. premiere]; James Helme Sutcliffe, "London," *ON* XXXVIII (Dec. 7, 1974), 36 [on British stage premiere].

Ba-Ta-Clan, opera in one act by Stephen Oliver, after Offenbach's opera buffa (1855, Paris); libretto (Eng) by the composer, after Ludovic Halévy's text. Composed 1988.

This satire on French life takes place in a mythical Oriental kingdom.

The work is set for four characters and male chorus.

Battle of Bothwell Brigg, The, Scottish romance in two acts by Henry Rowley Bishop; libretto (Eng) by Charles Farley, after Scott's *Old Morality* (1817). First performance May 22, 1820, London, Covent Garden.

Old Morality, who cleans old gravestones for a living, recounts the story of the battle between the Covenanters and the Cavaliers in 1679.

LIBRETTO: English (London: J. Lowndes, 1820).

Battle of Hexham, The, or, Days of Old, comic opera in three acts by Samuel Arnold; libretto (Eng) by George Colman Jr. First performance August 11, 1789, London, Little Theatre in the Haymarket, with John Bannister (Gondibert), Mrs. Goodall (Adeline), and Mrs. S. Kemble (Queen Margaret). First U.S. performance March 20, 1794, New York, with new accompaniments by Peter A. van Hagen Sr.; November 7, 1803, Boston; and April 1812, Philadelphia, Federal Street Theatre.

The setting is Northumberland at the time of the War of the Roses. In order to be with her beloved, Gondibert, Adeline dresses up as a young man. Gondibert rescues Queen Margaret and her young son Henry.

SCORE: vs (London: Longman & Broderip, n.d.).
LIBRETTO: English (Dublin: P. Byrne, 1790; Boston: n.p,. 1803).

Baucis and Philemon, or, The Wandering Deities, opera by Peter Prelleur; libretto (Eng) after La Fontaine. First performance April 7, 1740, London, New Wells Theatre.

The story is based on the mythological couple, who unknowingly entertain Jupiter and are thereby granted anything they want.

Set as *Philemon und Baucis* by J. C. Kaffka (1792, Augsburg); and *Philémon et Baucis* by C. Gounod (1860, Paris).

SCORE: vs, overture (in full score), songs, and duets (London: author, [1740?]).

Bayou Legend, A, opera in three acts by William Grant Still; libretto (Eng) by Verna Arvey. Composed in 1941. First performance November 11, 1974, Jackson, Mississippi, Opera/South, with Juanita Waller (Aurore), Barbara Conrad (Clothilde), John Miles (Bazile), and Robert Mosley (Leonce); conducted by Leonard de Paur. Revived June 15, 1981, WNET television, Opera/South, with Gary Burgess (Bazile), Carmen Balthrop (Aurore), and Raeschelle Potter (Clothilde); conducted by de Paur.

The story concerns a man, Leonce, who has been rejected by Clothilde. Clothilde is interested instead in Bazile, who agrees to marry her when she tells him she is pregnant, despite the fact he does not love her. Bazile falls in love with a spirit, Aurore, who warns him that Clothilde has lied to him. Clothilde accuses Bazile of witchcraft, and Bazile is hanged. When his spirit leaves his body to join Aurore, the Father Lestant declares that a miracle has taken place. Clothilde then confesses that she lied to Leonce and tries to get him to marry her; he refuses.

For a detailed description, see Kornick/*RAO*, 299–301.

Major roles: Clothilde (sop), Father Lestant (bass), Leonce (bar), Bazile (ten), and Aurore (sop).

The regional atmosphere is portrayed musically by a dance segment in the third act.

SCORE: fs (Los Angeles?: author?, 1941).
BIBLIOGRAPHY: Richard F. Shepard, "TV: Still's Opera of the Southland, 'A Bayou Legend,'" *NYT* (June 15, 1991), C, 24 [on television revival].

Bays's Opera, ballad opera in three acts; libretto (Eng) by Gabriel Odingsells. First performance March 30, 1730, London, Theatre-Royal, with Mr. Cibber Jr. (Bays), Mrs. Butler (Arabella), Mrs. Shireburn (Belinda), Mrs. Roberts (Cantato), Richard Charke (Tragedo), Miss Raster (Dulceda), and Mr. Berry (Pantomime).

Major roles: Bays; Arabella; Cantato, usurper of the Empire of Wit; Tragedo, lawful heir, in love with Dulceda; Dulceda, Cantato's daughter, in love with Tragedo; and Pantomime, pretender to the Throne of Wit.

LIBRETTO: English (London: J. Roberts, 1730); repr. ed. Rubsamen/*BO*, vol. 9, *The Influence of Pantomime and Harlequinade* (1974).

Beach of Falesá, The, opera in three acts by Alun Hoddinott; libretto (Eng) by Glyn Jones, after Robert Louis Stevenson's short story. First performance March 26, 1974, Cardiff, New Theatre, Welsh National Opera, with Delme Bryn-Jones (Wiltshire), Geraint Evans (Case), Sandra Browne (Uma), and Edward Byles (Father Galuchet); conducted by Richard Armstrong; produced by Michael Geliot; designed by Alexander McPherson.

The story is set in the South Seas and centers on John Wiltshire and Case, two European traders. Case undercuts Wiltshire by convincing him to marry Uma, a half-caste, and then says that she was promised to a native chief. Father Galuchet, a priest, helps the wronged Wiltshire destroy a voodoo shrine that helped Case control the natives. After Case confesses to killing previous traders, Wiltshire kills him.

Major roles: Wiltshire (bar), Case (bar), Uma (mezzo), and Father Galuchet (ten).
SCORE: vs (London: Oxford University Press, 1974).
BIBLIOGRAPHY: review, *MT* CXV (1974), 207.
SCORE: vs (London: Oxford University Press, 1974).

Bear, The, "extravaganza" in one act by William Walton; libretto (Eng) by Paul Dehn and the composer, after Anton Chekhov's play (1888). First performance June 3, 1967, Aldeburgh Festival, with Monica Sinclair (Madame Popova), John Shaw (Grigory Stepanovitch Smirnov), and Norman Lumsden (Luka); conducted by James Lockhart; produced by Colin Graham. First U.S. performance August 15, 1968, Aspen, Colorado, Aspen Music School Workshop, with Cynthia Bedford (Madame Popova), Stephen Rowland (Smirnov), and Ferenz Gall (Luka); conducted by Leonard Slatkin; directed by Madeleine Milhaud.

The setting is Madame Popova's house in the country in 1888. A young widow, Madame Popova, is bothered by her neighbor, Smirnov, who claims that her late husband owed him money. An argument between the young woman and Smirnov leads to a duel, but before anything serious happens, the couple start to enjoy each other's company. The work ends with a kiss between the two, witnessed by the servant Luka, who has come to break up the "fight."

For a plot summary, see K/*KOB*, 1134–35; K/*NKOB*, 955–56; Eaton/*OP* II, 249–50.

Major roles: Madame Yeliena Ivanovna Popova (mezzo); Grigory Stepanovitch Smirnov (bar); and Luka, Popova's old servant (bass).

The work uses musical quotes from composers such as Puccini, Britten, and Stravinsky at appropriate moments for comic effect.

For other settings see *The Boor* and *The Brute*.
SCORE: vs, German-English (London: Oxford University Press, [1968]).
LIBRETTO: English (London: Oxford, [1967]).
BIBLIOGRAPHY: Barbara Haddad, "Aspen," *ON* XXXIII (Oct. 12, 1968), 26 [on U.S. premiere]; William Mann, review, *The Times* (London) (June 5, 1967), 6 [on premiere].

Beast and Superbeast, four comic operas in one act by Jorge Martín; librettos (Eng) by Andrew Joffe, after the collection of stories *Beasts and Superbeasts* (1914) by Saki. First performance March 8, 1996, Bethesda, Maryland, Other Opera Company. First New York performance June 22, 1996, American Chamber Opera Company, Dicapo Theater; with Lynn Norris (the girl), Daniel Rawe (the aunt), Bethany Reeves (Conradin); narrated by Leslie Churchill Ward (Clovis Sangrail); conducted by Douglas Anderson.

Two Interlopers
When two enemies are trapped in the forest, they finally decide to forget their differences, only to be attacked by a pack of wolves.

Sredni Vashtar
A youth, Conradin, gives his pet ferret godlike features, to the extent that the animal rids the boy of Mrs. DeRopp, Conradin's strict guardian.

The Mappined Life
Life in the city is compared to animals living in a zoo. It features a young girl's musings, which are occasionally interrupted by her aunt and uncle.

Tobermory
To the horror of the guests at a country house, Tobermory, a cat that has been taught to speak, repeats what the guests and host have been saying about each other. Performed separately April 18, 1993, Eugene, Oregon, University of Oregon, School of Music.

Another setting of *Sredni Vashtar* is by Alastair Cassels-Brown (comp. 1983).
BIBLIOGRAPHY: Shirley Fleming, "A 'Beast' of Marked Superiority," *New York Post* (June 24, 1996), 33 [on New York premiere]; Allan Kozinn, review, *NYT* (June 24, 1996), C, 12 [on New York premiere]; Joseph McLellan, review, *Washington Post* (Mar. 9, 1996) [on premiere].

Beatrice, opera in three acts by Lee Hoiby; libretto (Eng) by Marcia Nardi, after Maurice Maeterlinck's *Soeur Béatrice* (1901). First performance October 23, 1959, Louisville, Kentucky.

The story concerns a young nun during the Middle Ages who is disgraced but then redeemed through mystical intervention.
DISCOGRAPHY: A. Nossaman, B. Bounell, R. Lohr, N. Thomas, R. Fischer, D. Clenny, E. Johnson, M. Treitz, Louisville Orchestra; cond. M. Bomhard, LOU 603 (1960, 2 LPs, mono).

Beatrice Cenci, opera in three acts by Berthold Goldschmidt; libretto (Eng) by Martin Esslin, after Percy Bysshe Shelley's *The Cenci* (1819). First performance (excerpts) 1952, BBC. First complete performance August 30, 1994, Berlin, with Roberta Alexander (Beatrice) and Simon Estes (Francesco Cenci).

The historically-based story is set in Rome, 1599. Faced by her father Francesco's increasing abuse of her and her family, Beatrice and Lucrezia, her mistreated stepmother, plan his murder, urged on by Orsino, Beatrice's former suitor and now a clergyman. Orsino abandons them when their plot is discovered, and the women are condemned to death.

For a detailed plot description, see K/*NKOB*, 276–77.

Major roles: Count Francesco Cenci (bass-bar); Lucrezia, his second wife (mezzo); Beatrice Cenci (sop); and Orsino, a prelate (ten).

The third act includes the pensive solo by the imprisoned Beatrice, "False Friend, Willst Thou Smile or Weep."

See *The Cenci* for other settings.
BIBLIOGRAPHY: Paul Banks, The Case of 'Beatrice Cenci,'" *Opera* XLV (Apr. 1988), 426–32; James Helme Sutcliffe, "Berlin," *ON* LIX (Mar. 18, 1995), 42 [on first full perf.].
DISCOGRAPHY: Alexander, D. Jones, Estes, Berlin Radio Chorus, German Sym.; cond. L. Zagrosek, Sony S2K-66836 (2 CDs), rev. C. J. Luten, *ON* LX (Jan. 20, 1996), 33.

Beauty and the Beast, opera in one act by Vittorio Giannini; libretto (Eng) by Robert A. Simon, after the French fairy tale by Mme. Leprince de Beaumont, *La belle et la bête*. First performance (concert) November 24, 1938, CBS radio. First stage performance February 14, 1946, Hartford, Connecticut, Julius Hartt School of Music.

In a family of three sisters, the spoiled first and second daughters badger their father for fine clothing, while Beauty asks only for a red rose. The father picks the flower in the garden of the Beast, who becomes furious and demands that, as punishment, the father hand over Beauty. The father reluctantly agrees. After a stay at the castle Beauty flees but, dreaming that the Beast is lonely, returns to him, finding that her love has changed him back into the handsome prince he once was.

For a detailed description, see Eaton/*OP* I, 168.

Major roles: the father (bar), Beauty (sop), and the Beast (ten).

SCORE: vs (New York: G. Ricordi & Co., [1951]).

Beauty and the Beast, opera in one act by Jeremiah Murray; libretto (Eng) by the composer, after Leprince de Beaumont. First performance May 8, 1974, New York, Public Opera Theater, with Kate Hurney (Beauty), Walter Hook (the Beast), Norman Phillips (the father), and Marjorie Minnis and Martha Thigpen (Beauty's sisters); conducted by the composer (at the piano); produced by Louis Galterio.

BIBLIOGRAPHY: Peter G. Davis, "'Beauty and Beast,' New Opera, Evokes 19th-Century Style," *NYT* (June 14, 1974), 34 [on premiere]; Frank Merkling, "New York," *ON* (Sept. 1974), 55 [on premiere].

Beauty and the Beast, opera in three acts by Frank DiGiacomo; libretto (Eng) by the composer and Emil P. Edmon, after Leprince de Beaumont First performance May 24, 1974, Syracuse, Regent Theatre, with Christine Kemperer (Beauty) and William Black (the Beast/Prince); conducted by Erwin Vrooman; designed, directed by the conductor.

Major roles: Beauty (sop) and the Beast/Prince (bar).

LIBRETTO: French-English (Toronto: Arcana Editions, 1987).

BIBLIOGRAPHY: E. Thomas Glasgow, review, *ON* (Sept. 1974), 55 [on premiere].

DISCOGRAPHY: C. Kemperer, W. Black, R. McCullough, G. Ross, D. Miller, Syracuse Sym. Orch.; cond. G. Sheldon, 20th Century, CEJS 1011–1013 (1976, Los Angeles, 3 LPs).

Beauty and the Beast, opera in two acts by Stephen Oliver; libretto (Eng) by the composer, translated from the Italian version of Carlo Collodi, after Leprince de Beaumont. First performance July 26, 1984, Batignano Festival (in Italian); conducted by Nicholas Kraemer, as *La bella e la bestia*. First performance (in English) June 21, 1985, London, St. John's Smith Square, with Anne Mason (Beauty), Robert Dean (the Beast), Linda MacLeod (the fairy), and Henry Herford (the father); conducted by Graeme Jenkins. First U.S. performance June 11, 1987, St. Louis, Opera Theatre, with Victoria Livengood (Beauty) and John Brandstetter (the Beast).

In this variation of the fairy tale, the father is a poor merchant with three daughters. The two older ones pester him to buy them new dresses, while the youngest, Beauty, his favorite, asks only for a single rose. When the father seeks shelter at night in a forest, he enters the Beast's estate, and when the father plucks a rose before he leaves, the enraged creature demands one of the daughters as recompense. Beauty comes to live with the beast but refuses to marry him. The Beast allows her to return home to see her father, who is ill, on the condition that she return within seven days. When she returns after the allotted time, she discovers that the Beast is dying of a broken heart.

Roles: the younger sister (col sop), the elder sister (mezzo), Beauty (mezzo), the fairy (sop), the Beast (bar), and the merchant (bass-bar).

SCORE: vs (Ital-Eng) (London: Novello, 1987).

BIBLIOGRAPHY: Winton Dean, review, *MT* CXXVI (1985), 475 [on British premiere]; Andrew Porter, "Musical Events," *NY* LXIII (July 6, 1987), 59–60 [on U.S. premiere].

Beauty and the Beast, children's opera in one act by Michael Easton; libretto (Eng) by Colin Duckworth, after Leprince de Beaumont. First performance 1989, Melbourne.

In this updated version of the French tale, a businessman sets out on a solo journey to aid his ailing business. His plane crash lands in the garden of the Beast. To win his freedom, the man agrees to send one of his daughters, Beauty, to be the Beast's friend. When a crisis occurs, the Beast's true identity, that of a prince, is revealed to Beauty, much to the annoyance of her sisters.

The many other settings of the story include those by Stephen Glover (ca. 1868); R. Murray Schafer, for voice and string quartet (1980); R. Moran's *Desert of Roses** (1992, Houston); and Philip Glass's *La belle et la bête*, to a French text and based on Jean Cocteau's screenplay for the 1946 film (1995, Brooklyn, N.Y.). See also *Zemire and Azor.*

Beauty Stone, The, romantic musical drama in three acts by Arthur S. Sullivan; libretto (Eng) by Arthur Wing Pinero; lyrics by Joseph Comyns Carr. First performance May 28, 1898, London, Savoy Theatre, with Walter Passmore (the Devil), Ruth Vincent (Laine), Pauline Jordan (Saïda), George Devoll (Philip of Mirlemont), Henry Lytton (Laine's father), and Rosina Brandram (Laine's mother); conducted by the composer.

The crippled Laine receives a stone from the Devil that makes her beautiful. In her new state she wins the heart of Philip of Mirlemont, a Flemish lord. The scorned mistress of Philip, Saïda, gets hold of the stone and changes Laine back into her crippled state. But when Philip returns from battle, he has become blind and thinks of his beloved as the beautiful woman he left behind.
SCORE: vs (London: Chappell; New York: Boosey, 1898).
LIBRETTO: English ([London]: Chappell & Co.; New York: Boosey & Co., [1898]).
DISCOGRAPHY: Soloists and orchestra of the performance group Prince Consort; Chorus of the Gilbert and Sullivan Society of Edinburgh; cond. D. Lyle, SHE 579/80 Pearl (1984).

Beckoning Fair One, The, opera in two acts by Gerald Kechley; libretto (Eng). First performance November 30, 1954, Seattle, University of Washington, Playhouse.

Bedouins, The, or, The Arabs of the Desert, comic opera in three acts by John Stevenson; libretto (Eng) by Eyles Irwin. First performance May 1, 1801, Dublin, Crow Street.
LIBRETTO: English ([Dublin: Graisberry and Campbell], 1802).

Bee-Hive, The, musical farce in two acts by Charles Edward Horn; libretto (Eng) by John G. Millingen, after Pigault-Lebrun's *Les rivaux d'eux mêmes*. First performance January 19, 1811, London, Lyceum Theatre.
LIBRETTO: English (London: W. H. Watt, 1811).

Before Breakfast, operatic farce by John Barnett; libretto (Eng) by R. B. Peake. First performance August 31, 1826, London, English Opera House.

Before Breakfast, opera in one act by Thomas Pasatieri; libretto (Eng) by Frank Corsaro, after Eugene O'Neill's monologue. First performance October 9, 1980, New York, New York City Opera, with Marilyn Zschau (the woman); conducted by Imre Pallo; produced by Frank Corsaro; designed by Lloyd Evans.

The story concerns a woman, once a marathon dancer but now a waitress, who drives her husband to suicide.

Role: the woman (sop).

Another setting of the story is E. Chisholm's *Dark Sonnet.**

BIBLIOGRAPHY: Donal Henahan, "Opera: 'An American Trilogy,' 3 One-Act Works," *NYT* (Oct. 10, 1980) [on premiere]; Robert Jacobson, "New York," *ON* XLV (Dec. 20, 1980), 42 [on premiere]; Dorle Soria, "An American Trilogy," *MA* XXX (Oct. 1980), 9–11.

Beggar's Love (A Little Girl at Play), opera in one act by Franklin Patterson; libretto (Eng) by Tyndall Gray and the composer. First performance December 8, 1929, New York, Ambassador Hotel.

The work is set in a contemporary American city slum. The young Peg scorns the love of the crippled Peter in favor of his indolent brother Nick. Unable to bear the situation, Peter ties up his brother, and when Peg returns, he stabs her.

Major roles: Peg (sop); Peter (bar); and Nick (ten).

Originally called *A Little Girl at Play: A Tragedy of the Slums.*

SCORE: vs (Boston and New York: C. C. Birchard & Co., 1930).

Beggar's Opera, The, ballad opera in three acts, arranged, adapted, with airs by John Pepusch; libretto (Eng) by John Gay. First performance January 29, 1728, London, Lincoln's Inn Fields Theatre (63 performances), with Lavinia Fenton (Polly Peachum), Thomas Walker (Macheath), John Hippisley (Peachum), and Mrs. Martin (Mrs. Peachum); produced by John Rich. Revised version by Thomas Linley, January 29, 1777, London, Drury Lane Theatre, with John Moody (Peachum), Mr. Bansby (Lockit), Joseph Vernon (Macheath), Mrs. Love (Mrs. Peachum), Mrs. Smith (Polly Peachum), and Mrs. Wrighten (Lucy Lockit). First U.S. performance December 3, 1750, New York, Nassau Street Theatre.

Modern versions include one by Frederic Austin: June 5, 1920, Hammersmith, London, Lyric Theatre, with Sylvia Nelis (Polly), Austin (Peachum), Violet Marquesita (Lucy), and Frederick Ranalow (Macheath); conducted by Eugene Goossens; produced by Nigel Playfair; it ran for 1,463 nights. Edward J. Dent's version received its first performance on May 22, 1944, Birmingham, England, Big Top. Revived September 1982, New York, Juilliard Theatre Center, with Denise Woods (Lucy); conducted by Ronald Braunstein; directed by Eve Shapiro.

Benjamin Britten's recomposition, with a libretto by Tyrone Guthrie, was first given on May 24, 1948, Cambridge, Arts Theatre, with Rose Hill (Lucy), Nancy Evans (Polly), and Peter Pears (Macheath); conducted by Britten; same version March 24, 1950, New York, Juilliard School, with Gladys Kuchta (Mrs. Peachum), Rosemary Kuhlmann (Polly), Eileen Schauler (Lucy), and John Drury (Macheath). Manfred Bukofzer's version appeared on April 6, 1954, New York, Columbia University, Brander Matthews Theater; conducted by Willard Rhodes.

Arthur Bliss wrote the score for the 1953 film version, directed by Peter Brook, which starred Laurence Olivier (Macheath), Hugh Griffiths (the Beggar), Stanley Holloway (Lockit), Dorothy Tutin (Lucy), and Jennifer Vyvyan. William Bolcom completed a version begun by Darius Milhaud; first performed January 31, 1979, Minneapolis, Tyrone Guthrie Theater.

A new performing version (see Discography) was made by Richard Bonynge and Douglas Gamley in 1981, updating or discarding the irrelevant text and using a full-size orchestra: "In preparing this new version of the music, we have constantly borne in mind that the work was originally presented as a popular entertainment" and that the major roles of Polly, Lucy, and Macheath "all require operatic voices," so that these parts are indeed sung by singers of the caliber of Kiri Te Kanawa, James Morris, and Joan Sutherland.

In the eighteenth-century setting, the Beggar introduces the work, making reference to the rivalry of the two main ladies of the plot, Polly and Lucy, both in love with Macheath. In the first act, Polly, daughter of Peachum, head of the beggars, weds her robber lover Macheath. Polly's parents are furious that she has married a thief and threaten to inform on him. When Polly tells Macheath of the danger, he hides in a brothel but is arrested, betrayed by Peachum. Polly visits Macheath in jail and meets Lucy, daughter of Lockit, the police chief; Macheath, it seems, has also married Lucy. After the ladies quarrel, Lucy helps Macheath escape. But, betrayed again, Macheath's freedom is short-lived; he is recaptured and sentenced to be hanged. Just before he is to be executed, he is saved by a pardon from the Queen herself.

For a detailed plot description, see K/*NKOB*, 237–40.

Major roles: Macheath (high bar); Lockit, the jailer (bass-bar); Lucy, Lockit's daughter (mezzo); Peachum, a fence (bass); Polly, his daughter (mezzo); Mrs. Peachum (sop); and the Beggar (speaking role).

Pepusch took most of the songs from *Pills to Purge Melancholy*, a collection by Thomas D'Urfey, published 1682–1724 (Dent edition, intro.). The sixty-nine airs include twenty-eight English ballads, twenty-three songs based on Irish, French, and Scotch tunes, and eleven on the works of Purcell, John Barrett, Jeremiah Clarke, G. F. Handel, Henry Carey, Bononcini, and John Eccles; the remaining eight may come from works by Geminiani, Pepusch, Frescobali, Lewis Ramondon, and John Wilford.

Eighteenth-century parodies include *The Fool's Opera* (1731), *Macheath in the Shades** (1735, London), *The Beggar's Pantomime, or, The Contending Columbines* (1736), *Macheath Turn'd Pyrate** (1737), and *The Bow-Street Opera** (1773). K. Weill's *Die Dreigroschenoper* (1928, Berlin), with the text adapted by B. Brecht, is the most famous twentieth-century treatment of the story; it was revived in a highly successful English version by M. Blitzstein in 1954, as *The Threepenny Opera.**

SCORE: overture, music for songs (unaccompanied) (London: J. and R. Tonson, 1765); vs ed. Edward J. Dent (London: Oxford University Press, 1954); fs (Oxford and New York: Oxford University Press, 1990).

LIBRETTO: English (London: John Watts, 1728); repr. ed. Rubsamen/*BO*, vol. 1, *The Beggar's Opera, Imitated and Parodied* (1974); rev. version (London: John Bell, 1777).

BIBLIOGRAPHY: Andrew Porter, "Musical Events," *NY* LVIII (Sept. 27, 1982), 134, 136; Robert Sabin, "Juilliard School Presents Britten's Beggar's Opera," *MA* LXX (Apr. 1950).

DISCOGRAPHY: F. Austin version (1920): Prietto, Westbury, Lipton, Camburn, McAlpine, Noble, Jones; chorus and instrumental ensemble; cond. R. Austin, London A4245 (2 LPs); B. Britten version (1948): A. Collins, A. Murray, P. Langdon, R. Lloyd; cond. S. Bedford, Argo 2-4368850-2 (2 CDs); D. Stevens version (1978): A. Jenkins, S. Minty, M. Cable, E. Lane, P. Clark, N. Rogers, E. Fleet, J. Noble, P. Hall, V. Midley, Accademia Monteverdiana; cond. D. Stevens, Koch Schwann 2 (2 CDs); Bonynge-Gamley version (1981): Te Kanawa, Morris, Sutherland, Lansbury, Marks, Resnik, Dean, Horden, Mitchell; National Philharmonic Orch.; cond. Bonynge, LDR 72008 (2 LPs).

VIDEO: music arr. Jeremy Barlow: S. Daltrey, R. Ashe, I. Blair, C. Hall, S. Johns, P. Routledge, P. Bayliss, English Baroque Soloists; cond. J. E. Gardiner, dir. J. Miller, perf. 1990, BBC television, Philips LD 070 408-1.

Beggar's Wedding, The, "a new opera" in three acts (ballad opera); libretto (Eng) by Charles Coffey. First performance March 24, 1729, Dublin, Smock Alley; May 29,

1729, London, with Mr. Smith (Alderman Quorum), Mr. Hulett (Chaunter), Mr. Chardin (Hunter), Mrs. Thomas (Mrs. Chaunter), Mrs. Nokes (Tippet), and Mrs. Mountford (Phebe). Also performed as *Phebe, or, The Beggar's Wedding*, in one act, June 13, 1729, London, Drury Lane Theatre, with Mr. Fielding (Justice Quorum), Mr. Bridgewater (Chaunter), Mr. Roberts (Hunter), Mrs. Shireburn (Mrs. Chaunter), Mrs. Heron (Tippet), and Mrs. Raftor (Phebe).

The story presents beggars in a positive light and includes a speech by the beggar king Chaunter, in which he extols the virtues of his way of life.

Major roles: Alderman Quorum, justice of the peace; Chaunter, king of the beggars; Hunter, his reputed son; Phebe, Quorum's reputed daughter; Mrs. Chaunter, queen of the beggars; and Tippet, maid to Phebe.

LIBRETTOS: English (London: James and John Knapton, 1729); English, as *Phebe* (London: J. and J. Knapton, 1729); repr. eds. Rubsamen/*BO*, vol. 22 (1974).

Beginning of the Day, The, children's opera by Anne Boyd; libretto (Eng). Composed 1980.

Be Glad Then America, a Decent Entertainment from the Thirteen Colonies, opera-oratorio in two acts by John La Montaine; libretto (Eng) by the composer, after documents from the American Revolution. First performance February 6, 1976, University Park, Pennsylvania, Pennsylvania State University, with Richard Lewis (George III), Donald Gramm (the Town Crier), and Odetta (Muse for America); conducted by Sarah Caldwell.

The work covers the founding of the United States as seen through the eyes of the colonists. It covers events such as the Stamp Act, the Battle of Lexington, and the signing of the Constitution. Each event is introduced by the Town Crier. He and King George III are the two characters that appear throughout the piece.

For a detailed description, see Kornick/*RAO*, 162–63.

Major roles: Town Crier (ten), King George III (ten), and Muse for America (mezzo).

The work quotes two musical pieces from the Revolutionary era, William Billings's hymn "Chester" and his "An Anthem for Fast Days," which includes the line "Be Glad, then, America." It was composed for the Penn State bicentennial.

SCORE: vs from holograph (Hollywood: P. J. Sifler, 1975).

LIBRETTO: English (University Park, Pa.: Pennsylvania State University Press, 1976).

BIBLIOGRAPHY: Allen Hughes, review, *NYT* (Feb. 8, 1976), 45 [on premiere].

Begum, The, "Hindoo comic opera" in two acts by Reginald De Koven; libretto (Eng) by Harry B. Smith. First performance November 21, 1887, New York, Fifth Avenue Theatre, with Mathilde Cottrelly (the Begum) and De Wolf Hopper (Howja-Dhu).

The Eastern ruler has a sure way to get rid of her husband when she begins to find him uninteresting—she makes him commander in chief of the army, declares war, and sends him off to his doom. Her plans are thwarted when her latest spouse, Howja-Dhu, has the audacity to defeat the enemy and return home unscathed.

LIBRETTO: English (Chicago: Blakely Printing Co., 1887).

Behold the Sun, opera in three acts by Alexander Goehr; libretto (Eng) by John McGrath and the composer. First performance, in German, in a shortened version, April 19, 1985, Duisburg, Deutsche Oper am Rhein, as *Die Wiedertäufer*; conducted by Hiroshi Wakasugi.

The story concerns the uprising by the Anabaptists in Münster in 1534. Two Dutch Anabaptists, Matthys, an idealist, and Bokelson, a conniver, try to organize their adherents, supported by the Berninck family. Opposing them is the Prince Bishop, who is afraid that the movement, which seeks a better world, will upset the social order. The Anabaptists, successful at first, are ultimately betrayed and massacred. The visionary Divara expresses their Utopian hopes as the work ends.

Major roles: Matthys (bar), Bokelson (ten), the Prince Bishop (bar), Divara (sop), and Christian Berninck (col sop).

The work, in which the chorus plays an important role, combines the devices of eighteenth-century figured bass and fugue with twentieth-century harmony. Among its highlights is Christian's aria "Behold the Sun."

SCORE: vs (Eng-Ger) (London: Schott; New York: Schott Music, 1985).

BIBLIOGRAPHY: Elizabeth Forbes, "Duisburg," *ON* L (Aug. 1985), 40–41 [on premiere]

Belisa, opera in one act by Albert Biales; libretto (Eng) by the composer, after Federico García-Lorca's play *Amor de Don Perlimplín con Belisa en su jardín* (1931). First performance January 29, 1989, St. Paul, Minnesota, Five College Interim Opera Project.

Don Perlimplin, a rich, older man, has married the young Belisa. In order to keep her happy, he invents a young lover who writes her poetry. Unable to live up to the ideal he has created or admit that he is the author of the poems, Perlimplin kills himself.

Also set by V. Rieti, as *Don Perlimplin** (1952, Urbana, Ill.); W. Fortner, as *In seinem Garten liebt Don Perlimplín Belisa* (1962, Schwetzingen); B. Sulzer, the same (1984, Linz); and C. Susa, as *The Love of Don Perlimplin** (1984, Purchase, N.Y.).

Bell, The, radio opera in one act by John Purser; libretto (Eng) by J. W. R. Purser (the composer's father). First performance December 27, 1972, BBC radio.

Belle, Le, or, Andre Goes Commercial, opera in one act by Louis Kroll; libretto (Eng). First performance September 30, 1935, New York, Pleasant Little Theater.

Bell Tower, The (Der Glockenturm), opera in one act by Ernst Krenek; libretto (Eng-Ger) by the composer, after a story by Herman Melville. First performance March 17, 1957, Urbana, Illinois, University of Illinois, School of Music, Lincoln Hall, with Donna Sue Burton (Una) and Manfred Capell (Bannadonna); conducted by John Garvey; produced by Ludwig Zirner.

In this horror story the mad genius Bannadonna makes a great bell for the city. In a rage after the workmen have tried to flee, Bannadonna kills Giovanni, his faithful helper. The workmen now believe that Giovanni's blood is in the bell. The assistant's daughter, Una, comes to the tower and falls under Bannadonna's spell. When she awakes from her trance, she tries to kill the madman, but he turns her to stone. She kills him nonetheless, and when the bell is struck, it breaks, revealing human flesh and the face of Una on its surface.

For a detailed description, see Eaton/*OP* I, 168–69

Major roles: Bannadonna (bar), Giovanni (bar), and Una (sop).

The score contains twelve-tone harmony, and much of the writing is declamatory, with orchestral interludes between the scenes.

BIBLIOGRAPHY: Claude Palisca, "Krenek's Campanile," *ON* XXI (Apr. 15, 1957), 15.

Bell Tower, The, music drama by Robert Haskins; libretto (Eng) by Allen Koppenhaver and the composer, after Melville. Composed 1976.

SCORE: ms score, signed holograph (photocopy, 1976, NYPL).

Belly Bag, The, chamber opera in one act by Michael Ball; libretto (Eng) by Alan Garner, after a medieval fragment. Composed 1992.

The setting is Alderley. Because a witch's leather bag is draining all the milk from the village cattle by night, the witch is summoned before the Bishop. Their meeting, however, only makes the Bishop humbler and wiser.

Bellyful, chamber opera in one act by Felix Werder; libretto (Eng) by Leonard Radic, after the Bible. Composed 1975. Not performed.

Belphegor, or, The Wishes, comic operatic afterpiece by François Barthelemon; libretto (Eng) by Miles Peter Andrews, after J. F. Guichard and N. Castet's *Le bûcheron, ou, Les trois souhaits*, set by Philidor (1763, Paris). First performance March 16, 1778, London, Drury Lane Theatre.

A devil, Belphegor, gives Booze and his wife, Dame Din, three wishes. When the wife chooses two wishes foolishly, the husband has to use the third to undo them.

For a description, see Fiske/*ETM*, 419–20.
SCORE: vs (London, 1778).
LIBRETTO: English ([Dublin]: The Booksellers, 1788).

Belshazzar's Feast, sacred opera by John Henry Griesbach; libretto (Eng), after the Bible. Composed 1835. Revised as an oratorio, under the title *Daniel*. First performance in this version June 30, 1854, London.

A setting of the story of the Babylonian ruler, whose defeat is predicted by Daniel.

Belshazzar's Feast, opera-cantata by George F. Root; libretto (Eng) by Benjamin Franklin Edmands, after the Bible. Composed ca. 1853. Revised as *Daniel, or, The Captivity and Restoration*, sacred cantata in three parts, 1853, with music by Root and William Bradbury; text by Chauncey Marvin Cady and Fanny Crosby.

Story also set by G. F. Handel, as *Belshazzar* (1745, London); as *Belsazer*, by F. Werder (1988, Dortmund, Ger.).
SCORE: as *Daniel* (New York: Mason Bros., 1853).
LIBRETTO: English, as *Daniel* (New York: Mason Bros., 1853).

Benevolent Tar, The, or, The Miller's Daughter, opera in one act by Charles Dibdin; libretto (Eng) by the composer. First performance 1785, London, Royal Circus.

Benito Cereno. See **An American Triptych.**

Benjamin, opera in a prologue and two acts by John Carbon; libretto (Eng) by Sarah White. First performance April 23, 1987, Lancaster, Pennsylvania, Franklin and Marshall College.

The story focuses on events in Benjamin Franklin's life.
SCORE: vs (Santa Barbara: California Philharmonic Association, 1987).

Bennelong, puppet opera in thirteen scenes by Barry Conyngham; libretto (Eng) by Murray Copland. First performance April 21, 1988, Groningen, Netherlands, State Theatre.

The action is narrated by two soloists (sop, ten), who tell the story of Captain Phillip, Australia's first governor; Phillip teaches Bennelong, his aboriginal captive, the "superiority" of Western thinking. To that end the captain takes Bennelong on a trip to London, where Bennelong is confused and disillusioned by what he sees. Coming back to Australia, Bennelong finds that his own society will no longer accept him, and, as he becomes drunk and starts to hallucinate, he is killed by a mysterious spear.
SCORE: vs (London: Universal Edition, 1987).

Benyowsky, or, The Exiles of Kamschatka, operatic play in three acts by Matthew King, Thomas Cooke, Michael Kelly, Barham Livius, and John Stevenson; libretto (Eng) by James Kenney, after Kotzebue. First performance March 16, 1826, London, Drury Lane Theatre.

Set by Victor Pelissier as *Count Benyowsky*, a play with music (1799, New York). LIBRETTO: English (London: Longman et al., 1826).

Berta, or, The Gnome of Hartsberg, romantic opera in two acts by Henry Smart; libretto (Eng) by Edward Fitzball. First performance May 26, 1855, London, Haymarket Theatre, with Mr. Weiss (Valouri), Sims Reeves (Michael), Mr. Manvers (Koff), Mr. W. Warren (Isaac), Mr. Hains (Corporal Strutz), Mr. Farquharson (burgomaster of Hartzberg), Mrs. Sims Reeves (Berta), and Miss Harriet Gordon (Nannetta).
LIBRETTO: English (London: Chappell Music, 1855).

Bertha, opera in one act by Ned Rorem; libretto (Eng) by Kenneth Koch, after his play of the same name. First performance November 26, 1973, New York, Alice Tully Hall, with Beverly Wolff (Queen Bertha); conducted by James Holmes. Revived (concert) March 1, 1981, New York, Golden Fleece; conducted by John Klingberg; directed by Lou Rodgers.

Set in and around the royal residence in Oslo, the story is a surrealistic treatment of the "mad" Queen Bertha of Norway, who launches an attack on Scotland, has her own teacher beheaded, and dismisses her council when the advisers object. At her death, she is acclaimed by her loyal subjects.

For a detailed description, see Eaton/*OP* II, 250.

Major roles: Bertha (mezzo) and counselor (bass).
SCORE: vs (New York: Boosey & Hawkes, [1973]).
BIBLIOGRAPHY: Peter Davis, "Short Operas: 2 by Golden Fleece," *NYT* (March 2, 1981) [on 1981 revival]; Robert Jacobson, "New York," *ON* XXXVIII (Jan. 19, 1974), 25–26 [on premiere].

Bethlehem, choral drama in two acts by Rutland Boughton; libretto (Eng) by the composer after the Coventry Nativity Play and traditional carols. First performance December 28, 1915, Street (near Glastonbury), England, Crispin Hall.
SCORE: vs (London, J. Curwen & Sons, 1920).

Better Sort, The, or, The Girl of Spirit, "an operatical, comical farce" (ballad opera); libretto (Eng) attributed to William Hill Brown. Composed 1789. First performance November 8, 1985, Worcester, Massachusetts, American Antiquarian Society, conducted by David P. McKay.

The farce is set in the Boston house of Mrs. Sententious, wife of a prosperous merchant. Peter Lovemuch is anxious to have his daughter, Mira, marry the old and supposedly wealthy Alonzo. Mira, in turn, wishes to marry the penniless Harry Truelove. Jenny helps the young lovers by revealing that Alonzo has lost his money and conniving to have Harry win the lottery.

For a description, see Virga/*AO*, 149–52.

Roles: Harry Truelove, "entertains a passion for *Mira*; Mr. Sententious, "a man of good sense"; Peter Lovemuch, an old man, "in love with *Alonzo*'s money"; Alonzo Hazard, "in love with *Mira*'s fortune"; Captain Flash, "a British subject—who loves to *belittle* America, and to talk about English politicks"; Yorick, "a good natured Yankee"; Jenny, friend of Mira; Mrs. Sententious, who "thinks if one has a fortune, one ought to enjoy it—and as she has money, the best way is to set up for one of the *better sort*"; and Mira, daughter of Lovemuch, "has some esteem for *Harry*, and is a 'girl of *spirit*.'" LIBRETTO: English (Boston: Isaiah Thomas and Co., 1789); repr. ed. Rubsamen/*BO*, vol. 28, *American Ballad Operas* (1974).

Between Two Worlds (The Dybbuk), opera by Shulamit Ran; libretto (Eng) by Charles Kondek, after S. Ansky's drama (1920). First performance June 20, 1997, Chicago, Lyric Opera Center, with Mary Jane Kania (Leya), Matthew Polezani (Khonnon), Jessie Raven (Freyde), Robin Blitch Wiper (Gittel), and Mark McCrory (Reb Azriel); conducted by Arthur Fagen; directed by Jonathan Eaton; designed by Danila Korogodsky.

In this telling of the Jewish fable, a woman, Leya, is possessed by the soul (dybbuk) of her dead fiancé, Khonnon; she can be freed only through exorcism.

The composer blends elements of a Hasidic lament and klezmer folk dance with the more traditional arioso in a score accompanied by a chamber orchestra. The voices of the departed are amplified to contrast with those of the living.

See *The Dybbuk* for other settings.
BIBLIOGRAPHY: John Van Rhein, "Chicago," *ON* LXII (Nov. 1997), 56 [on premiere].

Beyond Belief, opera in one act by Thomas Canning. First performance May 14, 1956, Rochester, New York, Eastman School of Music; conducted by Howard Hanson.

The satirical text concerns the atomic age and creating consciousness via science.
BIBLIOGRAPHY: review, *NYT* (May 15, 1956), 26 [on premiere].

Bianca, comic opera in one act by Henry Hadley; libretto (Eng) by Grant Stewart, after Carlo Goldoni's *La locandiera*. First performance October 15, 1918, New York, Park Theatre, with Maggie Teyte (Bianca), Howard White (Il Conte della Terramonte), Henri Scott (Il Cavaliere del Ruggio), Carl Formes (Fabricio), and Craig Campbell (Il Marchese d'Amalfi); conducted by the composer.

The work is set at an inn near Florence in 1760. Bianca, mistress of the inn, is the object of affection of the rivals Terramonte and Amalfi. When her servant, Fabricio, stops the two from fighting, she chooses him for her husband, rejecting also the suit of the woman-hating Cavaliere del Ruggio, whom she has charmed.

Major roles: Bianca (sop), Il Cavaliere del Ruggio (bass), Il Conte della Terramonte (bar), Il Marchese d'Amalfi (ten), Fabricio (bar), Pietro (bass), and Carlo (ten).

Among the highlights is the duet of Bianca and Fabricio, "Against My Will."
See Hipsher/*AO*, 233–34, for a description.

Other settings include *La locandiera* by A. Lamotte-Foucher (1798, Lucca); J. S. Mayr (1800, Venice); G. Farinelli (1808, Milan); E. Usiglio (1861, Turin); M. Persico (1941, Milan); and M. Thiriet (1960, Paris).
SCORE: vs (New York: Harold Flammer, 1918).

Bianca, the Bravo's Bride, "grand original legendary opera" in four acts by Michael Balfe; libretto (Eng) by John Palgrave Simpson, after M. G. Lewis's *Rugantino*. First performance December 6, 1860, London, Covent Garden, with Alberto Lawrence (Matteo Visconti), Henry Wharton (Count Malespina), Henry Corri (Memmino), A. St. Albyn (Beppo), Charles Lyall (Contarini), Mr. Wallworth (Montalto), Mr. Friend (Salviati), Mr. Chapman (Montereale), Mr. Grattan (Michele), W. Harrison (Forestpada), Louisa Pyne (Bianca), and Anna Thirlwall (Zeffirina).
SCORE: ms fs, mostly autograph (1860, British Library, MS. Add. 29356, 29357).
LIBRETTO: English (London: Covent Garden, [1860?]).

Big Black Box, The, comic opera in one act by Sam Morgenstern; libretto (Eng) by Francis Steegmuller, after an article in a Philippine newspaper. First performance February 13, 1968, New York, Metropolitan Opera Studio.

The poor lawyer Manuel is in love with Onita, daughter of the rich Don Fausto and Dona Clara, the girl's duenna. He attends a ball at Don Augustin's house, during which two drunk sailors bring in a large box supposedly containing a gift for the host. When it is opened, Don Augustin and the others are horrified at what they see.

The box is finally brought to Don Fausto, who fears he is being hunted by an enemy whom he has cheated. Onita and Dona Clara convince Don Fausto to call in Manuel, who is the only one in the town able to read the writing on the box. Manuel instructs the villagers to meet him at the church the next day. The "body" in the box turns out to be a statue of St. John the Baptist, sent as a gift, and the embarrassed Don Fausto is forced to give his daughter's hand in marriage to the wise Manuel.

For a detailed description, see Eaton/*OP* II, 251.

Roles: Don Augustin (bar), Onita (sop), Dona Clara (mezzo), Manuel (ten), sailors (ten, bass), and Don Fausto (bass).

Biko, opera by Priti Paintal; libretto (Eng) by Richard Fawkes. First performance May 29, 1992, Birmingham; June 10, 1992, London, English National Opera, with Daniel Washington (Biko), Hyacinth Nicholls (Biko's wife), Angela Caesar (woman), Gerard Quinn (security policeman), Stephen Richardson (Donald Woods), and Damon Evans (Thomas); conducted by Timothy Lole.

The story concerns the arrest and murder of the South African civil rights leader Steven Biko. In this treatment Biko's idealism is contrasted by the impatience of the militant Thomas. The other protagonists include Biko's wife, a security policeman who arrests Biko, and a sympathetic white newspaper editor, Donald Woods.

The music includes spirituals (whose use was criticized by the reviewers as inauthentic, as was the work's lack of passion and mostly nonoperatic style).
BIBLIOGRAPHY: John Allison, review, *Opera* XLIII (Aug. 1992), 990–91 [on London premiere]; Paul Griffiths, "The Black Death," *TLS* no. 4653 (June 5, 1992), 19 [on premiere].

Bilby's Doll, opera in three acts by Carlisle Floyd; libretto (Eng) by the composer after the novel by Esther Forbes *A Mirror for Witches* (1928). First performance February 27, 1976, Houston, Houston Grand Opera, with Catherine Malfitano (Doll Bilby), Alan Titus (Titus Thumb), Thomas Paul (Jared Bilby), Joy Davidson (Hannah Bilby), and Tom Fox (Mister Zelley); conducted by Christopher Keene; directed by David Pountney; designed by Ming Cho Lee.

The setting is seventeenth-century Massachusetts. When Deacon Thumb suggests that his son Titus wed Doll, Jared Bilby's adopted daughter, Hannah, Bilby's wife, causes trouble by suggesting that Doll, born to a couple burned as witches, is herself evil. Hannah also blames Doll when Bilby dies, but she is cleared by the clergyman Mister Zelley. Visiting Bilby's grave, Doll meets a handsome young stranger, and, taking his arrival as a sign, she weds him secretly. Doll is accused of witchcraft when twin sisters have convulsions. Titus and Zelley try to save her by offering to marry her, but she discloses that she already has a husband and is pregnant. Zelley realizes that her husband is, in fact, his own faithless son Shad, although he convinces Doll that her husband was the demon lover she had hoped to meet at Bilby's grave.

Major roles: Jared Bilby (ten), Titus Thumb (bar), Deacon Thumb (ten), Mister Zelley (bass-bar), Doll Bilby (sop), and Hannah Bilby (mezzo).

For a detailed description, see Kornick/*RAO*, 102–3.
SCORE: vs (New York: E. Schuberth, 1897).
BIBLIOGRAPHY: Allen Hughes, review, *NYT* (Feb. 29, 1976), I, 45 [on premiere].

Billy Budd, opera in a prologue, four acts, and an epilogue by Benjamin Britten; libretto (Eng) by E. M. Forster and Eric Crozier, after Herman Melville's story (1891, pub. 1924). First performance December 1, 1951, London, Covent Garden, with Theodor Uppman (Billy), Frederick Dalberg (Claggart), Peter Pears (Captain Vere), and Geraint Evans (Mr. Flint); conducted by the composer. First U.S. performance October 7, 1952, NBC-TV, with Theodor Uppman (Billy), Leon Lishner (Claggart), Andrew McKinley (Captain Vere), and Paul Ukena (Mr. Flint); conducted by Peter Herman Adler; designed by John Piper. First U.S. stage performance December 7, 1952, Bloomington, Indiana University School of Music, with Jack Gilaspy (Billy), Donald Vogel (Claggart), Eugene Bayless (Captain Vere), and James Cockrun (Mr. Flint); conducted by Ernst Hoffman.

Revised into a two-act version with prologue and epilogue, November 13, 1960, BBC, with Pears, J. Ward, and Langdon; conducted by the composer; first stage performance January 9, 1964, London, Covent Garden, with Lewis, Kerns, and Robinson; conducted by Georg Solti. First U.S. performance of revised version January 4, 1966 (concert), New York, American Opera Society; November 6, 1970 (staged), Chicago, Lyric Opera, with Uppman (Billy), Evans (Claggart), Richard Lewis (Captain Vere), Andrea Velis (Squeak), John Walker (Novice), Robert Thomas (Red Whiskers), and Dennis Wicks (Dansker); conducted by Bruno Bartoletti.

The setting is the English warship *Indomitable* during the Napoleonic Wars in 1797. The story concerns the young idealistic sailor Billy, who is taken off his ship, the *Rights o' Man*, and is forced into service on the *Indomitable*, along with Red Whiskers and Arthur Jones. Although popular with his shipmates and admired by Captain Vere, his innocence, exuberance, and naïveté cause him to be the target of the sadistic master-at-arms, John Claggart. Claggart instructs Squeak to make Billy feel uncomfortable and, using the Novice and Dansker to further his treachery, sets the stage for Billy's destruction. Billy's stutter prevents him from defending himself against Claggart's false charges of mutiny, and in an uncontrolled rage at the injustice, Billy strikes his tormentor dead. Captain Vere, although believing Billy innocent of willful murder, allows him to be sentenced to death. As Billy is about to be hanged, he exclaims, "Starry Vere, God Bless You." Vere recalls these events in the prologue and epilogue, in which he is shown as a haunted old man.

For a detailed plot synopsis and musical analysis, see K/*KOB*, 1184–93; K/*NKOB*, 111–17; Eaton/*OP* I, 36–37; *COH*, ed. Cooke and Reed (see Bibliography).

Major roles: Captain Edward Fairfax Vere (ten); Billy Budd (bar); John Claggart (bass); Squeak, the ship's corporal (ten); Novice (ten); Red Whiskers, an impressed sailor (ten); Mr. Flint, sailing master (bar); and Dansker, an old sailor (bass).

The opera is particularly effective in its striking choruses, for example, "This Is the Moment," during the battle with the French. Another highlight is the passacaglia-like duet between Billy and Dansker to end act 2, "For Jemmy-Legs Is Down on You." The opera is also noteworthy for its absence of any female roles. Britten uses different tonalities to represent various characters, events, and themes (see *COH*, 87–110). The work has been described as being symphonic in design (it was originally written in four acts), with act 1 as the exposition, act 2 as the slow movement, act 3 as the scherzo, and act 4 as the finale (see *COH*, 86–87).

The story was also set by G. F. Ghedini (1949, Venice).

BIBLIOGRAPHY: Mervyn Cooke and Philip Reed, *Benjamin Britten: Billy Budd, COH* (Cambridge: Cambridge University Press, 1993); Quaintance Eaton, "Billy's Bow," *ON* XLIII (Mar. 31, 1979), 28, 30; John W. Freeman, "Chicago," *ON* XXXV (Dec. 19, 26, 1970), 36 [on U.S. revival]; Clifford Hindley, "Britten's Billy Budd. The 'Interview Chords' Again," *MQ* 49/1 (1963), 99–126; Edward Lockspeiser, "Britten's Billy Budd Has Premiere," *MA* LXXII (Jan. 1, 1952), 3; Paul Nettl, review, *ON* XVII (Feb. 16, 1953), 10–11 [on U.S. stage premiere]; Gary Schmidgall, "Epitaph for Innocence," *ON* XLIV (Apr. 19, 1980), 21–22, 24–27; James Helme Sutcliffe, "The Infinite Sea," *ON* XLVIII (Apr. 14, 1984), 17–18, 43; Stephen Wadsworth, "The Go-Between," *ON* XLIV (Apr. 19, 1980), 11–12, 14; Arnold Whittall, "A War and a Wedding: Two Modern British Weddings," *ML* LV (1994), 299–306.

DISCOGRAPHY: P. Pears, T. Uppman, F. Dalberg, H. Alan, G. Evans, Royal Opera House Orchestra and Chorus; cond. B. Britten (Dec. 1, 1951, premiere), VAI Audio 3-VAIA 1034–3 (3 CDs); Pears, Glossop, Shirley-Quirk, Luxon, Langdon, Brannigan, London Sym. Orch. and Ambrosian Singers; cond. Britten, London 3 417428-2 (3 CDs); (rev. version) Pears, Dempsey, Tear, R. Bowman, Glossop, Shirley-Quirk, Drake, D. Bowman, Bryn-Jones, Langdon, Kelly, Brannigan, Boys from Wadsworth School, Ambrosian Opera Chorus and London Sym. Orch.; cond. Britten (1968), London OSA-1390 (3 CDs).

VIDEO: Allen, Langridge, Van Allan, English National Opera; cond. Atherton, Home Vision BIL 01 1 VHS.

Bird Catcher, The, comic burletta by V. de Cleeve; libretto (Eng). First performance 1799, London, Drury Lane Theatre, with Mr. Grimaldi (Peter).

The bird catcher is Robin, who, along with Peter, a fisherman, loves the watercress seller Nancy. In order to undermine Robin's chances Peter enlists the help of the unscrupulous bailiff Snatchem, but he in turn is charmed by Nancy and helps Robin pay a debt he owed Peter.

For a description, see Fiske/*ETM*, 579.

Bird in the Bush, A, opera in one act by Herbert Bielawa; libretto (Eng) by Warren Kliewer. First performance July 10, 1962, Los Angeles, University of Southern California.

A lonely widow, Magdalene Forensic, nurses a sickly sparrow back to health and lavishes affection on it. The bird escapes, and when Magdalene recaptures it with great difficulty, she destroys the bird; she is brought to the brink of madness by her efforts and the need to care for her senile mother.

For a detailed description, see Summers/*OOA*, 54–56.

Major roles: Magdalene Forensic (dram mezzo/sop); Natura Magen, her mother (alto); and Stanley Sullivan, a policeman (bass-bar/bass).

Birds, The, extravaganza in one act by Elizabeth Maconchy; libretto (Eng) by the composer, after Aristophanes (414 B.C.). First performance June 5, 1968, London, Bishop's Stortford College.

Fugitive Athenians convince the birds to create a city in the clouds. The city is situated to prevent the smoke of sacrifices by mortals from reaching the gods, and the smoke is blocked until the gods give in to the demands of the birds.

Other settings of the Aristophanes text are W. Braunfels's *Die Vögel* (1920, Munich); and Lejaren Hiller's "musical" *The Birds*, to a text by Walter Kerr (1958, Urbana, Ill.). See also the following entries.

SCORE: vs (New York and London: Boosey and Hawkes, [1974]).

Birds, The, musical fantasy by Halim El-Dabh; libretto (Eng) by the composer, after Aristophanes. Composed 1988.

Birds, The, opera by David Ahlstrom; libretto (Eng), after Aristophanes. First performance May 5, 1990, San Francisco.
    Scored for jazz ensemble.

Birds of a Feather, or, Buzz and Mum, burletta by John Moorehead and Thomas Attwood; libretto (Eng) possibly by John Moorehead. First performance July 25, 1796, London, Sadler's Wells.
LIBRETTO: English (London: Scatcherd . . . and Smeeton, 1796).

Birth-Day, The, or, The Prince of Arragon, opera in two acts by Samuel Arnold; libretto (Eng) by John O'Keeffe. First performance August 12, 1783, London, Little Theatre in the Haymarket.
    Composed for the Prince of Wales's coming-of-age.
SCORE: vs (London: author, n.d.).
LIBRETTO: English (London: T. Cadell, 1783).

Birthday, The, or, The Arcadian Contest, pastoral opera by Thomas Carter; anonymous libretto (Eng). First performance 1787, London, Royalty Theatre.

Birth/Day: The Frankenstein Musical, opera by Neil Wolfe; libretto (Eng) by Ron Troutman, after Mary Shelley. First performance October 15, 1993, Dallas, Hickory Street Annex, Deep Ellum Opera Company, with Tim Worley (Igor), Gaitley Mathews (Dr. Frankenstein), and Brenda Box Bristol; conducted by Mathews; directed by David McClinton.
    A treatment of the familiar tale of Frankenstein and his monstrous creation.
BIBLIOGRAPHY: John Briggs, "Dallas," *ON* (Feb. 19, 1994), 35 [on premiere].

Birthday of the Bank, The, comic opera in one act by Leonard Lehrman; libretto (Eng) by the composer, after Anton Chekhov's farce *Jubilee* (1891). First performance August 3, 1988, Glens Falls, New York, Lake George Opera Festival.
SCORE: ms vs, holograph (1988, NYPL).

Birthday of the Infanta, The, opera in one act by Ronald Nelson; libretto (Eng) by the composer, after Oscar Wilde. First performance May 14, 1956, Rochester, New York, Eastman School of Music; conducted by Howard Hanson.
    A dwarf, captured in the woods, is given to the Spanish Infanta on the occasion of her eighteenth birthday. He falls in love with her, only to die of a broken heart when, upon seeing himself in a mirror, he realizes how ugly he is.
    Major roles: the Infanta (sop); Mara, her guardian (mezzo/alto); and the dwarf (bar).
BIBLIOGRAPHY: review, *NYT* (May 15, 1956), 26 [on premiere].

Birthday of the Infanta, The, children's opera in one act by Richard Stoker; libretto (Eng) by S. Vincent, after Oscar Wilde. First performance July 12, 1963, London, St. Pancras Town Hall.
    Another setting is A. Zemlinsky's *Der Zwerg* (1922, Cologne).

Birth of Arthur, The, choral drama in two acts by Rutland Boughton; libretto (Eng) by Reginald R. Buckley and the composer. Composed 1909. First performance August 16, 1920, Glastonbury.

Part one of Boughton's Arthurian cycle, which also includes *The Round Table** (1916), *The Lily Maid** (1934), *Galahad** (comp. 1944, not perf.), and *Avalon** (1945, not perf.).

Birth of Hercules, The, pastoral by Thomas Augustine Arne; libretto (Eng) by William Shirley. Composed 1763. Its planned premiere at Covent Garden did not take place. The work was written in honor of the birth of the Prince of Wales.

Birth of the Poet, The, "an opera" by Peter Gordon; libretto (Eng) by Kathy Acker. First performance April 1984, Rotterdam. First U.S. performance December 4, 1985, Brooklyn, New York, Brooklyn Academy of Music Next Wave Festival, with Zach Grenier (Ali/Hinkley), Jan Leslie Harding (Cynthia), Max Jacobs (Propertius), and Valda Setterfield (lady with the whip); directed by Richard Foreman.

The plot is a cartoonish, erotic presentation of three "traumatic" events in world history: New York in the future as a nuclear power plant explodes, the late Roman Empire, and modern Iran.

BIBLIOGRAPHY: John Rockwell, review, *NYT* (Dec. 5, 1985), III, 17 [on U.S. premiere].
VIDEO: U.S. premiere (2 videocassettes, NYPL).

Bishop's Horse, The, children's opera in one act by David Ahlstrom; libretto (Eng), after a thirteenth-century story. First performance May 19, 1984, San Francisco.

Bitter-Sweet, "operette" in three acts by Noël Coward; libretto and lyrics (Eng) by the composer; orchestrated by De Orellana. First performance (tryout) July 2, 1929, Manchester, Palace Theatre; July 12, 1929, London, His Majesty's Theatre, with Peggy Wood (Sari/Sarah), George Metaxa (Carl), and Alan Napier (Lord Shayne); conducted by Reginald Burston. First U.S. performance November 5, 1929, New York, Ziegfeld Theatre, with Evelyn Laye (Sari/Sarah); conducted by Arthur Jones. Revived winter 1988, London, New Sadler's Wells Opera, with Valerie Masterson (Sari/Sarah).

The story, presented in flashback by the heroine, concerns an English socialite, Sarah, who falls in love with her music teacher, Carl Linden. Together they elope to Vienna, where he dies in a duel with a rival. Sarah returns to London as a famous singer, calling herself Sari Linden, and she marries Lord Shayne, while never forgetting her first love.

For a description, see Traubner/*O*, 339–41.

The memorable numbers include Sari's "Zigeuner," a mock gypsy piece; "I'll See You Again," which Sari sings first as a duet with Carl and then alone, at the end of the work; the drinking song "Tokay"; and "If Love Were All," sung by Manon, a café singer.

SCORE: vs (London, New York: Chappell, 1929).
LIBRETTO: English (London: M. Secker, 1929).
BIBLIOGRAPHY: Richard Traubner, review, *ON* LIII (July 1988), 53 [on revival].

Blackamoor Wash'd White, The, comic opera by Charles Dibdin; libretto (Eng) by Henry Bate. First performance February 1, 1776, London, Drury Lane Theatre, with Mrs. Wrighten and Mrs. Siddons (Julia).

Young Frederick, in love with Julia, wins access to the house of the rich Sir Oliver Oldfish, her father. By donning blackface, since the old man has decided to substitute black workers for his former white servants, Frederick is therefore able not only to enter the house but to elope with Julia.

For a detailed description, see Fiske/*ETM 2*, 375–76.

The work was a failure because of the claque arranged against the librettist, rather than the admittedly poor quality and offensive nature of the text.

Black Crook, The, "an original magical and spectacular drama in four acts," consisting of music by Thomas Baker, the ballet *La biche au bois*, and the melodrama in four acts, *The Black Crook* by Charles M. Barras. First performance September 12, 1866, New York, Niblo's Gardens, with E. B. Holmes (Zamiel), C. H. Morton (the Black Crook), G. C. Boniface (Rudolf), Annie Kemp Bowler (Stalacta), and Rose Morton (Amina). It ran for 475 performances. The many revivals included 1871, New York, with music by Giuseppe Operti.

Barras's story is an adaptation of Weber's *Der Freischütz*. The arch fiend is called Zamiel, and he convinces the Black Crook, Hertzog, to collect a human soul every twelfth month just before midnight. Hertzog frees the imprisoned painter Rudolf, who does not realize that Hertzog is after his soul. When Rudolf saves a dove, it turns out to be Stalacta, Queen of the Golden Realm, who saves him from his fate and unites him with the woman he loves, Amina.

For descriptions, see Bordman/*AMT*, 18–20; Root/*APSM*, 79–96.

The five-hour spectacle is considered the first American musical comedy. It came about because the ballet was supposed to have been performed at the Academy, which had just burned down, and its impresarios, Henry C. Jarrett and Harry Palmer, convinced William Wheatley, manager of Niblo's Gardens, to combine the two works.
LIBRETTO: English (Buffalo: Rockwell, Baker, & Hill, 1866).

Black Crook, The, "grand opéra-bouffe féerie" in four acts by Frederic Clay and George Jacobi; libretto (Eng) by Harry Paulton and Joseph Paulton, after Théodor Cogniard's *La biche au bois*. First performance December 23, 1872, London, Alhambra Theatre. Revised version December 3, 1881, London, Alhambra.

Black Epic, opera-pageant by Halim El-Dabh; libretto (Eng) by the composer. Composed 1968. Not performed.

The work presents a history of African people in the United States.

Black Rider, rock opera in twelve parts and a prologue; music and lyrics by Tom Waits; libretto (Eng) by William Burroughs. First performance March 31, 1990, Hamburg, Thalia Theater, with Dominique Horwitz (Pegleg), Stefan Kurt (Wilhelm), and Annette Paulmann (Käthchen); directed and designed by Robert Wilson. First U.S. performance December 1993, Brooklyn, New York, Brooklyn Academy of Music, with the same leads.

The story is inspired by Weber's opera *Der Freischütz* (1821, Berlin). Unlike the Weber, however, there is no happy ending. The hero, Wilhelm, is charmed and taken in by the devilish Pegleg, mistakenly shoots his beloved, Käthchen, and goes mad.

The dialogue is in rhymed German, while the songs are in English. Davis describes the style of the music as "a cross between Andrew Lloyd Webber and Kurt Weill . . . [that] mainly reeks of the beer hall," and Rockwell, as "*Der Freischütz* meets *Cabaret*, with a dash of *The Rocky Horror Picture Show* on the side" (see Bibliography). It has received a number of performances since its premiere.

Among the musical highlights is Pegleg's seductive "Come on Along with Me."

Part two of Robert Wilson's rock opera trilogy, which includes *Alice** (1992, Hamburg) and *Time Rocker** (1997, Paris).
TEXTS: English-German, Robert Wilson, *The Black Rider: The Casting of the Magic Bullets*, theater program, songs ([Hamburg]: Thalia Theater, 1990).
BIBLIOGRAPHY: Marge Betley, "New York City," *ON* (Feb. 19, 1994), 36 [on U.S. premiere]; Peter Davis, "American Gothic," *New York* (Dec. 6, 1993), 128 [on premiere]; Stephen

Holden, "When Tragedy Becomes the Bitter Food of Satire," *NYT* (Nov. 22, 1993), C, 11 [on U.S. premiere]; John Rockwell, "The Black Rider Rides Again," *ON* (Nov. 1993), 28–29 [on U.S. premiere]; Edward Rothstein, "'Black Rider' Gives Old Songs a Bitter Twist," *NYT* (Dec. 5, 1993), C, 37 [on U.S. premiere].

Black River, a Wisconsin Idyll, grand opera in a prologue and three acts by Conrad Susa; libretto (Eng) by Richard Street and the composer, after Michael Lesy's *Wisconsin Death Trip*. First performance October 6, 1975, St. Paul, Minnesota Opera. Revised version (1976) February 27, 1981, St. Paul.

The work is set in Wisconsin at the turn of the century and concerns three women. The first is Pauline L'Allemand, a former opera singer who is in a mental hospital. She imagines her earlier triumphs, as two other women relive their plights, the lonely wife of the judge who committed Pauline to the institution, and the judge's daughter, left a widow at a young age.

SCORE: holograph score (Boston: E. C. Schirmer Co., 1976).

BIBLIOGRAPHY: Andrew Porter, "Musical Events," *NY* LV (Aug. 27, 1979), 84.

Black Roses, opera in one act by Erik Chisholm; libretto (Eng) by the composer, after T. S. Eliot. First performance July 6, 1954, New York, Cherry Lane Theater.

Part 2 of the *Murder in Three Keys** trilogy; see also *Dark Sonnet** and *Simoon.**

Black Sea Follies, musical theater piece in two acts by Stanley Silverman, after Shostakovich; libretto (Eng) by Paul Schmidt. First performance August 6, 1986, Stockbridge, Massachusetts, Lenox Arts Center, with David Chandler (Shostakovich) and Alan Scarfe (Stalin).

The work is a mixture of tragedy and farce and involves Joseph Stalin and Dmitri Shostakovich, with the composer reminiscing in the 1970s, just before his death, about his persecution by the Russian dictator.

BIBLIOGRAPHY: Harlow Loomis Robinson, review, *MA/HiFi* XXXVI (Dec. 1986), 18–19 [on premiere]; John Simon, review, *New York* XX (Jan. 12, 1987), 49–50 [on premiere].

Black Spider, The, opera in three acts by Judith Weir; libretto (Eng) by the composer, after the novel *Die schwarze Spinne* (1842) by Jeremias Gotthelf and a news report from the *Times* (July 2, 1983). First performance March 6, 1985, Canterbury, England.

In order to complete the impossible task of building a road to the castle in one month, a town enlists the help of the Devil. As a reward the Devil gets the next child born in the village. When the newborn of a woman just arrived in the town is christened before the Devil can touch it, he takes his revenge by turning the woman into a black spider, which brings illness and ruin.

The Gotthelf story was also set in its German original by J. Matthias Hauer (1932, perf. 1966, Vienna); W. Burkhardt (1949, Zurich); and H. Sutermeister (1936, Bern).

SCORE: vs (London: Novello, 1989).

Black Vulture, The, or, The Wheel of Death, romantic burletta by George Rodwell; libretto (Eng) by Edward Fitzball. First performance October 4, 1830, London, Adelphi Theatre.

Black Water, opera in two acts by John Duffy; libretto (Eng) by Joyce Oates, after her novella of the same name (1992). First performance April 27, 1997, Philadelphia, American Music Theatre Festival, with Karen Burlingame (Kelly) and Patrick Mason (the Senator); conducted by Alan Johnson.

The story unfolds at a July 4 party and concerns an idealistic young girl infatuated with an attractive liberal senator. She goes off with him by car and drowns accidentally. The plot's resemblance to the Chappaquiddick incident that involved Senator Ted Kennedy and a young female aide is barely disguised.
BIBLIOGRAPHY: Robert Baxter, "Philadelphia," *Opera* (Sept. 1997), 1056–57 [on premiere]; James R. Oestreich, "Subject, Chappaquiddick," *NYT* (May 3, 1997), I, 21 [on premiere]; Patrick J. Smith, "Philadelphia," *ON* LXII (Aug. 1997), 41 [on premiere].

Black Widow, opera in three acts by Thomas Pasatieri; libretto (Eng) by the composer, after Miguel de Unamuno's short story *Dos madres*. First performance March 2, 1972, Seattle, with Joanna Simon (Raquel), Evelyn Mandac (Berta), Theodor Uppman (Juan), and David Lloyd and Jennie Tourel (Berta's parents); conducted by Henry Holt; produced by Lofti Mansouri.
Raquel, a beautiful young widow, is desperate to have a child. Juan, her lover, marries the young Berta and agrees, against his will, to give Raquel any child born from the marriage. In a surreal twist, Juan kills himself after giving up the child, and the triumphant Raquel takes over the care of Berta, who has become insane, and gives Berta enough money to marry again.
For a detailed description, see Eaton/*OP* II, 48–49.
Roles: Raquel (mezzo/sop); Berta (sop); Juan (bar); Doña Marta, Berta's mother (mezzo); and Don Pedro, Berta's father (bar).
The Spanish locale is reflected in some of the rhythms and embellishments.
SCORE: vs (New York: Belwin Mills, 1977).
BIBLIOGRAPHY: Frank J. Warnke, *ON* XXXVI (Apr. 8, 1972), 30 [on premiere].

Blake, opera by Leslie Adams; libretto (Eng) by Daniel Mayers, after an 1857 novel by Martin Delany, *Blake: or, The Huts of America* (1859). First performance (staged excerpts) April 11, May 12, 1985, Oberlin, Ohio, Oberlin Conservatory of Music. First full performances September 1991, Cleveland and Knoxville, with Curtis Rayam (Blake) and Martina Arroyo/Delcina Stevenson (Miranda); directed by David Farrar.
The plot concerns the relationship between a slave family, Blake, Miranda, his wife, and their son, and the white family who owns the plantation. When Miranda is sold to another plantation, a slave revolt ensues as Blake tries to find his wife.
Major roles: Blake, steward of a plantation (ten); and Miranda, his wife (sop).
BIBLIOGRAPHY: Rosalyn M. Story, "Positively Martina," *ON* LVI (Sept. 1991), 27–28.

Blanche de Nevers, opera in four acts by Michael Balfe; libretto (Eng) by John Brougham, after his *The Duke's Motto*, itself based on *Le bossu* (1858) by Paul Féval. First performance November 21, 1863, London, Covent Garden, with W. Harrison (Capt. Henri de Lagardère), W. H. Weiss (Prince de Gonzagues), A. St. Albyn (Philip of Orléans), Henry Corri (Cocardasse), J. Rouse (Peyrolles), Aynsley Cook (Aesop), Charles Lyall (Navailles), Mr. Arthur (Chavernay), Louisa Pyne (Blanche de Nevers), Emma Heywood (Princess de Gonzagues), and Anna Hiles (Zillah).
The villain of the piece is Gonzagues.
For the correct year of the premiere, see Eric W. White, *A Register of First Performances* (London: Society for Theatre Research, 1983), 81. The score also carries the year 1863.
SCORE: ms fs, partly autograph (1863, British Library, Add. MS. 29361, 29362).
LIBRETTO: English (London: Covent Garden, 1863?).

Bleeding Heart of Timpanogas, opera in three acts by William F. Hanson; libretto (Eng) by the composer, after E. L. Roberts. First performance April 7, 1939, Provo, Utah, Brigham Young University, College Hall.

The work centers on a cave on Mount Timpanogas, which contains a sizable stalactite in the shape of a human heart.

SCORE: vs ([n.p.] 1937; LCCN: 84-53817).

Blennerhasset, radio opera in one act by Vittorio Giannini; libretto (Eng) by Philip Roll and Norman Corwin. First performance November 22, 1939, CBS radio. First performance (stage) April 12, 1940, New York, Institute of Musical Art.

The story takes place in 1806, near Blennerhasset, an island near Parkersburg, West Virginia. Stephen is a follower of Aaron Burr and his plan to set up a new republic in the Southwest. Stephen, after parting from Madeleine, his fiancée, gathers his troops on the island. Madeleine, mistakenly believing General Wilkinson to be an ally, tells him of Stephen's hiding place on Blennerhasset. Wilkinson, who has turned against Burr, sends the militia to capture Stephen and his band. The wounded Stephen returns to Madeleine and dies in her arms, and Aaron Burr's cause is defeated.

Major roles: Stephen (ten), Madeleine (sop), and Wilkinson (bar).

Blessed Wilderness, The, opera by Jack Kilpatrick; libretto (Eng) by the composer. First performance April 18, 1959, Dallas, Southern Methodist University; conducted by Victor Allesandro.

The work is concerned with the eviction of the Cherokees from their Georgia homes in the 1830s and their resettlement in the area that is now Oklahoma.

The music echoes the composer's Cherokee heritage.

BIBLIOGRAPHY: "Opera Bows in Texas," *NYT* (Apr. 20, 1959) [on premiere]; preview, *NYT* (Mar. 20, 1959), 36.

Blind, The. See **The Dissolute Punished.**

Blind Beggar of Bethnal Green, The, or, A Receipt for Beauty, opera in one act by Thomas A. Arne; libretto (Eng) by Robert Dodsley. First performance April 3, 1741, London, Drury Lane Theatre.

LIBRETTO: English (London: Author, [1741]; Boston: Oliver & Munroe, 1803).

Blind Beggar's Daughter, The, ballad opera for young people of all ages by Geoffrey Bush; libretto (Eng) by Sheila Bathurst and the composer. First performance January 21, 1954, Farnham, England. Revised in 1964.

The work is set in 1285, twenty years after the Battle of Evesham. Bess, daughter of the blind beggar, sets out to find her fortune on the open road. She meets a knight at an inn in Romford, who wishes to marry her despite the objections of his kinsmen.

SCORE: vs (London: Elkin, [1953]).

Blind Girl, The, or, A Receipt for Beauty, comic opera in three acts by William Reeve and Joseph Mazzinghi; libretto (Eng) by Thomas Morton. First performance April 22, 1801, London, Covent Garden.

SCORE: vs (London, ca. 1801).

LIBRETTO: English (Boston: Oliver & Munroe, 1803).

Blind Man's Bluff, masque for soprano and mime by Peter Maxwell Davies; libretto (Lat and Eng) by the composer, freely based on Georg Büchner's play *Leonce und Lena* (1836). First performance May 29, 1972, London.

This masque of puzzling identities is based on the final scene of Büchner's play and on English nursery rhymes. The boy king sings a nursery rhyme on the theme of things not being what they seem, then demands to know the jester's identity. In response the jester introduces a mirror-dance for his two personae, dancer and mime, whom he afterward presents to the king as prince and princess. When the players take off masks to reveal themselves as prince and princess, the king abdicates and dies. The jester performs a mad solo that brings on painfully bright light; it blinds the dancer and the mime but restores the king's resurrected ghost.

Blind Raferty, opera in one act by Joan Trimble; libretto (Eng) by Cedric Cliffe. First performance May 22, 1957, London, BBC television; conducted by Stanford Robinson. BIBLIOGRAPHY: review, *MT* XCVIII (July 1957), 385 [on premiere].

Blind Witness News, opera by Ben Yarmolinsky; libretto (Eng) by Charles Bernstein. First performance December 7, 1990, New York, American Opera Projects, Blue Door Studio, with Rondi Charleston, James Javore, Suzanna Guzman, and Lynn Randolph; Elizabeth Rodgers and Steve Tyler, synthesizers; conducted by Robert Black; directed by Grethe Barrett Holby.

Set as a local television newscast (the title is a word play on ABC's "Eyewitness News"), the work features two news anchors who present stories in various musical ways, including a financial report in the style of a Gilbert and Sullivan patter song and the weather as a florid bel canto aria.
BIBLIOGRAPHY: Allan Kozinn, review, *NYT* (Dec. 9, 1990), I, 83 [on premiere].

Blockheads, The, or, Fortunate Contractor, pastiche opera in two acts; libretto (Eng) possibly by Noah Bisbee, after Mrs. Mercy Warren's play. First performance possibly 1782, New York.

The text is a criticism of the French support for the American colonists during the Revolution, with blockheads, i.e., mannequins, representing politically foolish people. The characters include Old Shaver, a barber and seller of wigs, and various allegorical personages.
For a description, see Virga/*AO*, 255–60.
LIBRETTO: English (Boston: John Gill, 1776; New York and London: G. Kearsley, 1782).

Blodwen (White Flower), opera in three acts by Joseph Parry; libretto (Eng) by David Rowlands. First performance June 20, 1878, Swansea, Wales.
SCORE: vs, in Welsh and English (Swansea: J. Parry, [1878?]).

Blond Eckbert, opera in two acts by Judith Weir; libretto (Eng) by the composer, after Ludwig Tieck's *Der blonde Eckbert* (1797). First performance August 14, 1994, Santa Fe, Santa Fe Opera, with Emily Golden (Berthe), James Michael McGuire (Blond Eckbert), Elizabeth Futral (the bird), Brad Cresswell (Walther/Hugo/old woman), and Franco Pomponi (the dog); conducted by George Manahan; directed by Francesca Zambello.

The setting is the Harz Mountains. Eckbert and his wife, Berthe, live in isolation. When they are visited during a storm by Walther, a friend of Eckbert's, Berthe recounts her younger years, including having run away from home, taken jeweled eggs from an old woman she met in the forest, and returning to her parents, only to discover that they have died. Walther seems to know Berthe's story very well, arousing Eckbert's jealousy. Becoming ever more jealous, Eckbert kills Walther while they are hunting. Berthe, who has been taken ill recalling the events from her past, dies. Driven into seclusion by his murderous deed, Eckbert goes back to the old woman's house and discovers the terrible truth about his wife's identity, that she was his sister.

For a detailed plot description, see K*INKOB*, 977–78.

Major roles: a bird (sop), Berthe (mezzo), Walther (ten); and Blond Eckbert (bar).
BIBLIOGRAPHY: Bernard Holland, "A Judith Weir Opera in Which Truth Is Harmful to Health," *NYT* (Aug. 16, 1994), C, 15, 18 [on premiere].

Blonde Donna, The, or, The Fiesta of Santa Barbara, comic opera in three acts by Ernest Carter; libretto (Eng) by the composer. First performance December 8, 1931, Brooklyn, New York, Little Theater.

The work concerns the romance of the "Blonde Donna" and Marinus. It is set in 1824, in Santa Barbara, California. Padre Bonifacio and Marina, the "Blonde Donna," defuse an uprising by the Mission Indians.

Major roles: Padre Bonifacio (bass); Tellacus (bar-buffo); the commandant of the Presidio (bass-bar); Marinus (ten); Señora Blanca, a rich widow (alto); and Marina, her blond daughter (sop).
SCORE: vs (New York: Composers Press, [1936]).
LIBRETTO: English, typewritten (n.p, ca. 1930; LCCN: 84-96732).

Blood Moon, chamber opera in three acts by Norman Dello Joio; libretto (Eng) by Gale Hoffman. First performance September 18, 1961, San Francisco, War Memorial Opera House, with Mary Costa (Ninette Lafont), Irene Dalis (Cleo Lafont), Albert Lance (Raymond Bardac), Keith Engen (Alexandre Dumas), Claude Heater (Tom Henney), Andrew Foldi (Mr. Parker), Dorothy Cole (Madame Bardac), and Marguerite Gignac (Edmee LeBlanc); conducted by Leopold Ludwig; produced by Dino Yannopoulos.

The story is inspired by the nineteenth-century actress Ada Mencken, an octoroon, who was in love with a white man, with devastating results for the heroine.

The work contains traditional set pieces.
BIBLIOGRAPHY: A. Boucher, "San Francisco," *ON* XXVI (Oct. 28, 1961), 29 [on premiere]; A. Frankenstein, "San Francisco," *Opera* XII (Nov. 1961), 706–8 [on premiere].

Blood Wedding, opera in three acts by Hale Smith; libretto (Eng), after García-Lorca's tragedy *Bodas de sangre* (1933). First performance 1953, Cleveland, Karamu House.

A young girl runs away with her former fiancé on her wedding day. This precipitates the fight in which both men are killed.

Blood Wedding, opera in two acts by Nicola LeFanu; libretto (Eng) by Deborah Levy, after García Lorca. First performance October 26, 1992, London, Jacob Street Studios, with Quentin Hayes (Leonardo), Annemarie Sand (the groom's mother), Philip Sheffield (the groom), and Yvette Bonner (the young girl).

The fears of a bridegroom's mother come true when the young girl her son is supposed to wed runs off with Leonardo, her former fiancé. Both men die in the ensuing fight.

Also set by W. Fortner, as *Die Bluthochzeit* (1957, Cologne); S. Szokolay, as *Vérnász* (1966, Wuppertal); and J. José, as *Bodas de sangre* (1979, Buenos Aires).
BIBLIOGRAPHY: Guy Richards, review, *Tempo,* No. 184 (Mar. 1993), 60–61 [on premiere].

Blue-Beard, or, Female Curiosity, "dramatick romance," with music by Michael Kelly, and several numbers from Grétry's *Raoul Barbe-bleue* (1789, Paris); libretto (Eng) by George Colman Jr., after Charles Perrault's fairy tale *Barbe-bleue* from *Les contes de ma mère l'Oye* (1697). First performance January 16, 1798, Drury Lane Theatre, London, with Miss De Camp (Irene), Mrs. Crouch (Fatima), Mr. Bannister, Mrs. Bland,

and Richard Suett. First American performance May 24, 1799, Philadelphia, with "new accompaniments by Mr. Reinagle." It enjoyed 120 American performances.

In the Colman version the oft-married villain, a Turk, attempts to kills Fatima, his latest wife, for disobeying his order not to look behind the door that hides her predecessors' remains. She is saved by the virtuous Selim, who kills Blue-Beard.

Despite Kelly's protestations that the score contained only his music, with the exception of two numbers, the overture was very close to Grétry's original, as was the finale (see the Porter edition, xxii; the introduction, xxi–xxiv, provides a detailed analysis of the music and text).

SCORES: vs (London: Longman and Broderip, 1798; Philadelphia, New York, and Baltimore: B. Carr, J. Hewitt, J. Carr); repr. ed. Susan L. Porter, *NAMT*, vol. 1 (1994).

LIBRETTOS: English (London: Cadell, Davies, 1794, 1798; New York: Columbian Press, 1795); repr. ed. *NAMT*, vol. 1 (1994).

BIBLIOGRAPHY: Susan L. Porter, "The Locked Room, or, Blue Beard as Barometer," *AM* 8 (Spring 1990), 54–70.

Bluebeard Repaired, operatic extravaganza in one act, an adaptation of Jacques Offenbach's operetta *Barbe-bleue* (1866, Paris), with music arranged by James Howard Tully; text (Eng) adapted by Henry Bellingham. First performance June 2, 1866, London, Olympic Theatre.

Other settings of the story include those by K. F. Baumgarten (pantomime, 1791, London); P. Dukas, as *Ariane et Barbe-bleue* (1907, Paris); B. Bartók, as *A Kékszakállú herceg vára* (Bluebeard's Castle) (1918, Budapest); and E. N. von Reznicek, as *Ritter Blaubart* (1920, Vienna and Leipzig).

LIBRETTO: English (London: T. H. Lacy, 1866?).

Blue Flame, musical fairy tale in four scenes by Alan Hovhaness; libretto (Eng) by the composer. First performance December 15, 1959, San Antonio, Municipal Auditorium.

SCORE: sketches (n.p., 1959; LCCN: 611-2305).

Blue Monday (135th Street), jazz opera "ala Afro-American" in one act by George Gershwin; libretto (Eng) by Buddy De Sylva, adapted by George Bassman; orchestrated by W. H. Vodery. First performance August 28, 1922, New York, Globe Theater as the opening for the second act of George White's *Scandals of 1922*. Retitled *135th Street* in 1925, with new orchestration by Ferde Grofé; first performance (concert) December 29, 1925, New York, Carnegie Hall. Revived 1984, Swiss Radio-Television, with Daniel Washington (Tom), La Verne Williams (Vi), Howard Haskin (Joe), and Raymond Bazemore (Sam); directed by David Freeman. Also March 14, 1994, Brooklyn, New York, Brooklyn College Opera, with Jesteena Walters (Vi), Thomas Young (Joe), and Phumzile Sojola (Sam).

The tragic story unfolds in a black saloon uptown. Tom, a singer at the saloon, wants Vi, the jealous girlfriend of the gambler Joe. Vi rejects Tom's advances, and he subsequently makes Vi believe, falsely, that Joe is carrying on with another woman. When Joe, who has confided in Sam, the bartender, refuses to show her a telegram he has received, she shoots him, only to learn that it said that he did not need to visit his mother, since she had been dead for three years.

Major roles: Joe (ten), Vi (sop), Sam (bar), and Tom (bar).

The work contains, among its songs, "Blue Monday Blues."

SCORE: vs, excerpts (Secaucus, N.J.: Warner Brothers, 1993).

BIBLIOGRAPHY: Will Crutchfield, preview, *NYT* (Aug. 3, 1984) [on broadcast of 1984 revival]; Edward Rothstein, review, *NYT* (Mar. 14, 1994), C, 14 [on 1994 revival].

Blue Peter, The, comic opera in one act by Cecil Armstrong Gibbs; libretto (Eng) by Albert Patrick Herbert. First performance December 11, 1923, London, Royal College of Music.
SCORE: ms fs (Royal College of Music); vs (London, 1925).

Blues in the Subway, "jazz" opera in one act by Alonzo Levister; text (Eng). First performance September 27, 1958, New York, Loew's Sheridan Theatre.
The work's three principals are a drunk, a girl, and a boy.
BIBLIOGRAPHY: John S. Wilson, review, *NYT* (Sept. 29, 1958), 32 [on premiere].

Blue Star, opera in one act by Judith Dvorkin; libretto (Eng) by the composer. First performance December 5, 1983, New York, Lincoln Center, Bruno Walter Auditorium, After Dinner Opera Company; conducted by Conrad Strasser.

Blue Wing, opera in three acts by Gerard Tonning; libretto (Eng). First performance May 18, 1917, Seattle, Moore Theater.

Boarding House, The, or, Five Hours at Brighton, musical farce in two acts by Charles Edward Horn; libretto (Eng) by Samuel Beazley Jr. First performance August 26, 1811, London, Lyceum Theatre. First U.S. performance June 5, 1812, New York.
LIBRETTO: English (London: C. Chapple, 1811; New York: The Longworths, 1812).

Boarding School, The, or, The Sham Captain, opera (ballad opera); libretto (Eng) by Charles Coffey, after Thomas D'Urfey's *Love for Money, or, The Boarding School* (1691). First performance January 29, 1733, London, Drury Lane Theatre, with Mr. Griffin (Alderman Nincompoop), Mr. Berry (Ned Brag), Mr. Shepherd (Zachary Brag), Mr. Oates (Coupee), Mr. Stopelaer (Warble), Mr. Harper (Lady Termagant), Mrs. Raftor (Miss Jenny), Mrs. Chark (Miss Molly), Mrs. Mullart (Backstitch), and Miss Mann (Tarnish).
The work is set in Chelsea.
LIBRETTO: English, with unaccompanied melodies (London: J. Watts, 1733); repr. ed. Rubsamen/*BO*, vol. 11, *Farce, Broad or Satirical* (1974).

Boatswain's Mate, The, comic opera in one act by Ethel Smyth; libretto (Eng) by the composer, after a story by William Wymark Jacobs, *Captains All*. First performance January 28, 1916, London, Shaftesbury Theatre, with Rosina Buckman (Mrs. Waters), Courtice Pounds (Harry Benn), and Frederick Ranalow (Ned Travers).
The title character of the opera, Harry Benn, is a conceited former boatswain who is trying to win the hand of Mrs. Waters, his landlady and owner of the Beehive Inn. He hatches a plan to have his new acquaintance, Travers, pretend to be a burglar and scare Mrs. Waters. Frightened, she will turn to Benn, who will "save" her from the "burglar's" clutches. The plan backfires when Mrs. Waters, instead of being afraid, grabs her gun and locks Travers in a cupboard. She then gets rid of her original suitor and turns her attentions to the reformed "burglar," who becomes her husband and takes over as landlord of the inn.
Major roles: Harry Benn (ten), Mrs. Waters (sop), and Travers (bar).
SCORE: vs (London: Forsyth Bros., 1915).

Boccaccio's Nightingale, opera in three acts by Lester Trimble; libretto (Eng) by George Maxim Ross, after Boccaccio's *Decameron* (1351–1353). Composed 1962. Revised 1983.

Filostrato narrates the story. Caterina is in love with Ricciardo, whom she has known from childhood, but her mother, Giacomina, wishes her to marry the Count, whom her father, Lizio, hates. As a signal to her lover, Caterina leaves a candle on her balcony. He comes to her room, but the candle that Caterina left is taken by the Count to be an invitation to join her; the Count's way, however, is blocked by the Friar. After the ensuing confusion the father, who discovers Caterina and Ricciardo together, gives his consent to their marriage.

For a detailed description, see Eaton/*OP* II, 251–52.

Major roles: Caterina (sop), Ricciardo (ten), Giacomina (mezzo), the Count (bar), the Friar (ten), and Lizio (bass).

Bohemian Girl, The, opera in three acts by Michael Balfe; libretto (Eng) by Alfred Bunn, after the ballet-pantomime *La Gipsy* (1839) of St. Georges, which was based on Miguel Cervantes' *La gitanella* (ca. 1614). First performance November 27, 1843, London, Drury Lane Theatre. First U.S. performance November 2, 1844, New York, Park Theatre. Revived 1951, London, Covent Garden; conducted by Sir Thomas Beecham. Also summer 1978, Colorado (in Beecham's version), with Peter Strummer (Devilshoof), Vinson Cole/Alan Kays, Leigh Munro/Marianna Christos, Alice Garrott (Gypsy queen), and Will Roy (the father); conducted by Donald P. Jenkins; November 19, 1993, New York, Hunter College, Kaye Playhouse, Dessoff Choir and Mannes Orchestra, with Lauren Flanigan (Arline), Joseph Corteggiano (Count Arnheim), Richard Holmes (Devilshoof), Ronald Naiditch (Florestein), Richard Slade (Thaddeus), and Marianne Cornetti (Gypsy queen); conducted by Cal Stewart Kellogg.

The story takes place in Pressburg, Austria (now Bratislava), in the eighteenth century. Arline, Count Arnheim's daughter, is kidnapped and raised by Gypsies after her father imprisons Devilshoof, their head, after he refuses to toast the Emperor's health. Arline longs for Thaddeus, who has joined the Gypsies and has raised her. When she is put into prison for stealing because of the machinations of the queen of the Gypsies, who is also in love with Thaddeus, Arline's father recognizes her since she is wearing his medallion. Thaddeus turns out to be a Polish nobleman, making him suitable for her to marry.

For a detailed plot description, see K/*NKOB*, 18–19.

Major roles: Thaddeus (ten); Arline (sop); Devilshoof, chief of the Gypsies (bass); Count Arnheim, governor of Pressburg (bar); Florestein, his nephew (ten); and the Gypsy queen (sop).

The opera ran for 100 nights at its London premiere. The famous "I Dreamt That I Dwelt in Marble Halls" is one of the opera's highlights, as are the canonic "Though Ev'ry Hope Be Fled" and the duet "This is Thy Deed."

The Gypsy Blonde was a musical based on Balfe's work; the music was adapted by Kenneth Jones; lyrics by Frank Gabrielson; June 25, 1934, New York, Lyric Theater. William S. Gilbert's *The Merry Zingara, or, The Tipsy Gipsy & the Pipsy Wipsy & the Dipsy Fopsy* (1868) was a parody of the work.

SCORES: fs ms, autograph (1843, British Library, MS. Add. 29335); vs ([New York], Wm. C. Bryant & Co.: Evening Post Steam Printers, 1871; New York: G. Schirmer, 1902).

LIBRETTOS: English (London: Johnson, [1843?]); W. S. Gilbert's parody (London: Phillips, [1868]).

BIBLIOGRAPHY: B. L. Scherer, review, *ON* LVIII (Feb. 19, 1994), 36 [on 1993 revival].

DISCOGRAPHY: N. Thomas, B. Cullen, P. Power, RTE Philharmonic Choir, National Sym. of Ireland; cond. R. Bonynge, Argo 433324–2 (2 CDs); rev. B. L. Scherer, "Recordings," *ON* LVII (Oct. 1992), 44.

Bohemians, The, rock opera by Bob Kirschner, after Puccini's *La bohème*; lyrics (Eng) by Diane Brown and Lizzie Olesker, after Henry Murger's novel *Scènes de la vie de bohème* (1847–1849). First performance June 1, 1990, New York, Paradise Opera, with William Badgett (Rudy Rolando), Max Jaffe (Leo), Jon E. Edwards (Fillmore), Diane Brown (Mimi), and Lizzie Olesker (Lola); directed by Erica K. Brown.

The work is set in a decaying New York City, 1999. Rodolfo has become Rudy Rolando, a poet; Mimi assembles trash and makes sculpture from it. Marcello, now called Leo, is also a sculptor, and his girlfriend, the erstwhile Musetta, is a punk rock singer by the name of Lola. Schaunard has become Fillmore.

When Mimi falls prey to an unnamed illness, only Lola stays to care for her. Leo goes for a doctor and Fillmore sells his coat, as in the Puccini opera. Unlike its namesake, however, the work has an upbeat ending with a full-blown dance number and Mimi rising from the dead.

*Rent** by Larson (1995) is another setting of the story.
BIBLIOGRAPHY: Allan Kozinn, "'Bohème' as 'Bohemians': It Rocks," *NYT* (June 5, 1990), C, 14 [on premiere].

Bok Choy Variations, opera by Evan Chen, libretto (Eng) by Fifi Servoss, Keith Huff, and Erick Simonson. First performance June 10, 1995, St. Paul, Ordway Music Theatre, with Jason Ma (Da Wei), Alan Muraoka (Lee), Edmund Eng (Zhanguo), Scott Watanabe (Fong), Chloe Stewart (May), Linda Balgord (Sophia), and Christine Toy (mother of Da Wei/May); conducted by Jeffrey Lewis.

The work centers on the lives of four young men from their days as children in communist China to their adulthood in the United States. At the center is the composer Da Wei, who falls in love with the young student May and also has a fling with Sophia, an American woman.
BIBLIOGRAPHY: Michael Anthony, "St. Paul," *ON* LX (Oct. 1995), 52 [on premiere].

Bon Appétit!, monologue in one act by Lee Hoiby; libretto (Eng) by Mark Shulgasser, after Julia Child. First performance March 8, 1989, Washington, D.C., Kennedy Center.

A comic culinary extravaganza that uses the wit and antics of the famed television chef; the "plot" concerns a segment of her show on making gateau au chocolat.

The work is scored for mezzo, with piano accompaniment, and it serves as a curtain-raiser for *The Italian Lesson.**

Bondman, The, opera in three acts by Michael Balfe; libretto (Eng) by Alfred Bunn, after Mélesville's *Le Chevalier de Saint-Georges* (1840). First performance December 11, 1846, London, Drury Lane Theatre, with Mr. Weiss (Marquis de Vernon), Mr. Rafter (Count Floreville), H. Horncastle (Viscount Morlière), and Emma Romer (Julie Corinne).

The hero, an illegitimate son of a white man and a black woman slave, is based on the real-life Chevalier de St. Georges, a musician, who becomes successful through his talents.
SCORE: ms fs, autograph (1846, British Library, MS. Add. 29346, 29347); vs (London: Chappell, n.d.).
LIBRETTO: English (London: W. S. Johnson and Chappell, [1846?]).

Bondocani, Il, or, The Caliph Robber, "serio-comic music drama" in three acts by Thomas Attwood and John Moorehead; libretto (Eng) by Thomas Dibdin, after the *Thousand and One Nights*. First performance November 15, 1800, London, Covent Garden, with Mr. Hodgkinson (Haroun Alraschid), Mr. Hogg (Chebib), Mr. Martin

(Hassan), Mr. Tyler (Hazeb), Mr. Jefferson (Cadi of Bagdat), Mr. Wilmot (Mahoud), Mr. Robinson (Coreb), Mr. Shapter (captain of the guard), Mrs. Hodgkinson (Selima), and Miss Brett (Darina). First U.S. performance December 11, 1801, Philadelphia.

The work is set in ancient Baghdad, called "Bagdat" in the libretto. It concerns the ruler Haroun Alraschid, who wanders around the city at night in disguise to see what his subjects are up to.

Roles: Haroun Alraschid, caliph of Bagdat; Chebib, a "decayed" merchant; Abdalla, his son; Hassan, a young courtier; Hazeb, father of Selima; Mesrour, principal officer; cadi of Bagdat; Mahoud, one of the guards; Coreb, an old slave; captain of the guard; Selima, imprisoned in the seraglio as Camira; and Darina, Chebib's daughter.

The music includes part of the finale of Mozart's *Die Zauberflöte*.

SCORE: vs (London: Goulding, Phipps, & D'Maine, n.d.).

LIBRETTO: English (London: T. N. Longman and O. Rees, 1801; New York: D. Longworth, 1805).

Boney Quillen, opera-pantomime in three scenes by Herbert Haufrecht; libretto (Eng) by the composer. First performance August 18, 1951, Chichester, New York, Folk Festival of the Catskills.

Boney Quillen works at a lumber camp. After an argument with the foreman he quits his job and gets into various fights. He then goes to work for Farmer Brown but quits that job, too, and disappears.

Major roles: Boney Quillen (ten), the foreman (speaking), the bartender (bar), Farmer Brown (bar), and Mrs. B. (alto).

SCORE: vs (New York: Broude, 1953).

Boor, The, opera in one act by Mark Bucci; libretto (Eng) by Eugene Haun, after A. Anton Chekhov's play *The Bear* (1888). First performance December 29, 1949, New York, Finch College; June 15, 1950, New York, After Dinner Opera, Master Theatre, with Geraldine Hamburg, Lawrence Avery, Lee Cash; Lillian Frengut (piano); conducted by Alexander Main.

BIBLIOGRAPHY: H. C. S., "After Dinner Troupe Offers Three Operas," *NYT* (June 15, 1950), 41 [on 1950 performance].

Boor, The, opera in one act by Myron S. Fink; libretto (Eng) by Bonnie Fink, after Chekhov. First performance February 14, 1955, St. Louis, Jefferson Hotel, Ivory Room. SCORE: vs (n.p., 1962; LCCN: 85-40715).

Boor, The, opera buffa in one act by Dominick Argento; libretto (Eng) by John [Olon] Scrymgeour, after Chekhov. First performance May 6, 1957, Rochester, New York, Eastman School of Music, with Barbara Altman (the widow) and William Duvall (the boor); conducted by Frederick Fennell; directed by Leonard Treash. Revivals include August 1985, Lake George, New York, Lake George Opera Festival, with Pamela South (the widow), Joseph Evans (the servant), and David Barron (the boor); conducted by Joseph De Rugeriis.

A grieving widow is put upon by her neighbor, a boor, who is a creditor of her late husband. She threatens to shoot him when he comes to collect a debt and challenges the man to a duel. The boor, moved by her determination, admits that he has fallen in love with her. The widow relents and accepts his offer of marriage.

For a detailed description, see Eaton/*OP* I, 170–71.

Major roles: the widow (sop), the boor (bass-bar), and the servant (ten).

SCORE: vs (New York: Boosey & Hawkes, 1960).
BIBLIOGRAPHY: review, "Two Operas at Festival," *NYT* (May 7, 1957), 40 [on premiere]; Mary Ellis Peltz, "Ninth Fool, First Boor," *ON* XX (Nov. 11, 1957), 18 [on premiere]; John Rockwell, "Review," *NYT* (Aug. 22, 1985), C, 24 [on 1985 revival].

Boor, The, opera in one act by Ulysses Kay; libretto (Eng) by Ulysses Kay, after the translation by Vladimir Ussachevsky of Chekhov's play. First performance April 3, 1968, Lexington, University of Kentucky.

When Grigory Stepanovitch Smirnov, a landowner, tries to collect on a debt, he is rebuffed by the debtor's widow, Elena Ivanovna Popova. She challenges Smirnov to a duel and then cajoles him into teaching her how to shoot. In the ensuing lesson the couple fall in love, and her servant, Luka, returns to find not chaos but the onetime adversaries planning to marry.

For a description, see Eaton/*OP* II, 252–53.

Major roles: Elena Ivanovna Popova (sop), Grigory Stepanovitch Smirnov (bar), and Luka (ten).
SCORE: ms ([1955], photocopy, NYPL; LC, LCCN: 65-74636).

Boor, The, opera in one act by Donald Grantham; libretto (Eng) by the composer, after Chekhov. First performance February 1989, Austin, Texas, University of Texas Opera Theater.

In this treatment of the famous story, Smirnov comes to collect payment from the widowed Madame Popova in order to pay his property taxes. The two argue, and Smirnov also turns on the two elderly servants, Luka and Anna. After she slaps his face, Smirnov challenges Madame Popova to a duel. Since she does not know how to shoot a pistol, Smirnov agrees to teach her but destroys a picture of her late husband in the process. The two find their dislike turning to love, and they marry.

For a detailed description, see Summers/*OOA*, 136–37.

Major roles: Yelena Ivanovna Popova (sop); Grigory Stepanovitch Smirnov (bar); Luka, Popova's servant (ten); Anna, Luka's wife (mezzo).

Other treatments of the story include A. Walbrunn's *Das Ungeheuer* (1914, Karlsruhe); K. Stierlin's *Der Bär* (1938, Osnabrück); L. Moss's *The Brute** (1961, New Haven); E. Dressel's *Der Bär* (1963, Radio Bern); W. Walton's *The Bear** (1967, Aldeburgh); and T. Beversdorf's *The Hooligan** (comp. 1969).

Borderline, The, opera in one act by Wilfred Mellers; libretto (Eng) by David Holbrooke. First performance June 4, 1959, London, Opera Performers, with Norman Tattersall (Eaper Weeper), Andrew Gold (Willy Wood), Edna Graham (Jenny Weeper), Lisle Jones (Solomon Grundy), and Bryan Drake (Farmer Makepile); conducted by Michael Pilkington; produced by Eric Simon.

The setting is a village. The "borderline" of the title refers to the point between childhood and adulthood.
BIBLIOGRAPHY: S. B. [Stanley Bayliss], review, *MT* C (Aug. 1959), 434 [on premiere].

Boston Baked Beans, "a New England opera piccola" in one act by Gail Kubik; libretto (Eng) by the composer. First performance March 9, 1952, New York, Modern Museum of Art, with Shirlee Emmons (Clementine) and Lee Cass (John Harvard); conducted by Frederic Waldman. First British performance January 7, 1953, London, BBC radio; conducted by the composer.

John Harvard, born in Boston, goes out West to mine for gold and become wealthy and meets Clementine, daughter of a miner. Although he at first pays little attention to her, Clementine is able to make him fall in love with her when she discovers that he has a passion for Boston baked beans, which she cooks for him.

For a plot description, see Summers/*OOA*, 189–90.

Roles: Clementine (lyric sop) and John Harvard (bass).

The work is scored for two singers and four instruments.

SCORE: vs (Ital-Eng) (New York: Chappell, 1956).

Bottle Imp, The, operatic romance in two acts by George Rodwell; libretto (Eng) by Richard B. Peake. First performance July 7, 1828, London, Lyceum Theatre.
LIBRETTO: English (London: Sherwood, Gilbert, and Piper, [1828?]).

Bottle Imp, The, opera in three acts by Peter Whiton; libretto (Eng) by William Meredith, after Robert Louis Stevenson. First performance April 10, 1958, Wilton, Connecticut, Wilton Playshop; conducted by Sheldon Soffer.
LIBRETTO: English (New London, Conn.: Meredith, [195?]).

Bottle of Champagne, The, operetta in one act by Henry Rowley Bishop; libretto by Edward Fitzball. First performance July 27, 1832, London, Vauxhall Gardens.
LIBRETTO: English ([London]: Published for the proprietors, [n.d.]).

Bourville Castle, or, The Gallic Orphan, comic opera by Benjamin Carr; orchestral accompaniments by Victor Pelissier; libretto (Eng) by John Blair Linn. First performance January 16, 1797, New York, John Street Theatre.

Bouvard and Pécuchet, opera in a prologue and three acts by Denis Aplvor; libretto (Eng) by the composer, after Gustave Flaubert's unfinished novel *Bouvard et Pécuchet* (1881). Composed 1971–1974.

The story centers on two clerks who meet and realize they have similar views. When they pool their resources to buy a farm, they try to implement their beliefs.

Bow Down, music theater piece by Harrison Birtwistle; text (Eng) by Tony Harrison, after versions of the ballad *The Two Sisters*. First performance July 5, 1977, London, National Theatre at Cottesloe Theatre, directed by Walter Donohue; conducted by Dominic Muldowney.

The work, in which the dark sister kills the fair sister, is set for five actors and four musicians. The music is fashioned from three basic intervals.

Bow-Street Opera, The, opera in three acts, after John Pepusch, "written on the plan of *The Beggar's Opera* [1728], all the most celebrated songs of which are parodies, and the whole piece adapted to modern times, manners, and characters"; libretto (Eng), after John Gay. First performance 1773, London, Covent Garden (possibly).
LIBRETTO: English (London: T. Mariner, [1773], repr. ed. Rubsamen/*BO*, vol. 1, *The Beggar's Opera, Imitated and Parodied* (1974).

Box, The, opera in three acts by Charles Hamm; libretto (Eng) by Allan Turpin. First performance February 4, 1961, New Orleans, Tulane University, Dixon Hall, with Helen Hougham Hamm, Maurine Mullin, Pat Ward, Edith Judkins, Sarah Mantel, Arthur Schoenberger, Jack Davis, Jack Wilson, and Marion Boling; conducted and produced by the composer.

Box, The, opera in one act by Charles G. Eakin; libretto (Eng) by the composer, after Anton Chekhov. First performance January 26, 1968, New York, Marymount Manhattan College, Mannes College Opera Production Workshop, with Richard Firmin, Betsy Norden, Frederick McDonald, Suzanne Cogan, and Patricia Brooker; conducted by Paul Berl.

The story concerns a music box, handed from person to person, whose noise drives people crazy. Among its possessors are Isabelle, a young girl, who gives it to the doctor. He passes it on to John, a janitor, who bestows it on the Prima Donna.

Major roles: Isabelle (sop), a doctor (ten), John (bass), and a Prima Donna (sop).
SCORE: vs, holograph (1966, NYPL).
BIBLIOGRAPHY: Harold C. Schonberg, "Music: Mannes Workshop Presents New Operas," *NYT* (Jan. 27, 1968), 18 [on premiere].

Boxes, radio opera in two parts by Michael Sahl; libretto (Eng) by Eric Salzman and the composer. First performance 1981–1982, New York, WKCR.

Boy from the Catacombs, The, church opera in two acts by Alan Ridout; libretto (Eng) by F. H. Wilkinson. First performance 1965, Canterbury, England, Canterbury Cathedral.

Boy of Santillane, The, or, Gil Blas and the Robbers of Asturia, musical play by Thomas S. Cooke and Jonathan Blewitt; libretto (Eng) by George Macfarren after Le Sage's *Histoire de Gil Blas de Santillane*. First performance April 16, 1827, London, Drury Lane Theatre.
LIBRETTO: English (London: J. and W. Jackson, 1827; London: J. Cumberland, [1837?]).

Boy Who Grew Too Fast, The, children's opera in one act by Gian Carlo Menotti; libretto (Eng) by the composer. First performance September 24, 1982, Wilmington, Delaware, OperaDelaware, with Frank Reynolds (Dr. Shrink), Joy Vandever (Nurse Proctor), Denise Coffey (Miss Hope), Philip Peterson (Poponel), Alan Wagner (the terrorist), and Sara Hagopian (Poponel's mother); conducted by Evelyn Swensson.

The story concerns a boy of nine who has just moved to town. He is mocked by his classmates because of his great size and his name, Poponel Skosvodmonit. His new teacher, Miss Hope, directs him to Dr. Shrink, who has invented a shrinking machine. The price for a cure is high—the boy must conform to everyone else's actions. When a terrorist, Mad Dog, comes to the school and demands a hostage, Poponel is the only volunteer. His courageous act makes him grow until he overcomes the terrorist.
BIBLIOGRAPHY: Jerry Floyd, "Reports: U.S.," *ON* XLVII (Dec. 4, 1982), 41–42 [on premiere]; Daniel Webster, "Menotti's Newest Opera Is a Nearly Perfect One, *Philadelphia Inquirer* (Sept. 25, 1982), C, 7 [on premiere].

Brain Opera, digital event in three parts by Tod Machover; "libretto" (Eng) by Marvin Minsky. First "performance" July 23, 1996, New York, Lincoln Center, Festival '96, lobby of the Juilliard School, with Teresa Marrin and Maribeth Back (electronic devices) and Anne Azema and Lorraine Hunt (taped singing); conducted by the composer.

The work consists of three parts; in the first, visitors wander through a "mind forest," in which electronic devices take down their impressions. In the second part, these responses are collected and combined with spoken dialogue and live feedback from the Internet. In the last part, this amalgam is combined further with prerecorded music and projected images. Consequently, no performance is ever the same. The text, presented during the last part, consists of short pronouncements concerning the nature of the mind.

BIBLIOGRAPHY: Yahlin Chang, "Roll Over, Beethoven," *Newsweek* (July 29, 1996), 71; Andrew Essex, "Mind Games," *NY* LXXII (July 22, 1996), 24–25; Alex Ross, "Composers Wanted, No Experience Needed," *NYT* (July 25, 1994), C, 13, 16 [on "premiere"].

Brandy Is My True Love's Name, "operatic western" in one act by Martin Kalmanoff; libretto (Eng) by Atra Baer. First performance June 17, 1953, New York, American Lyric Theatre.

The music is based on the simple folk song sung by Josh White.
BIBLIOGRAPHY: review, *Musical Courier,* CXLVII (July 1953), 13.

Brazen Bust, The, "melo-drama" in two acts by Henry Rowley Bishop; libretto (Eng) by Charles Kemble. First performance May 29, 1813, London, Covent Garden.

Roles: the King, the Miller, Richard, Peggy, Joe, Clump, Kate, and a clown.

The overture performed at the premiere was from *The Aethiop.**
SCORE: ms fs, autograph (British Library, Add. MS. 27706).

Breakfast Waltzes, bagatelle opera in one act by Harold Blumenfeld; libretto (Eng) by Charles Kondek, after Ferenc Molnár's sketch *The Witch*. Composed 1991. First performance July 12, 1997, Des Moines, Iowa, Des Moines Metro Opera Summer Festival.

The setting is the Viennese apartment of a successful actress ca. 1900. The actress's stagestruck maid, who is reading from her employer's script, goes to answer the doorbell. The visitor is the wife of Fritz, the actress's secretary-bookkeeper. The wife accuses the actress of having an affair with Fritz, but the actress convinces her that she is wrong. After the wife departs, the actress goes to rouse Fritz, who is asleep in her bedroom. As he prepares to leave, he mistakenly thinks the maid is in love with him after he hears her reading from the script. He starts to kiss the maid, whereupon the actress enters, followed by the wife, who has returned unexpectedly. The three women become furious with the unfaithful Fritz, who is thrown out of the apartment. Now alone, the women laugh at the ridiculousness of the situation.

For a detailed description, see Summers/*OOA*, 59–60.

Roles: the maid (sop), the actress (mezzo), the wife (mezzo/alto), and Fritz (ten).
SCORE: fs, vs holograph, 1991 (St. Louis, Mo.: MMB Music, 1991; NYPL).

Brian Boru, romantic Irish opera in three acts by Julian Edwards; libretto (Eng) by Stanlislaus Stangé. First performance October 19, 1896, New York.

Brickdust Man, The, operatic dialogue by Charles Dibdin; libretto (Eng) by Isaac Bickerstaffe. First performance 1772, London, Sadler's Wells. Revived 1960s, London, Opera Da Camera; orchestrated by Roger Fiske; also April 1992, London.

The work has two characters, John, who sells brick dust, and Moll, who sells milk and who was jilted by John. They eventually iron out their differences and agree to get married.

For a detailed description, see Fiske/*ETM*, 292–94.

This is the only Dibdin dialogue with an overture.
DISCOGRAPHY: Y. Barclay, K. West, instrumentalists; cond. P. Holman, "Opera Restor'd," orch. R. Fiske and P. Holman, Hyperion CDA 66608 (1992, London).

Bridal Ring, The, melodrama in two acts by Henry Condell and Victor Pelissier; libretto (Eng) by Frederick Reynolds. First performance October 16, 1810, London, Covent Garden. First U.S. performance February 10, 1812, Philadelphia.
LIBRETTO: English (New York: D. Longworth, 1812).

Bride Comes to Yellow Sky, The, opera in four scenes by Roger Nixon; libretto (Eng) by Ray B. West Jr., after Stephen Crane's short story (1898). First performance February 20, 1968, Charleston, Illinois, Eastern Illinois University. Revised version March 22, 1969, San Francisco, San Francisco State College.

The setting is Texas in the nineteenth century. The male protagonists are Sheriff Jack Potter and Scratchy Wilson, an old frontier gunfighter. When Potter brings his new bride to the town of Yellow Sky, Wilson realizes that the old ways are gone, after Potter refuses the former's challenge to a duel.

Roles: the bride (sop), Jack Potter (ten), the saloon keeper (bar), the drummer (bar), and Scratchy Wilson (bass).

SCORE; fs (n.p., 1967; LCCN: 85-64583).

Bride Elect, The, comic opera in three acts by John Philip Sousa; libretto (Eng) by the composer. First performance December 27, 1897, New Haven, Connecticut, with Albert Hart (King Papagallo), Frank Pollock (Guido), Lillian Carlsmith (Bianca), Christine MacDonald (Minutezza), Nella Bergen (La Pastoralla), and Emma Lackey (Rosamonda); conducted by John McGhie.

The work is set on the island of Capri. After a pet goat dies, war breaks out between two kingdoms. The victor, King Papagallo XII of Tiberio, demands that Princess Minutezza of Capri, the loser in the conflict, become his bride. She, however, is in love with Guido, the King's nephew. Minutezza has La Pastoralla, a female brigand, kidnap Papagallo. Queen Bianca, believing that her daughter, Minutezza, has been kidnapped instead, arranges to have the captives freed. In the end Minutezza and Guido are allowed to wed, and Papagallo agrees to wed the widowed Bianca.

The work includes among its highlights "The Bride Elect March," part of the second-act finale, "The Dogs of War," and the lullaby "The Snow Baby," sung by Minutezza.

SCORE: vs (Cincinnati: John Church Co., 1897).

DISCOGRAPHY: selections, arr. for band, U.S. Marine Corps, USMB CD-3 (3 CDs).

Bride from Pluto, The, children's opera in one act by Gian Carlo Menotti; libretto (Eng) by the composer. First performance April 14, 1982, Washington, D.C., Terrance Theater, with Pamela Hinchman (the queen), Nicholas Karousatos (Billy), Robert Keefe (Billy's father), and Dana Krueger (Billy's mother), and Camille Rosso (Rosie); conducted by Lorenzo Ricci Muti; choreographed by Helen Anne Barcay.

The spoiled son of a tailor, Billy, demands much more than his parents can afford. After his father throws him out of the house, he sees a spaceship in his backyard, carrying the Queen of Pluto, who has been looking throughout the galaxy for a husband. Her choice is Billy, whom she offers anything he wants on the condition that she replace his heart and soul with an electronic gadget. His friend Rosie saves him from such a fate by fashioning a substitute mechanical groom.

BIBLIOGRAPHY: Joseph McLellan, "Operatic Encounter: Menotti's 'Pluto' Premieres Here," *Washington Post* (Apr. 15, 1982), D, 1; Michael Mott, "Washington," *Opera* XXXIII (1982), 1058–60 [on premiere].

Bride of Dionysus, The, opera in three acts by Donald Tovey; libretto (Eng) by Robert Calverley Trevelyan. First performance April 23, 1929, Edinburgh.

A setting of the Ariadne story.

Tovey began working on the opera in 1897. It was his only stage work.

SCORE: ms, fs (Reid Music Library, University of Edinburgh).

Bride of Fortune, The, opera in three acts by Gillian Whitehead; libretto (Eng) by Anna Maria dell'Oso. First performance February 18, 1991, His Majesty's Theatre, Perth, Australia.
LIBRETTO: English (Sydney, Australia: Pellinor, 1991).

Bride of Song, The, opera in one act by Julius Benedict; libretto (Eng) by Henry Brougham Farnie. First performance December 3, 1864, London, Covent Garden, with Anna Thirlwall, Fanny Huddart, Henry Haigh, and Alberto Lawrence; conducted by Alfred Mellon.
    The composer's last operatic work, it has four soloists and no chorus.
SCORE: vs (London: Cramer, Wood, [ca. 1870]).

Brideship, The, opera by Robert Turner; libretto (Eng). First performance December 12, 1967, Vancouver.
BIBLIOGRAPHY: "New Canadian Music," *Musicanada* VII (Dec. 1967), 5.

Brides of Venice, The, grand opera in two acts by Julius Benedict; libretto (Eng) by Alfred Bunn and the composer. First performance April 22, 1844, London, Drury Lane Theatre, with Emma Romer; conducted by William Harrison.
    The work includes the cavatina "O Memory Cease to Grieve Me."
LIBRETTO: English (London: Johnson, [1844?]).

Bride Stripped Bare of Her Bachelors, Even, opera in three acts by Charles Shere; libretto (Eng) by the composer, after M. Duchamp's notes and painting *La mariée mise à nu.* First performance (partial), as *The Box of 1914,* January 30, 1981, San Francisco, Conservatory; December 1, 1984, Oakland, California, Mills College.
SCORE: fs, as *Box of 1914* (Berkeley, Calif.: Ear Press, 1981).

Brief Candle, "micro-opera" in three acts by William Mayer; libretto (Eng) by Milton Feist. First performance May 22, 1967, New York, New School Opera Workshop.
    The six-minute work consists of a chorus commenting on the life of a girl; her part is mimed.
SCORE: vs (Bryn Mawr, Pa.: T. Presser Co., 1971).
DISCOGRAPHY: soloists, Princeton Chamber Ensemble; cond. Weisberg, Desto 6430 (1 LP).

Britain's Brave Tars!!, or, All for St. Paul's, musical farce in one act by Thomas Attwood; libretto (Eng) by John O'Keeffe. First performance December 19, 1797, London, Covent Garden.

Britain's Glory, or, A Trip to Portsmouth, afterpiece in one act, partial pastiche by Samuel Arnold; libretto (Eng) by J. Roberts (Mr. Benson?). First performance August 18, 1794, London, Little Theatre in the Haymarket.
LIBRETTO: English (London: J. Barker, 1794).

Britannia, opera by John Frederick Lampe; libretto (Eng) by Thomas Lediard. First performance November 16, 1732, London, Little Theatre, with Cecilia Young (Britannia), Mrs. Seedo (Victory/Concord/Peace), and Gustav Waltz (Mars/Honour).
    For a detailed musical description, see Fiske/*ETM*, 134–35 .

Britannia, or, The Royal Lovers, wedding masque by Henry Carey; libretto (Eng) by George Lillo. First performance possibly February 1734, London.
    A revision of *The Happy Nuptials** (1733), written for the marriage of Princess Anne and William IV, the Prince of Orange, which was delayed and finally took place on March 15, 1734.

LIBRETTO: English, as *Britannia and Batavia* (London: J. Gray, 1740).

Britannia, or, Love and Glory, serenata by Thomas Augustine Arne; libretto (Eng) by Thomas Phillips. First performance March 21, 1734, London, Drury Lane Theatre.

The libretto mentions fourteen numbers. The work is lost.

Britannia, patriotic masque in two acts by Thomas Augustine Arne; libretto (Eng) by David Mallett. First performance May 9, 1755, London, Drury Lane Theatre.
SCORE: ss (London: I. Walsh, [1755]).
LIBRETTO: English (London: A. Millar, 1755).

Britannia Preserv'd, masque in one act by Stephen Oliver; libretto (Eng) by A. N. Wilson. First performance May 30, 1984, London, Hampton Court.

The masque examines British architecture from medieval times to the present; among the buildings is St. Paul's Cathedral.

Roles: four principal singers and mixed chorus.

Britannia triumphans, masque in one act by William Lawes; libretto (Eng) by William Davenant. First performance London, Whitehall, Masquing House, January 7, 1638.
SCORE: ms (Bodleian Mus. Sch. B.2); fs, ed. Murray Lefkowitz (Paris: Editions du Centre National de la Recherche Scientifique, 1970).
LIBRETTO: English (London: Thomas Walkley, 1637).

British Enchanters, The, or, No Magic Like Love, semi-opera in five acts by William Corbett; libretto (Eng) by George Granville. First performance February 21, 1706, London, Queen's Theatre, Haymarket.
LIBRETTO: English (London: J. Tonson, 1706).

British Fortitude, opera in one act by William Reeve; libretto (Eng) by James C. Cross. First performance April 29, 1794, London, Covent Garden.
SCORE: vs (London, ca. 1794).
LIBRETTO: English (London: J. Roach, 1794).

British Sailor, The, opera by William Boyton; libretto (Eng) by "Mr. Bernard." First performance May 22, 1789, London, Covent Garden.

Attwood's *Poor Soldier** (1795, London) may be another setting.

Britons, Strike Home, or, The Sailor's Rehearsal, ballad opera; libretto (Eng) by Edward Phillips. First performance December 31, 1739, London, Theatre Royal, with Mr. Winstone (Sir John Freehold), Mr. Berry (Captain Briton), Charles Macklin (Lieutenant Meanwell), Mr. Turbutt (Mr. Export), Henry Woodward (Dapperwit), Mr. Taswell (Father Dominique), Mr. Marten (Capstern), Mr. Ridout (Foremast), Mr. Yates (Bowspirit), and Mrs. Clive (Miss Kitty).

The patriotic story takes place on the *St. Joseph*, a ship taken from the Spanish.
LIBRETTO: English (London: J. Watts, 1739); repr. ed. Rubsamen/*BO*, vol. 2, *Historical and Patriotic Subjects* (1974).

Broken Gold, The, ballad opera in two acts by Charles Dibdin; libretto (Eng) by the composer. First performance February 8, 1806, London, Covent Garden.
SCORE: vs (London: Bland & Wellers, [n.d.]).
LIBRETTO: English (London: T. Woodfall, 1806).

Broken Pitcher, The. See **The Amorous Judge.**

Broken Promises, or, The Colonel, the Captain, and the Corporal, ballad opera by William Hawes; libretto (Eng) by Samuel J. Arnold. First performance July 6, 1825, London, English Opera House, with Catherine Stephens (Polly).

The work consists mainly of borrowings from Weber, Cherubini, and Meyerbeer, among others.

For a description of the music, see Theodore Fenner, *Opera in London* (Carbondalle, Ill.: University of Illinois Press, 1994), 480–82.

Broken Strings, opera in one act by Param Vir; libretto (Eng) by David Rudkin, after the traditional Buddhist story *Guttil Jatak*. First performance May 11, 1992, Amsterdam. First British performance July 11, 1996, London, Almeida Opera; conducted by Markus Stenz. Performed together with *Snatched by the Gods*.*

When the office of Player to the King is open, the young Musil is sure that he will be chosen to fill the post, but he is rejected by the judges. The aged, almost blind Guttil steps forward, and although the strings of his instrument break one by one, he continues to make beautiful music and to make magical creatures appear. When Musil tries to play after breaking his strings, he is not able to duplicate the old man's achievement.

For a plot description, see K*INKOB*, 917–18.

Major roles: the King (bass), Musil (ten), and Guttil (bass).

Bronwen, opera in three acts by Joseph Holbrooke; libretto (Eng) by Thomas Evelyn Ellis, after Welsh legends in *The Mabinogion*. First performance February 1, 1929, Huddersfield, Carl Rosa Company.

The third part of the trilogy *The Cauldron of Annwn** (see also *The Children of Don* and *Dylan*), this work includes characters that are reincarnations of those in the first two parts. Bronwen represents Elan, while Caradoc, who spurns her attentions, parallels Gwydion. Bronwen marries Matholoc (new to the trilogy) and gives birth to Gwern (Dylan). Bronwen and Matholoc gain control of the cauldron, which again wreaks havoc on all who come into contact with it.

SCORE: overture, miniature score (London: Goodwin & Tabb, [between 1929 and 1936]).

Bronze Horse, The, or, The Spell of the Cloud King, "musical drama" in two acts by George Rodwell; libretto (Eng) by Edward Fitzball, after Scribe's libretto for Auber's *Le cheval de bronze* (Paris, 1835). First performance December 14, 1835, London, Covent Garden.

The music was also partially adapted from Auber's opera.

SCORE: vs. (London, ca. 1835).

LIBRETTO: English (London: J. Duncombe, 183?).

Brother and Sister, "petit opera" in two acts by William Reeve and Henry Rowley Bishop; libretto (Eng) by William Dimond, after Joseph Patrat's comedy *L'heureuse erreur*. First performance February 1, 1815, London, Covent Garden. First U.S. performance January 5, 1816, New York.

LIBRETTOS: English (London: R. S. Kirby, 1829; New York: E. Murden, 1822).

Brother Joe, opera in two acts by Lehman Engel; libretto (Eng). First performance May 28, 1953, Cleveland, Karamu Theater.

Brothers, The, opera in one act by George Antheil; libretto (Eng) by the composer. First performance July 28, 1954, Denver, University of Denver.

A modern treatment of the story of Cain and Abel.

Brownings Go to Italy, The, opera in one act by Eleanor Everest Freer; libretto (Eng) by G. A. Hawkins-Ambler. First performance May 11, 1938, Chicago, Chicago Arts Club.

Brute, The, comic opera in one act by Lawrence Moss; libretto (Eng) by Eric Bentley, after Anton Chekhov's *The Bear* (1888). First performance July 29, 1961, New Haven, Connecticut, Yale Summer School of Music.

In this version of the Chekhov story, "the brute" refers to Smirnov, who comes to demand payment for the oats purchased by the late husband of the widow Popova for his horse "Toby." The widow asks Smirnov to teach her how to shoot her husband's pistols, so that she can kill Smirnov. The couple argues but, as her servant Luka comes in to stop the trouble, he sees the two have become quite fond of each other.

For a detailed description, see Eaton/*OP* II, 253.

Major roles: the widow Popova (sop), Grigory S. Smirnov (bar), and Luka (ten).

For other settings see *The Bear* and *The Boor.*

SCORE: vs (Bryn Mawr, Pa.: Theodore Presser, 1967).

Brutus of Alba, or, Augusta's Triumph, "new opera" (semi-opera) by Daniel Purcell, Henry Playford, and Samuel Scott; libretto (Eng) probably by George Powell and John Verbruggen. First performance October 1696, London, Dorset Garden.

LIBRETTO: English (London: S. Briscoe, 1697).

Bubbles, opera in one act by Hubert Bath; libretto (Eng), after Lady Isabella Augusta Gregory's play *Spreading the News* (1904). First performance November 26, 1923, Belfast.

Building of Bamba, The, "Irish mythological opera" by Henry Cowell; libretto (Eng) by John O. Variam. First performance August 18, 1917, Halcyon, California.

Bundle Man, The, chamber opera in two acts by Marshall Cold; libretto (Eng) by Ilsa Gilbert. First performance March 18, 1993, New York, Theater for the New City, with the composer (the Bundle Man), Steven Goldstein, Stephen Kahn, and Daryl Henriksen; conducted by Mimi Stern-Wolfe; produced by Tom O'Horgan.

In the mock Absurdist story, the Christlike Bundle Man, musically identified by "What Child Is This?" and "We Three Kings," is killed by the three other characters.

The music consists of various modern styles and includes hints of Menotti, Stravinsky, and Richard Strauss. The title role is a countertenor part.

BIBLIOGRAPHY: James R. Oestreich, "A New Opera Plays with Absurdism," *NYT* (March 22, 1993), C, 15 [on premiere].

Buoso's Ghost, opera by Michael Ching. First performance February 16, 1996, Pittsburgh, Byham Theater. First full performance January 25, 1997, Memphis, Tennessee, Opera Memphis, with John Dougherty (Simone), Kristopher Irmiter (Schicchi), Patti Jo Stevens (Zita), and Kent Fleshman (Betto).

A sequel to Puccini's *Gianni Schicchi*, the work opens with Rinuccio and Lauretta preparing to get married and Gianni Schicchi sorting out the effects of Buoso's house. Schicchi discovers that Buoso's relatives poisoned him. When they return and accuse Schicchi of having poisoned Buoso, Schicchi lets each one know that he is aware of the truth and tricks them into giving their part of the inheritance to him.

The Magistrate arrives and hears Schicchi's story that he was coming to thank Buoso for including him in his will, only to discover the relatives feeding Buoso all kinds of food; the Magistrate then discovers a note (written by Schicchi) saying that Buoso had poisoned himself; the relatives realize that they have been duped once more. They are

about to do away with Schicchi when there is a lightning bolt and a voice exclaims that it is the ghost of Buoso and that the relatives had better leave before the ghost rises from the dead to haunt them. They all run out except Zita, who declines Schicchi's offer of wine, reminding them that it is poisoned, and goes to fetch some unadulterated beverage. Gianni Schicchi turns to the audience, saying that since the composer has dared to appear on the same evening as Puccini [*Buoso* was performed together with *Gianni Schicchi*], "let us send him to hell or grant him, like me, Extenuating Circumstances" (from the synopsis by Shaun Townshend, Opera Memphis home page).
BIBLIOGRAPHY: William Marsh, review, *ON* LXI (Apr. 5, 1997), 48–49 [on first full performance]; Candy Williams, review, *Tribune-Review* (Pittsburgh) (Feb. 16, 1996), D, 10 [on premiere].

Burgomaster of Saardam, The, or, The Two Peters, musical drama in two acts by Henry Rowley Bishop; libretto (Eng) by Frederick Reynolds. First performance September 23, 1818, London.
The two Peters are Peter I, the Russian Tsar, and Peter, a young Dutch ship carpenter with whom the ruler switches identities in order to see how regular citizens live.
Another setting is A. Lortzing's *Zar und Zimmermann, oder, Die zwei Peter* (1837, Leipzig). Shield's *The Czar** (1790, London) also involves the two Peters.

Burning Bright, opera in three acts by Frank Lewin; libretto (Eng) by the composer, after John Steinbeck's play. First performance November 5, 1993, New Haven, Yale School of Music, Woolsey Hall, with Charles Damsel (Joe Saul), Sherry Overholt (Mordeen), and Rinde Eckert (Victor); conducted by Raymond Harvey.
When Mordeen Saul finds out her husband, Joe, cannot father a child, she secretly gets impregnated by the younger Victor. Driven at first to kill him, the husband realizes that his wife got pregnant because of her great love for him and her great wish to bear him a child.
BIBLIOGRAPHY: L. E. Auld, ed., *Burning Bright: the Genesis of an Opera* (Guilford, Conn.: Lyrica Society, 1985); Gilbert Mott, "New Haven," *ON* LVIII (Feb. 5, 1994), 40 [on premiere].

Burning Fiery Furnace, The, second parable by Benjamin Britten; libretto (Eng) by William Plomer, from the Book of Daniel. First performance June 9, 1966, Aldeburgh Festival, Orford Church, with Peter Pears (Nebuchadnezzar), Bryan Drake (astrologer), Robert Tear (Misael), Victor Godfrey (Azarias), John Shirley-Quirk (Ananias), and Peter Leeming (the herald). First U.S. performance June 25, 1967, Katonah, New York, Caramoor Festival, with Andrea Velis.
The familiar biblical story concerns the three Israelites who stand against Nebuchadnezzar. The astrologer convinces the Babylonian king that the Israelites should be killed when they refuse to eat Babylonian food or worship the image of the Babylonian god. When the three are unhurt in the fiery furnace, Nebuchadnezzar sets them free and converts to their religion.
For a detailed plot synopsis and musical analysis, see K/*KOB*, 1227–30; K/*NKOB*, 133–34; Eaton/*OP* II, 254.
Major roles: Nebuchadnezzar (ten); the three Israelites: Misael (Shadrach, in Babylonian, ten), Ananias (Meshach, bar), and Azarias (Abednego, bass); the herald (bar); and the astrologer (bar).
The work uses a formalized performance style, and the score employs plainsong as its point of departure. Second of the *Three Church Parables*. See also *Curlew River* and *The Prodigal Son*.
SCORES: vs, fs (London: Faber, 1968, 1966).

LIBRETTO: performance libretto, with prod. notes by Colin Graham (London: Faber, 1966).
BIBLIOGRAPHY: Charles Osborne, "Britten's Festival," *NYT* (June 10, 1966) [on premiere].
DISCOGRAPHY: Pears, Tear, Drake, Shirley-Quirk, Dean, Leeming, Adeney, Sanders, Brenner, Aronowitz, Marjoram, Ellis, Blades, Ledger; cond. Britten and Tunnard, London OSA-1163 (1 CD).

Burning House, The, fantasy opera in one act by Alan Hovhaness; libretto (Eng) by the composer. First performance August 24, 1964, Gatlinburg, Tennessee, Hunter Hills Theater, Summer Music Festival, with Fiona Fuerstner and San Son Candelaria (dancers) and Vashek Pazdera and Samuel Ramey (vocal soloists); conducted by Robert Schaaf.
The piece is set in "the Universe." Vahaken defeats Death and the Demon. Alone, he dubs himself fire, fashions a burning house, and ends up in outer space along with countless burning suns.
For a detailed description, see Eaton/*OP* II, 254–55.
Major roles: Vahaken (bar), Death (bar), Demon (dancer), and Life-and-Death (dancer).
SCORES: condensed score (New York: C. F. Peters, 1962; London: Faber Music, [1968, 1966]; vs (London: Faber Music, [1966]).
BIBLIOGRAPHY: Allen Hughes, "Tennessee Debut for Opera-Ballet," *NYT* (Aug. 25, 1964), 29 [on premiere].
DISCOGRAPHY: London OSA 1163 (OS 26049) (1968, stereo LP).

Bus to Stockport and Other Stories, theater piece by Eric Valinsky and Peter Schubert; text (Eng), after John Cage's *Silence* and *A Year from Monday*. First performance February 20, 1986, New York, Opera Uptown; directed by Rhonda Rubinson.
The work presents Cage's views on random order and indeterminacy.
BIBLIOGRAPHY: Tim Page, "Stage: Musical Homage to Works of John Cage," *NY* (Feb. 24, 1986), C, 13 [on premiere].

Butterfly Girl and Mirage Boy, chamber dance-opera by Herbert Owen Reed; libretto (Eng) by Hartley Alexander and F. W. Coggan. First performance February 8, 1985, Brooklyn, New York.

Buxom Joan, all-sung burletta in one act by Rayner Taylor; libretto (Eng) by Thomas Willet, after William Congreve's play *Love for Love*. First performance June 26, 1778, London, Little Theatre in the Haymarket. First U.S. performance January 30, 1801, Philadelphia, New (Chestnut Street) Theatre. Revived January 6, 1975, New York, Fraunces Tavern, After Dinner Theater, with Stephanie Sundine (mother), Susan Gayle (Joan), Dennis Williams (tinker), Rafael LaManna (tailor), James Javore (soldier), and Christopher Greene (sailor); conducted by Gregory Sandow; produced by Beth Flusser.
The setting is Deptford, London. Buxom Joan is courted by four men, the tinker, the tailor, the soldier, and the sailor, the last of which she really loves. Despite her mother's advice she rejects the first three, and when she accepts the sailor's offer of marriage, he joins the tinker and soldier to go off and fight for their country (the tailor does not join them, having demurred because of cowardice). She is able to bear the loss because of her patriotism.
Roles: Buxom Joan (sop); her mother (sop); Tom, a tinker (ten); Snip, a tailor (ten); Bluff, a soldier (bass); and Ben, a sailor (ten).
SCORE: vs, ed. and realized by Gregory Sandow (Bryn Mawr, Pa.: Theodore Presser, [1975]).

By Gemini, opera in a prologue and two acts by Murray Baylor; libretto (Eng). First performance March 2, 1949, Galesburg, Illinois, Knox College Theater.

C

Cabaret Opera, A, chamber opera by William Russo; libretto (Eng) after E. E. Cummings, Gertrude Stein, W. H. Auden, Ezra Pound, et al. First performance 1970, New York. Performed as *The Alice B. Toklas Hashish Fudge Review*, December 8, 1977, New York.

Cabildo, opera in one act by Amy Beach; libretto (Eng) by Nan Bagby Stephens. Composed 1932. First performance February 27, 1945, Athens, Georgia, University of Georgia. First professional performance May 13, 1995, New York, Alice Tully Hall (concert).

The story concerns the pirate Jean Lafitte, who was jailed in the Cabildo (once the governor's palace) but who escaped in order to aid Andrew Jackson to defend New Orleans against the British during the War of 1812. Among a modern group of visitors viewing Lafitte's cell is Mary, who imagines that Lafitte's beloved, Lady Valerie, came back from the dead to help him escape.

BIBLIOGRAPHY: Cori Ellison, "A Woman's Work Well Done," *NYT* (May 7, 1995), II, 29. DISCOGRAPHY: Flanigan, Hellekant, Griffey, Groves, E. Perry, Paul, N.Y. Concert Singers; cond. R. Wilson, Delos DE–3170; rev. John W. Freeman, *ON* LX (Apr. 13, 1996), 34.

Cabinet, The, comic opera in three acts by William Reeve, John Moorehead, John Braham, Domenico Corri, and John Davy; libretto (Eng) by Thomas Dibdin after the old ballad *The Golden Bull.* First performance February 9, 1802, London, Covent Garden, with Mr. Emery (Count Curvoso), Mr. Incledon (Lorenzo), Mr. Braham (Prince Orlando), Mr. Fawcett (Whimsiculo), Mr. Blanchard (Marquis de Grand Chateau), Mr. Simmons (Manikin), Mrs. H. Johnson/Miss Wheatley (Constantia), Signora Storace (Floretta), Mrs. Atkins (Leonora), Mrs. Powell (Doralice), Mrs. Dibdin (Crudelia), and Mrs. Mattocks (Curiosa). First U.S. performance March 28, 1807, Philadelphia.

In the plot Lorenzo, son of Count Curvoso, is in love with Leonora, while Prince Orlando and the rich old Marquis de Grand Chateau have their sights on Constantia, the Count's daughter. Meanwhile, Crudelia is in love with Prince Orlando.

SCORE: vs (London, ca. 1802).
LIBRETTO: English (New York: Longworth, 1806).

Cabin in the Sky, musical fantasy by Vernon Duke; libretto (Eng) by Lynn Root; lyrics by John Latouche. First performance October 25, 1940, New York, Martin Beck Theatre, with Ethel Waters (Petunia Jackson), Dooley Wilson ("Little Joe"), Todd Duncan (the Lord's General), and Rex Ingram (Lucifer Jr.); staged by George Balanchine. Revived January 1964, New York.

Petunia Jackson prays that her no-good husband will be spared, and the Good Lord consents to give him six months to show he is worthy. Things seem to be going well until Lucifer Jr. interferes, and provokes Joe into shooting his devoted wife. The good-hearted Petunia, arriving at the pearly gates, convinces the Good Lord to let her erring husband in, also.

The show, which featured choreography by George Balanchine, ran for twenty weeks. It includes the famed "Taking a Chance on Love," sung by Petunia.

The 1943 movie, directed by Vincente Minelli, starred Louis Armstrong, John Bubbles, Ethel Waters, Eddie Anderson, and Lena Horne.

LIBRETTO: English (New York: n.p., [1940?]).

BIBLIOGRAPHY: Margo Jefferson, "Using Black English Well (or Not)," *NYT* (Jan. 15, 1997), C, 11, 16 [includes discussion of movie version].

DISCOGRAPHY: cast of New York revival, Capitol W2073 (1964, 1 LP).

Cady of Bagdad, The, comic opera in three acts by Thomas Linley Jr.; libretto (Eng) by Abraham Portal, after the text by Lemonnier for Monsigny's and Gluck's *Le cadi dupé* (1761, Paris). First performance February 19, 1778, London, Drury Lane Theatre.

In this story, supposedly set from the *Thousand and One Nights*, Selima (Zelmire in the French) attempts to take revenge on the Cady because of his philandering. She pretends to love him, saying that she is the daughter of the dyer Omar, whose daughter is, in fact, quite ugly. When the Cady realizes the deception, he decides that his one wife, Fatime, whom he had ignored in favor of Selima, is pretty enough to keep his interest. Selima is left alone with her young lover, Abdullah (originally Nouradin).

SCORE: ms fs (British Library, M.S. Add. 29297).

LIBRETTO: English, excerpts (London: G. Kearsley, 1778).

Caedmar, Celtic opera in one act by Granville Bantock; libretto (Eng) by the composer. First performance (concert) July 12, 1892, London, Royal Academy of Music. First performance (stage) October 18, 1893, London, Crystal Palace.

The work is replete with Wagnerian elements.

Caernarvon Castle, or, The Birth of the Prince of Wales, "entertainment" in two acts by Thomas Attwood; libretto (Eng) by John Rose. First performance August 12, 1793, London, Haymarket Theatre.

SCORE: vs (London: Preston & Son, [1793]).

LIBRETTO: English, "sull'aria" (London: William Lane, 1793).

Caffres, The, or, Buried Alive, opera by John Davy; libretto (Eng) by Edmund John Eyre. First performance June 2, 1802, London, Covent Garden.

Cage, The, opera in one act by George Thaddeus Jones; libretto (Eng) by Leo Brady. First performance April 1959, Washington, D.C., Catholic University; shown on May 1, 1959, New York, NBC television.

Cain and Abel, opera by Ned Rorem; libretto (Eng) by Paul Goodman. Composed ca. 1946. Not performed.

Caleb Quotem and His Wife. See Throw Physic to the Dogs!

California Mystery Park, "soundtheater" (opera) by Carson Kievman. Composed 1980. First performance (excerpts) April 21, 1993, New York, American Opera Projects, with Ron Raines, Diane Kesling, and Stephanie Park.

The plot, set in postwar America, deals with the tensions between a World War II veteran and his Japanese daughter.

The work includes simultaneous recitation and singing among the characters.

SCORE: fs, excerpts ([New York]: Associated Music Publishers, 1980).
BIBLIOGRAPHY: Alex Ross, review, *NYT* (Apr. 24, 1993), A, 17 [on premiere].

Caliph of Bagdad, The, "an original oriental, operatic extravaganza," with "music composed, selected, and arranged" by Frank Musgrave; libretto (Eng) by William Brough, after the *Thousand and One Nights.* First performance December 26, 1867, London, Royal Strand Theatre, with Ada Swanborough (Haroun Alraschid), Gaston Murray (Mesrour), Thomas Thorne (Mahoud), David James (the Cadi), Elise Holt (Hassan), H. J. Turner (Chebib), Miss E. Johnstone (Abdallah), Mr. Imrie (captain of the guards), Miss Newton (Darina), and Miss Ada Harland (Camira).

The plot concerns Haroun Alraschid, the eighth-century Caliph of Bagdad and hero of many of the stories of the *Thousand and One Nights,* and Darina, daughter of the once prosperous Chebib. Chebib is now in debt to the Cadi. One night a stranger comes to Chebib's house and proposes that Darina marry him that evening. She agrees, and when the Cadi arrives at the door and demands to be paid, the stranger reveals his true identity, that of the Caliph, and punishes the evil Cadi.

The story was also set by A. Boieldieu, as *Le calife de Bagdad* (1800, Paris); and by M. García, as *Il califfo di Bagdad* (1813, Naples).
LIBRETTO: English (London: T. H. Lacy, ca. 1867).

Caliph's Clock, The, opera in three acts by Leo Kraft; libretto (Eng) by Joseph Machlis. First performance March 30, 1951, New York, Pauline Edwards Hall, Queens College Opera Workshop, with William Werbell, Jeanne London, Charles Ahlers, Michael Basile, and Helen Toby Feit; conducted by George Petitpas.

The fanciful story concerns a daring salesman from Hartford who sells a special clock to the caliph.
BIBLIOGRAPHY: C. H., "Queens Students Offer New Opera," *NYT* (Mar. 31, 1951), 8.

Calling of Mother Ann, The, opera in one act by Leonard Kastle; libretto (Eng) by the composer. First performance June 21, 1985, Hancock Shaker Village, Massachusetts.

A work about the Shakers. See also *The Journey of Mother Ann.*

Calvary, religious music drama in one act by Thomas Pasatieri; libretto (Eng) taken word-for-word from the play of Yeats. First performance April 7, 1971, Bellevue, Washington, St. Thomas Episcopal Church, Seattle Festival Opera, with Clayne Robison (Christ), Gerald Thorsen (Judas), and Archie Drake (Lazarus); conducted by Henry Holt; directed by Robert De Simone.

The religious text examines humankind's relationship to the Divine and vice versa. It also includes a religious confrontation between Jesus and Lazarus and Jesus and Judas.

Major roles: Christ (bar), Judas (ten), and Lazarus (bass).
SCORE: vs ([New York]: Belwin-Mills, [1972]).

Calypso, masque in three acts by Thomas Butler; libretto (Eng) by Richard Cumberland. First performance March 20, 1779, London, Covent Garden.
LIBRETTO: English (Dublin: Price [etc.], 1779; London: T. Evans, 1779).

Calypso, or, Love and Enchantment, serio-comic opera by Tommaso Giordani; libretto (Eng) by Robert Houlton. First performance April 1785, Dublin, Theatre Royal.

Calypso and Telemachus, grand opera in three acts by John Ernest Galliard; libretto (Eng) by John Hughes, after Fénelon's *Télémaque* (1699). First performance May 14,

1712, London, Haymarket, with Margherita de L'Epine (Calypso), Mrs. Barbier (Telemachus), Signora Manina (Eucharis), and Leveridge (Proteus).

Grieving over the departure of Ulysses, Calypso is thrilled when his son, Telemachus, arrives at her island. She tells him that Ulysses is dead in order to hold his attention, but he becomes enamored of Eucharis, who is herself desired by the sea god Proteus. The lovers are kept apart by the jealousy of both Calypso and Proteus, but Minerva saves Telemachus from death and returns him to Ithaca.

The work was given only five times.

SCORE: vs ([London: J. Walsh & J. Hare, 1712]).

LIBRETTO: English (London: E. Sanger, 1712).

Cambro-Britons, historical opera in three acts by Samuel Arnold; libretto (Eng) by James Boaden, after Lewis. First performance July 21, 1798, London, Little Theatre in the Haymarket, with John Johnstone.

The plot concerns the war between Edward I and Llewellyn, the Prince of Wales (d. 1882) in the thirteenth century. It is the first operatic treatment of a Welsh subject.

See Fiske/*ETM*, 283, for a detailed description.

LIBRETTO: English (London: G. G. and J. Robinson, 1798).

Camille, opera in a prologue and three acts by Hamilton Forrest; libretto (Eng) by the composer, after Alexandre Dumas's *La dame aux camélias* (1852). First performance December 10, 1930, Chicago, Civic Opera, with Mary Garden (Camille) and Charles Hackett (Armand); conducted by Emil Cooper.

The tragedy of Camille, a beautiful courtesan who unselfishly gives up her beloved, Armand, when his family disapproves. He returns only at the end as she is dying.

Other settings of the story include Dalayrac's comic *Camille, ou, Le souterrain* (1791, Paris); Verdi's *La Traviata* (1853, Venice); and M. Delmas's opéra-comique *Camille* (1921, Paris).

LIBRETTO: English (New York: F. Rullman, 1930).

Camp, The, musical entertainment in two acts by Thomas Linley Sr.; libretto (Eng) by Richard Tickell, a revision of Richard B. Sheridan's work. First performance October 15, 1778, London, Drury Lane Theatre, with Mr. Bannister (the serjeant [sic]), Mrs. Wrighten, Mrs. Fawcett (first recruit), Mr. Holcroft (2d recruit), Miss Walpole, and Mr. Webster. First U.S. performance December 15, 1806, Charleston, South Carolina.

The painter O'Daub, who has come to the camp at Coxheath, is misheard by some locals as talking against royalty and is arrested as a spy.

Based on "many [airs and trios]" from *The Royal Merchant,** according to the 1778 vocal score.

SCORE: vs (London: Samuel & Ann Thompson, [1778]).

LIBRETTO: English (London: [n.p.], 1795).

Campaign, The, or, Love in the East Indies, comic opera in three acts by William Shield; libretto (Eng) by Robert Jephson and N. Barry. First performance January 30, 1784, Dublin, Smock Alley; May 12, 1785, London, Covent Garden. Revised as *Love and War.**

The music included parts by Tenducci, with the overture by Haydn.

LIBRETTO: English, in *The Plays of Robert Jephson*, ed. Temple James Maynard (New York: Garland, 1980).

Cancelling Dark, The, radio opera in one act by Christopher Whelen; libretto (Eng) by Vernon Scannell. First performance December 5, 1954, London, BBC, Third Programme.

Candide, originally a comic operetta in two acts by Leonard Bernstein; book (Eng) by Lillian Hellman; lyrics by Richard Wilbur; additional lyrics by John Latouche and Dorothy Parker, after the novel by Voltaire. First performance October 29, 1956, Boston, Colonial Theater, with Barbara Cook (Cunegonde), Irra Petina (Old Lady), Robert Rounseville (Candide), and Max Adrian (Pangloss); conducted by Samuel Krachmalnick; directed by Tyrone Guthrie; same production December 1, 1956, New York, Martin Beck Theatre. First British performance April 30, 1959, London, Saville Theatre, with Mary Costa (Cunegonde), Edith Coates (Old Lady), and Denis Quilley (Candide).
"CHELSEA" VERSION: reduced to one act, with libretto (Eng) by Hugh Wheeler, lyrics by Richard Wilbur, Stephen Sondheim, and John Latouche, December 20, 1973, Brooklyn, New York, Chelsea Theatre; conducted by John Mauceri; directed by Harold Prince; March 8, 1974, New York, Broadway Theatre.

In this version the Wheeler book replaced Hellman's and followed the Voltaire original more closely. Stephen Sondheim supplied new lyrics for some of the songs, and several numbers were cut from the 1956 version. John Mauceri supervised the musical changes, and Hershy Kay reorchestrated the score for thirteen instruments.
"OPERA HOUSE VERSION": in two acts, with book adapted from Voltaire by Hugh Wheeler, lyrics by Richard Wilbur, additional lyrics by Stephen Sondheim and John Latouche, orchestrated by John Mauceri. First performance of this version October 13, 1982, New York, City Opera, with David Eisler (Candide), Erie Mills (Cunegonde), Deborah Darr (Paquette), Scott Reeve (Maximilian), Jack Harrold (Baron/Grand Inquisitor, etc.), John Lankston (Voltaire, etc.), and Muriel Costa-Greenspon (Old Lady); conducted by John Mauceri.

This version restored all the music, including some that had never been heard before; the work was expanded again into two acts. John Mauceri's new orchestration was based on that of the 1956 version. The order of the scenes and music was changed significantly.
"FINAL REVISED VERSION" (the last version approved by the composer). Performed 1988, Scottish Opera; December 1989 (concert), London; conducted by Bernstein (see DG recording, which includes a history by Andrew Porter of all the versions).

In this version, supervised by John Mauceri, there was a return to the scene sequence of the original Hellman text. It kept some of Wheeler's additions; libretto revisions were by John Wells. Among the musical restorations were Martin's "Words, Words, Words" ("Laughing Song") of act 2, added to a 1971 performance but cut from the opera house version.

In the satirical plot, which begins in Westphalia, the young and idealistic Candide believes his teacher, the philosopher Dr. Pangloss, when Pangloss explains that "This is the Best of All Possible Worlds." Pangloss encourages Candide to marry Cunegonde, and their feelings are expressed in the duet "Oh Happy We." Their plans are stymied when a civil war breaks out, and Cunegonde is abducted. Candide begins his travels, during which he meets Pangloss, who tells him that Cunegonde has been killed. Pangloss seemingly dies at the hands of the Spanish Inquisition in Lisbon for his optimism; his punishment is described by the bitingly sardonic chorus piece "Auto-da-Fé" ("What a Day"). Candide visits Paris, where he discovers Cunegonde as a "kept" woman. Candide, Cunegonde, and an Old Lady are kidnapped and sent to the New World as slaves, where they are separated. Candide amasses a fortune in Eldorado and tries to find Cunegonde once again. After a shipwreck he discovers his beloved in Venice and returns with her to Westphalia, where they meet Pangloss, miraculously still alive. Abandoning Pangloss's philosophy, he and Cunegonde vow to "Make Our Garden Grow."

For a detailed description, see Gänzl/*BBM*, 166–71; K/*NKOB*, 62–64.

Major roles: Candide (ten); Dr. Pangloss (bar); Cunegonde (sop); Maximilian, Cunegonde's brother (bar); Paquette, the maid (mezzo); and Old Lady (mezzo).

The musical highlights, which are found in all of the versions, include the brilliant overture in sonata form, often performed as a concert piece; the bravura aria "Glitter and Be Gay" (also a concert perennial), which is a parody of Marguerite's "Jewel Song" in Gounod's *Faust*—it is sung by Cunegonde in the Paris scene; and the beautiful and expansive C-major finale of the work, "Make Our Garden Grow," for the principals and chorus.

Earlier settings of the Voltaire include the vaudevilles *Candide et Cunégonde* (1837, Paris); and *Candide, ou, Tout est pour le mieux* (1848, Paris); and the opera-ballet *Kandida* by L. Knipper (comp. 1926–1927).

SCORE: vs, operetta version (New York: G. Schirmer, [1958]); vs (New York: Schirmer Books, 1976); score, opera house version, 1989 ([New York]: Jalni/Boosey & Hawkes, 1994).
LIBRETTO: English, operetta version (New York: Random House, 1957).
BIBLIOGRAPHY: Robert Jacobson, "Reports: U.S.," *ON* XLVII (Jan. 1, 1983), 38 [on 1982 "premiere"]; Andrew Porter, "Musical Events," *NY* LVIII (Nov. 1, 1982), 152–53 [on 1982 version]; David Patrick Stearns, "*Candide* Redux," *ON* LVI (Aug. 1991), 12–14.
DISCOGRAPHY: 1982 opera house version: E. Mills, D. Eisler, J. Lankston, New York City Opera Orch. and Chorus; cond. J. Mauceri, New World NW-340/41-1 (2 LPs), NW-340/41-2 (2 CDs), NW-340/41-4 (tape); "final revised version": J. Anderson, C. Ludwig, J. Hadley, N. Gedda, A. Green, D. Jones, K. Ollmann, London Sym.; cond. Bernstein, DG 429734-2 (1989, London, 2 CDs), rev. Patrick J. Stearns, "Recordings," *ON* LVI (Oct. 1991), 40–41.
VIDEO: Hadley, Anderson, Green, Ludwig, Gedda, Jones, Ollman, London Sym. Orch.; cond. Bernstein, DG VHS 072 423-3.

Candle, The, opera in one act by Philip M. Slates; libretto (Eng) by the composer. First performance July 26, 1956, Athens, Ohio, University of Ohio, Ewing Hall.

Canterbury Pilgrims, The, opera in three acts by Charles Stanford; libretto (Eng) by Gilbert A. A'Beckett. First performance April 28, 1884, London, Drury Lane Theatre, with Clara Perry (Cicely), Ben Davies (Hubert), Barrington Foote (Hal o' the Chepe), William Ludwig (Sir Christopher), Marian Burton (Dame Margery), and George Snazelle (Geoffrey); conducted by the composer.

The story, which does not follow the Chaucer version, involves a pilgrimage from London to the shrine of St. Thomas and includes the travails of two young lovers, Cicely and Hubert, who are able to stay together, despite the opposition of their parents.
SCORE: vs (London: Boosey, [1884?]; [Leipzig: Roder]).

Canterbury Pilgrims, The, opera in four acts by Reginald De Koven; libretto (Eng) by Percy Mackaye, after Chaucer. First performance March 8, 1917, New York, Metropolitan Opera, with Edith Mason (the prioress), Johannes Sembach (Chaucer), Margarete Ober (Alisoun), Basil Ruysdael (the miller), Albert Reiss (King Richard II), and Giulio Rossi (the host); conducted by Artur Bodanzky.

In the story, set in 1387 in England, Alisoun, the Wife of Bath, is looking for a sixth husband. She falls in love with the poet, who has his eye on the prioress. The Wife bets that she can get the prioress's brooch, a feat that will allow her to marry Chaucer. She does, and Chaucer, desperate, appeals to King Richard for help. He says that the Wife must marry a miller, and Chaucer is left to pursue the prioress.

Major roles: Chaucer (ten); Alisoun, the Wife of Bath (mezzo), the prioress (sop); the miller (bass); King Richard II (ten).

SCORE: vs (New York: Macmillan Co., 1916).

LIBRETTO: English (Cincinnati: John Church Co., 1916).

Canterbury Tale, A, opera by Betty Roe; libretto (Eng), after Chaucer. First performance October 9, 1986, Oakham, East Leicestershire, England, East Midlands Opera.

Canterbury Tales, The, opera in three acts by Erik Chisholm; libretto (Eng) by the composer, after Geoffrey Chaucer. Composed 1961–1962.

Act 1: **The Wyf of Bathes Tale,** composed 1962.

Act 2: **The Pardoner's Tale.*** First performance November 1961, Cape Town, Little Theatre.

Act 3: **The Nonnes Preestes Tale,** composed 1961.

The work is notable for its employment of ars nova and twelve-tone techniques and fourteenth-century tunes.

BIBLIOGRAPHY: G. Pulvermacher, "Chaucer into Opera," *Opera* XIII (1962), 187–88.

Canterville Ghost, The, children's opera in one act by Martin Kalmanoff; libretto (Eng), after Oscar Wilde. First performance March 11, 1967, New York, Judson Hall.

Capitan, El, comic opera in three acts by John Philip Sousa; libretto (Eng) by Charles Klein; lyrics by the composer and Tom Frost. First performance April 13, 1896, Boston, Tremont Theater with DeWolf Hopper (Don Enrico Medigua/El Capitan), Alfred Klein (Pozzo), T. S. Guise (Dom Luiz Cazarro), and Edna Wallace Hopper (Estrelda); April 20, 1896, New York, Broadway Theater, with the same cast. First British performance July 10, 1899, London, Lyric Theatre. Revived January 10, 1965, New York, Columbia University; conducted by Howard Shanet; and November 19, 1976, New York, Pace University, Eastern Opera Theater.

When El Capitan, the leader of a band of rebels in Peru, dies, the viceroy, Don Enrico Medigua, the only person who knows the leader is dead, assumes his identity. As El Capitan he meets and falls in love with Estrelda, daughter of Dom Luiz Cazarro, former viceroy of Peru. When Don Enrico assumes the identity of the viceroy once again, he is forced to give up Estrelda, since he is already married to Princess Marghanza.

Among its musical highlights are the title song, set as a march, and the duet of El Capitan and Estrelda that opens act 3, "Sweetheart, I'm Waiting."

Major roles: Princess Marghanza, wife of Don Enrico Medigua (mezzo); Isabel, their daughter (sop); Don Enrico Medigua, viceroy of Peru (ten); Dom Luiz Cazarro, ex-viceroy; Estrelda, Don Cazarro's daughter (mezzo); and Senor Amabile Pozzo, chamberlain of Peru (ten).

TEXT AND SCORE: vs (Cincinnati: John Church, 1896); repr. ed. Paul Bierley, *NAMT*, vol. 14 (1994).

BIBLIOGRAPHY: review, *NYT* (Jan. 11, 1965), 29 [on Columbia revival]; Jennifer Dunning, "Places for Operatic Insurrections," *NYT* (Nov. 19, 1976), C, 13.

Capitoline Venus, The, opera in one act by Ulysses Kay; libretto (Eng) by Judith Dvorkin, after a story by Mark Twain. First performance March 12, 1971, Quincy, Illinois, University of Illinois Opera Group.

In this satirical play about gullibility and set in Rome in the late 1800s, George Arnold exacts revenge over his friends who believe in the existence of giants in the Bible. He has a stone giant made, buried, and "discovered."

Major roles: George Arnold (ten), Mary Phillips (sop), and Mr. Phillips (bass).

Capocchio and Dorinna, "mock Italian opera" in one act by Rayner Taylor after *The Temple of Dullness**; libretto (Eng) by Rayner Taylor. First performance January 20, 1793, Annapolis, Maryland, Assembly Room.

The work was advertised in the *Maryland Gazette* of January 14, 1793, as consisting of "recitative, airs and duets."

Caponsacchi, opera in two acts by Richard Hageman; libretto (Eng) by Arthur Goodrich, after Robert Browning's poem *The Ring and the Book.* First performance February 4, 1937, New York, Metropolitan Opera, with Mario Chamlee (Caponsacchi), Lawrence Tibbett (Guido), and Helen Jepson (Pompilia); conducted by the composer. First performed as *Tragödie in Arezzo* (1932, Freiburg), in a German version by Werner Wolf.

The work takes place in 1698 Italy. Caponsacchi, a young priest, attempts, unsuccessfully, to shield Pompilia from her brutal husband, Guido. Accusing her of adultery, Guido kills her and is charged with murder.

SCORE: vs, English-German (Berlin: Edition Adler, 1931).

Cappemakers, The, music drama in two acts by John Taverner; libretto (Eng), after the York Mystery Plays. First performance June 14, 1964, Charleston Manor, Sussex, Sussex Festival. Revised for the stage, July 8, 1965, London, Royal Academy of Music; conducted by the composer; produced by Pauline Stuart.

BIBLIOGRAPHY: review, *MO* LXXXVIII (Sept. 1965), 715 [on stage premiere]; H. D. R., "Student Performances," *Opera* XVI (Sept. 1965), 680 [on stage premiere].

Capricious Lovers, The, comic opera in two acts by George Rush; libretto (Eng) by Robert Lloyd, after Charles Favart's *Le caprice amoureux, ou, Ninette à la cour,* set as a pastiche by Duni et al. (1755). First performance November 28, 1764, London, Drury Lane Theatre. Performed as an afterpiece, in two acts, March 2, 1765, London.

A prince, in disguise, tries to turn a country girl, Phoebe, into a lady and get her to forget her lover, but the prince's efforts do not succeed.

For a detailed description, see Fiske/*ETM,* 345–46.

Also set by T. Giordani, as *Phillis at Court** (1767, Dublin); J. Hiller, as *Lottchen am Hofe* (1767, Leipzig); and T. A. Arne, as *Phoebe at Court** (1776).

LIBRETTO: English, opera version (London: R. Withy et al., 1764); afterpiece version (London: R. Withy et al., 1765).

Captain Jinks of the Horse Marines, comic opera in three acts by Jack Beeson; libretto (Eng) by Sheldon Harnick, after a play by Clyde Fitch (1902). First performance September 20, 1975, Kansas City, Lyric Theater, with Carol Wilcox (Aurelia Trentoni), Robert Owen Jones (Captain Jinks), Carolyne James (Mrs. Gee), George Livings (the reporter), and Eugene Green (Colonel Mapleson); conducted by Russell Patterson.

The story, which takes place in New York City in the early 1870s, concerns Captain Jinks, an opera fan who bets that he can seduce Aurelia. Trentoni, a member of Colonel

Mapleson's opera company in New York at the turn of the century. The captain falls in love with the singer instead and, after complications, the story ends happily.

Major roles: Colonel Mapleson (basso cantante), Jonathan Jinks (ten), Mrs. Gee (alto/pianist), and Aurelia Trentoni (col sop).
SCORE: vs (New York: Boosey & Hawkes, 1983).
BIBLIOGRAPHY: Marshall Bialosky, "Dramatic Music: Jack Beeson," *MLA Notes* (Sept. 1985), 167–69; Ethan C. Mordden, "Kansas City," *ON* XL (Nov. 1975), 50 [on premiere].
DISCOGRAPHY: C. Wilcox, R. Jones, E. Green, G. Livings, K. Harmon, W. Latimer, Kansas City Philharmonic; cond. R. Patterson (1976), RCA ARL2-1727 (2 LPs); rev. Winthrop Sargent, *NY* LIII (Mar. 28, 1977), 109; same version on tape, Desto 7222/3.

Captain Lovelock, opera in one act by John Duke; libretto (Eng) by the composer, after Ludvig Holberg's play *The Changed Bridegroom*. First performance August 18, 1953, Hudson Falls, New York, Hudson Falls High School; February 20, 1954, New York, New York College of Music Opera Workshop, Carl Fischer Hall; conducted by Siegfried Landau.

After the widowed Terentia visits the city, she becomes determined to better her situation and marry a young military officer. Her daughters go to Madame Kirsten, a marriage broker, and arrange for Pernille, the maid, to pretend to be the dashing Captain Lovelock. Terentia comes to Madame Kirsten and is tricked into believing she has met her ideal husband. Only after Captain Lovelock is revealed to be Pernille does the humiliated Terentia realizes the foolishness of her plans.

For a detailed description, see Summers/*OOA*, 99–100.

Roles: Terentia (mezzo); Pernille (sop); Kirsten (mezzo/alto); and Leonora and Laurentia, Terentia's daughters (sop).
SCORE: vs (New York: C. Fischer, 1964).
BIBLIOGRAPHY: R. P., review, *NYT* (Feb. 21, 1956), 36 [on New York premiere].

Captain's Parrot, The, opera by Alexander Brent-Smith; libretto (Eng) by W. W. Jacobs, based on his *The Grey Parrot*. Composed ca. 1950.

The work is scored for thirteen characters and chorus, with a chamber orchestra.
SCORE: vs (London: Novello, [1950]).
LIBRETTO: English (London: Novello, [1950]).

Captive, The, pastiche of thirteen numbers by Charles Dibdin, Baldassare Galuppi, Gioacchino Cocchi, Leo Vinci, Vincenzo Ciampi, Matteo Vento, and Egidio Duni; text by Isaac Bickerstaffe, after Dryden's *Don Sebastian*. First performance June 21, 1769, London, Haymarket Theatre.

The story concerns the young Spaniard Ferdinand, who has been taken prisoner by a Turkish admiral and is given as a present to the Cadi. He is, like his later counterpart Pedrillo (in Mozart's *Die Entführung aus dem Serail*), made a gardener in the Cadi's house, and he falls in love with the Cadi's daughter, Zorayde. They plan to flee but are intercepted by the jealous stepmother, Fatime. The couple is saved, however, when the Cadi learns that his criminal activities have been uncovered, and the whole family escapes by ship.
LIBRETTO: English (London: W. Griffen, 1769; Georgetown [D.C.]: William Rind, Jr., 1810).

Captive, The, opera in one act by Peter Wishart; libretto (Eng) by Don Roberts. First performance June 29, 1960, Birmingham, England, Barber Institute.
LIBRETTO: English (n.p.: Hinrichsen Edition, [1960]).

Captive of Spilburg, The, opera in two acts by John Dussek and Michael Kelly, an adaptation of Dalayrac's *Camille* (1791, Paris); libretto (Eng) by Prince Hoare, after Marsollier's text, itself an adaptation of Mme. de Genlis's *Adèle et Théodore*. First performance November 14, 1798, London, Drury Lane, with Mrs. Crouch (Eugenia) and Michael Kelly (Canzemar). First U.S. performance March 25, 1801, New York, Park Theatre.

After Eugenia marries Korowitz secretly, his nephew Canzemar rescues her from bandits. Not knowing of the marriage, the nephew tries, but fails, to seduce her and releases her only when she promises not to tell of his actions. The husband, not receiving an explanation of where his wife has been and therefore suspecting her of infidelity, throws her into a dungeon, but the situation is resolved happily at the end.
LIBRETTO: English (London: Machell Stace and J. Hatchard, 1799).

Caractacus, opera by Thomas Augustine Arne; libretto (Eng) by George Colman Sr., after a tragedy by William Mason. First performance December 6, 1776, London, Covent Garden.

The music, which consisted of twenty-one numbers, is lost.

Set as a cantata by Edward Elgar (1898, Leeds).
LIBRETTO: English (York: R. Horsfield and J. Dodsley, London, 1777).

Caravan, The, or, The Driver and His Dog, "grand serio comic opera" in two acts by William Reeve; libretto (Eng) by Frederick Reynolds. First performance December 5, 1803, London, Drury Lane Theatre. First U.S. performance March 23, 1810, Philadelphia, Chestnut Street Theatre.
SCORE: vs (London, ca. 1803).
LIBRETTO: English (London: J. & J. Robinson, [1803]).

Caritas, opera in two continuous acts by Robert Saxon; libretto (Eng) by Arnold Wesker, after his play of the same name. First performance November 21, 1991, Wakefield, England, Wakefield Opera House.

The setting is Norfolk, England, July 1377. Despite the pleas of her fiancé Robert and her family, Christine Carpenter decides to become an anchoress, to be locked in a cell within the walls of the church. When she believes she has seen a divine vision, a priest warns her that she is seeing illusions created by the Devil. An itinerant priest, passing through the town, calls for the people to support the Peasants' Revolt, and when Christine begs to be let out of her cell, the Bishop turns down her plea. Robert joins the peasants, and Christine, left alone, goes insane.

Roles: Christine (sop); Bishop Henry of Norwich (bass-bar); Robert Lonle, Christine's fiancé (ten); Agnes, Christine's mother (mezzo); William, Christine's father (bass-bar); Richard Lonle, Robert's father (bass); Mathew, Christine's parish priest (ten); tax collector (ten); and Matilde, village gossip (mezzo).
DISCOGRAPHY: E. Davies; J. Best; C. Ventris; other soloists; English Northern Philharmonia; cond. D. Masson, 13502 Collins Classics (1 CD, 1992).

Carmen Jones, "a version of 'Carmen' for colored singers," after Georges Bizet's *Carmen* (1875, Paris), with new orchestral arrangements by Robert Russell Bennett; libretto (Eng) by Oscar Hammerstein II, after Meilhac and Halévy's text. First performance December 2, 1943, New York, Broadway Theatre, with Muriel Smith/Muriel Rahn (Carmen), Luther Saxon/Napoleon Reed (Joe), Carlotta Franzell/Elton J. Warren (Cindy Lou), and Glenn Bryant (Husky Miller); conducted by Joseph Littau; choreographed by Eugene Loring; choral direction by Robert Shaw; produced by Billy Rose.

This version is set in the United States in 1943 and with mostly black characters. Carmen Jones works in a parachute factory during World War II. The Don-José character she seduces is Joe, a black corporal. Carmen and Joe flee to Chicago, where Carmen meets Husky Miller, a successful boxer, an updating of Bizet's Escamillo. Joe's former love is Cindy Lou, Micaëla in the Bizet. The bull arena is a sports stadium, outside which Carmen meets her end.

Among the numbers are "Dat's Love" (the Habanera), "You Talk Jus' like My Maw" (Micaëla's song), "Dis Flower" (Flower Song), "Stan' Up an' Fight" (Toreador Song), and the quintet "Whizzin' Away along de Track" (the Card Song).

The work was very successful in its time, running for 503 performances. It was made into a movie in 1954 with Dorothy Dandridge (whose singing was dubbed by Marilyn Horne) and Harry Belafonte as the leads.

In his 1945 preface to *Carmen Jones* (vi), Hammerstein pointed out that "all the melodies—with a few very minor exceptions—are sung in their accustomed order," and the elimination of the recitatives was not taking a great liberty but rather kept with Bizet's original version, with spoken dialogue.

Other English treatments of *Carmen* include the parodies *Carmen, or, Soldiers and Seville-ians* by M. B. Leavitt's Grand English Operatic Burlesque Company (1880, New York); the burlesque *Carmen up to Date* by M. Lutz (1890, Liverpool); J. Corigliano's *Naked Carmen** (1970); and M. Ashman's *José's Carmen** (London, 1984).
SCORE: chorus score, selections (1943, photocopy of copyist's ms, NYPL); vs, selections ([New York]: Williamson Music, Milwaukee, Wisc., [1991], 1943).
LIBRETTO: English (New York: A. A. Knopf, 1945).
DISCOGRAPHY: M. Smith, L. Saxon, C. Franzell, G. Glenn, J. Hawkins, Carmen Jones Orch.; Carmen Jones Chorus; cond. J. Littau, Decca ED-904 (1955?, 1 LP), DL 79021 (1992, 1 CD); orig. prod., M. Smith, L. Saxon, E. J. Warren, AEI-CD045 (1998, 1 CD).

Carnival of Venice, The, comic opera by Thomas Linley Sr.; libretto (Eng) by Richard Tickell. First performance December 13, 1781, London, Drury Lane Theatre, with Mrs. Cargill and Miss Anna Maria Phillips.

The work includes the ballad "Young Lubin was a Shepherd Boy." Another piece, "The Song of Thy Love," was used in Storace's *The Haunted Tower** (1789, London).
SCORE: vs (London: Samuel, Ann, and Pete Thompson, n.d.).
LIBRETTO: English (London: n.p., 1781).

Carrion Crow, The, opera in one act by Grant Fletcher; libretto (Eng) by Frances Wells, after a radio play by John Jacob Niles. First performance March 20, 1953, Bloomington, Illinois, Illinois Wesleyan University.

The poor tailor Ebenezer Botts, frustrated by his wife, Pansy, her father, Grandpaw, the bank collector, Gathe Geezle, the loafer, Enoch Alsop, and the local politician, Snitch Crochett, decides to take his anger out on a noisy crow. He shoots but misses the bird, killing the family sow, Annabelle, instead.

For a detailed description, see Eaton/*OP* II, 257.

Major roles: Ebenezer Botts (ten), Snitch Crochett (ten), Enoch Alsop (bar), Gathe Geezle (bar), Pansy Botts (sop), and Grandpaw (ten).
SCORE: vs holograph, 1950 (NYPL, photocopy).

Carry Nation, opera in a prologue and two acts by Douglas Moore; libretto (Eng) by William North Jayme. First performance April 28, 1966, Lawrence, Kansas, University of Kansas, Murphy Hall, with Beverly Wolff (Carry), John Reardon (her husband), Kenneth Smith (her father), and Patricia Brooks (her mother); conducted by Robert Baustian; directed by Lewin Goff. The work was commissioned by and written for the centennial of the founding of the University of Kansas. It was revived in March 1968, New York, City Opera, with Beverly Wolff, Ellen Faull, and Julian Patrick; conducted by Samuel Krachmalnick.

The story, told in a series of flashbacks, is a treatment of the early life of Carry Nation, daughter of a strict religious father and a mother who is failing mentally. Carry dedicates her life to the abolition of alcohol after her husband, Charles, dies from excessive drinking.

For a detailed description, see Eaton/*OP* II, 57–58.

Major roles: Carry (mezzo); Charles Lloyd, her husband (bar); the father (bass-bar); and the mother (sop).

BIBLIOGRAPHY: Frank Merkling, review, *ON* XXX (June 4, 1966), 24 [on premiere]; Theodore Strongin, "Opera by Moore Bows in Kansas," *NYT* (Apr. 30, 1966), 18 [on premiere].
DISCOGRAPHY: Wolff, City Opera, Desto DC-6463/5.

Casanova's Homecoming, opera buffa in three acts by Dominick Argento; libretto (Eng) by the composer, after Casanova's *L'histoire de ma vie*. First performance April 12, 1985 (as *Casanova*), St. Paul, Minnesota Opera and St. Paul Chamber Orchestra, Ordway Music Theatre, with Julian Patrick (Casanova), Susanne Marsee (Bellino/Teresa), Elaine Bonazzi (Madame d'Urfé), Carol Gutknecht (Giulietta), Douglas Perry (Marquis de Lisle), and Michele McBride (Barbara); conducted by Scott Bergeson. First New York performance November 2, 1985, City Opera.

The story opens in the first week of Carnival season in 1774 in Venice. The aging Casanova has come home and proceeds to seduce Bellino, a singer who is supposedly a castrato but is, in reality, a beautiful woman named Teresa, who has donned a disguise to further her operatic career, as Casanova has guessed. He uses his new love to seduce the mad Madame d'Urfé, who wishes to be reborn as a man; during his escapade with her he steals her jewels, which he offers as a dowry for Barbara, his poor godchild, who turns out to be his daughter.

Major roles: Casanova (bar), Lorenzo (bar), Gabrielle (ten), Madame d'Urfé (alto), Giulietta (sop), and Barbara (sop).

The work includes, in a nod to its setting, borrowings from Jommelli's *Demofoonte*, and act 1, scene 2 is set in the opera house during a performance.

SCORE: vs (New York: Boosey & Hawkes, 1985).
LIBRETTO: English (New York: Boosey & Hawkes, [1985].
BIBLIOGRAPHY: Peter G. Davis, "Casanova's Latest Conquest," *New York Magazine* (Nov. 18, 1985), 92–93 [on New York premiere]; Donal Henahan, review, *NYT* (Nov. 3, 1985), I, 87 [on New York premiere]; Robert Jacobson, "St. Paul," *ON* L (July 1985), 34 [on premiere].

Casino Paradise, "opera for singing actors" by William Bolcom; libretto (Eng) by Arnold Weinstein. First performance April 8, 1989, Philadelphia, Play and Plays Theatre. Revived June 14, 1992, New York, the Ballroom, with Eddie Korbich (the son), Joan Morris (Cis Fergeson/nurse), and Andre De Shields (J. J. Fergeson); conducted by Roger Trefousse; composer, piano; Eric Valinsky, synthesizer; visuals by Larry Rivers.

The story deals with corruption and capitalism in a southern city and centers on the tycoon J. J. Fergeson and his offspring. In the end, the nurse gets the family's money.

The work has twenty set pieces.

BIBLIOGRAPHY: Bernard Holland, "American Opera Finds a Home at the Nightclub," *NYT* (June 16, 1992), C, 13 [on revival]; Martin Mayer, "Bolcom's Cabaret Opera," *Opera* XLIII (Sept. 1992), 1044 [on revival].

Casket, The, comic opera by Michael Rophino Lacy, after Mozart's *Idomeneo* (1781, Munich); libretto (Eng), after the play *Les premièrs amours*. First performance March 10, 1829, London, Drury Lane Theatre.

Cask of Amontillado, The, opera in one act by Charles Hamm; libretto (Eng) by the composer, after Edgar Allan Poe's tale. First performance March 1, 1953, Cincinnati, Cincinnati Conservatory.

Cask of Amontillado, The, opera in one act by Julia Perry; libretto (Eng) by the composer and Virginia Card, after Poe. First performance November 20, 1954, New York, Columbia University, McMillin Theater.

Cask of Amontillado, The, opera by Aldo Provenzano; libretto (Eng) by Seymour Reiter, after Poe. First performance April 26, 1968, Rochester, New York, Eastman School of Music.
SCORE: ms, ca. 1984 (n.p., n.d.; LCCN: 84-106284).

Cask of Amontillado, The, chamber opera in one act by Russell Currie; libretto (Eng) by Carl Laanes, after Poe. First performance April 3, 1982, New York, Bronx Arts Ensemble; conducted by the composer.
    In this tale of revenge, the poor Montresor, last descendant of a noble family, tricks Fortunato, who has insulted Montresor's family, into going into the family wine cellar, once a crypt, to sample some rare amontillado. Montresor chains the now inebriated Fortunato to the crypt wall and seals up the entrance.
    For a description, see Summers/*OOA*, 88–89.
    Roles: Montresor (bass-bar/ten) and Fortunato (ten).
    Part 1 of a trilogy of operas on stories by Poe. See also *Dream within a Dream* (1984) and *Ligeia* (1987).
SCORE: ms score, signed holograph (1982, photocopy, NYPL).

Cask of Amontillado, The, opera in one act by Stewart Copeland; libretto (Eng) by David Bamberger, after Poe. Composed 1993.

Castaway, opera in one act by Lennox Berkeley; libretto (Eng) by Paul Dehn, after Homer's *Odyssey* (sixth book). First performance June 3, 1967, Aldeburgh Festival, with Geoffrey Chard (Odysseus), Patricia Clark (Princess Nausicaa), Jean Allister (Queen Arete), James Atkins (King Alcinous), Malcolm Rivers (Laodamas), and Kenneth MacDonald (Demodocus); conducted by Meredith Davies.
    The story takes up Odysseus' shipwreck on the island of Scheria, where he is found by Princess Nausicaa, daughter of King Alcinous and Queen Arete. She falls in love with him immediately and is crushed to learn his real identity at a palace banquet, which he reveals after the blind minstrel Demodocus sings a song praising Odysseus' feats at Troy and lamenting his supposed death. The Greek hero sails away at daybreak on his voyage home to be reunited with his wife, Penelope, and Nausicaa is left alone, praying for his safe journey.
    Major roles: Odysseus (bar); Nausicaa (sop); Queen Arete (alto); King Alcinous (bass); Laodamas, Nausicaa's brother (bar); and Demodocus, a blind minstrel (ten).

Companion piece to *A Dinner Engagement.**
SCORE: vs (London: J. & W. Chester, [1970]).
BIBLIOGRAPHY: W. Mann, review, *The Times* (London) (June 5, 1967), 6 [on premiere].

Castle Agrazant, opera in two acts by Ralph Lyford; libretto (Eng) by the composer. First performance April 29, 1926, Cincinnati, with Olga Forrai (Isabeau), Forrest Lamont (Richard of Agrazant), and Howard Preston (Geoffrey of Lisiac); conducted by the composer.

The work takes place in 1290 during the last Crusade in northern France. The religious Richard of Agrazant leaves his young wife, Isabeau, to join the Crusade. In his absence Count Lisiac, a former suitor of Isabeau, tries to woo her and, failing, lies to her that Richard has been killed in the fighting. He then seizes Isabeau.

During a festival in the Hall of Lisiac, which Isabeau is forced to attend, a group of vagabonds performs. The ensemble is made up of Richard and his supporters, but Isabeau is gravely wounded in the resulting fighting, in which Lisiac is killed. Richard brings the dying Isabeau to a forest and, as he tells her of his love for her and of his experiences in the Holy Land, she dies.

For a detailed description, see Hipsher/*AO*, 306–8.

Major roles: Isabeau (sop); Richard of Agrazant, a Crusader (ten); Geoffrey of Lisiac, rejected suitor of Isabeau (bar); and Knight of Lisiac (bar).
SCORE: vs (Cincinnati: Ralph Lyford, 1922).

Castle Grim, opera by George Benjamin Allen; libretto (Eng). First performance 1865, London.

Castle of Andalusia, The, opera in three acts by Samuel Arnold; libretto (Eng) by John O'Keeffe, an alteration of *The Banditti** (1781, London). First performance November 2, 1782, London, Covent Garden, with Mr. Wilson (Don Scipio), Mr. Reinhold (Don Caesar/Captain Ramirez), Mr. Mattocks (Fernando), Mr. Fearon (Don Juan), Mrs. Kennedy (Alphonso), Mr. Edwin (Pedrillo), Miss Harper (Victoria), Miss Sestini (Lorenza), Miss Platt (Isabella), and Mrs. Wilson (Catilina). First U.S. performance April 21, 1788, New York, as *The Banditti*. First performance as *The Castle of Andalusia* February 17, 1794, Philadelphia.

The work is set in Spain.

For a description of the music and borrowings, see Fiske/*ETM*, 454–55, 600.

Highlights include Victoria's "Ah Solitude Take My Distress" in act 1.
SCORES: facsimile ed. vs, manuscript libretto (London: J. Bland, 1782), intro. by Robert Hoskins (London: Stainer & Bell, 1991).
LIBRETTO: English (London: John Bland, [1782]; London: T. Cadell, 1783); repr. ed. *English Opera and Masque*, vol. 5 (London: Stainer & Bell, 1991).

Castle of Aymon, The, or, The Four Brothers, opera in three acts by Michael Balfe, after his *Les quatre fils Aymon* (July 15, 1844, Paris); libretto (Eng) by Gilbert A. A'Beckett, a translation of Leuven and Brunswick's text. First performance November 20, 1844, London, Princess's Theatre.

Castle of Sorrento, The, "comick opera" in two acts by Thomas Attwood; libretto (Eng) by Henry Heartwell, after Alexandre Duval's *Le prisonnier, ou, La rassemblance*, set by Della Maria (1798, Paris). First performance July 13, 1799, London, Haymarket Theatre. First U.S. performance April 13, 1801, Boston.

The music was adapted by Attwood from his *The Prisoner** (1792), and the work was shortened from three acts to two.

Roles: Murville, Sorrento, Blinval, Germain, Belmont, and Rosina.
SCORE: vs (London: Goulding, Phipps & D'Almaine, [1799]).
LIBRETTO: English (London: Cadell and Davies, 1799).

Cat, The, opera in one act by Alan Ridout; libretto (Eng) by J. and N. Platt, after Aesop. First performance 1971, Berkshire, New York.

Cat and the Moon, The, opera in one act by Thomas Putsché; libretto (Eng) by the composer, after a play by W. B. Yeats. First performance May 22, 1960, Hartford, Connecticut. Also January 26, 1968, New York, Marymount Manhattan College, Mannes Opera Production Workshop, with Catherine Owens (Saint Colman), Calvin Matzke (blind beggar), and David Dodds (lame beggar); conducted by Paul Berl.

The allegorical story concerns two beggars, one blind and one lame, who are offered the chance either to regain sight and ability to walk or to enter the blessed state.
SCORE: fs ([New York: Seesaw Music Corp., 1974]).
BIBLIOGRAPHY: Harold C. Schonberg, "Music: Mannes Workshop Presents New Operas," *NYT* (Jan. 27, 1968), 18 [on New York premiere].
DISCOGRAPHY: E. Charleston, T. MacBone, J. Mack; Contemporary Chamber Players of the University of Chicago; cond. R. Shapey, Composers Recordings CRI SD 245.

Catch Him Who Can, musical farce in two acts by James Hook; libretto (Eng) by Theodore Edward Hook. First performance June 12, 1806, London, Little Theatre in the Haymarket. First U.S. performance March 8, 1809, Philadelphia.
LIBRETTO: English (London: C. and R. Baldwin, 1806).

Cat Cinderella, The, "favola in musica" in three acts by Roberto De Simone; libretto (Eng) by the composer, after G. Basile's 1636 version of the Cinderella story. First performance August 26, 1988, Edinburgh.
LIBRETTO: Italian (Turin: E. Einaudi, 1977).

Cathedral, The, comic opera in two acts by Larry Spivack; libretto (Eng) by Paul David White. First performance May 15, 1986, New York, Center for Contemporary Opera.

The setting is the Thirty Years' War.

Catherine, or, The Austrian Captive, musical drama in three acts by Lord Burghersh; libretto (Eng), after Cobb's libretto for Storace's *The Siege of Belgrade** (1791). First performance November 6, 1830, London, King's Theatre, Haymarket, by students of the Royal College of Music.

Originally performed as *L'assedio di Belgrade*, April 15, 1830, Florence, the composer's residence.

Catherine Grey, opera in three acts by Michael Balfe; libretto (Eng) by George Linley. First performance May 27, 1837, London, Drury Lane Theatre, with Emma Romer (Elizabeth I) and Michael Balfe.

The work is set during the reign of Elizabeth I.

Major roles: Catherine (sop), Cecil (ten), Elizabeth (sop), Hertford (bass), Lord Grey (bass), and Warner (bass).

An example of an "all-sung" English opera, the work includes Elizabeth's Italianate cabaletta "Hence! Thou Art Base, Perfidious Slave."

SCORES: ms fs (autograph, British Library, Add. MS. 29, 329–30); vocal excerpts: "Look Forth My Fairest" (New York: James L. Hewitt, [1837?]); "Not for Me" (New York: Atwill's Music Saloon [184?]); "Oh! I Could Love Him" (New York: Atwill's Music Saloon, [184?]); "Still to Be with Thee I Love" (New York, Firth & Hall, [184?]; "Sweet Peace, True Harbinger" (New York: Atwill's Music Saloon, [184?]).

Catherine Parr, opera in one act by Anthony Collins; libretto (Eng) after Maurice Baring's drama. First performance May 9, 1949, New York, NBC. First stage performance May 4, 1950, Hopkinton, New Hampshire, Meadow Hearth Theater. First British performance March 1, 1962, London, Barnes Music Club, with Donald Francke (Henry VIII), Barbara Lane (Catherine Parr), and Margaret Royle (a page); produced by Frederick Wilkinson.

The work concerns Henry VIII and his last wife.
BIBLIOGRAPHY: Stanley Sadie, review, *Opera* XIII (May 1962), 347 [on British premiere].

Catiline Conspiracy, The, opera in two acts by Iain Hamilton; libretto (Eng) by the composer, after Ben Jonson's tragedy (1611). First performance March 16, 1974, Stirling, Scotland, Scottish Opera, MacRobert Centre.

The story treats the conspiracy organized by Catiline to topple the Roman government, a plot uncovered by Cicero.
SCORE: vs (Bryn Mawr, Pa.: T. Presser, 1975).
BIBLIOGRAPHY: review, *MT* CXV (May 1974), 411–12; review, *Opera* XXV (Mar. 1974), 187; *ON* XXXVIII (June 1974), 194.

Cat in the Box, opera by Robert Miller; libretto (Eng) by Anthony and Nicholas Keene. First performance (excerpt) April 21, 1993, New York, American Opera Project.

In the work the barrier between two couples viewing television, the first at home, the second as part of a commercial, begins to fall apart.
BIBLIOGRAPHY: Alex Ross, review, *NYT* (Apr. 24, 1993) [on premiere].

Cats' Corner, children's opera in one act by Dennis Riley; libretto (Eng) by Joseph Pazillo. Composed 1983.

Cattarina, or, Friends at Court, comic opera in two acts by Frederic Clay; libretto (Eng) by Robert Reece. First performance August 17, 1874, Manchester, Prince's Theatre.

Cat Who Went to Heaven, The, opera in one act by Geoffrey Bush; libretto (Eng) by the composer, after Elizabeth Coatsworth. First performance December 9, 1976, Croydon, London.

The text is inspired by a Buddhist story.

Cauldron of Annwn (Annwyn), The, trilogy of operas by Joseph Holbrooke, with texts by Thomas Evelyn Ellis, after Welsh myths from *The Mabinogion*. It consists of *The Children of Don** (part 1; first perf. 1912), *Dylan** (part 2; comp. 1909; first perf. 1914), and *Bronwen** (part 3; comp. 1920; first perf. 1929).

The trilogy is set in mythical times. The magical cauldron of the goddess Caridwen links the three operas. It gives off fumes that intensify emotions to such an extent that they become violent obsessions.

For a detailed discussion of the cycle, whose music employs leitmotifs and Welsh melodies and is through-composed, see George Lowe, *Josef Holbrooke and His Work* (London: Kegan Paul, Trench, Trubner, and Co., 1920), 239–76.

LIBRETTO: English, in Ellis's *The Cauldron of Annwn* (London: T. W. Laurie, 1922).

Cave, The, "documentary video music theater" in three acts with music by Steve Reich; video and screen design by Beryl Korot. First performance May 1993, Vienna Festival. First British performance August 1993, London, Royal Festival Hall. First U.S. performance October 13, 1993, Brooklyn, New York, Brooklyn Academy of Music, Steve Reich Ensemble, with Cheryl Bensman Rowe, Marion Beckenstein, James Bassi, and Hugo Munday.

The focus of the work is the Cave of the Machpelah in Hebron on the West Bank, a place sacred to Jews, Christians, and Muslims. To create the work three groups were asked to define what the biblical characters Abraham, Sarah, Isaac, Hagar, and Ishmael, meant to them. The first act has the responses of Israeli Jews, the second, those of Palestinian Muslims, and the third, Americans. There is no formal libretto, and the music alternates between sections that are based on speech and those that are freely composed.

The singers are two sopranos, tenor, and baritone.
LIBRETTO: text and commentary (New York: Boosey & Hawkes, 1993).
BIBLIOGRAPHY: John Rockwell, "In Vienna, It Ain't Just Wiener Schnitzel," *NYT* (May 26, 1993), C, 13 [on premiere]; Edward Rothstein, "Complex Delving into Myth," *NYT* (Oct. 15, 1993), C, 3 [on U.S. premiere]; K. Robert Schwarz, "Witnesses," *ON* LVIII (Oct. 1993), 28–30, 58.
DISCOGRAPHY: Reich et al.; cond. P. Hillier, Nonesuch 79327-2 (3 CDs).

Cave of Trophonius, The, opera in two acts by Stephen Storace; libretto (Eng) by Prince Hoare (not an adaptation of the 1785 Salieri setting, according to Fiske/*ETM*, 511). First performance May 3, 1791, London, Drury Lane Theatre, with Mrs. Crouch, Anna Crouch, and Richard Suett.

The two daughters of Aristo, who are opposites in character, switch personalities when they enter the cave of Trophonius.

Also set by Antonio Salieri, as *La grotta di Trofonio* (1785, Vienna).
LIBRETTO: English, songs (1791, London).

Cavern, The, or, The Outlaws, comic opera by John Stevenson; libretto (Eng) by Sarah Isdell. First performance April 22, 1825, Dublin, Theatre Royal, Hawkins Street.

Celebration, The, comic opera in one act by Lowndes Maury; libretto (Eng). Composed 1955.
SCORE: vs ([n.p., n.d.]; LCCN: 84-114311).

Cenci, The, opera in eight scenes by Havergal Brian; libretto (Eng), after Shelley's play. Composed 1951–1952. First performance December 12, 1997, London, Millennium Sinfonia, with Helen Field (Beatrice) and David Wilson-Johnson (Count Cenci).

The story, set in 1599 Rome, concerns the real-life Beatrice Cenci, executed, along with her stepmother, Lucretia, for killing her father, the evil Count Francesco Cenci.

A highlight of the work is Beatrice's Farewell.

Also set by R. S. Coke (see next entry) and B. Goldschmidt, as *Beatrice Cenci*.*
SCORE: vs ([London]: United Music, [1986?]).

Cenci, The, opera in three acts by Roger Sacheverell Coke; libretto (Eng) by the composer, after Shelley's tragedy. First performance November 5, 1959, London, Scala Theatre, with Patricia Bartlett, Ronald Firmager, and Frank Sale; conducted by Eugene Goossens; directed by Oscar Fritz Schuh.

Chains of the Heart, The, or, Slave by Choice, opera in three acts by William Reeve and Joseph Mazzinghi; libretto (Eng) by Prince Hoare, after Marsollier's *Gulnare, ou, L'esclave persane* for Dalayrac (1798, Paris). First performance December 9, 1801, London, Covent Garden, with John Braham (Bensalla). First U.S. performance February 1, 1804, New York.

A slave girl in love with her master is put up for sale because he is in need of money. She contrives to get the money and stay with her beloved.

Other settings include F. Süssmayr's *Gülnare* (1800, Vienna).

SCORE: vs (London, ca. 1801).

LIBRETTOS: English (London: Rickady, 1801; New York: D. Longworth, 1804).

Chakravaka-Bird, The, song drama for radio by Anthony Gilbert; libretto (Eng) by the composer, after the translation by A. K. Ramanujan of poems by Mahadevi. First performance January 14, 1982, London, BBC.

Roles: mezzo, tenor, countertenor, and baritone/speaking.

Challenge, The, opera in three acts by Thomas S. Cooke, an arrangement of Hérold's *Le pré aux clercs* (1832, Paris); libretto (Eng) by Henry M. Milner, after Planard's text. First performance April 1, 1834, London, Covent Garden.

Chamber-Maid, The, ballad opera in one act; libretto (Eng) by Edward Phillips. First performance February 10, 1730, London, Theatre-Royal.

LIBRETTO: English (London: J. Watts, 1730).

Chanticleer, opera in one act by Seymour Barab; libretto (Eng) by M. C. Richards, after Chaucer's *The Nun's Priest's Tale* in the *Canterbury Tales* (1400). First performance August 4, 1956, Aspen, Colorado, with Adele Addison (Pertelote), Anna Julia Hoyt (the widow), Thomas Fitzpatrick, and Carl White (the Fox); conducted by Jan Behr; produced by John Newfield.

The devious Mr. Fox, looking for a meal, tricks the vain rooster Chanticleer, and, when his guard is down, carries the bird away. Pertelote, the rooster's favorite wife, enlists the aid of the turkey Gobbler, who distracts Mr. Fox enough to get him to drop Chanticleer. The two would-be victims take refuge in a tree, and Mrs. Fox scolds her husband for relinquishing their meal. Chanticleer is then lectured by Gobbler not to let the former's vanity get him into further trouble, and Mr. Fox is pummeled by the widow, who owns the animals.

Roles: Chanticleer (ten), Pertelote (sop), the widow (mezzo), Fox (bar).

SCORE: vs (New York: Boosey & Hawkes, [1964]).

BIBLIOGRAPHY: Emma Brady Rogers, "Aspen Novelties," *ON* XXI (Nov. 19, 1956), 15 [on premiere].

Chanticleer, opera in one act by Joyce Barthelson; libretto (Eng) by the composer, after Chaucer. First performance April 15, 1967, New York.

Another setting of the Chaucer tale (see the preceding entry).

Major roles: narrator (speaking), Chanticleer (ten), Pertelote (sop), Gobbler (bass), Mr. Fox (ten), and Mrs. Fox (alto).

SCORE: vs ([n.p., 1966], LCCN: 84-57787).

LIBRETTO: English, typescript (carbon, 1966, LCCN: 85-63518).

Chaos, opera in twenty-five scenes by Michael Gordon; libretto (Eng) by Matthew Maguire. Composed 1994.

With the help of Marie and Pierre Curie, Anna and Lorenz, a husband-and-wife team of scientists, break into the Zone of Chaos—a world consisting of fractal imagery and fantastic happenings. Dr. Aguabone, the head of the Institute of Science, feels deeply threatened by Anna and Lorenz's discovery of chaos, withdraws their research funding, and has them imprisoned. The pair counter by using the science of chaos to escape and in the end create a wild storm of activity.

Chapel in Lyonesse, The, dramatic scene by Rutland Boughton; libretto (Eng) by the composer, after William Morris. First performance August 1914, Glastonbury, England, Assembly Rooms.

Boughton later used the music in *Galahad*.*

Chaplet, The, musical entertainment in two acts by William Boyce; libretto (Eng) by Moses Mendez. First performance December 2, 1749, London, Drury Lane Theatre, with Miss Morris (Laura), Mrs. Clive (Pastora), and John Beard (Damon). First U.S. performance June 4, 1767, Philadelphia, Southwark Theatre.

The innocent shepherdess Laura and Pastora, a shepherdess experienced in the ways of love, both pine for Damon, who does not believe in marriage. In the end, however, Damon is forced to wed Laura, because she will not give in to him without a ring.

Among the numbers is "Contented All Day."

SCORE: vs ([London]: Jus. Walsh, [n.d.]).

LIBRETTO: English (London: M. Cowper, 1749).

ChaplinOperas, "operatic filmspiel" by Benedict Mason for solo singers, chorus, and large ensemble. Composed 1988. First performance autumn 1992, Strasbourg. First British performance July 24, 1993, London, Queen Elizabeth Hall.

The work combines three early Charlie Chaplin shorts, *Easy Street*, *The Immigrant*, and *The Adventurer*.

The second part, "The Immigrant," is set in a New York restaurant, where Chaplin, playing a penniless refugee, is intimidated by an enormous waiter, and the gulf between the two is underscored by having the singer's text in Russian.

Cast: mezzo and bass-bar.

Characteristics Man, The. See **Patria, no. 1**.

Charcoal Burner, The, radio opera by Thomas Wilson; libretto (Eng) by Edwin Morgan, after George Almar. First performance March 16, 1969, BBC, Scotland.

The setting is the Quantock Hills in 1789. John Walford, a charcoal burner, is in love with Anne Rice but obsessed with another woman. When he kills the object of his obsession, he is caught and sentenced to die. The work closes with a farewell duet between the condemned man and his first love.

Major roles: John Walford (ten) and Anne Rice (sop).

Charity Begins at Home, musical sketch by Alfred Cellier; libretto (Eng) by Benjamin Charles Stephenson. First performance February 7, 1872, London, Gallery of Illustration.

LIBRETTO: English (London: n.p., [ca. 1888]).

Charity Boy, The, short opera by William Reeve; libretto (Eng) by James C. Cross. First performance November 5, 1796, London, Drury Lane Theatre.

Charivari, chamber opera in nine movements by Peter Westergaard; libretto (Eng) by the composer. First performance May 13, 1953, Cambridge, Massachusetts, Sanders Theater.

Charlatan, The, comic opera in three acts by John Philip Sousa; libretto (Eng) by Charles Klein. First performance August 29, 1898, Montreal, with De Wolf Hopper (Demidoff), Edmund Stanley (Prince Boris), Alfred Klein (Gogol), George W. Barnum (Captain Peshofki), Arthur Cunningham (Grand Duke), Harry P. Stone (Koreff), C. Arthur (Skobeloff), Nella Bergen (Anna), Alice Judson (Katrinka), Katherine Carlisle (Sophie), and Adine Bouviere (Grand Duchess); conducted by Paul Steindorff.

In the story Prince Boris must marry someone from his own social class or give up his inheritance. He is tricked into wedding Anna, the daughter of a charlatan, Demidoff, by Gogol, Boris's uncle, who passes the girl off as Princess Ruchkowski, but then the real princess turns up with the Grand Duke. Demidoff reveals the plot to the Grand Duke, who promises to get the czar to help Prince Boris.
SCORE: vs (Cincinnati: John Church, 1898).

Charlie's Uncle, comic opera in one act by David Ahlstrom; libretto (Eng) by the composer. First performance April 23, 1954, Columbus, Ohio.

Charlotte's Web, children's opera by Lee Ahlin; libretto (Eng), after E. B. White. First performance October 20, 1988, St. Petersburg, Florida, American Stage.

Charlotte's Web, children's opera in one act by Charles Strouse; libretto (Eng) by Joseph Robinette, lyrics by the composer, after E. B. White's book. First performance February 17, 1989, Wilmington, Delaware, OperaDelaware.

Charter Oak, The, opera by Burton Leavitt; libretto (Eng) by Nason Leavitt. Composed ca. 1885.

The work is a satire on the implementation of Connecticut's blue laws and also pokes fun at the early General Assemblies.

The music, except for a grand march (at Yale), is lost. A copy of the text exists.
LIBRETTO: English (Hartford, Conn.: New England Home Print, 1895 [1892]).
BIBLIOGRAPHY: Robert A. Hamilton, "Historical Opera Eludes Searchers," *NYT* (Sept. 1, 1985), XXIII, 1.

Chatterton, opera in three acts by Gerard Victory; libretto (Eng) by the composer, after de Vigny's drama (1835). First performance (concert) January 28, 1971, Paris, ORTF.

The story concerns an imaginary incident that took place in the poet Thomas Chatterton's life. In order to make a living he changes his name and rents rooms from a prosperous businessman, whose sympathetic wife, Kitty, develops a fondness for him. When Chatterton writes to the Lord Mayor of London in hopes of obtaining a position, his true identity is revealed by onetime friends. The Lord Mayor's reply is an insult, as it offers him the post of valet. The poet's despondency is deepened by a newspaper article accusing him of plagiarism. He kills himself with poison, and Kitty, who has come to comfort him, dies of a broken heart.

Also set by Leoncavallo (1896, Rome).

Chekhov Trilogy, A, three operas by Richard Wargo; libretto (Eng) by the composer, after tales by Anton Chekhov. First performance of the trilogy July 28, 1990, Chautauqua, New York; conducted by Gary Magby:

    The Seduction of a Lady*
    A Visit to the Country*
    The Music Shop*
BIBLIOGRAPHY: E. Thomas Glasgow, "Chautauqua," *ON* LV (Dec. 22, 1990), 38–39 [on premiere]; Herman Trotter, "Chautauqua," *MA* CXI (Jan. 1991), 62 [on premiere].

Chelm, comic folk fantasy in one act by Robert Strassburg; libretto (Eng) by the composer, after Sholem Aleichem. First performance December 11, 1955, White Plains, New York, Westchester Community College, Little Theatre; January 28, 1956, New York, 92nd Street Y, Opera Theater of Westchester, with Ray Smolover, Norman Atkins, Jacqueline Langee, Edith Gordon, and Alice Richmond; conducted by Eugene Kusmiak.

The work is set in a mythical Jewish town in Poland.
BIBLIOGRAPHY: review, *NYT* (Jan. 30, 1956), 23 [on New York performance].

Chelsea Pensioner, The, comic opera in two acts by Charles Dibdin; libretto (Eng) by the composer. First performance May 6, 1779, London, Covent Garden.

Cherokee, The, opera in three acts by Stephen Storace; libretto (Eng) by James Cobb. First performance December 20, 1794, London, Drury Lane Theatre, with Michael Kelly (Colonel Blandford), Mrs. Crouch (Zelipha), Mrs. Bland (Winifred), John Bannister (Jack Average), and Nancy Storace. Revised as *Algonah** by Michael Kelly (1802). First U.S. performance June 24, 1799, Boston, Haymarket Theatre.

The opera is set in the American West. Colonel Blandford leads an expedition to stop the fighting between two rival Cherokee groups, the leaders of whom want the mysterious Zelipha. She is, in fact, an Englishwoman, who, with her young son, Henry, and her Welsh maid, Winifred, are living under assumed names. When one of the Indian leaders, Malooko, seizes Henry with the aim of getting his mother to come to the Cherokee camp, the boy is saved by a Cherokee friendly to the British. Zelipha turns out to be Mrs. Blandford. The two are captured by the Indians but are rescued in the end. A subplot involves Jack Average, who comes to wed Eleanor, his betrothed, and who looks after Henry when he is freed from Malooko.

For a detailed description, see Fiske/*ETM,* 529–30.

The overture is from Storace's *Gli sposi malcontenti* (1785, Vienna). There are also borrowings from Sarti and Bianchi.
SCORE: vs (London: J. Dale, 1791?); vs, "The Little Bird" (Philadelphia: John Aitken, n.d.).
LIBRETTO: English (London: J. Dale., 1794?).

Chicken Little, children's opera in one act by Thomas Benjamin; libretto (Eng) by Elaine Gerdine, after the fable. First performance June 6, 1985, Houston, Texas Opera Theater.
SCORE: vs (New York: American Music Center, 1985).

Chieftain, The, comic opera in two acts by Arthur S. Sullivan; libretto (Eng) by F. C. Burnand. First performance December 12, 1894, London, Savoy Theatre, with Courtice Pounds (Count Vasques de Gonzago), Walter Passmore (Peter Adolphus Grigg), Scott Fische (Ferdinand de Roxas), Richard Temple (Sancho), and Rosina Brandram

(Inez de Roxas). First U.S. performance September 9, 1895, New York, Abbey's Theatre, with Francis Wilson.

A British tourist, Mr. Grigg, is kidnapped by Spanish outlaws, whose chief is a woman disguised as a man; she falls in love with her captive, only to have the tourist's wife show up inconveniently.

The work was a revision of *The Contrabandista** (1867, London).
SCORE: vs (London: Boosey & Co., 1895).
DISCOGRAPHY: D. Adams, Sawston Village College Operatic Society Rare Recorded Editions SRRE 181-182 (2 LPs).

Child, The, opera by José Raoul Bernardo; libretto (Eng) by the composer, after José Martí's poem *La niña*. First performance August 8, 1974, Albany, State University at Albany, with Joan Patenaude (Maria, the Child), Dorothy Danner (the Child in the dream sequences), Jeanie Barnes and Dorothy Setian (her sisters), Nancy Williams and John Stevens (her parents), and Harry Danner (the poet); conducted by Paul Callaway.

A girl in the repressive society of Victorian Spain finds love with Harry Danner, a poet, but in the end, because of his familial duty, he must reject her in favor of marriage to a noblewoman.

Major roles: the Child, Maria (sop, dancer); her sisters; her parents; and the poet (ten).
BIBLIOGRAPHY: E. Thomas Glasgow, "Glens Falls, N.Y.," *ON* XXXIX (Oct. 1974), 50.

Childhood Miracle, A, opera in one act by Ned Rorem; libretto (Eng) by Elliott Stein, after an idea from Nathaniel Hawthorne's *The Snow Image*. First performance May 10, 1955, New York, Carl Fischer Hall, Punch Opera.

Emma visits her sister on a wintry day. The father goes off on an errand, and the two daughters, Peony and Violet, go out to build a snowman. The snowman becomes a "brother" for Violet, and although the father forces the girls to return to the house, they rush out into the gathering storm. By the time the parents find them, they have become frozen statues, like their "brother."

For a detailed description, see Eaton/*OP* I, 174.

Major roles: Peony (sop), Violet (mezzo), Snowman (ten), Aunt Emma (mezzo), mother (alto), and father (bass-bar).
SCORE: vs (New York: Southern Music, [1972]).
BIBLIOGRAPHY: Raymond Ericson, "Rorem, Rogers Works," *MA* LXXV (June 1955), 13–14 [on premiere].

Child of the Mountain, or, The Deserted Mother, opera in three acts by Anthony Philip Heinrich. First performance February 10, 1821, Philadelphia, Walnut Theatre.

Child of the Wreck, The, musical play by Thomas S. Cooke; libretto (Eng) by James Robinson Planché. First performance October 7, 1837, London, Drury Lane Theatre.
LIBRETTO: English (London, ca. 1837).

Children in the Wood, The, comic opera in two acts by Samuel Arnold; libretto (Eng) by Thomas Morton. First performance October 1, 1793, London, Little Theatre in the Haymarket, with Jack Bannister (Walter). It was given 132 times from its premiere up to 1800. First U.S. performance November 24, 1795, Old American Company, Philadelphia, Southwark Theatre, with Benjamin Carr (Lord Alford). Its American run totaled 124 performances.

The original grim story concerns two children who are abandoned and left to die because of their cruel uncle. In Morton's version, comic characters and a happy ending are added.

For an analysis of the music and text, see Porter's edition, xiii–xx.

The overture includes a Turkish march. Among the numbers in the style of grand opera are the da capo duet "Young Simon" and the work's only recitative, "Great Sir, Consider." The American premiere included additional songs by Benjamin Carr.

SCORE AND LIBRETTO: vs (London: Longman and Broderip, 1795); English libretto (London: n.p., 1794; New York: Robertson and Gowan, for Benjamin Gomez, 1795); repr. ed. Susan L. Porter, *NAMT*, vol. 1 (1994).

Children of Don, The, opera in a prologue and three acts by Joseph Holbrooke; libretto (Eng) by Thomas Evelyn Ellis, part 1 of the trilogy *The Cauldron of Annwn,** after Welsh legends in *The Mabinogion* (along with Holbrooke's *Dylan,** 1914, and *Bronwen,** 1929). First performance June 15, 1912, London, London Opera House.

The king of Annwn (Hades), Arawn, the keeper of the magical cauldron, is challenged by Gwydion, the son of the nature goddess Don. Gwydion kills the priests and Arawn and seizes the cauldron, bringing disaster upon himself and others. Among those affected are his half-sister, Elan, whose love he rejects; his brother Govannion, who falls in love with but then kills the maiden Goewin, the cauldron's attendant; and Math, leader of the Druids, whom Gwydion kills.

Major roles: Don (sop), Goewin (sop), Elan (alto), Gwydion (bar), Math (bar), Arawn (ten), and Govannion (bass).

Children's Crusade, The, church opera in one act by Alan Ridout; libretto (Eng) by D. Holbrook, after B. Brecht. First performance 1968, Canterbury, Canterbury Cathedral.

Chilkoot Maiden, The, opera in one act by Eleanor Everest Freer; libretto (Eng) by the composer. First performance fall 1927, Skagaway, Alabama.

The story deals with the Thlingit legend that each time a white man crosses the summit of White Pass, the snow is melted by a Chinook wind, touching off a devastating avalanche.

SCORE: vs (Milwaukee, Wis.: Wm. A. Kaun Music Co., [1926]).

Chinchilla, opera in three acts by Myron Fink; libretto (Eng) by Donald Moreland. First performance January 18, 1986, Binghamton, New York, the Forum Theatre, with Sharon Harrison (Delia Ashton), Jake Gardner (Nick Ashton), Richard Leech (Ramon Castillan), and Cynthia Clarey (Chichi Castillan); conducted by Duane Skrabalak.

On the eve of the departure of Ramon Castillan, a Latin-American diplomat, and his wife, Chichi, for their homeland, their friends, Nick and Delia Ashton, plan a farewell party. Ramon and Nick buy a chinchilla coat for each of their wives but also for their mistresses, who in fact are Chichi and Delia. The arrival of the furrier, Fyodor, to collect his money for the coats, brings the secrets into the open. The problem of the extra two coats is solved when Ramon gives one coat to Mrs. Betterbotham, a guest at the party and a former lover of his, and the husbands buy the fourth for Solange, Delia's maid, who is to be wed to Fyodor. The couples eventually make up, and the evening ends happily.

Major roles: Delia Ashton (sop), Nick Ashton (bar), Ramon Castillan (ten), Chichi Castillan (mezzo), Fyodor Kropotkin (bass), Mrs. Betterbotham (mezzo), and Solange (sop).

BIBLIOGRAPHY: L. Kerner, review, *HiFi/MA* XXXVI (June 1986), 41–42 [on premiere].

Chinese Canticle, opera in three scenes by Richard Stoker; libretto (Eng) by the composer, after Ssu-ma Ch'ien's *Records of the Historian.* First performance October 24, 1991, London, Purcell Room.

Chip and His Dog, opera in two scenes for children by Gian Carlo Menotti; libretto (Eng) by the composer. First performance May 5, 1979, Guelph, Ontario, Guelph Spring Festival, Canadian Children's Opera Chorus, Toronto, with David Coulter (Chip), Andrea Kuzmich (the dog), and Laura Zarins (the princess); conducted by Derek Holman. First U.S. performance May 1980, Charleston, South Carolina, Spoleto Festival USA.

Set in a mythical kingdom, the action concerns Chip, a poor boy, who tries to earn a living by making musical instruments but is hampered by the changing tastes of musicians. He is forced to sell his dog to the king, who presents it to his daughter in order to cheer her up. Eventually, the princess agrees to marry Chip in order to keep the affection of the dog, who misses its master.

Major roles: Chip (sop), Chip's dog (mime), and the princess (sop).

SCORE: vs (New York: G. Schirmer, 1979).

Chipita Rodríguez, opera in two acts by Larry Weiner; libretto (Eng) by Leo Carrillo and John Wilson. First performance April 3, 1982, Corpus Christi, Texas, Corpus Christi Symphony.

About a woman hanged in Texas in 1863 for murdering a horse trader.

Choice of Apollo, The, masque by William Yates; libretto (Eng) by John Potter. First performance March 11, 1765, London, Little Theatre in the Haymarket.

The work begins with Britannia at the banks of the Thames. She sends the sister Arts of Poetry, Painting, and Music to get advice from Apollo on how to "fill each distant Nation with Surprise."

See Fiske/*ETM*, 316 for a detailed description.

SCORE: ms fs (Library, Royal College of Music, 645).

Choleric Fathers, The, comic opera in three acts by William Shield; libretto (Eng) by Thomas Holcroft. First performance November 10, 1785, London, Covent Garden, with Mrs. Bannister, Mrs. Martyr, and William Parke.

For a detailed description of the music, see Fiske/*ETM*, 462–65.

SCORE: vs (London: Longman and Broderip, 1785; repr. ed. Wyton, Huntingdon, Cambs: King's Music, [1991]).

LIBRETTO: English (London: G. G. J. and J. Robinson, 1785).

Christina Romana, chamber opera in two acts by Libby Larsen; libretto (Eng) by Vern Sutton. First performance May 13, 1988, Minneapolis, University of Minnesota.

Christina's World, chamber opera in one act by Ross Edwards; libretto (Eng) by Dorothy Hewett. First performance 1983, Sydney, Australia.

Scored for two mezzo-sopranos, tenor, and baritone, chamber ensemble, and tape.

Christmas Carol, A, television opera in one act by Bernard Hermann; libretto (Eng) by Maxwell Anderson, after Charles Dickens. First performance December 23, 1954, New York, CBS television.

SCORE: vs (New York: Chappell, [n.d.]).

Christmas Carol, A, television opera by Edwin Coleman; libretto (Eng) by Margaret Burns Harris, after Dickens. First performance December 24, 1962, London, BBC television.

Christmas Carol, A, opera in one act by Gregory Sandow; libretto (Eng) by the composer, after Dickens. First performance December 21, 1977, Stratford, Connecticut, Eastern Opera Theater.
SCORE: vs (Borough Green, Kent: Novello, 1981).

Christmas Carol, A, opera in two acts by Thea Musgrave; libretto (Eng) by the composer, after Dickens. First performance December 7, 1979, Norfolk, Virginia, Virginia Opera Association, with Frederick Burchinal (Scrooge), Carolyne James (Mrs. Cratchit), Howard Bender (Ben Scrooge), Kathryn Montgomery (Belle), James Bartlett (Tiny Tim), and Jerold Norman (Bob Cratchit); conducted by Peter Mark. First British performance December 14, 1981, London, Royal Opera House, with Frederick Burchinal (Scrooge), Elizabeth Bainbridge (Mrs. Cratchit), Robin Leggate (Bob Cratchit), and Murray Melvin (Spirit of Christmas); conducted by Peter Mark.

A condensed setting of Dickens's famous tale. The miserly Scrooge is convinced, through a series of visions on Christmas Eve, to mend his ways and help his assistant, the struggling Bob Cratchit, and Cratchit's large family. The work includes a scene (act 1/6) in which the young Scrooge (Ben) abandons his beloved, Belle Fezziwig, and another (act 2/4) in which the Cratchits mourn the loss of Tiny Tim.

Major roles: Scrooge (bar), Ben Scrooge (bar), Spirit of Christmas (dancer), Mrs. Cratchit (mezzo), Bob Cratchit (ten), Belle Fezziwig (sop), Marley's Ghost (speaking), and Tiny Tim (boy performer).

The work is scored for a minimum of twelve performers. The three Spirits of Christmas are combined into one part, and Marley's Ghost is cast as an actor. The vocal highlights include a setting of "God Rest Ye Merry Gentlemen" in the finale, the number "All the Bells of London Town," and the quartet of the Cratchit family as they mourn Tiny Tim.
SCORE: vs (Borough Green, Kent: Novello, 1981).
BIBLIOGRAPHY: Martin Dreyer, "Opera," *MT* CXXII (1982), 116 [on British premiere]; Noel Goodwin, "London," *ON* XLVI (Apr. 3, 1982), 30 [on British premiere]; Robert Jacobson, "Norfolk," *ON* XLIV (Mar. 29, 1980), 26 [on premiere]; Rodney Milnes, "Dickens into Opera," *MT* CXXI (1981), 818–20.
DISCOGRAPHY: Peterson, Montgomery, James, Burchinal, Norman, Bender, Randolph, Virginia Opera; cond. Mark, Moss Opera Group MMG-302 (3); rev. John W. Freeman, "Records," *ON* XLV (Nov. 22, 1980), 44.

Christmas Carol, A, opera by Lee Hoiby; libretto (Eng) by Dennis Powers and Laird Williamson, after Dickens. First performance December 2, 1987, San Francisco, American Conservatory Theater.

Other versions include those by J. Cikker, as *Mr. Scrooge* (1963, Kassel); D. Gray (1960); L. Liviabella, as *Canto di natale* (1963); M. Kalmanoff, as *Mister Scrooge** (1966, New York); and J. Cohen (1970).

Christmas Rose, The, children's opera in three scenes by Frank Bridge; libretto (Eng) by Margaret Kemp-Welch and Constance Cotterell after a children's play. Composed 1919–1929. First performance December 8, 1931, London, Parry Opera Theatre, Royal College of Music; conducted by the composer. Revived December 1979 (concert), BBC, Welsh Symphony Orchestra, conducted by Guy Woolfenden.

The work takes place in Bethlehem. Miriam and Reuben, against the wishes of their shepherd father, follow him to Bethlehem to witness the birth of Christ. Despairing that they have no gift to give the Christ child, the children begin to weep, whereupon a rose sprouts from the snow-covered spot on which Miriam's tears have fallen.

Roles: Miriam (sop) and Reuben (mezzo); their father, a shepherd (bass-bar); two shepherds (ten, bar).
SCORE: vs (London: Augener, [c. 1931]).
BIBLIOGRAPHY: "Royal College of Music," *MT* LXXIII (Jan. 1932), 65 [on premiere].
DISCOGRAPHY: soloists, Chelsea Opera Group; cond. H. Williams, Pearl 9582 (1 CD).

Christmas Tale, A, opera in one act by Eleanor Everest Freer; libretto (Eng) by Barrett H. Clark, after the French play of Maurice Bouchor (1895). First performance December 27, 1929, Houston; December 19, 1936, Chicago, Chicago Women's Club.
SCORE: vs (Milwaukee: Wm. A. Kaun Music Co., [1928]).

Christmas Tale, The, opera by Charles Dibdin; libretto (Eng) by David Garrick. First performance December 27, 1773, London, Drury Lane Theatre.
SCORE: vs (London: Longman, Lukey, and Co. . . . and J. Johnston, [1774]).

Christopher Columbus, children's opera in one act by Martin Kalmanoff; libretto (Eng) by the composer, after J. Forscher. First performance March 1976, New York, tour of Producers' Association.

Other operas on the explorer include those by P. Ottoboni (1690, Rome); F. Morlacchi (1828, Genoa); R. Carnicier (1831, Madrid); A. Franchetti, *Cristoforo Colombo* (1892, Genoa); E. Dressel, *Armer Kolumbus* (1928, Kassel); D. Milhaud, *Christophe Colombo* (1930, Berlin); S. Vassilenko, *Khristofor Kolumb* (1939, Moscow); W. Böhme, *Kolumbus* (1950, Reichenbach); and P. Glass, *The Voyage** (1992, New York).

Christopher Sly, chamber opera in three acts by Thomas Eastwood; libretto (Eng) by Ronald F. Duncan, after Shakespeare's *The Taming of the Shrew*. (1544) First performance January 24, 1960, London, Royal Court, English Opera Group, with Jacqueline Delman, April Cantelo, John Kentish, Julian Moyle, Joseph Ward, Forbes Robinson, and Kevin Miller; conducted by Harry Newstone; directed by Colin Graham.

Christopher Sly, comic opera in two scenes and an interlude by Dominick Argento; libretto (Eng) by John Manlove, after Shakespeare. First performance May 31, 1963, Minneapolis, University of Minnesota; conducted by William Johnson.

The work takes place in sixteenth-century England. The drunken tinker Christopher Sly, hounded by his creditors, Peter Turph and Henry Pimpernell, and Marion Hacket, hostess of the alehouse, is picked up by a Lord and his guests. To make a joke at the hapless Christopher's expense, the Lord puts Sly in his bed and, when the tinker awakes, convinces him that Sly is the owner of the sumptuous quarters. Sly eventually catches on and, when left by himself, flees with all of the Lord's valuables and his two mistresses.

For a detailed description, see Eaton/*OP* II, 259–60.
Major roles: Christopher Sly, a tinker (bass-bar); Peter Turph, a tailor (ten); Henry Pimpernell, a smith (bass-bar); Marion Hacket (mezzo); and Lord (ten).
SCORE: vs (New York: Boosey & Hawkes, [1968]).
BIBLIOGRAPHY: Peter G. Davis, review, *New York* XX (Feb. 9, 1987), 89–90.

Chronicles, or, Vignettes of Passion, opera in one act by Gerald Frank Muller; libretto (Eng) by the composer. First performance October 1977, Rockville, Maryland, Montgomery College.

The setting is the present. Three women live in an apartment complex with a common courtyard. They reflect on their beloveds as they exchange greetings; Samantha thinks of Charlie, Vera of Charles, and Eloise of Chuck. When a male visitor enters the courtyard, the three women realize, angrily, that he is the same man courting all of them but using variations of his name for each.

For a description, see Summers/*OOA*, 226–27.

Roles: Vera (sop), Samantha (sop), and Eloise (mezzo/alto).

Chrononhotonthologos, burlesque opera in one act by Henry Carey, "the most tragical tragedy, that ever was tragedized by any company of tragedians"; libretto (Eng) by the composer. First performance February 22, 1734, London, Little Theatre in the Haymarket. First U.S. performance March 20, 1777, New York.

The characters include Chrononhotonthologos, king of Queerummania; Queen Dollalolla; the solemn Aldiborontiphoscophornia; and the genial Rigdumfunnidos. The later two names were appropriated by Sir Walter Scott for James and John Ballantyne, Scott's publishers.

Also known as *The Tragedy of Chrononhotonthologos*.

SCORE: vs (London: J. Shuckburg, L. Gilliver, and J. Jackson, n.d.).

LIBRETTO: English (London, 1734; London: Lister, 1787); American ed. (New York: D. Longworth, 1808); 1734 ed. repr. Rubsamen/*BO*, vol. 5, *Satire, Burlesque, Protest, and Ridicule*, part 1 (1974).

Cimarrón, El (The Fugitive Slave), "recital for four musicians" in two parts by Hans Werner Henze; libretto (Ger) by Hans Magnus Enzensberger, after Miguel Barnet's narrative of Esteban Montejo, *The Autobiography of a Runaway Slave*. First performance (in an English version by Christopher Keene) June 22, 1970, Aldeburgh Festival, with William Pearson, Karlheinz Zöller, Leo Brouwer, and Stomu Yamash'ta. First U.S. performance March 27, 1971, University of Pittsburgh.

The work consists of fifteen episodes involving four musicians: the singer, flute, guitar, and percussion. It presents the recollections of a 104-year-old runaway slave. The music contains passages that are half spoken and half sung, with some quartertone writing.

For a detailed description, see Eaton/*OP* II, 260–61.

Role: Esteban (bar).

LIBRETTO: German (Mainz: Schott, 1971).

BIBLIOGRAPHY: Carsten Wolfgang Becker, "Current Chronicle. Berlin," *MQ* LVII (1971), 314–15; David Matthews, "Henze's *El Cimarrón*," *Tempo* XCIV (Autumn 1970) [on premiere].

DISCOGRAPHY: Pearson, DG 2707.050; P. Yoder, M. Faust, R. Evers, M. Ardeleanu, Koch Schwann 2-314.030.

Cinderella, or, The Fairy and the Little Glass Slipper, opera in three acts, an adaptation by Michael Rophino Lacy of G. Rossini's *La Cenerentola* (1817, Rome); libretto (Eng) by the composer and G. Pons, after J. Ferretti, itself based on the Perrault fairy tale. First performance April 13, 1830, London, Covent Garden, with Mr. Wood (Prince Felix), Mr. Penson (Baron Pumpolino), Mr. Stansbury (Alidoro/Dandini), Mr. Morley (Pedro), Miss Paton (Cinderella), Miss Cawse (Clorinda/Fairy Queen), and Miss Hughes (Tisbe); conducted by Lacy. First U.S. performance January 24, 1831, New York, Park Theatre, with Mrs. Austin (Cinderella). It was performed more than fifty times during its first season in New York.

In the Lacy version, the Fairy Godmother becomes the Fairy Queen, and the royal suitor is called Prince Felix. Cinderella's stepsisters are Clorinda and Tisbe, who join with their father, Baron Pumpolino, in mistreating the heroine, called Angiolina. The Prince, who is looking for a wife, changes places with Dandini, his valet. Cinderella is aided in attending the ball by Alidoro, the Prince's tutor, and the Fairy Queen, and after she flees, she is found again by the prince by means of the glass slipper and the assistance of the Fairy Queen.

The work also includes music from Rossini's *Maometto II*, *Armida*, and *Guillaume Tell*. For a musical and textual analysis, see the Graziano edition, xiii–xxvi.

Another adaptation of the Rossini was made by Charles Edward Horn and performed on December 20, 1832, New York, Park Theatre. *Cinderella in Salerno** is yet another adaptation.

SCORE: vs (New York: Bourne, 1831?); repr. ed. John Graziano, *NAMT*, vol. 3 (1994).
LIBRETTO: English (London: T. H. Lacy, [1830?]); repr. ed. New York: S. French, [1856?]); repr. ed. John Graziano, *NAMT*, vol. 3 (1994).

Cinderella, "a little opera for big children, or, a big opera for little children," fairy opera in four acts by John Farmer; libretto (Eng) by Henry S. Leigh. First performance December 1883, Harrow, England.
SCORE: vs (Harrow, England: J. C. Wilbee, [1882]).

Cinderella, fairy tale opera in two acts by Jack Jarrett; libretto (Eng) by the composer. First performance 1956, Gainesville, Florida, University of Florida.

Cinderella, children's opera in two acts by Peter Maxwell Davies; libretto (Eng) by the composer. First performance June 21, 1980, Kirkwall, Scotland. First U.S. performance April 1982, Washington, D.C., Sheridan School.

In this version Cinderella is played by an au pair girl who has to care for the spoiled children of the Widow Grumble. Cinderella finds happiness through the powers of a magical cat.
SCORE: vs (London: Chester Music, 1980).
LIBRETTO: English (London and New York: Chester Music, 1980).

Cinderella, opera in one act by Michael Easton; libretto (Eng) by Colin Duckworth. Composed 1989.

In this retelling of the familiar children's story, Cinderella's father is a troubled inventor, and she is aided by Snuffles, the family dog.

Cinderella, or, The Vindication of Sloth, children's opera in one act by Stephen Oliver; libretto (Eng) by the composer. Composed 1991.

In this novel treatment of the fairy tale, the fat and lazy Cinderella resists the Devil's temptations and refuses to go to the ball because it is too much of a bother for her. Her sloth is rewarded as midnight strikes, and the palace explodes.

Cast: four children.

Cinderella in Salerno, children's opera in three acts by Raymond Walker; libretto (Eng) by William Beaumont. Composed 1976.

An arrangement of Rossini's *La Cenerentola* (1817, Rome).

Michael Kelly's pantomime *Cinderella, or, The Little Glass Slipper* appeared in London (1804) and Philadelphia (1806). The story was presented as the musical *Cin-*

derella by Richard Rodgers and Oscar Hammerstein II and broadcast on CBS television on March 31, 1957, with Julie Andrews in the title role.
SCORE: vs (Borough Green, Kent: Novello, [1976]).

Cinthia and Endimion, or, The Loves of the Deities, "new opera" in five acts by Daniel Purcell; libretto (Eng) by Thomas D'Urfey. First performance December 1696, London, Drury Lane Theatre.

Circassian Bride, The, opera in three acts by Henry Rowley Bishop; libretto (Eng) by Charles Ward. First performance February 23, 1809, London, Drury Lane Theatre, with Mr. Mathews (Dory), Mrs. Mountain (Rachael), and Miss Lyon (Erminia).
    The score was destroyed in the fire that swept Drury Lane the day after the premiere, but Bishop rewrote it from memory.
SCORE: ms fs, overture, some of the music, mostly autograph (ca. 1809, British Library, Add. MS. 27700); vs (London: L. Lavenu, [1809]).
LIBRETTO: English (London: Lowndes and Hobbs, [1809?]).

Circe, dramatic opera in five acts by John Bannister; libretto (Eng) by Charles Davenant. First performance March 1677, London, Dorset Garden.
    The music is lost.
LIBRETTO: English (London: Richard Tonson . . . , 1677).

Circe, opera by John Galliard; libretto (Eng) by Charles Davenant. First performance April 11, 1719, London, with Mr. Pack and Mrs. Thurmond.
SCORE: vs, "Sit on the Troubled Ocean's Face"; "Fairest if Thou Can'st Be Kind"; "Let Nature Henceforward Neglect" (all London., ca. 1720).

Circe, masque in three parts by William Hayes; anonymous libretto (Eng). Composed 1742. First performance (private) May 1749, Aston, Holte Bridgeman's Gardens.
    Major roles: Shepherd (sop/ten), Virtue (sop), Pleasure (sop), and Circe (sop).
    One air, "Ye Swains Who Possess the Rich Treasure," sung by Circe, was published in *London Magazine* (Nov. 1744).
BIBLIOGRAPHY: Simon Heighes, *The Lives and Works of William and Philip Hayes* (New York: Garland, 1995), 229–32.

Circe, radio opera in one act by Gerard Victory; libretto (Eng) by the composer. First performance September 22, 1972, Dublin, RTE.

Circumstances Alter Cases, comic operetta by Alfred B. Sedgwick; libretto (Eng) by the composer, "after the French of Francis Tourte." First performance 1876, New York?
    The story revolves around Mademoiselle Angôt, a French native forced to get work in New York as a ballerina when her parents die, having lost all their money and property. She adopts the name of Madame Angôt and is courted by a young lawyer who attempts to get back her fortune. These events occur before the opening of the actual operetta. Old Mr. Slyfox, father of the young lawyer, is aghast that his son wants to marry a person he thinks is merely a dancer and penniless. Learning about her fortune, the greedy old Slyfox tries to make her his wife, but she rejects him and resolves not to marry his son, either.
    Roles: Mr. Felix Slyfox, an old Boston lawyer; and Madame Angôt, prima ballerina of the Ballet de l'Opéra.
SCORE: vs (New York: De Witt Publishing House, 1876); repr. ed. Michael Meckna, *NAMT*, vol. 7 (1994).
LIBRETTO: the same.

Circus, The, tragic opera in one act by Edward Chudacoff; libretto (Eng) by Daniel Waldron. First performance July 2, 1953, Interlochen, Michigan, National Music Camp. SCORE: vs ([n.p., n.d.]; LCCN: 84-77361).

City Workers, operatic parody by Neil Weisensel; libretto (Eng) by Michael Cavanagh. First performance June 1, 1995, Victoria, British Columbia, Pacific Opera Victoria, with Ian Funk (Al).

The work makes funs of operatic conventions. Its chief character, Al, is a smart, strong, yet sensitive crew foreman.

BIBLIOGRAPHY: Robert Jordan, "Victoria, B.C.," *ON* LX (Sept. 1995), 62 [on premiere].

Civilization & Its Discontents, "bedroom opera" in one act by Michael Sahl and Eric Salzman; libretto (Eng) by the composers. First performance May 19, 1977, New York, American Musical and Dramatic Academy, with Karl Patrick Krause (Carlos Arachnid), Candice Earley (Jill Goodheart), Timothy Jerome (Derek Dude), and Paul Binotto (Jeremy Jive).

Derek Dude, a media person, goes to a bar with Jill Goodheart, his girlfriend, but they have a fight, and he storms out. Jeremy Jive, a theatrical agent, takes Jill back to the apartment he shares with Derek. Finding the couple there, Derek is first angry but then discovers that he and Jeremy are involved in the same business deal. Thus ignored, Jill threatens to kill herself with an electric knife. She is rescued by Carlos Arachnid, owner of the Bide-a-Wee Club, who takes her and the two men to his establishment.

Major roles: Jill Goodheart, an aspiring actress and singer (sop); Jeremy Jive, theatrical agent (ten); Carlos Arachnid, guru of club Bide-a-Wee (ten); and Derek Dude, Jill's boyfriend, ad agency type (bar).

The work is written in an opera-buffa style and contains set pieces.

SCORE: vs (New York: G. Schirmer, 1985).

DISCOGRAPHY: Krause, Earley, Parry, Binotto, Nonesuch N-78009.

CIVIL warS, the, Act V: The Rome Section, opera in a prologue and three scenes by Philip Glass; libretto (Eng, Lat, It) by Robert Wilson and Maita di Niscemi; designed by Wilson. First performance March 25, 1984, Rome, Teatro dell'Opera, with Harlan Foss (Lincoln). First U.S. performance May 20, 1984, New York, Opera Repertory Theatre.

Act V is the final act of a twelve-hour multimedia project by Wilson that was to have been presented at the 1984 Olympics in Los Angeles. Only *Act V* has been performed.

The action of *Act V*, set in Rome, concentrates on leaders of the civil wars in Italy and the United States, including Garibaldi, Lincoln, and Lee. Hercules arrives to assist humankind in its quest for peace and defeats destruction, whereupon he returns to heaven.

For a detailed description, see Kornick/*RAO*, 114–16.

Major roles: Abe Lincoln (bar), Earth Mother/Mrs. Lincoln (alto), Snow Owl/Almena (sop), Garibaldi (ten), and Hercules (bass).

LIBRETTO: Italian, of *Act V* ([Rome]: Edizioni del Teatro dell'Opera, [1984]).

Clair de Lune, romantic fantasy in three acts by Libby Larsen; libretto (Eng) by Patricia Hampl. First performance February 22, 1985, Little Rock, Arkansas, Opera Theatre, with Susan Peterson (Clair), Stephen Markuson (Henri), Barry Ellison (Richard), and Michele McBride (Kathleen); conducted by Benton Hess.

Clair, a former aviatrix, now almost fifty, spends much of her time reliving her aviation triumphs. Her ex-husband, Henri, comes to convince her to sell her airplane, the Clair de Lune, and she is subsequently visited by her young lover, Richard, and Kathleen, his new bride. Clair, defeated from both sides, is cajoled into selling her beloved airplane.

Roles: Clair (sop), Kathleen (sop), Henri (bass-bar), Richard (bar).

The work includes themes of a dozen works with a "moon" theme, such as Beethoven's "Moonlight" Sonata. The centerpiece of the opera is the aria set to Debussy's *Clair de Lune*, accompanied by solo piano.

BIBLIOGRAPHY: Eric E. Harrison, "Little Rock," *ON* XLIX (April 13, 1985), 41 [on premiere].

Clandestine Marriage, The, opera in three acts by Peter Wishart; libretto (Eng) by Don Roberts, after David Garrick and George Colman Sr.'s play. First performance June 8, 1971, London, Guildhall School of Music.

BIBLIOGRAPHY: "Guildhall School of Music," *MO* XCIV (Aug. 1971), 553 [on premiere]; Harold Rosenthal, "Student Performance," *Opera* XXII (Sept. 1971), 842 [on premiere].

Clari, or, The Maid of Milan, opera in three acts by Henry Rowley Bishop; libretto (Eng) by John Howard Payne, after Marmontel's tale *Laurette*. First performance May 8, 1823, London, Covent Garden. First U.S. performance November 12, 1823, New York, Park Theatre. Its sequel was *Home Sweet Home, or, The Rantz des Vaches.**

Clari contains the famous songs "Home Sweet Home" (from Bishop's 1816 *Who Wants a Wife?**), which was quoted in Donizetti's *Anna Bolena* (1830), and "Lo, Here, the Gentle Lark" (from his 1819 music to *The Comedy of Errors*).

LIBRETTO: English (London: J. Miller, 1823).

Clarissa, opera in two acts by Robin Holloway; libretto (Eng) by the composer, after Richardson's novel *Clarissa Harlowe* (1748). Composed 1976. First performance May 18, 1990, London, Coliseum, with Vivian Tierney (Clarissa) and Graeme Mattheson-Bruce (Lovelace); conducted by Oliver Knussen; directed by David Pountney.

The setting is eighteenth-century England. The young and innocent Clarissa is saved from being forced into an arranged marriage by her uncaring family, only to be put into a London brothel by her temporary savior, the attractive but unscrupulous Lovelace. She escapes for a time but is recaptured by Lovelace, who rapes her. She refuses his offer of marriage and, left alone, dies.

Major roles: Clarissa (sop); Lovelace (ten); and Anna, her confidante (col sop).

The composer used extracts from the opera for his *Clarissa Symphony*.

BIBLIOGRAPHY: Robert Hartford, "Live Performance," *MT* CXXXI (Aug. 1990), 434–35 [on premiere].

Clarkstown Witch, The, opera in two acts by Lionel Novak; libretto (Eng), after Hawthorne's *Feathertop*. First performance July 11, 1959, Piermont, New York, Rockland Lyric Theater.

See *Feathertop* and *The Scarecrow* for other settings of the story.

Claudia Legare, opera in three acts by Robert Ward; libretto (Eng) by Bernard Stambler, after Ibsen's *Hedda Gabler* (1890). First performance April 14, 1978, Minneapolis, Minnesota Opera Company, with Barbara Brandt (Claudia), Marsha Hunter (Daphne), John Brandstetter (Orlando); conducted by Philip Brunelle.

The setting is Charleston, South Carolina, after the Civil War. Claudia Legare, newly married to George Lowndes, remembers both her previous romance with Orlando and her beloved and strong father, General Legare. Orlando, together with Daphne Grayson, an old acquaintance of Claudia, has a plan to rebuild the South through industry rather than plantations. George is upset that Orlando's plans will make George's plantation worthless. Orlando's plan, meanwhile, has received the approval of Colonel Blagden, who tries to seduce Claudia, to no avail. Bitter about their past romance and disgusted that Orlando cannot match the memory of her father, Claudia goads Orlando, a reformed alcoholic, into drinking and suggests he shoot himself. He does, killing himself, and Blagden tells Claudia that he knows she was responsible for Orlando's death. Trapped, Claudia shoots herself.

For a detailed description, see Kornick/*RAO*, 318–20.

Major roles: George Lowndes (ten), Claudia Legare Lowndes (sop), Orlando Beaumont (bar), Daphne Grayson (sop), and Colonel Blagden (bass-bar).

See E. Harper's *Hedda Gabler* (1985, Glasgow) for another setting.

BIBLIOGRAPHY: Harold C. Schonberg, "Opera: Premiere of 'Claudia Legare,'" *NYT* (Apr. 17, 1978), C, 22.

Cleopatra's Night, opera in two acts by Henry Hadley; libretto (Eng) by Alice L. Pollock, after Gautier's *Une nuit de Cléopâtre*. First performance January 31, 1920, New York, with Frances Alda (Cleopatra), Orville Harrold (Meiamoun), Jeanne Gordon (Mardion), and Vincenzo Reschiglian (Mark Antony); conducted by Gennaro Papi.

Meiamoun, in love with Cleopatra, spends the night with the queen, knowing that he must die at dawn. When the sun rises, Cleopatra begs him to stay with her and live. He refuses, drinks the poisoned wine, and dies. Mark Antony, who has been away, enters the palace. When Mardion, in love with Meiamoun, finds out that he loved Cleopatra, she kills herself.

Major roles: Cleopatra, Queen of Egypt (sop); Meiamoun, a young Egyptian (ten); Mark Antony (bar); and Mardion, a maid of Cleopatra (mezzo).

The musical highlights include Cleopatra's "My Veins Seem Filled with Glowing Quicksilver" and the Oriental Dances.

SCORE: vs (Boston: Oliver Ditson Co., 1920).

LIBRETTO: English (Boston: Oliver Ditson Co., 1920).

BIBLIOGRAPHY: Richard Aldrich, "The Opera," *NYT* (Feb. 1, 1920), 21 [on premiere].

Climbing Boy, The, "comic drama with music" in three acts by William Hawes; libretto (Eng) by Richard Peake. Composed ca. 1834.

LIBRETTO: English (London: J. Miller, 1834).

Clock, The, opera in two acts and an epilogue by Vittorio Rieti; libretto (Eng) by Claire Nicholas. Composed 1960.

The dominating New England matriarch Mathilda Malone has driven away Doda, wife of her son Richard, who is suspected of having taken along a valuable necklace. Martha, Richard's sister, discovers that her mother, whom she had thought to be very ill, is playing cards with the young Dickie, a mischievous neighborhood child. Dickie keeps defeating the older woman at cards and claims as his prize the clock.

When Richard, who now lives with his mother, tries to wind the clock, he finds the necklace inside (placed there by a mysterious figure earlier in the opera). Dickie runs back to the boardinghouse where he lives with his mother, none other than Doda. She tells the boy how Richard, ashamed of his family's treatment of her, had sent her the necklace as consolation. Mathilda sends her daughter and family away, and Dickie refuses his grandmother's request that he return to her. The matriarch and Richard are left alone at the house, and Mathilda realizes that her gamble of hiding the necklace has not paid off.

For a detailed description, see Eaton/*OP* II, 261–62.

Major roles: Mathilda (alto), Richard (bar), Martha (mezzo), Dickie (mezzo), and Doda (sop).

LIBRETTO: English, typescript (ca. 1960, NYPL).

Clytemnestra, tragic opera in two acts by Peter Wishart; libretto (Eng) by Don Roberts. First performance February 13, 1974, London, Collegiate Theatre, with Maureen Lehane (Clytemnestra).

BIBLIOGRAPHY: Winton Dean, "Clytemnestra," *MT* CXV (Apr. 1974), 321 [on premiere]; Arthur Jacobs, "Clytemnestra," *Opera* XXV (May 1974), 456–57 [on premiere].

Cobler, The, or, A Wife of Ten Thousand, ballad opera in two acts, an adaptation by Charles Dibdin of Philidor's *Blaise le savetier* (1759, Paris); libretto (Eng) by Dibdin, after Sedaine's text. First performance December 9, 1774, London, Drury Lane Theatre.

The work is set in an alehouse, and the title character is saved from debt by the wiles of his wife.

LIBRETTO: English (London: T. Becket, 1774).

Cobler of Castlebury, The, musical farce in two acts by William Shield; libretto (Eng) by Henry Bate. First performance August 17, 1778, London, Haymarket Theatre.

Performed once.

LIBRETTO: English (London: G. Kearsley, [1799]).

Cobler's Opera, The, ballad opera; libretto (Eng) by Lacy Ryan. First performance April 26, 1728, London, Lincoln's Inn Fields, with Mr. Hall (Melton), Mr. Hippissley (Pyefleet/cobler), Mr. Laguerre (Harry Pyefleet), Mrs. Egleton (Peg Welfleet), and Miss Warren (Jenny Melton).

The setting is Billingsgate Fish Market. Melton, an oyster man, is in love with Peg Welfleet, a fishwoman, who is in love with Harry Pyefleet, son of Pyefleet, owner of an oyster vessel. He, in turn, loves Jenny Melton.

LIBRETTO: English, with airs (London, 1729); repr. Rubsamen/*BO*, vol. 14 (1974).

Cockcrow, children's opera in one act by Julia Smith; libretto (Eng) by Contance d'Arcy Mackay. First performance April 22, 1954, Austin, Texas, Driskill Hotel.

Coffee House, The, ballad opera in one act by Henry Carey and Henry Burgess; libretto (Eng) by James Miller, after Rousseau's *Le café*. First performance January 26, 1738, London, Drury Lane Theatre.

A look at the goings-on at a coffeehouse, with patrons playing board games, ill-informed discussions of politics, and so on.

SCORE: vs (London: J. Watts, 1737).

Coiners, The, or, The Soldier's Oath, opera by Michael Rophino Lacy, after Auber's *Le serment, ou, Les faux monnoyeurs* (1832, Paris); libretto (Eng), after Scribe and Mazères. First performance March 23, 1833, London, Covent Garden.

Colomba, opera in four acts by Alexander Mackenzie; libretto (Eng) by Francis Hueffer, after Prosper Mérimée's work (1841). First performance April 9, 1883, London, Drury Lane Theatre. Revised version in three acts; libretto by Claude Aveling; first performance December 3, 1912, London, Her Majesty's Theatre.

The setting is Corsica. While Orso is studying in England, his father is murdered by members of a family with whom his relatives have had an ongoing feud. On his return Orso is urged by his sister Colomba, a beautiful, but revenge-seeking, young woman, to avenge their father's killing. Although Orso is at first hesitant to do so, he begins to change his mind, and when he is ambushed by the sons of the assassin, he kills them and seeks safety in the hills. He is saved from being declared an outlaw when his English fiancée and her father, Colonel Nevill, speak in his defense.

This was the composer's first opera, and it was not well received because of its seemingly Wagnerian elements.

SCORE: vs (London: Novello, Ewer & Co. [etc.], [n.d.]).

Colonel Jonathan the Saint, "comedy of Reconstruction in four acts and an interlude of waltzes" by Dominick Argento; libretto (Eng) by John Olon-Scrymgeour. Composed 1961. First performance December 31, 1971, Denver, Loretto Heights College, Denver Lyric Opera; conducted by Norman Johnson.

Set just after the Civil War in Tidewater County, Maryland, the story centers on the partially burned mansion Lyoness. Colonel Jonathan Gilourin, a Union soldier, returns to the house, which has been turned into a hotel by Allegra Harper and Daisy, her niece. The house's owner, Sabrina, Daisy's sister, returns after failing to find her husband. The colonel, who strongly resembles Sabrina's husband, falls in love with the widow and persuades her to marry him. Together they rebuild the house, but Sabrina is increasingly drawn to the world of ghosts, where she encounters the spirit of her first husband.

For a detailed description, see Eaton/*OP* II, 61–62.

Major roles: Allegra Harper (sop), Daisy (mezzo), Jonathan Gilourin (ten), and Sabrina (sop).

Columba, opera in three acts by Kenneth Leighton; libretto (Eng) by Edwin Morgan. First performance June 16, 1981, Glasgow.

The work concerns the early Christian hero Columba (525–597), who is exiled from his native Ireland after a battle brought on by his unlawful copying of a Bible. He tries to convert the Picts in Scotland but runs into the opposition of Broichan, the Archdruid, who worships the pagan powers of nature.

Cast: four main characters and chorus.

Columbine, opera in three acts by Mary Davis; libretto (Eng) by Joanna Sampson. First performance April 23, 1973, Boulder, Colorado, Civic Opera.

Columbine String Quartet Tonight!, The, musical theater piece in two acts by Stanley Silverman; libretto (Eng) by Richard Foreman. First performance July 2, 1981, Stockbridge, Massachusetts, Lenox Arts Center.

Columbus, or, The Discovery of America, melodrama in three acts, with music by Alexander Reinagle; libretto (Eng) by Thomas Morton, after his play, itself partially after Marmontel's *Les Incas*. First performance (selections) January 30, 1797, Philadelphia. Also 1797, New York, with music by James Hewitt; and 1800, Boston, with music by Peter van Hagen.

LIBRETTO: English (London: W. Miller, 1792).

Columbus, or, The New World, opera by Homer Moore; libretto (Eng) by the composer. First performance 1903, St. Louis, with the composer (Columbus) and Charles Kunkel at the piano.

About the discovery of the Americas.

Other settings in English concerning Columbus include E. Stokes's *The Further Voyages of the Santa Maria** (comp. 1984); and P. Glass's *The Voyage** (1992, New York).

Combat Zone, opera by Richard Arnell; libretto (Eng) by the composer. First performance April 27, 1969, Hempstead, New York, Hofstra College.

Come and Go. See **Past Tense**.

Comedy of Errors, opera in five acts by Henry Rowley Bishop; libretto (Eng) by Frederick Reynolds after Shakespeare's play (1593). First performance December 11, 1819, London, Covent Garden.

Richard Rodgers's musical *Boys from Syracuse* (1978) is another setting.

SCORE: vs (London: Goulding, D'Almaine, Potter & Co., [n.d.]).

LIBRETTO: English (printed promptbook: London: Sampson Low, 1819).

Comet, The, or, He Would Be a Philosopher, ballad opera by James Hewitt; libretto (Eng) by William Milns. First performance February 1, 1797, New York, Old American Company.

LIBRETTO: English (New York: C. Smith, 1797).

Coming through Slaughter, opera by Mike Westbrook; libretto (Eng) by Michael Morris, after Michael Ondaatje's novel. First performance August 12, 1994, London, Queen Elizabeth Hall, with Wills Morgan (Buddy Bolden).

The work concerns the difficult life of jazz trombonist Buddy Bolden.

BIBLIOGRAPHY: Nick Kimberley, review, *Opera* XLV (Oct. 1994), 1219–20 [on premiere].

Command Performance, "opera concerto" in four acts by Robert Middleton; libretto (Eng) by Harold Wendell Smith. First performance November 11, 1961, Poughkeepsie, New York, Vassar College, Students Hall, with Blanche Thebom, Doris Yarick, Patricia Brooks, Robert Trehy, Ezio Flagello, Thomas Hayward, and James Billings; conducted by Middleton; produced by Sarah Caldwell.

Composed for the centennial of Vassar College.

LIBRETTO: English ([Boston: n.p., 1961?]).

Commedia, opera in four acts by Edward Cowie; libretto (Eng) by the composer. First performance (in German), as *Kommödianten*, June 10, 1979, Kassel, Staatstheater. First performance in English February 17, 1982, London, Sadler's Wells.

The work, using characters from the commedia dell'arte, mixes comedy and tragedy.

Roles: Columbine (sop), Harlequin (ten), Doctor (ten/counterten), Pantalone (bass), Brighella (bar), and Duchess (alto).

BIBLIOGRAPHY: Edward Cowie, review, *Opera* XXX (1979), 534–35.

Commission, The, "operatic episode" by Henry Cowell; libretto (Eng) by Colin McPhee. Composed 1954, in piano score with indications for orchestration. First performance, with orchestration by Henry Bloch, September 26, 1992, Woodstock, New York, Overlook Lyric Theatre, Bearsville Theatre, with Charles Sokolowski (Jonathan) and Frances Pallozzi (Julia), Corin Salon (Angela), and Lawrence Asher (Orlando); conducted by Bloch.

The plot, called a "roman à clef" by Cowell's widow, Sydney Cowell, has a composer (Cowell himself) create a work on commission from Affiliated Composers, Inc., headed by Angela (Claire Reis, founder of the League of Composers). The reluctant conductor, Orlando (Dmitri Mitropoulos), rehearses the work.
BIBLIOGRAPHY: Shirley Fleming, "Woodstock, NY," *ON* LVII (Dec. 19, 1992), 42 [on premiere].

Committee, The, comic opera in one act by Matt Doran; libretto (Eng) by Bettina Mae Dobrin. First performance March 15, 1958, New York, Columbia University, McMillin Theatre, with Patricia Brooks (the secretary) and James Tippey (the candidate); conducted by Joseph Liebling.
The story takes place in the office of a music department "in any large American university." A doctoral candidate is comforted by the pretty department secretary as he waits for his oral examination.
SCORE: vs ([n.p., n.d.]; LCCN: 84-69441).
BIBLIOGRAPHY: Edward Downes, "Satirical Opera Sung at Columbia," *NYT* (Mar. 17, 1958), 21 [on premiere].

Computer Marriage, A, comic opera in three acts by Ross Lee Finney; libretto (Eng) by the composer. Composed 1989.
The fantastic plot concerns the seventeenth-century astronomer Johannes Kepler, who, thrown into the future, plans to design the perfect wife by using modern machines, including, of course, computers. Among the other characters are Kepler's attractive housekeeper, who would like to have the scientist for herself.
BIBLIOGRAPHY: Ross Lee Finney, *Profile of a Lifetime* (New York: C. F. Peters), 231–34.

Comus, masque in three acts, with songs by Henry Lawes; text (Eng) by John Milton. First performance September 29, 1634, Ludlow Castle. First U.S. performance March 9, 1770, Philadelphia, Southwark Theatre.
SCORE: fs, ed. E. H. Visiak, Hubert J. Foss (Bloomsbury [London]: Nonesuch Press, 1937); vs, ed. Frank Bridge (London: Novello, 1956).
BIBLIOGRAPHY: John S. Diekhoff, comp., *A Maske at Ludlow: Essays on Milton's Comus* [with songs by Lawes] (Cleveland: Case Western Reserve University, 1968).
DISCOGRAPHY: Ritchie, Morison, Herbert, Gerlin, hpchd, St. Anthony Singers, and L'Oiseau-Lyre Orchestral Ensemble; cond. Lewis (1971), L'Oiseau-Lyre London 50070–71 (2 LPs), OLS 140–141 (2 CDs).

Comus, masque in three acts by Thomas Augustine Arne; libretto (Eng) by John Dalton, after Milton. First performance March 4, 1738, London, Drury Lane Theatre, with James Quin (Comus), Mrs. Cibber (the Lady), John Beard (Bacchanal/Attendant Spirit), Mrs. Clive (Euphrosyne), and Mrs. Arne (the Pastoral Nymph and Sabrina). First U.S. performance September 11, 1848, New York, Burtons Theatre, music of Lawes, Handel, and Arne arranged by George Loder.
In this mythological tale a Lady, left in the woods by her brothers to find food, is persuaded by Comus, in the disguise of a shepherd, to come to his palace. When the brothers discover that their sister has been placed under a spell, they are aided by a spirit, who gives them a magic potion to counteract the spell Comus has placed on their sibling. At a feast Comus tries to get the lady to drink the potion but is prevented from doing so by the brothers, and Sabrina, nymph of the river Severn, breaks Comus's spell. Virtue triumphs.

For a detailed musical description, see Fiske/*ETM,* 179–89.

Milton's text was also set by Stephen Oliver (1968, not perf.).

SCORES: fs, ms (British Museum, 1738: Add. MS. 11518); octavo score (London: R. Dodsley et al., 1738); quarto score (London: J. Simpson, [ca. 1750]); vs (London: Harrison & Co., [ca. 1785]); ed. Julian Herbage (London: Stainer & Bell, 1951).

LIBRETTOS: English (London: R. Dodsley et al., 1738; London: T. Lowndes, 1772).

DISCOGRAPHY: M. Ritchie, E. Morison, W. Herbert, R. Gerlin; cond. A. Lewis (1954, Herbage ed.); Editions de l'Oiseau-Lyre, OLS 50070–71.

Comus, masque in two acts, an adaptation by Henry Rowley Bishop, after Arne (see preceding entry); libretto (Eng), after Milton. First performance April 28, 1815, London, Covent Garden.

The arrangement, according to the 1815 libretto, contained "original music by Handel and Arne, with additions by Bishop; the overture by Cherubini, the dances by Mr. Ware."

LIBRETTO: English (London: J. Miller, 1815).

Condemned, The, choral opera in one act by Marc Blitzstein; libretto (Eng) by the composer. Composed 1932. Not performed.

Inspired by the Sacco and Vanzetti case of 1921, the opera, set in the Death House, focuses on four characters, each sung by a choral group: the Wife (two sop, one alto part); the Condemned (four-part male voices); the Friend (two bass parts); and the Priest (two ten parts).

For a description and compositional history, see Gordon/*MM,* 77–81.

Blitzstein's hopes for a first performance in the Soviet Union did not materialize. His second operatic treatment of the subject, *Sacco and Vanzetti,** was not completed.

Confessions of a Justified Sinner, The, opera in three acts by Thomas Wilson; libretto (Eng) by John Currie, after James Hogg. First performance June 15, 1976, York, Theatre Royal.

The story treats satanic possession in nineteenth-century Scotland.

Confidence Man, The, comic fable in two acts by George Rochberg; libretto (Eng) by Gene Rochberg after Herman Melville's novel. First performance August 1982, Santa Fe, Santa Fe Opera, with Neil Rosenshein (China), Sunny Joy Langton (Annabella); Brent Ellis (the Confidence Man); Deborah Cook (Angel of Bright Future), Michael Fiacco (Orchis), and Carolyne James (Mrs. Orchis); conducted by William Harwood.

The story is based on an episode from the Melville novel, chapter 40, "The Story of China Aster." It is an allegorical treatment of the theme of "faith and trust in mankind." The Confidence Man tells the story, in which China Aster, a poor candle maker, ignores the advice of Annabella, his wife, and, egged on by the Angel of Bright Future, accepts a loan from Orchis, a rich friend. China becomes penniless trying to repay it, and dies in misery, leaving his wife to bemoan his fate.

For a description, see Kornick/*RAO,* 241–44.

Major roles: Confidence Man (bar), China Aster (ten), Annabella, his wife (sop), Orchis (ten), Old Plain Talk (bass), and the Angel of Bright Future (sop).

The score contains traditional arias, duets, and ensembles, alternating with arioso passages.

SCORE: vs (Bryn Mawr, Pennsylvania: T. Presser Co., 1982).

BIBLIOGRAPHY: Jack Belsom, "Santa Fe: A Premiere and an Absorbing Repertory," *Opera* XXXIII (Festival 1982), 119–20; Robert Jacobson, review, *ON* XLVII (Nov. 1982), 38 [on premiere]; Andrew Porter, "A Frail Bark," *NY* LVIII (Aug. 16, 1982), 66–67 [on premiere].

Conjurer, "pop opera" in one act by Michael Sahl; libretto (Eng) by the composer. First performance June 1, 1975, New York, Public Theater; directed by Joseph Papp.

Conjur Moon, opera in three acts by Timothy Cameron Lloyd; orchestration by John Clifton; libretto (Eng) by David Thomas Lloyd, after Howard Richardson's play *Dark of the Moon* (1944). First performance May 17, 1979, Houston. Revived as *Witch Boy*, May 6, 1988, New York, Juilliard School; June 27, 1991, New York, Reimann Opera Theatre.

The story centers on a witch boy and his ill-fated love for a mortal woman.
BIBLIOGRAPHY: Arlo McKinnon Jr., review, *ON* LVI (Oct. 1991), 46 [on 1991 performance].

Conquistador, The, opera in a prologue, three acts, and epilogue by Myron Fink; libretto (Eng) by Donald Moreland. First performance March 1, 1997, San Diego, San Diego Opera, with Jerry Hadley (Don Luis de Carvajal), Elizabeth Hynes (Doña Elena de Robles), Adria Firestone (Doña Francisca de Matos), Louis Otey (Don Alvaro), Vivica Genaux (Isabel de Matos), Kenneth Cox (Bernardino de Sahagún), and John Duykers (Dr. Lobo Guerrero); conducted by Karen Keltner; directed by Sharon Ott; designed by Kent Dorsey.

In a story based on historical figures, Don Luis de Carvajal, a Spanish explorer and son of a Jewish family, settles in Mexico and falls in love with Doña Elena, niece of the viceroy, Don Alvaro. Luis raises the ire of the Spanish settlers when he supports the efforts of the friar Bernardino de Sahagún to educate the Indians rather than simply to enslave them. Fearing Luis's power, the viceroy and Dr. Lobo Guerrero, the chief inquisitor, learn of Don Luis's family and the fact that they, including his sister, Doña Francisca de Matos, still practice Judaism secretly. The pair succeed in bringing down the explorer, who dies in prison, and his loved ones, who are burned at the stake.
BIBLIOGRAPHY: Daniel Cariaga, "San Diego," *ON* LXII (July 1997), 44 [on premiere]; Rodney Milnes, "San Diego," *Opera* (July 1997), 797–99 [on premiere].

Consolations of Scholarship, The, "music-drama [in two acts] in the form of a Yüan (Chinese 13th/14th century) opera" by Judith Weir; libretto (Eng) by the composer, after *The Chao Family Orphan* and *A Stratagem of Interlocking Rings*. First performance May 5, 1985, Durham, England, Durham University, with Linda Hirst; conducted by Odaline de la Martinez.

The work tells of the devious General K'an, who plots to kill the noble Chao Tun, a government official. Chao's wife escapes with their infant son but then dies. The son, upon reaching adulthood, learns of his father's fate and warns the Emperor of the general's evil. The story is presented again in Weir's *Night at the Chinese Opera** (1989).

The work is scored for mezzo-soprano and instrumental ensemble (oboe, clarinet, bassoon, horn, violin, violoncello, piano, and percussion).
SCORE: facsimile score (London: Novello, 1991).
DISCOGRAPHY: L. Hirst; cond. O. de la Martinez, Novello Records 109 (1989), reissued as Cala Records CACD 88040 (1995, 1 CD).

Conspiracy of Pontiac, The, opera by Charles Mayer; libretto (Eng), after Francis Parkman. First performance January 27, 1887, Detroit, Brush Theatre.

Constance, opera in one act by Frederic Clay; libretto (Eng) by Thomas William Robertson. First performance January 23, 1865, London, Covent Garden.
SCORE: vs (London: Metzler & Co., [n.d.]).

Constant Maid, The, or, Poll of Plympton, musical entertainment in two parts by Thomas Carter; libretto (Eng) by John O'Keeffe. First performance January 16, 1788, London, Royal Circus.
SCORE: vs (London: J. Jarvis, 1787).

Consul, The, musical drama in three acts by Gian Carlo Menotti; libretto (Eng) by the composer. First performance March 1, 1950, Philadelphia, Shubert Theatre, with Patricia Neway (Magda), Marie Powers (the mother), Gloria Lane (the secretary), Maria Marlo (the foreign woman), Cornell MacNeil (John Sorel), Leon Lishner (the secret police agent), and Andrew McKinley (the magician); conducted by Lehman Engel. The production moved to the Ethel Barrymore Theatre in New York on March 15, 1950, with the same cast. First British performance February 7, 1951, London, Cambridge Theatre, with members of the original cast and Anna Pollak (the secretary); conducted by Thomas Schippers.

The action takes place "somewhere in Europe," the present. John Sorel has fled his country to save his life and wants his wife, Magda, his baby, and his mother to escape, also. Magda goes to the consulate to get the necessary papers but is frustrated by the red tape and the coldness of the secretary. After questioning by a secret agent, the death of her baby and mother-in-law, and the frustrations at the consulate, where the Consul is unable and unwilling to help her, Magda kills herself. John, her husband, who has returned home to take her away, finds her body and is arrested by the police.

For detailed descriptions, see Eaton/*OP* I, 44–45; K/*KOB*, 1346–51; K/*NKOB*, 458–60.

Major roles: John Sorel (bar), Magda Sorel (sop), the mother (alto), the secretary (mezzo), and the secret agent (bass).

The opera was extremely successful, and Menotti won the Pulitzer Prize for music and the New York Drama Critics Award for the best musical play. It was translated into twelve languages.

Among its compelling pieces are Magda's aria of despair, "To This We've Come," and her "Lullaby."
SCORE: vs (New York: G. Schirmer, 1995).
BIBLIOGRAPHY: Robert Sabin, "Menotti's The Consul Begins New York Run on Broadway," *MA* LII (Mar. 15, 1950), 7.

Contrabandista, The, or, The Law of the Ladrones, comic opera in two acts by Arthur S. Sullivan; libretto (Eng) by F. C. Burnand, an adaptation of Scribe's text for Auber's *L'ambassadrice* (1836, Paris). First performance December 18, 1867, London, St. George's Hall, with J. A. Shaw (Mr. Grigg) and Lucy Franklein (Inez de Roxas).

Set in Spain, the story concerns the British tourist Mr. Grigg, who is forced to lead a band of outlaws. It includes a bolero and cachucha to add local color.

The work was revived and expanded as *The Chieftain** (1894, London). J. P. Sousa's *The Smugglers*, with a text by Wilson J. Vance (1882, Philadelphia), is an adaptation of the original version.
SCORE: vs (London: Boosey, [1867]).
LIBRETTO : English ([London: J. Mallett, 1867]).

Contract, The, comic opera by John Stevenson and Philip Cogan; libretto (Eng) by Robert Houlton. First performance May 14, 1782, Dublin, Smock Alley. Revived as *The Double Stratagem*, May 19, 1784, Dublin, Capel Street Theatre.

Contrivances, The, "ballad opera" in one act by Henry Carey; libretto (Eng) by the composer. First performance June 20, 1729, London, Drury Lane Theatre. The performance of August 20, 1715 (as *The Contrivances, or, More Ways than One*), also in London, at the same theater, contained almost no music. First U.S. performance April 20, 1767, Philadelphia, Southwark Theatre.

The dashing hero Rovewell tricks the dull father in order to elope with the daughter. During the course of his deception Rovewell disguises himself as a country girl and his servant, Robin, as, among other characters, a lawyer.

The 1729 version had thirteen songs.
SCORE: vs (London: author, 1729).
LIBRETTO: English (Dublin: Sarah Cotter, [1761?]).

Conversion, The, opera in one act by Felix Werder; libretto (Eng) after Frank Wedekind. Composed 1973.

Cooper, The, comic opera in two acts by Thomas Augustine Arne; libretto (Eng) probably by the composer, after Audinot and Quétant's text (after Lafontaine) for *Le tonnelier*, set by Gossec (1765, Paris) and others. First performance June 10, 1772, London. First U.S. performance April 3, 1793, Boston.

The plot concerns the cooper, Old Martin, and the young Colin, both in love with Martin's ward, Fanny. In the end the young man is successful.

Major roles: Fanny (sop), Colin (ten), and Old Martin (bar).
SCORE: vs (London: William Napier, [1772]).
LIBRETTO: English, in *A Collection of the Most Esteemed Farces and Entertainments Performed on the British Stage*, vol. 6 (Edinburgh: S. Doig & W. Anderson, 1792), 217–37.
DISCOGRAPHY: Intimate Opera Co., cond. Antony Hopkins; adapted by Joseph Horovitz, Saga XID 5015 (195?, 1 LP).

Cop and the Anthem, The, opera in one act by Steve Cohen; libretto (Eng) by Alison Hubbard, after O. Henry. First performance June 11, 1982, New York, New York University Opera Studio.

Soapy, a vagrant, dreads the approaching winter and plans to receive warm housing, courtesy of the city, by getting arrested for a minor offense and put into a warm cell. His first attempts fail; when he refuses to pay for a meal, the waiters throw him onto the street; in subsequent tries, his friend Slim is arrested instead. Finally, Soapy is drawn to a church when he hears a choir performing an anthem inside and vows to reform. He is then arrested by a policeman on the charge of loitering.

For a detailed description, see Summers/*OOA*, 78–80.
Major roles: Soapy (bass-bar) and Slim (ten).
SCORE: ms score, holograph (1980, photocopy, NYPL).

Cornish Miners, The, melodrama in two acts by George Rodwell; libretto (Eng) by Richard Brinsley Peake. First performance July 2, 1827, London, Lyceum Theatre.

Corn King, The, opera in a prologue and two acts by Brian Easdale; libretto (Eng) by Naomi Mitchison, after her novel *The Corn King and the Spring Queen* (1931). First performance November 21, 1950, London, Paddington Hall Theatre.

Cortez, or, The Conquest of Mexico, opera in three acts by Henry Rowley Bishop; libretto (Eng) by James R. Planché, after William Prescott. First performance November 5, 1823, London.

When the troops of Cortez mutiny, he is aided by the Tlascalans, who have become his allies. A Tlascalan once saved by Cortez alerts Cortez to a plot against his life. Cortez is then able to rescue Mariana, a Mexican girl who has aided the Spanish.
LIBRETTO: English (London: J. Lowndes, [1823?]).

Costaso, opera in three acts by William Grant Still; libretto (Eng) by Verna Arvey. Composed 1954. First performance (excerpts) April 1989, Flagstaff, Arizona, University of Northern Arizona. First performance May 23, 1992, Pasadena, California, John Muir High School.
SCORE: vs (LCCN: 84-100688).

Cottage Festival, The, or, A Day in Wales, comic opera in one act by Tommaso Giordani; libretto (Eng) by Leonard MacNally. First performance November 28, 1796, Dublin, Theatre Royal.

Cottagers, The, opera in three acts, possibly by William Shield; libretto (Eng) by George Saville Carey. First performance 1766, London.
LIBRETTO: English (London, 1766); English (2d ed., London: Author, 1788).

Cottagers, The, ballad opera in one act by James Hewitt; anonymous libretto (Eng). First performance May 6, 1801, New York, Park Theatre.

Council of Ten, The, "Venetian water romance" by William Reeve; libretto (Eng) by Charles Dibdin Jr. First performance June 3, 1811, London, Sadler's Wells.
SCORE: vs (London, ca. 1811).

Countdown, computer-assisted opera in one act by Christopher Yavelow; libretto (Eng) by Laura Harrington. First performance February 12, 1987, Boston, Boston Lyric Opera.
    About the launching of a nuclear missile and the expected retaliation.

Country of the Blind, The, chamber opera in one act by Mark-Anthony Turnage; libretto (Eng) by Clare Venables, after a story by H. G. Wells. First performance June 13, 1997, Aldeburgh Festival, English National Opera Contemporary Opera Studio; conducted by Nicholas Kok.
    The story concerns a mountaineer who stumbles upon a community in which all the residents are blind.
BIBLIOGRAPHY: Andrew Clements, review, *The Guardian* (June 16, 1997), I, 2, and *Opera* XLVIII (Aug. 1997), 892–95 [on premiere]; Bernard Holland, "In the Shadow of Britten," *NYT* (June 21, 1997), A, 13 [on premiere].

Court and Cottage, operetta in one act by Frederic Clay; libretto (Eng) by Frederick Taylor. First performance March 22, 1862, London, Covent Garden.

Court Masque, The, or, Richmond in the Olden Time, opera by William Dawes, an arrangement of Hérold's *Le pré aux clercs* (1832, Paris); libretto (Eng) by James R. Planché, after Planard's text. First performance September 9, 1833, London, Adelphi Theatre.

Court of Alexander, The, all-sung afterpiece in two acts by John A. Fisher; libretto (Eng) by George Alexander Stevens. First performance January 5, 1770, London, Covent Garden.
    The work, which concerns Alexander the Great, is a burlesque of the historical operas of Handel and Metastasio, not, as *The London Stage* thought, of Nathaniel Lee's *The Rival Queens,* according to Fiske/*ETM*, 321.

LIBRETTO: English (London: T. Waller, [1770]).

Courtship of Camilla, The, opera in one act by Ruth Schonthal; libretto (Eng), after A. A. Milne's *The Ugly Duckling*. Composed 1980.
SCORE: vs (New York: American Music Center, 1980).

Courtship of Miles Standish, The, opera in three acts by Florence Ewart; libretto (Eng) by the composer, after Longfellow. First performance (concert) May 1931, Melbourne, Australia, New Conservatorium.

Miles Standish, captain of the settlement at Plymouth, has his friend John Alden woo Priscilla Mullins on his behalf. When Priscilla falls in love with John, Standish graciously steps aside.

Courtship of Miles Standish, The, opera in three acts by Timothy Spelman; libretto (Eng) by the composer, after Longfellow. Composed 1941.

Covenanters, The, Scottish ballad opera in two acts by Edward J. Loder; libretto (Eng) by Thomas Dibdin. First performance August 10, 1835, London, English Opera House, with Mr. Wilson (Donald Graeme), Mr. Williams (Allan Hamilton), Mr. J. Bland (Allaster Wilson), Mr. O. Smith (Sampson Harvey), Mr. Hemming (Captain Clobberton), Mr. McIan (Ross), Mr. Paulo (Atkins), Mr. Bowman (Hewson), Mr. Brunton (Sandy), Mr. Maitland (Captain Stirling), Miss P. Horton (Mary Hamilton), and Mrs. Griffith (Luckie Graeme).

The work is a late example of a pastiche using Scottish tunes (see Biddlecombe/ *EO*, 60).
LIBRETTO: English (London: J. Duncombe, [183?]).

Cowherd and the Sky Maiden, The, opera in two acts by John Verrall; libretto (Eng) by Esther Shepherd, after a Chinese drama. First performance January 17, 1952, Seattle, University of Washington, University Playhouse.
LIBRETTO: English (San Jose, Calif.: Pacific Rim, [1950]).

Cox and Box, or The Long-Lost Brothers, operetta in one act by Arthur S. Sullivan; libretto (Eng) by F. C. Burnand, after J. Maddison Morton's farce *Box and Cox* (1848). First performance May 11, 1867, London, Adelphi Theatre, with M. G. Du Maurier (Box), Harold Power (Cox), and Arthur Blunt (Sergeant Bouncer). First U.S. performance August 13, 1875, New York.

Two men, Mr. Cox and Mr. Box, unwittingly rent the same room from an unscrupulous landlord, Bouncer, who is able to carry on the trickery since one of the tenants works during the day, and the other during the night. The scheme comes to light when Mr. Cox and Mr. Box show up at the room at the same time.

Roles: James John Cox, a journeyman hatter (bar); John James Box, a journeyman printer (ten); and Sergeant Bouncer (bar).
SCORE: vs (London and New York: Boosey, 1866?; [London: Henderson et al., n.d.]).
LIBRETTO: English (London and New York: S. French, [180?]).
DISCOGRAPHY: D'Oyly Carte Opera Company, New Sym. Orch. of London; cond. I. Godfrey, London 417355-2 (2 CDs).
VIDEO: Ambrosian Opera Chorus; cond. McCarthy; London Symphony Orchestra; cond. A. Faris; dir. D. Alden, Goldcrest Films International, Opera World, VHS TRI-10V (1982 performance); rev. F. Paul Driscoll, *ON* LXII (Oct. 1997), 65.

Cradle Will Rock, The, opera in two acts by Marc Blitzstein; libretto (Eng) by the composer. First performance (concert) June 16, 1937, New York, Venice Theater, with

Howard da Silva (Larry Foreman), Will Geer (Mr. Mister), and Olive Stanton (the Moll); directed by Orson Welles. First performance in orchestra version November 24, 1947, New York, Carnegie Hall, with da Silva (Larry Foreman), Geer (Mr. Mister), and Estelle Loring (the Moll); conducted by Leonard Bernstein. First staged performance February 11, 1960, New York, City Center, with Tammy Grimes (the Moll) and da Silva (Larry Foreman); conducted by Lehman Engel; directed by da Silva. Revived May 1978, New York, Lyric Theatre.

The opera is a morality play. The scene opens in "Steeltown, USA," in 1931, during a union drive. The police mistakenly arrest the Liberty Committee, whose members are the elite of the town. They are hauled off to night court, along with the moll and the druggist.

The unionist Larry Foreman is brought into court; his speech had driven the cops to arrest the Liberty Committee in error; they had been listening to his speech with great displeasure. Mr. Mister, head of the family that owns the town and the steel factory, tries to buy off Larry Foreman, but his efforts are staunchly refused, and the union drive turns out to be a great success.

The work aroused much negative criticism at its premiere and at subsequent revivals, mostly because of the implications of its text. Among its critics is Ewen (*AMT*, 98–100), who calls it not an opera but a "glaring euphemism" and "political musical play" (99). For a nonjudgmental description, see Gordon/*MM*, 137–41, 162–66, 309–15, 465–69, and passim.

LIBRETTO: English (New York: Random House, [1938]).

DISCOGRAPHY: cast of 1937 Mercury Theatre production (abridged) of Orson Welles, narrator, pno accompaniment by composer, American Legacy Records T1001 (1938, orig. released as Musicraft Album 18); Peters, Andrews, Orbach, Bova, Theater Four, Kingsley, pno (1964), CRI SD-266 (2), reissue of MGM No. 4289–2 OC.

Craftsman, The, or, Weekly Journalist, ballad opera; libretto (Eng) by John Mottley. First performance October 15, 1728, London, Little Theatre in the Haymarket.
LIBRETTO: English (London: J. Roberts, 1728).

Crazy to Kill, detective opera in one act by John Beckwith; libretto (Eng) by James Reaney, after Ann Cardwell's novel. First performance May 11, 1989, Guelph, Ontario, with Jean Stillwell (Agatha) and Paul Massel (Detective Fry).

In the story, set in a private asylum near Ontario in the 1930s, Detective Fry is assisted in his search for a serial killer by Agatha Lawson, one of the patients.

The score blends popular music styles of the 1930s with more modern ones and features Agatha's ballad, which concludes the opera.
LIBRETTO: English (Guelph, Ont.: Guelph Spring Festival, 1988).

Creation, The, church opera in seven scenes by Alan Ridout; libretto (Eng) by Patric Dickinson, after Genesis. First performance 1973, Ely, England, Ely Cathedral.

Creation of the World, The, comic opera in one act by James Penberthy; libretto (Eng) by Gwen Harwood. Composed 1990.

Crescent Eyebrows, "concert opera" in one act by Judith Dvorkin; libretto (Eng). First performance January 8, 1956, New York, Town Hall.

Cricket on the Heart, The, opera in three acts by Alexander Campbell Mackenzie; libretto (Eng) by Julian R. Sturgis, after Charles Dickens's tale. First performance June

6, 1914, London, Royal Academy of Music. Revised as a light opera August 13, 1923, Glasgow, Royal Theatre.

Crier by Night, The, opera in one act by Edgar Bainton; libretto (Eng) by G. Bottomley. Composed 1919. First performance August 8, 1942, ABC.

Crimson Bird, The, opera in one act by Frederic Enebach; libretto (Eng) by Richard Strawn, after Marie de France's *Lai de Freine*. First performance April 19, 1979, Crawfordsville, Indiana, Wabash College.

The setting is medieval France. Two lords own adjacent houses, separated by fields and a wall. When one marries, his wife meets the other lord; the two fall in love. The husband catches his wife waiting at the window for her lover. To allay his suspicions, she explains that she is waiting for the nightingale's song. The husband has his servants catch the bird, and he kills it. In despair the wife sends the lifeless creature to her lover, along with an explanatory note. He puts the bird in a jeweled gold casket to remember his lost love.

For a description, see Summers/*OOA*, 105–6.

Major roles; the lady (sop); Chevalier I, her husband (bass-bar); Chevalier II, her lover (ten); and Compere, the narrator (bass-bar).

SCORE: ms vs, holograph (1979, photocopy, NYPL).

Crisis, The, or, Love and Fear, comic opera afterpiece in two acts by William Shield; libretto (Eng) by Thomas Holcroft. First performance May 1, 1778, London, Drury Lane Theatre.

Critic, The, or, An Opera Rehearsed, opera in two acts by Charles Stanford; libretto (Eng) by Lewis C. James, after Richard Sheridan's play (1779). First performance January 14, 1916, London, Shaftesbury Theatre, with Robert Maitland, Frank Mullings, Percy Heming, and Frederick Ranalow; conducted by Eugene Goossens.

The setting is a theater, and the action unfolds during the rehearsal of an opera.

Main characters: Puff, the composer; the critic, Sneer (speaking); the assistant prompter, Mr. Hopkins (speaking); the conductor; the cast of the opera: Tilburina (sop); the Governor of Tilbury Fort (bar), and the Spaniard Don Ferolo Whiskerandos (ten).

The score includes musical quotes from Handel and Beethoven.

Critic upon Critic, "a dramatic medley" (ballad opera) in three acts; libretto (Eng) by Leonard MacNally. First performance 1792, London, Covent Garden, with Mr. Quick (Attic), Mr. Macready (Tickler), Mr. Edwin (Scribble), Mr. Wilson (Sir Swindle Mac Subtle), Mrs. Martyr (Miss Crotchet), Mrs. Webb (Mrs. Bully), and Miss Green (Miss Plausible).

LIBRETTO: English, 2d ed. (London: J. Almon, 1792); repr. ed. R/*BO*, vol. 6, *Satire, Burlesque, Protest, and Ridicule*, part 2 (1974).

Cross and the Crescent, The, opera in four acts by Colin MacAlpin; anonymous libretto after John Davidson's version in English of François Coppée's play *Pour la couronne*. First performance November 22, 1903, London, Covent Garden.

Crossing, The, opera in one act by John Metcalf; libretto (Eng) by the composer, after Geoff Gilham's play. First performance September 20, 1984, Cardiff, Chapter Arts Centre, Music Theatre Ensemble, with John Rath (George Grosz), Alison Truefitt

(Käthe), Belinda Neave (the Woman), and Frank Roselaar-Green (the Sailor); conducted by Wyn Davies.

The work examines a chance meeting of the German painter George Grosz and another passenger on a ship crossing the Atlantic to the United States in 1933. The meeting leads to emotional conflict for the artist.

In addition to lyrical set pieces for Grosz and Käthe, there are mimed and danced sections for the other two members of the cast.

BIBLIOGRAPHY: Malcolm Boyd, "Wales," *MT* CXXVI (Jan. 1985), 41 [on premiere].

Crucible, The, concert drama by Richard Hageman; libretto (Eng). First performance February 4, 1943, Los Angeles.

Crucible, The, opera in four acts by Robert Ward; libretto (Eng) by Bernard Stambler, after the play by Arthur Miller (1952). First performance October 26, 1961, New York, City Opera, with Eunice Alberts (Rebecca Nurse), Frances Bible (Elizabeth Proctor), Patricia Brooks (Abigail Williams), Norman Kelley (Rev. Samuel Parris), Chester Ludgin (John Proctor), Ken Neate (Judge Danforth), and Norman Treigle (Rev. John Hale); conducted by Emerson Buckley; directed by Allen Fletcher. It was revived in March 1968, in New York, City Opera. First British performance June 6, 1984, London, Abbey Opera at Bloomsbury Theatre, with Alexander Gauld (John Proctor) and Alice Hyde (Abigail Williams); conducted by Antony Shelley.

The opera is set during the witch hunts in Salem in 1692. Among its victims are Rebecca Nurse and John Proctor, respected members of the community. Rebecca is accused of witchcraft by the greedy Thomas Putnam, to get her family's land, and John by Abigail Williams, his vengeful mistress, after she is dismissed by John's wife, Elizabeth, and renounced by John. The rigid Judge Danforth orders Rebecca and John to be hanged, despite pleas for leniency from Reverend Hale and Reverend Parris, Abigail's uncle.

For detailed descriptions, see *C/MS*, 76–92; Eaton/*OP* II, 64–65.

Major roles: John Proctor (bar), Elizabeth Proctor (mezzo), Abigail Williams (sop), Rebecca Nurse (alto), Judge Danforth (ten), John Hale (bass), Samuel Parris (ten), and Tituba (alto).

Arthur Miller's text is an allegory for the McCarthy "witch hunts" for supposed Communists in American society in the 1950s. Witchcraft is also treated in Cadman's *A Witch of Salem**; the slave Tituba, Abigail's companion who claims to have met with the Devil, appears as Tibuda in Cadman's work.

SCORE: vs score, English-German (n.p.: Highgate Press, [1963]).

LIBRETTO: English ([n.p.]: Highgate Press, 1961).

BIBLIOGRAPHY: Andrew Clements, "Fringe and Student Performances: The Crucible," *Opera* XXXV (1984), 1043–44 [on British premiere].

DISCOGRAPHY: Ebert, Kelley, Wynder, P. Brooks, Farr, Ukena, Alberts, Malas, Stern, Ludgin, Macurdy, Bible, New York City Opera Orch.; cond. E. Buckley, Albany Troy 025-26-2 (2 CDs, originally released as CRI 168); rev. Paul Kresh, *Classical* II (Nov. 1990), 64.

Crusade, The, musical drama in three acts by William Shield; libretto (Eng) by Frederic Reynolds. First performance May 7, 1790, London, Covent Garden.

SCORE: fs (London, 1790).

LIBRETTO: English (London: Longman and Broderip, 1790).

Crusaders, The, grand opera in three acts by Julius Benedict; libretto (Eng) by Alfred Bunn. First performance February 26, 1846, London, Drury Lane Theatre, with Mr.

Howell (Conrade), W. Harrison (Bohemond), Mr. Borrani (Raymond), H. Horncastle (Amaury), S. Jones (Sanserre), Mr. Morgan (Martel), Mr. Weiss (William), Mr. Stretton (Hassan), D. W. King (Ismaël), T. Matthews (Melech), Miss Romer (Alméa), Miss Rainforth (Iseult), and Miss Fitzjames (Bertha); conducted by William Harrison.

Six numbers of the work survive.

LIBRETTO: English (London: W. S. Johnson, 1846).

Cry of Clytaemnestra, The, opera in one act by John Eaton; libretto (Eng) by Patrick Creagh, after Aeschylus. First performance March 1, 1980, Bloomington, Indiana University Opera Theater, with Paula Redd (Clytaemnestra); conducted by Thomas Baldner.

Through visions Clytaemnestra recalls her daughter Iphigenia's sacrifice, and she thinks of her husband, Agamemnon, in Troy, and his affair with Cassandra. When she awakens from her last vision, Clytaemnestra realizes that she has decided to kill her husband. Beacons in the horizon indicate his arrival, and she leaves to greet him.

Major roles: Clytaemnestra, Agamemnon, and Cassandra.

The score, which uses a chamber orchestra, combines microtonal writing and a moderate dissonance with lyrical passages. Donal Henahan described it as "another one of those imitative efforts, supposedly in the style of Berg . . . . [employing] all the clichés of Viennese Expressionism" (see below).

BIBLIOGRAPHY: Donal Henahan, "Opera: Double Local Debut of One-Acters in Brooklyn," *NYT* (Nov. 15, 1980), 13 [on New York premiere]; Andrew Porter, "Musical Events," *NY* LVI (Mar. 31, 1980), 94–95 [on premiere]; John Von Rhein, "Reports: U.S.," *ON* XLIV (May 1980), 36 [on premiere].

Cubana, La (The Cuban Woman), "a cruel and obscene vaudeville" in five scenes by Hans Werner Henze; libretto (Ger) by Hans Magnus Enzensberger, after Miguel Barnet's novel *La canción de Rachel.* First performance March 4, 1974, New York, WNET, in English; libretto and lyrics by Mel Mandel, with Lee Venora (young Rachel); Lili Darvas (older Rachel); and Alan Titus (trio of men in Rachel's life). First stage performance May 28, 1975, Munich.

The action centers around the aged Rachel, once a famous music hall singer and actress, as she relives her past through a series of flashbacks, while Ofelia, her maid, warns that revolution is breaking out nearby.

For a detailed description, see Eaton/*OP* II, 66–67.

Major roles: young Rachel, a beauty in the cabaret (sop); Rachel's lovers: Eusebio, a rich young man (bar), Paco, an artist (bar), and Federico, a student (bar); old Rachel (speaking role); Lucile, a young whore (mezzo); Alberto/Yarini (ten); Don Alfonso, a circus director (bass-bar); El Cimarrón, a former slave (bass-bar); a critic/theater director (ten); and Ofelia, Rachel's maid (sop).

The music contains melodic writing as well as dissonance, dialogue, and *Sprechstimme.*

SCORE: vs, ed. Wilfried Steinbrenner (Mainz: B. Schott's Söhne; New York: Schott, 1974).

BIBLIOGRAPHY: Bernard Jacobson, "Henze's 'La Cubana,'" *Opera* XXIX (1978), 953–56; the same, "TV," *ON* XXXVIII (Mar. 16, 1974), 25 [on premiere].

Cue 67, opera by Michael Ching; libretto (Eng) by Sandra Bernhard. First performance February 8, 1992, Richmond, Virginia, Virginia Opera, with Christine Akre (Anne/Ariel), Michael Caldwell (Michael/Prospero), and David Maze (Gerry); conducted by the composer.

In a blending of reality and the supernatural, a theater company attempts to put on Shakespeare's *The Tempest*. Anne, who is supposed to play the part of Ariel, is killed by falling scenery during a rehearsal, which bring on nightmares for the stage director, Gerry, Anne's former boyfriend.

The works combines orchestral sounds with those of a saxophone and synthesizer.
BIBLIOGRAPHY: Sorab Modi, "Richmond," *ON* LVI (Apr. 11, 1992), 48 [on premiere].

Cumberland Fair, jamboree in one act by Alec Wilder; text (Eng) by Arnold Sundgaard. First performance May 22, 1953, Montclair, New Jersey, Montclair State College.

The setting is Sycamore Hill, near the Cumberland Fair, on an October day. The characters include the haughty Polly, Reuben Ranzo, a rural prince charming, and the Cinderella-like Phoebe. Ben Blake and Billy Barlow also make an appearance.
SCORE: vs (New York: Hollis Music, [1953]).

Cunning Man, The, "musical entertainment, imitated and adapted to the original music," English version of J.-J. Rousseau's *Le devin du village* (1752, Paris) by Charles Burney; libretto (Eng) by Burney. First performance November 21, 1766, London, Drury Lane Theatre, with Mr. Champness. Revived October 1979, Boston, Museum of Fine Arts.

A soothsayer helps Colette win back her beloved, Colin.
SCORE: vs (London: R. Bremner, [1766]).
LIBRETTO: English, 2d ed. (London: T. Becket and P. A. De Hondt, 1766).
DISCOGRAPHY: cond. C. Kaufman; SK 285 AFKA Records (1979, 1 LP).

Cupid and Death, masque in one act (five entries, three scenes), with music by Christopher Gibbons and Matthew Locke; text (Eng) by James Shirley. First performance (private) March 26, 1653, London; produced by Luke Channen. Revised version by Locke; performed 1659, London, Leicester Fields.

While Cupid and Death are staying in the same inn, the Chamberlain exchanges their arrows while the two are sleeping. Ignorant of this, Cupid shoots and kills a number of young lovers, while Death's missiles give renewed vigor to the old and sick, all of which horrifies Mother Nature. As punishment for his actions, the Chamberlain is struck by one of Death's arrows, compelling him make love to his trained apes. Mercury appears and restores order, Cupid is banished from court, and Death's powers are curtailed. The lovers who have been killed because of the prank are remembered in the concluding scene.

The work includes spoken dialogue, recitative, set songs, choruses, and ballet.

Major roles: Cupid and Death (speaking and dancing), Mother Nature (sop), Mercury (bass), and the Chamberlain (speaking and singing).

Among the numbers is Mercury's recitative "Hence, Ye Profane," set by Locke.
SCORE: ms, 1659 version (British Library, Add. MS. 17799); fs ed. Edward J. Dent, *Musica Britannica*, vol. 2 (London: Stainer and Bell, 1951); partial rescoring by Bishop (British Library, Add. MS. 17800).

Cupid and Psyche, opera in one act by Ashley Vernon; libretto (Eng) by Greta Hartwig. First performance July 27, 1956, Woodstock, New York, Byrdcliffe Theatre, Turnau Opera Players.
SCORE: vs (n.p, n.d.; LCCN: 84-115878).

Cupid's Revenge, "Arcadian pastoral" in two acts by James Hook; libretto (Eng) by Francis Gentleman, after John Hoadly's *Love's Revenge*. First performance July 27, 1772, London, Little Theatre in the Haymarket. First U.S. performance April 15, 1795, Charleston, South Carolina.

LIBRETTO: English (London: J. Bell, 1772).

Cure for a Scold, A, ballad opera in two acts; libretto (Eng) by James Worsdale, after John Lacy's *Sauny the Scot, or, The Taming of the Shrew*, itself after the Shakespeare play. First performance February 25, 1735, London, Drury Lane Theatre, with Mr. Shepard (Sir William Worthy), Mr. Mecklin (Mr. Manly), Mr. Este (Heartwell), Mr. Cross (Gainlove), Mrs. Clive (Peg), Mrs. Pritchard (Flora), and Mrs. Cross (Lucy).

The story is a version of Shakespeare's play *The Taming of the Shrew*.

LIBRETTO: English (London: Gilliver, [1735]); repr. ed. Rubsamen/*BO*, vol. 4, *The Medical and Legal Professions* (1974).

Curious Fern, The, comic opera in one act by Meyer Kupferman; libretto (Eng) by Alistair Reid. First performance June 5, 1957, New York, Master Institute Theatre, with Ellen Faull (the fern).

The work is set in England in 1894 and concerns two spinsters who own an intelligent fern.

Roles: Aunt Cynthia (sop); Aunt Lucy (mezzo); Matthew, their nephew (bar); Gloomy Domingo, an old man (ten/high bar); Mabel, his daughter (mezzo); and the fern (col sop).

SCORE: vs (New York: Mercury Music, 1956).

BIBLIOGRAPHY: Ross Parmenter, "Chamber Operas Given in Debuts," *NYT* (June 6, 1957), 34.

Curlew River, parable in one act by Benjamin Britten; libretto (Eng) by William Plomer, after the Japanese Noh play *Sumidagawa* by Jūro Motomasa. First performance June 13, 1964, Aldeburgh Festival, Orford Church, with Peter Pears (the mother), John Shirley-Quirk (the ferryman), Bryan Drake (the traveler), and Don Garrard (the Abbot); conducted by the composer; produced by Colin Graham. First U.S. performance June 26, 1966, Katonah, New York, Caramoor Festival, with Andrea Velis, Clatworthy, Ara Berberian.

A crazed mother seeks her lost son, and when she is taken to his grave, at the side of the Curlew River, he appears in a vision, and her madness disappears.

For detailed descriptions, see Eaton/*OP* II, 262–63; K/*KOB*, 1223–27; K/*NKOB*, 132–33.

Major roles: the mother (ten), the son (treble); the ferryman (bar); the traveler (bar); and the leader of the pilgrims (bass).

The work is performed by an all-male cast in a stylized manner based on the medieval religious drama. Plainsong takes the place of the traditional, ancient Japanese music. The orchestra is sparse, consisting of seven instruments.

One of Britten's *Three Church Parables*. See also *The Burning Fiery Furnace* and *The Prodigal Son*.

N. Scarim's *Sumidagawa** and C. Raybould's *The Sumida River** are other settings.

SCORES: vs, ss (London: Faber, 1964).

LIBRETTO: libretto with performance notes by Colin Graham (London: Faber, 1964).

BIBLIOGRAPHY: Quaintance Eaton, "Reports," *ON* XXXII (Dec. 30, 1967), 31 [on New York revival, November 27, 1967]; Charles Osborne, "Britten's Festival," *NYT* (July 5, 1964), II, 9 [on premiere].

DISCOGRAPHY: P. Pears, J. Shirley-Quirk, Drake, Blackburn, Webb, Adney, Sanders, Aronowitz, Knussen, Ellis, Blades, Ledgar; cond. Britten and Tunnard, London A4156 [OSA-1156] (2 CDs); M. Milhofer, M. Hargreaves, G. H. Jones, M. Evans, Guildhall Chamber Ensemble; cond. D. Angus, Koch-Schwann SCH 313972.

Currency Lass, The, or, My Native Girl, musical play in two acts; libretto (Eng) by Edward Geoghegan. First performance May 27, 1844, Sydney, Australia, Royal Victoria Theatre. Revived October 1966, Sydney, Jane Street Theatre.

The work, which concerns a native-born girl mistakenly thought to be Aboriginal, is a compilation of existing tunes.

SCORE: vs, ed. Roger Covell (Sydney: Currency Press, 1976).
BIBLIOGRAPHY: Helen Musa, *"The Currency Lass,"* in *A Companion to Theatre in Australia,* ed. Philip Parsons (Sydney: Currency Press, 1995), 178.

Curse of Mauvais-Air, The, mini-opera by Paul Reif; libretto (Eng) by the composer. First performance May 9, 1974, New York.

Composed for four singers and pianist-narrator.

SCORE: vs (New York: Seesaw Music, 1976).

Cymbia, or, The Magic Thimble, comic opera in three acts by Florian Pascal; libretto (Eng) by Harry Paulton. First performance March 21, 1883, London, Strand Theatre.

LIBRETTO: English (London: J. Williams, [189?]).

Cymon, "a dramatic romance" in a prologue, five acts, and an epilogue by Michael Arne; libretto (Eng) by David Garrick, after John Dryden's play *Cymon and Iphigenia.* First performance January 2, 1767, London, Drury Lane Theatre. First U.S. performance March 3, 1773, Philadelphia. Revived with a new overture and songs, London, January 17, 1778.

Cymon, a prince, is under the spell of Urganda, an enchantress. He becomes enamored of Sylvia, a shepherdess, and she is threatened with harm by her rival. Cymon and Sylvia are saved by the intervention of the magician Merlin, whose powers are stronger than those of Urganda.

Major roles: Cymon (ten), Urganda (sop), Sylvia (sop), and Merlin (ten).

This was Arne's greatest success. Its numbers include "This Cold Flinty Heart," "Yet Awhile Sweet Sleep," and "Oh Why Should I Sorrow."

SCORE: vs (London, [177-]; London: Longman and Broderip, [ca. 1785]).
LIBRETTO: English (London: T. Becket & P. A. DeHondt, 1767).

Cymon, adaptation in three acts by Henry Rowley Bishop of Arne's work (see preceding entry). First performance November 20, 1815, London, Covent Garden.

The work includes the trio of Daphne, Phoebe, and Linco in act 1, "Could You Never Yet Discover."

SCORE: ms autograph of overture, "additional Musick" (1815, British Museum, MS. Add. 30859); vs (London: Goulding, D'Almaine, Potter & Co., [1815?]).
LIBRETTO: English (London: John Miller, 1815).

Cynthia Parker, opera in three acts by Julia Smith; libretto (Eng) by Jan Fortune. First performance (excerpts) February 16, 1939, Denton, Texas, North Texas State University. Revised 1977. First complete performance December 5, 1985, Austin, Texas, University of Texas; directed by Robert De Simone.

The work is concerned with the clash of white and Native American culture and the sorrow it brings. Cynthia Parker, a white girl, abducted during the massacre of Parker's Fort and raised by the Comanches, stays with them for twenty-five years and becomes the wife of Peta Nacoma. She is recaptured by Captain L. S. Ross of the Texas Rangers during the Battle of Pease River.

SCORE: ms vs (New York: American Music Center, 1978).

Cyrano, opera in four acts by Walter Damrosch; libretto (Eng) by William J. Henderson, after Edmond Rostand's play *Cyrano de Bergerac* (1897). First performance (as *Cyrano de Bergerac*) February 27, 1913, New York, Metropolitan Opera, with Frances Alda (Roxane), Pasquale Amato (Cyrano), Maria Mattfeld (the duenna), Riccardo Martin (Christian), Albert Reiss (Ragueneau), Putnam Griswold (De Guiche), William Hinshaw (Le Bret), and Lambert Murphy (Montfleury); conducted by Alfred Hertz. Revised version February 20, 1941, New York, Carnegie Hall (concert).

The story of the long-nosed poet Cyrano de Bergerac, who helps the handsome, but dull-witted, Christian court the beautiful Roxane. Only when Cyrano is dying does Roxane discover that it was he who wrote her so eloquently and that she loves Cyrano in return.

Major roles: Roxane (sop), Cyrano de Bergerac (bar), the duenna (alto); Lise (sop), Christian (ten), Ragueneau (ten), De Guiche (bass), Le Bret (bass), and Montfleury (ten).

Also set by F. Alfano (1936, Rome); musical comedy setting by J. Dvorkin (1964, Winston-Salem, North Carolina). See also the following five entries.
SCORE: vs (New York: G. Schirmer, 1913).

Cyrano, "heroic comedy in music" in three acts by Jack Beeson; libretto (Eng) by Sheldon Harnick, after Rostand. First performance 1994, Hagen, Germany.

Cyrano de Bergerac, comic opera in three acts by Victor Herbert; libretto (Eng) by Stuart Reed, after Rostand; lyrics by Harry Bache Smith. First performance September 11, 1899, Montreal; September 11, 1899, New York, Knickerbocker Theatre, with Francis Wilson (Cyrano), Charles H. Bowers (Christian), and Lulu Glaser (Roxane); conducted by John McGhie; directed by A. M. Holbrooke.

For a detailed description, see Waters/*VH*, 153–56.
SCORE: vs (New York: M. Witmark, 1899).

Cyrano de Bergerac, opera in a prologue and three acts by Samuel D. Pokrass; libretto by Charles O. Locke, after Rostand. Composed 1932.
SCORE: vs, ms (1932, NYPL).

Cyrano de Bergerac, opera by Cecil Effinger; libretto (Eng) by Donald Sutherland, after Rostand. First performance July 21, 1968, Boulder, Colorado, University of Colorado.

Cyrano de Bergerac, opera by Jack Jarrett, after Rostand. First performance April 27, 1972, Greensboro, North Carolina, University of North Carolina at Greensboro.

Czar, The, comic opera in three acts by William Shield; libretto (Eng) by John O'Keeffe. First performance March 8, 1790, London, Covent Garden, with Charles Bannister (Peter I), Mr. Blanchard (Count Couvanski), John Johnstone (Colonel Lefort), Mr. Darley (Commodore Swivel), Mr. Quick (Justice Applejack), Mrs. Billington (Ottokesa), Mrs. Mountain (Mrs. Applejack), and Mrs. Martyr (Ellen). Also known as *The Czar Peter*.

The work is set in London and Deptford and concerns the Russian czar Peter, who works in disguise in the shipyard at Deptford.

A. Lortzing set the same story as *Zar und Zimmermann, oder, die zwei Peter* (1837, Leipzig). Both operas share the character of Lefort, the Russian ambassador. Another setting is H. R. Bishop's *The Burgomaster of Saardam** (1818, London).
LIBRETTO: English, in *The Dramatic Works of John O'Keeffe*, vol. 3, as *The Czar Peter* (London: author [T. Woodfall et al.], 1798).

D

Daelia, opera in one act by Hamilton Forrest; libretto (Eng) by the composer. First performance July 21, 1954, Interlochen, Michigan, National Music Camp.

Daisy, historical drama in two acts by Julia Smith; libretto (Eng) by Bertita Harding. First performance March 11, 1973, Miami, Greater Miami Opera Association.

The story follows the development of the U.S. Girl Scouts. Recovering from a divorce, Daisy makes the acquaintance of Sir Robert Baden-Powell, the founder of the Boy Scouts and Girl Guides. She begins the Girl Guiding group in her native Georgia, helped by Nina Pape. Daisy changes the name to the Girl Scouts, and the group grows into a nationwide organization. When Daisy learns that she has a fatal illness, she convinces Jane Rippin to hold a Girl Scouts conference in Briarcliff, New York. Daisy finds peace, knowing that the movement she started has aided thousands of young girls.

Major roles: Daisy Low (sop); Billow, Daisy's husband (ten); and Sir Robert Baden-Powell (bar).

For a detailed description, see Kornick/*RAO*, 286–88.

SCORE: vs ([n.p., 1972]; LCCN 84-96333).

Dalgerie, tragic opera in one act by James Penberthy; libretto (Eng) by Mary Durack, after her novel *Keep Him My Country*. First performance January 22, 1959, Perth, Australia, Somerville Auditorium. Also performed July 25, 1973, Sydney, Opera House, together with Sitsky's *The Fall of the House of Usher*,* the first operas to be staged there.

The love between an Aboriginal woman, Dalgerie, and Stan, her Caucasian boss, is forbidden by her tribal laws. Afflicted by leprosy, she asks to see him once more and dies in his arms.

Major roles: Dalgerie (sop) and Stan (bar).

BIBLIOGRAPHY: F. R. Blanks, review, *MT* CXIV (Oct. 1973), 1036 [on Sydney performance].

Damon and Phillida, ballad opera in one act; libretto (Eng) by Colley Cibber. First performance August 16, 1729, London, Little Theatre in the Haymarket, with Richard Clarke (Damon). First U.S. performance February 18, 1751, New York, Nassau Street Theatre.

The setting is the Arcadian Fields. Damon, who is opposed to marriage, is forced to propose to Phillida after she decides that she can live without him.

Roles: Arcas, a nobleman; Aegon, his friend; Corydon, an old shepherd; Phillida, daughter of Corydon; Cimon and Mopsus, simple brothers in love with Phillida; and Damon, an inconstant.

A successful revision of *Love in a Riddle** (1729, London).

LIBRETTOS: English (London: J. Watts, 1729; London, 1749); repr. ed. Rubsamen/*BO*, vol. 8, *Classical Subjects II: Pastoral and Comedy* (1974).

Damon and Phillida, ballad opera in one act, revised by Charles Dibdin; libretto (Eng) by Henry Carey, after Colley Cibber's text. First performance December 21, 1768, London, Drury Lane Theatre.

SCORE: vs, Dibdin version (London: C. & S. Thompson, n.d.).
LIBRETTO: English (London: J. and R. Tonson, 1765).

Dancing Master, The, opera in one act by Malcolm Arnold; libretto (Eng) by Joe Mendoza, after William Wycherly's *The Gentleman Dancing Master*. Composed 1952. First stage performance March 1, 1962, London, Barnes Music Club, with David Barrett (French dandy), Guelda Cunningham (Miranda), Fergus O'Kelly (Gerard); conducted by Lucy Reynolds.

This comedy of intrigues and misunderstandings concerns Miranda, the heroine, and her two suitors, a French dandy and Gerard, who disguises himself as a dancing master to win Miranda's affections.
BIBLIOGRAPHY: E. Chapman, "Malcolm Arnold's Opera," *Musical Events* XVII (Apr. 1962), 12; Stanley Sadie, review, *Opera* XIII (May 1962), 347 [on premiere].

Dangerous Liaisons, The, opera in two acts by Conrad Susa; libretto (Eng) by Philip Littell, after *Les liaisons dangereuses* by Pierre Choderlos de Laclos (1782). First performance September 10, 1994, San Francisco, San Francisco Opera, with Frederica von Stade (Marquise de Merteuil), Thomas Hampson (Vicomte de Valmont), Renée Fleming (Mme. de Tourvel), Judith Forst (Mme. de Volanges), and Johanna Meier (Mme. de Rosemonde); conducted by Donald Runnicles.

The aristocratic and unscrupulous Valmont, who prides himself in seducing women from all walks of life, sets out to conquer two women through the aid of the equally villainous Marquise de Merteuil. Although he is successful in his conquests and ruins the lives of his victims, Valmont is killed in a duel, and the Marquise's treachery is also uncovered.

Major roles: Marquise de Merteuil (mezzo), Mme. de Tourvel (sop), Mme. de Volanges (mezzo), Mme. de Rosemonde (sop), and Vicomte de Valmont (bar).

Also set by P. Swerts as *Les liaisons dangereuses* (1997, Antwerp).
BIBLIOGRAPHY: James R. Oestreich, "Operas on Willful Women and Pliable Men," *NYT* (Sept. 13, 1994), C, 15 [on premiere]; Stephanie von Buchau, review, *ON* LIX (Jan. 7, 1995), 39 [on premiere].

Dante and Beatrice, opera in three acts by Stephen Rowland Philpot; libretto (Eng) by W. J. Miller. First performance November 25, 1889, London, Gresham Hall (Brixton). SCORE: vs (London: Lowe & Brydone, 1893).

Danton and Robespierre, opera in three acts by John Eaton; libretto (Eng) by Patrick Creagh. First performance April 21, 1978, Bloomington, Indiana, Indiana University Opera Theater, with James Anderson/Michael Ballam (Danton), Timothy Noble/Robert McFarland (Robespierre), Gran Wilson (Camille), Edith Vanerette/Sally Wolf (Lucille), Mary Shearer/Debra Grodecki (Louise), and Nelda Nelson (Gabrielle); conducted by Thomas Baldner.

With the French Revolution as its backdrop, the opera highlights the conflict between the idealistic Danton and the mad realist Robespierre. After Danton's short retirement to the country during the Reign of Terror, led by Robespierre, Danton returns to the Assembly to urge moderation. The final, fruitless attempt at reconciliation between the two men ends with tragedy, and both are beheaded.

Major roles: Danton (ten); Robespierre (bass-bar); Camille Desmoulins (ten); Louise, Danton's mistress (sop); and Lucille (col sop).

The work uses a large orchestra; among the musical highlights is Robespierre's "O God, O Great Creator, Look Down on What We Do," sung to a chorale. When Robespierre tries to repeat this prayer after Danton's death, he sings terribly out of tune, a powerful effect.

Also set by G. von Einem (1947, Salzburg).

SCORE: ms score, holograph (1977, photocopy, NYPL).

LIBRETTO: English (Delaware Water Gap, Pa.: Shawnee Press, 1978).

BIBLIOGRAPHY: William Mootz, "Reports: U.S.," *ON* XLIII (Aug. 1978), 45-46 [on premiere]; Andrew Porter, "Musical Events: Enflam'd by Hope," *NY* LIV (May 22, 1978), 118–21 [on premiere].

DISCOGRAPHY: Shearer, Nelson, Vanerette, Anderson, Noble, Wilson, Langan, Indiana University Opera Theater; cond. Baldner, CRI IUS-421 (1978, Bloomington, Ind., 3 CDs); rev. John W. Freeman, "Records," *ON* XLV (Jan. 10, 1981), 29.

Daphne, or, The Pipes of Arcadia, comic opera in three acts by Arthur Bird; libretto (Eng) by Marguerite Merington. First performance (concert) April 1, 1895, New York, Hotel Astoria; (stage) December 13, 1897, New York.

LIBRETTO: English (New York: Century Co., 1896).

Daphne and Amintor, afterpiece, pastiche by Samuel Arnold; libretto (Eng) by Isaac Bickerstaffe, after G. de Saint-Foix's *L'oracle* and Susanna Cibber's translation (1752). First performance October 8, 1765, London, Drury Lane Theatre, with Joseph Vernon (Amintor) and Miss Wright (Daphne). First U.S. performance May 29, 1785, Charleston, South Carolina, Theatre in the City Exchange.

According to a prophecy, Amintor will have a happy life only if his wife-to-be believes that he is deaf, mute, and without feelings until after the marriage ceremony. Accordingly, his mother, a magician, picks for his prospective wife Daphne, and when she meets her intended, she does her best to get him interested in her, despite his seeming inattention.

For a description, see Fiske/*ETM*, 341–42.

LIBRETTO: English (London: Robert Bremnersche, 1765).

Darby's Return, comic sketch; libretto (Eng) by William Dunlap. First performance November 24, 1789, New York, New York Theatre.

According to the author, this was the sequel to John O'Keeffe's text for *The Poor Soldier*.*

The title character, having returned home to Ireland after traveling extensively, describes his experiences in Prussia, Austria, Turkey, and the United States, especially New York, where he observed the celebrations accompanying the adoption of the U.S. Constitution.

George Washington, who had just been elected president, was in the audience for the premiere.

For a description, see Virga/*AO*, 264–69.

LIBRETTO: English (New York: Hodge, Allen, and Campbell, 1789).

Darkened City, The, opera in three acts by Bernhard Heiden; libretto (Eng) by Robert Glynn Kelly. First performance February 1963, Bloomington, Indiana, Indiana University.

The plot stresses the themes of how individuals deal with crises and the miracle of the dead returning to life. Set in a fourteenth-century English city that is a shrine for pilgrims, it involves, as with its biblical counterpart, Lazarus, a councillor who succumbs to the plague but is restored to life. The widow of Lazarus must contend with a bevy of persistent suitors, as Penelope does in Monteverdi's *Il ritorno d'Ulisse in patria*. The widow meets her husband, who has been restored to life; he, meanwhile, has become a religious fanatic, which pits him against the town's practical mayor; when the light at the shrine dies out, so does the resurrected Lazarus.

Major roles: first mourner (alto); priest (bar); the mayor (bass); Lazarus (bar); the wife of Lazarus (sop); and first citizen, leader of the Penitents (bar).

The work uses Gregorian chant and leitmotifs.

Dark Pilgrimage, television opera in one act by Phyllis Tate; libretto (Eng) by David Franklin. First performance July 5, 1962, BBC television, with Margaret Tynes (Euralie) and Nigel Douglas (Mel).

In the updating of the Orpheus myth, the hero, Mel, a composer of classical music (and a white man), attempts to take his jazz-singing wife, Euralie, who is black, away from the club in which she sings, owned by Pluto.

The work includes nightclub numbers performed by the heroine, accompanied by a real jazz band.
BIBLIOGRAPHY: Arthur Jacobs, "On Television," *Opera* XIII (Sept. 1962), 636–37 [on premiere].

Dark Sonnet, opera in one act by Erik Chisholm; libretto (Eng) by the composer, after Eugene O'Neill's drama *Before Breakfast*. First performance October 20, 1952, Cape Town, South Africa. First U.S. performance July 6, 1954, New York.

Part one of the trilogy *Murder in Three Keys,** with *Black Roses** and *Simoon.**

Dark Waters, melodrama in one act by Ernst Krenek; libretto (Eng and Ger) by the composer. First performance May 2, 1951, Los Angeles, in English, University of Southern California. Performed in German as *Dunkle Wasser*, fall 1954, Darmstadt, Darmstadt International Holiday Courses of New Music; conducted by the composer.

The story is set on a riverboat. Joe, a poor bargeman, tries to better his life by smuggling diamonds for some gangsters, despite the warnings from his wife, Claire, and his son, Phil. A mysterious woman steals one of the diamonds and then turns her charm on Phil and Joe; Joe tells a policeman who has come to the boat that the girl is Joe's niece. When Joe shoots at his son, thinking that he has stolen the diamond, he hits the girl instead, killing her. She turns out to be the daughter of the rich Mendoza, head of the gangsters, and Joe is doomed.

For a detailed description, see Eaton/*OP* II, 264–65.

Major roles: Claire (alto), Joe (bar), Phil (ten), and the girl (sop).

There is no chorus, and the work is scored for chamber orchestra. The score contains dodecaphonic writing.
SCORE: fs, vs (Kassel: Bärenreiter, 1951).
BIBLIOGRAPHY: Horst Koegler, "*Dark Waters* in Darmstadt," *ON* XIX (Nov. 15, 1954), 23.

Darling Corie, folk drama in one act by Elie Siegmeister; libretto (Eng) by Lewis Allan. First performance February 18, 1954, Hempstead, New York, Hofstra College.

The work centers on the experiences of mountain folks.
SCORE: vs (New York: Chappell, [1954]).

Daughter of St. Mark, The, grand opera seria in four acts by Michael Balfe; libretto (Eng) by Alfred Bunn, after J. H. Vernoy de Saint-Georges's *La reine de Chypre*, set by Halévy (1841, Paris). First performance November 27, 1844, London, with Elizabeth Rainforth (Catarina). First U.S. performance June 18, 1855, New York, Park Theatre.

Catarina of Venice, in love with Adolphe, is forced by the evil Mocenigo to wed King Lusignan of Crete. Andrea, Catarina's uncle, reveals that she is the blameless daughter of Mocenigo, who had plotted against the king. The king then graciously gives her up.
SCORE: ms fs, autograph (1844, British Library, MS. Add. 29341–29343).
LIBRETTO: English (London: Johnson, [1844]).

Daughter of the Double Duke of Dingle, The, children's opera in one act by Dennis Arlan; libretto (Eng) by James Billings. First performance June 17, 1978, Katonah, New York, Caramoor Festival.

Daughter of the Forest, The, opera in one act by Arthur Nevin; libretto (Eng) by Randolph Hartley. First performance January 5, 1918, Chicago, Auditorium, with Frances Peralta (the daughter), Forrest Lamont (the lover), and James Goddard (the father); conducted by the composer.

The setting is western Pennsylvania at the time of the Civil War. The father, a trapper, has had to rear his daughter by himself, after the death of her mother. When the daughter becomes pregnant, she chooses to kill herself. Her lover, wanting to follow her in death, takes the father's advice and goes off to die nobly on the battlefield.
SCORE: vs (Cincinnati: J. Church, 1917).

David, opera by Robert P. Skilling; libretto (Eng). First performance (concert) May 3, 1951, New York, Broadway Temple, Washington Heights Methodist Church; conducted by the composer.

David, opera-oratorio in three acts by Edward M. Goldman; libretto (Eng) by the composer, after the Old Testament. Composed 1967.

About the biblical King David.

Other settings include D. Milhaud's *David* (1954, Jerusalem); and the children's opera by B. Burroughs (1968).
SCORE: vs, holograph (1967, photocopy, NYPL).

David and Bathsheba, opera in one act by David Barlow; libretto (Eng) by Ursula Vaughan Williams. First performance October 15, 1969, Newcastle upon Tyne, St. Thomas Church.

A setting of the biblical tale.

David Garrick, opera in three acts by Reginald Somerville; libretto (Eng) by the composer, after the play by Thomas William Robertson. First performance December 9, 1920, London, Covent Garden.

A treatment of the life of the eighteenth-century actor, playwright, and theater manager.

See also *Garrick* by A. Stoessel (1937, New York).
SCORE: vs (London: Ascherberg, Hopwood, & Crew, Ltd., [etc.], 1920).

David Rizzio, opera in three acts, with music by John Braham, Thomas S. Cooke, William Reeve, and Thomas Attwood (one song); libretto (Eng) by Ralph Hamilton; song texts by Charles Dibdin Jr. First performance June 17, 1820, London, Drury Lane Theatre.

A treatment of the story about the confidant of Mary, Queen of Scots.
LIBRETTO: English (London: J. Lowndes, 1820).

David Rizzio, grand opera in two acts by Mary Moore; libretto (Eng-It) by Emanuel Browne. First performance, as *Rizzio*, May 26, 1932, Los Angeles, Shrine Auditorium, with Rodolfo Hoyos (Lord Murray), Rosalie Barker Frye (Lady Argyle), William Wheatley (Lord Darnley), Alphonso Pedroza (Douglas), Lutar Hoobyar (David Rizzio), Dorothy Francis (Mary Stuart), and Frank Ellison (Lord Ruthven); conducted by Alberto Conti. Revived April 2, 1982, Los Angeles, University of Southern California, American Theatre of the Opera.

A setting of the story of the musician David Rizzio, who becomes the confidant of Mary, Queen of Scots. He is murdered through the efforts of Lord Darnley, Mary's husband, in order to isolate her.

Major roles: Lord Murray, chief inquisitor of the court (bar); Lady Argyle, sister of Mary Stuart (mezzo); Lord Darnley, royal consort of Mary Stuart (ten); David Rizzio, secretary of Mary Stuart (ten); Douglas, messenger for the banished lords (bass); Lord Ruthven, leader of the banished lords (bass); and Mary Stuart, queen of Scotland (sop).

Other operatic treatments of Rizzio's life include V. Capecalarp's *David Riccio* (1850); L. Canepa's *Davide Rizzio* (1872); D. Moor's *Rizzio* (1932); and T. Musgrave's *Mary, Queen of Scots** (1977).
SCORE: vs (San Bruno, Calif.: Wesley Webster, 1937; repr. New York: Da Capo Press, 1981).

David's Violin, an arrangement by Mark Slobin of the "opera" (musical drama) *Dovid's fiedele* by Sigmund Mogulesco and others (1897, New York; see below); text (Eng) by Slobin, a translation of Joseph Lateiner's Yiddish original. First performance 1976, Middletown, Connecticut, Wesleyan University; adapted for the stage by Tony Connor.

Set in a small Eastern European town, late nineteenth century, the "plot" concerns David's transition from a street musician, or *klezmer*, to a renowned virtuoso.

Major roles: David; Tevya, a wealthy merchant; Yankele, his son; Eve, his niece; Tabele, David's daughter; Itsele, a wealthy man; Tillie, his daughter; Keyla Beyla, a wealthy widow; and Bertie, her son.

An early interpreter of the title role was Max Rosenthal.

The score includes music by Abraham Goldfaden, Mark M. Warshawsky, Louis Friedsell, Joseph M. Rumshinsky, and Mogulesco. Among the numbers are selections from Goldfaden's opera *Die Zauberin*, and a lament, based on a Warsaw street musician's tune, which was highlighted in the 1936 film *Yidl mitn fidl*.
SCORE: performing edition, based on sheet music from the early twentieth century, ed. Mark Slobin, in *Yiddish Theater in America*, NAMT, vol. 11 (1994).
TEXT: 1914 version of text (printed in Przemyszl, Poland), performing ed., with an English text, by Mark Slobin, in *Yiddish Theater in America*, NAMT, vol. 11 (1994).

Dawn of the West, The, opera in four acts by Emil Enna; libretto (Eng). First performance November 7, 1915, Portland, Oregon.

Dawnpath, chamber opera in one act by Nicola LeFanu; libretto (Eng) by the composer. First performance September 29, 1977, London, Collegiate.

Drawn from two Native American legends, the story deals with the creation of the world.

Scored for two singers, five instrumentalists, and dancer.

Day at Rome, A, musical entertainment in two acts by Thomas Attwood; libretto (Eng) by Charles Smith. First performance October 17, 1798, London, Covent Garden. LIBRETTO: English (London: H. D. Symonds . . . and C. Cawthorne, 1798).

Day Return, opera in one act by Michael Head; libretto (Eng) by Nancy Bush. First performance April 1970, London, Mercury Theatre, Intimate Opera Company.

Dead, The, opera by Murray Boren; libretto (Eng) by Glen Nelson, after James Joyce. First performance October 1993, New York, Hell's Kitchen Opera. SCORE: ms score, holograph (1993, photocopy, NYPL).

Dead Alive, The, or, The Double Funeral, comic opera in two acts by Samuel Arnold; libretto (Eng) by John O'Keeffe. First performance June 16, 1781, London, Little Theatre in the Haymarket. First U.S. performance September 24, 1789, New York; February 19, 1790, Philadelphia, Southwark Theatre.
　　The story is similar to that of Weber's *Abu Hassan* of 1811, but it is set in London, rather than Baghdad. In the O'Keeffe version the young couple, Edward and Caroline, try to stave off their creditors, including Degagee, by having their rich relatives, Miss Hebe Wintertop and Sir Walter Weathercock, think that one of the young people has died, in order for the "surviving" spouse to receive "funeral" money. When Sir Walter asks about the deception: "Are you not asham'd to be alive?" Edward answers, "The truth is, sir, our money was departed, and our credit expir'd," to which Caroline adds, "And we could no longer have liv'd in earnest, had we not died in jest."
　　The original tale comes from the second part of *The Sleeper Awakened or, The Dead Alive* of the *Thousand and One Nights.*
SCORE: vs (New York: Old American Co., 1789).
LIBRETTO: English (Dublin: Booksellers, 1783; New York: Hodge, Allen, and Campbell, 1789; Philadelphia: Thomas H. Palmer, 1822).

De Amore, mini-opera in one act by Elaine Barkin; libretto (Eng, Sp, Provençal) by the composer, after Capellanus's treatise. First performance February 14, 1982, Oberlin, Ohio, Oberlin College Opera Theater; directed by Judith Layng.
　　Scored for four female and four male singer-speakers and ensemble.

Death Fetch, The, or, The Student of Göttingen, operatic romance by Charles Edward Horn; libretto (Eng) by J. B. Buckstone. First performance July 25, 1826, London, Lyceum Theatre. First U.S. performance June 15, 1829, New York, Bowery Theater.

Death in the Family, A, opera in three acts by William Mayer; libretto (Eng) by the composer, after James Agee's novel and Tad Mosel's play *All the Way Home*. First performance March 11, 1983, Minneapolis, Orpheum Theater, with Barbara Brandt (Mary), James E. McKeel Jr. (Jay), Mary Boyd Frederickson (Aunt Hannah), Linda Wilcox (Catherine), Gary Briggle (Andrew), John Andreasen (Ralph), and David Lancaster/Sean Forner (boy Rufus); conducted by Philip Brunelle.
　　The work is set in Knoxville, Tennessee, 1915. Jay Follett has come to see his father, who is ill, but Jay is killed in an auto accident. His family, including his wife, Mary, his four-year-old daughter, Catherine, and, in particular, his six-year-old son, Rufus, are left to deal with the significance of death.
SCORE: vs, holograph (photocopy, NYPL).

BIBLIOGRAPHY: Robert Jacobson, "Reports: U.S.," *ON* XLVII (June 1983), 38 [on premiere]; Andrew Porter, "Musical Events: Let's Make an Opera," *NY* LXII (July 14, 1986), 58, 60 [on June 1986 performance, St. Louis].

Death in Venice, opera in two acts by Benjamin Britten; libretto (Eng) by Myfanwy Piper, after the story by Thomas Mann. First performance June 16, 1973, Aldeburgh Festival, with Peter Pears (Gustav von Aschenbach), John Shirley-Quirk (the seven nemeses), Robert Huguenin (Tadzio), and Peter Leeming (the English Clerk); conducted by Steuart Bedford; produced by Colin Graham; choreographed by Frederick Ashton. First U.S. performance October 18, 1974, New York, Metropolitan Opera, with the same cast and Bryan Pitts (Tadzio) and Frederick Burchinal (the English Clerk).

An aging novelist, Gustav von Aschenbach, searches for inspiration for his work in Venice, where he becomes infatuated with Tadzio, a beautiful Polish boy he sees daily on the beach. Tormented by guilt and unable to confess his love, the novelist ignores the warnings about the plague that has been ravaging the city. Falling ill himself, he dies alone on the beach, as the object of his obsession runs away, unaware of his plight.

For a detailed plot synopsis and musical analysis, see *COH*, ed. Donald Mitchell (1987); and K*IKOB*, 1237–45; K*INKOB*, 138–41.

Major roles: Gustav von Aschenbach, a novelist (ten); Tadzio (dancer); Seven Nemeses: the Traveller, the Elderly Fop, the Old Gondolier, the Hotel Manager, the Hotel Barber, the Leader of the Players, and Dionysus (bar); Voice of Apollo (counterten); and the English Clerk (bar).

The various scenes of the opera are connected by interludes, and dance is an important aspect of the work; Tadzio, his family, and his friends are played by dancers, and there is no verbal communication between them and Aschenbach. The characters who lead Aschenbach toward his demise, the seven nemeses, are sung by one performer, a baritone.

SCORES: fs, vs (London: Faber, 1973).
LIBRETTO: English (London: Faber, 1973).
BIBLIOGRAPHY: Robert Jacobson, "Reports: U.S.," *ON* XXXIX (Dec. 7, 1974), 30 [on U.S. premiere]; George R. Marek, "Mann and Music," *ON* XXXIX (Dec. 14, 1974), 30–33; Eric Walter White, "The Voyage to Venice," *ON* XXXIX (Dec. 14, 1974), 15–19.
DISCOGRAPHY: P. Pears, J. Shirley-Quirk, P. Leeming, English Opera Group, English Chamber Orch.; cond. S. Bedford, London 425669-2 (1990, 2 CDs; reissue of 1974 recording).
VIDEO: Pears, Glyndebourne; cond. G. Jenkins, DEA04V 1 VHS.

Death of a Ghost, The, opera in one act by Jack Gottlieb; libretto (Eng) by the composer, after Oscar Wilde's *The Canterville Ghost*. First performance December 13, 1988, New York, Golden Fleece.

Death of Baldur, The, opera for young people in one act by David Bedford; libretto (Eng) by Terry Bagg and Marian Needham, after the Icelandic myth, "as told by Snorri Sturluson in the 'Prose Edda.'" First performance March 20, 1980, Elgin, Scotland.

Baldur, son of Odin and Fricka, dreams of his imminent death. Although his parents try to prevent it, Baldur is killed by his blind brother, Hodur, tricked by the evil Loki, who has disguised himself as an woman. When Odin sends the god Hermod to beg the goddess Hela to restore Baldur to the living, the plan is thwarted by the further machinations of Loki.

Major roles: Odin, chief god (bar); Fricka, his wife (sop); Baldur, their son (sop/treble); Hodur, his blind brother (bar); Loki, the evil god (sop/treble); Nanna, Baldur's wife (sop); Hela, goddess of the underworld (sop); Vala, the prophetess (sop); and Hermod, a god (bar).
SCORE: vs (London: Universal Edition, 1979).

Death of Captain Faulkner, The, afterpiece pastiche in one act by Samuel Arnold; libretto (Eng) probably by William Pearce. First performance May 6, 1795, London, Covent Garden.
LIBRETTO: English (London: Glindon and Co., 1795).

Death of Cuchulain, The, opera in one act by Jolyon Brettingham Smith; libretto (Eng), translated into German by Ursula Clemens, after the play of the same name by William Butler Yeats. Composed 1973.

The legendary Irish warrior, after many good acts and victories, meets his downfall when his foes devise, through magic, an imaginary foe whom he fights until he is mortally wounded. His widow, Emer, jumps into his grave and dies with him.

Major roles: Cuchulain, Gaelic hero (bar); Eithne Inguba, Cuchulain's young mistress (sop); Aoife, Scottish warrior queen (alto); and Emer, Cuchulain's wife (dancer).
SCORE: vs, English-German (Berlin: Bote & Bock, 1975).

Death of Dido, The, all-sung masque by John Pepusch, "Compos'd to musick, after the Italian manner"; libretto (Eng) by Barton Booth. First performance April 4, 1716, London, Drury Lane Theatre, with Mrs. Barbier as Aeneas.

A setting of the Dido and Aeneas story. Booth's libretto was also set by Arne, as *Dido and Aeneas.**
LIBRETTO: English (London: Bernard Lintott, 1716).

Death of Enkidu: Part I, chamber opera by Harry Somers; libretto (Eng) by M. Kinch, after the *Epic of Gilgamesh.* First performance December 7, 1977, Toronto.

The story concerns Enkidu, first an opponent and then a great friend of Gilgamesh. The gods decree Enkidu's death because he has taken part in the killing of the storm bull of heaven.

Death of King Philip, The, opera in one act by Paul Earls; libretto (Eng) by Romulus Linney, after his play. First performance March 26, 1976, Brookline, Massachusetts, New England Chamber Opera.

The story concerns Philip, Indian king of the Wampanoags in New England, who died in 1676 after leading a revolt known as King Philip's War against the English colonists.

Death of Klinghoffer, The, opera in three acts by John Adams; libretto (Eng) by Alice Goodman. First performance March 19, 1991, Brussels, Théâtre de la Monnaie, with Sanford Sylvan (Leon Klinghoffer), James Maddalena (the Captain), Stephanie Friedman (Omar), and Sheila Nadler (Marilyn Klinghoffer); conducted by Kent Nagano; directed by Peter Sellars; choreographed by Mark Morris; sets by George Tsypin. First U.S. performance September 1991, New York, Brooklyn Academy of Music, with Thomas Young.

A treatment of the 1985 Achille Lauro affair, in which Palestinians hijacked a Greek cruise ship and killed one of the passengers, Leon Klinghoffer, a wheelchair-bound American of Jewish descent, and threw his body overboard.

For a detailed description, see K/*NKOB,* 5–7.

Major roles: the Captain (bar); Omar, a terrorist (mezzo); Leon Klinghoffer (bar); and Marilyn Klinghoffer (alto).

At the premiere the various "sides," the Palestinians, Israelis, and passengers, wore the same costumes, and the roles were interchangeable. The work was widely criticized musically and for its perceived pro-Palestinian, anti-Jewish slant. The daughters of the Klinghoffers refused an invitation to attend the premiere. Wrote Edward Rothstein after the first New York performance (see below): "This ideological posing is morally tawdry, given the horrific events of 'Klinghoffer,' but its libretto is too confused and Mr. Adams's music too limited in range to really evoke the skewed sentiments it strains for."

Among the praised numbers is the moving scene for Marilyn Klinghoffer that closes the opera. When the work was recorded, the prologue, which, in its unflattering portrayal of a Jewish couple at home, was deemed particularly offensive, was deleted. The reviewer described the recorded version as a "latter-day Baroque opera-oratorio" (see below).

SCORES: fs of holograph (New York: Boosey & Hawkes, 1991?); vs (New York: Boosey & Hawkes, 1994).

BIBLIOGRAPHY: Patrick J. Smith, "Coming of Age," *ON* LV (June 1991), 48 [on premiere], and "The Birth of Klinghoffer," *ON* LV (Mar. 16, 1991), 21–22; Andrew Porter, "Musical Events," *NY* LXII (Sept. 30, 1991), 82–84 [on premiere]; Edward Rothstein, "'Klinghoffer' Sinks into Minimal Sea," *NYT* (Sept. 15, 1991), II, 25.

DISCOGRAPHY: Elektra Nonsesuch 79281-2 (1992, 2 CDs), J. Felty, S. Friedman, S. Nadler, T. Young, J. Maddalena, T. Hammons, Lyon Opera Orch. and English Opera Chorus; cond. K. Nagano; rev. K. Robert Schwarz, "*Klinghoffer* Recorded," I.S.A.M. *Newsletter* XXII (Spring 1993), 5.

Death of Lincoln, The, opera by Edwin London; libretto (Eng). Composed 1976. First performance 1988, Cleveland, Cleveland State University.

Death of the Virgin, The, opera in one act by Richard Owen; libretto (Eng) by Michael Straight, after the painting by Caravaggio. First performance (excerpts) January 1981, New York, Opera America Showcase. First complete performance March 31, 1983, New York. Revived March 18, 1987, New York, Lyric Opera.

The Cardinal, patron of the painter Caravaggio, argues with the artist about the content of a painting of the Virgin, which Caravaggio has based on Lena, a barmaid. The artist takes the work with him and refuses the Cardinal's demands to return it, whereupon he is thrown into prison. Lena, trying to win Caravaggio's release, gives back the painting and is cursed by Caravaggio for her actions.

Lena's drowned body is found, and Caravaggio, seeing the bloated body, paints *The Death of the Virgin*, using the body as a model. The fathers of the church for which the painting was made are unable to understand why the artist chose such a model and refuse to accept it. Caravaggio is left recalling Lena's love and inspiration to him.

For a detailed description, see Kornick/*RAO*, 218–20.

Major roles: the Cardinal (ten), Caravaggio (bar), and Lena (sop).

Death of Tintagiles, The, opera by Lawrance Collingwood; libretto (Eng) by Alfred Sutro, a translation of Maurice Maeterlinck's play *La mort de Tintagiles* (1894). First performance (concert) April 16, 1950, London, Sadler's Wells Theatre.

Death of Tintagiles, The, chamber opera in two acts by Gregory Sullivan Isaacs; libretto (Eng) by the composer, after Maeterlinck. First performance Indianola, Indiana, May 4, 1973.

SCORE: ms vs, holograph (1973, photocopy, NYPL).

December and May, operatic farce in two acts by Henry Rowley Bishop; libretto (Eng) by William Dimond, after Barnaby Brittle. First performance May 16, 1818, London. SCORE: ms fs (British Library, Add. MS. 36949).

Decision, The, opera in three acts by Thea Musgrave; libretto (Eng) by Maurice Lindsay, after a television play by Ken Taylor, itself based on a true incident. First performance November 30, 1967, London, Sadler's Wells, with Bryan Drake (John Brown), Gregory Dempsey (Wayson), George MacPherson (Brown's father), Stafford Dean (minister), Margaret Lensky (Kate), and Noreen Berry (her aunt); conducted by Leon Lovett; produced by Colin Graham.

Trapped in a mine accident, John Brown recalls the unhappy events of his life, including the decision of his girlfriend, Kate, to marry Wayson, the foreman of the mine. When Kate, pregnant, gives birth to a stillborn child, Wayson threatens to reveal her shame. She succumbs to a fever and her fear of disclosure. John is censored publicly by the minister.

The scene moves to the present, as Wayson tries to halt the rescue efforts, while John's fellow miners and his father continue their attempts to save him, and he has hallucinations of his father, Kate, her aunt, and the minister. Wayson makes the would-be rescuers leave, but, hearing knocking and giving in to his conscience, he goes against the manager's advice and rescues Brown. The miner dies, but Wayson, having repented, praises the memory of his dead rival.

For a detailed description, see Eaton/*OP* II, 72–73.

Major roles: John Brown (bar), Kate (mezzo), John's father (bass-bar), Wayson (ten), Kate's aunt (alto), the manager of the mine (bass), and the minister (bass).

The work, Musgrave's first full-length opera, contains serial writing.
LIBRETTO: English (London: J. & W. Chester, [1967]).
BIBLIOGRAPHY: review, *HiFi/MA* XVIII (Mar. 1968), 30–31 [on premiere].

Decius and Paulina, masque by John Galliard; libretto (Eng) by Lewis Theobald. First performance March 22, 1718, London, Lincoln's Inn Fields. Performed with the "comic-dramatick opera" *The Lady's Triumph.*
LIBRETTO: English (London: J. Browne, 1718).

Decorator, The, opera in one act by Russell Woollen; libretto (Eng) by P. Getlein. First performance April 1959, Washington, D.C., Catholic University of America; broadcast May 24, 1959, New York, NBC.

Decoy, The, or, The Harlot's Opera, ballad opera; libretto (Eng) by Henry Potter. First performance February 5, 1733, London, Goodman's Fields, with Mr. Lyon (Sir Francis Firebriecks), Mr. Stoppelaer (Mr. Xenadechy), Mr. Huddy (Sir Ralph Reformage), Mr. James (Sir Thomas Pairnails), Mr. Jenkins (Squire Spendthrift), Mr. Hulett (Mrs. Haverly), Mr. Pearce (Mrs. Clarkwell), Mrs. Williamson (Mrs. Frisk), and Miss Sandham (Betty Drostepate).

The setting is a London brothel; the work ends with the ladies of the night being sent to Brideswell Prison.

The "grotesque pantomime entertainment" *The Harlot's Progress, or, The Ridotto al Fresco*, with a text by Theophilus Cibber, was given at the Drury Lane Theatre on March 31, 1733.

LIBRETTO: English, with ballad airs (London, 1733); repr. Rubsamen/*BO*, vol. 3, *Harlots, Rakes, and Bawds* (1974).

Deed of Gift, The, comic opera in three acts; libretto (Eng) by Samuel Woodworth. First performance 1822, Boston, Federal Street Theatre.
LIBRETTO: English (New York: C. N. Baldwin, 1822).

Deep River, "native opera with jazz" in three acts by William Franke Harling; libretto (Eng) by Laurence Stallings. First performance September 18, 1926, Lancaster, Pennsylvania, Fulton Opera House; September 21, 1926, Philadelphia, Shubert Theatre, with Jules Bledsoe (Tizanne), Rose McClendon (Octavie), Bessie Allison (Sara), Luis Alberni (Brusard), Lottice Howell (Mugette), David Sager (Jules), Louisa Ronstadt (Mugette's mother), Antonio Salerno (Hercule), and Charlotte Murray (the Voodoo Queen); conducted by the composer; same cast October 4, 1926, New York, Imperial Theatre.
The first act is set at a café of the Theater Orleans. Brusard is upset that he has lost his mistress, and Jules brings the lovely Mugette to comfort Brusard. In the second act, set in the Place Congo, Mugette, ignoring her mother's warnings, attends a voodoo meeting and requests a voodoo charm to win the love of a Kentuckian, but the Voodoo Queen warns Mugette to give up her quest. She defies the advice and prays to God, which arouses the wrath of the voodoo devil worshipers.
In the last act, set at Hercule's Quadroon Ball, the prophecy is fulfilled.
For a detailed description, see Hipsher/*AO*, 254–56.

Deer Stalker, The, or, The Outlaw's Daughter, Scottish operatic melodrama by Edward J. Loder; libretto (Eng) by Mark Lemon. First performance April 12, 1841, London, English Opera House.
The work is based on Scottish airs.

Deirdre, opera in three acts by Healey Willan; libretto (Eng) by John Coulter, after the ancient Irish tale from the Ulster cycle. First performance (concert) April 20, 1946, CBC radio. First performance (stage) April 2, 1965, Toronto, MacMillan Theatre, Opera School of the Royal Conservatory of Music. Originally called *Deirdre of the Sorrows*.
In the story, which has similarities to the Tristan and Isolde legend, Deirdre is a foundling who has been raised in isolation by Levercham, her nurse, because of the prophecy at her birth that she would cause ruin and bloodshed. As she comes of age, Deirdre refuses to marry King Conochar, her guardian. Instead, she runs away with Naisi, an Ullah prince. The work ends with the deaths of the lovers and the end of King Conochar's kingdom, all of which was prophesied at her birth.
For a detailed description, see Clarke/*HW*, 124–34.
Major roles: Deirdre (sop); King Conochar (bar); Naisi (ten); and Levercham, Deirdre's nurse (alto).
SCORE: vs (Scarborough, Ont.: Berandol Music, 1972).

Deirdre, opera in one act by Leon Stein; libretto (Eng), after W. B. Yeats. First performance May 18, 1957, Chicago, University of Chicago, Chicago Club.

Deirdre in Exile, opera in one act by Fritz Hart; libretto (Eng) by the composer. First performance September 22, 1926, Melbourne, Australia, Playhouse.

Deirdre of the Sorrows, opera in three acts by Fritz Hart; libretto (Eng), after the play by John M. Synge (1910), itself based on the Irish legend. Composed 1916.

Deirdre of the Sorrows, lyric drama in one act by John Becker; libretto (Eng), after Synge. Composed 1945. First performance 1956–1957, Chicago, National Association of Teachers.

Deirdre of the Sorrows, tragic opera in three acts by Karl Rankl; libretto (Eng), after Synge. Composed 1951. Not performed.
  Also set by Hooper Brewster-Jones (comp. 1915–1916, unfin.).

Delicate King, The, miniature farce for television in one act by Louis Gruenberg; libretto (Eng) by the composer, after Alexandre Dumas fils. Composed 1955. Not performed.

Delinquents, The, opera in one act by Martin Kalmanoff; libretto (Eng) by the composer. First performance April 26, 1955, Philadelphia, Comic Opera.
  The story centers on a teenage couple whose only solution to their troubles is to commit suicide.

Della's Gift, drama in a prologue and two acts by Dan Welcher; libretto (Eng) by Paul Woodruff, after O. Henry's story *The Gift of the Magi*. First performance February 2, 1987, Austin, Texas, Texas Opera Theatre.
  In the modernization of O. Henry's tale, the wife is called Della, and the husband Jim. Della sells her beautiful hair in order to buy Jim a gold chain for his watch, and he sells his watch to buy her combs for her tresses. When they open each other's gift, they realize what has happened, but they are consoled by their love and the true meaning of Christmas. They pass the bored and rich Sheba and Solomon, owners of the wig made from Della's hair and the watch that recently belonged to Jim.
  Major roles: Della Young (sop) and Jim Young (bar).
  For a detailed description, see Kornick/*RAO*, 334–35.

Demon, The, or, The Mystic Branch, romantic opera in three acts by Henry Rowley Bishop, an adaptation of G. Meyerbeer's *Robert le diable* (1831, Paris); libretto (Eng) by Edward Fitzball and John B. Buckstone, after Scribe's text. First performance February 20, 1832, London, Drury Lane Theatre.
  The ghost of Robert's mother and Isabella, his beloved, save Robert from the devilish Bertram.
  Lacy's adaptation, *The Fiend Father,** was given a day later. See also *Robert the Devil.*

Demon Lover, The, opera in one act by Ron Nelson; libretto (Eng) by Sidney L. Berger. First performance June 1986, Dallas, Texas, Lyric Arts Festival.
  Lucinda Givens, a pious and distant woman, attends a revival meeting with a friend and is moved by the experience. Simon Price, an alcoholic, is teased by D. K. and Roy, who promise to give Simon alcohol if he can seduce the virtuous Lucinda. Discovering Lucinda's spiritual awakening, Simon seduces her disguised as a demon. When D. K. and Roy demand proof of the seduction, Simon returns to Lucinda, to find that she has fallen in love with him. Unable to cope with the situation, Simon flees. He returns when he has a change of heart and realizes he needs Lucinda, only to discover that she has hanged herself in order to search for him in the next world.
  For more on the plot, see Summers/*OOA*, 227–29.
  Major roles: Simon Price (ten), Lucinda Givens (sop), D. K. (ten), Roy (bar), and Dessie (mezzo).

Composed for the sesquicentennial of Texas.
SCORE: ms vs, holograph (1986, photocopy, NYPL).

Denmark Vesey, opera in three acts by Paul Bowles; libretto (Eng) by Charles-Henri Ford. First performance (act 1) 1937, New York.

The title character (1767–ca. 1822) was a freed black slave who planned a revolt in 1822 that never materialized but caused South Carolina to pass strict laws that limited sharply the education, travel, and occupations of free blacks and slaves alike.

Also set by Thomas Cabaniss (1987, Waterford, Conn.).

Dennis Cleveland, opera in the format of a talk show by Mikel Rouse; libretto (Eng) by the composer. First performance November 1996, New York, the Kitchen, with Rouse.

The title character is the host of a surreal talk show, in which he gets his guests to tell stories that uncover his own memories.

The music incorporates elements of rock opera; the work uses a synthesizer as its accompaniment.
BIBLIOGRAPHY: Jon Pareles, "Surreal Talk-Show Host Roams through an Opera," *NYT* (Nov. 4, 1996), A, 23.
DISCOGRAPHY: M. Rouse, singer/electronics, New World NW 80506-2 (1 CD); rev. William R. Braun, "Recordings," *ON* LXI (Jan. 25, 1997), 45.

Departure, The, opera in one act by Elizabeth Maconchy; libretto (Eng) by Anne Ridler. First performance December 16, 1962, London, Sadler's Wells, New Opera Company, with Catherine Wilson (the woman); conducted by Alan Boustead.

The action centers on a dialogue between a deceased woman and her grieving husband. It opens with a young wife sitting at her dressing table and seeing, outside, her husband attending her funeral; she thereby realizes that she has died. When her spouse returns, she sings to him of their first meeting. He can hear, but cannot see, her, and the two recall scenes of their brief life together, before they part forever.

Part of the trilogy of one-act operas, along with *The Three Strangers** and *The Sofa.**
BIBLIOGRAPHY: Edmund Tracy, "London Diary," *MT* CIV (Feb. 1963), 118 [on stage premiere].

Departure, The, tragic opera in three acts by Allan Davis; libretto (Eng) by the composer. First performance April 24, 1975, Montevallo, Alabama, University of Montevallo; conducted by Peter Paul Fuchs.

The opera takes place in New Orleans at the time of the Mardi Gras and involves elements of voodoo. The young Therese Villiers, feeling trapped in her marriage to Henri, an older man, sends Taffy, her maid, to get help from the Voodooiene to incapacitate Henri and allow Therese to flee with the gambler Toni, her lover. The Voodooiene demands money from Therese for the spell she has cast, but Therese refuses, since the spell has proved ineffective. Therese plans with Toni to drug her husband in order to escape, but the husband overhears her, and when she comes to offer him a glass of drugged wine, he confronts her. When he asks how she could abandon their dead son's grave, Therese screams that Geraud, one of Henri's acquaintances, is the real father, whereupon Henri becomes enraged and strangles Therese. He covers his face with a mask intended for Therese, and when Toni comes to meet his beloved, he assumes the masked figure is Therese. Only when Toni takes Therese's covered body to the cellar, does he discover the truth. The opera ends with Henri's heading for the Mardi Gras parade.

Major roles: Therese Villiers (sop), Toni (ten), Henri (bar), Taffy (mezzo), the Voodooiene (alto), and Geraud (bass-bar).
SCORE: vs, ms (1975, photocopy, NYPL).
BIBLIOGRAPHY: Allan Davis, "The Departure: A Composer's Search for a Lyric Theatre," *OJ* VIII/3 (1975), 22–28.

De Profundis, monodrama for baritone, percussion, and two string quartets by Larry Sitsky; text (Eng) by Gwen Harwood, after Oscar Wilde. First performance (concert) October 1, 1982, Canberra, School of Music. First stage performance April 8, 1987, Sydney, Australia, University of New South Wales.

Derby Day, comic opera in three acts by Albert Reynolds; libretto (Eng) by Alan Patrick Herbert. First performance February 24, 1932, Hammersmith, London, Lyric Theatre.
   The work is scored for nine characters, mixed chorus, and chamber orchestra.
SCORE: vs (London: Elkin, [1932]).
LIBRETTO: English (London: Methuen & Co. [1931]).

Deseret, or, A Saint's Afflictions, comic opera in three acts by Dudley Buck; libretto (Eng) by William Augustus Croffut. First performance October 11, 1880, New York, Fourteenth Street Theater.
   A lighthearted treatment of Brigham Young and his many wives. See next entry for a serious setting.
SCORE: vs (New York: Wm. Pond & Co., 1880).

Deseret, opera in three acts by Leonard Kastle; libretto (Eng) by Anne Howard Bailey. First performance January 1, 1961, New York television, with Judith Raskin (Ann Louisa), Mac Morgan (Chauncey Brice), Marjory McClung (Eliza Brice), Rosemary Kuhlmann (Sarah), Kenneth Smith (Brigham Young), and John Alexander (Captain James Dee); conducted by Peter Herman Adler; produced by Kirk Browning.
   The young Ann Louisa Brice has been promised by her parents as the twenty-fifth wife of Brigham Young. Although she knows the prophet is old, she is honored that he has chosen her. Her acceptance is shaken when she meets the young and lively Captain James Dee. Although she is attracted to him, she is determined to go through with her wedding to the prophet. When Dee interrupts a celebration before the wedding and kisses Ann passionately, the prophet realizes that she truly loves Dee. He agrees to let the young couple be the messenger beyond Deseret, the Mormon empire, and he returns to his first wife, Sarah.
   For a detailed description, see Eaton/*OP* I, 48–49.
   Major roles: Ann Louisa Brice (sop); Brigham Young (bar/bass-bar); Captain James Dee (ten); Eliza Brice, Ann's mother (sop); Chauncey Brice, her father (bar); and Sarah (mezzo/alto).
LIBRETTO: English (New York, 1959; repr. *MA* LXXX [Dec. 1960], 67–77).

Deserted Village, The, opera in three acts by John Glover; libretto (Eng) by Edmund Falconer, after Oliver Goldsmith's poem (1770). First performance 1880, London.
   In the work, set in a village, Auburn, in the eighteenth century, Nora, falls in love with Patrick, a poor local boy. He turns out to be the long-lost son of Squire Thornhill.
SCORE: vs (London: Duncan Davidson, [1880?]).

Deserter, The, comic opera in two acts by Charles Dibdin, an adaptation of Monsigny's *Le déserteur* (Paris, 1769), with two numbers by Philidor; libretto (Eng), after Sedaine.

First performance November 2, 1773, London, Drury Lane Theatre, with Mrs. Smith (Louisa), Mrs. Wrighten (Jenny), Mr. Vernon (Henry), Mrs. Love (Margaret), and Mr. Dibdin (Simkin). First U.S. performance June 8, 1787, New York, arranged by Victor Pelissier and Benjamin Carr.

The setting is a village near a French army camp. The plot involves a trick played on the soldier Henry by his former girlfriend, Jenny. Jenny circulates the story that Henry's intended, Louisa, has wed Simkin, a boor. When Henry is heard complaining about "desertion" by soldiers sent out to track down a real deserter, he is arrested and put into prison. He is rescued in the end by the faithful Louisa.

For a detailed description, see Fiske/*ETM,* 370.

SCORE: vs (London: Harrison, Cluse, [1800?]).

LIBRETTO: English (London: T. Becket, 1773; New York: Samuel Campbell, 1787).

Desert Flower, The, opera in three acts by Vincent Wallace; libretto (Eng) by Augustus Glossop Harris and Thomas John Williams, after *Jaguarita l'Indienne* by Vernoy de Saint-Georges and de Leuven, set by F. Halévy (1855, Paris). First performance October 12, 1863, London, Covent Garden. First U.S. performance January 13, 1868, New York, Academy of Music.

Desert of Roses, opera in two acts by Robert Moran; libretto (Eng) by Michael John LaChiusa. First performance February 20, 1992, Houston, Houston Grand Opera, with Stella Zambalis (the Woman), Heidi Jones (Sister One), Patricia Johnson (Sister Two), Eric Perkins (the Brother), Jayne West (the Girl), Kelly Anderson (the Father), and John Stephens (the Monster); conducted by John DeMain.

The story is a version of the tale of Beauty and the Beast. Here the Beast is called the Monster and is a Union soldier who enjoys killing in the extreme. He is imprisoned in a desert of roses, and he is redeemed through the love of the Girl in the part of Beauty.

The seven roles of this semiminimalist work include the Monster (bass-bar), the Girl (sop), the narrator (sop), Sister One (sop), Sister Two (sop), the Brother (ten), and the Father (bass-bar).

BIBLIOGRAPHY: William Albright, "Houston," *ON* LVII (July 1992), 41 [on premiere]; K. Robert Schwarz, "New York City," *ON* LIX (July 1994), 45–46 [on New York premiere]; Edward Rothstein, "An Avant-Garde Composer Produces a Sentimental Beauty and the Beast," *NYT* (Feb. 21, 1992), C, 3 [on premiere].

Désirée, comic opera in two acts by John Philip Sousa; libretto by Edward M. Taber, after John Maddison Morton's *Our Wife*. First performance May 1, 1884, Washington, D.C.

The work is set in France during the era of Richelieu.

SCORE: vs (Boston: White, Smith, 1882); restored, elaborated, and ed. Jerrold Fisher and William Martin (New York: Lyric Theatre, 1991).

DISCOGRAPHY: Pocono Pops; cond. Fisher, Amdec AMTC 101 (1993 live perf., 1 CD).

Desire under the Elms, opera in three acts by Edward Thomas; libretto (Eng) by Joseph Masteroff, after Eugene O'Neill's play (1924). First performance August 8, 1978, New London, Connecticut; revised version January 10, 1989, New York, City Center, with Judy Kaye (Abbie), Nicholas Solomon (Ephraim), and James Schwisow (Eben); conducted by Leigh Gibbs Gore.

All members of the Cabot family want to own the successful Cabot farm, which belonged to the mother of Eben Cabot. Meanwhile Eben's father, Ephraim, has married the scheming Abbie, who plans to get a claim on the farm by having a child with Ephraim.

She also seduces Eben, who is eager to get even with his father. When the child is born, Ephraim, knowing of Eben's affair, threatens to send his son away when the child is old enough to work on the farm. Abbie, afraid of losing Eben, kills the child and then admits it was Eden's. Eden, still drawn to Abbie, accepts partial blame for the baby's death and is arrested along with Abbie. The older Cabot is left alone with the farm.

Major roles: Eben Cabot (ten), Abbie (sop), and Ephraim Cabot (bass-bar).

For a detailed description, see Kornick/*RAO*, 311–13.

BIBLIOGRAPHY: Allan Kozinn, "Premiere of 'Desire,'" *NYT* (Jan. 13, 1989), C, 3.

Devil and Daniel Webster, The, opera in one act by Douglas Moore; libretto (Eng) by Stephen Vincent Benét, after his short story (1937). First performance May 18, 1939, New York, Martin Beck Theater, with John Gurney (Jabez Stone), Nancy McCord (Mary Stone), Lansing Hatfield (Daniel Webster), George Rasely (Mr. Scratch); conducted by Fritz Reiner; directed by John Houseman.

The opera is set in New Hampshire. It opens with the marriage of Jabez and Mary Stone. Mary comes from a very poor family, but Jabez has always, to everyone's surprise, done very well. The great Daniel Webster appears, as does another guest, a lawyer, Scratch, from Boston; he has a black collecting box under his arm, and his appearance horrifies Jabez. The neighbors now understand that Jabez Stone has sold his soul to the Devil and flee from his presence. Jabez explains to Mary, who has remained, why he made such a bargain. Daniel, who has heard everything, agrees to help the couple.

Webster challenges Scratch, the Devil, to a trial, whereupon Scratch convenes a jury of famed American traitors and renegades, and a severe judge, the one who presided at the Salem witch trials. After many difficulties Webster, through his oratorical gifts, is able to turn the tide and save Jabez. The Devil is driven out, and the people rejoice.

For a detailed description, see Eaton/*OP* I, 176–77.

Major roles: Jabez Stone (bass), Mary Stone (mezzo/sop); Daniel Webster (bar), and Mr. Scratch (ten).

SCORE: vs (New York: Boosey & Hawkes, [1943]).

LIBRETTO: English (New York and Toronto: Farrar & Rinehart [1939]).

BIBLIOGRAPHY: Howard Taubman, review, *NYT* (Apr. 6, 1959), 33 [on revival].

DISCOGRAPHY: Desto DST-6450.

Devil of a Duke, The, or, Trapolin's Vagaries, "farcical ballad opera"; libretto (Eng) by Robert Drury, after Nahum Tate's pantomime *A Duke and No Duke* (1684). First performance August 17, 1732, London, Drury Lane Theatre, with Mr. Roberts (Lavinio), Mr. Stopelaer (Brunetto), Mr. Paget (Barberino), Mr. Winstone (Alberto), Mr. Cross (Mago), Mr. Bridgewater (Trapolin), Miss Mears (Isabella), Miss Atherton (Prudentia), and Miss Raftor (Flametta).

A magician turns Trapolin, a servant, into the double of the real Duke of Florence. Confusion abounds when the real Duke returns.

LIBRETTOS: English, with music (London: Charles Corbett . . . and John Torbuck, 1732, 1733); repr. Rubsamen/*BO*, vols. 10 and 25 (1974).

Devil of a Lover, The, musical farce in two acts by Thomas Attwood; libretto (Eng) by George Moubray. First performance March 17, 1798, London, Covent Garden.

LIBRETTO: ms, English (Huntington Library, San Marino, Calif., Larpent 1199).

Devil's Bridge, The, operatic romance in three acts by Charles Horn, John Braham, and Domenico Corri; libretto (Eng) by Samuel J. Arnold. First performance May 6,

1812, London, Lyceum Theatre, Drury Lane Company. First U.S. performance July 4, 1815, New York.
LIBRETTO: English (New York: J. Longworth, 1817).

Devil's Brother, The, opera by George Alexander Lee, an adaptation of Auber's *Fra Diavolo* (1830, Paris); anonymous text (Eng). First performance February 1, 1831, London, Drury Lane; performed with a translation by Michael Rophino Lacy as *Fra Diavolo.**
SCORES: vs, "Daylight Love Is Pass'd Away" (New York: Dubios & Stodart, [ca. 1830]); "How Gaily Rows the Gondolier" (Boston: C. Bradlee, [183?]).

Devil's Disciple, The, opera in two acts by Joyce Barthelson; libretto (Eng) by the composer, after George Bernard Shaw. First performance November 4, 1977, White Plains, New York, Highlands School.

Devil's Elixir, The, or, The Shadowless Man, musical romance in two acts by George Rodwell; libretto (Eng) by Edward Fitzball, after E. T. A. Hoffmann's novel *Die Elixiere des Teufels* (1815). First performance April 20, 1829, London, Covent Garden.
SCORE: vs (London: Goulding and D'Almaine, 1829).
LIBRETTO: English (London: J. Cumberland, [1829]).

Devil's in It, The, comic opera in a prologue and three acts by Michael Balfe; libretto (Eng) by Alfred Bunn, after Charles Coffey's *The Devil to Pay* (see below). First performance July 26, 1852, London, Covent Garden. First U.S. performance December 17, 1852, New York, Park Theatre.
LIBRETTO: English (London: Harrison, Cluse, [1800?]).

Devil's Opera, The, opera in two acts by George Alexander Macfarren; libretto (Eng) by George Macfarren Sr. First performance August 13, 1838, London, Lyceum.
    The work is set in Venice, and local color is reflected in the use of a Venetian dance.
    See Biddlecombe/*EO*, 153, for a discussion of the music.
    Its musical highlights include "Queen of Cities" and the ballad "O Blame Me Not."
LIBRETTO: English (London: Chapman and Hall, [1838?]).

Devil Take Her, The, opera in one act by Arthur Benjamin; libretto (Eng) by Alan Collard and John B. Gordon; lyrics by Cedric Cliffe. First performance December 11, 1931, London, Royal College of Music. First U.S. performance February 13, 1941, New York, Juilliard School.
    The Poet is married to a beautiful woman who has been unable to speak since she was born. When a famous surgeon arrives, the Poet has him operate on the wife, who begins to talk and changes into a monster. In desperation, the Poet screams, "The Devil take her!" But the Prince of Darkness is no match for her either, and he and the Poet escape by means of a trap door. The newly talkative wife closes the opera with the moral "Be rather dumb than a scold like me."
    For a detailed description, see Eaton/*OP* I, 177–78.
    Major roles: the wife (mezzo), the Poet (ten), the Doctor (bass), and the Devil (bass).
SCORE: vs (London and New York: Boosey & Co., 1932).

Devil to Pay, The, or, The Wives Metamorphos'd, ballad opera in three acts, consisting of sixteen songs (one attributed to Seedo); text by Charles Coffey, with John Mottley, after the farce *Devil of a Wife, or A Comical Transformation* (1686) by Thomas Jevon, possibly with Thomas Shadwell. First performance August 6, 1731, London,

Drury Lane Theatre, with Mrs. Clive (Nell Jobson), Mr. Stopelaer (Sir John Loverule), Mr. Harper (Jobson), and Mrs. Mills (Lady Loverule). Revived in a one-act version, adapted by Theopholus Cibber, December 1, 1731, London, Goodman's Fields Theatre. First U.S. performance March 16, 1736, Charleston, South Carolina. The sequel was *The Merry Cobbler** (1735, London).

Two couples are the center of the action. Nell Jobson is married to a jealous village cobbler, while Sir John Loverule is constantly henpecked by his wife. When Lady Loverule refuses hospitality to a mysterious doctor, he is told to try to get accommodations at the cobbler's house, but the cobbler refuses, fearing that the stranger will try to seduce Nell. Angered, the stranger causes Nell and Lady Loverule to change places, and Jobson beats the woman he thinks to be his wife, while Sir John showers Nell with kindness.

Major roles: Sir John Loverule, "an honest country gentleman"; doctor; Lady Loverule, Sir John's wife; Jobson, "a psalm-singing cobler"; and Nell, Jobson's wife.

Other settings of the original are J. C. Standfuss's *Der Teufel ist los, oder Die verwandelten Weiber* (1752, Leipzig); J. A. Hiller's adaptation of the Standfuss version, as *Der Teufel ist los* (1766, Leipzig); and M. Balfe's *The Devil's in It** (1852, London). LIBRETTO: English (London: J. Watts, 1731); repr. Rubsamen/*BO*, vol. 10 (1974).

Devil upon Two Sticks, The, or, The Country Beau, ballad opera; libretto (Eng) by Charles Coffey. First performance April 16, 1729, London, Drury Lane Theatre.

Diable amoureux, Le, opera in one act by Robert Xavier Rodríguez; libretto (Eng) by the composer and Frans Boerlage, after Jacques Cazotte's story (1776). First performance (television) April 11, 1979, Dallas, KERA-TV.

The setting is a castle in Provence in the fourteenth century. Baron des Rouvières hosts an elegant banquet at his castle and announces the engagement of his son, Rogier, to Béatrice. As the guests begin to dance, the Devil appears in the guise of the beautiful Damietta and casts a spell that causes Rogier to fall in love with Damietta and the Baron and Béatrice to be drawn to each other. The Devil is eventually unmasked, and the Baron, knowing he must relinquish any feelings for Béatrice, blesses the betrothal of Béatrice and Rogier.

For a description, see Summers/*OOA*, 253–54.

Major roles: Baron des Rouvières (bass-bar), Rogier (ten), Béatrice (sop), and the Devil (mezzo).

SCORE: ms vs, excerpts (1977, signed photocopy, NYPL).

Diadesté, or, The Veiled Lady, opéra bouffe in two acts by Michael Balfe; libretto (Eng) by Edward Fitzball, after L. Pillet and Villain de St. Hilaire's text for F. Godefroid's opera *La diadesté, ou, La gageure arabe* (1836, Paris). First performance May 17, 1838, London, with Emma Romer, Fanny Healy, Miss Poole, Mr. Guibilei, John Templeton, and Henry Phillips.

The composer's first English comic opera.

SCORE: fs ms (1838, British Library, Add. MS 29333).

LIBRETTO: ms, ca. 1852, English (NYPL).

Dialogue between Jupiter and Cupid, A. See **The Dissolute Punished**.

Dialogues, Christmas opera in five scenes by Jon Bauman; libretto (Eng) by Sister Maura, after Psalm 51. First performance December 1987, Frostburg, Maryland, Frostburg State University.

Diamond Cut Diamond, or, Venetian Revels, comic opera in two acts by James Hook; libretto (Eng) by James Hook Jr. First performance May 23, 1797, London, Covent Garden.

Diarmid, opera in four acts by Hamish MacCunn; libretto (Eng) by the Duke of Argyll, after "heroic Celtic legends." First performance October 23, 1897, London, Covent Garden; conducted by the composer.

The title character, favored by the goddess Freya and invulnerable except for his heel (as with Achilles), is drawn to Grania, the young wife of King Fionn. When Diarmid is wounded by a thistle in the heel, Fionn lets him die rather than give him a healing magic potion.

Among the numbers are the act-one aria "Heavy Thy Burden, Diarmid," sung by Eila, the king's daughter, whose love Diarmid rejects.

LIBRETTO: English, in *Passages from the Past* (London: Hutchinson and Co., 1907).
BIBLIOGRAPHY: review, "Royal Carl Rosa Opera Company," *The Times* (London) (Oct. 25, 1897), 8 [on premiere].

Diary of a Madman, The, opera in one act by Humphrey Searle; libretto (Eng) by the composer, after Gogol's story (1835). First performance October 3, 1958, Berlin, as *Das Tagebuch eines Irrenden*. First British performance April 26, 1960, London, New Opera Company (at Sadler's Wells), with Alexander Young (Poprichin). First U.S. performance August 17, 1967, Aspen, Colorado, Aspen Music School, with Grayson Hirst (Poprichin); conducted by Walter Susskind.

The story follows the mental collapse of a clerk, Poprichin, who falls in love with Sophie, the daughter of his boss.

Major roles: Aksenti Ivanov Poprichin, the madman (ten); Sophie (sop); and department chief/director of an insane asylum (bar).

The serial work is scored for electronic music and orchestra.
BIBLIOGRAPHY: review, "Aspen Produces a Searle Opera," *NYT* (Aug. 19, 1967), 16 [on U.S. premiere]; John Warrack, review, *Opera* XI (June 1960), 442–44 [on British premiere].

Diary of an African-American, staged musical entertainment by Hannibal Peterson; text (Eng) by the composer. First performance (concert) October 31, 1991, New York, Abyssinian Baptist Church. First stage performance March 10, 1994, St. Paul, World Theatre, Minnesota Opera and Music-Theatre Group, with Peterson, Ann Sinclair, Byron Utley, and Brandon Martin; bassist Andy McCloud; drummer Cecil Brooks II; pianist-music director Rahn Burton.

The autobiographical story tells of an ailing trumpeter who arrives in Kenya, land of his ancestors, and receives a kalimba from a little boy. The instrument helps him to recover physically and spiritually, and he gives it to his own son when he returns to America.

The music contains elements of jazz, gospel, and blues.
BIBLIOGRAPHY: Michael Anthony, "St. Paul," *ON* LVIII (June 1994), 48 [on stage premiere]; Mike Joyce, review, *Washington Post* (July 3, 1995), C, 7.

Dice of Death, The, romantic opera in three acts by Edward Loder; libretto (Eng) by John Oxenford. First performance September 14, 1835, London, English Opera House.

Dido, arrangement by Charles Edward Horn of music by Rossini; libretto (Eng). First performance April 9, 1829, New York, Park Theatre.

Dido, Queen of Carthage, all-sung "serious" opera in three acts by Stephen Storace; libretto (Eng) by Prince Hoare, after Metastasio's *Didone abbandonata.* First performance May 23, 1792, London, King's Theatre in the Haymarket.

The work treats the story of Dido being abandoned by Aeneas. It follows opera seria conventions, with arias linked by recitative.

LIBRETTO: English, with the masque *Neptune's Prophecy* (London: n.p., 1792).

Dido and Aeneas, opera in a prologue and three acts by Henry Purcell; text (Eng) by Nahum Tate, after Book 4 of Virgil's *Aeneid* (19 B.C.). First known performance before December 1689, London, Josias Priest's School for Young Gentlewomen; first public performances about February 1700, February 9, 1704, and April 19, 1704, London, Lincoln's Inn Fields, as an interlude of the masque *The Loves of Dido and Aeneas.* First U.S. performance February 10, 1923, New York, Plaza Hotel.

The work centers on the tale of Queen Dido of Carthage, who falls in love with the Trojan hero Aeneas, who has escaped from Troy. The Witches, in their plan to bring about the ruin of Carthage and Dido, convince Aeneas that he must fulfill his duty and return to Italy. Deserted by Aeneas, Dido sings the famed and eloquent lament "When I Am Laid in Earth," constructed on a ground bass of five bars, ending with the sorrowful "Remember me"; she then expires.

For a detailed plot description, see K/*NKOB,* 610–12.

Major roles: Dido (sop); Aeneas (ten); Belinda, Dido's confidante (sop); sorceress (bar/mezzo); and false Mercury (alto).

SCORES: fs ed. G. A. Macfarren (London: Musical Antiquarian Society, 1841), ed. W. H. Cummings, III, Collected Edition (1889); vs ed. E. F. Rimbault (1872); vs, rev. ed. Ellen T. Harris (Oxford and New York: Oxford University Press, 1987).

BIBLIOGRAPHY: Ellen T. Harris, Henry Purcell's 'Dido and Aeneas (Oxford, 1987); the same, "Recitative and Aria in *Dido and Aeneas,*" in *Studies in the History of Music,* vol. 2 (New York: Broude, 1988).

DISCOGRAPHY: Yakar, Schmidt, Scharinger, Schoenberg Chorus, Concentus Musicus; cond. Harnoncourt, Teldec 6-42919; rev. John W. Freeman, "Records," *ON* XVLVIII (Apr. 14, 1984), 45; Troyanos, Palmer, Kern, Stilwell, Langridge, English Chamber Choir and Orch.; cond. Leppard, RCA ARL1-3021; Baker, Burrowes, Reynolds, Pears, Tear, London Opera Chorus, Aldeburgh Festival Strings; cond. Bedford, London OSA-1170; both rev. John W. Freeman, "Records," *ON* XLIII (Mar. 31, 1979), 40.

Dido and Aeneas, masque by Thomas Arne; libretto (Eng) by Barton Booth. First performance January 12, 1734, London.

Dido and Aeneas, comic opera by James Hook; libretto (Eng) possibly by Thomas Bridges. First performance July 24, 1771, London, Theatre in the Haymarket.

LIBRETTO: English (London: T. Davies, 1771).

Dido and Aeneas, opera in one act by Thomas Beveridge; libretto (Eng). First performance February 14, 1958, Boston, Fogg Art Museum.

The numerous operatic settings of the story include J. Pepusch's *The Death of Dido** (1716, London); and H. Berlioz's *Les Troyens à Carthage* (1863, Paris).

Diet, The, opera buffa in one act by Elmer Olenick; libretto (Eng) by Carl Gersuny and the composer. First performance March 22, 1984, New York, Golden Fleece Ltd.

The setting is a small town in America, the present. The very overweight Bertha is supposed to be a bridesmaid for Polly's upcoming wedding but cannot fit into her outfit. Bertha's attempts to lose weight by dieting are unsuccessful. As a last resort she visits a clinic, where she gets stuck in a steam cabinet. The repairman, Ralph, falls in love with Bertha and asks her to marry him. Her father finally agrees to the match. Since she is unable to fit into a wedding dress, Bertha wears an oversize bath towel instead for the ceremony.

For a detailed plot description, see Summers/*OOA*, 233–34.

Roles: Bertha (sop), Polly (alto), Ralph (ten), and the father (bar).

SCORE: ms, holograph (1979, photocopy, NYPL).

Different Fields, opera in one act by Mike Reid, orchestrated by Michael Ching; libretto (Eng) by Sarah Schlesinger. First performance February 7, 1996, New York, New Victory Theater, with Joseph Mahowald (Aaron), Amir Jamal Williams (Casey), Theresa Hamm-Smith (Casey's mother), Judith Engel (team owner), and William Walker (Bowen); conducted by Joshua Rosenblum.

The story concerns the football hero Aaron James, who has trouble dealing with the fame and money that his talents have brought him. He in turn takes a young, fatherless boy, Casey, under his wing.

When Aaron throws a play-off game because he cannot pay off his gambling debts, he admits his misdeed, leaves his team, and seeks the road to redemption.

Among the musical highlights is Aaron's "Bright November Morning."

BIBLIOGRAPHY: Edward Lewine, "The Opera That Is Football: Reid's Careers Meet on Broadway," *NYT* (Feb. 5, 1996), C, 3; Anthony Tommasini, "From Pop to an Opera on Football," *NYT* (Feb. 10, 1996), 15 [on premiere].

Dilettante, Il, burletta by James Hook; libretto (Eng). First performance August 22, 1772, London, Marylebone Gardens, with Charles Bannister.

LIBRETTO: English (London: n.p., 1772).

Dinner Engagement, A, opera in one act by Lennox Berkeley; libretto (Eng) by Paul Dehn. First performance June 17, 1954, Aldeburgh, Jubilee Hall, with Frederick Sharp (Earl of Dunmow), Emelie Hooke (Countess of Dunmow), April Cantelo (Susan), Flora Nielsen (Grand Duchess of Monteblanco), and Alexander Young (Prince Philippe); conducted by Vilem Tausky; produced by William Chappell; designed by Peter Snow. First U.S. performance 1958, Seattle, University of Washington.

An English noble, the Earl of Dunmow, and his wife, the Countess, who have fallen on hard times, have invited the well-to-do Grand Duchess and her son, Philippe, to dinner, in the hope that the son will fall in love with the couple's daughter, Susan. Things go wrong from the start, when the guests enter the dwelling through the back door. Philippe, however, is smitten by Susan and proposes marriage that very evening.

Major roles: Earl of Dunmow (bar), the Countess (sop), Mrs. Kneebone, their servant (alto), Grand Duchess of Monteblanco (alto), Philippe (ten), and Susan (sop).

The work includes a mock French folk song sung by Philippe.

SCORE: vs (London: Chester, [1955]).

BIBLIOGRAPHY: review, "Aldeburgh Festival," *The Times* (London) (June 18, 1954), 2 [on premiere].

Dioclesian (The Prophetess, or, The History of Dioclesian), "an English Opera" by Henry Purcell; libretto (Eng) by Thomas Betterton, after *The Prophetess* (1622) by John Fletcher and Philip Massinger. First performance June 1690, London, Dorset Garden Theatre, with Mr. Lewis (Diocles), Mr. Hull (Charinus), Mr. Whitfield (Maximinian), Mr. Clarke (Cosroe), Mrs. Bates (Delphia), Mrs. S. Kemble (Drusilla), and Mrs. Inchbald (Aurelia). First U.S. performance, as *Dioclesian* (concert), April 15, 1936, New York, Washington Square College.

The prophetess of the title is Delphia, who predicts that the Roman soldier Diocles will become the emperor. Her prediction comes true when Diocles slays Aper, the captain of the guards, who killed Numerianus, the late emperor. Diocles is declared the ruler by the Roman soldiers and renames himself Dioclesian, but he runs into trouble when he abandons the homely Drusilla, niece of Delphia, for the beautiful Aurelia; in revenge Delphia makes Aurelia fall in love with Maximinian, Diocles' nephew. When Diocles defeats the invading Persians, he restores their king, Cosroe, gives control of the empire to Maximinian, and promises to wed Drusilla. The work concludes with a final, self-contained masque, to celebrate Diocles' retirement. It has as its centerpiece the taming of the irascible Jove by Cupid.

Major roles: Charinus, Emperor of Rome; Diocles, afterward Dioclesian, private soldier, then Emperor; Maximinian, nephew to Diocles, then Emperor; Cosroe, King of Persia; Aper, murderer of Numerianus, the late emperor; Aurelia, sister of Charinus; Delphia, the Prophetess; Drusilla, Delphia's niece.

SCORES: fs, *The Works of Henry Purcell*, vol. 9, ed. J. Frederick Bridge and John Pointer, rev. Margaret Laurie (Borough Green, Sevenoaks, Kent: Novello, 1961, repr. 1979); vs ed. Margaret Laurie (Borough Green, Sevenoaks, Kent: Novello, 1983).

LIBRETTO: English, as *The Prophetess* (London: John Carr, for the author, 1691).

Dione, pastoral tragedy in five acts by Frederick Lampe; libretto (Eng), after John Gay's play (1720). First performance February 23, 1733, London, Little Theatre in the Haymarket, with Cecilia Young (Dione).

In Gay's setting, Dione is in love with Evander, who, unfortunately for her, loves Parthenia. Dione dresses herself as a boy to be near Evander, and when Evander thinks that Dione, in her disguise, is threatening Parthenia, he stabs Dione. In remorse Evander kills himself.

The music and libretto are lost.

TEXT: English, in *Gay, John. The Works of Mr. John Gay: Containing Poems on Several Occasions,* vol. 2 (Dublin: James Potts, 1770).

Dirce, or, The Fatal Urn, serious recitative drama by Charles Horne; libretto (Eng), after Metastasio's *Demofoonte.* First performance June 2, 1821, London, Drury Lane Theatre.

The story concerns Demophoon, the King of Cheronnesus, who selects Dirce for the annual sacrifice of a virgin to the gods, not knowing that she is secretly wed to his son, Timante.

One number from the opera is still extant.

Metastasio's text was set more than seventy times.

Directions, The, chamber opera in one act by Michael Torke; libretto (Eng). First performance August 6, 1986, Iraklion, Crete, Summer 86 Festival; conducted by Theodore Antoniou.

The work is scored for soprano, mezzo, tenor, and chorus.

Director, The, opera in one act by Felix Werder; libretto (Eng) by the composer. First performance June 7, 1980, Melbourne, Australia, University of Melbourne.

For bass voice (Director), soprano voice (Psalmist), flute, oboe, clarinet, horn, percussion, bass, and piano.
SCORE: facsimile score (Sydney, Australia: the Australian Music Centre, 1980).

Disappointed Impresario, The. See **The Unmusical Impresario.**

Disappointment, The, ballad opera in one act, "alter'd from a farce, after the manner of the BEGGAR'S OPERA"; libretto (Eng) by John Randall. First performance 1732, London, Theatre in the Haymarket, with Mr. Jones (Don Pedro), Mr. Warwell (F. Berrado), Mr. Giles (Teague), Mrs. Martin (Lady Pedro), and Mrs. Palms (Clara).
LIBRETTO: English (London: S. Slow, 1732).

Disappointment, The, or, The Force of Credulity, ballad opera, "a new American comic-opera of two acts"; libretto (Eng) by Andrew Barton. The planned premiere of April 20, 1767, in Philadelphia, was canceled. First performance, as *Treasure Hunt*, March 1937, Brooklyn, New York, Majestic Theatre. Score reconstructed by Samuel Adler (see vs, below), with the first performance April 7, 1976, Washington, D.C.
    The story, set in pre-Revolutionary Philadelphia, involves three practical jokers, Hum, Quadrant, and Parchment, who play a joke on Raccoon, taking into account his greedy nature. They dupe him into thinking a hidden chest contains a treasure. To their dismay, he discovers the box, removes the valuables inside, and replaces them with stones. In a subplot, Lucy, niece of Washball, one of Raccoon's friends, refuses her uncle's request to marry a suitor he has selected for her and elopes with the man she really loves. The opera ends with the uncle's accepting the inevitable.
    Major roles: the men: Hum, Parchment, Quadrant, Rattletrap, "a supposed conjurer," and Raccoon, "an old debauchee," Washball, "an avaritious old Barber," and Meanwell, a gentleman, in love with Washball's niece; the women: Moll Plackett, "a woman of the town, in keeping by Raccoon," and Miss Lucy, Washball's niece, in love with Meanwell.
    For a detailed description, see Sonneck/*SIMG*, 433–50 and Virga/*AO*, 17–23..
    The score consists of popular airs, including "Yankee Doodle," which Raccoon sings when he promises to take care of his beloved Moll Plackett after he finds the treasure.
    This was the first U.S. opera libretto to be printed (1767).
SCORE: vs, ed. Jerald C. Graue and Judith Layng, musical accompaniments and new overture by Samuel Adler, *Recent Researches in American Music*, vols. 3–4 (Madison, Wisc.: A-R Editions, 1976); critical ed. David Mays (Gainesville: University Presses of Florida, 1976).
LIBRETTO: English (New York: Samuel Taylor, 1767); three acts (Philadelphia: Francis Shallus, 1796); repr. of 1767 ed. Rubsamen/*BO*, vol. 28, *American Ballad Opera* (1974).
BIBLIOGRAPHY: John Graye, *NYT* (Sept. 22, 1976), 28 [on reconstruction]; *NYT* (Oct. 17, 1976), 19 [on performance].

Dismissed with Prejudice, opera in one act by Richard Owen; libretto (Eng) by the composer. Composed 1956.

Dissipation of Purely Sound, The, radiophonic opera for tape by Norma Beecroft. First performance 1988, Toronto, CKLN Radio.

Dissolute Punished, The, four one-act operas by Stephen Oliver; libretto (Eng) by the composer. First performance August 1972, Edinburgh, St. Mary's Hall.

A Dialogue between Jupiter and Cupid, after Thomas Heywood;
The Blind, after Maurice Maeterlinck's *Les aveugles* (1890);
The Fall of Miss Moss, after Katherine Mansfield;
Il dissoluto punito.

Distressed Knight, The, or, The Enchanted Lady, comic opera by Tommaso Giordani; libretto (Eng). First performance February 12, 1791, Dublin, Theatre Royal.

Diva, The, opera in one act by William Ferris; libretto (Eng) by John Vorrasi, after a scenario by the composer. First performance June 13, 1987, Chicago, Illinois, Chicago Opera Theater, New Works Showcase.

The setting is Island Bay, the present. Following a serious of disastrous farewell concerts, the Diva retires to her hometown. Despite opposition from Oliver Stark, the local music critic, the Diva agrees to make one last appearance at a benefit for the local conservatory, a move supported by David Brown, the Diva's first manager. The concert opens and includes the professional debut of Loretta Norris, the protégé of Stark; although she sings badly, she is greeted by much applause. The Diva is next and, overcome by emotion, has trouble continuing; annoyed, Stark storms out. The Diva then regains her composure and sings beautifully, making the audience and Brown ecstatic.

For a description, see Summers/*OOA*, 111–13.

Major roles: the Diva (sop), David Brown (ten), Loretta Norris (col sop), and Oliver Stark (bass).

Divertissement No. 3, "a lunchbag opera for paper bags and instruments" by Robert Moran. First "performance" October 31, 1971, London, BBC television.

The work consists of people in large paper bags walking up and down London Wall and around St. Paul's Cathedral, all the while making noises on toy instruments; the first "performance" engendered the annoyance of passing businesspeople and delight of the children who saw it.

BIBLIOGRAPHY: Keith Spence, "Television," *MT* CXII (1971), 1198 [on "premiere"].

Divina, La, opera buffa in one act by Thomas Pasatieri; libretto (Eng) by the composer. First performance March 16, 1966, New York, Juilliard School, with Linnie Mower (Madame Altina), Gwendolyn Killebrew (Cecily), Kerry McDevitt (Haemon), and Grayson Hirst (young conductor); conducted by Allan Lewis; produced by Christopher West.

Madame Altina, a diva who is getting on in years, is giving her "farewell" performance, which is none too soon for her beleaguered maid and Haemon, her manager. Alone with her thoughts in her dressing room, the diva begins to fear a future away from the limelight and attention. She thrills her audience and dismays her maid and manager when she announces that she will present another "farewell" the following week.

For a detailed description, see Eaton/*OP* II, 265–66.

Major roles: Madame Altina (col sop); Cecily, her maid (alto); Haemon, her manager (bar); and a young conductor (ten).

The second of the composer's triptych. The other two operas are *Padrevia** and *The Women.**

SCORE: vs, English-German (Bryn Mawr, Pa.: T. Presser, 1968).

Divorce, The, musical entertainment in two acts by James Hook; libretto (Eng) by Lady Dorothea Dubois. First performance? July 28, 1772, London, Marylebone Gardens.

Doctor and the Apothecary, The, musical entertainment in two acts by Stephen Storace, an adaptation of Dittersdorf's *Doktor und Apotheker* (1786, Vienna); libretto (Eng) by James Cobb, after the text by Gottlieb Stephanie the Younger, itself founded on the French play *L'apothicaire de Murcia.* First performance October 25, 1788, London, Drury Lane Theatre, with John Bannister (Juan), Mrs. Crouch (Anna), Richard Suett (Dr. Bilioso), and Mr. Parsons (the apothecary). First U.S. performance April 26, 1796, Charleston, South Carolina, City [Church Street] Theatre, arranged by B. Bergmann.

    In the story Carlos, the son of the doctor, is in love with Anna, the daughter of the apothecary. Unfortunately, the fathers are bitter enemies, and Anna's father wants her to marry the middle-aged Captain Sturmwald. The young lovers are saved with the help of Juan, who is interested in Isabella, Anna's companion. Carlos "marries" Anna in his disguise as the captain, and all ends happily for the young couple.

    Nine of the numbers are based on Dittersdorf's music, especially in act 1. The overture, unlike that of contemporary English works, is in one movement.

LIBRETTO: English (London: C. Dilly, 1788).

Doctor Faustus Lights the Lights, comic opera in three acts by Meyer Kupferman; libretto (Eng) by the composer, after Gertrude Stein's *Three Plays.* First performance April 5, 1953, Bronxville, New York, Sarah Lawrence College. Revised 1963.

    Also set as ballet by C. Wuorinen (1957).

SCORE: vs, excerpts, holograph (NYPL, photocopy).

Doctor Faustus Lights the Lights, opera in three acts by David Ahlstrom; libretto (Eng) by the composer, after Stein. First performance October 29, 1982, San Francisco, Voices/SF.

Doctor of Alcantara, The, opera in two acts by Julius Eichberg; libretto (Eng) by Benjamin E. Woolf. First performance April 7, 1862, Boston, Boston Museum.

    In the story Carlos, son of Balthazar, is in love with Isabella, the daughter of Doctor Paracelsus. After many mix-ups the pair come together and are allowed to wed.

    Major roles: Doctor Paracelsus (bar); his wife (sop); their daughter (sop); her fiancé (ten).

    The work is in the mold of Offenbach's operettas.

SCORE: vs (Boston: Oliver Ditson & Co., 1879); repr. ed. Charlotte R. Kaufman, *NAMT*, vol. 12 (1994).

LIBRETTO: English (Philadelphia, 1870).

Doctor of Myddfai, The, opera by Peter Maxwell Davies; libretto (Eng) by David Pountney, after a Welsh legend. First performance July 5, 1996, Cardiff, Welsh National Opera, with Paul Whelan (the doctor), Lisa Tyrrell (the child), and Gwynne Howell (the ruler); conducted by Richard Armstrong; directed by Pountney.

    The plot concerns the appearance in a country of a mysterious disease reminiscent of AIDS. A doctor arrives who possesses the cure. When people who are afflicted with the disease hear about this, they rush to him and in the process crush him to death. The doctor's daughter takes over his healing powers but compels the ruler, who is himself ill, to walk into a lake, which causes three girls to emerge chanting the magical cure.

BIBLIOGRAPHY: Tom Sutcliffe, "British Journal," *ON* LXI (Dec. 14, 1996), 71 [on premiere].

Doctor Ox's Experiment, opera in two acts by Gavin Bryars; libretto (Eng) by Blake Morrison, after Jules Verne. First performance (final scene) November 18, 1988, London, Queen Elizabeth Hall. First full performance June 25, 1997, BBC television; conducted by James Holmes; directed by David Pountney. First full stage performance scheduled for June 15, 1998, London, English National Opera, with Bonaventura Bottone (Dr. Ox); conducted by Holmes.

The surrealistic work, which contains traditional arias, choruses, and duets, concerns a small Flemish town coping with the deranged Dr. Ox and his experiment, filling the town's air with a mysterious gas.

Dolly Varden, comic opera in two acts by Julian Edwards; libretto (Eng) by Stanislaus Stangé, after Charles Dickens's *Barnaby Rudge* (1841). First performance 1901, London. First U.S. performance January 1, 1902, New York, Herald Square Theater, with Lulu Glaser (Dolly), Van Rensselaer Wheeler (Capt. Belleville), and Albert Parr (John Fairfax).

After Dolly Varden's guardian, John Fairfax, forces her to write a letter renouncing her love for Capt. Belleville, Dolly rewrites the missive to say she has her guardian's permission to wed Belleville and tricks Fairfax into delivering it to her beloved. SCORE: autograph fs (LCCN: 84-100870); vs (New York: M. Withmark & Sons, 1901).

Don Cristóbal and Rosita, operatic farce in one act by John Crawford; libretto (Eng) by the composer, after the *Retablillo de Don Cristóbal y Doña Rosita* of Federico García Lorca. First performance April 15, 1970, Wellesley, Massachusetts, Wellesley College.

The setting is an Andalusian village, early nineteenth century. The beautiful young Rosita is betrothed to the violent and grotesque Don Cristóbal and dreads the upcoming marriage, which her father favors. She would much rather marry Cocoliche, her young lover, but tells him she cannot. Another former lover, Currito, comes to the town and visits Rosita in her room. When Don Cristóbal appears, Rosita quickly hides the young man in her closet and does the same with Cocoliche when he appears also. The young men witness Don Cristóbal's attempts to court Rosita, and Currito, enraged, comes out of hiding and stabs his rival, only to discover that Don Cristóbal is really a life-sized puppet. Following a pretend funeral, Rosita and Cocoliche are united.

For a description, see Summers/*OOA*, 84–85.

Major roles: Rosita (sop), Don Cristóbal (buffo bar), Cocoliche (ten), Currito (bar), and Rosita's father (buffo bass). SCORE: ms vs (1970, photocopy, NYPL).

Don Fortunato, comic opera in one act by Hamilton Forrest; libretto (Eng) by the composer. First performance July 22, 1952, Interlochen, Michigan, National Music Camp.

Don Fulimone, or, The Lover with Two Mistresses, comic opera by Tommaso Giordani; libretto (Eng). First performance January 7, 1765, Dublin, Smock Alley.

Don Giovanni. See **The Libertine**.

Don John, or, The Two Violettas, operatic drama in three acts by Henry Rowley Bishop and William Ware; libretto (Eng) by Frederick Reynolds, after John Fletcher's comedy *The Chances* (possibly with Francis Beaumont; pub. 1647), itself based on one of Cervantes's *Novelas ejemplares* (1613). First performance February 20, 1821, London, Covent Garden.

The title refers to the coincidences that result in a number of difficulties for Constantia when she elopes with the Duke of Ferrara. The pair are aided by two Spanish gentlemen, Don John and Don Frederick, their landlady, Dame Gillian, and the wizard Peter Vecchio.

The music includes "Oh, What a Gay and Joyous Scene" (after Paisiello), and the finale of the third act is based on Mozart.
SCORE: ms fs (British Library, Add. MS. 36953); vs (London: Goulding, D'Almaine, Potter, [1820]).
LIBRETTO: English (London: J. Miller, 1821).

Don John of Austria, opera in three acts by Isaac Nathan; libretto (Eng) by Jacob L. Montefiore. First performance May 7, 1847, Sydney, Australia, Royal Victoria Theatre; conducted by the composer. First British performance September 12, 1997, London, Chelsea Opera Group; conducted by Daniel Jackson; produced by Philip Parr; directed by Jane Wildgoose.
The work is considered to be the first Australian opera to receive a complete performance in that country.

Don Juan de Mañara, opera in four acts by Eugene Goossens; libretto (Eng) by Arnold Bennett, after Dumas père (1836). First performance June 24, 1937, London, Covent Garden, with Lawrence Tibbett (Don Juan).
Don Juan, the hero (based on a historical character), follows a life of debauchery and associated intrigue. Along the way he gets involved in public flagellation, murder, and suicide. He is ultimately confronted with the ghosts of those who have died, whereupon he finally repents and joins a holy brotherhood.
The work, which was a failure, includes an impressive orchestral intermezzo between acts 3 and 4.
Also set by A. Enna (1925, Copenhagen).
SCORE: vs (London: J. & W. Chester, 1935).
BIBLIOGRAPHY: review, "World Premiere of Goossens Opera," *NYT* (June 25, 1937), 25.

Donkey, The, opera in one act by Stephen Oliver; libretto (Eng) by David Pountney. First performance September 20, 1973, Stirling, Scotland, MacRobert Centre.

Donna, La, opera in one act by Colin Brumby; libretto (Eng) by David Goddard. First performance July 2, 1988, Sydney, Australia, Opera Centre.

Don Perlimplin, opera in three acts by Vittorio Rieti; libretto (Sp) by the composer, after the play by Federico García Lorca, *Amor de Don Perlimplín con Belisa en su jardín* (1931); translated into English by James Graham Luján. First performance March 30, 1952, Urbana, Illinois, University of Illinois (concert); 1952, Paris (staged).
Set in Spain at the end of the eighteenth century, the story involves the rich Don Perlimplin, who has married the young Belisa. In order to keep her happy he invents a young lover who sends her flowers and writes her poetry. At the end he kills himself rather than reveal to her that he is in fact the lover, because he cannot live up to the ideal he has created.
Major roles: Don Perlimplin (bass) and Belisa (sop).
Also set by W. Fortner, as *In seinem Garten liebt Don Perlimplín Belisa* (1962, Schwetzingen); B. Maderna (1962, Radio Audizioni Italiane); B. Sulzer (1984, Linz); C. Susa, as *The Love of Don Perlimplin** (1984, Purchase, N. Y.); and A. Biales, as *Belisa** (1989, St. Paul, Minn.).
SCORE: vs, English, Italian, Spanish (New York: Associated Music Publishers, ca. 1949).

Don Quixote, all-sung afterpiece in one act by Samuel Arnold; libretto (Eng) by D. G. Piguenit, after Cervantes. First performance June 30, 1774, London, Marylebone Gardens.

Don Quixote, grand comic and spectacular opera in three acts by Frederic Clay; libretto (Eng) by Harry Paulton and A. Maltby, after Cervantes. First performance September 25, 1876, London, Alhambra.

Don Quixote, comic opera in three acts by Reginald De Koven; libretto (Eng) and lyrics by Harry B. Smith, after Cervantes. First performance November 18, 1889, Boston, Boston Ideal Opera Company.
SCORE: vs (New York: G. Schirmer and Leipzig: C. G. Roder, 1890).

Don Quixote, the Knight of the Woeful Countenance, or, The Humours of Sancho Panza, romantic burletta by George Rodwell; libretto (Eng) by J. B. Buckstone, after Cervantes. First performance January 7, 1833, London, Adelphi Theatre.
LIBRETTO: English (London: Richardson and Clarke, [1833?]).

Don Quixote, opera by Thomas J. Hewitt; libretto (Eng) by Fred Edmonds, after Cervantes. First performance 1909, London.
SCORE: vs (London: J. Curwen & Sons, [1909]).

Don Quixote de la Mancha, comic opera in two acts by Alfred Hill; libretto (Eng) by W. Beattie, after Cervantes. Composed 1904.

Don Quixote in England, ballad opera; libretto (Eng) by Henry Fielding, after Cervantes. First performance April 5, 1734, London, Little Theatre in the Haymarket, with Mr. Roberts (Don Quixote), Mr. Mullart (Sancho), Mr. Machen (Sir Thomas Loveland), Mr. Macklin (Squire Badger), Miss Atherton (Dorothea), and Mrs. Hide (Jezebel).
  The work takes place at an inn in a country borough. It includes fifteen airs.
  Among the many settings of the Cervantes tale are the incidental music by Purcell, Eccles, and others to Thomas D'Urfey's text (1694, London); *Harlequin and Quixote*, pantomime by W. Reeve (1797, London); vaudeville by B. Silvester (J. G. Noe, 1873, New York); musical entertainment by A. Neuendorff (in German, 1882, New York); J. Redding (1884, New York); operetta by G. Jacobi (1894, London); W. G. Kaufman (1903, New York); and *The Man of La Mancha*, musical by M. Leigh, text by J. Darion (1965, New York). See also *An Adventure of Don Quixote*.
LIBRETTO: English, with music (London: J. Watts, 1734); repr. ed. Rubsamen/*BO*, vol. 6, *Satire, Burlesque, Protest, and Ridicule*, part 2 (1974).

Don Raphael, ballad opera, arranged by James Hewitt; libretto (Eng), after George Walker. First performance 1804, New York.
  The work contains one song by Hewitt.

Don Sancho, or, The Student's Whim, ballad opera in two acts; libretto (Eng) by Elizabeth Boyd. First performance 1739, London.
  The setting is Oxford, in the University garden.
  Roles: Lord Lovewit, Jack Taste, and Joe Curious, Oxford students; and Don Sancho, "a reduc'd Nobleman highly esteem'd by the University for his great Learning and Piety, supported by a voluntary Contribution of the Collegians."
  Performed together with the masque *Minerva's Triumph*.
LIBRETTO: English (London: author, 1739); repr. Rubsamen/*BO*, vol. 10, *Magical Transformation and Necromancy* (1974).

Don Saverio, opera buffa by Thomas Arne; libretto (Eng) probably by the composer. First performance February 15, 1750, London, Drury Lane Theatre, with George Mattocks (Alonzo), Catherine Clive (Clarice), Miss Norris (Turkish lady), and John Beard (Don Saverio).

The action takes place in Naples. Alonzo, leaving his betrothed in Rome, romances Clarice, whose friend, the Turkish lady, is really Alonzo's intended in disguise. Don Saverio, foppish brother of Clarice, is extraneous to the plot but gets to sing five songs, including one in French.

Don't Call Me by My Right Name, opera by Joseph Fennimore; libretto (Eng) by the composer, after James Purdy's story. First performance October 1, 1975, New York, Carnegie Recital Hall.

Don't We All?, opera in one act by Burrill Phillips; libretto (Eng) by Alberta Phillips. First performance May 9, 1949, Rochester, New York, Eastman School of Music; conducted by Ward Woodbury.

A couple, Nell and Tom, are relaxing in the kitchen of their farm when they remember that the door needs to be bolted, and they start to argue about who should do it. They decide that the first to speak should have to secure the door. When their neighbors Amy and Ralph come, they cannot understand the silence and tease the other couple until they become furious. After the neighbors have left, Tom and Nell are about to forget about their quarrel until Nell recalls that Tom was the first to speak. Thus, reasons the husband, a man always loses an argument with a woman, ergo, "Don't we all?"

For a detailed description, see Eaton/*OP* I, 179–80.

Roles: Nell (alto), Tom (bar), Amy (sop), and Ralph (ten).

BIBLIOGRAPHY: review, "Chamber Operas at Eastman Fete," *NYT* (May 10, 1949), 28 [on premiere].

Doom-Kiss, The, legendary operatic entertainment in two acts by Henry Rowley Bishop; libretto (Eng) by Isaac Pocock. First performance October 29, 1832, London, Drury Lane Theatre.

SCORE: fs ms (British Library, Add. MS. 36960).

Door, The, opera in one act by Irving Mopper; libretto (Eng) by Margaret Matthews Hordyk, after the Robert Louis Stevenson story *The Sire de Malétroit's Door*. First performance December 2, 1956, Newark, New Jersey, Lauter Auditorium, as *The Sire de Maletroit's Door*.

When Alain, the Sire de Maletroit, discovers that his niece, Blanche, is smitten by a captain whom she has seen only in church, he decides to teach her a lesson. He decrees that she must marry the first man to come through his door. As the young soldier Denis is the first to enter, he is faced either with marrying the niece or being hanged. Denis bravely offers to die, although he has been taken with Blanche, who in turn asks him to marry her. When Alain reappears, he finds his niece in the arms of Denis and happily welcomes their marriage.

For a detailed description, see Eaton/*OP* I, 180.

Major roles: Alain (ten), Denis (bar), and Blanche (sop).

J. Duke's *Sire de Maledroit** and S. Barab's *The Maletroit Door** are other settings.

Dorian, multimedia opera by Herbert A. Deutsch; libretto (Eng) by Robert Kastenbaum, after Oscar Wilde's *The Picture of Dorian Gray*. First performance February 3, 1995, Garden City, New York, Hofstra University.

See *The Picture of Dorian Gray* for L. Liebermann's setting of the story.

BIBLIOGRAPHY: Barbara Delatiner, "Dorian Gray Takes to Stage," *NYT* (Jan. 29, 1995), XIII (Long Island issue), 13.

Doris, comic opera in three acts by Alfred Cellier; libretto (Eng) by Benjamin Charles Stephenson. First performance April 20, 1889, London, Lyric Theatre, with Annie Albu (Doris); conducted by Ivan Caryll. Revision of *Tower of London** (1879, Manchester).

The setting is London and concerns Doris Shelton, daughter of an alderman.
SCORE: vs ed. Ivan Caryll (London: Chappell, [ca. 1889]).

Dorothy, comic opera in three acts by Alfred Cellier; libretto (Eng) by Benjamin Charles Stephenson, a revision of *Nell Gwynne** (1876). First performance September 25, 1886, London, Gaiety, with Hayden Coffin (Geoffrey). First U.S. performance November 5, 1887, New York, Standard Theater, with Lillian Russell (Dorothy), Agnes Stone (her cousin), Harry Paulton, Eugene Oudin, John E. Brand, and William Hamilton.

When two young English ladies who are cousins take jobs as barmaids at a festival, they are swept off their feet by two customers. One of them, Geoffrey, prefers his newly discovered lady friend to the one his uncle has picked for him to wed, a woman called Dorothy, whom he has never met. In the end, to be sure, Dorothy and Geoffrey's new love are one and the same. Dorothy's cousin is allowed to wed her love, also.
SCORE: vs (London: Chappell, [1886]).
LIBRETTO: English (London: Chappell, [ca. 1887]).

Double Disappointment, The, ballad opera; libretto (Eng) by Moses Mendez. First performance March 18, 1746, London, Drury Lane Theatre, with Miss Young (Isabel), Mr. Barrington (Phelim O'Blunder), Mr. Collins (Gripe), and Mr. Lowe (Loveless).

The work includes the air "Balin a mona," set to an Irish tune and sung by Phelim.
LIBRETTO: English (London, 1746; London: F. and J. Noble, 1760); 1746 ed. repr. Rubsamen/*BO*, vol. 13, *Farce: Amorous Intrigue and Deception II* (1974).

Double Disguise, The, or, The Irish Chambermaid, comic opera in two acts by James Hook; libretto (Eng) by Harriet Horncastle (Hook). First performance March 8, 1784, London, Drury Lane Theatre, with Mr. Barrymore (Lord Hartweed) and Miss Phillips (Emily). First U.S. performance November 10, 1794, Charleston, City Theatre, arranged by R. Chateadun, Victor Pelissier; April 29, 1795, New York, John Street Theatre.
LIBRETTO: English (London: J. Bell, 1784).

Double Trouble, comedy in one act, with a prologue, epilogue, and two choral interludes by Richard Mohaupt; libretto (Eng) by Roger Maren, after Plautus's *Menaechmi*; German version by Louis A. Bornemisza, as *Zwillingskomödie*. First performance, in English, December 4, 1954, Louisville, Kentucky Opera, Columbia Auditorium, with Richard Dales (Hocus), William Pickett (Pocus), Margaret Pullian (Erotia), Charme Riesley (Cynthia), W. D. Elliott (Lucio), and Monas Herlan (Dr. Antibioticus); conducted by Moritz Bomhard.

The story concerns the twins Hocus and Pocus, the sons of Docus and Crocus. They were separated at an early age, and when they are reunited, trouble and confusion ensue.

For a detailed description, see Eaton/*OP* I, 180–81.

Major roles: Hocus (bass-bar); Pocus (bass-bar); Naggia, wife of Hocus (mezzo); Erotia, a courtesan (sop); Cynthia, Hocus's daughter (sop); Lucio, Cynthia's lover (ten); and Dr. Antibioticus, Lucio's father (ten).

The chorus introduces and offers ironic comments about the action.
SCORE: vs (Eng-Ger) (New York: Associated Music Publishers, 1954).

Dove of Peace, The, comic opera in three acts by Walter Damrosch; libretto (Eng) by Wallace Irwin. First performances October 15, 1912, Philadelphia; November 4, 1912, New York, with Frank Pollock (Willie) and Alice Yorke (Hildegarde).

The satirical work, which takes place in the nineteenth century, is set in Portsmouth, New Hampshire, Guam, and the U.S. Senate chamber. A clause in the will of the grandmother of Willie Perkins says that if the shy young man is kissed before he is twenty-five, peace will reign throughout the world. Willie, who is afraid of women, runs off to Guam, whereupon the Spanish-American War starts. When he finally kisses Hildegarde Tyler there, peace is restored. But all find that peace is a bore, and when a way is found to circumvent the clause in grandma's will (he had been kissed after the requisite age, because of the time difference), all are able to return to fighting.

Major roles: Hildegarde Tyler, a college girl (sop); Juanita Mendoza, Spanish exile at Guam (mezzo); Willie Petruchio Perkins, the "unkissed child of Peace" (ten); Arabella Smithson, "New England type of pert professional waitress" (alto); Hon. Terence Donnybrook, "a professional peace agitator" (bar); Capt. Paul Jones, navy hero (bar); Sir Hannibal Hobbs, British ambassador to Guam (bass); McGinnis, a bos'n (bass); and the vice president of the United States (ten).

The work was a failure and was not helped by the approaching war in Europe. SCORE: vs (New York: G. Schirmer, 1912).

Down by the Greenwood Side, dramatic pastorale in one act by Harrison Birtwistle; libretto (Eng) by Michael Nyman, after the traditional English Mummers' Play and the *Ballad of the Cruel Mother*. First performance May 8, 1969, Brighton Festival, with Jenny Hill and Music Theatre Ensemble; conducted by David Atherton. Revived June 14, 1984, London, Place Theatre, Endymion Ensemble, with Penelope Walmsley-Clark (Mrs. Green); conducted by John Whitfield

The story tells of St. George being killed and resurrected twice and Mrs. Green's narrative of how she killed her child.

Major roles: Mrs. Green (sop); actors: Father Christmas, St. George, Bold Slasher, Dr. Blood; and Jack Finney (mime).

Mrs. Green is the only singing part, while the other characters recite or chant their lines.
BIBLIOGRAPHY: review, *Opera* XXXV (Sept. 1984), 1045–46 [on revival].

Down in the Valley, folk opera in one act by Kurt Weill; libretto (Eng) by Arnold Sundgaard. First performance July 15, 1948, Bloomington, Indiana, University of Indiana, East Hall, with Marion Bell (Jennie Parsons), Aiken, James Welsh (Brack Weaver), Campbell, Carpenter, and Jones; conducted by Ernst Hoffmann; directed by Hans Busch. First British performance October 23, 1957, Bristol.

In this work, the leader of the chorus explains the action. Brack Weaver, jailed for murdering Thomas Bouché during a fight, escapes to be with Jennie Parsons, his beloved. The murder is shown in flashbacks. When Brack is convinced of Jennie's love, he gives himself up to face his punishment.

For a detailed description, see Eaton/*OP* I, 181–82

Major roles: Brack Weaver (ten), Jennie Parsons (sop), Thomas Bouché (bass), and Leader/Preacher (bar).

The work uses themes from American folk music. Originally conceived as a radio opera, it was reworked, with the bulk of the dialogue changed to recitative and melodrama. The folk song "Down in the Valley" recurs nineteen times, each instance being treated according to the demands of the dramatic situation. The opera is intended for nonprofessional performers.

SCORE: vs (New York: G. Schirmer, 1948).

DISCOGRAPHY: Davidson, Acito, Collup, Maby, Lang; cond. W. Gundlach, Fredonia Chamber Singers, Kammerchor der Universität Dortmund, Capriccio 60 020 (1 CD).

Dowser, The, pastoral in one act by Arnold Franchetti; libretto (Eng) by E. R. Mills. Composed 1956. Not performed.

Draagenfut Girl, opera in two acts by Meyer Kupferman; libretto (Eng) by the composer. First performance May 8, 1958, Bronxville, New York, Sarah Lawrence College.

A treatment of the Cinderella tale.

Dracula, opera in one act by Arnold Franchetti; libretto (Eng) by the composer, after Bram Stoker's novel (1897). Composed 1979.

Dracula!, "Victorian melodrama" by Carey Blyton; libretto by the composer, after Stoker. Composed 1983. First performance summer 1984, London.

The thirty-minute work is scored for narrator and unison voices, with piano accompaniment or music hall orchestra.

R. Peters's *Nosferatu** is another setting of the Dracula story (1993, Toronto).

SCORE: vs (Borough Green, Kent: Novello, 1983?).

Dracula Diary, The, chamber "opera macabre" in one act by Robert Moran; libretto (Eng) by James Skofield. First performance March 18, 1994, Houston, Houston Opera.

The opera concerns a vampire opera diva who is discovered by an impresario. The impresario, in turn, becomes her next victim.

The minimalist score features an organ and spooky sound effects.

DISCOGRAPHY: Knoop, Grove, Very, Maddalena, Sikon, Houston Opera Studio; cond. Holmquist, Catalyst 09026–6238–2 (premiere cast, 1994); rev. Patrick J. Smith, "Recordings," *ON* LIX (Jan. 7, 1995): 36.

Dragon, The, opera by George Alexander Lee, libretto (Eng) by John Morton. First performance August 4, 1834, London, English Opera House.

Dragon, The, fantasy opera in three acts by Deems Taylor; libretto (Eng) by the composer, after the play by Lady Gregory. First performance (piano accompaniment) February 6, 1958, New York, Hall of Fame Playhouse, New York University Workshop Chamber Orchestra, with Rita Fabel, Stanley Goldstein, Anatol Schlosser, Sandra Barnette, Violet Serwin, and Ralston Hill; Martha Pestalozzi and Louis Bagger, piano and organ; conducted by John Lovell; produced by William Vorenburg.

The story is a "fantasy about the days when there were kings in Ireland." The king is in mourning because he no longer gets the parcels of food brought by the suitors whom his daughter has rejected. Although the princess must marry because it has been foretold that she will be eaten by a dragon if she does not, she prefers that fate to being stuck with someone she does not love. Manus, the young King of Sorcha, comes to help the princess, in his disguise as a chef. When the dragon appears, Manus cuts out the beast's heart and replaces it with that of a squirrel, rendering the dragon harmless. The princess accepts Manus's offer of marriage, and all ends happily.

BIBLIOGRAPHY: Edward Downes, review, *NYT* (Feb. 7, 1958), 17 [on premiere].

Dragon of Wantley, The, "a burlesque opera" in three acts by John Frederick Lampe; libretto (Eng) by Henry Carey. First performance May 16, 1737, London, Haymarket, with Thomas Salway (Moore), Isabella Young (Margery), Esther Young (Mauxalinda), and Henry Reinhold (the dragon). It was parodied in the anonymous *The Pigeon-Pye*, published in 1738; the sequel was *Margery, or, A Worse Plague than the Dragon.**

Gubbins begs Moore, the hero, to protect his daughter Margery from a dragon. Another threat to Margery is Mauxalinda, one of Moore's discarded mistresses.

The work, which was very successful, satirized Handel's Italian works in particular and Italian opera in general, then current in London.

For a detailed description, see Fiske/*ETM*, 148–54.

Set as *The Dragon of Wantley, or, Harlequin and Mother Shipton*, a "grand Christmas pantomime," by Levey, with text by E. Blanchard (1870?).
LIBRETTO: English (London: John Wilcox, 1738).

Drama at Home, The, or, An Evening at Home, review in one act by Thomas German Reed; libretto (Eng) by James R. Planché. First performance April 8, 1844, London.

Dream Beach, musical theater piece in three acts by Michael Sahl; libretto (Eng) by Howard Pflanzer. First performance March 20, 1988, New York, Green Auditorium.

Dream Child, opera in two acts by Henry Mollicone; libretto (Eng) by Howard Richardson, after the play *La buanderie* by David Guerdon. Composed 1975.
SCORE: fs, holograph (New York: American Composers Alliance, 1975).

Dreamers, The, opera by David Conte; libretto (Eng) by Philip Littell. First performance August 1996, Sonoma, California, Sebastiani Theatre, with Shouvic Mondle (General Vallejo), Karen Connor, Sylvie Braitman, Antoine Garth, and Kevin Brackett; conducted by John Miner.

Written to celebrate the sesquicentennial of the city of Sonoma, the work centers on General Mariano Guadalupe Vallejo, who founded the city.
BIBLIOGRAPHY: Byron Belt, "Sonoma, CA," *ON* LXI (Dec. 28, 1996), 43 [on premiere].

Dreamkeepers, opera in two acts by David Carlson; libretto (Eng) by Aden Ross, after Ute traditions. First performance January 13, 1996, Salt Lake City, Utah, Capitol Theatre, with Ann Panagulias (Ela).

The story centers on the Ute Indians of eastern Utah. Ela Colorow, a contemporary Ute woman, comes back to the reservation where her seer grandmother is dying. Ela seeks her grandmother's help to save Ela's Anglo lover, Adam Wade, who has been seriously hurt in an automobile accident. Ela travels back to the spiritual world, where she confronts her own doubts and the travails of her people, personified by Sloane, a lawyer who is blocking land claims by her tribe. Ela returns to the regular world and is reunited with Adam, who has recovered.

Major roles: Ela Colorow (sop), grandmother (mezzo), Adam Wade (ten), and Sloane (bar).
BIBLIOGRAPHY: Peter Wynne, "Return of the Native," *ON* LX (Jan. 6, 1996), 28–29.
DISCOGRAPHY: symphonic sequences, Utah Sym.; cond. S. Robertson, New World Records 80496-2 (1997, Salt Lake City perf., 1 CD).

Dream of Valentino, The, opera in two acts by Dominick Argento; libretto (Eng) by Charles Nolte. First performance January 15, 1994, Washington, D.C., Washington Opera, with Robert Brubaker (Valentino), Suzanne Murphy (June Mathis), Julian Patrick (the Mogul), Joyce Castle (Alla Nazimova), Edrie Means (Jean Acker), Julia Anne Wolf (Natacha Rambova), and Dan Dressen (Marvin Heeno); conducted by Christopher Keene; directed by Ann-Margaret Pettersson.

The work is set in Hollywood in its early days. It opens with Valentino's funeral in 1926 and then examines his life, including his two marriages, and the evil effect of the Mogul, who wants to control him.

The title represents the dreams others have for the movie star, as well as Valentino's own.

BIBLIOGRAPHY: Edward Rothstein, "Clashing Keys for 'Valentino,'" *NYT* (Jan. 17, 1994), C, 11, 15 [on premiere]; and "The Bad Guy Is a Mogul? Find an Exit," *NYT* (Jan. 30, 1994), C, 27.

Dream Play, The, opera in one act by Timothy Sullivan; libretto (Eng) by the composer, after August Strindberg's work (1902). First performance May 11, 1988, Toronto, Texaco Opera Theatre.

Other settings of the Strindberg play include *Ein Traumspiel* by J. Weismann (1925, Duisburg) and A. Reimann (1965, Kiel), and M. Williamson's *The Growing Castle** (1968).

Dream Sequence '76, opera in two parts by Alvin Singleton; libretto (Eng) by the composer. First performance 1976, Graz, Austria.

For singers, actors, chamber orchestra, and tape.

Dreams in Spades, comic musical fantasy in one act by Serge Hovey; libretto (Eng) by the composer. First performance December 15, 1949, Philadelphia, Plays and Players Theatre.

Dream within a Dream, A, opera in one act by Russell Currie; libretto (Eng) by Robert Kornfeld, after Edgar Allan Poe's *The Fall of the House of Usher*. First performance (concert) April 29, 1984, Bronx, New York, Wave Hill. First stage performance June 15, 1985, Bronx Arts Ensemble, with James Rensink (Roderick), Mary Ann Hart (Lady Madeline), and Arturo Spinetti (the visitor). Revived June 10, 1988, New York, Symphony Space.

In this version, the news of Lady Madeline's death is conveyed during the visitor's first visit with Roderick Usher. Roderick then says that he wishes to leave Madeline's coffin in the underground vaults to make sure that she is really dead.

Part 2 of a trilogy of operas on stories by Poe. See also *The Cask of Amatillado* (1982) and *Ligeia* (1987).

LIBRETTO: English (Bronx, N.Y.: Bronx Society of Science and Letters, Bronx Community College, 1985).

BIBLIOGRAPHY: Will Crutchfield, "Opera: Bronx Arts Ensemble in 'Fall of the House of Usher,'" *NYT* (June 17, 1985), III, 14 [on 1985 performance].

Dress, The, opera comedy in one act by Mark Bucci; libretto (Eng) by the composer. First performance October 8, 1953, New York, 92nd Street Y, Kaufmann Concert Hall.

Vicki uses the rent money to buy herself a beautiful dress when her husband, David, is away. The dress is secured by a padlock, and while Vicki is showing the garment to her neighbor Sylvia, she loses the key. Her husband returns unexpectedly and finds the key. Only after he has gone to sleep is Vicki able to retrieve it, and she is left with the prospect of explaining her extravagant purchase the next day.

For a detailed description, see Eaton/*OP* I, 182.

Roles: Vicki (sop), David (bar), and Sylvia (sop).
SCORE: vs (New York: Chappell, 1956).
BIBLIOGRAPHY: review, "Music by Americans," *MA* LXXIV (Jan. 1, 1954), 14 [on premiere].

Dreyfus, opera by Morris Cotel, libretto (Eng) by Mordecai Newman. First performance January 17, 1985, Brooklyn, New York, Brooklyn Academy of Music, with James Rensink (Herzl), Allan Glassman (Capt. Alfred Dreyfus), Lynnen Yakes (Lucie Dreyfus), and Stephen O'Mara (Lieutenant Colonel Picquart); conducted by the composer. The work was also performed in 1993 in Bielefeld, Germany, and in Vienna, at the Staatsoper, on October 26, 1994.

The opera examines the decline of Dreyfus after his pardon and the parallel rise of Theodor Herzl, sent to Paris to cover the Dreyfus trial, and Herzl's development into an ardent Zionist.

The music for Herzl is partially based on the *Hatikvah.*

Another opera on the subject is *Dreyfus—Die Affäre* by J. Meier, with a libretto by G. R. Whyte (1994, Berlin).
BIBLIOGRAPHY: Donal Henahan, "The Opera: 'Dreyfus' Premieres," *NYT* (Jan. 19, 1985), C, 11 [on premiere].

Dr. Heidegger's Experiment. See *An American Triptych.*

Dr. Heidegger's Experiment, opera in one act by Sam Raphling; libretto (Eng), after Nathaniel Hawthorne's story *Dr. Heidegger's Experiment.* First performance February 18, 1956, New York, Greenwich House.

Dr. Heidegger's Fountain of Youth, chamber opera in one act by Jack Beeson; libretto (Eng) by Sheldon Harnick, after Hawthorne. First performance November 19, 1978, New York, with Carol Wilcox (Rachel Lockhart), Judith Christin (Hannah Moody), Grayson Hirst (Reuben Waterford), Robert Shiesley (Colonel Killigrew), Alfred Anderson (Dr. Heidegger), and Miranda Beeson (maid); conducted by Thomas Martin.

Dr. Heidegger invites four aged friends to his house. He shows them a liquid that supposedly comes from the Fountain of Youth and revives a forty-five-year-old rose that he has kept in a book. He then invites them to try the potion themselves. They do and feel young again; Rachel Lockhart flirts with Colonel Killigrew and Reuben Waterford, and Hannah Moody remembers her unrequited feelings for Waterford. The two men come to blows over Rachel and knock over the flask containing the fluid. After the potion spills on the floor, the rose withers, and the four grow old once again. While Dr. Heidegger concludes that he is glad that his youth is behind him, the four friends determine to go and find the Fountain of Youth themselves.

Roles: Rachel Lockhart, a widow (lyr sop); Hannah Moody, a spinster (mezzo); Reuben Waterford (ten); Colonel Killigrew (bar); Dr. Heidegger (bass/bass-bar); and a maid (speaking).

See P. Schwartz's *The Experiment* (1956, Gambier, Ohio) for another setting.
SCORE: vs (New York: Boosey & Hawkes, 1998).
BIBLIOGRAPHY: Peter G. Davis, "Opera: Bel Canto Troupe Offers Program of 3 One-Act Works," *NYT* (May 7, 1981), C, 20 [on revival].
DISCOGRAPHY: orig. cast, CRI SD406 (1 LP); reissued as Citadel Records CTD88125 (1 CD).

Drink of Eternity, The, opera-pageant by Halim El-Dabh; libretto (Eng) by the composer. First performance spring 1981, Washington, D.C., Georgetown University.

Dr. Jekyll and Mr. Hyde, opera in two acts by Frank D. Fragale; libretto (Eng) by W. Erich, after Robert Louis Stevenson's story *The Strange Case of Dr. Jekyll and Mr. Hyde.* First performance August 28, 1953, Berkeley, California, Garfield Theater.
BIBLIOGRAPHY: "Fragale Arrives," *International Musician* LII (Nov. 1953), 28 [on premiere].

Dr. Jekyll and Mr. Hyde, romantic opera in one act by Barry O'Neal; libretto (Eng) by Robin Jones, after Stevenson. Composed 1980.
   The brilliant Dr. Henry Jekyll is engaged to Joanna Enfield, sister of Richard Enfield, his best friend. Richard tells him that Sir Danvers Carew, another scientist, has disparaged Dr. Jekyll's work publicly. Jekyll has Carew come to his laboratory and drinks the potion he has developed; Jekyll turns into the murderous Mr. Hyde and kills Carew, the first of several victims. Changed back into Dr. Jekyll, he tries to tell Joanna and Richard about his plight but becomes Mr. Hyde in their presence and kills Richard. Transformed once more into Dr. Jekyll, the scientist poisons himself, realizing that his own death is the only solution.
   For a description, see Summers/*OOA,* 236–38.
   Major roles: Dr. Henry Jekyll (ten), Joanna Enfield (sop), and Richard Enfield (bar/bass-bar).
SCORE: ms vs, holograph (1980, photocopy, NYPL).

Dr. Musikus, opera for children in one act by Antony Hopkins; libretto (Eng) by the composer. First performance March 20, 1969, London, Arts Theatre.
   Dr. Musikus, a great composer, is finishing the last few bars of his 29th symphony. When a reporter visits him, the composer recounts four incidents from his early life. Thinking he is a medical doctor, a lady asks him to deal with her medical ills, which are cured by the power of his music. As the work ends, the ghosts of Schubert and Bach appear to join in an arrangement of Bach's "Jesu, Joy of Man's Desiring."
SCORE: vs (London, 1970).

Dr. Selavy's Magic Theatre, musical review by Stanley Silverman; libretto (Eng) by Richard Foreman; lyrics (Eng) by Tom Hendry. First performance August 12, 1972, Stockbridge, Massachusetts, Lenox Arts Center. Revived there January 1984.
LIBRETTO: English, typescript, 1984 (NYPL, photocopy).

Drumlin Legend, The, folk opera in three acts by Ernst Bacon; libretto (Eng) by Helena Carus. First performance May 4, 1949, New York, Columbia University, Brander Matthews Hall, with Frank Sherman Baker (the aviator), Joseph Scandin (Pennypacker), John Powell (the farmer), Ruth Krug (the mother), and Jean Swetland (Norah); conducted by Otto Luening.
   The plot centers around a sacred tree. Kelly, an aviator, now works as a gardener and is in love with Norah, the daughter of a farmer. Although Kelly wishes to return to flying, he has a change of heart after he is inducted into the mythical society in the hill country, or "the drumlins." He then prevents the nasty Pennypacker, who is pressuring Norah's father financially, from hacking down the tree.
BIBLIOGRAPHY: Olin Downes, "Columbia Offers 'Drumlin Legend,'" *NYT* (May 10, 1949), 29 [on premiere].

Duchess of Dantzic, The, comic opera in three acts by Ivan Caryll; libretto (Eng) by Henry Hamilton, after Sardou's *Madame Sans-Gêne*. First performance October 17, 1903, London, Lyric, with Evie Greene (the duchess), Courtice Pounds (Papillon), and Holbrook Blinn (Napoleon). First U.S. performance January 14, 1905, New York, Daly's.

Set at the court of Napoleon, the story features a laundress who becomes a duchess.

Sardou's text was also set by Giordano as *Madame Sans-Gêne* (1915, New York).

SCORE: vs (London: Chappell & Co., 1903).

Duchess of Malfi, The, opera in three acts by Stephen Oliver; libretto (Eng) by the composer, after John Webster's tragic play (ca. 1613). First performance November 23, 1971, Oxford, Playhouse, Oxford University Opera Club, with Oliver (Bosola). Revised version August 5, 1978, Santa Fe.

When the widowed duchess marries Antonio, her steward, she offends her brother Ferdinand, duke of Calabria, and the cardinal. As punishment she is imprisoned, and Bosola, in the employ of the cardinal, kills the duchess, her children, and Antonio.

BIBLIOGRAPHY: Quaintance Eaton, review, *Music Journal* XXXVI (Nov. 1978), 4–7.

Duchess of Malfi, The, opera in three acts by Stephen Douglas Burton; libretto (Eng) by Christopher Keene, after John Webster. First performance August 18, 1978, Vienna, Virginia, Wolftrap, with Roberta Palmer (Duchess), Neil Rosenshein (Antonio), and Judith Christin (Cariola); conducted by Christopher Keene.

The Duchess of Malfi, who has been widowed at a young age, is prevented from remarrying by her brothers. To see that she does not defy them and dishonor their family, the two brothers place a spy, Daniel de Bosola, in their sister's household. Ferdinand, the cardinal, has already treated Bosola dishonorably, and Bosola is in turn soon corrupted by his masters. The Duchess secretly weds her major domo, Antonio Bologna, who is beneath her socially. When her action is discovered, she is imprisoned and tortured, and Ferdinand is killed in a fight with Bosola.

This was the first American opera to have its premiere at Wolftrap.

BIBLIOGRAPHY: Charles Timbrell, review, *ON* XLIII (Nov. 1978), 79–80 [on premiere].

Duel, The, opera in one act by Al Carmines; libretto (Eng) by the composer. First performance June 28, 1974, Brooklyn, New York, Metropolitan Opera Studio.

About the duel between Aaron Burr and Alexander Hamilton.

BIBLIOGRAPHY: Raymond Ericson, review, *NYT* (Apr. 25, 1974), 48 [on premiere].

Duenna, The, or, The Double Elopement, comic opera in three acts, with music mostly by Thomas Linley Sr. and Jr.; libretto (Eng) by Richard B. Sheridan. First performance November 21, 1775, London, Covent Garden, with Miss Brown (Clara), Michael Leoni (Don Carlos), George Mattocks (Ferdinand), Isabella Mattocks (Louisa), Charles Dubellamy (Antonio), Mr. Wilson (Don Jerome), and John Quick (Mendoza). First U.S. performance July 10, 1786, New York, arranged by Thomas Bradford. Revived December 26, 1924, Hammersmith, with music arranged by Alfred Reynolds; March 7, 1962, BBC; March 16, 1976, London, Camden Festival.

The story is set in eighteenth-century Seville. Louisa, daughter of Don Jerome, is supposed to wed the aged and wealthy Isaac Mendoza, but she is in love with the young Antonio. She dons the disguise of Margaret, her duenna, and flees. During her flight she meets Ferdinand, her brother, who is attempting to elope with Clara d'Almazzo. Clara joins Louisa's scheme and finds refuge in a convent so that Louisa can pretend to be Clara. Margaret, passing herself off as Louisa, convinces the abandoned Mendoza to run off with her. In the meantime, the trickery has fooled even Ferdinand and Antonio, who almost come to blows when all of those involved show up at the convent. In the end, however, the identities are straightened out, and Don Jerome lets his children decide whom they will wed, and Mendoza marries the duenna.

For a detailed description, see Fiske/*ETM*, 414–19.

Roles: Don Jerome (bass); Louisa, his daughter (sop); Ferdinand, his son (ten); Margaret, Louisa's duenna (mezzo); Clara (sop); Isaac Mendoza (ten); Don Carlos, Mendoza's friend (ten); and Antonio (ten).

The work was extremely successful during its initial season and eclipsed *The Beggar's Opera** in number of performances. There were various pirated adaptations of the text, such as Thomas Ryder's *The Governess*, performed January 31, 1777, Dublin, Crow Street Theatre (see Fiske/*ETM*, 301).

The story was also set by S. Prokofiev, as *Betrothal in a Monastery* (1946, Leningrad); and R. Gerhard (see following entry). The characterization of the unwanted rich suitor as a Jewish stereotype continues in the Prokofiev and Gerhard settings.

SCORE: fs, overture, arr. A. Carse (London: Augener, [1941]); vs (London: C. and S. Thompson, [1775?]).

LIBRETTO: English (London: J. Wilkie et al, 1775; New York: James Humphreys Jr. & Valentine Nutter, 1779); Ryder version (Dublin: n.p., 1777).

Duenna, The, opera in three acts by Roberto Gerhard; libretto (Eng) by the composer and Christopher Hassall, after Sheridan's comedy. First performance February 23, 1949, BBC. First performance (concert) June 27, 1951, Wiesbaden, with Joan Cross (Luisa) and Peter Pears (Don Antonio). First British performance 1972, BBC. First stage performance, in a version by David Drew, January 21, 1992, Madrid, Teatro Lírico National, with David Rendall, Robin Leggate, and Richard Van Allan (Don Jerome); conducted by Antoni Ros Marbá. First British stage performance July 1992, Leeds, Opera North, with Gillian Knight (the duenna), Adrian Clarke (Don Antonio), Gordon Wilson (Don Ferdinand), Susan Chilcott (Donna Luisa), Pamela Helen Stephen (Donna Clara), Eric Roberts (Don Isaac), and Andrew Chore (Don Jerome); conducted by Ros Marbá.

The setting is Seville. Two couples are in love, Don Antonio and Donna Luisa, and Don Ferdinand and Donna Clara. Luisa, daughter of Don Jerome, is supposed to wed someone she has never met, and Clara's stepmother is planning to send the girl to a convent in order to seize her inheritance. True love wins out in the end with the help of the duenna, who scares off the potential suitor, Portuguese, by pretending to be Luisa.

For a detailed plot description, see K/*NKOB*, 241–43.

Major roles: Don Antonio (ten), Donna Luisa (sop), the duenna (mezzo), Don Ferdinand (bar), and Donna Clara (sop).

The work, which was not staged during the composer's lifetime, includes set pieces that display elements of Spanish folk music and contain themes signifying certain characters or dramatic situations.

SCORE: vs, ed. David Drew (London: Boosey & Hawkes, 1996).

BIBLIOGRAPHY: Robin Holloway, "Poised for Take-Off," *Spectator* XXVI (Feb. 22, 1992), 36 [on stage premiere]; Gerald Larner, "The Duenna," *Guardian* (Sept. 19, 1992), 29 [on Brit. premiere]; Anne Midgette, "Bielefeld," *ON* LVI (Dec. 24, 1994) [on Bielefeld revival]; Tom Sutcliffe, "British Journal," *ON* LVII (Jan. 16, 1993), 34 [on British stage premiere].

DISCOGRAPHY: E. Roberts, N. Archer, A. Clarke, S. Glanville, C. Powell, R. Van Allan, P. Wade, Opera North Chorus, English Northern Philharmonia; cond. A. Ros Marbá, Chandos

CHAN 95202 (2) (2 CDs); rev. Richard Traubner, "Recordings," *ON* LXII (July 1997), 37; Antony Bye, "Record Review," *Tempo* CCI (July 1997), 201.

Duke of Savoy, The, or, Wife and Mistress, musical play in three acts by Henry Rowley Bishop; libretto (Eng) by Frederick Reynolds, an adaptation of Marsollier's text for Dalayrac's *Les deux petits Savoyards* (1789, Paris). First performance September 29, 1817, London, Covent Garden.

Roles: Lealto, Podrida, and Ninette.

SCORE: ms fs, autograph (1817, British Library, Add. MS. 27708).

Duke or Devil, "farcical opera" in one act by Nicholas Gatty; libretto (Eng) by I. Gatty. First performance December 16, 1909, Manchester, England.

LIBRETTO: English (London: Novello & Co., 1912).

Dulcamara, or, The Little Duck and the Great Quack, burlesque opera, after Donizetti's *L'elisir d'amore* (1832, Milan); libretto (Eng) by William S. Gilbert, after the text by Felice Romani. First performance December 29, 1866, London, St. James Theatre, with Carlotta Addison (Adina) and Frank Matthews (the great quack). Revised for a performance December 1870, London, Opera Comique.

In this version of the Romani plot about a fake love potion, the quack is Dulcamara, a local doctor who tells his healthy patients that their imagined consumption can be cured by his inhalation process. Among his patients is the lovesick Nemorino (cast as a soprano), in love with Adina; Dulcamara convinces Nemorino that he needs treatment. In the end the characters find out they are all related, with Beppo turning out, incredibly, to be Dulcamara's mother.

The writing of the work came at the end of a libel trial in which a Dr. Hunter sued a journal after being accused of being a charlatan.

Major roles: Dulcamara, a little duck; the great quack; Beppo, his assistant; and Nemorino (sop).

For a detailed description, see Stedman/*WSG*, 35–38.

LIBRETTO: English, in *New and Original Extravaganzas* (Boston: J. W. Luce & Co., [1932]).

Dumb Wife, The, chamber opera in two acts by Louis Gruenberg; libretto (Eng) by the composer, after Anatole France's novel *Celui qui épousa une femme muette*, a dramatization of Rabelais. Composed 1922–1923.

Legal reasons barred the work from being performed until thirty years after Anatole France's death (in 1924).

SCORE: vs, holograph, 1922–1923 (NYPL, in ink, with typescript libretto).

Dumb Wife, The, opera in one act by Joseph Horovitz; libretto (Eng) by Peter Shaffer, after Rabelais. First performance 1953, Lowestoft, England, Intimate Opera Company. Revived January 10, 1972, Antwerp.

BIBLIOGRAPHY: C. Mason, review, *MT* XCV (Jan. 1954), 33 [on premiere].

Dunstan and the Devil, opera in a prologue and one act by Malcolm Williamson; libretto (Eng) by Geoffrey Dunn. First performance May 19, 1967, Cookham, Festival Society.

The work is set in the tenth century and concerns Saint Dunstan, the eventual Archbishop of Canterbury, and his meetings with the Devil. Before he is born, Heorstan and Keondrud, his parents, come to Glastonbury church for a blessing. The father's candle is burned out, but the mother's is rekindled, a sign that the unborn Dunstan will lead a holy life.

Although he is urged to take up a religious calling, Dunstan, a gifted goldsmith, is, as a young man, constantly tempted by worldly concerns and people, including a lady who admires his work. When Dunstan's uncle Alphege tries to get him onto his appointed path, the Devil hurls a boulder at the pair, but it is deflected by angels. Dunstan begins to make objects for the church, while his former lady love enlists the help of the Devil to recapture her beloved. She suddenly repents and is forgiven by Dunstan, who then takes after his nemesis. The Devil disguises himself as various animals. When he enters the shape of a fox, Dunstan grabs him with hot pincers, thus defeating him.

For a detailed description, see Eaton/*OP* II, 267–68.

Major roles: Dunstan (ten), the Devil (bass), Alphege (bar), and the lady (sop).

Dybbuk, The, music drama in three acts by David Tamkin; libretto (Eng) by Alex Tamkin, after the play of S. Ansky (pseud.). First performance October 4, 1951, New York, City Center, with Patricia Neway (Leah), Shirley Russell (Gittel), Frances Bible (Frade), Mack Harrell (Rabbi Azrael), and Robert Rounseville (Chanon); conducted by Joseph Rosenstock; choreographed by Sophie Maslow.

Chanon, entranced by the Jewish Kabala, looks for a way to become rich so that he can marry his beloved, Leah. His efforts lead to his death, but his spirit enters the body of Leah as a dybbuk.

The work includes passages from the Song of Songs.

SCORE: vs (New York: Boosey & Hawkes, 1985).

LIBRETTO: English (New York: n.p., n.d.).

BIBLIOGRAPHY: review, *NYT* (Oct. 5, 1951), 23 [on premiere]; review, *Opera* II (Dec. 5, 1951), 704–5 [on premiere].

Dybbuk, The, opera in four acts by Joel Mandelbaum; libretto (Eng) by the composer, after Ansky. First performance May 24, 1972, New York. Revised 1978.

Dybbuk, The, opera by Frank DiGiacomo; libretto (Eng) by the composer, after Ansky. First performance May 19, 1978, New York.

Also set by L. Rocca, as *Il Dibuk* (1934, Milan); K. Füssel, as *Der Dybuk* (1970, Karlsruhe); L. Bernstein, as *The Dybbuk*, a ballet (1974, New York); and S. Ran, as *Between Two Worlds** (1997, Chicago). George Gershwin never fulfilled his 1929 commission from the Metropolitan Opera to write a work called *The Dybbuk*.

Dylan, Son of the Wave, opera in three acts by Joseph Holbrooke; libretto (Eng) by Thomas Evelyn Ellis, after Welsh legends in *The Mabinogion*; second part of his Welsh trilogy, *The Cauldron of Annwn*, consisting also of *The Children of Don** (1912) and *Bronwen** (1929). First performance July 4, 1914, London, Drury Lane Theatre.

The story begins twenty years after the conclusion of *The Children of Don.** Elan believes that her son, Dylan, fathered by Lyd, the sea king, has been killed by Gwydion. When Dylan returns to her as a grown man, Govannion, Gwydion's brother, kills Dylan, believing that Gwydion is Dylan's father. To avenge his son's death, Lyd brings the fury of the sea down on Govannion and the castle in which he had sought shelter.

SCORE: fs (London, Novello and Co., [191?]).

Dynamite Tonite, actors' opera in two acts by William Bolcom; libretto (Eng) by Arnold Weinstein. First performance December 21, 1963, New York, Actors' Studio.

For unspecified voices and chamber ensemble.

SCORE: ms fs (New York: American Music Center, 1963).

E

E. & O. Line, "electronic blues opera" by Anne LeBaron; libretto (Eng) by Thulani Davis, after the story of Orpheus and Eurydice. First performance June 28, 1996, Annandale, Virginia, Ernst Theater, Opera Americana.

The opera tells the story of the Eurydice legend from the point of view of the heroine. It is updated and set in a small Southern town. Charon's ferry has become a train, and Hades is the Dreamtime Cafe.

The work is set for four solo voices, twelve instruments, six-part mixed blues and gospel chorus, women's jazz and blues trio, and taped sounds.
SCORE: ms fs (New York: American Music Center, 1991).
DISCOGRAPHY: selections; cond. LeBaron, Mode MOD 42 (1987, Library of Congress).

Early Dawn, opera in three acts by Normand Lockwood; libretto (Eng) by R. Russell Porter. First performance August 7, 1961, Denver, University of Denver, Little Theater.

The setting is the eve of the Civil War. Miriam, the daughter of Jeb and Mary, is drawn to Jeff, the family's adopted son, even though he was born in the South and she is an abolitionist. As Miriam and Jeff plan their wedding, the Civil War breaks out. When Jeb refuses to enlist, Miriam betrays him to the authorities. Although she changes her mind and tries to save him, aided by her brother Joel and her father, Jeff is hanged, and Jeb is killed by the frenzied mob.

Earth Mother, The, tragic opera in three acts by James Penberthy; libretto (Eng) by the composer and D. Stuart. Composed 1957–1958.

The story concerns two Aboriginals who marry, only to find out that they are half-siblings.

Earthquake, The, or, The Spectre of the Nile, "burletta operatic spectacle" in three acts by George Rodwell; libretto (Eng) by Edward Fitzball. First performance December 15, 1828, London, Adelphi Theatre; cast (for 1829 performance): Mr. Gallott (Orchus), Mr. Sinclair (Palmedo), Mr. T. P. Cooke (Galzetto), Mr. Yates (Doctor Kaliboss), Mr. Wilkinson (Pagnag), Mr. Morris (Bussiris), Mr. Sanders (Ibad), Miss Graddon (Alethe), and Mrs. Yates (Orynthe).

Major roles: Orchus, pretend sorcerer; Palmedo, young Athenian soldier; Galzetto, his Egyptian slave; Doctor Kaliboss, inventor of the elixir of life; Pagnag, keeper of golden beetles; Bussiris; Ibad; Alethe, Christian maid, captive; Orynthe, Doctor Kaliboss's slave and intended wife.
SCORE: vs (London, ca. 1828).
LIBRETTO: English (London: J. Cumberland, [183?]).

Earth-Trapped, chamber dance-opera in one scene by Herbert Owen Reed; libretto (Eng) by the composer, adapted from Manito masks (American Indian spirit legends) by Hartley Alexander. First performance (concert) February 24, 1962, East Lansing,

Michigan, Michigan State University, Music Auditorium. First stage performance May 23, 1970, San Francisco, Western Opera.
SCORE: holograph (New York: Mills Music, 1960).

East and West, opera by Ian McQueen; libretto (Eng) by Jonathan Moore. First performance July 18, 1995, London; with Fiona Kimm (Iolanda), Quentin Hayes (Benno), and Lynne Davies (Amira); directed by Jonathan Moore.

The story centers on the difficulties and animosity encountered by a family of Moslem Bosnians who are guest workers in a West German mining town, with a subplot of a romantic attraction between Iolanda and Benno, her brother-in-law.
BIBLIOGRAPHY: Jeffrey Joseph, "Reviews," *MT* CXXXVI (Sept. 1995), 512–13 [on premiere].

Eastward in Eden, opera in three acts by Jan Meyerowitz; libretto (Eng) by Dorothy Gardner, after her play of the same name. First performance November 16, 1951, Detroit, Wayne University, Wayne University Theatre, with Virginia Person (Emily Dickinson) and Amasa Tiffany (Rev. Dr. Charles Wadsworth); conducted by Walter Poole; directed by Leonard Leone. Act 2 (The Meeting) performed August 28, 1956, Oglebay Park, West Virginia, directed by Boris Goldovsky.

The work focuses on the life of Emily Dickinson. It includes, in the second act, the poet's meeting with the Reverend Mr. Wadsworth. The title of the opera was subsequently changed to *Emily Dickinson*.
BIBLIOGRAPHY: Owen Rachleff, "Oglebay Fortnight," *ON* XXI (Nov. 19, 1956), 21 [on act 2, "The Meeting"]; review, *MA* LXXIV (June 1954), 9 [on New York premiere]; review, "New American Opera Unveiled in Detroit," *NYT* (Nov. 17, 1951), 10 [on premiere].

Echo, The, opera in one act by Franklin Patterson; libretto (Eng) by the composer. First performance June 9, 1926, Portland, Oregon, Oregon Civic Auditorium, Portland Symphony Orchestra, with Forrest Lamont (Theudas), Marie Rappold (Acantha), Marjorie Dodge (Yfel), and Lawrence Tibbett (Cunnan); conducted by Walter Henry Rothwell.

The setting is a great cave, inhabited only by Acantha, who has been banished to this desolate island. She rescues Theudas, and the two fall in love. The two resist the efforts of the elfin people, led by Yfel and Cunnan, and leave the island by boat.
SCORE: vs (New York: G. Schirmer, 1922).

Echoes of the Shining Prince, opera in one act by Seth Cooper; libretto (Eng) by Elizabeth Aldrich, after Murasaki Shikibu's *The Tale of the Genji*. First performance April 26, 1985, New York, Merkin Hall, with Donna Wade and Fusako Yoshida; conducted by the composer.

The work blends Eastern and Western cultures in its flute and koto accompaniment (played by the conductor and one of the two singers), whose music includes sliding between pitches and quasi-modal vocal lines.
BIBLIOGRAPHY: Bernard Holland, "Concert: Spectra Arts Offers Opera," *NYT* (May 2, 1985), III, 16 [on premiere].

Edgar and Emily, opera in one act by Ernst Toch; libretto (Eng) by the composer, after Christian Morgenstern. First performance April 22, 1965, New York, Mannes College of Music. A revision of his *Egon und Emilie* (1928, Mainz).

The setting is a living room in the present. Emily, unable to get a response from her partner, Edgar, becomes furious and leaves the room. Edgar then recites the old proverb to the audience: speech is silver, but silence is gold.

Roles: Emily (col sop) and Edgar (speaking).
SCORE: vs (New York: Associated Music Publishers, 1958).
BIBLIOGRAPHY: review, *NYT* (Apr. 22, 1965), 26 [on premiere].

Edgar and Emmeline, entertainment in two acts by Michael Arne; libretto (Eng) by John Hawkesworth. First performance January 31, 1761, London, Drury Lane Theatre. First U.S. performance March 9, 1770, Philadelphia, Southwark Theatre.

The work takes place in Windsor Forest and concerns the meeting of the title characters, Edgar, who is dressed as a woman, and Emmeline, passing herself off as a man.
LIBRETTO: English (London: Longman et al., 1809).

Education of the Girlchild, opera by Meredith Monk; libretto (Eng) and choreography by the composer. First performance spring 1973, New York, Cathedral of St. John the Divine, members of The House, including Meredith Monk, Monica Moseley, Lanny Harrison, Blondell Cummings, Lee Nagrin, and Coco Pekelis; November 1973, Brooklyn.

Scored for six voices, electronic organ, and piano.
BIBLIOGRAPHY: John Rockwell, review, *ON* XXXIX (Feb. 2, 1974), 24 [on Brooklyn perf.].

Edward John Eyre, opera in one act by Barry Conyngham; libretto (Eng) by Meredith Oakes and selections from Eyre's *Journals of Expeditions of Discovery* (1845). First performance May 1, 1971, Sydney, Australia, University of New South Wales.

The work covers Eyre's journey of 1840–1841 through the desert of southwest Australia. Eyre is accompanied on the difficult expedition by one aboriginal guide only, named Wylie.
DISCOGRAPHY: soloists, University of New South Wales Opera Orch. and Chorus; cond. R. Covell, His Master's Voice OASD–7562 (1973, 1 LP).

Edwin and Angelina, or, The Banditti, opera in three acts by Victor Pelissier; libretto (Eng) by Elihu Hubbard Smith, after Oliver Goldsmith's ballad (1764). First performance December 19, 1796, New York, John Street Theatre, with Mr. Hodgkinson (Sifrid), Mr. Tyler (Edwin), Mr. Martin (Ethelbert), and Mrs. Hodgkinson (Angelina).

The complex plot is set in northern England. The wealthy Ethelbert, upon reaching adulthood, shuns and then imprisons the poor Sifrid, his childhood friend. Ethelbert also kidnaps Emma, Sifrid's beloved. Sifrid, believing Emma to be dead, escapes and forms a group of bandits. Ethelbert then tries to seduce Angelina, beloved of the knight Edwin, who has become a hermit because Angelina has rejected him. Eventually Sifrid captures Ethelbert but releases him when the latter promises to restore Emma to him. Edwin and Angelina are also reunited.

For a detailed description, see Sonneck/*SIMG*, 474–77. Sonneck describes the work as the first American opera (474).

Two numbers survive, including "The Bird When Summer Charms No More," sung by Angelina.

Goldsmith's ballad was also set by John Stevenson, together with J. Clifton (1815).
LIBRETTO: English (New York: T. & J. Swords, 1797).

Egg, The, operatic riddle in one act by Gian Carlo Menotti; libretto (Eng) by the composer. First performance June 17, 1976, Washington, D.C., Washington Cathedral, with Matthew Murray (Manuel), Anastasios Vrenios (St. Simeon Stylites), and Esther Hinds (the Basilissa); conducted by Paul Callaway.

The allegorical story on the meaning of life is set in the Byzantine Empire in the fifth century. An angel gives an egg to St. Simeon Stylites, who has lived on top of a 60-foot-high pole for thirty years. The egg, which is supposed to contain the meaning of life, is later found by St. Simeon's nephew, Manuel, who gives it to the Basilissa, the empress of Byzantium. She and her court are unable to open it, and so Manuel is thrown out of court. He then gives it to a mother and her starving child, whereupon the egg is opened; it saves the child's life.

BIBLIOGRAPHY: Donal Henahan, "Opera: Double Local Debut of One-Acters in Brooklyn," *NYT* (Nov. 15, 1980), 13 [on New York premiere]; Charles Timbrell, "Reports: U.S.," *ON* XLI (Oct. 1976), 64 [on premiere].

Egypt, opera in three acts by William J. McCoy; libretto (Eng) by the composer. First performance (two acts) September 17, 1921, Berkeley, California, Music Festival.

A setting of the Antony and Cleopatra story, the work opens in Tarsus. Called to answer about her treachery to Rome, Cleopatra instead charms Antony and returns with him to her palace in Alexandria. When her fleet is destroyed at Actium, she retreats to her tomb. Antony dies of his wounds, and Cleopatra, pretending to agree to terms offered by Octavian, dies by the bite of an asp.

SCORE: vs (n.p., n.d.; LCCN: 84-178253).

Egyptian Festival, The, opera in three acts by Charles Florio; libretto (Eng) by Andrew Franklin. First performance March 11, 1800, London, Drury Lane Theatre, with Raymond (Mustapha Muley Bey), Charles Holland (Ali Hassan), Charles Kemble (Murteza), Mme. Mara (Zemira), Mrs. Bland (Nigra), and John Bannister Jr. (Longbow).

LIBRETTO: English (London: J. Ridgway, 1800).

Eight Songs for a Mad King, monodrama in eight parts by Peter Maxwell Davies; libretto (Eng) by Randolph Stow, after King George III's miniature organ that played eight tunes. First performance April 22, 1969, London, Pierrot Players. First U.S. performance July 1970, Aspen, Colorado, Contemporary Music Conference, with Julius Eastman.

The "plot" consists of a monologue by the King as he listens to his birds perform. The dialogue includes actual words uttered by the British monarch and snatches of music from pieces such as Handel's *Messiah.*

For a detailed description, see Eaton/*OP* II, 268–69.

Role: King George III (bass-bar).

BIBLIOGRAPHY: Quaintance Eaton, "Aspen," *ON* XXXV (Sept. 19, 1970), 27 [on U.S. premiere].

Eighth Wonder, The, opera in fifteen scenes by Alan John; libretto (Eng) by the composer and Dennis Watkins. First performance October 14, 1995, Sydney, Australia, with David Hobson, Donald Shanks, and Clare Gormley; conducted by Richard Gill.

About the controversies surrounding the building of the Sydney Opera House.

SCORE: vs (Sydney: Pellinor, 1995).

BIBLIOGRAPHY: John Cargher, "Sydney," *ON* LX (Feb. 17, 1996), 50 [on premiere].

Einstein on the Beach, opera in four acts by Philip Glass, libretto (Eng) by the composer and Robert Wilson, and spoken text by Christopher Knowles, Lucinda Childs, and Samuel M. Johnson; designed by Robert Wilson. First performance July 25, 1976, Avignon Festival. First U.S. performance November 21, 1976, New York, Metropolitan Opera House, with Lucinda Childs and Sheryl L. Sutton; produced by Gilbert Helmsley; choreographed by Andrew deGroat.

The minimalist opera consists of repetitive harmonies and rhythmic patterns that accompany the stage tableaux of Wilson. The tableaux themselves employ four repeating visual images, those of trains, a trial, a spaceship, and Albert Einstein. Einstein often observes the action while he plays his violin. Each "act" is connected by "knee plays," that is, intermezzi.

For a detailed description, see K*INKOB*, 255–56.

This is the first of Glass's series of "portrait" operas; the others are *Satyagraha** (1980) and *Akhnaten** (1984).

The work was parodied by Peter Schickele in his *Prelude to Einstein on the Fritz** (1989).
BIBLIOGRAPHY: Clive Barnes, "'Einstein on the Beach' Transforms Boredom into Memorable Theater," *NYT* (Nov. 23, 1976), 40 [on U.S. premiere].
DISCOGRAPHY: Philip Glass Ensemble; cond. M. Riesman, CBS M4K 38875 (1979, 4 LPs); the same, Elektra Nonesuch 79323-2 (1993, 3 CDs).

Ekkehard, opera in four acts by Florence Ewart; libretto (Eng) by the composer, after Joseph Viktor von Scheffel's novel (1857). First performance (excerpt) November 23, 1923, Melbourne, Australia, Queen's Hall.

The story, set in the tenth century, concerns the young monk Ekkehard, who becomes a tutor of the Duchess, a young widow. The two become attracted to each other, with unhappy results, after which Ekkehard becomes a hermit.

The work uses leitmotifs to represent the emotions of the characters.

Also set by J. J. Abert (1878, Berlin).

eL/Aficionado, opera in one act by Robert Ashley; libretto (Eng) by the composer. First performance 1988, Marseilles. First U.S. performance (concert) October 9, 1991, New York, Merkin Concert Hall, with Thomas Buckner (the Agent), and Robert Ashley, Sam Ashley, and Jacqueline Humbert (Interrogators); Blue Gene Tyranny and Joseph Kubera, pianos.

Continuing the life of the Junior, Jr., an Agent, this work features Interrogators challenging the Agent via various types of musical dialogue.

Part 4 of the tetralogy *Now Eleanor's Idea.**
BIBLIOGRAPHY: Edward Rothstein, "A Mysterious 'Television Opera,'" *NYT* (Oct. 11, 1991), C, 30 [on U.S. premiere].
DISCOGRAPHY: T. Buckner, R. Ashley, T. Hamilton, S. Ashley, J. Humbert, Lovely Music 1004 (1995, 1 CD).

Elanda and Eclipse, opera in two acts by Guy Halahan; libretto (Eng) by the composer. First performance September 12, 1957, London, with Doreen Murray, Johanna Peters, Alan Bratfield, John Stoddart, and Norman Tattersall; conducted by Eric Stanley; produced by John Copley.
BIBLIOGRAPHY: G. Montagu, *London Music* XXII (Nov. 1957), 45 [on premiere].

Eleanor of Aquitaine, opera in two acts by Gillian Whitehead; libretto (Eng) by Fleur Adcock. First performance (act 2) October 1967, Sydney, Australia, Opera Centre.

See C. Floyd's *Flower and the Hawk* (1972, Jacksonville, Fla.) for another treatment of Eleanor.

Election, The, musical interlude in one act by François Hippolyte Barthelemon; libretto (Eng) by Miles Peter Andrews. First performance October 19, 1774, London, Drury Lane Theatre.

The text was written as an attack on candidates who accept bribes.

Election, The, comic opera in three acts by Charles Horn; libretto (Eng) by Samuel J. Arnold, after Joanna Baillie's play. First performance June 7, 1817, London, Lyceum.

Electrification of the Soviet Union, The, opera in two acts by Nigel Osborne; libretto (Eng) by Craig Raine, after Boris Pasternak's novella *The Last Summer* and his verse novel *Spectorsky* (1931). First performance October 5, 1987, Glyndebourne, with Elizabeth Laurence (Anna Arild), Linda Hirst (Natasha), Anna Steiger (Sashka), Jonathan Veira (Lemokh), Henry Herford (Boris Pasternak), and Omar Ebrahim (Serezha Spectorsky); conducted by Elgar Howarth; produced by Peter Sellars.

The "plot," which begins and ends with Boris Pasternak, centers on the historical "electrification" of the USSR, played out in the tensions between various groups, including the inactive artist Serezha Spectorsky, who works as a tutor, and the active revolutionaries Natasha and Lemokh. It also examines Serezha's involvement with two women, Anna Arild, a governess, and Sashka, a prostitute.

Major roles: Boris Pasternak (bar); Serezha Spectorsky (bar); Anna Arild (sop); Sashka (sop); Natasha, Serezha's sister (mezzo); and Lemokh (speaking).
LIBRETTO: English (London and Boston: Faber and Faber, 1986).
BIBLIOGRAPHY: Arthur Jacobs, "'The Electrification of the Soviet Union,'" *Opera* XXXVIII (Dec. 1987), 1449–51 [on premiere]; Anthony Marks, "Glyndebourne," *MT* CXXVIII (Dec. 1987), 707–08 [on premiere].

Elegy for Young Lovers, opera in three acts by Hans Werner Henze; libretto (Ger) by Ludwig Landgraf, Werner Schachtel, and the composer, as *Elegie für junge Liebende*, after the English text by W. H. Auden and Chester Kallman. First performance (in German) May 20, 1961, Schwetzingen Festival, with Eva-Maria Rogner (Hilda), Dietrich Fischer-Dieskau (Mittenhofer), Karl Christian Kohn (Dr. Reischmann), Friedrich Lenz (Toni), Lillian Bennigsen (Caroline), and Ingeborg Bremert (Elisabeth); conducted by Heinrich Bender; produced by the composer. First performance with English text July 13, 1961, Glyndebourne, with Elisabeth Söderström, Dorothy Dorrow, Kerstin Meyer, André Turp, Carlos Alexander, and Thomas Hemsley; conducted by John Pritchard; produced by Günther Rennert. First U.S. performance April 29, 1965, Juilliard School, with Lorna Haywood and Janet Wagner (Caroline), Rita Shane (Hilda), Jack Davison (Mittenhofer), and Robert Jones (Toni); conducted by Christopher West.

The story concerns the great poet Gregor Mittenhofer, who looks for inspiration in the tragedies of others. He goes to the "Schwarzer Adler" Inn in the Alps every year to be moved by the despair of Hilda Mack, still waiting for the return of her husband, who vanished on their honeymoon forty years ago. When the husband is found frozen in a glacier, the poet turns to the young lovers, Toni, his stepson, and Elisabeth. They meet their deaths at the Hammerhorn Mountain, having been sent there by the poet. He then writes his "Elegy for Young Lovers," which he reads to the audience as the opera ends.

For detailed descriptions, see Eaton/*OP* II, 81–82; K/*KOB*, 921–26; K/*NKOB*, 344–46.

Major roles: Gregor Mittenhofer, poet (bar); Hilda Mack, a widow (col sop); Toni, Mittenhofer's stepson (ten); Elisabeth (sop); Caroline, Countess of Kirchstetten and secretary of Mittenhofer (alto); Elisabeth Zimmer (sop); and Dr. Wilhelm Reischmann, a doctor and father of Toni (bass).
SCORE: English-German vs (Mainz: B. Schott's Söhne, 1961; rev. ed. 1989).

BIBLIOGRAPHY: Martin Bernheimer, "Current Chronicle. Munich," *MQ* XLVIII (1962), 118–20, and "New York," *Opera* XVI (1965), 572–73; Frank Martin, "New York Novelties," *ON* XXX (Sept. 25, 1965), 22 [on U.S. premiere]; Hans Werner Henze, "On Writing 'Elegy for Young Lovers,'" *Opera* XII (1961), 433–34; Andrew Porter, "Elegy for Young Lovers," *MT* CII (1961), 418–19 [on Glyndebourne premiere].

Elephant's Child, The, children's opera by Daron Hagen; libretto (Eng) by the composer, after Rudyard Kipling. Composed 1994.

Roles: for six male voices a cappella (or mixed chorus a cappella).

Elephant Steps, "a fearful radio show" by Stanley Silverman; libretto (Eng) by Richard Foreman; electronic music realized by Pril Smiley. First performance August 7, 1968, Lenox, Massachusetts, Tanglewood Music Festival, Berkshire Music Center Fellowship Program; conducted by Michael Tilson Thomas. First New York performance April 24, 1970, Hunter College; conducted by Károly Köpe.

The surrealistic story concerns Hartman, who is ill; Hannah, his wife; Max; Otto; and the Doctor. They are trying to understand Reinhardt, whose house all but Hartman can enter. Hartman, finding refuge in his kitchen with the Scrubwoman, dreams that Elephant Angels have told him to use a ladder to get to Reinhardt's house. He does and sees the mysterious Reinhardt jumping around the room seven times. Hartman is thereby "illuminated."

For a detailed description, see Eaton/*OP* II, 269.

Major roles: Hartman (bass), Max (ten), Dr. Worms (ten), Scrubwoman (sop), Hannah (sop), Otto (bar), and Elephant Angels (sop, alto).

BIBLIOGRAPHY: Harold C. Schonberg, "Music: But Is It Opera?," *NYT* (Apr. 25, 1970), 32 [on New York premiere]; "Opera: Spinning the Dial," *Time*.LXCII (Aug. 16, 1968), 48 [on premiere].
DISCOGRAPHY: S. Belling, K. Altman, M. Sokol, P. Steele, L. Enstad, R. Gagnon, L. Marshall, L. Rix; cond. M. T. Thomas, Columbia M2X-33044 (2 LPs).

Elfrida, "dramatic poem" in five acts by Thomas Arne; libretto (Eng) by George Colman Sr., after William Mason's poem (1751). First performance November 21, 1772, London, Covent Garden, with Mr. Smith (Athelwold), Mr. Bensley (Edgar), Mrs. Mattocks (Albina), and Miss Catley (Elfrida).

The setting is Saxon times. Edgar, King of England, becomes enamored of Elfrida and kills her husband, Athelwold. Elfrida escapes Edgar's clutches by becoming a nun.

For a detailed description, see Fiske/*ETM*, 364–65.

All the vocal parts are for female singers.

El Greco, opera in three acts by William Harper; libretto (Eng) by Bernardo Solano. First performance September 24, 1993, New York, Playhouse 91, with Daryl Henriksen (El Greco), Veronica Tyler (Teresa), and Gabriel Barre (Archbishop Quiroga); designed by Tom O'Horgan.

The work offers a look at events in the life of the famous Renaissance painter, especially his difficult relationship with his son, Jorge Manuel; his assistant, Preboste; his menacing patron, Archbishop Quiroga; and the feminist mystic, Teresa. It includes the coming to life of some of his most famous tableaux, such as *The Burial of Count Orgaz* and *Toledo.*

BIBLIOGRAPHY: Alex Ross, "Linking Distant Strife to That of Modern Times," *NYT* (Sept. 27, 1993), C, 15 [on premiere].

Eliza, opera in three acts by Thomas A. Arne; libretto (Eng) by Richard Rolt. First performance May 29, 1754, London, Little Theatre in the Haymarket.

The title character is Queen Elizabeth, but she never appears in the piece. It is a patriotic offering, during which war and peace are talked about, and it includes a representation of the Spanish Armada. Its lack of any real plot and excessive length probably contributed to its failure, despite its fine music.

For a detailed description, see Fiske/*ETM*, 239–42.

SCORE: vs (London: John Walsh, [1758]); vs (London: Harrison & Co., n.d.).

Elizabeth and Leicester, opera in one act by Edwin S. Lindsey; libretto (Eng) by the composer. First performance April 21, 1936, Chattanooga, Tennessee, University of Chattanooga, John A. Patten Memorial Chapel.

BIBLIOGRAPHY: "Opera in Chattanooga," *NYT* (Apr. 22, 1936), 29 [on premiere].

Ellen, opera in two acts by Alec Wilder; libretto (Eng) by William Engvick. Composed 1955.

Eloise and Abelard, opera in three acts by Gerard Victory; libretto (Eng) by the composer. First performance (excerpts) 1973, RTE, Dublin.

A setting of the Abelard and Heloise story.

See also *Abelard and Heloise* by Ward (1982, Charlotte, N.C.).

Elphi Bey, or, The Arab's Faith, musical drama in three acts, with numbers by Thomas Attwood; libretto (Eng) by Ralph Hamilton. First performance April 17, 1817, London, Drury Lane Theatre.

LIBRETTO: English (London: W. Clowes, 1817).

Embarkation, The, musical entertainment in two acts by William Reeve; libretto (Eng) by Andrew Franklin. First performance October 3, 1799, London, Drury Lane Theatre.

SCORE: vs (London: Goulding, Phipps & D'Almaine, [1799]).

Embrace the Monster, opera by Ken Valitsky; libretto (Eng) by Lydia Lunch. First performance (excerpt) April 21, 1993, New York, American Opera Projects, with Dora Ohrenstein.

The pop-inspired work deals with domestic and political violence.

BIBLIOGRAPHY: Alex Ross, "American Operas in Progress," *NYT* (April 24, 1993) [on first performance].

Emerald Isle, or, The Caves of Carrig-Cleena, comic opera in two acts by Arthur S. Sullivan; completed by Edward German; libretto (Eng) by Basil Hood. First performance April 27, 1901, London, Savoy Theatre, with Henry A. Lytton (Pat Murphy), Robert Evett (Terence O'Brien), Walter Passmore (Professor Bunn), and Rosina Brandram (Countess of Newtown). First U.S. performance September 1, 1902, New York, Herald Square Theatre, with Jefferson de Angelis (Professor Bunn).

The plot, set in Ireland about 1800, concerns an Irish rebel who wins the heart of the daughter of the Lord Lieutenant of Ireland.

Among the highlights is Terence's song "I'm Descended from Brian Boru," one of the few items completely composed and scored by Sullivan.

SCORE: vs (London and New York: Chappell, 1901).

LIBRETTO: English (1900).

Emma, opera in three acts by Murray Boren; libretto (Eng) by Eric Samuelsen, after an incident in Mormon history. First performance January 26, 1984, Provo, Utah, Brigham Young University, with Susan Alexander (Emma). Revised version July 10, 1992, New York, Hell's Kitchen Opera; conducted by the composer.

The story concerns Emma Smith, after her husband, Joseph Smith Jr., founder of the Mormon Church, is killed in Illinois. Although the church leaders decide to go west to avoid further persecution, Emma decides to stay.

SCORE: fs ms, 1983 (NYPL, photocopy).

BIBLIOGRAPHY: Allan Kozinn, review, *NYT* (July 14, 1992), C, 15 [on rev. version]; Dorothy Stowe, "Provo, Utah," *ON* XLVIII (Mar. 31, 1984), 39–40 [on premiere].

Emmeline, opera in two acts by Tobias Picker; libretto (Eng) by J. D. McClatchy, after the novel (1980) by Judith Rossner. First performance July 27, 1996, Santa Fe, Santa Fe Opera, with Patricia Racette (Emmeline), Victor Ledbetter (Maguire), Anne-Marie Owens (Aunt Hannah), Curt Peterson (Matthew), Herbert Perry (Pastor Avery), Kevin Langan (Emmeline's father), and Melanie Sarakatsannis (Sophie); conducted by George Manahan; produced by Francesca Zambello.

The true story concerns Emmeline Mosher, a young girl who comes to work at a Lowell, Massachusetts mill in 1841 and is seduced by, and bears the child of, Maguire, the foreman. Disgraced by her situation, she gives away the child, whom she believes is a girl, and reconstructs her life, marrying Matthew Gurney, a younger man. But at her mother's funeral her Aunt Hannah reveals the awful truth; the young man Emmeline has married is in fact her abandoned son. The horrified community, led by the rigid Pastor Avery, condemns the pair. Matthew flees, but the strong-willed Emmeline vows to stay.

Major roles: Emmeline (sop); Maguire (bar); Aunt Hannah (mezzo); Matthew (ten); Pastor Avery (bass); and Sophie, a friend of Emmeline (sop).

The melody of "Rock of Ages" is included during the wedding scene.

BIBLIOGRAPHY: Glenn Giffin, "Santa Fe, NM," *ON* LXI (Dec. 14, 1996), 64–65 [on premiere]; Allan Kozinn, "Tragedy and Deadly Sins under a Wet Desert Sky," *NYT* (Aug. 5, 1996), C, 15, 16 [on premiere].

DISCOGRAPHY: Racette, Owens, Peterson, Ledbetter, Perry, Langan, Santa Fe Opera; cond. Manahan, recording of premiere, Albany Records 284-85 (2 CDs).

Emperor and the Nightingale, The, opera in three acts by Susan Bingham; libretto (Eng), after Hans Christian Andersen's tale *The Nightingale*. First performance June 1982, New Haven, Connecticut.

See *The Nightingale* for other settings.

Emperor Jones, The, opera in a prologue and two acts by Louis Gruenberg; libretto (Eng) by Kathleen de Jaffa, after Eugene O'Neill's play (1920). First performance January 7, 1933, New York, Metropolitan Opera, with Lawrence Tibbett (Brutus Jones), Marek Windheim (Henry Smithers), Pearl Besuner (old native woman), and Helmsley Winfield (witch doctor); conducted by Tulio Serafin; directed by Alexander Sanine. Revived 1951, Rome; conducted by Serafin. Also February 9, 1979, Detroit, Music Hall, Michigan Opera Theatre, with David Arnold/Andrew Smith (Brutus Jones), Daniel Bottess (Henry Smithers), Frances Brockington (old native woman), Clifford Fears (Congo witch doctor); conducted by Robert Willoughby Jones; directed by Rhoda Levine.

Set on an island in the Caribbean, the story involves an ex-Pullman porter, Brutus Jones, who is also an escaped convict. He has made himself emperor of the islanders but angered many along his way to power. Among his enemies is the Iago-like Cockney trader Henry Smithers. Warned that the people are about to revolt, Jones flees to the jungle, where he is tortured by hallucinations about his past victims. Discovered by the witch doctor, he kills himself.

Major roles: Brutus Jones (bar); Henry Smithers, a Cockney trader (ten); old native woman (sop); and the Congo witch doctor (dancer).

Among the opera's numbers is the spiritual "Standin' in the Need of Prayer," and much of the vocal writing is presented in monologue. Drum rhythms are prominent in the orchestra, and there are several choral interludes. A proposed television showing of the opera in 1950 was canceled because of its possible offense to African Americans. Andrew Porter, writing about its revival in Detroit in 1979 (see Bibliography), found its language "pretty offensive still" and compared it musically to Schoenberg's monodrama *Erwartung* (1924, Prague).

SCORE: English-German vs (Newton Centre, Mass.: GunMar Music, 1990, 1959).

LIBRETTO: English (New York: F. Rullman, 1932).

BIBLIOGRAPHY: Hans Heinsheimer, "Emperor Resurrexit," *ON* XLIII (Feb. 10, 1979), 15–21 [on 1979 revival]; Andrew Porter, review, *NY* LV (Mar. 1979), 115–17 [on 1979 revival].

Emperor Norton, opera in one act by Henry Mollicone; libretto (Eng) by John S. Bowman. First performance May 14, 1981, San Francisco.

Roles: soprano, mezzo-soprano, tenor, and baritone.

Scored for piano, violin, and cello.

Emperor of the Moon, farce by Michael Arne; libretto (Eng), after Aphra Behn. First performance March 22, 1777, London, Patagonian Theatre. First U.S. performance (excerpts) February 17, 1952, New York, Municipal Broadway Center.

Also pantomime by Peter Prelleur, October 15, 1735, London, Goodman's Fields.

Emperor's New Clothes, The, opera in one act for young audiences by Douglas Moore; libretto (Eng) by Raymond Abrashkin, after Hans Christian Andersen. First performance (concert) February 19, 1949, New York, Carnegie Hall.

The story of the vain emperor who is bamboozled by his tailors until an innocent child asks his father why the ruler is not wearing any garments.

Roles: narrator (speaking), child (speaking), the emperor (ten), the prime minister (bar), the father (speaking), his son (speaking), and two tailors (ten).

Emperor's New Clothes, The, opera in one act by Libby Larsen; libretto (Eng) by Timothy Mason, after Andersen. First performance October 13, 1979, Minneapolis.

Emperor's New Clothes, The, unfinished opera by Roger Sessions; libretto (Eng) by Andrew Porter, after Andersen. Composed 1978–1984.

Emperor's New Clothes, The, opera in one act by Judith Dvorkin; libretto (Eng) by the composer, after Andersen. First performance September 1989, New York, Singing Theater.

SCORE: ms score, holograph (1989, photocopy, NYPL).

Empty Bottle, The, opera in three acts by Martin Kalmanoff; libretto (Eng) by Atra Baer. First performance (radio) April 3, 1966, New York, Judson Hall; conducted by

Siegfried Landau. First stage performance July 19, 1991, New York, Amato Opera Theatre, with Garth Taylor (Silvio), Helen Van Tine (his mother), Alicia Alexander (Maria), Sarah Hill (Antonia), and David Kantley (Vincenzo).

The opera is set in Little Italy in the 1930s and deals with the final days and death of Silvio, a gangster from Sicily.

SCORE: vs holograph (NYPL, photocopy).

BIBLIOGRAPHY: Joel Hoenig, "New York," *ON* XXX (May 7, 1966), 23 [on premiere]; Arlo McKinnon Jr., "New York City," *ON* XLVI (Oct. 1991), 46 [on stage premiere].

Empty Places, music theater piece by Laurie Anderson. First performance June 8, 1989, Charleston, South Carolina, Spoleto Festival.

BIBLIOGRAPHY: Laurie Anderson, *Empty Places: A Performance* (New York: Harper Perennial, 1991).

VIDEO: L. Anderson, voice, instruments, computer animation, Brooklyn Academy of Music Opera House, Oct. 4, 1989 (NYPL).

Enchanted Canary, The, children's opera in one act by Noel Stevens; libretto (Eng) by Andrew Oerke. First performance March 18, 1961, Bemidji, Minnesota, Bemidji State College. Also April 1967, Tampa, University of Tampa.

The prince, who wants to be an artist, ignores pressure from Lord Tubby, his father, and his intended bride, Lady Gaga, and goes off to find the princess, trapped in an orange by a witch.

BIBLIOGRAPHY: Joseph Truncale, *Opera Digest* III/2 (1983), 24–25.

Enchanted Garden, The, opera in one act by Thomas Dunhill; libretto (Eng) by the composer. First performance March 1928, London, Royal College of Music.

SCORE: vs (London, Stainer & Bell, Ltd., 1925).

Enchanted Garden, The, children's opera by Robert Shaughnessy; libretto (Eng) by William M. Peterson. Composed 1972.

SCORE: condensed score (n.p., LCCN: 84-114012).

Enchanted Horse, The, or, The Eastern Lovers, opera in three acts by Jonathan Jones. First performance September 30, 1844, New York, Park Theatre, with the composer in the role of the prince.

Enchanted Kiss, The, opera in one act by Robert Russell Bennett; libretto (Eng) by Robert A. Simon, after a short story by O. Henry. First performance (radio, excerpts) December 30, 1945, New York, Mutual Network.

Enchanted Pear Tree, The, comic opera in one act by Hall Overton; libretto (Eng) by John Thompson, after Boccaccio's *Decameron*. First performance February 7, 1950, New York, Juilliard Opera Theatre.

SCORE: vs (New York: American Composers Alliance, 1949).

Enchanted Wood, The, afterpiece by Samuel Arnold; anonymous libretto (Eng). First performance July 25, 1792, London, Little Theatre in the Haymarket.

Una has to choose between the handsome, but self-centered, Ethelred or the kind, but deformed, Julian. Orion helps her by putting her beaus into a magic cauldron, which reverses their physical characteristics.

For a detailed description, see Fiske/*ETM*, 560–61.

SCORE: vs (London: Smart, n.d.).

Enchanter, The, or, Love and Magic, dramatic afterpiece in one act by John Christopher Smith; libretto (Eng) by David Garrick. First performance December 13, 1760, London, Drury Lane Theatre, with Michael Leoni (Kaliel), Thomas Lowe (Zoreb), and Mrs. Vincent (Zaida).

The exotic setting has Zaida as its heroine. She must fend off the advances of Moroc, an enchanter, who attempts to wreck her romance with Zoreb. Moroc in fact does Zoreb in, but Zoreb is revived by Kaliel, Moroc's assistant, who uses the enchanter's magic wand.

For a description, see Fiske/*ETM*, 246–47.

Comic opera version by Tommaso Giordani, January 17, 1765, Dublin, Smock Alley Theatre.

SCORE: fs (London: J. Walsh, [n.d.]).

LIBRETTO: English (London: J. and R. Tonson, 1760).

Enchanter, The, opera-ballet in three acts by Joseph Holbrooke; libretto (Eng) by Douglas Malloch, after Max Rabinoff. First performance, as *The Enchanted Garden*, spring 1915, Chicago, Auditorium Theatre.

The work blends elements of opera, ballet, and mime.

SCORE: vs, as *The Wizard* (London, 1914).

Enchantress, The, or, The Happy Island, musical entertainment by Tommaso Giordani; libretto (Eng) by Anna Maria Edwards. First performance December 31, 1783, Dublin, English Opera House.

LIBRETTO: English (Dublin: H. Colbert, 1787).

Enchantress, The, opera in four acts by Michael Balfe; libretto (Eng) by Alfred Bunn, after the French text of Vernoy de Saint-Georges. First performance May 14, 1845, London, Drury Lane Theatre, with Anna Thillon (Stella), Mr. Weiss (Duke d'Aquila), and William Harrison (Sylvio). First U.S. performance January 31, 1846, Philadelphia, Walnut Street Theater; May 25, 1846, New York, Chatham Theater; March 26, 1849, New York, Broadway Theatre (billed as the first American performance using the 1849 libretto).

Among the highlights is Stella's "Who Has Not Heard," which includes elements of melodrama.

SCORE: fs ms, mostly autograph (1845, British Library, MS. Add. 29344, 29345).

LIBRETTO: English (London: W. S. Johnson, [1845?]; New York: Douglas, [1849]).

Endymion, opera in a prologue, two parts, and an epilogue by John Henry Antill; libretto (Eng) by the composer, after the allegory by John Keats (1817). Composed 1924. First performance July 22, 1953, Sydney, Australia, Tivoli Theatre, New South Wales National Opera Company; conducted by the composer.

About the love of Endymion for the moon goddess.

Endymion, opera-ballet in five scenes by Robert Russell Bennett; libretto (Eng) by Robert A. Simon, after a poem by Bernard le Bovier de Fontenelle. Composed 1927. First performance April 5, 1935, Rochester, Eastman School of Music; conducted by Howard Hanson.

The story concerns the unrequited love of Endymion for the goddess Diana.

S. Coleridge-Taylor's cantata *Endymion's Dream* (1910, Brighton) is another setting.

BIBLIOGRAPHY: review, *NYT* (Apr. 6, 1935), 11 [on premiere].

Engaged, or, Cheviot's Choice, comic opera in three acts, with music by Arthur S. Sullivan; libretto (Eng) from William S. Gilbert's play *Engaged!* (1877), adapted by George Rowell and Kenneth Mobbs. First performance March 27, 1962, Bristol, England, Victoria Rooms. First U.S. performance 1965, New York, Village Light Opera. Revived May 2, 1984, New York, Village Light Opera, with Martha Jean Stener (debutante) and Lawrence Adams (Cheviot Hill); conducted by Ronald W. Noll; directed by Jennifer Stock.

The tightwad Cheviot Hill proposes to every girl whose acquaintance he makes, including a scheming debutante.

The music is based on Sullivan's *The Grand Duke,* The Sorcerer,* Thespis,* Utopia Limited,** and *Di Ballo* (overture).

SCORE: vs (London: Chappell, [1963]).

LIBRETTO: English (London: Chappell, 1963).

BIBLIOGRAPHY: Stephen Holden, "Music: Village Light Opera's 'Engaged!'" *NYT* (May 3, 1984), III, 17 [on revival].

English Cat, The, "a story for singers and instrumentalists" by Hans Werner Henze; libretto (Eng) by Edward Bond, after Balzac's *Peines de coeur d'une chatte anglaise* (1840). First performance, in German, as *Die englische Katze*, June 2, 1983, Schwetzingen, Schlosstheater, in a translation by Ken Bartlett, with Roland Bracht (Arnold), Elisabeth Glauser (Babette), Inga Nielsen (Minette), Regina Marheinek (Louise), Martin Finke (Lord Puff), and Wolfgang Schöne (Tom); conducted by Dennis Russell Davies. First U.S. performance (in English) July 28, 1985, Santa Fe, with Inga Nielsen (Minette), Scott Reeve (Tom), Michael Myers (Lord Puff), Kurt Link (Arnold), and Kathryn Gamberoni (Louise); staged by Charles Ludlam. First British performance (in English) August 21, 1987, Edinburgh, Leigh Theatre, with Susan Roberts (Minette), Erin James (Babette), and Neil Jenkins (Lord Puff); conducted by David Shallon.

The satirical story centers around a community of cats and other animals that dress and act like human beings. It opens on the impending marriage of the aged Lord Puff, president of the Royal Society for the Preservation of Rats, to Minette. This union is opposed by the devious Arnold, Puff's nephew, who is in love with Minette himself.

The marriage finally takes place. Tom returns after a stint in the marines and tries to get Minette to run off with him, but they are apprehended by the Royal Society, and Tom is put on trial. He is freed after the disclosure that he is the long-lost son of Lord Fairport and is therefore the richest cat in England. He then turns his attentions to Babette, Minette's sister, and is about to sign a will giving Babette his entire fortune when he is stabbed by Lucian, who then tells the Royal Society that Tom killed himself. Tom's money thereby reverts to the society, and the opera ends with Louise, a mouse who had become an honorary cat, declaring that she has lost her trust in the cat species.

For a detailed description, see K*INKOB*, 352–54.

Major roles: Lord Puff (ten); Arnold, his nephew (bass); Tom (bar); Minette (sop); Babette, her sister (mezzo); Louise, a mouse (sop); and Lucian, a fox (ten).

The score, despite its occasional dissonance, is written in a neoclassical style and is very melodious.

SCORE: English-German vs (Mainz and New York: Schott, 1983).

BIBLIOGRAPHY: Noël Goodwin, "In Review," *ON* LII (Mar. 12, 1988), 40 [on British premiere]; Horst Koegler, "Reports: Foreign," *ON* XLVIII (Aug. 1983), 42 [on premiere]; Andrew Porter, "Musical Events: Melodious Cats," *NY* LXI (Sept. 2, 1985), 58–59 [on U.S.

premiere]; John Rockwell, "Opera in Santa Fe, Henze's 'English Cat,'" *NYT* (July 29, 1985) [on U.S. premiere].
DISCOGRAPHY: soloists, Parnassus Orch. London; cond. M. Stenz, Wergo WER 6204–2—WER 6205-2 (1989 performance, Berlin, 2 CDs).

English Eccentrics, The, chamber opera in two acts by Malcolm Williamson; libretto (Eng) by Geoffrey Dunn, after Edith Sitwell's work (1933). First performance June 11, 1964, Aldeburgh Festival, Jubilee Hall, with April Cantelo (Princess Caraboo); conducted by Meredith Davies; produced by William Chappell.

The work examines a group of eccentric characters and their decline. Among them are the once wealthy Sarah Whitehead, who is unable to deal with her financial decline; Beau Brummell, a former judge of fashion reduced to living in a boardinghouse; and Princess Caraboo, in reality Mary Barker, who passes herself off as an exotic princess.

English Fleet in 1342, The, historical comic opera in three acts by John Braham; libretto (Eng) by Thomas J. Dibdin. First performance December 14, 1803, London, Covent Garden. First U.S. performance April 26, 1819, New York, Park Theatre.

Among the characters are De Mountfort, Robert of Artois, Oliver de Clisson, John de Montauban, Valentin, Captain Fitzwater, the Bishop of Leon, Jane of Flanders, Adela, Katherine, and Isabel.
SCORE: vs (London: M. P. Corri & Co., 1802?).
LIBRETTO: English (London: Longman et al., 1805).

English Lesson, An, "opera-happening" in one act by Gabriel Charpentier; libretto (Eng) by the composer. First performance August 3, 1968, Stratford, Ontario, National Festival Orchestra; conducted by Lawrence Smith.

Englishmen in India, comic opera in three acts by Henry Rowley Bishop; libretto (Eng) by William Dimond. First performance January 27, 1827, London, Drury Lane Theatre.

Roles: Tancred, Tom Tape, Gulnare, Poplin, Sally, Dorrington, and the Count.
SCORE: ms fs, autograph (1827, British Library, Add. MS. 27720).

Enraged Musician, The. See Ut Pictora Poesis!

Entente Cordiale, postwar comedy in one act by Ethel Smyth; libretto (Eng) by the composer. First performance July 22, 1925, London, Royal Conservatory of Music, with Gwyneth Edwards (Jeanne Arcot), Winifred Burton (Emma Iggins), Robert Gwynne (Erb Iggins), Dunstan Hart (Bill Baylis), and Charles Draper (Charles Arcot).

A lighthearted treatment of the First World War.
SCORE: fs (London: Curwen, 1925).

Ephelia, opera by Harry Lawrence Freeman; libretto (Eng) by the composer. First performance February 9, 1893, Denver.

The work is lost.

Ephesian Matron, The, or, The Widow's Tears, "comic serenata, after the manner of the Italian" in one act by Charles Dibdin; libretto (Eng) by Isaac Bickerstaffe, after Petronius's *Satyricon*. First performance May 12, 1769, London, Ranelagh House, with Mrs. Sophia Baddley (the Matron) and Dibdin (the centurion). Modern revivals include March 13, 1963, London, Royal College of Music; produced by Dennis Arundell; 1971, London; and April 1992, London.

The setting is ancient Rome. A seemingly desolate widow, grieving at her husband's tomb, receives great comfort from the centurion guarding the unburied bodies outside her husband's mausoleum.

For a description, see Fiske/*ETM*, 354–55.

SCORE: vs (London: J. Johnston, n.d.).

BIBLIOGRAPHY: Arthur Jacobs, "Student and Amateur Performances," *Opera* XIV (May 1963), 354 [on 1963 revival]; review, *MT* CXII (1971), 318.

DISCOGRAPHY: B. Mills, J. Streeton, M. Padmore, A. Knight, instrumentalists; cond. P. Holman, "Opera Restor'd," orch. R. Fiske and Holman, Hyperion CDA 66608 (1992, 1 CD).

Epilogue, musical drama in one act by Michael Dansicker; libretto (Eng) by Sarah Schlesinger. Composed 1980.

SCORE: ms vs, holograph (1980, NYPL).

Equation, The, opera in one act by Geoffrey Bush; libretto (Eng) by the composer, after John Drinkwater's play *X=0.* First performance January 11, 1968, London, All Saints, Margaret Street, Sacred Music-Drama Society.

The setting is the time of the Roman siege of Jerusalem in A.D. 70. Two pairs of friends find themselves on opposite sides. Marcus and Junius are idealistic Roman officers, and Simon and David are members of the fanatical Resistance, who believe that a Jewish victory will bring peace and fulfill the vision of Isaiah that "the lion shall lie down with the lamb, and a little child shall lead them."

As the work ends, the Roman Marcus and the Jew Simon have each lost his friend (killed by their opposite numbers) and have discovered that in all wars, regardless of the motive or the place, there can be only one solution to the equation "X equals nothing."

SCORE: vs (London: Elkin, [1967]).

Erode the Great, pageant opera in two acts by John La Montaine; libretto (Eng) by the composer, after the Bible, medieval miracle plays, and the Latin liturgy. First performance December 31, 1969, Washington, D.C.

The plot is a telling of the birth of Christ. The action takes place at Herod's palace and sites near Jerusalem.

Roles: narrator (speaking); Herod the Great (bar); Lightfoot, a messenger (ten); Jaspur, King of Tarsus (ten); Melchior, King of Anatoly (bar); Balthazar, King of Saba (bass); Mary (sop); young angel (ten); Gabriel (ten); two counselors (ten, bar); demon (ten); and Joseph (silent).

Part of the composer's Christmas trilogy; see also *Novellis, Novellis* (1961) and *The Shephardes Playe* (1967).

SCORE: vs (Hollywood: Paul J. Sifler, 1969).

Eros and Psyche, opera in three acts by Conrad Cummings; libretto (Eng) by the composer. First performance November 16, 1983, Oberlin, Ohio, Oberlin College, with Salvatore Campagne (Eros), Ann Panagulias (Psyche), Melisssa Malde/Adriana Repetto (Venus), and Todd Thomas (Zephyr).

The story from Greek myth is that of the god Eros, who falls in love with the mortal Psyche. In the end they are allowed to marry, and Psyche becomes immortal, despite the interference of Venus, the jealous mother of Eros.

Major roles: Eros (ten), Psyche (sop), Venus (sop), and Zephyr (bar).

The opera is written in an eighteenth-century style, and its Baroque-sized orchestra includes a harpsichord.

The story was also set by Tadeusz Kassern (1954, unfin.).
BIBLIOGRAPHY: Philippa Kiraly, "Oberlin (Ohio)," *Opera* XXXV (1984), 391–93 [on premiere].

Errors, chamber opera by Andrew Wilson-Dickson; libretto (Eng) by Roger Warren, after Shakespeare's *Comedy of Errors.* First performance September 18, 1980, Leicester, England, Leicester University at Haymarket Studio.
BIBLIOGRAPHY: Elizabeth Forbes, review, *Opera* XXXI (Sept. 1980), 950 [on premiere].

Escape from Liberty, The, opera by Robert Doellner; libretto (Eng). First performance April 1, 1948, Hartford, Connecticut, Avery Memorial Hall.

Escapes, The, or, The Water-Carrier, musical entertainment in two acts by Thomas Attwood; libretto (Eng) by Thomas Holcroft, after Bouilly's text for Cherubini's *Les deux journées* (1800, Paris). First performance October 14, 1801, London, Covent Garden.
The story, set in 1647 Paris, has as its background the frictions between Cardinal Mazarin and the Paris parliament. It concerns a water carrier and his family who hide a parliamentarian and his wife from the Cardinal's police.
Attwood's score includes music by L. Cherubini.

Escorial, The, opera in one act by Marvin David Levy; libretto (Eng) by the composer and Lionel Abel, after the play by Michel de Ghelderode (1928). First performance May 4, 1958, New York, "Music in Our Time," Lexington Avenue Young Men's and Young Women's Hebrew Association, Kaufman Concert Hall, with Robert Rue (the King), Loren Driscoll (Folial), and Roy Lazarus (the monk); conducted by Margaret Hillis.
The demented King has forbidden the monk to let the bells toll, and the Queen, driven to despair, has sought love at the hands of the court jester, Folial. The King, having found out, poisons the Queen and makes Folial perform a farce for the ruler's amusement. The jester tells the tale of the beggar who becomes a king and then grabs the monarch's crown from his head, making them both equal. The monk comes to inform everyone that the Queen has died, whereupon the King has Folial strangled.
For a detailed description, see Eaton/*OP* I, 184–85.
Major roles: the King (bar), Folial (ten), and the monk (bass).
Also set by Carmine Coppola (not perf.).
BIBLIOGRAPHY: Ross Parmenter, "Music: Opera Premiere," *NYT* (May 5, 1958), 26.

Esmeralda, opera in four acts by Arthur Goring Thomas; libretto (Eng) by T. J. H. Marzials and Alberto Randegger, after Victor Hugo's novel *Notre-Dame de Paris* (1831). First performance March 26, 1883, London, Drury Lane Theatre. First U.S. performance November 19, 1900, New York.
The story concerns Esmeralda, a beautiful gypsy girl, who is in love with Captain Phoebus and desired by the evil archdeacon, Claude Frollo. When she is condemned to death as a witch for refusing Frollo's advances, Quasimodo, the hunchbacked bell ringer who is devoted to her, intervenes.
Other settings of Hugo's story include L. Bertin (1836, Paris); A. Mazzucato (1838, Mantua); A. Dargomyzhsky (1847, Moscow); F. Campagna (1869, St. Petersburg); F. Pedrell, as *Quasimodo* (1875, Barcelona); and F. Schmidt (1914, Vienna). English settings include G. Rodwell's *Quasimodo** (1836, London); and W. Fry's *Notre-Dame of Paris** (1864, Philadelphia).
SCORE: vs (London: Boosey & Co., n.d.; New York: W. A. Pond, [188?]).

LIBRETTO: English (London?: n.p., 1883?).

Esther, opera in two acts by Fritz Hart; libretto (Eng) by the composer, after the Book of Esther. Composed 1923.

The story was also set by Awrel Hughes, in Welsh, as *Esther a Serch yw'r doctor* (1965); see following entries for other settings.

Esther, opera in five acts by Jacob Knoller; libretto (Eng) by the composer, after the Book of Esther. Composed ca. 1941, based on his German version (1930). First (?) performance February 17, 1950, New York.

The tale of Esther, who saves her people from the evil Haman.

Roles: Xerxes (Ahasuerus), King of Persia (bass); Haman (bar); Seres, his wife (alto); Maardokai, leader of the Israelites in Susa (bass); and Esther, his niece (sop). SCORE: vs, manuscript, Eng-Ger (1941, NYPL; LCCN: 84-106872).

Esther, biblical opera in three acts by Jan Meyerowitz; libretto (Eng) by Langston Hughes, after early rabbinical commentaries, the Book of Esther, and the Racine play (1689). First performance March 17, 1957, University of Illinois, Lincoln Hall Theater, with Elaine Quint (Esther); conducted and produced by Ludwig Zirner.

The Persian king Ahasuerus has married Esther, a Hebrew, but he does not know she is Jewish. She has kept her religion a secret on the advice of her uncle Mordecai, but she reveals her identity to the king when his evil adviser Haman plots to destroy all the Jews in Persia. The king respects Esther for her courage and hangs Haman on the gallows the wicked adviser had erected for Esther's coreligionists.

For a detailed description, see Eaton/*OP* I, 58–59.

Major roles: Esther (sop), Ahasuerus (bass-bar), Mordecai (ten), and Haman (bar). BIBLIOGRAPHY: Ruth Berges, "Esther for Urbana," *ON* XXI (Mar. 11, 1957), 14 [on premiere]; Claude Palisca, review, *ON* XXI (Apr. 15, 1957), 15 [on premiere].

Esther, opera in two acts by Eva Noel Harvey; libretto (Eng) by the composer, after the Book of Esther. Composed 1974.

Major roles: Esther (col sop), Ahasuerus (ten), Haman (bar), and Mordecai (bar). SCORE: vs (Johannesburg: Dramatic, Artistic and Literary Rights Organisation, 1974).

Esther, "a vaudeville megillah" by Elizabeth Swados; libretto (Eng) by Elie Wiesel and the composer, after the Book of Esther. First performance February 28, 1988, New York, 92nd Street Y, Mosaic Theater; directed by the composer. SCORE: vs ed. Michael Sottile (New York: Broadway Play, 1989).

Esther, opera in three acts by Hugo Weisgall; libretto (Eng) by Charles Kondek, after the Book of Esther. First performance October 8, 1993, New York, New York City Opera, with Lauren Flanigan (Esther) and Eugene Perry (Xerxes); conducted by Joseph Colaneri; directed by Christopher Mattaliano; designed by Jerome Sirlin.

A treatment of the story of Esther, wife of King Xerxes, and her help in freeing the Jews from bondage in Persia.

The traditionally shaped opera uses a full-sized orchestra and includes a formal ballet.

BIBLIOGRAPHY: Martin Bernheimer, review, *Los Angeles Times* (Oct. 11, 1993), F, 3 [on premiere]; Edward Rothstein, review, *NYT* (Oct. 11, 1993), C, 11 [on premiere]; Mark Swed, "New York City," *ON* LVIII (Dec. 25, 1993), 34–35 [on premiere].

Esther and Cousin Mordecai, folk opera in four acts by Evelyn La Rue Pittman; libretto (Eng) by the composer, after the biblical story. First performance May 8, 1957, Paris. First U.S. performance (excerpts) September 26, 1962, New York, Carnegie Hall. SCORE: vs (n.p., n.d.; LCCN: 84-109525).

Estranged, "parlor opera" in one act by Alfred B. Sedgwick, after Verdi's *Il trovatore* (1853, Rome); text (Eng) adapted from Charles Sears Lancaster's comedietta *Advice to Husbands.* First performance 1876, New York?

The plot concerns Frank Trevor, who has been deceived into thinking that he killed a man and that his bride of just six months has been unfaithful to him. Returning from service in the army, Frank unknowingly saves his wife from an attacker and discovers his innocence and that of his wife.

Roles: General Leslie; Frank Trevor, known as Colonel Rasileigh; and Mrs. Trevor, Leslie's daughter.
SCORE AND LIBRETTO: vs (New York: Robert M. De Witt, 1876); repr. ed. Michael Meckna, *NAMT,* vol. 7 (1994).

Eternal Road, The, biblical drama in a prologue and three acts by Kurt Weill; libretto (Eng) by Ludwig Lewisohn; additional lyrics by Charles Alan; a revision of Franz Werfel's four-act text for the original version, *Der Weg der Verheissung* (1935, un-perf.). First performance of the Lewisohn version January 7, 1937, New York, Manhattan Opera House, with Sam Jaffe (the Adversary), Lotte Lenya (Miriam/witch of Endor), and Sidney Lumet (son of the Estranged One); conducted by Isaac Van Grove and Leo Kopp; directed by Max Reinhardt; produced by Meyer Weisgal. A moderate success but financial disaster, it ran for 153 performances. Revised as *Propheten* by David Drew; first performance May 28, 1998, Vienna; conducted by Dennis Russell Davies. Original version revived in an abridged concert version, as *Kings and Prophecies,* October 4, 1998, New York, Avery Fisher Hall; conducted by Leon Botstein.

The work opens in a small synagogue; a rabbi tells his congregants, who are seeking shelter from a pogrom, of the history of the Israelites, including the stories of Abraham, Moses, Ruth, and David, through the Diaspora. The congregation is forced to leave the sanctuary at the end by a group of soldiers, but they are heartened by visions of the Messiah.

Major roles (singing): the Rabbi (bar), Eliezer (bar), White Angel (ten), Abraham (bar), Rachel (sop), Joseph (bar), Moses (bar), Miriam (sop), Voice of God (bar), Angel of Death (bass), Ruth (mezzo), Boaz (bar), Saul (bar), David (ten), Solomon (bar), and Jeremiah (bar), speaking: the Estranged One and his son, the Adversary, and the witch of Endor.

Parts of *The Eternal Road* were used by Weill for two more works on Jewish subjects, *We Will Never Die* (1943), which tried to raise awareness about the extermination of the Jews—it was directed by Moss Hart and produced by Billy Rose, with a text by Ben Hecht; and *A Flag Is Born* (1946)—with a text by Hecht and directed by Luther Adler—in support of a Jewish homeland in Palestine. The history of the three works is examined by Stephen J. Whitfield in "The Politics of Pageantry, 1936–1946," *American Jewish History* LXXXIV (Sept. 1, 1996), 221–51.

The Jewish experience in Palestine is treated in Jacob Weinberg's *Hechalutz (The Pioneers),* given in 1926 in Jerusalem (excerpts) and in 1934 in New York (complete).

Ethan Frome, lyric opera in three acts and an epilogue by Douglas Allanbrook; libretto (Eng) by John Clinton Hunt, after Edith Wharton's novel (1911). Composed

1952. First performance 1981, Opera America Showcase. First full performance November 13, 1998, Cambridge, Massachusetts, Harvard-Radcliffe Dramatic Club.

The story of the unhappy hero, his nagging, hypochondriacal wife, Zeena, and her cousin, Mattie, with whom Frome falls in love, with disastrous results.
LIBRETTO: English, typescript (ca. 1950, NYPL, photocopy).

Ethan Frome, opera in two acts by John Beall; libretto (Eng) by Jack Held, after Wharton. First performance November 18, 1997, Morgantown, West Virginia, West Virginia University Opera Theater.
SCORE: vs, fs (New York: American Music Center, 1997).

Eugene Aram, opera in four acts by Granville Bantock; libretto (Eng), after Edward Bulwer-Lytton's novel *Eugene Aram* and Thomas Hood's poem *The Dream of Eugene Aram*. Composed 1892. Not completed.

A schoolmaster resorts to crime when he becomes poor and is tortured by his guilty conscience thereafter.

Europeras 1 & 2, "opera" in two unrelated parts by John Cage, after music by Mozart, Puccini, and others. First performance December 12, 1987, Frankfurt, Schauspielhaus. First U.S. performance July 14, 1988, Purchase, New York, Pepsico Summerfare, Frankfurt Opera; conducted by Gary Bertini.

Musically, the work involves a collection of operatic fragments by past composers, sung by performers wearing costumes that may or may not be related to the original costumes or vocal types. Ballet dancers enter and exit during the proceedings, and the scenery includes panels of past composers, animals, and birds. There are twelve alternative plots described in the program accompanying the performance, but none of them is enacted onstage. The various aspects of the work were composed through chance methods, employing Andrew Culver's *I Ching* computer program.
SCORE: scenario (New York: Henmar Press, 1988).
BIBLIOGRAPHY: John Rockwell, review, *NYT* (July 16, 1988), 11 [on U.S. premiere].

Europeras 3 & 4, "operas" by John Cage. First performance June 17, 1990, London, Almeida Theatre; directed by Andrew Culver. First U.S. performance November 13 and 14, Long Beach, California, Long Beach Opera, Convention Center Theater; directed by Culver.

Europera 3 is scored for six singers, two pianists, and six players; *Europera 4* is for two singers, player, and pianist. The singers compete against recordings of singers of the past, and the pianists play bits and pieces of Liszt opera transcriptions. The performing parts are generated by chance methods, employing Culver's *I Ching* computer program.
DISCOGRAPHY: V. Ray, B. Pezzone, pianos; cond. A. Culver, Mode 38–39 (1995, 2 CDs).
BIBLIOGRAPHY: Daniel Cariaga, review, *ON* LVIII (Feb. 5, 1994), 41 [on U.S. premiere]; Keith Potter, "Almeida's Operas," *MT* CXXXI (Sept. 1990), 495–96 [on premiere].

Europera 5, "opera" by John Cage. First performance April 18, 1991, Buffalo, New York, SUNY-Buffalo, Slee Hall.

The sixty-minute piece is scored for two singers, pianist, director, television set, radio, and Victrola. The singers each perform five arias, and the piano plays arrangements of the arias.

For a detailed discussion of *Europeras 1–5*, see William Fetterman, *John Cage's Theatre Pieces* (Amsterdam: Overseas Publishing Association, 1996), 167–87.

DISCOGRAPHY: M. Herr, G. Burgess, Y. Mikhashoff, J. Williams, D. Metz, Mode 36 (1 CD).

Eurydice, "a farce: as it was d-mned" (ballad opera); libretto (Eng) by Henry Fielding. First performance 1743?, London, Drury Lane Theatre.

Roles: Pluto, Orpheus, Proserpine, Eurydice, Charon, and ghosts.
LIBRETTO: English, in *Miscellanies*, vol. 2 (Dublin: John Smith, 1743); repr. ed. Rubsamen/*BO*, vol. 7, *Classical Subjects I: Satire and Burlesque* (1974).

Evangeline, "musical comedy" by Edward Everett Rice, script by J. Cheever Goodwin. First performance New York, July 27, 1874, New York, with Ione Burke (Evangeline) and Connie Thompson (Gabriel). Successful revival June 4, 1876, New York, Daly's, with Eliza Weathersby (Gabriel), and Lizzie Harold (Evangeline).

The story is a travesty of Henry Wadsworth Longfellow's narrative poem *Evangeline* (1847). Its heroine, Evangeline, and her lover, Gabriel, end up together, after being pursued by, among things, a heifer.

The "Heifer Dance" was one of the most popular parts of the work, and the musical itself became one of the most popular musicals of the last two decades of the nineteenth century.
SCORE AND LIBRETTO: vs (New York: T. B. Harms & Co., 1877 [1886?]); promptbook (1874); repr. ed. Richard Jackson, *NAMT*, vol. 13 (1994).

Evangeline, dramatic opera in three acts by Otto Luening; libretto (Eng) by the composer, after Longfellow. First performance May 10, 1948, New York, Columbia University, Brander Matthews Theater, with Teresa Stich (Evangeline), Alfred Kunz (Gabriel), and Josh Wheeler (Felicien); conducted by the composer. Revived February 8, 1985, New York, After Dinner Opera Company.

The story, set in Nova Scotia in the 1700s, follows selected themes from Longfellow's narrative, in which Evangeline and her lover, Gabriel, are forced to part when the British throw the Acadians out of Nova Scotia. They are reunited only years later, when Evangeline nurses the dying Gabriel during an epidemic in Philadelphia.

Major roles: Evangeline Bellefontaine (sop), Gabriel Lajeunesse (ten), and Father Felicien (bass).
SCORE: vs (New York, London, and Frankfurt: C. F. Peters, 1974).
BIBLIOGRAPHY: Olin Downes, "Opera by Luening Has Its Premiere," *NYT* (May 6, 1948), 31; review, *NYT* (Feb. 13, 1985), II, 22 [on revival].

Evening for Three, An, opera in one act by Gerard Victory; libretto (Eng) by the composer, after Lotte Ingrisch. First performance (concert) July 19, 1976, RTE, Dublin. First stage performance May 17, 1980, Dublin, Carroll's.

Even unto Bethlehem, opera in four scenes by Fritz Hart; libretto (Eng) by the composer. First performance December 20, 1943, Honolulu, Academy of Arts.

Eve of Adam, The, operatic romance in one act by John Duffy. First performance June 1, 1955, Interlaken, Massachusetts, Stockbridge School.

Eve of St. John, The, opera in one act by Alexander Mackenzie; libretto (Eng) by Eleanor Farjeon. First performance April 16, 1924, Liverpool.

The work examines the phenomenon of midsummer madness in reference to love, as in *A Midsummer Night's Dream.**

LIBRETTO: English (London: Ascherberg, Hepwood & Crew, 1925).

Everyman, choral opera in a prologue and four acts by William Lester; libretto (Eng) by the composer after the medieval morality play. First performance April 24, 1927, Chicago, Biennial Convention of the National Federation of Music Clubs; conducted by the composer.

Death is told to find Everyman and tell him that he is about to die. After receiving the news, Everyman is refused aid by Fellowship, Kindred, and Goods. He is, however, supported by Good Deeds, Knowledge, and Confession, among others, with Good Deeds staying with Everyman as his earthly existence comes to an end.

See also the next entry, *Reverend Everyman,* and *The Summoning of Everyman.*
SCORE: vs (New York and Birmingham, Engl.: J. Fischer & Bro., 1927).

Everyman, opera in one act by Vaclav Nelhybel; libretto (Eng), after a medieval morality play. First performance October 30, 1974, Memphis, Tennessee.
SCORE: ms score, photocopy (Hackensack, N.J.: Barta Music Co., 1979).

Ever Young, The, opera in five scenes by Rutland Boughton; libretto (Eng) by the composer. Composed 1929. First performance September 9, 1935, Bath, Pavilion.

Evil Eye, The, "a legend of the Levant: a romantic musical drama" in two acts by George Rodwell; libretto (Eng) by Richard B. Peake. First performance August 18, 1831, London, Adelphi.
LIBRETTO: English (London: T. H. Lacy, [1831?]).

Evita, all-sung rock opera in two acts by Andrew Lloyd Webber; libretto (Eng) by Tim Rice. First performance June 21, 1978, London, Prince Edward Theatre, with Julie Covington (Evita). First U.S. performance September 25, 1979, New York, Broadway Theatre, with Patti LuPone (Evita), Bob Gunton (Péron), and Mandy Patinkin (Che Guevara); directed by Harold Prince. The New York production ran for 1,567 nights.

The events of Eva (Evita) Péron's life are recounted by the ever-present and mocking Che Guevara, her revolutionary countryman. Act 1 opens in a movie theater in 1952 with the announcement of her death and returns to her humble beginnings as Eva Duarte in a small Argentinian town, her career as an easy woman and obscure actress, and her increasing fame, which culminates in her marriage to the Argentinian strongman Juan Péron in 1945. In act 2 Evita, catering especially to the workers and the poor, becomes extremely powerful politically but is blocked from becoming vice president. The work ends with her death from cancer at the age of thirty-three.

The chorus is present in most of the scenes, clothed in the garb appropriate to the action unfolding, as with the demonstrations against Péron or the grieving populace mourning the death of the almost deified Evita.

Among the musical highlights are Evita's "Don't Cry for Me, Argentina" and the imaginary confrontation of Che and Evita, "Waltz for Eva and Che."

The work was made into a movie in 1996, with Madonna in the title role, Jonathan Pryce as Péron, and Antonio Banderas as Che.
SCORE: vs (Melville, N.Y.: Leeds Music Corp., [1979]).
LIBRETTO: English (London: Elm Tree Books, 1978).
DISCOGRAPHY: J. Covington, London Philharmonic Orch.; cond. A. Bowles, MCA Records, MCA2-11003 (1976, London, 2 LPs); P. LuPone, M. Patinkin, B. Gunton, MCA Records, MCAD2-11007 (1979, Universal City, Calif., 2 LPs).

Excitement at the Circus, children's opera in one act by Allan Blank; libretto (Eng) by Irving Leitner. First performance spring 1969, Paterson, New Jersey.

Exile, The, melodramatic opera in three acts by Joseph Mazzinghi; libretto (Eng) by Frederick Reynolds, after Sophie Cottin's *Elisabeth, ou, Les exilés de Sibérie*. First performance November 10, 1808, London, Covent Garden. First U.S. performance April 27, 1810, New York, Park Theatre.

Set at the time of Empress Elizabeth of Russia, the story concerns Count Ulrick, who is exiled to Siberia. His daughter, Alexina, travels to Moscow in search of a pardon and is aided by Romanoff, who is in disguise. Alexina is successful and weds Romanoff.
LIBRETTO: English (Charleston, S.C.: J. Maxwell, 1810).

Experiment, The, chamber opera in one act by Paul Schwartz; libretto (Eng) by Kathryn Schwartz, after Nathaniel Hawthorne's short story *Dr. Heidegger's Experiment*. First performance January 27, 1956, Gambier, Ohio, Baldwin-Wallace College. Revived 1971.

The wise Dr. Heidegger promises to make his friends young again if they promise that they will not repeat the mistakes they made when they were young. The friends protest that, of course, they have learned from their errors. When they drink water from a supposed Fountain of Youth, they proceed to behave foolishly.

Major roles: Dr. Heidegger (bar); Widow Wycherly, a faded beauty (sop); Colonel Killigrew, an old wastrel (ten); Melbourne, a poor former merchant (bar); and Gascoigne, a failed politician (bass).

See *Dr. Heidegger's Experiment* and *Dr. Heidegger's Fountain of Youth* for other settings.
BIBLIOGRAPHY: Mario Alch, "The Experiment—Paul Schwartz," *OJ* IV (1971), 25–26.

Exposition of a Picture, The, conversation in one act by Stephen Oliver; libretto (Eng) by the composer. First performance June 24, 1986, London, Royal Academy of Arts.

Two painters meet at a museum in about 1850 in front of a painting of Mary Magdalene. The artists are, in fact, from operas by Puccini: one is Marcello, from *La bohème*, and the other an old Italian whose beloved was named Tosca.

Cast: ten and bar.
The work is scored for string quartet.

Eye of Horus, The, mono-opera in one act by Halim El-Dabh; libretto (Eng) by the composer. First performance spring 1967, Boston.

Eyes and No Eyes, or, The Art of Seeing, comic opera in three acts by Thomas German Reed; libretto (Eng) by William S. Gilbert after Hans Christian Andersen's *The Emperor's New Clothes*. First performance July 5, 1875, London, St. George's Hall. The opera was rescored by "Florian Pascal" (Joseph Benjamin Williams) for a performance in 1896.

In the satirical plot, twin brothers Pierrot and Arlequin are in love with Clochette and Columbine. Cassandre, the girls' uncle, is in love with the elderly coquette Nicolette. Clochette and Columbine claim that they have a cloak that can be seen only by genuine lovers. In the end, the brothers, now chastened, give up flirting.

Roles: Cassandre (bass), Columbine (mezzo), Clochette (sop), Arlequin (bar), Pierrot (ten), and Nicolette (alto/mezzo).

For an analysis, see Stedman/*GBS*, 44–47.
LIBRETTO: English, for "Pascal" setting (London: J. Williams); Stedman/*GBS*, 199–254.

F

Fables, "five very short operas" by Ned Rorem; libretto (Eng) by Marianne Moore, a translation of poems from Jean de La Fontaine's *Fables* (1668–1694). First performance May 21, 1971, Martin, Tennessee, University of Tennessee, Fine Arts Building; conducted by Marilyn Jewett.

The work is based on La Fontaine's *The Lion in Love, The Sun and the Frogs, The Bird Wounded by an Arrow, The Fox and the Grapes,* and *The Animals Sick with the Plague.*

It is set for a minimum of three singers, chorus, and mimes ad libitum, accompanied by piano.

SCORE: vs (New York: Boosey & Hawkes, [1974]).

Fables, chamber opera in two acts by Hugh Aitken; libretto (Eng) by the composer, after Jean de La Fontaine's *Fables* (1668–1694). First performance November 1, 1975, Washington, D.C., Library of Congress, New York Chamber Soloists.

The work is based on ten of Aesop's fables, *The Cicada and the Ant, The Oak and the Reed, The Wolf and the Lamb, The Pilgrims and the Oyster, The Companions of Odysseus, The Raven and the Fox, The Meeting Held by the Rats, The Cat and the Two Sparrows, The Animals Sick with the Plague,* and *Death and the Woodcutter.*

For a detailed description, see Kornick/*RAO*, 12–14.

SCORE: vs (n.p., 1974).

Face on the Barroom Floor, The, opera in one act by Henry Mollicone; libretto (Eng) by John S. Bowman, after the ballad by H. Antoine D'Arcy. First performance July 22, 1978, Central City, Colorado, Opera House; it was written for the 100th anniversary of the opera house.

The story is a western American parable of the true tale of a woman's face that was painted on the floor of the Teller House Saloon in the 1930s. Two young people, Larry and Isabelle, enter a bar and hear about the story of the face of Madeline from Tom, the bartender. Madeline was killed during a fight between Matt and John. Isabelle, Larry, and Tom assume the identity of the characters of the tale. When they come back to the present, the drama takes a tragic turn when Isabelle is killed in a fight between Tom, Isabelle's secret lover, and Larry.

For a detailed description, see Kornick/*RAO*, 198–200.

Roles: Isabelle/Madeline (sop), Larry/Matt (ten), and Tom/John (bar).

The work is scored for three voices, with piano, flute, and violoncello.

SCORE: vs (Melville, N.Y.: Belwin-Mills, 1979).

BIBLIOGRAPHY: Andrew Porter, "Musical Events," *NY* LV (Aug. 27, 1979), 84–85 [on 1979 revival].

DISCOGRAPHY: McGiffin, McCauley, Holloway, Lenichek (flute), Banks (cello), Mollicone (piano). CRI SD–442; rev. Eric Dalheim, *American Music* I/3 (1983), 110; John W. Freeman, "Records," *ON* XLV (Apr. 11, 1981), 52.

Fahrenheit 451, opera in one act by Benton Broadstock; libretto (Eng) by Ray Bradbury, after his novel (1953). Composed 1992.

The action takes place in a futuristic society in which people are forbidden to read books, and firemen start conflagrations to burn the offending tomes. One such fireman, Montag, changes his mind after reading a contraband book and, after being forced to incinerate his newly acquired "treasures," escapes and finds refuge with a group called the "book people."

The work uses an electronic score on compact disc.

Ray Bradbury's story was also made into a successful movie, starring Oskar Werner and Julie Christie (1966).

Failing Kansas, quasi-opera by Mikel Rouse; libretto (Eng) by the composer, after Truman Capote's *In Cold Blood* (1969). First performance February 3, 1995, New York, the Kitchen; revived March 22, 1997, St. Louis, New Music Circle, Steinberg Auditorium, with Mikel Rouse.

The work is performed by one person and concerns the murder of a Kansas farm family by two ex-convicts, who are eventually captured and executed for their crime. BIBLIOGRAPHY: Jeff Daniel, "Redefining Opera: 'Failing Kansas,'" *St. Louis Post-Dispatch* (Mar. 20, 1995), 19, and "Bloody Crime in Kansas Makes Interesting Opera," *St. Louis Post-Dispatch* (Mar. 26, 1995), E, 4 [on revival]; Edward Rothstein, "Capote's 'In Cold Blood' as Basis of a Quasi Opera," *NYT* (Feb. 6, 1995), C, 12 [on premiere].

Fair American, The, opera in three acts by Thomas Carter; libretto (Eng) by Frederick Pilon. First performance May 18, 1782, London, Drury Lane Theatre. First U.S. performance November 9, 1789, New York, John Street Theatre, with Anna Phillips (Angelica).

The "Fair American" of the title, Angelica, is saved by a British officer.
LIBRETTO: English (London: T. Evans, 1782).

Fairies, The, opera in a prologue and three acts by John Christopher Smith; libretto (Eng) by David Garrick, after Shakespeare's *A Midsummer Night's Dream* (1596), with additional text from Milton, Waller, Lansdown, Dryden, Hammond, and others. First performance February 3, 1755, London, Drury Lane Theatre. First U.S. performance May 29, 1786, New York.

An adaptation of the Shakespeare play minus the comic sections.

For a detailed description, see Fiske/*ETM*, 243–46.

The overture comes from Smith's *Daphne* (1744), a pastoral.
SCORE: vs (London: Printed for I. Walsh, [1755]).

Fairies' Revelry, The, operatic cantata ("summer night fantasy") by Richard Kieserling for soprano solo and three-part solo chorus. Composed 1924.
SCORE: vs (Philadelphia: Theodore Presser Co., 1924).

Fairies' Revels, The, or, Love in the Highlands, burletta in one act by Samuel Arnold; libretto (Eng) by John Fawcett, after Thomas Moore's poem *The Ring*. First performance August 14, 1802, London, Little Theatre in the Haymarket.

The work includes the famous "Bluebells of Scotland."
LIBRETTO: English (London: Woodfall, 1802).

Fair Means or Foul, opera in one act for a young audience by Seymour Barab; libretto (Eng) by the composer. Composed 1983.

The Prince, a contemplative sort, is threatened by the evil Regent, who intends to keep the young man from ascending the throne. The plan is foiled, however, by the determined Princess.

Roles: the Princess (sop), the Fairy Godmother (sop), the governess (mezzo), the Prince (ten), and the Penultimate Plenipotentiary (bar).

SCORE: vs (New York: G. Schirmer, 1984).

Fair Peruvian, The, comic opera in three acts by James Hook; anonymous libretto (Eng), after Marmontel's text for Grétry's *L'amitié à l'épreuve* (1770, Fontainebleau). First performance March 18, 1786, London, Covent Garden, with Mrs. Billington (Coraly). Also known under the title *The Peruvian*.

The story involves the Peruvian girl Coraly, who has been brought to England by an English sailor. When he goes on another voyage, he leaves Coraly with his friend Belville. After she falls in love with Belville, the sailor, on his return, graciously gives up his claims to her.

SCORE: vs (London: S., A., & P. Thompson, n.d.).

LIBRETTO: English, as *The Peruvian* (London: J. Bell, 1786).

Fair Rosamond, opera in four acts by John Barnett; libretto (Eng) by C. Z. Barnett. First performance February 28, 1837, London, Drury Lane Theatre, with Emma Romer (Rosamond).

The story centers on a liaison between Rosamond and King Henry II. Rosamond learns her lover's true identity only at the coronation. When Queen Eleanor finds out about the affair, she intends to kill Rosamond but is stopped from doing so at the last moment.

For a description, see Biddlecombe/*EO*, 82–83, passim.

This grandiose work includes a five-part madrigal in the fourth act, "Merrily Wake Music's Measure."

The plot was used earlier by J. Addison in his *Rosamond,** set by T. Clayton (1707, London), and by T. A. Arne (1733, London). F. C. Burnand's *Fair Rosamond, or, The Maze, the Maid, and the Monarch!* (1862, London) is a satirical treatment of the story.

SCORE: vs (London: Cramer & Co. [n.d.]).

LIBRETTO: English (London: John Duncombe, [1837]).

Fair Traders, The, boys' opera in three scenes by Hugo Cole; libretto (Eng) by the composer. First performance August 30, 1971, Wokingham, England, Town Hall.

Fairy Favour, The, masque in one act by J. C. Bach; libretto (Eng) by Thomas Hull. First performance January 31, 1767, London, Covent Garden, with Tom Linley (Puck).

The cast consists of children. In the story, Titania's "boy," Puck, who has disappeared, turns up in a castle near the Thames.

The work, which is Bach's only original stage work in English, was written for a visit to the theater of the future Prince Regent when he was four years old. Only the libretto survives.

Also a pantomime with text probably by James Wrighten (1790).

LIBRETTO: English (London: J. Cooper, 1766).

Fairy Festival, The, all-sung masque in one act by Thomas Attwood; libretto (Eng) by John Rose. First performance May 13, 1797, London, Drury Lane Theatre, with Miss Leake and Miss Wentworth.

Fairy Lake, The, adaptation by George Alexander Lee of Auber's *Le lac des fées* (1839, Paris); libretto (Eng), after Scribe and Mélesville. First performance October 26, 1839, London, Drury Lane Theatre.

Another version of the Auber work, with additional music by Hérold, Marschner, and Mercadante, with an English text by C. Selby, appeared on May 13, 1839, London, Strand Theatre.

Fairyland, opera in three acts by Horatio Parker; libretto (Eng) by Brian Hooker. First performance July 1, 1915, Los Angeles, with Marcella Craft (Rosamund), Ralph Errolle (Auburn), William Wade Hinshaw (Corvain), Albert Reiss (Robin), and Kathleen Howard (Myriel); conducted by Alfred Hertz.

The work is set in Central Europe in the thirteenth century. Rosamund, a novice, falls in love with King Auburn, who gives up his crown to Abbess Myriel. His brother Corvain strikes him, leaving him for dead. Auburn is saved by the fairies and meets Rosamund once again. When they are seized by Corvain and Myriel, now his ally, and are condemned to be burned at the stake, throngs of fairies rush in and save the pair, who then rule over their domain.

Roles: Auburn, King, then Prince of Fairyland (heroic ten); Corvain, his brother (bass); Myriel, the Abbess (mezzo); Rosamund (high sop); and Robin (lyric ten).
SCORE: vs (New York: G. Schirmer, 1914; New Haven, Conn.: Yale University Press, 1915).
LIBRETTO: English (New Haven, Conn.: Yale University Press, 1915).

Fairy Oak, The, opera in three acts by Henry Forbes; libretto (Eng) by Henry C. Coape (or Edward Fitzball). First performance October 18, 1845, London, Drury Lane Theatre.

Fairy Prince, The, afterpiece by Thomas Arne; libretto (Eng) by George Colman Sr., after Ben Jonson's court masque *Oberon, the Fairy Prince* (1611). First performance November 12, 1771, London.
SCORE: vs (London: Welcker, [1771]).
LIBRETTO: English (London: T. Becket, 1771).

Fairy Queen, The, ballet-opera in a prologue and five acts by Henry Purcell; anonymous libretto (Eng), possibly by Elkanah Settle, adapted from Shakespeare's *A Midsummer Night's Dream* (1596). First performance May 2, 1692, London, Dorset Gardens, with Mrs. Aliff, Mrs. Dyer, Mr. Freeman, Mrs. Butler, Mr. Pate, and Mr. Reading. First U.S. performance April 30, 1932, San Francisco, Palace of the Legion of Honor.

The work adds to Shakespeare's characters a host of strange creatures, including nymphs and monkeys and gods and goddesses, not to mention Chinese dancers and the four seasons. The character of Theseus is represented by the Duke, who wishes his daughter Hermia to wed Demetrius. In the end Titania and Oberon persuade the Duke to allow Hermia to wed Lysander, and they call on Juno to bless the lovers.

Major roles (actors): the Duke (Theseus), Hermia, Demetrius, Lysander, Puck, Oberon, and Titania; (singers): the drunken poet (bar); Night (sop); Sleep (bass); Idyllic love (sop); Corydon, a shepherd (bar); Mopsa, a shepherdess (sop); Phoebus Apollo (ten); Juno (sop); and Hymen (bass).

The piece consists of a series of arias and dances.

SCORES: fs ed. J. S. Shedlock (1903), as vol. 23, *Collected Works* (1914), rev. ed. Anthony Lewis, *The Works of Henry Purcell*, vol. 12 (London: Novello and Co., 1968); vs (Borough Green, Sevenoaks, Kent: Novello, 1966).
BIBLIOGRAPHY: *Purcell's The Fairy Queen . . . A Photographic Record by Edward Mandinian*, with preface by Edward J. Dent, articles by Constant Lambert and Michael Ayrton (London: John Lehmann, 1948); Roger Savage, "The Shakespeare–Purcell Fairy Queen: A Defence and Commendation," *Early Music* I/4 (1973), 200–21.
DISCOGRAPHY: B. Bonney, S. McNair, E. von Magnus-Harnoncourt, Concentus Musicus Wien; cond. N. Harnoncourt, Teldec (1995, 2 CDs); L. Hunt, C. Pierard, S. Bickley, H. Crook, M. Padmore, R. Wistreich, D. Wilson-Johnson, Schütz Choir of London, London Classical Players; cond. R. Norrington, EMI Classics CDCB 55234 (1994, London, 1 CD).

Fairy Tale, The, afterpiece pastiche in two acts by Michael Arne, after John Christopher Smith's *The Fairies** (1755, London), epilogue songs by Samuel Arnold; libretto by George Colman Sr., based on David Garrick's version for Smith, after Shakespeare's *A Midsummer Night's Dream*. First performance July 18, 1777, London, Haymarket. The work contains five numbers by Arne.

Falcon, The, chamber opera in one act by Hugo Cole; libretto (Eng) by Norman Platt, after Boccaccio. First performance August 29, 1968, Bath, Shawford Mill.

Fallen Fairies, The, opera in two acts by Edward German; libretto (Eng) by William S. Gilbert. First performance December 15, 1909, London, Garrick Theatre.

Fall of Algiers, The, grand opera in three acts by Henry Rowley Bishop; libretto (Eng) by C. E. Walter, after John Payne. First performance January 19, 1825, London, Drury Lane Theatre, with Catherine Stephens (Lauretta). First U.S. performance July 4, 1827, Philadelphia, New (Chestnut Street) Theatre.
   The plot is a mixture of Mozart's *Die Entführung aus dem Serail* and Rossini's *L'Italiana in Algeri*. The story concerns the young hero Algernon Rockwardine, whose wife, Amanda, has been captured by pirates and is now in the seraglio of the Bey of Algiers, Orasmin. In an effort to free his wife, Algernon is captured and made a slave. After an escape attempt with a ladder fails, the couple seems doomed until the intervention of Algernon's father, Admiral Rockwardine, whose forces capture the city of Algiers.
   The characters include the bumbling Timothy Tourist, the spirited Lauretta, and the Osmin-like Mahmoud.
   Musical exoticism is especially evident in "Loud Let the Moorish Tambour Sound," the finale for act 1, and "While Thus with Friendship's Warm Caress," the finale for act 2, both in the instrumentation (long drum, cymbals, triangle, and "timpano—or side drum") and in the martial character of the music itself.
   Roles: Algernon, Lauretta, Amanda, Orasmin, Zaida, Timothy, Cogi, Omar, and Selim.
SCORE: ms fs, autograph (British Library, Add. MS. 27718); vs (London: Goulding, D'Almaine, & Co., [1825]).
LIBRETTO: English (London: J. Cumberland, [1825?]).

Fall of Miss Moss, The. See The Dissolute Punished.

Fall of the City, The, music drama in one act by James Cohn; libretto (Eng), after Archibald MacLeish's work of the same name (1937). First performance July 29, 1955, Athens, Ohio, Ohio University, Ewing Auditorium.
   The story of an unnamed city in which the fearful residents accept domination by a tyrant whose power is illusory.

SCORE: vs (n.p., n.d.; LCCN: 84-71041).

Fall of the House of Usher, The, opera in three scenes by Avery Claflin; libretto (Eng) by the composer, after the story by Edgar Allan Poe. Composed 1921.

Fall of the House of Usher, unfinished opera by Roger Sessions; libretto (Eng) by Samuel A. Eliot Jr., after Poe. Composed 1925.

Fall of the House of Usher, The, opera in one act by Clarence Loomis; libretto (Eng), after Poe. First performance January 11, 1941, Indianapolis.

Fall of the House of Usher, The, opera in five scenes by Morris Hutchins Ruger; libretto (Eng) by Francis Millington, after Poe. First performance April 15, 1953, Los Angeles, Wilshire Ebel Theater.
BIBLIOGRAPHY: "America," *Opera* IV (Aug. 1953), 493 [on premiere].

Fall of the House of Usher, The, opera in one act by Larry Sitsky; libretto (Eng) by Gwen Harwood, after Poe. First performance August 18, 1965, Hobart, Australia, Hobart Festival. Also performed July 25, 1973, Sydney, Opera House, together with *Dalgerie,** the first operas to be staged there.
        The Narrator comes to the house of Roderick Usher, his Friend. Roderick, almost insane, is caring for Madeline, his twin sister, who is terminally ill and to whom he is extremely close. When she dies (or so it appears), she is buried, and her brother goes mad. The Narrator reads to his demented friend, while strange noises are heard through-out the house. They are being made by Madeline, who was in fact buried alive. She seizes her brother, and the two are brought together again in death, which brings about the fall of the house of Usher.
        Major roles: Narrator (ten), Roderick Usher (bar), and Madeline (sop).
        The music includes ten 12-note rows.
SCORE: vs (Sydney: G. Ricordi & Co., 1974).

Fall of the House of Usher, The, opera in one act by Gregory Sandow; libretto (Eng) by Thomas M. Disch, after Poe. First performance February 3, 1979, New York.

Fall of the House of Usher, The, chamber opera in two acts by Philip Glass; libretto (Eng) by Arthur Yorinks, after Poe. First performance May 29, 1988, Louisville, Ken-tucky, Kentucky Opera-American Repertory Theatre, with David Trombley (William), Dwayne Croft (Roderick Usher), and Sharon Baker (Madeline); conducted by Richard Pittman; directed by Richard Foreman.
        In this treatment of the famous Poe tale, the audience has to decide whether the story is real or a hallucination and decide about the relationships among the narrator (William), his friend Roderick Usher, and Roderick's dying sister, Madeline, whether she has been buried alive, whether the house is a living, evil entity, and whether super-natural forces are at work.
        The work is scored for chamber orchestra and synthesizer.
LIBRETTO: English (Bryn Mawr, Pa.: Theodore Presser, 1988).
BIBLIOGRAPHY: Peter G. Davis, review, *New York* XXII (July 31, 1989), 65 [on 1989 performance]; William Mootz, "Louisville," *ON* LIII (Oct. 1988), 46 [on premiere].

False Alarms, or, My Cousin, comic opera in three (two) acts by John Addison, John Braham, and Matthew Peter King; libretto (Eng) by James Kenney. First performance

January 12, 1807, London, Drury Lane Theatre, with Mr. Wroughton (Sir Damon Gayland), Mrs. Mountain (Lady Gayland), and Miss Duncan (Caroline Sedley). First U.S. performance February 6, 1809, Boston, Federal Street Theatre.

In the story Miss Carolyn Sedley saves the marriage of the jealous Sir Damon Gayland and his young wife by means of tricks and disguises.

LIBRETTO: English (New York: D. Longworth, 1807).

False and True, or, The Irishman in Italy, afterpiece in three acts by Samuel Arnold; libretto (Eng) by George Moultrie. First performance August 11, 1798, London, Little Theatre in the Haymarket.

LIBRETTO: English (London: J. Bell, 1798).

False Guardians Outwitted, The, ballad opera; libretto (Eng) by William Goodall. First performance 1740, London.

The setting is Sir Toby's house.

Roles: Sir Toby Lovewealth, uncle and guardian to Dorinda; Lord Varnish, a silly fop, in love with Miss Gaylove; Mr. Rickitt, uncle to Gaylove, in love with Dorinda; Christiano, son to Sir Toby, in love with Miss Gaylove; Captain Swagger, a great bully, in love with Dorinda; Harry, servant to Gaylove, in love with Kitty; Corporal Standsalt, the captain's follower; Dorinda, niece and ward to Sir Toby, in love with Gaylove; Miss Gaylove, sister to Gaylove, in love with Christiano; Kitty, servant to Dorinda, in love with Harry.

LIBRETTO: English, in *The True Englishman's Miscellany* (London: author, 1740).

False Messiah, The, opera in two acts by Bruce Adolphe; libretto (Eng) by Mel Gordon. First performance April 9, 1983, New York, 92nd Street Y; conducted by Amy Kaiser.

The work concerns Shabbethai Zevi, who lived from 1626 to 1676.

SCORE: vs, holograph, 1982 (NYPL, photocopy).

Family Affair, A, opera by Julian Grant; libretto (Eng) by Nick Dear, after his translation of A. N. Ostrovsky. First performance July 1993, London, Almeida Theatre.

The story concerns a wealthy Moscow merchant whose declaration of bankruptcy to confound his creditors leads to his own downfall.

BIBLIOGRAPHY: Michael Blake, review, *Tempo*, No. 186 (Sept. 1993), 53 [on premiere].

Family Jars, The, operatic farce by George Perry; libretto (Eng) by J. Lunn. First performance August 26, 1822, London, Haymarket.

Family Man, The, opera for one singer by Leonard Lehrman; libretto (Eng) by the composer, after a story by Mikhail Sholokhov. First performance (concert) January 11, 1984, New York, Stern College, Koch Auditorium, with Ronald Edwards; Lehrman, piano. First stage performance June 1985, New York, Golden Fleece.

About a family's destruction in 1920s Russia.

SCORE: ms vs, holograph (photocopy, 1984, NYPL).

Family Papers, chamber opera by Charles Wood; libretto (Eng), after Charles Dickens's *Martin Chuzzlewit*, Chapter 4 (1844). First performance February 12, 1924, London, Royal College of Music.

BIBLIOGRAPHY: Ian Copley, "Two Dickensian Chamber Operas," *Dickensian* LXIX (May 1973), 102–4.

Family Quarrels, opera by William Reeve, John Braham, and John Moorehead; libretto (Eng) by Thomas Dibdin. First performance December 18, 1802, London, Covent Garden, with Mr. Munden (Sir Peppercorn Crabstick), Charles Incledon (Foxglove), Mr. Simmons (Squire Supplejack), Mr. Braham (Charles Supplejack), Miss Chapman (Lady Patience Crabstick), Miss Waddy (Caroline Crabstick), Nancy Storace (Susan), Mrs. Davenport (Mrs. Supplejack), Mrs. Dibdin (Kitty), and Isabella Mattocks (Lady Selina Sugarcane).

The setting is a village that contains the mansions of the wealthy and quarrelsome Crabstick and Supplejack families.

SCORE: vs (London, ca. 1802).
LIBRETTO: English (New York: Longworth, 1806).

Fan, The, comic opera in two acts by Lee Goldstein; libretto (Eng) by Charles Kondek, after Carlo Goldoni's *Il ventaglio.* First performance June 17, 1989, Chicago, Blackstone Theatre, Lyric Opera Center for American Artists.

The fan, owned by Candidia, breaks, and getting it fixed causes all sorts of problems. When Candida gives it to her beloved Evarist to have fixed, he takes it to Susannah, and his actions are noticed by Candida, who suspects they are lovers. Evarist gives it to Nina to give back to Candida, and Coronato and Crispino, admirers of Nina, conclude wrongly that Nina loves Evarist. Candida, feeling that she has been betrayed, consents to marry the Baron. Despite all the complications, all turns out well in the end.

For a detailed description, see Kornick/*RAO,* 127–29.

Major roles: Candida (sop), Nina (mezzo), Count Rocca Marina (ten), Signor Evarist (ten), and Crispino (ten).

Fancy'd Queen, The, ballad opera; libretto (Eng) by Robert Drury. First performance August 14, 1733, London, Drury Lane Theatre.
LIBRETTO: English (London: C. Corbett, 1733).

Fand, monodrama in one act by James Wilson; libretto (Eng) by the composer. First performance August 26, 1975, Kilkenny, Ireland, St. Canice's Cathedral.

Fanny Robin, opera in one act by Edward Harper; libretto (Eng) by the composer, "from episodes in Thomas Hardy's novel *Far from the Madding Crowd* [1874], from his Wessex poems, the metrical psalmody of Sternhold and Hopkins, and traditional English folk songs with additional material by Roger Savage" (according to the 1979 vocal score). First performance February 5, 1975, Edinburgh, University Opera Club.

The story concerns the episode from Hardy in which Fanny Robin, a servant girl, is pursued and then deserted by a handsome sergeant, Frank Troy.

Major roles: Fanny Robin (sop), Sergeant Frank Troy (bar), and presenter (speaking).

Another treatment of the Hardy novel is by Alva Henderson (not perf.).

SCORE: vs (London: Oxford University Press, 1979).
DISCOGRAPHY: Scottish Opera Chorus; cond. R. Horn, Oxford University Press OUP 200 (1980, London).

Fantastics, The, romantic opera in three acts by Fritz Hart; libretto (Eng), after Edmond Rostand. Composed 1918.

Fantasy in Delft, opera in one act by Henry F. Gilbert; libretto (Eng) by Thomas P. Robinson. Composed 1919.

The work is set in Delft, Holland, in the seventeenth century. In the fantasy, Delft pottery figures, including two bright young girls, spring to life following a new moon. The girls get the better of their proper old aunt and start seeing two local youths.

The opera was rejected by the Metropolitan, and conductor Gino Marinuzzi's interest in the piece ended when he left the Chicago Opera in 1919.

Farewell Supper, The, chamber opera in one act by Frederic Hart; libretto (Eng) by Francis Barnard, after Arthur Schnitzler's *Abschiedssouper*. First performance February 3, 1984, Brooklyn, New York, Brooklyn College.
BIBLIOGRAPHY: "New Operas and Premieres," *Central Opera* XXV (1984), 6.

Far Harbour, opera in two acts by Baldwin Bergersen; libretto (Eng) by William Archibald. First performance January 22, 1948, New York, Hunter College Playhouse.

Farinelli, seriocomic opera in two acts by John Barnett; libretto (Eng) by C. Z. Barnett. First performance February 8, 1839, London, Drury Lane Theatre, with Mr. Balfe (Farinelli), Mr. Stretton (Philip V), Mr. Giubilei (Don Gil Polo), Mr. Franks (Theodore), Miss Romer (Elizabeth Farnese), and Miss Poole (Leonora/Geraldine Polo).

A treatment of the castrato's life. Another opera on the singer is H. Zumpe's *Farinelli* (1886, Hamburg).
LIBRETTO: English (London: J. Duncombe & Co., [1839?]).

Farmer, The, comic opera in two acts by William Shield; libretto (Eng) by John O'Keeffe, after his *The Plague of Riches*. First performance October 31, 1787, London, Covent Garden, with Mr. Hull (Colonel Dormont), Mr. Johnstone (Valentine), Mr. Thompson (Lawyer Fairly/Farmer Stubble), Charles Bannister (Farmer Blackberry), Mr. Edwin (Jemmy Jumps), Mr. Rock (Counsellor Flummery), Mrs. Mountain (Louisa), Mrs. Mattocks (Betty Blackberrry), and Mrs. Martyr (Molly Maybush). First U.S. performance October 18, 1790, Richmond, Virginia, West-Bignall.

The work begins on a farm in Kent and concludes in London. The plot involves the pitfalls of borrowing money.

For a detailed description, see Fiske/*ETM*, 467–68.

The overture is by Tommaso Giordani. There are also borrowings from Mozart and Paisiello. Shield's numbers include "The Ploughboy." Another highlight is the patter song "Gad a Mercy," sung by the comical Jemmy Jumps, a maker of stays.
LIBRETTOS: English (London: Longman & Broderip, n.d.; [Boston]: Apollo Press, [1794]).

Farmer and the Nymph, The, lyric legend in one act by Alexander Tcherepnin; libretto by Giovanni Cardelli, after Siao Yu. First performance August 13, 1952, Aspen, Colorado, with Anne Bollinger (the nymph), Leslie Chabay (the farmer), and Richard Leach (the narrator).

A lonely farmer weds a nymph, who is forced to leave him after twenty years.

The work uses the pentatonic scale to emphasize the simplicity of the story.
SCORE: vs (London: Boosey & Hawkes, 1972).
BIBLIOGRAPHY: Quaintance Eaton, "Aspen," *MA* LXXII (Sept. 1952), 6 [on premiere].

Farmer's Wife, The, comic opera in three acts by Henry Rowley Bishop, with John Davy, William Reeve, John Addison, Thomas Welsh, and H. Condell; libretto (Eng) by Charles Dibdin Jr. First performance February 1, 1814, London, Covent Garden. First U.S. performance September 26, 1814, New York, Park Theatre.
LIBRETTO: English (London: G. and S. Robinson, 1814).

Fashionable Lady, The, or, Harlequin's Opera, ballad opera; libretto (Eng) by James Ralph. First performance April 2, 1730, London, Goodman's Fields, with Mr. Penkethman (Mr. Ballad), W. Giffard (Mr. Meanwell), Mr. Bullock (Mr. Modely), Mr. Lacey (Mr. Drama), W. Williams (Mr. Merit), Mrs. Thomas (Mr. Smooth), Mr. Huddy (Captain Hackum), Mr. Smith (Mr. Whim), Mr. Collet (Mr. Trifle), Mrs. Mountford (Mrs. Foible), Mrs. Giffard (Mrs. Sprightly), Mrs. Palmer (Prattle), and Mr. Birney Jr. (Harlequin).

The thin plot pits drama against ballad opera in the setting of a rehearsal. It makes fun both of ballad opera and the artificiality of Italian opera.

For a detailed description, see Sonneck/*SIMG*, 429–33; he finds that this work bears a faint resemblance to the *Beggar's Opera** but says that the Ralph text is much more obscene.

The sixty-eight airs include the popular ballads "A Cobler There Was" and "An Old Woman Poor and Blind."
LIBRETTO: English (London: J. Watts, 1730); repr. Rubsamen/*BO*, vol. 9 (1974).

Fast Asleep, or, The Opiate, musical farce in two acts by Thomas Attwood; libretto (Eng) by Samuel Birch, after a play by James Powell. First performance, as *Fast Asleep*, November 27, 1797 (October 28 in some sources), London, Drury Lane Theatre.

The setting is Florence; the story involves a young man who drinks an opiate by mistake and falls asleep in the company of his beloved.
LIBRETTO: English, ms, as *The Opiate* (1797, Larpent 1182); see Dougald MacMillan, comp., *Catalogue of the Larpent Plays in the Huntington Library* (San Marino, Calif., 1939), 196.

Fatal Oath, The, melodrama in one act by Boris Koutzen; libretto (Eng) by the composer, after Honoré de Balzac's *La grande Bretèche*. First performance May 25, 1955, New York, Manhattan School of Music, Opera Workshop, with Geraldine Kullman (Rosalie), Margaret Turnley (Countess de Merret), Brent Williams (De Feredia), Robert Falk (Count de Merret), and Harold Orback (Gorenslat); conducted by Hugh Ross; produced by John Brownlee.

In the story the unhappily married Countess de Merret seeks love with De Feredia, a Spanish nobleman, with disastrous results.

For other settings, see *La grande Bretèche* and *The Secret*.
BIBLIOGRAPHY: Howard Taubman, review, *NYT* (May 26, 1955), 26 [on premiere].

Father of the Child, Christmas opera in one act by Seymour Barab; libretto (Eng) by the composer, after the play by William Gibson. First performance October 7, 1985, Bayside, New York, After Dinner Opera.

In order to save Mary from Satan, the angel Gabriel comes to Earth in human form. Joseph, who doubts the Holy Conception, demands that Gabriel perform a miracle in order to convince him. When Satan tries to sabotage the miracle, Gabriel sacrifices himself to allow it to occur.

Fathers, The, or, The Good Natur'd Man, comic opera; libretto (Eng) by Henry Fielding. First performance November 30, 1778, London, Covent Garden.

One song, "While the Sweet Blushing Spring," is by Michael Arne.
LIBRETTO: English, rev. R. B. Sheridan (London: T. Cadell, 1778).

Fat Tuesday, jazz opera in two acts by Sol Berkowitz; libretto (Eng) by James Lipton. First performance August 11, 1956, Tamiment, Pennsylvania, Tamiment Playhouse.

Faun in the Forest, A, opera in one act by Gerald Cockshott; libretto (Eng) by the composer. First performance August 9, 1959, Westport, Connecticut, After Dinner Opera Company, White Barn Theater, with Jeanne Beauvais, Norman Myrvik, and Francis Barnard; Emanuel Levenson, piano.

In this satire the Lady sits waiting for her lover, Sir Hugo the Dull, who is an unsuccessful dragon hunter. While Hugo is proposing, the Faun, whose entrance is noted musically by a quote from Debussy's tone poem, arrives and captures the Lady's interest. The Faun arranges to give Sir Hugo his piccolo for catching dragons, while Sir Hugo surrenders the Lady.

For a detailed description, see Eaton/*OP* II, 273.

Major roles: the Lady (sop), Sir Hugo (ten), and the Faun (bass-bar).

SCORE: vs (New York: Boosey & Hawkes, [1974]).

BIBLIOGRAPHY: John Briggs, "One-Act Operas," *NYT* (Aug. 10, 1959), 24 [on premiere].

Faust, television opera (monodrama) by John J. Becker; libretto (Eng) by Bayard Taylor, after Goethe. Composed 1951. First performance (concert) April 8, 1965, Los Angeles.

The work is written for tenor.

Faust and Marguerite. See **Mephistopheles**.

Faust Counter Faust, opera by John Gessner; libretto (Eng) by Wesley Balk, after Goethe. First performance January 30, 1971, Minneapolis, Center Opera. Also April 1, 1971, San Francisco, San Francisco Opera; conducted by Philip Brunelle.

A mental patient, believing himself to be Faust, is forced to listen to extracts from various settings of the Goethe work, including those by Gounod, Berlioz, and Boito.

BIBLIOGRAPHY: Donal Henahan, review, *NYT* (Aug. 6, 1971), 14 [on New York premiere].

Faustus, romantic drama in three acts by Henry Rowley Bishop, Thomas Cooke, and Charles Edward Horn; libretto (Eng) by George Soane, after Goethe. First performance May 16, 1825, London, Drury Lane Theatre, with Catherine Stephens (Adine).

The work begins with the overture from Weber's *Euryanthe* (1823, Vienna).

Among the characters are Adine, Orsini, the Count, Faust, Wagner, and Lucetta.

Other English treatments of the Goethe work include *Mephistopheles, or Faust and Marguerite*** by Meyer Lutz (1855, Surrey); *Faust and Marguerite,* "travestie" in one act by F. C. Burnand (ca. 1864); *Faust and Gretchen,* operetta by Moritz Heuzenroeder (1883, Adelaide); *Faust Up-to-Date,* burlesque by Lutz (1888, London); and *Henry Faust*** by G. S. Isaacs (1993, Forest Park, Ill.). Also German setting by Havergal Brian, as *Faust* (comp. 1954–1956).

SCORE: ms fs, autograph (1825, British Library, Add. MS. 27719); vs (London: Goulding & D'Almaine, 1825?).

LIBRETTO: English (London: J. Miller, 1825).

Fayette, or, Bush Revels, "original Australian comic opera" in three acts by George Benjamin Allen; libretto (Eng) by James B. Stephens. First performance 1892, Brisbane?

LIBRETTO: English (Brisbane: Watson, Ferguson, 1892).

Fay-Yen-Fah. See **The Land of Happiness**.

Feast of Samhain, The, comic opera in three acts by Erik Chisholm; libretto (Eng) by the composer, after James Stephen's *The Isle of Youth*. Composed 1941.

SCORE: text and music (Glasgow: W. MacLellan, [1942]).

Feather Cloak, The, opera by George Barati; libretto (Eng), after Katherine M. Yates. Composed 1970.

Feathertop, opera in two acts by Joyce Barthelson; libretto (Eng) by the composer, after a story by Nathaniel Hawthorne. First performance (concert) January 26, 1968, New York.

The mischievous witch Mother Rigby brings to life a scarecrow, who is mistaken for Lord Feathertop. The scarecrow, in his human guise, seeks the hand of Polly Gookin. The only people who see through the deception are the children and Daniel, Polly's beloved. Polly is on the verge of accepting the scarecrow's hand when his true identity is revealed by a special mirror.

For a detailed description, see Eaton/*OP* II, 86–87.

Major roles: Mother Rigby (mezzo), Judge Gookin (bass), Polly Gookin (lyr sop), Lord Feathertop (ten), and Daniel (bar).

Feathertop, opera by Edward Barnes; libretto (Eng) by Maurice Valency, after Nathaniel Hawthorne. First performance February 7, 1980, New York, Juilliard American Opera Center, with Ruth Jacobson (the servant) and J. Patrick Raftery (Major Whitby); conducted by Richard Dufallo; directed by H. Wesley Balk. Expanded to three acts; first performance April 30, 1982, Minneapolis, Gutherie Theater, with John Brandstetter (Feathertop) and Judith Christin (the Witch); conducted by Philip Brunelle.

N. Lockwood's *Scarecrow** (1945, New York) is another setting of the story.

BIBLIOGRAPHY: Peter G. Davis, "Juilliard Presents Premiere of 'Feathertop,'" *NYT* (Feb. 9, 1980), 14 [on premiere]; M. A. Feldman, "U.S.," *ON* XLVII (Sept. 1982), 42, 44 [on 1982 premiere]; Robert Jacobson, "U.S.," *ON* XLIV (June 1980), 34–35 [on premiere].

Fee First, comic opera in one act ("a medical musical") by Matt Doran; libretto (Eng) by the composer. First performance April 27, 1973, Los Angeles, Mount St. Mary's College.

The setting is a physician's waiting room, the present. In this satire, Dr. Norman is more concerned about his golf game than his patients, tranquilizing the complaining patients with the help of his nurse, Miss Harper, and scolding another, Mr. Clemons, for bleeding on the carpet.

For a detailed description, see Summers/*OOA*, 98–99.

Roles: Dr. Leonard Norman (bass-bar/bar); Miss Harper (sop); and Mr. Clemons, an elderly patient (ten).

SCORE: ms (1973, photocopy, NYPL).

Felipe, opera in three acts by Hugh Aitken; libretto (Eng) by the composer and Laura Tapia, after Cervantes's *El celoso extremeño.* Composed 1981.

Felix, or, The Festival of Roses, opera in two acts by Meyer Lutz; libretto (Eng) by John Oxenford. First performance October 23, 1865, London, Gaiety Theatre, with E. Connell (Prince of Provence), Elliot Galer (Count Felix), Gaston Smith (Bailie), Mr. Bentley (Lucas), H. Hayes (Bertrand), Susan Galton (Countess of Martigne), Blanche Galton (Amelia), and Fanny Reeves (Jeannette).

LIBRETTO: English (London: Metzler, [1865?]).

Female Parson, The, or, Beau in the Sudds, "an opera" (ballad opera); libretto (Eng) by Charles Coffey. First performance April 27, 1730, London, Little Theatre in the Haymarket.

The setting is London.

Major roles: Sir Quibble Quibus, "an old debauch'd Justice of the Peace"; Captain Noble, an officer in love with Lady Quibus; Lady Quibus; Miss Lure, "a jilt of the town, kept by the Justice"; and Pinner, maid and confidante to Lady Quibus.

LIBRETTO: English (London, 1730); repr. ed. Rubsamen/*BO*, vol. 3, *Harlots, Rakes, and Bawds* (1974).

Female Rake, The, or, Modern Fine Lady, ballad opera; libretto (Eng) by Joseph Dorman. First performance April 26, 1736, London, New Theatre in the Haymarket, with Mr. Pullen (Lord Fashion), Mr. Turner (Sir George Friendly), Mr. Freeman (Clerimont), Mr. Smith (Townly/Sir Harry Trueman), Mr. Williams (Dapper), Mr. Lowder (George), Mr. Adams (James), Miss Jones (Libertina), Mrs. Eaton (Sylvia), Mrs. Mills (Celia), and Mrs. Talbot (Phillis).

The title page includes a quotation from Pope:

Men, some to Business, some to Pleasure take,

But, ev'ry Woman is, at Heart, a Rake.

LIBRETTO: English (London: J. Dormer . . . , 1736); repr. ed. Rubsamen/*BO*, vol. 6, *Satire, Burlesque, Protest, and Ridicule*, II (1974).

Fencing Master, The, comic opera in three acts by Reginald De Koven; libretto (Eng) by Harry Bache Smith. First performance November 14, 1892, New York, Casino Theatre, with Marie Tempest (Francesca), Hubert Wilke (Fortunio), Grace Golden (Countess Filippa), Charles Hopper (Galeazzo Visconti), and Jerome Sykes (the astrologer).

The story, set in fifteenth-century Milan and Venice, centers on Francesca, daughter of the fencing master, who disguises herself as a boy, but she is in love with Fortunio, heir to the dukedom of Milan but left penniless by Galeazzo Visconti. Not knowing her sex, Fortunio has fallen in love with Countess Filippa, and when he reveals his plans to run off with his beloved, Francesca betrays him. Enraged, Fortunio challenges "him" to a duel and learns Francesca's real identity when she is wounded. Fortunio then realizes that he really loves Francesca, and his fortune is restored when the duke and his astrologer are defeated.

LIBRETTO: English (Buffalo: Baker, Jones, 1892).

Fennimore and Gerda, opera in eleven scenes by Frederick Delius; libretto (Ger) by the composer, after Jens Peter Jacobsen's novel *Niels Lyhne* (1880); English version by Philip Heseltine. First performance October 21, 1919, Frankfurt, Opernhaus, in German. First British performance (concert) March 27, 1962, BBC Third Programme, with Sybil Michelow (Fennimore), John Cameron (Niels), Max Worthley (Erik), and Jeannette Sinclair (Gerda); conducted by Stanford Robinson. First British stage performance 1968, Hammersmith, London, Hammersmith Municipal Opera; revived summer 1983, Edinburgh Festival. First U.S. performance June 1981, St. Louis, Opera Theatre, with Kathryn Bouleyn (Fennimore), Stephen Dickson (Niels), David Bankston (Erik), and Kathryn Gamberoni (Gerda); conducted by Christopher Keene.

Set in Denmark, the story centers on Niels, who, despite his feelings for Fennimore, stands by as Fennimore weds Erik, an artist and Niels's best friend. Admitting that her marriage was a mistake, Fennimore finds that she is still drawn to Niels, and he has the same feelings for her. When Erik is thrown from a cart and killed, however, Fennimore, filled with a sense of guilt, turns away from Niels and banishes him from her house. Three years pass, during which Niels returns to the farm where he spent his childhood. He meets Gerda, daughter of a local councillor, and when he proposes marriage, she happily accepts his offer.

Major roles: Niels Lyhne, a writer (bar); Erik Refstrup, his cousin (ten); Fennimore, daughter of Consul Claudi (sop); and Gerda (sop).

Delius's last opera contains beautiful music, but it is hampered by a weak text. The eleven scenes, or "pictures," are connected by descriptive musical interludes. Delius added the two "Gerda" scenes (10 and 11) because he felt that the work, which originally ended with Fennimore's casting off Niels, was incomplete and too gloomy.

SCORE: fs (London and New York: Boosey & Hawkes, 1989).
BIBLIOGRAPHY: Deryck Cooke, "Broadcast Opera," *Opera* XIII (May 1962), 352 [on British premiere]; Robert Jacobson, "Reports: U.S.," *ON* XLVI (Oct. 1981), 31; Nicholas Kenyon, "Musical Events: Pictures from the Midwest," *NY* LXXVII (June 29, 1981), 70.
DISCOGRAPHY: Söderström, Tear, Cook, Danish Radio Chorus and Sym.; cond. Davies, Angel SBLX-3835 (2).

Ferryman's Daughter, The, "opera of the 18th-century Thames Waterside for schools" by Alan Bush; libretto by Nancy Bush. First performance March 6, 1964, Letchworth, England, St. Christopher's School.

In order to get security for his daughter, Jenny, the aging Mr. Wilkins, a Thames waterman, wants her to marry a waterman, but she prefers her current suitor, Tom Starling, a young farmer. To Jenny's dismay, Mr. Wilkins announces that the winner of the annual race for the championship of the river will also win her hand and his boat.

Tom's rival, Nat, a conceited waterman, is sure he will win. Although nobody gives Tom a chance, he asks if he may compete and is allowed to enter. Jenny asks the help of Mrs. Patchett, a fisherman's wife, who knows that Nat is very fond of periwinkles. Before the race begins, she tempts Nat into devouring a hefty amount, and, having eaten too many, Nat loses the race to Tom.

The work is scored for five solo voices and chorus.

Fête at Coqueville, The, opera in one act by Alan Rea; libretto by Betty Iocavetti, after a story by Zola. First performance April 11, 1976, Fresno, California, Opera Association.

The setting is Coqueville, France, ca. 1860. Two families that inhabit the small fishing village have been enemies for generations. This state of affairs seems to doom the love of Margot, the daughter of La Queue Floche, the mayor, and Delphin Mahe, a fisherman, since Margot and Delphin are members of the opposing families. One day one of Delphin's long-lost boats appears, filled with wine, which the village's inhabitants proceed to consume. Their inebriation brings about feelings of friendliness toward one another. When the fisherman Mouchel visits the village to find out why the deliveries of fish have stopped, he finds that all of the townspeople are asleep on the beach. A fête is arranged to celebrate the new friendships and the upcoming nuptials of Margot and Delphin.

For a detailed description, see Summers/*OOA*, 249–50.

Major roles: La Queue Floche (bar), Margot (sop), Delphin Mahe, (ten), and Mouchel (bar).

Fête Galante, "dance-dream" (opera) in one act by Ethel Smyth; libretto (Eng) by Edward Shanks, after the story by Maurice Baring. First performance June 4, 1923,

Birmingham, England, British National Opera Company, with Dorothy Orsay (the queen), Muriel Gough (Columbine), Joseph Yates (the king), Sumner Austin (Pierrot), Harry Sennett (Harlequin), and Geoffrey Dams (the lover).
SCORE: fs (Vienna: Universal, 1923).

Feudal Times, musical drama in two acts by Michael Kelly; libretto (Eng) by George Colman Jr.. First performance January 19, 1799, London. First U.S. performance March 20, 1809, Boston, Federal Street Theatre.

Fiend-Father, The, or, Robert of Normandy, grand romantic opera in three acts by Michael Rophino Lacy, an adaptation of G. Meyerbeer's *Robert-le-diable* (1831, Paris); libretto (Eng) by Lacy, after Scribe and Delavigne. First performance February 21, 1832, London, Covent Garden.
    Bishop's version, *The Demon,** appeared a day earlier, also in London.
    Also known under the title *Robert the Devil, or, The Fiend-Father.* See, in addition, *Robert the Devil.*
LIBRETTO: English (London: T. H. Lacy, [183?]).

Fiery Tales, comic opera in one act by Larry Sitsky; libretto (Eng) by Gwen Harwood, after Chaucer's *Canterbury Tales* and Boccaccio's *Decameron.* First performance March 23, 1976, Adelaide, Australia, Adelaide Festival.
SCORE: vs (New York: Seesaw Music, 1992).

Fifth for Bridge, A, opera in one act by Robert Sheldon; libretto (Eng) by Hitchcock. First performance December 3, 1961, San Francisco, San Francisco Conservatory of Music.

Final Alice, opera by David Del Tredici; libretto (Eng), after the last two chapters of Lewis Carroll's *Alice in Wonderland* and other texts. First performance (concert) October 7, 1976, Chicago.
    Another setting by the composer of a Carroll text is the one-act *Dum Dee Tweedle* (composed 1990–1992).
SCORE: fs (New York: Boosey & Hawkes, [1978]).
DISCOGRAPHY: Hendricks, Chicago Symphony, cond. Solti, London LDR-71018, rev. John W. Freeman, "Records," *ON* XLVI (Dec. 19, 1981), 44.

Final Ingredient, The, television opera in one act by David Amram; libretto (Eng) by Arnold Weinstein, after a television play by Reginald Rose (1959), based on a true story. First performance April 11, 1965, New York, Directions '65, ABC television, with Elaine Bonazzi, William Covington, Richard Frisch, Ezio Flagello, and Alan Baker; conducted by the composer.
    The opera is set in a Nazi concentration camp, Bergen Belsen, in 1944, and the "final ingredient" is the egg needed to make matzohs for a secret celebration of Passover. The prisoner who obtains the egg from a bird's nest is killed for his deed.
    The music is built on the three-note motive sounded by the English horn at the beginning of the opera.
LIBRETTO: English (see Discography).
BIBLIOGRAPHY: Walter Carlson, "Add a Touch of Bitters," *NYT* (Apr. 11, 1965), II, 21 [preview]; Theodore Strongin, review, *NYT* (Apr. 12, 1965), 71 [on premiere].

DISCOGRAPHY: Endich, Bonazzi, Kova, Covington, Sopher, Flagello, Smith, Frisch, Baker; cond. the composer, Premier 1056 (1965 broadcast, 1 CD, with libretto); rev. Jane L. Komarov, *ON* LX (Feb. 8, 1997), 40.

Findings, The, radio opera in one act by Christopher Whelen; libretto (Eng) by the composer. First performance July 16, 1972, London, BBC, Radio 3.

Finn and the Black Hag, children's opera in two acts by Raymond Warren; libretto (Eng) by Janet McNeil. First performance December 11, 1959, Belfast.
SCORE: piano-conductor score (London: Novello, [1962]).

Fionn and Terra, grand opera in two acts by Learmont Drysdale; libretto (Eng) by the Duke of Argyll. Composed 1909; scoring completed by David Stephen after Drysdale's death.
       The work was scheduled for Oscar Hammerstein's London Opera House, but its planned premiere was abandoned when the hall closed in 1912.
LIBRETTO: English (Edinburgh: W. Cuthbertson, 1912).

Fire and Water, comic opera in two acts by Samuel Arnold; libretto (Eng) by Miles Peter Andrews. First performance July 8, 1780, London, Little Theatre in the Haymarket.
LIBRETTO: English (London: T. Cadell, 1780).

Fire on the Wind, opera in two acts by Colin Brumby; libretto (Eng) by the composer, after Anthony Coburn. First performance (excerpts) September 25, 1991, Brisbane, Australia.

First Christmas, The, opera in one act by John Henry Antill; libretto (Eng) by Pat Flowers. First performance December 25, 1969, Sydney, Australia, Australian television.

Fisherman, The, opera in two acts by Tom Scott; libretto (Eng), after Oscar Wilde. Composed 1956.

Fisherman and His Wife, The, children's opera in two acts by Gunther Schuller; libretto (Eng) by John Updike, after the Grimm fairy tale. First performance May 7, 1970, Boston, Opera Company of Boston, with David Lloyd (the fisherman), Muriel Greenspon (his wife), Donald Gramm (the fish), and Louise Budd (the cat); conducted by the composer.
       A simple fisherman is convinced by his wife to ask for more and more favors from a great fish he has captured and thrown back into the sea. When the wife asks to play God, she and her husband are reduced to their original poor state. They remain happy, however.
       For a detailed description, see Eaton/*OP* II, 275.
       Roles: the fish (bass-bar), the fisherman (ten), the wife (mezzo), and the cat (sop).
BIBLIOGRAPHY: Raymond Ericson, "Opera: Grimm Fairy Tale," *NYT* (May 9, 1970), 15 [on premiere].

Fisherman and His Wife, The, opera in one act by Susan Bingham; libretto (Eng) by the composer, after the Brothers Grimm. Completed 1987.
       Also set by E. Rapoport (not perf.)

Fisherman Called Peter, A, biblical opera in one act by Richard Owen; libretto (Eng) by the composer. First performance March 14, 1965, Carmel, New York. Revived October 8, 1967, New York, St. James Presbyterian Church, with Arthur Thompson (Simon), Ray Lawrence (John the Baptist), and Adele Addison (Deborah); conducted by Abraham Kaplan.

The story concerns Simon, called Peter, who hears the preaching of Jesus and is convinced to follow him.

SCORE: vs, holograph, 1965 (NYPL, photocopy).

BIBLIOGRAPHY: review, "Owen Opera Sung in Harlem Church," *NYT* (Oct. 9, 1967) [on premiere].

DISCOGRAPHY: L. Owen, Neson, Doggett, Hermann, Van Vrooman, Reardon, Chorus and Orch.; cond. Egermann, Serenus 12027, rev. John W. Freeman, "Records," *ON* XXXV (Apr. 10, 1971), 34.

Fisherman's Wife, The, fairy-tale opera in one act by Leon Stein; libretto (Eng) by Roslyn Rosen, after the Brothers Grimm. First performance January 10, 1955, St. Joseph, Michigan.

Fit for a King, "opera-travesty" in a prologue and one act by Martin Kalmanoff; libretto (Eng) by Atra Baer, after *The Emperor's New Clothes* of Hans Christian Andersen. First performance (broadcast) February 13, 1949, New York, WNYC. First performance (staged) June 21, 1950, New York, Master Theatre; conducted by Georgette Palmer; piano accompaniment by the composer and Laverne Gustafson.

Uncle Adrian, a disillusioned children's host on Radio Station WROT, gives the familiar tale a nasty twist. To his surprise, the station rewards him with a bigger contract.

SCORES: fs, ms (n.p., 1948; LCCN: 51-25769); vs, ms ([New York?], 1948, LCCN: 51-30593).

BIBLIOGRAPHY: H. C. S., review, *NYT* (June 22, 1950), 33 [on stage premiere].

Five Shaggy-Dog Operas, opera in five parts by Tom Johnson; libretto (Eng) by the composer. First performance September 15, 1978, New York.

The work consists of *Door, Window, Drawers, Dryer,* and *Box.*

Flaming Arrow, The, or, The Shaft of Ku'pish-ta-ya, "Indian intermezzo" in one act by Mary Moore; libretto (Eng) by Sarah Pratt Carr. First performance March 27, 1922, San Francisco, Century Club, with Emilie Lancel, Easton Kent, and Marion Vecki; conducted by the composer. Revised as *The Shaft of Ku'pish-ta-ya* and performed November 25, 1927, Los Angeles.

Set in the nineteenth century, the story involves the Zuni chief O-ko-mo-bo, whose land has been stricken with a drought. Ka-mi-ah, a young Hopi brave, asks for the hand of his childhood friend Lo-lu-na, daughter of O-ko-mo-bo. The chief gives his consent if the rains come before the moon leaves the rim of the hillside; if not, the young warrior must die by a poisoned arrow. The rain arrives, and the lovers are united.

For a description, see Hipsher/*AO*, 329–30.

Among the musical devices is the use of the five-tone scale.

Flapper, The, jazz opera in four acts by Harry Lawrence Freeman; libretto by the composer. Composed 1929.

The setting is a broker's office and the Ritz-Carlton Hotel in New York.

Originally called *American Romance.*

Flash in the Pan, ballad opera by James Hewitt; libretto (Eng) by William Milns. First performance April 20, 1798, New York, with Miss Broadhurst.
SCORE: vs, excerpt: "When the Old Heathen Gods" ([New York: J. Jewitt, 1798]).

Flax into Gold, the Story of Rumpelstiltskin, children's opera in three scenes by Hugo Cole; libretto (Eng) by Catherine Storr. First performance 1966, Oxford.
SCORE: vs (London: Chappell, 1963).

Flitch of Bacon, The, comic opera (afterpiece) with music composed and arranged by William Shield; libretto (Eng) by Henry Bate. First performance August 17, 1778, London, Little Theatre in the Haymarket, with Mr. Brett (Greville), John Edwin (Tipple), Charles Bannister (Capt. Wilson), Miss Harper (Eliza), and Mr. Parsons (Major Benbow). First American performance October 30, 1780, New York, Theatre Royal (John Street Theatre), with a cast taken from members of the occupying British army of General Howe. First professional U.S. performance September 27, 1785, New York, John Street Theatre.

A young couple, Eliza and Captain Greville, make amends for their elopement one year and one day earlier by becoming the winners, in the contest for the happiest married couple in the area, of a flitch of bacon. They are awarded the prize by Justice Benbow, Eliza's father, and they also receive Eliza's dowry after Major Benbow discovers that he has been duped by Captain Wilson, a friend of the couple, into pursuing a woman that was really the disguised Eliza, his niece.

Major roles: Captain Wilson (bass), Eliza (sop), Captain Greville (ten), Justice Benbow (speaking), and Major Benbow (bass).

Among the borrowings is "No: 'Twas Neither Shape nor Feature," in act 1, scene 3; it is based on J. C. Bach's arrangement of Michele Mortellari's "Io ti lascio."
SCORE: vs (London: William Napier [1778], with second violin and harpsichord); the Bach aria is reproduced in *The Collected Works of J. C. Bach*, vol. 25, *Works with English Texts*, ed. Ernest Warburton (New York: Garland, 1990).

Flood, The (Noah and the Flood), musical play by Igor Stravinsky; text (Eng) by Robert Craft, after the York and Chester mystery plays and Genesis. First performance June 14, 1962, CBS television; conducted by Robert Craft; choreographed by George Balanchine. First stage performance April 30, 1963, Hamburg, Staatsoper.

Like Benjamin Britten's *Noyes Flood,** also based on the Chester mystery play, this work treats the biblical story of Noah and the Flood.

Roles: singing: Satan (ten), God (2 bass); speaking: Noah, Noah's wife, Noah's sons, narrator, and caller.

The score, which uses serial technique, calls for solo voices, actors, and orchestra; its mimed and danced sections are "The Building of the Ark" and "The Flood." The work ends with "The Covenant of the Rainbow," which consists of "The Word of God," sung by two basses to represent God; a melodrama by Noah; return of the instrumental introduction; an aria by Lucifer; and a Sanctus, sung by the chorus.
SCORE: vs, English-German (London and New York: Boosey & Hawkes, 1963).
BIBLIOGRAPHY: John Ardoin, "'Noah and the Flood' Premiered on CBS-TV," *MA* LXXXII (July 1962), 20; Richard Franko Goldman, review, *MQ* XLVIII (1962), 514–17 [on premiere].

Flora, opera in two acts, "being the farce of the country-wake, alter'd after the manner of the BEGGAR'S OPERA"; libretto (Eng) by John Hippisley, after Thomas Dogget's *The Country-Wake* (1696). First performance April 17, 1729, London, Lincoln's Inn Fields, with John Hippisley (Sir Thomas Testy), Mr. Walker (Friendly), H. Bullock (Dick), Mr. Laguerre (Hob), Mr. Hall (Old Hob), Mrs. Chantrel (Flora), Mrs. Kilby (Betty), and Mrs. Egleton (Hob's mother). First American performance February 18, 1735, Charleston, Charleston Street Theatre.

The setting is Somersetshire "one sultry summer's day."

Roles: Sir Thomas Testy, uncle and guardian to Flora; Friendly, a gentleman in love with Flora; Dick, an impudent fellow, his man; Hob, a simple country fellow; Old Hob, his father; Flora, niece to Sir Thomas, in love with Friendly; Betty, her maid and confident [sic]; and Hob's mother.

SCORE: vs (London: A. Bettesworth, C. Hitch, and T. Wood, 1732).

LIBRETTO: English (London: T. Wood, 1729), repr. Rubsamen/*BO*, vol. 16 (1974).

Flora, or, Hob in the Well, opera by William Bates, with seven songs by John Hippisley, from *Flora* (see preceding entry) and Bates's overture and eight new songs. First performance April 25, 1770, London, Covent Garden.

The simple plot, set in the English countryside, has Hob falling into the well. When his mother pulls him out, she thinks he is a monster because of his appearance.

LIBRETTOS: English ([London, 178?]; London: J. Parsons, 1794).

Florence Nightingale, opera in three acts by D. M. Williams; libretto (Eng). First performance May 4, 1943, New York, St. Bartholomew's Community House.

Florimel, or, Love's Revenge, dramatic pastoral in two acts by Maurice Greene; libretto (Eng) by John Hoadly. First performance 1734, Winchester, Farnham Castle.

The work is set in Arcadia and concerns the lovers Myrtillo and Florimel, a shepherd and shepherdess, and the trouble caused by Cupid and a Satyr.

In later performances Myrtillo was sung by a countertenor.

Roles: Myrtillo (sop), Florimel (sop), Cupid (sop), and Satyr (bass).

SCORE: ms fs (British Library, King's Music Library, MS. 22 d.14; Add. 5325); facsimile of 22 d.14, ed. H. Diack Johnstone (London: Stainer & Bell, 1995).

LIBRETTO: English (London, 1734); facsimile (London: Stainer & Bell, 1995).

Florizel and Perdita, or, The Winter's Tale, opera by William Boyce (one song by Michael Arne); libretto (Eng) by David Garrick, after Shakespeare. First performance January 21, 1756, London, Drury Lane Theatre.

Flower and Hawk, monodrama in one scene by Carlisle Floyd; libretto (Eng) by the composer. First performance May 16, 1972, Jacksonville, Florida, Civic Auditorium, Jacksonville Symphony, with Phyllis Curtin (Eleanor); conducted by Willis Page.

The story centers on Eleanor of Aquitaine during her imprisonment in Salisbury Tower by King Henry II, her second husband. Her despair is relieved as she remembers the good and bad parts of her life, as wife of Louis VII of France, the death of her son Richard the Lion-Hearted, her time with her troubadour lover when she was the Duchess of Aquitaine, and her humiliation because of Rosamond, the mistress of Henry. The tolling of the bells from the tower, indicating that Henry has died, signals her freedom.

The title refers to Eleanor's seal.

For a detailed description, see Eaton/*OP* II, 276.

The music includes her lovely prayer for Richard, "O Holy Mother of God."

Role: Eleanor of Aquitaine (sop).

SCORE: vs (New York: Belwin-Mills, 1977).

Flower Queen, The, or, The Coronation of the Rose, opera-cantata in two parts by George F. Root; libretto (Eng) by Frances J. Crosby. First performance March 11, 1853, New York, Abbott's Spingler Institute.

The moralistic work concerns a recluse restored to the world by flower children.
SCORE: vs (New York: Mason & Law, 1852).

Flowers, opera by John Hardy; libretto (Eng) by the composer and Heledd Wyn-Hardy, after Ed Harris's *Flowers of the Dead Red Sea* (1991). First performance March 18, 1994, Cardiff, Music Theatre Wales, with Michael Bundy (Mock) and Gareth Lloyd (Joe).

The story concerns the deteriorating position of craftsmen, in this case, butchers.
BIBLIOGRAPHY: Kenneth Loveland, review, *Opera* XLV (May 1994), 622–23 [on premiere].

Fly, opera in two acts by Barry Conyngham; libretto (Eng) by Murray Copland. First performance August 25, 1984, Melbourne, Australia, Victorian Arts Centre, State Theatre.

The story, set in the early twentieth century, centers around Lawrence Hargrave, an inventor, who has shunned turning his findings into profit-making ventures because of his past. The second act is set on a steamer in 1876, with Hargrave as a young man. He is part of an expedition up the Fly River in New Guinea, where he is so repulsed by the jealousy and greed of the expedition's leader, D'Albertis, that he vows to devote himself only to research. The second scene returns the action back to the present. Mrs. Hargrave has started to accept her husband's lack of ambition. But when she receives news that their son has died in the fighting at Gallipoli, Hargrave, numbed by grief, retreats into his work.

Major roles: Maggie Hargrave (mezzo); Lawrence Hargrave (ten); their daughters, Margaret and Olive Hargrave (sop); and D'Albertis, a naturalist (bar).

Flying Dutchman, The, or, The Phantom Ship, nautical drama in three acts by George Rodwell; libretto (Eng) by Edward Fitzball, after an account from *Blackwood's Magazine*, according to Fitzball. First performance January 1, 1827, London, Adelphi Theatre. First U.S. performance April 9, 1827, New York.

Vanderecken, in league with Rockalda, "an evil spirit," is the accursed captain of the "Flying Dutchman." Other characters include Lestelle; Capt. Peppercoal; Smutta, a slave; Lieutenant Mowdrey; Lucy; and Toby Varnish.

The work preceded by sixteen years its more famous namesake, Richard Wagner's *Der fliegende Holländer* (1843, Dresden). Pierre L. P. Dietsch's *Le vaisseau-fantôme*, once thought to be based solely on Wagner's scenario but in fact coming from several sources (see the Millington article), appeared in 1842 in Paris. Another setting of the story is *Vanderecken, or, The Flying Dutchman* (1886, London), with a text by Tom Taylor.
LIBRETTO: English (London: J. Cumberland, n.d.; New York: S. French, [185?]).
BIBLIOGRAPHY: Bernd Laroche, *Der fliegende Holländer: Wirkung und Wandlung* (New York: P. Lang, 1993): includes Rodwell's libretto; Barry Millington, "'The Flying Dutchman,' 'Le vaisseau fantôme' and Other Nautical Yarns," *MT* CXXVII (1986), 131–35.

Follies and Fancies, opera in one act by Judith Shatin Allen; libretto (Eng) by Gloria Russo. First performance June 14, 1987, New York, Tomi Theater, Golden Fleece Ltd., with Veronica Burke (Magdelon), Mark Amspoker (La Grange), Kevin Kennedy (Mascarille), Lauren Lipson (Marrotte), and Wilbur Lewis (the father); conducted by Jerome Shannon.

Set in the eighteenth century, the work concerns a country girl who comes to Paris and adopts the conceited airs of her acquaintances. She is put in her place by La Grange, her longtime lover, who through a ruse shows her how silly she has been.

Roles: Magdelon; La Grange; Mascarille, La Grange's conniving assistant; Marrotte, a maid; and Magdelon's father.
BIBLIOGRAPHY: Michael Kimmelman, review, *NYT* (June 18, 1987), C, 17 [on premiere].

Follies of a Night, comic opera in two acts by Virginia Gabriel; libretto (Eng) by James R. Planché, after *Charlot* by Lockroy, Anicet-Bourgeois, and L. E. Vanderburch. First performance ca. 1870, London.

Roles: Chartres, Druggendraft, Pierre Palliot, Duchess of Chartres, Duval, Duroc, Brissac, and Antoine.
LIBRETTO: English (London: J. B. Cramer, [18??]).

Fontainbleau, or, Our Way in France, comic opera in three acts by William Shield; libretto (Eng) by John O'Keeffe. First performance November 16, 1784, London, Covent Garden, with Charles Incledon (Lord Winlowe), Mr. Wernitzer (Col. Epaulette), Mr. Wilson (Sir John Bull), Mr. Edwin (Tally Ho), Mr. Johnstone (Henry), Mr. Lewis (Lackland), Mrs. Webb (Lady Bull), Mrs. Billington (Rosa), Miss Wheeler (Celia), Mrs. Mattocks (Miss Dolly Bull), Mrs. Kennedy (Mrs. Casey), and Mrs. Martyr (Nannette). First U.S. performance March 9, 1785, Charleston, South Carolina, Charleston Theatre.

The hero is forced to visit France in the mistaken belief that he has killed somebody in a duel.

For a description of the music, see Fiske/*ETM*, 462–65.

The overture is a combination of several French melodies.
SCORE: vs (London: Dublin: Booksellers, 1789).
LIBRETTO: English, in *The Dramatic Works of John O'Keeffe*, vol. 2 (London: author [T. Woodfall et al.], 1798).

Fool, The, chamber opera in two scenes by Harry Somers; libretto (Eng) by Michael Fram. First performance November 15, 1956, Toronto.

Fool's Opera, The, or, The Taste of the Age, ballad opera; libretto (Eng) by "Mat. Medley" (Anthony Aston). First performance March (?) 1731, Oxford, with Mr. Aston Sr. (Poet), Mr. Aston Jr. (Fool), Mrs. Motteux (Lady), and Mrs. Smith (maid).

The work, a parody of *The Beggar's Opera,** is set in a hall.
LIBRETTO: English (London: T. Payne, [1731]); repr. ed. Rubsamen/*BO*, vol. 1, *The Beggar's Opera, Imitated and Parodied* (1974).

Forced Marriage, The, opera in four acts by Fritz Hart; libretto (Eng), after Molière's *Le mariage forcé* (1664). Composed 1928.

The aged Sganarelle withdraws his proposal of marriage to a young girl but is forced by the girl's brother to proceed with the nuptials.

Foreign Experiences, opera by Robert Ashley; libretto (Eng) by the composer. Composed 1987. Second part of the four-opera cycle *Now Eleanor's Idea.** First performance, as part of the cycle, November 15, 1994, Brooklyn, New York, Brooklyn Academy of Music.
BIBLIOGRAPHY: Bernard Holland, "When a Composer Turns Opera Upside Down," *NYT* (Nov. 21, 1994), C, 10.

For England, Ho!, "melodramatic opera" in two acts by Henry Rowley Bishop; libretto (Eng) by Isaac Pocock. First performance December 15, 1813, London, Covent Garden, with Welsh. First U.S. performance April 5, 1815, New York, arranged by Charles Gilfert, as *Freedom Ho.*

Roles: Lisette, Michael, Jerome, Enrico, Captain Laurel, Jaques, Tom Tough, and three sailors.
SCORE: ms fs (ca. 1813, British Library, Add. MS. 27704).
LIBRETTO: English (New York: D. Longworth, 1815).

Forest, The, tragic opera in one act by Ethel Smyth; libretto (Ger-Eng) by the composer and Henry Brewster, as *Der Wald*; conducted by Carl Muck. First performance (in German) April 9, 1902, Berlin. First performance in English, as *The Forest*, July 18, 1902, London, Covent Garden, with Katharina Lohse (Röschen), Olive Fremstad (Iolanthe), Alois Pennarini (Heinrich), and David Bispham (Rudolf); conducted by Otto Lohse. First U.S. performance, as *Der Wald*, March 11, 1903, New York, Metropolitan Opera; conducted by Alfred Hertz.
The work is composed in the German Romantic style.
SCORE: vs, English-German (Mainz: B. Schott's Söhne, 1902).

Forest, The, opera in seven acts by David Byrne; orchestrated by Jimmie Haskell; libretto (Eng) by Heiner Müller and Darryl Pinckney, after the *Epic of Gilgamesh*. First performance October 1988, West Berlin. First U.S. performance December 3, 1988, Brooklyn, New York, with Martin Wuttke (Gilgamesh), Howie Seago (Enkidu), Geno Lechner (the whore), and Eva Maria Meineke (Gilgamesh's mother); directed by Robert Wilson; conducted by Haskell; choreographed by Suzushi Hanayagi.
A treatment of the legend of half-mortal Gilgamesh, who is befriended by the wild man Enkidu.
Other settings of the legend include those by Harry Somers, as *The Death of Enkidu** (1977, Toronto); and Philip Glass, *The Flower of Youth* (1992, London).

Foresters, The, or, Twenty-Five Years Since, opera in three acts by Edward Loder; libretto (Eng) by Thomas J. Serle. First performance October 19, 1838, London, Covent Garden.

Forest Rose, The, or, American Farmers, pastoral opera in two acts by John Davies; libretto (Eng) by Samuel Woodworth. First performance October 7, 1825, New York.
LIBRETTO: English (New York: Circulating Library and Dramatic Repository, 1825).

Fortress, The, "melo-drama" in three acts by James Hook; libretto (Eng) by Theodore Edward Hook, after Pixérécourt's *La fortresse du Danube*. First performance July 16, 1807, London, Little Theatre in the Haymarket.
LIBRETTO: English (London: Samuel Tipper, 1807).

Fortunate Isles, The, or, The Triumphs of Britannia, allegorical and national masque, partly adapted, by Henry Rowley Bishop; libretto (Eng) by James R. Planché. First performance February 12, 1840, London, Covent Garden, with Miss Vestris.
SCORE: ms fs (1840, British Library, Add. MS. 27729).

Fortunato, tragic farce in three scenes by Miriam Gideon; libretto (Eng) by Frederick Ewen, after a play by Serafin and Joaquin Quintero. Composed 1954–1956.
The setting is Madrid in the early twentieth century. After a young couple, Alberto and Constanza, are defrauded by Don Victorio, they swear not to be taken in again. They therefore turn down the pleas of the poor Fortunato, who has a large family to support. He is eventually forced to take a job as a target for the champion sharpshooter Amaranta at the circus.

For a detailed description, see Summers/*OOA*, 128–29.

Major roles: Fortunato, a clerk (bar); Alberto, a young architect (bar); Constanza, his wife (sop); Don Victorio, a panhandler (ten); and Amaranta, a champion sharpshooter (alto).

SCORE: vs (n.p., 1954–1956; LCCN: 70-217060).

Fortune of Saint Macabre, The, opera seria in one act by Roger Hannay; libretto (Eng) by R. Bonnard. First performance March 21, 1964, Moorhead, Minnesota, Concordia College.

Fortune's Favorites, comic opera in one act by Seymour Barab; libretto (Eng) by the composer, after Saki's short story *Baker's Dozen*. First performance June 19, 1982, New York, After Dinner Opera.

Former lovers, Richard and Emily, find themselves seated together at a crowded restaurant. Since they are superstitious, they believe that this has happened because fate wished to throw them together for a second chance. Since both of them have lost their spouses, and together they have twelve, not thirteen, children (Richard having miscounted!), they resolve to wed.

Major roles: Richard (bar) and Emily (mezzo).

For a detailed description, see Kornick/*RAO*, 40–41.

Fortune Teller, The, comic opera in three acts by Victor Herbert; libretto (Eng) by Harry Bache Smith. First performance (preparatory) September 14, 1898, Toronto, Grand Opera House; and September 19, 1898, Buffalo, Star Theatre. First official performance September 26, 1898, New York, Wallack's Theatre, with Alice Nielsen (Irma/Musette), Joseph Herbert (Count Berezowski), Eugene Cowles (Sandor), and Frank Rushworth (Captain Ladislas); conducted by Paul Steindorff; directed by Julian Mitchell. First British performance April 9, 1901, London, Shaftesbury Theatre, with Nielsen in the title role.

In this tale of mixed-up identities, Irma, an unhappy heiress, bears a strong resemblance to Musette, a gypsy fortune teller. Irma is betrothed, unhappily, to Count Berezowski, although she loves Ladislas, a Hungarian hussar. Musette is courted by Sandor, a gypsy musician. Irma ultimately finds happiness with the help of Musette and a Hungarian military victory.

The musical highlights include Irma's "Always Do as People Say You Should," which opens the work, and the famous quintets "Romany Life" and "Czardas."

For a detailed description, see Waters/*VH*, 136–40.

SCORE: condensed score (New York: Witmark, [1950]); vs (London: E. Ascherberg; New York: M. Witmark, 1899).

LIBRETTO: English (New York: Wittmark, 1898).

Fortunio and His Seven Gifted Servants, operatic extravaganza in four scenes by Francis T. S. Darley; libretto (Eng), after James R. Planché's play (1843), itself based on a nursery tale by Aulnoy. First performance March 26, 1883, Philadelphia.

Fortunio is really the disguised Myrtine, daughter of Baron Dunove. She kills a dragon with the help of seven servants. Princess Vindicta, sister of King Alfourite, then claims that Fortunio has proposed to her and wants the throne for "himself." Thereupon Fortunio reveals her true identity and weds the king herself.

The composer is identified in some sources as "Sully."

Major roles: Fortunio (sop), Baron Dunove (bass), the dragon (bass), Princess Vindicta (mezzo), and King Alfourite (ten).
SCORE: vs (Philadelphia: J. M. Stoddart & Co., 1883).
LIBRETTO: English (New York and Philadelphia: J. M. Stoddart, 1883).

Forty Thieves, grand operatic romance in two acts by Michael Kelly; libretto (Eng) by George Colman Jr., after Richard Brinsley Sheridan's *Arabian Night's Entertainment,* based on the *Thousand and One Nights.* First performance April 8, 1806, London, Drury Lane Theatre. First U.S. performance December 18, 1807, Charleston, South Carolina, Charleston Theatre.

Found Objects, chamber opera in one act by Roger Trefousse; libretto (Eng) by the composer. First performance January 6, 1991, New York, Mannes College of Music, with Carola Glaser, Susan Taplinger, Natalie Arduino, Rodrick Dixon, Jonathan Kline, and Constantinos Yiannoudes; conducted by the composer; staged by Paul Echols.
    The story recounts a summer trip from New York to Maine during which three characters discuss the changes in the scenery and the "found objects," that is, items such as road signs, overheard conversations, and radio jingles.
    The work is scored for six singers representing the three personae. The music includes arias and motets for six voices.
BIBLIOGRAPHY: James R. Oestreich, review, *NYT* (Jan. 10, 1991), C, 13 [on premiere].

Foundling of the Forest, The, opera in three acts, music partly by Michael Kelly; libretto (Eng) by William Dimond. First performance 1809, London.
LIBRETTO: English (London: Longman, Hurst, Rees, and Orme, 1809).

Fountain of Youth, The, comic opera by Alfred Reynolds; libretto (Eng) by the composer. Composed 1931. Not performed.
SCORE: vs (London: Elkin & Co., [1931]).

Four Note Opera, The, one-act spoof on opera by Tom Johnson; libretto (Eng) by the composer. First performance May 16, 1972, New York, Cubiculo Theater.
    This farce, for soprano, alto, tenor, baritone, and bass, contains music that is built on four notes: A, B, D, E. It ends in mass suicide, when the singers are immobilized, and the music slowly stops.
    For a detailed description, see Eaton/*OP* II, 276–77.
    The composer (see below) admits that his work "was greatly influenced by Luigi Pirandello's *Six Characters in Search of an Author.* My characters . . . were constantly aware that they were only performers, that they were being manipulated by an author, and that their destiny was to be obedient to a score."
SCORE: vs (New York: Associated Music Publishers, 1973).
LIBRETTO: English, typescript (1972?, NYPL).
BIBLIOGRAPHY: Tom Johnson, "At Home Abroad," *ON* LIX (Oct. 1994), 34.

Four Saints in Three Acts, opera in a prelude and four acts by Virgil Thomson; libretto (Eng) by Gertrude Stein. First performance (concert) May 20, 1933, Ann Arbor, Michigan, Hill Auditorium. First performance (stage) February 8, 1934, Hartford, Connecticut, produced by the Society of Friends and Enemies of Modern Music, at the opening of Avery Memorial Theatre, with an all-black cast, with Altonell Hines (Commère), Abner Dorsey (Compère), Edward Matthews (St. Ignatius), Beatrice Robinson Waye (St. Theresa I), Bruce Howard (St. Theresa II), Bertha Fitzhugh Baker (St. Settlement), and

Embry Bonner (St. Chavez); conducted by Alexander Smallens; directed and choreo-graphed by Frederick Ashton. Same production February 20, 1934, New York. Revived January 1996, Houston, with Marietta Simpson (Commère), Wilbur Pauley (Compère), Sanford Sylvan (St. Ignatius), Ashley Putnam (St. Theresa I), Suzanna Guzman (St. Theresa II), Nicole Heaston (St. Settlement); conducted by Dennis Russell Davies; directed by Robert Wilson. Same production August 1, 1996, New York, Lincoln Center Festival 96.

The opera was conceived for a cast of seven black figures. The "plot," such as it is, involves fictional, but typical, incidents in the lives of St. Theresa of Avila and St. Ignatius Loyola and of the imaginary St. Settlement and St. Chavez.

For detailed descriptions, see Eaton/*OP* I, 69; K/*KOB*, 1324–26; K/*NKOB*, 822–23.

Major roles: St. Theresa I (sop), St. Theresa II (mezzo), St. Ignatius (bar), St. Settlement (sop), Commère (mezzo), Compère (bass), and St. Chavez (ten).

The work is full of surrealistic moments, set pieces, accompanied recitative, and parlando. Its seemingly simple style is in reality quite sophisticated.

SCORES: vs (New York: Music Press, 19??; New York: G. Schirmer, 1948).
LIBRETTO: English (Paris: W. A. Bradley, [1933]; New York: Random House, 1934).
BIBLIOGRAPHY: Paul Griffiths, "The Deadly Saints," *NY* LXXI (Nov. 13, 1995), 86–87 [on 1996 Houston revival]; Anthony Tommasini, *Virgil Thomson* (New York: W. W. Norton, 1997), 240–67, passim.
DISCOGRAPHY: cond. Thomson, RCA Victor LCT 1139 (1954); Dale, Bradley, Quivar, Allen, Matthews, Brown, Thompson, Orch. of Our Time; cond. Thome, Nonesuch 79035 (1982, 2 CDs), rev. John W. Freeman, "Records," *ON* XLVII (Feb. 26, 1983), 44.

Four-Score: An Opera of Opposites, opera in two acts by Harold Blumenfeld; li-bretto (Eng) by Charles Kondak, after Johann Nestroy's *Das Haus der Temperamente* (1837). Composed 1984. First performance (concert, excerpts) March 3, 1989, Cincin-nati, University of Cincinnati Conservatory of Music, Opera Studio.

Fourth Day, Fifth Tale, The, opera in one act by David Ahlstrom; libretto (Eng) by the composer, after Boccaccio's *The Decameron.* Composed 1961.

Isabetta remembers a former lover, Lorenzo, and her brother, Rustico. She recalls that Lorenzo disappeared and came to her in a dream, recounting that Rustico had killed him. The lovers sing of their everlasting love and bewail Rustico's treachery.

For a description, see Summers/*OOA*, 5–6.

Roles: Isabetta (sop) and Lorenzo (ten).

SCORE: ms, holograph (photocopy, NYPL).

Fourth of July, or, The Sailor's Festival, opera in one act; anonymous libretto (Eng). First performance July 4, 1788, Philadelphia, Southwark Theatre.

Fourth of July, or, The Temple of American Independence, allegorical musical drama by Victor Pelissier; anonymous libretto (Eng). First performance July 4, 1799, New York, Park Theatre.

Four-Thousand Dollars, opera by Tom Turner; libretto (Eng) by Vance Bourjaily. First performance July 29, 1969, Iowa City, University of Iowa, Macbride Auditorium; conducted by James Dixon.

In the story, set in a Georgia swamp, two men come to blows over $4,000 worth of construction company scrip, the winnings of a poker game. Both are interested in the same local beauty, and the men come to untimely ends by the opera's close.

BIBLIOGRAPHY: "Bourjaily Opera Opens . . . to Mixed Reviews," *NYT* (July 31, 1969), 26.

Fox, The, opera in one act by Leslie Kondorossy; libretto (Eng) by Shawn Hall, after Kalman Mikszath's novel. First performance January 28, 1961, Cleveland.

Two sisters, Carol and Margie, are lamenting the fact that their wealthy aunt, recently deceased, has left them only a decrepit stuffed fox in her will. A robber arrives and demands money; the sisters have only the fox, which the thief seizes. Feeling how heavy it is, he slits it open, whereupon a cache of jewels falls out. He chloroforms the sisters but then, feeling guilty, puts them gently on the sofa and tries to mend the torn animal. They awake, and when their uncle Joe arrives and asks for the fox in return for a good deal of money, they happily accept, suspecting that Joe knows what was hidden in the animal.

For a description, see Summers/*OOA*, 181–82.

Roles: Carol (sop), Margie (mezzo), Uncle Joe (bar), and the robber (pantomime).

Foxy Quiller, comic opera in three acts by Reginald De Koven; libretto (Eng) by Harry B. Smith. First performance November 5, 1900, New York, Broadway Theater, with W. G. Stewart (Ned Royster), Grace Cameron (Daphne), Louis Cassavant (Abel Gudgeon), and Adolph Zink (the thief).

When Ned Royster, a young sailor, is the victim of a thief, Abel Gudgeon, the father of Ned's fiancée, Daphne, hires the wily Foxy Quiller to find the perpetrator. Although the money turns up in Quiller's luggage, he is saved from imprisonment when the real thief admits his guilt.

A sequel to *The Highwayman** (1897).

SCORE: vs (New York: E. Schuberth, 1900).

Fra Diavolo, or, The Inn of Terracina, opera in three acts by Michael Rophino Lacy, after Auber's work (1830, Paris); libretto (Eng) by Lacy, after the text by Scribe. First performance November 3, 1831, London, Covent Garden.

The story concerns the robber Fra Diavolo, who dons the disguise of a marquis and seduces the daughter of an innkeeper while planning an elaborate jewel robbery.

Another arrangement was Lee's *The Devil's Brother,** which appeared in February of 1831; also the musical burletta, after Scribe's text, *Wanted, a Brigand, or, A Visit from Fra-Diavolo* by George Stansbury and Mary A'Beckett (1838, London); and "a new and original burlesque burletta" by H. J. Byron, as *Fra Diavolo!, or, The Beauty and the Brigands* (1858, London).

LIBRETTO: English (London: J. Miller, 1833).

Francis the First, grand opera by Edward J. Loder; libretto (Eng) by McKinlan. First performance November 6, 1838, London, Drury Lane Theatre.

The work, which includes a number of songs composed earlier by Loder, features the once-famous ballad "The Old House at Home."

François Villon, opera in three acts by Maurice Baron; libretto (Eng). First performance (radio, excerpts) April 14, 1940, New York, NBC.

About the fifteenth-century French poet.

Frankenstein, opera in three acts by Gregory Sandow; libretto (Eng) by Thomas N. Disch, after Mary Shelley's *Frankenstein* (1818). First performance August 7, 1980, Glens Falls, New York.

About the scientist Dr. Frankenstein and the monster he creates.

Frankenstein, or, A Bolt from the Blue, Victorian melodrama for schools by Carey Blyton; libretto (Eng) by the composer, after Shelley. Composed 1987.

The forty-minute work has a cast of narrator and unison voices, with piano and optional flexible instrumentation for a "music-hall" sound.
SCORE: vs (London: Novello, 1989).

Frankenstein: The Modern Prometheus, musical drama in three acts by Libby Larsen; libretto (Eng) by the composer, after Shelley. First performance May 25, 1990, St. Paul, Minnesota.
    Roles: soprano, mezzo-soprano, two tenors, two basses, and boy soprano.

Frankie, children's opera by Alan John; libretto (Eng) by David Holman. First performance April 8, 1987, Adelaide, State Opera of South Australia; conducted by Peter Deane.
    About a racially prejudiced gang of inner-city youth.
BIBLIOGRAPHY: Elizabeth Silsbury, review, *Opera* XXXVIII (Oct. 1987), 1158 [on premiere].

Franklin's Tale, The, opera in one act by Noel Sokoloff; libretto (Eng) by Ted Hart, after Chaucer's tale. First performance November 10, 1961, Baton Rouge, Louisiana, Louisiana State University, University Theater.
    While the kindly Arveragus is away, his wife, Dorigena, is courted by Aurelius. Dorigena jokingly says that she will give in to Aurelius only if all the rocks have been removed from the coast of Brittany. Aurelius enlists the help of the magician Cedasus to achieve this. Arveragus, learning of his wife's silly promise, tells her to honor it, but Aurelius, overhearing the two, releases Dorigena from her vow.
    For a detailed description, see Eaton/*OP* II, 277.
    Major roles: Arveragus (bass), Dorigena (sop), Aurelius (ten), and Cedasus (bass-bar).

Freak Show, The, opera in one act by Clifford Taylor; libretto (Eng) by Edward Lind. Composed 1975.
    The setting is a "seedy amusement park, ca. 1925." Six freaks who are part of the show lament that they are missing the seventh member of their troupe, the man of stone. The scene switches to a mother and her son at a restaurant; they are to be joined by the father, a cold man who has little patience for his family. When he arrives, he voices his displeasure with his wife and son. The action returns to the amusement park, where the freak show is about to begin. The unhappy family is part of the audience, and the father, cajoled by the devil, who is disguised as a carnival barker, is driven to shoot his family. He is changed into the man of stone, the missing part of the performing troupe.
    For a detailed description, see Summers/*OOA*, 292–94.
    Major roles: the father (bass-bar/bar), the mother (sop), the son (ten), the barker (bass-bar).
SCORE: ms fs, holograph (1975, photocopy, NYPL); vs (New York: American Composers Alliance, 1975).

Frederick Douglass, opera in three acts by Dorothy Rudd Moore; libretto (Eng) by the composer. First performance June 28, 1985, New York, Aaron Davis Hall, Opera Ebony; conducted by Warren Wilson.

Frederick Douglass, opera in three acts by Ulysses Kay; libretto (Eng) by Donald Dorr. First performance April 14, 1991, Newark, New Jersey, Symphony Hall, New Jersey State Opera, with Kevin Maynor (Douglass), Klara Barlow (Helen), and Gregory Rahming (Howard); conducted by Alfredo Silipigni.
    The plot concerns the second marriage of the abolitionist orator to a white woman and his basically innocent involvement in the collapse of a bank.

Major roles: Douglass (bass-bar); Helen, his wife (sop); and Howard, his son (bar).
The score is filled with melodies based on nineteenth-century Americana tunes and
Haitian folk music.
BIBLIOGRAPHY: Michael Redmond, review, *ON* LVI (Aug. 1991), 42 [on premiere].

Frederick the Great, or, The Heart of a Soldier, afterpiece in three acts by Thomas
Cooke; libretto (Eng) by Samuel J. Arnold. First performance August 4, 1814, Lon-
don, Lyceum.
LIBRETTO: English (London: J. Miller, 1815).

Free and Easy, comic opera in two acts by John Addison, libretto (Eng) by Samuel J.
Arnold. First performance September 16, 1816, London.
LIBRETTO: English (London: J. Cumberland & Son, [n.d.]).

Freebooters, The, "grand serio-comick opera, " an arrangement by William Hawes of
Paer's *I fuorusciti di Firenze* (1802, Dresden); libretto (Eng) translated by Hampden
Napier from Anelli's text. First performance August 20, 1827, London, Lyceum Theatre.

Uberto, who has been banished from Florence by his opponent, Edoarde, heads a
group of bandits who live in the Alps. They capture Isabella, wife of Edoarde, and
when Edoarde finds the camp and attempts to flee with her, they are stopped by Uberto.
Uberto magnanimously decides to spare Edoarde's life at the request of Isabella, who
turns out to be his daughter. Uberto and his men are then pardoned.
LIBRETTO: English (London: S. G. Fairbrother, [n.d.]).

Free Knights, The, or, The Edict of Charlemagne, dramatic opera in three acts by
Joseph Mazzinghi; libretto (Eng) by Frederick Reynolds. First performance February
8, 1810, London, Covent Garden. First U.S. performance May 13, 1810, New York,
Pearl Theatre, with Mr. Egerton (Prince Palatine), Mr. Young (Abbot of Corbey), Mr.
Blanchard (Baron Ravensburg), Mr. Incledon (Count Roland), Mr. C. Kemble
(Ravensburg), Mrs. Davenport (Countess Roland), Mrs. Dickons (Ulrica), and Mrs. H.
Johnston (Agness).
LIBRETTO: English (New York: David Longworth, 1810).

Free Lance, The, operatic spoof in two acts by John Philip Sousa; libretto (Eng) by
Harry B. Smith. First performance 1905, Philadelphia; April 16, 1906, New York,
New Amsterdam, with Albert Hart (the Duke of Graftiana), George Tallman (Florian/
Prince Florian), Nella Bergen (Princess Yolanda), Jeanette Lowrie (Griselda), Felix
Haney (the Emperor of Bragadocia), and Joseph Cawthorn (Sigmund Lump); con-
ducted by the composer. Revived in Philadelphia in 1979.

Florian, son of the Duke of Graftiana, balks at his father's attempts to have him
wed Yolanda, who is the daughter of the emperor of Bragadocia. She flees and changes
places with Griselda, a goose girl, while Florian, not knowing of this switch, takes the
place of Sigmund Lump, the goatherd husband of Griselda.
The work closed after thirty-five performances in New York. It includes the stir-
ring march that ends the work, "Drums Are Beating."
SCORE: vs (Cincinnati, 1906).

Freischütz, Der, "a new muse-sick-all and see-nick performance from the new German uproar. By the celebrated funnybear," a "travestie" of Weber's *Der Freischütz*
(1821, Berlin), by "Septimus Globus, Esq." First performance 1824; probably the same
as *Der Fryshot, or Number Seven*, May 26, 1825, Edinburgh.

LIBRETTO: English (London: C. Baldwyn, 1824).

Freischütz, Der, an adaptation, with additional music, by Henry Rowley Bishop of Weber; libretto (Eng) adapted by George Soane, after Friedrich Kind's text. First performance November 10, 1824, London, Drury Lane Theatre.

Freshwater, opera in one act by Eric Valinsky; libretto (Eng), after Virginia Woolf's comedy. First performance October 19, 1984, New York, Opera Uptown.

Frida, opera in two acts by Robert Xavier Rodríguez; libretto (Eng and Sp) by Hilary Blecher; lyrics and monologues by Migdalia Cruz. First performance April 11, 1991, Philadelphia, American Music Theater Festival. Revised version June 3, 1993, Houston, Houston Opera.
    A treatment of the life of the Mexican artist Frida Kahlo and her tortured relationship with her artist husband Diego Rivera.

Fridiof's Saga, children's opera in one act by David Bedford; libretto (Eng) by Terry Bragg, after an Icelandic saga. First performance 1981, Elgin, Scotland, Gordonstoun School.
    See also E. E. Freer's *Frithiof.*
DISCOGRAPHY: excerpt, "First and Foremost," Apollo Saxophone Quartet, Argo 443903-2ZH (1995, London, 1 CD).

Fridolin, operatic burletta in three acts by Frank Romer; libretto (Eng) by Mark Lemon. First performance December 1, 1840, London, National English Opera, Prince's Theatre, with Emma Romer.
    The work, a family affair (the composer was Emma Romer's brother, and the librettist her brother-in-law), was withdrawn after eight performances.
LIBRETTO: English (London: James Pattie, [1840]).

Friend Fritz, comic opera by Julian Edwards; libretto (Eng), after Emile Erckmann and P. A. Chatrian's novel (1846). First performance January 26, 1893, New York.
    Fritz, who seems to be a lifelong bachelor, falls in love with Suzel, the daughter of one of his tenants, through the efforts of Rabbi David, a professional matchmaker.
    Also set by P. Mascagni as *L'amico Fritz* (1891, Rome).

Friend in Need, A, musical entertainment by Michael Kelly; libretto (Eng) by Prince Hoare. First performance February 2, 1797, London, Drury Lane Theatre.
SCORE: vs (London: Dale, [1797]).

Friends and Dinosaurs, children's opera by Charles Shadle; libretto (Eng). First performance May 20, 1989, Needham, Massachusetts, Longwood Opera; summer 1990, Glens Falls, New York, Lake George Opera Festival.

Frieze of Life, The, chamber opera in one act by Edward Applebaum; libretto (Eng) by Julia Garza, after paintings of Edvard Munch. First performance January 29, 1983, Newport Beach, California.

Frithiof, opera in two acts by Eleanor Everest Freer; libretto (Eng) by Clement Shaw, after Esaias Tegnér's *Frithiofs Saga* (1825). First performance April 11, 1929, Chicago, Illinois Women's Athletic Club; (concert) February 1, 1931, Chicago, Studebaker Theater.
    The work is based on a Norse legend.
SCORE: vs (Milwaukee, Wisc.: William A. Koun Music Co., 1928).

Fritzi, opera-bagatelle in one act by Harold Blumenfeld; libretto (Eng) by Charles Kondek. Composed 1979. First performance November 3, 1988, Chicago, Chicago Opera Theater.

Frog-Hopping, chamber opera in one act by William Boswell; libretto (Eng) by Robert Salomon. First performance February 5, 1982, Brooklyn, Brooklyn College Opera Theater.

Frog Man, The, chamber opera by Alan Hovhaness; libretto (Eng) by the composer. Composed 1987.

Frogs of Windham, The, comic opera in three acts by Burton E. Leavitt; libretto (Eng) by Nason W. Leavitt. Composed ca. 1891. First (?) performance 1983, Windham, Connecticut, Windham Theater Guild.

The story is set in the Connecticut town of Windham, where the residents take up arms when they hear a terrible commotion during the night. The commotion is the result of frogs escaping a dried-up pond located in the center of the town.

LIBRETTO: English (New Haven, Conn.: J. J. Kiernan, 1891).
BIBLIOGRAPHY: Robert A. Hamilton, "Historical Opera Eludes Searchers," *NYT* (Sept. 1, 1985), XXIII, 1.

From the Towers of the Moon, opera in one act by Robert Moran; libretto (Eng) by John Michael LaChiusa, after the legend of Kaguyahme. First performance March 27, 1992, St. Paul, Minnesota Opera, with Elisabeth Comeaux (the Girl/Moon Goddess), John Andreasen (the Peasant), Miriam Langsjoen (the Wife), Peter Halverson (the Emperor), Antonia Fusaro (the Emperor's Mother), Hugh Givens (the Minister of War), and Thomas Schumacher (the Grand Consul); conducted by Jack Gaughan.

The story concerns the Japanese legend of the immortal Moon Goddess, who is given to a childless couple to end their grief and provide them with love.

BIBLIOGRAPHY: Charles Morton, "St. Paul," *ON* LVII (Sept. 1992), 63–64 [on premiere].

Frozen Lake, The, arrangement by George W. Reeve of Auber's *La neige* (1823, Paris); libretto (Eng) by James R. Planché, after Scribe and Delavigne's text. First performance November 26, 1824, London, Covent Garden.

Frustration, "mini-opera" parody in one act by Sheldon Harnick of Debussy's *Pelléas et Mélisande* (1902, Paris); libretto (Eng) by the composer. First performance 1968, Washington, D.C., Smithsonian Institution. First New York performance May 1981, New York, Bel Canto Opera; conducted by Maria Waldman.

The six-minute work concerns two lovers who meet in the forest, with the character of Pelléas changed mysteriously into an old woman; the two get nowhere and go off in an attempt to change Pelléas back into a young woman.

Roles: Mélisande (sop/mezzo), Pelléas (mezzo/alto).

The work is scored for two female voices, violin, clarinet, and piano.

SCORE: performing score (Bryn Mawr, Pa.: T. Presser, 1973).
BIBLIOGRAPHY: Peter G. Davis, "Opera: Bel Canto Troupe Offers Program of 3 One-Act Works," *NYT* (May 7, 1981), C, 20 [on New York premiere].

Fugitives, The, opera in three acts by Carlisle Floyd; libretto (Eng) by the composer. First performance April 17, 1951, Tallahassee, Opperman Hall, Florida State.

Full Circle, opera in one act by Robin Orr; libretto (Eng) by Sydney G. Smith. First performance April 10, 1968, Perth, Scotland, Scottish National Opera.

The story of an unemployed man during the Depression who becomes a thief out of desperation and in the end kills a policeman.

The work was composed as a companion piece for Stravinsky's *L'histoire du soldat.* It is similarly scored for the same instruments and viola.

SCORE: vs (London: International Music Co., [1968]).

BIBLIOGRAPHY: R. Crichton, "Perth," *MT* CIX (June 1968), 561 [on premiere].

Full Moon in March, opera in one act by John Harbison; libretto (Eng) by the composer, after the play by W. B. Yeats (1935). First performance April 30, 1979, Boston, Boston Musica Viva, Sanders Theater, with D'Anna Fortunato (the Queen), David Arnold (the Swineherd), and Cheryl Cobb and Kim Scown (the attendants); conducted by Richard Pittman. First British performance April 7, 1983, London, New Opera Company, Blooms-bury Theatre, with Fiona Kimm (the Queen), Michael Rippon (the Swineherd), and Laureen Livingstone and Richard Steele (the attendants); conducted by Leon Lovett.

In an operatic plot reminiscent of Richard Strauss's *Salome* (1905) and Giacomo Puccini's *Turandot* (1926), the Queen has offered herself in marriage to the man who can move her by his song. To date, no suitor has succeeded. When a crude swineherd comes forth, she realizes that he is the one she has been seeking, but she is so revolted by his appearance that she has him beheaded before he can sing. A dancer, miming the Queen, then dances before the severed head and enacts a type of ritual consummation; the Queen admits that her cold world has been transformed.

Major roles: the Queen (sop) and the Swineherd (bar).

The work, for a small orchestral group, contains exotic musical effects through its use of incantational rhythms and prepared-piano sonorities.

SCORE: vs (New York: Associated Music Publishers, 1983).

BIBLIOGRAPHY: Debra Cash, "Boston," *ON* XLIII (July 1979), 32 [on premiere]; Martin Dreyer, "New Opera Company," *MT* CXXIV (June 1983), 375 [on British premiere]; Maurice Dunmore, "Reports: Foreign," *ON* XLVIII (July 1983), 40–41 [on British premiere]; Harold Rosenthal, "A Full Moon in March," *Opera* (June 1985), 672–73 [on British premiere].

DISCOGRAPHY: Fortunato, Arnold, Cobb, Scown, Boston Musica Viva; cond. R. Pittman CRI SD 454; rev. John W. Freeman, "Records," *ON* XLIX (Mar. 16, 1983), 44.

Funeral of Jan Palach, The, fantasy opera in one act by Connie Beckley; libretto (Eng) by David Shapiro. First performance December 7, 1990, New York, American Opera Projects, Blue Door Studio, with David Frye (Palach), Jane Shaulis (Palach's mother), Harlan Foss (man), and Margaret Bishop (woman); conducted by Robert Black; Jayn Rosenfeld and Debi Pellkofer, flutists; directed by Grethe Barrett Holby.

The work centers on the Czechoslovakian dissident who killed himself during the uprising in 1968 against Soviet rule. Palach speaks from the grave while his mother laments, and a man and woman, in the fashion of a Greek chorus, comment on the events.

BIBLIOGRAPHY: Allan Kozinn, review, *NYT* (Dec, 9, 1990), I, 83 [on premiere].

Further Voyages of the Santa Maria, The, opera in three acts by Eric Stokes; libretto (Eng) by Alvin Greenberg. Composed 1984.

The story concerns the ghost of Columbus, who joins the crews of spaceships called the Santa Maria.

See *Columbus* for other settings about the explorer.

G

Gagliarda of a Merry Plague, opera in one act by Lazare Saminsky; libretto (Eng) by the composer, after Edgar Allan Poe's *The Masque of the Red Death*. First performance February 2, 1925, New York, Times Square Theater.

A prince and his friends flee to a secluded castle to escape a devastating plague, only to fall victim to it when the Red Death infiltrates their revelries.

Gainsborough, romantic opera in three acts by Albert Coates; libretto (Eng) by Cecil Reginald Grundy. First performance April 20, 1941, Los Angeles, University of California, Royce Hall, as *Gainsborough's Duchess*.

The plot is described as "an episode in the life of Thomas Gainsborough" in the vocal score.

SCORE: vs (London?: n.p., 1939; LCCN: 42-12370).

Galahad, music drama in four scenes by Rutland Boughton; libretto (Eng) by the composer. Composed 1943–1944. Unperformed.

The work was part four of the composer's Arthurian cycle and included *The Chapel in Lyonesse** as its second scene.

Gale, opera in one act by Ethel Leginska; libretto (Eng) by Catherine A. Dawson-Scott and Henry Dawson Lowry, after Dawson-Scott's novel (1922). First performance November 23, 1935, Chicago, Civic Opera House, with John Charles Thomas, conducted by the composer.

The setting is the Cornish seaside.

SCORE: ms vs, as *The Haunting* (holograph, NYPL).

Galileo Galilei, opera in three acts by Ezra Laderman; libretto (Eng) by Joe Darion. First performance February 3, 1979, Binghamton, New York, Forum, Tri-Cities Opera.

The opera is told in a series of flashbacks by the old and blind Galileo. He recalls his research and subsequent trial for heresy, during which he was protected by Cardinals Bellarmine and Barberini. He also remembers his daughters and his mistress, Lavinia, and the new charges of heresy that led to his forced confession. Discharged from prison because of his age and infirmity, Galileo has an old friend take his book to be published in Holland.

Major roles: Galileo (bass-bar), the friend (mezzo), Cardinal Bellarmine (bar), Cardinal Barberini (ten), and the interrogator (ten).

For a detailed description, see Kornick/*RAO*, 165–67.

The dissonant and contrapuntal work is a revision of the oratorio *The Trials of Galileo* (1967, New York).

SCORE: vs (New York: Oxford University Press, 1978).
LIBRETTO: English (New York: Oxford University Press, 1978).

Gallantry, "soap opera" in one act by Douglas Moore; libretto (Eng) by Arnold Sundgaard. First performance March 19, 1958, New York, Columbia University, Brander

Matthews Theater, with Bonnie Murray, David Atkinson, Joseph Sopher, and Cecilia Ward; conducted by Emerson Buckley; produced by Day Tuttle.

In this farcical treatment of television soap operas, the action takes place in an operating room. The surgeon loves the anesthetist, who loves the patient undergoing the operation. Commercials interrupt the critical moments.

Roles: announcer (mezzo), Dr. Gregg (bar), Lola (sop), and Donald (ten).

For a detailed description, see Eaton/*OP* I, 186–87.

SCORE: vs (New York: G. Schirmer, [1958]).

BIBLIOGRAPHY: H. C. S., "Moore's Opera, 'Gallantry,' in Premiere," *NYT* (March 20, 1958), 34.

Gambrinus, King of Lager Beer, "diabolical musical, comical, and nonsensical Ethiopian burlesque," music by Alfred B. Sedgwick, text (Eng) by Frank Dumont. First performance July 21, 1876, Jackson, Michigan, with James T. Gulick (Gambrinus), Lew Benedict (Switzerkase), Frank Dumont (Belzebub), Ben Standway (Splutter), D. H. Smith (Kniphauser), and Frank List (Gretchen).

In this comical treatment of the Faust legend, the poor Gambrinus, unsuccessful in his pursuit of the beautiful Gretchen, is promised thirty years of good living if he gives his soul to Belzebub, the Devil, after the thirty years have elapsed. When Belzebub comes for Gambrinus, the Devil is fooled into seizing Switzerkase instead.

Major roles: Gambrinus, a poor woodchopper; Switzerkase; King of the Lunch Fiends; Belzebub, demon of the Black Forest; Gretchen, fair maid of the village; and Kniphauser, her father, fond of beer and wine.

The eleven musical numbers include Gambrinus's lively song "Drink! Drink! Banish Dull Care!" (no. 9).

SCORE: vs (words and music) (New York: De Witt Publishing House, 1876); repr. ed. Michael Meckna, *NAMT*, vol. 7 (1994).

Game of Cards, opera in one act by Arnold Franchetti; libretto (Eng) by Max Weber. First performance (concert) March 20, 1955, Hartford, Connecticut, Hartt College of Music. First performance (stage) May 5, 1956, Hartford, Burns School Auditorium; conducted by Moshe Paranov.

The antiwar story concerns arrival of peace at the end of the Thirty Years' War; three soldiers, stationed at an inn, play a game of cards.

Part 3 of a trilogy of works about war, consisting also of *The Princess** and *The Maypole.**

SCORE: vs ([n.p., 1963]; LCCN: 73-206131).

BIBLIOGRAPHY: Ross Parmenter, "2 One-Act Operas Sung at Hartford," *NYT* (May 10, 1956), 27 [on premiere].

Game of Chance, A, opera in one act by Seymour Barab; libretto (Eng) by Evelyn Manacher Draper, after the play *All on a Summer's Day* by Florence Ryerson and Colin Clements. First performance January 11, 1957, Rock Island, Illinois, Augustana College, Potter Hall. First British performance March 13, 1963, London, Royal College of Music, with Barbara Budmani, Patricia Thomas, Cynthia Bateman, and James Richards; conducted by Richard Austin; produced by Douglas Craig.

Three young women who are neighbors are granted their dearest wish by a representative, but they find their wishes are not enough: the one who asked for a fortune now misses her friends; the second, who wanted to be famous, now needs love; the woman who wished for love finds marriage has brought her only unending work.

Roles: first neighbor (sop), second neighbor (sop), third neighbor (mezzo), and the representative (bass-bar).

For a detailed description, see Eaton/*OP* I, 187.

SCORE: vs ([New York]: Boosey & Hawkes, 1960).

BIBLIOGRAPHY: Arthur Jacobs, "Student and Amateur Performances," *Opera* (May 1963) 354–55 [on British premiere].

Garden, The, melodrama by Stephen Oliver; libretto (Eng) by the composer. First performance, as *Il giardino*, July 27, 1977, Batignano, Italy. First performance as *The Garden* April 17, 1980, London, Wigmore Hall.

The story concerns a woman sitting in a garden, who is visited by a man who commiserates with her on her husband's death. It gradually appears that he knows more about that death than she would like. But in the end, it is he who is disconcerted.

The work is scored for soprano and tenor with lute and viola da gamba or string quartet and harpsichord.

SCORE: vs, Italian-English, ed. Peter Washtell (Borough Green, Kent: Novello, 1984).

Garden of Artemis, The, or, Apollo's Revels, "tableau chantant in the antique manner" (mythological opera) in one act by Daniel Pinkham; libretto (Eng) by Robert Hillyer. First performance 1948, Cambridge, Massachusetts.

The young Clorinda, desired by Apollo, is changed into a flower by Artemis, goddess of virgins. Other young women who have been changed do not mind their pursuit by Apollo, who changes them back into women. He also promises to do the same for Clorinda.

Roles: Clorinda (sop), Artemis (mezzo/alto), and Apollo (bar).

For a detailed description, see Eaton/*OP* II, 278.

SCORE: solo voices, women's chorus, flute, clarinet, violin, viola, and violoncello (n.p., n.d.; LCCN: 84-90905).

Garden of Mystery, The, opera in one act by Charles Wakefield Cadman; libretto (Eng) by Nelle Eberhart, after the story *Rappaccini's Daughter* by Nathaniel Hawthorne. First performance March 20, 1925, New York. Revived February 16, 1996, New York, American Chamber Opera Company, with George Walker (Dr. Rappaccini), Helen Cadmus (Beatrice), Yvonne de Treville (Bianca), Ernest Davis (Giovanni), and Hubert Linscott (Enrico); conducted by Douglas Anderson.

Dr. Rappaccini has raised his daughter, Beatrice, on the poisonous plants of his mysterious garden, making her breath lethal. Giovanni, a neighbor, falls in love with her and gets an antidote to counteract the poisons. When Giovanni begins to berate her and she discovers that he is immune to the poison, the despondent Beatrice drinks the antidote herself, knowing that it will kill her.

See *Rappaccini's Daughter* for other settings.

LIBRETTO: English (New York and Birmingham, England: J. Fischer & Bros., 1925).

Gardens of Adonis, The, opera in three scenes by Hugo Weisgall; libretto (Eng) by John Olon-Scrymgeour, after Shakespeare's *Venus and Adonis*. Composed 1959; revised 1977–1981. First performance September 12, 1992, Omaha, Nebraska, Opera/ Omaha, with Melanie Helton (Venus), Jon Garrison (Adonis), Eric McLuskey (Martial), Jayne West (Zoë), Rebecca Privitera (Cupid), Malcolm Rivers (Tydeus), and Kristine Jepson (Death); conducted by Hal France.

In the plot, set in modern America, Adonis and his friend Martial come upon a middle-aged Venus in her swimming pool. Adonis is taken with her, but his life is ended by the abrupt appearance of Death.

Major roles: Venus (sop); Adonis (ten); Martial (bar); Zoë, Venus's maid (sop); Tydeus, the gardener (bass-bar); Cupid (sop); and Death (mezzo).

BIBLIOGRAPHY: James R. Oestreich, "Love's Labors Exercised in a Series in Omaha," *NYT* (Sept. 24, 1992) [on premiere]; Robert G. Ruetz, "Omaha," *ON* LVII (Jan. 2, 1993), 40–41 [on premiere]; Bruce Saylor, "Pursuit of Beauty," *ON* LVII (Sept. 1992), 28, 30–31.

Garibaldi, or, The Rival Patriots, opera in two acts by Frederick Cowen; libretto (Eng) by Rosalind Cowen. First performance (private) 1860, London.

Garni Sands, opera in two acts by George Dreyfus; libretto (Eng) by Frank Kellaway. Composed 1965. First performance August 12, 1972, Sydney, Australia, University of New South Wales. First U.S. performance May 11, 1975, New York, Bel Canto Opera, with John Sayers (convict lover), Lee Winston (another convict), and Howard Nevison (Narrator).

The story involves a colonial farming family that gives work to a group of convicts, and the resulting tragedy when the daughter of the family falls in love with one of the prisoners.

The Narrator tells the story and acts as a type of Greek chorus.

SCORE: vs ([Melbourne]: Allans Music, [1974?]).

BIBLIOGRAPHY: Robert Sherman, "Bel Canto Offers the Australian 'Garni Sands,'" *NYT* (May 12, 1975), 39 [on U.S. premiere].

Garrick, opera in three acts by Albert Stoessel; libretto (Eng) by Robert A. Simon, after the play *David Garrick*. First performance February 24, 1937, New York, Juilliard School, with Gean Greenwell (Colly Cibber), Donald Dickson (David Garrick), Alice George (Julia Paulding), Albert Gifford (Harry Marchmont), Glenn Darwin (Lord Darnley), and Pauline Pierce (Peg Woffington); conducted by the composer.

The work takes place in London about 1744 and concerns the life of David Garrick. Among the characters are Lord Darnley; Colley Cibber; Peg Woffington, a former love of Garrick; Harry Marchmont, Garrick's friend and rival; and Julia Paulding, a secret admirer whom he finally meets.

Another setting of his life is Somerville's *David Garrick** (1920).

SCORE: vs (New York: J. Fischer & Bros., 1937).

BIBLIOGRAPHY: Olin Downes, "Juilliard School Presents 'Garrick,'" *NYT* (Feb. 21, 1937) [on premiere].

Gasconado the Great, "a tragi-comi [sic], political, whimsical opera"; libretto (Eng) by James Worsdale. First performance 1759, London.

The work is set in a palace.

Roles: Gasconado, Lord Roland, Gripewell, Harlequin, Punch, Scaramouch, Pierro, Alecto, Megera, and Pampaline.

LIBRETTO: English (London: author, 1759); repr. ed. Rubsamen/*BO*, vol. 14, *Topical and Nautical Operas* (1974).

Gate, The, scenic oratorio in two parts by Max Brand; libretto (Eng) by Frederick Faust (pseud. of Brand). First performance May 23, 1944, New York, Metropolitan Opera House.

For soloists, chorus, orchestra, actors, and narrator.

LIBRETTO: English (New York: Associated Music Publishers, [1944]).

Gawain, opera in two acts by Harrison Birtwistle; libretto (Eng) by David Harsent, after an anonymous late fourteenth-century poem. First performance May 30, 1991, London, Covent Garden, with Marie Angel (Morgan le Fay), Elizabeth Laurence (Lady de Hautdesert), Richard Greager (Arthur), Penelope Walmsley-Clark (Guinevere), John Tomlinson (Bertilak de Hautdesert/the Green Knight), and François Le Roux (Gawain); conducted by Elgar Howarth. Revised version April 14, 1994, London, Covent Garden.

In the story, the enchantress Morgan le Fay is jealous of the love between Arthur and Guinevere. Morgan has as her earthly counterpart Lady de Hautdesert, whose husband, Bertilak de Hautdesert, is paralleled in the supernatural world by the Green Knight. The enchantress brings chaos to Arthur's court, as she tempts Gawain, Arthur's nephew, to battle the Green Knight, who is beheaded but survives.

For a detailed plot description, see K/*NKOB*, 72–74.

Major roles: Gawain (bar), Lady de Hautdesert (mezzo), Morgan le Fay (sop), the Green Knight/Bertilak de Hautdesert (bar), Fool (bar), Arthur (ten), Guinevere (sop), Baldwin (ten), Agravain (bar), and Ywain (ten).

LIBRETTO: English (London: Universal, 1991).

BIBLIOGRAPHY: R. Addlington, "Birtwistle's 'Gawain,'" *MT* CXXXV (July 1994), 463; Antony Bye, "Live Performance," *MT* CXXXII (May 1991), 231, 233 [on premiere]; Andrew Clements, "'Gawain,' an Opera about People," *Opera* XLII (1991), 874–79; Winton Dean, "Birtwistle's 'Gawain,'" *Opera* XLV (June 1994), 749–52; Wilfrid Mellers, "Music for Everyman," *TLS* (June 14, 1991), 18 [on premiere].

DISCOGRAPHY: rev. version: Angel, P. Walmsley-Clark, Howells, Greager, F. Le Roux, J. Tomlinson, Chorus and Orch. of the Royal Opera House; cond. E. Howarth, Collins Classics 70412; rev. Jonathan Cross, "Record Reviews," *Tempo* CC (April 1997), 53–54; Patrick J. Smith, "Recordings," *ON* LXII (Oct. 1997), 40.

Gay Deceivers, or, More Laugh than Love, farce in two acts, an adaptation by William Hawes and Michael Kelly of Grétry's *Les événéments imprévus* (1799, Versailles); translation by George Colman Jr. of Thomas d'Hèle's libretto. First performance August 22, 1804, London, Little Theatre in the Haymarket.

LIBRETTO: English (London: M. Kelly, [1804?]; London: J. Cawthorn, [etc.], 1808).

Gay Musketeers, The, "romantic comedy opera" in three acts by Maurice Baron. Composed 1925.

SCORE: vs: ([n.p.], 1925; LCCN: 84-57194).

LIBRETTO: English ([n.p.], 1925; LCCN: 84-109794).

Geisha, The, "a story of a tea house: Japanese musical play" in two acts by Sidney Jones; libretto (Eng) by Owen Hall (Jimmy Davis), after P. Loti's *Madame Chrysanthème* (1887); lyrics by Harry Greenbank. First performance April 25, 1896, London, Daly's, with Rutland Barrington (Marquis Imari), Hayden Coffin (Fairfax), and Marie Tempest (the geisha). First U.S. performance September 9, 1896, New York, Daly's.

Of particular interest to the history of opera is that the story is similar to that of Puccini's *Madama Butterfly* (1904), with the English Lieutenant Reginald Fairfax as Pinkerton's counterpart. It was Jones's most popular work; it ran for 760 performances in London, 160 in New York. Another setting of an opera with a Japanese theme is Aldo Franchetti's tragedy *Namiko-San** (1925, Chicago).

SCORE: vs (London: Hopwood & Crew, 1896).

LIBRETTO: English (London: Hopwood & Crew, 1896; New York: Chasmer-Winchell, 1896); Italian, as *La geisha, L'istoria di una casa di the* (Rome: Tipografia C. Luci, 1905).

General, The, opera in one act by Felix Werder; libretto (Eng) by Leonard Radic. Composed 1966.

Generous Free-Mason, The, or, The Constant Lady, with the Humours of Squire Noodle, and His Man Doodle, "a tragi-comi-farcical ballad opera in three acts"; libretto (Eng) by William R. Chetwood. First performance August 20, 1730, London, Bartholomew Fair. Also performed December 28, 1730, London, Theatre in the Haymarket.

The work is set in Tunis.

Major roles: Amurath, King of Tunis; Mizra, High-Admiral; Sebastian, an English gentleman; Zelmana, Queen of Tunis; Maria, an English lady; Sir Jasper Moody; Caelia his daughter; Cleremont, her lover; Lettice, her maid; and Davy, Cleremont's man.

The work includes "Neptune, Tritons, Turks, &c."

LIBRETTO: English (London: J. Roberts, 1731); repr. ed. Rubsamen/*BO*, vol. 11, *Farce, Broad or Satirical* (1974).

Genesis, "cassation for audience and instruments" (children's opera) by Malcolm Williamson; libretto (Eng) by the composer. First performance April 23, 1973, London.

The work requires three singing-acting groups and three instrument-playing groups, accompanied by a piano or organ.

"Conceived as a simple method of teaching children of all ages the mechanics of opera."

SCORE: vs ([London]: J. Weinberger, [1971]; Frankfurt/Main: Heros Musikverlag, [1971]).

Genevieve, or, The Maid of Switzerland, romantic drama in one act by George Macfarren; libretto (Eng) by Mrs. Cornwell Baron-Wilson. First performance November 3, 1834, London, English Opera House.

LIBRETTO: English, prompter's copy ([London?: n.p., 183-?]).

Gentleman in Black, The, "original musical legend" in two acts by Frederic Clay; libretto (Eng) by William S. Gilbert. First performance May 26, 1870, London, Covent Garden.

LIBRETTO: English (London: T. H. Lacy, [1870?]).

Gentleman's Island (Robinsonade), opera buffa in one act by Joseph Horovitz; libretto (Eng) by Gordon Snell, after William S. Gilbert's *Etiquette*. First performance December 14, 1958, London, Arts Council Drawing Room, with Stephen Manton and Bruce Boyce; conducted by the composer; produced by Douglas Craig. First U.S. performance August 9, 1959, Westport, Connecticut, White Barn Theater, Intimate Opera Company, with Manton and Boyce; conducted by the composer.

The satirical work concerns two English gentlemen stranded on a South Sea island; the subtitle is a reference to Daniel Defoe's classic. They at first do not speak to each other, since, as gentlemen, they have not been properly introduced. But when they both think out loud, they learn that they have a mutual acquaintance, one Robinson. Time passes, and a search party appears, led by Robinson. But since the group consists of convicts, the gentlemen refuse their help. Left alone, they stop speaking to each other and go off to their separate areas.

Roles: Mr. Gray (ten) and Mr. Somers (bar).

SCORE: vs, English-German (London: J. & W. Chester, [1960]).

BIBLIOGRAPHY: review, *NYT* (Aug. 8, 1959), 83 [on U.S. premiere].

Gentlemen, Be Seated!, musical entertainment in two acts by Jerome Moross; libretto (Eng) by Edward Eager and the composer. First performance October 10, 1963, New York, with Dick Shawn (Mister Interlocutor), Avon Long (Mister Tambo), Carol Brice (Harriet Tubman), Alice Ghostley (Belle Boyd), Cholly Atkins (Mister Bones), and Bernard Addison (Mister Banjo); conducted by Emerson Buckley.

The work presents a history of the Civil War via a minstrel show. Among the episodes are the "Picnic at Manassas" and "Atlanta to the Sea." The musical highlights include "The Ballad of Belle Boyd" and "This Isn't a Gentleman's War."

SCORE: vs (n.p., [1967]; LCCN: 85-61210).

LIBRETTO: English (New York: L. Kroll Agency, [1964]).

BIBLIOGRAPHY: Harold C. Schonberg, "Opera: 'Gentlemen' at the City Center," *NYT* (Oct. 11, 1963), 42 [on premiere].

Gentlemen in Waiting, opera in one act by Thomas Booth; libretto (Eng) by the composer. First performance December 20, 1967, New York, Carnegie Recital Hall, with David Griffith, Mike Connally, Dan Shook, and David Foster; composer at the piano.

The setting is a maternity ward with a group of four expectant fathers and their reactions to their new infants' arrivals.

Roles: man 1 (ten), man 2 (bar), man 3 (ten/high bar), and man 4 (bass).

SCORE: vs (n.p. [1967]; LCCN: 85-61210).

BIBLIOGRAPHY: Raymond Ericson, "Latest Opera Topic: Expectant Fathers," *NYT* (Dec. 21, 1967), 42 [on premiere].

Gentle Shepherd, The, "a Scots pastoral comedy" in five acts, consisting of twenty-one ballad airs; text (Eng) by Allan Ramsay. First performance January 29, 1729, Edinburgh, Taylor's Theatre; revised as *Patie and Peggy, or, The Fair Foundling** (1730, London). First U.S. performance January 7, 1786, New York, John Street Theatre.

The nobleman's son Patie dons the disguise of a shepherd so that he can spend time with Peggy, a simple country girl. Peggy, it turns out, is noble-born herself.

Roles: Sir William Worthy; Patie, the gentle shepherd; Roger, a rich young shepherd; Symon and Glaud, two old shepherds; Bauldy, a clown; Peggy, thought to be Glaud's niece; Jenny, Glaud's daughter; Mause, an old woman; Elspa, Symon's wife; Madge, Glaud's sister.

LIBRETTOS: English (Edinburgh: Tho. Ruddiman for the author; London: Thomas Longman and James M'Ewin; Glasgow: Alexander Carmichael, 1725); English, with music (London, 1775; repr. ed. Rubsamen/*BO*, vol. 6, *Satire, Burlesque, Protest, and Ridicule II* [1974]); English (Glasgow: D. Allan, Dickson's Closs; Edinburgh: J. Murray; and London: C. Elliot, Strand, 1788).

Gentle Shepherd, The, pastoral comedy in one act by Thomas Linley Sr.; libretto (Eng) by Richard Tickell, after Allan Ramsay's text (see preceding entry). First performance October 29, 1781, London, Drury Lane Theatre.

SCORE: vs (London: Harrison, Cluse, [1800?]).

Gentle Spirit, A, chamber opera in one act by John Taverner; libretto (Eng) by Gerard McLarnon, after a short story by Dostoyevsky. First performance June 6, 1977, Bath.

The setting is the late nineteenth century. A Russian pawnbroker is grieving for his wife, who has killed herself, because of her husband's insensitivity, by throwing herself from the window of their apartment. As he sits beside her lifeless body, he wonders why she committed suicide, as the action goes back to important happenings in their marriage.

Roles: the wife (sop) and the husband (ten).

The serial work is scored for two singers, tape, and thirteen instrumentalists.

SCORE: vs (London: Chester, 1979).

Geraldine, or, The Lover's Well, opera by Michael Balfe, after his opera *Le puits d'amour* (1843, Paris); libretto (Eng) by Gilbert A. A'Beckett, after the text by Scribe and A. de Leuven. First performance August 14, 1843, London, Princess's Theatre.

Gettysburg, opera in one act by Morris Hutchen Ruger; libretto (Eng). First performance September 23, 1938, Los Angeles, Hollywood Bowl.

Ghosts: Live from Galilee, opera by Genji Ito; libretto (Eng) by Edgar Nkosi White. First performance February 16, 1993, New York, La Mama E.T.C., with Lynnard E. Williams (Clarence), Phyllis Nunn (Donna Lee), Nancy Anderson (Ruby Bates), Judy Brady (Clarence's mother), Charles Britt (the sheriff), and Jonathan Goldstein (Leibowitz).

The historically-based story concerns the last surviving member of the Scottsboro boys, Clarence Norris, who escapes from prison rather than face death on the false charge of raping two white women in Scottsboro, Alabama, in 1931. He and his girlfriend, Donna Lee, go to the apartment of his New York lawyer, Leibowitz, who unsuccessfully defended Norris and his companions. Norris is recaptured but eventually pardoned by the George-Wallace-like sheriff.

The music, which includes blues and country sections, uses a synthesizer and guitar.

BIBLIOGRAPHY: Alex Ross, "A Racial Wrong Portrayed in Blues," *NYT* (Feb. 17, 1993), C, 13 [on premiere].

Ghosts of Versailles, The, grand opera buffa in two acts by John Corigliano; libretto (Eng) by William M. Hoffman, suggested by Beaumarchais's *La mère coupable*. First performance December 23, 1991, New York, Metropolitan Opera, with Teresa Stratas (Marie Antoinette), Judith Christin (Susanna), Renée Fleming (Rosina), Tracy Dahl (Florestine), Stella Zambalis (Cherubino), Marilyn Horne (Samira), Graham Clark (Bégearss), Gino Quilico (Figaro), Peter Kazaras (Count Almaviva), Neil Rosenshein (Léon), and Håkan Hagegård (Beaumarchais); conducted by James Levine.

The ghosts of the court of Louis XVI gather to hear a new opera by Beaumarchais's ghost. The opera is set in Paris in autumn 1793. Count Almaviva is trapped with his family in France; he hopes to sell Marie Antoinette's necklace in order to buy the doomed queen's freedom and take her to the New World. In their way stands the evil Bégearss, who demands the necklace and the hand of Florestine, the illegitimate daughter of Almaviva (Florestine loves Léon, the illegitimate offspring of Rosina and Cherubino).

When Bégearss tries to block the escape of the Almavivas from prison, he is foiled by Figaro and Beaumarchais, who have donned the guise of executioners; he is sent to be executed. Figaro guides Almaviva, Rosina, Léon, Florestine, and Susanna to safety in the New World. But as Beaumarchais is about to release Marie Antoinette, she refuses, unwilling to change history, which would mean losing him. The two are reunited as ghosts, and Beaumarchais puts the necklace around her neck.

Major roles: Marie Antoinette (sop), Susanna (sop), Rosina (sop), Cherubino (sop), Florestine (sop), Count Almaviva (ten), Léon (ten), Bégearss (ten), Beaumarchais (bar), and Figaro (bar).

The work includes a cavatina and cabaletta by the Egyptian singer Samira, a role that is perhaps a nod to Baba the Turk in Stravinsky's 1951 *The Rake's Progress.**
SCORE: vs (New York and Milwaukee: G. Schirmer).
LIBRETTO: English (New York and Milwaukee: G. Schirmer).
VIDEO: Hagegård, Stratas, New York Metropolitan Opera; cond. J. Levine.
BIBLIOGRAPHY: *ON* LVI (Jan. 4, 1992): Michael C. Nott, "The Long Road to Versailles," 8–11, 49; Joel Honig, "The Ghosts of Azilum," 12–15; William M. Hoffman, "Ghost Writer," 16, 18–20, 48; Philip Kennicott, "Mother Love," 22–25; Patrick J. Smith, *"The Ghosts of Versailles*: A Preview," *ON* LVI (Dec. 21, 1991), 24–25.

Giant's Garden, The, opera in two acts by Sherman Krane; libretto (Eng), after Oscar Wilde. First performance March 12, 1960, Norfolk, Virginia, College of William and Mary, Blair Jr. High School Auditorium.

Giants in the Earth, opera in three acts by Douglas Moore; libretto (Eng) by Arnold Sundgaard, after the novel by Ole E. Rölvaag (1927). First performance March 28, 1951, New York, Brander Matthews Theater, Columbia Opera Workshop, with Josh Wheeler (Per Hansa), Brenda Miller (Beret), Viviane Bauer (Sorrine), Helen Dautrich (Kjersti), and James Cosenza (Henry); conducted by Willard Rhodes. Revised version April 4, 1974, Grand Forks, North Dakota, Opera Company of the University of North Dakota, with Chester Ludgin (Per Hansa), Eileen Schauler (Beret), Margaret S. Gunderson (Sorrine), Katherine Lee (Kjersti), and William Franke (Henry); conducted by Philip Hisey.

The story centers on the Norwegian immigrants Per Hansa and his wife, Beret, who come to the Dakota plains to make a new life for themselves, joining their countrymen Hans Olsa and his wife, Sorrine; Syvert and his wife, Kjersti; and Henry, whose sweetheart has refused to join him; he eventually marries Dagmar. Per is determined to succeed, but Beret wants to return to Norway. The families face a series of natural disasters, and Beret starts to lose her mind, believing she has been punished for abandoning her parents in her homeland. Per wants his newborn son baptized, but Beret refuses to let the boy be baptized with the name Victorious. When the child becomes sick, she sends her husband out in a raging storm to find a preacher for the boy, discovering too late that she has sent Per to his death.

Major roles: Per Hansa (bar), Beret (sop), Hans Olsa (bass-bar), Sorrine (alto), Syvert (ten), Kjersti (sop), and Henry (ten).

For a detailed description, see Eaton/*OP* I, 73.

The work received the Pulitzer Prize in 1951.
BIBLIOGRAPHY: Gimi Beni, review, *OJ* VII/2 (1974), 35–37 [on rev. version]; Olin Downes, "New Moore Opera Is Presented Here," *NYT* (Mar. 29, 1951, 25.

Gibraltar, comic opera by Tommaso Giordani; libretto (Eng) by Robert Houlton. First performance December 18, 1783, Dublin, English Opera House.

Gift, The, children's opera in one act by Alan Ridout; libretto (Eng) by Allan Wicks, after Christina Rossetti's *Goblin Market.* First performance 1971, Canterbury Cathedral.

Gift of Song, A, Christmas opera in one act by Mary E. Caldwell; libretto (Eng) by the composer. First performance December 3, 1961, Pasadena, California.

The story involves the composition of the famous "Silent Night." After Karl Gruber sings the song to the Ambassador of Prussia at the choir school in Salzburg, the choirmaster visits the Gruber home to uncover the original.

For a detailed description, see Eaton/*OP* II, 278–79.

Major roles: Karl Franz Felix, young son of the composer (sop); Analisa, his older sister (sop); Papa Gruber (bar); Mama Gruber (mezzo); Choirmaster Herr Doktor Geheimrat, the Prussian ambassador (bar); and Choirmaster Wilhelm (ten).

SCORE: vs (New York: Boosey & Hawkes, 1961).

Gift of the Magi, The, opera in one act by Ruth Taylor Magney; libretto (Eng) by the composer, after the story by O. Henry. First performance April 16, 1964, Minneapolis.

A poor young couple, in order to buy gifts for each other, sell their most precious possessions, the wife, Della, her long hair, and the husband, James, his watch. Their gifts to each other are a fancy comb for the long hair that no longer adorns Della's head and a fob for the watch James no longer owns.

For a detailed description, see Eaton/*OP* II, 279.

Roles: Della Young (sop), James Dillingham Young (bar), and Mme. Sophronie (alto).

Gift of the Magi, The, opera by Susan Bingham; libretto (Eng) by the composer, after O. Henry. First performance December 1, 1984, New Haven, Connecticut, Chancel Opera Company.

Gift of the Magi, The, opera in one act by Richard Brown; libretto (Eng) by Nancy Grobe, after O. Henry. Completed 1985.

Gift of the Magi, The, chamber opera in one act by Betsy Warren; libretto (Eng) by David McCord, after O. Henry. First performance 1985, New Orleans.

Also musical by Richard Adler (1978).

SCORES: fs, vs (New York: American Music Center, 1985).

Gilded Cage, The, opera in one act by Benjamin Lees; libretto (Eng) by Alastair Reid. First performance November 1964, New York, Museum of Modern Art.

Gilt-Edged Kid, The, opera in one act by George Dreyfus; libretto (Eng) by Lynne Strahan. First performance April 11, 1976, Melbourne, Australia.

A satire on political leadership in Australia.

SCORE: vs (Melbourne: Allans Music, [1976]).

Giovanni, the Sculptor, romantic comic opera in three acts by Alfred Hill; libretto (Eng) by Harriet Callan. First performance August 3, 1914, Sydney, Australia.

The story centers on the talented country lad Giovanni, who comes to Florence, where his love for Princess Violetta is rejected. He despairs until his first love, Amina, finds him.

SCORE: vs, ed. Haydn Reeder and Royston Gustavson (Parkville, Australia: Centre for Studies in Australian Music, University of Melbourne, 1994).

Giovanni in London, or, The Libertine Reclaimed, "an operatic extravaganza in two acts"; libretto (Eng) by William T. Montcrieff. First performance 1817, London, Olympic Pavilion.

Don Giovanni, thrown out of hell because of his antics, joins London society.

The work includes Mozart's music, as well as some by John Whitaker.

Major roles: Don Giovanni, Deputy English, Leporello, Mrs. English, and Mrs. Leporello.

See also Bishop's *The Libertine* (1817, London).

LIBRETTO: English (London: J. Miller, 1818).

Gipsey Prince, The, comic opera by Michael Kelly; libretto (Eng) by Thomas Moore. First performance July 24, 1801, London, Theatre Royal, Haymarket.

Gipsies, The, comic opera in two acts by Samuel Arnold; libretto (Eng) by Charles Dibdin, possibly after C. Favart's *La bohémienne,* a French version of the libretto (1755, Paris) for R. di Capua's *La zingara* (1753, Paris; but see below). First performance August 3, 1778, London, Little Theatre in the Haymarket.
　　The Dibdin-Favart connection is denied by Loewenberg (*Annals,* 223).
LIBRETTO: English (London: T. Cadell, 1778).

Gipsy's Warning, The, opera in two acts by Julius Benedict; libretto (Eng) by George Linley and Richard B. Peake. First performance April 19, 1838, London, Drury Lane Theatre, with Emma Romer.
LIBRETTO: English (London: W. Wright, [183?]).

Girl and the Unicorn, The, children's opera in three parts by Stephen Oliver; libretto (Eng) by the composer. First performance December 9, 1978, London, Church of St. James Norland.
　　In this parable, the townspeople, egged on by a Sinister Woman, believe they can catch the unicorn living in the forest if they use a mute girl as bait. The unicorn is thereby captured and exploited by the people, until it dies. In the course of trying to protect the animal, the girl finds her voice.
SCORE: vs (Borough Green: Novello, 1984).

Girls of Holland, The, fantastic light opera by Reginald De Koven; libretto (Eng) by Stanislaus Stangé. First performance November 18, 1907, New York, Lyric Theatre, with Harry Fairleigh (Dr. Franz), Vera Michelena (Ariella), and Edward M. Tavor (Snowdrop).
　　Dr. Franz hopes to win the hand of Frau Van Biere's niece by showing that his new elixir works. With the assistance of Ariella, a cousin of Mephisto, Dr. Franz brings the statue of Snowdrop to life. When the revived statue goes after the niece, he is changed back to stone.

Give Me Liberty or Give Me Death, children's opera in one act by Martin Kalmanoff; libretto (Eng) by R. K. Adams. First performance January 2, 1975, New York, Producer's Association.

Glittering Gate, The, opera in one act by Peggy Glanville-Hicks; libretto (Eng) by Lord Edward Dunsany. First performance May 14, 1959, New York, YMHA, Kaufmann Concert Hall, with Robert Price (Bill) and David Smith (Jim); conducted by Newell Jenkins; staged by James Price; designed by Robert Mitchell.
　　When Jim and Bill, two burglars, end up at the Gate of Heaven, they are discouraged. The place is filled with empty beer bottles, to the chagrin of Jim, a drunk. After discussing their desires, the men open the gate. To their further consternation, they are met by nothing but a star-studded empty space.
　　Roles: Bill, a burglar (ten); and Jim, a burglar and a drunk (bar).
　　For a detailed description, see Eaton/*OP* II, 281–82.
BIBLIOGRAPHY: Howard Taubman, "Opera: Two Premieres," *NYT* (May 15, 1959), 25.

Gloriana, opera in three acts by Benjamin Britten; libretto (Eng) by William Plomer, after Lytton Strachey's *Elizabeth and Essex* (1928). The work was commissioned for the coronation of Queen Elizabeth II in 1953. First performance June 8, 1953, London,

Covent Garden, with the queen in attendance, with Joan Cross (Elizabeth), Jennifer Vyvyan (Penelope Rich), Monica Sinclair (Frances), Peter Pears (Essex), Geraint Evans (Mountjoy), Arnold Matters (Cecil), and Frederick Dalberg (Raleigh); conducted by John Pritchard; produced by Basil Coleman; designed by John Piper; choreographed by John Cranko. First U.S. performance May 8, 1956, Cincinnati, with Inge Borkh (Elizabeth), Suzanne Danco (Penelope), Nell Rankin (Frances), John Alexander (Essex), and Theodor Uppman (Mountjoy); conducted by Joseph Krips.

The opera examines events from the later years of the reign of Queen Elizabeth I and focuses on her relationship with the Earl of Essex. Essex, one of her favorites, asks permission to lead an army against the rebel Tyrone in Ireland. When Essex returns to England after having failed in his endeavor, he has lost the Queen's favor. Elizabeth, urged on by Cecil, her minister, believes Essex has betrayed her. Essex, despite his wife Frances's pleas, is sentenced to death at the urging of Cecil and because of the insolent arguments of Lady Rich, Essex's sister. The opera ends as Elizabeth prepares for death.

For detailed synopses and musical and textual analyses, see Eaton/*OP* II, 99–100; *ENOG* 24 (1983), 75–100; K/*KOB*, 1194–1201; K/*NKOB*, 118–22.

Major roles: Elizabeth I (sop); Robert Devereux, the Earl of Essex (ten); Frances, Countess of Essex (mezzo); Charles Blount, Lord Mountjoy (bar); Penelope (Lady Rich), sister to Essex (sop); Sir Robert Cecil, Secretary of the Council (bar); and Sir Walter Raleigh, Captain of the Guard (bar).

In light of the event for which it was composed, the choice of the opera's plot was quite odd. The work was not very successful, although it fared better in more recent revivals.

Other operas on the subject of Queen Elizabeth I include S. Pavesi's *Elisabetta, regina d'Inghilterra* (1810, Turin); G. Rossini's work of the same name (1815, Naples); G. Donizetti's *Roberto Devereux* (1837, Naples); and W. Fortner's *Elisabeth Tudor* (1972, Berlin).

SCORE: vs (London and New York: Boosey & Hawkes, 1953).
LIBRETTO: English, in *ENOG* 24 (1983), 103–25.
BIBLIOGRAPHY: Paul Banks, ed., *Britten's* Gloriana: *Essays and Sources*, Aldeburgh Studies in Music, vol. 1 (Woodbridge, Suffolk: Boydell Press, 1993).
DISCOGRAPHY: J. Barstow, D. Jones, P. Langridge, J. M. Ainsley, J. Shirley-Quirk, B. Terfel, Welsh National Opera Orch. and Chorus; cond. C. Mackerras, Argo 2-440213-2 (2 CDs).
VIDEO: S. Walker, E. Vaughan, A. Rolfe, R. Van Allan, English National Opera; cond. M. Elder, Virgin VHS VVD 344.

Glorious First of June, The, pastiche by Stephen Storace; libretto (Eng) by James Cobb et al. First performance July 2, 1794, London, Drury Lane Theatre, with Nancy Storace (Margaretta). Revised as *Cape St. Vincent, or, British Valour Triumphant*, March 1797, London, Drury Lane Theatre.

William and Robin sign up for duty in Lord Howe's fleet, but before they depart, Robin gives a purse of money to Susan, William's betrothed, for her to give to Margaretta. Margaretta, in turn, has seen William at Susan's abode and suspects that the two are carrying on an affair. The misunderstandings are resolved, and when the two sailors return after the glorious British victory, all celebrate jubilantly.

The work was written to celebrate the victory of Admiral Howe over the French fleet at Ushant on June 1, 1794.

See Fiske/*ETM*, 527–28 for a detailed description.

Among the numbers is "When Britain First at Heav'n's Command," known today by the name "Rule Britannia," which ends the work; it was originally used in Arne's *Alfred** (1740).
SCORE: vs (London: Printed for J. Dale, [1795]).

Glory Coach, The, opera in three acts by Francis Barnard; libretto (Eng) by the composer, after the *Wakefield Mystery Plays* by the Wakefield Master. First performance March 28, 1982, New York, First Presbyterian Church.

Goat in Chelm, A, opera in one act by Abraham Binder; libretto (Eng) by the composer, after Sholem Aleichem. First performance (concert) March 20, 1960, New York, 92nd Street Y, with Lawrence Davidson, Louise DeComier, Michael Kermoyan, Lawrence Avery, Shirley Russell, Nico Castel, and Joan Caplan; conducted by Maurice Levine.

Goddess of Truth, The, comic opera by Julian Edwards; libretto (Eng) by Stanislaus Stangé. First performance February 26, 1896, New York, Abbey Theatre.
A treatment of the Pygmalion legend.

Godfather Death, opera in three acts by Jan Meyerowitz; libretto (Eng) by Peter John Stephens. First performance June 2, 1961, Brooklyn, New York, Brooklyn College Opera Workshop; conducted by Siegmund Levarie.
The young Aegidius, aided by Death, dies when he disobeys his new benefactor.
BIBLIOGRAPHY: Raymond Ericson, review, *NYT* (June 8, 1961), 39 [on premiere].

Godiva, opera in three acts by Martin Kalmanoff; libretto (Eng) by Atra Baer. First performance (radio) February 15, 1953, New York, WNYC.
The story traces the destruction of a woman's marriage through societal pressures.
SCORE: ms vs, holograph (1952, photocopy, NYPL).

Going, The, opera in one act by Mark Beall; libretto (Eng). First performance November 7, 1987, Cincinnati, University of Cincinnati, Contemporary Music Ensemble.

Golden Apple, The, opera in two acts by Jerome Moross; libretto (Eng) by John Latouche, after Homer's *The Iliad* and *The Odyssey*. First performance March 11, 1954, New York, Phoenix Theatre, with Kaye Ballard (Helen), Jonathan Lucas (Paris), Stephen Douglass (Ulysses), and Priscilla Gillette (Penelope); conducted by Hugh Ross.
The plot is set in turn-of-the-century America. Paris, a traveling salesman, absconds with Helen, wife of Sheriff Menelaus. A neighbor, Ulysses, tracks them down and defeats Paris in a boxing match. The victor then returns home to his faithful wife, Penelope.
The highlights include Helen's ballad "Lazy Afternoon."
LIBRETTO: English (New York: Random House, [1954]).
BIBLIOGRAPHY: Brooks Atkinson, review, *NYT* (Mar. 12, 1954), 15 [on premiere].

Golden Bird, The, opera by William Russo; libretto (Eng) by Albert Williams and the composer, after *Der goldene Vogel* by the Brothers Grimm. Composed 1984.
For narrator, solo voices, and orchestra.
SCORE: vs (Newton Centre, Mass.: GunMar Music, [1992?].

Golden Butterfly, The, comic opera by Reginald De Koven; libretto (Eng) by Harry Bache Smith. First performance October 12, 1908, New York, Broadway Theatre, with Walter Percival (Franz), Louis Harrison (Baron von Affenkoff), Grace Van Studdiford (Ilma Walden), and Louis Cassavant (the prince); conducted by the composer.

The story involves Franz, a composer, who comes to Paris to make his fortune. Baron von Affenkoff, who claims that Franz has forgotten his true love, Ilma, invites her to sing in his new opera, called *The Butterfly*, on the condition that she marry him. Franz, believing that he should not stand in the way of his beloved's career, pretends to be a Russian prince. When the real prince shows up and threatens to arrest Franz for his deception, he learns of the reason for the disguise. It turns out that Baron von Affenkoff's opera is really Franz's, which the Baron had stolen. Franz and Ilma are reunited.

Golden Child, Christmas opera in three acts by Philip Bezanson; libretto (Eng) by Paul Engle. First performance July 28, 1959, Iowa City, Iowa, as *Western Child.* Revised as *Golden Child*, December 16, 1960, Hallmark Hall of Fame, with Patricia Neway, Brenda Lewis, Jerome Hines, and Stephen Douglass; conducted by Herbert Grossman.

A Nativity story that takes place in Sutter's Fort at the time of the Gold Rush. The birth of a child in a manger rings peace to the world of the goldminers.
LIBRETTO: English (Kansas City, Missouri: Hallmark Cards, 1960).
BIBLIOGRAPHY: Harold C. Schonberg, "TV: A Christmas Opera," *NYT* (Dec. 17, 1960), 47.

Golden Crane, The, opera "for young people's theatre" by Don Henry Kay; libretto (Eng) by Gwen Harwood, after a Japanese folktale by Tohr Yamaguchi. Composed 1985.
SCORE: fs, autograph (Australian Music Centre Library); rehearsal score (197?, photocopy, University of Tasmania).

Golden Crucible, The, opera by Jack Kilpatrick; libretto (Eng). First performance 1959, Pittsburgh.

Golden Fleece, The, or, Jason in Colchis and Medea in Corinth, extravaganza in one act by Thomas German Reed; libretto (Eng) by James R. Planché. First performance March 24, 1845, London, Haymarket Theatre.
Also operetta by Louis Kroll (1915).

Golden Lion, The, opera in two acts by Gerald Kechley; libretto (Eng) by Elwyn Kechley. First performance April 28, 1959, University of Washington, Seattle. Revised 1959.

Set in ninth-century Byzantium, the story concerns the struggle between two parties to choose an empress for Theophilus, the hedonistic emperor. On one side are the Patriarch John and the Empress-Dowager, with the young Casia as their candidate. They are opposed by the false monk Amos, who supports Theodora.

Through Amos's trickery Theophilus gives the apple, symbolic of his final choice of a wife, to Theodora, causing Casia to enter a nunnery. The good-hearted Theodora, learning of Amos's machinations, vows to give up her throne, but Theophilus, gaining understanding at last, vows to rule justly with Theodora as his wife and Michael, their son, as his heir.

For a detailed description, see Eaton/*OP* II, 101.
Major roles: Theophilus (bar), Theodora (sop/mezzo), Amos (ten), Casia (sop), John (bass), and Empress-Dowager (mezzo).

Golden Pippen, The, pastiche burletta, compiled by John Abraham Fischer; libretto (Eng) by Kane O'Hara. First performance February 6, 1773, London, Covent Garden.

The story concerns the Judgment of Paris, during which Juno and Pallas accuse Venus of cheating at cards.
LIBRETTO: English, in *Two Burlettas*, ed. Phyllis T. Dircks (New York: Garland, 1987).

Golden Ring, The, fairy opera in three acts by Frederic Clay; libretto (Eng) by G. R. Sims. First performance December 3, 1883, London, Alhambra.

Golden Vanity, The, vaudeville for boys and piano by Benjamin Britten; text by Colin Graham (Eng), after the old English ballad. First performance June 3, 1967, Aldeburgh Festival.

This work, designed to be performed by children, tells of the cabin boy who rescues his ship from a thieving pirate vessel, only to be cheated out of his reward by the dishonest captain and bosun of his ship.

Major roles: the boy (treble), the captain (alto), and the bosun (treble).
SCORE: vs (Eng-Ger) (London: Faber: New York: G. Schirmer, [1967]).
BIBLIOGRAPHY: W. Mann, review, *The Times* (London) (June 5, 1967), 6 [on premiere].

Golden Web, The, opera in three acts; music by Arthur Goring Thomas, completed by Sidney P. Waddington; libretto (Eng) by Frederick Corder and B. C. Stephenson. First performance February 15, 1893, Liverpool.
SCORE: vs (London [etc.]: Chappell & Co., n.d.).

Goldilocks and the Three Bears, chamber opera by Judith Lang Zaimont; libretto (Eng) by Doris L. Kosloff, after the children's fairy tale. First performance January 5, 1986, Chappaqua, New York.

Golem, The, opera by Lazar Weiner; libretto (Eng) by Raymond Smolover, after Halper Leivick's play *Goylem*. First performance January 13, 1957, White Plains, New York, Opera Theatre of Westchester. First performance with orchestration by the composer and David Finko May 2, 1981, New York, 92nd Street Y, with Judith Raskin, Robert Paul Abelson, Bernard Fitch, Eugene Green, and Nadia Bach; conducted by Amy Kaiser; directed by Dan Bredemann.

The story is that of the golem of Jewish lore, a living being made from a mound of clay to serve its creator and fight against attacks from enemies of the Jews.
SCORE: ms score, holograph (1957, NYPL).
BIBLIOGRAPHY: Edward Rothstein, review, *NYT* (May 1, 1981), C, 3 [on orch. version].

Golem, The, opera in four acts by Abraham Ellstein; libretto (Eng) by the composer and Sylvia Regan, after Leivick, adapted by Joseph Buloff. First performance November 1961, Boston (preview); March 22, 1962, New York, City Opera.
SCORE: ms vs (1957, holograph, NYPL; [n.p.], 1962], LCCN: 84-110666).
LIBRETTO: English, typescript (Harvard University, Harvard Depository SC 260); English (New York: Program Pub. Co., 1962?).

Golem, The, grand opera in three acts by Larry Sitsky; libretto (Eng) by Gwen Harwood, after Leivick. Composed 1980. Excerpts performed 1984, Sydney. First complete performance October 14, 1993, Sydney.

Among the orchestral interludes are "The Golem Rises" and "Death of Rachel."
SCORE: vs, orch. interludes (New York: Seesaw Music, 1990).
LIBRETTO: English (Sydney, Australia: Pellinor, 1993).

Golem, chamber opera in a prelude and a legend by John Casken; libretto (Eng) by the composer and Pierre Audi, after Leivick. First performance June 28, 1989, London, Almeida Opera, with Patricia Rozario (Miriam), Christopher Robson (Ometh), John Hull (the golem), and Adrian Clarke (the Maharal); conducted by Richard Bernas. First U.S. performance September 21, 1990, Omaha, Nebraska, Opera/Omaha, with Terry Hodges (the Maharal), Gordon Holleman (the golem), Jayne West (Miriam), and Douglas Stevens (Ometh); conducted by Richard Pittman.

The story, which unfolds in a series of flashbacks, concerns the Maharal, a six-teenth-century rabbi who breathes life into a clay figure, the golem. The Maharal ignores the advice of the Prometheus-like Ometh, and the golem becomes all too human, desiring Miriam, the rabbi's wife. By mistake the golem, intended to protect the persecuted, kills one of the townspeople who have tried to gain freedom. The rabbi is then forced to destroy his creation.

For a detailed plot description, see K/*NKOB*, 149–50.

Major roles: the Maharal (bar), the golem (bass-bar), Miriam (sop), and Ometh (counterten).

Also set by Stanley Silverman as a musical play (comp. 1984).

SCORE: vs (London and New York: Schott, 1991).

LIBRETTO: English (London and New York: Schott, 1991).

BIBLIOGRAPHY: Andrew Porter, "Musical Events," *NY* LXVI (Nov. 12, 1990), 109–10 [on U.S. premiere]; Tom Sutcliffe, review, *The Guardian* (June 30, 1989), 32 [on premiere]. DISCOGRAPHY: Rozario, Robson, Clarke, Hall, Music Projects/London; cond. Bernas; Virgin Classics VCD 7 91204 (1991, 2 CDs); rev. Patrick J. Smith, "Recordings, *ON* LVI (Mar. 14, 1992), 35.

Gondoliers, The, or The King of Barataria, comic opera in two acts by Arthur S. Sullivan; libretto (Eng) by William S. Gilbert. First performance December 7, 1889, London, Savoy Theatre, with Frank Wyatt (Duke of Plaza-Toro), Wallace Brownlow (Luiz), W. H. Denny (Don Alhambra), Courtice Pounds (Marco Palmieri), Rutland Barrington (Giuseppe Palmieri), Rosina Brandram (Duchess of Plaza Toro), Decima Moore (Casilda), and Miss Bernard (Inez). The London production ran for 554 nights. First U.S. performance January 7, 1890, New York, New Park Theatre. The New York run was a failure.

The work, set in Venice, satirizes democratic equality. The heir to the throne of Barataria was abducted as an infant by Don Alhambra del Bolero, the Grand Inquisitor, and put in the care of a gondolier. The throne is now vacant, so Don Alhambra seeks out the sons of the gondolier, Marco and Giuseppe Palmieri, to determine which is the real heir to the throne of Barataria. Since such a determination is proving difficult, the young gondoliers rule jointly until the matter can be resolved, leaving their sweethearts, Gianetta and Tessa, behind. When the two women arrive in Barataria, they learn that the heir was promised as an infant as the future husband of Casilda, daughter of the Duke and Duchess of Plaza-Toro. Casilda, however, loves Luiz, servant to the Duke. In the end, however, it turns out, conveniently, that Luiz is the rightful heir, having been switched with the son of the prince's nurse.

Major roles: the Duke of Plaza-Toro, a grandee of Spain (bar); Luiz, his attendant (ten); Don Alhambra del Bolero, the Grand Inquisitor (bass-bar); Marco Palmieri (ten) and Giuseppe Palmieri (bar), Venetian gondoliers; the Duchess of Plaza Toro (alto); Casilda, her daughter (sop); Inez, the King's foster mother (alto).

SCORE: vs (London: Chappell & Co., 1890; Cincinnati, John Church Co., 1890).

LIBRETTO: English (Cincinnati: The John Church Co., 1889).

DISCOGRAPHY: J. Reed, K. Sandford, D'Oyly Carte Opera Company, London GON60C (2 CDs); G. Evans, A. Young, O. Brannigan, R. Lewis, Pro Arte Orch., Glyndebourne Festival Chorus; cond. N. Sargent, EMI Classics 2-CODMB 64394 (2 CDs).

Goodbye to the Clown, opera in one act by Ezra Laderman; libretto (Eng) by Ernest Kinoy. First performance May 22, 1960, New York, 92nd Street Y, Neway Opera Theatre; conducted by Charles Wilson; directed by Patricia Neway.

The fatherless Peggy has a clown who entertains and reminds her of the stories told to her by her father. Her mother, discouraged by Peggy's behavior, sends the girl to her room despite the protestations of Uncle George. Peggy then hears her relatives converse and realizes for the first time that her father is dead and that the clown is his emissary to help her understand and mature. Since she no longer needs the clown, he disappears, and Peggy goes to sleep, full of a new maturity.

For a detailed description, see Eaton/*OP* II, 280.

Major roles: Peggy (sop), the mother (mezzo), the clown (bar), and Uncle George (bass).

BIBLIOGRAPHY: Eric Salzman, review, *NYT* (May 23, 1960), 37 [on premiere].

Good Friday 1663, television opera by Mike Westbrook and Kate Westbrook; libretto (Eng) by Helen Simpson. First performance March 12, 1995, London, Channel 4, with Kate Westbrook (Belinda).

The young heroine, Belinda, is represented musically by a jazz-like style, while the somber Parson Snakepeace is portrayed by standard, solemn music.

BIBLIOGRAPHY: Jeffrey Joseph, review, *MT* CXXXVI (May 1995), 254–55 [on premiere].

Good Life, A, opera in one act by Stanley Silverman; libretto (Eng) by J. Moss. First performance April 1986, Washington, D.C., Kennedy Center.

Goodman Brown, opera by Harold Fink; libretto (Eng) by Edward J. Megroth, after Nathaniel Hawthorne's short story *Young Goodman Brown*. First performance April 9, 1968, Painesville, Ohio, Lake Erie College; conducted by the composer.

A telling of the story of the young Puritan who, resisting the seductive pull of the devil, discovers that his wife, Faith, has been drawn into the devil's cult.

See also *Young Goodman Brown*.

SCORE: vs (Painesville, Ohio: Lake Erie College Press, 1968).

Good Soldier Schweik, The, opera in two acts by Robert Kurka; libretto (Eng) by Lewis Allan, after Jaroslav Hašek's novel. Orchestration completed by Hershy Kay. First performance (posthumous) April 23, 1958, New York, City Center, with Norman Kelley (Schweik), Mary LeSawyer (Mrs. Muller), Helen Baisley (Katy Wendler), Ruth Hobart (Baroness von Botzenheim), Emile Renan, Jack De Lon (Brettschneider), Emile Renan (army doctor), David Atkinson (Lt. Henry Lukash), and Chester Watson (Palivec); conducted by Julius Rudel; produced by Carmen Capalbo.

This satire, set in Bohemia before and during the First World War, concerns Schweik, who, hearing of the assassination of Archduke Ferdinand at Sarajevo, is arrested for making harmless political remarks; considered an idiot by a team of psychiatrists, he is sent to an insane asylum. In his short stay there he volunteers for duty in the army and is eventually sent to the front, where he wanders off while on patrol.

Major roles: Joseph Schweik (ten); Brettschneider, a secret policeman (ten); Lt. Lukash (bar); Palivec (bar); Baroness von Botzenheim (alto); army doctor (ten); and Mrs. Muller (sop).

For a detailed description, see Eaton/*OP* I, 76–77.

The work includes sections in blues style and Czech drinking songs and the amusing "Psychiatrists' Trio" and "Army Doctor's Song."

Another setting of the story is *Il buon soldato* by G. Turchi (1962, Milan).

BIBLIOGRAPHY: Anson B. Cutts, review, *ON* XXX (Apr. 2, 1965), 35 [on 1965 revival in Minneapolis]; Quaintance Eaton, review, *ON* XXXII (Dec. 30, 1967), 31 [on New York revival, Nov. 1967]; Howard Taubman, "Opera: Kurka's 'Schweik,'" *NYT* (Apr. 24, 1958), 36 [on premiere].

Good Tidings from the Holy Beast, opera in one act by Dan Locklair; libretto (Eng), after the *Chester Miracle Cycle.* First performance December 21, 1978, Lincoln, Nebraska, First Plymouth Congregational Church.

A telling of the Nativity story.

Major roles: Maria (sop) and Joseph (bar).

Goose Girl, The, opera in four acts for young people by Thomas Pasatieri; libretto (Eng) by the composer, after the fairy tale by the Brothers Grimm. First performance February 15, 1981, Fort Worth, Texas.

A princess leaves for her wedding in the company of her lady-in-waiting, a horse that talks, and a magic linen that can grant three wishes. The servant steals the linen and uses the first wish to make herself a princess. She kills the horse and turns the real princess into a goose girl. But the king, overhearing the servant's wicked machinations, gets the linen back and restores it to the real princess, who restores the horse to life.

Also an operetta by Seymour Barab, as *Who Am I?* (1971, Tempe, Arizona).

SCORE: vs (New York: G. Schirmer, 1982).

Gooseherd and the Goblin, The, children's opera in one act by Julia Smith; libretto (Eng) by J. F. Royle. First performance February 22, 1947, New York, Municipal Broadcasting Station.

Governess, The, opera in one act by Charles Mallett; libretto (Eng) by Roxanne Houston. First performance October 18, 1954, London, St. Pancras Town Hall; conducted by Colin Davis.

Goya, opera in three acts by Gian Carlo Menotti; libretto (Eng) by the composer. First performance November 28, 1986, Washington, D.C., Washington Opera, PBS television, with Plácido Domingo (Goya), Victoria Vergara (Duchess of Alba), and Karen Huffstodt (Queen Maria Luisa); conducted by Rafael Frühbeck de Burgos; produced by Gian Carlo Menotti. Revised 1991.

The plot tells of the artist's affair with the beautiful Duchess of Alba, whom he first meets in a common pub, where she is disguised as a servant girl. In the midst of his affair Goya becomes deaf, and the Duchess is poisoned by her arch enemy, Queen Maria Luisa. As an old man Goya ponders the meaning of life and his art.

SCORE: vs (New York: G. Schirmer, 1995).

BIBLIOGRAPHY: Irvin Molotsky, "Making an Operatic Hero Out of Goya," *NYT* (Nov. 9, 1986), II, 19; David Patrick Stearns, "The Man behind the Artist," *ON* LI (Nov. 1986), 15–18, and review, *ON* LI (Mar. 14, 1987), 38 [on premiere].

Grace of Todd, The, opera in one act by Gordon Crosse; libretto (Eng) by David Rudkin. First performance June 7, 1969, Aldeburgh, with April Cantelo (the lady), Robert Tear (Todd), Neil Howlett (Shard), Carl Duggan (Bowring), Malcolm Ribers (Furlong), David Hartley (Millichip), and John Winfield (Pratt); conducted by David Atherton; produced by Colin Graham.

The clumsy and not-too-bright Todd must contend with the bragging of Second Lieutenant Pratt and Lance Corporal Shard. Unable to pass any of the tests or cross the river, Todd starts to daydream, imagining that his comrades Millichip and Bowring are offering him gifts. The gifts are intended, instead, for the Lady, who is standing behind him.

When Todd is aroused from his musings, he becomes wild and runs into the corporal like a bull. Todd is locked up.

For a detailed description, see Eaton/*OP* II, 281.

Major roles: Second Lieutenant Pratt (ten), Lance Corporal Shard (bar), Private Todd (ten/high bar), Private Bowring (ten), Private Furlong (bar/bass), Private Millichip (bass), the Lady (sop/mezzo), Bowring's girl (sop), Furlong's girl (sop), and Millichip's girl (sop).

LIBRETTO: English (London: Oxford University Press, 1969).

Graces, The, intermezzo in one act by Charles Dibdin; libretto (Eng) by the composer. First performance 1782, London, Royal Circus.

Three nymphs tie up Cupid after he tries to seduce them.

LIBRETTO: English (London: G. Kearsly, 1782).

Graciosa and Percinet, "original fairy extravaganza" in one act; libretto (Eng) by James R. Planché, after the nursery tale *Gracieuse et Percinet* by Countess d'Aulnoy. First performance 1845, London.

The work is a musical with "popular and borrowed" airs.

LIBRETTO: English, from the promptbook (London: Fairbrother, Strange, 1845).

Graduation Ode, comic opera in three acts by Raymond Warren; libretto (Eng) by Janet McNeil. First performance November 20, 1963, Belfast, King George VI Hall.

SCORE: vs (London, 1963).

Grand Duke, The, or, The Statutory Duel, comic opera in two acts by Arthur S. Sullivan; libretto (Eng) by William S. Gilbert (his last for Sullivan). First performance March 7, 1896, London, Savoy Theatre, with Walter Passmore (Rudolph, the Grand Duke), Charles Kenningham (Ernest Dummkopf), Rutland Barrington (Ludwig), Scott Russell (Dr. Tannhäuser), Emmie Owen (the Princess of Monte Carlo), and Rosina Brandram (the Baroness von Krakenfeldt). This production ran for 123 nights. First U.S. performance April 7, 1937, New York.

The story takes place in the make-believe German duchy of Pfennig Halbpfenning in 1750. Dueling has been banned, and in its place adversaries draw a card; whoever draws the lower card is legally deceased, with his assets going to the winner. When Ludwig, an actor in the theatrical troupe of Ernest Dummkopf, wins such a duel against Grand Duke Rudolph, he becomes much sought after as a husband. Among his "suitors" are Lisa, his own fiancée, Julia Jellicoe, the not-so-young Baroness von Krakenfeldt, scheduled to wed the Grand Duke, and the Princess of Monte Carlo, a woman to whom Rudolph was pledged when they were both children.

Amid all the confusion Dr. Tannhäuser finds that the law that cost the Duke his holdings was interpreted incorrectly; Ludwig was actually the loser, since his card, the ace, should have been counted as the low card. The various couples originally meant for each other get back together, and the work ends happily.

Grande Bretèche, La, opera in one act by Avery Claflin; libretto (Eng) by Roswell George Mills, after Honoré de Balzac's story. First performance February 3, 1957, NBC radio.

SCORE: orchestral parts (ca. 1947, photocopy, NYPL).

DISCOGRAPHY: Composers Recordings CRI 108X (1957, 1 LP).

Grande Bretèche, La, opera in one act by Stanley Hollingsworth; libretto (Eng) by the composer, after Balzac. First performance February 10, 1957, New York, NBC television, Opera Theater, with Gloria Lane, Hugh Thompson, Adelaide Bishop, Gimi Beni, and Davis Cunningham; conducted by Peter H. Adler; produced by John Schwartz.

The story concerns an unhappily married countess and her ill-fated love for a Spanish nobleman.

The story was also set by B. Koutzen, as *The Fatal Oath** (1955, New York); Val Patacchi as *The Secret** (1955); and A. Tansman, as *Le serment* (1955, Brussels).
BIBLIOGRAPHY: Barbara Land, "A Composer Serious about Television Music," *NYT* (Feb. 12, 1957), 11.

Grand Slam, parody in one act by Ashley Vernon; libretto (Eng) by Greta Hartwig. First performance June 25, 1955, Stamford, Connecticut.

Grant, Warden of the Plains, opera by Murray Adaskin; libretto (Eng). First performance May 31, 1967, Winnipeg, Manitoba.

Gran Uile, or, The Island Queen, opera by Samuel Lover; libretto (Eng). First performance February 9, 1832, Dublin.

Gray Mare's Best Horse, The, burletta in three acts, with music arranged by Rayner Taylor; libretto (Eng) by Henry Fielding. First performance July 1731, London, King's Theatre, Haymarket. First U.S. performance January 24, 1793, Annapolis, Maryland.

The work concerns married life and includes "A Breakfast Scene a Month after Marriage."

Great McPorridge Disaster, The, opera in one act by Stephen Oliver; libretto (Eng) by the composer. First performance May 1976, Bath.

Greatshot, cabaret opera in two acts by William Bolcom; libretto (Eng) by Arnold Weinstein. First performance May 15, 1969, New Haven, Connecticut.

The story concerns an incident in the life of the "beat" novelist William Burroughs.

Great Stone Face, The, opera in a prologue and five scenes by Martin Kalmanoff; libretto (Eng) by the composer, after Nathaniel Hawthorne's story. First performance November 14, 1968, Muncie, Indiana, Ball State University.

Believing his mother's prophecy that a child born in his valley will become the greatest man of his time and resemble the Great Stone Face, Ernest seeks in vain for the person to fill that role. When he reaches old age, Ernest realizes that he, the Man of Character, is the person his mother was talking about.

For a detailed description, see Eaton/*OP* II, 282.

Major roles: Ernest as a boy (boy sop), Ernest as an adult (bar), his mother (mezzo), Mr. Gathergold/Poet (ten), Old Blood and Thunder/Husband and Philanthropist (bass), and Old Stony Phiz/Professor (bar).

Greek, opera in two acts by Mark-Anthony Turnage; libretto (Eng) by the composer and Jonathan Moore, after a play by Steven Berkoff (1979), based on the Oedipus myth. First performance June 17, 1988, Munich, Carl-Orff Saal, with Quentin Hayes (Eddy). First British performance September 1990, London, Coliseum. First U.S. performance July 23, 1998, Aspen, Colorado, Wheeler Opera House, Aspen Music Festival.

The setting is the East End of London in the late twentieth century. Eddy, coming from a working-class family, enters the world of free enterprise but is unable to adjust to the system. In a petty argument he kills the Café Manager and marries the man's wife. He finally achieves respectability and makes peace with his parents. To end the continued plague of greed and self-interest that governs his country, Eddy solves the riddle of the two lesbians guarding the "Sphynx" outside the city. He returns triumphant, only to learn from his parents that he was adopted during the war and that, in fact, his wife is also his mother.

For a detailed plot description, see K/*NKOB*, 841–42.

Major roles: Eddy (high bar), Café Manager (bar), and his wife (mezzo).

Among the musical highlights are the ensemble "We Only Love" and the concluding "Exit from Paradise to Heaven!" sung by Eddy.

SCORE: vs (London and New York: Schott, 1990).

BIBLIOGRAPHY: Tom Sutcliffe, "Riddle of an East End Oedipus," *Guardian* (Sept. 29, 1990), 21 [on British premiere].

DISCOGRAPHY: F. Kimm, H. Charnock, Q. Hayes, R. Suart, Greek Ensemble; cond. R. Bernas, Argo 440 368 2 (1 CD), rev. Stephen Johnson, *Opera* XLVI (Jan. 1995), 121–22.

Greek Kalends, The, children's opera in two acts by Alan Ridout; libretto (Eng) by J. H. Oldham. First performance 1956, Tunbridge Wells, England.

Greek Passion, The, opera in two acts by Bohuslav Martinů; libretto (Eng) by the composer, after Jonathan Griffin's English translation of Nikos Kazantzakis's novel *Christ Recrucified*. First performance, in English, June 9, 1961, Zurich, Stadttheater, with Sandra Warfield (Katerina), Heinz Borst (Fotis), James Pease (Grigoris), and Glade Peterson (Manolios); conducted by Paul Sacher; produced by Herbert Graf. First performance in German, June 1971, Zurich. First U.S. performance April 26, 1981, New York, Metropolitan Opera, Indiana University School of Music, with Timothy Noble (Grigoris), David Rampy (Panait), Rebecca Field (Katerina), and Daniel Brewer (Manolios); conducted by Bryan Balkwill. First British performance April 29, 1981, Cardiff, Welsh National Opera, with John Mitchinson (Manolios), Richard Van Allan (Grigoris), Helen Field (Katerina), and Arthur Davies (Yannakos); conducted by Charles Mackerras.

Martinů's last opera was written with a performance at Covent Garden in mind (where it was presented in 1985). The libretto exists in English and German versions, and the story is set on a stony, barren mountain in Greece in the early part of the twentieth century.

The plot intertwines the themes of villagers chosen for the annual Passion play and the plight of refugees uprooted by the Turks. The shepherd Manolios is chosen to play Christ, the young widow Katerina is cast as Mary Magdalene, the violent Panait, who is secretly in love with Katerina, is to play Judas, and the kind Yannakos, a peddler, is to be Peter. Manolios and Katerina urge the villagers to accept the refugees, as does the priest Fotis, against the opposition of another priest, Grigoris. As the story unfolds, Manolios is killed by a group of villagers, led by the jealous Panait. They have been stirred up by Grigoris and the village elders, who fear that Manolios has begun to take his role too seriously.

For plot synopses and descriptions, see K/*KOB*, 1303–7; K/*NKOB*, 426–28; Eaton/ *OP* II, 101–3.

Major roles: Katerina (sop); Grigoris (bass-bar); Manolios (ten); Fotis (bass-bar); Panait (ten); and Yannakos, a peddler (ten).

BIBLIOGRAPHY: Peter G. Davis, "Opera: Indiana University's 'Greek Passion,'" *NYT* (Sept. 28, 1981), C, 20 [on U.S. premiere]; Winton Dean, "Reports," *Opera* XXXII (1981), 744-46 [on British premiere]; Elisabeth Forbes, "Music in London," *MT* CXXVI (1985),

107; Nicolas Kenyon, "Musical Events," *NY* LVII (May 18, 1981), 166 [on the Indiana premiere]; Brian Large, "Martinů's 'Greek Passion,'" *Opera* XXXII (1981), 344–49 [on British premiere]; John Warrack, "Martinů's New Opera at Zurich," *Opera* XII (1961), 510–12.
DISCOGRAPHY: Cullis, Field, Savory, Mitchinson, Lawton, Tomlinson, Czech Philharmonic Chorus, Brno State Phil; cond. Mackerras, Supraphon 1116-3611/2 (1981; 2 LPs, in English); rev. John W. Freeman, *ON* XLVI (Mar. 6, 1982), 37.

Green Mansions, radio opera by Louis Gruenberg; libretto (Eng), after W. H. Hudson. First performance October 17, 1937, Columbia Broadcasting Company.
Set in the tropics of South America, the tale concerns Mr. Abel and his ill-fated love for the bird girl Rima.

Grenadier, The, dialogue opera by Charles Dibdin; libretto (Eng) possibly by David Garrick. First performance April 19, 1773, London, Sadler's Wells, with Thomas Lowe. Revived April 1992, London.
Ralph fears, rightly, that Jenny, his beloved, has taken up with a grenadier. Ralph catches her with the soldier but gives way when threatened by the grenadier's sword.
DISCOGRAPHY: S. Bisatt, K. West, A. Mayor, instrumentalists; cond. P. Holman, "Opera Restor'd," orch. Holman, Hyperion CDA 66608 (1992, London).

Gretna Green, comic opera in two acts, arranged by Samuel Arnold; libretto (Eng) by Charles Stuart and John O'Keeffe. First performance August 28, 1783, London, Little Theatre in the Haymarket. First U.S. performance March 11, 1803, Philadelphia, Chestnut Street Theatre.
Arnold wrote a new overture after Scottish tunes.
SCORE: vs (London: John Preston, [1782]).

Greysteel, or, The Bearsarks Come to Surnadale, opera in one act by Nicholas Gatty; libretto (Eng) by Reginald Gatty, after G. W. Dasent's translation of the Icelandic saga *Gisli, the Soursop*. First performance March 1, 1906, Sheffield; revived in two acts March 23, 1938, London, Sadler's Wells.

Griffelkin, fairy tale opera in three acts by Lukas Foss; libretto (Eng) by Alastair Reid. First performance November 6, 1955, New York, NBC television, with Adelaide Bishop (Griffelkin), Mignon Dunn, Andrew McKinley, and Lee Cass; conducted by Peter Herman Adler. First performance (stage) November 6, 1956, Lenox, Massachusetts, Tanglewood, Theatre Concert Hall, with Regina Sarfaty (Griffelkin's grandmother) and Mildred Allen (Griffelkin); conducted by the composer; directed by Boris Goldovsky. Revised version October 7, 1993, New York, New York State Theater, City Opera, with Robin Tabachnik (Griffelkin), Diana Daniele (Griffelkin's grandmother), and Helen Yu (little girl); conducted by Scott Bergeson; directed by Jonathan Pape; designed by Jerome Sirlin.
The story concerns a child devil who is sent out into the world by his grandmother to create as much trouble as he can in twenty-four hours. When, by the end of his trip, he begins to use his magic for more humane purposes, he is cut adrift by his fellow devils.
Major roles: the grandmother (alto); Griffelkin, a young devil (sop); and the little girl (mezzo).
SCORE: vs (New York: C. Fischer, 1990).
BIBLIOGRAPHY: Edward Rothstein, "A Little Devil Who Was Too Good," *NYT* (Oct. 9, 1993), A, 13 [on premiere of rev. version]; Laura Tappen Safford, "Tanglewood Imps," *ON* XIX (Nov. 15, 1956), 15 [on stage premiere].

Grimm Duo, A, two one-act operas by Paul Earls; libretto (Eng), after the Brothers Grimm. First performance December 31, 1976, Boston, New England Chamber Players. Consists of *The Dog and Sparrow* and *The Brementown Musicians.*

The first work is scored for mezzo soprano, narrator (bass), and chamber ensemble; the second is for soprano, alto, tenor, bass, instruments, and speaking voices on tape. SCORE: ms score, holograph (1976, signed photocopy, NYPL).

Grinning at the Devil (Aria to Ariel), opera in two acts by James Wilson; libretto (Eng) by Elsa Gress. First performance February 28, 1989, Copenhagen, Riddersalen Theatre.

Based on the life of the Danish writer Karen Bixen, the work concerns Tania and her love affair with Denys in Africa. At a party in New York attended by celebrities, she reflects on her time with her deceased lover. LIBRETTO: English-Danish (Copenhagen: Henrik Nebelong, 1989).

Grove, The, semi-opera by Daniel Purcell; libretto (Eng) by John Oldmixon. First performance February 19, 1700, London, Drury Lane Theatre.

A group of Greek nobles have found a grove on the Gulf of Venice. While most of them decide to return to Thrace, one couple decides to stay.

Growing Castle, The, opera in two acts by Malcolm Williamson; libretto (Eng) by the composer, after Strindberg's *Dream Play.* First performance August 13, 1968, Dynevor Castle, Wales, with Benjamin Luxon (Axel), Geoffrey Chard (the Lawyer), and Jennifer Vyvyan (Agnes); conducted by the composer. First U.S. performance July 3, 1970, Katonah, New York, Caramoor Festival, with Clarice Carson (Agnes), Brent Ellis, Nancy Williams, and William Metcalf.

Agnes, a daughter of the gods, comes down from the heavens to see what earthly life is like. She encounters the Officer and his dying Mother, on whom she takes pity, and dons the disguise of a janitress, whose painful shawl allows her to empathize with humans. She marries the Lawyer, but she begins to hate him and is rescued by the Officer. Agnes comes to realize that love is suffering.

Major roles: Agnes (sop), the Mother (mezzo), the Officer (bar), and the Lawyer (bar). There are a total of twenty-eight roles, all of which may be performed by these four singers.

For a detailed description, see Eaton/*OP* II, 103–4. BIBLIOGRAPHY: "An Opera Is Sung in Welsh Castle," *NYT* (Aug. 15, 1968), 46 [on premiere].

Grub Street Opera, The, ballad opera, with new music, by Anthony Bowles; libretto (Eng), after Henry Fielding. First performance May 30, 1986, New York, Soho Repertory.

Grub-Street Opera, The, ballad opera; libretto (Eng) by Henry Fielding. First performance 1731, London, New Theatre in the Haymarket.

The work contains sixty-five songs. *The Welsh Opera** was, according to the libretto, an earlier, unauthorized version. LIBRETTO: English (London: [E. Raynor], 1731); repr. ed. Edgar V. Roberts, *Regents Restoration Drama Series* (Lincoln, Nebr.: University of Nebraska Press, [1968]).

Guacamayo's Old Song and Dance, opera by John Oliver; libretto (Eng) by Melissa Cameron. First performance February 26, 1991, Toronto, Tanenbaum Opera Centre, with Valerie Gonzalez, Wendy Nielsen, Norine Burgess, Gary Rideout, Robert Milne; conducted by Richard Bradshaw; produced by François Racine.

The work, set in Guatemala, takes its story from old Mayan tales about defeating gods who have been deceitful. Three tales are recounted by five contemporary Guatemalans, who themselves have been oppressed.

BIBLIOGRAPHY: Urjo Kareda, "Toronto," *ON* LV (May 1991), 54 [on premiere].

Guardian Outwitted, The, comic opera in three acts by Thomas Arne; libretto (Eng) probably by the composer. First performance December 12, 1764, London, Covent Garden, with George Mattocks (Lord Planwell), John Beard (Sir British Blunt), Edward Shuter (Sir Liquorish Trapgold), Charlotte Brent (Flirtilla), Isabella Hallam (Lady Julia), Miss Miller (Pinup), and Miss Wainright (Maukin).

The piece is set in London.

SCORES: vs (London: Robert Bremner, [1764]); overture ed. Gwilym Beechey ([London]: Oxford University Press, [1973]).

LIBRETTO: English (London: J. & R. Tomson, 1764).

Guest of Honor, A, "ragtime opera" in one act by Scott Joplin; libretto (Eng) by the composer. First performance 1903, St. Louis.

The score is lost (see bibliography), and the content of the plot is unknown. The work consists of twelve rags.

BIBLIOGRAPHY: Edward A. Berlin, "On the Trail of *A Guest of Honor:* In Search of Scott Joplin's Lost Opera," in *A Celebration of American Music: Words and Music in Honor of H. Wiley Hitchcock,* ed. Richard A. Crawford et al. (Ann Arbor, Mich., 1990), 51–65.

Guide to the Life Expectancy of a Rose, A, operatic fantasy in one act by Vivian Fine. First performance February 7, 1959, New York, Donnell Library, Composers Forum, with Bethany Beardslee and William McGrath; conducted by Carlos Surinach; staged by Martha Graham.

The text is based on the garden page of the *New York Times.*

Scored for five voices and chamber ensemble.

BIBLIOGRAPHY: J. L. B., "Composers Forum Offers New Opera," *NYT* (Feb. 9, 1959), 24 [preview].

Guido Ferranti, tragic opera in one act by Jane Van Etten; libretto (Eng) Elsie M. Wilbor, after Oscar Wilde's *The Duchess of Padua.* First performance December 29, 1914, Chicago, Auditorium Theater, Century Opera Company, with Hazel Eden (Beatrice) and Worthe Faulkner (Guido Ferranti); conducted by Agide Jacchia.

The beautiful young Beatrice is married to an old and tyrannical duke. When she falls in love with Guido Ferranti, she plans to murder her husband. Guido has similar plans, but when he hears that Beatrice has indeed killed her spouse, he rejects her, whereupon she claims that it was he who killed the duke.

LIBRETTO: English (Chicago: Clayton F. Summy, 1915).

Guillaume Tell, opera in four acts, an adaptation by Henry Rowley Bishop of Rossini's work (1829, Paris); libretto (Eng) translated by Alfred Bunn, after Etienne de Jouy, Bis, and Marrast. First performance December 3, 1838, London, Drury Lane Theatre.

See also *Hofer, or, The Tell of the Tyrol.**

Guillem the Troubadour, opera in four acts by Alexander Mackenzie; libretto (Eng) by Francis Hueffer. First performance June 8, 1886, London, Drury Lane Theatre.

A telling of the ill-fated love affair between Guillem de Cabestanh and the wife of a Provençal noble.

Guilt of Lillian Sloan, The, opera in two acts by William Neil; libretto (Eng) by Frank Galati and the composer, after the murder trial of Edith Thompson and Frederick Bywaters (1922). First performance June 6, 1986, Chicago, Lyric Opera, with Donald Kasch (Owen Evans).

The lovers Lillian Sloan and Owen Evans are on trial for murdering Lillian's husband, Howard Sloan. Flashbacks cover the sequence of events that led to the unhappy wife's getting Evans, a young sailor, to help with her husband's murder. In the end it is revealed that Lillian herself killed Howard Sloan, without help from Evans. Both lovers are then hanged.

Major roles: Lillian Sloan (sop), Owen Evans (ten), Solicitor General (bar), Howard Sloan (bass), defense attorney Sitwell (ten), Judge Cassel (bar), and Lillian's mother (mezzo).

For a detailed description, see Kornick/*RAO*, 214–16.
BIBLIOGRAPHY: Andrew Porter, "Musical Events: Let's Make an Opera," *NY* LXII (July 14, 1986), 60–61 [on premiere].

Gulliver, opera for young audiences in three acts by Victoria Bond; libretto (Eng) by Moses Goldberg, after Jonathan Swift. First performance (concert) March 17, 1988, Louisville, Stage One. First performance there 1989. Revived (excerpts) March 27, 1997, New York, Greenwich House, with Robert Osborne.

A telling of the voyages of Gulliver to fantastic lands.

Other settings include the composer's *Travels** (1995, Roanoke, Va.); and *Gulliver*, a mixed-media work, with music by Elliot Kaplan, Frank Lewin, and Easley Blackwood (1975, Minneapolis).

Gustavus III, or, The Masked Ball, opera by Thomas S. Cooke, an arrangement of Auber's *Gustave III, ou, Le bal masqué* (1833, Paris); libretto (Eng) by James R. Planché, after Scribe's text. First performance November 13, 1833, London, Covent Garden. First U.S. performance July 21, 1834, New York.

A treatment of the eighteenth-century Swedish king and his assassination.

Later versions are S. Mercadante's *Il reggente* (1843, Turin) and G. Verdi's *Un ballo in maschera* (1859, Rome).
LIBRETTO: English (London: D'Almaine, [1833?]).

Gustavus Vasa. See The Hero of the North.

Guy Mannering, or, The Gipsy's Prophecy, musical play in three acts by Thomas Attwood and Henry Rowley Bishop; libretto by Daniel Terry, after Sir Walter Scott's novel (1815). First performance March 12, 1816, London, Covent Garden, with Miss Matthews (Julia), Mr. Abbott (Mannering), and Mr. Duruset (Henry Bertram).

The setting is Scotland. On Guy Mannering's visit to the home of the laird of Ellangowan, a son, Henry Bertram, is born. The boy disappears, and the parents die brokenhearted. When Mannering returns from a stay in India, he is followed by a Captain Brown, who, identified by a gypsy, turns out to be the missing Bertram. The young man, restored to his fortune, is able to marry Julia, Mannering's daughter.

The music, according to the score, includes "several well-known Scottish airs." Among the numbers is the air "Be Mine, Dear Maid."
SCORE: ms fs (British Library, Add. MS. 36945); vs (London: Goulding, D'Almaine, Potter, & Co., n.d.).

H

Haddon Hall, comic opera in two acts by Arthur S. Sullivan; libretto (Eng) by Sydney Grundy. First performance September 24, 1892, London, Savoy Theatre, with Courtice Pounds (John Manners), Richard Green (Sir George Vernon), Lucille Hill (Dorothy Vernon), Rutland Barrington (Rupert), and Rosina Brandram (Lady Vernon). It ran for 214 performances.

The historically-based story is updated from the sixteenth century to the Cromwell era. The proper Miss Dorothy Vernon, an English heiress, elopes with a Catholic boy, John Manners, to the consternation of her family and Rupert, Dorothy's intended.

For a description, see Jacobs/*AS*, 345–47.

Among the changes in Sullivan's style is the long second-act finale, with continuous music and lack of spoken dialogue.

SCORE: vs (London: Chappell; New York: Boosey, 1892).
LIBRETTO: English (London: Chappell; New York: Novello, Ewer, 1892).

Haircut, opera in one act by Sam Morgenstern; libretto (Eng) by Jan Henry, after Ring Lardner's story. First performance May 2, 1969, New York, Metropolitan Opera Studio.

The village barber, Whitey, recounts to the circus man the cruelties of the town bully, Jim Kendall. Among Kendall's mean tricks is leaving his family marooned outside the circus, and they gain admittance only through the efforts of the kindhearted Doc Stair. Kendall, already annoyed, is further enraged when the doctor seems solicitous to Julie Gregg, to whom Kendall is also attracted. Kendall, faking the doctor's voice, arranges a meeting with Julie by telephone. She therefore does not understand the doctor's apparent coolness when they meet. The next morning another of Kendall's victims, the homeless Paul, rushes in to say that Kendall was shot by accident and Mrs. Kendall accuses him of murder. Paul, considering fleeing, stays to face his accusers on the advice of Whitey. Julie, meanwhile, discovers that Doc is in fact married to a hopeless invalid; she therefore understands more deeply his seeming indifference to her.

For a detailed description, see Eaton/*OP* II, 282–83.

Major roles: Whitey (bass-bar), Julie Gregg (sop), Jim Kendall (bar), Doc Stair (bar), and Paul (ten).

Half Magic in King Arthur's Court, children's opera in one act by Martin Kalmanoff; libretto (Eng) by E. Eager. First performance May 17, 1963, Walding River, New York, Walding River High School.

Hamlet, opera in three acts by Humphrey Searle; libretto (Eng) by the composer, a shortened version of the Shakespeare text, translated into German by Hans Keller and Paul Hamburger, after August Wilhelm von Schlegel's version. First performance, in German, March 5, 1968, Hamburg, Staatsoper, with Sylvia Anderson (Ophelia), Kerstin Meyer (Gertrude), Ronald Dowd (Claudius), Tom Krause (Hamlet), Toni Blankenheim (Polonius), and Willi Hartmann (Laertes); conducted by Matthias Kuntzsch;

directed by August Everding. First British performance, in English, April 18, 1969, London, Covent Garden, with Victor Braun (Hamlet), Anne Howells (Ophelia), Patricia Johnson (Gertrude), Dowd (Claudius), and David Hughes (Laertes); conducted by Edward Downes.

The setting sticks very closely to the Shakespeare version, with six minor characters deleted and the play reduced to three acts. The music is written in a twelve-tone idiom, and the characters have themes that are based on basic series. The work opens with an orchestral section to evoke the ghost. Among the highlights is Ophelia's dramatic mad scene, written in a modernistic folk-song style.

Major roles: Ophelia (sop); Gertrude, the Queen (mezzo); Claudius (ten); Hamlet (bar); Polonius (bar); and Laertes (ten).

SCORE: vs, German-English (London: Faber, 1971).

BIBLIOGRAPHY: Frank Granville Barker, "Reports," *ON* XXXIII (June 14, 1969), 31 [on British premiere]; Andrew Porter, "Reports," *MT* CIX (1968), 457–58 [on premiere]; James Helme Sutcliffe, "Reports: Foreign," *ON* XXXII (Apr. 20, 1968), 29 [on premiere]; Stephen Walsh, "Two *Hamlets*," *Tempo* (Summer 1969), 6–12 [on Searle and Szokolay versions].

Hamlet, opera in three acts by Sergius Kagen; libretto (Eng), after Shakespeare. First performance November 9, 1962, Baltimore, Peabody Conservatory.

Hamlet Travestie, tragic-comic burlesque opera in two acts, with music arranged by John Bray; libretto (Eng) by John Poole. First performance January 24, 1811, London, New Theatre. First U.S. performance March 7, 1812, Philadelphia, Chestnut Street Theatre, with Bray (Hamlet).

The work opens with a soliloquy to the tune "Derry Down."

Among the many other settings of the Shakespeare play are those by F. Gasparini, *Ambleto* (1705, Venice); D. Scarlatti, *Amleto* (1715, Rome); L. Caruso (1789, Florence); G. Andreozzi, *Amleto* (1792, Padua); J. Schuster's "Karrikatur" (1809, Vienna); S. Mercadante, *Amleto* (1822, Milan); M. Maretzek (1843, Brünn); A. Buzzolla (1848, Venice); A. Stadtfeld, *Hamlet* (1857, Darmstadt); F. Faccio, *Amleto* (1865, Genoa); A. Thomas (1868, Paris); J. Hopp, with the parody *Hammlet* [*sic*] (1874, Vienna); A. Hignard (1888, Nantes); E. Keurvels (1891, incidental music); P. L. Atherton and E. H. Abbott, with the musical burlesque *Hamlet, Prince of Denmark* (1893, Cambridge, Mass.); L. Heward (1916, unfin.); J. Kalnins, *Hamlets* (1936, Riga); P. Reif, *Mad Hamlet** (comp. 1966); S. Szokolay, *Hamlet* (1968, Budapest); H. U. Engelmann, *Ophelia* (1969, Hanover); P. I. Bentoiu, *Hamlet* (1971, Bucharest); W. Rihm, *Hamletmaschine* (1987, West Berlin); and C. Kievman (unfin., 1987).

LIBRETTO: English (London: Richardson, 1810; New York: David Longworth, 1811).

Hand of Bridge, A, comedy in one act by Samuel Barber; libretto (Eng) by Gian Carlo Menotti. First performance (concert) April 14, 1959, New York, Waldorf Astoria, with Patricia Neway (Geraldine) and William Lewis (Bill); first performance (staged) June 17, 1959, Spoleto, Italy, Festival of Two Worlds, with Ellen Miville (Sally), Lewis (Bill), (Geraldine), and René Miville (David); conducted by Richard Feist. First U.S. performance (stage) April 6, 1960, New York, Mannes College of Music.

Two bored couples play their customary game of bridge and fantasize during the proceedings. The entire work lasts about nine minutes and is set for four voices and chamber orchestra.

Roles: David, a businessman (bar); Geraldine, his wife (sop); Bill, a lawyer (ten); and Sally, Bill's wife (alto).

For a detailed description, see Eaton/*OP* II, 283.

SCORE: vs (New York: G. Schirmer, [1960]), rev. Victor Yellin, *Notes* XVIII/4 (1961), 641.

DISCOGRAPHY: Gregg Smith Singers, Adirondack Chamber Orch.; cond. Smith, Premier PRCD-1009; rev. C. J. Luten, "Recordings," *ON* LVI (Jan. 18, 1992), 37.

Hands across the Sky, opera in one act by Antony Hopkins; libretto (Eng) by Gordon Snell. First performance July 8, 1959, Cheltenham, England, Town Hall.

BIBLIOGRAPHY: J. P. Austen, "English Understatement," *ON* XXIV (Oct. 3, 1959), 22 [on premiere].

Hanging Judge, The (The Inevitable Hour), opera in three acts by Normand Lockwood; libretto (Eng) by Russell Porter. First performance March 6, 1964, Denver, University of Denver.

The work is set on the American frontier in 1861. Minister Shannon has urged in vain that his town ignore the evilness of Bardwell and his gang. In the face of rising violence Shannon accepts two pistols from Rheba, the town prostitute, and shoots one of Bardwell's hoodlums in self-defense, thereby becoming a "hanging judge." As the fighting of the Civil War approaches the area, the governor asks that all swear allegiance to the Union, and when Raleigh, Shannon's friend, defies the order and asks Shannon to give up his judgeship in protest, Shannon declares his friend to be a traitor. The minister is made a colonel and is sent to a western fort with the aim of protecting the Indians but, urged on by Rheba, orders a massacre at the Indian camp and kills four prisoners himself. Only Rheba comes to witness his court-martial, and when he realizes that it was she who gave him wrong advice, he kills her.

For a detailed description, see Eaton/*OP* II, 107–8.

Major roles: Brother Shannon (bar); Elizabeth, his wife (mezzo); Rheba (sop/mezzo); and Raleigh (bar/bass).

BIBLIOGRAPHY: E. B. Rogers, "Denver's West," *ON* XXVIII (May 2, 1964), 26 [on premiere]; A. Young, "Colorado," *MA* LXXXIV (May 1964), 18 [on premiere].

Hangman, Hangman!, chamber opera in one act by Leonardo Balada; libretto (Eng) by the composer, after a traditional cowboy song. First performance (in Catalonian) October 10, 1982, Barcelona. First U.S. performance October 8, 1983, Pittsburgh, Carnegie-Mellon University, with François Clemmons (Johnny), Lee Cass (narrator/bartender), David Orcutt (the sheriff), Gerald Sell (the hangman), Donna Zapola (the sweetheart), Michael Wieser (the father), and Jennifer Song (the mother); conducted by Werner Torkanowsky.

The tale concerns a young man, Johnny, who is to die because of a minor crime; he has been abandoned by his family and friends. Just as he is about to be hanged, he sees his parents and his sweetheart ride up; he assumes they are buying his release. Unfortunately, Johnny has been mean to them for years, and so they have come to see him swing from the gallows. Just before the execution, however, a wealthy landowner buys Johnny's release; the crowd and his family, seeing his change of luck, cheer.

Roles: Johnny (ten), mother (alto), father (bass), sweetheart (sop), sheriff (bass), narrator/bartender (speaking), and man from audience (speaking).

The work is written for a narrator, five singers, and two actors, accompanied by a small instrumental ensemble.

SCORE: vs (New York: G. Schirmer, 1987).
BIBLIOGRAPHY: Robert Croan, review, *ON* XLVIII (Dec. 10, 1983), 72 [on U.S. premiere].

Hannah, opera in a prologue and three acts by Leonard Lehrman; libretto (Eng) by the composer and Orel Odinov. First performance May 22, 1980, Mannheim-Seckenheim, Germany; December 26, 1989, New York, WBAI-FM radio.

About the sister of Judah Maccabee.

The composer describes the piece as "my anti-war feminist Chanukah opera," in his "What Is Jewish Opera," *OJ* XXIX (June 1, 1996), 56–61.
SCORE: vs, holograph (1979, copy, NYPL).

Hannah Hewitt, or, The Female Crusoe, afterpiece in two acts by Charles Dibdin; libretto (Eng) by the composer. First performance May 7, 1798, London, Drury Lane Theatre.

Hansel and Gretel, children's opera in one act by Marla Stoddard; libretto (Eng) by the composer, after the tale by the Brothers Grimm. First performance February 1986, Arcata, California, Humbolt State University, Children's Theater.

Hansel & Gretel & Ted & Alice, operatic spoof in one act by "P.D.Q. Bach" (Peter Schickele); libretto (Eng) by the composer. First performance March 1972, Dallas.

A takeoff on E. Humperdinck's opera *Hänsel und Gretel* (1893, Weimar) and the movie *Bob & Carol & Ted & Alice* (1969).

Other settings include J. F. Reichardt's *Hänschen und Gretchen* (1772, Leipzig).

HAPP, or, Orpheus in Clover, micro-opera in one act by Eric Stokes; libretto (Eng) by the composer. First performance October 11, 1977, Minneapolis.

The lyrics of the work gradually spell out "Happy Birthday."

Happy Arcadia, opera in one act by Frederic Clay; libretto (Eng) by William S. Gilbert. First performance October 28, 1872, London, Gallery of Illustration.

The Arcadians include Daphne, her husband, Colin, their daughter, Chloe, and Strephon, Chloe's suitor. They are tired of their unending happiness but lie about their plight when the handsome Lycidas comes to court Chloe. Another visitor is Astrologos, a "blighted bogy" who leaves magic articles, each of which can grant its owner one wish. Using their wishes, the Arcadians exchange identities and get a new set of wishes to free themselves from their "curse."

Roles: Strephon, a happy Arcadian, betrothed to Chloe; Lycidas, the handsomest man in the world; Colin, a virtuous old peasant, father of Chloe; Daphne, an elderly Arcadian, Chloe's mother; Chloe, a happy Arcadian, betrothed to Strephon; Astrologos, a "blighted bogy."

For a detailed description, see Stedman/*GBS*, 39–44.
LIBRETTOS: English (London: J. Williams; New York: Schuberth, 1896); Stedman, *GBS*, 167–97.

Happy Captive, The, opera by John Galliard; libretto (Eng) by Lewis Theobald, after Cervantes. First performance April 16, 1741, London, Little Theatre in the Haymarket.

The music for Galliard's last operatic work is lost. The text was used for Arne's *The Temple of Dullness** (1745, London).

Happy Disguise, The, comic opera by Tommaso Giordani; libretto (Eng) by Wally Chamberlain Oulton. First performance January 7, 1784, Dublin, English Opera House.

Happy End, "melodrama with songs" in three acts, an adaptation by Michael Feingold of Kurt Weill's work (1929, Berlin); book and lyrics (Eng) by Feingold, after Elisabeth Hauptmann and Bertolt Brecht. First performance (professional) April 6, 1972, New Haven, Connecticut, Yale Repertory Theatre; conducted by Thomas Fay; directed by Michael Posnick. Revivals include April 26, 1977, Brooklyn, New York, Chelsea Theater Center, with Meryl Streep (Lillian Holiday) and Bob Gunton (Bill Cracker); February 17, 1995, Baltimore, Center Stage; conducted by Mark Bennett; directed by Irene Lewis.

The sparse plot revolves around a young Salvation Army worker, Lillian Holiday, who is trying to protect the souls of a group of gangsters. She falls in love with Bill Cracker, owner of the Chicago dance hall in which the criminals meet, led by Dr. Nakamura. In the end she converts Bill and his "colleagues."

Major roles: Bill Cracker, a gangster (high bar); Sam Wurlitzer (bar); Dr. Nakamura (bar); Lady in Grey (mezzo); Lieutenant Lillian Holiday (sop); and Sister Jane (mezzo).

The creators of the piece intended to capture the spirit and success of *The Three-penny Opera,** but the discord accompanying its creation and its tumultuous first production led to its early exit from the repertory. The musical highlights include the "Bilbao Song" and the "Sailors' Tango" (act 1), and "Surabaya Johnny" (act 3).

The Feingold version, a free adaptation of the text that maintains Brecht's lyrics in a "more or less literal translation" (see 1972 libretto, ix), revived interest in the work.

The plot has similarities to that of Frank Loesser's musical *Guys and Dolls* (1950), based on Damon Runyon's 1932 short story *The Idyll of Sarah Brown.* Gustave Kerker's *The Belle of New York* (1897, New York), with a text by Hugh Morton, features a Salvation Army heroine trying to reform a wayward young man.

SCORE: fs, adaptation, lyrics Michael Feingold; music ed. Alan Boustead "in accordance with the composer's mss" (London: Universal Edition, 1981).

LIBRETTO: English, transl. and ed. M. Feingold (London and New York: Methuen, 1972).

BIBLIOGRAPHY: Clive Barnes, review, *NYT* (Apr. 27, 1977), C, 17 [on 1977 revival].

Happy Families, comic opera in three acts by Thomas Dunhill; libretto (Eng) by Rose Fyleman. First performance November 1, 1933, Guildford, England.

SCORE: vs (London: J. B. Cramer, [1933]).

Happy Hypocrite, The, opera in one act by William Masland; libretto (Eng) by the composer, after the tale by Max Beerbohm. Composed 1978.

The setting is London and Kensington, spring 1818. The evil Lord George Hell falls in love with Jenny Mere, a young entertainer. She declines his offer of marriage because she wants to wed a man with a saintly face and thinks his exudes evilness. He goes to a mask dealer, Mr. Aeneas, and buys a mask to transform his visage. Hell tracks Jenny down, and she falls in love with the now saintly-looking man, agreeing to marry him. His former mistress, La Gambogi, finds him and, after he refuses to go back with her to London, rips off his mask. To her astonishment, she sees that his face has been transformed into the good person he has become. La Gambogi departs, knowing she has lost.

For a description, see Summers/*OOA,* 209–11.

Major roles: Lord George Hell (bar), La Gambogi (mezzo), Jenny Mere (sop), and Mr. Aeneas (bar).

SCORE: ms vs, holograph (1978, photocopy, NYPL).

Happy Lovers, The, or, The Beau Metamorphos'd, opera (ballad opera); libretto (Eng) by Henry Ward. First performance 1736, London, Lincoln's-Inn Fields, with Mr.

Bullock (Sir Timothy Careful), Mr. Ward (Modish), Mr. Hemskirk (Constant), and Mrs. Forrester (Celia).

Constant and the foppish Modish are both in love with Celia, daughter of Sir Timothy Careful.

LIBRETTO: English (London: S. Slow, 1736; Edinburgh: R. Drummond, 1745); repr. ed. (1736) Rubsamen/*BO*, vol. 13, *Farce, Amorous Intrigue and Deception II* (1974).

Happy Nuptials, The, masque by Henry Carey; libretto (Eng) by the composer. First performance November 24, 1733, London, Goodman's Fields. Revised as *Britannia, or, The Royal Lovers.**

Composed for the impending marriage of Princess Anne and the Prince of Orange, which was postponed until March 15, 1734; ergo the revision and new title.

Happy Prince, The, opera in one act by Malcolm Williamson; libretto (Eng) by the composer, after Oscar Wilde. First performance May 22, 1965, Farnham Festival, England, with April Cantelo (swallow). First U.S. performance August 25, 1967, Newport, Rhode Island, Metropolitan Opera Festival, Concert Hall, with David Plettner (the Prince, acted), Mathew Patterson (the swallow, acted), Nancy Williams (the Prince, sung), and Gail Robinson (the swallow, sung); conducted by David Stivender.

The statue of the Happy Prince, encrusted by jewels, is saddened by the actions of the city's residents, and so he tells a swallow to use the jewels to help others in need throughout the world. Eventually exhausted by his chores, the bird dies, and the Prince's leaden heart breaks. The citizens, seeing that the statue has become shabby, take it down and attempt to burn it together with the body of the bird. The heart of the Prince, however, will not be consumed, and angels arrive to inform the populace that the city's most valuable possessions are the heart and the swallow.

Roles: the swallow (sop), the Prince (sop), the mayor (alto), the seamstress (mezzo), her son (sop), the author (mezzo/alto), the matchgirl (sop), and a rich girl (sop).

For a detailed description, see Eaton/*OP* II, 283–84.

Also set by V. Raines (not perf.).

BIBLIOGRAPHY: Harold C. Schonberg, review, *NYT* (Aug. 26, 1967), 31 [on U.S. premiere].

Hard Times, opera in two acts and twenty-six scenes by Geoffrey Burgon; libretto by the composer, based on the novel by Charles Dickens. Composed 1991.

The modernized version of the story is set in Coketown, an industrial area, in which Gradgrind, an educator, runs a model school where students are taught to learn "facts" and are forbidden to use their imagination. Gradgrind discovers his children Louise and Tom trying to glimpse Sleary's circus. Bounderby, an associate of Gradgrind, wants to marry Louise. Although she is disgusted by him, she eventually accepts his proposal, since she has been brainwashed by her father's educational system into thinking that she has no choice. Harthouse, an admirer of Louise, cannot understand her decision.

Tom, meanwhile, gets into trouble for gambling. Harthouse offers to help him, but Tom is too much in debt and, suspected of robbing a bank, escapes arrest and flees the country by ship. Although Louise tells her father that she loves Harthouse, her training leaves her unable to change her situation and join Tom.

Harlot and the Monk, The, opera in one act by Craig Bohmler; libretto (Eng) by James Howley, after an eighth-century Indian play. First performance February 1985, Atlanta, Banff Centre for the Arts.

Harlot's Progress, The. See **The Decoy.**

Harmfulness of Tobacco, The, mono-opera by Martin Kalmanoff; libretto (Eng) by Eric Bentley, after Anton Chekhov. First performance March 22, 1979, New York, Alice Tully Hall.
SCORE: vs, holograph (1977, NYPL).

Harmoonia, opera in one act by Stephen Paulus; libretto (Eng) by M. D. Browne. First performance February 23, 1991, Muscatine, Louisiana, Central Middle Auditorium.

Harold, opera in four acts by George Marshall-Hall; libretto (Eng) by the composer. Composed before 1888. First performance (one scene) February 2, 1888, London.
About the last Saxon king.

Harold, or, The Norman Conquest, opera in three acts by Frederic Cowen; libretto (Eng) by Edward Malet. First performance June 8, 1895, London, Covent Garden, with Emma Albani (Edith), Louise Messlinger (Adela), Philip Brozel (Harold), and David Bispham (William of Normandy); conducted by the composer.
SCORE: vs (London: J. Williams; New York: E. Schuberth [J. F. H. Meyer], 1895).
LIBRETTO: English (London: J. Skirven, [1788]).

Haroun al Raschid. See *The Aethiop.*

Haroun Alraschid, opera in three acts by Henry Rowley Bishop; libretto (Eng) by William Dimond. First performance January 11, 1813, London, Covent Garden. A revision of *The Aethiop** (1812, London).
The title character is the famous ruler of Bagdad from the *Thousand and One Nights.* The work includes the lovesick young man featured later in Peter Cornelius's *Der Barbier von Bagdad* (1858, Weimar), Noureddin (ten), who sings an echo-recitative and air, "Who Threads the Gloom by Moonlight Hour." Another highlight is Selidor's song "Go, Mystical Flow'r to My Lady-Love."
SCORE: copyist's score, four arias, 1813: "Go, Mystical Flow'r," "Farewell, Farewell, the Golden Day," "Who Threads the Gloom" ("thrids" in the ms), and "Now Fill the Air" (British Library, Add. MS. 36963).

Harpies, The, fantasy opera in one act by Marc Blitzstein; libretto (Eng) by the composer. Composed 1931. First performance May 25, 1953, New York, Manhattan School of Music, with Vilma Georgiou, Stamford Nishimura, Nassrine Mobite, Cornelia Nobles, Paulyn Warren, Kenneth Lane, Paul Ingegneri, and Coleridge-Taylor Parkinson; conducted by Hugh Ross.
A treatment of the Greek legend in which the blind oracle Phineus is tormented by the harpies, until they are dispersed by the Argonauts, led by Jason.
The work is set for eight singers and chamber ensemble.
BIBLIOGRAPHY: Howard Taubman, review, *NYT* (May 26, 1953) [on premiere].
DISCOGRAPHY: R. Rees, T. Bogdan, E. Najera, Adirondack Co., Gregg Smith Singers; cond. G. Smith, Premier PRCD 1009 (1991, 1 CD).

Harriet, the Woman Called Moses, opera in two acts by Thea Musgrave. First performance March 1, 1985, Norfolk, Virginia, with Cynthia Haymon (Harriet), Alteouise DeVaughn (Rit), Ben Holt (Josiah), Barry Craft (Preston), and Jay Willoughby (the master); conducted by Peter Mark. Revised in one-act version as *The Story of Harriet Tubman*; first performance October 24, 1990, Milwaukee, with Kevin Maynor, Sheila

Tate (Harriet), Rochelle Ellis (Harriet's mother), and Richard Hobson (Josiah); conducted by Tim Rolek.

The opera focuses on a string of vignettes, connected by a narrative, outlining the life of the escaped slave Harriet Tubman, who became a "conductor" on the Underground Railroad, which was used to bring southern slaves to freedom in the North. In this treatment of her story, having found safety in the North under the protection of Mr. Garrett, a Quaker, Harriet remembers the events of her life. She runs away from the plantation after her kind master dies and his drunken son Preston takes control, and the cruel overseer is no longer restrained. After she finds her way North, Harriet returns to the South to help other slaves escape, despite her desire to stay in the North with Josiah, her lover. Among those she rescues are Rit, her mother, Ben, her father, and Benjie, her brother. When they try to reach the Canadian border and safety, Preston, who has pursued them, shoots at Harriet but kills Josiah, who has been shielding her. She and her family vow to continue their fight for freedom and happiness.

Major roles: Harriet (sop); Rit, Harriet's mother (mezzo); Josiah, Harriet's lover (bar); the master (bar); Preston (ten); the overseer (ten); Benjie (ten), Ben (bass); and Mr. Garrett (bass).

The musical highlights of the abbreviated version include the spiritual "Deep River" and the "Juba" dance scene.

BIBLIOGRAPHY: Robert Jacobson, "Norfolk," *ON* XLIV (June 1985), 35–36 [on premiere]; Lawrence Singer, "Milwaukee," *ON* LV (Jan. 19, 1991), 40.

Harriet Tubman, opera by Leo Edwards; libretto (Eng). First performance November 9, 1986, New York, Opera Ebony; May 1988, New York, Mannes College of Music.

Harrison Loved His Umbrella, "musical cartoon for children" in one act by Stanley Hollingsworth; libretto (Eng) by Rhoda Levine, after her book (1964). First performance May 27, 1981, Charleston, South Carolina.

In this fantasy the title character refuses to part with his umbrella, much to the consternation of the town's parents, whose children do the same. Matters improve when Harrison transfers his affections to a yo-yo.

For a description, see Kornick/*RAO*, 149–50.

Harry le Roi, "heroic pastoral burletta" in one act by Henry Rowley Bishop; libretto (Eng) by Isaac Pocock, after Robert Dodsley's *The King and the Miller of Mansfield*. First performance July 2, 1813, London, Covent Garden.

SCORE: ms fs, autograph (1813, British Library, Add. MS. 27705).

Hartford Bridge, or, The Skirts of the Camp, "operatic farce" in two acts by William Shield; libretto (Eng) by William Pearce. First performance November 3, 1792, London, Covent Garden, with Mr. Munden (Peregrine Forester), Charles Incledon (Captain Fieldair), and Mrs. Clendining (Clara). First U.S. performance May 30, 1794, Philadelphia, Chestnut Street Theatre.

The work is set in a military camp near the bridge of the title. Its many musical quotations include borrowings from Gluck's ballet *Don Juan* (1761) and Paisiello's opera *La molinara* (1789, Naples), and a Russian folk song used later by Glinka in the orchestral work *Kamarinskaya* (1848).

For a detailed description, see Fiske/*ETM*, 550–51.

SCORE: vs (London: Longman & Broderip, n.d.).

LIBRETTO: English (Dublin: P. Byrne, 1793; London: Longman et al., 1809).

Harvest, The, opera in three acts by Vittorio Giannini; libretto (Eng) by Karl Klasder and the composer. First performance November 25, 1961, Chicago, Lyric Opera, with Marilyn Horne (Lora), William Wilderman (Sam), Geraint Evans (Lem), Richard Carl Knoll (Mark), Robert Schmorr (Grandpa Jones), and Jeffrey Wolfe (Jason); conducted by the composer; directed by Herbert Machiz.

The setting is the American Southwest, ca. 1900. It concerns the turmoil and yearnings of a struggling family.

SCORE: vs (New York: C. Ricordi, [1961]).

Harvest Home, The, comic afterpiece opera in two acts by Charles Dibdin; libretto (Eng) by the composer. First performance May 16, 1787, London, Little Theatre in the Haymarket.

The work was performed only seven times.

SCORE: vs (London: Preston, n.d.).
LIBRETTO: English (London: Harrison, 1787).

Harvey Milk, "biographical opera based on fact and fiction" in three acts by Stewart Wallace; libretto (Eng) by Michael Korie. First performance January 21, 1995, Houston, Houston Grand Opera, with Robert Orth (Harvey Milk), Raymond Very (Dan White), Juliana Gondek (Dianne Feinstein), Robynne Redmon (Anne Kronenberg), Bradley Williams (Scott Smith), and Gidon Saks (George Moscone). Revised version November 27, 1996 (the eighteenth anniversary of the killings), San Francisco, Orpheum Theater, with Orth, Very, Gondek, Saks, and James Maddalena (Messenger).

The story concerns the life of Harvey Milk, a gay city supervisor in San Francisco, who was gunned down, along with George Moscone, the mayor, on November 27, 1978. Their killer was Dan White, a former policeman and fellow supervisor, who was convicted of the deed.

The opera begins with Milk's killing and then flashes back to his childhood in New York, beginning with his trip as a fifteen-year-old by himself to the Metropolitan Opera, where he wonders about a group of "men without wives." When he follows them to Central Park, the youngster is entrapped and arrested by a plainclothes policeman, which leads him to confront his own sexuality and the hostility of others to those who are different, his fighting back, which is urged upon him by his friend Scott Smith, and, ultimately, his murder.

Major roles: Harvey Milk (bar), Dan White (ten), George Moscone (bass), Scott Smith (ten), Dianne Feinstein (sop), Henry Wong (male sop), Messenger (bar), and Anne Kronenberg (mezzo).

The music is a mixture of many styles and includes elements of jazz, American folk music, medieval polyphony, and Middle Eastern liturgical music. In a move to unify the opera emotionally and musically, the lead singers, except for the portrayer of Milk, have two or three other roles. The soprano who sings Dianne Feinstein, for example, is also cast as "Mama" and "Hooker," while Dan White is grouped with the "Man in Trench Coat" and the "Cop."

BIBLIOGRAPHY: Martin Bernheimer, "San Francisco," *ON* XLVIII (Mar. 1997), 291–92 [on San Francisco revival]; Tim Golden, "A Gay Camelot Goes Home to Find It's True," *NYT* (Nov. 30, 1996), 19, 20 [on San Francisco revival]; Bernard Holland, "No, Wishing Won't Make Operas Good," *NYT* (April 30, 1995), C, 29; Barry Millington, "Performance," *MT* (April 1995), 208–9 [on premiere]; Edward Rothstein, review, *NYT* (Jan. 23, 1995), C, 11 [on premiere].

DISCOGRAPHY: Bishop, Grove, Gondek, Orth, Jacobs, Very, Maddalena, San Francisco Opera; cond. Runnicles, Teldec 0630-15856 (2 CDs).

Haste to the Wedding, comic opera by George Grossmith; libretto (Eng) by William S. Gilbert, after Labiche's *Un chapeau de paille d'Italie* and Gilbert's own *The Wedding March* (1873). First performance July 27, 1892, London, Criterion Theatre, with Frank Wyatt, Lionel Brough, and Grossmith (Cousin Foodle).

A prospective bridegroom is forced, on the day of his wedding, to find a replacement hat for a female acquaintance when his horse eats her original straw hat, all this to prevent her husband from becoming jealous.

The work was a failure.

LIBRETTO: English, in *Original Comic Operas Written by W. S. Gilbert;* English (London: Chappell, [1900?]); (London: Chatto & Windus, 1911).

Haunted Castle, The, musical entertainment in two acts by Tommaso Giordani; libretto (Eng) by Walley Chamberlain Oulton. First performance December 18, 1783, Dublin, English Opera House.

LIBRETTO: English (Dublin: R. Marchbank, 1785).

Haunted Tower, The, comic opera in three acts, music "selected, adapted and composed" by Stephen Storace; libretto (Eng) by James Cobb. First performance November 24, 1789, London, Drury Lane Theatre, with Nancy Storace (Adela), Anna Maria Crouch (Lady Elinor), Michael Kelly (Oakland), John Bannister (Edward), Robert Baddeley (Charles), Charles Digum (Robert), and Thomas Sedgwick (Charles). First U.S. performances April 24, 1793, Charleston, South Carolina, Charleston Theatre; January 7, 1795, New York.

The plot, set in the time of William the Conqueror, concerns Lord William, son of Baron Oakland, who has been unjustly exiled. In his place the king has put a boor, whose son, the not so bright Edward, wishes to wed Adela but has been slated to marry Lady Elinor de Courcy. Elinor, in turn, is secretly in love with Sir Palomede, in reality Lord William. William and Elinor pass themselves off as a jester and Cicely, a maid. Adela, meanwhile, has been accepted as Lady Elinor, and plans to marry Edward before everyone's real identities are revealed.

William is recognized by Hugo, one of his father's old servants, and he gains access to the castle. After scaring the dishonest help by pretending that the tower is haunted, he regains his title and weds the real Elinor. Adela and Edwin marry, also.

For a detailed description, see Fiske/*ETM,* 501–8.

Major roles: the false Baron Oakland (nonsinging); Robert, his servant (ten); Charles, another servant (bass); Lord William (ten); Lady Elinor de Courcy (sop); Edward (bar); and Adela (sop).

Among the work's several borrowings are "The Song of Thy Love," from Linley's *The Carnival of Venice** (1781, London); and pieces by Paisiello, Martini, and Purcell.

SCORE: vs (London: Longman & Broderip, [ca. 1790]).

LIBRETTO: English (Dublin: P. Burne and J. Jones, [n.d.]).

BIBLIOGRAPHY: Jane Girdham, *English Opera in Late Eighteenth-Century London* (Oxford: Clarendon Press, 1997), 137–53.

Have You Heard, Do You Know?, divertimento in seven scenes by Louise Talma; libretto (Eng) by the composer. First performance January 18, 1981, New York, Whitney Museum of Art.

The setting is a house in Queens or Brooklyn Heights at breakfast and involves a couple's conversation, which is interrupted by their neighbor Mildred, who drops in to gossip.

Roles: Fred, a young businessman (ten); Della, his wife (sop); and Mildred, a friend (mezzo).

DISCOGRAPHY: S. Davenny Wyner, B. Martin, P. Sperry; cond. A. Weisberg, MHS 7308K (1 LP).

Haydn's Head, opera in one act by Larry Baker; libretto (Eng). First performance July 30, 1987, Cleveland, Opera Cleveland, Al Fresco Festival.

Haymakers, The, operatic cantata in two parts by George F. Root; libretto (Eng) by the composer. First performance January 10, 1860, Chicago, Musical Union.

The work, concerning farm society in the Midwest, is completely sung.

SCORE: vs (Boston: Mason Brothers, 1857); repr. ed. Dennis R. Martin, *Recent Researches in American Music*, vols. 9–10 (Madison, Wisc.: A-R Editions, 1984).

LIBRETTO: English (New York: Mason Brothers, 1860).

DISCOGRAPHY: pt. 2: E. Rose, F. McKinley, North Texas State University, New World Records NW 234 (1978).

Hazel Kirke, opera in four acts by Mark Houston; libretto (Eng), after the play by Steele MacKaye (1880). First performance August 7, 1987, Glens Falls, New York, Lake George Opera, with Karen Hunt (Hazel Kirke), Harlan Foss (Dunstan Kirke), Victoria Livengood (Hazel's mother), David Eisler (Arthur), George Massey (Hazel's intended), and Rosalind Elias (Arthur's mother); conducted by Hal France.

Dunstan Kirke insists that Hazel, his virtuous daughter, who is in love with Arthur, marry someone else instead. When she refuses, he banishes her, only to be struck by blindness as a punishment.

BIBLIOGRAPHY: B. A. Nilsson, "Glens Falls," *ON* LII (Nov. 1987), 53–54 [on premiere].

Headless Horseman, The, school opera in one act by Douglas Moore; libretto (Eng) by Stephen Vincent Benét, after Washington Irving's *The Legend of Sleepy Hollow*. First performance March 4, 1937, Bronxville, New York.

About the schoolteacher Ichabod Crane, whose rival for the hand of Katrina Van Tassel, Brom Van Brunt, masquerades as a headless horseman and runs Ichabod out of town.

Hearing, opera in five scenes by Ned Rorem; libretto (Eng) by James Holmes, after poems by Kenneth Koch. First performance (concert) March 15, 1977, New York, Christ and St. Stephen's Church, with the Gregg Smith Singers; conducted by Smith.

A young woman rejects the attentions of a young man in favor of an older gentleman. He is attracted to her, and the two go off together. This makes the older man's lady friend unhappy, as well as the young man. The deserted lady manages to win back the older gentleman, and the young woman, now rejected, becomes interested in the young man.

Roles: a lady in lilac (sop), a jealous gentleman (ten), a poetic lady (mezzo), and a young man with a French horn (bar).

The text is a dramatization of Koch's poems set as the song cycle *Hearing* by the composer in 1966. The work is scored for singers and seven instruments.

Heart of Midlothian, The, musical drama in three acts by Henry Rowley Bishop; libretto (Eng) by Daniel Terry, after Scott's novel (1818). First performance April 17, 1819, London, Covent Garden.

See next entry for the plot.

Major roles: Effie, Jeanie, Madge, and Staunton.

SCORE: ms fs, autograph (1819, British Library, Add. MS. 27711).

LIBRETTO: English (London: William Stockdale, 1819).

Heart of Midlothian, The, opera in three acts, an adaptation by Edward Loder of Carafa's *La prison d'Edimbourg* (1833, Paris); libretto (Eng) by Captain Rafter, after Scribe and Planard's text, itself based on Scott. First performance April 18, 1849, London, Princess's Theatre, with Herr Mengis (Duke of Argyle), Charles Braham (George Staunton), Miss Poole (Jeanie Deans), Miss Lanza (Effie Deans), and Mme. Nau (Madge Wildfire); conducted by Loder.

The setting is Edinburgh in the eighteenth century. Effie Deans has been sentenced to death for killing her illegitimate child, the son of George Staunton, who had seduced her. She is confined in the prison known as the "Heart of Midlothian." Her half sister, Jeanie, with the help of the Duke of Argyle, obtains a pardon for Effie from Queen Caroline, and Effie marries Staunton. Staunton is ultimately shot by a gypsy boy, his illegitimate son, who was in fact not killed by Effie years before but raised by the mother of Madge Wildfire, another of Staunton's conquests.

See the preceding entry and *Jeanie Deans* (1894) for other settings.

LIBRETTO: English (London: Charles Jefferys, n.d.).

Hearts on Fire, opera in one act by Roger Ames; libretto (Eng) by Laura Harrington. First performance May 11, 1995, Minneapolis, New Music Theater Ensemble, with Susan Lamberg (Claire), Ruth MacKensie (Mae), Bradley Greenwald (Tommy), and James Bohn; conducted by Thomas Linker; directed by Ben Krywosz; Linker (keyboards) and Shane Oslund (guitar).

The young Claire must cope with her depressive mother, Mae, who will not leave the house and thinks sex and love are evil. Claire becomes involved with Tommy, a contemporary, and the older Simon Rivers. Eventually she discovers that Claire's father shot his wife's lover and then himself many years ago. Mae drowns herself in the river, thereby freeing her daughter from her emotional burdens.

The score includes spoken dialogue, speeches, arias, and ensembles. It ends with a muted vocal quartet.

BIBLIOGRAPHY: Michael Anthony, "Minneapolis," *ON* LX (Sept. 1995), 62–63 [on premiere].

Heaven Ablaze in His Breast, opera in one act by Judith Weir; libretto (Eng) by the composer, after E. T. A. Hoffmann's *Der Sandmann* (1816). First performance October 5, 1989, Basildon, Essex, England, Towngate.

The story concerns the troubled Nathanael, tormented by his father's death, and the evil lawyer Coppelius, who is transformed into the barometer seller Coppola. Nathanael is captivated by the beautiful but distant Olimpia, daughter of Professor Spalanzani. She turns out to be a clockwork automaton. Returning to Clara, his first love, Nathanael is driven to madness and tries to throw her over a parapet. She is saved by her brother, but Nathanael, lured by the voice of Coppelius, jumps to his death.

Elements of the story may be found in Offenbach's *Les contes d'Hoffmann* (1881, Paris).

The worlds of ballet and opera are melded, whereby the singers are required to dance, and the dancers to sing.

Heavenfields, children's opera by Glenn Buhr; libretto (Eng). First performance June 1, 1995, Victoria, British Columbia, Pacific Opera Victoria, with Amanda Leigh (Lucretia) and Jay Bowen (Lobquin the Leprechaun).
BIBLIOGRAPHY: Robert Jordan, "Victoria, B.C.," *ON* LX (Sept. 1995), 61 [on premiere]).

Hedda Gabler, opera in a prologue and three acts by Edward Harper; libretto (Eng) by the composer based mainly on the translation of Ibsen's play by Michael Meyer. First performance June 5, 1985, Glasgow, King's Theatre, with Kathryn Harries (Hedda), Robert Dean (Tesman), Anne Mason (Mrs. Elvsted), William Neill (Loevberg), and Rodney Macann (Judge Brack); conducted by Diego Masson.
The title character, bored by her professor husband, George Tesman, schemes to ruin his rival, Loevberg, whose success, nurtured by Mrs. Elvsted, threatens Hedda's comfortable life. She traps Loevberg into killing himself but is then open to blackmail by Judge Brack, who knows what she has done. Her only solution is to shoot herself.
Among the musical highlights are a duet between Hedda and Loevberg.
See R. Ward's *Claudia Legare* (1978, Minneapolis) for another setting.
LIBRETTO: English (Oxford: Oxford University Press, Music Dept., 1985).
BIBLIOGRAPHY: Noel Goodwin, "Glasgow," *ON* L (Sept. 1985), 57–58 [on premiere]; Edward Harper, "An Ibsen Opera," *MT* CXXVI (1985), 334–37.

Heir of Vironi, or, Honesty the Best Policy, "operatic piece" in two acts by Henry Rowley Bishop, with Whitaker; libretto (Eng) by Isaac Pocock. First performance February 27, 1817, London, with Catherine Stephens.
The characters include Roberto, Ribaldi, Laurina, Phillipe, and Count Alberti.
SCORE: ms fs, autograph (1817, British Library, MS. Add. 27707).

Helena's Husband, opera in one act by Louis Gruenberg; libretto (Eng) by Philip Moeller, after his play. Composed 1938.
The work is based on Helen of Troy.
SCORE: ms score, holograph, ink (19??, NYPL).
LIBRETTO: English, typescript (carbon copy), holograph in ink (1938, NYPL).

Helen in Egypt, opera in one act by Jonathan Elkus; libretto by Jere Knight, after a poem by Hilda Doolittle. First performance November 30, 1970, Milwaukee, University of Wisconsin, Opera Theater.
In this version of the Greek myth, Ares claims he started the Trojan War, not Helen. Helen, now in exile, meets Achilles, and they become lovers.
Roles: Helen (sop), Ares (bar), and Achilles (ten).

Helen Retires, opera in three acts by George Antheil; libretto (Eng) by John Erskine, after his novel *The Private Life of Helen of Troy.* First performance February 28, 1934, New York, Juilliard School, with Marvel Biddle (Helen), Julius Heuhn (Achilles), Gean Greenwell (Eteoneus), Mordecai Bauman (Menelaos), Roland Partridge (Paris); conducted by Albert Stoessel.
This satirical treatment of the story of Helen of Troy begins, after the death of Helen's husband, Menelaos. In her quest for someone she can love, Helen searches for the ghost of Achilles on the Island of the Blest. She woos him back to life but eventually decides that they must go their separate ways before their love dies. Helen sends Achilles back to take his place among the ghosts. Believing that she has exhausted the

possibilities of life, she decides to wait for death, until a young fisherman appears, whereupon she decides not to die after all.

The text is a metrical spoof on ancient Greek verse, which is accompanied by Viennese waltzes.

LIBRETTO: English (Indianapolis and New York: Bobbs-Merrill Co., 1934).

Hello Out There, chamber opera in one act by Jack Beeson; libretto (Eng) by the composer, after William Saroyan's tragedy. First performance May 27, 1954, New York, Columbia University, Brander Matthews Theater, with Lena Gabrieli, Stephanie Turash, Ralph Farnsworth, Marvin Worden, and Lorenzo Herrera; conducted by Willard Rhodes; staged by Felix Brentano. First British performance June 4, 1963, London, Park Lane Opera Group, St. Pancras Town Hall, with Rhiannon James and Neil Howlett; conducted by Alan Boustead.

When a young man is arrested and jailed for raping the wife of a town resident, he convinces the jail's cook, a young girl, to fetch her father's gun in order to defend himself against the enraged husband and describes the happy life they will have once he has escaped. While the girl is gone, the husband and his friends appear. Not believing the young man's protestations that the wife is a slut, the husband shoots the young man. The girl returns to see the brutal end to her dreams of escape and happiness.

For a detailed description, see Eaton/*OP* I, 188–89.

Major roles: the girl (sop), the young man (bar), and the husband (ten).

SCORE: vs (New York: Mills Music, 1960).

BIBLIOGRAPHY: Olin Downes, "Columbia Stages Two New Operas," *NYT* (May 28, 1954), 18 [on premiere]; Harold Rosenthal, "London Opera Diary," *Opera* XIV (Aug. 1963), 567 [on British premiere].

DISCOGRAPHY: G. Gabrieli, J. Reardon, M. Worden, Columbia Chamber Orch.; cond. F. Waldman, Columbia ML 5265 (1958, 1 LP); the same, Desto DST 6451 (1965, 1 LP); reissued as Bay Cities BCD 1034 (1991, 1 CD).

Hell's Angels, chamber opera in two acts by Nigel Osborne; libretto (Eng) by David Freeman, after Oskar Panizza's play *Das Liebeskonzil*. First performance January 6, 1986, London, Opera Factory; conducted by Diego Masson; directed by David Freeman.

An allegorical treatment of the AIDS epidemic via an imagined punishment through syphilis of the members of the court of the Borgia Pope Alexander VI in 1494. Despite its historical and religious characters, the work, according to the libretto, "deals in myth and superstition rather than history or religion."

Among the characters are, from Heaven and Hell: Satan (bass), Salome (high sop), Helen of Troy (sop), Heloise (sop), Agrippina (sop), and Jesus (ten); from Earth, 1494: Pope Alexander VI (ten), Cesare Borgia (bass-bar), and Lucrezia Borgia (sop); and from Earth, today: the Pope (ten), the foreign minister (bass-bar), and the puppetmaster (bass).

LIBRETTO: English (London: Universal Edition, 1986).

Heloise and Abelard, opera in three acts by Charles M. Wilson; libretto (Eng) by Eugene Benson. First performance September 8, 1973, Toronto, O'Keefe Centre, Canadian Opera Company.

A treatment of the medieval lovers.

The work uses a prepared tape.

Heloise and Abelard, opera in two acts by Peter Tahourdin; libretto (Eng) by the composer. Composed 1991.

Scored for soprano, tenor, baritone, and chamber ensemble.

Also dramatic cantata by Elizabeth Maconchy (comp. 1978). See *Abelard and Eloise* for another setting.

LIBRETTO: English (Sydney: Pellinor, 1993).

Help, Help, the Globolinks!, opera in one act "for children and those who like children" by Gian Carlo Menotti; libretto (Eng) by the composer. First performance December 19, 1968, Hamburg, with William Workman (Tony), Edith Mathis (Emily), Arlene Saunders (Madame Euterpova), Ursula Boese (Penelope Newkirk), Franz Grundheber (Mr. Lavender-Gas), Noel Mangin (Dr. Turtlespit), Kurt Marschner (Timothy), and Raymond Wolansky (Dr. Stone); conducted by Mathias Lutzsch. First U.S. performance August 1, 1969, Santa Fe, with John Reardon, Marguerite Willauer, and Judith Blegen; conducted by Gustav Meier.

Set in contemporary America, the story concerns a busload of children who are stranded when the bus breaks down. It is surrounded by unearthly globolinks, who are driven back only by musical sounds. As a child goes off to get help, the remaining children are saved by the intervention of good music.

For a detailed description, see Eaton/*OP* II, 284–85.

Major roles: Emily (sop); Madame Euterpova, the music teacher (sop); Dr. Stone, Dean of St. Paul's School (high bar); Tony, the bus driver (bar); Timothy, the school janitor (ten); Miss Penelope Newkirk, the mathematics teacher (mezzo); Mr. Lavender-Gas, the literature professor (bar); and Dr. Turtlespit, the science professor (bass).

A simple vocal line and standard harmonies are typical of the score, set along with several electronic passages.

SCORE: vs (New York: G. Schirmer, 1969).

BIBLIOGRAPHY: review, *HiFi/MA* XIX (Nov. 1969), 25ff. [on U.S. premiere]; Winthrop Sargeant, review, *NY* XLV (Jan. 3, 1970), 44 [on U.S. premiere]; Harold C. Schonberg, "Menotti's Globolinks Invade Santa Fe," *NYT* (Aug. 18, 1969), 28 [on U.S. premiere].

Helvellyn, opera in four acts by George A. Macfarren; libretto (Eng) by John Oxenford, after Salomon Mosenthal's play *Der Sonnwendhof* (1857). First performance November 3, 1864, London, Covent Garden.

Monica, a widow, has inherited the Sonnwendhof, run by her foreman, Valentin, whom she wishes to wed. Her plans are interrupted by the appearance of the young Anna, who asks for shelter and attracts Valentin's interest. Anna rejects him, saying that she is cursed since her father has been labeled an arsonist. Monica, at first angered by Valentin's change of heart, relents and supports the two lovers. And when Anna's father turns out to be innocent and the real criminal dies, Anna and Valentin are united.

LIBRETTO: English (London: Cramer, [1864?]).

Henri Quatre, or, Paris in the Olden Times, musical romance in three acts by Henry Rowley Bishop; libretto (Eng) by Thomas Morton. First performance April 23, 1820, London, Covent Garden.

The duet "Oh, What a Gay and Joyous Scene" comes from Paisiello, and the act 3 finale from Mozart.

SCORE: ms fs (British Library, Add. MS. 36951).

Henrique, or, The Love Pilgrim, opera in three acts by William Michael Rooke; libretto (Eng) by John Thomas Haines. First performance May 2, 1839, London, Covent Garden.

Henry and Emma, or, The Nut-Brown Maid, all-sung "musical drama" by Thomas Arne; libretto (Eng) by Henry Bate Dudley, after Matthew Prior's poem *The Nut-Brown Maid.* First performance March 31, 1749, London, Covent Garden.

The son of an earl wins the love of a maid when he disguises himself as a man in exile and she agrees to marry him despite the hardships she thinks he must face.

LIBRETTO: English (London: T. Davies, 1774).

Henry Faust, one-character opera in three acts by Gregory Sullivan Isaacs; libretto (Eng) by the composer, after Goethe's *Faust.* First performance April 11, 1993, Forest Park, Illinois, Circle Theater.

SCORE: ms score, holograph (1993; photocopy, NYPL).

Heracles, opera in three acts by John Eaton; libretto (Eng) by Michael Fried, after Sophocles' *The Women of Trachis* and Seneca's *Hercules Oetaeus.* First performance (radio) October 10, 1968, RAI, Turin, Italy. First stage performance May 15, 1972, Bloomington, Indiana University.

After Heracles is victorious against King Erytus, he is deceived by his supposed friend Lichas into thinking that Iole, the dead king's daughter, is intended to bear him a child, since he hears a prophecy that the virgin daughter of an enemy will give birth to heroic sons from a son of Zeus. Deianira, wife of Heracles, believes that if she puts drops of blood from the slain zephyr Nessus on a robe, they will cause Heracles to love only her. She entrusts Lichas with the robe, but when she learns that the blood has made the robe deadly, she tries to warn Lichas; it is too late, however; horrified, she kills herself. Hyllus, the son of Heracles and Deianira, discovers the treachery of Lichas, aided by Iole. Lichas, attempting to escape, is killed by a bolt of lightning. The dying Heracles realizes that the prophecy will come true if Hyllus weds Iole.

For a detailed description, see Eaton/*OP* II, 109–10.

Major roles: Heracles (bar), Lichas (ten), Hyllus (ten), Deianira (mezzo), and Iole (sop).

Hercules, musical drama in three acts by George Frideric Handel; libretto (Eng) by Thomas Broughton, after Sophocles' *The Women of Trachis* and Ovid's *Metamorphoses.* First performance January 5, 1745, London (concert), with Henry Reinhold (Hercules), Miss Robinson (Dejanira), Elisabeth Duparc (Iole), John Beard (Hyllus), and Susanna Cibber (Lichas).

Dejanira is awaiting the return of Hercules, her husband, while their son Hyllus resolves to find his father. When Hercules appears he brings with him the captive princess Iole, whom Dejanira suspects of being involved with her husband. Dejanira gives Hercules a robe she had obtained from Nessus, killed long ago by Hercules, a garment she believes will revive Hercules's interest in her. The robe turns out to be poisonous, and Hercules dies agonizingly. Wracked by guilt, Dejanira is consoled by a priest, who says Hercules has been carried off to be with the gods on Olympus.

For a discussion of the work's genre and the reasons for its failure in 1745 and afterwards, see the article by Gilman listed below. He finds that *Hercules,* lying "ge-

nerically somewhere between oratorio and opera in text, score, and performance" (49), and between English and Italian opera, satisfied neither opera nor oratorio enthusiasts.
SCORE: vs (London: Novello, Ewer, [1877]).
BIBLIOGRAPHY: Todd S. Gilman, "Primary Sources: Handel's *Hercules* and Its Semiosis," *MQ* LXXXI (Fall 1997), 449–81.
DISCOGRAPHY: J. Smith, S. Walker, C. Denley, A. Rolfe, J. Tomlinson, P. Savidge, Monteverdi Choir, English Baroque Soloists; cond. J. E. Gardiner, Archiv ARC-423137-2 (1983, Hamburg, 2 LPs).

Hermann, or, The Broken Spear, musical drama in two acts by John Thomson; anonymous libretto (Eng). First performance October 27, 1834, London, Lyceum, with Henry Phillips (Hermann) and Harriet Waylett (Margaret).
    The music exhibits touches of Mozart and Weber.
SCORE: ms vs (1834, British Library, Add. MS. 33816–33818).

Hermione, The, or, Valour's Triumph, musical piece in one act by Thomas Attwood; libretto (Eng) by Thomas Dibdin. First performance London, April 5, 1800, London.

Hermiston, opera in three acts by Robin Orr; libretto (Eng) by Bill Bryden, after Robert Louis Stevenson's unfinished novel *Weir of Hermiston* (1896). First performance August 27, 1975, Edinburgh, King's Theatre.
    After Archie Weir protests his father's harshness at shipping off prisoners to be hanged, he is sent off to the family estate in Hermiston. When he finds out that his friend Frank has raped Archie's beloved, Christina, Archie becomes enraged and kills Frank. He is then sentenced to death by hanging.
    Major roles: Archie Weir (bar); Lord Hermiston, his father (bass); Frank (ten); and Christina (sop).

Hero, The, comic opera in three acts by Gian Carlo Menotti; libretto (Eng) by the composer. First performance June 1, 1976, Philadelphia, Opera Company of Philadelphia, with Nancy Shade (Barbara), Dominic Cossa (David), Diane Curry (Mildred), and David Griffith (Dr. Brainkoff); conducted by Christopher Keene.
    The plot concerns a man in Revenville, Pennsylvania, David Murphy, who has become famous because he has slept for ten years. He awakens just before he is about to break the world record for sleeping, and his wife, Mildred, and the town are in a state of panic because they see their chance to capitalize on his achievement jeopardized.
    Major roles: Barbara, David Murphy's cousin (sop); Mildred Murphy (mezzo); David Murphy, her husband (bar); and Dr. Brainkoff (ten).
BIBLIOGRAPHY: James Felton, "Menotti Creates a Delicious Opera for Bicentennial," *The Evening Bulletin*, Philadelphia (June 2, 1976), 21 [on premiere]; Robert Jacobson, "Reports: U.S.," *ON* XLI (Aug. 1976), 36–37 [on premiere].

Hero, The, television opera by Mark Bucci; libretto (Eng) by the composer, after Frank D. Gilroy's *Far Rockaway*. First performance September 24, 1965, New York.

Hero and Leander, operatic burletta in two acts by William Reeve; libretto (Eng) by Isaac Jackman. First performance 1787, London, Royalty Theatre, Goodman's Fields.
    A setting of the Greek myth about the tragic lovers.

LIBRETTO: English (London: J. Murray, 1787); in *The British Drama*, vol. 11 (London: J. Dicks, 1872).

Hero of the North, The, or, Gustavas Vasa, "historical musical drama" in five acts by Michael Kelly; libretto (Eng) by William Dimond. First performance February 19, 1803, London, Drury Lane Theatre. First U.S. performance April 2, 1804, Philadelphia, Chestnut Street Theatre.

The work is about the sixteenth-century Swedish king who led a victorious revolt against the ruling Danes. The setting is Dalecarlia, "a Northern Province in Sweden."

Major roles: Gustavus, Christiern, Arvida, Peterson, Laertes, Anderson, Sivard, Arnoldus, Christina, Augusta, Gustava, and Marina.

Presented as *Gustavas Vasa*, November 29, 1810, London, Covent Garden.
LIBRETTO: English, as *The Hero of the North* (London: 1803, Barker); as *Gustavas Vasa* (New York: Longworths, at the Dramatic Repository, Shakespeare-Gallery, Jan. 1812).

Herod, Do Your Worst, chamber Nativity opera by Bryan Kelly; libretto (Eng) by John Fuller. Composed 1968.

A contemporary setting of the story of the Nativity.

Another setting involving Herod and Jesus is Gabriel von Wayditch's *Jesus before Herod*, to a Hungarian text, translated into English for its posthumous premiere (1979, San Diego).

Heroes of the Lakes, a Tribute to the Brave, comic opera in two acts; anonymous libretto (Eng). First performance October 1, 1813, Baltimore.

About the Battle of Lake Erie.

He's Coming (via Slumborough, Snoozleton & Snoreham), opera in one act by Thomas German Reed; libretto by F. C. Burnand. First performance May 17, 1874, London, St. George's Hall.

Hester Prynne, opera in three acts by Avery Claflin; libretto (Eng) by Dorothea Claflin, after *The Scarlet Letter* by Nathaniel Hawthorne. First performance December 15, 1934, Hartford (one scene).

See *The Scarlet Letter* for other settings of Hawthorne's story.
SCORE: ms vs, selections (New York: American Composers Alliance, 1954).

He Who Gets Slapped, opera in three acts by Robert Ward; libretto (Eng) by Bernard Stambler, after Andreyev's play. First performance May 17, 1956, New York, Juilliard School, as *Pantaloon*, with Paul Ukena (Pantaloon), Regina Sarfaty (Zinida), and Ewan Harbrecht (Consuelo); conducted by Rudolph Thomas. Revised 1973.

A failed gentleman asks to be part of a circus that has come to town. The owner, Briquet, agrees to let the stranger play the part of Pantaloon, "he who gets slapped." The stranger intervenes in the lives of the circus people and prevents the fake Count Mancini from marrying off his daughter Consuelo, in love with the bareback rider Bezano, to the old Baron Regnard. Zinida, wife of Briquet and enamored herself of Bezano, discloses the clown's past failure at the end, but he succeeds in ruining the plans of various schemers and giving hope to the young lovers.

For a detailed description, see Eaton/*OP* I, 79.

Major roles: Count Mancini (ten), Briquet (bass-bar), Zinida (sop), Pantaloon (bar), Consuelo (sop), Bezano (ten), and Baron Regnard (bass-bar).

SCORE: vs (New York, 1961).
LIBRETTO: English (New York: Highgate Press, 1959).
BIBLIOGRAPHY: Howard Taubman, "Opera: 'Pantaloon' Has Its Premiere," *NYT* (May 18, 1956), 20 [on premiere].

Higglety Pigglety Pop!, or, There Must Be More to Life, fantasy opera in one act by Oliver Knussen; libretto (Eng) by Maurice Sendak and the composer. First performance (incomplete) October 13, 1984, Glyndebourne; preliminary version (Aug. 5, 1985, Glyndebourne); final version June 5, 1990, Los Angeles, Music Center.

Jennie, a Sealyham terrier, is certain that life contains more than creature comforts. She leave her elegant home and finds adventure with a Pig-in-Sandwich Board, a Cat-Milkman, a parlor maid, and a friendly Lion. At the conclusion she achieves her ambition by becoming a leading lady in the Mother Goose World Theater.
LIBRETTO: English (London: Faber, 19??).
BIBLIOGRAPHY: Martin Bernheimer, "Some Sonic Sendak at the Music Center," *Los Angeles Times* (June 9, 1990), F, 5 [on Los Angeles premiere].
VIDEO: Hetherington, Munro, Rhys-Williams, Buchan, Rees, Hardy, Gallacher, Jenkins, Richardson, London Sinfonietta, Glyndebourne Festival; cond. Knussen, Teldec 4509-97966-6; rev. Patrick J. Smith, *ON* LIX (Apr. 1, 1995), 52.

Highland Fair, The, or, Union of the Clans, Scottish ballad opera; libretto (Eng) by Joseph Mitchell. First performance March 20, 1731, London, Drury Lane Theatre, with Mr. Mills Jr. (Charles), Mr. Harper (Donald), Mr. Paget (Duncan), Mr. Fielding (Alaster), Mrs. Robert (Davy), Miss Vaughan (Jeany), and Mrs. Thurmond (Maggy).

The majority of the tunes come from Allan Ramsay's collection *The Tea-Table Miscellany* (1724, London).
LIBRETTO: English, with ballad airs (London, 1731); repr. Rubsamen/*BO*, vol. 25 , *Scottish Ballad Operas II: History and Politics* (1974).

Highland Reel, The, comic opera in four acts by William Shield; libretto (Eng) by John O'Keeffe. First performance November 6, 1788, London, Covent Garden, with Mr. Aickin (Laird of Coll), Mr. Powell (Laird of Raasay), Mr. Quick (McGillpin), Mr. Johnstone (Sandy), Mr. Bannister (Sergeant Jack), and Miss Reynolds (Jenny). First U.S. performance February 11, 1793, Charleston, South Carolina, Charleston Theatre.

The work takes place in Coll and Raasay. It concerns the orphaned Jenny, who has been brought up by the mean-spirited McGillpin, a steward. She falls in love with Sandy, a peasant (in reality the son of the Laird of Coll). Sandy is about to be taken away by a recruiting sergeant when the Laird of Coll appears and rescues the lovers.

Its music includes a march borrowed from Handel's *Judas Maccabeus* and Scottish airs.
SCORE: short score (London: Longman & Broderip, ca. 1788).
LIBRETTO: English (London: Longman and Broderip, [1788?]; New York: John Harrison, 1794).

Highwayman, The, romantic comic opera in three acts by Reginald De Koven; book (Eng) by Harry B. Smith. First performance December 13, 1897, New York, with Edwin White (Sir John Hawkhurst), Joseph O'Hara (Dick Fitzgerald), Hilda Clark (Lady Constance), and Jerome Sykes (Foxy Quiller). The work was revived on May 2, 1917, New York, 44th Street Theatre, for twenty-two performances.

The action takes place in England at the close of the eighteenth century. Dick Fitzgerald has been brought to financial ruin by Sir John Hawkhurst in a game of chance. In order to support himself Fitzgerald becomes a highwayman named Captain Scarlet. He falls in love with Lady Constance and receives a pardon, but they are thwarted by Hawkhurst, who steals the reprieve, which is taken back at gunpoint by Lady Constance. Comic relief is provided by Foxy Quiller, the constable.

Major roles: Dick Fitzgerald, an Irish soldier of fortune (ten); Lady Constance, a belle of the court (sop); Sir John Hawkhurst, a government attaché (bass); and Foxy Quiller, a constable (bar).

The composer's *Foxy Quiller** (1900) is a sequel.

SCORE AND LIBRETTO: vs (New York: T. B. Harms & Co., 1898); unpublished typescript, 1897 (Waltham, Mass.: Brandeis University); repr. ed. Orly Krasner, *NAMT*, vol. 15 (1994).

Highway 1, U.S.A., melodrama in one act by William Grant Still; libretto (Eng) by Verna Arvey. First performance March 11, 1963, Miami, University of Miami.

Nate, raised by his brother, Bob, and by Mary, Bob's wife, leads a dissolute life despite the efforts of the couple to support him and give him a chance to finish his education. Mary, embittered, tells Aunt Lou of her hatred of Nate. After returning home once again Nate makes a play for Mary. When she resists, he stabs her. Thinking that Mary is dead, Bob shifts the blame to himself and says that he attacked his wife. But Mary survives and says that it was Nate who tried to kill her. Bob finally refuses to help Nate anymore, and Nate is taken away. Bob pledges to Mary that they will have a better life.

Major roles: Mary (sop), Bob (bar), Nate (ten), and Aunt Lou (mezzo/sop).

For a detailed description, see Kornick/*RAO*, 301–3.

Hindenburg, "documentary video opera," with music by Steve Reich; video by Beryl Korot. First performance (excerpt) June 23, 1997, Bonn, Oper der Stadt Bonn. First complete performance May 26, 1998, Charleston, South Carolina, Spoleto USA Festival; conducted by Bradley Lubman.

The work examines the election of Paul von Hindenburg as president of Germany in 1925, the crash of the giant airship *Hindenburg,* named in his honor, in 1937 in Lakehurst, New Jersey, and the subsequent world war.

Hindenburg is set for five voices, chamber ensemble, and large video projection screen.

Hipopera: Mod Traviata, Mod Faust, Mod Carmen, Mod Aïda, work in four acts by Martin Kalmanoff; libretto (Eng) by the composer. First performance (of *Mod Traviata*) May 4, 1972, "Mike Douglas Show"; *Mod Carmen, Mod Traviata*, April 9, 1977, Boise, Idaho, Boise State University.

The music is based on Verdi's *La Traviata* and *Aïda*, Gounod's *Faust*, and Bizet's *Carmen.*

Hippolytus, opera in two acts by Learmont Drysdale; libretto (Eng) by Gilbert Murray, a translation of Euripides' tragedy. First performance December 1905, Glasgow, Athenaeum.

A treatment of Phaedra's ill-fated love for Hippolytus.

Hired Hand, The, opera in one act by Robert Milano; libretto (Eng), after Robert Frost's poem *The Death of the Hired Man* (1914). First performance March 23, 1959,

New York, Carl Fischer Hall, with Lucille Perret (the wife), Peter Johl (the farmer), and Buddy Nadler (the narrator); conducted by Jerome L. Keller.

A farmer and his wife argue whether to take back an old hired hand who has returned to ask for work. When the farmer goes to tell the man of their decision, he discovers that the aged hand has died.

BIBLIOGRAPHY: Eric Salzman, "1-Act Opera Based on Poem by Frost," *NYT* (Mar. 24, 1959) [on premiere].

His Excellency, comic opera in two acts by F. Osmond Carr; libretto (Eng) by William S. Gilbert. First performance 1894, London. First U.S. performance October 14, 1895, New York, Broadway Theater.

The story concerns a joke-playing governor who chooses a commoner as his target, only to discover that his victim is the disguised king.

SCORE: vs (London: J. Williams; New York: E. Schuberth, 1894).

LIBRETTO: English (New York: T. B. Harms, [1894]).

His Majesty, or, The Court of Vingolia, comic opera in two acts by Alexander Mackenzie; libretto (Eng) by F. C. Burnand and R. C. Lehmann, with additional lyrics by Adrian Ross. First performance February 20, 1897, London, Savoy Theatre, with George Grossmith (King Ferdinand).

Complications ensue when King Ferdinand, who has been betrothed to Lucilla Chloris, falls in love with Felice, a peasant, and Lucilla, arriving for her arranged marriage, prefers Prince Max of Baluria.

Hit or Miss, comic opera in two acts by Charles Smith; libretto (Eng) by Isaac Pocock. First performance February 26, 1810, London, Lyceum. First U.S. performance December 5, 1810, New York.

H.M.S. Pinafore, or, The Lass That Loved a Sailor, nautical comic opera in two acts by Arthur S. Sullivan; libretto (Eng) by William S. Gilbert. First performance May 25, 1878, London, Opéra Comique, with George Grossmith (the Rt. Hon. Sir Joseph Porter), Rutland Barrington (Captain Corcoran), George Power (Ralph Rackstraw), Richard Temple (Dick Deadeye), Emma Howson (Josephine), Jessie Bond (Hebe), and Harriet Everard (Little Buttercup). The pair's first great success. First U.S. performance (in a pirated and altered version) November 25, 1878, Boston. First U.S. performance in the original London version December 1, 1879, New York, Fifth Avenue Theatre; conducted by the composer.

A satire on class distinctions, the plot involves mistaken identities. Ralph Rackstraw, a lowly seaman, is forbidden from marrying Josephine, daughter of Captain Corcoran, Ralph's commander. The Rt. Hon. Sir Joseph Porter, First Lord of the Admiralty, also has his eye on Josephine. Ralph's position is further complicated by the evil machinations of Dick Deadeye, another sailor. Everything is set right at the end, when Little Buttercup reveals that Ralph is of elevated birth after all. He was switched when he was born with Captain Corcoran, who is really just a commoner. Ralph, now a captain, is free to marry Josephine, suddenly of a lower station, and the Admiral is consoled by the attentions of Hebe, his cousin.

Major roles: the Rt. Hon. Sir Joseph Porter, K.C.B., First Lord of the Admiralty (bar); Captain Corcoran, commander of the *Pinafore* (bar); Ralph Rackstraw, able seaman (ten); Dick Deadeye, able seaman (bass); Josephine, the captain's daughter (sop); Hebe, Sir Joseph's first cousin (mezzo); and Mrs. Cripps, called Little Buttercup (alto).

Among the many well-known songs are "I'm Called Little Buttercup," the rousing "A British Tar" (act 1), and Ralph's plaintive "Farewell My Own" (act 2).

DISCOGRAPHY: M. Green, E. Halman, R. Walker, L. Osborn, L. Rands, M. Harding, D. Fancourt, J. Gillingham, R. Flynn, D'Oyly Carte Opera Co.; cond. I. Godfrey, Richmond/London RS 62003 (2 LPs); G. Baker, J. Cameron, R. Lewis, Pro Arte Orch., Glyndebourne Festival Chorus; cond. M. Sargent, EMI Classics 2-CDMB 64397 (2 CDs); F. Palmer, R. Evans, M. Schade, T. Allen, R. Suart, D. Adams, Welsh National Opera Orch. and Chorus; cond. C. Mackerras, Telarc CD 80374 (1 CD).

Hob's Opera. See **Flora.**

Hofer, or, The Tell of the Tyrol, historical opera in three acts, an adaptation by Henry Rowley Bishop of Gioacchino Rossini's *Guillaume Tell* (1829, Paris); libretto (Eng) translated by James R. Planché, after E. de Jouy and Bis's text. First performance May 1, 1830, London, Drury Lane Theatre. First U.S. performance September 19, 1831, New York. A version by Fitzball was performed in 1832 in London.

A telling of the story of Andreas Hofer, a Tyrolean hero along the lines of William Tell. Other characters include Donay and Job Spokewoppen, two traitors; Josephine, a young orphan; and Marie, Hofer's wife.

See *Guillaume Tell* for another version. *The Archers** is yet another setting of the story of William Tell.

SCORE: vs (London: D'Almaine, [1830]).

LIBRETTO: English, Fitzball version (London: J. Cumberland, [1832]; New York: Samuel French, 1856).

Holly from the Bongs, Nativity opera in one act by Gordon Crosse; libretto (Eng) by Alan Garner. First performance December 9, 1974, Manchester, England.

Holy Blood and Crescent Moon, opera in two acts by Stewart Copeland; libretto (Eng) by Susan Shirwen. First performance October 10, 1989, Cleveland, Cleveland Opera, with Edward J. Crafts (Grand Wazir), Gloria Parker (Dahlia), Tom Emlyn Williams (the Imam), Douglas Stevens (Abdullah), Joe Garrison (Edmund), Maria Berg (Eleanor), and James Rensink (King Tancred); conducted by Imre Pallo; directed by David Bamberger.

The work, set in the Holy Land during the Crusades, concerns the doomed love of the Frankish king, Edmund, and Dahlia, daughter of the Grand Wazir.

BIBLIOGRAPHY: John Rockwell, review, *NYT* (Oct. 12, 1989), C, 26 [on premiere].

Holy Devil, The, opera in three acts by Nicolas Nabokov; libretto (Eng) by Stephen Spender and the composer. First performance April 18, 1958, Louisville, Kentucky Opera Association, with Richard Dales (deputy), William Pickett (the Prince), Russell Hammar (the Grand Duke), Joel Ebersole (the doctor), Robert Fischer (Rasputin), Audrey Nossaman (the Empress), Audrey Sanborn (Anna), and Larry St. Claire (the Czarevich); conducted by Moritz Bomhard. Revised and expanded into three acts, with a text by Frederick Goldbeck, as *Der Tod des Grigori Rasputin*, November 27, 1959, Cologne, with Denise Duval, Hanna Ludwig, Frans Andersson, Hans Schachtschneider, and Albert Weikenmeier; conducted by Joseph Rosenstock; produced by Günther Rennert.

A treatment of the life of the Russian monk Rasputin, culminating with his murder.

The music includes traces of themes from popular music of the period and from the Russian Orthodox liturgy.

SCORE: vs, as *Rasputin's End* (Paris, 1959).
DISCOGRAPHY: Members of the Kentucky Opera Assn; Louisville Orch.; cond. M. Bomhard, Louisville Phil. Society, LOU-594 (1959, Louisville, Ky.).

Home, Sweet Home, or, The Rantz des Vaches, opera in three acts by Henry Rowley Bishop; libretto (Eng) by Isaac Pocock. First performance March 19, 1829, London, Covent Garden; a sequel to *Clari.**

Roles: Florine, Lisette, Claudine, Edward, Mme. Germance, La Roche, and Natz.

Joseph Weigl's *Schweizerfamilie* (1809, Vienna) was given as *The Swiss Family, or Home, Sweet Home*, June 27, 1828, London, Surrey Theatre, with the text translated by Charles Somerset.
SCORE: ms fs, autograph (1828–29, British Library, MS. Add. 27724).
LIBRETTO: English (London: Kirby, 1829).

Honest Frauds, musical farce in two acts by Charles Edward Horn; libretto (Eng) by J. Lunn. First performance July 29, 1830, London, Little Theatre in the Haymarket.

Honest Yorkshireman, The, ballad opera in one act, arranged and composed by Henry Carey; libretto (Eng) by Carey. First performance July 15, 1735, London, Little Theatre in the Haymarket. First American performance March 2, 1753, New York.

Arabella is supposed to wed a man of her father's choosing, a Yorkshireman. The intended bridegroom is intercepted, however, by Gaylove, Arabella's beloved, who convinces him to change his clothes into something more "fashionable," which allows Gaylove to appear at his beloved's house in the hoodwinked man's clothing and pass himself off as Arabella's future husband.

For a detailed description, see Fiske/*ETM*, 123–24.
LIBRETTO: English (London, 1736); repr. Rubsamen/*BO*, vol. 27 (1974).

Honey Moon, The, comic opera by William Linley; libretto (Eng) by the composer. First performance January 7, 1797, London, Drury Lane Theatre, with Mr. Kelly (Sir George Orbit), Mr. Suett (Sir William Wellbred), Mr. Palmer (Captain Belmont), Miss Pope (Lady Wellbred), Miss Leake (Emmeline), Miss Arne (Dorinda), Miss De Camp (Floretta), and Mrs. Bland (Dina).
LIBRETTO: English (London: C. Lowndes, 1797).

Honey Moon, The, comedy in five acts, an arrangement of *Matrimony,** by James Hewitt and Michael Kelly; libretto (Eng) by James Tobin. First performance January 31, 1805, London, Drury Lane Theatre, with John Bannister (Rolando), Mr. Collins (Jaquez), Mr. Bartley (Montalban), Miss Duncan (Juliana), Miss Mellon (Volante), and Miss De Camp (Zamora); May 17, 1805, New York.

The setting is Madrid.

Major roles: Duke of Aranza, in love with Juliana; Count Montalban, in love with Volante; Rolando, rejected by Juliana; Balthazar, a painter; Jaquez, Aranza's servant; and Juliana, Volante, and Zamora, Balthazar's daughters.
LIBRETTO: English (London: Longman et al., 1805; Philadelphia: E. Bronson, 1805).

Hooligan, The, opera in one act by Thomas Beversdorf; libretto (Eng), after Anton Chekhov's *The Bear*. Composed 1969.

Hoosier Tale, A, opera in three acts by Walter Kaufmann; libretto (Eng) by the composer. First performance July 30, 1966, Bloomington, Indiana, Indiana University; conducted by the composer.

The plot, centering on the conflicts between Indians and settlers in Indiana at the beginning of the nineteenth century, follows the unhappy story of William Conner, a white trader, and Mekinges Anderson, his Indian wife. They are separated when Mekinges is forced to go with her tribe, according to tribal law, and Conner is ordered to stay in Indiana by the U.S. government.

The work includes musical quotations from "Yankee Doodle Dandy" and "The Star Spangled Banner." It was composed for the 150th anniversary of Indiana's statehood.
BIBLIOGRAPHY: Allen Hughes, review, *NYT* (July 29, 1966), 20.

Hopitu (Hopi People), opera in one act by Lois Albright; libretto (Eng) by Milo William Billingsley, after Hopi legends. First performance (concert) February 16, 1955, New York, Carnegie Hall, with Angelene Collins, Charles Curtis, Robert Morris, and James Ellington, the Lois Albright Vocal Ensemble, and a company of Hopi Indian singers; conducted by the composer.

The work is based on Hopi Indian chants.
SCORE: vs (n.p., n.d.).
BIBLIOGRAPHY: review, "'Hopitu' Opera Sung," *NYT* (Feb. 17, 1955), 22 [on premiere].

Hopper's Wife, opera by Stewart Wallace; libretto (Eng) by Michael Korie. First performance June 14, 1997, Long Beach, California, Long Beach Opera, Carpenter Theatre, with Juliana Gondek (Hedda), Lucy Schaufer (Ava), and Chris Pedro Trakas (Hopper); conducted by Michael Barrett.

The work, which includes episodes of nudity and pornography, concerns the abused wife of artist Edward Hopper; she is transformed into the columnist Hedda Hopper. The story also involves the actress Ava Gardner, as well as other real and imagined personages.
BIBLIOGRAPHY: Daniel Cariaga, "Long Beach," *ON* LXII (Oct. 1997), 48 [on premiere]; Mark Swed, "'Hopper's Wife'—Not for the Faint of Art," *Los Angeles Times* (June 16, 1997), F, 1 [on premiere].

Horspfal, opera in two acts by Eric Stokes; libretto (Eng) by Alvin Greenberg. First performance February 15, 1969, Minneapolis, Center Opera Association, Tyrone Guthrie Theater, with James Bower (the Indian) and Sarita Roche (Betsy Ross); conducted by Thomas Nee; directed by H. Wesley Balk.

The story covers the unhappy experiences of the Indian with the white invaders. He has to deal with Betsy Ross, who talks about racial purity, a preacher (represented by film clips of John Wayne), and others.

The name of the opera is a combination of horse opera and the Parsifal-like main character.

For a detailed description, see Eaton/*OP* II, 112–13.

Major roles: Indian (bar) and Crows (sop, sop/mezzo, ten, bar); Betsy Ross (sop).
BIBLIOGRAPHY: Harold C. Schonberg, review, *NYT* (Feb. 17, 1969), 30 [on premiere].

Hoshi-San, grand opera in three acts by Wassili Leps; libretto (Eng) by John Luther Long. First performance May 21, 1909, Philadelphia, Operatic Society, with Isabel Buchanan (Hoshi-San), Frederick Freemantel (Ji-Saburo); conducted by the composer.

The setting is Japan in 1688. Hoshi-San, a dancer, has been imprisoned for falling in love with the daimyo Ji-Saburo, who has gone off to war. Ji-Saburo returns, but he has been blinded by his compatriots for choosing love over honor. As he and Hoshi-San try to escape, they are surrounded by samurai warriors, who force them into the desert to die.

For a detailed description, see Hipsher/*AO*, 292–94.
LIBRETTO: English (Philadelphia: George T. Haly, 1909).

Hospital for Fools, An, ballad opera by Thomas Arne; libretto (Eng) by James Miller. First performance November 15, 1739, London, Drury Lane Theatre. Given only twice.
LIBRETTO: English (London: Harrison, 1781).

Hotel, opera in two parts by Orlando Gough; libretto (Eng) by Caryl Churchill. First performance April 24, 1997, London, Second Stride at The Place, with Jenny Miller, Richard Chew, Wayne Ellington, Gabrielle McNaughton, and Colin Poole; choreographed by Ian Spink; designed by Lucy Bevan.

In part 1, "Eight Rooms," six couples (including two adulterers), two individuals, and a human television set enter the same hotel room, unpack, and go to bed, without taking note of anyone else around them. They awake the next morning and have breakfast.

In the second part, "Two Nights," parts of two diaries are sung and danced by the two protagonists.
BIBLIOGRAPHY: Rodney Milnes, "Hotel," *Opera* (July 1997), 866–67 [on premiere].

Hotel Eden, chamber opera in three acts by Henry Mollicone; libretto (Eng) by Judith Fein, after the Book of Genesis. First performance November 25, 1989, San Jose, California, Opera San José; conducted by Barbara Day Turner. Revived June 1995, New York, New York University, Reimann Opera Theater; conducted by Michel Singher; directed by Nancy Rhodes.

The plot, set at the Hotel Eden, concerns three difficult marriages drawn from the Bible but given a feminist viewpoint. Act 1 involves Adam and Eve, who check into the hotel and meet Lilith, Adam's angry first wife. In the second, Mr. and Mrs. Noah arrive, whereupon Mr. Noah gets drunk, causing his wife to find solace with the staff. In the third, the aged and childless Abraham and Sarah visit the hotel for some rest to find, happily, that Sarah is pregnant.

Scored for chamber ensemble, the work includes elements of rock, jazz, and the American musical theater.
BIBLIOGRAPHY: Martin Bernheimer, review, *Los Angeles Times* (Nov. 29, 1989), F, 3 [on premiere]; William Ratliff, *ON* LIV (Feb. 17, 1990), 44 [on premiere].

Hotel for Criminals, satire in two acts by Stanley Silverman; libretto (Eng) by Richard Foreman, after Louis Feulliade's series of silent crime films. First performance August 14, 1974, Lenox, Massachusetts, Lenox Arts Center.

The setting is Paris just before the outbreak of World War I. The action centers on the movie criminal Fantomas; Judex, the detective pursuing him; the lovers Max and Helen; the sexy Irma Vep; and the daughter of Fantomas, Helene, with whom Judex has fallen in love.

Major roles: Max Beauchamp (ten), Fantomas (bar), Judex (bass), Helene (sop), and Irma Vep (mezzo).

For a detailed description, see Kornick/*RAO*, 283–84.
SCORE: vs, ms (1974) (NYPL, photocopy).
LIBRETTO: English, in Richard Foreman, *Love & Science: Selected Music-Theatre Texts* (New York: Theatre Communications Group, 1991).

Houdini, "circus opera" by Peter Schat; libretto (Eng) by Adrian Mitchell. First performance August 4, 1979, Aspen, Colorado.

SCORE: vs (Amsterdam: Donemus, [1977]).

Hound of Heaven, The, sacred music drama by Humphrey John Stewart; libretto (Eng) by Francis Thompson. First performance April 24, 1924, San Francisco.
SCORE: vs (New York: J. Fischer & Brother, 1924).

House to Be Sold, A, comic opera in two acts by Michael Kelly, after Dalayrac's *Maison à vendre* (1800, Paris); libretto (Eng) by James Cobb, after A. Duval's text. First performance November 17, 1802, London, Drury Lane Theatre. First U.S. performance May 25, 1803, New York, Park Theatre.

Hovel, The, afterpiece in two acts by Samuel Arnold; libretto (Eng). First performance May 23, 1797, London, Drury Lane Theatre.

Howard, opera in one act by John David Earnest; libretto (Eng) by Tray Christopher. First performance March 1987, New York, Golden Fleece.

In this fanciful treatment of the final days of Howard Hughes, Howard, confined to a white room, escapes through the window when he is left unguarded. He meets people from various stages of his life, including his family and an old hag, who says that his life and death are just like everyone else's. At the end he is again sitting in the white room.

For a description, see Summers/*OOA*, 101–3.

Major roles: Howard (bar), mother (sop), Auntie (mezzo), starlet (sop), and guard 4/hag (male voice).
SCORE: ms vs, holograph (1980, photocopy, NYPL).

How to Be Happy, afterpiece in five acts by Samuel Arnold; libretto (Eng) by George Brewer. First performance August 9, 1794, London, Little Theatre in the Haymarket.

How to Make Love, opera in one act by Lawrence Widdoes; libretto (Eng) by C. C. Widdoes. First performance January 13, 1994, New York, Columbia University, Kathryn Bache Miller Theatre, with Laura Hemphill (Sharon), Elena Commendador and Alan Hineline (mannequins), Bejun Mehta (street musician), Tony Dillon (shop proprietor), Kyle Pfortmiller (sex-book author), Elizabeth Weigle (his companion), and Lawrence Harris (the masher); conducted by Glen Cortese; designed by Adam Mead Faletti; directed by Pamela Cederquist.

The story centers around Sharon, a young saleswoman, who makes up for her lack of a love life through fantasies engendered by how-to-do-it books on sex that include mannequins that come to life. All the while she has to fend off the unwanted attentions of a group of male admirers.
SCORE: orchestral score, ms (copy; NYPL).
BIBLIOGRAPHY: Bernard Holland, "Of Romance, Sex and Fashion," *NYT* (Jan. 15, 1994), I, 11 [on premiere].

Huckleberry Finn, opera in two acts by Hall Overton; libretto (Eng) by the composer and Judith Stampfer, after Mark Twain. First performance May 20, 1971, New York, Juilliard School, with David Hall (Huck), Pamela Hebert (Miss Watson), Lenus Carlson (Huck's father), David Wilder (the King), and William Bumstead (the Duke); conducted by Dennis Russell Davies; directed by William Woodman.

The story covers Huck and Jim rafting down the river and how the King and the Duke separate the boys from their dinner and a community from its money.
BIBLIOGRAPHY: Frank Merkling, "New York," *ON* XXXVI (Sept. 1971), 22 [on premiere]; Winthrop Sergeant, "Huckleberry Hash," *NY* XLVII (May 29, 1971), 57 [on premiere].

Hugh the Drover, romantic ballad opera in two acts by Ralph Vaughan Williams; libretto (Eng) by Harold Child. First performance July 4, 1924, London, Royal College of Music. First professional performance 1924, London, His Majesty's Theatre, with Mary Lewis, Tudor Davies, and Frederic Collier; conducted by Malcolm Sargent. First U.S. performance February 21, 1928, Washington, D.C. Revised in 1959.

This tale, set in the Cotswolds in about 1812, involves winning the day against all odds. Hugh, a drover, fights a boxing match with John the butcher for the hand of the lovely Mary, daughter of the constable. Despite the uneven match, Hugh is victorious in the end. He is accused of being a spy for the French and put in the stocks, but when the sergeant comes to take him away, the law officer recognizes him and takes away John in his stead, leaving Hugh with Mary.

For a detailed plot synopsis, see K/*KOB*, 1119–21; K/*NKOB*, 845–46.

Major roles: Hugh (ten), John (bass-bar), and Mary (sop).

The work employs genuine English folk songs and a psalm-tune. Among the highlights is "A Song of the Road," which Hugh sings to Mary when they first meet.
SCORES: vs (London: Curwen [1951]); rev. ed. London: J. Curwen, New York: G. Schirmer, 1977).

Humorous Lieutenant, The, or, Alexander's Successors, musical play in three acts by Henry Rowley Bishop; libretto (Eng) by Frederick Reynolds, after Beaumont and Fletcher. First performance January 18, 1817, London, Covent Garden.

Roles: Eudocia, Phocyon, the Lieutenant, and Sinon.
SCORE: ms fs, autograph (1817, British Library, Add. MS. 27710).

Hundred Nights, The. See Jenny, or, The Hundred Nights.

Hunted, The, historical drama in one act by Martin Mailman; libretto (Eng) by the composer, after the play by Morton Fine and David Friedkin. First performance April 27, 1959, Rochester, New York, Eastman School; conducted by Frederick Fennell; directed by Leonard Treash.

The work is set in Kansas shortly after the American Civil War. Clay Chandler comes to the home of Ellen and her father, Landry, saying that he is fleeing from Hesse's band of outlaws and is being sought by them because he has informed on them in an anonymous letter to the sheriff. They agree to hide him and, when Hesse arrives, tell him that Clay is no longer in their home. Clay is seen by Mrs. Tilbert, the local gossip, however, and Ellen is forced to say that Clay is one of the father's Civil War comrades. Clay goes to testify at the trial of one of the captured outlaws and is freed after giving evidence, while the outlaw is hanged. Landry accuses Clay of cowardice for dragging Ellen into the deception but, remembering his own desertion during the war, supports Ellen's desire to help Clay. Hesse comes looking for Clay and is about to shoot him when Landry points a rifle at the outlaw. Hesse shoots Landry, killing him, and Clay shoots Hesse.

For a description, see Summers/*OOA*, 205–6.

Roles: Ellen Landry (sop), Clay Chandler (ten), Vance Landry (bass-bar), Mrs. Tilbert (alto/mezzo), and Hesse (bar).
BIBLIOGRAPHY: review, "Rochester Fete Begins," *NYT* (Apr. 28, 1959), 41 [on premiere].

Hunted The, opera in one act by Dwight Gustafson; libretto (Eng). First performance May 26, 1960, Greenville, South Carolina, Bob Jones University.

Hunter of the Alps, The, comic opera in three acts by Michael Kelly; libretto (Eng) by William Dimond. First performance July 3, 1804, London, Little Theatre in the Haymarket. First U.S. performance, arranged by James Hewitt, May 22, 1805, New York, Park Theatre.

Hunting of the Snark, The, children's entertainment in one act by Ezra Laderman; text (Eng), after the poem of Lewis Carroll. First performance (concert) March 25, 1961, New York, Hunter College. First stage performance April 13, 1978, New York.

The characters of the work, in searching for the snark, an unknown creature, actually explore their own relationships. They find the snark at the end, only to discover that he is really a boojum, and when a snark turns out to be a boojum, it disappears.

Hunting of the Snark, The, children's opera in one act by James Wilson; libretto (Eng), after Lewis Carroll. First performance January 5, 1965, Dublin, Royal Irish Academy of Music.

Hunting of the Snark, The, opera by Edwin Roberts; libretto (Eng) by Bill Tchkirides, after Lewis Carroll. First performance September 9, 1971, New York.
BIBLIOGRAPHY: A. Hughes, review, *NYT* (Sept. 10, 1971), 71 [on premiere].

Hunt the Slipper, musical farce in two acts by Samuel Arnold; libretto (Eng) by Henry Ryder Knapp. First performance August 21, 1784, London, Little Theatre in the Haymarket. First U.S. performance May 31, 1795, New York, Park Theatre.
LIBRETTO: English ([Dublin]: Booksellers, 1792).

Hurlothrumbo, or, The Super-Natural, burlesque by Samuel Johnson; libretto (Eng) by the composer. First performance March 29, 1729, London, Little Theatre in the Haymarket, with Johnson (Lord Flame).

The nonsensical plot's title character's full name is "King Soarentherial, Dologodelmo, Hurlothrumbo."
LIBRETTO: English (London: T. Walker and J. Schuckburgh, 1729).

Hydrogen Jukebox, The, music theater in two acts by Philip Glass; libretto (Eng) by Allen Ginsberg. First performance (concert) April 22, 1990, Philadelphia. First performance (stage) May 26, 1990, Charleston, Spoleto Festival USA; conducted by Martin Goldray.

This work treats such subjects as the Middle East, nuclear war, a dying planet, and the Iran-contra scandal. The title comes from Ginsberg's poetry: "listening to the crack of doom on the hydrogen jukebox."

It is set for six vocalists and chamber ensemble.
BIBLIOGRAPHY: Peter G. Davis, review, *New York* XXIV (May 27, 1991), 69.

Hymen, operatic interlude by Michael Arne; libretto (Eng) by Allen. First performance January 23, 1764, London, Drury Lane Theatre.

I

I Am . . . in Search of John Clare, opera by Robin Grant; libretto (Eng), after John Clare's poetry and prose. First performance November 12, 1994, London, Royal Northern College of Music, The Daily Telegraph Theatre, with Daniel Hoadley and Thomas Guthrie (the young and old Clare, respectively); conducted by Jonathan Brett; produced and designed by Jennifer Hamilton.

The story is based on John Clare, a nineteenth-century rural poet from Northamptonshire, who spent the last decades of his life in insane asylums.

BIBLIOGRAPHY: Michael Kennedy, review, *Opera* XLVI (Jan. 1995), 113–14 [on premiere].

I Am the Way, "scenes from the life of Christ" in four acts by Jerome Hines, orchestrated by Ralph Hermann; libretto (Eng) by the composer. First performance March 24, 1959, South Orange, New Jersey, with the composer (Jesus Christ). First professional performance April 7, 1968, New York, Metropolitan Opera House, with Hines, Ezio Flagello, Carlotta Ordassy, Nedda Casei, Calvin Marsh, and Chris LaChona; conducted by Ralph Hermann.

The derivative music, which has many similarities to nineteenth-century opera, includes Christ's aria that ends act 2, a setting of the Lord's Prayer.

The composer, a leading bass at the Metropolitan Opera for many years, intended this work to be the first part of a trilogy.

SCORE: vs ([n.p., 1967]; LCCN: 84-67708).

LIBRETTO: Russian-English, for July 7, 1993, performance in Moscow (Moscow: Bolshoi Theater, [1993]).

BIBLIOGRAPHY: Donal Henahan, "Jerome Hines's Opera Has Premiere," *NYT* (Apr. 18, 1968), 56 [on professional premiere].

Ib and Little Christina, "picture in three panels" by Franco Leoni; libretto (Eng) by Basil Hood, after the story by Hans Christian Andersen. First performance November 14, 1901, London, Savoy.

LIBRETTO: English (London: Chappell, 1901); promptbook, typescript (NYPL).

I Can't Stand Wagner, opera in one act by Seymour Barab; libretto (Eng) by the composer, after the story *Floyd and the Eumenides* by Evelyn E. Smith. First performance December 12, 1986, New York, Singer's Forum.

When a composer's masterpiece, "The Zeus Symphony," receives its premiere in Athens, it is praised by all but its namesake. Zeus's distaste for the atonal score makes him send the Three Furies after the hapless composer.

SCORE: vs (New York: American Music Center, 1985).

Icarus, "sky opera" by Paul Earls; libretto (Eng) by Ian Strasfogel. First performance, in German, as *Ikarus*, September 25, 1982, Linz, Austria. First U.S. performance (in English) May 30, 1984, Cambridge, Massachusetts, Musica Viva, MIT Center for Advanced Visual Studies, with Nelda Nelson (Pasiphaë), Timothy Noble (Daedalus), and Joseph Olefirowicz (Icarus); lighting design by Günther Schneider-Siemssen; directed by Ian Strasfogel.

A treatment of the Icarus myth, in which Icarus and Daedalus, his father, flee from Crete using wings of feather and wax. Icarus disregards his father's warning and comes too close to the sun, whereupon the wings melt and he falls into the sea.
BIBLIOGRAPHY: Debra Cash, "Boston," *ON* XLVIII (1984), 60 [on U.S. premiere].

Ice Break, The, opera in twenty-nine scenes by Michael Tippett; libretto (Eng) by the composer. First performance July 7, 1977, London, Covent Garden, with Heather Harper (Nadia), Beverly Vaughn (Hannah), John Shirley-Quirk (Lev), Tom McDonell (Yuri), and Clyde Walker (Olympion); conducted by Colin Davis. First U.S. performance 1979, Boston; conducted by Sarah Caldwell.

Surviving for twenty years in a prison camp, Lev leaves for a new life and, at the airport, is reunited with his wife, Nadia, and their now grown son, Yuri. At the airport they meet Hannah, Nadia's friend, who is black and who has gone to see the black "champion" Olympion, who is surrounded by his fan club. When a riot occurs, Olympion and Gayle, Yuri's girlfriend, are killed, Yuri is near death, and Nadia succumbs. A psychedelic interlude takes place that involves the messenger Astron, who the people believe is God, despite Astron's protestations. A young doctor operates on Yuri and saves him, and Yuri is reunited with his father.

For detailed synopses and analyses, see K/*KOB*, 1154–56; K/*NKOB*, 837–39.

Major roles: Lev (bass); Nadia, his wife (lyr sop); Gayle (dramatic sop); Hannah, her friend, who is black (mezzo); Olympion, a black champion (ten); Yuri (bar); Astron, the messenger (sung by two people: lyric mezzo and high ten/counter ten); and Luke, a young doctor (ten).
SCORE: vs (London and New York: Schott, 1977).
LIBRETTO: English, in *ENOG* 29 (1985), 127–41.
BIBLIOGRAPHY: Frank Granville Barker, review, *ON* XLII (Oct. 1977), 57 [on premiere]; Jane Birkhead, "Dramatic Music," *MLA Notes* XXXVII (Dec. 1980), 427–28; Kemp/*Tippett*, 462–74; Leslie East, "Stereotypes and Rebirth," *ENOG* 29, 115–26.

Ida, or, The Guardian Storks, opera by Henry Leslie; libretto (Eng) by John Palgrave Simpson. First performance November 15, 1865, London, Covent Garden.

Idea, The, children's operetta by Gustav Holst; libretto (Eng) by Fritz B. Hart. Composed ca. 1896. Not performed.

Idiots First, fable in one act by Marc Blitzstein; composed 1962–1964; completed by Leonard Lehrman; libretto (Eng) by Blitzstein, after Bernard Malamud. First performance March 14, 1976, Bloomington, Indiana, Marc Blitzstein Opera Company, with *Karla**; January 22, 1978, New York, Bel Canto Opera, with Ronald Edwards (Mendel) and Stephen Colantti (Itzak); Georgianna Pappas, piano.

Mendel is warned by Ginzberg, the messenger of death, that he is about to die. To raise the train fare to send his simple son, Itzak, on a train to be with relatives in California, Mendel asks for help, but without success. He gets a new coat from a poor rabbi to pawn for the fare. After interference from Ginzberg, Itzak is allowed to board the train. Mendel returns to the gate and dies, alone.

For a detailed description, see Kornick/*RAO*, 68–69.

Major roles: Mendel (bar), Itzak (ten), and Ginzberg (bar).

Part of the *Tales of Malamud*,* together with *Karla.**
BIBLIOGRAPHY: Peter G. Davis, "2 'Malamud' Operas of Blitzstein Given," *NYT* (Jan. 18, 1978), C, 19 [on N.Y. premiere].

Idle Rumor, An, comic opera in one act by Dennis Busch; libretto (Eng) by the composer. Composed 1986.

For two sopranos, tenor, baritone, and chamber string orchestra.

SCORE: ms score, holograph (1986, photocopy, NYPL).

Idol's Eye, The, comic opera in three acts by Victor Herbert; libretto (Eng) by Harry B. Smith. A sequel to *The Wizard of the Nile.** First performance September 20, 1897, Troy, New York; repeated October 25, 1897, New York, Broadway Theatre, with Frank Daniels (Abel Conn), Maurice Darcy (Ned Winner), Alf C. Whelan (Jamie McSnuffy), Will Danforth (Don Pablo Tabasco), and Helen Redmond (Maraquita); conducted by Frank Pallma; directed by Julian Mitchell.

The story is set in India. It concerns the theft of a sacred ruby from an Indian idol by McSnuffy, a down-on-his-luck Scotsman whose life has been saved by Conn, a balloonist. The gem has the power to make its possessor beloved by everyone who comes into contact with that person. Its counterpart, also desired by all, is a jewel with the power to generate hatred. The love gem is eventually secured by Ned, an American novelist who needs money to wed his beloved Maraquita, daughter of the wealthy Don Pablo Tabasco, a Cuban planter traveling through India.

For a detailed description, see Waters/*VH*, 129–32.

The musical highlights include Don Pablo's Cuban Song" (act 1) and the choral "Entrance of the Brahmins" (act 1) and the "Song of the Priestess" of act 2.

SCORE: vs (New York: E. Schuberth, 1897).

Iernin, opera in three acts by George Lloyd; libretto (Eng) by William Lloyd. First performance November 6, 1934, Penzance, England.

DISCOGRAPHY: BBC Singers and Concert Orch.; cond. G. Lloyd, Albany Records 3-TROY 121–23 (rec. Nov. 1984, Golders Green Hippodrome; prod. 1994, Albany, N.Y., 3 CDs).

If the Cap Fits, opera in one act by Geoffrey Bush; libretto (Eng) by the composer, after Molière's *Les précieuses ridicules.* First performance July 10, 1956, Cheltenham, England, Intimate Opera Company.

The spoiled Madelaine expects to attract an appropriate suitor because of her position and therefore turns away a prospective husband she deems to be too plain. He returns in disguise and captures her attention.

For a detailed description, see Summers/*OOA*, 71–72.

Roles: Madelaine (sop); Mr. Grange, a rejected suitor (ten); and Madelaine's father (bar/bass-bar).

SCORE: vs (London: Augener; New York: Galaxy Music Corp., [1964]).

Ile, opera in one act by Beatrice Laufer; libretto (Eng), after the play of the same name (1917) by Eugene O'Neill. First performance April 28, 1957, New York. Revived 1977, New Haven, Connecticut, Yale School of Music; directed by Phyllis Curtin; 1988, Shanghai, Eugene O'Neill Festival.

The story concerns a sea captain who is so obsessed with whaling that his wife suffers enormously and his crew threatens mutiny.

I Like It to Be a Play, conversational chamber opera in one act by Charles Shere; libretto (Eng), after Gertrude Stein. First performance February 6, 1989, San Francisco, Hartley Martin Gallery.

Part 2 of a trilogy set to plays by Stein; see also *Ladies Voices* and *What Happened.*
SCORE: fs (Berkeley, Calif.: Fallen Leaf Press, 1996).

Illusion, The, or, The Trances of Nourjahad, "an oriental romance" in three acts by
Michael Kelly; libretto (Eng) by Samuel J. Arnold, "founded on a Persian tale written
by Mrs. Sheridan." First performance 1813, London.

One of the various settings of tales from the *Thousand and One Nights*, this is a
treatment of the *Sleeper Awakened*, as in Weber's *Abu Hassan* (1811, Munich); G.
Meyerbeer's *Wirth und Gast* (1813, Stuttgart); E. Loder's *Nourjahad** (1834); C.
Packer's *Sadak and Kalasra** (1835, London); and P. Cornelius's *Der Barbier von
Bagdad* (1858, Weimar).
LIBRETTO: English (London: J. Barker, 1813).

Illustrious Stranger, The, or, Married and Buried, operatic farce in two acts by
Isaac Nathan; libretto (Eng) by James Kenney and J. G. Millingen. First performance
October 1827, London, Drury Lane Theatre.
LIBRETTO: English (London: William Kenneth, 1827).

Illustrious Traveller, The, or, The Forges of Kanzel, melodrama in two acts; libretto
(Eng) by Frederick Reynolds. First performance February 3, 1818, London, Covent
Garden.
SCORE: ms fs (British Library, Add. MS. 36949).

I Love My Voice: The First Neurotic Opera, monodrama in one act by Donald Arlington; libretto (Eng) by Stephen Holt. First performance May 18, 1978, New York,
Riverside Church.

Immigrants, The, opera in three acts by Frederick Converse; libretto (Eng) by Percy
Mackaye. Composed ca. 1914.

The work is set in New York in the early twentieth century.

Immortal Hour, The, opera in two acts by Rutland Boughton; libretto (Eng) by "Fiona
Macleod" (William Sharp). First performance August 26, 1914, Glastonbury, with Irene
Lemon (Etain), Arthur Jordan (Midir), Frederic Austin (Eochaidh), the composer (standing in for an ill singer, in the part of Dalua), Muriel Boughton (Spirit Voice), Neville
Strutt (Manus), Agnes Thomas (Maive), and Arthur Trowbridge (Old Bard); conducted
by Kennedy Scott. First U.S. performance April 6, 1926, New York, Grove Street Theater, with John Gurney; conducted by Alberto Bimboni.

In the story Etain, a fairy, meets King Eochaidh, a mortal, through the machinations
of the outcast Dalua, Lord of Shadow. Etain and Eochaidh fall in love and marry. After
a year of wedded bliss the couple is visited by a stranger, Midir, the fairy prince, who
puts Etain under a trance so that she follows him to the Land of Heart's Desire. Dalua
touches Eochaidh, which kills him, and thereby grants his wish not to have his happiness fade.

For a detailed plot synopsis and a musical analysis, see K/*KOB*, 1128–30; K/*NKOB*,
96–97.

Major roles: Dalua (bar), Etain (sop), Eochaidh (bar), Spirit Voice (mezzo), Manus
(bass), Maive (alto), Old Bard (bass), and Midir (ten).

The work was wildly successful when it was revived on October 13, 1922, and by 1932 had seen more than 500 performances in London. Its 1953 revival in London, however, was a failure.

SCORE: vs (London: Stainer & Bell, 1920).

DISCOGRAPHY: Dawson, Taylor, Davies, Wilson-Johnson, Kennedy, Bryson, Mitchell Choir, English Chamber Orch.; cond. Melville, Hyperion A-66101/2 (2 LPs); rev. John W. Freeman, "Records," *ON* XLIX (Mar. 2, 1985), 36.

Implications of Melissa, chamber opera in one act by Philip Carlsen; libretto (Eng) by the composer. First performance February 5, 1982, Brooklyn, New York, Brooklyn College Opera.

In the Absurdist plot, three characters represent the three sides of one personality and undergo a wide variety of emotions.

Scored for soprano, mezzo, tenor, and chamber ensemble.

SCORE: holograph ms score (1982, NYPL).

Importance of Being Earnest, The, opera in three acts by Erik Chisholm; libretto (Eng) by the composer, after Oscar Wilde. Composed 1963.

Impossible Forest, The, opera in two acts by Alec Wilder; libretto (Eng) by Marshall Barer. First performance July 13, 1958, Westport, Connecticut.

Improvement (Don Leaves Linda), television opera in four acts by Robert Ashley; libretto (Eng) by the composer. Composed 1986. First performance October 7, 1991, New York, Merkin Concert Hall, with Jacqueline Humbold (Linda), Thomas Buckner (Mr. Payne), Joan La Barbara (Now Eleanor), Sam Ashley (Junior, Jr.), Adam Klein (the Doctor), Amy X. Neuburg (Mr. Payne's Mother), and the composer (Narrator).

In the "plot" Don leaves Linda to teach at a small college, and Linda meets Mr. Payne.

Roles: Linda (singer); Don; Mr. Payne, Linda's companion (singer); Now Eleanor (sop); Junior, Jr. (singer); the Doctor (singer); Mr. Payne's Mother (singer); and Narrator (singer).

Scored for soloists, narrator, and electronic tape.

First episode of the quartet of television operas *Now Eleanor's Idea** (comp. 1986–1989).

BIBLIOGRAPHY: Bernard Holland, "When a Composer Turns Opera Upside Down," *NYT* (Nov 21, 1994), C. 10; Jon Pareles, review, *NYT* (Oct. 12, 1991), A, 22 [on premiere].

DISCOGRAPHY: Humbert, Neuburg, Buckner, S. Ashley, Klein, R. Ashley, Elektra/Nonesuch 79289-2 (1992, 2 CDs).

In a Garden, opera in one act by Meyer Kupferman; libretto (Eng), after Gertrude Stein's *First Reader*. First performance December 29, 1949, New York; June 15, 1950, New York, After Dinner Opera, Master Theatre, with Sylvia Stahlman, Burton Trimble, and James Beni; Georgette Palmer (piano); conducted by Alexander Main.

In this satire the young Lucy dreams that she is a queen and is courted by two boys, Philip, and Kit Raccoon the First. To help her decide which of them to accept, the boys fight and kill each other. Lucy is left alone but with the crowns of the two boys.

For a detailed description, see Eaton/*OP* I, 191.

Roles: Lucy Willow (sop), Philip Hall (ten), and Kit Raccoon the First (bar).

SCORE: vs (New York: Mercury Music Corp., 1951).

BIBLIOGRAPHY: H. C. S., "After Dinner Troupe Offers Three Operas," *NYT* (June 15, 1950), 41 [on 1950 performance].

Incident at Owl Creek, radio opera in one act by Christopher Whelen; libretto (Eng) by the composer, after Ambrose Bierce's story from his *Tales of Soldiers and Civilians* (1891). First performance May 26, 1969, BBC radio.

A southern plantation owner, about to be hanged by Union soldiers, imagines that he has escaped. His reverie is ended when the noose tightens around his neck.

T. Musgrave's *Occurrence at Owl Creek** (1982) is another setting.

Incognita, opera in three acts by Egon Wellesz; libretto (Eng) by Elizabeth Mackenzie, after William Congreve's novel (1691). First performance December 5, 1951, Oxford, Town Hall, Oxford University Opera Club.

A tale of mistaken identities.

Also set by C. Lecoq as *Le coeur et la main* (1882, Paris).

SCORE: vs ([n.p.] 1950; LCCN: 60-2003).

BIBLIOGRAPHY: Arthur Jacobs, review, *MA* LXXII (Feb. 1952) [on premiere].

In Dahomey, musical comedy in three acts by Will Marion Cook; libretto (Eng) by Jesse A. Shipp; lyrics by Paul Laurence Dunbar. First performance September 12, 1902, Stamford, Connecticut; February 18, 1903, New York, New York Theatre, with George Walker (Rareback Pinkerton) and Bert Williams (Shylock Homestead).

A group of black entrepreneurs from Boston try to fleece other unsuspecting and poor American blacks into investing in a scheme to colonize Africa. The fast-talking Rareback dupes the simple Shylock Homestead into parting with his money, but Rareback's excesses raise the ire of even the mild-mannered "investor."

The work represented the first full-length musical written by African Americans and with an African-American cast to be presented at a major Broadway music house. It drew mild praise from the white press and was fairly successful in London, including a performance at Buckingham Palace. It was given more than 1,100 times in the United States and England from 1902 to 1906.

SCORE: vs, *The Music and Scripts,* In Dahomey, ed. Thomas L. Riis, *Recent Researches in American Music*, vol. 25 (Madison, Wisc.: A-R Editions, 1996); includes songs added or substituted in later productions.

BIBLIOGRAPHY: Thomas L. Riis, *More Than Just Minstrel Shows* (Brooklyn, N.Y.: Institute for Studies in American Music, 1992), 48–56.

Indian Princess, The, or, La Belle Sauvage, "operatic melo-drame" in three acts by John Bray; libretto (Eng) by James Nelson Barker. First performance April 6, 1808, Philadelphia, Chestnut Street Theatre, with Mr. Rutherford (Captain Smith), Mr. Wood (Lieutenant Rolfe), Mr. Serson (Powhatan), and Mrs. Wilmot (Pocahontas). First British performance December 15, 1820, London, Drury Lane Theatre, as *Pocahontas*.

The opera covers the love story of John Smith and Pocahontas, the "Indian Princess" of the title and daughter of Powhatan.

SCORE: vs (Philadelphia: G. E. Blake, 1808); repr. ed. H. Wiley Hitchcock, in *Earlier American Music*, no. 11 (New York: Da Capo Press, 1972); includes 1808 libretto.

BIBLIOG. PHY: H. Wiley Hitchcock, "An Early American Melodrama: *The Indian Princess* of J. N. Barker and John Bray," *MLA Notes* XX (June 1955), 375–88.

DISCOGRAPHY: J. Otten, J. Porrello, R. Anderson, J. M. Ousley, M. Best, S. Belling, D. Vanderline, Federal Music Society Opera Co., cond. John Baldon, New World 232 (1 LP).

Indian Puzzle, An, opera in one act by Thomas German Reed; libretto (Eng) by Gilbert A. A'Beckett. First performance February 28, 1876, London, St. George's Hall.

Indian Queen, The, semi-opera in five acts by Henry Purcell (the final masque, the Masque of Hymen, was written by Daniel Purcell after his brother's death); libretto (Eng) by John Dryden and Robert Howard, after Dryden's *Indian Emperor* (1665). First performance probably late autumn 1695, London, Drury Lane Theatre, with George Powell (Montezuma), Richard Leveridge (Ismeron), Mr. Bowen (the God of Dreams), and Mrs. Knight (Zempoalla).

The setting is Mexico at the time of the Incas. In the geographically skewered story, Montezuma, as a reward for defeating the Mexicans, asks to wed Orazia, daughter of the Inca king. The king is so angered by Montezuma's request that the latter flees and seeks safety with the Mexicans. While he is there, Zempoalla, the Mexican queen, is discovered to have in fact usurped the throne from Montezuma's mother. After the Mexicans seize Orazia and her father, Montezuma intervenes to save them from execution, aided by the Mexican prince Acacis, also in love with Orazia, who kills himself. It turns out that the Inca king is in fact also the King of the Mexicans, and Montezuma and Orazia are allowed to wed. In despair Zempoalla kills herself.

The musical numbers are in four scenes, the prologue, a masque in act 2, an incantation in act 3, and a sacrificial scene in act 5. The concluding masque is by Daniel Purcell.

SCORE: ms fs (after 1696, British Library, Add. MS 31449).
LIBRETTO: English, Dryden's text, in Robert Howard, *Four New Plays* (London: Henry Herringman, 1665).
DISCOGRAPHY: C. Bott, E. Kirkby, J. Ainsley, J. Podger, G. Finley, H. Parker, D. Thomas, S. Berridge, T. Williams, Academy of Ancient Music; cond. C. Hogwood, L'Oiseau-Lyre 444339-2.

Ines de Castro, opera in three acts by Thomas Pasatieri; libretto (Eng) by Bernard Stambler. First performance March 30, 1976, Baltimore, Lyric Opera Company, with Evelyn Mandac (Ines de Castro), Richard Stilwell (Pedro), James Morris (King Alfonso), Lili Chookasian (Queen Beatrix), Sheila Nadler (Dona Bianca); conducted by Christopher Keene; produced by Tito Capobianco; directed by Rosa Ponselle.

The work focuses on the story of Ines (Inés, d. 1355), the doomed mistress of Pedro, the crown prince of Portugal.

The story was also set by F. Bianchi (1794, Naples); Zingarelli (1798, Milan); G. Persiani (1835, Naples); R. Coelho; and J. MacMillan (1996; see next entry).
BIBLIOGRAPHY: Harold C. Schonberg, review, *NYT* (Apr. 1, 1976), 28 [on premiere].

Inés de Castro, opera in two acts by James MacMillan; libretto (Eng) by the composer, after a play by John Clifford. First performance August 23, 1996, Edinburgh, Scottish Opera, with Helen Field (Inés), Jeffrey Lawton (Pedro), Anne Collins (Nurse/Old Woman), Jacek Strauch (Pacheco), Stafford Dean (King of Portugal), Elizabeth Byrne (Bianca), and Christopher Purves (the executioner); conducted by Richard Armstrong; produced by Jonathan Moore.

Inés, the mistress of Pedro, the Crown Prince, has borne him children, which pains Bianca, Pedro's infertile wife, and worries his father, the King. Pacheco, the King's adviser, kills Inés, her children, and the Nurse. Now mad with grief, Pedro worships Inés's begowned corpse and carries out his bloody revenge when he becomes king.

Among the musical devices are the unifying chorale of act 1, with a four-note motto. The motto reappears in the second act.

BIBLIOGRAPHY: Tom Sutcliffe, "British Journal," *ON* LXI (Dec. 14, 1996), 71 [on premiere]; Ronald Weitzman, "First Performances," *Tempo* CXCIX (Jan. 1997), 29–32.

Inevitable Hour, The. See **The Hanging Judge.**

Infidelio, opera in seven scenes by Elisabeth Lutyens; libretto (Eng) by T. E. Ranselm (the composer's pseudonym). First performance April 17, 1973, London, Sadler's Wells.

The work examines a girl's suicide via the unfolding of her unhappy love affair.

BIBLIOGRAPHY: Winton Dean, review, *MT* CXIV (June 1973), 618 [on premiere]; Rodney Milnes, review, *Opera* XXIV (June 1973), 545–47 [on premiere].

Inkle and Yarico, or, The Benevolent Maid, comic opera in three acts by Samuel Arnold; libretto (Eng) by George Colman Jr., after Richard Steele's essay in *The Spectator* (1711) First performance August 4, 1787, London, Little Theatre in the Haymarket, with John Bannister (Inkle), Mr. Davies (Campley), Mrs. Kemble (Yarico), Mrs. Bannister (Narcissa), Mr. Parsons (Sir Christopher Curry), Mr. Edwin (Trudge), and Miss George (Wowski). First U.S. performance July 6, 1789, New York, John Street Theatre.

The setting is "on the Main of America" and then Barbados. The plot concerns a beautiful Indian girl, Yarico, who meets Inkle, a young English merchant who is fleeing his Indian pursuers. After she hides him in a cave, feeds him, and falls in love with him, he repays her kindness by bringing her back to his ship and trying to sell her into slavery, a move that is halted by his intended client, Sir Christopher Curry, the Governor. In the end Inkle agrees to wed Yarico, mainly because his fiancée, Narcissa, the Governor's daughter, has decided to marry the more noble Captain Campley.

Colman's text is considered to be the first English play to denounce slavery, which was being debated at the time in England. It also includes the Cockney character Trudge, Inkle's servant, and Wowski, the black servant of Yarico. These two also marry at the end.

For a detailed description, see Fiske/*ETM,* 476–80.

Major roles: Inkle (ten), Yarico (sop), Narcissa (sop), Trudge (bar), Wowski (sop), and Captain Campley (bar).

Set as a Singspiel by F. Kauer, as *Inkle und Yariko* (1807, Vienna).

SCORES: vs (London: Longman & Broderip, 1787?; [Boston]: William P. Blake et al., 1794).

LIBRETTOS: English (London: G. G. J. and J. Robinson, [1787]; [Boston]: Apollo Press, 1794; Philadelphia: Enoch Story, [1793]); repr. of 1787 London version in Rubsamen/*BO*, vol. 28, *American Ballad Operas* (1974).

Inland Woman, The, opera in one act by Erik Chisholm; libretto (Eng) by the composer, after Mary Lavin. First performance October 21, 1953, Cape Town, South Africa.

BIBLIOGRAPHY: "South Africa," *Opera* V (Oct. 1954), 629–30 [on premiere].

In Memoriam . . . Kit Carson, opera by Robert Ashley; libretto (Eng) by the composer. First performance 1964, Ann Arbor, Michigan; December 10, 1971, Oakland, California, Mills College.

Chance composition for eight instruments or performers, or groups of instruments and/or performers.

SCORE: fs, with performance instructions (Baltimore: Smith; Sonic Art Editions, 1990).

Inner Voices, opera by David Barnett; libretto (Eng) by Josephine Barnett. First performance December 17, 1972, New York.

Inner Voices, chamber opera in ten scenes by Brian Howard; libretto (Eng), by Louis Nowra. First performance February 25, 1977, Sydney, Australia. First British performance April 7, 1985, London, New Opera Company, Bloomsbury Theatre, with Malcolm Rivers (Mirovich), Lyndon Terracini (Ivan), Laureen Livingstone (Princess Ali), Jane Metcalfe (Anne), and Alexander Gauld (Vladimir); conducted by Howard Williams; directed by Anthony Besch.

The story, set in Russia, concerns the idiot Ivan, the heir to the throne at the time of Catherine the Great. In order to prevent him from succeeding her, Catherine has him imprisoned. Ivan's guardian, Mirovich, an army officer, has other plans. He wants to make Ivan the Emperor but control him himself. When Catherine dies, Ivan becomes the emperor and imprisons his former tormenters.

LIBRETTO: English (with music) (Sydney, Australia: Currency Press, 1977).

BIBLIOGRAPHY: Martin Dreyer, "New Opera Company" *MT* CXXIV (1983), 375 [on premiere]; Harold Rosenthal, "Inner Voices," *Opera* XXXVI (1985), 674 [on British premiere].

In Possession, operetta in one act by Frederic Clay; libretto (Eng) by Robert Reece. First performance June 20, 1871, London, Gallery of Illustration.

Inquest of Love, The, opera in two acts by Jonathan Harvey; libretto (Eng) by the composer and David Rudkin. First performance June 5, 1993, London, English National Opera, with Linda McLeod (Ann), Peter Coleman-Wright (John), Helen Field (Elspeth), Richard Van Allan (the Abbot), and Barry Banks (Josh); conducted by Mark Elder; directed by David Pountney.

The Abbot presides at a wedding, during which the bride is shot by a mysterious woman. The story is retold from several different viewpoints, each with different music, including a purely orchestral version during which the stage action is presented in mime. Reconciliation is achieved in the afterlife.

LIBRETTO: English (London: Faber Music, 1992, 1993).

BIBLIOGRAPHY: George Hall, "Harvey's Inquest of Love," *MO* CXVI (Sept. 1993), 297 [on premiere]; John Warnaby, "Inquest of Love: A Second View," *MO* CXVI (Oct. 1993), 326–27 [on premiere].

Insect Comedy, The, opera in three acts by Martin Kalmanoff; libretto (Eng) by Lewis Allan, after the play *Insect Life* (1923) by Karel and Josef Čapek. Composed 1977. First performance May 20, 1993, New York, Hunter College, Kaye Playhouse, with Stephen Kechulius (the Vagrant), Steven Tharp, Amy Goldstein, and Karen Burlingame; conducted by Richard Marshall; directed by Lou Galterio

In this antiwar story, the Vagrant, disillusioned by his fellow human beings, gets drunk and takes a rest in a field outside the city. In his drunken haze the swarming insects around him take on human characteristics. The Vagrant, believing he has learned much about humans from watching the insects, tries to share his knowledge with the world by returning to civilization, but he dies before he can do so.

For a detailed description, see Eaton/*OP* II, 115–16.

Roles: Vagrant (bar), Professor (ten), Felix (ten), Iris (sop), Chrysalis (sop), Chneumon fly (bar), Beetle (bass), Mrs. Beetle (mezzo), Cricket (ten), Mrs. Cricket (mezzo), and Scientist (ten).

The musical highlights include the "Iris" aria in act 1.

SCORE: ms vs (New York: American Music Center, 1977?).

BIBLIOGRAPHY: John Freeman, "New York City," *ON* LVIII (Oct. 1993), 40 [on premiere]; James R. Oestreich, "'The Insect Comedy,'" *NYT* (May 29, 1993), A, 14 [on premiere].

Inspector General, The, opera in three acts by Eugene Zador; libretto (Ger) by the composer, as *Der Revisor*, after Gogol's play (1836). Composed 1928; not performed. Revised and reorchestrated, with an English text by George Mead. First performance, in the revised version, in two acts (in English), June 11, 1971, Torrance, California, El Camino College.

The story concerns a corrupt mayor and his advisers, who expect an inspector to visit their town in disguise. Khlestakoff, a minor civil servant from St. Petersburg, is stranded there and, mistaken for the official, takes advantage of the situation. Although his real identity is discovered by the nosy postmaster, he escapes before he is unmasked; just as the town officials are in a rage about being deceived, the genuine inspector shows up.

Major roles: Khlestakoff, the impostor (ten); the Burgomaster (bass); Maria, daughter of the Burgomaster (sop); and the postmaster (bar).

The story was also set by W. Egk, as *Der Revisor* (1957, Schwetzingen).

BIBLIOGRAPHY: Clifford Reims, *"The Inspector General,"* *OJ* IV (1971), 15–16.

Institution of the Garter, The, or, Arthur's Round Table Restored, all-sung afterpiece in three parts by Charles Dibdin; libretto (Eng) by David Garrick, after Gilbert West. First performance October 28, 1771, London, Drury Lane Theatre, with Miss Hopkins (the Black Prince).

The setting is Windsor at the time of Edward III.

LIBRETTO: English (London: Printed for T. Becket and P. A. DeHondt . . . , 1771).

Intelligence Park, The, opera in three acts by Gerald Barry; libretto (Eng) by Vincent Deane. First performance July 6, 1990, London, Almeida Theatre, Opera Factory.

SCORE: vs, five chorales (Oxford and New York: Oxford University Press, 1991).

Intelligent Systems, multimedia opera in two acts by Carson Kievman; libretto (Eng) by the composer. First performance October 20, 1984, Baden-Baden, Germany.

SCORE: fs, orchestral suite (New York: Intelligent Co. Publishers, 1983).

In the Beginning, church opera in two acts by Raymond Warren; libretto (Eng) by the composer after the Bible and John Milton's *Paradise Lost*. First performance July 22, 1982, Bristol, Clifton Cathedral.

In the Drought, opera in four scenes by John Joubert; libretto (Eng) by Adolph Wood. First performance October 20, 1956, Johannesburg.

Elsie, the young wife of Jakobus Rey, is anxiously awaiting her lover Harry Mitchell, an English prospector. When he arrives he begs her to flee with him, but Elsie refuses, since she fears and pities her husband, and she is reminded by the ever-present

Bible on her table that she is breaking one of the Commandments. When Elsie's cousin Ottilie arrives, Harry takes his leave. Ottilie, along with other members of the family and the Predikant, a minister of the Dutch Reformed Church, resolves to tell Jakobus of his wife's unfaithfulness. Jakobus tries to blot out the incident from his family's record, and because of his actions the drought that has ravaged the land is broken.

The score includes ten singing parts and chamber orchestra.

SCORE: vs (n.p., n.d.; LCCN: 84-49957).

In the House of Crossed Desires, chamber opera by John Woolrich; libretto (Eng) by Marina Warner. First performance July 6, 1996, Cheltenham, England, Everyman Theatre; staged by Michael McCarthy.

The story concerns a magician who is love with his young niece and therefore dresses her as a boy to prevent other males from paying attention to her.

BIBLIOGRAPHY: Andrew Clements, review, *Guardian* (July 9, 1996), II, 9 [on premiere].

In the Name of Culture, chamber opera in one act by Alberto Bimboni; libretto (Eng) by Norma Frizelle Stolzenbach. First performance May 9, 1949, Rochester, New York, Eastman School of Music; conducted by the composer.

The story is a satirical look at a meeting of a women's club.

The score includes an imitation of a Chopin nocturne and a mock radio male quartet.

BIBLIOGRAPHY: "Chamber Operas at Eastman Fete," *NYT* (May 10, 1949), 28 [on premiere].

In the Pasha's Garden, opera in one act by John Seymour; libretto (Eng) by Henry C. Tracy, after a story by H. G. Dwight. First performance January 24, 1935, New York, Metropolitan Opera, with Helen Jepson (Hélène), Frederick Jagel (Etienne), Lawrence Tibbett (the Pasha), Marek Windheim (Zümbül Agha), and Arthur Anderson (Shaban); conducted by Ettore Panizza; directed by Wilhelm von Wymetal Jr.

Major roles: Hélène (sop), Etienne (ten), the Pasha (bar), Zümbül Agha (ten), and Shaban (bass).

Intimate Immensity, "staged media poem" by Morton Subotnick; text (Eng). First performance July 1997, New York, La Guardia Theater, with Joan La Barbara, Thomas Buckner, and I Nyoman Wente (Balinese dancer).

For two vocalists, Balinese dancer, video, electronic device, and two "playerless" pianos.

BIBLIOGRAPHY: Paul Griffiths, "Indeed, It's a Long Journey," *NYT* (Jul. 18, 1997), C, 7, and "A Festival's Promise Unfulfilled," *NYT* (Aug. 3, 1997), 25 [on premiere]; Mark Swed, "Medium Needs a Massage: Opera Review," *Los Angeles Times* (July 29, 1997), F, 1 [on Los Angeles premiere].

Intriguing Chambermaid, The, comedy (ballad opera) in two acts; libretto (Eng) by Henry Fielding, after Regnard's *Retour imprévu*. First performance 1734, London, Drury Lane Theatre.

The work revolves around a calculating chambermaid.

LIBRETTO: English (London, 1734); repr. ed. Rubsamen/*BO*, vol. 12, *Farce: Amorous Intrigue and Deception*, I (1974).

Introductions and Good-Byes, nine-minute opera by Lukas Foss; libretto (Eng) by Gian Carlo Menotti. First performance (concert) May 5, 1960, New York. First performance (stage) June 1960, Spoleto, Italy, Festival of the Two Worlds. First British performance June 4, 1963, London, Park Lane Opera Group, St. Pancras Town Hall

The "plot" consists of the comments of nine guests invited to a cocktail party; their remarks are vocalized by a quartet seated in the orchestra pit.

For a detailed description, see Eaton/*OP* II, 285.

Roles: the host (bar), the nine guests (actors or dancers), and vocal quartet (SATB).
SCORE: vs (New York: C. Fischer, [1961]).
BIBLIOGRAPHY: Harold Rosenthal, "London Opera Diary," *Opera* XIV (Aug. 1963), 567 [on British premiere].

Intruder, The, opera in one act by Robert Starer; libretto (Eng) by Mary Anne Pryor. First performance December 4, 1956, New York, Punch Opera, with Patricia Conner (Edna), Judith Hoyt, Sadie McCollum, Richard Roussilo, and Gert Spero; produced by Rex Wilder.

The setting is a New England farmhouse. A young roustabout comes into the life of a widow and her two daughters.
BIBLIOGRAPHY: Frank Merkling, review, *ON* XXI (Dec. 31, 1956), 15 [on premiere].

Intruder, The, opera in one act by James Feldman; libretto (Eng) by Gary Stotcals, after Maurice Maeterlinck's *L'intruse* (1890). First performance February 10, 1984, Berea, Ohio, Baldwin-Wallace College, Conservatory of Music.

The symbolist plot deals with the inevitability of death.

Invincibles, The, musical farce in two acts by George Alexander Lee; libretto (Eng) by Thomas Morton. First performance February 28, 1828, London, Covent Garden.

The setting is the south of France.
LIBRETTOS: English (London: J. Cumberland, [1828]; New York: Wm. Van Norden, 1829).

Invisible Girl, The, operatic farce in one act by James Hook; libretto (Eng) by Theodore Edward Hook. First performance April 28, 1806, London, Drury Lane Theatre. First U.S. performance January 26, 1807, New York, Park Theatre.

Iolan. See **The Pipe of Desire.**

Iolanthe, or, The Peer and the Peri, fairy opera in two acts by Arthur S. Sullivan; libretto (Eng) by William S. Gilbert. First performance November 25, 1882, London, Savoy Theatre, with George Grossmith (Lord Chancellor), Rutland Barrington (Earl of Mountararat), Durward Lely (Earl Tolloller), Charles Manners (Private Willis), Richard Temple (Strephon), Jessie Bond (Iolanthe), Leonora Braham (Phyllis), and Alice Barnett (Queen of the Fairies). The work opened simultaneously in New York, at the Standard Theatre. The London run lasted 398 performances. First U.S. performance November 25, 1882, New York, Standard Theatre, with W. T. Carleton (Strephon), J. H. Ryley (Lord Chancellor), and Marie Jansen (Iolanthe).

The setting is an Arcadian landscape in Westminster. The story follows the life of the fairy Iolanthe, who has been banished by the Queen of the Fairies because she has married a mortal. Her son, Strephon, is love with the shepherdess Phyllis, but he cannot marry because he is half mortal and half fairy. In the end, however, true love wins out, as the Queen of the Fairies lends a hand.

Major roles: the Lord Chancellor (bar); the Earl of Mountararat (bar); Earl Tolloller (ten); Private Willis, a member of the Grenadier Guards (bass-bar); Strephon, an Arcadian shepherd (bar); Queen of the Fairies (alto); Iolanthe, a fairy and Strephon's mother (mezzo); and Phyllis, an Arcadian shepherdess (sop).

For a detailed description, see Stedman/*WSG*, 200–8.

Also set, as a serious opera, by Tchaikovsky, as *Iolanta* (*Yolanta*) (1892, St. Petersburg); parodies include one by Davison Dalziel (1883, Chicago).
SCORE: vs (New York: Hitchcock, 1882).
LIBRETTO: English (New York and Philadelphia: J. M. Stoddart; Philadelphia: Marshall & Co., 1882).
VIDEO: D. Hammond-Stroud, K. Flowers, Ambrosian Opera Chorus, London Sym. Orch.; cond. A. Faris; staged by D. Pountney, Goldcrest Films International, Opera World, VHS IOL-10V (1982 performance); rev. F. Paul Driscoll, *ON* LXII (Oct. 1997), 65.

I Rise in Flame, Cried the Phoenix, opera in one act by Thomas J. Flanagan; libretto (Eng), after Tennessee Williams's play. First performance February 7, 1980, New York, Golden Fleece Ltd., with John Jellison (Lawrence), Lucille Sullam (Frieda), and Sally Ann Sward (Bertha); John Klingberg, piano accompaniment.

About the last days of D. H. Lawrence.
BIBLIOGRAPHY: Allen Hughes, "Opera: Based on Tennessee Williams Play, *NYT* (Feb. 9, 1980), 45 [on premiere].

Irish Legacy, The, afterpiece by Samuel Arnold; libretto (Eng) by the composer. First performance June 26, 1797, London, Little Theatre in the Haymarket.

Irish Mimic, The, or, Blunders at Brighton, musical entertainment in two acts by William Shield; libretto (Eng) by John O'Keeffe. First performance April 23, 1795, London, Covent Garden.
LIBRETTO: English (London: T. N. Longman, 1795).

Irish Tar, The, or, Which Is the Girl, musical piece in one act by Thomas Attwood; libretto (Eng) by Wally C. Oulton. First performance August 24, 1797, London, Theatre Royal, Haymarket.

Irmelin, opera in three acts by Frederick Delius; libretto (Eng) by the composer. Composed 1890–1892. First performance May 4, 1953, Oxford, New Theatre, with Edna Graham (Irmelin), Thomas Round (Nils), Arthur Copley (the King), and George Hancock (Rolf); conducted by Thomas Beecham; produced by Dennis Arundell.

The story concerns the Princess Irmelin, who is waiting for her true love and has rejected the suitors that her father, the king, has put forth. Nils, in reality a prince who has been placed under a spell by the band of the robber Rolf, comes dressed as a swineherd. Nils is also looking for the perfect woman. Having been advised that he will discover such a woman at the end of a silver stream, he goes there and finds Irmelin.

For a detailed description, see Eaton/*OP* II, 118.
Major roles: Irmelin (sop), the king (bass), Nils (ten), and Rolf (bass-bar).
SCORE: vs (London: Hawkes & Son, and New York: Boosey & Hawkes, 1953).
BIBLIOGRAPHY: Andrew Porter, review, *MT* XCIV (1953), 275 [on premiere].
DISCOGRAPHY: Hannan, Mitchinson, Rippon, Cook, Schilling, Taylor, BBC Singers and Concert Orch.; cond. N. Del Mar, BBC CD 30002.

Irmengarda, opera by Leonhard Emil Bach; libretto (Eng) by W. Beatty-Kingston. First performance December 8, 1892, London, Covent Garden.

SCORE: vs (Leipzig: E. Hatzfeld et al., 1892).

Iron Chest, The, play with music in three acts by Stephen Storace; libretto (Eng) by George Colman Jr., after William Godwin's novel *Things As They Are, or, The Adventures of Caleb Williams* (1794). First performance March 12, 1796, London, Drury Lane Theatre, with John Philip Kemble (Sir Edward), John Bannister (Wilford), Nancy Storace (Barbara), Miss Farren (Helen), and Mr. Kelly (Orson). First U.S. performance April 17, 1797, Philadelphia, Chestnut Street Theatre.

The story centers on Wilford, an honest young man from a poor family, who becomes the servant and confidant of the reclusive Sir Edward Mortimer. Wilford learns that his master once killed the uncle of Helen, his beloved, and when he tries to find evidence of the secret, he is caught. Trying to flee, Wilford is stopped by the robber Orson, who, on Sir Edward's orders, frames Wilford by hiding jewelry in his luggage. Wilford refuses to divulge his master's secret, thereby receiving Sir Edward's gratitude. When Sir Edward suffers a stroke after his half brother uncovers the secret, Wilford marries Barbara, daughter of the poacher Rawbold.

For a detailed description, see Fiske/*ETM*, 533–36.

The work includes "Sweet Little Barbara" (no. 5), a setting of "Se vuol ballare" from Mozart's *Le nozze di Figaro*, first used by Storace in Six Easy and Progressive Sonatinas (1791).

LIBRETTO: English (London: Cadell and Davies, 1796); repr. in *Revolution and Romanticism, 1789–1834* (Oxford: Woodstock Books, 1989).

BIBLIOGRAPHY: Jane Girdham, *English Opera in Late Eighteenth-Century London* (Oxford: Clarendon Press, 1997), 189–98.

Iron Man, The, opera in two acts by Malcolm Fox; libretto (Eng) by Sue Rider and Jim Vilé, after the story of the same name by Ted Hughes. First performance April 11, 1987, Adelaide, Australia, State Opera, with Dushyant Kumar (Iron Man); conducted by Brian Stacey.

The Iron Man is created after lightning hits a beach full of discarded pieces of metal. The next morning he is discovered by two children and by several angry adults, whose cars he has consumed. The children dig a hole to trap him but regret their actions when the adults bury him in the earth. After he escapes, the children find an effective way for him to survive; they advise him to live in the local scrap-metal yard, where he can eat whatever he wishes. The Iron Man gratefully accepts their solution, which astounds the adults. Later on, when a Space Being lands on Earth and attacks the planet, the Iron Man returns the kindness shown him by the children by defeating it. Peace for the earth results.

BIBLIOGRAPHY: Elizabeth Silsbury, review, *Opera* XXXVIII (Oct. 1987), 1158 [on premiere].

Isaac Levi, opera in one act by Frederick Piket; libretto (Eng) by Raymond Smolover. First performance December 11, 1955, White Plains, New York, Westchester Opera Theater; January 28, 1956, New York, 92nd Street Y, Opera Theatre of Westchester, with Ray Smolover (Isaac), Norman Atkins, Jacqueline Langee, Edith Gordon, and Alice Richmond; conducted by Eugene Kusmiak.

The story deals with the problems confronting contemporary Jews, including intermarriage and loss of faith.

BIBLIOGRAPHY: review, *MA* LXXVI (Feb. 15, 1956), 208 [on premiere]; review, *NYT* (Jan. 30, 1956), 23 [on New York premiere].

Isabella's Fortune, comic opera in one act by William Russo; libretto (Eng) by Albert Williams. First performance September 11, 1974, New York, Commedia Company of Chicago, together with *Pedrolino's Revenge.**

The work, based on the commedia dell'arte, combines elements of jazz, rock, Italian madrigals, and musical comedy.

BIBLIOGRAPHY: Harold C. Schonberg, "Opera: Updating Commedia dell'Arte," *NYT* (Sept. 13, 1974), C, 31 [on premiere].

Isidore de Merida, or, The Devil's Creek, revival of Stephen Storace's *The Pirates** (1792, London), with new text; additional music by John Braham, Saverio Mercadante, and Giuseppe Balducci; revised orchestration by Thomas Cooke. First performance November 21, 1827, London, Drury Lane Theatre. Also performed June 9, 1828, New York, with music arranged by Charles Edward Horn.

SCORE: vs, "Smile, Fair Signoras" (London: Clementi, [182?]).

Isis and Osiris, lyric drama by Elisabeth Lutyens; libretto (Eng) by the composer after Plutarch. First performance November 26, 1976, London, Morley College.

The work, which celebrates the seasons and, at the same time, life and death, includes choral dances. It is scored for solo soprano.

SCORE: fs, facsimile (London: Olivan Press, Universal Edition, 1989, 1969).

Island, The, opera in one act by William Russo; libretto (Eng) by A. Mitchell. First performance July 13, 1963, BBC.

The work examines the effect of a developed society on an indigenous population.

Islanders, The, opera in three acts by Charles Dibdin; libretto (Eng) by the composer, after Saint-Foix. First performance November 25, 1780, London, Covent Garden, with Charles Frederick Reinhold (Yanko) and Mrs. Kennedy (Ora). Revised as *The Marriage Act** (1781).

Spaniards and Indians inhabit an island off the American coast. The Indian hero and heroine are Yanko and Ora, who are in love.

For a detailed description, see Fiske/*ETM*, 430.

Island God, The, opera in one act by Gian Carlo Menotti; libretto (It) by the composer, after Gordon S. Mumford's *An Island God* (1897). First performance, in an English translation by Fleming McLeish, February 20, 1942, New York, Metropolitan Opera, with Leonard Warren (Ilo), Astrid Varnay (Telea), Raoul Jobin (Luca), and Norman Cordon (a Greek god); conducted by Ettore Panizza; directed by Lothar Wallerstein.

The setting is a Mediterranean island. After Telea deserts her husband, Ilo, for Luca, a fisherman, Ilo demolishes the temple he was reconstructing for an island god.

Withdrawn by the composer after the premiere season.

LIBRETTO: English (New York: G. Ricordi & Co., 1942).

Island of St. Marguerite, The, opera in two acts by Thomas Shaw; libretto (Eng) by John St. John, after Voltaire's *L'anecdote sur l'homme au masque de fer* (1764). First performance November 13, 1789, London, Drury Lane Theatre, with Michael Kelly (Man in the Iron Mask). March 28, 1800, Charleston, South Carolina, Charleston Theatre.

In the story, the prisoner in the iron mask is freed by the mob, who destroys the castle in which he was confined. The Temple of Liberty springs from the rubble.

The work includes borrowings from *Le nozze di Figaro* and a Haydn sonata.

For a detailed description, see Fiske/*ETM*, 505–6.

LIBRETTO: English (London: J. Debrett, 1789).

Island of Tomorrow, The, chamber opera in one act by Myron Fink; libretto (Eng) by Lou Rodgers. First performance June 19, 1986, New York, Golden Fleece Ltd.; conducted by Stephen-Francis Vasa.

The work, set in a waiting room on Ellis Island in 1912, concerns a group of immigrants and a judge who must determine their fate.

BIBLIOGRAPHY: Bernard Holland, review, *NYT* (June 22, 1986), I, 44 [on premiere].

Island Princess, The, or, Generous Portuguese, opera in a prologue and five acts by Daniel Purcell, with additions by Richard Leveridge (four songs) and Jeremiah Clarke (all of the instrumental music); libretto (Eng) by Peter Motteux, after John Fletcher's comedy. First performance January 1699, London, Drury Lane Theatre.

In the plot, set in the Spice Islands in the East Indies, Armusia, a Portuguese of noble birth, is engaged to marry Quisara, sister of the Island King. The pair are unjustly accused of various crimes and condemned to die, but at the last moment the truth is revealed, and the work ends happily.

See Fiske/*ETM*, 11–12 for a detailed description.

SCORE: ms fs (British Museum, 1698, Add. MS 15318, in Clarke's hand).

Isle of Youth, The. See **The Feast of Samhain.**

Isolt of the White Hands, opera in four acts by Fritz Hart; libretto (Eng) by E. A. Robinson. Composed 1933.

Israelites in Egypt, The, or, The Passage of the Red Sea, dramatic opera-oratorio by Michael Rophino Lacy, after Handel's *Israel in Egypt* (1739, London) and Rossini's *Mosè in Egitto* (1818, Naples); libretto (Eng) by Lacy. First performance February 22, 1833, London, Covent Garden. First U.S. performance October 31, 1842, New York.

LIBRETTO: English (London: Kenneth, [1833?]).

Italian Lesson, The, monodrama in one act by Lee Hoiby; libretto (Eng) by Mark Shulgasser, after Ruth Draper. First performance (concert) July 1982, Newport, Rhode Island, Newport Music Festival. First stage performance January 18, 1985, Baltimore, Baltimore Opera, with Jean Stapleton (the woman); conducted by Henry Mollicone.

The parody centers on a New York society matron who tries to arrange her busy social life in the midst of taking an Italian lesson.

Role: woman (sop/mezzo).

Composed to follow the curtain-raiser *Bon Appetit!**

BIBLIOGRAPHY: David Patrick Stearns, "Baltimore," *ON* XLIX (Apr. 13, 1985), 43 [on stage premiere].

Italian Villagers, The, comic opera in three acts by William Shield; libretto (Eng) by Prince Hoare. First performance April 25, 1797, London, Covent Garden.

The setting is Italy during the Renaissance. The story revolves around Valentine, who is in love with Isabel.

It Began at Breakfast, opera in one act by Robert Elmore; libretto (Eng). First performance February 18, 1941, Philadelphia.

Ivanhoe, or, The Knight Templar, musical drama by John Parry; libretto (Eng) by Samuel Beazley Jr., after Sir Walter Scott's novel (1819). First performance March 2, 1820, London, Drury Lane Theatre.

The work uses music from Storace. Among its highlights is "The Lullaby."
LIBRETTO: English (London: W. Smith, 1820).

Ivanhoe, grand opera in five acts by Arthur S. Sullivan; libretto (Eng) by Julian R. Sturgis, after Scott. First performance January 31, 1891, London, with Ben Davies (Ivanhoe), Eugène Oudin (Bois-Gilbert), Esther Palliser (Rowena), Margaret MacIntyne (Rebecca), and Avon Saxon (Friar Tuck). The work was composed for the inauguration of the Royal English Opera House at Cambridge Circus. It ran for 160 performances.

In this treatment of the story Ivanhoe and Lady Rowena are in love, but Rowena's guardian, Cedric, wants her to wed someone with royal blood. De Bracy and Bois-Gilbert, two knights Templar, attend a tournament and are so taken by the appearance of Rowena and Rebecca, a Jewish girl, that they kidnap them and also Cedric and Isaac, father of Rebecca. The victims are imprisoned in the castle of Torquilstone, which Ivanhoe attacks. When the errant knights escape with Rebecca, Ivanhoe catches up with them and challenges Bois-Gilbert to a duel, in which Bois-Gilbert is killed. King Richard the Lionhearted disbands the Templars and allows Ivanhoe and Rowena to wed.

Major roles: Ivanhoe (ten), Lady Rowena (sop), Cedric (bar), De Bracy (ten), Bois-Gilbert (bar), Rebecca (sop), Isaac (bar), and King Richard (bass).

Other settings of the Ivanhoe story include Parry's work (1820; see previous entry); *Ivanhoé*, pastiche of Rossini operas (1826, Paris), adapted by M. R. Lacy as *The Maid of Judah** (1829, London); H. Marschner, *Der Templer und die Jüdin* (1829, Leipzig); G. Pacini, *Ivanhoe* (Venice, 1832); O. Nicolai, *Il templario* (1841, Turin); and Pisani, *Rebecca* (1865). William Brough set the text to *Ivanhoe*, "an extravaganza in two acts"; it uses popular and borrowed airs (1850).
SCORE: vs (London: Chappell, 1891?).

I Was Looking at the Ceiling and Then I Saw the Sky, "song-play" in two acts by John Adams; libretto (Eng) by June Jordan. First performance May 11, 1995, Berkeley, California, Zellerbach Playhouse, with the Paul Dresher Ensemble; conducted by Grant Gershon; directed by Peter Sellars.

Set in Los Angeles in the 1990s, the story concerns residents of the inner city and their efforts to cope with their difficult situations. They include the preacher David, who defends Dewain after he is arrested by Mike for stealing. Dewain faces a long prison sentence, since he is a repeat offender.

Roles: David, a black Baptist minister; Leila, a black graduate student; Consuelo, an undocumented immigrant mother of two from El Salvador; Mike, a white cop and community activist; Dewain, a black reformed gang leader; Tiffany, a white television crime news reporter; and Rick, a Vietnamese American Legal Aid defense attorney.
LIBRETTO: English (New York: Scribner, 1995).

J

Jack and Roberta, opera in two acts by Thomas Cain; libretto (Eng) by the composer, after the play by Eugène Ionesco, *Jacques, ou, La soumission* (1953). First performance January 16, 1981, Riverside, Maryland, Prince George's Civic Opera; performed there as *Jack: The Submission*, January 24, 1982.
LIBRETTO: English (London: Printed for the Composer, [1975]).

Jack and the Beanstalk, "a fairy opera for children" in three acts by Louis Gruenberg; libretto (Eng) by John Erskine. First performance November 19, 1931, New York, Juilliard School of Music, with Mary Katherine Atkins (Jack), Beatrice Hegt (the mother), Pearl Besuner (the princess), and Raymond Middleton (the giant); conducted by Albert Stoessel. Revised version February 10, 1940, Brooklyn, New York, Brooklyn Academy of Music, with Alma Milstead (Jack), Marion Selee (the mother), Cecile Sherman (the princess), and Howard Laramy (the giant); Jack Radunski, piano.

A setting of the famous children's story.

The premiere was such a triumph that the opera then ran for another two weeks at the 44th Street Theater.
SCORE: ms score (1930, holograph, NYPL); vs (Boston: C. C. Birchard, 1930).
LIBRETTO: English (Indianapolis, The Bobbs-Merrill Company, 1931).
BIBLIOGRAPHY: review, *NYT* (Feb. 11, 1940), 50 [on rev. version].

Jack Benny Show, The, multimedia opera by John Moran, after the television series. First performance 1988, New York, Symphony Space.

Jackie O, pop opera in one act by Michael Daugherty; libretto (Eng) by Wayne Koestenbaum. First performance March 14, 1997, Houston, Wortham Theater Center, Houston Opera Studio, with Nicole Heaston (Jackie O), Eric Owens (Aristotle Onassis), Stephanie Novacek (Maria Callas), and Daniel Belcher (Andy Warhol); conducted by Christopher Larkin.

Inspired by the life of Jacqueline Kennedy Onassis, the ninety-minute work presents events that are "based on history, but are largely imaginary or metaphorical," according to the librettist. Included are the imagined duet of reconciliation between Jackie and Maria Callas after Jackie marries Onassis and a duet between Jackie and the ghost of her assassinated husband.
BIBLIOGRAPHY: William Albright, "Houston," *ON* LXII (July 1997), 43–44 [on premiere]; David Patrick Stearns, review, *BBC Music Magazine* (June 1997), 16 [on premiere].
DISCOGRAPHY: N. Heaston, E. Owens, S. Novacek, Houston Grand Opera; cond. C. Larkin, London 455 591-2 ZH (1 CD).

Jack of Newbury, opera in three acts with masque by James Hook; libretto (Eng) by James Hook Jr. First performance May 6, 1795, London, Drury Lane Theatre, with Miss Leake.

The work was concluded by a masque in honor of the marriage of the Prince and Princess of Wales.
SCORE: vs (London: Composer, [1795]).

Jack Sheppard, drama by George Rodwell; libretto (Eng) by John B. Buckstone, after William Harrison Ainsworth. First performance October 28, 1839, London, Adelphi Theatre.

Jacob and the Indians, opera in three acts by Ezra Laderman; libretto (Eng) by Ernest Kinoy, after Stephen Vincent Benét. First performance July 26, 1957, Woodstock, New York, Turnau Opera Players, with William Nahr (Jacob), Lucille Sullam (Naomi), and Harold Johnson (the merchant); designed by Tom de Gaetani; Jackson Wiley and Barbara Owens, pianos.

The time is before the American Revolution. A young Jewish scholar comes from Germany to Philadelphia. In order to make a living and marry Naomi, the daughter of a successful merchant, Jacob begins to trade with the Indians and live in the wilderness, an experience that helps him to develop as a person.

The music includes a Hasidic dance.

BIBLIOGRAPHY: Jan Maguire, review, *ON* XXII (Nov. 11, 1957), 24 [on premiere].

Jacob's Room, chamber opera in one act by Morton Subotnick; libretto (Eng), after Virginia Woolf, Nicholas Gage, Elie Wiesel, and Plato; video imagery by Steina and Woody Vasulke. First performance November 2, 1987, St. Paul, Minnesota. First complete performance, in three acts, April 20, 1993, Philadelphia, Klein Branch of the Jewish Community Centers of Greater Philadelphia, American Music Theater Festival, with Joan La Barbara (Mother/Guide), Thomas Buckner (reader), and Erika Duke-Kirkpatrick (cello); directed by Herbert Blau and John Alleyne. Originally a piece for soprano and string quartet (see below).

The work, written as a memorial to the Holocaust, is a commentary on universal suffering; it quotes from, among other texts, Woolf's *Jacob's Room* (1922), Plato's *Phaedrus*, Wiesel's *Night* (1958), and Gage's *Eleni* (1983), a memoir of the Greek civil war.

Composed initially for soprano and string quartet (1984), it was rescored for singer, cello, and computer-generated sounds (1987); and then for one singer, speaker, electronically-generated sounds, and video projections (1992). In this version the speaker recites passages from Woolf and Plato in the background.

BIBLIOGRAPHY: Allan Kozinn, "New Sounds," *NYT* (Mar. 10, 1992), C, 14 [on rev. version], and "Holocaust Memorials Can Also Be Operas," *NYT* (Apr. 22, 1993), C, 17 [on premiere of theater version].

DISCOGRAPHY: J. La Barbara and E. Duke, Wergo WER 2014-50 (1987 version).

Jailer, The, opera in one act by Dwight Gustafson; libretto (Eng) by the composer. First performance June 27, 1954, Greenville, South Carolina, Bob Jones University.

Jamie and Anna, "Scots pastoral" in one act by William Reeve; libretto (Eng). First performance ca. 1801, London.

SCORE: vs (London, ca. 1801).

Jane Annie, or, The Good Conduct Prize, comic opera in two acts by Ernest Ford; libretto (Eng) by James M. Barrie and Arthur Conan Doyle. First performance May 3, 1893, London, Savoy Theatre, with Rutland Barrington (a proctor), Lawrence Grindley (Sims), Rosina Brandram (Miss Sims), and Dorothy Vane (Jane Annie).

Despite the illustrious librettists, the work was a flop.

SCORE: vs (London: Chappell & Co., 1893).

LIBRETTO: English (London: Chappell & Co., 1893).

Jane Heir, satirical opera by Peter Healey; libretto (Eng) by the composer, after Charlotte Brontë's novel. First performance April 28, 1989, New York, Performance Space, Mesopotamian Opera, with Peter Healey (Jane) and Janet Norquist (St. John); conducted by Richard Gordon-Berg.

This spoof takes up the story where the Brontë tale ends. Rochester has died, and Jane has gone mad. Chester and Livia Servermoor have managed to become administrators of Rochester's estate. St. John arrives to take Jane to a warmer climate. The situation leads to the "famous signature sextet," a takeoff on Donizetti's *Lucia di Lammermoor* (1835, Naples).

The music work includes passages that evoke the music of Verdi and Handel, as well as that of Andrew Lloyd Webber.

BIBLIOGRAPHY: Will Crutchfield, review *NYT* (April 30, 1989), I, 64 [on premiere].

VIDEO: recording of April 30, 1989 performance (2 tapes, NYPL).

Jealous Cellist and Other Acts of Misconduct, The, opera in two acts by Eric Stokes; libretto (Eng) by Alvin Greenberg. First performance February 2, 1979, Minneapolis, Minnesota Opera.

The science fiction love story concerns two groups of people who are suddenly switched in terms of place and time.

Jealous Clown, The, ballad opera; libretto (Eng) by Thomas Gataker. First performance December 16, 1730, London, Goodman's Fields.

LIBRETTO: English (London, 1730); repr. Rubsamen/*BO*, vol. 12, *Farce: Amorous Intrigue and Deception*, I (1974).

Jeanie Deans, opera in four acts by Hamish MacCunn; libretto (Eng) by Joseph Bennett, after Sir Walter Scott's *Heart of Midlothian* (1818). First performance November 15, 1894, Edinburgh. Revived February 9, 1986, Opera West at Gaiety Theatre, with Paula Bott (Jeanie Deans), Philip Doghan (Staunton), Isabel Fitch (Lady Suffolk), Linda Hibberd (Queen Caroline), James Nicol (John, Duke of Argyle), Marilyn de Blieck (Madge Wildfire), and Una Buchanan (Effie); conducted by Raymond Bramwell; produced by de Blieck.

Jeanie Deans is a Scottish farmer's daughter, who travels, at great danger, to London in order to get a royal pardon for Effie, her half-sister, who has been wrongly accused of killing her illegitimate baby, fathered by Staunton, who has also seduced Madge Wildfire. Jeanie is successful, with the help of John, Duke of Argyle, in obtaining a pardon from Queen Caroline.

The work includes effective solos, ensembles, and choruses and uses Scottish folk music.

The Heart of Midlothian* (1819, 1849) is another setting of the story.

SCORE: vs (London: Mathias & Strickland, 1894).

BIBLIOGRAPHY: Arthur Jacobs, "Jeanie Deans," *Opera* XXXVII (1986), 592 (on 1986 revival).

Jenny, or, The Hundred Nights, fable in one act by Hugo Weisgall; libretto (Eng) by John Hollander, after the Noh play *Sotoba Komachi*, translated by Yukio Mishima. First performance April 22, 1976, New York, Juilliard School, American Opera Theater, with Penelope Daner (Jenny) and Ronald Hudlund (George); conducted by Bruce Ferden.

George, a photographer, comes across Jenny, an old hag of 99, in the park. She tells him that whoever perceives her as the beauty she once was will die. She recounts the tale of her suitor, whom she promised to wed if he courted her for 100 nights. George is drawn into the story and starts to tell Jenny how beautiful she is, but she reminds him of the consequences, and he regains his senses. He is unable, however, to keep his mind in the present and, calling Jenny beautiful, dies.

For a detailed description, see Kornick/*RAO*, 328–30.

Major roles: Jenny (sop) and George (bar).

BIBLIOGRAPHY: Harold C. Schonberg, review, *NYT* (Apr. 23, 1976), 26 [on premiere].

Jenny Lind, musical play by Dai-Keong Lee, a revision of *Phineas and the Nightingale**; libretto (Eng), after P. T. Barnum's *Recollections* (1878). Composed 1981.

Jeremiah, opera in four acts by Myron Fink; libretto (Eng) by Earlene Hawley. First performance May 25, 1962, Binghamton, New York, Tri-Cities Opera, Harpur College Auditorium. Revived April 23, 24, 29, 30, 1983, Binghamton, New York, the Forum, with Catherine Allard/Marilyn Altman (Rebecca Stephens), Janet Parker/Melissa Thorburn (Deborah Carter), Randolph Messing/Terry Chafee Shirk (Jeremiah Stephens), and Bruce Reed/Richard Leech (Samuel Stephens); conducted by Peyton Hibbitt/Duane Skrabalak.

The story is set around 1880 in rural southern Illinois, near the Ozark Mountains. The fanatical Jeremiah Stephens, after fighting with his wife, Rebecca, seeks consolation in the arms of the young schoolteacher who lives with them, Deborah Carter. Samuel, Jeremiah's son, is also taken with the young lady. When Deborah confesses before the congregation that she has sinned, they accuse Samuel of being her secret lover. The son reveals that it is Jeremiah who has in fact sinned, but the elder Stephens says he is above the judgment of the congregants. Left alone, Jeremiah reads the passage in the Bible about the sacrifice of Isaac. When Samuel comes to his father to make amends, Jeremiah, now mad, strangles his son.

For a detailed description, see Eaton/*OP* II, 120–21.

Major roles: Jeremiah Stephens (bar), Rebecca Stephens (sop), Samuel Stephens (ten), and Deborah Carter (mezzo).

SCORE: vs ([n.p., 1962]; LCCN: 84-89456).

BIBLIOGRAPHY: review, *NYT* (May 27, 1962), 51 [on premiere].

Jericho Road, opera in two acts by Pietro Aria; libretto (Eng) by Isabel Harriss Barr, after the Bible. First performance March 12, 1969, Philadelphia, Philadelphia Grand Opera.

Aria calls the work a "symbol of enlightenment and renewal" (see Ericson article).

BIBLIOGRAPHY: Raymond Ericson, "Long Road," *NYT* (Mar. 9, 1969), II, 19, 32.

Jessie Tree, The, church opera in one act by Elizabeth Maconchy; libretto (Eng) by Anne Ridler. First performance October 7, 1970, Dorchester Festival, Dorchester Abbey, with Philip Langridge.

Jessy Lea, "opera di camera" in two acts by George Macfarren; libretto (Eng) by John Oxenford, after Scribe's *Le philtre*, set by Auber (1831, Paris). First performance November 2, 1863, London, Gallery of Illustration. Revived June 4, 1988, London, Morley Opera at King's College, with Diane Atherton (Jessy) and Kathryn Hide (the gypsy girl); conducted by Stuart Hutchinson.

Jessy Lea, a local belle, has as her rival a gypsy girl.

SCORE: vs (London: Novello, Ewer & Co., [n.d.]).

BIBLIOGRAPHY: Arthur Jacobs, "Cradled among the Reeds: Two Victorian Operettas," *MT* CXXIX (May 1988), 234–35 [on revival].

Jest of Hahalaba, The, chamber opera in one act by Morris Cotel; libretto (Eng), after a play by Lord Dunsany. Composed 1961.

The work is set in the study of Sir Arthur on December 31, 1928.

SCORE: vs, ms (1961, NYPL, photocopy).

Jesus Christ Superstar, rock opera in two acts by Andrew Lloyd Webber; libretto (Eng) by Tim Rice. First performance October 12, 1971, New York, Mark Hellinger Theater, with Jeff Fenholt (Jesus), Ben Vereen (Judas Iscariot), Barry Denen (Pilate), and Yvonne Elliman (Mary Magdalene); conducted by Marc Pressel; directed by Tom O'Horgan.

The story is a retelling, in modern terms and language, of the last week of Jesus.

Among its numbers are the title song, sung by the chorus, and Mary Magdalene's "I Don't Know How to Love Him."

The work, which was criticized as being both anti-Semitic and sacrilegious, was successful. It was issued as a rock LP album before coming to the stage.

BIBLIOGRAPHY: Clive Barnes, "Theater: Christ's Passion Transported to the Stage in Guise of Serious Pop," *NYT* (Oct. 13, 1971), 40 [on premiere]; Lawrence Van Gelder, "Two Jewish Organizations Are Critical of 'Superstar,'" *NYT*, the same.

Jewel Box, The, or, a Mirror Remade, opera in two acts, with music by W. A. Mozart, arranged by Paul Griffiths; libretto (Eng) by Griffiths. First performance February 19, 1991, Nottingham, Opera North; conducted by Elgar Howarth. First U.S. performance 1991, Vienna, Virginia, Wolf Trap. First complete U.S. performance June 19, 1996, New York, American Opera Musical Theater Company, John Jay Theater, with Tammy Hensrud-Kerian (the Composer), Mary Paul (the Singer), Janet Momjian (Colombina), and Gary Lehman (Pantalone); conducted by Thomas Conlin; directed by Theodore Mann. Shortened version as *The Small Jewel Box** (1995, New York).

In this work the past is merged with the present. Four commedia dell'arte characters are stuck in the make-believe world of an unfinished opera buffa. They are able to transcend their time and get in touch with a composer from the past (Mozart); he falls in love with Colombina, whose attentions are also sought by Pedrolino, while at the same time being pressed by his father and others of his time to finish his own work. The Composer ultimately brings both worlds together by making a masterpiece incorporating the characters from the two.

The work uses music from the unfinished *Il sposo deluso* (1783) and *Die Zauberflöte* (1791). It is set in Singspiel style, with dialogue connecting Mozart's music.

BIBLIOGRAPHY: Paul Griffiths, "Filling 'The Jewel Box,'" *Opera* XLII (Jan. 1991), 24–27; Rodney Milnes, "Jewels in a Setting," *Opera* XLII (April 1991), 382–84 [on premiere]; James Oestreich, "A New Mozart Opera with Him in It? Sort Of," *NYT* (June 22, 1996), 14.

Jewel Merchants, The, comic opera in one act by Louis Cheslock; libretto (Eng) by James B. Cabell. First performance February 26, 1940, Baltimore.

Jewess, The, "grand operatic drama" in three acts by Thomas Cooke, adapted from Halévy's *La Juive* (1835, Paris); libretto (Eng) by James R. Planché, after Scribe's text. First performance November 16, 1835, London, Drury Lane Theatre.

Rachel, daughter of the Jewish goldsmith Eléazer, is attracted to Samuel, one of her father's workers whom she takes to be a fellow Jew but is really Prince Léopold in disguise. Eudoxia, Léopold's wife, convinces Rachel to deny any involvement with Léopold. Cardinal de Brogni, who has persecuted the Jews in the city, offers to save Rachel's life and his own if Eléazer renounces his faith; Eléazer reminds the prelate that the Cardinal's daughter, who has disappeared, was rescued by a Jew many years ago during a fire. Rachel also refuses to give up her faith and dies, whereupon Eléazer reveals that Rachel was really the Cardinal's daughter.

LIBRETTO: English (London: Porter and Wright, 1835).

Joan, or, The Brigands of Bluegoria, comic opera by Ernest Ford; libretto (Eng) by R. Martin. First performance June 9, 1890, London, Opera Comique.

Joan, opera in one act by Al Carmines; libretto (Eng) by the composer. First performance November 21, 1971, New York, Judson Memorial Church.
     This modern setting of the Joan of Arc story includes elements of the musical.
BIBLIOGRAPHY: Mel Gussow, review, *NYT* (Dec. 14, 1971), 55.

Joan of Arc, grand opera in three acts by Michael Balfe; libretto (Eng) by Edward Fitzball, after Robert Southey. First performance November 30, 1837, London, Drury Lane Theatre, with Emma Romer (Joan) and Mr. Baker (Charles VII).
     Other characters are Madelon, Dunois, Renaud, St. Catherine, Agnes, and Beauvais.
SCORE: fs ms, partly autograph (1837, British Library, Add. MS. 29331, 29332).
LIBRETTO: English (London: Wright, [1837]).

Joan of Arc, "historical music drama" in a prologue, three acts, and seven *tableaux vivants* by Raymond Rôze; libretto (Eng) by the composer. First performance November 1, 1913, London, Covent Garden, Raymond Rôze English Opera Season.

Joan of Arc, opera in one act by Eleanor Everest Freer; libretto (Eng) by the composer. First performance (stage) December 3, 1929, Chicago, Junior Friends of Art.
     A treatment of the French heroine, concentrating on her call to serve the Lord.
SCORE: vs (Milwaukee: William A. Jaun, [1929]).

Joan of Arc, church opera in one act by Geoffrey Burgon; libretto (Eng) by Susan Hill. Composed 1970.
     The work treats the story of the French fifteenth-century heroine, her claim of hearing voices, and her trial for heresy and witchcraft.
     The composer derived the music of the voices that Joan hears from two pieces of plainchant, one for the Epiphany, the day on which she was born, and the second for the Magnificat. The secular *L'homme armé* is also incorporated into the score.

Jocasta, opera in two acts by Ruth Schonthal; libretto (Eng) by the composer, after Helene Cicoux. First performance (excerpts) October 25, 1996, New York, Cornelia Conally Center.
     A treatment of the Oedipus story from the point of view of his mother.

Joe Hill, opera in two acts by Alan Bush; libretto (Eng) by Barrie Stavis, after his play *The Man Who Never Died*. First performance, in German, September 29, 1970, East Berlin, Staatsoper, with Erich Siebenschuh (Joe), Herbert Rössler (Ed Rowan), Nelly Ailakova (Mary Weber), Horst Hiestermann (Tom Sharpe/Scott McBride), and Siegfried Vogel (Alexander Marshall).
     The politically charged plot involves the execution of the Swedish-born labor agitator Joe Hill in 1915 in Salt Lake City for the murder of a prominent citizen. Hill is characterized here as the victim of the courts, and John T. Moody, a boss of the copper mine, has him framed for murder when his attempts to have Hill killed are unsuccessful.
     The score includes four of Hill's protest songs.
BIBLIOGRAPHY: James Helme Sutcliffe, review, *NYT* (Oct. 1, 1970), 54 [on premiere].

John Barleycorn, ballad opera in three acts for narrator and chorus by Bruce Montgomery; libretto (Eng) by Mary Fairclough. Composed 1962.
     The story of the work is based, like Robert Burns's poem, on a mythical character. It concerns the plot of his neighbors to kill Sir John Barleycorn during the harvest season. The scheme fails, and John forgives his tormenters.

SCORE: vs (London: Novello, [1962]).
LIBRETTO: English (London: Novello, [1962]).

John Brown, opera in three acts by Kirke Mechem; libretto (Eng) by the composer. Composed 1989.

The opera covers the events leading up to and surrounding the abortive attack by abolitionist John Brown and his followers in 1859 on the U.S. arsenal in Harper's Ferry, Virginia. Brown confides to Frederick Douglas that he, like Moses, has been chosen by God to lead the slaves to freedom. He is sentenced to execution by hanging for his deeds, and as the opera ends, Douglas proclaims, "You cannot bury him! As long as men love freedom, John Brown will never die."

John Hooten, opera in one act by William Russo; libretto (Eng) by the composer, after Shakespeare's *Othello*. First performance January 1963, London, BBC. First stage performance January 12, 1967, Chicago, Crane High School.

Based on Shakespeare's play, the work is set in the modern era.

Johnny and the Mohawks, children's opera in one act by Elizabeth Maconchy; libretto (Eng) by the composer. First performance March 1970, London, Francis Holland School.
SCORE: vs (London: Oxford University Press, [1970]).

John of Paris, comic opera in two acts by Henry Rowley Bishop, arranged and expanded from Boieldieu's *Jean de Paris* (1812, Paris); libretto by Isaac Pocock, after Saint-Just. First performance November 12, 1814, London, Covent Garden. First U.S. performance November 25, 1816, New York.
SCORE: vs (London, Goulding, D'Almaine, Potter, & Co. [n.d.]); *A March & Pastoral Dance* (New York: W. Dubois, [ca. 1820]).

John Socman, opera in three acts by George Lloyd; libretto (Eng) by William Lloyd. First performance May 15, 1951, Bristol, Hippodrome, Carl Rosa Opera Company.

The setting is England in 1415. Richard, an archer, returns from the Battle of Agincourt and discovers that his intended, Sybil, is being forced to marry John Socman, a magistrate, to save her father, Warner, from being labeled a heretic. The young lovers are spared when it turns out that Socman already has a wife.

Major roles: John Socman (bar), Richard (ten), Sybil (sop), and Warner (bass).
SCORE: vs (n.p., 1951).
BIBLIOGRAPHY: Harold D. Rosenthal, review, *Opera* II (1951), 421–23 [on premiere].

Johnson Preserv'd, chamber opera in three acts by Richard Stoker; libretto (Eng) by Jill Watt, after verses by Boswell. First performance 1967.

The work describes a meeting between the famous doctor and Boswell, his biographer. A misunderstanding leads Johnson to marry Mrs. Thrale, his landlady.
SCORE: vs (London: Peters, 1971).

Jolly Roger, The, or, The Admiral's Daughter, comic opera in three acts by Walter Leigh; libretto (Eng) by Scobie Mackenzie and V. C. Clinton-Baddeley. First performance February 13, 1933, Manchester, England.

Jonah, opera in two or three acts by Jack Beeson, "to be played, danced and sung"; libretto (Eng) by the composer, after Paul Goodman's play. Composed 1948–1950.

Jonah, opera-cantata by Hugo Cole; libretto (Eng) by the composer, after the Bible. Composed 1967.

Scored for nineteen roles, chorus, and orchestra.
SCORE: vs (Sevenoaks, Kent: Novello, [1967]).

Jonathan Postfree, or, The Honest Yankee, ballad opera in three acts; libretto (Eng) by Lazarus Beach. First performance 1807, New York.
LIBRETTO: English (New York: David Longworth, 1803).

Jongleur de Notre Dame, Le, masque by Peter Maxwell Davies; libretto (Latin and English) by the composer, after a medieval French legend. First performance June 18, 1978, Kirkwall, Scotland.
The work is based on the old French legend of the simple juggler who enters a monastery as a novice. Unable to compete with the other brothers (all performed by the musicians in the group) in designing gifts for the Virgin (a role performed by the female violinist in the group), he can offer as a gift only his juggling talent, which, nonetheless, moves the Virgin.
Cast: abbot (bar) and mime (juggler).
Also set by J. Massenet (1902, Monte Carlo).
SCORE: vs (London: Chester Music, 1978).

Joringel and the Songflowers, children's opera in one act by Margaret Garwood; libretto (Eng) by the composer, after the Brothers Grimm. First performance February 25, 1987, Roxborough, Pennsylvania.

Jōruri, opera in three acts by Minoru Miki; libretto (Eng) by Colin Graham, after Monzaemon Chikamatsu's puppet play. First performance May 30, 1985, St. Louis, Opera Theatre of St. Louis, with Faith Esham, John Brandstetter, Andrew Wentzel, and Mallory Walker; conducted by Joseph Rescigno.
The work, which contains elements of Kabuki, concerns the struggle between loyalty and the pull of human emotions.
SCORE: ms vs (1984, photocopy, NYPL).
BIBLIOGRAPHY: Andrew Porter, "Musical Events," *NY* LXI (July 1, 1985), 88ff. [on premiere]; James Wierzbicki, "St. Louis," *ON* L (Sept. 1985), 50–51 [on premiere].

José's Carmen, arrangement of Georges Bizet's *Carmen* by Mike Ashman; libretto (Eng) adapted from the French text. First performance November 22, 1984, London, Welsh National Opera, Cross Keys College, with Henry Newman (Escamillo).
The work is a condensation of the original score, and it is written for four singers and a pianist.
BIBLIOGRAPHY: "José's Carmen," *Opera* XXXV (1984), 211–12 [on premiere].

Journey, The, opera by John Metcalf; libretto (Eng) by John Hope Mason, partially inspired by *I Ching.* First performance June 12, 1981, Cardiff, Sherman Theatre, Wales National Opera, with Julian Moyle (the Story Teller), Lesley Garrett (Nicola), Menai Davies (Gwen), Timothy German (Scott), and Henry Newman (Craig); conducted by Anthony Hose; produced by John Eaton; designed by Peter Mumford.
The journey of the title is an imaginary one, and the music is in a serial style.
BIBLIOGRAPHY: Malcolm Boyd, review, *MT* CXXII (June 1981), 369–71.

Journey of Edith Wharton, The, "opera-biographica" in a prologue, two acts, and an epilogue by Roger Hannay; libretto (Eng), after Robert Graves. First performance 1988 (excerpts), Chapel Hill, University of North Carolina, Opera Workshop. Revised into one act, as *Scenes from a Literary Life,* 1990 (not perf.).

Journey of Mother Ann, The, opera in one act by Leonard Kastle; libretto (Eng) by the composer. First performance January 22, 1987, Albany, New York.

An opera about the Shakers. See also *The Calling of Mother Ann* (1985).

Jovial Crew, The, ballad opera; libretto (Eng) by Edward Roome, after Richard Brome's comedy (1641). First performance February 8, 1731, London, Drury Lane Theatre.

In this sympathetic treatment of beggars, the story involves young women who run away from home and travel dressed as beggars.

LIBRETTO: English (London: J. Watts, 1731); repr. Rubsamen/*BO*, vol. 17, *Country Operas III: Sentimental and Moral Comedies* (1974).

Jovial Crew, The, ballad opera, a revision by William Bates of the 1731 version (see preceding entry). First performance February 14, 1760, London, Covent Garden, with Miss Brent (Rachel), Mr. Beard, Mr. Lowe, and Mr. Mattocks. Retitled *The Ladies Frolick** (1770, London).

For a description, see Fiske/*ETM*, 397–99.

LIBRETTO: English (London: J. and R. Tonson, 1760).

Juan, or, The Libertine, opera by William Alwyn; libretto (Eng) by the composer. Composed 1969.

Jubilee, afterpiece in two parts by Charles Dibdin; libretto (Eng) by Isaac Bickerstaffe et al., after David Garrick's Shakespeare entertainment at Stratford. First performance October 14, 1769, London, Ranelagh Gardens. First U.S. performance June 1, 1795, Philadelphia, Chestnut Street Theatre.

The work was extremely popular in its time.

LIBRETTO: English, "Songs, Choruses, &c" (London: T. Becket and P. A. De Hondt, 1770).

Jubilee, opera in three acts by Ulysses Kay; libretto (Eng) by Donald Dorr, after Margaret Walker's novel (1966); November 20, 1976, Jackson, Mississippi, Opera/South.

The opera opens in 1859, as the Georgia plantation owner John Dutton holds a party to celebrate the engagement of his daughter Lillian to Kevin MacDougal, a young schoolteacher. Dutton has another daughter, Vyry, by his slave mistress, but he forbids her marriage to Randall Ware, a free black and father of her son, Jim.

In 1860, attempting to escape to the North, Vyry is captured and flogged. Since Ware does not know what happened, he assumes she has abandoned him on their flight to the North. At the end of the Civil War John Dutton is dead, poisoned by his cook, Mandy; Kevin has been killed in battle; and Lillian has become mentally unhinged after being attacked by a looter. Since Vyry has been left alone and does not know the whereabouts of Ware, she agrees to marry Innis Brown, a former slave. During a celebration of the community Ware returns and demands that he be given custody of Jim. His anger disappears when Vyry explains what has happened to her; she agrees to let Ware take their son north for a better life, and Vyry and Innis, having grown to love each other, plan their life together.

For a detailed description, see Kornick/*RAO*, 156–58.

Major roles: Lillian Dutton (sop), Vyry (mezzo), Innis Brown (ten), Randall Ware (bar), Kevin MacDougal (ten), and John Dutton (bass).

Judas Tree, The, "musical drama of Judas Iscariot" by Peter Dickinson; text (Eng) by Thomas Blackburn. First performance May 27, 1965, London.

The work is concerned with Judas Iscariot, who hanged himself because he could not bear the guilt he felt over betraying Christ. The first scene of this work opens with Judas lying prone in a state of complete withdrawal. Pilate, a detached observer, comments on Judas's situation and suggests that "without contraries there is no progression" and that the actions of Judas also furthered the kingdom of God.

The dark side of divine imagination is represented in the final scene of the work, which features a Nazi Kommandant.

The cast includes five speaking parts, two tenors, chorus, and a chamber orchestra. The work is intended for church production.

SCORE: vs (London: Novello, [1967]).

LIBRETTO: English (London: Novello, [1965]).

Judgment, The, opera in three acts by Meyer Kupferman; libretto (Eng) by P. Freeman. Composed 1966. Not performed.

A treatment of the story of Lot.

Judgment Day, opera in one act by Paul Berl; libretto (Eng) by Michael Pollon. First performance May 28, 1951, New York, Mannes Music School Opera Workshop, with Ingrid Hallberg/Lois McCauley (Hannah), Robert Price (Dr. Hopewell), Norman Atkins (Crumpin), Anthony Costa (Crunch), Newton Gammon (Pastor), and Grace Hoffman (Hopewell's mother).

The plot, which takes place in seventeenth-century New England, involves an innocent young woman who is accused of witchcraft but is exonerated in the end, with her villainous accuser committing suicide.

BIBLIOGRAPHY: Olin Downes, review, *NYT* (May 29, 1951), 20 [on premiere].

Judgment of Hercules, The, masque by Maurice Greene; libretto (Eng) probably by John Hoadly. First performance before 1740, London?

Hercules must choose between Virtue and Pleasure and selects the latter.

The music is lost.

Judgment of Paris, The, pastoral masque in one act by John Eccles; libretto (Eng) by William Congreve. First performance March 21, 1701, London, Dorset Gardens.

A telling of the Greek myth, in which Paris must judge who is the most beautiful, with his decision leading to untold woes, including the Trojan War.

See following two entries for other settings of Congreve's text.

SCORE: vs (London: John Walsh & John Hare, 1702); repr. ed. Richard Platt (Tunbridge Wells, England: R. Macnutt, 1984).

LIBRETTO: English, Purcell, Eccles, and Finger versions (London: Jacob Tonson, 1701).

Judgment of Paris, The, pastoral masque in one act by Gottfried Finger; libretto (Eng) by William Congreve. First performance no later than March 28, 1701, London, Dorset Garden.

LIBRETTO: English, Purcell, Eccles, and Finger versions (London: Jacob Tonson, 1701).

Judgment of Paris, The, pastoral masque in one act by Daniel Purcell; libretto (Eng) by William Congreve. First performance April 11, 1701, London.

SCORE: vs (London: I. Walsh, [1700]).

LIBRETTO: English, Purcell, Eccles, and Finger versions (London: Jacob Tonson, 1701).

Judgment of Paris, The, pastoral ballad opera in one act; anonymous libretto (Eng). First performance May 4, 1731, London, Lincoln's Inn Fields.

LIBRETTO: English (London, J. Roberts, 1731).

Judgment of Paris, The, masque by Thomas Arne; libretto (Eng) by William Congreve. First performance March 12, 1742, London, Drury Lane Theatre, with John Beard (Paris), Thomas Lowe (Mercury), Mrs. Arne (Venus), Mrs. Clive (Pallas), and Mrs. Edwards (Juno). Expanded version April 3, 1759, London, Covent Garden.
For a detailed description, see Fiske/*ETM*, 194–98.
Also an entertainment, with music by Seedo and text by John Weaver (1733, London).
SCORE: facsimile, ed. Ian Spink, *Musica Britannica*, vol. 42 (London: Stainer and Bell, 1978).

Judgment of Paris, The, burletta in two acts by François-Hippolyte Barthelemon; libretto (Eng) by Ralph Schomberg. First performance 1768, London, Theatre Royal in the Haymarket.
LIBRETTO: English (London: T. Becket and P. A. De Hondt, 1768).

Judgment of St. Francis, The, opera in one act by Nicolas Flagello; libretto (Eng) by Armand Aulicino. First performance March 18/19, 1966, New York, Manhattan School of Music, with Emilio Beleval/Lindsey Bergan (Francis), Marc Belfort/Richard Clark (his father), Jane Judge/Judith De Paul (his mother), and John Brownlee (Bishop Guido); conducted by Anton Coppola; directed by Carlton Gauld.
The story, told in flashbacks, deals with the 1207 trial of Francis (Francesco), before Guido II, bishop of Assisi. Francis has been accused by his rich father of stealing his money to rebuild a local church. The bishop rules that money, if stolen, cannot be used, even for sacred purposes.
Major roles: Francis (ten); Madonna Pica, his mother (sop); Clara (lyric sop); Pietro, Francis's father (bar); a priest (bass); and the bishop (bass).
For a detailed description, see Eaton/*OP* II, 288.
The work, described as "in rondo," contains four scenes in the episcopal palace, with three intervening episodes consisting of flashbacks.
BIBLIOGRAPHY: Joel Hoenig, "New York," *ON* XXX (May 7, 1966), 22 [on premiere]; Allen Hughes, "A Flagello Opera," *NYT* (Mar. 19, 1966), 18 [on premiere].

Judith, lyric drama in three acts by George W. Chadwick; libretto (Eng) by William Chauncy Langdon, after the Book of Judith. First performance (concert) September 26, 1901, Worcester, Massachusetts, Worcester Festival.
In this version the widowed Judith, offering herself to the Assyrian army commander Holofernes in order to save her people, cuts off his head and takes it back to Ozias, the leader of the Israelite camp.
Roles: Judith (mezzo), Achior (ten), Holofernes (bar), Ozias (bass), and sentinel (ten).
SCORE: vs (New York: G. Schirmer, [1901]); repr. ed. H. Wiley Hitchcock, *Early American Music*, vol. 3 (New York: Da Capo, 1972).

Judith, opera in one act by Eugene Goossens; libretto (Eng) by Arnold Bennett, after the Old Testament story. First performance June 25, 1929, London, Covent Garden, with Göta Ljungberg (Judith).
The Assyrian army general Holofernes imprisons Achior, an Ammonite, for having advised the warrior not to attack the Judean city of Bethulia. The beautiful Judith, chosen by her people to save the city, comes with her servant Haggith to speak with Holofernes and wins the freedom of Achior. Bagoas, Holofernes's chief eunuch, is delighted by Judith's appearance, and Holofernes is determined to seduce Judith. Invited to dine with Holofernes, she gets him drunk, and, as he is incapacitated, she kills him.

SCORE: vs (London: J. &. W. Chester, [1929]).
LIBRETTO: English (London: J. &. W. Chester, [1929]).

Judith, opera in one act by Douglas Smith; libretto (Eng) by Pauline Smolin, after the Book of Judith. First performance September 4, 1982, Cincinnati.

Judith and Holofernes, opera in three acts by Myron S. Fink; libretto (Eng) by Donald Moreland, after Giradoux's play. First performance (concert) February 4, 1978, Purchase, New York, SUNY, with Eileen Schauler (Judith) and Arthur Burrows (Holofernes).

The plot focuses on the complex relationship of the title characters.

Also opera by Ian McQueen, as *Judith och Holofernes* (1987, Vadstena, Sweden), in English as *Line of Terror**; puppet opera in one act by David Lang (1990, Munich).
SCORE: ms vs, holograph (1977, photocopy, signed, NYPL).

Juggler of Our Lady, The, opera in one act by Ulysses Kay; libretto (Eng) by Alexander King. First performance February 3, 1962, New Orleans.

The juggler Colin, stranded after a fair, seeks refuge in a church. When he cannot sleep, he comes into the chapel and is taken by the statue of the Virgin. Since he has nothing to give, he offers his talents as a juggler and performs his act. He falls asleep exhausted, and the statue bends over to bless him. The suspicious monks who have been watching him are nonplussed.

Major roles: Colin (ten); Martin, companion of Colin (bar); and Chrysostom and Nicodemus, monks (ten, bar).

For a detailed description, see Eaton/*OP* II, 289.
SCORE: fs (copy: [New York]: Pembroke Music, 1978).

Julia, light opera in three acts by Roger Quilter; libretto (Eng) by Jeffrey Lambourne. First performance December 3, 1936, London, Covent Garden; conducted by Albert Coates.

The story is a fictionalized account of the romance between the artist George Morland and Anne Ward, sister of the engraver James Ward.
SCORE: vs, as *Love at the Inn* (London: Ascherberg, Hopwood & Crew, 1949).

Julian, drama in five scenes by Charles Fussell; libretto (Eng), after Gustav Flaubert. First performance April 15, 1972, Winston-Salem, North Carolina.

Julian, the Apostate Caesar, opera in three acts by Lazare Saminsky; libretto (Eng) by the composer. Composed 1933–1938.

The work is set in the fourth century A.D. in Ephesus and Antioch. It concerns the Roman emperor Julian, who renounced Christianity upon becoming emperor.

Major roles: Caesar Julian, nephew of Constantine (bar); Ayreneh, Julian's wife (sop); Agneh, her sister, a Christian nun (mezzo); Paullinus, a Christian presbyter (bass-bar); Jovian, the Roman commander (ten); and Maximas, high priest of the Sun God (ten).
SCORE: vs, as *The Defeat of Caesar Julian (Christus Vincit)* (London: J. & W. Chester, 1959).

Julius Caesar Jones, children's opera in two acts by Malcolm Williamson; libretto (Eng) by Geoffrey Dunn. First performance January 4, 1966, London, Jannetta Cochrane Theatre, Finchley Children's Music Group, with April Cantelo and Anna Pollak; produced by William Chappell; designed by Peter Rice.

At a party given by the Everetts the children go off and play their own game, which takes place on a Polynesian island ruled by the strict Julius Caesar Jones. When Ambrose gives the secret sign away to his father, his playmates "condemn" him to death.

Called back to the party, all the children break out of the fantasy except Ambrose, who has fainted. Discovering this, the parents are shocked and distressed.

Roles: adults: Mr. Everett (bar); Mrs. Everett (sop); and Mrs. Whyley, Mrs. Everett's sister (mezzo); children: John, Elizabeth, and Ambrose Everett (treble, sop, treble); Susan Whyley (mezzo); and Harven, Ambrose's friend (treble); fantasy children and animals: Aloma (mezzo), Jess (sop), Babs (sop), Julius Caesar Jones (boy mezzo/bar), Silas Gapteeth (treble), the leopard (mezzo), Toomie (treble), Bimbo (treble), and tortoise (silent).

For a detailed description, see Eaton/*OP* II, 289–90.

Jumping Frog of Calaveras County, The, comic opera in one act by Lukas Foss; ibretto (Eng) by Jean Karsavina, after Mark Twain's story *The Celebrated Jumping Frog of Calaveras County.* First performance May 18, 1950, Bloomington, Indiana, Indiana University, with Alton E. Wilder, Lou Herber, and Charles Campbell; conducted by Ernst Hoffman.

Jim Smiley brags about the exploits of his amazing frog, Dan'l Webster, which is capable of jumping farther than any other frog in the county. His audience consists of Lulu, the town belle, and Uncle Henry, owner of the bar. During the discussion the Stranger comes in and, skeptical of Jim's claims, challenges him to a frog race. He then asks Jim to find another frog to take part in the race and, while Jim is gone, fills Dan'l Webster with quail shot.

The scene switches to the public square, on which the race is to take place. The various townspeople lay bets on Dan'l, but when the race begins, he is unable to move. The Stranger begins to leave with his winnings, but Jim, discovering the quail shot, wrests the money away from the Stranger and drives him out of the county.

For a detailed description, see Eaton/*OP* I, 192–93.

Major roles: Jim Smiley (ten), Uncle Henry (bar), Lulu (mezzo), and the Stranger (bass).

BIBLIOGRAPHY: Paul Nettl, "Indiana University," *MA* LXX (May 1950), 11 [on premiere].

Junípero Serra, opera in one act by Wells Hively; libretto (Eng) by the composer. First performance March 28, 1953, Palma de Mallorca, Spain.

The work is set at a mission in San Carlos Borromeo, Monterey, California, in June 1780.

Roles: Junípero Sera, president, Franciscan enterprises, California (bass); Felipe de Neve, governor of California (ten); Juan Crospi, associate of Serra (bar); Marguerita, Indian convert (sop); Domingo, an Indian convert (ten); Fortún, a corporal (ten); Diego, an Indian outlaw (bar); Matilaha, an old pagan Indian (mezzo).

The music contains two authentic mission melodies.

SCORE: copyist's score (1953, NYPL).

Juniper Tree: A Tragic Household Tale, The, play with music by Wendy Kesselman; libretto (Eng) by the composer, after the Brothers Grimm. First performance July 7, 1982, Lenox, Massachusetts, Lenox Arts Center Music Theater Group.

See the following entry for the plot.

LIBRETTO: English (New York: S. French, 1982, 1985).

Juniper Tree, The, children's opera by Philip Glass and Robert Moran; libretto (Eng) by Arthur Yorinks, after the Brothers Grimm. First performance December 11, 1985, Cambridge, Massachusetts, American Repertory Theater, with Lynn Torgove (the son), Ruby Hinds (the stepmother), Sanford Sylvan (the father), Jayne West (the first wife), and Janet Brown (the daughter); conducted by Robert Pittman.

The gruesome story, which includes murder and cannibalism, concerns a couple who desire a child desperately. The wife, however, dies when giving birth to their son and the father remarries. The second wife, after bearing a daughter, is so jealous of the memory of the first wife that she kills the boy and makes her daughter believe that the young woman was responsible for the boy's death. The daughter buries his bones near a juniper tree. His soul enters a bird attached to the tree, and the bird drops a millstone on the stepmother, which kills her. The son is thereby reborn and rejoins his family, taking the place of the evil stepmother.

Written in a quasi-minimalist style.

Major roles: the father (bar), the mother (sop), the son (sop), the daughter (sop), and the stepmother (mezzo).

BIBLIOGRAPHY: John Rockwell, review, *NYT* (Dec. 15, 1985), I, 103 [on premiere].

Juniper Tree, The, chamber opera in one act by Andrew Toovey; libretto by Dic Edwards, after the Brothers Grimm. First performance July 27, 1993, Broomhill, Kent.

In this version, the stepmother is spared and offered the hope of redemption.

BIBLIOGRAPHY: Andrew Porter, review, *Opera* XLIV (Oct. 1993), 1245–46 [on premiere].

Juniper Tree, The, opera by Roderick Watkins; libretto (Eng) by Patricia Debney, after the Brothers Grimm. First performance April 1997, Munich, Biennale. First British performance June 30, 1997, London, Almeida Theatre, Almeida Opera, with Louise Mott (Marlinchen), Robert Poulton, (father), and Timothy Webb (the boy); conducted by Markus Stenz; produced by Michael Vale.

BIBLIOGRAPHY: Max Loppert, review, *Opera* (Sept. 1997), 1098–1101 [on premiere]; Andrew Clements, review, *Opera* XLVIII (Sept. 1997), 112–14 [on British premiere].

Jupiter, or, The Cobbler and the King, comic opera in two acts by Julian Edwards; libretto (Eng) by Harry B. Smith. First performance April 14, 1892, New York.

Jupiter and Alcmena, comic opera in three acts by Charles Dibdin; libretto (Eng) by the composer, after Dryden's *Amphitryon*. First performance October 27, 1781, London, Covent Garden.

In the story Jupiter seduces Alcmena in the guise of Amphitryon, her husband.

The work was an abysmal failure and received only two performances.

Also burletta, as *The Burletta of Errors, or, Jupiter and Alcmena*, to a text by James R. Planché (1820, London), after Dryden.

Justice, or, The Caliph and the Cobbler, musical drama in three acts by Charles Horne; libretto (Eng) by John S. Faucit. First performance November 28, 1820, London, Drury Lane Theatre.

LIBRETTO: ms, promptbook (ca. 1820, NYPL).

Just in Time, opera in three acts by Thomas Carter; libretto (Eng) by Thomas Hurlstone. First performance May 10, 1792, London, Covent Garden, with Mr. Fawcett (Doctor Camomile), Charles Incledon (Melville), Mr. Munden (Stave), and Miss Dahl (Augusta)

The newly rich Sir Solomon Oddly, formerly a grocer, wishes his daughter Augusta to marry Doctor Camomile, a quack who is after Oddly's fortune. Augusta herself is in love with Melville. She is saved from marrying Camomile when he turns out to have a wife, Maria, who has been staying in the cottage of the young parish clerk Stave.

For a detailed description, see Fiske/*ETM*, 549–50.

K

Kabballah, chamber opera in seven movements by Stewart Wallace; libretto (Eng, Hebrew, etc.) by Michael Korie. First performance November 16, 1989, Brooklyn, New York, Brooklyn Academy of Music.

The text is a combination of Hebrew, Aramaic, German, Spanish, and English.

SCORE: vs, ms (1989, photocopy, NYPL).

DISCOGRAPHY: Koch CD 370 482 H1.

Kafka's Chimp, opera by John Metcalf; libretto (Eng) by Mark Morris. First performance August 1, 1996, Banff, Alberta, with Steven Horst (Red Peter), Michael Douglas Jones (the scientist), and Frances Pappas (the lady).

In this comedy, Red Peter, a chimp from the African Gold Coast, is dragged back to Europe. In order to escape being placed in a zoo, he tries to become human and succeeds in part, only to have his animal background appear from time to time. By the end Peter gains a lady friend, and the scientist who tries to display him starts acting like a chimp.

Major roles: Red Peter (bar), the scientist (ten), and the lady (sop).

BIBLIOGRAPHY: Norbert Ruebsaat, "Banff" *ON* LXI (Dec. 14, 1996), 62 [on premiere].

Kais, opera in four acts by William Reeve and John Braham; libretto (Eng) by Isaac Brandon, after I. Disraeli's romance *Mejnoun and Leila*. First performance February 11, 1808, London, Drury Lane Theatre.

LIBRETTO: English (London: Murray, 1808).

Kalamona and the Four Winds, children's opera in one act by Leslie Kondorossy; libretto (Eng) by Shawn Hall, after a Hungarian fairy tale. First performance September 12, 1971, Cleveland, Shawn Hall.

SCORE: vs (Cleveland: Hermes Music, [1972]).

Kamouraska, opera in three acts by Charles Wilson; libretto (Eng) by the composer, after Anne Hébert's work (1973). First performance (concert) November 3, 1979, Toronto, Comus Music Theatre Studio.

Karla, opera in one act by Leonard Lehrman; libretto (Eng) by the composer, after Bernard Malamud's *Notes from a Lady at a Dinner Party*. First performance, as *Notes from a Lady*, August 3, 1974, Ithaca, New York. First professional performance March 7, 1976, Bloomington, Indiana; also January 14, 1978, New York, Bel Canto Opera, with Stephen Owen (Clem), Allan H. Glassman (Max), and Valerie Saalbach (Karla); conducted by Randal Hoey; Georgianna Pappas, piano.

The story involves the morals or lack of them of the affluent set. A young architect, Ralph Lewin, and his wife, Ada, are invited to the home of Ralph's mentor, Clem Harris, an older professor of architecture at Columbia University. Clem and his wife, Karla, are giving a party in honor of Max Adler, the brilliant former student of Ralph and Clem. At the party Ralph flirts with Karla, who is much younger than her husband, and plans to meet her at a motel later. As the evening progresses, however, Karla becomes upset and tries to pass a note to Ralph. She drops it, and it is picked up by Shirley, a divorced secretary who was supposed to be Ralph's date, but she gives the missive to Ralph without reading it. Karla, it turns out, is six months pregnant.

For a detailed description, see Summers/*OOA*, 195–97.

Major roles: Karla Harris (sop); Clem Harris, a professor of architecture (bass-bar); Ralph Lewin (ten); Ada Lewin, his wife (mezzo); Shirley Fisher, Clem's secretary (mezzo/alto); and Max Adler, a former student (bar).

Part of the *Tales of Malamud*, together with Blitzstein's *Idiots First*.*
SCORE: vs (Bryn Mawr, Pa.: T. Presser, 1975).
BIBLIOGRAPHY: Peter G. Davis, "2 'Malamud' Operas," *NYT* (Jan. 18, 1978), C, 19 [on N.Y. premiere].

Keolanthe (Këolanthé), or, The Unearthly Bride, opera in two acts by Michael Balfe; libretto (Eng) by Edward Fitzball. First performance March 9, 1841, London, Lyceum, with Lina Roser (Keolanthe).

The story involves a young Italian student and the title character, an ancient Egyptian princess.
SCORE: piano score, overture (London: Cramer, Addison, & Beale, [184?]).

Key Money, opera in one act by Michael Head; libretto (Eng) by Nancy Bush. First performance April 1970, London, Mercury Theatre, Intimate Opera Company.

Killing No Murder, farce in two acts by James Hook; libretto (Eng) by Theodore Edward Hook. First performance probably August 21, 1809, London, Little Theatre in the Haymarket.
LIBRETTO: English (London: S. Tipper, 1809; New York: D. Longworth, 1809).

King, The, opera in five acts by Fritz Hart; libretto (Eng) by the composer, after S. Phillips. Composed 1921.

King Alfred and the Cakes, opera in one act by Nicholas Gatty; libretto (Eng) by Reginald Gatty. First performance December 10, 1930, London, Royal College of Music.

King Arthur, or, The British Worthy, "a dramatick opera" in a prologue, five acts, and an epilogue by Henry Purcell; words (Eng) by John Dryden, a sequel to *Albion and Albanius** (1685). First performance May or June 1691, London, Dorset Gardens, with Mr. Betterton (Arthur), Mr. Williams (Oswald), Mr. Kynaston (Merlin), Mr. Sandford (Osmond), Mrs. Bracegirdle (Emmeline), Mrs. Butler (Philidel), and Mr. Bowman (Grimbald). First U.S. performance April 25, 1800, New York, Park Theatre. Revivals include a new version by Colin Graham and Philip Ledger; first performance October 19, 1970, Norwich Festival, English Opera Group. Another revival December 17, 1970, Edinburgh, English Opera Group, with April Cantelo (Emmeline), Benjamin Luxon (Arthur), Denis Dowling (Merlin), and Michael Rippon (Grimbald); conducted by Philip Ledger.

In this tale of the Arthurian legend, King Arthur battles with the Saxon Oswald, king of Kent, for his kingdom and for the freedom of the beautiful Emmeline, wife of Arthur. Each side is aided by sorcerers and spirits, with Osmond and Grimbald assisting Oswald and with Merlin and Philidel helping Arthur. Arthur is victorious in the end and, after defeating the Saxons, forgives Oswald for his treachery.

Major roles: King Arthur, Oswald, Osmond, Merlin, and Emmeline (all speaking); and Philidel (sop) and Grimbald (bar).

The main protagonists have speaking parts (parts that are sung in modern revivals). The chief vocalists are the spirits Philidel and Grimbald, who also speak, in a departure from the common semi-opera. Among the musical highlights are the battle air and chorus of the Britons in the first act, "Come if You Dare, Our Trumpets Sound"; the second-act "Hither This Way," led by Philidel; the magnificent "What Power Art Thou," sung in the Frost Scene of the third act by the Cold Genius; the immense passacaglia of act 4, "How Happy the Lover," constructed on a ground bass of four bars; and, in the celebratory act 5 after Arthur's victory, the bass aria "Ye Blust'ring Brethren of the Skies."

There are at least thirty operas on the subject of King Arthur, including E. Chausson's posthumous *Le roi Arthus* (1903, Brussels).

SCORES: fs, ed. Dennis Arundell, *The Works of Henry Purcell*, vol. 26 (London, 1928); rev. ed. Margaret Laurie (London: Novello and Co., 1971); vs ed. Margaret Laurie (Borough Green, Sevenoaks, Kent: Novello, 1972).
LIBRETTO: English (London: Jacob Tonson, 1691).
BIBLIOGRAPHY: Colin Graham, "*King Arthur* Revised and Revived," *Opera* XXI (1970), 904–10; Alan Swanson, "Edinburgh," *ON* XXXV (Feb. 13, 1971), 30–31.
DISCOGRAPHY: B. Bannatyne-Scott, English Concert; cond. T. Pinnock, Archiv 435 490-2 (1991); rev. Jonathan Freeman Attwood, *MT* CXXXIII (Jan. 1993), 41; V. Gens, C. McFadden, S. Piau, S. Waters, M. Padmore, I. Paton, J. Best, P. Salomaa, F. Bazola; Les Arts Florissants; cond. W. Christie, Erato (Atlantic Classics) 98535-2 (1995, 2 CDs); rev. Roland Graeme, "Recordings," *OJ* XII (Summer 1996).

King Charles II, opera in two acts by George Macfarren; libretto (Eng) by Desmond L. Ryan, after John H. Payne's comedy. First performance October 27, 1849, London, Princess's Theatre.
LIBRETTO: English (London: Chappell, Cramer, Beale, [185?]).

Kingdom Come, opera in one act by Wilton Mason; libretto (Eng). First performance August 17, 1953, Boone, North Carolina, Administration Hall, Appalachian State Teachers College.

Kingdom for a Cow, A, musical play by Kurt Weill; book (Eng) by Reginald Arkell; lyrics by Desmond Carter. First performance June 28, 1935, London, Savoy Theatre. Restored German version first performed March 23, 1990, Düsseldorf, Tonhalle.

This satire is set in an imaginary Caribbean island consisting of the countries of Santa Maria and Ucqua. The arms dealer Leslie Jones tries to ply his trade by inciting war between the two nations. Mendez, the president of Santa Maria and a pacifist, nevertheless accepts Jones's money by buying weapons he does not intend to use. Jones, with the support of General Conchas, propels the two countries toward war. Caught in between are Juan and Juanita, villagers who plan to get married. Juan, although drafted into Santa Maria's army, refuses to fight and instead beats up the General. When Juan is sent before a firing squad for his actions, he is saved because the weapons the soldiers use to shoot him have been rendered powerless. The General, realizing the benefits of peace, spares Juan and allows him to wed Juanita.

Major roles: Leslie Jones (bar), President Mendez (ten buffo), General Conchas (high bar), Juan (lyr ten), and Juanita (lyr sop).

The work, based on Weill's unfinished operetta *Der Kuhhandel*, to a text by Robert Vambery, ran for only three weeks in London. Weill used some of the music for later works, for example the opening theme of "September Song." The original libretto of

Vambery was revised in 1977 and a performance version created by Lys Symonette; this version was first performed in 1990 .
DISCOGRAPHY: restored German version, excerpts, E. Büchner, L. Peacock, C. Schotenröhr, W. Raffeiner, O. Hillebrandt, Kölner Rundfunkorchester; cond. J. Latham-König, Capriccio CD 60-013-1.

Kingdom of the Birds, The. See **The Wonders in the Sun**.

King Hal, romantic opera in three acts by Humphrey John Stewart; libretto (Eng) by Daniel O'Connell, revised by Allan Dunn. First performance scheduled for 1906 in San Francisco, with Joseph D. Redding (the King), Mrs. Dickman, Mrs. Clarence Eddy, Mrs. Mary Wyman Willis, Donald Grant, and Elmer De Pue, but the fire destroyed the performing materials, including the orchestral score, the band parts, and the sets. Performed 1911, San Francisco.

The work is set in the time of Henry VIII. Leonard is in love with Phyllis, but her father, Bardolph, owner of the Star and Garter Inn, is against the match. The King comes in disguise to the inn and woos the girl, whereupon Leonard strikes him, a capital offense. Leonard flees into the forest with the outlaws, who capture Robert, and he betrays them all to the King's guards. Phyllis begs for mercy, the King relents, and Robert, the constable of Windsor, is forced to wed the widow Dorothy as punishment.

Roles: King Hal (bar); Leonard, a forester (ten); Bardolph, landlord of the Star and Garter Inn, Windsor (bass); Ralph, chief of the outlaws (bass); Dickson, outlaw (ten); Robert (ten); Phyllis, daughter of Bardolph (sop); Dorothy, widow (mezzo); and Elizabeth, Bardolph's wife (alto).

Also known as *Bluff King Hal.*
SCORE: vs (New York: J. Fischer, 1911).

King Harald, opera in three acts by Anders Emile; libretto (Eng) by Cleveland Wilson. First performance January 7, 1948, New York, Hunter College.

King Harald's Saga, "grand opera" in three acts for solo soprano by Judith Weir; libretto (Eng) by the composer, after the Icelandic saga *Heimskringal.* First performance May 17, 1979, Dumfries, Scotland, Dumfries Music Club.

The story concerns the Norwegian invasion of England by King Harald "Hardradi," resulting in defeat for the invaders at the Battle of Stamford Bridge. Nineteen days later the Normans triumphed at the Battle of Hastings.

The soprano sings eight roles.
DISCOGRAPHY: J. Manning, Cala Records CACD 88040 (1995, 1 CD).

King Kong, "an African jazz opera" by Todd Matshikiza; book (Eng) by Harry Bloom; lyrics by Pat Williams. Composed 1961.
LIBRETTO: English (London: Collins, 1961).

King of Cadonia, The, musical play by Sidney Jones; book (Eng) by Frederick Lonsdale; lyrics (Eng) by Adrian Ross. First performance September 3, 1908, London, Prince of Wales, with Gracie Leigh (Malitza) and Bertram Wallis. First U.S. performance January 10, 1910, New York, Daly's Theatre, with Marguerite Clark, William Norris, and Robert Dempster.

A king disguises himself as a commoner and goes among his people to find out their opinion of him.

The work ran for 330 performances in London. Its two-week New York run included additions by Jerome Kern.
SCORE: vs (London: Keith, Prowse, 1908).
LIBRETTO: English (London: Keith, Prowse, & Co., 1908).

King of Cats, The, opera in one act by Harold Oliver; libretto by Eleanor Keats, after a story by Stephen Vincent Benét. Composed 1976.

The setting is New York, the present or recent past. A visiting conductor, Monsieur Thibault, is admired by all kinds of society women, including Princess Kauarda, which makes her companion, Tommy, extremely jealous. At a party thrown by Mrs. Dingle, the Princess and the conductor meet and are drawn to each other. Desperate, Tommy, who has noticed that the conductor resembles a cat, consults an occult specialist, Billy Strange. Strange tells him the tale of the "King of the Cats," which he instructs Tommy to recite at the next party that Thibault attends. The ensuing get-together is an engagement party for Thibault and the Princess. When Tommy recites his story, Thibault becomes increasingly upset and exclaims that he is, in fact, the king of the cats, and vanishes up the chimney in a cloud of smoke.

For a description, see Summers/*OOA*, 235–36.

Major roles: Tommy Brooks (ten), Princess Kauarda (col sop), Monsieur Thibault (male dancer/speaking role), and Mrs. Dingle (mezzo/alto).
SCORE: ms score, holograph (1976, photocopy, NYPL).

King of Hearts, television opera in one act by Michael Torke; libretto (Eng) by Chris Rawlence. First performance February 26, 1995, BBC, Channel 4, with Hilton McCrae (Charles), Lynne Davies (Helen), and Omar Ebrahim (Antoine). First U.S. (and stage) performance July 27, 1996, Aspen, Colorado, Wheeler Opera House, with Scott Wyatt (Antoine), Sarah Turner (Helen), and Alfred Walker III (Charles); conducted by the composer; directed by Edward Berkeley.

The story centers on Antoine, a shy and inhibited physics teacher who is receiving analysis from Charles. Helen, a fellow teacher of Antoine, is Charles's wife. She too feels that her life is without romance. When Antoine finds Helen's purse, which has been stolen, the two are thrown together and, by the end, become lovers, thereby excluding Charles.

Major roles: Antoine (ten), Helen (sop), and Charles (bass).
BIBLIOGRAPHY: Glenn Giffin, "Aspen, CO," *ON* LXI (Dec. 14, 1996), 64–65 [on U.S. premiere]; Jeffrey Josephs, "The Little Picture Show," *MT* CXXXVI (May 1995), 254–55 [on premiere].

King of the Clouds, children's opera in one act by Michael Ching and Hugh Moffat; libretto (Eng). First performance January 18, 1993, Dayton, Ohio, Dayton Opera. Tour by New Orleans Opera, September 1993.

About the problems faced by ordinary people.
BIBLIOGRAPHY: Frank Gagnard, "'Kid Opera' in the Key of Life," *Times-Picayune* (Sept. 18, 1993), E, 1 [on tour].

King of the Golden River, opera for children in two acts and three scenes by Colin Hand; libretto by (Eng) Edwin H. Alton, freely adapted from the story by John Ruskin. Composed 1969.

Three brothers, Hans, Schwartz, and Gluck, live in the country of Styria, some time in the legendary past. Hans and Schwartz work the land, and Gluck, the youngest of the three, looks after the cottage and does the cooking and is often treated badly by his siblings. One evening he is visited by a mysterious stranger. The elder brothers dismiss him rudely, and their actions bring disaster to the land. The stranger appears again and tells Gluck that a river may be turned to gold by casting three drops of holy water into it. The journey is hard and dangerous, and the two elder brothers fail because of their selfishness. Gluck, however, is successful and returns his land to its former wealth.

King of the Golden River, opera in one act by Elizabeth Maconchy; libretto (Eng) by Anne Ridler, after John Ruskin. First performance October 29, 1975, Oxford, University Church of St. Mary.

King of the Other Country, The, chamber opera in one act by Gillian Whitehead; libretto (Eng) by Fleur Adcock. First performance June 5, 1984, Sydney, Australia, New South Wales Conservatorium.

King Pepin's Campaign, opera burlesque in two acts by Thomas Arne; libretto (Eng) by William Shirley. First performance April 15, 1745, London, Drury Lane Theatre.
    The story concerns the adventures of the king with a group of amorous nuns.
    The libretto mentions nineteen numbers, but the work is lost.

King Priam, opera in three acts by Michael Tippett; libretto (Eng) by the composer, after Homer's *Iliad*. First performance May 29, 1962, London, Covent Garden, with Marie Collier (Hecuba), Josephine Veasey (Andromache), Margreta Elkins (Helen), Richard Lewis (Achilles), Forbes Robinson (King Priam), Victor Godfrey (Hector), John Dobson (Paris), John Lanigan (Hermes), and Noreen Berry (Nurse); conducted by John Pritchard; directed by Sam Wanamaker.
    King Priam, at Hecuba's urging, decides to have his infant son Paris killed because the Old Man has prophesied that Paris will be responsible for Priam's death. Priam is not unhappy, however, when he learns that the child's life has been spared; he is being raised by a shepherd. Hector and Priam then take Paris to Troy, where Paris and Hector argue. Paris subsequently takes Helen from Sparta. The act closes with the Judgment of Paris, arranged by Hermes, in which Paris chooses Aphrodite (really Helen) over Hera and Athene as the most beautiful, thereby earning the hatred of the other two goddesses.
    During the Trojan War Achilles sulks in his tent while his countrymen are being routed by the Trojans. The Trojans' effort is made less effective by the continuing quarreling of Hector and Paris. When Patroclus dons Achilles' armor, he is slain by Hector, who in turn is killed by the avenging Achilles. Moved by Priam's grief, Achilles surrenders the body of Hector to Priam. The king is killed at the altar by Neoptolomus, the son of Achilles, and the opera ends.
    For detailed plot synopses, see Eaton/*OP* II, 128–29; K/*KOB*, 1145–49; K/*NKOB*, 832–33.
    Major roles: Priam, King of Troy (bass-bar); Hecuba, his wife (sop); Old Man (bass); Hector, eldest son of Priam and Hecuba (bar); the young Paris, second son of Priam (sop); the older Paris (ten); Helen, wife of King Menelaus of Sparta (mezzo); Hermes (ten); Achilles, a Greek hero (ten); and Patroclus, friend of Achilles (light bar).

Also set by James Wilson (comp. 1987–1992).
SCORE: vs, German-English (London: Schott; New York: Associated Music Publishers, [1962]).
LIBRETTO: English, in *ENOG* 29 (1985), 73–92.
BIBLIOGRAPHY: Andrew Clements, "Music for an Epic," *ENOG* 29, 65–72; Robert L. Jacobs, "Opera," *MR* XXIII (Aug. 1962), 251–52 [on premiere]; Kemp/*Tippett*, 354–70; Michael Tippett, "'King Priam'—Some Questions Answered," *Opera* XIII (May 1962), 297–99.
DISCOGRAPHY: H. Harper, F. Palmer, Y. Minton, R. Tear, P. Langridge, T. Allen, N. Bailey, S. Roberts, London Sinfonietta, cond. D. Atherton, London LDR-73006 (3 LPs); rev. John W. Freeman, "Records," *ON* XLVI (May 1982), 44; reissued as Chandos CHAN 9406 (CD).
VIDEO: Walker, Mason, Macann, Price, Kent Opera; cond. R. Norrington (1985), Home Vision KIN02; rev. Harvey E. Phillips, "Videocassettes," *ON* LIII (April 15, 1989), 40.

King Rene's Daughter, opera in one act by Julian Edwards; libretto (Eng) by the composer, after Henrik Hertz. First performance November 23, 1893, New York, Hermann's Theatre, with Eleanor Mayo (Iolanthe) and Charles Bassett (Tristan).

Count Tristan arrives at court to wed Iolanthe, daughter of King Rene, but falls in love with a blind girl and wishes to wed her instead. He discovers, happily, that she is Iolanthe.

Also set by Henry Smart as a cantata (comp. 1833); opera by Tchaikovsky, as *Iolanta* (1892, St. Petersburg).

King's Breakfast, The, opera in one scene by Joyce Barthelson; libretto (Eng) by the composer, a free adaptation of Maurice Baring's *Catherine Parr*. First performance April 6, 1973, Atlantic City, New Jersey, National Federation of Music Clubs.

The breakfast of Henry VIII and Catherine Parr, his sixth wife, is marred by her jealousy of her predecessors. Because the couple both love music, harmony is restored briefly, again to be disrupted by an argument over the color of the horse of Alexander the Great, at which point Henry threatens Catherine with the fate that met some of his earlier wives. Henry is again soothed by music.

For a detailed description, see Eaton/*OP* II, 291.

Major roles: Henry VIII (bar) and Queen Catherine Parr (sop).

King's Henchman, The, opera in three acts by Deems Taylor; libretto (Eng) by Edna St. Vincent Millay. First performance February 17, 1927, New York, Metropolitan Opera, with Florence Easton (Aelfrida), Edward Johnson (Aethelwold), Lawrence Tibbett (Eadgar), Louis D'Angelo (Ordgar), William Gustafson (Maccus), and Merle Alcock (Ase); conducted by Tulio Serafin.

The setting is the west of England in the tenth century. Eadgar of Wessex, the English king, sends Aethelwold to gain the hand of the Princess Aelfrida for him. Instead, Aethelwold weds the princess himself but tells the king that she is quite ugly. When the king visits the pair and discovers how pretty she really is, Aethelwold, guilt-ridden, kills himself.

Major roles: Eadgar (bar); Aethelwold (ten); Princess Aelfrida (sop); Ordgar, Thane of Devon, her father (bass); Maccus, Aelfrida's master of the horses (bass); and Ase, Aelfrida's servant (mezzo).
SCORE: vs (New York: J. Fischer & Bro., 1926).

King's Price, The, opera by Alick MacLean; libretto (Eng) by Sheridan Ross. First performance April 29, 1904, London, Royalty Theatre.

King's Proxy, The, or, Judge for Yourself, comic opera in three acts by Thomas Cooke; libretto (Eng) by Samuel J. Arnold. First performance August 19, 1815, London, Lyceum.

The story is a comic treatment of Edgar, the tenth-century English king, his paramour, Elfrida, and her murdered husband, Athelwold.

T. A. Arne's *Elfrida** (1772, London) is a serious setting of the story, as is Paisiello's *Elfrida* (1792, Naples). See also D. Taylor's *The King's Henchman.*
LIBRETTO: English (London: J. Miller, 1815).

King's Twelve Moons, The, chamber opera in one act by Joelle Wallach; libretto (Eng), after the Brothers Grimm's *Twelve Dancing Princesses.* First performance 1989, New York.

The work is scored for one male and four female voices.
SCORE: ms fs (New York: American Music Center, 1989).

King Who Saved Himself from Being Saved, The, opera in one act by Philip Hagemann; libretto (Eng). First performance April 4, 1987, Chico, California. Revived February 1997, New York, Manhattan School of Music, National Opera Association.

Kiss, The, video-duet by Michael Nyman; text (Eng). First performance October 13, 1984, London, Channel 4.

Kisses for a Quid, opera in one act by Felix Werder; libretto (Eng) by A. Marshall. First performance March 23, 1961, Melbourne, Australia, Queen's Theatre.

Knee Plays, the, entr'actes ("the American section") by David Byrne for *the CIVIL warS** of Philip Glass; libretto (Eng) by the composer. First performance April 27, 1984, Minneapolis.

The interludes consist of thirteen vignettes in the style of Asian theater; there is no singing, and the work is held together by a dance ensemble that manipulates the "characters," that is, a tree, a boat, and a book. The text consists of narration unconnected to the stage action.
LIBRETTO: English (Minneapolis: Walker Art Center, 1984).
BIBLIOGRAPHY: M. A. Feldman, "Minneapolis/St. Paul," *ON* XLIX (Nov. 1984), 50–51 [on premiere].

Knickerbockers, The, comic opera in three acts by Reginald De Koven; libretto (Eng) by Harry Bache Smith. First performance May 29, 1893, New York, Garden Theatre, with W. H. Macdonald (Miles Bradford), Camille D'Arville (Katrina), Edwin W. Hoff (Hendrick), Jessie Bartlett Davis (Priscilla), and Henry Clay Barnabee (the governor).

After Miles Bradford, having arrived in New Amsterdam, helps another Puritan escape, he is accused of being a spy. His friend Hendrick convinces Miles to avoid arrest by passing himself off as Priscilla, betrothed of Hendrick. Priscilla's father, the governor, is told of the plot and sends his soldiers to arrest Miles, but they capture the real Priscilla instead, despite her protests. Priscilla, meanwhile, is able to disguise herself as a soldier and catch the attention of Katrina, daughter of the governor. All turns out happily in the end, however, as identities are straightened out. Katrina marries Miles, and Priscilla weds Hendrick.

Roles: Peter Stuyvesant, Governor of New Amsterdam (bar); Antony van Corlear, his trumpeter (bar); Diedrick Schermerhorn, a burgomaster (bass); Hendrick, his son (ten); Miles Bradford, a Puritan captain (ten); Katrina, the Governor's daughter (sop); Priscilla, a Puritan damsel (mezzo); Dame Stuyvesant (mezzo); Captain van Wart (ten); and Barbara, a maid (sop).

Some of the characters also appear in treatments of Washington Irving's *Legend of Sleepy Hollow* (1819), A. Lora's *The Legend of Sleepy Hollow* (not perf.), and D. Moore's *The Headless Horseman** (1937, Bronxville, New York).
SCORE: vs (New York: G. Schirmer, 1892).
LIBRETTO: English (Chicago: Smith, 1891).

Knife, The, opera in two acts by Daniel Jones; libretto (Eng) by the composer. First performance December 2, 1963, London, Sadler's Wells, with Frank Olegario (black man); conducted by the composer.

A black man is saved from a lynching when a white man confesses to the crime that the former was accused of committing.
BIBLIOGRAPHY: A. Stewart, "Daniel Jones's Opera," *MT* CIV (1963), 790 [on premiere].

Knight of Snowdoun, The, musical drama in three acts by Henry Rowley Bishop; libretto (Eng) by Thomas Morton, after Sir Walter Scott's The *Lady of the Lake* (1810). First performance February 5, 1811, London, Covent Garden. First U.S. performance June 12, 1811, New York, Park Theatre.

The work is set in Scotland. James V, disguised as James Fitz-James, receives shelter in what turns out to be his enemy Roderick Dhu's house. Ellen, daughter of the outlawed James of Douglas, is the unwilling fiancée of Roderick. When Roderick is killed in an uprising against James, Ellen successfully pleads with the ruler to spare her father's life and to be allowed to marry her beloved, Malcolm Graeme.

See *The Lady of the Lake* for other settings.
SCORE: ms fs (1811, British Library, Add. MS 36940).
LIBRETTO: English (London: Sharpe and Hailes, 1811).

Knight of the Leopard, The, opera in three acts by Michael Balfe; libretto (Eng) by Arthur Matthison, after Sir Walter Scott's *The Talisman* (1825). First performance (as *Il talismano*, in an Italian version by Giuseppe Zaffira) June 11, 1874, London, Drury Lane Theatre, with William Carlton (Richard Coeur de Lion), Joseph Maas (Sir Kenneth), William Hamilton (Emir Sheerkohf), Miss Beaumont (Berengaria), and Miss Clara Louise Kellogg (Edith Plantagenet). First performance (in English) January 15, 1891, Liverpool. First U.S. performance February 10, 1875, New York.

The work is set in the Holy Land and involves a disguised Scottish knight known as Sir Kenneth, or, the Knight of the Leopard, who is fighting for Richard Coeur de Lion. Things are going badly for the Crusaders because of arguments among the various rulers and Richard's illness. Kenneth meets Emir Sheerkohf, at first an enemy who becomes a friend, and the emir, returning in the guise of a physician, gives Richard a healing talisman. Kenneth, disgraced for having been duped into courting Berengaria, Richard's wife, regains his honor for saving Richard from being assassinated. When Kenneth is revealed to be of noble birth, he is allowed to wed his beloved, the royal Edith Plantagenet.

Major roles: Richard Coeur de Lion (bar), Kenneth (ten), Emir Sheerkohf (bass), Berengaria (sop), and Edith Plantagenet (sop).

Other settings of Scott's novel include H. R. Bishop's *The Talisman** (1826); G. Pacini's *Il talismano* (1829); and A. Adam's *Richard en Palestine* (1844, Paris).

SCORE: ms fs, mostly autograph (British Library, Add. MS. 33535A, B).
LIBRETTO: English-Italian (London: J. Mapelson, [1875?]).

Knights of the Cross, The, or, The Hermit's Prophecy, musical romance in three acts by Henry Rowley Bishop, partially based on Boieldieu's *Charles de France* (1816, Paris); libretto (Eng) by Samuel Beazley, after Sir Walter Scott's *The Talisman* (1825). First performance May 29, 1826, London, Drury Lane Theatre.

The story concerns Sir Kenneth, the Scottish knight who aids Richard during the Crusades and wins the love of Edith Plantagenet.

Roles: Blondel, Edith, and Sir Kenneth.

The overture is based on that of *The Humorous Lieutenant** and Beethoven's overture to *Fidelio*.
SCORE: ms fs, autograph (1826, British Library, Add. MS. 27719).
LIBRETTO: English (London: J. Cumberland, [n.d.]).

Knot Garden, The, opera in three acts by Michael Tippett; libretto (Eng) by the composer. First performance December 2, 1970, London, Covent Garden, with Josephine Barstow (Gayle), Jill Gomez (Flora), Yvonne Minton (Thea), Robert Tear (Dov), Raimund Herincx (Faber), Thomas Carey, and Thomas Helmsley; conducted by Colin Davis; produced by Peter Hall. First U.S. performance February 22, 1974, Evanston, Illinois, Northwestern University. Chamber ensemble version by Merion Bowen, 1984, London, Royal Court Theatre, Opera Factory/London Sinfonietta; conducted by Howard Williams.

Faber and Thea have asked the analyst Mangus to treat Flora, their ward, but Mangus quickly sees that the real problem lies in the relationship between Faber and Thea. The group is joined by a homosexual couple, Mel, a black writer, and Dov, a white musician, and then by Thea's sister Denise, a "dedicated freedom fighter" who has been tortured. In order to resolve the various problems, Mangus devises a number of activities, such as a charade based on *The Tempest* that includes the turning of the symbolic knot garden (hence the opera's title). In the end Mel joins with Denise, the marriage of Faber and Thea is strengthened, Flora gains independence and maturity, and Dov leaves alone on a journey of self-discovery.

For detailed plot synopses, see Eaton/*OP* II, 130–31; K/*KOB*, 1149–53; K/*NKOB*, 835–37.

Major roles: Faber, a civil engineer (bar); Thea, his wife, a gardener (mezzo); Flora, their daughter (sop); Mel, a black writer in his twenties (bar); Dov, a white musician (ten); Denise, Flora's sister (sop); and Mangus, an analyst (bar).

This was Tippett's first opera to be performed in the United States. It includes a duet between Mel and Denise that has as its basis the civil rights song "We Shall Overcome" and Flora's singing of a selection from Schubert's *Die schöne Müllerin*, both in the second act.
LIBRETTO: English (London: Schott, [1969]).
BIBLIOGRAPHY: Meirion Bowen, "A Tempest of Our Time," *ENOG* 29, 93–98; Kemp/*Tippett*, 402–31; Anthony Lewis, review, *NYT* (Dec. 4, 1970), 56 [on premiere].

Koanga, lyric drama in three acts by Frederick Delius; libretto (Eng) by the composer and Charles Francis Keary, after George Washington Cable's novel *The Grandissimes* (1880). Composed 1895–1897. First performance (concert, incomplete), May 30, 1899,

London, St. James's Hall. First full stage performance March 30, 1904, Elberfeld, Stadttheater, in a German translation by Jelka Delius, with Rose Kaiser (Palmyra) and Clarence Whitehall (Koanga); conducted by Fritz Cassirer. First British performance September 23, 1935, in an English version by Jelka Delius, London, Covent Garden, with Oda Slobodskaya (Palmyra) and John Brownlee (Koanga); conducted by Thomas Beecham. First U.S. performance December 18, 1970, Washington, D.C., Opera Society, with Eugene Holmes (Koanga), Claudia Lindsey (Palmyra), William McDonald (Simon Perez), Will Roy (Don José Martinez), and Joyce Gerber (Clotilda); conducted by Paul Callaway. Revised by Douglas Craig and Andrew Page for 1972 production, London, Sadler's Wells.

The story, told by Uncle Joe, an old slave, is set on an eighteenth-century plantation on the Mississippi River. Koanga, an African prince, has been brought to the plantation of Don José Martinez to wed the mulatto Palmyra. She in turn is desired by Simon Perez, the overseer. The girl is kidnapped by the overseer at her wedding to Koanga, who escapes to the forest. In revenge, Koanga and a voodoo priest bring down a plague on the plantation. Koanga kills the pursuing Perez but dies himself in the fight. Palmyra, in despair, kills herself with Koanga's spear.

Major roles: Koanga (bar), Palmyra (sop), Simon Perez (ten), Clotilda (alto), and Don José Martinez (bass).

The chorus plays a vital role in this work.

For a detailed plot synopsis and musical analysis, see Eaton/*OP* II, 132; and K/ *KOB*, 1113–16.

SCORE: vs, ed. Eric Fenby (London: Boosey & Hawkes, 1935); rev. libretto by Douglas Craig and Andrew Page (London and New York: Boosey & Hawkes [1974]).

LIBRETTO: English (rev. by Thomas Beecham and Edward Agate ([London]: Boosey & Hawkes, [1962?], 1935).

BIBLIOGRAPHY: Irving Lowens, "Washington," *MT* CXXII (1971), 265 [on U.S. premiere]; Harold C. Schonberg, "Opera: Neglected 'Koanga' of Frederick Delius," *NYT* (Dec. 20, 1970), 54 [on U.S. premiere]; Florence Stevenson, "Koanga," *ON* XXXV (Dec. 19, 1970), 34–35.

Kumana, opera in one act (five scenes) by Ernest Kanitz; libretto (Eng) by Jane Marshall. Completed March 1953.

The orphan of American missionaries, Kumana, raised by the residents of the Pacific island called Kumana, goes to live with her wealthy aunt Rosalie Smith when the island is selected for atomic tests. Her simple upbringing makes her unequipped to deal with the intricacies of her aunt's society, and when a baby is left on Smith's doorstep, everyone assumes that it is Kumana's, including Tom, her aunt's gardener, to whom Kumana had proposed after asking Andrew, fiancé of Kumana's cousin Gwen. In the end the rich Roger agrees to wed Kumana and bring up the child, and Tom pretends to be the father's baby to spare any further embarrassment.

Major roles: Tom (bar), Kumana (sop), Rosalie Smith (sop), Gwen (alto), Andrew (ten), and Robert (bass).

For a detailed description, see Eaton/*OP* II, 134.

SCORE: vs, holograph (1953, photocopy, NYPL).

Kykunkor, the Witch, dance opera based on African tunes by Asadata Dafora Horton; libretto (Eng). First performance May 7, 1934, New York, Unity Theatre Studio.

L

Labyrinth, The, "opera—a one-act riddle" by Gian Carlo Menotti; libretto (Eng) by the composer. First performance March 3, 1963, NBC, TV Opera Theater, with Elaine Bonazzi (the Spy), Robert White (the old Chess Player), John Reardon (the groom), Judith Raskin (the bride), Beverly Wolff (the executive director), Frank Porretta (the astronaut), Leon Lishner (Death/desk clerk), John West (Death's assistant), and Eugene Green (Italian opera singer); conducted by Herbert Grossman.

The symbolic plot involves a bride and groom on their honeymoon at a hotel who cannot find the key to their room. The action revolves around the groom's fruitless attempts to locate the key or get assistance in retrieving it.

The music, mostly in parlando style, contains three ariettas, including the bride's song of reminiscence, and two duets for the bride and groom.
BIBLIOGRAPHY: Paul Hume, "New Menotti Opera Shines in TV Debut," *Washington Post* (Mar. 4, 1963), B, 4.

Ladies Frolick, The, ballad opera, with new overture and six new songs by William Bates; libretto (Eng) by James Love, an abridged version of *The Jovial Crew*.* First performance May 7, 1770, London, Drury Lane Theatre.
LIBRETTO: English (London: Longman, Lukey & Co., [1770]).

Ladies Voices, opera in one act by Vernon Martin; libretto (Eng), after Gertrude Stein. First performance June 3, 1956, Norman, Oklahoma, University of Oklahoma.

The satirical "story" consists of a mass of non sequiturs uttered by the performers.
For a detailed description, see Eaton/*OP* II, 293.
Roles: two sopranos and two mezzo/altos.

Ladies Voices (The Repercussive Sojourn), opera by Carson Kievman; libretto (Eng) by the composer, after Stein. Composed 1973–1974.

For women's voices, trumpet, shakuhachi, koto, and four percussionists.
SCORE: ms score, signed holograph (1974, holograph, NYPL).

Ladies Voices, chamber opera in a prologue and four acts by Charles Shere; libretto (Eng), after Stein. First performance October 30, 1987, Berkeley, California, Berkeley Arts Center.

Part 1 of a trilogy set to plays by Stein; see also *I Like It to Be A Play, What Happened.*
SCORE: fs (Berkeley, Calif.: Fallen Leaf Press, 1996).

Ladle, The, dialogue opera by Charles Dibdin; libretto (Eng) by the composer, after the poem by Matthew Prior. First performance April 14, 1773, London, Sadler's Wells.

The work is composed for three characters.
SCORE: vs (London: Longman, Lukey, and Co. and John Johnston, [177?]).

Lad of the Hills, or, The Wicklow Gold Mine, comic opera in three acts by William Shield; libretto (Eng) by John O'Keeffe. First performance April 9, 1796, London, Covent Garden. Also performed as *The Wicklow Mountains,** October 7, 1796.

When the hero of the work uncovers several pieces of gold in the Wicklow Mountains outside Dublin, the authorities think he has stolen them.

LIBRETTO: English, as *The Wicklow Mountains* (Dublin: John Whitworth, 1797).

Lady and the Devil, The, musical drama in two acts by Michael Kelly; libretto (Eng) by William Dimond. First performance May 3, 1820, London, Drury Lane Theatre. LIBRETTO: English (London: R. S. Kirby, [1820?]).

Lady Dolly, romantic comic opera by Alfred Hill; libretto (Eng) by Margery Browne. First performance March 31, 1900, Sydney, Australia, Palace Theatre.

The slight plot concerns ghosts.

Lady from Colorado, The, opera in two acts by Robert Ward; libretto (Eng) by Bernard Stambler, after the novel by Homer Croy (1957). First performance July 3, 1964, Central City, Colorado, Central City Opera, with Mignon Dunn (Eve St. John), Mary Ellen Pracht (Katie), Davis Cunningham (Lord Moon), Promise Paul (Jack Spaniard), and Chester Ludgin (Jeff Stafford); conducted by Emerson Buckley; directed by Christopher West; choreographed by Helen Tamiris. Revised as *Lady Kate** (1994).

The setting is Elkhorn, Colorado in the 1870s. The story centers on an Irish immigrant washerwoman, Katie Lawder, who marries the expatriate English nobleman Cecil Moon. After Moon's father dies the couple visits England but, since Kate, now Lady Kate, does not fit in with the British nobility, they come back to Colorado and become ranchers. Despite the machinations of Jack Spaniard, Moon is elected to the State Senate.

Major roles: Katie Lawder (sop); Lord Moon, her husband (ten); Eve St. John, Katie's friend (mezzo); Jeff Stafford, a frontiersman (bar); and Jack Spaniard (bar).

Among the highlights is a paean to the center of much of the action, the first-act "Out Here in Colorado."
BIBLIOGRAPHY: "World Premiere for Ward Opera," *NYT* (July 5, 1964), 42.

Lady in the Dark, musical play in two acts by Kurt Weill; libretto (Eng) by Moss Hart; lyrics by Ira Gershwin. First performance December 30, 1941, Boston, Colonial Theatre; January 23, 1941, New York, Alvin Theatre, with Gertrude Lawrence (Liza Elliott), Bert Lytell (Kendall Nesbitt), Danny Kaye (Randall Paxton), Victor Mature (Randy Curtis), Donald Randolph (Dr. Brooks), and Macdonald Carey (Charlie Johnson); conducted by Maurice Abravanel. The work was revised and extended by David Loud and John Mauceri; first performance of this version August 1988, Edinburgh Festival; conducted by Mauceri.

A successful but unhappy female magazine editor, Liza Elliott, has trouble choosing which of four men is most suitable for her: Kendall Nesbitt, her married benefactor and publisher; the shallow film star Randy Curtis; Randall Paxton, a photographer; or her advertising manager, the bluff Charlie Johnson.

Through the help of a psychiatrist, Dr. Brooks, she interprets a series of four dreams she has about them and about various parts of her life. She finds that it is Charlie whom she really loves.

Major roles: Liza Elliott (high mezzo), Kendall Nesbitt (bar), Randy Curtis (bar), Randall Paxton (high bar), and Charlie Johnson (bar).

Most of the music occurs in the four dream sequences, where it is continuous. Among the highlights are Liza's jazz-infused "One Life to Live," part of the first sequence, "Glamour Dream"; "The Saga of Jenny," in the third, "Circus Dream"; and "My Ship," which comprises the fourth. "Circus Dream" also includes the patter song "Tschaikowsky," sung by Randall Paxton, who spits out the names of forty-nine Russian composers in the space of forty or so seconds.

SCORE: vs, ed. Albert Sirmay (New York: Chappell, [1941]).
LIBRETTO: English (New York: Random House, [1941]).
BIBLIOGRAPHY: "Boston by Wire," *NYT* (Jan. 5, 1941), IX, 1, 2 [on Boston premiere];
Brooks Atkinson, "The Play in Review," *NYT* (Jan. 24, 1941), 14 [on New York premiere]).
DISCOGRAPHY: R. Stevens, A. Green, J. Reardon; cond. L. Engel, Sony/CBS MHL-62869; incl. excerpts with Danny Kaye (ca. 1963, studio version; rereleased 1997).

Lady Kate, opera in two acts by Robert Ward, a revision of *The Lady from Colorado**
(1964); libretto (Eng) by Bernard Stambler, after Croy. First performance June 8, 1994,
Wooster, Ohio, Freedlander Theatre, Ohio Light Opera, with Emily Martin (Katie),
Bradley Howard (Lord Cecil Moon), Patti Jo Stevens (Eve St. John), and Dennis Jesse
(Jack Spaniard); conducted by Steven Byess; directed by James Stuart; choreographed
by Carol Hageman. Same cast January 22, 1995, Durham, North Carolina, Triangle
Opera Theatre; conducted by Scott Tilley; choreographed by Lara Hamblen.
   In this revision, the comic bad guy, Jack Spaniard, has added importance. Colorado's
desire to become a state is also one of the elements of the story.
BIBLIOGRAPHY: Carl J. Halperin, "Durham, N.C.," *ON* LIX (April 15, 1995), 40–41;
"Wooster," *Opera* XLVI (Jan. 1995), 67 [on premiere].

Lady of Ephesus, The, chamber opera by Raymond Warren; libretto (Eng). First performance February 16, 1959, Belfast.

Lady of Light, opera-oratorio by Alan Hovhaness; libretto (Eng) by the composer.
First performance (concert) 1974, Montana.
SCORE: fs, vs (New York: C. F. Peters Corp., [1969]).

Lady of Longford, The, opera in one act by Leonhard Emil Bach; original English
libretto (Eng) by A. G. Harris and F. E. Weatherly; translated into Italian by G. A.
Mazzucato for the premiere, July 21, 1894, London, Covent Garden. Revived April 20,
1896, London, Drury Lane Theatre, in the English version.
   Roles: Countess Longford, Count Longford, and Muriel.
SCORE: vs (London: E. Ascherberg & Co., 1894).
LIBRETTO: German (London: Ascherberg & Co., n.d.).

Lady of the Castle, chamber opera in three acts by Mira Spektor; libretto (Eng) by
Andrea Balis, after the play by Lea Goldberg. First performance February 4, 1982,
New York, Theater for the New City.
   The work concerns the Holocaust.
SCORE: vs, holograph (New York: American Music Center, 1982).

Lady of the Inn, The, opera in three acts by Peter Wishart; libretto (Eng) by Don
Roberts, after Carlo Goldoni. First performance June 17, 1983, Reading, England, Reading University, with Maureen Lehane.
   The story takes place in Turenne in the Middle Ages.

Lady of the Lake, The, or, The Knight of Snowdoun, "melo-dramatic romance"
arranged by William Francis; libretto (Eng) by Edmund John Eyre, after Sir Walter
Scott. First performance January 15, 1811, Edinburgh. First U.S. performance January
1, 1812, Philadelphia, Chestnut Street Theatre.

Lady of the Lake, The, romantic opera in a prologue and three acts by Karl Schmidt;
libretto (Eng) by Wallace Taylor Hughes, after Scott. First performance December 6,
1931, Chicago, Fortnightly Club, American Opera Society.

The setting is Scotland in 1100. James V, disguised as James Fitz-James, takes refuge in what turns out to be the house of his enemy Roderick Dhu. Ellen, daughter of the outlawed James of Douglas, is Roderick's reluctant fiancée. When Roderick is killed in an uprising against James, Ellen successfully pleads with the ruler to spare her father's life and to be allowed to marry her beloved, Malcolm Graeme.

Roles: James V, King of Scotland (ten); Roderick Dhu, chieftain of Clan-Alpine (bar); Lord James of Douglas (bass); Malcolm Graeme, a youth (ten); Alan Bane, a bard and prophet (ten); John de Brent, a captain (bar); Ellen, daughter of Douglas (sop); Margaret, mother of Roderick (alto).

The story was also set by H. R. Bishop as *The Knight of Snowdoun** (1811, London); by W. Francis (1811, see previous entry); by James Sanderson, with a text by Thomas Dibdin, as a "grand dramatic romance" (1811); by G. Rossini as *La donna del lago* (1819, Naples); as a pastiche by L. de Corvey (1825); and by V. von Püttlingen (1829).

Lady of the Lake, The, opera in one act by Elie Siegmeister; libretto (Eng) by Edward Mabley, after Bernard Malamud. First performance October 5, 1985, New York, 92nd Street Y, Kaufmann Auditorium, with James Javore and Sharon Cooner; conducted by Amy Kaiser.

In this story an American tourist, Henry Blumberg, visits an island at Lake Maggiore in Italy, where he meets and falls in love with Isabella, the daughter of Ernesto, an Italian caretaker; both Henry and Isabella conceal their Jewish identity. He disregards the *pensione* owner's warning to stay away from the family and meets Isabella again. When Henry asks Isabella to marry him, she tears off her blouse to reveal her concentration camp number and runs away, before Henry can admit to her that he is Jewish also.

Roles: Henry Blumberg (bar); Isabella (sop); Ernesto (bass); and the padrona, owner of a *pensione* (mezzo).
BIBLIOGRAPHY: Byron Belt, review, *ON* L (Jan. 4, 1985), 42–43 [on premiere]; Will Crutchfield, review, *NYT* (Oct 7, 1985), C, 18 [on premiere].

Lady of the Manor, The, comic opera in three acts by James Hook; libretto (Eng) by William Kendrick, after Charles Johnson's *The Country Lasses* (1715). First performance November 23, 1778, London, Covent Garden, with Miss Vernon (Laura) and Mr. Vernon (Wildman).

The plot involves two society youths who court two farm girls, who, in reality, are their suitors' social equals. Manly marries Flora, in reality Lady Lucy, without knowing her true identity. The other young man, Wildman, pursues Laura, who is actually Mrs. Townley. In the course of his pursuit he fights a duel with a "rival," who is in fact Mrs. Townley, disguised as a man.
SCORE: overture (London: Harrison, Cluse, ca. 1800).
LIBRETTO: English (London: E. and C. Dilly . . . J. Wilkie et al., 1778).

Lady Rohesia, comic opera in one act by Antony Hopkins; libretto (Eng) by the composer, after R. H. Barham's *Ingoldsby Legends* (1837–1840). First performance March 17, 1948, London, Sadler's Wells.

The title character leaves her deathbed to scold her husband for turning his affections to the maid. In the sequel, it is the husband who is dying, while the wife becomes interested in the priest. The prompter keeps the action going.

Roles: Lady Rohesia (sop), the husband (bar), the maid (sop), the priest (ten), and the prompter (bar).
SCORE: vs (London: Chester, 1947).

Lady's Triumph, The, "comick-dramatic opera"; libretto (Eng) by Elkanah Settle. First performance March 22, 1718, London, Lincoln's Inn Fields.
Performed with Galliard's masque *Decius and Paulina.**
LIBRETTO: English (London: J. Browne, 1718).

Lake, The, chamber opera by Barbara Pentland; libretto (Eng) by Dorothy Livesay. First performance March 3, 1954, Vancouver.

Lake of Menteith, The, opera in one act by Harold Noble; libretto (Eng) by David Harris. First performance August 13, 1967, London, BBC radio.

Lallah Rookh, or, The Cashmerian Minstrel, opera by Charles Edward Horn; libretto (Eng) by M. J. Sullivan, after Thomas Moore. First performance 1818, Dublin, Theatre Royal.
Other settings of Moore's work include D. Kashin's *The One-Day Reign of Nourmahal* (comp. 1817); G. Spontini's *Nurmahal* (1822, Berlin); F. David's *Lallah-Roukh* (1862, Paris); A. Rubinstein's *The Veiled Prophet* (1881); and C. Stanford's *The Veiled Prophet of Khorassan** (1881, Hanover). William Brough's "burlesque and pantomime" *Lalla Rookh, or, The Princess, the Peri, & the Troubadour* appeared in 1857 (London).

Lamentable Reign of Charles the Last, The, "pantopera" in one act by George Dreyfus; libretto (Eng) by Tim Robertson. First performance March 23, 1976, Adelaide, Australia, Scott Theatre, Festival of the Arts; conducted by Myer Fredman.
The work is a musical representation of a political cartoon.

Lamentations. See **Three Lamentations**.

Lamentations of Doctor Faustus, The, a "little conceit for music" by Mark Hewitt; libretto (Eng), after Goethe. First performance November 12, 1994, London, Royal Northern College of Music, the Daily Telegraph Theatre, with Davis Usher (Faust) and Alan Beck (the Devil); conducted by Timothy Redmond; produced by Sasha French; designed by Jonathan French.
This version of the Faust story opens with the clock's striking midnight. The first half of the work is a monologue for Faust, cast here as a baritone.
In the second half Faust is cast as a contestant in a quiz show, with Faust having to contend with the trickery of the Devil as the host of the show. The work ends with Faust again in his study, informed by the narrator that he has to live with his soul, which is wanted neither by Hell nor by Heaven.
BIBLIOGRAPHY: Michael Kennedy, review, *Opera* XLVI (Jan. 1995), 113–14 [on premiere].

Lament of Kamuela, The, multimedia science fiction by Jon Appleton; libretto (Eng) by the composer. First performance August 10, 1983, Hanover, New Hampshire.
The work is scored for four voices, live electronics, rock band, string quartet, shamisen, slides, film, and video.

Lancelot, opera in two acts by Iain Hamilton; libretto (Eng) by the composer, after Thomas Malory's cycle *Le morte d'Arthur* (1470). First performance August 24, 1985, Arundel, England, Arundel Castle.

Landara, opera in three acts by Efrem Zimbalist; libretto (Eng) by Bernice Kenyon. First performance April 6, 1956, Philadelphia.
SCORE: vs (n.p., n.d.; LCCN: 84-171223).

Land between the Rivers, The, opera in two acts by Carl van Buskirk; libretto (Eng), after Robert Penn Warren's *The Ballad of Billie Potts*. First performance May 18, 1956, Bloomington, Indiana, Indiana University, with Donald Vogel, and William Yeats; conducted by Wolfgang Vacano; produced by Hans Busch.

Land of Happiness, The, music drama by Joseph Redding; libretto (Eng) by Charles Templeton Crocker, after his play. First performance August 4, 1917, San Francisco, Bohemian Club. Revised as the French grand opera *Fay-Yen-Fah* (1925, Monte Carlo; 1926, San Francisco).

The story involves a young Chinese nobleman, Shiunin, who bests the wicked fox god and is able to wed Fay-Yen-Fah, the daughter of the viceroy.
SCORE: vs (San Francisco: Bohemian Club, [1917]).

Land of Heart's Desire, The, opera in one act by Fritz Hart; libretto (Eng), after William Butler Yeats. Composed 1914.

Land of the Misty Water, The, opera in three acts by Charles Wakefield Cadman; libretto (Eng) by Nelle Eberhart, after Francis La Flesche's story. Composed 1909–1912. Not performed.

Revised as *Ramala* (1938).
SCORE: as *Ramala*, vs ms, holograph (1938, NYPL).

Landsdown Castle, or, The Sorcerer of Tewkesbury, operetta in two acts by Gustav Holst; libretto (Eng) by A. C. Cunningham. First performance (concert) February 7, 1893, Cheltenham, Corn Exchange; conducted by D'Arcy de Ferrars; Holst (piano).

The work, set at the time of Henry VIII, concerns a sorcerer and a magic mirror.

Last Day, monologue by Ned Rorem; libretto (Eng) by Jay Harrison. First performance May 27, 1967, New York, New School Opera Workshop.

The work involves the thoughts of a prisoner who has been condemned to die.

It is scored for voice, string quartet, woodwind quartet, and piano.
BIBLIOGRAPHY: John W. Freeman, review, *ON* XXXII (Sept. 23, 1967), 21 [on premiere].

Last Days of Pompeii, The, or, Seventeen Hundred Years Ago, historical burletta by George Rodwell; libretto (Eng) by J. B. Buckstone, after Edward Bulwer-Lytton's work. First performance December 15, 1834, London, Adelphi Theatre.

Last Leaf, The, opera in one act by Alva Henderson; libretto (Eng) by the composer, after O. Henry's story. First performance June 17, 1979, Saratoga, California.

Deserted by her lover, Edward, for another woman, Cathy, a painter, becomes ill and takes to her bed, saying that she will die when the last leaf falls from the tree outside her window. Mr. Behrman, an older painter who has become Cathy's friend, overhears the conversation. The next morning, after a severe storm, Cathy sees that the leaf is still there. She does not know that the leaf was painted by Mr. Behrman during the storm, during which he caught pneumonia and died shortly afterwards.

For a description, see Summers/*OOA*, 145–46.

Major roles: Cathy (sop); Helen, her friend (mezzo); and Mr. Behrman (bass/bar).
BIBLIOGRAPHY: William Ratliff, review, *ON* XLIV (Sept. 1979), 58 [on premiere].

Last Lover, The, morality play in one act by Robert Starer; libretto (Eng) by Gail Godwin, after legends about a woman called Pelagia. First performance August 2, 1975, Katonah, New York, Caramoor Festival. Revived March 1985, St. Michael's

Church, American Chamber Opera Company, with Margaret Astrup (Pelagia); conducted by Douglas Anderson.

Pelagia, who has led a dissolute life, attempts to seduce the holy man Veronus. Her failure leads her to admire the holy life, and she rejects the advances of the Seducer (the devil) and enters a monastery as a monk. Pelagia, as a monk, offers advice to a nun, who is then taken away by the Seducer. Pelagia is blamed for the seduction and, refusing to defend herself, is banished to a cave.

For a detailed description, see Kornick/*RAO*, 297–98.

Major roles: Pelagia (mezzo), Veronus/the Seducer (bar), and the young nun/Pelagia's maid (sop).

SCORE: vs (Melville, N.Y.: MCA Music, [1977]).

BIBLIOGRAPHY: Peter G. Davis, "'Last Lover' Premiere Is Sung Zestfully," *NYT* (Aug. 4, 1975), 14; Gail Godwin, "A Novelist Sings a Different Tune," *NYT* (Dec. 15, 1985), VI, 59, 62, 67; Andrew Porter, "Musical Events," *NY* LXI (April 8, 1985), 60–61 [on 1985 revival].

Last of the Mohicans, The, opera in two acts by Alva Henderson; libretto (Eng) by Janet Lewis, after James Fenimore Cooper. First performance June 12, 1976, Wilmington, Delaware, Wilmington Opera Society.

The story is told in flashback of the death of the lovely girl Cora and Uncas, the "last of the Mohicans," secretly in love with her. Cora and her sister, Alice, are on their way to Fort William Henry, commanded by Munro, their father, and they are accompanied by Heyward, their guardian, who is in love with Alice, and the bitter Magua, once a great chieftain but now Munro's servant. Magua abandons the group, but they find help from the Mohican chief Chingatchgook, Uncas, his son, and Hawkeye, a white man living with the Indians.

The group reaches the fort, but it is soon attacked and overwhelmed by the French, led by General Montcalm. The occupants, including the girls and their father, are allowed to leave, but they are attacked by Magua and a band of followers, who slaughter all but the two girls, whom Magua takes as his prisoners. Heyward escapes and convinces Chingatchgook, Uncas, and Hawkeye to help him rescue the women. In the rescue attempt Cora is killed by her captors, and Uncas by Magua, but Hawkeye then shoots Magua. The scene returns to the present, with Hawkeye's promising to stay with Chingatchgook.

Major roles: Cora (sop), Uncas (ten), Hawkeye (bar), Magua (bar), and Heyward (ten).

For a detailed description, see Kornick/*RAO*, 139–41.

The story was also set by Paul Hastings as *L'ultimo dei Mohicani* (1916, Florence).

Last Puppet, The, opera in one act by Anthony Strilko; libretto (Eng) by Harry Duncan, after a play by Grace Dorcas Ruthenburg. First performance December 1963, New York, National Opera Association.

When the puppet maker Kolar must use the advance money for his wife's funeral instead of for making the puppet ordered by the Margrave of Moonbourne, he is in despair. His daughter Tilda, unable to sell their possessions to the Old Clothes Man for more money, decides to play the puppet herself. She is blocked by her father, who takes on the role of the puppet, and he is taken away in the procession.

For a detailed description, see Eaton/*OP* II, 295–96.

Major roles: Karl Kolar (bar), Tilda (sop), and Old Clothes Man (ten).

Last Savage, The, "opéra-bouffe" in three acts by Gian Carlo Menotti; libretto (Fr) by the composer. First performance, in French, as *Le dernier sauvage*, October 22, 1963,

Paris, Opéra-Comique, with Mady Mesplé (Kitty), Gabriel Bacquier (Abdul), Xavier Depraz (Mr. Scattergood), Adriana Maliponte (Sardula), and Michele Molese (Kodana); conducted by Serge Baudo. First U.S. performance, in an English version by the composer, January 23, 1964, New York, Metropolitan Opera, with Roberta Peters (Kitty), Teresa Stratas (Sardula), Morley Meredith (Scattergood), and George London (Abdul); conducted by Thomas Schippers.

The satirical story is set in Chicago and in India. It concerns Kitty, a rich young woman and daughter of the millionaire Scattergood, who is passionately interested in anthropology. She accompanies her parents to India, where they constantly confuse the real with the fake. Prince Kodana, the son of the Maharajah and Maharani, is taken with Kitty, but she refuses to marry him unless she finds the "last savage," the abominable snowman of the Himalayas. The prince therefore gets a poor stable boy, Abdul, originally in love with the maid Sardula, to dress up as the "snowman." Kitty, deceived, marries the peasant but insists that her father provide the couple's simple abode with all the modern comforts.

For detailed descriptions, see C/*MS*, 201–21; Eaton/*OP* II, 135.

Major roles: Kitty (sop), Abdul (bar), Sardula (sop), Prince Kodana (ten), Mr. Scattergood (bass-bar), Maharajah of Rajaputana (bass), and Maharani of Rajaputana (alto).
SCORE: vs English-Italian (New York: Belwin-Mills, 1963, 1973).
LIBRETTO: English (New York: F. Colombo, [1964]).

Law of Java, The, musical drama in three acts by Henry Rowley Bishop; libretto (Eng) by George Colman Jr. First performance May 11, 1822, London, Covent Garden.

The work includes several arrangements of music from other operas.
SCORES: ms fs (British Library, Add. MS. 36955); vs (London: Goulding, D'Almaine, Potter, & Co., [ca. 1822]).
LIBRETTO: English (London: J. Miller, 1822).

Law versus Love, comic opera in one act by George Linley; libretto (Eng) by James R. Planché. First performance December 6, 1862, London, Princess's Theatre.
LIBRETTO: English (London: T. H. Lacy, [186?]).

Leah Kleschna, grand opera by Harry Lawrence Freeman; libretto (Eng) by the composer, after the play by Charles McLellan. Composed 1930.

Leap Year, musical duality by Alfred B. Sedgwick, an adaptation of J. Offenbach's *Geneviève de Brabant* (1859, Paris). First performance 1875, New York.

In order to hold on to his inheritance, the nasty Adolphus must get married. His cousin Clementine uses the occasion of leap year to maneuver her reluctant beau into proposing.
Roles: Adolphus and Clementine.
The music consists of six songs.
SCORE: vs (New York: Robert M. De Witt, 1875); repr. ed. Michael Meckna (1994).

Ledge, The, chamber opera in one act by Richard Rodney Bennett; libretto (Eng) by Adrian Mitchell. First performance September 12, 1961, London, Sadler's Wells, with Gerald English (Joe), John Cameron (the other man), and Dorothy Dorrow (the wife); conducted by Alexander Gibson; produced by John Blatchley.

Joe, clinging to a ledge, is determined to jump and ignores the pleas of a man who had a similar experience. His wife's entreaties are also in vain until she starts to laugh at one of his comments. Her outburst brings him back to his senses, and he leaves the precipice slowly.

For a detailed description, see Eaton/*OP* II, 296.

Major roles: Joe (ten), the other man (bar), and the wife (sop).
BIBLIOGRAPHY: Arthur Jacobs, review, *Opera* XII (Oct. 1961), 670–72 [on premiere].

Legend, The, lyric tragedy in one act by Joseph Carl Breil; libretto (Eng) by Jacques Byrne. First performance March 12, 1919, New York, Metropolitan Opera, with Rosa Ponselle (Carmelita), Paul Althouse (Stephen Pauloff), Louis D'Angelo (Stackareff), and Kathleen Howard (Marta); conducted by Roberto Moranzoni.

The setting is in the Balkan "Muscovadia" and concerns Count Stackareff, who is a bandit by day known as Black Lorenzo. Carmelita, the Count's daughter, is in love with Stephen Pauloff, a Hussar commander. A local legend has it that whoever opens the door at the inn will die within a year. Stephen does so, and when Stephen, in the course of his duty, goes to arrest the Count because of his criminal activities, Carmelita shoots Stephen. She is then shot by the Hussar's soldiers.

Major roles: Carmelita (sop), Stephen Pauloff (ten), Stackareff (bar), and Marta (mezzo).
SCORE: vs (New York, Melbourne, and Toronto: Chappell & Co., 1919).

Legend, The, opera by Bain Murray; libretto (Eng) by Janet Lewis, after her novel *The Invasion*. First performance May 8, 1987, Cleveland, Cleveland State University.

The story concerns the romance between Neengay, daughter of an Ojibway war chief, and John Johnstone, an Irishman.
LIBRETTO: English (Santa Barbara, Calif.: J. Daniel, 1987).

Légende Provençale, opera in three acts by Mary Moore; libretto (Eng-Fr) by Eleanor Flaig. Composed 1929–1938. The full score is lost.

Taking place in the fifteenth century, the story concerns an evil sorcerer, Drascovie, who causes the hero, Amiel, to kill himself and causes Amiel's beloved, Rozanne, to die. The lovers' souls meet above the funeral procession of the young woman. The work ends with the love duet "Redeeming Love and Vanquished Death," set against the "Dona eis requiem" of the monks.

Rozanne's act 3 aria was performed in French as "L'étoile du soir" with orchestra, conducted by James Sample, in April 1941.

The work was originally entitled *Macabre*.

Legend of Sleepy Hollow, opera by Robert Haskins; libretto (Eng) by Allen. J. Koppenhaver, after Washington Irving's story. Composed 1976.

Set in pre-Revolutionary New York, the story concerns the hapless schoolmaster Ichabod Crane and his encounter with his romantic rival, dressed as a ghostly figure.
See also *The Headless Horseman* and *Sleepy Hollow*.
LIBRETTO: typescript, holograph (1976, photocopy, NYPL).

Legend of Spain, A, opera in one act by Eleanor Everest Freer; libretto (Eng) by the composer. First performance June 19, 1931, Milwaukee.

The story concerns the town of Archcedona at the time of Ferdinand and Isabella.

Legend of the Piper, The, opera in one act by Eleanor Everest Freer; libretto by Josephine P. Peabody, after her play *The Piper*. First performance February 24, 1925, South Bend, Indiana, Progress Club, with Julia M. Rode (the Piper); conducted by Olive Maine.

In this treatment of the famed story, the Pied Piper lures the children away when, instead of being given the promised thousand guilders for ridding Hamelin of rats, he is offered only fifteen.

SCORE: vs (Boston: C. C. Birchard & Co., [1922]).

Legend of Wiwaste, The, opera by S. Earle Blakeslee; libretto (Eng) by the composer, after a Dakota Sioux legend. First performance April 25, 1924, Ontario, California, with Tsianina Redfeather Blackstone (Wiwaste). Revived 1927, Los Angeles, Hollywood Bowl, and 1966 and 1970, as *Red Cloud.*

The work, set before the arrival of the Europeans, deals with Native American courting and marriage customs. The Romantic score incorporates elements of Native American music, including authentic melodies and rhythmic figures, into its style.

Legends Three, opera in one act by Martin Kalmanoff; libretto (Eng) by the composer, after M. Brenner. First performance November 11, 1969, New York, Jewish Heritage Theater.

Lenz, opera in one act by Larry Sitsky; libretto (Eng) by Gwen Harwood, after Georg Büchner's novella. First performance March 14, 1974, Sydney, Australia, Opera House.

The story concerns the German poet and protégé of Goethe, Jakob Lenz (1751–1792), and opens in Waldbach in 1771, where he falls in love with Friederike von Brion, Goethe's mistress, and his strange behavior leads to his forced departure. Showing the first signs of his madness, Lenz is cared for by Christoph Kaufmann. He then comes under the care of the pastor Oberlin, and his fits of madness increase. He is eventually locked up after he attempts suicide.

Major roles: Jakob Lenz (ten), Friederike von Brion (mezzo), Christoph Kaufmann (bar), and Oberlin (bass).

Another setting of the Büchner tale is *Jakob Lenz,* by W. Rihm (1979, Hamburg).

Leo, the Royal Cadet, "entirely new and original Canadian military opera" in four acts by Oscar F. Telgmann; libretto (Eng) by George Frederick Cameron. First performance July 11, 1889, Kingston, Ontario, Martin's Opera House.

The work traces the career of the title character, including his battle with the Zulus. LIBRETTO: English, ms (1889?, National Library of Canada).

Leonora, lyrical drama in three acts by William Fry; libretto (Eng) by Joseph Reese Fry, after Edward Bulwer-Lytton's novel *The Lady of Lyons* (1838). First performance June 4, 1845, Philadelphia, Chestnut Street Theatre, with P. Ritchings (Valdor), Edward Seguin (Montalvo), Mr. Brinton (Alfrerez), Mr. Frazer (Julio), Mrs. Seguin (Leonora), and Miss Ince (Mariana); conducted by the composer. It ran for sixteen performances. The work was revived in May 1929 in a concert version by Otto Kinkeldey, in New York. Staged revival January 31, 1987, New York, Fashion Institute of Technology, Bel Canto Opera, in an edition by David Kelleher.

The setting is Spain at the time of the conquest of the Americas.

Fry claimed that it was the first grand opera by an American-born composer. The music itself is in the style of Bellini.
SCORE: vs (New York: E. Ferrett, 1846).
BIBLIOGRAPHY: B. L. Scherer, "New York," *ON* LI (June 1987), 52 [on 1987 revival].

Leper, The, "tabloid grand opera" in one act by Mary Moore; libretto (Eng) by Dudley Burrows. Composed 1912. Concert performance (date unknown).

The story concerns two characters who sacrifice everything to benefit each other.

Leper King, The, music-dance-drama by Alan Hovhaness; libretto (Eng) by the composer. First performance 1969, Chicago.
SCORE: vs (New York, C. F. Peters Corp., 1967).

Leper's Flute, The, opera in four acts by Ernest Bryson; libretto (Eng) by Ian Duncan Colvin, after his novel. First performance October 15, 1926, Glasgow.
SCORE: vs (London: Goodwin & Tabb, 1926).

Lessons, The, opera by Robert Ashley; libretto (Eng). First performance 1981, New York. May be performed as part of *Perfect Lives.**

Lestocq, or, The Fête of the Hermitage, historical opera in three acts, adaptation by Thomas S. Cooke of Auber's *Lestocq, ou, L'intrigue et l'amour* (1834, Paris); libretto (Eng) by George Macfarren, after Scribe's text. First performance February 21, 1835, London, Covent Garden.
LIBRETTO: English (London: J. Cumberland, [1835?]).

Lethe, or, Aesop in the Shades, satirical afterpiece opera by Thomas Arne; libretto (Eng) by David Garrick. First performance January 18, 1749, London, Drury Lane Theatre.
    In this satire, Pluto allows certain members of London society to drink the waters of forgetfulness at the river Lethe. They are also encouraged to inform Aesop, the barman at the Lethe, about their wishes, thereby revealing their weaknesses.
    The work includes songs by Boyce.
LIBRETTO: English (London: Paul Vaillant . . . , 1749).

Let My People Go, church opera in two acts by Raymond Warren; libretto (Eng) by the composer, after the Bible and spirituals. First performance March 22, 1972, Liverpool, Metropolitan Cathedral.

Let's Build a Nut House, chamber opera in one act by Robert Moran; libretto (Eng). First performance April 19, 1969, San Jose, State College.
    Written in memory of Paul Hindemith, a play on his *Wir bauen eine Stadt* (Let's Build a Town) (1930, Berlin).

Let's Make an Opera!/The Little Sweep, "entertainment for young people" in three acts by Benjamin Britten; libretto (Eng) by Eric Crozier. First performance June 14, 1949, Aldeburgh Festival, with Gladys Parr (Miss Baggott), Elizabeth Parry (Rowan), Max Worthley (Clem), and Norman Lumsden (Black Bob); conducted by Norman Del Mar. First U.S. performance March 22, 1950, St. Louis, Kiel Opera House; conducted by Stanley Chapple.
    In the first two acts a group of six children and five adults discuss the possibility of writing and presenting an opera. The third act is the opera itself, called *The Little Sweep*.
    The Little Sweep
    The story is set in 1810 and focuses on a nine-year-old chimney sweep who becomes stuck in a chimney on his first job. He is rescued from the nasty sweep master, Black Bob, by a group of well-to-do children.
    For detailed descriptions, see Eaton/*OP* I, 194–95; K/*KOB*, 1180–83; K/*NKOB*, 110–11.
    Major roles: Miss Baggott, the housekeeper (alto); Black Bob, the sweep master (bass); Clem, Black Bob's assistant (ten); Rowan, the nursery maid (sop); Juliet Brook,

the conductor of the opera (sop); Sam, the new sweep boy (treble); Gay Brook (treble); Sophie Brook (sop); John Crome (treble); Tina Crome (sop); and Hugh Crome (treble).
LIBRETTO: English (London and New York: Boosey & Hawkes, [1949]).
SCORE: vs, of *The Little Sweep* (London and New York: Boosey & Hawkes, [1965]).
BIBLIOGRAPHY: Cecil Smith, "Educators Conference Hears Britten Opera for Children," *MA* LXX (Apr. 16, 1950), 16, 50 [on U.S. premiere].

Letter for Queen Victoria, A, opera in four acts by Alan Lloyd; libretto (Eng) by Robert Wilson. First performance June 15, 1974, Spoleto, Italy; December 5, 1974, Paris.
    Composed for alto, flute, and string quartet.
LIBRETTO: English-French (Paris: Festival d'Automne, 1974).

Letter from an Astrologer, jazz opera by Paul Knopf; libretto (Eng) by the composer. First performance March 13, 1976, New York, Carnegie Recital Hall, with Evelyn Blakey and Toney Watkins; composer, piano; Duke Cleamons, bass.
    An astrologer is able to control people through his predictions, with the help of his young female assistant, Bags. He tries to get the aid of a pastor and his flock to make an alcoholic skeptic believe his utterances.
    The music employs various types of jazz, including ragtime.
BIBLIOGRAPHY: Robert Palmer, review, *NYT* (Mar. 14, 1976), 49 [on premiere].

Letters, Riddles, and Writs, opera in one act by Michael Nyman and Robert Lepage; libretto (Eng) by Jeremy Newsom, after Leopold and W. A. Mozart's letters. Originally part of the BBC series *Not Mozart*, for the commemoration of the bicentenary of Mozart's death, November 10, 1991. First stage performance June 24, 1992, London, Shaw Theatre, Endymion Ensemble, with Jonathan Peter Kenny (Mozart) and Martin Nelson (Leopold/Sarastro); designed by David Blight; produced by David Meyer.
    An examination of Mozart's difficult relationship with his father through the father–son letters and a set of riddles by Mozart for the 1782 Carnival.
    The music is also based on that of W. A. Mozart, and the work is set for countertenor, bass, and chamber ensemble.
    Roles: Mozart (counterten) and Leopold/Sarastro (bass).
BIBLIOGRAPHY: S. Pettitt, review, *Opera* XLIII (Sept. 1992), 1116 [on stage premiere].

Letters to Leo, opera in one act by James Wilson; libretto (Eng) by the composer, after Vincent van Gogh. First performance November 26, 1984, Dublin, St. Stephen's Church.
    Role: baritone.

Letter to Emily, A, opera in one act by Lockrem Johnson; libretto (Eng) by the composer, after Robert Hupton's play *Consider the Lilies*. First performance April 24, 1951, Seattle, Cornish College. Revised version July 26, 1951, Interlochen, Michigan.
    Despite her harsh father's ridicule, Emily Dickinson secretly sends some of her poems to Colonel Higginson, a critic living in Boston. When Higginson invites the shy Emily to Boston, she goes at the urging of her sister Lavinia. Once in Boston Emily discovers that Higginson does not really appreciate her work and, reminded of her father's criticisms, retreats back into her shell.
    For a detailed description, see Eaton/*OP* I, 193–94.
    Major roles: Emily Dickinson (sop); Lavinia, her sister (mezzo); Edward Dickinson, her father (bass-bar); and Colonel Higginson (bar).
    The mostly diatonic score contains some mild dissonances.

Letty, the Basket-Maker, opera in a prologue and three acts by Michael Balfe; libretto (Eng) by J. P. Simpson. First performance June 14, 1871, London, Gaiety Theatre.

A revision of *The Devil's In It** (1852).

Major roles: a magician, Bridget, the Count, Herman, the Countess, Albert, Letty, a fiddler, and a music-master.

SCORE: fs ms, autograph, incomplete (British Library, Add. MS. 33536); vs (London, 1871).

Liar, Liar, "opera for children, teachers and other grown-ups" by Sam Raphling; libretto (Eng) by James Vernon Hatch. Composed 1972.

SCORE: vs ([Hastings-on-Hudson, N.Y.]): General Music Pub. Co., [1972]).

Libertine, The, operatic drama in two acts by Henry Rowley Bishop, an adaptation of Mozart's *Don Giovanni* (1787, Prague); text translated from the Italian of Da Ponte by Isaac Pocock. First performance May 20, 1817, London, Covent Garden, with Charles Kemble (the Don) and John Liston (Leporello)

The plot is almost identical to the Da Ponte setting, and the dialogue is a word-for-word translation.

A comical version of the story is Thomas Dibdin's two-act burletta *Don Giovanni, or, A Spectre on Horseback,* "a comic, heroic, operatic, tragic, pantomimic, burletta-spectacular extravaganza" in two acts, first performed in 1817 in London, Royal Circus. Among its characters are, in addition to Don Giovanni, Don Octavio, Leporello, and Donna Anna, Lobsteretta, Shrimperina, and Contadine.

Other settings in English include William Hawes's version (1830, London); Bishop's *Giovanni in London, or, The Libertine Reclaimed** (1817, London); Meyer Lutz's three-act *Don Juan,* a "gaiety burlesque," to a libretto by Adrian Ross and J. T. Tanner (London, 1893); Raymond Walker and William Beaumont's *The Marble Guest,* school opera in four acts, after Mozart (1966); and W. Alwyn's *Juan, or, The Libertine** (comp. 1969).

SCORE: vs (London: Goulding, D'Almaine, Potter, 1817).

LIBRETTOS: English, Dibdin and Pocock versions (London: J. Miller, 1817; New York: D. Longworth, 1818); Ross-Tanner version (London: E. Ascherberg and New York: E. Schuberth, 1894); Walker-Beaumont version (London: Novello, [1966].

Liberty Hall, or, A Test of Good Fellowship, comic opera in two acts by Charles Dibdin; libretto (Eng) by the composer. First performance February 8, 1785, London, Drury Lane Theatre.

LIBRETTO: English (London: G. Kearsley, 1785).

Life, Death, and Renovation of Tom Thumb, burletta by Charles Dibdin; libretto (Eng) by the composer, after Henry Fielding. First performance March 28, 1785, London, Royal Circus.

LIBRETTO: English ([London]: [n.p.], 1785).

Life Goes to a Party, opera in one act by Robert Middleton; libretto (Eng) by the composer. First performance August 13, 1948, Lenox, Massachusetts, Tanglewood.

Lifework of Juan Diaz, The, opera by Lawrence Rapchak; libretto (Eng) by Carl J. Ratner, after a short story by Ray Bradbury. First performance April 1990, Chicago, Chamber Opera Chicago.

Ligeia, opera fantasy in two acts by Russell Currie; libretto (Eng) by Robert Kornfeld, after Poe. First performance April 5, 1987, Riverdale, New Jersey, YM-YWHA.

The title character, a mysterious dark beauty, weds a young aristocrat but then becomes ill and dies. When her distraught husband weds again, his new wife, the blond Lady Rowena, also takes ill and dies; however, she comes back to life on her bier, revived by the spirit of Ligeia.

Part 3 of a trilogy of operas on stories by Poe. See also *The Cask of Amatillado* (1982) and *Dream within a Dream* (1984).

Ligeia, opera by Augusta Read Thomas; libretto (Eng) by Leslie Dunton-Downer, after Poe. First performance (amateur) February 20, 1994, Baltimore, Peabody Conservatory, Peabody Camerata, with Monica Reinagel (Ligeia), Jenny Elliott (Rowena), Jennifer Davison (Virginia Clemm), and Geoffrey Parrish (Poe); conducted by Gene Young. First professional performance May 19, 1994, Evian, France, Evian Music Festival; conducted by Mstislav Rostropovich; directed by Roger Brunyate. First professional U.S. performance July 29, 1995, Aspen, Wheeler Opera House.

The work blends Poe's story with elements of his own life and includes his first and second wives, the thirteen-year-old Virginia Clemm and the strong-willed Rowena Trevanion. Poe is promised continued inspiration by his muse, the Mephistophelian Ligeia, in exchange for his devotion to her, an arrangement that is threatened by Rowena.

LIBRETTO: English (Bryn Mawr, Pa.: T. Presser, 1994).
BIBLIOGRAPHY: Mark Carrington, "'Ligeia': Poe's Muse Put to Music," *Washington Post* (Feb. 24, 1994), C, 2 [on premiere]; Eleanor Keats, "Exotic 'Ligeia' a Ringing Success," *Denver Post* (July 31, 1995), F, 3 [on Aspen premiere].

Light from St. Agnes, A, lyric tragedy in one act by W. Franke Harling; libretto (Eng) by Minnie Maddern Fiske. First performance December 26, 1925, Chicago, Civic Opera, with Rosa Raisa ('Toinette), George Baklanoff (Michel Kerouac), and Forrest Lamont (Père Bertrand); conducted by Giorgio Polacco.

The wanton 'Toinette is standing at the coffin of Agnes Deveiaux, a devoted nun, who has left the woman a diamond crucifix. The drunk Michel enters and wants to steal Agnes's cross. When 'Toinette rings the bell of the convent to warn of the theft, Michel stabs her. As she dies, the crucifix appears on her breast. Michel slinks away.
SCORE: vs (New York: R. L. Huntzinger, 1925).
BIBLIOGRAPHY: "New Operas Out West," *NYT* (Jan. 10, 1926), VII, 6 [summary of reviews on premiere].

Lighthouse, The, chamber opera in a prologue and one act by Peter Maxwell Davies; libretto (Eng) by the composer. First performance September 2, 1980, Edinburgh, Moray House, with Neil Mackie (Sandy/Officer 1), Michael Rippon (Blazes/Officer 2), and David Wilson Johnson (Arthur/Officer 3); conducted by Richard Dufallo. First U.S. performance May 15, 1985, Philadelphia, Academy of Vocal Arts, with Robert Rowland, David Neal, and Todd Thomas; conducted by Theodore Antoniou.

Based on an actual occurrence, the story opens on a courtroom inquiry into the strange disappearance of three lighthouse attendants in the Western Islands of Scotland in 1900. It then proceeds to a reenactment of the event according to the composer's interpretation of it.

Roles: Sandy/Officer 1 (ten), Blazes/Officer 2 (bar), and Arthur/voice of cards/ Officer 3 (bass).
SCORE: vs (London: J. & W. Chester, 1982).

BIBLIOGRAPHY: Donal Henahan, "Opera: 'Lighthouse,'" *NYT* (Dec. 1, 1985) [on New York premiere]; Gary Schmidgall, "Philadelphia," *ON* L (July 1985), 36 [on U.S. premiere].

Light of Asia, The, "sacred legend" in three acts by Isadore de Lara; libretto (Eng) by W. Beatty-Kingston, after Sir Edwin Arnold's poem (1879). First performance June 11, 1892, London, Covent Garden. First composed as a cantata.

About the fifth-century Prince Guatama of India, the founder of Buddhism.

SCORE: vs, cantata version (London: Novello, Ewer [between 1886–1899]).

Light of the Harem, opera in three acts by Arthur Goring Thomas; libretto (Eng) by C. Harrison, after Thomas Moore. First performance November 7, 1879, London, Royal Academy of Music.

Light Opera, The, a "ritual of healing with tools and weapons" by Charlie Morrow; text from ancient Hebrew and Maori sources. First performance June 6, 1983, New York, Western Wind.

Like a Window, opera by Elisabeth Lutyens; libretto (Eng) by the composer, after letters of Vincent van Gogh. First performance (concert) November 24, 1977, London, BBC.

Lilith, opera by Deborah Drattell; libretto (Eng) by David Steven Cohen, after the Midrash. The first performance was scheduled for June 4, 1997, New York, Dicapo Opera Theater but was canceled because of a labor dispute. First performance (concert) August 16, 1998, Cooperstown, New York, Glimmerglass Opera.

The action opens at the funeral of Adam, at which the children of Adam and Eve meet those of Adam and Lilith, his first wife, who left the Garden of Eden because she refused to be subservient to him. It follows the strife between Lilith and Eve and ends with neither gaining the upper hand but each growing to understand and accept the other.

Also set by H. Weisgall, as *Lillith** (1934, not perf.).

BIBLIOGRAPHY: Susan Josephs, "Lilith's Dark Song," *Jewish Week* (May 30, 1997), 39; Allan Kozinn, "All about Eve and Adam's Ex, a Demon," *NYT* (June 1, 1997), II, 29, 34.

Lilla, operatic drama, with parts of Joseph Weigl's *Die Schweizerfamilie* (1809, Vienna), with a text (Eng) by James R. Planché. First performance October 21, 1825, London, Covent Garden.

Lilliput, afterpiece by Samuel Arnold; libretto (Eng) by David Garrick, after Jonathan Swift's *Gulliver's Travels*. First performance May 15, 1777, London, Little Theatre in the Haymarket.

LIBRETTO: English (London: P. Vaillant, 1757).

Lillith, opera in one act by Hugo Weisgall; libretto (Eng), after Lois Elman. Composed 1934.

SCORE: fs, vs ([n.p.], 1934, 1933–34; LCCN: 65-77560, 65-7756).

Lilly, The. See **Zululand.**

Lily, opera in three acts by Leon Kirchner; libretto (Eng) by the composer, after Saul Bellow's novel *Henderson the Rain King*. First performance April 14, 1977, New York, New York City Opera, with Ara Berberian (Henderson), George Shirley (Romilayu),

Geanie Faulkner (Princess Mtalba), Joy Blackett (Queen Willatale), and Susan Belling (Lily); conducted by the composer; directed by Tom O'Horgan.

Gene Henderson, an American millionaire, has come to Africa to find "the way to live." Trying to remove a group of frogs that are destroying an African tribe's water supply, Henderson unknowingly destroys the Arnewi's water supply as well. He recalls his second wife, Lily, throughout the action.

Major roles: Gene Henderson (bass); Romilayu (ten); Princess Mtalba, of the Arnewi (col sop); Queen Willatale, of the Arnewi (mezzo); Lily, Henderson's wife (col sop).

BIBLIOGRAPHY: Hans Heinsheimer, "Zeroing In," *ON* XLI (Apr. 16, 1977), 13–15; Andrew Porter, "Musical Events," *NY* LIII (May 2, 1977), 124–27 [on premiere].

SCORE: vs (New York: Associated Music Publishers, ca. 1977).

Lily Maid, The, opera in two acts by Rutland Boughton; libretto (Eng) by the composer. First performance September 10, 1934, Stroud, Gloucestershire, Church Room, with Nellie Palliser (Elaine) and Augustus Milner (Lancelot); conducted by the composer.

Among the musical highlights is Elaine's closing aria.

Part 3 of the Arthurian cycle, which also includes *The Birth of Arthur** (1920), *The Round Table** (1916), *Galahad** (comp. 1944), and *Avalon** (comp. 1945).

BIBLIOGRAPHY: review, *The Times* (London) (Sept. 11, 1934), 10 [on premiere].

Lily of Killarney, The, opera in three acts by Julius Benedict; libretto (Eng) by John Oxenford and Dion Boucicault, after Boucicault's drama *Colleen Bawn* (1860). First performance February 8, 1862, London, Covent Garden, with Louisa Pyne (Eily O'Connor), Charles Santley (Danny Mann), and William Harrison; conducted by Alfred Mellon. First U.S. performance November 20, 1867, Philadelphia.

After Hardress Cregan weds Eily O'Connor clandestinely, Mr. Corrigan, his widowed mother's landlord, threatens that unless the son marries Ann Shute, an heiress, Corrigan will make Mrs. Cregan marry him to repay her debt. Faced by this prospect, Hardress tries to make his bride give him the marriage certificate, but she is urged by Myles na Coppaleen, who loves her, and the parish priest to hold on to the paper. Danny Mann, a boatman and Hardress's friend, offers to help him by eliminating Eily. Danny tells Hardress that the signal he should use is to send the boatman his glove. After a quarrel between the Cregans, Mrs. Cregan, at Danny's urging, sends him her son's glove, unaware of its significance. Danny confronts Eily at the lake and threatens to kill her unless she gives him the marriage certificate. When she refuses, he shoves her into the lake. Myles, who is hunting, fires at what he thinks is an otter. It is really Danny, and as he dies, he implicates Hardress in Eily's murder. Eily, meanwhile, has been rescued by Myles.

Corrigan disrupts the wedding ceremony of Hardress and Ann Shute and orders the accompanying soldiers to take him into custody for having arranged Eily's supposed murder. Mrs. Cregan states that she sent the glove to Danny, and the arrival of a very alive Eily and Myles clears Hardress of murder charges. Hardress then declares before the assembled throng that he is married to Eily, and the generous Ann Shute pays off the Cregans' debts to Corrigan.

For a detailed plot description, see K/*NKOB*, 37–38

Major roles: Hardress Cregan (ten), Eily O'Connor (sop), Mrs. Cregan (alto), Corrigan (bass), Ann Shute (sop), Myles na Coppaleen (ten), Father Tom (bass), and Danny Mann (bar).

SCORE: vs (London and New York: Boosey [187?]).

LIBRETTOS: English (London: Copyright Protection Office, 1879; Boston: Ditson, [18??]).

Lima Beans, comic opera in one act by Douglas Townsend; libretto (Eng), after Alfred Kreymborg's play (1925). First performance January 7, 1956, New York.
LIBRETTO: English (New York: S. French; London: S. French, Ltd., [1925]).
BIBLIOGRAPHY: review, *Musical Courier* CLIII (Feb. 1956), 79 [on premiere].

Linco's Travels, theater work by Michael Arne, with J. Vernon; libretto (Eng) by David Garrick. First performance April 6, 1767, London, Drury Lane Theatre. First U.S. performance December 17, 1791, Philadelphia, Kenna Company.
LIBRETTO: English ([n.p.], [1767]).

Line of Terror, opera in one act by Ian McQueen, an English version of his *Judith och Holofernes* (1987, Vadstena, Sweden); libretto (Eng), after the Book of Judith. First performance July 14, 1993, London, Almeida Theatre, with Virginia Kerr (Judith), Richard Halton (Holofernes), and Andrew Watts (Achior).
A modernized treatment of the biblical story.
BIBLIOGRAPHY: Rodney Milnes, review, *Opera* XLIV (Sept. 1993), 1108 [on premiere].

Linnet from the Leaf, The, music theater work by Elisabeth Lutyens; libretto (Eng) by the composer. First performance (concert) November 11, 1979, London, BBC.
The work is a condemnation of racism.

Lion, The, children's opera in two acts by Arnold Franchetti; libretto (Eng) by Ruth Howard Sanderson and Marie Franchetti. First performance (private) December 16, 1950, New London, Connecticut, Williams Memorial Institute. First public performance July 12, 1953, Westport, Connecticut, White Barn Theatre, with James Mattinely (the lion), Lena Sinagulia and Amelia Haas (the princesses), Helen Hubbard (their mother), and Samuel Bertsche (trainer/narrator); conducted by Raymond Hanson; directed by Ralph Pendleton.
In the plot an escaped circus lion wants to be a household pet, since he hates crowds and has trouble sleeping on noisy trains. He wanders into the bedroom of the princesses and tells them his sad tale. He ends up back at the circus after being drawn there by the smell of good food.
BIBLIOGRAPHY: Harold C. Schonberg, "Crowd-Hating Lion Star of New Opera," *NYT* (July 13, 1953).

Lion and Androcles, The, children's opera in one act by John Eaton; libretto (Eng) by E. Walter and D. Anderson, after the fable by Aeneas Silvius. First performance May 1, 1974, Indianapolis, P.S. No. 47.

Lionel and Clarissa, opera in three acts by Charles Dibdin, including music by other composers; libretto (Eng) by Isaac Bickerstaffe. First performance February 25, 1768, London, Covent Garden, with George Mattocks (Lionel), Miss Macken (Clarissa), Mr. Dyer (Jessamy), Mrs. Baker (Diana), Mr. Shuter (Colonel Oldboy), and Mr. Mahon (Harman). Revised as *Lionel and Clarissa, or, The School for Fathers,* February 8, 1770, London, Covent Garden, with Mr. Vernon (Lionel), Mrs. Baddeley (Clarissa), Dibdin (Jessamy), Mrs. Wrighten (Diana), Mr. Parsons (Colonel Oldboy), and Mr. Fawcett (Harman). Revised version by Henry Rowley Bishop, May 3, 1814, London, Covent Garden. First American performance December 14, 1772, Philadelphia, Southwark Theatre.
In this familiar plot Colonel Oldboy wants his son, Mr. Jessamy, to wed Clarissa, daughter of Sir Flowerdale. Clarissa, in turn, loves Lionel. The young couple's problems are solved when the visiting Harman elopes with Jessamy's sister, Diana, obligating Sir Flowerdale to accept his daughter Clarissa's choice of a husband.

For a detailed description, see Fiske/*ETM*, 355–57 (1770 version) and 603-5 (1768 version).

Major roles: Colonel Oldboy (ten), Mr. Jessamy (ten), Clarissa (sop), Harman (ten), and Diana (sop).

Among the musical highlights are Clarissa's "Immortal Powers" (act 1) and Diana's "Ladies, Ladies" (act 2), both by Dibdin. Other composers represented include Arne, Galuppi, Scolari, and Vento. Dibdin composed all three finales.
SCORE: vs (London: John Johnston, n.d.).
LIBRETTO: English (London: J. Johnston, [1770?]; Philadelphia: Matthew Cary, 1794).
DISCOGRAPHY: excerpts, O. Groves, W. Temple, Hammersmith Lyric Theatre Orch.; cond. A. Reynolds, Pearl PEA 9917 (from 1925 HMV recording; 1 CD, mono).

Lion, the Witch, and the Wardrobe, The, children's opera in four acts by John McCabe; libretto (Eng) by Gerald Larner, after C. S. Lewis's book (1950). First performance April 29, 1969, Manchester, England, Manchester Cathedral. First U.S. performance March 9, 1990, Wilmington, Delaware.

For two adults and nine or more children.
SCORE: vs (London: Novello, 1971).

Little Beggars, The, chamber ballad opera in one act; music arranged by Max Saunders; libretto (Eng) by Caryl Brahms and Ned Sherrin. First performance March 20, 1958, London, BBC television, with Alec McCowen (Mack).

An updating of the *Beggar's Opera** to an East End bomb-site in the 1950s.
BIBLIOGRAPHY: review, *The Times* (London) (Mar. 21, 1958), 3 [on premiere].

Little Billy, nautical opera in one act for children by Michael Hurd; libretto (Eng) by the composer, using the poem of William Makepeace Thackeray. First performance March 25, 1964, Stroud, England.

Little Billy is the youngest of three Bristol sailors who run out of provisions. He is saved at the last moment from being eaten by the other two.
LIBRETTO: English (London: Novello, [1966]).

Little Mermaid, The, opera in two acts for schools and young people by Anne Boyd; libretto (Eng) by Robin Lee, after Hans Christian Andersen. Composed 1978. First performance 1986, Sydney, Australian Opera.

The story concerns a mermaid who wants to be human.

Also set by W. Maliszewski as *Syrena* (1928); by M. More (1951); and by D. Harris (comp. 1985–1990).
SCORE: vs (London: Faber, 1978; New York: G. Schirmer, 1980).

Little Nightmare Music, A, "opera in one irrevocable act" by "P. D. Q. Bach" (Peter Schickele); libretto (Eng) by the composer. First performance December 27, 1982, New York, Carnegie Hall.

The story is a spoof of Peter Shaffer's play *Amadeus*, in which Salieri is shown to have destroyed Mozart out of jealousy. It includes the added characters of P. D. Q. Bach and Schlafer, the playwright, whom Salieri tries to poison but ends up poisoning Mozart by mistake because of his bumbling servant, P. D. Q Bach.

For a detailed description, see Kornick/*RAO*, 272–73.

Major roles: Antonio Salieri, a successful composer (bar); Peter Schlafer, a mysterious writer (ten); Wolfgang Amadeus Mozart, a not so successful composer (silent); and P. D. Q. Bach, a servant (silent).

The music is based almost entirely on Mozart's *Eine kleine Nachtmusik*. The title is also a not-so-veiled reference to the very successful operatic musical *A Little Night Music* by Stephen Sondheim (1973, New York). It includes the duet "Uh oh—" and the finale, "What hutzpah!"

SCORE: vs (Bryn Mawr, Pa.: T. Presser, 1984).

DISCOGRAPHY: B. Ford, J. Billings, G. Tarack (violin), New York Pick-Up Ensemble; cond. P. Schickele, Vanguard 78448 (1983, New York, 1 CD).

Little Redinka, children's opera in one act by Michael Easton; libretto (Eng) by Alan Hopgood. First performance 1991, Melbourne, Australia, Victoria State Opera.

In this version of the children's story, Little Red Riding Hood takes an airplane to Melbourne, Australia. During the flight she discovers that the seemingly nice Mr. Wolf is really an international jewel thief. He is apprehended through the efforts of a French policeman and a sharp airline hostess.

Little Red Riding Hood, opera by Mary A'Beckett; libretto (Eng) by the composer, after the Brothers Grimm. First performance August 1842, London, Surrey Gardens Theatre.

Little Red Riding Hood, children's opera in one act by Seymour Barab; libretto (Eng) by the composer, after the Brothers Grimm. First performance 1958, San Francisco; October 13, 1962, New York, Carl Fischer Hall.

A retelling of the classic children's tale.

Roles: Little Red Riding Hood (sop), mother/grandmother (mezzo), and wolf/woodsman (bar).

SCORE: vs ([New York]: Boosey & Hawkes, 1965).

Little Stories in Tomorrow's Paper, opera in one act by Seymour Barab; libretto (Eng) by the composer. First performance June 14, 1979, New York.

When two murderers who are hiding in a forest meet a stranger, they assume he is a fellow criminal. They determine to punish him when they find that the man has not committed any crimes.

Little Sweep, The. See **Let's Make an Opera!**

Little Tycoon, The, comic opera in two acts by Willard Spenser; libretto (Eng) by the composer. First performance January 1885, Philadelphia, with R. E. Graham (Knickerbocker), Carrie M. Dietrich (Violet), E. H. Van Veghten (Lord Dolphin), and W. S. Rising (Alvin). First New York performance March 29, 1885, Standard Theater, with the original cast; it ran until June.

The simple plot concerns Alvin, who pretends to be a Japanese nobleman in order to impress his fiancée Violet's snobbish, but dumb, father, General Knickerbocker. Knickerbocker's scheme to marry his daughter off to an English lord flounder when Alvin appears at Knickerbocker's mansion in the guise of "His Royal Highness Sham, the Great Tycoon of Japan" (Spenser copyrighted the work a full three years before *The Mikado*) and makes the father forget about his previous plans for his daughter's marriage.

The work was quite successful in Philadelphia, where it ran for over two months; its New York run was not so successful, but it toured through the United States for several years. Its most popular number was the waltz "Love Comes Like a Summer Sigh."

See Bordman/*AMT*, 85–86, for a detailed plot and description.

SCORE: vs (New York: Gottsberger, 1882).

LIBRETTO: English (Philadelphia: W. H. Keyser, 1886).

Little Women, opera in two acts by Eleanor Everest Freer; libretto (Eng) by the composer, after Louisa May Alcott. First performance April 2, 1934, Chicago, Musician's Club of Women, with Frances Coates Grace.

A treatment of the famous story of the March sisters, led by the heroine, the literary-minded Jo.

A two-act setting by Mark Adamo, with a text by the composer, was performed on March 13, 1998, Houston, Houston Grand Opera.

Livery Rake, The, ballad opera; libretto (Eng) by Edward Phillips. First performance May 5, 1733, London, Drury Lane Theatre.

LIBRETTO: English (London: J. Watts, 1733); repr. ed. Rubsamen/*BO*, vol. 16, *Country Operas II: Farcical Humor and Stratagem* (1974).

Living Solid Face, chamber dance-opera by Herbert Owen Reed; libretto (Eng) by Hartley Alexander and F. W. Coggan. First performance (concert) February 24, 1962, East Lansing, Michigan. First stage performance February 10, 1976, Brookings, South Dakota.

Lizzie Borden, "a family portrait" in three acts by Jack Beeson; libretto (Eng) by Kenward Elmslie, after a scenario by Richard Plant with the subtitle *A Family Portrait in Three Acts.* First performance March 25, 1965, New York, City Opera, with Brenda Lewis (Lizzie Borden), Ellen Faull (Abigail Borden), Anne Elgar (Margret Borden), Herbert Beattie (Andrew Borden), Richard Fredericks (Captain Jason MacFarlane), and Richard Krause (Reverend Harrington); conducted by Anton Coppola; directed by Nikos Psacharopoulos. Revivals include July 1990, Cooperstown, New York, Glimmgerglass Opera; March 1999, New York, City Opera (scheduled).

The work is based on the case of Lizzie Borden, tried and acquitted of the ax murder of her father and stepmother. It is set in Fall River, Massachusetts, in the 1890s. In this treatment of the story, Lizzie tries to aid her sister Margret to escape their dreadful existence with their tight-fisted banker father, Andrew, and his mean-spirited second wife, Abigail, called Abbie. Lizzie helps Margret elope with Captain Jason MacFarlane, after Andrew denies the couple permission to wed, insisting that Jason marry Lizzie instead.

When Abbie catches Lizzie daydreaming in her mother's wedding dress, Lizzie realizes that she is now left alone with her father and stepmother. Abbie taunts Lizzie and treats her like a servant. After Abbie leaves to take a nap, the unhinged Lizzie enters her bedroom with an ax and kills her. When the father returns, he meets a similar fate.

The last scene opens several years later. Lizzie, despite her acquittal by the jury, is shunned by her neighbors, and her donations are refused by Reverend Harrington's congregation. The opera closes with the children's taunting verses ringing in her ears.

For a detailed description, see Eaton/*OP* II, 139–40.

Roles: Lizzie (mezzo); Andrew Borden, her father (bass-bar); Abigail (Abbie), her stepmother (col sop); Margret, her sister (sop); Captain Jason MacFarlane (bar); and Reverend Harrington (ten).

The dramatic score, containing through-composed sections and set pieces, employs both twentieth-century expressionistic passages and nineteenth-century American folk styles, including hymn tunes harmonized dissonantly and a lighthearted ballad (Abbie's Bird Song). Among the other musical highlights are the two act 2 quintets of the principals, Lizzie's Mad Scene to end the act, and her Dressing Scene of act 3.

See also *The Passion of Lizzie Borden* by M. Spektor (1986). Morton Gould's ballet *Fall River Legend* (1947, New York) is another setting of the story.

SCORE: ([New York]: Boosey and Hawkes, [1967]).
BIBLIOGRAPHY: Jack Beeson, "The Autobiography of Lizzie Borden," *OJ* IV/1 (1986–87), 15–42; review, *Opera* XVI (July 1965), 494; Howard Klein, "World Premiere of 'Lizzie Borden,'" *NYT* (Mar. 26, 1965), 29.
DISCOGRAPHY: Faull, Lewis, Elgar, Fredericks, Beattie, Krause, Chorus and Orch. of New York City Opera; cond. Coppola, Desto D455/7 (3 LPs); reissued as CRI CD 694 (1995, 2 CDs).

Lizzie Strotter (a Modern Lysistrata), or, The Women War on War (with a Sideswipe at High Fashion), opera in one act by Martin Kalmanoff; libretto (Eng) by the composer, after Aristophanes' *Lysistrata*. First performance March 6–7, 1958, Des Moines, Iowa, Drake University.

The setting is the meeting room of a women's club, the present. Lizzie Strotter, the head of the group, together with her sister, Lottie, plan to get all women's clubs in the United States to bring an end to war by declaring a moratorium on sex unless the men comply. The women invite their Russian counterparts, led by Madame Grabski. When this strategy fails to produce results, the women use their second plan, to wear mididresses and chemises only. Learning this, the men give up.

For a description, see Summers/*OOA*, 166–67.

Major roles: Lizzie Strotter (sop), Lottie Strotter (sop), Aurelia (alto), and Madame Grabski (sop).

SCORE: vs (New York: Operation Opera, 1958).

Loafer and the Loaf, The, opera in one act by Henry Leland Clarke; libretto (Eng) by Evelyn Sharp. First performance May 1, 1956, Los Angeles.

The setting is "any old street in the city that never was, not yet." The Loafer purloins a loaf from the Baker Boy's cart and is apprehended by the Prosperous Citizen but is defended by the Poet's Wife, because she thinks the Loafer may also be a poet. He turns out, in fact, to be not only a poet but her husband as well, and the Baker's Boy, who was to be blamed for all the shenanigans, mollifies the assemblage with cream cakes.

For a detailed description, see Eaton/*OP* I, 195–96.

Roles: Baker's Boy (sop), the Loafer (ten), Prosperous Citizen (bar), Poet's Wife (mezzo), the watchman (bass), and the minstrel (mime).

SCORE: vs, holograph (1957, photocopy, NYPL).

Loca, La, opera in three acts by Gian Carlo Menotti; libretto (Eng) by the composer. First performance June 3, 1979, San Diego, San Diego Opera, with Beverly Sills (Queen Juana), Susanne Marsee (Doña Manuela), Joseph Evans (Miguel de Denia), Robert Hale (Ximenes de Cisneros), and John Bröcheler (Felipe/Fernando/Carlos V); conducted by Calvin Simmons; directed by Tito Capobianco. Also September 16, 1979, New York, City Opera, with a similar cast. Revised 1982, Spoleto, Italy; first U.S. performance June 1, 1984, Charleston, South Carolina, Spoleto Festival U.S.A., with Adriana Vanelli (Juana) and Louis Otey (Felipe/King /Fernando/Carlos); conducted by Herbert Gietzen.

Set in Spain in the sixteenth century, the tragic story follows Queen Juana of Castile and Léon, called "la loca" (the Mad), and her betrayal by her father, her husband, and her son.

Major roles: Queen Juana la Loca (sop); her father, Fernando/her husband, Felipe (Philip)/her son, Carlos (bar); Doña Manuela (mezzo); Miguel de Denia (ten); and Ximenes de Cisneros, Bishop of Toledo (bar).

A vocal highlight of the work is Juana's lullaby, which she sings to the dying Philip at the end of act 1.

SCORE: vs (New York: G. Schirmer, [1979]).
BIBLIOGRAPHY: Robert Jacobson, review, *ON* XLIV (Dec. 8, 1979), 27 [on New York premiere]; Tim Page, review, *NYT* (June 3, 1984), I, 61 [on U.S. premiere of rev. version]; Harold C. Schonberg, review, *NYT* (Sept. 17, 1979), C, 13 [on New York premiere].

Lock and Key, musical farce in two acts by William Shield; libretto (Eng) by Prince Hoare. First performance February 2, 1796, London, Covent Garden. First U.S. performance July 7, 1796, Hartford, Connecticut, Old American Theatre.

The story concerns an old guardian, who locks up his young charge to keep her from marrying.

The overture is by William T. Parke.
SCORE: vs (London: Preston & Son, [1796]).
LIBRETTO: English (London: T. N. Longman, 1797; New York: David Longworth, 1806).

Lodge of Shadows, The, music drama in one act by Samuel Adler; libretto (Eng) by Jarold Ramsey. Composed 1973. First performance May 3, 1988, Fort Worth, Texas.

Scored for baritone solo, dancers, and orchestra.
SCORE: fs (New York: C. Fischer, [1977]).

Lodger, The, melodrama in two acts by Phyllis Tate; libretto (Eng) by David Franklin, after the novel by Mrs. Belloc-Lowndes (1913). First performance July 16, 1960, London, with Jean Evans (Emma Bunting), David Bowman (the Lodger), William McCue (John Bunting), and John Wakefield (Joe Chandler); conducted by Myers Foggin; produced by Dorothy Pattinson.

The story is based on a character along the lines of Jack the Ripper.
BIBLIOGRAPHY: Harold D. Rosenthal, "Royal Academy of Music, London," *Opera* XI (Sept. 1960), 648–49 [on premiere].

Lodoiska, opera (pastiche) in three acts by Stephen Storace, after Cherubini, Kreutzer, and Andreozzi (see below); libretto (Eng) by John Philip Kemble, after Dejaure's text for Cherubini (1791, Paris). First performance June 9, 1794, London, Drury Lane Theatre, with Mr. Kelly (Count Floreski), Mr. Palmer (Baron Lovinski), Mr. Barrymore (Kera Khan), and Mrs. Crouch (Lodoiska). First U.S. performance March 3, 1806, Boston, Federal Street Theatre. Storace's version was arranged by Henry Rowley Bishop, October 15, 1816, London, Covent Garden.

In this rescue opera, the Polish prince Count Floreski searches for Lodoiska, princess of Altanno, in order to marry her. She has been imprisoned by another suitor, the evil Baron Lovinski. The Tartars, led by Kera Khan, attack the castle in which she is imprisoned, and Kera Khan kills the Baron in a hand-to-hand fight. The Tartars then release Lodoiska and Floreski, whom they have captured, because of his kindly actions toward them previously.

The three settings on which the Storace version is based are those by L. Cherubini (1791, Paris); K. Kreutzer (1791, Paris); and G. Andreozzi (1796). Other settings of the story include J. S. Mayr (1796, Venice), L. Caruso (1798, Rome), F. Paer (1804, Bologna), Curmi (1846), and Succo (1849).
LIBRETTO: English (Boston: W. Blagrove/Greenough et al., 1807; London: Longman et al., 1809).

Logan Rock, The, comic opera in three acts by Inglis Gundry; libretto (Eng) by the composer, after William Bottrell. First performance August 15, 1956, Porthcurno, England, Minack Theatre.

Long Christmas Dinner, opera in one act by Paul Hindemith; libretto (Ger and Eng versions) by the composer and Thornton Wilder, after Wilder's tale. First performance December 17, 1961, Mannheim, Nationaltheater (in German) as *Das lange Weihnachtsmahl*, with Elisabeth Thoma, Eva-Maria Molner, Getrud Schretter-Petersik, Petrina Kruss, Erika Ahsbahs, Thomas Tipton, Jean Cox, Frederick Dalberg, and Georg Völker; conducted by the composer; directed by Hans Schüler. First U.S. performance (in English) March 13–16, 1963, New York, Juilliard School; conducted by the composer (March 13–14), and by Jorge Mester (March 15–16).

The story, beginning in the dining room of the Bayard home at Christmas, covers ninety dinners in the Bayard household.

For detailed descriptions, see Eaton/*OP* II, 294; K/*NKOB*, 366–67.

Major roles: Lucia (sop), Mother Bayard (alto), Roderick (bar), Brandon (bass), Charles (ten), Genevieve (mezzo), and Leonora (high sop).

The music comprises a series of short set pieces that flow into each other, and the work is unified by the use of the Christmas song "God Rest Ye Merry Gentlemen" at the beginning and end. It covers ninety years of the Bayard family and stresses the themes of love and conflict of the generations and the things that hold the family's life together.

SCORE: vs ed. composer (Ger-Eng) (Mainz: B. Schott's Söhne, 1961).

LIBRETTO: the same.

BIBLIOGRAPHY: Everett Helm, "Reviews," *MA* LXXXIII (May 1963), 20 [on U.S. premiere]; Horst Koegler, "Reports," *Opera* XIII (1962), 178 [on premiere]; Norbert J. Schneider, "Thorton Wilder und Paul Hindemith. Zu ihrem Briefwechsel annlässlich der Entstehung von The Long Christmas Dinner," *Hindemith Jahrbuch* XI (1982), 137–88; Hugo Weisgall, "Current Chronicle," *MQ* XLIX (July 1963), 369–401 [on 1963 premiere].

Long Island Dreamer. See *Three Lamentations*.

Long Odds, The, burletta by Charles Dibdin; libretto (Eng) by the composer. First performance November 13, 1783, London, Royal Circus.

Long Way, The, opera by Alec Wilder; libretto by Arnold Sundgaard. First performance June 3, 1955, Nyack, New York.

Lord Arthur Savile's Crime, opera in one act by Geoffrey Bush; libretto (Eng) by the composer, after the story by Oscar Wilde (1891). First performance December 5, 1972, London, Guildhall School.

Lord Batemen, or, Picotee's Pledge, comic opera in two acts by Edward Solomon; libretto (Eng) by Henry P. Stephens. First performance 1882, London, Gaiety.

Also burlesque, with text by Henry J. Byron (1869, London).

SCORE: vs (Philadelphia: J. M. Stoddart, 1882).

Lord Bateman, romantic ballad opera in three acts by Arnold Forster; libretto (Eng) by Jan Sharp, after Charles Dickens's *The Loving Ballad of Lord Bateman*. First performance March 11, 1958, London, Cecil Sharp House, with Heather Goddin, Noel Banke, and Peter Hemmings; conducted by Alan Boustead; produced by Colin Graham.

SCORE: vs (London: Novello, [1960]).

Lord Byron, opera in three scenes by Jack Graham; libretto (Eng) by Norbert Engels and James Lewis Cassaday. First performance December 17, 1926, South Bend, Indiana, University Theater, for the theater's opening.

A treatment of Byron's life.

Most of the lyrics come from his poems.

Lord Byron, opera in three acts by Virgil Thomson; libretto (Eng) by Jack Larson. First performance April 20, 1972, New York, Juilliard School, with Grayson Hirst (Lord Byron), Carolyn Val-Schmidt (Lady Augusta Leigh), Lynne Wickenden (Lady Byron), Barrie Smith (Lady Melbourne), and Lenus Carlson (Thomas Moore); conducted by Gerhard Samuel; directed by John Houseman. The composer revised and cut the work for its publication in 1975 and again for its revival on December 7, 1985, New York, New York Repertory Theatre, with Paul Spencer Adkins (Byron); conducted by Leigh Gibbs Gore; directed by Nancy Rhodes.

The work opens with a chorus of London people mourning the death of the English poet Byron and then reviews his life in the following scenes, especially his involvement with his estranged wife, Annabella Milbanke, and his half sister, Augusta Leigh. When the poet Thomas Moore gives Byron's memoirs to Augusta, she has the memoirs burned. The Dean of Westminster Abbey does not want Byron honored, but the ghosts of the great poets buried in the Abbey welcome Byron as one of their own.

For a detailed plot description, see K/*NKOB*, 826–27.

Major roles: Lord Byron (ten); Lady Byron, orig. Annabella Milbanke (mezzo); Augusta Leigh (sop); and Thomas Moore, the poet (bar).

SCORE: vs, ms ([n.p., 1971]; LCCN: 84-171113).

BIBLIOGRAPHY: Andrew Porter, review *NY* LIII (Jan. 17, 1977), 106–8 [on recording of premiere]; John Rockwell, review, *NYT* (Dec. 9, 1985) [on revival].

Lord Byron's Love Letter, opera in one act by Raffaello de Banfield; libretto (Eng) by Tennessee Williams. First performance January 17, 1955, New Orleans, Tulane University, with Patricia Neway (the grandmother), Gertrude Ribla (the spinster), Cecilia Ward, and James Stuart; conducted by Nicola Rescigno; produced by James Elliott.

The story, set in New Orleans, concerns a spinster and her grandmother, who received a letter as a young girl from Lord Byron. The pair live off the proceeds of the tourists who pay to see the letter. During Mardi Gras two coarse tourists steal the note, after which the grandmother reveals that Lord Byron was, in fact, the spinster's grandfather.

For a detailed description, see Eaton/*OP* I, 196.

Roles: the old woman (sop/mezzo), the matron (alto), the husband (ten), and the spinster (sop); in the pantomime: a middle-aged woman, a young girl, and a handsome young man (Lord Byron).

SCORE: vs (New York: G. Ricordi [1955, 1960]).

DISCOGRAPHY: A. Varnay, G. Ribla, N. Carruba, M. Carlin, Academy Sym. Orch.; cond. N. Rescigno, RCA Victor LM 2258 (1958).

Lord of the Isles, The, or, The Gathering of the Clans, romantic national opera by George Rodwell; libretto (Eng) by Edward Fitzball, after Sir Walter Scott's poem (1815). First performance November 20, 1834, London, Surrey Theatre, with Mr. Archer (Robert Bruce), Mr. Wilson (Ronald), Mr. Morley (Lord of Lorn), Mr. Maitland (Lord Edward), Miss Land (Lady Isabel), and Miss Mayoss (Edith of Lorn).

Set against the story of Robert Bruce's return to Scotland in 1307, the work involves Edith of Lorn, who is in love with Lord Ronald, Lord of the Isles. Although she becomes his fiancée, he is in love with Isabel, Bruce's sister. After Edith risks her life to save Bruce and Ronald, Ronald realizes that he really loves her.

SCORE: vs (London, ca. 1834).

LIBRETTO: English (London: Dramatic Author's Society, 1834).

Lord of the Manor, The, comic opera in three acts by William Jackson; libretto (Eng) by General John Burgoyne, after Marmontel's *Silvain*, set by Grétry (1770, Paris). First performance December 27, 1780, London, with Charles Bannister (Rashly), Miss Farren (Sophia), Miss Prudom (Annette), Mr. Palmer (Contrast), Mrs. Wrighten (Peggy), and Mr. Vernon (Truemore). Revised version with music by Henry Rowley Bishop, John Davy, J. C. Doyle, William Reeve, and R. Welsh; libretto revised by Thomas Dibdin Jr.; first performance October 24, 1812, London, Covent Garden.

The lord of the manor is unaware that his son, whom he banished from his estate a long time ago, has returned and is living under the name of "Rashly." A widower, Rashly has two daughters, Sophia and Annette; Sophia is pursued by Contrast, the lord's younger son. Sophia herself is in love with Truemore, whom Contrast tries to have drafted into the army. Truemore is saved by the intercession of Peggy, the daughters' maid, when Peggy convinces Corporal Drill to take Contrast instead. After Contrast deserts, he is brought before the lord for punishment. When the lord finds out that the pretty young ladies he has been seeing in the park are actually his granddaughters, he forgives both Contrast and Rashly.

For a detailed description, see Fiske/*ETM*, 442–45.

The work includes "Encompass'd in an Angel's Frame," in which Rashly remembers his dead wife.

SCORE: vs (London: John Preston, [1781]).
LIBRETTO: English (Philadelphia: Henry Taylor, 1791).

Lorenzaccio, opera in three acts by Colin Brumby; libretto (Eng) by the composer, after Alfred de Musset. First performance (excerpts) October 29, 1986, Sydney, Australia.

The work is set in Florence during the Renaissance.

SCORE: ms fs (Sydney: Australian Music Centre, [1988?]).

Loretta, a Tale of Seville, opera in three acts by Louis Lavenu; libretto (Eng) by Alfred Bunn. First performance November 9, 1846, London, Drury Lane Theatre, with Mr. W. Harrison (Don Carlos), Mr. D. W. King (Ferdinand), Mr. Morgan (Varaez), Mr. Hodges (Cordova), Mr. S. Jones (Don Henriquez), Mr. Borrani (Philippo), Mr. Weiss (Don Juanito), Anna Bishop (Loretta), and Miss Poole (Florinda).

A version of the Don Juan story, in which the now repentant Don Carlos meets Loretta, one of his victims, several years after their encounter.

LIBRETTO: English (London: W. S. Johnston, [1846?]).

Losers, The, "contemporary opera" in two acts by Harold Farberman; libretto (Eng) by Barbara Fried. First performance March 26, 1971, New York, Juilliard School, Juilliard American Opera Center, with Barbara Shuttleworth (Donna), Julia Lansford (Marie), Lenus Carlson (Buzz), John Seabury (Joker), and Michael Warren (Bo); conducted by the composer; directed by John Houseman; choreographed by Patricia Birch.

The work, set in California, has as its keynote "hedonistic violence," in the words of reviewer Frank Merkling. It includes rapes, beatings, murder, and a gang initiation. The orchestra features percussion and winds and a jazz quartet. The libretto uses hip language, as well as four- and five-letter words; the title refers to the male protagonists.

SCORE: vs, holograph (New York: General Music, 1968).
BIBLIOGRAPHY: "New York," *ON* XXXV (May 15, 1971), 22 [on premiere].

Lost Child, The, television opera in three acts by Godfrey Ridout; libretto (Eng) by John Reid, after a Christmas tale. First performance 1975, CBS television.

Lost in the Stars, musical tragedy in two acts by Kurt Weill; libretto (Eng) by Maxwell Anderson, after Alan Paton's novel *Cry the Beloved Country.* First performance October 30, 1949, New York, Music Box Theatre, with Todd Duncan (Stephen Kumalo), Gertrude Jeanette (Grace Kumalo), Julian Mayfield (Absalom), Inez Matthews (Irina), and Leslie Banks (James Jarvis); conducted by Maurice Levine; directed by Maurice Levine. It ran for 273 performances. Subsequent revivals have not been successful.

The story of the fateful interaction of a white and a black family in the South Africa of 1949. Parson Stephen Kumalo goes to Johannesburg to find his son, Absalom, when he and his wife have received no news from him. Absalom has fallen into rough company, and in order to get money to support himself and his pregnant girlfriend, Irina, he kills Arthur Jarvis, a young white liberal, during a holdup. Absalom is sentenced to death for his crime. As Absalom is about to die, James Jarvis, the conservative father of the murder victim, comes to the older Kumalo's house, where the fathers both mourn for their lost sons.

Major roles: Leader (ten/high bar), Stephen Kumalo (bar), Linda (singer-dancer), Irina (mezzo), and Alex (boy sop).

SCORE: vs (New York: Chappell, 1950).

DISCOGRAPHY: original cast (excerpts): T. Duncan, conducted by M. Levine, MCAD-10302 (CD); A. Woodley, G. Hopkins, C. Clarey, C. Woods, Orch. of St. Luke's Concert Chorale of New York; cond. J. Rudel, MusicMasters Classics CD 01612-67100-2 (2 CDs).

Lottery, The, ballad opera, with music arranged and partially composed by Mr. Seedo; libretto (Eng) by Henry Fielding. First performance January 1, 1732, London, Theatre Royal, with Mrs. Clive (Chloe).

Two confidence men target the innocent and seemingly rich Chloe, with one of them offering to marry her. Their plans fall through when she turns out to have little money, having talked about her fortune on the assumption that she would win the lottery, which, of course, she does not.

The music includes selections from Handel.

LIBRETTO: English (London: Lister, 1788).

Louis XIV, opera by Homer Moore; libretto (Eng) by the composer. First performance February 16, 1917, St. Louis, Odeon, with Marguerita Beriza, Augusta Lenska, Henri Scott, and Florencio Constantino.

LIBRETTO: English, mimeograph copy (ca. 1917; LCCN: 84-101458)

Louis Riel, historical opera in three acts by Harry Somers; libretto (Eng, Fr, Cree, Lat) by Mavor Moore and Jacques Languirand. First performance September 23, 1967, Toronto, Canadian Opera, O'Keefe Centre, with Bernard Turgeon (Riel), Joseph Rouleau (Bishop Taché), Cornelis Opthof (Sir John Macdonald), Roxalana Roslaf (Marguerite), Patricia Rideout (Riel's mother), and Mary Morrison (Sara, Riel's sister); conducted by Victor Feldbrill; staged by Leon Major.

The story concerns the spokesman of the Métis, descendants of the French settlers and Indians. It opens in 1869, at Fort Garry (now Winnipeg). Riel, reviled by some and considered a martyr by others, leads a movement to set up a nation independent of the Ontario government. He is supported in his efforts by Bishop Taché and opposed by the double-dealing and cynical Sir John Macdonald. Riel, having led his followers in failed uprisings in Manitoba in 1869 and 1884, is convicted of treason and hanged in 1885.

The work combines atonality, folk-songlike sections, popular songs, traditional arias, and electronic sounds. Its musical highlights include a setting of the popular song "We'll

Hang Him up the River," set against a mob scene, the folk song "The Buffalo Hunt," used as a background for an Indian scene, and Marguerite's lullaby to her child, "Kuyas" (act 3), an Indian tribal song with a text in Cree.
BIBLIOGRAPHY: Brian Cherney, "Louis Riel," in *Harry Somers* (Toronto and Buffalo: University of Toronto Press, 1975), 129–40; Raymond Ericson, "'Louis Riel,' Music Drama, Presented in Toronto," *NYT* (Sept. 25, 1967), 55 [on premiere].
DISCOGRAPHY: premiere cast, Centrediscs CMC 24/26 (3 CDs).

Love and Madness, tragicomedy in five acts by Samuel Arnold; libretto (Eng) by Francis G. Waldron, after Shakespeare and Fletcher's *Two Noble Kinsmen*. First performance September 21, 1795, London, Little Theatre in the Haymarket.
    The work concerns two knights who vie for the love of a woman.

Love and Money, or, The Fair Caledonian, afterpiece ballad opera in two acts by Samuel Arnold; libretto (Eng) by R. Benson. First performance August 28, 1795, London, Little Theatre in the Haymarket, with Miss De Camp. First U.S. performance October 10, 1797, Boston.
LIBRETTO: English (New York: D. Longworth, 1813).

Love and Psyche, musical myth in two acts by Linder Chlarson; libretto (Eng) by the composer. Composed 1978.
    The work is set in Greece just after the Trojan War.
SCORE: ms score, holograph (1978, photocopy, NYPL).

Love and Revenge, or, The Vintner Outwitted, "an opera" (ballad opera); libretto (Eng) by Thomas Cooke. First performance 1729, London?, with Mr. Wells (Heartfree), Mr. Mullart (Rovewell), Mr. Lacey (Trueman), Mr. Fielding (Brainworm), Mr. Stoppelaer (Mulligrub), Mr. Dove (Shameless), Mrs. Mullart (Bellamira), Mrs. Clarke (Charlot), Miss Wood (Louisa), Mrs. Reynolds (Mother Pearce), and Mrs. Nokes (Mrs. Mulligrub).
    The setting is London. In the story, Rovewell loves Bellamira, a courtesan, while Louisa loves Rovewell. Trueman and Charlot are also in love.
LIBRETTO: English (London, 1729); repr. ed. Rubsamen/*BO*, vol. 3, *Harlots, Rakes, and Bawds* (1974).

Love and War, comic opera in two acts by William Shield; libretto (Eng) by John O'Keeffe. First performance March 12, 1787, London, Covent Garden.
    A revision of *The Campaign.**
LIBRETTO: English (London: T. Cadell, 1787).

Love at First Sight, or, The Wit of a Woman, ballad opera in two acts; libretto (Eng) by Joseph Yarrow. First performance 1742, London.
LIBRETTO: English (London: T. Gent, 1742); repr. Rubsamen/*BO*, vol. 27, *York Ballad Operas and Yorkshiremen* (1974).

Love at First Sight, ballad opera in two acts; libretto (Eng) by Thomas King. First performance October 17, 1763, London, Drury Lane Theatre.
LIBRETTO: English (London: T. Becket and P. A. De Hondt, 1763).

Love Burns, chamber opera in two acts by Graeme Koehne; libretto by Louis Nowra. First performance 1992, Adelaide, Australia, Festival of the Arts.

Love Charm, The, or, The Village Coquette, comic opera in two acts by Henry Rowley Bishop, an adaptation of Auber's *Le philtre* (1831, Paris); libretto (Eng) by James

R. Planché, after Scribe. First performance November 3, 1831, London, Drury Lane Theatre.

Another version is *The Love Spell*,* arranged by Horn.

Love, Death, and High Notes, comedy in one act by Claude White; libretto (Eng) by Linda Brovsky. First performance October 1, 1988, St. Louis, Missouri, Parkway Central High School, Opera Theatre of St. Louis.

Paula and David are rehearsing a new opera with Jeffrey, the set designer, and the opera coach. They act out the final scene but discover that the last page is missing. In the interim they fill in their own ending and use the standard clichés of opera. The last page is found, and the rehearsal comes to an end.

For a detailed description, see Kornick/*RAO*, 335–36.

Major roles: Paula (sop); Lynn, the stage director (mezzo); David (ten); and Jeffrey (bar).

Love Finds the Way, comic opera in three acts by Thomas Augustine Arne, A. M. G. Sacchini, and J. A. Fisher; libretto (Eng) by Thomas Hull, after Arthur Murphy's *The School for Guardians* (1767). First performance November 18, 1777, London, Covent Garden.

Love in a Blaze, comic opera by (Sir) John Stevenson and Philip Cogan; libretto (Eng) by Joseph Atkinson. First performance May 29, 1799, Dublin, Crown Street.

Love in a Camp, or, Patrick in Prussia, comic opera in two acts by William Shield; libretto (Eng) by John O'Keeffe. First performance February 17, 1786, London, Covent Garden, with M. Davies (Marshall), Mr. Wilson (Father Luke), Mr. Johnstone (Captain Patrick), M. W. Palmer (Rupert), Mr. Cubitt (Olmutz), Mr. Quick (Quiz), John Edwin (Darby), Mrs. Bannister (Norah), Mrs. Martyr (Flora), and Mrs. Webb (Mabel Flourish). A sequel to *The Poor Soldier.**

The setting is a Prussian camp near Breslau. The story picks up the adventures of Patrick and Darby, who join the Prussian army and are followed by Norah, Patrick's beloved.

In the sequel Patrick is sung by a tenor; John Johnstone, the Dermot of *The Poor Soldier*, created the role at the premiere.

SCORE: vs (London: Longman & Broderip, [1786]).

Love in a Riddle, pastoral ballad opera, songs arranged by Henry Carey; libretto (Eng) by Colley Cibber. First performance January 7, 1729, London, Drury Lane Theatre.

The setting is Arcadia, and the dialogue is in blank verse.

When the work failed, it was revised as *Damon and Phillida** (1729, London), with better results. It includes a sung epilogue, set to Carey's "Sally in Our Alley."

LIBRETTO: English (London: J. Watts, [1729]); repr. Rubsamen/*BO*, vol. 7, *Classical Subjects II: Pastoral and Comedy* (1974).

Love in a Village, comic opera in three acts by Thomas Arne; libretto (Eng) by Isaac Bickerstaffe. A revision of *The Village Opera** (1729). First performance December 8, 1762, London, Covent Garden, with Mr. Mattocks (Young Meadows), Mr. Shuter (Justice Woodcock), Mr. Beard (Hawthorn), Miss Brent (Rosetta), and Miss Hallam (Lucinda). First American performance June 9, 1766, Philadelphia, Society Hill. Revived 1952, Aldeburgh; conducted by Charles Oldham; December 7, 1984, New York, Opera Shop of the Vineyard, with Lucille Patton, Maria Welker, and David Kelleg; conducted by James Kurtz; directed by Joseph LoSchiavo.

Lucinda, daughter of Justice Woodcock, and Rosetta, daughter of Sir Nicholas Wiseacre, conspire to marry the men of their own choosing. Rosetta disguises herself as Lucinda's maid, and Young Meadows, her beloved, is in the guise of a gardener.

Music partially composed (19 numbers, 6 of them written for this work) by Arne, with 24 by 15 other composers, including Handel and Boyce. For a description, see Fiske/*ETM*, 327–32.
SCORE: vs (London: I. Walsh, [1763]; London: Longman & Co., 1769).
LIBRETTO: English (Philadelphia: M. Carey, 1794).
BIBLIOGRAPHY: Tim Page, "An Ancestor of Operetta Revived," NYT (Dec. 2, 1984), II, 19 [on U.S. revival].

Love in Disguise, comic opera by Tommaso Giordani; libretto (Eng) by H. Lucas. First performance April 24, 1766, Dublin, Smock Alley.

Love in the City, comic opera in two acts by Charles Dibdin; libretto (Eng) by Isaac Bickerstaffe. First performance February 21, 1767, London, Covent Garden. It was reduced to *The Romp** (1781), an afterpiece.

The work is a parody of Arne's *Love in a Village** and includes music by G. Cocchi, Barthelemon, Galuppi, Jommelli, and Pergolesi.
LIBRETTO: English (London: W. Griffin, 1767).

Love in the East, or, Adventures of Twelve Hours, comic opera in three acts by Thomas Linley; libretto (Eng) by James Cobb. First performance February 25, 1788, London, Drury Lane Theatre.

The work is set in India.
SCORE: vs (London: Samuel, Ann, & Peter Thompson).
LIBRETTO: English (Dublin: Printed by W. Porter for Messrs. Wilkinson, Burnet [etc.]; London: J. Jarvis, 1788).

Love in Transit, opera in one act by Richard Arnell; libretto (Eng) by Hal Burton. First performance February 27, 1958, London, Guildhall School of Music.
SCORE: vs ([n.p.] [195-]; LCCN: 60-2394).

Love in Wrinkles, or, The Russian Stratagem, comic opera in two acts by Michael Rophino Lacy, after Fétis's opera *Le vielle* (1826, Paris); libretto (Eng), after Scribe and Delavigne's text. First performance December 4, 1828, London, Drury Lane Theatre, with John Braham.

Another version is J. Blewitt's *My Old Woman** (1829).

Love Laughs at Locksmiths, operatic farce in two acts by Michael Kelly, after Méhul's *Une folie* (1803, Paris); libretto (Eng) by George Colman Jr., after J. N. Bouilly's text for Méhul. First performance July 25, 1803, London, Haymarket. First U.S. performance May 23, 1804, New York, Federal Street Theatre.

The overture is by Henry Condell, and the work includes the trio "No, No I Doubt You Much," adapted by Kelly from Méhul's music.
SCORE: vs (London, 1803); repr. ed. Stoddard Lincoln (New York: Da Capo Press, 1979).

Love Laughs at Locksmiths, comic opera in one act by Joseph Carl Breil; libretto (Eng) by the composer. First performance October 27, 1910, Portsmouth, Maine.

Love Life, vaudeville in two acts by Kurt Weill; libretto (Eng) by Alan Jay Lerner. First performance October 7, 1948, New York, 46th Street Theater, with Nanette Fabray (Susan) and Ray Middleton (Sam). The show ran for 252 performances.

The story follows the married life of Sam and Susan Cooper through 150 years of American history, beginning in 1791. In the second act, which is set in the present, the marriage is undergoing great strains and seems about to break up; it is saved by a minstrel show.

Major roles: Susan Cooper (sop) and Sam Cooper (bass-bar).

The musical highlights include the duet "Here I'll Stay" and Susan's "Green-Up Time."
SCORE: ms vs, holography (1947, photocopy, NYPL).
LIBRETTO: English, typescript (1948?, carbon copy, NYPL).

Love of Don Perlimplin, The, opera in one act by Conrad Susa; libretto (Eng) by the composer and Richard Street, after Federico García Lorca's play *Amor de Don Perlimplín con Belisa en su jardín* (1931). First performance August 2, 1984, Purchase, New York, Pepsico Summerfare, with David Malis (Don Perlimplin), Ruth Ann Swenson (Belisa), and Nancy Gustafson (Belisa's mother); conducted by Andrew Meltzer; directed by David Alden.

The aging Don Perlimplin earns his young bride's love by bringing about his own death.

Also set by V. Rieti, as *Don Belisa** (1952, Urbana, Ill.); W. Fortner as *In seinem Garten liebt Don Perlimplin Belisa* (1962, Schwetzingen); B. Sulzer, the same (1984, Linz); and A. Biales, as *Belisa** (1989, St. Paul, Minn.).
BIBLIOGRAPHY: Robert Jacobson, "Purchase, N.Y.," *ON* XLIX (Dec. 8, 1984), 46–47 [on premiere].

Lover His Own Rival, The, ballad opera; libretto (Eng) by Abraham Langford. First performance February 10, 1736, London, New Theatre, Goodman's Fields.

The work, which is set in London, concerns a clever maid whose plotting precipitates the events of the opera.

Among the seventeen airs is one by John Stanley.
LIBRETTO: English (London: J. Watts, 1736); repr. Rubsamen/*BO*, vol. 12 (1974).

Lover's Knot, The, opera by Simon Bucharoff; libretto (Eng) by Cora Bennett-Stephenson. First performance January 15, 1916, Chicago, Chicago Opera Company, Auditorium, with Myrna Sharlow (Sylvia), Augusta Lenska (Beatrice), George Hamlin (Walter), and Graham Marr (Edward); conducted by Marcel Charlier.

The setting is Norfolk, Virginia, about 1870. Walter, who has tried to forget about Beatrice, his beloved, by traveling extensively, returns home. He finds that she is entertaining a northern friend, Sylvia, at her home, and his attempts at courtesy are mistaken for romantic interest. This arouses the anger of Walter's friend, Edward, Beatrice's brother, who is, himself, interested in Sylvia. Annoyed by the turn of events, Sylvia disguises herself as a man and pretends to make love to Beatrice, in full view of Edward and Walter. The two "lovers" reveal their true identities, and the lovers return to each other.
SCORE: vs (London: Schirmer, [1916]).

Lover's Opera, The, ballad opera; libretto (Eng) by William R. Chetwood. First performance May 14, 1729, London, Theatre-Royal.

The work includes songs by Richard Charke.
LIBRETTO: English (London: A. Dodd, 1729); repr. ed. Rubsamen/*BO*, vol. 12, *Farce: Amorous Intrigue and Deception* I (1974).

Love's Alarms, opera by Edward Fitzwilliam; libretto (Eng) by the composer. First performance November 17, 1853, London, Theatre in the Haymarket.

Love's Dream, "petite opera" in two acts, with music arranged by M. Moss; libretto (Eng) by Samuel Beazley, after Scribe and Aumer's vaudeville *La somnambule* (1816). First performance July 5, 1821/revival 1831, both London, Theatre Royal, English Opera House, with Mr. Grove/F. Matthews (Mr. Dormer), Mr. Pearman/J. Bland (Henry Morton), Mr. Wrench (Frederick Easy), Mr. Harley/J. Russell (Simon), Mr. Morley/Mr. Aldridge (lawyer), Miss Kelly (Cecilia Dormer), and Mrs. Bryan/Miss Pincott (Maria).

The sleepwalking Cecilia, engaged to Frederick, is allowed to wed her beloved, Henry.

See also *La sonnambula*, Bishop's arrangement (1833, London) of Bellini's opera.

LIBRETTOS: English (London: J. Lowndes, 1821; London: J. Duncombe & Co., [1831?]).

Love's Labour's Lost, comedy in six scenes by Nicolas Nabokov; libretto (Eng) by W. H. Auden and Chester Kallman, after Shakespeare's play. First performance February 7, 1973, Brussels, Théâtre de la Monnaie, Deutsche Oper, in a German translation by Claus H. Henneberg, as *Verlor'ne Liebesmüh'*.

King Ferdinand of Navarre, together with two of his friends, swear off women for three years. Their plans are derailed by the appearance of the princess of Navarre and her ladies, who capture the hearts of the men.

The music parodies various musical styles, including those of Beethoven, Wagner, and Weill.

SCORE: vs, English-German (Wiesbaden: Bote & Bock, 1973).

Love's Labour's Lost, opera in two acts by Geoffrey Bush; libretto (Eng) by the composer, after Shakespeare's play. Composed 1988.

Other settings by Adrian Beecham (comp. 1934) and Ray Leslee (1986, Buffalo, N.Y.).

Loves of Mars and Venus, The, "all-sung" masque in a prologue and three acts by John Eccles; text (Eng) by Peter Motteux. First performance November 1696, London, Lincoln's Inn Fields Theatre.

The masque was written to be inserted into the farce *The Anatomist, or, The Shame Doctor* by Edward Ravenscroft. The music of the prologue and third act are by Gottfried Finger.

LIBRETTOS: English (London: n.p., 1696; London: A. Bettesworth and F. Clay, 1722).

Love Spell, The, or, The Flirts of the Village, adaptation by Charles E. Horn of Auber's two-act opera *Le philtre* (1831, Paris); libretto (Eng), after Scribe. First performance October 27, 1831, London, Olympic Theatre.

Another version is *The Love Charm,** arranged by Bishop (Nov. 3, 1831, London).

Love's Sacrifice, pastoral opera in one act by George Chadwick; libretto (Eng) by David K. Stevens. First performance February 1, 1923, Chicago, Playhouse.

SCORE: vs (Boston: C. C. Birchard & Co., 1917).

Love's Triumph, opera in one act by Carlo Cesarini, Giovanni del Violone, and Francisco Gasparini; libretto (Eng) by Peter Anthony Motteux, after *La pastorella* by Cardinal Ottoboni. First performance February 26, 1708, London, Queen's Theatre, Haymarket, with Mr. Leveridge (Neralbo) and Miss L'Epine (Olindo).

Each of the composers wrote one act.

LIBRETTO: English (London: J. Tonson, 1708).

Love's Triumph, comic opera in three acts by Vincent Wallace; libretto by James R. Planché, after Mélesville and Laya's comedy *Le portrait vivant* (1842). First performance November 3, 1862, London, Covent Garden, with Louisa Pyne (Mme. de Valois/ Theresa), William Harrison (Marquis de Pons), W. H. Weiss (Count de Canillac), Aynsley Cook (Baron Duretrete), Laura Baxter (Henri, Viscomte de Verneuil), Henry Corri (Mynherr van Groot), and George Perren (Adolph Savigny).

For a musical description, see Biddlecombe/*EO*, 138–39.

The work includes the aria "O Rank, Thou Hast Thy Shackles" and the ballad "Lovely, Longing, and Beloved."

SCORES: fs, ms (British Library, Add. MS. 37211–3); vs (London: Addison & Lucas, [n.d.]; New York: W. Hall; London: Addison & Lucas, 1862).
LIBRETTO: English (New York: W. Hall and London: Addison & Lucas, [1862?]).

Loving/Toi, opera in one act with electronic sound by R. Murray Schafer; text (Eng) by the composer; French translation by Gabriel Charpentier. First performance February 3, 1966, CBC TV French Network, Montreal. First stage performance March 11, 1978, Toronto.

Taking the two official languages of Canada as its cue, the work concerns the relationship between a woman (who speaks English) and a man (who speaks French). Also involved are several aspects of the female personality, Modesty, Vanity, and Eros, roles sung in English; and Ishtar, sung in French.

Roles: male and female speaking roles, Modesty (sop), Vanity (mezzo), Eros (mezzo), and Ishtar (mezzo).
SCORE: (Toronto: Berandol Music, [1979])

Lowland Sea, The, opera in one act by Alec Wilder; libretto (Eng) by Arnold Sundgaard. First performance May 8, 1952, Montclair, New Jersey.

The work is slanted toward being performed by school and community groups. Set in Scarlet Town about 1845, it centers around Dorie Davis, who reluctantly weds the widower Nathaniel, after her beloved Johnny Dee's ship sinks. When Johnny returns, Dorie sends him away, despite the fact that she still loves him.

Major roles: Dorie Davis (sop/mezzo), Johnny Dee (bar), Nathaniel Hazard (ten), and Captain Jesse (bass-bar).

Lucille, opera by Silas Gamaliel Pratt; libretto (Eng). First performance March 14, 1887, Chicago, Columbia Theater.

A revision of his early opera *Antonio.**

LIBRETTO: English (Chicago: Skeen & Stuart Stationery Co., 1887).

Luck of Ginger Coffey, The, opera by Raymond Pannell; libretto (Eng) by Ronald Hambleton, after Brian Moore's novel (1960). First performance September 1967, Toronto, O'Keefe Center for the Performing Arts, Canadian Opera, with Harry Theyard (Ginger Coffey), Mignon Dunn (Veronica, his wife), Doreen Millman (their daughter), and William Pickett (Gerry); conducted by Samuel Krachmalnick.

The story, updated from the 1940s to the present and given an upbeat ending, follows the fortunes of the unlikable Ginger Coffey, an out-of-work Irish immigrant, who comes to Canada with his family to change his luck.

The music contains a variety of styles, including serialism, jazz, and rock 'n' roll, and opens with a *Tosca*-like scene in which Ginger's running commentary is punctuated by the strains of a boys' choir in the background.
BIBLIOGRAPHY: Donal Henahan, "'Luck of Ginger Coffey' Staged as Opera by Canadian Troupe," *NYT* (Sept. 17, 1967), 84 [on premiere].

Lucky Discovery, The, ballad opera; libretto (Eng) by John Arthur. First performance 1738, London.
LIBRETTO: English (York: Author, 1737).

Lucky Dollar, The, opera in one act by Ernest Kanitz; libretto (Eng) by Ann Stanford. First performance 1958, Los Angeles, University of California.

A girl, after eating a meal at Joe's café, is unable to pay and tries to sneak out, but she is stopped by the proprietor. The Engineer, witnessing the events, has Joe hire the girl as a waitress. She brings prosperity to the café, and the owner starts to fall in love with her. When, at the suggestion of the Engineer, the girl bets most of her savings on the dollar jackpot, she loses; only when she wagers her lucky dollar does she win. She takes her money and leaves.

For a detailed description, see Eaton/*OP* II, 297.

Roles: Joe (ten), the girl (sop), and the Engineer (bar).

Lucky-Peter's Journey, opera in three acts by Malcolm Williamson; libretto (Eng) by E. Tracy, after August Strindberg's play (1880). First performance August 13, 1968, Dynevor Castle, Wales, Dynevor Festival; December 18, 1969, London, Coliseum, with April Cantelo (Nisse), Jennifer Vyvyan (Nilla), Geoffrey Chard (Peter), Shirley Chapman (Lisa), Aileen Fischer (Good Fairy), and John Delaney (Loki); conducted by John Baker.

The Good Fairy visits young Peter on Christmas Eve and grants him anything he wants. He learns, however, that love is the greatest gift.
LIBRETTO: English (London: J. Weinberger, 1969).
BIBLIOGRAPHY: M. Williamson, "'Lucky-Peter's Journey,'" *MT* CX (Dec. 1969), 1227–31.

Lucky Star, The, comic opera in three acts, a version of *The Merry Monarch*,* itself an adaptation of E. Chabrier's *L'étoile* (1877, Paris), with new music by Ivan Caryll; new dialogue by C. H. E. Brookfield and new lyrics by Adrian Ross and Aubrey Hoppwood, after Leterrier and Vanloo. First performance January 7, 1899, London, Savoy Theatre, with Walter Passmore (King Oluf), Ruth Vincent (the Princess), and Emmie Owen (Lazuli).

King Oluf, who is very superstitious, learns from Siroco, his astrologer, that the king will live only as long as Lazuli, who has been chosen to be a sacrifice. Lazuli quickly earns a reprieve.
SCORE: vs (London: Chappell, [1899?]).

Lucy's Lapses, opera in one act by Christopher Drobny; libretto (Eng) by Laura Harrington. First performance August 20, 1987, New York, Playwright Horizons; April 27, 1990, Portland, Oregon, Winningstad Theatre.

A story about the elderly.

Lurline, opera in three acts by Vincent Wallace; libretto (Eng) by Edward Fitzball. First performance February 23, 1860, London, Covent Garden, with Louisa Pyne (Lurline), Charles Santley (Rhineberg), and William Harrison (Rudolph). The work enjoyed quite a success on English stages. First U.S. performance June 1, 1863, Cambridge, Massachusetts (concert).

The title character, a nymph, falls in love with Count Rudolph and, putting him under a spell, gets him to join her in her cave under the Rhine River. She presents him with a magical ring, and Rhineberg, her father, gives him a treasure chest. When Rudolph returns home for a brief stay, Ghiva, his former fiancée, seizes the ring and tosses it into the Rhine, where it is retrieved by the gnome Zeelick. Zeelick then gives it to Lurline, causing her to think that Rudolph has deserted her. Lurline is infuriated until she learns that Rudolph's friends have planned to kill him and seize the treasure. She uses her harp to kill the would-be assassins, and Rudolph returns to her.

Major roles: Lurline (sop), Count Rudolph (ten), River King (bar), Ghiva (mezzo), and Zeelick (bass).

The scene at the bottom of the Rhine precedes the one in Richard Wagner's *Das Rheingold* by nine years. *Lurline* was also noteworthy for its groundbreaking effects and large-scale scenes.

For a description of the music, see Biddlecombe/*EO*, 133–34.

Other settings include a "grand romantic spectacle," *Lurline, or, The Revolt of the Naiades*, with a text by J. S. Dalrymple (lib. pub. 184?, Boston); I. Lachner, *Loreley* (1846, Munich); F. Mendelssohn, *Die Loreley* (fragments performed 1851, Leipzig); M. Bruch, *Die Loreley* (1863, Mannheim); A. Catalani, *Elda* (1880, Turin), revived as *Loreley* (1890, Turin); Mohr, as *Loreley* (1884); F. Pacius, *Die Loreley* (1887, Helsinki); E. Naumann, *Loreley* (1889, Berlin); and H. Sommer (1891, Brunswick).
SCORE: vs (London: Cramer, [186?]).
LIBRETTO: English (London: Published and sold in the [Royal English Opera] Theatre, [1860]; New York: William Hall & Son, 1859; Baker & Godwin, 1861).

Lycidas, "musical entertainment" in one act by William Jackson; libretto (Eng) by the composer, after Milton. First performance November 4, 1767, London, Covent Garden.

Lyneia, opera in two acts by William Clifton Byrd; libretto (Eng). First performance January 20, 1949, Cincinnati, University of Cincinnati, Wilson Auditorium; conducted by the composer.
BIBLIOGRAPHY: C. L. Shockley, "Native Opera in Cincinnati," *ON* XIII (Apr. 25, 1949), 28–29 [on premiere].

Lysistrata, opera in one act by Joyce Barthelson; libretto (Eng), after Aristophanes. First performance March 27, 1981, New York, New York University Opera Studio; conducted by Thomas Martin.

Unhappy because of the work they must do while their husbands are fighting the Spartans, the Athenian women, led by Lysistrata, vow to deny their husbands conjugal benefits when they return from the fighting and hide in the Acropolis. The Spartan women agree to treat their men the same way. The efforts of the women are successful; the Magistrate announces that the men on both sides have agreed to sign a peace treaty immediately.

Major roles: Lysistrata, wife of Theodosius (sop); Myrrhine, wife of Kinesius (sop); Kalonike, wife of Polydorus (mezzo); Magistrate of Athens (bar); Theodosius, husband of Lysistrata (ten); Kinesius, husband of Myrrhine (bar); Polydorus, husband of Kalonike (bar).

Also play in music by Wilfrid Mellers (1948, not perf.).
BIBLIOGRAPHY: review, *HiFi/MA* XXII (Aug. 1981), 26 [on premiere].

Lysistrata & the War, comic opera "in the musical style of Mozart" by Robert Fink; libretto (Eng) by the composer, after Aristophanes. First performance 1967, Detroit, Wayne State University. Revised, with a new ending, 1979.

The work was originally conceived as a protest against the Vietnam War. In its revised version, according to the score, it is a "commentary on modern times."
SCORE: vs (Saskatoon, Saskatchewan: Greenwich-Meridian 1979).
LIBRETTO: English (Saskatoon, Saskatchewan: Greenwich, 1996).

M

Ma Barker, chamber opera in three acts by John Eaton; libretto (Eng) by Arthur Gold. Composed 1957.
SCORE: vs ([New York: G. Schirmer, 1957?]).

Macbeth, semi-opera in five acts by Matthew Locke and Robert Johnson; libretto (Eng) by William Davenant, after Shakespeare's play (1606) and Thomas Middleton's *The Witch* (1610). First performance February 18 (?), 1673, London, Dorset Theatre.

In Davenant's version the parts of Macduff and Lady Macduff are expanded, and some of the minor characters are dropped.

See following entries for the settings of Davenant's text by Eccles and Leveridge; the three versions are described by Fiske/*ETM*, 26–29; see also Fiske, "The *Macbeth* Music," *ML* XLV (April 1964), 114–25; Robert E. Moore, "The Music to *Macbeth*," *MQ* XLVII (Jan. 1961), 22–40.

Macbeth, semi-opera in five acts by John Eccles; libretto (Eng); libretto (Eng) by William Davenant, after Shakespeare and Middleton. First performance 1696, London.
SCORE: ms, Eccles version (autograph, British Library, Add. MS. 12219).

Macbeth, semi-opera in five acts, with music by Richard Leveridge; libretto (Eng) by William Davenant, after Shakespeare and Thomas Middleton. First performance November 21, 1702, London, Drury Lane Theatre, with Leveridge (Hecate).

Leveridge's music was long attributed to Locke, who had made the first setting of Davenant's text. The work includes songs from Middleton's play, with music by Johnson. Leveridge's version was used until 1875.
SCORES: ms (Cambridge, Fitzwilliam Museum); score of songs, airs, choruses ed. Boyce, attrib. Locke (London: Birchall, 18??); vs (London and New York: Boosey and Co., [18??]).

Macbeth, opera in three acts by Lawrance Collingwood; libretto (Eng) by the composer, after Shakespeare's play (1606). Excerpts, concert, November 10, 1927, London, Queen's Hall. First complete performance April 12, 1934, London, Sadler's Wells.

Macbeth, opera in three acts by Edward M. Goldman; libretto (Eng) by the composer, after Shakespeare. Composed 1961.
SCORE: ms vs (1961, photocopy, NYPL).

Macbeth, opera in one act by Sidney Halpern; libretto (Eng) by the composer, after Shakespeare. First performance April 4, 1965, New York, Off-Broadway Opera Company.

Other musical settings of Shakespeare's play include H.-A.-B. Chélard (1827, Paris); L. A. Piccinni (1829, Paris); G. Verdi (1847, Milan); W. Taubert (1858, Berlin); L. Rossi, *Biorn* (1877, London); E. Bloch (1910, Paris); A. Goedicke (1944); N. Gatty (ca. 1947); and H. Koppel (1970, Copenhagen). Also Samuel Arnold's incidental music (1778, London); and Trisha Ward's rock musical *Nightshriek* (1986, London).

Macheath in the Shades, "serio-comi-farcical-Elysian ballad opera" in two acts, a parody of *The Beggar's Opera** (1728). First performance 1735, London, Covent Garden.

In this version Macheath, Polly, and several of the prostitutes find themselves in Hades, where they meet such immortals as Alexander the Great, Cleopatra, and Ben Jonson.

Macheath Turn'd Pyrate, or, Polly in India, ballad opera; anonymous libretto (Eng). First performance May 30, 1737, London, Little Theatre in the Haymarket.

A parody of *The Beggar's Opera*.*

Madame Adare, opera in one act by Stanley Silverman; libretto (Eng) by Richard Foreman. First performance October 9, 1980, New York, New York City Opera, with Carol Gutknecht (Madame Adare), Richard Cross (Dr. Hoffman), James Billings (agent), Harris Poor (the devil), Nico Castel (Diaghilev), David Rae Smith (the interviewer), and Lewis White (the director); conducted by Brian Salesky; directed by Foreman.

The satirical plot involves Madame Adare, a diva, who has difficulty deciding whether she should become a singer in the fashion of Barbra Streisand or Maria Callas. She decides to have a career in both styles after she shoots her psychiatrist, Dr. Hoffman.

Major roles: Madame Adare (sop) and Dr. Hoffman (bass-bar).

SCORE: fs, holograph (New York: G. Schirmer, 1980).

BIBLIOGRAPHY: Donal Henahan, review, *NYT* (Oct. 10, 1980), C, 14 [on premiere]; Robert Jacobson, "North America," *ON* XLV (Dec. 20, 1980), 42 [on premiere]; Dorle J. Soria, preview, *MA* XXX (Oct. 1980), 37–38.

Mad Captain, The, ballad opera in one act; libretto (Eng) by Robert Drury. First performance March 5, 1733, London, Goodman's Fields.

LIBRETTO: English (London: Charles Corbett, 1733); repr. ed. Rubsamen/*BO*, vol. 12, *Farce: Amorous Intrigue and Deception* I (1974).

Madeleine, or, The Magic Kiss, comic opera in three acts by Julian Edwards; libretto (Eng) by Stanislaus Stangé. First performance July 31, 1894, New York.

Madeleine, lyric opera in one act by Victor Herbert; libretto (Eng) by Grant Stewart, after the French play *Je dîne chez ma mère* by Decourcelle and Thibaut. First performance January 24, 1914, New York, Metropolitan Opera, with Frances Alda (Madeleine), Lenora Sparkes (Nichette), Antonio Pini-Corsi (Chevalier de Mauprat), Paul Althouse (François), and Andrés de Segurola (Didier); conducted by Giorgio Polacco. Revived January 1984, Nevada City; conducted by Monroe Kanouse.

On New Year's Day in 1770 the famous soprano Madeleine Fleury of the Paris Opéra asks her male admirers to join her, but each declines, saying he wishes to be with his mother. When Didier, a poor artist, invites her to dine with him and his mother, she decides to spend the day with her own mother.

Major roles: Madeleine Fleury (sop); Nichette, her maid (sop); Chevalier de Mauprat (bass); François, Duc d'Esterre (ten); and Didier, a painter (bass).

For a detailed description, see Hipsher/*AO*, 264–65; and Waters/*VH*, 394–400.

SCORE: fs, vs (New York: G. Schirmer, 1913).

BIBLIOGRAPHY: Glenn Loney, "U.S.: Reports," *ON* XLVIII (May 1984), 45 [on revival]; Edward Hagelin Pearson, "Victor Herbert's 'Madeleine,'" *OQ* XIII (Summer 1997), 59–75.

Mad Hamlet, melodrama in three acts by Paul Reif; libretto (Eng) by Robert Corcoran, after Shakespeare's play. Composed 1965.

Mad House, The, ballad opera; libretto (Eng) by Robert Baker. First performance 1737, London, Lincoln's Inn Fields.

LIBRETTO: English (London: T. Cooper, 1737); repr. ed. Rubsamen/*BO*, vol. 4, *The Medical and Legal Professions* (1974).

Madman, The, afterpiece, all-sung pastiche by Samuel Arnold; libretto (Eng). First performance August 28, 1770, London, Marylebone Gardens.

Madness and Sorrow, monodrama by Daron Hagen; libretto (Eng) by the composer, after various sources, including mental hospital records. First performance January 31, 1997, Tacoma, Washington, Tacoma Chamber Players, with Paul Sperry.

Madrigal Opera, A, chamber opera in one act by Philip Glass; libretto, unspecified. First performance, as *Attaca—A Madrigal Opera,* June 25, 1980, Amsterdam, Carré Theater, with a text by the composer and Robert Malasch.

The plotless work is scored for six voices, violin, and viola.

Also given 1981, New York, as *The Panther*, with a Rilke poem as the text; and 1985, Los Angeles, as *A Madrigal Opera*, with a text by Len Jenkins.

Maggie. See **An American Triptych.**

Magi, The, opera in one act by John La Montaine; libretto (Eng) by the composer. First performance Washington, D.C., National Cathedral, December 27, 1967.

Magic Barrel, The, unfinished opera in one act by Marc Blitzstein; libretto (Eng) by the composer, after Bernard Malamud. Composed 1962–1964.

The story concerns a rabbinical student, Leo Finkle, who, wishing to find a spouse, goes to the marriage broker Pinye Salzman. Rejecting all of Pinye's candidates, Leo, seemingly by accident, finds among Pinye's photographs one of a woman he finds appealing. She turns out to be Pinye's wayward daughter.

Magic Beanstalk, The, children's opera in one act by Martin Kalmanoff; libretto (Eng) by James Cahalan. First performance 1976, Monticello, New York, Delano Playhouse.

Magic Bonbons, The, opera in eight scenes by Allan Blank; libretto (Eng) by the composer, after L. Frank Baum. Composed 1983.

Magic Chair, The, opera in one act by Eugene Zador; libretto (Eng) by George Jellinek, after Ferenc Karinthy. First performance May 14, 1966, Baton Rouge.

Magic Fan, The, or, The Filip on the Nose, operetta in one act by Henry Rowley Bishop; libretto (Eng) by Edward Fitzball. First performance June 18, 1832, London, Vauxhall Gardens.

Magic Fishbone, The, children's opera by Tom Chapin; text (Eng) by Alice Elliot; lyrics by Michael Mark. First performance October 8, 1988, New York, On Stage Productions. LIBRETTO: English (Woodstock, Illinois: Dramatic Publishing, 1990).

Magic Flute, The, adaptation by Charles Edward Horn of Mozart's *Die Zauberflöte* (1791, Vienna); libretto (Eng), after the text by Emanuel Schikaneder. First performance April 17, 1833, New York, Park Theatre.

Magic Fountain, The, lyric drama in three acts by Frederick Delius; libretto (Eng) by the composer. Composed 1893–1895. First performance (broadcast) November 20, 1977, London, BBC, with John Mitchinson (Solano), Katherine Pring (Watawa), Norman Welsby (Wapanacki), and Richard Angas (Talum Hadjo); conducted by Norman Del Mar.

The work is set in Florida and concerns the legend of the Fountain of Youth sought by the Spanish explorer Ponce de Léon. In this version, the hero is Solano, who is washed ashore and found by Seminole Indians. They give him Princess Watawa as a guide, and the two fall in love. She warns him not to drink the water of a fountain they have found because it is poisonous. When he refuses to listen, she throws herself into the fountain and dies. Seeing her sacrifice, he plunges in after her, to provide a *Tristan*-type ending.

Major roles: Solano (ten), Watawa (sop), Wapanacki (bass), and Talum (bass).

The opera contains part of the composer's *Florida Suite* and a leitmotif for Watawa from *Sea Drift*. The love duet between Watawa and Solano is one of the musical highlights of the work.

SCORE: vs ed. Eric Fenby (London: Boosey & Hawkes, 1979).
BIBLIOGRAPHY: Christopher Redwood, review, *MT* CXVIII (1977), 909 [on premiere].
DISCOGRAPHY: Pring, Mitchinson, Welsby, Angas, BBC Singers and Concert Orch.; cond. N. Del Mar. Arabesque 8121 (2) and Atrium BBC-2001; rev. John W. Freeman, "Records," *ON* XLV (Apr. 11, 1981), 52 [rereleased on CD, BBC CD 30002].

Magic Girdle, The, burletta in two parts by François Hippolyte Barthelemon; libretto (Eng) by George Savile Carey, after Rousseau. First performance July 17, 1770, London, Marylebone Gardens.

Magic Horn, The, "new grand operatic romantic fairy burlesque extravaganza" by George Alexander Lee, an adaptation of Weber's *Oberon**; libretto (Eng) by Charles Dance, after Planché's text. First performance 1846, London.
LIBRETTO: English (London: W. Grogan, [1846?]).

Magician, The, opera in one act by Alun Hoddinott; libretto (Eng) by John Morgan. First performance February 1976, Welsh radio, as *Murder, the Magician*, with Geraint Evans (Sesto), Elizabeth Gale (Adriana), Ian Caley (Angelo), and the Welsh Philharmonia Orchestra; conducted by Eric Wetherall. First stage performance April 1976, Cardiff, University College Cardiff Opera Workshop, with Kelvin Thomas (Sesto), Linda Coombes (Adriana), and Maldwyn Davies (Angelo); conducted by Clifford Bunford.

Roles: Sesto, the magician (bar); Adriana, his wife (sop); Angelo, his assistant (ten).
SCORE: vs (London: Oxford University Press, 1978).

Magician No Conjuror, The, comic opera in three acts by Joseph Mazzinghi; libretto (Eng) by Robert Merry. First performance Covent Garden, 1792.

Magic Land of Opera, The, children's opera in one act by Martin Kalmanoff; libretto (Eng) by the composer. First performance 1972, New York.

Magic Laurel Tree, The, opera for children by Eusebia S. Hunkins; libretto (Eng) by Emily E. Hammood, after the medieval French fairy tale *Les douze princesses dansantes*. First performance July 12, 1974, Shaker Heights, Cleveland, Laurel School of the Theatre.
SCORE: ms vs (1974, photocopy, NYPL).

Magic Minstrel, The, "aqua drama" by William Reeve; libretto (Eng) by Charles Dibdin Jr. First performance Whitsunday, 1808, London, Sadler's Wells.
SCORE: vs (London: G. Goulding, [1792]).

Magic Mirror, The, unfinished opera in one act by Gustav Holst; libretto (Eng) by Fritz B. Hart, after George Macdonald's *Phantastes*. Composed 1896. Not performed.

Magic Opal, The, opera in two acts by Isaac Albéniz; libretto (Eng) by Arthur Law. First performance January 19, 1893, London, Lyric Theatre.
LIBRETTO: English (London: J. Williams, 1911).

Magic Trumpet, The, musical fairy tale for children by Gerard Victory; libretto (Eng) by the composer. First performance January 25, 1974, Dublin, RTE, RTE Symphony.

Magnet, The, all-sung afterpiece by Samuel Arnold; libretto (Eng). First performance June 27, 1771, London, Marylebone Gardens.
LIBRETTO: English (London: T. Becket, 1771).

Magnifica, La, opera in one act by Timothy Spelman; libretto (Eng) by Leolyn Louise Everett. Composed 1920.
The work takes place in South America during its colonial period.

Magpie or the Maid, The, melodrama in three acts by Henry Rowley Bishop; libretto (Eng) by Isaac Pocock, after *La pie voleuse* (1815) by T. Badouin d'Aubigny and L.-C. Caigniez. First performance September 15, 1815, London, Covent Garden.
The story concerns a maid who is falsely accused of stealing a silver spoon; the thief is discovered to be a magpie.
Other settings include the musical entertainment *The Maid and the Magpye, or, Which Is the Thief?*, with music by Henry Smart and text by Samuel J. Arnold (1815, London); Bishop's *Ninetta** (1830, London); and the burletta, with overture and incidental music by W. H. Montgomery and text by Henry J. Byron, *The Maid and the Magpie* (1858, London), after Rossini's *La gazza ladra* (1817, Milan).
LIBRETTO: English (London: J. Miller, 1815).

Mahmoud, opera in three acts by Stephen Storace, completed by Michael Kelly and others; libretto (Eng) by Prince Hoare, after the *Thousand and One Nights*. First performance April 30, 1796, London, Drury Lane Theatre, with John Braham (Noureddin), Charles Kemble (Mahmoud), Michael Kelly, Nancy Storace, and Jack Bannister.
The title character is a speaking role. Noureddin (ten) is his younger brother.
For a description, see Fiske/*ETM*, 538–39.
The music by Storace is mostly from his *Gli sposi malcontenti* (1785, Vienna), set here as "From Tears Unavailing, "Follow, Follow, Boldly Enter," "To Arms," and "At Your Feet Thus Lowly Bending." The work also includes "Safe in the Word," set to music from Haydn's *Orlando Paladino* (1782, Esterháza), and "Health to Your Highness," from Paisiello's *I zingari in fiera* (1789, Naples).
LIBRETTO: English (London: n.p., 1796; rev. Wyton, Huntington: King's Music, [1898?]).

Maid Marian, or, The Huntress of Arlingford, "legendary opera" in three acts by Henry Rowley Bishop; libretto (Eng) by James R. Planché, after the satirical novel by Thomas L. Peacock (1822). First performance December 3, 1822, London, Covent Garden. First U.S. performance January 9, 1824, New York, as *Maid Marian, or, the Merry Days of Robin Hood.*
The work features Maid Marian, Robin Hood, Friar Tuck, and Prince John.
SCORE: ms fs (1822, British Library, Add. MS. 36956).
LIBRETTO: English (London: J. Lowndes, [1822]).

Maid Marian, comic opera in three acts by Reginald De Koven; libretto (Eng) by Harry B. Smith. First performance January 27, 1902, New York, Garden Theatre, with Frank Rushworth (Robin Hood), Grace Van Studdiford (Maid Marion), Henry Clay

Barnabee (Sheriff of Nottingham), Will Fitzgerald (Guy of Gisbourne), and W. H. MacDonald (Little John). This was a sequel to his *Robin Hood** (1890, Chicago).

The story opens with Robin Hood's being sent by King Richard to the Crusades, leaving Maid Marion alone to fend off the advances of the Sheriff of Nottingham, acting for Guy of Gisbourne. Little John and other members of Robin's band take Marion to join Robin, but she becomes a prisoner of the Saracens, and Robin and his followers are also captured after they are betrayed by the Sheriff. The lovers escape back to England and bring the Sheriff and his cronies to justice.

Also set by Colin Campbell (not perf.).

Maid of Artois, The, opera in three acts by Michael Balfe; libretto (Eng) by Alfred Bunn. First performance May 26, 1836, London, Drury Lane Theatre, with Maria Malibran and Henry Phillips. Revived October 8, 1846, London, Drury Lane Theatre, with additional music by Balfe. First U.S. performance November 5, 1847, New York.

The characters include the Marquis, Jules, Coralie, Isoline, Count Sulnier, Synnelet, Ninka, and Martin.

The title role was created for Malibran.

SCORE: ms fs, autograph (1836, British Library, Add. MS. 29327, 29328).

LIBRETTO: English (London: W. S. Johnson, [1846?]).

Maid of Honour, The, opera in three acts by Michael Balfe; libretto (Eng) by Edward Fitzball. First performance December 20, 1847, London, Drury Lane Theatre, with Sims Reeves (Lyonnel).

Lady Henriette, maid of honor to the Queen, disguises herself as a country girl and is hired by Lyonnel to be his servant.

Major roles: Lady Henriette, Alison, Sir Tristram, Lyonnel, Walter, and the Queen.

The text is on the same subject as Friedrich von Flotow's *Martha* (November 25, 1847, Vienna).

SCORE: ms fs, autograph (1847, British Library, Add. MS. 29348, 29349).

Maid of Judah, The, or, The Knights Templars, serious opera in three acts by Michael Rophino Lacy, after Rossini's pastiche *Ivanhoé* (1826, Paris); libretto (Eng) by Lacy, after the text by E. Deschamps and G. G. de Wailly, itself based on Scott's novel *Ivanhoe*. First performance March 7, 1829, London, Covent Garden. First U.S. performance February 27, 1832, New York.

A treatment of the story of Ivanhoe and Rebecca.

See Cooke's *The Jewess* and Sullivan's *Ivanhoe* for other settings.

LIBRETTO: English (London: J. Cumberland, [182?]).

Maid of Plymouth, The, comic opera in two acts by T. Pearsall Thorne; libretto (Eng) by Clay M. Greene. First performance 1893, New York.

SCORE: vs (New York: T. B. Harms & Co., 1893).

Maid of Saxony, The, or, Who's the Traitor, opera in three acts by Charles Edward Horn; libretto (Eng) by George P. Morris, after Maria Edgeworth. First performance May 23, 1842, New York, Park Theatre.

LIBRETTO: English, in *Poems by George P. Morris* (New York: C. Scribner, 1854).

Maid of the Mill, The, pastiche comic opera in three acts, arranged by Samuel Arnold (from the music of eighteen composers, including J. C. Bach); libretto (Eng) by Isaac Bickerstaffe, after Samuel Richardson's *Pamela* (1740). First performance January 31, 1765, London, Covent Garden, with Miss Brent (Patty), Miss Hallam (Theodosia), Mr.

Beard (Giles), and Mr. Mattocks (Lord Ainsworth). First American performance May 4, 1769, New York, John Street Theatre.

In this version of the story, Patty, daughter of the local miller, is the heroine. She is employed by Lord Ainsworth, who is jealous of the farmer Giles's attentions to Patty. Patty is jealous of Theodosia, who, Patty thinks, is in love with Ainsworth. In the end Patty and Ainsworth realize they love each other.

Arnold's first stage work (using four of his own numbers), it is the first English piece to have concerted music to accompany action on the stage. It includes an aria by J. C. Bach from his opera *Orione* (1763, London), here as Patty's "Trust Me, Would You Taste True Pleasure," in act 2, scene 5; and the duet by Patty and Lord Ainsworth in act 3, scene 10, "My Life, My Joy, My Blessing" (newly composed).

See below for other settings.

SCORE: vs (London: Robert Bremner, [1765]); 2 Bach numbers repr. *The Collected Works of J. C. Bach*, vol. 25, *Works with English Texts*, ed. Ernest Warburton (New York: Garland, 1990).
LIBRETTO: English (London: J. Newbery, 1765).

Maid of the Mill, The, comic opera in three acts by Tommaso Giordani; libretto (Eng) by Isaac Bickerstaffe, after Richardson's *Pamela* (1740). First performance March 26, 1765, Dublin, Smock Alley.
LIBRETTO: English (Dublin: Author, 1765).

Maid of the Mill, The, ballad opera in three acts by Henry Rowley Bishop, after Arnold's work (see above); libretto (Eng) by Isaac Bickerstaffe. First performance October 18, 1814, London, Covent Garden.

Maid of the Oaks, The, dramatic entertainment in five acts by François Hippolyte Barthelemon; libretto (Eng) by General John Burgoyne, after Marmontel's text for Grétry's *Silvain*. First performance November 5, 1774, London, Drury Lane Theatre, with Joseph Vernon and Mrs. Barthelemon. An expansion of the version presented June 9, 1774, at the marriage of the Earl of Derby at the Oaks, near Epson, England. First U.S. performance May 23, 1796, Philadelphia, Chestnut Street Theatre.

As Sir Harry Groveby prepares to marry Maria, he has a discussion with the painter and the architect about the entertainment scheduled for the upcoming festivities.

For a detailed description, see Fiske/*ETM*, 380–81.
LIBRETTO: English (London: T. Becket, 1774).

Maid of the Vale, The, comic opera in three acts by Michael Arne; libretto (Eng) by Thomas Holcroft, after Goldoni's *La buona figliuola*, itself after Richardson's *Pamela*. First performance February 15, 1775, London, Smock Alley.

See *The Maid of the Mill* for other settings.
LIBRETTO: English (Dublin: C. Jenkins, 1775).

Make Me a Willow Cabin, operatic scena by Richard Stoker; libretto (Eng) by the composer, after Shakespeare. First performance February 14, 1973, London, Purcell Room.
BIBLIOGRAPHY: B. Orr, review, *Composer* XLIX (autumn 1973), 31 [on premiere].

Making of the Representative for Planet 8, The, opera in three acts by Philip Glass; libretto (Eng) by Doris Lessing, after her novel *Canopus in Argos: Archives*. First performance July 8, 1988, Houston, Worthey Center, Cullen Theater, with Harlan Foss (Doeg), Timothy Breese (Johor), Louise Edeiken (Alsi), and Jason Alexander (Nooni); conducted by John DeMain. First British performance November 9, 1988, London.

In this allegorical and symbolic tale, the residents of the once-idyllic Planet 8 have learned that their world is doomed because of an approaching Ice Age, brought on by an alteration of the planet's orbit. They hope for salvation from their protectors, the Canopeans, represented by Johor, who urges the people to build a wall around the planet. The fate of the people is mirrored by the lives of Alsi and Nooni and Doeg, the leader, who has little to offer his people. With most of the people having died, the surviving souls and knowledge combine in one "representative for Planet 8."

Major roles: Johor (bass), Doeg (bar), Alsi (sop), and Nooni (ten).

For a detailed description, see Kornick/*RAO*, 122–24.

LIBRETTO: English (Bryn Mawr, Pa: Dunvagen Music, 1988).

Malady of Love, opera in one act by Lehman Engel; libretto (Eng) by Lewis Allen. First performance May 27, 1954, New York, Columbia University, Brander Matthews Theatre, with Ruth Fleming, Stephanie Turash, and Warren Galjour; conducted by Willard Rhodes; staged by Felix Brentano.

Emily Brown, a young woman obsessed by thoughts of the opposite sex, seeks relief at the office of the young and naive Dr. Barlow. After she reveals her dreams and fantasies to him, he becomes upset. She confesses the obvious, that she is in love with him. He agrees to become part of her cure by marrying her.

For a detailed description, see Eaton/*OP* I, 197.

Roles: Emily Brown (sop); Dr. Stanley Barlow, a psychoanalyst (bar); and two dancers for dream sequence.

BIBLIOGRAPHY: Olin Downes, review, *NYT* (May 28, 1954), 18 [on premiere]; Irving Kolodin, "The Spring Crop of New Premieres," *Saturday Review* XXXVII (June 12, 1954), 28.

Maletroit Door, The, or, Sire de Maletroit, opera in one act by Seymour Barab; libretto (Eng) by Martha England, after Robert Louis Stevenson's *The Sire de Malétroit's Door*. First performance January 28, 1960, New York, Manhattan School of Music Opera Workshop, Hunter College, with Johanna Meier; conducted by Hugh Ross.

I. Mopper's *The Door** and J. Duke's *Sire de Maledroit** are other settings.

BIBLIOGRAPHY: Harold Schonberg, review, *NYT* (Jan. 29, 1960), 15 [on premiere].

Malvina, "national ballad opera" by George Alexander Lee; libretto (Eng) by George Macfarren. First performance January 28, 1826, London, Drury Lane Theatre.

The work contains a variation of the Scottish tune "Roy's Wife of Aldivalloch" and is the last English opera of the time to use a specific Irish melody. See Biddlecombe/ *EO* for an explanation of its attribution to Lee rather than Thomas Cooke (p. 75) and for a description (p. 60).

LIBRETTO: English (London: Jackson and Macfarren, [1826]).

Malvolio, opera in three acts by Fritz Hart; libretto (Eng), after Shakespeare's *Twelfth Night* (1600). Composed 1913. First performance (act 1) December 5, 1919, Melbourne, Australia, Playhouse.

Manaclas, pastoral by Johann Christian Bach; libretto (Eng) by James Harris. First performance August 22 or 24, 1764, Salisbury, England, Salisbury Festival.

The work used arias from Bach's *Orione* (1763, London) and *Zanaida* (1763, London) and new two choruses.

Mañana, television opera in one act by Arthur Benjamin; libretto (Eng) by Caryl Brahms and Giovanni Foa, after *Under the Juniper Tree* by Brahms. First performance February 1, 1956, London, BBC, with Heather Harper; conducted by John Pritchard.

Mandarin, The, "Chinese comic opera" in three acts by Reginald De Koven; libretto (Eng) by Harry B. Smith. First performance November 2, 1896, New York, Herald Square Theatre, with George Honey (the mandarin), G. C. Boniface Jr. (Fan-Tan), and Bertha Waltzinger (Fan-Tan's wife).

Wanting to seduce the wife of the carpenter Fan-Tan, the mandarin disguises himself as the husband. The carpenter, meanwhile, is wanted by the police, so when they come to Fan-Tan's home, they arrest the mandarin instead, and Fan-Tan is taken to the mandarin's home by servants of the mandarin, who think the carpenter is their master. The mandarin has twelve wives, and when Fan-Tan's own wife joins the group, Fan-Tan is scheduled to die because of a law forbidding a man from having thirteen wives. He is saved from his fate when the real mandarin reveals his deception.
LIBRETTO: English (n.p., 1896).

Mandarin, The, opera buffa in three acts "in the fashion of a zarzuela" by Jonathan Elkus; libretto (Eng) by Richard Franko Goldman, after *O mandarim* by José Maria Eça de Queiroz. First performance October 26, 1967, New York.

Teodoro, a poor Lisbon clerk, makes a deal with the Devil to get a fortune from the Mandarin, who dies, but his ghost follows Teodoro to Peking.

Roles: Teodoro (ten), the Devil (bar), Madame Camiloff (mezzo), and General Camiloff (bass).
LIBRETTO: English (New York: Carl Fischer, 1969).

Man from Tuscany, The, opera in two acts by Antony Hopkins; libretto (Eng) by Christopher Hassall. First performance July 20, 1951, Canterbury, Canterbury Cathedral, Chapter House.

Man from Venus, The, opera in one act by Philip Cannon; libretto (Eng) by Jacqueline Laidlaw. First performance December 5, 1966, Waltham Abbey, Essex, England, Town Hall, with Gavin Walton (Nicolas).

A suburban matron tries to marry off her daughter to a foolish young man deemed to have a good future. The mother's plans are put on hold with the appearance of a strange creature.

The score includes electronically-produced sounds to represent the "man from Venus."
BIBLIOGRAPHY: Arthur Jacobs, review, *Opera* XVIII (Jan. 1967), 81 [on premiere].

Manhattan Book of the Dead, The, opera in two acts by David First. First performance April 27, 1995, New York, La Mama E.T.C., with Thomas Buckner (singer), and Pascal Benichou and Cavin Bodouin (dancers); conducted by Petr Kotik; choreographed by Gloria McLean; television images and recorded voice by Ching Valdes-Aran, David Gearey, and Patricia Smith.

The work follows its sole character from watching his friends die to coming to terms with the inevitable. It uses recorded voices and television images.
BIBLIOGRAPHY: Bernard Holland, "Taking Death and Survival and Making Them into an Opera," *NYT* (May 1, 1995), C, 12 [on premiere].

Maniac, The, or, The Swiss Banditti, serio-comic opera in three acts by Henry Rowley Bishop; libretto (Eng) by Samuel J. Arnold. First performance March 13, 1810, London, Lyceum.

The title character is a young woman who has been led astray by a lover, a situation that breaks her father's heart and causes his death. As a result she becomes very distraught. Things improve by the end, however.
SCORE: ms fs (1810, British Library, Add. MS. 35938, 35939); selections (London, 1810).
LIBRETTO: English: (London: Lowndes and Hobbs, [1810?]).

Man of Feeling, A, opera in one act by Stephen Oliver; libretto (Eng) by the composer, after Arthur Schnitzler's *Der Empfindsame.* First performance November 17, 1980, London, Islington, King's Head Theatre Club.
    The action centers on an opera singer and Fritz, a sensitive soul. Fritz kills himself when she leaves him, and their affair is detailed in a letter read by a friend following Fritz's death.
    All of the roles are sung by a soprano and baritone.
SCORE: vs (Borough Green: Novello, 1983).

Man on a Bearskin Rug, The, comic opera in one act by Paul Ramsier; libretto (Eng) by James Elward. First performance April 13, 1969, Aberdeen, South Dakota, Northern State Teachers College, with John Reardon (Henry), Nancy Dussault (Doris), and Ruth Kobart (Mrs. Le Moine).
    A young man, Henry, argues with his fiancée, Doris, after a party. She leaves, and Mrs. Le Moine, the landlady, comes in with a big box containing a white bearskin rug. When they put it down on the floor, Mrs. Le Moine becomes amorous. Doris comes back and, seeing what is going on, becomes very jealous. Mrs. Le Moine leaves, and when she returns, Doris and Henry are kissing. She says that the rug belongs to Stanley and takes it away. Doris's mood changes, and she starts to harangue Henry again.
    Roles: Henry (bar); Doris (sop); and Mrs. Le Moine, his landlady (alto).
SCORE: vs (Boosey & Hawkes, 1963).

Manson Family, The, multimedia opera by John Moran; libretto (Eng) by the composer. First performance July 17, 1990, New York, Alice Tully Hall, Lincoln Center's Serious Fun Festival.
    The work is based on the 1969 killings of the actress Sharon Tate and others and the murder trial of Charles Manson and his female followers, known as his "family."
    The score includes a musical collage, with various sound effects, and dialogue taken from the trial itself.
BIBLIOGRAPHY: John Baskett, "Over the Edge," *ON* LVI (Mar. 14, 1992), 22–24 [interview with composer]; John Rockwell, review, *NYT* (Jul. 22, 1990), 1 [on premiere].
DISCOGRAPHY: Roache, Moran, Iggy Pop, Point Music/Philips 432967-2 (1992, 1 CD).

Man Who Corrupted Hadleyville, The, opera by Robert Nelson; libretto (Eng) by Kate Pogue. Composed 1986.
SCORE: ms vs, holograph (1986, photocopy, NYPL).

Man Who Mistook His Wife for a Hat, The, opera in one act by Michael Nyman; libretto (Eng) by Christopher Rawlence, after a medical case history by Oliver Sacks. First performance October 27, 1986, London, Institute of Contemporary Arts, with Emile Belcourt (Dr. S), Frederick Westcott (Dr. P), and Sarah Leonard (Mrs. P); conducted by the composer. First U.S. performance October 1, 1987, Philadelphia, WHYY-TV, Forum Theatre.
    The work is based on the case study by Dr. Sacks of a musician suffering from visual agnosia, or "mental blindness"; in the opera he is called "Dr. P."

Roles: Dr. S (ten), Dr. P (bar), and Mrs. P (sop).
BIBLIOGRAPHY: Robert Baxter, review, *ON* LII (Jan. 30, 1988), 34 [on U.S. premiere].
DISCOGRAPHY: Belcourt, Leonard, Westcott; cond. Nyman, CBS MK44669 (1987, London, 2 CDs).

Man with Footsoles of Wind, The, chamber opera in three acts by Kevin Volans; libretto (Eng) by Roger Clarke, after a conception by Bruce Chatwin in *The Songlines* and inspired by Arthur Rimbaud's autobiographical *Un saison en enfers* (1873). First performance, as *The Man Who Strides the Wind*, July 2, 1993, London, Contemporary Opera Studio, Almeida Opera, with Thomas Randle (Rimbaud); conducted by David Parry; directed by Peter Mumford; choreographed by Siobhan Davies.

The first act concentrates on the beginning and end of Rimbaud's life, and his relationship with his sister and mother. The second and third, set in the Ethiopian desert, concern an imaginary conversation of Rimbaud taking place on an imaginary journey.

Roles: Arthur Rimbaud (ten); Arthur as a boy (treble); Madame Rimbaud, his mother (sop); Isabelle Rimbaud, his sister (sop); captain of the African steamer (speaking); and Djami, Rimbaud's African servant (bar).
BIBLIOGRAPHY: Michael Blake, review, *Tempo*, No. 186 (Sept. 1993), 52–53 [on premiere].

Man without a Country, The, opera in two acts by Walter Damrosch; libretto (Eng) by Arthur Guiterman, after a story by Edward Everett Hale; scenario by the composer. First performance May 12, 1937, New York, Metropolitan Opera, with Helen Traubel (Mary Rutledge), Arthur Carron (Philip Nolan), George Rasely (Harman Blennerhassett), Joseph Royer (Aaron Burr), John Gurney (Colonel Morgan), Nicholas Massue (Parke), Lodovico Oliviero (Fairfax), Wilfred Engelman (Pinckney), and George Cehanovsky (Reeve); conducted by the composer.

The story concerns Philip Nolan, a U.S. navy officer who is put on trial for his connection to Aaron Burr's treason. In a fit of anger Nolan curses his native country and says he never wants to hear its name again. As punishment he is moved from vessel to vessel without being allowed to land or hear anything about the United States. Nolan becomes a fierce patriot and fights bravely for his native land during the War of 1812 but dies without receiving his official pardon.

Major roles: Mary Rutledge (sop), Philip Nolan (ten), Harman Blennerhassett (ten), Aaron Burr (bar), Colonel Morgan (bass), Parke (ten), Fairfax (ten), Pinckney (bar), and Reeve (bar).
SCORE: vs (New York: G. Schirmer, 1937).

Many Moons, opera in one act by Celius Dougherty; libretto (Eng) by the composer, after James Thurber. First performance December 6, 1962, Poughkeepsie, New York.

The Princess Lenore becomes sick after eating too many raspberry tarts. Her cure lies in the powers of the moon, so, at the Jester's suggestion, a tiny moon is created for her, which helps her get better.

Many Moons, opera by Robert Kapilow; libretto (Eng) by Hilary Blecher, after James Thurber's story. First performance January 18, 1997, Princeton, New Jersey, Richardson Auditorium; conducted by the composer.

See preceding entry for the story.

Roles: the jester (mezzo), the young boy (boy sop), Princess Lenore (sop), the doctor (bar), the king (bar), the Lord Chamberlain (bass-bar), the wizard (ten), the goldsmith (bass-bar), the assistant goldsmith (sop), and the mathematician (sop).

Marco Polo, opera in one act by Tan Dun; libretto (Eng) by Paul Griffiths. First performance May 7, 1996, Munich, Biennale. First U.S. performance November 8, 1997, New York, City Opera, with Adam Klein (Polo), Christine Abraham (Sheherezada/ Mahler/ Queen), Rod Nelman (Kublai Khan), Stephen Bryant (Dante/Shakespeare), Susan Botti (Water), and Chen Shi-Zheng (Rustichello/Li Po); directed by Martha Clarke.

Described as an "opera within an opera," the work is an imaginary presentation of Marco Polo's journey from Venice to China, which is thought of as a search for dreams.

It incorporates elements of Western avant-garde music with those of the Peking Opera, Kabuki, and Indonesian shadow theater. The cast is divided into four types: memory: Polo (ten); beings: Marco (mezzo); Kublai Khan (bass); nature: Water (sop); and shadows: Rustichello/Li Po (Peking Opera singer); Sheherezada/Mahler/Queen (mezzo); Dante/Shakespeare (bar). To the Western instruments are added "world instruments" such as Tibetan bells, singing bowls, and horns.

Among borrowings from classical music are snatches of *Das Lied von der Erde* to parallel the character of Mahler.
BIBLIOGRAPHY: Patrick J. Smith, "Marco Polo's Voyage to a World of Ideas," *NYT* (Nov. 11, 1997), E, 5 [on U.S. premiere].
DISCOGRAPHY: Botti, Warren, Montano, Young, Briant, Gong, Chen, Cappella Amsterdam, Netherlands Radio Phil.; cond. Tan Dun, SRCR1881/82 Sony Classical (2 CDs, 1997); rev. Patrick J. Smith, "Recordings," *ON* LXII (Dec. 20, 1997), 38.

Margery, or, A Worse Plague than the Dragon, opera by John Frederick Lampe; libretto (Eng) by Henry Carey. First performance December 9, 1738, London, Covent Garden, with Isabella (Young) Lampe (Margery), Esther Young (Mauxalinda), and Thomas Salway (Moore); the sequel to *The Dragon of Wantley*.*

When Margery's bridegroom, Moore, runs off on his wedding night to find a former lover, Mauxalinda, Margery's father, Gubbins, saves his daughter's honor by marrying Mauxalinda himself.

Unlike *The Dragon of Wantley*, this opera was a failure.
SCORE: vs (London: John Wilcox, 1739).
LIBRETTO: English (John Wilcox, 1739).

Maria Elena, opera in one act by Thomas Pasatieri; libretto (Eng) by the composer. First performance April 6, 1983, Tucson, Arizona Opera Theatre, with Majo Carroll (Maria), Sherry Rutherford (Luisa), and Jerold Siena (Silva); conducted by Richard Woitach.

In a series of flashbacks the imprisoned Maria sees the events of her life unfold before her. When her husband, Salvador, dies, she is convinced by her friend Rosa to stop mourning and live in the country.
BIBLIOGRAPHY: Kenneth La Fave, review, *ON* XLVIII (July 1983), 38 [on premiere].

Maria Golovin, opera in three acts by Gian Carlo Menotti; libretto (Eng) by the composer. First performance August 20, 1958, Brussels, Théâtre de l'Exposition (in Italian), with Franca Duval (Maria Golovin), Patricia Neway (the mother), Ruth Kobart (Agata), Richard Cross (Donato), and Herbert Handt (Dr. Zuckertanz); conducted by Peter Herman Adler; produced by the composer. First U.S. performance (in English) November 5, 1958, New York, Martin Beck Theater, with a similar cast.

The plot is set in a small frontier town about 1919. It opens with Maria Golovin's awaiting her husband's return from a prisoner-of-war camp. She is spending the summer with her son and his tutor, Dr. Zuckertanz, in the villa of a young blind man, Donato. Donato lives there with his mother. Maria and the young man are attracted to each other and begin an affair, but his jealousy and possessiveness lead him to violence. He is fooled by his mother into thinking he has shot Maria and goes into hiding.

Major roles: Maria (sop), Dr. Zuckertanz (ten), Donato (bass-bar), and his mother (alto).

For a detailed description, see Eaton/*OP* I, 95–96.

SCORE: vs, Italian-English (New York: Belwin-Mills, 1958, 1959, 1978).

BIBLIOGRAPHY: Howard Taubman, "Don't Say 'Opera,'" *NYT* (Nov. 30, 1958), II, 11.

Maria Malibran, opera in three acts by Robert Russell Bennett; libretto (Eng) by Robert A. Simon. First performance April 8, 1935, New York, Juilliard School, with Helen Marshall/Josephine Antoine (Maria Malibran), Allen Stewart (Philip), and Risë Stevens (Cornelia Bayard); conducted by Albert Stoessel; directed by Alfredo Valenti.

A fictionalized account of the short, unhappy stay of the singer in New York in 1827, during which she meets her first love, Philip, who is now engaged to someone else.

The work includes the folk song "Home, Sweet Home" and the aria "Una voce poco fa" by Rossini.

BIBLIOGRAPHY: Howard Taubman, "'Maria Malibran' Sung in Premiere," *NYT* (Apr. 9, 1935), 24.

Marian, comic opera in two acts by William Shield; libretto (Eng) by Frances Brooke. First performance May 22, 1788, London, Covent Garden, with Mrs. Billington (Marian). First U.S. performance April 4, 1798, Philadelphia, Chestnut Street Theatre.

Marian's mother prevents her from wedding Edward, since her intended's family is poorer than hers. When Edward's family comes into money, the lovers are allowed to wed.

For a description, see Fiske/*ETM*, 467–68.

SCORE: vs (London: Longman & Broderip, [1788]).

LIBRETTO: English (London, 1788).

Marie, the Foundling of the Lake, adaptation by Edward Loder of Hérold's *Marie* (1826, Paris); libretto (Eng), after Planard's text. First performance January 18, 1849, London, Princess's Theatre.

Marilyn, opera in two acts by Ezra Laderman; libretto (Eng) by Norman Rosten after his book *Marilyn: The Untold Story*. First performance October 6, 1993, New York, New York City Opera, with Kathryn Gamberoni (Marilyn Monroe), Susanne Marsee (Rose), Michael Rees Davis (Senator), Philip Cokorinos (Rick), and Ron Baker (psychiatrist); conducted by Hal France; designed by Jerome Sirlin.

On the actress and American icon Marilyn Monroe at the end of her life, in 1962, with flashbacks to her childhood and her mother, Rick, her ex-husband (a combination of Monroe's three actual husbands), and her confrontation with the Senator who has abandoned her after their affair.

The score includes contemporary musical references such as a theme from "Hooray for Hollywood" and elements of pop and jazz.

Monroe's life is also examined in L. Ferrero's opera *Marilyn* (1980, Rome).

BIBLIOGRAPHY: Edward Rothstein, "New Milieu for Monroe," *NYT* (Oct. 8, 1993), C, 3.

Mariners, The, musical entertainment in two acts by Thomas Attwood, including music by Mozart; libretto (Eng) by Samuel Birch. First performance May 10, 1793, London, Haymarket Theatre, with Thomas Sedgwick.

The work includes the music of Sarastro's "In diesen heil'gen Hallen" from *Die Zauberflöte*. The overture is by Thomas Shaw.
SCORE: vs (London: Longman & Broderip, n.d.).

Mario and the Magician, opera in one act by Stephen Oliver; libretto (Eng) by the composer, after the novella by Thomas Mann (1929). First performance, in Italian, as *Mario ed il mago*, August 6, 1988, Batignano, Italy. First performance, in English, as *Mario and the Magician*, May 3, 1989, Milwaukee.

The work takes place in an Italian hotel. A German mother is arguing with a citizen over bathing rules, and she is fined by the mayor because her daughter has been bathing without any clothes on. The action then moves to the magic show, which Cipolla holds in the hotel and hypnotizes the guests.

Mario and the Magician, opera in three acts by Harry Somers; libretto (Eng) by Rod Anderson, after Mann. First performance May 19, 1992, Toronto, Elgin Theatre, with David Rampy (Cipolla), Theodore Baerg (Stefan), and Benoit Boutet (Mario).

The story revolves around the rise of Fascism in Italy and is set at an Italian hotel in a small town, Torre di Venera in 1928. Stefan, the narrator, recounts his Italian holiday during which he encounters a Mephistophelian magician, Cipolla, who hypnotizes the tourists, and Mario, a waiter, who presents obstacles to Cipolla's success.
BIBLIOGRAPHY: Paul Griffiths, "Musical Events," *NY* LXVIII (June 8, 1992), 71–73 [on premiere]; Urjo Kareda, "Toronto," *ON* LVII (Nov. 1992), 53 [on premiere].

Mario and the Magician, opera by Francis Thorne; libretto (Eng) by J. D. McClatchy, after Mann. First performance March 12, 1994, Brooklyn College Opera, George Gershwin Theater, with David Parsons (Cipolla) and Thomas Ballard (Mario); conducted by Richard Barrett; directed by Donna Vaughn.

In this Faustian story, set in Fascist Italy, Cipolla, the magician, sells his soul in order to obtain power and knowledge and is opposed by Mario, a waiter.

Also set by J. Vajda (1988, Budapest).
BIBLIOGRAPHY: Edward Rothstein, review, *NYT* (Mar. 14, 1994), C, 14 [on premiere].

Marita and Her Heart's Desire, children's opera in one act by Bruce Adolphe; libretto (Eng) by Louise Gikow. First performance January 27, 1995, New York, John Jay Theater; narrated by Michele Mariana. Performed with the composer's *The Amazing Adventure of Alvin Allegretto*.*

A young city girl sets off with a group of animals to ask the moon to grant her fondest wish.
BIBLIOGRAPHY: Edward Rothstein, review, *NYT* (January 31, 1995), C, 14 [on premiere].

Maritana, opera in three acts by Vincent Wallace; libretto (Eng) by Edward Fitzball, after the French *Don César de Bazan* (1844) by d'Ennery and Dumanoir. First performance November 15, 1845, London, Drury Lane Theatre, with Emma Romer (Maritana) and William Harrison (Don Caesar). First U.S. performances November 9, 1846, Philadelphia; May 4, 1848, New York, Bowery Theatre.

The setting is early nineteenth-century Madrid. Don José, who is trying to impress the Spanish Queen, gets Don Caesar to wed Maritana, a street singer, just before he is to be executed. Don José also insinuates to the Queen that the King has shown more than a passing interest in Maritana. The schemer's plans are thwarted when Don Caesar's execution proves to be a mock one, and he comes back for his new wife. Don José is killed by Don Caesar before he can betray the King, and Maritana and her noble husband have a happy life together.

For detailed descriptions, see Biddlecombe/*EO*, 132–33; K/*NKOB*, 952–53.

Major roles: Don José (bar), Maritana (sop), the Queen (sop), Don Caesar (ten), and the King (bass).

Among the highlights are Maritana's "Scenes That Are Brightest" and Don José's "In Happy Moments."

Also set by Massenet as *Don César de Bazan* (1872, Paris).

LIBRETTOS: English (London: W. S. Johnson, [184?]; Boston: Castle Square Theatre, [1896]).

Markheim, dramatic sketch in one act by Philip Napier Miles; libretto (Eng) by the composer, after Robert Louis Stevenson's story. First performance February 10, 1923, London, Metropolitan Theatre (concert). First stage performance October 13, 1924, Clifton (near Bristol).

Markheim, opera in one act by Carlisle Floyd; libretto (Eng) by the composer, after the story of Robert Louis Stevenson. First performance March 31, 1966, New Orleans, New Orleans Opera, with Norman Treigle (Markheim), Alan Crofoot (Josiah Creach), William Diard (the Stranger), and Audrey Schuh (Tess); conducted by Knud Andersson.

The setting is 1880s London. The down-on-his-luck Markheim visits an old pawnshop on Christmas Eve. After he kills Creach, the owner, he meets the Stranger, who offers him unlimited pleasure if he is willing to commit one more crime. He must kill the maid Tess, for she is returning to the store and will discover Markheim's crime. Instead, Markheim confesses and has Tess call the police. The opera ends with a chorus singing "Gloria in excelsis Deo."

Roles: Josiah Creach (ten), Markheim (bass-bar), Tess (sop), and the Stranger (ten).

SCORE: vs (New York: Boosey & Hawkes, 1968).

BIBLIOGRAPHY: Jack Belsom, review, *ON* XXX (May 7, 1966), 22 [on premiere].

DISCOGRAPHY: A. Schuh, N. Treigle, A. Crofoot, W. Diard, New Orleans Opera; cond. K. Andersson, VAI Audio 1107 (1966); rev. Patrick J. Smith, *ON* LX (Oct. 1995), 46.

Marko the Miser, children's opera in one act by Thea Musgrave; libretto (Eng) by the composer and F. Samson, after A. A. Afanasyev. First performance 1963, Farnham, Surrey, England.

Marquesa of O, The, opera in one act by Elie Siegmeister; libretto (Eng) by Norman Rosten, after Kleist's novella (1808). Composed 1982.

When the widowed Julietta, a marquise, discovers to her horror that she is pregnant, which she cannot explain, she appeals publicly for the father to reveal himself so that she can marry him and save her reputation. He turns out to be Count F, who had rescued her from a rampaging group of Russian soldiers, only to take advantage of her when she fainted. She forgives him after he shows true repentance and love.

Marriage Act, The, afterpiece in two acts by Charles Dibdin; libretto (Eng) by the composer. First performance September 17, 1781, London, Covent Garden.

Originally performed as the opera *The Islanders** (1780).

LIBRETTO: English (London: G. Kearsley, 1781).

Marriage Counselor, The, opera in one act by Matt Doran; libretto (Eng) by the composer. First performance March 12, 1977, Los Angeles.

Marriage Machine, The, opera in one act by Colin Brunby; libretto (Eng) by the composer. First performance January 28, 1972, Sydney, Australia.

Marriage of Aude, lyric opera in three scenes by Bernard Rogers; libretto (Eng) by Charles Rodda, after *The Song of Roland.* First performance May 22, 1931, Rochester, New York, Eastman School of Music; conducted by Emmanuel Balaban.

The setting is Charlemagne's palace. Aude comes to the palace to find news about her missing fiancé, Roland. The king orders Duke Naimes to tell her the bad news. Naimes describes how Roland was wounded in battle. When a knight brings Roland's sword and a mourning robe, Aude realizes that Roland is dead; she takes his sword and raises it above her head. As it shatters, she falls down dead.

Marriage-Office, The (The Device), afterpiece by William Bates; libretto (Eng) by Richards. First performance May 5, 1777, London, Covent Garden.

Marriage of Figaro, The, comic opera in three acts, partial arrangement by Henry Rowley Bishop of Mozart's *Le nozze di Figaro* (1786, Vienna); libretto (Eng) by John Fawcett and Daniel Terry, after Thomas Holcroft and Beaumarchais. First performance March 6, 1819, London, Covent Garden, with Mary Anne Paton (Susanna). First U.S. performance of this version May 10, 1824, New York.

The work includes the same characters as Mozart's opera, with the addition of Fiorella (Fiorello) from Rossini's *Il barbiere di Seviglia.*

Another musical adaptation was made by Charles Edward Horn and performed on January 21, 1828, New York, Park Theatre.

SCORE: ms fs, autograph (1819, British Library, Add. MS. 27712); vs (London: Goulding, D'Almaine, Potter, [between 1819 and 1823]).

Marriage of Oceanus and Brittania, The, "allegorical fiction, really declaring England's riches, glory, and puissance by sea: to be represented in Musick, Dances, and proper Scenes"; music and text (Eng) by Richard Flecknoe. Composed ca. 1659. Although the libretto was published, there is no recorded performance.

The music itself is lost.

LIBRETTO: English ([London: n.p.], 1659).

Marriage Proposal, opera in one act by Jeremiah Murray; libretto (Eng) by the composer, after Anton Chekhov's play (1889). First performance February 1, 1973, New York, Clark Center, with Kate Hurney (Natasha), Ray Harrell (the father), and Henry Grossman (the suitor).

The work uses musical quotes from Verdi, Bernstein, and Tchaikovsky for comic effect.

BIBLIOGRAPHY: L. Kerner, "New York," *ON* XXXVII (Mar. 24, 1973), 33 [on premiere].

Marriage Proposal, The, opera in one act by Paul Goldstaub; libretto (Eng) by the composer, after Chekhov. First performance (concert) May 25, 1978, Mankato, Minnesota, Mankato State University.

The nervous Lomov comes to propose to Natasha, daughter of his neighbor, Chubukov, but when she appears, not knowing why he has come, he loses his nerve and they start to argue, with the father finally throwing him out of the house. Natasha gets her father to bring Lomov back to the house, but the young people again argue, and Lomov faints. Feeling that Lomov is the last prospect for Natasha, Chubukov gets them to set a wedding date between arguments.

For a description, see Summers/*OOA*, 131–32.
Roles: Lomov (ten), Natasha (sop), and Chubukov (bass-bar/bass).

Marriages between Zones 3, 4, and 5, opera in two acts by Paul Alan Barker; libretto (Eng) by the composer, after Doris Lessing's novel *Canopus in Argos: Archives*. First performance April 10, 1985, London, Opera Viva, with Christine Barker (new Queen), Julie Wilde (ex-Queen), John Oakley-Tucker (narrator); conducted by Christopher Willis.

The parable concerns the brutal King of Zone 4 and his wives and ex-wives.
BIBLIOGRAPHY: Rodney Milnes, review, *Opera* XXXVI (June 1985), 707–8 [on premiere].

Marriages between Zones 3, 4, and 5, opera in two acts by Philip Glass; libretto (Eng) by Doris Lessing, after her novel (1980). First performance May 10, 1997, in a German translation by Saskia M. Wesnigk, May 10, 1997, Heidelberg, Germany; conducted by Thomas Kalb; directed by Brigitta Trommler.

The work concerns the battle of the sexes in three different cultures.

Married Men Go to Hell (The Devil Takes a Wife), opera in three acts by Arnold Franchetti; libretto (Eng) by E. Willheim, after Machiavelli. Composed 1975.

Martin's Lie, opera in one act by Gian Carlo Menotti; libretto (Eng) by the composer. First performance June 3, 1964, Bath, England, Bristol Cathedral, with William McAlpine (Father Cornelius), Noreen Berry (Naninga), Donald McIntyre (the stranger), Otakar Kraus (the sheriff), and Michael Wennink (Martin); conducted by Lawrence Leonard. First U.S. performance June 17, 1976, Washington Cathedral, with Simon Jackson (Martin), Gene Tucker (Father Cornelius), Richard Dirksen (the stranger), Dana Krueger (Naninga), and Gimi Beni (the sheriff); conducted by Paul Callaway.

The work is set in St. Isadore's orphanage in the fourteenth century. Martin is an orphan living in the small home, run by a loving housekeeper, Naninga, and a kind monk, Father Cornelius. Alone in the kitchen at night, Martin gives refuge to a stranger who, finding out that Martin is obsessed with finding his father, claims to be his parent. When the boy lies to the sheriff to protect the stranger, who is really a fugitive from justice, he is threatened with torture and dies of fright.
BIBLIOGRAPHY: review, *NYT* (June 5, 1964), 25; Charles Timbrell, "Reports: U.S.," *ON* XLI (Oct. 1976), 64 [on U.S. premiere].

Martyr, The, grand opera in two acts by Harry Lawrence Freeman; libretto (Eng) by the composer. First performance September 1893, Denver, German Theatre; October, 1893, Chicago, World's Columbia Exposition, with Abram Williamson (Pharaoh), Adah Roberts (Mariamum), William Carey (Platonus), Edward Bennett (Rei), and Ida Williamson (Shirah); conducted by the composer. Revived May 7, 1947, Carnegie Hall, Negro Grand Opera Company, with Muriel Rahn, Bettye Voorhees, Loys Price, and Paul Robinson; conducted by the composer.

The Egyptian nobleman Platonus is imprisoned by his countrymen after converting to Judaism. He rejects the pleas of his fiancée, Shirah, and reaffirms his faith. Rei, the high priest, condemns Platonus to death, and the Queen, rejecting Shirah's pleas, allows the sentence to be carried out.

Martyrdom of St. Magnus, The, opera in nine scenes by Peter Maxwell Davies; libretto (Eng) by the composer, after George Mackay Brown's novel. First performance June 18, 1977, Kirkwall, in the Orkney Islands, with Neil Mackie (Magnus/King of Norway), Michael Rippon and Brian Rayner-Cooke (the baritone roles), Ian Comboy

(Bishop of Orkney), and Mary Thomas (Blind Mary); conducted by the composer. First U.S. performance June 29, 1978, Central City, Colorado, with Paul Sperry (Magnus), Jan DeGaetani (Blind Mary), and Werner Klemperer; conducted by Richard Dufallo.

The work begins and ends with Blind Mary. The action follows Magnus, a pacifist hero, who is murdered by his cousin, Earl Hakon. At the conclusion Mary regains her sight through a miracle, which occurs at the tomb of St. Magnus.

Four male singers and a mezzo soprano sing several different roles, accompanied by ten instrumentalists.

SCORE: vs (London and New York: Boosey & Hawkes, 1977).

BIBLIOGRAPHY: Noel Goodwin, "Reports: Foreign," *ON* XLII (Sept. 1977), 61-62.

Martyred, The, opera in two acts by James Wade; libretto (Eng) by the composer, after the novel (1964) by Richard E. Kim and a drama by Kim Ki-pal. First performance April 8, 1970, Seoul, South Korea.

The setting is Pyong-yang, Korea, 1950, during the Korean War. A young South Korean officer, Captain Park, returns home to find that his estranged father, a minister, has been murdered, after being betrayed by Reverend Shin, according to the captured Major Jung. With the imminent approach of the Communist forces, Shin, trying to deal with his guilt, remains behind to offer comfort to the city's inhabitants.

For a detailed description, see Eaton/*OP* II, 300–1.

Major roles: Reverend Shin (bar), Captain Park (ten), Colonel Chang (bar), Major Jung (bass), and Mrs. Hann (mezzo).

Mary, Queen of Scots, opera in three acts by Thea Musgrave; libretto (Eng) by the composer, after Amalia Elguera's play *Moray.* First performance September 6, 1977, Edinburgh, Edinburgh International Festival, with Catherine Wilson (Mary), David Hillman (Darnley), Gregory Dempsey (Bothwell), Jake Gardner (James Stewart), and Stafford Dean (Riccio); conducted by the composer; produced by Colin Graham. First U.S. performance March 29, 1978, Norfolk, Virginia, Virginia Opera, with Ashley Putnam (Mary), Jake Gardner (James Stewart), Barry Busse (Bothwell), and John Garrison (Darnley); conducted by Peter Mark; directed by David Farrar. First New York performance March 1, 1981, New York, City Opera, with the same principals, except for Richard Fredericks as James Stewart and Rico Serbo as Darnley.

The opera examines Mary's life beginning in 1561, when she leaves France for Scotland, having become a widow, and ends in 1568, when she is forced to flee to England. On her arrival in Scotland she is met by her half brother, the Protestant James Stewart, and Bothwell, a Scottish baron. Bothwell, who clashes with David Riccio, Mary's favorite adviser, is forced to leave court, and James Stewart, who is against her marriage to the Catholic Lord Darnley, departs in anger. The marriage to Darnley proves to be a disaster. The ambitious Darnley, at the urging of his confederates to gain more power and convinced that Riccio is the father of Mary's child, has Riccio murdered. Mary turns to Bothwell for help, and he has Darnley killed, after which Mary loses the support of the people. She must go to England, where she becomes a prisoner of Elizabeth I.

Major roles: Mary, Queen of Scots (sop); James Stewart, Earl of Moray (bar); James Hepburn, Earl of Bothwell (ten); Henry Stuart, Lord Darnley (ten); and David Riccio/ Cardinal Beaton (bass-bar).

Among the musical highlights are Mary's act 1 "The Three Stars of My Firmament," in which she thinks of Bothwell, James Stewart, and Darnley; the act 2 duet between Mary and James, which is preceded by James's aria "Now I Shall Rule!" and Mary's "Alone, Alone, I Stand Alone."

Aspects of Mary's life have been treated in operas by P. Casella (1813); F. S. Mercadante (1821); F. J. Fétis, *Marie Stuart en Ecosse* (1823, Paris); C. Coccia, *Maria Stuarda* (1828, Milan); Grazioli (1828); G. Donizetti, *Maria Stuarda* (1834, Naples); L. Niedermeier, *Marie Stuart* (1844, Paris); J. L. Duprato, *Marie Stuart au chateau de Lochleven* (1863, unperf.); V. Capecalarp, *David Riccio* (1850); L. Canepa, *Davide Rizzio* (1872); C. Palumbo (1874); F. March, monodrama, *Mary Stuart, Queen of Scots* (1875); R. Lavello (1895); D. Moor, *Rizzio* 1932); W. Hiller, *An diesem heutigen Tage* (1973); Virani (1974); and S. Slonimsky, *Mariya Styuart* (1981, Leningrad). See also *David Rizzio, Mary Stuart,* and *Rizzio.*

See John Watts, "Other Operas about Mary Stuart," *Donizetti Society Journal* III (1977), 265–67.

SCORE: vs (Borough Green, Kent: Novello, [1978]).

BIBLIOGRAPHY: Noel Goodwin, review, *ON* XLII (Nov. 1977), 66–67 [on premiere]; Donal Henahan, review, *NYT* (March 2, 1981), C, 18 [on New York premiere]; Robert Jacobson, "News from: Norfolk," *ON* XLII (June 1978), 32 [on U.S. premiere]; Andrew Porter, review, *NY* LIV (May 1, 1978), 136 [on U.S. premiere].

DISCOGRAPHY: Putnam, Garrison, Busse, Gardner, Bell, Virginia Opera Assoc., cond. Mark, Moss Music Group MMG-301 (3); rev. John W. Freeman, "Records," *ON* XLIV (Nov. 1979), 58.

Mary Dyer, opera in three acts by Richard Owen; libretto (Eng) by the composer, after trial documents, diaries, and letters. First performance June 12, 1976, Suffern, New York, Eastern Opera Company, Hudson Valley Philharmonic. Also February 4, 1979, New York.

The fictional story, based on historical events, centers on the persecution in Massachusetts of the Quakers. The victims include Mary Dyer of Rhode Island, who has been put in prison and is released on the condition that she not return to Massachusetts. When Mary does return to protest the impending death of another Quaker, Robinson, she is again imprisoned. The governor offers to spare her and even Robinson; she refuses, since he will not repeal the law allowing the persecution of the Quakers. Robinson is hanged, and then Mary.

Major roles: Mary Dyer (sop), Governor John Endicott (bar), and Magistrate Norton (ten).

For a detailed description, see Kornick/*RAO*, 220–22.

SCORE: vs, holograph, 1976 (NYPL, photocopy).

Mary of Egypt, opera in two acts by John Taverner; libretto (Eng) by Mother Thekla. First performance June 24, 1992, Aldeburgh, with Patricia Rozario (Mary), Stephen Varcoe (Zossima), and Chloe Goodchild (narrator); conducted by Lionel Friend.

The story concerns the once dissolute Mary, who meets the holy man Zossima. She abandons her earlier ways for a life of meditation and denial in the Egyptian desert, and her devotion teaches humility to Zossima.

Major roles: Mary (sop), Zossima (bar), and narrator (sop).

The work is built musically around the ancient Byzantine hymn "Awed by Thy Beauty."

BIBLIOGRAPHY: John Koopman, "Aldeburgh," *ON* LVII (Nov. 1992), 58 [on premiere].

Mary Stuart, opera by Bain Murray; libretto (Eng) by the composer. First performance March 1, 1991, Cleveland, Cleveland State University, with Joan Peterson (Mary).

A sympathetic portrayal of the Scottish queen.

BIBLIOGRAPHY: Frank Hruby, review, *MA* CXI (July 1991), 38 [on premiere].

Mary Surratt, opera in one act by Gerald Muller; libretto (Eng) by the composer. First performance October 28, 1989, Fort Washington, Maryland, Harmony Hall, with Jennifer Muller (Mary) and Eugene Galvin (Booth).

A treatment of the story of Mary Surratt, who was convicted and hanged for her supposed involvement in the plot to kill Abraham Lincoln. The opera covers events taking place on the day of the assassination, in which Booth and his friends visit Mary's boardinghouse.

Major roles: Mary Surratt (sop) and John Booth (bar).

BIBLIOGRAPHY: Jeanne Spaeth, review, *Washington Post* (Oct. 30, 1989), B, 10 [on premiere].

Masaniello, or, The Dumb Girl of Portici, adaptation by Thomas S. Cooke and Barham Livius, of Auber's *La muette de Portici* (1828, Paris); libretto (Eng) by James Kenney, after the text of Scribe and Delavigne. First performance May 4, 1829, London, Drury Lane Theatre.

The setting is Portici and Naples in 1647. Discovering that his sister Fenella has been seduced by Alfonso, son of the Duke of Arcos, Masaniello, a fisherman, vows revenge. Princess Elvira, who has wed Alfonso, rejects him when she finds out what he has done. Masaniello leads a rebellion of the peasants of Portici, but when the revolt gets out of hand, he helps Elvira and Alfonso escape. The Duke mounts a counterattack against the rebels, and Masaniello is killed trying to aid Elvira. Asking Elvira to forgive Alfonso for his past actions, Fenella kills herself as Mount Vesuvius erupts.

The story was also set by M. Carafa (1827, Paris), S. Pavesi (1831), and J. Napoli (1953, Milan). See the previous entry for another version.

LIBRETTO: English (London: E. Moxon, 1831).

Masaniello, the Fisherman of Naples, opera in five acts by Henry Rowley Bishop; libretto (Eng) by George Soane, after the play of Henry M. Milner (1824). First performance February 17, 1825, London, Drury Lane Theatre.

Cooke's adaptation (preceding entry) is another version of the story.

LIBRETTO: English (London: J. Miller, 1825).

Mask of Evil, The, opera in one act by Henry Mollicone; libretto (Eng) by Kate Pogue. First performance April 30, 1982, Minneapolis, Minnesota Opera.

SCORE: vs, holograph, 1982 (NYPL, photocopy).

Mask of Orpheus, The, lyric tragedy in three acts by Harrison Birtwistle; libretto (Eng) by Peter Zinovieff. First performance May 21, 1986, London, English National Opera, with Philip Langridge, Nigel Robson, Jean Rigby, Ethna Robinson, Tom McDonnell, Rodney Macann, Marie Angel, and Richard Angas; conducted by Elgar Howarth and Paul Daniel.

Each of the three acts looks at one aspect of the Orpheus and Euridice story, and each of the three major characters is portrayed by three performers representing the various sides of the role.

For detailed descriptions, see *K/KOB*, 1249–54; *K/NKOB*, 67–71.

Major roles: Orpheus: the man, the hero, the myth/Hades (ten, mime, ten); Euridice: the woman, the hero, the myth/Persephone (mezzo, mime); and Aristaeus: the man, the hero, the myth/Charon (bass-bar/mime).

The score includes sections of electronic music.

SCORE: vs, fs (Vienna: Universal Edition, 1984?).

LIBRETTO: English, the same.

Mason of Buda, The, nautical burletta in two acts by George Rodwell; libretto (Eng) by James R. Planché, after Scribe's setting for Auber's *Le maçon* (1825). First performance October 1, 1828, London, Adelphi Theatre.
LIBRETTO: English (London: J. Cumberland, [1828]).

Masque of Angels, The, opera in one act by Dominick Argento; libretto (Eng) by John Olon-Scrymgeour. First performance January 9, 1964, Minneapolis, Tyrone Guthrie Theater, Center Opera Company; conducted by Thomas Nee.

The setting is a present-day church. Several angels have come to inspect the goings-on, and they attempt to help out with a romance between a young couple, Ann and John. The head angel, Metatron, is concerned about the reduced number of dancers, and an embittered Spinster and frustrated old Professor offer advice to the young people. The mission is successful when John and Ann kiss, and the group prepares for its next assignment, helping the marriages of heads of state.

Major roles: Metatron (bar); Sandolfon, his aide-de-camp (ten); Sadriel, company clerk (ten); Jeremiel, an angel (ten); Raguel, another angel (bar); John, a young man (ten); Ann, a young woman (sop); the Spinster (mezzo); and the Professor (bass).

For a detailed description, see Eaton/*OP* II, 301–2.
SCORE: vs (New York: Boosey & Hawkes, 1964?).
BIBLIOGRAPHY: "Twin Cities Critics Praise New Opera," *NYT* (Jan. 11, 1964), 15 [on premiere].

Masque of Clouds, The, opera in three acts by Tom Johnson; libretto (Eng) by the composer and Robert Kushner. First performance October 10, 1975, New York, the Kitchen.

Major roles: the Sun (ten), the Lake (mezzo), the Forest (bar), and the Clouds (2 col sop).

The work is a masque in the Baroque style.
BIBLIOGRAPHY: Tom Johnson, "At Home Abroad," *ON* LIX (Oct. 1994), 34–35.

Masque of Pandora, The, grand opera by Alfred Cellier; libretto (Eng) by B. C. Stephenson, after Longfellow. First performance January 10, 1881, Boston, Boston Theatre, Blanche Roosevelt English Opera Company.
LIBRETTO: English (Boston: Houghton Mifflin, 1881).

Masque of Pandora, The, opera in one act by Eleanor Everest Freer; libretto (Eng) by the composer, after Longfellow. First performance (concert) October 24, 1933, Chicago.
Also presented as a masque, with music by Alfred Cellier (1881).

Masque of War and Peace, The, opera by Hamish MacCunn; libretto (Eng) by Louis Napoleon Parker. First performance February 13, 1900, London, Her Majesty's.
SCORE: vs (London: Chappell & Co., Ltd., 1900).

Massimilliano, the Court Jester, or, The Love of a Caliban, romantic opera in one act by Eleanor Everest Freer; libretto (Eng) by Elia W. Peattie. First performance January 19, 1926, Lincoln, Nebraska, with Arthur Seymour (Lord Pietro), Charles Cline (Lord Ascanio), John Becker (Massimilliano), Alberta Morris (Lady Lucrezia), and Marie McCormick (Lady Margherita); conducted by Clarence Bawden.

The setting is Venice in the fifteenth century. Massimilliano, the court jester, secretly loves the noble Lady Lucrezia, daughter of Pietro, a doge. Because she is attracted to the voice of a Venetian gondolier, really Massimilliano in disguise, who serenades her each night, she puts off Lord Ascanio's request for marriage, saying she will give her decision at a birthday celebration. When she asks that the person who has serenaded her so

beautifully reveal his identity, she is horrified when it turns out to be Massimilliano. Seeing her look of loathing after he kisses her, Massimilliano stabs himself.
SCORE: vs (n.p., n.d.; LCCN: 85-61617).

Master Valiant, opera in three acts by Martin Shaw; libretto (Eng) by Barclay Baron. First performance June 1936, London, Crystal Palace.

Matched and Mated, opera in one act by Thomas German Reed; libretto (Eng) by F. C. Burnand. First performance November 6, 1876, London, St. George's Hall.

Match for a Widow, A, or, The Frolics of Fancy, comic opera in three acts by Charles Dibdin; libretto (Eng) by Joseph Atkinson, after Joseph Patrat's *L'heureuse erreur.* First performance 1788, London.
LIBRETTO: English (London: C. Dilly et al., 1788).

Mathew in the School of Life, "sci-fi techno-opera" by John Moran; libretto (Eng). First performance October 7, 1994, New York, Ridge Theater, the Kitchen.
   The plot unfolds on a distant space station, sometime in the future and involves Mathew, an android who is given human feelings and knowledge over the span of four days, from Maundy Thursday to Easter Sunday, à la Parsifal but in a much lighter and tongue-in-cheek vein.
BIBLIOGRAPHY: Bernard Holland, "An Opera for Soloists Who Click and Whir," *NYT* (Oct. 7, 1994), C, 27 [on premiere]; Stephen Holden, "It Ain't Over Till the Robot Lip-Synchs," *NYT* (Oct. 6, 1995), C, 30.

Matilda of Hungary, opera in three acts by Vincent Wallace; libretto (Eng) by Alfred Bunn. First performance February 22, 1847, London, Drury Lane Theatre, with Mr. Borrani (Count Magnus) and Miss Romer (Matilda).
   Matilda, the Hungarian queen, is admired by the power-seeking Count Magnus.
   The work, which contains Italian elements, is considered one of Wallace's weaker ventures (see Biddlecombe/*EO*, 31, 133, and passim).
LIBRETTO: English (London: Cramer, Beale, [1847?]).

Matinee Idyll, A, opera in one act by Hamilton Forrest; libretto (Eng) by the composer. First performance August 17, 1954, Interlochen, Michigan.

Matrimony, petite opera in two acts, an adaptation by Matthew Peter King of Dalayrac's *Adolphe et Clara, ou, Les deux prisonniers* (1799, Paris), "the overture and music, entirely new"; libretto (Eng) by James Kenney, after Marsollier's text. First performance November 20, 1804, London, Drury Lane Theatre, with Mr. Dowton (Baron de Limburg), Mr. Elliston (Delaval), John Johnstone (O'Cloghorty), and Dorothy Jordan (Clara). First U.S. performance May 17, 1805, New York, Park Theatre, in an arrangement by James Hewitt, as *The Honey Moon.**
LIBRETTO: English (London: Longman et al., 1804; New York: Longworth, 1805).

Maureen O'Mara, opera in three acts by Cyril Scott; libretto (Eng) by the composer. Composed 1946.

Mayakovsky and the Sun, opera by Melanie Daiken; libretto (Eng), after Vladimir Mayakovsky. First performance September 1, 1971, Edinburgh Festival, Music Theatre Ensemble; conducted by Alexander Goehr.
BIBLIOGRAPHY: review, *World Music* XIII/3 (1971), 85 [on premiere].

May Day, or, The Little Gipsy, operatic afterpiece in one act by Thomas Arne; libretto (Eng) by David Garrick. First performance October 28, 1775, London, Drury Lane Theatre, with Harriet Abrams.

The setting is a village green. The title character tells fortunes to the villagers; she herself is, in fact, a resident of the town who is unable to marry William, her beloved, because of her father's disapproval. In the end, however, she has her way.
LIBRETTO: English (London: T. Becket, 1775).

May Day in Town, or, New-York in an Uproar, comic opera in two acts "with music compiled from the most eminent Masters"; libretto (Eng) by Royall Tyler. First performance May 19, 1787, New York, James Street Theatre, Old American Company.

The work was performed only once.

Mayerling, tragic opera in three acts by Henry Rauscher Humphreys; libretto (Eng) by the composer. First performance November 16, 1957, Cincinnati, Conservatory of Music, with Carolyn Goodbar, Miriam Broderick, John Lankston, and John Vian; conducted by William Byrd; produced by Wilfred Engleman.

The story concerns the doomed affair between Archduke Rudolf, the crown prince of Austria, and his mistress.

Also opera by Kurt List (not perf.).
SCORE: vs (Cincinnati: Willis Music, [1959]).

Mayor of Casterbridge, The, opera in three acts by Peter Tranchell; libretto (Eng) by the composer and Peter Bentley, after the novel (1886) by Thomas Hardy. First performance July 30, 1951, Cambridge, England, Arts Theatre.

The plot is a compression of Hardy's story.

Maypole, The, opera in one act by Arnold Franchetti; libretto (Eng) by E. R. Mills. First performance July 6, 1952, Westport, Connecticut, White Barn.

Part 2 of a trilogy about war that includes *The Princess** (1952) and *The Game of Cards** (1955).

McTeague, opera in two acts by William Bolcom; libretto (Eng) by Arnold Weinstein and Robert Altman, after the novel of the same name by Frank Norris (1900). First performance November 3, 1992, Chicago, Lyric Opera, with Catherine Malfitano (Trina Sieppe), Ben Heppner (McTeague), Timothy Nolen (Marcus Schouler), and Emily Golden (Maria Macapa); conducted by Dennis Russell Davies; designed by Yuri Kuper.

The work is set in 1899 in San Francisco. It concerns a self-taught dentist who rises to the top socially, only to lose everything; his wife, Trina, who is obsessed with gold; his friend Marcus Schouler, who is obsessed with Trina and therefore betrays his friend; and the immigrant servant Maria Macapa. McTeague recalls his happier existence via hallucinatory flashbacks, as he spends his last hours in Death Valley.

Major roles: McTeague (heldenten); Trina Sieppe, his wife (sop); Marcus Schouler, McTeague's best friend (bar); and Maria Macapa, a cleaning woman.
SCORE: vs (Milwaukee: E. B. Marks, 1992, 1995).
BIBLIOGRAPHY: *ON* LVII (Nov. 1992): Nancy Malitz, "Synthesizer," 14–16, 30; Carrie Rickey, "Tarnishing the Gilded Age: Robert Altman Directs *McTeague,*" 18, 20, 22; Donald Pizer, "Fool's Gold," 24–25; Edward Rothstein, "'McTeague' Just Wants to Be Loved," *NYT* (Nov. 1992), II, 25 [on premiere]; John von Rhein, "Chicago," *ON* LVII (Feb. 27, 1993), 37–38 [on premiere].

Meal, The, opera in one act by Violet Archer; libretto (Eng) by Rowland Holt Wilson. First performance October 19, 1985, Edmonton, Alberta, Citadel Theatre, with Larry Benson and John Mitchell; conducted by William Shookhoff.

Meanwhile, Back at Cinderella's, comic opera in four scenes by Denis Arlan; libretto (Eng) by James Billings. First performance New York, May 5, 1976, New York Lyric Opera.

In a spoof of the Cinderella story, it is Cinderella, here presented as ugly and nasty, who refuses her family's request to go to the ball until threatened by her godfather. When she meets the Prince, also a disgusting character, the two find that they have a lot in common. Cinderella leaves the ball without her shoes, because they hurt. The sisters also leave their shoes at the ball so that their suitors will bring them to the girls at home. The suitors ask for the sisters' hands in marriage, and the Prince, though late, comes to claim Cinderella for his wife.

For a detailed description, see Kornick/*RAO*, 34–36.

Major roles: narrator (mezzo); Cinderella Nabgratz (mezzo); Harold, the herald (ten); Prince Dimmly (ten); Filbert Nabgratz, father of Cinderella (bass); Ariadne and Daphne Nabgratz, Cinderella's stepsisters (sop); Fairy Godfather (bar).

SCORE: ms vs (New York: American Music Center, 1971).

BIBLIOGRAPHY: Raymond Ericson, "Opera: Cinderella Spoof," *NYT* (May 15, 1976), 15 [on premiere].

Medea, opera in one act by Jonathan Elkus; libretto (Eng) by the composer, after Euripides. First performance November 13, 1970, Milwaukee, University of Wisconsin, Opera Theater.

Medea, opera in two acts by Alva Henderson; libretto (Eng) by the composer, after Robinson Jeffers's adaptation of Euripides' tragedy. First performance November 29, 1972, San Diego, San Diego Opera, with Irene Dalis (Medea), Glade Peterson (Jason), and Samuel Van Dusen (Creon); conducted by Walter Herbert; directed by Gita Hager.

Jason has returned to Corinth with the coveted Golden Fleece, and as a reward Creon grants him the hand of his daughter; Jason thus abandons Medea, who has borne him two sons and helped him get the Golden Fleece. In revenge Medea sends the Nurse with the two sons and bridal gifts to Jason's new wife, a golden wreath and veil that turn to fire when the wife puts them on, killing her and consuming Creon's palace. Although the children escape, Medea kills them with her own hands and gives their corpses to Jason. He tries to kill her in vain and returns to his ship, which has started to rot.

Major roles: Medea (mezzo), Jason (ten), Creon (bass), and the Nurse (mezzo).

For a detailed description, see Kornick/*RAO*, 142–43.

The title character is onstage during the entire opera.

Medea, opera in two acts by Ray Luke; libretto (Eng) by Carveth Osterhaus, after Euripides. First performance May 3, 1979, Boston.

Medea, opera in three acts by Gavin Bryars; libretto (Eng, Fr, and Greek) by Robert Wilson, after Euripides. First performance (in French) October 23, 1984, Lyons, Opéra, with Yvonne Kenny (Medea) and Louis Otey (Jason).

Major roles: Medea (sop) and Jason (bar).

The composer uses tuned percussion, oboes, and saxophones instead of violins.

BIBLIOGRAPHY: Charles Pitt, review, *HiFi/MA* XXXV (Aug. 1985), 31 [on premiere].

Medea, opera in one act by Felix Werder; libretto (Eng) by the composer, after Euripides. First performance September 17, 1985, Melbourne, Australia, College of Advanced Education.

Medea in Corinth, musical drama in one act by Benjamin Lees; libretto (Eng), after Jeffers's adaptation of Euripides. First performance January 10, 1971, London. First U.S. performance May 1974, CBS.

In this setting of the story, Medea and her sons have been banished so that Jason can wed the daughter of King Creon of Corinth. In revenge Medea sends the new bride a poisoned robe; Medea then kills her own children, fathered by Jason.

Major roles: Medea (mezzo), Creon (bass-bar/bass), and Jason (bar).

The work is scored for soloists, wind quintet, and timpani.

Among the other settings of the Medea story are Cavalli's *Giasone* (1649, Venice); A. Gianettini's *Medea in Atene* (1675, Venice); J. S. Kusser's *Jason* (1692, Brunswick); M.-A. Charpentier's *Médée* (1693, Paris); J.-F. Salomon's *Médée et Jason* (1713, Paris); J. C. Smith's *Medea* (1761, not perf.); Cherubini's *Médée* (1797, Paris); J. S. Mayr's *Medea in Corinto* (1813, Naples); G. Pacini's *Medea* (1843, Palermo); Milhaud's *Médée* (1939, Antwerp); and B. A. Zimmermann's *Medea* (1970, not completed).

SCORE: vs (New York: Boosey & Hawkes, 1985).

Medium, The, tragedy in two acts by Gian Carlo Menotti; libretto (Eng) by the composer. First performance May 8, 1946, New York, Columbia University, Brander Matthews Theater, with Evelyn Keller (Monica), Claramae Turner (Madame Flora), Leo Coleman (Toby), Beverly Dame (Mrs. Gobineau), Jacques La Rochelle (Mr. Gobineau), and Virginia Beeler (Mrs. Nolan); conducted by Otto Luening. First British performance April 29, 1948, London, Aldwych Theatre. Revised February 18, 1947, New York, Heckscher Theater, with Evelyn Keller (Monica), Marie Powers (Madame Flora), Leo Coleman (Toby), Beverly Dame (Mrs. Gobineau), Paul Kwartin (Mr. Gobineau), and Virginia Beeler (Mrs. Nolan); conducted by Jacques Barzun. The production moved to the Ethel Barrymore Theatre on May 1, 1947, with the same cast for the revision, except Frank Rogier as Mr. Gobineau and Emmanuel Balaban as the conductor.

Madame Flora, a medium, with the help of her daughter, Monica, and Toby, a mute servant, tries to cheat her clients through faked seances. She is touched herself by a hand during one of the sessions, a happening that she cannot explain. Driven to desperation by this turn of events, she shoots at a figure hiding in a booth. It is Tony, who, terrified, has hidden himself, and he dies as she asks him if he was the presence she sensed during the seance.

For detailed plot synopses, see K/*KOB,* 1343–45; K/*NKOB,* 456–57.

Roles: Monica, daughter of Madame Flora (sop); Toby (silent); Madame Flora (alto); Mrs. Gobineau (sop); Mr. Gobineau (bar); and Mrs. Nolan (mezzo).

The opera's highlights includes "At Last the Hour Has Come," sung by Baba, "The Black Swan," and "Monica's Waltz."

SCORE: vs, fs (New York: G. Schirmer, [1947], 1978).

LIBRETTO: English (New York: G. Schirmer, 1967).

DISCOGRAPHY: Keller, Cotlow, Powers, Dame, Mastice, Rogier; cond. Balaban, Columbia SL154 (1 LP); Resnik, Blegen, Derr, Carlson, Patrick, Opera Soc. of Washington; cond. Mester, Columbia MS-7387 (1 LP); Bedi, Ragains, Castle, Landin, Van DeGraff; cond. Rapchak, Chicago Opera Theater Orch., Cedille 034 (1 CD).

VIDEO: M. Powers, A. M. Alberghetti, L. Coleman, B. Dame, B. Kibler, D. Morgan, Symphony Orch. of Rome Radio Italiana; cond. T. Schippers, VAI-OP-4 Video Arts International (1984, New York).

Medium, The, monodrama for mezzo-soprano by Peter Maxwell Davies; libretto (Eng) by the composer. First performance June 21, 1981, Stromness, Kirkwall, Scotland. SCORE: vs (London and New York: Boosey & Hawkes, 1981, 1983).

Melita, opera in one act by Charles Camilleri; libretto (Eng) by Ursula Vaughan Williams, after a Maltese folk legend. First performance November 28, 1968, Belfast, Aquinas Hall.
  The story concerns Melita, who is unhappy at the prospect of marrying a stranger. The situation changes with the help of a magical golden ring.

Mellstock Quire, The, opera in one act by Edward Harper; libretto (Eng) by R. Savage, after Thomas Hardy's *Under the Greenwood Tree* (1872). First performance February 10, 1988, Edinburgh, George Square Theatre.
  The story concerns the pretty schoolmistress Fancy Day; she is pursued by various suitors, including Dick Dewy, who, along with his father, has been ousted from his position as a musician at the church because of the new organ.

Menaced Assassin, The, opera by Jeremy Peyton Jones; libretto (Eng), after Edgar Allan Poe. First performance May 1989, London, Donmar Warehouse Theatre.

Menna, opera in three acts by Arwel Hughes; libretto (Eng) by Wyn Griffith, after an old Welsh legend. First performance November 9, 1953, Cardiff, Wales, Sophia Gardens, Welsh National Opera, with Richard Lewis (Gwyn), Roderick Jones (Ivan), Patti Lewis (Gaynor), Elsie Morison (Menna), Phyllis Ash-Child (Atys), and Clifford Bunford (groomsman); conducted by the composer; produced by Anthony Besch; designed by Rosemary Vercoe.
  An engaged couple, Gwyn and Menna, defy fate and carve their names on a dead tree the day before they are to be wed. The old crone Atys curses the village because she has not been invited to attend the nuptials. In accordance with custom, Menna hides, to be found by the groomsman for the ceremony. Unfortunately, she disappears permanently. Many years later Gwyn, who has become mad, still waits by the tree for his beloved. When lightning strikes the tree, it shows Menna's wedding dress. Gwyn, throwing himself on the gown, expires.

Men of Blackmoor, The, opera in six scenes by Alan Bush; libretto (Eng) by Nancy Bush. First performance November 18, 1956, Weimar, in a German translation by Marianne Graefe, as *Die Männer von Blackmoor*.
SCORE: vs (London, J. Williams, [1959]).
LIBRETTO: English (London: J. Williams, [1959]).

Mephistopheles, or, Faust and Marguerite, romantic opera in three acts by Meyer Lutz; libretto (Eng) by Henri Drayton, after Goethe. First performance May 16, 1855, Surrey, England.
  See *Faust* for other settings.
LIBRETTO: English (London: J. K. Chapman, 1855).

Merchant of Venice, The, masque in four acts by Adrian Welles Beecham; libretto (Eng) by the composer (?), after Shakespeare's play. First performance September 18, 1922, Brighton, England, Grand Theatre.

La Violette's *Shylock** (1930, Chicago) is another English setting of the play.

Mer de Glace, opera in a prologue and seven scenes by Richard Meale; libretto (Eng) by David Malouf. First performance October 3, 1991, Sydney, Australia.
DISCOGRAPHY: excerpts, ABC 446 477-2.

Mermaid, The, opera in three acts by Margaret More; libretto (Eng) by Claudine Currey, after the story *The Little Mermaid* by Hans Christian Andersen; September 4, 1951, Birmingham, England, Moseley Institute.

Mermaid in Lock No. 7, The, opera in one act by Elie Siegmeister; libretto (Eng) by Edward Mabley. First performance July 20, 1958, Pittsburgh, Point State Park.

A young sailor, Jack, son of Cap'n Swabby, who tends to the lock, is saved by Liz, a mermaid, who falls in love with him. He deserts her for the singer Monongahela Sal. Cap'n Swabby meets the mermaid, who has come to look for his son. Despite his misgivings, the father sends Liz to the nightclub. When Sal turns the crowd against the stranger, the mermaid convinces Jack to go back with her to the water.

For a detailed description, see Eaton/*OP* II, 302–3.

Roles: Cap'n Swabby (bass-bar), Bonny Jack (lyr bar), Liz (lyr sop), and Monongahela Sal (alto).
SCORE: vs (New York: C. F. Peters, 1958).

Merrie England, light opera in two acts by Edward German; libretto (Eng) by Basil Hood. First performance April 2, 1902, London, Savoy Theatre. First U.S. performance (concert) April 13, 1956, New York, Hunter College. Revived August 10, 1960, London, Sadler's Wells, with Anna Pollak (Queen Elizabeth), John Carolan (Raleigh), John Hargreaves (Essex), and Joan Stuart (Bessie Throckmorton); conducted by James Robertson.

The story concerns the rivalry between the Earl of Essex and Sir Walter Raleigh to win favor of Queen Elizabeth I. When the Queen finds out that Raleigh is really in love with Bessie Throckmorton, she tries to have her rival killed, but the scheme goes awry because of Essex's machinations.

Major roles: Queen Elizabeth I (alto), Sir Walter Raleigh (ten), Bessie Throckmorton (sop), and the Earl of Essex (bar).

Among the musical highlights are the ballads "The English Rose," "O Peaceful England," and "The Yeomen of England."
BIBLIOGRAPHY: William S. Mann, "Sadler's Wells," *Opera* XI (Sept. 1960), 645–47 [on 1960 revival].
DISCOGRAPHY: McAlpine, Bronhill, Glossop, Sinclair, Kern, Williams Singers and Orch.; cond. M. Collins, Chant du Monde (2 CDs).

Merry Benedicts, The, comic opera by Maurice Arnold; libretto (Eng). First performance 1896, Brooklyn, New York.

Merry Cobler, The, ballad opera in one act; libretto (Eng) by Charles Coffey. First performance May 6, 1735, London, Drury Lane Theatre, with Mr. Salway (Sir John Loverule), Mr. Harper (Jobson), Mrs. Pritchard (Lady Loverule), Miss Oats (Lucy), and Mrs. Clive (Nell).

The work, set in a country village, was a sequel to *The Devil to Pay** (1731, London).

LIBRETTO: English (London, 1735); repr. Rubsamen/*BO*, vol. 10, *Farce: Magical Transformation and Necromancy* (1974).

Merry Duchess, The, "sporting comic opera" in two acts by Frederic Clay; libretto (Eng) by George R. Sims. First performance April 23, 1883, London, Royalty. First U.S. performance September 1883, New York, Standard, with John Nash (the jockey), Selina Dolaro (the Duchess), and Henry E. Dixey (Brabazon Sykes).

The plot concerns a jockey who courts and wins the heart of the Duchess of Epson Downs, after the villain, Brabazon Sykes, fails to poison her horse.

LIBRETTO: English (London: Chappell, [188?]; New York: J. J. Little, [1883?]).

Merry Freaks in Troublous Times, comic opera in two acts by Isaac Nathan; libretto (Eng) by Charles Nagel. First performance (excerpts) May 29, 1843, Sydney, Australia, Royal Hotel.

This was the first original opera composed in Australia; Nathan's *Don John** (1847) has the claim as the first opera composed and given a complete performance in Australia.

SCORE: vs, overture, pts, holograph (photocopy, National Library of Australia, [1843–44?]).

Merry Gardner, The, comic opera in two acts by Victor Pelissier; libretto (Eng) by William Dunlap, after a French text. First performance February 3, 1801, New York, Park Theatre.

Among the numbers is "At First How Humble."

Merry Monarch, The, comic opera in three acts, an adaptation by John Philip Sousa of E. Chabrier's *L'étoile* (1877, Paris); libretto (Eng) by John Cheever Goodwin and Woolson Morse of the text by Leterrier and Vanloo. First performance August 18, 1890, New York, Broadway Theatre, with Francis Wilson (King Anso IV), Marie Jansen (Lazuli), and Charles Plunkett (Sirocco). Performed in London as *The Lucky Star** (1899, London).

King Anso IV needs an annual human sacrifice, so he chooses the street vendor Lazuli. Complications arise when the monarch's astrologer Sirocco reveals that the horoscopes of both the king and the would-be sacrifice are so closely linked that the death of one will cause the demise of the other. The king and his advisers then try to keep Lazuli alive, for obvious reasons.

LIBRETTO: English (New York: T. B. Harms, 1890).

Merrymount, opera in two acts by David Stanley Smith; libretto (Eng) by Lee Wilson Dodd, after Hawthorne's tale *The Maypole of Merry Mount*. Composed 1912–1913.

The setting is Merrymount, Massachusetts, at the time of the Puritans. Alain de Rouzie, a member of the settlement, is in love with Rachel Palfrey, daughter of the strict governor of Plymouth, who considers the settlement blasphemous. Because of the father's disapproval, the two seek shelter in Merry Mount, where they are welcomed by Sir Thomas Morton. They are imprisoned after the witch Goody Price and Rachel's Puritan lover stir up the populace against them. A sympathetic woman frees the couple, but they are captured by the governor of Plymouth and his men. Alain is banished to France, thus separating the lovers forever.

Merry Mount, opera in two acts by Howard Hanson; libretto (Eng) by Richard L. Stokes, after Hawthorne. First performance (concert) May 20, 1933, Ann Arbor, Michigan. First performance (stage) February 10, 1934, New York, Metropolitan Opera, with Lawrence Tibbett (Bradford), Gladys Swarthout (Plentiful Tewke), Arthur Anderson (Elder Tewke), Marek Windheim (Jack Prence), Göta Ljungberg (Lady Marigold/

Astoreth), Louis D'Angelo (Thomas Morton), and Edward Johnson (Sir Gower Lackland/Lucifer). Revived 1964, San Antonio, with Beverly Sills (Lady Marigold) and Brian Sullivan (Bradford).

Set in a Puritan enclave, near present-day Quincy, Massachusetts, 1630, the story concerns Wrestling Bradford, a Puritan pastor, and the rival Cavaliers. Bradford has rejected the hand of Plentiful Tewke, daughter of another Puritan, Elder Tewke. When Prence is whipped for joining the revelries of the Cavaliers, Lady Marigold and her party arrive, and she stops the punishment. Bradford is immediately attracted to her, only to become enraged after he discovers that she is engaged to Sir Gower Lackland. Bradford leads a band of Puritans, who destroy the Cavalier stronghold, Merry Mount.

When Bradford orders Marigold's release after she is captured, he attempts to embrace her, whereupon her husband tries to free her and is killed. Marigold is kept confined to prevent her from telling other English colonists what has happened. Bradford, chided for abandoning Plentiful Tewke, seeks refuge in sleep; he dreams that Gower is Lucifer and Marigold is Astoreth. In order to possess her, he agrees to curse New England and sign Lucifer's book, thereby getting the mark of Satan on his forehead. After he awakes, Bradford recounts his dreams to Plentiful Tewke, and they go back to the Puritan village, which has been destroyed by an Indian attack. When Bradford tells the others of his dreams, Marigold is condemned as a witch and sentenced to be burned. Revealing that he has the sign of the devil on his forehead, Bradford grabs Marigold and pulls her into the burning church, which had been set afire during the Indian attack.

For a detailed description, see Hipsher/*AO*, 241–44.

Major roles: Wrestling Bradford (bar); Lady Marigold Sandys/Astoreth (sop); Thomas Morton, her uncle (bar); Sir Gower Lackland/Lucifer (ten); Plentiful Tewke (mezzo); Elder Tewke, her father (bass); and Jack Prence, a mountebank (ten).
SCORE: vs (New York: Harms, 1933).

Merry Wives of Windsor, The, comic opera by Charles Edward Horn, with J. Parry, S. Webbe, et al.; libretto (Eng) by Frederick Reynolds, after Shakespeare's play. First performance February 20, 1824, London, Drury Lane Theatre.

Metamenagerie, "department store window opera" by Robert Moran; text (Eng). Composed 1974.

Metamorphoses, afterpiece in two acts by Charles Dibdin; libretto (Eng) by the composer, after Molière's *Le sicilien* and *George Dandin*. First performance August 26, 1776, London, Little Theatre in the Haymarket.

Metamorphosis, opera by William Jackson; libretto (Eng) by the composer, with lyrics by Richard Tickell. First performance December 5, 1783, London, Drury Lane Theatre, with Elizabeth Wrighten and Anna Phillips.

Metamorphosis, opera in three acts by Michael White; libretto (Eng) by Milton Goldberg, after Franz Kafka's story. First performance May 3, 1968, Philadelphia, Theater of the Living Arts, Civic Center; conducted by Maurice Kaplow.

The story is that of Gregor's change from a man into an insect. In the first act his family complains about him except for his sister, Grete, who has sympathy for his plight. The second act is about the trouble Gregor's condition for his family. It includes Grete's "For Whom Do the Bells Toll." In the third act, when the lodgers threaten to move out if nothing is done about Gregor, his family lets him starve to death. The family mourns him with a dance to a requiem, and the opera concludes with the charwoman disposing of Gregor's remains, which have been placed in a trash can.

Each act is preceded by an electronic preface. There are six main characters.

The work, for chamber ensemble, employs the techniques of Sprechstimme and musical elements ranging from jazz and serialism to Lutheran chorales and electronic music.
BIBLIOGRAPHY: Donald Chittum, "Current Chronicle: Philadelphia," *MQ* LV (1969), 91–95 [musical analysis]; Allen Hughes, review, *NYT* (May 5, 1968), 84 [on premiere].

Metamorphosis, opera in two acts by Brian Howard; libretto (Eng) by Steven Berkoff and the composer, after Kafka. First performance September 30, 1983, Melbourne.

Metamorphosis, opera by Thomas Beversdorf; libretto (Eng), after Kafka. Composed 1968.

Metamorphosis of the Beggar's Opera, The, ballad opera; libretto (Eng). First performance March 11, 1730, London, Little Theatre in the Haymarket.

In this parody of *The Beggar's Opera*,* the performing parts are reversed, with the male parts played by women and the female parts by men.

Midas, "new burletta" in three acts, consisting of popular tunes; libretto (Eng) by Kane O'Hara. First performance January 22, 1762, Dublin, Crow Street Theatre; two acts, February 22, 1764, London, Covent Garden, as an "English burletta." First American performance November 24, 1769, Philadelphia, Southwark Theatre.

In the story Apollo, exiled from Olympus, dons the disguise of Pol, a shepherd. Midas organizes a singing contest between Pol and Pan for the hand of Nysa, and when he makes Pan the winner, Pol sheds his disguise and puts asses' ears on the unfortunate Midas.

For an analysis, see Fiske/*ETM*, 318–21.

A parody of Italian opera seria, it also made fun of the masque.
LIBRETTOS: English, ms (National Library of Ireland, Dublin, MSS. 92449, 9250); English (Dublin, 1762; London: G. Kearsley et al., 1764); repr. eds. Rubsamen/*BO*, vol. 23, *Irish Ballad Operas and Burlesques II* (1974); two-act version (London: W. Griffin, 1766), repr. ed. P. T. Dircks (New York: AMS Press, 1992).

Midnight Angel, The, opera in two acts by David Carlson; libretto (Eng) by Peter Beagle, after O. Henry's short story. First performance June 1, 1993, St. Louis, Opera Theatre, with Elaine Bonazzi (Lady Neville), Katherine Terrell (Contessa dei Candini), Mary Margaret Sapp (Margaret Leval), Christine Abraham (Angeline/Death), James Maddalena (Capt. Richard Compson), Tracey Welborn (Henry), Brad Cresswell (John Lorimond), and John Stephens (the butler); conducted by Stewart Robertson; directed by Linda Brovsky.

The setting is Edwardian England. The conceited and bored Lady Neville invites Death to be the guest of honor at her glittering ball. Her special guest arrives at midnight in a guise that surprises all of those in attendance.
BIBLIOGRAPHY: Charles Morton, "St. Louis," *ON* LVIII (Oct. 1993), 45 [on premiere].

Midnight Duel, The, lyric radio drama in one act by Leslie Kondorossy; libretto (Eng) by the composer and Shawn Hall (Elizabeth Davis), after an anonymous story, translated by C. E. Kulin. First performance March 29, 1955, Cleveland.

In a love triangle, MacCooper is in love with Dorothy, wife of Harral, his best friend, although she is faithful to her husband. When Harral loses heavily at cards with MacCooper, the latter proposes that they play one more hand. If Harral wins, he will owe nothing. If he loses, however, Dorothy will have to go with MacCooper. When MacCooper wins, Harral refuses to honor the agreement, whereby MacCooper challenges him to a duel at midnight. The two masked figures meet and MacCooper mortally wounds his opponent. When the masks are removed, the dying person is revealed to be Dorothy, who has drugged her husband and taken his place, believing that the two friends would not carry out the duel. Dorothy expires, and the distraught MacCooper shoots himself.

For a detailed description, see Summers/*OOA*, 182–84.

Major roles: Dorothy (sop), Harral (ten), and MacCooper (bar).

Midnight Wanderers, comic opera in two acts by William Shield; libretto (Eng) by William Pearce. First performance February 25, 1793, London, Covent Garden, with Mrs. Clendining and Mrs. Martyr. First U.S. performance June 1, 1796, Philadelphia, Chestnut Street Theatre.

The setting is "the mountains of Biscay."

The overture is from Naumann's *Amphion* (1778, Stockholm), and there is also music by Grétry and Paisiello.

SCORE: parts (London: Longman & Broderip, [1793]).

LIBRETTO: English (London: T. N. Longman, 1793).

Midsummer Madness, comic opera in three acts by Cecil Armstrong Gibbs; libretto (Eng) by Clifford Bax. First performance July 3, 1924, Hammersmith, London, Lyric Theatre; conducted by Alfred Reynolds.

SCORE: vs (London: J. Curwen, 1924).

LIBRETTO: English (London: E. Benn, 1923).

Midsummer Marriage, The, opera in three acts by Michael Tippett; libretto (Eng) by the composer. First performance January 27, 1955, London, Covent Garden, with Joan Sutherland (Jenifer), Adele Leigh (Bella), Oralia Dominguez (Sosostris), Richard Lewis (Mark), John Lanigan (Jack), Otakar Kraus (King Fisher), and Frederick Dalberg (Ancient); conducted by John Pritchard; produced by Christopher West. First U.S. performance October 15, 1983, San Francisco, San Francisco Opera, with Dennis Bailey (Mark), Mary Jane Johnson (Jenifer), Raimund Herincx (King Fisher), Sheri Greenawald (Bella), Ryland Davies (Jack), Sheila Nadler (Sosostris), and Leslie Richards and Kevin Lanigan (the Ancients); conducted by David Agler.

With similarities to *Die Zauberflöte*, the plot concerns two couples, Mark and Jenifer, who seek to wed but must prove themselves worthy before getting married, and the simpler Bella and Jack. Matters for the first couple are complicated by Jenifer's businessman father, who opposes the union. Much of the action is played out against the background of an unending English midsummer, made mysterious by Sosostris, a seer, and a group of Ancients. The action is brought to a head in the second act—the Ritual Dances show in ballet the conflict between the sexes. In the end Mark and Jenifer obtain the self-knowledge to make them ready for marriage.

For detailed plot summaries, see K/*KOB*, 1136–45; K/*NKOB*, 828–32.

Major roles: Mark, a young man of unknown background (ten); Jenifer, his intended (sop); King Fisher, Jenifer's father, a businessman (bar); Bella, his secretary (sop); Jack, Bella's boyfriend (ten); and Sosostris, a clairvoyant (alto).

SCORE: vs (London: Schott, New York: Associated Music Publishers, 1954).

LIBRETTO: English, in *ENOG* 29 (1985), 25–52.

BIBLIOGRAPHY: S. von Buchau, review, *ON* XLVIII (Jan. 1984), 38 [on U.S. premiere]; *ENOG* 29: P. Driver, "A Ritual of Renewal," 19–24, J. L. Davies, "'A Visionary Night,'" 65–72; Kemp/*Tippett*, 209–77; A. Whittall, "A War and a Wedding," *ML* LV (1974), 299–306.

DISCOGRAPHY: Sutherland, Lewis, Coates, Kraus, Leigh, Lanigan, Sinclair; cond. Pritchard, Gala GL 100.524 (1955, Covent Garden, 2 CDs).

Midsummer Night's Dream, A, all-sung afterpiece with music by Charles Burney (three songs by Michael Arne); libretto (Eng) by David Garrick and George Colman Sr., after Shakespeare's play (1596). First performance November 23, 1763, London, Drury Lane Theatre, with Miss Wright. Two-act version as *The Fairy Tale.**

Midsummer Night's Dream, A, "opera," with music "composed and arranged" by Henry Rowley Bishop; libretto (Eng) by Frederick Reynolds, after Shakespeare. First performance January 17, 1816, London, Covent Garden.

The work includes borrowings from Arne, Benjamin Cooke, Stevens, Smith, and Battishill.

SCORE: fs ms (1816, British Library, Add. MS. 86944).

Midsummer Night's Dream, A, opera in three acts by Benjamin Britten; libretto (Eng) by the composer and Peter Pears, after Shakespeare. First performance June 11, 1960, Aldeburgh, with Alfred Deller (Oberon), Jennifer Vyvyan (Tytania), April Cantelo (Helena), Marjorie Thomas (Hermia), Thomas Hemsley (Demetrius), Joseph Ward (Starveling), George Maran (Lysander), Peter Pears (Flute), Owen Brannigan (Bottom), Norman Lumsden (Quince), David Kelley (Snug), Edward Byles (Snout), and Leonide Massine Jr. (Puck); conducted by the composer; produced by John Cranko; designed by John Piper and Carl Toms. First Covent Garden performance February 2, 1961, with Russell Oberlin (Oberon), Joan Carlyle (Tytania), Nicholas Chagrin (Puck), Geraint Evans (Bottom), Michael Langdon (Quince), John Lanigan (Flute), André Turp (Lysander), Joseph Ward (Starveling), Kenneth Macdonald (Snout); conducted by Georg Solti; produced by John Gielgud. First U.S. performance October 10, 1961, San Francisco, San Francisco War Memorial, with Russell Oberlin (Oberon), Mary Costa (Titania), Joy Coghill (Puck), Herbert Handt (Flute), Raymond Manton (Snout), Keith Engen (Quince), Andrew Foldi (Snug), and Geraint Evans (Bottom); conducted by Silvio Varviso; designed by Harry Horner.

The story is a close rendition of the Shakespeare original (with five acts trimmed to three and the insertion of one line, which explains that Hermia is being forced to wed Demetrius). It eliminates the first act and starts with the second, the forest at night. Oberon, quarreling with his queen, wants Puck to drug Tytania, so she will fall in love with the first being she sees when she awakes. He can thereby have the "lovely boy stolen from an Indian king" for himself. The opera ends with the reconciliation of the king and his wife.

The characters fall into three groups and are delineated by the orchestration: (1) the fairies, including Oberon, Tytania, and Puck; (2) the lovers, who include Lysander and Demetrius, both of whom desire Hermia, who loves Lysander; and Helena, who loves Demetrius; (3) the rustics, Bottom, to whom Tytania is drawn when she is put under a spell, Quince, Flute, Snug, Snout, and Starveling.

The work includes the playlet *Pyramus and Thisbe* in the third act, a parody of various devices found in Romantic opera, in which the rustics take all the parts, male, female, and nonhuman, that is, a wall. To emphasize the otherworldliness and importance of the part, Britten scores Oberon for a countertenor. The pivotal role of Puck is for an actor whose part has no singing.

For detailed plot synopses and analyses, see *K/KOB,* 1214–22; *K/NKOB,* 128–31.

Major roles: Oberon, King of the Fairies (counterten); Tytania, Queen of the Fairies (col sop); Puck (speaking role, acrobat); Theseus, Duke of Athens (bass); Demetrius (bar); Lysander (ten); Hermia (mezzo), in love with Lysander; Helena (sop), in love with Demetrius; Bottom, a weaver (bass-bar); Quince, a carpenter (bass); Flute, a bellows-maker (ten); Snug, a joiner (bass); Snout, a tinker (ten); Starveling, a tailor (bar).

See also *Fairy Queen, Pyramus and Thisbe*, and *Oberon*.

Also set by Dennis Arundell (comp. 1930).

BIBLIOGRAPHY: Mervyn Cooke, "Britten and Shakespeare," *ML* LXXIV (1993), 246–68; Alfred Frankenstein, review, *Opera* XII (Dec. 1961), 791 [on U.S. premiere]; Howard Taubman, review, *NYT* (June 13, 1960), 33 [on premiere] and "Britten's 'Dream,'" *NYT* (June 19, 1960), II, 9; John Warrack, review, *Opera* XII (Mar. 1961), 201–5 [on London premiere].

DISCOGRAPHY: E. Harwood, J. Veasey, H. Watts, A. Deller, P. Pears, J. Shirley-Quirk, London Sym. Orch. and Chorus; cond. Britten, London 42556-3 (2 CDs); S. McNair, R. Philogene, J. Watson, B. Asawa, J. M. Ainsley, P. Whelan, R. Lloyd, London Sym.; cond. C. Davis, Philips 454122 (2 CDs); rev. Sarah Bryan Miller, "Recordings," *ON* LXI (Jan. 25, 1997), 42.

VIDEO: Cotrubas, Bowman, Appelgren, Lott, Glyndebourne Festival Chorus, London Phil. Orch.; cond. Haitink, Castle VHS CV1 2008 (1981, Glyndebourne); rev. Harvey E. Phillips, "Videocassettes," *ON* LIII (July 1988), 45; Jon Alan Conrad, "Video," *ON* LX (Oct. 1995), 61.

Mighty Casey, The, "baseball opera" in three scenes by William Schuman; libretto (Eng) by Jeremy Gury. First performance May 4, 1951, Hartford, Connecticut. Revivals include July 25, 1986, Cooperstown, New York, Glimmerglass Opera Theater, with Paul Jackel (Casey), Erwin Densen (the manager), Carla Cortner (Merry), and Brian Steele (the watchman); conducted by Charles Schneider; December 12, 1990, New York, Juilliard School, with Stacey Robinson (Casey), Andrew Parks (the manager), Catherine Thorpe (Merry), and Franco Pomponi (the watchman); conducted by Gerard Schwarz.

The piece is set in Mudville, U.S.A., "not so long ago, a brilliant afternoon in early autumn." The mighty Casey comes to bat in the bottom of the ninth inning, his team about to lose unless he does something spectacular, as he has done in the past. It is not to be—the mighty Casey strikes out! His girl, Merry, and a fan come to offer comfort.

For a detailed description, see Eaton/*OP* I, 202.

Major roles: Merry (sop); Thatcher, the Centerville catcher (bar); Fireball Snedeker, the Centerville pitcher (bar); Casey (actor/dancer, in pantomime); the manager (bar); Charlie, a fan; Umpire Buttenheiser (bar); and the watchman (bar).

The text includes Ernest L. Thayer's poem *Casey at the Bat*, the closing lines of which are used for a sorrowful chorale at the end of the work. The watchman serves as narrator of the unfolding events. The cantata version (1976) is entitled *Casey at the Bat*.

SCORE: vs (New York: G. Schirmer, [1954], 1985).

BIBLIOGRAPHY: Paul Hume, review of score, *MLA Notes* XII (June 1955), 485–86; Tim Page, "Opera: Schuman's 'Mighty Casey,' Sung in the Baseball Capital," *NYT* (July 27, 1986), 39 [on 1986 revival].

DISCOGRAPHY: R. Rees, T. Bogdan, R. Muenz, Gregg Smith Singers, Adirondack Chamber Orch.; cond. Smith, Premier PRCD-1009 (1 CD); rev. C. J. Luten, "Recordings," *ON* LVI (Jan. 18, 1992), 37.

Mikado, The, or, The Town of Titipu, "Japanese" opera in two acts by Arthur S. Sullivan; libretto (Eng) by William S. Gilbert. First performance March 14, 1885, London, Savoy Theatre, with Richard Temple (the Mikado), Durward Lely (Nanki-Poo), George Grossmith (Ko-Ko), Rutland Barrington (Pooh-Bah), F. Bovill (Pish-Tush), Leonora Braham (Yum-Yum), Jessie Bond (Pitti-Sing), Sybil Grey (Peep-Bo), and Rosina Brandram (Katisha); the production ran for 672 nights. First U.S. performance July 6, 1885, Chicago, and various New York theaters in later July and August, including the superior D'Oyly Carte version on August 24, New York, Fifth Avenue Theatre, with F. Federici (the Mikado), Courtice Pounds (Nanki-Poo), F. Billington (Pooh-Bah), George Thorne (Ko-Ko), Geraldine Ulmar (Yum-Yum), and Elsie Cameron (Katisha); directed by Richard Barker; this production received 250 performances. The countless modern revivals include many by opera companies, for example, in May 1981, Chicago, Lyric Opera, directed by Peter Sellars, with Neil Rosenshein (Nanki-Poo), Michelle Harman-Gulick (Yum-Yum), Sharon Graham (Pitti-Sing), Dan Sullivan (Pish-Tush), William Wildermann (Pooh-Bah), Donald Adams (the Mikado), and John Reed (Ko-Ko); conducted by Craig Smith.

The work is set in the mythical Titipu in Japan. In order to escape the amorous advances of the elderly Katisha, Nanki-Poo, son of the Mikado, has disguised himself and roamed Japan. When he comes to Titipu, he falls in love with Yum-Yum, fiancée of Ko-Ko, the Lord High Executioner, who has his position because he has been condemned to death for flirting and cannot execute anyone before he himself is beheaded. Eventually, Nanki-Poo consents to be beheaded if he can win the hand of Yum-Yum. He is spared when Ko-Ko, Pitti-Sing, and Pooh-Bah make the emperor believe that a beheading has taken place. Ko-Ko accepts the hand of Katisha, Nanki-Poo's disappointed admirer.

Major roles: the Mikado of Japan (bass-bar); Nanki-Poo, his son (ten); Ko-Ko, Lord High Executioner of Titipu (bar); Pooh-Bah, Lord High Everything Else (bass-bar); Pish-Tush, a noble Lord (bar); Yum-Yum (sop), Pitti-Sing (mezzo), and Peep-Bo (sop), three sisters and wards of Ko-Ko; Katisha, an elderly lady in love with Nanki-Poo (alto).

Among the many brilliant numbers in this work, considered one of the greatest of all operettas, are Yum-Yum's beautiful "The Sun Whose Rays," Nanki-Poo's ballad-like "A Wand'ring Minstrel I," the duet "The Flowers That Bloom in the Spring" of Nanki-Poo and Ko-Ko, Ko-Ko's plaintive "Willow, Tit-Willow," and the sisters' trio "Three Little Maids from School." The plot capitalizes on the British fascination with Japanese artifacts. A Japanese woman was brought in before the premiere to teach the cast proper mannerisms, makeup, and fan manipulation.

For a detailed description, see Stedman/*WSG*, 223–35; Traubner/*O*, 169–76.
BIBLIOGRAPHY: Andrew Porter, review, *NY* LVII (May 30, 1981), 92-95 [on Sellars revival]; Paul Selley, "The Japanese March in 'The Mikado,'" *MT* CXXVI (1984), 454–56. VIDEO: Baron, Donkin, Str. Home Vision; M. Green, D'Oyly Carte Opera, London Sym. Orch., MIK03V 1 VHS; Revill, Collins, Flowers, J. Stewart, Ambrosian Opera Chorus; cond. McCarthy; London Sym. Orch.; cond. A. Faris, Goldcrest Films International, Opera World, VHS MIK-10V (1982 performance); rev. F. Paul Driscoll, *ON* LXII (Oct. 1997), 65.

Mikhoels the Wise, opera in two acts by Bruce Adolphe; libretto (Eng) by Mel Gordon. First performance May 8, 1982, New York, 92nd Street Y.

The work deals with the life of Solomon Mikhailovich Mikhoels, a Russian Yiddish actor.
SCORE: vs, holograph (New York: American Composers Alliance, 1981).

Mildred's Well, "a romance of the Middle Ages," opera in one act by Thomas German Reed; libretto (Eng) by F. C. Burnand. First performance May 5, 1873, London, Gallery of Illustration.

Milesian, The, comic opera in two acts by Thomas Carter; libretto (Eng) by Isaac Jackman. First performance March 20, 1777, London, Drury Lane Theatre.

The work centers on a talkative Irish sea captain.
LIBRETTO: English (London: J. Wilkie, 1777).

Miller and His Men, The, "melo-drama" in two acts by Henry Rowley Bishop; libretto (Eng) by Isaac Pocock. First performance October 21, 1813, London, Covent Garden. First U.S. performance July 4, 1814, New York, Park Theatre, with Mr. Chapman (Kelmar), Miss Booth (Claudine), Mr. Abbott (Lothair), Mr. Farley (Grindoff, later Wolf), Mrs. Egerton (Ravina), Mr. Vining (Count Frederick Friberg), and Miss Carew (Claudine).

Kelmar, an old cottager, wants his daughter Claudine to marry Grindoff, a miller, but she is in love with the young peasant Lothair. Grindoff, under the name of Wolf, heads a band of robbers and draws Lothair into his circle. When Claudine is kidnapped, Count Frederick intervenes, aided by Ravina, Grindoff's mistress, and Lothair saves Claudine by receiving the blow meant for her.

Also one-act burlesque, with music by Henry J. Byron and text by Francis Talfourd (1860, London).

SCORES: ms fs, autograph (ca. 1813, British Library, Add. MS. 27703); vs (London: Goulding et al., ca. 1815).

LIBRETTOS: English (London: Chapple, 1813; New York: David Longworth, 1818); modern ed. in *Hiss the Villain*, ed. Michael R. Booth (London: Eyre & Spottiswoode, 1964), 41–86.

Mines of Sulphur, The, opera in three acts by Richard Rodney Bennett; libretto (Eng) by Beverley Cross. First performance February 24, 1965, London, Sadler's Wells, with Frank Olegario (Braxton), Joyce Blackham (Rosalind), Gregory Dempsey (Boconnion), Gwyn Griffiths (Tovey), Harold Blackburn (Sherrin), Catherine Wilson (Jenny), Ann Howard (Leda), David Hillman (Fenney), David Bowman (Tooley), and John Fryatt (Trim); conducted by Colin Davis; produced by Colin Graham. First U.S. performance January 17, 1968, New York, Juilliard School, with Alan Ord (Braxton), Barbara Shuttleworth (Rosalind), Robert Jones (Boconnion), Muneo Okawa (Tovey), Robert Shiesley (Sherrin), Evelyn Mandac (Jenny), Janet Wagner (Leda), Michael Best (Fenney), Arthur Thompson (Tooley), and Hal Watters (Trim); conducted by Jean Morel; directed by John Houseman.

Set in the great hall of a decaying English manor house in the eighteenth century, the work concerns a play within a play. A group of gypsies murder a wealthy old man and take over his manor house. Their leader, Boconnion, invites a company of traveling players to spend the night in the house in exchange for performing a play. The play tells the story of what, in fact, has happened at the house—a wealthy man is killed by his young wife and valet. When he attempts at dawn to steal the players' wagon, lock them in the house, and kill them, he finds that Jenny, the troupe's leading lady, is sick with the plague.

The opera gets its title from Shakespeare's *Othello*, act 3, scene 3: "Dangerous conceits are in their natures poisons/ Which at first are scarce found to distaste,/ But with a little act upon the blood/ Burn like the mines of sulphur."

The dramatic score is written in a twelve-tone style and employs elements such as ostinato and a jarring horn call to emphasize the atmosphere and goings-on of the plot.

SCORE: vs ([London]: Universal Edition, [1965]).

BIBLIOGRAPHY: Noël Goodwin, "'The Mines of Sulphur.' Noël Goodwin Questions Richard Rodney Bennett," *Opera* XVI (1965), 85; Charles Osborne, review, *NYT* (Feb. 25, 1965), 24 [on premiere]; review, *NYT* (Jan. 18, 1968), 48 [on U.S. premiere]; "Taut, Fierce Plot in New Opera," *The Times* (London) (Feb. 25, 1965), 16 [on premiere].

Minette Fontaine, opera in three acts by William Grant Still; libretto (Eng) by Verna Arvey. First performance October 24, 1984, Baton Rouge, Baton Rouge Opera.

The setting is New Orleans, 1880. The diva Minette wants the wealthy planter Diron for herself, despite the fact that he is engaged to Clarice, Diron's daughter. Minette achieves her goal by enlisting the aid of the voodoo priestess Marie. When Lucien, Minette's cousin, convinces Diron that Minette has used voodoo to get him to fall in love with her, Diron suffers a stroke.

For a detailed description, see Kornick/*RAO*, 303–4.

Major roles: Minette Fontaine (sop), Diron Hachard (ten), Clarice de Noyan (sop), Lucien Fontaine (bass-bar), and Marie Laveau (alto).

Among the musical highlights are a voodoo dance and the duet of Diron and Clarice, "My Beloved."

SCORE: vs (n.p., 1959; LCCN: 84-73291).

Mink Stockings, The, opera in one act by Paul Marshall; libretto (Eng) by the composer. First performance February 12, 1961, Columbus, Ohio, Ohio State University; conducted by the composer; produced by Theron McClure.

Minna, or, The Fall from the Cliff, comic opera by Isidore de Lara; libretto (Eng) by H. S. Edwards. First performance 1866, London, Crystal Palace.

Minstrel's Return, The, or, The Sultan's Jubilee, musical interlude by Fourness Rolfe; libretto (Eng) by the composer. First performance March 22, 1855, Newcastle upon Tyne, Theatre Royal.

Minutes till Midnight, opera in three acts by Robert Ward; libretto (Eng) by the composer and Daniel Lang. First performance June 4, 1982, Miami, Greater Miami Opera, with Thomas Stewart and Evelyn Lear; conducted by Emerson Buckley.

Discouraged by the lethal power of nuclear energy, Emil, important in its development, decides not to continue working on defense projects. He is approached by Amory, who tries to convince him that the country needs cosmic energy to defend itself against hostile powers. Emil, at first working on the project, resigns when he realizes that it is too deadly, as does Chris, one of his protégés. When Chris joins the antiwar protesters, he is shot, and Emil is further distraught by news of his wife's death. Ignoring Amory's entreaties to continue with the search for the cosmic formula, Emil sends the formula to an international science journal, so that all the world's scientists and leaders will have access to it, not just one country.

Major roles: Emil (bar); Chris (ten); Julie, Emil's assistant and girlfriend of Chris (sop); Margo, Emil's wife (mezzo); and Amory (bass-bar).

For a detailed description, see Kornick/*RAO*, 321–22.

SCORE: vs (N[ew] Y[ork]: Highgate Press, 1982).

LIBRETTO: English ([New York]: Highgate Press, 1982).

BIBLIOGRAPHY: Andrew Porter, review, *NY* LVI (June 21, 1982), 106 [on premiere].

Miracle, The, television opera in one act by James Penberthy; libretto (Eng) by the composer. First performance March 28, 1964, Perth, Australia, Winthrop Hall.

Miracle of Flanders, The, television opera in one act by Louis Gruenberg; libretto (Eng), after Honoré de Balzac. Composed 1954. Not performed.

Miracle of Nemirov, The, chamber opera in one act by Faye-Ellen Silverman; libretto (Eng) by the composer, after I. L. Peretz's short story. Composed 1974.

The work is scored for singers, instruments, and tape, which is based on a traditional Talmudic reciting formula.

Miranda and the Dark Young Man, opera in one act by Elie Siegmeister; libretto (Eng) by Edward Eager. First performance May 9, 1956, Hartford, Connecticut.; conducted by Moshe Paranov.

In order to aid the young Miranda against her overprotective father, Aunt Nan concocts a plan. She feeds the father made-up tales of Miranda's meeting with the mysterious, dark young man who comes by the house daily. The until-now innocent young man, confronted by the father's accusations, decides to meet the willing lady and make some of the accusations true.

For a detailed description, see Eaton/*OP* I, 202–3.

Roles: Miranda (sop), her father (bass-bar), Aunt Nan (mezzo), the dark young man (bar/ten), and the fair young man/middle-aged man (nonspeaking).

BIBLIOGRAPHY: Ross Parmenter, review, *NYT* (May 10, 1956), 27 [on premiere].

Mirror for the Sky, A, folk opera by Gail Kubik; libretto (Eng) by Jessamyn West. First performance May 23, 1939, Eugene, Oregon.

Based on the life of the naturalist John James Audubon.

LIBRETTO: English (New York: Harcourt, Brace, [1948].

Mischance, The, dialogue by Charles Dibdin; libretto (Eng) by the composer, after *The Barber of Bagdad*, from the *Thousand and One Nights*. First performance July 12, 1773, London, Sadler's Wells, with Thomas Lowe.

The work was set for three characters, two female and one male.

LIBRETTO: English (London: John Johnston, and Longman, Lukey & Co., [1773?]).

Misper, children's opera by John Lunn; libretto (Eng) by Stephen Plaice. First performance February 28, 1997, Glyndebourne, East Sussex Academy of Music Orchestra, with Omar Ebrahim (Chinese philosopher), Ben Davies (chief bully), Mary King, and Melanie Pappenheim; conducted by Andrea Quinn; directed by Stephen Langridge.

In the work a twelfth-century Chinese philosopher is ordered by the emperor to compose a book on the future. Through an accident he is hurled into the present, where he is unable to help a young boy who is being bullied by a gang. Things work out with the help of a brave young girl, and the philosopher goes back to his own century. The title of the opera is derived from the British police jargon for missing person, i.e., "misper," the appellation given to the philosopher when he lands in contemporary England.

BIBLIOGRAPHY: "Misper," *Opera* XLVIII (May 1997), 593–94 [on premiere].

Miss Chicken Little, musical fable in one act by opera by Alec Wilder; libretto (Eng) by William Engvick. First performance December 27, 1954, New York, CBS television.

Miss Donnithorne's Maggot, music-theater piece by Peter Maxwell Davies; libretto (Eng) by Randolph Stow. First performance March 9, 1974, Adelaide, Australia.

The work is for mezzo-soprano and instrumental ensemble.

SCORE: fs (London and New York: Boosey & Hawkes, [1977]).

Miss Havisham's Fire, or, An Investigation into the Unusual and Violent Death of Aurelia Havisham on the Seventeenth of April in the Year Eighteen-Sixty, opera in a prologue, two acts, and an epilogue by Dominick Argento; libretto (Eng) by John Olon-Scrymgeour, after a character in Charles Dickens's novel *Great Expectations*. First performance March 22, 1979, New York, New York City Opera, with Rita Shane and Gianna Rolandi (the old and young Miss Havisham), Susanne Marsee (Estella), Alan Titus (Pip), Elaine Bonazzi (Nanny), Paul Ukena (Orlick), and John Lankston

(Bentley Drummle); conducted by Julius Rudel; directed by H. Wesley Balk; designed by John Conklin.

The epilogue was expanded as *Miss Havisham's Wedding Night* (1981; see next entry).

The setting is Satis House, its gardens, and surroundings, in Essex, England, from 1810 to 1860. Miss Havisham, having been jilted on her wedding day by her intended, lives for fifty years in the seclusion of her home in her wedding dress. The dress catches fire, and she dies. The plot takes the form of an inquest on this event, conducted by Miss Havisham's solicitor, Jaggers. Other Dickens characters, the four Pockets, Camilla, Georgina, cousin Raymond, Estella, Sarah, Pip, Orlick, Drummle, and the added character, Miss Havisham's nanny, appear during the course of the opera.

For a description, see Kornick/*RAO*, 24–27.

Major roles: Aurelia Havisham (col sop); Estella Drummle, Miss Havisham's adopted daughter (mezzo); Jaggers (bass), Bentley Drummle, Estella's husband (ten); Pip (bar); Orlick, the caretaker (bass); and Nanny (sop).

SCORE: vs ([New York]: Boosey & Hawkes, 1987).

LIBRETTO: English ([New York]: Boosey & Hawkes, [1979]).

BIBLIOGRAPHY: Hans Heinsheimer, "Great Expectations," *ON* LXIII (Mar. 24, 1979), 34–35, and "Miss Havisham's Fire," *Playbill* (Apr. 1979), 6, 8, 10, 12; Robert Jacobson, "Reports: U.S.," *ON* XLIII (June 1979), 39–40; Patrick Smith, "Reports: New York," *Opera* XXX (1979), 587–88 [on premiere].

Miss Havisham's Wedding Night, opera monodrama in one act by Dominick Argento, expanded epilogue of *Miss Havisham's Fire**; libretto (Eng) by John Olon-Scrymgeour, after Dickens. First performance May 1, 1981, Minneapolis, Minneapolis Opera, Tyrone Guthrie Theater, with Rita Shane (Miss Havisham); conducted by Philip Brunelle.

The setting is Satis House, Essex, England, 1850. The work opens on Miss Havisham's wedding day. Awaiting the event, she receives a note from her intended calling the marriage off and vows never to leave her dwelling or remove her wedding dress.

For a description, see Kornick/*RAO*, 27–28.

Major role: Aurelia Havisham (sop).

SCORE: vs (New York?: Boosey & Hawkes, 1987).

Mississippi Legend, opera in two acts by Jacques Wolfe; libretto (Eng) by Roark Bradford, after his play of the same name. First performance April 24, 1951, New York, Village Opera Company, with Donald Johnston (John Henry); conducted by Daniel Vandersall.

The story concerns the Paul Bunyon-like John Henry, who lives in Mississippi.

The work contains folk tunes occasionally given a jazzy accompaniment. It first appeared as a musical on Broadway in 1939.

BIBLIOGRAPHY: Harold C. Schonberg, "Wolfe Folk Opera Is Unveiled Here," *NYT* (Apr. 25, 1951), 33 [on premiere].

Miss Julie, opera in two acts by Ned Rorem; libretto (Eng) by Kenward Elmslie, after the play by August Strindberg. First performance November 4, 1965, New York, City Opera, with Marguerite Willauer (Julie), Donald Gramm (John), Elaine Bonazzi (Christine), and Richard Krause (Niels); conducted by Robert Zeller. Revised version April 5, 1979, New York, New York University, New York Lyric Opera, with Judith James and William Dansby; conducted by Peter Leonard. Revived April 4, 1979, New York, New York University Theater, New York Lyric Opera, with Beverly Morgan (Julie), Veronica August (Christine), and Ronald Madden (John).

The setting is a country estate in Sweden in the 1880s during the summer. The story concerns Miss Julie, daughter of the Count, and her fiancé, Niels, who breaks off their engagement after a quarrel. She then takes up with John, her father's valet, who is the fiancé of Christine, the cook. When the bizarre relationship is thwarted by the return of the Count, Julie prepares to kill herself.

Major roles: Julie (sop), Niels (ten), John (bass-bar), and Christine (mezzo).

SCORE: vs (New York: Boosey & Hawkes, 1965).

BIBLIOGRAPHY: Peter G. Davis, "'Miss Julie' by Ned Rorem Is Revived by Lyric Opera," *NYT* (Apr. 7, 1979), 14; Thomas P. Lanier, "New York," *ON* XLIV (July 1979), 36 [on revival]; Frank Merkling, "New York," *ON* XXX (Dec. 18, 1965), 29 [on premiere]; Harold Schonberg, "Opera: 'Miss Julie' at City Center," *NYT* (Nov. 5, 1965), 32 [on premiere].

DISCOGRAPHY: excerpts: James, August, Madden, New York Lyric Opera; cond. Leonard, Z Press PS-1338 (Battery Records); rev. James W. Freeman, "Records," *ON* XLV (Apr. 11, 1981), 52; complete: T. Fried, P. Torre, Manhattan School of Music; cond. D. Gilbert (1994, live), Newport Classic 401 421-8142 (2 CDs).

Miss Julie, opera in two acts by William Alwyn; libretto (Eng) by the composer, after Strindberg. First performance January 23, 1979, London, Kingsway Hall, with Jill Gomez (Miss Julie), John Mitchinson (Ulrik), Benjamin Luxon (Jean); conducted by Vilem Tausky. Revived October 15, 1997, Norwich, England, Theatre Royal, with Judith Howarth (Miss Julie), Karl Daymond (Jean), and Ian Caley (Ulrik).

See previous entry for the plot.

Major roles: Miss Julie (sop); Kristin, the cook (mezzo); Ulrik, the gamekeeper (ten); and Jean, the cook's valet (bar).

Also set by A. Bibalo, as *Frøken Julie* (1975, Århus, Denmark); and I. Kuusisto (1994, Vaasa, Finland).

BIBLIOGRAPHY: John Allison, review, *Opera* XLVIII (Dec. 1997), 1499–1500 [on revival].

DISCOGRAPHY: J. Gomez, D. Jones, J. Mitchinson, B. Luxon; Philharmonia Orch.; cond. V. Tausky, Lyrita SRCD 2218-1 (rec. 1979, London; prod. 1992, Burnham Bucks., Engl., 2 CDs).

Miss Lucy in Town, ballad farce by Thomas Arne; libretto (Eng) by Henry Fielding. First performance May 6, 1742, London, Drury Lane Theatre. Revived as *The Country Madcap in London*, June 10, 1770, London, Drury Lane Theatre.

Mistake, The, chamber opera in one act by Jonathan B. Sheffer; libretto (Eng) by Stephen Wadsworth. First performance August 16, 1981, Denver, Central City Opera.

The story is about a soprano's travails, and it takes place during the intermission of a concert. Ariel has made a mistake during the first half of her concert. She agonizes during the intermission as to what caused her miscue, but she is unable to find the reason, and, in addition, she has an argument with Sandy, her boyfriend. Before she returns to the stage, however, she regains her control after being comforted by Walter, her manager, and reconciling with Sandy, and walks out with renewed confidence.

Major roles: Ariel (lyric sop), America (mezzo), Elena (lyric mezzo), Walter (ten), Sandy (bar), and Frank (bass-bar).

Mistakes of a Day, The, operatic afterpiece in two acts by John W. Callcott; libretto (Eng) possibly by J. H. Colls. First performance 1787, Norwich, England.

Roles: Sir Nicholas Avaro, Fitzgig, Hardy, Belvil[l]e, and Louisa.

The work includes the song "The Sail-Yards Whistle in the Wind," sung by Hardy.

SCORE: ms fs, autograph (1785, British Library, Add. MS. 27638).

LIBRETTO: English (Larpent 760, Huntington Library, San Marino, Calif.)

Mistress into Maid, opera in two acts by Vernon Duke; libretto (Eng) by the composer, after Pushkin's *Tales of Belkin*. First performance December 12, 1958, Santa Barbara, California, University of California, Opera Theater, with Shirley Eisley, Dorothy Westral, Kay McCracken, Nancy Adams, Charles Buffrum, Archie Deake, and Carl Zytowski; conducted by Stefan Krayk; produced by Zytowski.

Moby Dick, opera in two acts by James Low; libretto (Eng) by Brainerd Duffield, after Melville's novel. First performance September 2, 1955, Idylwild, California, Idylwild Opera Workshop; conducted by Milton Young; produced by Howard Banks.

Moby Dick, opera in two acts by Richard Brooks; libretto (Eng) by the composer after Melville. Composed 1987.
SCORE: overture (New York: American Composers Alliance, 1987).

Moby Dick, opera-oratorio in three acts by Solomon Epstein; libretto (Eng) by Joyce Adler and the composer, after Herman Melville. Composed 1989.
    Also set as a cantata by B. Herrmann (1940, New York); unfinished opera by L. De Costa (n.d.); opera by H. D. Hewitt (n.d.).
SCORE: ms score (1989, NYPL).

Mock Catalani in Little Puddleton, The, musical burletta by Charles Nagel; libretto (Eng) by the composer. First performance May 4, 1842, Sydney, Australia, Royal Victoria Theatre.
LIBRETTO: English (broadside) (Sydney: n.p., 1842).

Mock Doctor, The, or, The Dumb Lady Cur'd, ballad opera in one or two acts; libretto (Eng) by Henry Fielding, after Molière's *Le médecin malgré lui*. First performance June 26, 1732, London, Drury Lane Theatre, with Mr. Shepherd (Sir Jasper), Mr. Stopelaer (Leander), Miss Raftor (Dorcas), and Miss Williams (Charlotte). First American performance April 30, 1750, New York, Kean and Murray.
    The penniless Leander is able to marry Charlotte, daughter of Sir Jasper, after she pretends to be unable to speak and is "cured" by a mock doctor, assisted by Leander. Leander inherits his uncle's fortune, thereby pacifying his new father-in-law.
LIBRETTO: English, with ballad airs (London: J. Watts, 1732); repr. ed. Rubsamen/*BO*, vol. 4, *The Medical and Legal Professions* (1974).

Mock Lawyer, The, ballad opera in one act; libretto (Eng) by Edward Phillips. First performance April 27, 1733, London, Covent Garden, with Mr. Hall (Justice Lovelaw), Thomas Salway (Valentine), Mr. Hippisley (Cheatly), Mr. Chapman (Feignwell), Mr. Aston (Dash), Miss Norsa (Laetitia), and Miss Bincks (Betty).
    The mock lawyer in this story is Valentine.
    Roles: Justice Lovelaw, Laetitia's father; Valentine, in love with Laetitia; Cheatly, an attorney; Feignwell, Valentine's servant; Dash, Lovelaw's clerk; Laetitia; and Betty, her maid.
LIBRETTO: English (London: T. Astley, 1733); repr. ed. Rubsamen/*BO*, vol. 4, *The Medical and Legal Professions* (1974).

Modern Painters, opera in seven scenes by David Lang; libretto (Eng) by Manuela Hoelterhoff. First performance July 29, 1995, Santa Fe, Santa Fe Opera, with François Le Roux (Ruskin), Ann Panagulias (Effie, his wife), Sheila Nadler (his mother), and Mark Thomsen (John Everett Millais); conducted by George Manahan.
    The opera's seven scenes correspond to the criteria of value the artist John Ruskin put forth in his book *The Seven Lamps of Architecture*. It includes vignettes from his

life, including his overbearing mother, marriage to a child bride, conflicts with various artists, and his madness.

An orchestral interlude is played between each scene. The opera includes an adaptation of the composer's "Anvil Chorus" for solo percussionist in its opening section.
BIBLIOGRAPHY: Paul Griffiths, "Musical Events, Blank Canvas," *NY* LXXI (Sept. 11, 1995), 98–99 [on premiere]; James R. Oestreich, "Ruskin, at Full Cry in a New Form" *NYT* (Aug. 7, 1995), C, 9, 12 [on premiere]; John Russell, "Stalking a Man of Words with Music," *NYT* (July 23, 1995), H, 27 [on premiere]; Patrick J. Smith, "Santa Fe," *ON* LX (Oct. 1995), 50–51 [on premiere].

Moment of War, A, opera in one act by Richard Owen; libretto (Eng) by the composer. Composed 1958. First performance November 1964, Buenos Aires.

Momus Turn'd Fabulist, or, Vulcan's Wedding, ballad opera in three acts; libretto (Eng) by Ebenezer Forrest, after Fuzelier and Legrand's *Momus fabuliste, ou, Les noces de Vulcain*. First performance December 3, 1729, London, Lincoln's Inn Fields, with Mr. Milward (Jupiter), Mr. Morgan (Neptune), Mr. Salway (Apollo), Mr. Walker (Mars), Mr. Hippisley (Plutus), Mr. Hall (Vulcan), Mr. Ray (Mercury), Mr. Hulett (Momus), Mrs. Egleton (Juno), and Mrs. Cantrell (Venus).

The satirical story has a mythological setting.
LIBRETTO: English, with music (London: J. Watts, 1729); repr. ed. Rubsamen/*BO*, vol. 7, *Classical Subjects I: Satire and Burlesque* (1974).

Mona, opera in three acts by Horatio Parker; libretto (Eng) by Brian Hooker. First performance March 14, 1912, New York, Metropolitan Opera, with Louise Homer (Mona), Riccardo Martin (Quintus), Rita Fornia (Enya), Herbert Witherspoon (Arth), William Hinshaw (Gloom), Albert Reiss (Nial), Lambert Murphy (Caradoc), Putnam Griswold (Roman governor), and Basil Ruysdael (old man); conducted by Alfred Hertz.

The setting is Britain during the time of the Roman occupation. Mona is the leader of a revolt against Roman rule, and she kills Quintus, her lover, who is really Gwynn, son of the Roman governor, because she thinks, wrongly, that he is a traitor to her cause.

Roles: Mona, princess of Britain (mezzo); Quintus (ten); Enya (sop); Arth (bass); Gloom (bar); Nial (ten); Caradoc (ten); Roman governor (bass); and old man (bass).
SCORE: orchestral parts (New York: G. Schirmer, 1912).
LIBRETTO: English (New York: G. Schirmer, 1911).

Monkey Opera, The, or, The Making of a Soliloquy, opera by Roger Trefousse; libretto by Jane DeLynn. First performance April 17, 1982, Brooklyn, New York, Brooklyn Academy of Music.
SCORE: ms, holograph (1982, photocopy, NYPL).

Monkey See, Monkey Do, opera for children in one act by Robert Xavier Rodríguez; libretto (Eng and Sp) by Mary Duren and the composer, after a Mexican folktale. First performance February 18, 1987, Dallas, Dallas Opera.

The setting is a Mexican village. Antonio, an organ grinder, is extremely fond of his monkey. Perdito, a young sombrero maker, wishes to wed Antonio's daughter, Maria. When the monkey runs away, the whole town goes in search of him, but other monkeys steal all of Perdito's hats and hide, with Antonio's monkey, in a tree. When Perdito notices that the monkeys imitate all his actions, he throws his hat to the ground, whereupon the monkey tosses all of the filched sombreros onto the ground. Perdito's cleverness earns him fame and gratitude from the rest of the town.

Major roles: Perdito, sombrero salesman (ten); Maria, his fiancée (sop); and Antonio, an organ grinder and Maria's father (bass).

The score includes quotes from Mexican folk pieces such as the "Chapanecas" and "El jarabe tapatio." The work can be performed by singing actors or by puppets and singers (or tape).

SCORE: vs (New York: G. Schirmer, 1987, 1995).

Monkey's Paw, The, melodrama in one act by Charles Hamm; libretto (Eng) by the composer, after a short story by William Wymark Jacobs. First performance May 2, 1952, Cincinnati, Conservatory of Music.

Monkey's Paw, The, opera in one act by Sidney Halpern; libretto (Eng) by the composer, after Jacobs. First performance April 4, 1965, New York, Off-Broadway Opera Company.

Monkey's Paw, The, chamber opera in three scenes by William P. Alexander; libretto (Eng) by the composer, after Jacobs. First performance November 13, 1972, Edinboro, Pennsylvania, Edinboro State College.

Major Morris visits an old friend, Wade, and his family. Morris has brought a monkey's paw that can grant three wishes, but when Wade buys the paw, Morris cautions that since the paw is cursed, the wishes must be made with great care. Wade first wishes for a great deal of money; the next day a member of his son's firm comes to present a check to the family; the son has died, and the money is meant as compensation. Mrs. Wade begs her husband to use the second wish to bring their son back to life; he reluctantly agrees, only to use his third wish to have the money back rather than their son.

For a description, see Summers/*OOA*, 7–8.

Major roles: Mr. Wade (bar), Mrs. Wade (sop), John Wade (ten), and Major Morris (bar).

SCORE: ms vs, holograph (1991, photocopy, NYPL).

Monk of Toledo, The, grand opera in a prologue and three acts by E. Bruce Knowlton; libretto (Eng) by the composer. First performance May 10, 1926, Portland, Oregon, with J. McMillan Muir (Francisca), Leon Delmond (Henri), Gladys Brumbaugh (Marie Violet); conducted by the composer.

The opera takes place between 1814 and 1854. Told in flashback, it opens with the monk Francisca at prayer. He tells his story, which begins at Cannes, France, after Napoleon has escaped from Elba and landed. Colonel Violet finds out that his sister, Marie, now a serving girl, has been insulted by Henri, one of his soldiers. In a rage he kills Henri and flees to a monastery. In the last act, set in the present, Francisca insists that he is Colonel Violet and faints. An old woman enters and she is Marie, who has looked for her brother since he disappeared; when he awakens, he recognizes his sibling.

For a detailed description, see Hipsher/*AO*, 286–88.

Monster Bed, The, comic opera in one act by Stefania Maria de Kenessey; libretto (Eng) by Billy Aronson, after the book by Jeanne Willis. First performance December 4, 1990, New York, New School for Research.

A young monster, Dennis, is afraid to go to sleep because he fears humans will seize him, although his mother tells him that they do not exist.

SCORE: ms score, holograph (1990, photocopy, NYPL).

Montezuma, opera in three acts by Roger Sessions; libretto (Eng) by Giuseppe Antonio Borgese, after the memoirs of Bernal Diaz del Castillo. First performance April 19, 1964, West Berlin, Deutsche Oper, in German, with Ernst Krukowski (Bernal Diaz del Castillo, the Old), William Dooley (Hernán Cortez), Loren Driscoll (Pedro de Alvarado), Manfred Röhrl (Fray Olmedo de la Merced, the Young), Karl Ernst Mercker (Bernal Diaz del Castillo, the Young), Annabelle Bernard (Malinche), Helmut Melchert (Montezuma), Barry McDaniel (Cuauhtemoc), Martin Vantin (Cacamatzin), and Martti Talvela (Teuhtlilli). First U.S. performance April 1, 1976, Boston, Opera Company of Boston, with Brent Ellis (Cortez), Richard Lewis (Montezuma), and Phyllis Bryn-Julson; conducted by Sarah Caldwell. Revived February 19, 1982, New York, Juilliard School; conducted by Frederik Prausnitz; directed by Ian Strasfogel; designed by Ming Cho Lee.

The story examines the meeting of Montezuma with the Spanish conquistadores in 1519, led by Cortez, Montezuma's imprisonment, and his death at the hands of a hostile Aztec crowd in 1520. It is narrated by Bernal Diaz, one of Cortez's soldiers, as an old man.

In the first act the Spanish land on the coast near Vera Cruz and build a settlement. Cortez is drawn to the beautiful Aztec woman Malinche, who hails him as the foretold white god of peace, Quetzalcoatl. Malinche, now Cortez's mistress, converts and takes the name of Doña Marina. As the second act opens, Bernal describes the Spanish killing of the Aztecs at Cholula, after discovering that Montezuma had planned to attack them. Eventually, Cortez meets Montezuma at his palace, and the two leaders seem to have various common interests, but Alvarado, Cortez's second in command, is hostile and wants only to acquire Aztec gold. On the other side, Cuauhtemoc, a young Aztec noble, is openly suspicious of the Spanish and foments distrust among the other Aztecs. He calls Malinche a Spanish whore and tries to kill her, and in the melee that follows Alvarado slays one of the Aztec nobles, the Lord of Tacuba. Cuauhtemoc and most of the royal retinue are able to escape, leaving only Montezuma behind. Cortez reluctantly agrees to imprison him.

Things come to a head in act 3, when Alvarado, in charge of guarding the royal palace while Cortez is away, leads a massacre of the defenseless Aztec natives. Cortez, realizing that any hopes of peace have been ended, also prepares for battle. Montezuma makes a last attempt to forestall the fighting and praises Malinche as a "mixer of seeds." As he speaks, he is the target of stones and spears thrown by his angry countrymen, who rush off to declare Cuauhtemoc as their new king. The mortally injured Montezuma, hoping for a better time in the future, dies in Malinche's arms.

Roles: Bernal Diaz del Castillo, the Old, narrator (bar); Hernán Cortez (bar); Pedro de Alvarado (ten); Fray Olmedo de la Merced, the Young (ten); Bernal Diaz del Castillo, the Young (ten); Malinche, slave girl, formerly a princess (sop); Montezuma, Aztec emperor (ten); Cuauhtemoc (bar); Cacamatzin, Lord of Texoco (ten); Netzahualcoyotl, an old priest (bass); and Teuhtlilli, ambassador of Montezuma (ten).

BIBLIOGRAPHY: John Rockwell, "Sessions 'Montezuma' Comes to U.S.," *NYT* (Apr. 2, 1976), 24; "Sessions's Opera Stirs Berliners," *NYT* (Apr. 21, 1964), 43 [on premiere]; Michael Steinberg, "Enter Montezuma," *ON* XL (Apr. 3, 1976), 10–16; *NYT* (Apr. 20, 1964), 32; *NYT* (Apr. 21, 1964), 43.

Montezuma's Death, opera in one act by Linder Chlarson; libretto (Eng) by the composer. First performance June 11, 1982, New York, New York University Opera Studio.

A telling of the defeat and death of Montezuma at the hands of Cortes and his forces.

Major roles: Fernando Cortes (ten), Geronimo de Aguilar (bass-bar), Dona Marina (mezzo), and Montezuma (ten).

Other settings of the Montezuma story include Frederick Gleason's *Montezuma* (comp. 1885, not perf.); and W. Rihm's *Die Eroberung von Mexico* (1992, Hamburg).

Month in the Country, A. See **Natalia Petrovna.**

Montrose, or, The Children of the Mist, opera in three acts by Henry Rowley Bishop, Ware, and Watson; libretto (Eng) by Isaac Pocock, after Sir Walter Scott's *The Legend of Montrose* (1820). First performance February 14, 1822, London, Covent Garden.
    The work includes famous Scottish airs.
SCORE: ms fs (1822, British Library, Add. MS. 36954).

Moon and Sixpence, The, opera in three acts by John Gardner; libretto (Eng) by Patrick Terry, after Somerset Maugham's novel. First performance May 24, 1957, London, Sadler's Wells, with Elizabeth Fretwell (Blanche), Anna Pollak (Mrs. Strickland), and Owen Brannigan (Charles Strickland); conducted by Alexander Gibson; produced by Peter Hall.
    The story of an ordinary stockbroker, Charles Strickland, who deserts his wife and family in London to become a painter in Tahiti.

Moon Flowers, opera in one act by Richard Arnell; libretto (Eng) by the composer. First performance July 23, 1959, Kent, Kentish Opera Group.
LIBRETTO: English ([n.p.], [1959]; LCCN: 62-39407).

Moon Maiden, The, chamber opera in one act by Rutland Boughton; libretto (Eng) by Marie Stopes, after a Japanese Noh play. First performance April 23, 1918, Glastonbury, Assembly Rooms.

Moonrakers, The, "cassation for audience and orchestra" in one act by Malcolm Williamson. First performance April 22, 1967, Brighton, England. First U.S. performance July 31, 1969, New York, Central Park, Adventure Playground.
    A seven-minute "participation" opera that involves any number of people selected from the audience and an orchestra; the plot concerns smugglers, policemen, and villagers. There are no set roles.
SCORE: vs (London: J. Weinberger, [1967]).
BIBLIOGRAPHY: Steven V. Roberts, review, *NYT* (Aug. 1, 1969), 36 [on U.S. premiere].

Moorish Maid, A, or, The Queen of the Riffs, comic opera in two acts by Alfred Hill; libretto (Eng) by John Youlin Burch. First performance June 26, 1905, Auckland, New Zealand, with Rosina Buckman (La Zara).
    The setting is a fictional desert world and centers around La Zara, the title character.

Moralities, three scenic cantatas by Hans Werner Henze; libretto (Eng) by W. H. Auden, after Aesop's fables. First performance May 18, 1968, Cincinnati, Musical Festival Association.
    Scored for speaker, alto, bass, mixed chorus, and orchestra.
SCORE: vs, English-German (Mainz: B. Schott's Söhne; New York: Schott Music Corp., [1969]).

Morning, Noon, and Night, comic opera by George Perry; libretto (Eng) by Thomas J. Dibdin. First performance September 9, 1822, London, Haymarket.
LIBRETTO: English (London: Simpkin and Marshall, 1822).

Moro, or, The Painter of Antwerp, grand opera in a prologue and three acts by Michael Balfe; libretto (Eng) by William A. Barrett, a translation and adaptation of Piave's text for Balfe's *Pittore e duca* (1854, Trieste). First performance January 22, 1882, London, Her Majesty's Theatre.
LIBRETTO: English (as *The Painter of Antwerp*; London: J. B. Cramer, 1882).

Morvoren, opera in two acts by Philip Cannon; libretto (Eng) by Maisie Radford, after a Cornish legend. First performance July 15, 1964, London, Royal College of Music.

Most Happy Fella, The, "extended musical comedy" in three acts by Frank Loesser; libretto (Eng) by the composer, after Sidney Howard's play *They Knew What They Wanted* (1924); orchestrated by Don Walker. First performance May 3, 1956, New York, Imperial Theatre, with Robert Weede (Tony), Jo Sullivan (Rosabella), Art Lund (Joe), Susan Johnson (Cleo), and Shorty Long (Herman).

The story is set in the Napa Valley in California in 1927. Tony, a middle-aged winemaker, falls in love with a young waitress, Rosabella, whom he has seen in a San Francisco restaurant. Beginning a correspondence with her, he sends her a photograph of Joe, his handsome young hired hand, fearing that she would reject him if she were to see his picture instead. Rosabella comes to the vineyard and meets Joe, who quickly tells her the truth. She is about to leave when she discovers that Tony has been injured; feeling sorry for him, she decides to stay and marry him. Unable to resist Joe during her new husband's convalescence, Rosabella has a short affair with Joe and becomes pregnant. She tries to leave in order to spare Tony; at first enraged, he puts aside his anger to accept her and raise the unborn child as his own.

This partially operatic work has only fifteen minutes of spoken dialogue and more than forty musical numbers. Much of its operatic writing may be found in Tony's part; the score also includes Rosabella's ballad "Somebody, Somewhere" and the popular male quartet "Standing on the Corner."
SCORE: vs (New York: Frank, [1957]).
LIBRETTO: English, in *Theatre Arts* (New York) XLII (Oct. 1958), 36–53.
DISCOGRAPHY: orig. cast, Columbia 03L 240 (1956), reissued as Sony S2K 48010 (2 CDs).

Most Important Man, The, opera in three acts by Gian Carlo Menotti; libretto (Eng) by the composer. First performance March 12, 1971, New York, City Opera, with Eugene Holmes (Toimé Ukamba), Harry Theyard (Arnek), Beverly Wolff (Leona), Joanna Bruno (Cora), Delores Jones (Mrs. Agebda Akawasi), Richard Stilwell (Eric Rupert); conducted by Christopher Keene. (The premiere was scheduled for March 7, but that performance was considered a preview). Revised for performance January 17, 1972, Trieste.

The action is set in colonial Africa during this century. Toimé Ukamba hopes to become "the most important man" when he discovers a formula to change the world and flees into the bush with his wife, Cora, daughter of Dr. Arnek, his white mentor. He is thwarted by the "white state" and Dr. Arnek. Toimé dies, disgraced, leaving Dr. Arnek as the most important man, since only he now knows the formula.

Major roles: Toimé Ukamba (bar); Dr. Otto Arnek (ten); Leona, Arnek's wife (mezzo); Cora, his daughter (sop); Mrs. Agebda Akawasi, a native leader (sop); and Eric Rupert, Arnek's young white assistant (bar).
BIBLIOGRAPHY: Harriet Johnson, "'Important Man' in Premiere," *New York Post* (Mar. 13, 1971), 21; Harold C. Schonberg, "The Opera: Menotti's 'Most Important Man,'" *NYT* (Mar. 14, 1971), 71 [on premiere]; review, *NY* XLVII (Mar. 20, 1971), 132 [on premiere].

Mother, The, fantasy in one act by Joseph Wood; libretto (Eng) by Hurd Hatfield, after H. C. Andersen. First performance December 9, 1942, New York, Juilliard School.

Mother, The, opera in one act by Stanley Hollingsworth; libretto (Eng) by the composer and John Fandel, after Andersen. First performance March 29, 1954, Philadelphia, Curtis Institute.

In this fantasy Death comes dressed as the Old Man and takes Anna's ill child with him. The mother goes after him and is aided in finding him by Night, the Blackthorn, and the Lake, for whom she weeps copiously. When she finally meets up with Death, he convinces her to leave her child with him, since the boy would have suffered greatly. Anna returns to the land of the living.

For a detailed plot description, see Eaton/*OP* II, 303–4.

Roles: Anna (sop), Old Man (Death) (bass-bar), Night (mezzo), the Blackthorn (ten), the Lake (col sop), the old woman (mezzo).

SCORE: vs (New York: G. Ricordi & Co., 1961).

Mother and Child, opera in one act by Lee McClure; libretto (Eng) by Ron Whyte. First performance May 23, 1990, New York, St. John the Divine; conducted by Bill Grossman.

The story concerns a mother who must deal with her newborn's physical disabilities.

BIBLIOGRAPHY: Bernard Holland, "Posthumous Premiere," *NYT* (May 29, 1990), C, 14.

Mother Goose, or, The Golden Egg, "pantomimical operatic romance" by William Henry Ware; libretto (Eng) by Thomas Dibdin. First performance December 26, 1806, London. First U.S. performance March 3, 1809, Charleston, South Carolina, Charleston Theatre.

Mother of Three Sons, The, dance opera by Leroy Jenkins; libretto (Eng) by Ann T. Greene (Eng); directed and choreographed by Bill T. Jones. First performance May 1990, Munich Biennale Festival. First U.S. performance October 19, 1991, New York, City Opera, with Ruby Hinds (the Mother), Leonard Cruz (man-with-no-boat), Bill T. Jones (the River), and Batatunde (drums).

The story centers on a woman's driving desire to have male children, and it takes its inspiration from sub-Saharan folk tales. The Mother leaves her husband, the Water, after she bears a daughter, whom she kills, and becomes the lover of the River, who promises to give her sons. But when the sons are maimed, through her carelessness, she abandons them and, by the end, brings pain and death to herself and her offspring.

Only the Mother, among the singers, appears onstage. The rest of the singers are offstage, and the plot is enacted by dancers, while the drama is moved forward by the narrator and singers. An African drummer adds rhythmic vibrancy and mood.

BIBLIOGRAPHY: Edward Rothstein, "Bill T. Jones's 'Mother of Three Sons,'" *NYT* (Oct. 21, 1991), C, 13 [on premiere]; Robert Sandla, "Terra Nova," *ON* LVI (Oct. 1991), 32-33, 56; Gene Santoro, "Ol' Man River Meets His Mate," *NYT* (Oct. 13, 1991), II, 23, 38; Barrymore Laurence Scherer, "In Review," *ON* LVI (Jan. 18, 1992), 41, 45 [on U.S. premiere].

Mother of Us All, The, opera in two acts by Virgil Thomson; libretto (Eng) by Gertrude Stein. First performance May 7, 1947, New York, Columbia University, Brander Matthews Hall, with Dorothy Dow (Susan B. Anthony), Ruth Krug (Indiana Elliot), Teresa Stich (Henrietta M.), Robert Grooters (Virgil T.), William Horne (Jo the Loiterer), Bertram Rowe (Daniel Webster), and Carolyn Blakeslee (Angel More); conducted by Otto Luening; directed by John Taras.

The work is a pageant around the life and political ideals of the suffragette Susan B. Anthony and contains real and imagined characters.

For detailed plot synopses, see K/*KOB*, 1326–30; K/*NKOB*, 456–57.

Major roles: Susan B. Anthony (sop); Anne, her confidante (alto); Daniel Webster (bass); Andrew Johnson (ten); Thaddeus Stevens (ten); Angel More, Daniel Webster's sweetheart (sop); John Adams (ten); Constance Fletcher (mezzo); Lillian Russell (sop);

Gertrude S., a cheerful, middle-aged woman (sop); Virgil T., a pleasant master of ceremonies (bar); Ulysses S. Grant (bar); and Donald Gallup (bar).

Among the highlights is the hymnlike "Lead Kindly Light."

SCORE: vs (New York: G. Schirmer, 19??).

BIBLIOGRAPHY: Olin Downes, "New Stein Opera," *NYT* (May 8, 1947), 30 [on premiere].

DISCOGRAPHY: Dunn, Godfrey, Orvath, Maxwell, Putnam, Vanni, Beck, Atherton, Booth, Ives, Lewis, Perry, Loewengart, Santa Fe Opera; cond. R. Leppard, New World Records NW-288/9 (2).

Mountain Blood, grand opera in three acts by Franklin Patterson; libretto (Eng) by the composer, after Joseph Hergesheimer's novel (1915). Composed 1926.

The story concerns the nouveaux riches of Virginia and the descendants of the Highlanders.

LIBRETTO: English, typewritten (1926, LCCN: 84-195513).

Mountaineers, The, opera in three acts by Samuel Arnold; libretto (Eng) by George Colman Jr., after Cervantes's *Don Quixote*. First performance August 3, 1793, London, Little Theatre in the Haymarket, with John Kemble (Octavian). First U.S. performance April 6, 1795, Boston, Federal Street Theatre.

In this story, combined from two in the Cervantes, a captive escapes from imprisonment in Algiers to the mountains, joined by a Moorish girl, Zorayda, who has become a Christian.

For a detailed description, see Fiske/*ETM*, 561–62.

SCORE: vs (London: Preston & Son, n.d.).

LIBRETTO: English (London: J. Debrett, 1795; Boston: William P. Blake, 1796).

Mountain Sylph, The, opera in two acts by John Barnett; libretto (Eng) by T. J. Thackeray, after the ballet *La sylphide* (1832). First performance August 25, 1834, London, Lyceum, with Emma Romer (Aeolia), Mr. Wilson (Donald), Miss Somerville (Jessie), and Henry Philips (Hela); conducted by William Hawes.

Donald, betrothed to Jessie, is really in love with the sylph Aeolia, a situation brought to light by the evil Hela, who plots revenge when berated by Donald. The lovers run off during the marriage ceremony, but Aeolia is saved from death by the Sylphid queen, who turns Aeolia into a human.

For a detailed plot and musical description, see Biddlecombe/*EO*, 78–82.

The music plays an important part in characterizations and plot development.

"Burlesque burletta" by Betsey Fry, as *The Area Sylph* (London, 18??).

LIBRETTO: English (New York: J. Kennedy, 1835).

Mountebanks, The, comic opera in two acts by Alfred Cellier; libretto (Eng) by William S. Gilbert. First performance January 4, 1892, London, Lyric Theatre, with J. Robertson and Geraldine Ulmar. First U.S. performance January 11, 1892, Garden Theater, with Hayden Coffin and Lillian Russell.

The story concerns a magic potion that lets those who imbibe it become the people they pretend to be.

LIBRETTO: English (London: Chappell; New York: Novello, 1892).

Mourning Becomes Electra, opera in three acts by Marvin David Levy; libretto (Eng) by Henry Butler, after the play by Eugene O'Neill. First performance March 17, 1967, New York, Metropolitan Opera, with Marie Collier (Christine Mannon), Evelyn Lear (Lavinia Mannon), Raymond Michalski (Jed), Sherrill Milnes (Adam Brant), Ron

Bottcher (Peter Niles), Lilian Sukis (Helen Niles), John Macurdy (General Ezra Mannon), and John Reardon (Orin Mannon); conducted by Zubin Mehta; designed by Boris Aronson. Revised version October 1998, Chicago, Lyric Opera.

The story is a recasting of the *Oresteia* of Aeschylus, with the setting moved to a New England seaport in 1865. The first act is called "The Homecoming." Christine Mannon, the Clytemnestra character, is awaiting the return of her husband, General Ezra Mannon, from the Civil War. During his absence she has taken Adam Brant, a sea captain (and illegitimate cousin of her husband) as her lover (the Aegisthus role). She plots to get rid of her husband on his return, and when, after an argument, he has a heart attack, Christine gives him poison instead of his medicine. Their daughter, the Elektra-like Lavinia, hears her father accuse the mother of poisoning him.

In the second act, "The Hunted," Orin (Orestes), who secretly harbors incestuous feelings for his sister, returns, having been wounded in the fighting. Peter and Helen Niles, also sister and brother, visit the Mannon family on a condolence call, Peter being in love with Lavinia, and Helen attracted to Orin. After their departure Lavinia tells Orin of her mother's actions, and the enraged man swears to avenge his father's killing. The siblings follow their mother to her rendezvous with Brant on his ship, and when the mother leaves, Orin stabs Brant. When her children tell her that they know of her guilt and that Brant has been slain, she kills herself. Lavinia and Orin tell their servant Jed to inform everyone that their mother died from grief over her husband's passing.

The final act is call "The Haunted." It is a year later, and Lavinia and Orin have returned from a long holiday. They are visited by Peter and Helen Niles, who still hope that they can wed the respective siblings. When Lavinia expresses interest in Peter, and they embrace, Orin becomes enraged and sends Peter away. Helen is also dismissed. With his feelings for Lavinia and his confusion with all that has happened, Orin accepts the pistol that Lavinia has given him and shoots himself. Although Peter still hopes to wed Lavinia, she refers to him as "Adam." Realizing the hopelessness of the situation, Peter departs, leaving Lavinia alone with her ghosts and guilt, as the last surviving Mannon.

For detailed descriptions, see *C/MS*, 271–90; Eaton/*OP* II, 162–63.

Major roles: Christine Mannon (sop); Lavinia Mannon (sop); Adam Brant (bar); Peter Niles (bar); Helen Niles (sop); General Ezra Mannon (bass-bar); Orin Mannon (bar/ten); and Jed, a servant (bass).
LIBRETTO: English ([New York]: Boosey and Hawkes, [1967]).
BIBLIOGRAPHY: Harold C. Schonberg, review, *NYT* (Mar. 18, 1967), 17 [on premiere].

Moustique, opera in three acts by Henri Kowalski; libretto (Eng) by Marcus Clarke. Composed 1881. First performance 1883, Brussels, Alcazar Royal; July 2, 1889 (excerpts), Sydney, Australia, Opera House.

Mouth of the Nile, The, or, The Glorious First of August, musical entertainment in one act by Thomas Attwood; libretto (Eng) by Thomas Dibdin. First performance October 25, 1798, London, Covent Garden. First U.S. performance May 13, 1799, New York, Park Theatre.
SCORE: vs (London: Goulding, Phipps & D'Almaine, n.d.).

Movie Opera (Prevue), chamber opera in one act by Jack Gottlieb; libretto (Eng) by the composer. First performance June 19, 1986, New York, Golden Fleece Ltd.

About a cabaret singer.
BIBLIOGRAPHY: Bernard Holland, review, *NYT* (June 22, 1986), I, 44 [on premiere].

M.P., or, The Blue Stocking, comic opera in three acts by Thomas Moore and Charles Horn (overture, orchestration); libretto (Eng) by Thomas Moore. First performance September 9, 1811, London, Lyceum Theatre. First U.S. performance June 6, 1812, New York, Park Theatre.
LIBRETTO: English (New York: Longworths, 1812).

Mr. and Mrs. Discobbolos, chamber opera in two acts by Peter Westergaard; libretto (Eng) by the composer, after Edward Lear's poem. First performance March 21, 1966, New York, Columbia University, American Chamber Opera.
When Mr. and Mrs. Discobbolos are picnicking, they become fearful and decide to remain where they are, atop a wall. After having twelve children, they find their situation hopeless, and Mr. Discobbolos blows himself and his entire family up.
Roles: Mrs. Discobbolos (sop) and Mr. Discobbolos (ten).
A parody of grand opera, the work lasts seventeen minutes.
SCORE: vs (New York: A. Broude, [1968]).
DISCOGRAPHY: V. Lamoree, J. Litten, Group for Contemporary Music at Columbia; cond. H. Sollberger, CRI SD-271 (1971, 1 LP).

Mr. Bellamy Comes Home, opera in three acts by Hill Rivington; libretto (Eng) by Martin R. Holmes. First performance October 13, 1950, London, Fortune Theatre.
Two suitors, a patriot and a traitor, pursue an English country maid.
BIBLIOGRAPHY: review, *The Times* (London) (Oct. 14, 1950), 8 [on premiere].

Mr. Pepys, "ballad-opera" in three acts by Martin Shaw; libretto (Eng) by Clifford Bax. First performance February 11, 1926, London, Everyman Theatre.
SCORE: vs (London, J. B. Cramer & Co., Ltd., 1926).
LIBRETTO: English (New York: S. French; London: S. French Ltd., 1927).

Mr. Punch, "operatic entertainment for young people" by Michael Hurd; libretto (Eng) by the composer. First performance April 3, 1970, Göteburg, Sweden, Götabergsskolan.
Also set by Derek Healey (comp. 1969).
SCORE: fs (Sevenoaks, Kent: Novello, [1971]).

Mr. Scrooge, children's opera in one act by Martin Kalmanoff; libretto (Eng) by G. Lebowitz, after Charles Dickens's *A Christmas Carol*. First performance December 3, 1966, New York, Judson Hall.

Mrs. Dalloway, opera in two acts by Libby Larsen; libretto (Eng) by Bonnie Grice, after the novel by Virginia Woolf (1925). First performance July 22, 1993, Cleveland, Lyric Opera, with Mary Elizabeth Poore (Clarissa), Garry Briggle (Septimus), and Richard Lewis (Peter Walsh); conducted by Benton Hess; staged by Michael McConnell.
The plot centers on a day's events in the life of Clarissa Dalloway, a member of English society. She is entertaining the visiting Peter Walsh, whom she had once rejected despite the fact that she loved him, because of his possessive nature. Clarissa's story is presented, together with that of the shell-shocked Septimus.
Major roles: Clarissa Dalloway (sop), Septimus (ten), and Peter Walsh (ten).
Scored for chamber instruments and electronic tape.
BIBLIOGRAPHY: Donald Rosenberg, review, *ON* LVIII (Nov. 1993), 45–46 [on premiere].

Mrs. Farmer's Daughter, opera by Jack Eric Williams; libretto (Eng). First performance July 1983, Purchase, New York, Summerfare. Revised version 1984, Philadelphia, American Music Theater Festival, with Sharon Scruggs.
About the difficult life of actress Frances Farmer.

Much Ado about Nothing, opera in four acts by Charles Stanford; libretto (Eng) by Julian R. Sturgis, after Shakespeare's play (1599). First performance May 30, 1901, London, Covent Garden, with Suzanne Adams (Hero), Marie Brema (Beatrice), Walter Hyde, John Coates (Claudio), David Bispham, and Putnam Griswold (Leonato); conducted by Mancinelli. Revived November 1, 1965, Wexford, Ireland, Wexford Festival; conducted by Courtney Kenny.

The opera closed after two performances at Covent Garden.

The text, the Beatrice and Benedict story, is a rhymed version of Shakespeare's work. The opera was criticized from the very beginning for its lack of imagination and vitality (and the Larner review on its revival restates this).

Its few highlights include Claudio's serenade to Hero in act 2, and Claudio's rejection of Hero at the act 3 wedding ceremony.

Other settings of the Shakespeare play include *Béatrice et Bénédict* of Berlioz (1862, Paris); *Viel Lärm um nichts* of H. Heinrich (1956, Frankfurt/Oder); and T. Khrennikov's parody *Much Ado about Hearts* (1972, Moscow).
SCORE: vs (London and New York: Boosey & Co., 1901).
BIBLIOGRAPHY: Gerald Larner, "'Wexford," *Opera* XVI (1965), 67–68 [on revival].

Muirgheís, "the first Irish opera," in three acts, by O'Brien Butler; libretto (Eng) by Nora Chesson; translated into Gaelic by T. O'Donoghue. First performance December 7, 1903, Dublin.
SCORE: vs, Gaelic-English (New York: Breitkopf & Härtel, 1910).

Mulligan Guard Ball, The, musical drama in one act by David Braham; text (Eng) by Ned Harrigan. First performance January 13, 1879, New York, Theatre Comique, with Harrigan (Dan Mulligan), Tony Hart (Tommy Mulligan), Nellie Jones (Katy), Annie Mack (Bridget Lochmuller), and Harry Fisher (Gustavus Lochmuller). It ran for 100 nights. Revived and expanded into two acts (1883) and three acts (1892).

Dan Mulligan runs into trouble planning the annual ball that carries his name when he discovers that it is booked for the same hall and time as an event by a black group, the Skidmore Guards. A solution is reached when the blacks agree to stage their festivities upstairs. A second problem for Dan is that his son Tommy is in love with Katy, daughter of the German immigrant Lochmullers, and the mothers despise each other. When the youngsters elope, the fathers, Dan and Gustavus, prepare to do battle, but the differences between the families are smoothed out when the newly married couple come back home.

The work opened two days before *H.M.S. Pinafore** made its New York debut. It was the first in a series of Mulligan works, all having a set cast of characters. Among its numbers are "The Mulligan Guard Ball Quadrille," which serves as the overture and, with an obvious nod to its Irish characters, "The Harp That Once Thro' Tara's Halls." The black angle is portrayed in the "Skidmore Fancy Ball."
SCORE/LIBRETTO: English; contemporary sheet music, score and parts, typed libretto (libretto, NYPL); repr. ed. Katherine K. Preston, *NAMT*, vol. 10 (1994).

Murder in Three Keys, trilogy of operas by Erik Chisholm; libretto (Eng) by the composer. First performance of trilogy July 6, 1954, New York, Cherry Lane Theatre; conducted by Rex Wilder. **Black Roses**: Harriet Hill (Alice), Martha Moore (Mary), John Miller (Bertie), Willard Pierce (Charlie), Carolyn Burns (Annabella), Fred Patrick (Sammy), and Charles Oliver (Joe); **Dark Sonnet**: Ellen Brehm (Mrs. Rowland); and **Simoon**: Jane Cramer (Biskra), John Miller (Yusuf), Richard Roussin (Guimard), and Harriet Hill (voice).

Black Roses, opera in one act; libretto (Eng), after T. S. Eliot.

Dark Sonnet, opera in one act; libretto (Eng), after Eugene O'Neill's *Before Breakfast.* The story was also set by Thomas Pasatieri as *Before Breakfast.**

The story, set in Greenwich Village during the Depression, concerns a wife of loose morals, Mrs. Rowland, who lambastes her husband in the next room.

Simoon, opera in one act; libretto (Eng), after August Strindberg.

BIBLIOGRAPHY: Howard Taubman, "'A Trilogy of Terror' Bows," *NYT* (July 7, 1954), 23.

Murder of Comrade Sharik, The, comic satire in a prologue and two acts by William Bergsma; libretto (Eng) by the composer, after Mikhail Bulgakov's novel *Heart of a Dog,* translated by Mirra Ginsburg. First performance 1973, Seattle. Revised 1978. First performance Brooklyn, New York, April 10, 1986.

When Dr. Danielov is angered by opposition from the Tenants Committee in his building, he uses his experimentation with sex transplants on a dog, Sharik, who turns into a human being. Sharik proceeds to spout party propaganda and fall in love with Darya, the doctor's cook. Stymied, the doctor calls on Stalin, one of his satisfied patients, to assist him in regaining control of his household, but Stalin refuses to interfere, opening the door to Sharik's increasing domination. With the help of Blumenthal, the doctor is able to operate on Sharik. Accused of murdering Sharik, the doctor produces his "patient" as he changes him back into a dog once again.

For a detailed description, see Kornick/*RAO*, 58–60.

Major roles: Sharik (ten), Dr. Danielov (bar), Blumenthal (bass), and Darya Petrovna (mezzo).

Music Critic, The, opera by John Henry Antill; libretto (Eng) by the composer. First performance 1953, Sydney, Australia.

Music Hath Mischief, The, radio opera in one act by Gerard Victory; libretto (Eng) by the composer. First performance October 29, 1967, Dublin, RTE. First stage performance December 3, 1968, Dublin, Grand Opera Society, RTE Symphony Orchestra with Patricia McCarry (the wife), William Young (the husband), Patrick Ring (the postman); conducted by Napoleone Annovazzi.

A couple's wedded bliss is threatened on their tenth anniversary when the postman delivers a strange music box, which brings on a series of misfortunes. When they toss the box out of the window, their luck seems to change. Unfortunately, the box hits the postman, who returns with the box's creator, who turns out to be the god of fortune. He has orchestrated the entire episode for his own entertainment.

BIBLIOGRAPHY: W. H. A. Williams, "Dublin," *ON* (Feb. 1, 1969), 32 [on stage premiere].

Musicians of Bremen, The, "a not-so-Grimm modern musical fairy tale" by Alfred Balkin, orchestration by Ken Morgan; lyrics and book (Eng) by the composer. Composed 1972.

Another setting is D. Arlan's *Ballad of the Bremen Band.**

SCORE: vs (Fort Lauderdale, Fla.: Now View Music, 1982).

Music Mad, dramatic sketch by James Hook; libretto (Eng) by Theodore Edward Hook. First performance August 27, 1807, London, Little Theatre in the Haymarket.

LIBRETTO: English (New York: Longworths, 1812).

Music Robber, The, comic opera in two acts by Isaac Van Grove; libretto (Eng) by Richard L. Stokes. First performance July 4, 1926, Cincinnati, Zoological Gardens Opera Company, with Forrest Lamont (Wolfgang Amadeus Mozart), Kathryne Browne (Constanze

Mozart), Raymond Koch (Franz Sussmayer), Howard Preston (Count Johann von Walsegg), and Benjamin Groban (Emanuel Schikaneder); conducted by the composer.

In this fanciful story, Mozart, already sick, has just finished *The Magic Flute*. When Count von Walsegg hears Mozart tell Constanze that he has heard ghostly voices tell him to write a Requiem, Walsegg steals the manuscript after Mozart completes it. Walsegg is forced by, among others, Beethoven, to reveal his fraud, and Mozart becomes happy once more!

Music Shop, The, opera in one act by Richard Wargo; libretto (Eng) by the composer based on Anton Chekhov's sketch *Forgot*. First performance October 1985, St. Paul, Minnesota, Midwest Opera Theater. Fall 1990 performance with Brent Weber (Ivan Stepanovich), Perry Ward (Dimitri, the shopkeeper), Kathlyn Fries (Masha), and Elizabeth Huling (Ivan's wife).

When the forgetful Ivan Stepanovich comes to buy his wife some sheet music but has failed to write down the name of the piece, the shopkeeper and his assistant, Masha, sing an array of melodies, including Mozart's "Alleluia" and "My Bonny Lies Over the Ocean."

Major roles: Masha (sop), Dimitri Petrovsky (bar), Ivan Stepanovich (ten), and the wife (mezzo).

Part of *A Chekhov Trilogy.**

Music with Roots in the Aether, television opera by Robert Ashley; libretto (Eng) by the composer. First performance 1976, Paris, Festival d'Automne.

The work consists of video portraits of seven composers: David Behrman, Philip Glass, Alvin Lucier, Gordon Mumma, Pauline Oliveros, Terry Riley, and Robert Ashley. VIDEO: Lovely Music (1976, New York).

Muskrat Lullaby, opera in three scenes by Edward Barnes; libretto (Eng) by the composer, after the book *Mama Don't Allow* (1984) by Thacher Hurd. First performance 1989, Los Angeles, Music Center Opera Education Program.

For soloists, narrator/pianist, and audience as the chorus.
SCORE: ms vs (St. Louis: MMB Music, 1989).

My Aunt, operatic farce by John Addison; libretto (Eng) by Samuel J. Arnold. First performance August 1, 1815, London, Lyceum.
LIBRETTO: English (Boston: C. Callender, 1820).

My Brother Called, music drama by Robert Ashley; libretto (Eng) by the composer. First performance November 1988, Chicago. First New York performance January 18, 1990, New York, Merkin Concert Hall, with Thomas Buckner.

An agent at a café observes passersby and is aided by a fellow agent, or "brother."
The action is continued in *eL Aficionado.**
BIBLIOGRAPHY: Howard Reich, "'Brother' Premieres on Enchanting Note," *Chicago Tribune* (Nov. 3, 1988), 7; John Rockwell, "Premiere of Ashley's 'Brother,'" *NYT* (Jan. 21, 1990), I, 49.

My Grandmother, musical farce in two acts by Stephen Storace; libretto (Eng) by Prince Hoare. First performance December 16, 1793, London, Little Theatre in the Haymarket, with Richard Suett (Dicky Gossip), Jack Bannister (Vapour), and Nancy Storace (Florella). First U.S. performance April 27, 1795, Philadelphia, Chestnut Street Theatre.

One of the characters, a village barber, is based on the title character of the Barber of Bagdad from *The Arabian Nights*. In the present setting, the young hero, Vapour, is smitten by the picture of a girl dressed in a long-ago style. He becomes so disheveled in his passion that he goes to the barber, Dicky Gossip, whose slowness and loquacious-ness drive him to distraction. His friend Medley dresses his own daughter Florella to look like the girl in the portrait and ensnare Vapour.

For a detailed description, see Fiske/*ETM*, 521–22.

The overture comes from Storace's *Venus and Adonis** (1793, London).

LIBRETTO: English (London: E. Powell, 1795; New York: D. Longworth, 1806).

My Heart's in the Highlands, opera in two acts by David Ahlstrom; libretto (Eng) by the composer, after William Saroyan's play (1939). Composed 1955.

The work takes place in Fresno, California, in 1914. See next entry for another setting.

SCORE: ms vs (1955, photocopy, NYPL).

My Heart's in the Highlands, chamber opera in two acts by Jack Beeson; libretto (Eng) by the composer, after Saroyan. First performance March 17, 1970, NET, with Gerard Harrington (Johnny), Lili Chookasian (the grandmother), Alan Crofoot (the father), Spiro Malas (the grocer), and Ken Smith (Jasper MacGregor); conducted by Peter Herman Adler. First performance (stage) October 25, 1988, New York, Columbia University, Kathryn Bache Miller Theatre, with Ara Berberian/Peter Loehle, John Schackelford, Stephen Owen, Adam Plotch, Maro Partamian, and Michael Kutner; conducted by Richard Marshall.

The story tells of a poor Armenian-American family in 1914 in Fresno, California, through the eyes of the nine-year-old son, Johnny, who lives with his father, Ben Alex-ander, a failed poet, and his grandmother, who speaks (and sings) only in Armenian. The family barely gets by with food bought on credit from Kosak, a grocer. The trio invites the ailing Jasper MacGregor, an old actor who has run away from an old age home, to stay with them. He is brought back to the home, whereupon things worsen for the Alexanders, but he returns once more. When he dies after entertaining the family and neighbors with a reading of Shakespeare, a young couple comes to take over the house, and the Alexander family is evicted.

For a detailed description, see Eaton/*OP* II, 163–64.

Major roles: Ben Alexander (ten), Jasper MacGregor (bass-bar), Johnny (boy sop), Mr. Kosak (deep bass), and the grandmother (alto).

SCORE: vs (New York: Boosey & Hawkes, 1973).

BIBLIOGRAPHY: Frank Merkling, review, *ON* XXXIV (Apr. 4, 1970), 32 [on premiere].

My Kinsman, Major Molineux, opera in one act by Bruce Saylor; libretto (Eng) by Cary Plotkin, after Nathaniel Hawthorne. First performance August 28, 1976, Pitts-burgh, Pennsylvania Opera Festival, Winchester-Thurston Theater.

The work is set in a colonial town during the time of the American Revolution. The young Englishman Robin comes to a colonial town where a wealthy relative, Major Molineux, the King's governor, has promised to aid him. When there is no trace of Molineux, Robin is left to his own devices, and a rebellion breaks out. Molineux be-lieves that Robin, caught in the middle, has joined the rebellion, and as Molineux is exiled, Robin is truly left alone.

For a detailed description, see Kornick/*RAO*, 268–69.

Major roles: Robin (ten) and Major Molineux (bar).

My Lady Molly, comic opera in two acts by Sidney Jones; libretto (Eng) by G. J. Jessop, Percy Greenbank, and C. H. Taylor. First performance March 14, 1903, Lon-don, Terry's, with Sybil Arundale (Captain Romney) and Decima Moore.

The story, set in the eighteenth century, concerns a young woman who passes herself off as an army captain.
SCORE: vs (London: Keith, Prowse; Boston, B. F. Wood Music Co., 1902).
LIBRETTO: English (London: Keith, Prowse, 1902).

My Love, My Umbrella, comic opera by Kevin O'Connell; libretto (Eng) by James Conway, after John McGahern. First performance November 14, 1997, Belfast.
About the love life, carried on under an umbrella, of a young man just come to Dublin.

My Old Woman, musical comedy in three acts by Jonathan Blewitt, an adaptation of Fétis's *La vieille* (1826, Paris); libretto (Eng) by George Macfarren, after Scribe and Delavigne's text. First performance January 14, 1829, London, Surrey Theatre.
An earlier arrangement was Lacy's *Love in Wrinkles** (1828).
LIBRETTO: English (London: J. Cumberland, [1829?]).

My Own Lover, operatic farce by George Rodwell; libretto (Eng) by the composer. First performance January 11, 1832, London, Drury Lane Theatre.
LIBRETTO: English ([London: W. Reynolds], 1832).

Myrtillo, pastoral interlude, "composed after the Italian manner" by John Pepusch; libretto (Eng) by Colley Cibber. First performance November 5, 1715, London, Drury Lane Theatre, with Margherita de L'Epine (Myrtillo).
LIBRETTO: English (London: Henry Lintot, 1736).

Myshkin, television opera in one act by John Eaton; libretto (Eng) by Patrick Creagh, after Dostoyevsky's *The Idiot.* First performance April 23, 1973, New York, PBS.
The title character's mental stability is echoed in the music, with the orchestra tuned in quarter tones, while his madness is represented by electronic music tuned in sixth tones.

Mysteries of the Castle, The, musical drama in three acts by William Shield; libretto (Eng) by Miles Peter Andrews and Frederick Reynolds, inspired by Ann Ward Radcliffe's *The Mysteries of Eudolpho.* First performance January 31, 1795, London, Covent Garden. First U.S. performance April 15, 1796, Boston, Federal Street Theatre.
The setting is Sicily. Julia, who is threatened by the evil Count, is saved by an underground passage that leads to a castle.

Mystic Fortress, The, radio opera in one act by Leslie Kondorossy; libretto (Eng) by the composer. First performance June 12, 1955, Cleveland, WSRS.

Mystic Trumpeter, The, opera in one act by Robert Starer; libretto (Eng), after Walt Whitman. First performance February 4, 1983, Brooklyn, New York, Brooklyn College.

My Uncle, operetta by John Addison; libretto (Eng) by Samuel Beazley. First performance June 23, 1817, London, Lyceum.

My Walking Photograph, "musical duality" in one act by Alfred B. Sedgwick, an adaptation of Lecocq's *La fille de Madame Angot* (1872, Brussels); libretto (Eng) by the composer. First performance 1876, Chicago?
The courtship of the music teacher Mr. Robson to a young widow is brought to an end when his wife discovers his wandering and starts a flirtation of her own.
Roles: Mr. Richard Robson, teacher of music; and Mrs. Richard Robson, his wife.
SCORE: vs (Chicago: Dramatic Publishing Co., 1876); repr. ed. Michael Meckna, *NAMT,* vol. 7 (1974).

N

Naboth's Vineyard, dramatic madrigal by Alexander Goehr; libretto (narrative in English, arias in Latin), after the Old Testament, Book of Kings 1, 21. First performance July 16, 1968, London. First U.S. performance June 30, 1970, Aspen, Colorado, with Jacqueline Pierce, Melvin Novick, and James Selway.

King Ahab wants to have Naboth's vineyards. Ahab's wife, Jezebel, has Naboth stoned to death when he refuses to give them up. The Lord reserves punishment not for Ahab but for his descendants.

The work is set for three vocalists (alto, ten, bass) and small ensemble (six players).

Part 1 of the *Triptych,** which also includes *Shadowplay** (1970) and *Sonata about Jerusalem** (1971).
SCORE: fs, English-German (London: Schott; New York: Schott Music Corp., [1973]).
BIBLIOGRAPHY: Quaintance Eaton, "Aspen," *ON* XXXV (Sept. 19, 1970), 27 [on U.S. premiere]; Philip Kennicott, "Composer's Page," *ON* LVI (Dec. 7, 1991), 48, 70.

Nada, opera by Harry L. Freeman; libretto (Eng) by the composer. First performance (concert, excerpts) 1900, Cleveland. Revised (1941–1944) as *Nada and the Lily*, part of the *Zululand** trilogy.

Nadeshda, romantic opera in four acts by Arthur Goring Thomas; libretto (Eng) by Julian Sturgis. First performance April 16, 1885, London, Drury Lane.
SCORE: vs (London: Boosey; New York: W. A. Pond, [ca. 1885]).

Naked Carmen, "electric rock opera" in one act by John Corigliano and David Hess, after Bizet's *Carmen* (1875, Paris). Composed 1970.

The work employs synthesizers, rock and opera singers, and amplified instruments.
DISCOGRAPHY: M. Moore, W. Walker, Detroit Sym., Mercury SRM 1-604 (1 LP).

Naked Revolution, multimedia opera by Dave Soldier; libretto (Eng) by Maita di Niscemi. First performance October 11, 1997, New York, the Kitchen, with Tony Boutté (the cabdriver), Robert Osborne (the general), and Jimmy Justice (the citizen); conducted by Richard Auldon Clark; artistic concept by Vitaly Komar and Alexander Melamid; directed by David Herskovits.

The work, which stresses the theme that all revolutions eventually fade away and are replaced by others, opens with a Russian immigrant cab driver explaining his disturbing dreams to his psychiatrist. In the fantasy that follows, revolutionaries such as Washington, Lenin, and Isadora Duncan meet and put forth their beliefs.

The score includes elements of country music, dance, and choral writing.
BIBLIOGRAPHY: Anthony Tommasini, "Opera with Washington and Lenin? Revolutionary!," *NYT* (Oct. 14, 1997), E, 5 [on premiere].

Namiko-San, tragic opera by Aldo Franchetti; libretto (Eng) by the composer, after Leo Duran's *The Daymio*. First performance December 11, 1925, Chicago, with Richard Bonelli (Yiro Danyemon), Tamaki Miura (Namiko-San), Theodore Ritch (Yasui), Alice D'Hermanoy (Towa-San), and Vittorio Revisan (Sato); conducted by the composer.

The setting is medieval Japan. The sixteen-year-old Namiko-San is the geisha of the fierce Yiro Danyemon, warrior prince of the province. He has declared that anyone stealing rice from his plantation will be put to death. Yasui, a poor young monk, asks Namiko-San for something to eat when he stops by her modest hut, which is near the temple of Nikko. The two immediately become drawn to each other, and when Yasui hears Yiro's bugle call, he prepares to flee, aware that the prince hates monks. Before Yasui departs, Namiko-San makes him promise that he will return and take her away; her signal will be hanging out a red lantern to indicate that the coast is clear.

The jealous Yiro arrives, dragging in Towa-San, an old woman who has been captured for stealing a bit of rice. Namiko-San, with the help of Sato, her gardener, helps the woman to escape, but Yiro discovers evidence of Yasui's meal and finds his rosary. After forcing Namiko-San to reveal her plans, Yiro hides and waits for the monk's return. When he does, Yiro steps forward and, inadvertently, stabs Namiko-San, who has stepped between the two men. She dies in Yasui's arms.

For a detailed description, see Hipsher/*AO*, 186–88.

Tamaki Miura, a famous Japanese singer who sang the title role, requested that Franchetti compose an opera with a role to complement her role as Madama Butterfly. This opera was the result.

SCORE: vs, manuscript (n.p., 1938; LCCN: 84-190937).

Nancy, or, The Parting Lovers, all-sung afterpiece by Henry Carey; libretto (Eng) by the composer. First performance December 1, 1739, London, Covent Garden. Revived as *True Blue, or, The Press Gang.*

Nancy is separated from her beloved, True Blue, when he is forced into a press gang for a British man-of-war by Lieutenant Dreadnaught. At the end she is comforted by her father.

For a detailed description, see Fiske/*ETM*, 155–56.

Nancy Brown, operetta by Henry Hadley; libretto (Eng) by Frederic Ranken and George Broadhurst. First performance February 16, 1903, New York, Bijou, with Marie Cahill.

In the story Nancy Brown is a marriage broker who comes to the impoverished country of Bally Hoo and brightens its financial future by supplying a wealthy, but unmarried, heiress.

The work includes the interpolation "Under the Bamboo Tree," written by Bob Cole, and the newly-composed "Congo Love Song," by Cole and Johnson; both were vehicles for Cahill.

LIBRETTO: English (New York, Jos. Stern & Co., 1903).

Narcissa, or, The Cost of Empire, grand opera in four acts by Mary Moore; libretto (Eng) by Sarah Pratt Carr. First performance April 22, 1912, Seattle, Moore Theatre, with Luella Chilson-Ohrman (Narcissa), Charles Hargreaves (Marcus Whitman), Frederick Warford (Yellow Serpent), Harold Spaulding (Elijah), Albert Gilette (Delaware Tom), Frederick Levin (Dr. John McLaughlin), and Ruth Scott Laidlaw (Siskadee); conducted by the composer.

The setting is upstate New York and the Oregon territory in the 1830s. Marcus Whitman, a missionary from upstate New York, brings his fiancée, Narcissa, to the West to continue his efforts at converting the Indians. They are befriended by Yellow Serpent and Elijah, his son. When white settlers kill Elijah in California, a group of Indians, led by Delaware Tom, kill Marcus and Narcissa before Dr. McLaughlin, head of the station, can bring aid. Siskadee, Elijah's lover, mourns her friends' passing, and Yellow Serpent swears vengeance against the killers of his friends.

For a description, see Hipsher/*AO*, 331–32; Smith/*MCM*, 70–83.

Major roles: Marcus Whitman (ten); Elijah (ten); Yellow Serpent (bar); Delaware Tom (bar); Dr. John McLaughlin, Chief Factor of the Hudson Bay Company (bass); Narcissa Prentiss (dramatic sop); and Siskadee, Indian princess (alto).

The opera's creators made a conscious attempt to portray the Indians in a positive light, stating in the foreword that "an effort has been made to give the Indian sympathetic treatment. Misunderstood, defrauded, outraged, his relations with Americans make that chapter in our history one of growing shame."

The music contains Indian themes and rhythms. Among the highlights are the hymn "Yes, My Native Land I Love Thee," which the congregation sings to Marcus and Narcissa as they prepare for their journey at the end of act 1; Narcissa's prayer and lullaby at the opening of act 3; and Elijah's ballad "When Camas Bloom," also in act 3.
SCORE: vs (New York: M. Witmark & Sons, 1912).

Narensky, or, The Road to Yaroslaf, "serio-comic" opera in three acts by Charles Edward Horn, John Braham, and William Reeve; libretto (Eng) by Charles Armitage Brown. First performance January 11, 1814, London, Drury Lane Theatre.

The overture was composed by Reeve.
LIBRETTO: English (London: J. Cawthorn, 1814).

Natalia Petrovna, opera in two acts by Lee Hoiby; libretto (Eng) by William Ball, after Turgenev's *A Month in the Country*. First performance October 8, 1964, New York, New York City Opera Company, with Richard Cross (Rakitin), Maria Dornya (Natalia), John McCollum (Arkady), Anthony Rudel (Kolia), Sandra Darling (Vera), Muriel Greenspon (Anna), Patricia Brooks (Lisaveta), and John Reardon (Arkady); conducted by Julius Rudel; directed by William Ball. Revived as *A Month in the Country*, January 1981, Boston.

The bored Countess Natalia Petrovna Islaeva, wife of a country landowner, Arkady Sergeitch Islaev, is enamored of Alexei Alexeivitch Belaev, summer tutor to the couple's son Kolia. Natalia accuses Vera Alexandrovna, Natalia's orphaned niece, of being involved with the tutor, who in turn grows increasingly passionate about Natalia and is forced to leave. Natalia's husband suspects that Mihail Mihailovitch Rakitin, an author in love with Natalia, is her only paramour. Natalia's jealousy over Vera drives the girl into the arms of a silly old suitor, and Lisaveta Bogdanovna, companion to Natalia's mother-in-law, Anna Semyonovna, flees also.

Major roles: Mihail Mihailovitch (bass-bar), Natalia Petrovna Islaeva (sop), Arkady Sergeitch Islaev (ten), Vera Alexandrovna (lyric sop), Lisaveta Bogdanovna (sop), and Anna Semyonovna (mezzo).

For a detailed description, see Eaton/*OP* II, 165–66.
SCORE: (New York: Boosey and Hawkes, 1967).
BIBLIOGRAPHY: Harold C. Schonberg, review, *NYT* (Oct. 9, 1964), 33 [on premiere].

Nathan the Wise, poetic drama in three acts by Leslie Kondorossy; libretto (Eng) by Shawn Hall, after Lessing's *Nathan der Weise* (1779). First performance 1969, Cleveland.

The setting is Jerusalem during the Crusades. The plot centers on the Jewish trader Nathan, whose wisdom and ecumenism earn him the respect and friendship of Sultan Saladin, a Muslim. Nathan's adopted daughter turns out to be the sister of the knight who has fallen in love with her, and both are the children of Sultan Saladin's dead brother and his Christian wife.

Native Land, or, The Return from Slavery, opera in three acts by Henry Rowley Bishop, a partial adaptation of G. Rossini's *Tancredi* (1813, Venice); libretto (Eng) by William Dimond, after G. Rossi. First performance February 10, 1824, London, Covent Garden, with Mr. Sinclair (Aurelio di Montalo), Mr. Farren (Giuseppo), Mr. Cooper (Tancredi), and Miss Paton (Clymante).

Aurelio, a nobleman from Genoa, is captured by Barbary pirates and is unable to contact his beloved, Clymante, because Giuseppo, his guard, destroys his letters. In the end Aurelio is freed, with the help of Tancredi, and rejoins Clymante.

LIBRETTO: English (London: Printed for R. S. Kirby, 1824; New York: E. M. Murden, 1824).

Nativity, The, opera in a prologue and three scenes by Fritz Hart; libretto (Eng), after old sources. Composed 1931.

Nativity, "Christmas canticle for the Child" by Norman Dello Joio; libretto (Eng) by William Gibson. First performance December 4, 1987, Midland, Michigan.

SCORE: vs (New York: Associated Music Publishers, 1990).

Nativity according to St. Luke, The, musical drama in seven scenes by Randall Thompson; libretto (Eng). First performance December 12, 1961, Cambridge, Massachusetts.

SCORE: vs (Boston: E. C. Schirmer, [1961]).

Natoma, romantic opera in three acts by Victor Herbert; libretto (Eng) by Joseph D. Redding. First performance February 25, 1911, Philadelphia, with Mary Garden (Natoma), John McCormack (Lieut. Paul Merrill), Gustave Huberdeau (Don Francisco), Hector Dufranne (Father Peralta), Mario Sammarco (Alvarado), Lillian Grenville (Barbara), Frank Preisch (Castro), and Constantin Nicolay (Kagama); conducted by Cleofonte Campanini; directed by Fernand Almanz. The production opened on February 25, 1911, at the Metropolitan Opera House in New York.

The setting is the Spanish-controlled Santa Cruz and Santa Barbara, 1820. Alvarado, a young and hot-tempered Spaniard, wants to marry Barbara, the only child of the wealthy Don Francisco, and thereby get control of Don Francisco's estate. Natoma, a pure-blooded Indian and once Barbara's playmate and handmaiden, is captivated by the newly arrived U.S. Lieutenant Paul Merrill, but he falls in love with Barbara when he meets her. The half-breed Castro plans with Alvarado to kidnap Barbara, aided by Kagama, but just as they are to seize Barbara at a dance, Natoma stabs Alvarado, killing him. Father Peralta grants Natoma sanctuary despite the murder.

Roles: Kagama, friend of Castro (bass); Pico (ten); Don Francisco de la Guerra, noble Spaniard (bass); Father Peralta (bass); Juan Bautista Alvarado, a young Spaniard (bar); José Castro, a half-breed (bar); Paul Merrill, U.S. lieutenant (ten); Barbara de la Guerra, daughter of Don Francisco (sop); Natoma, an Indian girl (sop).

For a detailed description, see Hipsher/*AO*, 260–64; and Waters/*VH*, 375–91.

Among the musical highlights are Paul and Natoma's scene and Barbara's "Oh, Wondrous Night!" of act 1 and the Dagger Dance and Natoma's soliloquy of act 2. The effective music was hampered by a weak text, and the critics were extremely harsh toward the work after its New York performance. Nonetheless, it received numerous performances in the next three years, being abandoned thereafter. It was Herbert's first grand opera.

SCORE: vs (New York: G. Schirmer, 1911).

Naughty Marietta, comic opera in two acts by Victor Herbert; libretto (Eng) by R. J. Young. First performance October 24, 1910, Syracuse, Werling Opera House; November 7, 1910, New York, with Emma Trentini (Marietta), Orville Harrold (Captain Dick),

Edward Martindel (Etienne), Marie Duchêne (Adah), Harry Cooper (Simon), and Kate
Elinore (Lizette); directed by Jacques Coini.

The setting is eighteenth-century Louisiana. Marietta d'Altena, a young woman
from a noble Italian family, has come to America to get away from her unhappy marriage. She meets Captain Dick, who is searching for the pirate Bras Priqué. Marietta
and Dick find themselves drawn to each other. Another arrival is Adah, mistress of
Etienne Grandet, whose father is the lieutenant governor. Adah loves Etienne, but he
has lost interest in her. Etienne is drawn to Marietta when he hears her sing the "Italian
Street Song." Dick admits that he too has fallen in love with Marietta, and he also is
able to woo her unencumbered when Etienne, conveniently, turns out to be the pirate
Dick was searching for. The work ends with the famous "Ah, Sweet Mystery of Life."

Bordman calls this piece "the American masterwork of the era" (Bordman/*AMT*,
261). It is still revived today.

For a detailed description, see Gänzl/*BBM*, 24–29; Waters/*VH*, 355–63.
SCORE: vs (New York: Witmark, 1910).
DISCOGRAPHY: R. Young, J. Blazer, E. Green, L. Harrington, W. Turnage, Catholic Uni-
versity of America, A Cappella Choir, Millennium Chamber Orch.; cond. J. Morris, N 026
Smithsonian Collection (1981, 3 LPs).
VIDEO: P. Munsel, A. Drake, Video Artists International 72004 VAI (1993, Fort Lee, N.J.).

Nausicaa, opera in three acts, a prologue, and interludes by Peggy Glanville-Hicks;
libretto (Eng) by Robert Graves, after his novel *Homer's Daughter.* First performance
August 19, 1961, Athens, with Teresa Stratas (Nausicaa), Sophia Steffan (Queen Arete),
Edward Ruhl (Phemius), Michalis Heliotis (Antinous), John Modenos (Aethon), Spiro
Malas (King Alcinous), George Tsantikos (Clytoneus), and George Monsios
(Eurymachus); conducted by Carlos Surinach; produced by John Butler.

The setting is a Greek city-state in western Sicily, ca. eighth century B.C., and the
story is a variation of the *Odyssey*, with a woman as its creator, not Homer. The Penelope of the tale is Nausicaa, and Odysseus is Aethon, a Cretan who has been shipwrecked. Nausicaa is the daughter of Alcinous, King of Drepanum; he leaves to search
for his lost son Laodamus, leaving his wife, his daughter, and his young son Clytoneus
behind. In his absence Nausicaa is besieged by suitors. Aethon appears, and he and
Nausicaa fall in love. When Queen Arete sets up a shooting contest for the next day to
determine who will wed Nausicaa, the lovers are married secretly that night. During
the contest Aethon is triumphant and kills every suitor. Nausicaa spares the life of
Phemius, a minstrel who had joined a plot by the suitors to overthrow the palace. In
return he is required to sing only her version of the Penelope tale.

For a detailed description, see Eaton/*OP* II, 166–67.
Major roles: Nausicaa (lyr sop), Aethon (bar), Phemius (ten), Clytoneus (ten), Queen
Arete (mezzo), and Antinous and Eurymachus, suitors (ten, bar).
DISCOGRAPHY: T. Stratas, S. Steffan, J. Modenos, S. Malas, Athens Sym. Orch. and
Chorus; cond. C. Surinach, Athens Festival, 1961, Composers Recordings CRI 175 (1964,
1 LP); reissued as CRI SRD 695 (1995, 1 CD).

Nautch Girl, The, or, The Rajah of Chutneypore, "new Indian comic opera" in two
acts by Edward Solomon; libretto (Eng) by George Dance; lyrics by Dance and Frank
Desprez. First performance June 30, 1891, London, Savoy Theatre, with Jessie Bond
(Hollee Beebee), Courtice Pounds (Indru), and Rutland Barrington (Punka).

The work is set in India. Indru, son of Punka, the rajah of Chutneypore, is in love with
Hollee Beebee, a nautch dancer. Since the lovers are of different castes, they are forbidden

from marrying. Indru tries to solve the problem by renouncing his caste; unfortunately, his beloved is at the same time raised to the Brahmin caste, making the two unequal again. Hollee then departs for Europe, leaving Indru and Punka behind to deal with scheming relatives and Bumbo, an idol who has come to life to retrieve his diamond eye.
SCORE: vs (London: Chappell, 1891).

Naval Pillar, The, or, Britannia Triumphant, musical interlude (pastiche) by John Moorehead, John Calcott, and Thomas Linley; libretto (Eng) by Thomas Dibdin. First performance October 7, 1799, London, Covent Garden. First U.S. performance April 23, 1800, Philadelphia, Chestnut Street Theatre.
    The patriotic work includes a finale based on "The Star-Spangled Banner" but described here as an "old air."
LIBRETTO: English (London, ca. 1799).

Necklace, The, opera in one act by Wayne Bohrnstedt; libretto (Eng) by Lucile March. First performance March 12, 1956, Redlands, California.

Neither, operatic monodrama in one act by Morton Feldman; text (Eng) consists of the poem of the same name by Samuel Beckett. First performance May 13, 1977, Rome, with Martha Hanneman; conducted by Marcello Panni. First U.S. performance November 1978, New York, Manhattan School of Music.
    The plotless work uses as its libretto the sixteen lines of Beckett's poem.
SCORE: vs (Vienna: Universal Edition, 1977).

Nell, ballad opera in two acts and an epilogue by Alison Bauld; libretto (Eng) by the composer. First performance June 1, 1988, London, Midsummer Opera at Donmar Warehouse.
    The setting is inland Australia. In order to escape her poor family's wretched existence, their simple daughter, Nell, has a child by a stranger and sees the world differently thereafter; when he suggests that they escape together, she declines.
BIBLIOGRAPHY: Noël Goodwin, review, *Opera* XXXIX (Aug. 1988), 1009–10 [on premiere].

Nell Gwynne, comic opera by Alfred Cellier; libretto (Eng) by H. B. Farnie, after *Rochester* by Moncrieff. First performance October 16, 1878, Manchester, Prince's Theatre.
    Revised as *Dorothy** (1886).

Nelson, opera in three acts by Lennox Berkeley; libretto (Eng) by Alan Pryce-Jones. First performance September 22, 1954, London, Sadler's Wells, with Victoria Elliott, Anna Pollak (Lady Nelson), Sheila Rex, Robert Thomas, Arnold Matters (Sir William Hamilton), David Ward (Hardy), and Stanley Clarkson; conducted by Vilem Tausky; produced by George Devine.
    The British Embassy in Naples is celebrating Lord Nelson's great Nile victory at a party hosted by Sir William, the British ambassador, and Lady Emma Hamilton, his wife. When Nelson enters, he seems terribly saddened, and a fortune-teller predicts his future unhappiness. Nelson seeks solace with Emma Hamilton, and the two, drawn to each other, give vent to their intense feelings.
    When Nelson returns to London, Lord Minto forces him to choose either his career or Emma. Reluctantly, he agrees to leave her, and, at a Portsmouth inn, his friend Hardy tells him he has made the right decision. Emma also comes to see him off. Nelson dies during the Battle of Trafalgar, which ends with a great victory for England. Hardy recounts the details of Nelson's final moments to Emma, and she remembers their love with joy, as the opera comes to a close.

Major roles: Sir William Hamilton (bar), Lady Emma Hamilton (sop), Lord Nelson (ten), Lady Nelson (mezzo), Lord Minto (bass-bar), and Hardy (bass).

Netly Abbey, comic opera in two acts by William Shield, with the overture and one song by William Parke, finale by William Howard; libretto (Eng) by William Pearce. First performance April 10, 1794, London, Covent Garden, with Mrs. Martyr and Charles Incledon. First U.S. performance December 8, 1800, Philadelphia, Chestnut Street Theatre.

The work concerns the navy, and the title refers to a Gothic ruin.

SCORE: vs (London: Longman & Broderip, n.d.).

LIBRETTO: English, in Elizabeth Simpson, ed., *A Collection of Farces*, vol. 3 (London, 1815).

New Don Juan!, A, "operatical, satirical, poetical, egotistical, melo-dramatical, extravaganzical, but strictly moral burletta" in two acts by George Rodwell; libretto (Eng) by J. B. Buckstone, after Byron's poem. First performance 1828, London, Adelphi Theatre.

LIBRETTO: English, 2d ed. (London: T. Richardson, [1828?]).

Newest Opera in the World, The, improvisatory opera by H. Wesley Balk; libretto (Eng) by Philip Brunelle. First performance May 12, 1974, Minneapolis, Minnesota Opera.

The musical style, settings, and plot change for each performance, since they are determined by spinning wheels of fortune.

BIBLIOGRAPHY: M. A. Feldman, review, *ON* XXXIX (Sept. 1974), 54–55 [on premiere].

New Spain, or, Love in Mexico, afterpiece in three acts by Samuel Arnold; libretto (Eng) by John Scawen. First performance July 16, 1790, London, Little Theatre in the Haymarket, with Mrs. Goodall and Miss Fontenelle.

In the story Leonora messes up her planned elopement by showing up at the wrong place. Her intended, Don Garcia, goes to New Mexico in despair, thinking he has been deserted. Leonora follows him with her servant Flora, and both are disguised as men. Leonora joins the army and has worked her way up to the rank of Lieutenant-Governor. In her new position she wins back her beloved Don Garcia.

LIBRETTO: English (Dublin: P. Wogan [et al.], 1790).

New World, "an opera about what Columbus did to the 'Indians'" in one or two acts by Leonard Lehrman; libretto (Eng) by the composer. First performance (concert) October 12, 1991, New York, Lincoln Center Library, After Dinner Opera Company.

New Year, opera in three acts by Michael Tippett; libretto (Eng) by the composer. First performance October 27, 1989, Houston, Grand Opera, with Krister St. Hill (Donny), Peter Kazaras (Pelegrin), Richetta Manager (Regan), Jane Shaulis (Nan), Richard Schiappa (narrator), Helen Field (Jo Ann), and James Maddalena (Merlin); conducted by John DeMain; choreographed by Bill T. Jones. First British performance Glyndebourne, July 1, 1990, with the same cast, except for Philip Langridge (Pelegrin) and Nigel Robson (narrator); conducted by Andrew Davis.

The fantasy plot concerns Pelegrin, a space pilot from "Nowhere Tomorrow," who comes to Earth on New Year's Eve to assist the agoraphobic Jo Ann, who wants to be a doctor. At the end she departs from her room to take on "Terror Town."

For a detailed plot description, see K/*NKOB*, 839–41.

Roles: Jo Ann (sop); Donny, her brother (bar); Nan, their foster mother (mezzo); Pelegrin (ten); Merlin, a computer wizard (bar); narrator (male singer); and Regan, Pelegrin and Merlin's boss (sop).

The score exhibits the influence of the Broadway musical and pop music, for example, a rap duet for two electric guitars, three saxophones, and jazz percussion.

SCORE: vs (London and New York: Schott, 1989).
LIBRETTO: English (London: Schott, 1989).
BIBLIOGRAPHY: Noël Goodwin, "Glyndebourne," *ON* LV (Jan. 19, 1991), 48 [on British premiere]; Andrew Porter, review, *NY* LXV (Nov. 20, 1989), 114–17 [on premiere].

Night, opera in one act by Hugo Weisgall; libretto (Eng), after Sholem Asch's play (1921). Composed 1932.
SCORE: fs (n.p., 193?; LCCN: 64-59680).

Night at the Chinese Opera, A, opera in three acts by Judith Weir; libretto (Eng) by the composer, after the Chinese drama *The Chao Family Orphan* (thirteenth century). First performance July 8, 1987, Cheltenham, England, Kent Opera, with Michael Chance (the General). First U.S. performance 1989, Santa Fe.

The setting is China in the thirteenth century. The work, centering around an ancient Chinese play, combines Orientalisms with Western operatic genres. It concerns Chao Sun, an explorer and mapmaker, who is exiled from Loyan, his native city. His son Chao Lin is given the task of constructing a canal, and among his workers is a group of actors, who present a play, *The Chao Family Orphan,* which tells of a young man who is left an orphan through the machinations of the evil General Tu-an-Ku, who unknowingly adopts the boy. When the son reaches adulthood, he discovers the truth about his parents' demise and vows to avenge them. When the play is complete, Chao Lin receives praise for his canal. While examining his work, he learns from an old woman of his own father's fate and begins his plans for revenge.

For a detailed plot description, see K/*NKOB*, 974–76.

The play forms the plot of Weir's *The Consolations of Scholarship.**

Night before the Wedding and the Wedding Night, The, comic opera in two acts, a partial adaptation and enlargement by Henry Rowley Bishop of Boieldieu's *Les deux nuits* (1829, Paris); libretto (Eng) by Edward Fitzball, after Scribe and Bouilly. First performance November 17, 1829, London, Covent Garden, with Lionel Lorimer (Lord Fingar), Valentine Acton (Sir Edward), Miss Betti (Rose), Mr. Blakfort (Villars), Mr. Duncar (Alford), Miss Carill (Jocelyn), Mr. Salgar (Woodstock), Le Constable (Justice Rigid), Mr. Strun (Portlock), Mr. Jakmann (Torpid), and Mr. Neville (Valter).
SCORE: ms fs (1829, British Library, Add. MS. 27725, 27728).

Night Blooming Cereus, chamber opera in two acts by John Beckwith; libretto (Eng) by James Reaney. First performance March 4, 1959, Toronto, CBS radio. First performance (stage) April 5, 1960, Toronto, Hart House.

Night Dancers, The, or, The Wills, opera in two acts by Edward J. Loder; libretto (Eng) by George Soane, after a German legend. First performance October 28, 1846, London, Princess's, with H. Haigh (Albert), Madame Palmieri (Giselle), and H. Corri (Fridolin).

In a story faintly echoed by the later *Lohengrin* (1850), Giselle has a dream on the eve of her wedding that her betrothed, Albert, is really a prince, thereby smashing her hopes for happiness. His true identity is uncovered by the nosy Fridolin, and, despondent, Giselle begins to die. Albert also wishes for death to join his beloved, but she begs him to keep on living and remember her. Giselle now wakes up and realizes this was all a bad dream.

For a detailed examination of the plot and music, see Biddlecombe/*EO*, 88–91.

Nightingale, The, opera in three acts by Joseph Clokey; libretto (Eng) by Willis K. Jones, after *The Nightingale* by Hans Christian Andersen. First performance December 12, 1925, Miami, University of Miami.

Nightingale, The, opera in a prologue and one act by Bernard Rogers; libretto (Eng) by the composer, after Andersen. First performance (concert) May 10, 1955, New York, Punch Opera. First performance (stage) May 6, 1957, Rochester, New York, Eastman School of Music, Kilbourne Hall, with Carol Dawn Moyer; conducted by Frederick Fennell; directed by Leonard Treash.

The beautiful Nightingale is brought to the Chinese emperor's court to perform a wondrous song, but it is soon replaced by a mechanical bird, a gift from the Japanese emperor. When the Chinese emperor becomes deathly ill, the mechanical bird, now broken, has no effect on the monarch's impending demise; the real Nightingale, however, begins to sing, and Death is banished, bringing the emperor back to health.

For a detailed description, see Eaton/*OP* I, 203.

Major roles: the Nightingale (sop) and the emperor of China (bar/bass-bar).
BIBLIOGRAPHY: Mary Ellis Peltz, review, *ON* XXII (Nov. 11, 1957), 18 [on stage premiere].

Nightingale, children's opera in two acts by Charles Strouse; libretto (Eng) by the composer, after Andersen. First performance April 16, 1982, Vienna, Virginia, Wolf Trap.

The story concerns the powerful Emperor of China, who has become bored by his beautiful Nightingale. The bird returns to the forest, after its place is taken by a bejeweled mechanical bird. The Emperor is about to die when the Nightingale and a young maid return to save him and bring rejoicing to all of China.
SCORE: vs (New York: G. Schirmer, 1982).
BIBLIOGRAPHY: Jerry Floyd, review, *ON* XLVII (July 1982), 32 [on premiere].

Nightingale and the Rose, The, radio opera in one act by George Lessner; libretto (Eng), after Oscar Wilde's story. First performance April 25, 1942, NBC radio, NBC Symphony.

Nightingale and the Rose, The, fairy tale opera in one act by Margaret Garwood; libretto (Eng) by the composer, after Wilde. First performance October 21, 1973, Chester, Pennsylvania, Widener College, Pennsylvania Opera Company.

In despair that Stefan has rejected her for the fickle Narcissa, Rossignol agrees to help Stefan find the perfect rose in order to satisfy Narcissa. His task is impossible, because the garden has not had roses for many years. When Rossignol's grandmother, a witch, reveals that roses will bloom only if Rossignol dies, she sacrifices herself for her beloved. Stefan picks the rose that has just bloomed, but Narcissa rejects him anyway.

For a detailed description, see Kornick/*RAO*, 108–9.

Major roles: Rossignol (sop), Stefan (ten), Narcissa (sop), and grandmother (mezzo).

Nightingale and the Rose, The, chamber opera in one act by Elena Firsova, after the original Russian version, *Solovey i roza* (1991); libretto (Eng), after Wilde and Christina Rossetti. First performance July 8, 1994, London, Almeida Theatre.
BIBLIOGRAPHY: Malcolm Miller, review, *Tempo* CXC (Sept. 1994), 30–31 [on premiere].

Nightingale, Inc., comic opera in one act by Michael Colgrass; libretto (Eng) by the composer. First performance March 13, 1975, Urbana, Illinois.

Nightingale's Apprentice, The, story opera for children and adults in one act by Ann Silsbee; libretto (Eng) by the composer. First performance April 13, 1984, Ithaca, New York, Troika Association.

A clock maker's young apprentice is assisted in her tasks by a nightingale.

Night in Old Paris, A, opera in one act by Henry Hadley; libretto (Eng) by Frederick Truesdell, after Glen MacDonough's play. First performance (private) December 14, 1924, New York. First performance (public) January 22, 1930, New York, NBC radio.

SCORE: ms fs, holograph (1924, NYPL).

Night in the Puszta, A, opera in one act by Leslie Kondorossy; libretto (Eng) by the composer. First performance June 28, 1953, Cleveland, Auditorium.

The work takes place in the Magyar lowlands.

Nightmare Abbey, opera by Douglas Allanbrook; libretto (Eng), after Thomas Peacock's novel. Composed 1960.

Night of the Moonspell, opera in three acts by Elie Siegmeister; libretto (Eng) by Edward Mabley, after Shakespeare's *Midsummer Night's Dream*. First performance November 14, 1976, Shreveport, Louisiana.

In this version of the Shakespeare play, Oberon and Titania are replaced by the King and Queen of the Mardi Gras, Theseus and Hippolyte become the Colonel and Josephine, wealthy owners of a plantation, and Puck is Robin, a young black man who practices voodoo. Robin's spell goes awry, and various mismatched couples result, including Margaret and Anthony (Hermia and Lysander in the Shakespeare) and Holly and David (Helena and Demetrius). Nic Mazette, a weaver, is the contemporary equivalent of Bottom.

Major roles: Margaret (sop), Anthony (bar), Holly (sop), David (ten), Robin (ten), King and Queen of the Mardi Gras (bar, mezzo), and Nic Mazette (bass-bar).

For a detailed description, see Kornick/*RAO*, 280–81.

Night Passage, opera in one act by Robert Moran. First performance April 27, 1995, Seattle, University of Washington, Meany Theatre, Seattle Men's Chorus.

The story, set in England in 1895, concerns the flight of 600 gay men after learning of Oscar Wilde's arrest on charges of practicing homosexuality.

Nights of Annabel Lee, opera by Lou Rodgers; libretto (Eng) by the composer. First performance December 13, 1996, New York, Golden Fleece Ltd.

The work concerns Edgar Allan Poe and his young wife, Virginia Clemm, whose death inspires his famous poem.

Night's Surprise, A, opera in one act by Thomas German Reed; libretto (Eng) by West Cromer (A. Law). First performance February 12, 1877, London, St. George's Hall.

Nigredo Hotel, opera in one act by Nic Gotham; libretto (Eng) by Ann-Marie MacDonald. First performance 1992, Stratford, Ontario, Tarragon Theatre. First stage performance June 1, 1995, Victoria, British Columbia, Pacific Opera Victoria, McPherson Playhouse, with Sharie Saunders (Sophie) and Claude Robitaille (Raymond).

The setting is a seedy hotel room and concerns Sophie, the slatternly owner of the hotel, and Raymond, a young surgeon.

The score, while following the format of traditional opera, shows a strong influence of jazz.

BIBLIOGRAPHY: Robert Jordan, "Victoria," *ON* LX (Sept. 1995), 61–62 [on stage premiere]).

Nina, operatic afterpiece in one act by William Shield and William Thomas Parke, an adaptation of N.-M. Dalayrac's *Nina, ou, La folle par amour* (1786, Paris); libretto (Eng) by John Wolcott, from the French text of B. J. Marsolier. First performance April 24, 1787, London, Covent Garden, with Margaret Martyr. First U.S. performance February 4, 1805, New York, Park Theatre (with a libretto by William Dunlop).

The story is based on the character of Maria in Sterne's *Sentimental Journey*. Also set by G. Paisiello (1789, Caserta).

LIBRETTO: English (London: Longman and Broderip, [1787?]).

Nine Rivers from Jordan, opera in a prologue and three acts by Hugo Weisgall; libretto (Eng) by Denis Johnston. First performance October 9, 1968, New York, City Opera, with Julian Patrick (Don), Joshua Hecht (Sergeant Abe Goldberg), Paul Huddleston (Judas-God), Eileen Schauler (Lot's Wife/Pietà/Eve), John Stewart (Andrew), and Nico Castel (one of the Apostles); conducted by Gustav Meier; directed by Vlado Habunek.

The story is told as a series of flashbacks, when Abe Goldberg, an American sergeant, comes across a man at the grave of "D. R. Hanwell." Goldberg remembers the story of Hanwell. During World War II a British soldier, Don Hanwell, who is on duty near the Dead Sea, sees an apparition of the Salt Woman, who warns him not to have a gun or kill anyone during the war. He follows her warning and therefore lets a German soldier, Otto Suder, escape.

The scene shifts to a trial of the leaders of the Todenwald concentration camp, at which Suder is a guard. The judgment declares that we are all responsible for the war. Feeling guilty at having let Suder escape, Don Hanwell decides to kill him with a bomb. Hanwell again meets up with the German, who then tries to convince the other English soldiers, including Copperhead Kelly, Don's friend, that Don is really a Nazi spy. Copperhead and the others believe him, but Suder is killed when he tries to throw Don's bomb. Don, dying, asks God for the reason he was betrayed; God answers, through Copperhead's voice, that all people are responsible for their own lives and areas that they cannot control; and even though humanity is guilty, it is not damned.

Major roles: Don Hanwell (bar), Abe Goldberg (bar), Salt Woman (sop), Copperhead Kelly (bar/ten), and Otto Suder (ten).
LIBRETTO: English (Bryn Mawr, Pa.: Theodore Presser, 1969).
BIBLIOGRAPHY: Frank Merkling, "Reports: U.S.," *ON* (Nov. 23, 1968), 22 [on premiere]; Harold C. Schonberg, "Opera: 'Nine Rivers from Jordan' Has Premiere," *NYT* (Oct. 10, 1968), 62; Winthrop Sargeant, review, *NY* XLIV (Oct. 19, 1968), 218 [on premiere].

Ninetta, or, The Maid of Palaiseau, comic opera in three acts, an adaptation by Henry Rowley Bishop of Rossini's *La gazza ladra* (1817, Milan); libretto (Eng) by Edward Fitzball, after G. Gheradini's text, based on *La pie voleuse* by Caigniez and d'Aubigny. First performance February 4, 1830, London, Covent Garden. Revived in a two-act version, as *The Maid of Palaiseau*, October 13, 1838, London, Drury Lane Theatre.

In the tale Ninetta, a young serving girl, is accused of taking a silver spoon from the house in which she works, after she rebuffs the advances of the master. Sentenced to death for her "crime," she is saved when the actual thief is discovered to be a magpie.

See Bishop's *The Magpie or the Maid* (1815, London) for another setting.
LIBRETTO: English (London: J. Ebers, [1830]).

Ninth Statue, The, or, The Irishman in Bagdad, musical romance in two acts by Charles Edward Horn; libretto (Eng), after the *Thousand and One Nights*. First performance November 29, 1814, London, Drury Lane Theatre.
LIBRETTO: English (London: John Miller, 1814).

Nixon in China, opera in three acts by John Adams; libretto (Eng) by Alice Goodman. First performance October 23, 1987, Houston, Houston Grand Opera, with Sanford Sylvan (Chou En-lai), James Maddalena (Richard Nixon), Thomas Hammons (Henry Kissinger), John Duykers (Mao Tse-tung), Carolann Page (Pat Nixon), and Trudy Ellen Craney (Chiang Ch'ing); conducted by John DeMain. First British performance September 1, 1988, Edinburgh, Houston Grand Opera production; conducted by the composer. The Houston premiere was preceded by a concert preview on May 25, 1987, San Francisco, Herbst Theater, with the same cast, except for Ronald Gerard as Kissinger.

The story is based on the first visit of then-president Richard M. Nixon, Pat, his wife, and Henry Kissinger, the secretary of state, to mainland China in February 1972, where they meet Mao Tse-tung, his wife, Chiang Ch'ing, and Chou En-lai.

Major roles: Chou En-lai (bar), Richard Nixon (bar), Henry Kissinger (bass), Mao Tse-tung (ten), Pat Nixon (sop), and Chiang Ch'ing (Mme. Mao) (sop).

The minimalist score includes coloratura-like writing for Mme. Mao and a "Red Detachment of Women" ballet, choreographed for the premiere by Mark Morris, in which Kissinger plays an evil landlord, and Pat Nixon tries to rescue the mistreated heroine.
BIBLIOGRAPHY: William Albright, review, *ON* LII (Apr. 9, 1988), 34–36 [on premiere]; Martin Bernheimer, "America: Nixon in Progress," *Opera* XXXVIII (1987), 1022–23 [on concert preview]; Patrick J. Smith, "Inner Landscape," *ON* LIV (July 1989), 20–22.
DISCOGRAPHY: orig. cast: Page, Craney, Maddalena, Sylvan, Duykers, Hammons, Orch. of St. Luke's; cond. De Waart, Elektra/Nonesuch 79177–1 (3 CDs), 79177–4 (2 tapes); rev. John W. Freeman, "Recordings," *ON* LIII (July 1988), 42.

Noah, opera in two acts by Michael Sahl and Eric Salzman; libretto (Eng) by the composers. First performance February 10, 1978, Brooklyn, New York, Pratt Institute.

In this treatment of the story of Noah, Godthefather [*sic*] plans to destroy the city of Atlantis because of the corruption of its residents. Noah, who, with his family, lives apart from the throngs, starts to build an ark when he hears of the impending calamity. During the deluge, Godthefather appears and promises to lead Noah and his group to safety if Noah signs the covenant. After Noah agrees, he is shown the new Atlantis, where he and his family prosper and rule the natives. When he is 600 years old, Noah is faced by a revolt of his resentful subjects, and when Shem, his son, sides with them, Noah is stricken and expires.

See also *The Flood*.*
BIBLIOGRAPHY: Tim Page, review, *NYT* (Mar. 12, 1987), C, 24 [on revival].

Noah and the Stowaway, opera in one act by Martin Kalmanoff; libretto (Eng) by Atra Baer, after the Bible. First performance (concert) February 18, 1951, New York, WNYC. First stage performance October 12, 1952, New York, Provincetown Theater.

In this futuristic version of the biblical story, a stowaway wreaks havoc on the ark.

Noble Outlaw, The, comic opera in three acts by Henry Rowley Bishop; libretto (Eng) by Mrs. Opie, after Fletcher's *The Pilgrim*. First performance April 7, 1815, London.
SCORE: ms fs (British Library, Add. MS. 36943).
LIBRETTO: English (London: Barker, 1815).

Noble Peasant, The, comic opera in three acts by William Shield; libretto (Eng) by Thomas Holcroft. First performance August 2, 1784, London, Theatre Royal. First U.S. performance May 8, 1795, Philadelphia, Southwark Theatre.

The love story is set in Saxon times.
SCORE: vs (London: William Napier, n.d.).
LIBRETTO: English (London: G. Robinson, 1784; Dublin: J. Exshaw, 1784).

Noble Pedlar, The, or, The Fortune Hunter, burletta in two parts by François Hippolyte Barthelemon; libretto (Eng) by George S. Carey. First performance August 21, 1770, London, Marylebone Gardens.
LIBRETTO: English (London: W. Nicoll, 1770).

No Cards, musical piece in one act by "L[ionel] Elliott" (Joseph Benjamin Williams); libretto (Eng) by William S. Gilbert. First performance March 29, 1869, London, Gallery of Illustration.

Miss Annabella Penrose, an heiress, lives with her aunt, Mrs. Pennythorne. Annabella is courted by Ellis Dee, an old bachelor, who is frightened off when Annabella is said to be penniless. She weds the poor Mr. Churchmouse instead.

SCORE: vs (London: J. Williams, [1901]).
LIBRETTO: English (London: J. Williams, [1902]).

Noelani, opera by George Barati; libretto (Eng). Composed 1968. First performance 1971, Aptos, California (?).

No. 11 Bus, music-theater work for mime, singers, dancers, and instrumental ensemble by Peter Maxwell Davies; text (Eng) by the composer. First performance March 20, 1984, London, Queen Elizabeth Hall; conducted by Günther Bauer-Schenk.

The supernatural fantasy, which is based on Tarot cards, features continuous music.
SCORE: miniature score (London: Chester Music, 1990).

No for an Answer, opera in two acts by Marc Blitzstein; libretto (Eng) by the composer. First performance January 5, 1941, New York, with Olive Deering (Clara Chase), Lloyd Gough (Paul Chase), Alfred Ryder (Max Kraus), Carol Channing (Bobbie), and Martin Wolfson (Nick Kyriakos).

The plot concerns a group of Greek-American workers, most of them unemployed, in a small town near a summer resort. They congregate in the Diogenes Club, which meets in a room attached to Nick Kyriakos's roadside diner. Among supporters of the Club are the liberal intellectual Paul Chase and his wife, Clara, who is the wealthy sister of a congressman.

The Club arouses the fear and hatred of the Resort Association of the area's hotel owners, who believe it will lead to the formation of a union. Joe, Nick's son, returns to his hometown, only to be killed, and the Club is set afire because of the efforts of the Resort Association. Nick and his friends are left with just their Club song, "No for an Answer," and their spirit with which to carry on.

For a detailed description, see Gordon/*MM*, 178–81, 190–98.

The chorus plays an essential role in the work, functioning, at times, like a traditional Greek chorus.
SCORE: ms vs (photostat; LCCN: 84-179945).
LIBRETTO: English (typed copy; New York: M. Blitzstein; William Morris Office, [1940]).
BIBLIOGRAPHY: Marc Blitzstein, "Of 'No for an Answer,'" *NYT* (Jan. 5, 1941), IX, 2.
DISCOGRAPHY: C. Channing, O. Deering, N. Green, H. Sundergard, C. Ruskin, M. Wolfson, L. Gough, C. Conway, B. Conway, M. Loring; Blitzstein, pno, Theme 103 (1941).

Noises, Sounds & Sweet Airs, opera by Michael Nyman; libretto (Eng), after Shakespeare's *The Tempest*. First performance December 7, 1994, Tokyo, with Catherine Bott, Hilary Summers, and Christopher Gillet; conducted by Robert Lepage. First British performance January 30, 1996, London, Royal Festival Hall.

First performed as the dance opera *La princesse de Milan*, July 24, 1991, Avignon.

None So Blind as Those Who Won't See, afterpiece in two acts by Samuel Arnold; libretto (Eng) by Charles Dibdin, after L. F. A. Dorvigny. First performance July 2, 1782, London, Little Theatre in the Haymarket.

No Neutral Ground, chamber opera in one act by William Edward Brandt; libretto (Eng) by the composer. First performance December 10, 1961, Pullman, Washington, Washington State University Opera Theater.

The setting is the Tennessee hills, spring 1861. The reclusive Jones lives in a cabin in the Tennessee hills. His solitude is disturbed by the Civil War, during which the young Sarah seeks his protection when attackers kill her parents during a raid. A wounded Union soldier is also granted refuge by the reluctant Jones, and Sarah returns the soldier to health. When Joe Sikes leads a group of raiders against the cabin, Joe, deciding that he can no longer avoid involvement, drives back the raiders.

For a description, see Summers/*OOA*, 62–63.

Major roles: Jones (bar), Sarah (sop), soldier (ten), and Joe Sikes (bass-bar/bar). SCORE: vs, holograph (1960, photocopy, NYPL).

Nordisa, opera in three acts by Frederick Corder; libretto (Eng) by the composer. First performance January 26, 1887, Liverpool, Royal Court, Carl Rosa Opera Company.

Nosferatu, chamber opera in one act by Randolph Peters; libretto (Eng) by Marilyn Powell. First performance December 8, 1993, Toronto, Canadian Opera Company.

This treatment of the Dracula legend includes Camilla, daughter of the title character.

No Song, No Supper, comic opera in two acts "chiefly composed" by Stephen Storace; libretto (Eng) by Prince Hoare. First performance April 16, 1790, London, Drury Lane Theatre, with Michael Kelly (Frederick) and Nancy Storace (Margaretta). First U.S. performance November 30, 1792, Philadelphia, Southwark Theatre.

The work opens on the Cornwall coast and involves Frederick and Robin, who have survived a shipwreck during a storm. They wish to wed their beloved ladies, Louisa Crop and Margaretta. Despite the efforts of a shady lawyer hoping to dupe Louisa's stepmother, the sailors prevail after they find a pot of gold washed ashore by the shipwreck.

The music includes a trio and a sextet from Storace's opera *Gli equivoci* (1786, Vienna) and pieces from Grétry's *L'épreuve villageoise*.

For a detailed description, see Fiske/*ETM*, 506–8.
SCORE: fs, ed. Roger Fiske, *Musica Britannica*, vol. 16 (London: Stainer and Bell, 1959). LIBRETTO: English (Dublin: P. Byrne, 1792; [Boston]: Belknap & Hall, 1794). BIBLIOGRAPHY: Jane Girdham, *English Opera in Late Eighteenth-Century London* (Oxford: Clarendon Press, 1997), 177–89.

Not a Spanish Kiss, comic opera in one act by Seymour Barab; libretto (Eng) by the composer. First performance 1977, New York, New York Singing Teachers Association; May 2, 1981, New York, Golden Fleece Ltd.

The satirical plot is set in Spain. Piero, a young, poor poet, is enamored of Betta, wife of the successful businessman Crispin, and asks to pay for a kiss, but Crispin demands that the young poet pay 1,000 pesetas for the privilege. When Piero says that he has only 750 pesetas, Crispin grudgingly agrees to lower the price. Husband and wife go off, planning how to spend the money, and Piero reveals that he has no money at all.

For a detailed description, see Kornick/*RAO*, 40–42.

Major roles: Betta (sop), Piero (ten), and Crispin (bar).
BIBLIOGRAPHY: Bernard Holland, review, *NYT* (May 7, 1981), C, 15 [on 1981 revival].

Not for Me, or, The New Apple of Discord, arrangement by William Hawes of L. Maurer's *Der neue Paris* (1826, Hanover); libretto (Eng) by Hampden Napier, a translation of the anonymous libretto. First performance August 23, 1828, London, Lyceum Theatre.

Nothing Superfluous, operatic farce in one act by George Alexander Lee; libretto (Eng) by C. Pelham Thompson. First performance June 1829, London, Haymarket Theatre, with Mr. Thompson (Selim), Mr. Brindal (Giaper), and Mrs. Corri (Gulnare).

The work is set in Constantinople. Among its characters are Selim, the sultan; Giafer, the grand vizir; and Gulnare.

LIBRETTO: English (London: J. Duncombe, [182?]).

Notre Dame des fleurs, mini-opera by Peter Maxwell Davies; libretto (Eng) by the composer. First performance March 17, 1973, London, Queen Elizabeth Hall.

Notre-Dame of Paris, grand opera in four acts by William Fry; libretto (Eng) by Joseph R. Fry, after Hugo's novel. First performance May 4, 1864, Philadelphia, American Academy of Music, with Compte Bouchard (Esmeralda), Jenny Kempton (Gudule), William Castle (De Chateaupers), S. C. Campbell (Dom Frollo), Edward Seguin (Quasimodo), and William Skaats (Florian); conducted by Theodore Thomas.

A treatment of Hugo's famous novel, which includes the act 4 chorus "Oh, Happy Day, Again the Bells of Notre Dame Ring Merrily."

G. Rodwell's *Quasimodo** (1836, London) and T. G. Thomas's *Esmeralda** (1883, London) are other English settings.

Notturno in La, or, As a Conductor Dreams, opera in two acts by Arnold Franchetti; libretto (Eng) by Louis Berrone, after Alfred de Musset. First performance October 20, 1966, Hartford, Connecticut, Trinity College.

The opera is scored for a large percussion ensemble and a violin.

No. 204, opera in one act by Thomas German Reed; libretto (Eng) by F. C. Burnand. First performance May 7, 1877, London, St. George's Hall.

Nourjahad, grand opera in three acts by Edward Loder; libretto (Eng) by Samuel J. Arnold, after his text for *Illusion, or, The Trances of Nourjahad** (1813), written for Michael Kelly. First performance July 21, 1834, London, English Opera House, with Henry Phillips (Nourjahad) and Emma Romer (Zulima).

A treatment of a tale from the *Thousand and One Nights*, along the lines of Weber's *Abu Hassan* (1811, Munich); G. Meyerbeer's *Wirth und Gast* (1813, Stuttgart); and P. Cornelius's *Der Barbier von Bagdad* (1858, Weimar).

Major roles: Nourjahad, Zulima, Hasem Shemzeddin, and Mandane.

SCORE: ms fs (ca. 1834, British Library, Add. 33802–33805).

Novellis, Novellis, pageant opera by John La Montaine; libretto (Eng) by the composer, after the Bible, two miracle plays, and the Latin liturgy. First performance December 24, 1961, Washington, D.C.

Part of the composer's Christmas trilogy; see also *Erode the Great* (1969) and *The Shephardes Playe* (1967).

SCORE: vs (New York: G. Schirmer, 1962).

Now Eleanor's Idea, cycle of four one-act operas by Robert Ashley, composed 1986–1989; libretto (Eng) by the composer:

    Improvement (Don Leaves Linda) (1986)
    Foreign Experiences (1987)
    el/ Aficionado (1988)
    Now Eleanor's Idea (1988)

First performance of cycle November 14–17, 1994, Brooklyn, New York, Brooklyn Academy of Music, narrated by the composer; electronics by Tom Hamilton.
BIBLIOGRAPHY: Bernard Holland, "When a Composer Turns Opera Upside Down," *NYT* (Nov. 21, 1994), C, 10 [on premiere of cycle].

Noye's Fludde, miracle play in one act by Benjamin Britten; libretto (Eng) from the Chester miracle play. First performance June 18, 1958, Aldeburgh, Orford Church, with Owen Brannigan (Noye), Gladys Parr (Mrs. Noye), and Trevor Anthony (the Voice of God); conducted by Charles Mackerras. First U.S. performance March 16, 1959, New York, Union Theological Seminary.

Following the biblical story, Noye (Noah) is told by the Voice of God to erect an ark and save his family and one pair of each animal from the impending Flood. After the Flood comes, Noye releases a dove that finds dry land. The occupants of the ark then leave its confines.

For plot synopses, see K/*KOB*, 1213–14; K/*NKOB*, 127–28.

Major roles: Noye (bar), Voice of God (speaking role), and Mrs. Noye (sop).

The score employs a children's orchestra and a professional one, and the congregation joins in for three hymns, "Lord Jesus, Think on Me," "Eternal Father, Strong to Save," and "The Spacious Firmament on High," based on Thomas Tallis's canon.

See also I. Stravinsky's *The Flood* and Sahl and Salzman's *Noah*.
LIBRETTOS: English (London and New York, Boosey and Hawkes, [1958]); stage guide (London and New York, Boosey and Hawkes, [1958]).
BIBLIOGRAPHY: Ross Parmenter, review, *NYT* (May 11, 1964), 38.

Numbered, The, opera in a prologue and two acts by Elisabeth Lutyens; libretto (Eng) by M. Volkonakis, after Elias Canetti's *Die Befristeten* (1964). Composed 1965–1967.

The story concerns a society whose inhabitants know when they are to die but are not allowed to reveal that information.

Nunnery, The, comic operatic afterpiece in two acts by William Shield; libretto (Eng) by William Pearce. First performance April 12, 1785, London, Covent Garden, with John Edwin.

For a description of the music, see Fiske/*ETM*, 465–66.
SCORE: vs (London: Longman & Broderip, [1785]).

Nun's Priest's Tale, The, opera in one act by Ross Lee Finney; libretto (Eng) by the composer, after Chaucer's *Canterbury Tales*. First performance August 1965, Hanover, New Hampshire.

A setting of the tale in which the fox catches the vain rooster Chanticleer, only to be tricked into releasing his prey.

The work is written for chamber orchestra and centers on the folk song "Fox Went out on a Chilly Night."

See *Chanticleer* for other settings.
SCORE: fs, for solo voices, chorus, chamber orch. (New York: Henmar Press, 1977).

Nymph of the Grotto, The, or, A Daughter's Vow, opera in three acts by George Alexander Lee and Giovanni Liverati; libretto (Eng) by William Dimond. First performance January 15, 1829, London, Covent Garden, with Mr. Fawcett (Baron of Mont Orguiel), Miss Jarman (Amadis), Mr. Wood (Hippolyte), Mrs. Chatterly (Marguerite de Valois), and Miss Cawse (Estelle de Ponthieu).
LIBRETTO: English (London: R. S. Kirby, 1829).

O

Oath of Bad Brown Bill, The, children's opera in two acts by Barry Conyngham; libretto (Eng) by Murray Copland, after Stephen Axelsen's book (1980). First performance January 6, 1985, Melbourne, Australia, Victorian Arts Centre, Playbox Theatre Company.

Major roles: Bess (sop), Jim (ten), Mick (bar), Reg (bass-bar), and Bill Bolter (boy sop).

SCORE: vs ([London]: Universal Edition, 1985).

Obelisk, The, opera in one act by Michael Easton; libretto (Eng) by the composer, after a short story by E. M. Forster. Composed 1984.

The failing marriage of a couple is saved during a stop at a dreary English seaside town when they encounter two sailors during a walk.

Oberon, or, The Charmed Horn, "romantic fairy tale" in two acts, music arranged and adapted by Thomas Cooke; libretto (Eng) by George Macfarren, after Wieland's poem. First performance March 27, 1826, London, Drury Lane Theatre, with Miss Vincent.

LIBRETTO: English (London: J. Tabby, 1826; New York: E. M. Murden, 1826).

Oberon, or, The Elf King's Oath, romantic fairy opera in three acts by Carl Maria von Weber; libretto (Eng) by James R. Planché, after William Sotheby's translation of C. M. Wieland's *Oberon* (1780) and the French romance *Huon de Bordeaux*. First performance April 12, 1826, London, Covent Garden, in English, with Mary Anne Paton (Rezia), John Braham (Huon), Lucia Elizabeth Vestris (Fatima), John Fawcett (Sherasmin), Charles Bland (Oberon), Harriet Cawse (Puck), and Mary Anne Goward (mermaid). First performance in German, translated by Theodor Hell, December 23, 1826, Leipzig. First U.S. performance October 9, 1828, New York, Park Theatre (in English), arranged by Charles Edward Horn.

The story opens in the fairy kingdom of Oberon and Titania, who have quarreled. Oberon will not be reconciled with his wife until he can be shown an example of a truly loving couple. Puck tells him of the French knight Huon de Bordeaux, who has insulted the Emperor Charlemagne and been banished until he makes Rezia, the daughter of the Caliph of Bagdad, his bride. Oberon causes Huon to dream of the lovely Rezia, and he immediately falls in love with her. In order to spirit her away, he is given a magic horn. Huon and Sherasmin, his squire, escape from Bagdad with Rezia and Fatima, her confidante, but lose the horn and are shipwrecked. The four are seized by pirates and sold as slaves to the Emir of Tunis, Almansor. The Emir attempts to seduce Rezia, and his wife to seduce Huon, but their overtures are refused, which leads to the young lovers' being condemned to death. Fortunately, Sherasmin finds the magic horn, and the four are saved. The lovers are returned to France, and Huon receives a pardon from Charlemagne. Oberon is convinced that he has found a faithful couple.

For a detailed plot description, see K/*KOB*, 140–46; K/*NKOB*, 962–65.

Major roles: Oberon, King of the Elves (ten); Titania, his wife (silent role); Puck (mezzo); Harun al Rashid, Caliph of Bagdad (speaking role); Rezia, his daughter (sop); Fatima, her confidante (sop); Almansor, Emir of Tunis (speaking role); Roschana, his wife (speaking role); Huon of Bordeaux (ten); Sherasmin, his squire (bar).

The opera, commissioned by Charles Kemble for a London performance, was very successful at its premiere and was heard thirty-one more times in London in its first season. Although occasionally performed today (usually in German), the opera has had limited success, probably as a result of its plodding text and complicated plot. The composer died less than two months after its premiere. Its magnificent overture, still played as a concert piece today, contains the magic horn call and features various themes of the opera's numbers. Other highlights include, in act 1, Oberon's "Fatal Vow" and Huon's "From Boyhood Trained"; in act 2, Rezia's "A Lonely Arab Maid" and "Ocean! Thou Mighty Monster," and the quartet of Huon, Sherasmin, Rezia, and Fatima, "Over the Dark Blue Waters"; and, in act 3, the finale "Hark! What Notes Are Swelling."

SCORES: ms fs, autograph, with two extra songs composed for Braham: "Yes, Even Love" and "Ruler of This Awful Hour" (1826, British Library, Add. MS. 27746–27748); fs (Berlin: Schlesinger'sche Buch- und Musikhandlung, ca. 1881; repr. Farnborough, Hants: Gregg, 1969).
LIBRETTO: English (London: Hunt and Clarke, 1826); repr. ed (London: Hutchinson, 1985).
BIBLIOGRAPHY: P. R. Kirby, "Weber's Operas in London, 1824–1826," *MQ* XXXII (1946), 333–53; Andrew Porter, review, *NY* LIV (Mar. 13, 1978), 118–22 [on New York revival]; Ernest Sanders, "Oberon and Zar und Zimmermann," *MQ* XL (1954), 521–32; Horst Seeger, "Das 'Original-Libretto' zum 'Oberon,'" *Musikbühne 76* (1976), 33–87; John Warrack, "Weber and 'Oberon,'" *Opera Annals* IV (1957), 65–72, "'Oberon' und der englische Geschmack," *Musikbühne 76* (1976), 15–31, and *Carl Maria von Weber*, 2d ed. (Cambridge: Engl.: Cambridge University Press, 1976), 321–44.

Oberon's Oath, or, The Paladin and the Princess, musical drama in two acts by John Parry; libretto (Eng) by Benjamin Thompson, after Sotheby's translation of Wieland. First performance May 21, 1816, London, Drury Lane Theatre.

Other settings of the story include the masque *Oberon, the Fairy Prince*, with a text by Ben Jonson (1611, Whitehall); P. Wranitzky, *Oberon* (1789; Vienna); F. Kunzen, *Holger Danske* (1789, Copenhagen); G. C. Grosheim, *Titania* (1792, Kassel); W. Reeve, *Harlequin and Oberon* (pantomime, 1796, London); and the anonymous "new grand comic Christmas pantomime" *Oberon, King of the Elves* (1858, London?).
LIBRETTO: English (London: J. Miller [B. M'Millan], 1816).

Occurrence at Owl Creek Bridge, An, radio opera by Thea Musgrave; libretto (Eng) by the composer, after the short story by Ambrose Bierce from his *Tales of Soldiers and Civilians* (1891). First performance September 14, 1982, BBC broadcast, with Jake Gardner (Peyton Farquhar) and Gayle Hunnicut (narrator/wife); conducted by the composer. First stage performance June 23, 1988, Bracknell.

The story, set at the time of the Civil War, is of Peyton Farquhar, a southern plantation owner who is condemned to death for trying to set fire to an important bridge. As he is about to be hanged by Union soldiers, he imagines that he has escaped and returned to his home. The tale ends as the noose kills him.

Roles: Peyton Farquhar (bar) and narrator/wife.

The work uses taped nature sounds as a background.

Whelen's *Incident at Owl Creek** (1969) is another setting.
BIBLIOGRAPHY: review, *ON* XLVII (Jan. 15, 1983), 6 [on premiere].

Octoroon, The, grand opera by Harry Lawrence Freeman; libretto (Eng) by the composer, after M. E. Braddon. Composed 1904. First performance 1931, CBS radio.

Odyssey, opera in one act by Alice Shields; libretto (Eng) by the composer. First performance August 1975, Glens Falls, New York, Lake George Opera Festival.
    The text is based in part on Homer's *Odyssey*, and the work is scored for tenor, bass-baritone, male chorus, and chamber orchestra.
SCORE: vs (New York: American Music Center, 1975).

Oedipus, music-dance drama in one act by Harry Partch; libretto (Eng) by the composer, after Yeats's version of Sophocles' *Oedipus tyrannus.* First performance, as *King Oedipus*, March 14, 1952, Oakland, California, Mills College. Revised version September 11, 1954, Sausalito, California.
    In the work spoken dialogue alternates with intoned vocal sections.

Oedipus Tex, "dramatic oratorio or opera in one cathartic act" by "P. D. Q. Bach" (Peter Schickele); libretto (Eng) by the composer, after Sophocles. First performance March 15, 1988, Minneapolis, Plymouth Music Series.
    The parody of the Greek tragedy centers on Oedipus Tex, a cowboy and the brother of Oedipus Rex. Along the way he shoots some strangers, solves a riddle by Big Foot, and settles down with the queen of the rodeo, Billie Jo Casta. Soon a plague infests the town, and Madam Peep, the fortune-teller, explains that Oedipus Tex is the cause of all the trouble. In despair Billie Jo hangs herself, and the repentant Tex gouges out his eyes with his wife's rhinestone barrettes. The action closes with the chorus singing "The Eyes of Texas Are upon You."
    For a detailed description, see Kornick/*RAO*, 273–74.
    Major roles: Oedipus Tex (bar), Billie Jo Casta (sop), Madam Peep (mezzo), and narrator (ten).

Of Age Tomorrow, operatic farce in two acts by Michael Kelly; libretto (Eng) by Thomas J. Dibdin, after August Kotzebue's *Der Wildfang.* First performance February 1, 1800, London, Drury Lane Theatre, with Mr. Bannister (Frederick Baron Willinhurst), Mr. Suett (Baron Piffeberg), Mr. Maddocks (Friz), Mrs. Sparks (Lady Brumback), Miss Hicks (Sophia), and Miss De Camp (Maria). First U.S. performance January 31, 1804, Boston, Federal Street Theatre.
    The setting is Germany, at a hotel.
LIBRETTO: English (London: J. Barker, 1805; Boston, John West, 1806).

Of Mice and Men, opera in three acts by Carlisle Floyd; libretto (Eng) by the composer, after John Steinbeck's novel and play. First performance January 22, 1970, Seattle, Seattle Opera, with Robert Moulson (Lennie), Julian Patrick (George), Harry Theyard (Curley), Carol Bayard (Curley's wife), Kerry McDevitt (Slim), and Gerald Thorsen (ballad singer); conducted by Anton Coppola; directed by Frank Corsaro.
    The story concerns two migrant workers, George and Lennie. They are fleeing from the police because the slow-witted, but dangerous, Lennie has again gotten into trouble. Lennie inadvertently kills the wife of Curley, the mean-spirited owner of the ranch where the migrants work. In the end George kills Lennie to save him from the avenging posse.
    For a detailed description, see Eaton/*OP* II, 170–72.
    Major roles: George (bass-bar), Lennie (ten), Curley (ten), Curley's wife (sop), Slim (bar), and ballad singer (ten).

This traditional work includes among its numbers a striking duet between Curley's wife and Lennie, before he kills her, and the closing duet between Lennie and George.
SCORE: vs ([New York]: Belwin-Mills, [1971]).
BIBLIOGRAPHY: Robert Commanday, "Steinbeck's 'Of Mice and Men' Goes Operatic," *NYT* (Feb. 1, 1970), II, 23, 36; *OJ* IV (Winter 1971), 5–32: Carlisle Floyd, "The Creation," Frank Corsaro, "The Direction," Henry Holt, "The Premiere," Julian Patrick, "The Performance," Thomas Martin, "The Second Production," Robert Moulson, "The Performance," Carol Bayard, "The Performance," Robert W. Holton, "The Publisher"; Frank J. Warnke, "Reports: U.S.," *ON* XXXIV (Mar. 14, 1970), 30–31 [on premiere].

Oh! This Love, or, The Masqueraders, comic opera in three acts by Matthew King; libretto (Eng) by James Kenney. First performance June 12, 1810, London, English Opera at the Lyceum. First U.S. performance February 26, 1812, New York, Park Theatre.
    The setting is Milan, with members of the English nobility as masqueraders.
SCORES: vs (London: Phipps, [18??]); vs, excerpts (New York: J. Paff's Music Store, [1812]).

O'Higgins of Chile, unfinished opera in three acts by Henry Cowell; libretto (Eng) by Elizabeth Lomax. Composed 1949. Left unorchestrated.
    About the Chilean hero Bernardo O'Higgins, in the years 1812 to 1822.

Oithona, dramatic poem in three parts by François Hippolyte Barthelemon; anonymous libretto (Eng), after James Macpherson's Ossianic epic. First performance March 3, 1768, London, Theatre Royal, Haymarket (two acts only).
    The setting is the second century A.D. Oithona is abducted and raped when her husband, Gaul, is off in battle. While the husband and his men seek to avenge his wife's disgrace, Oithona herself joins in the battle and is killed.
LIBRETTO: English (London: T. Becket and P. & A. de Hondt, 1768).

Oithona, opera by Edgar Leslie Bainton; libretto (Eng), after Ossian. First performance August 11, 1915, Glastonbury.

Olaf, grand opera in two acts by Howard Kirkpatrick; libretto (Eng) by the composer after Louise Cox's epic poem. First performance March 5, 1912, Lincoln, Nebraska.
    The setting is the ninth century. The countryside has been ravaged by a dragon to such an extent that the King has offered his daughter Erica's hand in marriage to the one who kills the beast. Sigurd, a knight, has failed in his many tries to summon up enough courage to do the task. Olaf, who has returned after many years in the Far East, slays the dragon and wins Erica.

Old Black Joe, opera in one act by Harry Rowe Shelley; libretto (Eng) by Clay M. Green. First performance (private) February 26, 1911, New York, "The Lambs" Theatrical Club, with an all-male cast.
    The minstrel show-like work is set on a southern plantation at the end of the Civil War and includes a version of Stephen Foster's famous "Old Black Joe."

Old Cloathsman, The, comic opera in three acts by Thomas Attwood; libretto (Eng) by Thomas Holcroft. First performance April 2, 1799, London, Covent Garden.
SCORE: vs (London: Goulding, Phipps & D'Almaine, n.d.).

Old Fools, or, Love's Stratagem, burletta by John Moorehead; libretto (Eng) by Charles Dibdin. First performance April 14, 1800, London, Sadler's Wells.

Old Maid and the Thief, The, "grotesque opera" in 14 scenes (three acts) by Gian Carlo Menotti; libretto (Eng) by the composer. First performance (NBC radio) April 22, 1939, with Mary Hoppel (Miss Todd), Margaret Daum (Laetitia), Dorothy Sarnoff (Miss Pinkerton), Robert Weede (Bob), and Joseph Curtin (narrator); conducted by Alberto Erede. First U.S. performance March 7, 1970, New York, City Opera. First British performance July 14, 1960, Orpington, Kent, Kentish Opera Group, with Moyna Cope (Miss Todd); conducted by Audrey Langford.

A middle-aged spinster, Miss Todd, lives with her young servant, Laetitia. As Miss Todd is entertaining her friend Miss Pinkerton, a young beggar comes to the door and persuades Miss Todd to let him stay the night.

The following day Miss Todd learns from her friend that a criminal fitting the description of her overnight guest has escaped from prison. But the old maid is entranced by the young man and, along with Laetitia, protects him. The two women rob a liquor store for money to give Bob, as the stranger is called. When he does not respond to her advances, Miss Todd calls the police, even though she has discovered that he is not the escaped convict. While she is summoning help, Bob and the young servant girl ransack the house and drive away in the spinster's car.

Major roles: Miss Todd (alto), Laetitia (sop), Miss Pinkerton (sop), and Bob (bar).

For a detailed description, see Eaton/*OP* I, 206.

SCORE: vs (New York: G. Ricordi & Co., 1942; New York: Franco Colombo, 1943).

BIBLIOGRAPHY: Andrew Porter, review, *Opera* XI (Sept. 1960), 651 [on British premiere].

DISCOGRAPHY: Hoppel, Daum, Sarnoff, Weede; cond. Erede, world premiere broadcast, April 22, 1939, [n.p.], Unique Opera Records UORC 141 [1972?]; M. Baker, J. Blegen, J. Reardon, A. Reynolds; cond. J. Mester; Teatro Verdi di Trieste, Mercury SR 90521 [1970].

Old Majestic, The, opera in two acts by Robert Xavier Rodríguez; libretto (Eng) by Mary Duren. First performance May 28, 1988, San Antonio, University of Texas.

The setting is the back stage of the great Majestic Theater in 1930. The Stock Market crash is paralleled in the lives of the performers by the introduction of talking movies and the end, therewith, of silent films.

The work includes snippets of popular old songs, parts of real vaudeville routines, and reminiscences of vaudevillians, including Eddie Cantor.

For a detailed description, see Kornick/*RAO*, 252–54.

Major roles: Nora Kelly, singer/dancer (sop); Madame Fifi, "show-biz veteran" (mezzo); Lou Ferren, comedian (ten); Ben Palmer, son of the theater owner (bar); Nelsoni, pompous magician (bass-bar); and Sammy May, aging comedian (bass).

Old Man Taught Wisdom, An, or, The Virgin Unmask'd, "a farce" (ballad opera) in one act; libretto (Eng) by Henry Fielding. First performance January 6, 1735, London, Drury Lane Theatre. First American performance, as *The Virgin Unmask'd*, April 22, 1751, New York, Kean and Murray.

A father presents his daughter, Lucy, with various suitors for her to marry, but she declines, wedding the footman instead.

LIBRETTO: English, with unaccompanied melodies (London: John Watts, 1735); repr. ed. Rubsamen/*BO,* vol. 11, *Farce, Broad or Satirical* (1974).

Old Pipes and the Dryad, chamber opera in one act by Alan Rea; libretto (Eng) by Betty Iacovetti, after a story by Frank R. Stockton. First performance February 20, 1980, Fresno, California.

SCORE: ms vs, holograph (1977, photocopy, NYPL).

Old Woman of Eighty, The, all-sung burletta by Charles Dibdin; libretto (Eng) by the composer. First performance 1777, London, Sadler's Wells. First U.S. performance February 28, 1797, Annapolis, Maryland.

Olympians, The, opera in three acts by Arthur Bliss; libretto (Eng) by John Boynton Priestly. First performance September 29, 1949, London, Covent Garden, with Margherita Grandi (Diana), Edith Coates (Mme. Bardeau), James Johnston (Hector), David Franklin (Mars), and Howell Glynne (Lavatte); conducted by Karl Rankl.

The gods of Olympus, now limited to having power once every hundred years, wander through the world as a troupe of players. They happen upon a town on Midsummer Night in 1836, where the parsimonious and well-to-do Lavatte has arranged to have his daughter Madeleine wed Baron de Craval, an old and distasteful man. Hector de Florac, a young poet, is in love with Madeleine, and when Lavatte hires the troupe to perform, the Olympians use their powers, which they have regained for this one night, to help the young people get engaged; the gods also distribute Lavatte's gold between the pair and the town's needy residents.

Roles: Madame Bardeau (mezzo), Joseph Lavatte (bass), Madeleine (sop), Hector de Florac (ten), Jean (bar), and Alfred (bar); and the Olympians: Jupiter (bar), Diana (sop), Bacchus (ten), Mars (bass-bar), and Mercury (dancer).
SCORE: vs (London: Novello, [1950]).

On Blue Mountain, folk opera in one act by Scott Eyerly; libretto (Eng) by the composer. First performance October 16, 1986, New York, Town Hall.

The work, set in the 1930s, concerns people in Appalachia.

Once in a While the Odd Thing Happens, opera in three acts by Paul Godfrey; libretto (Eng) by the composer. First performance September 18, 1990, London, Cottesloe Theatre, with Stephen Boxer (Auden), Michael Maloney (Britten), Deborah Meyer Findlay (Beata), Julian Wadham (Pears), and Hilary Dawson (Beth Britten).

The work begins with the meeting of W. H. Auden and Benjamin Britten in the 1930s and continues until the premiere of *Peter Grimes*, and it explains the relation between composer, poet, and singer. This play-like piece consists mostly of free verse, with music brought in only at the end of the second act: the *Frank Bridge Variations* and the opening of *Grimes*.
LIBRETTO: English (London: Methuen Drama; Portsmouth, N.H.: Heinemann, 1995).
BIBLIOGRAPHY: Peter Dickinson, review, *MT* CXXXII (Jan. 1991), 720 [on premiere].

Once upon a Moon, opera in two acts by Gerard Victory; libretto (Eng) by B. Roach. First performance June 1950, Dublin, Phoenix Hall.

Ondine, opera in three acts by Seymour Barab; libretto (Eng) by the composer, after the French play by Jean Giraudoux (1939), itself based on the 1811 tale *Undine* by de La Motte Fouqué. First performance (concert) March 24, 1995, New York, St. Peter's Church, Center for Contemporary Opera; conducted by Richard Marshall.

A treatment of the story of the underwater creature Ondine, who is loved by a knight and then betrayed by him.

See *Undine* for other settings.
BIBLIOGRAPHY: review, *Opera Today* (Feb. 1995), 1, 4 [on premiere].

One and the Same, scena by Elisabeth Lutyens; libretto (Eng) by the composer. First performance June 21, 1976, York, England.

One Christmas Long Ago, opera in a prelude and one act by William Mayer; libretto (Eng) by the composer, after Raymond MacDonald Alden's *Why the Chimes Rang.* First performance November 9, 1962, Muncie, Indiana, Ball State Teachers College.

Special bells in a church tower peal only when a good deed has been performed, despite the attempts of individuals to influence them. Among those trying to get the bells to ring are the countess, who surrenders her jewels; the sculptor, who relinquishes his self-portrait; the rich man, who gives up his gold; and the King, who surrenders his crown, all to no avail. The bells do ring, however, after a young boy remains outside in the cold during the night to take care of an old beggar woman.

For a detailed plot description, see Eaton/*OP* II, 306.

Roles: old man (bar), older brother (boy sop/sop), Parsley the page (high bar), beggar woman (mezzo), younger brother (boy sop/sop), sculptor /minister (ten), countess (sop), and the King (speaking).

SCORE: vs ([New York]: Galaxy Music, 1963).

One Man Show, comic opera in two acts by Nicholas Maw; libretto (Eng) by Arthur Jacobs, after Saki's story *The Background.* First performance November 12, 1964, London. Revised 1966. First U.S. performance 1975, Pittsburgh, Carnegie-Mellon University, Opera Workshop.

A man, Joe, has an unusual tattoo on his back, and the design is designated as a work of art. The art is "bought" by Maggie Dempster, who takes an interest in more than the tattoo but is rebuffed. The design is then sold to a British museum, whose director, Sir Horace Stringfellow, discovers the meaning of the work: it is "Joe," spelled backwards, which the director discovers by standing on his head.

Roles: Joe (bar), Maggie Dempster (mezzo), and Sir Horace Stringfellow (ten).

SCORE: vs (London and New York: Boosey & Hawkes, [1968]).

One Night of Cleopatra, television opera in one act by Louis Gruenberg; libretto (Eng) by the composer, after Théophile Gautier. Composed 1954. Not performed.

One O'Clock, or, The Knight and the Wood Daemon, grand romantic opera in three acts by Matthew King and Michael Kelly; libretto (Eng) by Matthew G. Lewis, after his play. First performance August 1, 1811, London, English Opera at the Lyceum.

Sequel to *The Wood Daemon** (1807, London).

LIBRETTOS: English (London: Lowndes and Hobbs [1811]; New York: D. Longworth, 1813).

One Thousand Airplanes on the Roof, "a science fiction music-drama" by Philip Glass; libretto (Eng) David Henry Hwang; designed by Jerome Sirlin. First performance July 15, 1988, Vienna, International Airport, Hangar No. 5.

The action centers around M, who remembers his meeting with extraterrestrial beings and their message to him, which said that nobody would believe him.

LIBRETTO: English, introd. John Howell (Salt Lake City, Utah: Peregrine Smith Books, 1989).

BIBLIOGRAPHY: Michael Walsh, review, *Time* CXXXII (Aug. 1, 1988), 58 [on premiere].

One Too Many, comedietta in one act by Frederick Cowen; libretto (Eng) by F. C. Burnand. First performance June 24, 1874, London, St. George's Hall.

SCORE: vs (London, 1898).

Only a Miracle, Christmas opera in one act by Seymour Barab; libretto (Eng) by the composer. Composed 1985.

The setting is in biblical times. Herod is searching for the Child and offers a substantial reward for information that will help find Him. The Landlord who refused shelter to Mary and Joseph suspects that they have been aided by his slave girl. He is willing to go to any lengths to find out the Child's whereabouts, and the slave girl is willing to do the same to prevent that. The Child now needs a miracle.

Roles: Sylphinia (sop), Soldier (ten), Landlord (bar), and messenger/King Herod (bass).

SCORE: vs (New York: G. Schirmer, 1985).

On the March, musical comedy in two acts by Frederic Clay, arranged by E. Solomon and J. Crook; libretto (Eng) by C. Clay, W. Yardley, and B. C. Stephenson. First performance May 18, 1896, Sheffield, England, Theatre Royal.

On the Razzle, opera in three acts by Robin Orr; libretto (Eng) by the composer, after Tom Stoppard's adaptation of Johann Nestroy's *Einen Jux will er sich machen.* First performance June 27, 1988, Glasgow, New Athenaeum.

Zangler, a grocer, brings along Marie, his niece, on a trip to Vienna, in order to keep her from seeing Sonders, her beloved. Zangler's efforts are, of course, in vain, especially after Sonders receives a large inheritance, which removes Zangler's argument that Sonders is poor and therefore a bad marriage prospect.

Major roles: Zangler (bass), Marie (sop), and Sonders (ten).

Opening, The, opera in one act by Alec Wilder; libretto (Eng) by Arnold Sundgaard. First performance May 19, 1969, Boston, New England Conservatory of Music.

A group is getting ready to put on the play *The Reason Why.* There has been a delay, however, because, according to the Prince, the leading lady, Marcia, has broken her ankle. Although he tries to fit the slipper on members of the audience, it fits only the usher. The injured Marcia comes to the stage and says that the play is over.

For a detailed plot description, see Eaton/*OP* II, 307.

Roles: Gerald, the author (bar); Antoinette, his wife (mezzo); Mrs. Dolly Filagree (mezzo); Ronnie (bar); Anne (sop/mezzo); Clarence (bar); Alastair Frontenac, a critic (ten); Trudi, his patient wife (sop/mezzo); Prince Charming (bar); usher (sop); and Marcia (nonspeaking).

Open the Gates, biblical opera in three acts by Dai-Keong Lee; libretto (Eng) by R. Payne. First performance February 22, 1951, New York.

The plot concerns the life of Mary Magdalene.

Open Window, The, opera in one act by David Ahlstrom; libretto (Eng) by the composer. First performance (concert) March 1, 1953, Cincinnati, Conservatory of Music.

Open Window, The, opera in one act by Malcolm Arnold; libretto (Eng) by Sydney Gilliat, after a short story by Saki. First performance December 14, 1956, BBC television. First stage performance April 24, 1958, Holton cum Beckering, England, Lincoln Opera Group.

BIBLIOGRAPHY: review, *Opera* XIII (Feb. 1962), 140.

Opera Cloak, The, comic opera in one act by Walter Damrosch; libretto (Eng) by Gretchen Damrosch Finletter. First performance November 3, 1942, New York, Broadway Theater, New York Opera Company.

Roles: Susan (sop), Mrs. Sweet (mezzo), Michael (ten), Ikey (bass), chauffeur (bar), Signor Martini (bar), and Rosa Martini (sop).

The work contains a brief musical reference to ragtime.

SCORE: vs , ms (1942, New York, NYPL).

Opera Flies, opera in three acts for young people by Halim El-Dabh; libretto (Eng) by the composer. First performance May 5, 1971, Washington, D.C., Hawthorne School of Washington, with members of the Hawthorne School; conducted by Russell Woollen.

The work takes as its inspiration the Kent State tragedy of May 4, 1970, in which four students were shot to death by members of the Ohio National Guard, who were called in to quell an anti-Vietnam War demonstration.

Although the characters have names not related to the actual students, that of Vekeero is based on Mary Vecchio, the young girl shown mourning over one of the dead students in a famous photograph of the event.

The composer was on the campus the day the shootings occurred. "Flies" refers to the students.

BIBLIOGRAPHY: Donal Henahan, "Kent State Composer Threads Tragedy into Opera," *NYT* (May 31, 1971), 10; Allen Hughes, "'Opera Flies' Pays a Four-Day Visit," *NYT* (June 4, 1971), 23 [on New York premiere].

Opera of Operas, The, or, Tom Thumb the Great, opera by Frederick Lampe; lyrics (Eng) by William Hatchett and Eliza Haywood, after Henry Fielding's *Tragedy of Tragedies*. First performance May 31, 1733, London, Little Theatre in the Haymarket, with Richard Arne (Tom Thumb).

LIBRETTO: English (London, 1733).

Opera of Operas, The, or, Tom Thumb the Great, opera in three acts by Thomas Arne. First performance October 29, 1733, at Lincoln's Inn Fields.

Arne's version of the satirical text was much more successful, so that Lampe countered with an afterpiece version on November 7 at Drury Lane.

Opera, Opera, comic opera in one act by Martin Kalmanoff; libretto (Eng) by the composer, after William Saroyan. First performance February 22, 1956, New York, After Dinner Opera Company.

The work is a spoof on operatic conventions.

Roles: young woman (sop), elderly lady (mezzo), sister (mezzo), boy (ten), young man (bar/low ten), and gorilla-like boy (bass).

SCORE: vs (New York: Fischer, 1956).

BIBLIOGRAPHY: Harold Schonberg, "Three One-Act Operas," *NYT* (Feb. 23, 1956), 33 [on premiere].

Ophelia of the Nine Mile Beach, comic opera in one act by James Penberthy; libretto (Eng) by the composer. First performance July 1965, Tasmania, Australia, Theatre Royale.

Ophelia, bored by her husband, Harold, tries to win the attention of her next-door neighbor, a poet considered lazy by the neighbors but always defended by Hannah, his loyal wife. When Ophelia's efforts to lure the poet fail, she jumps into the surf and cries for help. She rejects Harold's attempts to rescue her, hoping the poet will "save" her. Instead, Hannah appears and hits Ophelia, telling the mulling crowd to go home.

Roles: Ophelia (sop), Hannah (alto), the poet (silent), and Harold (ten).

Oracle, The, or, The Interrupted Sacrifice, opera in two acts, an adaptation by William Hawes of Winter's *Das unterbrochene Opferfest* (1796, Vienna); libretto (Eng) by Hampden Napier and Samuel J. Arnold, after Huber's text. First performance August 7, 1826, London, Lyceum Theatre.

The setting is Peru. Faulkland, an Englishman in the service of the king of the Incas, is supposed to wed the king's daughter. But he is accused of treason by his former fiancée, a Spanish lady, and a jealous army rival and sentenced to death. The plot comes to light, and Faulkland is permitted to wed his beloved.
SCORE: vs, quintet, "Farewell Yet Not Forever" (London: Welsh & Hawes, [1826?]).

Oracle, The, music drama in one act by Bernard Lees; libretto (Eng) by the composer. Composed 1955–1956. The planned television premiere was canceled because of financial reasons.

The story is a fantasy about a computer.

Ordeal of Osbert, The, comic opera in one act by Allan Davis; libretto (Eng) by the composer, after a short story by P. G. Wodehouse from his *Mr. Mulliner Speakes*. First performance summer 1949, Duxbury, Massachusetts, Plymouth Rock Center of Music and Art. First New York performance May 25, 1956, Third Street Music Settlement; conducted by the composer.

The setting is present-day London. Osbert, set to marry Mabel, is under threat from Mabel's former fiance, Bashford Braddock, not to go through with the wedding, and by Sir Petherick, Mabel's uncle, who promises to make Osbert's life miserable if he backs out of the marriage. Osbert is saved when two robbers trying to ransack his apartment begin to argue and knock each other unconscious. Osbert is perceived to be a great hero, his nemesis flees, and the uncle is satisfied.

For a detailed description, see Summers/*OOA*, 89–91.

Major roles: Mabel Petherick (sop), Osbert Mulliner (ten), Bashford Braddock (bar), and Sir Petherick (bass).
SCORE: ms vs, holograph (1949, photocopy, NYPL).
BIBLIOGRAPHY: R. P., "Music: Opera Workshop," *NYT* (May 25, 1956), 28 [on New York premiere].

Order of Good Cheer, The, ballad opera by Healey Willan; libretto (Eng) by John Murray, a translation of Louvigny de Montigny's *L'ordre du bon temps*. First performance, in French, May 25, 1928, Quebec, Château Frontenac; conducted by the composer.

The work is set in Port Royal in 1606, during the ascendancy of Champlain.

The music contains arrangements of French Canadian folk songs.

Orestes, dramatic opera in five acts by John Pepusch; libretto (Eng) by Lewis Theobald, after Davenant's *Circe*. First performance April 3, 1731, London, Lincoln's Inn Fields.
LIBRETTO: English (London: John Watts, 1731).

Oriana, romantic legend in three acts by Frederic Clay; libretto (Eng) by James Albery. First performance February 16, 1873, London, Globe Theatre.

Orpheus, burletta in two acts "introduced in the farce called A new rehearsal, or A peep behind the curtain" by François Hippolyte Barthelemon; libretto (Eng) by David Garrick. First performance October 23, 1767, London, Drury Lane Theatre.
SCORE: vs (London: Welcker, [1767]).

Orpheus, rock opera in one act by John Austin; libretto (Eng) by the composer. First performance March 10, 1967, Chicago.

Orpheus, chamber opera in six parts: prologue, parts 1 to 4, and postlude by Geoffrey Burgon; libretto (Eng) by Peter Porter. First performance July 17, 1982, Wells, England, Wells Cathedral.
The work traces the marriage of Orpheus to Eurydice, her demise, and his attempts to bring her back from the Underworld. A postlude ends the opera on a joyful note, as the chorus and soloists declare that the couple's love lives forever.
Roles: Eurydice (sop), Orpheus (ten), Charon (bar), and Hades (bass).
Another setting is Philip Glass's *Orphée* (1993, Brooklyn, New York), set to a French text.

Orpheus and Euridice, opera in one scene by Matthew Locke; libretto (Eng) by Elkanah Settle. First performance July 3 (?), 1673, London, Duke's, Dorset Gardens, in the fourth act of Settle's *The Empress of Morocco.*
The scene is performed by Orpheus, Pluto, Proserpine (spelled "Prosserpine" in the score), and one of the latter's attendants. It includes short arias, recitative, and a concluding chorus.
SCORE: ms (Oxford, Christ Church Library, no. 692).

Orpheus and Eurydice, dramatic musical entertainment by J. F. Lampe; libretto (Eng) by Lewis Theobald. First performance February 12, 1740, London, Covent Garden.
Lampe's music was used for a one-act pantomime with the same name by Henry Sommer in January 1740.
SCORE: vs, with music by Handel, etc. (London: Walsh, [1740]).

Orpheus Descending, opera by Bruce Saylor; libretto by J. D. McClatchy, after Tennessee Williams's play (1957). First performance June 10, 1994, Chicago, Northwestern University, Cahn Auditorium, Lyric Opera of Chicago, with Juliana Rambaldi (Lady), Victor Benedetti (Val), Teresa Fedea (Carol Cutrere), Stephen Morscheck (Jabe Torrance), and Emily Magee (Vee Talbott); conducted by Stewart Robinson; directed by Rhoda Levine.
In this nod to the Orpheus legend, Val Xavier, a reformed hustler who plays the guitar, comes to a dusty southern town in an attempt to start a new life. He is taken under the wing of the slightly mad Vee Talbott, wife of the sheriff, and he gets a job at the dry goods store, which is owned by the tragic and delicate Lady and Jabe Torrance, her gruff, crippled husband. Val and Lady fall in love, and he also attracts the unwanted attention of Carol, sister of one of Lady's old flames. Val refuses to heed Vee's warnings to leave town when he learns that Lady is pregnant with his child. As Lady rejoices at her "victory" over her brutal husband, Jabe comes downstairs and shoots her. Val, trying to escape, is killed by the pursuing sheriff and his men.
Major roles: Val Xavier (bar); Lady Torrance (sop); Jabe Torrance, her husband (bass-bar); Carol Cutrere (mezzo); and Vee Talbott (sop).

BIBLIOGRAPHY: Deborah S. Holloway, "Orpheus Ascending," *ON* LVIII (June 1994), 18–19 [preview]; Alex Ross, "The Orpheus Legend Puts on a Modern Face," *NYT* (June 13, 1994), C, 11 [on premiere]; John Von Rhein, "Chicago," *ON* LIX (Nov. 1994), 51–52 [on premiere].

Orpheus: Eurydice, chamber opera in two acts by John White; libretto (Eng) by Robin Barson. First performance April 6, 1976, London, Drama Centre.

The story concerns initiation rites; despite the title, it is not connected to the Greek legend.

Orpheus in Pecan Springs, opera in one act by William Latham; libretto (Eng) by Thomas Holliday. First performance December 4, 1980, Denton, Texas, North Texas State University.

The setting is rural Texas, 1883–1884. An outpost threatened by Indian attacks is led by Levi, whose wife, Hannah, has been unable to conceive. A ballad singer named Isaiah stops briefly at the colony and attracts Hannah's interest. He departs, and Hannah dreams that he has been attacked by Indians and is seriously wounded. Isaiah is rescued by a group from the colony. In the next scene Hannah is seen rocking her three-month-old baby, and Isaiah is recounting how he saved himself from being killed by the Indians by singing, as had Orpheus in Hades.

For a description, see Summers/*OOA*, 191–92.

Major roles: Isaiah (bar), Levi (ten), and Hannah (sop).

Orpheus II, "liturgy" in seven parts by Gabriel Charpentier; libretto (Eng) by the composer. First performance July 1972, Stratford, Ontario, Canada. A revision of the composer's *Orphée* (1969, Ottawa).

Osiris Ritual, The, opera by Halim El-Dabh; libretto (Eng) by the composer. First performance December 1972, Washington, D.C., Hawthorne School.

Part of the trilogy *Ptahmose and the Magic Spell*, which includes *Aton, the Ankh, and the Word** and *The Twelve Hours*.*

Osmyn and Daraxa, musical romance in two acts by Thomas Attwood; libretto (Eng) by James Boaden. First performance March 7, 1793, London, King's Theatre.

The work includes two selections from Mozart.

Osseo, romantic grand opera in three acts by Edith Noyes-Greene; libretto (Eng) by Lillie Fuller Mirriam. First performance 1917, Brookline, Massachusetts, Maud Freshel's Theater; also May 9, 1922, Boston, Jordan Hall.

Based on episodes in Native American history, it concerns the Nipnets, a tribe in what is now Massachusetts, before the arrival of Europeans.

Major roles: Osseo, an Indian hunter; Avano, an outsider; Wauchita, Osseo's wife; and Maynomis, the chief's daughter.

Otherwise Engaged, opera in one act by Allan Davis; libretto (Eng) by the composer. First performance April 23, 1958, New York, Sullivan Street Playhouse.

Other Wise Man, The, opera in one act by Isaac Van Grove; libretto (Eng) by the composer, after a story by Henry Van Dyke. First performance July 14, 1959, Bentonville, Arkansas.

The setting is Bethlehem and Jerusalem in the first part of the first century A.D. Artaban, a magi like the Three Wise Men, has bought three jewels for the newborn Christ, selling all his possessions to obtain them. In following the star to Bethlehem, Artaban sells one of the jewels to save an old Hebrew, then another to save a baby from Herod's soldiers. Searching for Jesus for thirty-three years, he finally arrives in Jerusalem on the day of the Crucifixion but has become ill and half blind. He sells his last jewel, a pearl, with which he had hoped to ransom Jesus, to save a young woman from Macedonian soldiers. When he reaches the Cross, he is wounded fatally and falls near the Cross. He cries out that he has failed, but a voice speaks, saying that he has, through his helping of the weakest, succeeded. Artaban dies in peace.

Major roles: Artaban (ten); Abgarus, his father (bass-bar); Atossa, his mother (mezzo/alto; Roxana, his younger sister (sop); old Hebrew (ten/high bar); and young mother of Bethlehem (mezzo/sop).

For a detailed description, see Eaton/*OP* II, 307–8.

Other Wise Man, The, opera in one act by Stefania de Kenessey; libretto (Eng) by Peter Wallace, after Van Dyke. First performance December 13, 1996, New York, Golden Fleece Ltd. Also May 10, 1998, New York, Mannes College of Music.

Another setting of the story of Artaban.

Otho Visconti, opera in three acts by Frederick Gleason; libretto (Eng) by the composer. First performance (posthumous premiere) June 4, 1907, Chicago, College Theater; conducted by Walter Keller.

Ouanga, opera by Clarence Cameron White; libretto (Eng) by John Frederick Matheus. First performance (concert) November 1932, Chicago; June 10, 1949, South Bend, Indiana. The work was revived on March 27, 1956, New York, Metropolitan Opera, National Negro Opera Foundation, with McHenry Boatwright (Dessalines), Juanita King (Defilée), Adelaide Boatner (Mougali), and Fritz Vincent (priest); and September 29, 1956, in New York, Carnegie Hall, with Boatwright (Dessalines), King (Defilée), and Carol Brice (Mougali).

Based on a true incident, the story concerns Jean-Jacques Dessalines, who in 1804 proclaimed himself emperor of Haiti and, convinced he was another Napoleon, ruled brutally and tried to abolish voodooism by brutal means. Within two years Dessalines fell at the hands of his own army.

Roles: Jean-Jacques Dessalines, Emperor of Haiti (bar); Defilée, former beloved (sop); Michel, Dessalines's servant (ten); Licite, a young peasant (sop); Mougali, voodoo priestess (alto); Le Bossal, Dessalines's aide (ten); Gerin, a general (ten); and Papaloi, voodoo priest (bar).

SCORE: vs ([Fort Wayne, Ind.: C. C. White], 1938; New York: S. Fox, [1955]).
LIBRETTO: English, typewritten copy (Charleston, W. Va., 1931; LCCN: 85-69634).

Our Island Home, comic opera in one act by Thomas German Reed; libretto (Eng) by William S. Gilbert. First performance June 20, 1870, London, Gallery of Illustration, with Thomas German Reed, Priscilla Reed, Fanny Holland, and Arthur Cecil (playing themselves), and Corney Green (Alfred Reed).

The setting is an island in the Indian Ocean, where the performers Mr. and Mrs. Reed, Miss Holland, and Arthur Cecil, have been marooned and are squabbling over their assigned plots of land. As in *The Pirates of Penzance*,* the young Alfred, son of Mr. and Mrs. Reed, has been apprenticed to a pirate as the result of an error. He becomes the sadistic Captain Bang, chief of the pirates. He is about to slaughter the inhabitants of the island, including his parents, when Arthur Cecil points out that the young man, now of age, is no longer bound to the terms of his pirate apprenticeship.

Roles: Mrs. German Reed; Mr. German Reed; Miss Fanny Holland; Mr. Arthur Cecil; and Captain Bang, a pirate chief, later Edward [Alfred] Reed.

For a detailed description, see Stedman/*GBS*, 32-34.

LIBRETTO: English, in Stedman/*GBS*, 107–66.

Our Man in Havana, opera in three acts by Malcolm Williamson; libretto (Eng) by Sidney Gilliat, after Graham Greene's novel. First performance July 2, 1963, Aldeburgh Festival, with Owen Brannigan (Dr. Hasselbacher), Raymond Nilsson (Bramble), Stanley Bevan (Lopez), Joyce Millward (Milly), Raymond Herincx (Segura), Eric Shilling (Hawthorne), April Cantelo (Beatrice), and David Bowman (Carter); conducted by James Loughran; produced by John Blatchley.

The setting of this farcical story is Cuba, just before Castro's takeover in 1959. "Our man" is Bramble, an Englishman who has settled in Havana and is barely getting by as a seller of vacuum cleaners. He is distressed that Milly, his sixteen-year-old daughter, has been charmed by the evil Segura, the police chief. In order to make ends meet and take Milly away from Segura, Bramble reluctantly accepts the offer of Hawthorne, the British Foreign Office representative, to be an English spy, and he is joined by a female spy, Beatrice, who becomes enamored of him. Bramble, however, makes up all of his activities, which, at first, raise the suspicions of Hawthorne and Beatrice but, surprisingly, start to represent actual people and events. Eventually, Bramble discovers that a murderer is after him, one Carter, and Dr. Hasselbacher, another reluctant spy, is killed after he tries to warn Bramble. When Segura comes to visit and asks for Milly's hand, Bramble gets him drunk so that he can deal with Carter. Unable to dispatch Carter at first, Bramble shoots and kills Carter after the latter fires at him. Bramble goes back to his home, where his next assignment is to deal with the inebriated Segura.

Major roles: Bramble (ten), Dr. Hasselbacher (bass), Milly (sop), Beatrice (sop), Segura (bar), Hawthorne (high bar), and Carter (bar).

For a detailed description, see Eaton/*OP* II, 175–76.

SCORE: vs (London: J. Weinberger, [1964]).

BIBLIOGRAPHY: Arthur Jacobs, "London Opera Diary," *Opera* XIV (Aug. 1963), 564–66 [on premiere].

Outcast, The, opera in two acts by Noa Ain; libretto (Eng) by the composer, after the story of Ruth. First full performance June 3, 1994, Houston, Houston Grand Opera's Opera New World Program, with Gail Hadani (Ruta), Ann Duquesnay (Ruta's mother), Eugene Perry (Gideon), Linda Thompson (Naomi), Felicia Coleman Evans (Inanna), and José Garcia (Boaz); conducted by Ward Holmquist, with jazz pianist Theo Saunders. Performed April 26, 1995, Brooklyn, New York, Brooklyn Academy of Music, Majestic Theater, with Clare Gormley (Ruta).

The story is a treatment of the story of Ruth, here called Ruta. Ruta tells her story to the protective Boaz in a series of flashbacks.

The score includes a blend of gospel, jazz, rock music, African folk music, and melodies in classical European style.

BIBLIOGRAPHY: William Albright, "Houston," *ON* LIX (Nov. 1994), 52 [on Houston premiere]; Susan Josephs, "Ruth Redux," *Jewish Week* (Apr. 21, 1995), 35 [preview of BAM performance].

Outcasts of Poker Flat, The, opera in one act by Stanworth R. Beckler; libretto (Eng) by Jon Pearce, after Brett Harte's short story (1869). First performance December 16, 1960, Stockton, California, College of the Pacific.

See next entry for the story.

Major roles: Tom Simpson, "the Innocent" (ten); Piney Woods (sop); the Duchess (mezzo); John Oakhurst (bar); and Mother Shipton (alto).

Outcasts of Poker Flat, The, opera in one act by Samuel Adler; libretto (Eng), after Harte. First performance June 8, 1962, Denton, Texas.

The outcasts are Gambler Oakhurst and Duchess, the madam of Poker Flat, thrown out of the town by the upstanding citizens. They have sought shelter at a hut, where they are joined by a young girl, Piney, and Innocent, a young man, who have run off together. The group's horses and packs are stolen during a snowstorm by Uncle Billy, the town drunk, and their situation becomes critical. When food runs low, Duchess gives her portion to Piney, and Innocent goes back to the town to seek help. In the meantime Oakhurst kills himself, and when Innocent returns, he finds that Duchess is also dead, and Piney is unconscious. Feeling guilty, the residents of the town bring back the outcasts to Poker Flat for proper burial.

For a detailed description, see Eaton/*OP* II, 308–9.

Major roles: Piney (sop), Duchess (mezzo), Innocent (ten), Oakhurst (bar), and Uncle Billy (bass).

Outcasts of Poker Flat, The, opera in four scenes by William MacSems; libretto (Eng), after Harte. Composed 1972.
SCORE: vs (n.p., [1972]; LCCN: 84-124539).

Out of Bondage, ballad opera; libretto (Eng) by Joseph Bradford. First performance March 20, 1876, Lynn, Massachusetts, Music Hall, with Emma Louise Hyers and Anna Madah Hyers.

The story, told from the slave's point of view, traces the journey from bondage to freedom.

The songs making up the music include "Angels Meet Me at the Cross-Road," "Did My Lord Deliber Daniel?," "Gwine to Ride up in de Chariot," "Nobody Knows What Trouble I See," and "Old Kentucky Home."
TEXT AND MUSIC: ms libretto (Washington, D.C.: Library of Congress); various nineteenth-century sheet-music songs, repr. ed. Eileen Southern, *NAMT*, vol. 9 (1974).

Out of Place, or, The Lake of Lausanne, operatic romance in two acts by William Reeve and John Braham; libretto (Eng) by Frederick Reynolds. First performance February 28, 1805, London, Covent Garden. First U.S. performance October 9, 1812, New York, Park Theatre.
SCORE: vs (London: Clementi & Co., ca. 1805).
LIBRETTO: English (New York: W. Turner, 1808).

Out of Sight, operetta in one act by Frederic Clay; libretto (Eng) by Benjamin Charles Stephenson. First performance February 1860, London.

Outpost, The, opera by John Hullah; anonymous libretto (Eng). First performance May 17, 1838, London, Covent Garden.

Out the Window, comic opera in one act by Seymour Barab; libretto (Eng) by the composer. First performance (concert) May 12, 1985, New York, After Dinner Opera, with Jocelyn Wilkes and Bill Bonecutter; Conrad Strasser (pno). Presented together with *Predators** under the designation "Tour de Farce."

A woman who has a terribly jealous husband tries to help her marital situation by getting her neighbor to pretend to have an affair with her in order to rid her husband of his jealousy. To her dismay, she discovers that the neighbor's wife is also extremely jealous.
BIBLIOGRAPHY: Bernard Holland, "Music: 'Farce" by Barab," *NYT* (May 16, 1985) [on premiere].

Owen Wingrave, opera in two acts by Benjamin Britten; libretto (Eng) by Myfanwy Piper, after Henry James's story (1892). First performance May 16, 1971, for television broadcast: U.S. (NET), Britain (BBC), with Heather Harper (Mrs. Coyle), Jennifer Vyvyan (Mrs. Julian), Sylvia Fisher (Miss Wingrave), Janet Baker (Kate), Peter Pears (Sir Philip), Benjamin Luxon (Owen Wingrave), John Shirley-Quirk (Spencer Coyle), and Nigel Douglas (Lechmere); conducted by the composer. First stage performance May 10, 1973, London, Covent Garden, with a similar cast; conducted by Steuart Bedford. First U.S. performance August 9, 1973, Santa Fe.

Echoing Britten's pacifist beliefs and, according to recent reevaluations (see McClatchie's article), his homosexuality, the story tells of a young man, Owen Wingrave, the last of his line, who rebels, ostensibly, against the military traditions of his family. He thereby offends his aunt, Miss Wingrave, his grandfather, Sir Philip, and his fiancée, Kate, who turn away from him despite his support from Spencer Coyle, his tutor. In order to prove his courage to Kate, Owen spends a night in the haunted room of his family's estate in which an ancestor was found dead without any wounds on his body. Next morning Owen, similarly, is discovered dead, without any visible cause of death.

For a detailed plot synopsis and musical analysis, see K/*KOB*, 1232–37; K/*NKOB*, 135–38.

Major roles: Owen Wingrave (bar), Miss Wingrave (sop), Sir Philip (ten), Kate (mezzo), Spencer Coyle (bass-bar), and Mrs. Coyle (sop).
SCORE: vs (London: Faber, [1973]).
LIBRETTO: English (London: Faber, 1973).
BIBLIOGRAPHY: Speight Jenkins, "TV: Owen Wingrave," *ON* XXXV (June 12, 1971), 27 [on premiere]; Stephen McClatchie, "Benjamin Britten, *Owen Wingrave* and the Politics of the Closet; or, 'He Shall Be Straightened out at Paramore,'" *Cambridge Opera Journal* VIII (1996), 59–75.
DISCOGRAPHY: Fisher, Vyvyan, Harper, Baker, Pears, Douglas, Luxon, Shirley-Quirk, Wadsworth School Boys' Choir, English Chamber Orch.; cond. Britten, London OSA 1291 (1972).

Oxford Act, The, ballad opera; libretto (Eng). First performance summer (?) 1733, Oxford, performed by a group of Oxford students.
LIBRETTO: English (London: L. Gulliver, 1733).

Ozmyn and Daraxa, musical romance in two acts by Thomas Attwood; libretto (Eng) by James Boaden. First performance March 7, 1793, London, Haymarket Theatre.

The work is set in Spain in the seventeenth century. It includes music by Mozart.
LIBRETTO: English ([London]: C. Lowndes, [1793?]).

P

Pacha's Bridal, The, opera in three acts by Frank Romer; libretto (Eng) by Mark Lemon. First performance September 8, 1836, London, English Opera House.
LIBRETTO: English (London: J. Duncombe, [1836?]).

Packet Boat, The, or, A Peep behind the Veil, musical farce in two acts by Thomas Attwood; libretto (Eng) by Samuel Birch. First performance May 13, 1794, London, Covent Garden.

Paddy Whack in Italia, Il, opera in one act by Samuel Lover; libretto (Eng) by the composer. First performance April 22, 1841, London, English Opera House.
LIBRETTO: English (London: J. Duncombe, [1841?]).

Padlock, The, comic opera in two acts by Charles Dibdin; libretto (Eng) by Isaac Bickerstaffe, after Cervantes's story *El celoso extremeño* from the *Novelas exemplares* (1613). First performance October 3, 1768, London, Drury Lane Theatre, with Mrs. Arne (Leonora), Mr. Vernon (Leander), Mr. Dibdin (Mungo), Mrs. Dorman (Ursula), and Mr. (Charles) Bannister (Don Diego).

The action, set in Salamanca, centers on the aging Don Diego, who is thinking of wedding Leonora, his ward. He gives six keys to the elderly confidante, Ursula, to safeguard his intended's virtue, and instructs Mungo, his black servant, to stay awake all night as an added precaution. When a young man, Leander, comes disguised as a lame beggar because he has learned that Leonora is quite beautiful, his entry is blocked by a sizable padlock affixed to the front door. Insulted that Diego did not trust her to protect Leonora, Ursula tells the "beggar" how he can get over the garden wall. When he removes his disguise, she becomes enamored of him, and he plays along with her to get access to Leonora. Don Diego returns without warning, but he realizes the folly of wanting to marry Leonora and steps aside for Leander.

For a detailed description, see Fiske/*ETM*, 350–53.
SCORE: vs (London: John Johnston for the author, n.d.).
LIBRETTO: English (London: Longman & Broderip, [1768?]).

Padrevia, opera in one act by Thomas Pasatieri; libretto (Eng) by the composer, after Giovanni Boccaccio's *Decamerone*. First performance November 18, 1967, Brooklyn, New York, with Joyce Mathis (Gismonda), Stanley Debel (Tancred), Grayson Hirst (Guiscardo), and Robert Gross (narrator); directed by Károly Köpe.

In order to keep his daughter Gismonda away from the world, King Tancred locks her up in his castle. She falls in love with Guiscardo, the young gardener, however, and when the king finds them together in bed, he throws the gardener into prison. When the gardener is killed, Gismonda takes poison.

Major roles: Gismonda, Princess of Padrevia (sop); Tancred, her father, King of Padrevia (bass-bar); Guiscardo, a gardener (ten); and narrator (speaking).

Part 3 of the composer's triptych. The other operas are *La Divina** and *The Women.**
SCORE: vs (Bryn Mawr, Pa.: T. Presser, 1971).

Padrone, The, opera by George W. Chadwick; libretto (Eng) by K. Stevens, after a scenario by the composer. Composed 1912. First performance (concert) September 1995, Warterbury, Connecticut, Thomaston Opera House, Waterbury Symphony Orchestra. First stage performance April 11, 1997, Boston, Northeastern University, Blackman Auditorium, New England Conservatory Opera Theatre; conducted by John Moriarity; staged by Marc Astafan.

The story concerns the then-contemporary practice of bringing impoverished Italian immigrants to this country who were then forced to work for their sponsor, the "padrone," until they paid off their debt.

BIBLIOGRAPHY: Frances Chamberlain, preview, *NYT* (Sept. 3, 1995), XIII (Conn. supplement), 15; Richard Dyer, review, *Boston Globe* (Apr. 12, 1997), C, 4 [on stage premiere].

Pageant of Darkness and Light, The, stage pageant in six episodes by Hamish MacCunn; libretto (Eng) by John Oxenham. Composed 1908.
SCORE: vs (London, 1908).

Paid Off. See **Three Instant Operas.**

Palace of Mirth, The, dialogue by Charles Dibdin. First performance 1772, London, Sadler's Wells.
SCORE: vs (London: John Johnston, [n.d.]).

Pan and Syrinx, masque by John Galliard; libretto (Eng) by Lewis Theobald. First performance January 14, 1718, London, Lincoln's Inn Fields, with Richard Leveridge (Pan) and Mrs. Barbier (Syrinx).

The god Pan pursues Syrinx, a nymph, who is eventually turned into a reed.

For a detailed description, see Fiske/*ETM*, 59–60.
SCORE: fs ms (1717, British Library, Add. MS. 31588); vs, "How Sweet the Warbling Linnet Sings," ed. L. Ring ([London]: Universal Edition, [1961]).

Pandora's Box, short opera for young people by Cecil Effinger; libretto (Eng) by Sally Monsour. First performance 1962, Boulder, Colorado, University of Colorado.

Pandora's Box, children's opera by in one act by Michael Cave; libretto by the composer and Judyth Walker Cave. First performance April 7, 1971, Los Angeles.
SCORE: ms fs, holograph (1971, photocopy, NYPL).

Panfilo and Lauretta. See **The Visitors.**

Panic, The, chamber opera in one act by David Sawyer; libretto (Eng) by Paul Godfrey. First performance 1991, London.

The work is scored for soprano, tenor, baritone, and bass, and chamber ensemble.

Pantagleize, opera in three acts by Robert Starer; libretto (Eng) by the composer, after Michel de Ghélerode. First performance April 7, 1973, Brooklyn, New York, Brooklyn College, with Grayson Hirst (Pantagleize); conducted by Károly Köpe.

The setting is a European city between wars. The innocent Pantagleize is used by a group of revolutionaries to foment an uprising by speaking their password, "What a lovely day." Four of the revolutionaries, Bianca, a poet, Bamboola, an Uncle Tom caricature, Innocenti, an intellectual going under the guise of a waiter, and Banger, who is lame and carries a machine gun, plan their enterprise in the café practically in the presence of Creep, a police spy. Pantagleize, oblivious to what is going on, thinks that the uproar that his words engendered is due to an imminent eclipse of the sun. He is seduced by Rachel, who then gives him a gun and convinces him to take over the imperial treasure at the State Bank. While he is away, Creep shoots Rachel. Pantagleize obtains the treasure after tricking General Macboom, but he and the real revolutionaries are eventually seized, tried, and condemned to death, Pantagleize not understanding to the end why he is being punished.

For a detailed description, see Eaton/*OP* II, 177–78.

Major roles: Pantagleize (ten), Rachel Silberchatz (mezzo), Creep (actor), Bamboola (bass), Bianca (col sop), and Innocenti (bar).

BIBLIOGRAPHY: Harvey E. Phillips, review, *ON* XXXVII (June 1973), 25 [on premiere].

Parabola and Circula, opera in one act by Marc Blitzstein; libretto (Eng) by George Whitsett. Composed 1929. Not performed.

The "plot," set in the "World of Forms," involves a loving couple, Parabola and Circula, and their adopted children, Rectangula and Intersecta. The family's peace is destroyed when doubts are raised by Prism, a friend of Parabola, and reinforced by Geodesa and Linea. Only too late does Parabola realize his error, by which time Circula has been undone.

For a description, see Gordon/*MM*, 51–52.

Roles: Parabola (bar), Circula (sop), Rectangula (ten), Intersecta (sop), Prism (ten), Geodesa (bass-bar), and Linea (alto).

Paradise Lost, "sacra rappresentazione" in two acts by Krzystof Penderecki; libretto (Eng) by Christopher Fry, after Milton's poem. First performance November 29, 1978, Chicago, Lyric Opera, with Arnold Moss (Milton), Ellen Shade (Eve), William Stone (Adam), Peter Van Ginkel (Satan), Paul Esswood (Death), Joy Davidson (Sin), Michael Ballam (Beelzebub), Melvin Lowry (Belial), James Schwisow (Gabriel), Alan Opie (Messias), and Frank Little (Michael); conducted by Bruno Bartoletti.

Among the players is the blind Milton (actor), who tells the story of original sin at the outset and then serves as narrator. Among the other characters are Adam, Eve, and Satan.

The work includes a chorus singing the first chorale of J. S. Bach's *St. John Passion*, "O grosse Lieb'," in translation.

Other settings include J.–F. Le Sueur's *Le mort d'Adam* (1809, Paris, after Klopstock's drama); G. Spontini (unfin., 1838); and A. Rubinstein (1856, perf. 1875, Düsseldorf).

BIBLIOGRAPHY: Hans Heinsheimer, "Paradise Regained," *ON* XLIII (Nov. 1978), 48, 50, 52, 55; Robert Jacobson, "Reports: U.S.," *ON* XLIII (Feb. 3, 1979), 32 [on premiere]; Andrew Porter, "Musical Events," *NY* LIV (Dec. 18, 1978), 88, 90, 91 [on premiere].

Paragraph, The, musical entertainment in two acts by John Braham; libretto (Eng) by Prince Hoare. First performance March 8, 1804, London. First U.S. performance November 23, 1804, Baltimore.

LIBRETTO: English (London: R. Phillips, 1804).

Pardoner's Tale, The, opera in one act by Erik Chisholm; libretto (Eng) by the composer, after Chaucer. First performance November 1961, Cape Town, South Africa.

Three friends meet at an inn to get drunk. When they hear bells tolling for a friend who has died, they plan to avenge him by killing Death. An old man directs them to Death in a room upstairs, where they find a chest full of gold. Two of them send the third out for wine, planning to kill him when he returns, so that they can have the gold themselves. They stab him when he comes back and drink the wine he has brought. They die, also, since their erstwhile friend had poisoned the wine, intending to keep the gold for himself.

Act 2 of the composer's *Canterbury Tales*.*

BIBLIOGRAPHY: review, *Opera* LXII (1961), 187–88 [on premiere].

Pardoner's Tale, The, chamber opera in one act by Noel Sokoloff; libretto (Eng) by Ted Hart, after Chaucer. Composed 1961.

Pardoner's Tale, The, opera in one act by Ernest Lubin; libretto (Eng) by Ted Hart, after Chaucer. First performance November 19, 1966, Denver.

Pardoner's Tale, The, opera in one act by John S. Davis; libretto (Eng), after Chaucer. First performance May 23, 1967, University of Arizona.

Pardoner's Tale, The, opera in one act by Alan Ridout; libretto (Eng) by Norman Platt, after Chaucer. First performance April 1, 1971, Canterbury, England, Marlowe Theatre, Kent Opera.

Parfait for Irene, A, comic opera in three acts by Walter Kaufmann; libretto (Eng) by the composer. First performance February 21, 1952, Bloomington, University of Indiana.
    A timid druggist eventually wins Irene, the girl of his dreams.
BIBLIOGRAPHY: Paul Nettl, review, *MA* LXXII (March 1952), 10 [on premiere].

Pariahs, The, opera in three acts by Leonard Kastle; libretto (Eng) by the composer. Composed 1966. First performance (excerpts) 1985, Albany.
    The plot concerns whaling.

Paris Doll, The, operatic comedy by Reginald De Koven; libretto (Eng) by Harry B. Smith. First performance September 14, 1897, Hartford, Connecticut, Parson's Theatre.

Parlour, The, opera in one act by Grace Williams; libretto (Eng) by the composer, after Maupassant's short story *En famille*. First performance May 5, 1966, Cardiff, New Theatre, Welsh National Opera, with Edith Coates (Grandmamma), Edward Byles (Papa), Noreen Berry (Mamma), Anne Pashley (Louisa), and Janet Hughes (Augusta); conducted by Bryan Balkwill; produced by John Moody; designed by Elizabeth Friendship. Revived July 9, 1993, Welsh College of Music and Drama, with Huw May (Papa), Kim-Marie Woodhouse (Mamma), Montserrat Pasco Tico (Grandmamma), Isobel Warnock (Louisa), and Justine Platts (Augusta); conducted by John Pryce-Jones.
    Set in a seaside town, the story revolves around a family who hope to ease their financial problems when the well-off Grandmamma dies. She seemingly obliges and passes away, only to come back to life after hearing her family discuss what they plan to do with her wealth once the neighbors have paid their condolences.
BIBLIOGRAPHY: Kenneth Loveland, review, *MO* CXVI (Aug. 1993), 263–64 [on revival].

Partisans, The, opera in two scenes by Inglis Gundry; libretto (Eng) by the composer. First performance May 28, 1946, London, St. Pancras Town Hall.
LIBRETTO: English (London: Hinrichsen, [1946]).

Pasqual Bruno, opera in three acts by John Liptrot Hatton; libretto (Eng) by Edward Fitzball, after Alexandre Dumas Sr. First performance, in a German translation by Joseph von Seyfried, March 2, 1844, Vienna, Kärntnertortheater.
    The setting is Sicily. Among the musical numbers is the song "Revenge."
    The work was a failure and was apparently never performed in England.

Passion and Resurrection, church opera in twelve scenes by Jonathan Harvey; libretto from the texts of Benedictine Latin church dramas, translated into English by

Michael Wadsworth. First performance Passiontide, March 21, 1981, Winchester, Winchester Cathedral; conducted by Martin Neary.

Major roles: Jesus (bar), Peter (bass), John (ten), Mary Magdalene (sop), Pilate (ten), and Judas (bass).

Passionate Man, A, opera in two acts by James Wilson; libretto (Eng) by Bruce Arnold. First performance June 21, 1995, Dublin, Trinity College; conducted by Colman Pearce.

The title character, Jonathan Swift, brings about the defeat of the Duke of Marlborough.
BIBLIOGRAPHY: Ian Fox, "Passionless Opera," *Opera* XLVI (Oct. 1995), 1207 [on premiere].

Passion of Jonathan Wade, The, opera in three acts by Carlisle Floyd; libretto (Eng) by the composer. First performance October 11, 1962, New York, New York City Opera, with Theodor Uppman (Jonathan Wade), Phyllis Curtin (Celia), Norman Treigle (Judge Townsend), Frank Poretta (Lucas Wardlaw), and Norman Kelley (Enoch Pratt); conducted by Julius Rudel; staged by Allen Fletcher. Revised version first performed January 18, 1991, Houston, Houston Grand Opera, Wortham Theater Center, with Dale Duesing (Wade), Sheryl Woods (Celia), Julian Patrick (Townsend), Debria Brown (Nicey), Joseph Evans (Wardlaw), John Duykers (Pratt), Donnie Ray Albert (James Bell), and Eric Perkins (Lt. Perkins); conducted by John DeMain.

The work is set in post–Civil War Columbia, South Carolina. Jonathan Wade, the miliary governor and a decent man, falls in love with Celia, a southern belle. Despite the objections of her father, Judge Brooks Townsend, she marries Wade, who is caught between the sinister forces of both the North and the South, represented by the fanatical northern politician Enoch Pratt and the southern ex-slaveholder Lucas Wardlaw. Unable to deal with the situation, Wade is about to flee to Brazil, when he is shot by an anonymous agent, who could come from either side.

Major roles: Jonathan Wade (bar); Celia, his wife (sop); Brooks Townsend, a southern judge (bass-bar); Nicey, Townsend's maid (alto); Lucas Wardlaw (ten); Enoch Pratt (ten); James Bell, a northern judge (bass-bar); and Lt. Perkins, Wade's assistant (ten).

The bitonal score is composed as a number opera and has arias and ensembles, as well as bits of local color, made-up spirituals, and folk songs.
LIBRETTO: English (New York: Boosey & Hawkes, [1990]).
BIBLIOGRAPHY: William Albright, "Passion Rekindled," *ON* LV (Jan. 5, 1991), 18–20; the same, "Houston," *ON* LV (June 1991), 46–47 [on 1991 revival]; Conrad Osborne, "New York," *MT* CIV (Feb. 1963), 120 [on premiere]; Robert Suro, "Opera's Revision Defines a Composer," *NYT* (Feb. 2, 1991), L, 13.

Passion of Lizzie Borden, The, "mosaic of memories" in one act by Mira J. Spektor; libretto (Eng), after Ruth Whitman's poem. First performance July 13, 1986, Buffalo, State University of New York. Also April 7, 1988, New York, Golden Fleece Ltd.

The work concerns the musings of the title character years after her acquittal.
BIBLIOGRAPHY: Will Crutchfield, review, *NYT* (Apr. 10, 1988), 59 [on N.Y. performance].

Passion of Oedipus, The, opera in two scenes by Roy Travis; libretto (Eng) by the composer, after Sophocles. First performance November 8, 1968, University of Southern California, Los Angeles, Royce Hall, with William Du Pre (Oedipus), Christina Krooskos (Jocasta), John Robert Dunlap (Creon), Richard Hale (old shepherd), William Farrel (Tiresias), Anna Levistki (the sphinx), and Cary Archer Smith (Laius); conducted by Jan Popper.

Oedipus's solving of the riddle of the sphinx at Thebes and his unwitting murder of his father are shown in a series of flashbacks.

The mostly atonal score includes some harmonic passages. The chorus has an active role in the development of the plot.

BIBLIOGRAPHY: Albert Goldberg, review, *ON* XXXIII (Dec. 28, 1968), 32 [on premiere]. DISCOGRAPHY: selections, M. Kehane, W. Du Pre; cond. Popper, Royal Philharmonic Orch. and Chorus, Orion ORS 73129 (1973, 1 LP].

Passion of Simple Simon, The, theater opera in three acts by Eric Salzman and Michael Sahl; libretto (Eng) by the composers. First performance February 1, 1979, New York, Theater for the New City. Revised as a radio opera, 1980, National Public Radio.

The protagonist is a sniper who kills joggers in New York's Central Park and subsequently becomes a punk-rock celebrity.

Passion of Vincent Van Gogh, The, opera in three acts by Christopher Yavelow; libretto (Eng) by the composer, after letters of van Gogh and official documents. First performance (abridged) April 14, 1984, Dallas, University of Texas.

LIBRETTO: English-German ([Cambridge, Mass.]: C. Yavelow, 1983).

Passion, Poison, and Petrifaction, farce in one act by Bruce Taub; libretto (Eng) by the composer, after George Bernard Shaw's play. First performance April 1, 1976, New York, Composers Ensemble.

Discovering that his wife, Lady Magnesia, has a lover, Adolphus Bastable, George Fitztollemache determines to stab his wife and hides in her bedchamber. When Adolphus enters, George feeds him poison. To save Adolphus, Lady Magnesia says she will become George's lover rather than his obedient servant and wife. The couple try to save Adolphus by feeding him lime, including plaster and a bust of Lady Magnesia, but the young man, instead, turns into a human statue. The landlord, police officer, and doctor rush in to see what the commotion is about. They are struck by a bolt of lightning and turned to ashes. Lady Magnesia and George, left alone, pledge their love and place the statue of Adolphus in the corner.

For a detailed description, see Kornick/*RAO*, 309–10.

Major roles: Lady Magnesia (sop), George Fitztollemache (bass), and Adolphus Bastable (ten).

Pastoral, opera in one act by James Galloway; libretto (Eng), after James Morley's play. First performance May 22, 1988, Albuquerque, Opera Southwest.

Past Tense, two one-act operas by Stephen Oliver; libretto (Eng) by the composer. First performance June 5, 1974, Huddersfield, England, School of Music, consisting of:

Old Times

Come and Go, after Samuel Beckett

Pathelin, "opera-entertainment" in one act by Wilfred Josephs; libretto (Eng) by Edward Marsh. Composed 1963.

The unscrupulous Pathelin, a lawyer who goes so far as to cheat a draper out of cloth for his clothing and then denies the whole thing, gets his comeuppance at a trial when his client, a shepherd accused of stealing from the same draper, gets out of paying his fee.

Patie and Peggy, or, The Fair Foundling, "Scottish" ballad opera in one act; libretto (Eng) by Theophilus Cibber, an adaptation of Ramsay's original text. First performance

probably May 1, 1730,** London, Drury Lane Theatre, with Mr. Williams (Sir William Worthy), Mrs. Roberts (Patie), Miss Raftor (Peggy), and Mr. Cibber Jr. (Roger).
The work was a revision of *The Gentle Shepherd** (1729, London).
**April 20 is listed as the first performance in *The London Stage*, vol. 3/1, ed. Arthur W. Scouten (Carbondale, Ill.: Southern Illinois University Press, 1960–61), 51. LIBRETTO: English (London: J. Watts, 1731); repr. Rubsamen/*BO*, vol. 24, *Scottish Ballad Operas I: Pastoral Comedies* (1974).

Patience, or, Bunthorne's Bride, comic opera in two acts by Arthur Sullivan; libretto (Eng) by William S. Gilbert. First performance April 23, 1881, London, Opéra Comique, with Richard Temple (Colonel Calverley), Frank Thornton (Major Murgatroyd), Durward Lely (Duke of Dunstable), George Grossmith (Reginald Bunthorne), Rutland Barrington (Archibald Grosvenor), Jessie Bond (Lady Angela), Julia Gwynne (Lady Saphir), May Fortescue (Lady Ella), Alice Barnett (Lady Jane), and Leonora Braham (Patience). First U.S. performance July 28, 1881, St. Louis, Uhrig's Cave; September 22, 1881, New York, Standard Theatre, with A. Wilkinson (Murgatroyd), J. H. Ryley (Bunthorne), James Barton (Grosvenor), and Carrie Burton (Patience).

The story satirizes the aesthetic craze of the 1880s with things pastoral. It concerns two poets, Bunthorne and Grosvenor, who are competing for the love of Patience, a milkmaid. Bunthorne is adored by twenty lovelorn maidens, while Patience, believing that real love must be utterly unselfish, shuns the love of Archibald Grosvenor, a childhood companion, who she feels is too perfect.

She agrees to marry Bunthorne because she dislikes him, and the twenty maidens turn their attentions to Grosvenor. Bunthorne forces Grosvenor to cut his hair, thereby making himself more ordinary and, therefore, suitable for Patience, whereupon she ends her engagement to Bunthorne. Bunthorne's only remaining admirer is the portly Lady Jane, but she is claimed by the Duke of Dunstable, who wants a plain wife, and Bunthorne is left without anyone to wed.

Major roles: Colonel Calverley (bar), Major Murgatroyd (bar), and the Duke of Dunstable (ten), officers of the Dragon Guards; Reginald Bunthorne, a "fleshy" poet (bar); Archibald Grosvenor (bar), an "idyllic" poet; the Lady Angela (mezzo), the Lady Saphir (mezzo), the Lady Ella (sop), and the Lady Jane (alto), rapturous maidens; and Patience, a dairy maid (sop).

For a detailed description, see Stedman/*WSG*, 181–85.
VIDEO: D. Hammond-Stroud, S. Dugdale, A. Collins, D. Adams, Ambrosian Opera Chorus; cond. McCarthy; London Sym. Orch.; cond. A. Faris, Goldcrest Films International, Opera World, VHS PAT-10V (1982 perf.); rev. F. Paul Driscoll, *ON* LXII (Oct. 1997), 65.

Patience and Sarah, opera in three acts by Paula M. Kimper; libretto (Eng) by Wende Persons, after the novel *Place for Us* (1969) by Isabel Miller. First performance (concert) June 1996, New York, American Opera Projects, with Lori Ann Philips (Patience), Elaine Valby (Sarah), Michael Hendrick (Edward White), and Barton Green (Daniel Peel). First stage performance July 10, 1998, New York, Lincoln Center Festival.

The story, set in the nineteenth century, concerns the relationship that develops between Patience White, a prosperous painter who lives with her brother Edward and his wife, and Sarah Dowling, the boyish blue-collar daughter of a neighbor. In the face of family objections that the women go west together, Sarah, dressed as a boy, travels alone and is befriended by Parson Daniel Peel. When Sarah returns to her home, she and Patience decide to go off together.

The score uses hymn tunes and includes set pieces such as arias, ballads, and duets.
BIBLIOGRAPHY: Allan Kozinn, "Two Women with Gumption," *NYT* (July 2, 1996), C, 16 [on concert premiere].

Patria, cycle of music-theater works (orig. trilogy) by R. Murray Schafer; libretto (Eng-Fr) by the composer, projected to include twelve works.
  The cycle focuses on ritual and figures of mythology, e.g., Ariadne (nos. 1, 2, 5).
  Patria, Prologue: The Princess of the Stars. First performance September 26, 1981, Heart Lake, near Brompton, Ontario.
  "Designed for performance at dawn on an autumn morning" (score, p. 4).
  The composer's version of creation, inspired by Native American myths.
SCORE: fs (Toronto: Arcana Editions, 1986).
  Patria, no. 1: Wolfman (formerly **The Characteristics Man**), "a work for the theatre." Composed 1966–1974. First performance 1974, Toronto; Nov. 21, 1987, Toronto, Shaw Festival.
SCORE: fs (Toronto: Berandol Music, 1978).
  Patria, no. 2: Requiems for the Party Girl, "a work for the stage." First performance August 23, 1972, Stratford, Ontario.
SCORE: (Toronto: Berandol Music, 1978).
  Patria, no. 3: The Greatest Show. First performance August 6, 1987, Petersborough, Ontario, Festival of the Arts.
  Patria, no. 4: The Black Theatre of Hermes Trismegistos. First performance March 9, 1989, Liège, Liège Festival.
SCORE: fs (Toronto: Arcana Editions, 1988).
  Patria, no. 5: The Crown of Ariadne. First performance (concert) March 2, 1992, Toronto.
  Patria, no. 6: RA. First performance May 4, 1983, Toronto, Science Center, Comus Music Theatre.
  For singers, actors, dancers, instruments, tape, and electronic sounds, with audience participation. Based on Egyptian mythology, it features the jackal-headed god Anubis.
SCORE: fs (Indian River, Ont.: Arcana Editions, 1989).
BIBLIOGRAPHY: R. Murray Schafer, *Patria and the Theatre of Confluence* (Indian River, Ont.: Arcana Editions, 1991).

Patrick, television opera in three acts by A. J. Potter; libretto (Eng) by Donagh McDonagh. First performance March 17, 1965, Dublin, RTE TV; conducted by Tibor Paul.

Patriot, The, tragic opera in one act by Julian Edwards; libretto (Eng) by Stanislaus Stangé. First performance November 23, 1908, New York. Revived July 25, 1975, Newport, Rhode Island, Newport Music Festival, The Breakers.
  The conspirators Enoch Crosby, Lajeunesse, Corey, and Manheim plan to kill George Washington. The plot fails when Marion, Manheim's daughter, secretly takes Washington's place. Manheim then unwittingly stabs Marion instead of his intended target.
  Roles: Manheim, a Tory farmer (bar); Marion (sop); George Washington (bar); Enoch Crosby, an English spy (ten); Lajeunesse (bar); and Corey (bar).
SCORE: vs (New York: M. Witmark & Sons, 1907).
BIBLIOGRAPHY: Harold C. Schonberg, review, *NYT* (July 26, 1975), 15 [on revival].

Patron, The, or, The Statesman's Opera, ballad opera in two acts; libretto (Eng) by Thomas Odell. First performance May 7, 1729, London, Little Theatre in the Haymarket, with Mr. Hulet (Lord Falcon), Mr. Giffard (Sir Holly Glee), Mr. Reynolds (Merit), and Mrs. Nokes (Peggy Lure).

The work was a stinging attack on Walpole, the prime minister at the time. The patron (Walpole) is called Lord Falcon; he ruins the life of Merit, a gentleman who depends on him for support.

LIBRETTO: English (London: John Clarke, 1729); repr. ed. Rubsamen/*BO*, vol. 3, *Harlots, Rakes, and Bawds* (1974).

Paul and Virginia, musical drama in two acts by William Reeve and Joseph Mazzinghi; libretto (Eng) by James Cobb. First performance May 1, 1800, London, Covent Garden. First U.S. performance March 18, 1803, Boston, Federal Street Theatre.

The setting is a desert island on which a pair of lovers is stranded.

The story was set as *Paul et Virginie* by R. Kreutzer (1791, Paris) and V. Massé (1876, Paris); and as *Paolo e Virginia* by P. C. Guglielmi (1817, Naples).

SCORE: vs (London, ca. 1800).

Paul Bunyan, opera in a prologue and two acts by Benjamin Britten; libretto (Eng) by W. H. Auden. First performance May 5, 1941, New York, Columbia University, with Helen Marshall (Tiny), William Hess (Inkslinger), Bliss Woodward (Hel Helson), Charles Cammock (Slim), Milton Warchoff (Paul Bunyan), and Mordecai Bauman (Narrator). Withdrawn from performance until its revival (excerpts) 1974, Aldeburgh Festival. Revised version February 1, 1976, BBC radio, with Norma Burrowes, Peter Pears, and George Hamilton IV; conducted by Steuart Bedford (concert); stage, June 4, 1976, Aldeburgh Festival, with Iris Saunders, Neil Jenkins, and Russell Smythe.

A musical fable, the story follows the progress of American settlers on the western frontier. The folk hero Paul Bunyan is the spiritual inspiration of the lumberman, one who is heard but not seen. The human characters include Hel Helson, "the man of brawn, but no brain," the highly intelligent Inkslinger, and the charmer Slim, who marries the boss's daughter.

Bunyan comes to a lumberjack camp and encounters four Swedish loggers, led by Hel Helson. Bunyan weds Carrie, but the marriage is unsuccessful, and Carrie goes back home, along with their young daughter, Tiny. When the mother dies soon after, Bunyan retrieves his daughter, who eventually marries Slim, the camp cook. Helson, jealous of Bunyan's position at the camp, tries to kill the giant, but he realizes he is no match and decides it is better to follow Bunyan's orders.

For a detailed plot synopsis, see K/*KOB*, 1157–60.

Major roles: the Narrator (bar/ten); the voice of Paul Bunyan (speaking role); Johnny Inkslinger, a bookkeeper (ten); Tiny, daughter of Paul Bunyan (sop); Hot Biscuit Slim, a good cook (ten); and Hel Helson, a foreman (bar).

The work includes ballads, character pieces, blues, and choruses.

SCORE: vs ([n.p.], 1941, LCCN: 84-141025; London: Faber, 1976).

LIBRETTO: English (London: Faber, 1976).

DISCOGRAPHY: Nelson, Jette, Herber, Hardy, Lawless, Bohn, Dressen, Sutton, Fristad, Wagner, Plymouth Music Series (Minnesota); cond. P. Brunelle, Virgin Classics VCD7-90710 (rec. May 1987, St. Paul, 2 CDs); rev. John W. Freeman, *ON* LIII (Dec. 24, 1988), 45.

Paul Clifford, musical drama in three acts by George Rodwell; libretto (Eng) by Edward Fitzball, after Bulwer-Lytton. First performance October 28, 1835, London, Covent Garden.

SCORE: vs (London, ca. 1835).
LIBRETTO: English (London: J. Duncombe & Co., [183?]).

Paul Laurence Dunbar, opera by Valerie Capers; libretto (Eng). First performance February 12, 1988, New York, Opera Ebony.

The work concerns the nineteenth-century poet, who was the son of former slaves.

Pauline, opera in four acts by Frederic Cowen; libretto (Eng) by Henry Hersee, after Bulwer Lytton's *The Lady of Lyons.* First performance November 22, 1876, London, Lyceum, with Charles Santley (Claude Melnotte), Carl Rosa Opera Company.

The poor Claude Melnotte, goaded by his friends Beausant and Glavis, attempts to win the hand of the haughty Pauline Deschapelles by pretending to be a nobleman. Claude and Pauline marry, and even after Pauline discovers the deception, she sticks by her husband. He volunteers for the army and acquits himself bravely, thereby bringing true honor upon himself.

Major roles: Pauline (sop), Claude Melnotte (bar), Beausant (bar), and Glavis (ten).

Pavilion, The, musical entertainment by William Linley; libretto (Eng) by the composer. First performance November 16, 1799, London, Drury Lane Theatre, with Michael Kelly (the Caliph) and Miss De Camp, Mrs. Bland, and Mrs. Crouch (Arab maidens). Performed later under the title *The Ring.*

The work is set in a harem.
SCORE: ms fs (British Library, Egerton 2494).

Pay Off, The, cabaret opera by William Russo; libretto (Eng) by Denise Declue. First performance February 16, 1984, Chicago.

Pay to My Order, or, A Chaste Salute, vaudeville by Charles Edward Horn; libretto (Eng) by James R. Planché and W. H. Armstrong. First performance July 9, 1827, London, Vauxhall Gardens.

Pearl of Iran, The, romantic opera in one act by Granville Bantock; libretto (Eng) by the composer. Composed 1894.
SCORE: vs (Leipzig, 1894).

Pearl Tree, The, opera in two acts by Edgar Leslie Bainton; libretto (Eng) by Robert Trevelyan. First performance May 20, 1944, Sydney, Australia, Conservatorium of Music Opera School; conducted by the composer.

The tale comes from a Hindu legend. The deity Krishna, a young boy at the time, displays his powers of magic by making a pearl from his mother, Yashoda, into a splendid tree. His love for Rahda, a village girl who had refused to give him a pearl, is rewarded at the end.

Major roles: Krishna (ten), Yashoda (alto), and Rahda (sop).

Peasant Boy, The, opera in three acts by Michael Kelly; libretto (Eng) by William Dimond. First performance 1811, London, Lyceum.
LIBRETTO: English (London: J. Barker, 1811; New York: The Longworths, 1811).

Peculiar Sam, or, The Underground Railroad, musical play; libretto (Eng) by Pauline Elizabeth Hopkins. First stage performance December 8, 1879, Boston, Young Men's Christian Union, with Sam Lucas (Sam).

The action centers on the slavery-to-freedom theme, with the slaves fleeing from their plantation and stopping along the way to Canada via the famed Underground Railroad. The leader is Peculiar Sam.

Among the famous songs that accompany the play are "Good Bye My Old Cabin Home," "Gospel Train," and "Home, Sweet Home."

TEXT AND MUSIC: ms libretto (Washington, D.C.: Library of Congress), various songs in nineteenth-century sheet music eds.; repr. ed. Eileen Southern, *NAMT*, vol. 9 (1994).

Pedrolino's Revenge, comic opera in one act by William Russo; libretto (Eng) by Jonathan Abarbanel. First performance September 11, 1974, New York, Commedia Company of Chicago, together with *Isabella's Fortune.**

The work, based on the commedia dell'arte, combines elements of jazz, rock, Italian madrigals, and musical comedy.

BIBLIOGRAPHY: Harold C. Schonberg, "Opera: Updating Commedia dell'Arte," *NYT* (Sept. 13, 1974), C, 31 [on premiere].

Peeping Tom of Coventry, comic opera in two acts by Samuel Arnold; libretto (Eng) by John O'Keeffe. First performance September 6, 1784, London, Little Theatre in the Haymarket. First U.S. performance February 18, 1793, Charleston, South Carolina, Charleston Theatre.

The story involves Lady Godiva, who is talked about but not seen, and the Mayor of Coventry, who makes advances to the title character's wife.

SCORE: vs (London: Harrison & Co., 1784).

LIBRETTO: English (London: Harrison, [1784]; New York: Addison B. Price, 1813); repr. of 1784 version in Rubsamen/*BO*, vol. 23, *Irish Ballad Operas and Burlesques*, II (1974).

Peleus and Thetis, masque in one act by William Boyce; libretto (Eng) by George Granville, after his *Poems* (1712). Performed by 1740, London.

The setting is the Caucasus Mountains, the site of Prometheus' imprisonment. Since he is known for his wisdom, Peleus comes to him for advice about a problem; Peleus, a mortal, is in love with Thetis, a nymph, a love that is not allowed. The problem is worsened by the fact that Jupiter is also interested in Thetis. Prometheus then tells Jupiter to let the lovers alone, for he knows that they are destined to be the parents of Achilles.

DISCOGRAPHY: P. Holman, Opera Restor'd, Hyperion Records 66935 (1997, 1 CD).

Peleus and Thetis, masque by William Hayes; libretto (Eng) by Granville, after his *Poems* (1712). Composed ca. 1749.

Major roles: Peleus (ten), Thetis (sop), Prometheus (bass), and Jupiter (alto).

BIBLIOGRAPHY: Simon Heighes, *The Lives and Works of William and Philip Hayes* (New York: Garland, 1995), 232–36.

Penelope, ballad opera in three acts; libretto (Eng) by Thomas Cooke and John Mottley. First performance May 8, 1728, London, Little Theatre in the Haymarket, with Mrs. Clarke (Penelope).

In this updating of the classical story, Penelope is the owner of the Royal Oak Ale-House in London. She is constantly being annoyed by suitors, including a tailor and butcher, since her soldier husband, Ulysses, has been away for twenty years because of the Marlborough Wars.

For a detailed description, see Fiske/*ETM*, 106–7.

LIBRETTO: English, with airs (London: Tho. Green et al., 1728); repr. ed. Rubsamen/*BO*, vol. 7, *Classical Subjects I: Satire and Burlesque* (1974).

Penitentes, The, opera in three acts by Thomas Pasatieri; libretto (Eng) by Anne Howard Bailey. First performance August 3, 1974, Aspen, Colorado, Wheeler Opera House, with David Britton (Felipe) and Wayne Turnage (John).

The Penitentes are a group of religious Mexican Indians in the Southwest, whose rituals include a reenactment of Christ's crucifixion on Easter Sunday. They are joined by a bored trio of Americans, the governor, Elena, his mistress, and John, Elena's former lover. Elena attempts to seduce Felipe, who has been chosen to represent Christ; seeking to redeem his self-worth, John takes Felipe's place, and the shamed Felipe hangs himself.
BIBLIOGRAPHY: Peter G. Davis, review, *NYT* (Aug. 5, 1974), 32 [on premiere].

Penny for a Song, comic opera in two acts by Richard Rodney Bennett; libretto (Eng) by Colin Graham, after the play by John Whiting. First performance October 31, 1967, London, Sadler's Wells, with John Fryatt (Sir Timothy Bellboys), Eric Shilling (Lamprett Bellboys), Joan Davies (Hester Bellboys), Margaret Neville (Dorcas Bellboys), Alan Charles (Edward Sterne), and Emile Belcourt (Hallam Matthews); conducted by Bryan Balkwill; produced by Colin Graham.

The opera is set in 1804, at Sir Timothy Bellboys's house in Dorset. Everyone is expecting an invasion by the French, led by Napoleon. Sir Timothy's plan is to pretend to be Napoleon and, if the French troops come to his house, tell them, in French, that they have lost the battle and are to return home. The invasion never takes place, although a few false alarms occur. A subplot is the romance of Dorcas Bellboys, Sir Timothy's daughter, and Edward Sterne, a hardened soldier.

Major roles: Sir Timothy Bellboys (ten); Dorcas Bellboys (sop); Lamprett Bellboys, his brother (bar); Hester Bellboys, his wife (mezzo); Hallam Matthews, a gentleman of leisure (ten); and Edward Sterne, a soldier (bar).
SCORE: fs ([London]: Universal Edition, [1967]).
BIBLIOGRAPHY: Peter Heyworth, "A Shiny 'Penny for a Song,'" *NYT* (Nov. 19, 1967), II, 38 [on premiere].

Pepito's Golden Flower, children's opera in one act by Mary Elizabeth Caldwell; orchestrated by Lauris Jones. First performance March 13, 1955, Pasadena, Civic Auditorium; conducted by Jones.

The story, set in 1812 at the Mission Santa Ynez, concerns Pepito, a young Mexican boy who rings the bells of the church. He is devastated when an earthquake destroys the bells and becomes mischievous, but all is put right when the new bells arrive.
BIBLIOGRAPHY: Juliette Laine, review, *ON* XIX (Apr. 18, 1955), 32 [on premiere].

Perfect Fool, The, opera in one act by Gustav Holst; libretto (Eng) by the composer. First performance May 14, 1923, London, Covent Garden, with Robert Parker (the Wizard), Edna Thornton (the Mother), Maggie Teyte (the Princess), Walter Hyde (the Troubadour), and Frederick Collier (the Traveller); conducted by Eugene Goossens. First U.S. performance March 20, 1962, Wichita, Kansas. Revived Winter 1972, Detroit, Ford Auditorium, Overture to Opera Company; conducted by Pierre Hetu.

The story has the Troubadour courting the Princess, in competition with the Traveller. She finally gives her hand to the Perfect Fool, who does not care in the least for her.

Roles: the Troubadour (ten), the Princess (sop), the Mother (alto), the Wizard (bar), the Traveller (bass), and the Perfect Fool (speaking part).

The Fool, who does not sing and says only one word, "No," during the entire opera, sleeps through most of the action, during which he wins the hand of a Princess and defeats the Wizard. He is aided by his mother, who lifts the love potion from the Wizard.

The opera makes fun of the traditional operatic conventions of Wagner and Verdi in particular, via the Wotan-like Traveller and the Troubadour, the latter singing a parody of the drinking song in *La Traviata*.
SCORE: vs (London: Novello, 1923).
BIBLIOGRAPHY: Jay Carr, "Detroit," *ON* XXXVI (Apr. 8, 1972), 31 [on U.S. revival]; "E. E.," "Opera in London. 'The Perfect Fool' at Covent Garden," *MT* LXIV (June 1, 1923), 423 [on premiere].

Perfect Lives (Private Parts), opera in seven episodes for television by Robert Ashley; libretto (Eng) by the composer. First performance (excerpts) December 26, 1978, New York, New York Dance Theatre Workshop; 1980 (complete), New York, the Kitchen. First British performance 1984, England.

The entertainers Raoul de Noget and Buddy, his friend, come to perform at The Perfect Lives Lounge in a small Midwestern town. They meet Isolde, nearing thirty and not yet married, and "D," her football-playing younger brother. "D" makes plans with his friend Ed, who is in love and planning to elope with Gwyn, to open the safe at the bank, along with Dwayne, another friend. Isolde creates a diversion, and the robbers make off with the money; Ed and the unsuspecting Gwyn, "D," and Dwayne end up somewhere in Indiana. Meanwhile, Eleanor, a teller at the bank, falls in love with Buddy. Back in town Isolde is left alone to ponder her future.

The work is scored for three solo voices and solo piano, all synchronized with prerecorded orchestral "beds."
LIBRETTO: English (New York: Archer Fields; San Francisco: Burning Books, 1991).
DISCOGRAPHY: R. Ashley, "Blue" Gene Tyranny (kbd), J. Kroesen and D. Van Tieghem (chorus, perc), Shorr (electronics), Lovely Music 2-LMC-413/4947 (tape); 3-LCD 49173 (CD).
VIDEO: "B." G. Tyranny, R. Ashley, J. Kroesen, D. Van Tieghem; dir. J. Sanborn, prod. C. Schoolman, P. Gordon, Lovely Music (1983, New York).

Pericles, grand opera by Alan Hovhaness; libretto (Eng) by the composer, after the play by Shakespeare (1609). Composed 1975. First performance (excerpts, concert) 1979, Shippensburg, Pennsylvania.

Perpetual, opera in one act by Ernest Kanitz; libretto (Eng) by Ellen Terry. First performance April 26, 1961, Los Angeles.

The setting is an antique mechanical music wagon that has three marionettes, in the eighteenth century. Three marionettes sing, spin, and stop, aligning themselves differently each time. During the first stop Colombina and Arlecchino wind up facing each other and sing a love duet; at the next turn, Colombina and Scaramuccio are opposite each other and sing a duet, while Arlecchino is jealous. The third time, they all face forward and complain since they are now alone.

Roles: Colombina (lyr sop), Arlecchino (lyr ten), and Scaramuccio (bass-bar).
SCORES: vs ([n.p., 1960]; LCCN: 84-70834); rev. vs (Bryn Mawr, Pa.: T. Presser Co., 1971).

Persephone, children's opera in three acts by Hugo Cole; libretto (Eng) by the composer. First performance July 14, 1955, London, Wimbledon High School.

Persian Hunters, The, or, The Rose of Gurgistan, seriocomic opera in three acts by Charles Edward Horn and George Perry (overture); libretto (Eng) by Thomas Noble. First performance August 13, 1817, London, Lyceum Theatre.
LIBRETTO: English (London: Sherwood, Neely, and Jones, 1817).

Peruvian, The. See **The Fair Peruvian.**

Pesceballo, Il, pastiche in one act by Francis James Child; libretto (Eng) translated from the Italian of Child and G. Sedgwick by James Russell Lowell. First performance (private) May 1862, Cambridge, Massachusetts; first performance (public) May 10, 1864, Boston, Chickering Hall.

The "plot" revolves around a hungry student from Harvard who has enough money in his pocket to buy only half a portion of food. The title song, "The Lay of the One Fishball," was still popular in the first decade of the twentieth century, when it was reproduced in *Heart Songs* (Boston: Chappell, 1909) and later publications.

The musical numbers include adaptations of arias from Rossini's *Il barbiere di Siviglia* and *La Cenerentola*, Donizetti's *Lucrezia Borgia*, *La Favorita*, and *Lucia di Lammermoor*, Mozart's *Die Zauberflöte* and *Don Giovanni*, and Bellini's *Norma*. The recitatives, by John Knowles Paine, are lost.

Interest in the work was revived when a reprint of the libretto appeared in 1899.
SCORE: ms short score (Harvard, Houghton Library, *45M-581F).
TEXT AND MUSIC: libretto, an annotated ed. owned by Charles E. Norton, with the composer listed as "Maestro Rossibelli-Donimozarti" (Cambridge, Mass.: Riverside Press, 1862); repr. ed. Dale Cockrell, *NAMT*, vol. 8 (1994).

Peter Grimes, opera in three acts by Benjamin Britten; libretto (Eng) by Montagu Slater, after the poem *The Borough* by George Crabbe (1810). First performance June 7, 1945, London, Sadler's Wells, with Joan Cross (Ellen), Edith Coates (Auntie), Peter Pears (Peter Grimes), Roderick Jones (Balstrode), Edmund Donlevy (Ned Keene), and Owen Brannigan (Swallow); conducted by Reginald Goodall; produced by Eric Crozier. First U.S. performance August 6, 1948, Tanglewood, Massachusetts, with Florence Manning (Ellen), Ellen Carleen (Auntie), William Horne (Peter), Robert Grey (Ned), Leonard Treash (Swallow), and James Pease (Balstrode); conducted by Leonard Bernstein; directed by Crozier and Frederic Cohen.

The setting is the Borough, a fishing village on the east coast of England, about 1830. The prologue is through composed and laced with dissonance. The coroner Swallow is holding an inquest at the Moot Hall of the Borough into the death of the reclusive Peter Grimes's apprentice at sea. Even though Grimes is acquitted, suspicions remain, and he is warned not to take on another boy. Only Ellen Orford, the widowed schoolmistress, is supportive of him, and the prologue concludes with their duet.

An atmospheric orchestral interlude connects the prologue to the first act (such interludes are used to connect the two scenes of each of the three acts). The "dawn" music heralds the beginning of a new day in the Borough and accompanies the choral singing, with the scene unfolding in five sections. In the first, the other fishermen reluctantly help Grimes pull his boat onto land; in the second, Hobson vociferously declines Ned Keene's request to find another apprentice; and the third, which interrupts Hobson's protestations, is Ellen's lyrical and extended arioso "Let Her among You without Fault Cast the First Stone," in which she defends Grimes. The fourth section is a massive fugal ensemble and chorus commenting on the oncoming storm, the music of which dominates the rest of the scene. In the last, Grimes and Balstrode undertake an extended dialogue that reveals Grimes's emotional conflicts, when he narrates the terrible events at sea, in "Picture What That Day Was Like" and his plan to find favor in the Borough by being successful: "They Listen to Money." He concludes, after Balstrode's departure, with the plaintive "What Harbour Shelters Peace?," in which he envisions a life with Ellen.

Another orchestral interlude, the "Storm," leads into the second scene, set at the Boar's Inn, run by Auntie, assisted by her "Nieces." The music includes strophic songs by Auntie and Balstrode, whose refrain includes the telling "We live and let live, and look, we keep our hands to ourselves." The good mood of the inn's inhabitants is ended by the appearance of Grimes, who sings his aria "Now the Great Bear and Pleiades." Auntie attempts to defuse the rising anger of the crowd, and, similarly, Ned Keene offers the round "Old Joe Has Gone Fishing." With the appearance of Hobson, Ellen, and the new apprentice, Grimes rushes off with the boy into the storm, after Ellen tells the lad that "Peter will take you home," which is taken up mockingly by the chorus.

Act 2 opens with a gentle orchestral interlude that includes a sparkling toccata. It is a bright Sunday morning, and everything seems in order. Ellen is with the new apprentice and is knitting him a garment. She becomes distraught when she notices that his coat is torn and that he has bruises and sadly tells the boy, "After the storm will come a sleep, like oceans deep," which parallels the Gloria being sung by the congregants of the nearby church. When Grimes enters, Ellen confronts him with his brutality, whereupon he strikes her and, as the church service ends, sings, "So be it—and God have mercy upon me." He leaves with the boy in tow, and the arriving villagers sense that "Grimes is at his exercise." Boles stirs up the crowd, who determine to punish Grimes, and Ellen's efforts to defend him are derided. A group, led by the Rector and Swallow, head off to Grimes's hut. The scene ends with the "trio" of the two Nieces, Auntie, and Ellen (the Nieces singing mostly in unison).

An orchestral passacaglia, the fourth interlude, leads into scene 2, which opens in Grimes's hut. He sings an extended monologue (built on the two-note motif of the foghorn), which ends with "in harbour still and deep." Hearing the approaching crowd, Grimes pushes the apprentice out the door, the lad falling to his death on the treacherous cliffs; Peter flees. The "rescue" party finds nothing in the hut and leaves.

Act 3, introduced by a moonlight-drenched interlude, is set again in the Borough street and beach, like the first scene of act 1. The inhabitants are enjoying themselves, both at the Moot Hall and at the Boar. Mrs. Sedley enters and tries to get Keene to help her prove that Peter Grimes is a killer; this section is accompanied by a Ländler played by an offstage orchestra. Sedley is left alone and, unseen by the arriving Ellen and Balstrode, hears the former sea captain declare that Grimes's boat is in dock but its owner is absent. Ellen admits that she has found the jersey she had knit for the young apprentice washed up on the beach, in her aria "Embroidery in Childhood Was a Luxury of Idleness." Balstrode tries to comfort her by suggesting that the two can still help Grimes. Mrs. Sedley conveys what she has heard to the crowd, who vociferously declare that "him who despises us we'll destroy" and end the scene with the fortissimo words describing the object of their wrath, "Peter Grimes!"

The sixth interlude, built on a dominant seventh chord, leads into the last scene. In a mad scene, a raving Grimes, accompanied by an offstage chorus and foghorn, rambles on about his life and the tragedies that have befallen him. When Ellen and Balstrode arrive, he fails to recognize Ellen when she tries to take him home. Balstrode, speaking his words, intervenes and tells Grimes to sail his boat out to sea and scuttle it; Peter agrees, and the three depart. The orchestra recapitulates the "dawn music" of the first act. The villagers, unsuccessful in their search for Grimes, have returned. Morning has come, and the chorus sings the music of the first act. Swallow peers out to sea and sees the sinking boat as reported by the coast guard, which arouses nobody's interest. Life in the Borough returns to normal, at least on the surface.

For musical analyses and plot descriptions, see *COH*, ed. Philip Brett (1983), *ENOG* 24 (1983); K/*KOB*, 1160–69; K/*NKOB*, 100–4.

Major roles: Peter Grimes (ten); Ellen Orford (sop); Captain Balstrode (bar); Auntie, landlady of "the Boar" (alto); Swallow, a lawyer (bass); Rev. Horace Adams, the rector (ten); and Hobson, the carrier (bass).

SCORE: fs ms (LC); vs (London and New York: Boosey & Hawkes, 1945); Paul Banks, ed., *The Making of* Peter Grimes, vol. 1, *The Facsimile of Britten's Composition Draft*, vol. 2, *Notes and Commentaries* (Aldeburgh: Boydell Press, 1996).

LIBRETTO: English (London, New York: Boosey & Hawkes, [1945]).

BIBLIOGRAPHY: Philip Brett, "Britten and Grimes," *MT* CXVIII (1977): 995–1000; Olin Downes, "Britten's 'Grimes' Unveiled at Lenox," *NYT* (Aug. 7, 1946), 18 [on U.S. premiere]; Gary Schmidgall, "Out of the Borough," *ON* XLII (Dec. 10, 1977), 11–15; Christopher Wintle, "The Living Conflict," *TLS* (Apr. 26, 1991), 15.

DISCOGRAPHY: Harper, Vickers, Summers, Royal Opera; cond. Davis, Philips 420975-1 PH3 (3 LPs), 420975–4 PH3 (3 CDs); Watson, Pears, Evans, Royal Opera; cond. Britten, London 414577–2 LH3 (3 CDs).

VIDEO: Vickers, Harper, Bailey, Royal Opera; cond. Davies, dir. J. Vernon, Castle VHS CVI 2015; Cairns, Langridge, Opie, ENO; cond. Atherton, dir. Gavin, Decca VHS 071 428–3.

Peter Homan's Dream, folk opera in two acts by Herbert Owen Reed; libretto (Eng) by John Jennings. First performance May 13, 1955, East Lansing, Michigan, Michigan State University.

The setting is Michigan in 1870. The work was originally called *Michigan's Dream* and was written for the centennial of Michigan State University in 1955.

SCORE: vs, holograph (New York: Mills Music, 1955).

Peter Ibbetson, opera in three acts by Deems Taylor; libretto (Eng) by the composer and Constance Collier, after Collier's play, itself founded on George du Maurier's novel (1892). First performance February 7, 1931, New York, Metropolitan Opera, with Lucrezia Bori (Duchess of Towers), Edward Johnson (Peter Ibbetson), and Lawrence Tibbett (Colonel Ibbetson); conducted by Tulio Serafin.

Peter Ibbetson draws a life sentence in Newgate Prison after killing his evil uncle, Colonel Ibbetson. He starts to lose his sense of reality while imprisoned and dreams of his past life, especially his childhood sweetheart, Mary. After forty years of incarceration, he is told that his beloved Mary has died. He too succumbs, whereupon the walls of the prison disappear, and Peter, young again, is reunited with her.

Major roles: Peter Ibbetson (ten); Colonel Ibbetson, his uncle (bar); and Mary, Duchess of Towers (sop).

SCORE: vs (New York: J. Fischer & Bro., 1930).

BIBLIOGRAPHY: E. Eulass, "American Opera at the Metropolitan," *ON* V (Feb. 3, 1941), 28.

Petrified Princess, The, puppet opera in one act by Richard Arnell; libretto (Eng) by Bryan Guiness. First performance May 5, 1959, London, BBC.

Petrov, light opera in two acts by Michael Easton; libretto (Eng) by the composer and Alan Hopgood, with additional lyrics by Michael Atkinson. First performance January 1992, Melbourne, Victorian Arts Centre.

The story concerns the scandal in Australia during the 1950s that was caused by the defection of Petrov.

Petruccio, opera in one act by Alick Maclean; libretto (Eng), after Shakespeare's *The Taming of the Shrew* (1594). First performance June 29, 1895, London, Covent Garden.

In the verismo style, it was first performed on a double bill with *Cavalleria rusticana*. See *The Taming of the Shrew* for other settings of the Shakespeare play.

Pet Shop, The, opera in one act by Vittorio Rieti; libretto (Eng) by Claire Nicolas, after a story by the composer. First performance April 14, 1958, New York, Mannes College, with Joan Wall, Sheila Bredach, and Edward Eriksen; conducted by Carl Bamberger; produced by Ralph Herbert.

Mrs. Camouflage has come to the pet shop to replace her departed dog, Mimi. The new pet must match her costume that she is to wear to the Dog and Dowager Parade. She is accompanied on her search by her daughter Trixie, who proceeds to fall in love with the handsome Mr. Canicular, owner of the shop, while the mother takes several dogs out for test walks. Mrs. Camouflage approves of the match between her daughter and Mr. Canicular when he turns out to be a judge at the style show.

For a detailed description, see Eaton/*OP* I, 209.

Roles: Mrs. Camouflage (alto), Trixie (sop), Mr. Canicular (ten), and dogs (three mimes).

Peveril of the Peak, musical drama in one act by Charles Edward Horn; libretto by Isaac Pocock, after Sir Walter Scott (1822). First performance October 21, 1826, London, Covent Garden.

Set during the period of the Popish Plot in England (1678), which cast suspicions on English Catholics, the story involves Julian Peveril, a Cavalier, who is in love with Alice, daughter of Bridgenorth, a Roundhead. Accused of treason, Julian and his father are absolved in the end, saved by the half-Moorish Fenella, who has fallen in love with Julian. SCORE: vs, chorus "Home, Home"; glee and chorus "Look Out, Look Out" (London: Welsh & Hawes, [1826?]).

Phaeton, radio opera by Alan Ridout; libretto (Eng) by Patric Dickinson. First performance 1974, BBC.

Phantom of the Opera, The, all-sung musical in a prologue and two acts by Andrew Lloyd Webber; book (Eng) by Richard Stilgoe and the composer, after the novel by Gaston Leroux (1911); lyrics by Charles Hart. First performance October 9, 1986, London, Her Majesty's Theatre, with Sarah Brightman (Christine), Steve Barton (Raoul), Michael Crawford (the Phantom), and Judy Kaye (Carlotta). First U.S. performance January 26, 1988, New York, Majestic Theatre, with the same leads; directed by Harold Prince; designed by Maria Björnson.

The setting is the Paris Opéra, 1881. A disfigured musician, who has become insane, wants a promising young singer to be given a starring role at the Opéra and kills all who stand in her way, including Carlotta, the reigning prima donna. Becoming desperate, the Phantom kidnaps his would-be protégée and takes her to the Labyrinth, his underground hideout. She is rescued by her beloved, Raoul, and the Phantom dies.

The derivative score skillfully combines elements of nineteenth-century opera with techniques and melodic devices of Broadway musicals. Among the highlights are the Phantom's "The Music of the Night" (act 1, scene 5); "All I Ask of You" (act 1, scene 10), sung by Raoul and Christine; and "The Point of No Return" (act 2, scene 7), with the Phantom and Christine. It includes spectacular stage effects, such as a giant chandelier crashing to the floor of the Opéra and killing Carlotta.

Also musical play, with music by Offenbach, arranged by Alastair MacNeill, text by Ken Hill (1994).

SCORE: vs, selections (Milwaukee, Wisc.: H. Leonard, 1987).

LIBRETTO: English, in George Perry, *The Complete Phantom of the Opera* (London: Pavilion, 1987).

BIBLIOGRAPHY: William A. Henry, review, *Time* CXXVIII (Oct. 27, 1986), 103 [on premiere]; Mimi Kramer, review, *NY* LXIV (Feb. 8, 1988), 97–98 [on U.S. premiere]; Barrymore Laurence Scherer, "In Review," *ON* LII (June 1988), 32 [on U.S. premiere].

DISCOGRAPHY: Crawford, Brightman; cond. M. Reed, 831-273-2 Polydor (1987, 2 CDs).

Pharnaces, grand opera in three acts by William Bates; libretto (Eng) by Thomas Hull, after Antonio Maria Lucchini's text for Porta's *Farnace* (1731, Bologna). First performance February 15, 1765, London, with Mr. Vernon (Pharnaces), Mrs. Vincent (Tamiris), Miss Rogers (Pharnaces's daughter), Mr. Giustinelli (Pompey), and Thomas Reinhold (Athridates).

The King of Sinope, Pharnaces, is out for revenge because he has been defeated by Pompey. Pharnaces, in turn, is the target of the Romans because they think he has seduced the daughter of the Roman general Athridates. They take Pharnaces's sister Selinda hostage, and Pompey falls in love with her. Athridates tries to kidnap Pharnaces's daughter, who is protected by Tamiris, her mother. When the child is discovered, Athridates's revenge turns to forgiveness when he realizes that Tamiris is, in fact, his long-lost daughter.

Pharnaces, "new English opera" by various composers; libretto (Eng) by Robert Houlton, after the text used for the 1765 *Pharnaces.** First performance May 8, 1783, London, Smock Alley, with Mr. Tenducci (Pharnaces), Miss Jameson (Aspasia), and Mr. Urbani (Pompey).

The work includes four arias by J. C. Bach: "Oh! Turn, Behold My Streaming Eyes" comes from *The Revenge of Athridates** (1766), and three new ones, all in act 1, are Pharnaces's "O Base Deceiver" in scene 4, Aspasia's "Forbear, My Sire, Thy Cruel Rage" in scene 7, and Pompey's "View Thy Danger" in scene 8.

Pharsalia, dramatic commentary in one act by Iain Hamilton; libretto (Eng) by the composer, after Lucan. First performance August 27, 1969, Edinburgh, Edinburgh Festival, Freemason's Hall.

The plotless work is set in Roman times and comments on the grief caused by civil war and the battle of Pharsalia, waged between Caesar and Pompey.

Roles: narrator (2 sop, alto, ten, bar, bass), Caesar (sung by the bar), and Pompey (sung by the ten).

Philander and Silvia, or, Love Crown'd at Last, pastoral opera by Benjamin Carr; libretto (Eng). First performance October 16, 1792, London, Sadler's Wells.

Philandering, or, The Rose Queen, comic opera in three acts by Charles Edward Horn and John Braham; libretto (Eng) by Samuel Beazley. First performance January 13, 1824, London, Drury Lane Theatre.

LIBRETTO: English (London: J. Miller, 1824).

Philip Marshall, opera in two acts by Seymour Barab; libretto (Eng) by the composer. First performance July 12, 1974, Chautauqua, New York, Chautauqua Opera Association, with Julia Lovett (Maritha), Theodor Uppman (Philip Marshall), David Griffith

(Jonathan), Suzanne Blum (Rosellen), and Ronald Holgate (Lucius); conducted by Wolfgang Schanzer; directed by Whitfield Lloyd-Schanzer.

The title character, a lieutenant in the Confederate army, returns home after he has recovered from his injuries to discover that despair and confusion abound. When he tries to help his loved ones, calamity is the result. He visits the Hannans, old family friends, and promises the mother that he will convince Jonathan, their pacifist son, to return home. Their daughter, Maritha, is in love with Philip but knows that he is bound to Rosellen, his fiancée. In his absence, however, Rosellen has become the mistress of Lucius, who runs a brothel. Jonathan, after an unsuccessful duel with Philip, kills himself. When Rosellen tries to return to Philip, Lucius kills her. In despair over what has happened, Philip leaves.

For a detailed description, see Eaton/*OP* II, 180–81.

Major roles: Maritha (sop); Philip (bar); Jonathan (ten); Mrs. Hannan (mezzo); Mr. Hannan (bass); Rosellen (sop); Lucius (bar); and Wellington, an old family servant (bass). BIBLIOGRAPHY: E. Thomas Glasgow, "Chautauqua," *ON* XXXIX (Oct. 1974), 50; Allen Hughes, "Premiere Held for Full-Length Barab Opera," *NYT* (July 17, 1974), 22.

Phillis at Court, comic opera in two acts by Tommaso Giordani; libretto (Eng) by R. Lloyd, after Charles Favart's text *Le caprice amoureux*, set by Duni et al. (1755, Paris). First performance February 25, 1767, Dublin.

The Capricious Lovers* (1764) and *Phoebe at Court** (1776) have the same story.

Phineas and the Nightingale, opera by Dai-Keong Lee; libretto (Eng) by Robert Healey, after P. T. Barnum's *Recollections*. Composed 1952.

Reworked as *Jenny Lind.**

Phoebe, pastoral in three acts by Maurice Greene; libretto (Eng) by John Hoadly. Composed 1747. First performance January 16, 1755, London, Mr. Ogle's Great Room, Dean St., Soho.

The work opens with two shepherds, Amyntas and Sylvio, discussing their amorous adventures. One of them, Sylvio, is really Phoebe, who has been spurned by her lover, Amyntas, and has come in disguise to be near him. The situation is complicated by the appearance of Celia, Amyntas's sister, who becomes interested in Sylvio. Celia, in turn, is pursued by the somewhat oafish peasant Linco. Celia, in despair at having been rejected by Sylvio, contemplates killing herself. When Amyntas discovers that his sister has a bracelet that he had given to Phoebe once upon a time, he becomes jealous after Celia reveals that Phoebe had given it to Sylvio. Amyntas challenges Sylvio to a duel, at which point Sylvio reverts to her identity as Phoebe.

For a detailed description, see Fiske/*ETM*, 200–3.

Phoebe at Court, opera by Thomas Arne; libretto (Eng) by the composer, after Charles Favart's *Ninette à la court*. First performance 1776, London, Little Theatre.

See *The Capricious Lovers* (1764) and *Phillis at Court* (1767) for other settings.

Phoenix Too Frequent, A, opera in one act by Stephen Oliver; libretto (Eng) by C. Fry. First performance June 1970, Oxford, Holywell Music Rooms.

Photographer, The, music-theater work in three acts by Philip Glass; libretto (Eng) by the composer and Rob Malasch. First performance May 30, 1982, Amsterdam, Netherlands Opera.

The work is based on the life of the renowned photographer Eadweard Muybridge, who was accused, tried, and acquitted of the murder of his wife's lover.
DISCOGRAPHY: excerpts, Zukofsky, violin; cond. Riesman, CBS FM 37849 (1983, 1 LP).

Photograph—1920, comedy in five acts by Martin Kalmanoff; libretto (Eng) by the composer, after Gertrude Stein. First performance July 27, 1971, Lake Placid, New York.
  The plotless work portrays the inner and outside personality of a character.
  Roles: Twin I (sop/mezzo) and Twin II (sop/mezzo).

Photograph, 1920, opera in five acts by Thomas Oboe Lee; libretto (Eng), after Stein. Composed 1978. Revised 1982.
SCORE; ms, holograph (1978, 1982, Brookline, Somerville, Mass., photocopy, NYPL).

Photo of the Colonel, The, opera in two acts by Humphrey Searle; libretto (Eng) by the composer, after Ionesco's play *Tueur sans gages* (1958). First performance (radio, in English) March 1964, London, BBC. First performance (stage, in German), as *Das Photo des Colonel*, June 3, 1964, Frankfurt, Opera House; directed by Hans Neugebauer.
  The work features the familiar Ionesco character of Bérenger, who comes to a "city of lights" that is a paradise except for one thing; there is a homicidal maniac on the loose. His victims include Dany, Bérenger's girlfriend. Since the police are so busy with traffic problems and other "important" duties, Bérenger is left to catch the killer himself. He is aided by his friend Edouard, who has a list of the killer's future victims. Bérenger eventually comes face-to-face with his prey, an unremarkable, slight person, who, nevertheless, defeats him.
  Major roles: Bérenger (ten), architect (bar), Dany (sop), the murderer (silent), and Edouard (high bar).
SCORE: vs, English, French, German (London: Schott, [1968]).
BIBLIOGRAPHY: N. Godwin, "The Photo of the Colonel," *Opera* XV (May 1964), 358–59 [on premiere]; Jean-Pierre Lenoir, review, *NYT* (June 4, 1964), 28 [on stage premiere]; R. Steyer, "Frankfurt," *Opera* XV (Aug. 1964), 550 [on stage premiere].

Photo-Op: Life in the Political Fast Lane, "opera on contemporary political 'discourse'" by Conrad Cummings; libretto (Eng) by James Siena. First performance May 21, 1990, New York, LaMama, with Margaret Bishop and Larry Adams (the candidates); produced by Bob McGrath.
  The work, inspired by the 1988 Presidential campaign, consists of two candidates reading their speeches over and over again; instrumental interludes separate the readings.
BIBLIOGRAPHY: Andrew Porter, review, *NY* LXVI (June 1990), 107 [on premiere]; John Rockwell, review, *NYT* (May 27, 1990), I, 58 [on premiere].
DISCOGRAPHY: Cummings Ensemble, CRI 627 (1990, 1 CD).

Phrases from Orpheus, multimedia opera by Charles Wilson; libretto (Eng), after poems by Douglas G. Jones (1967). First performance May 10, 1971, Guelph, Canada, Spring Festival.

Phyllis, "romantic opera" in two acts by Richard Henry Warren; libretto (Eng). First performance May 7, 1900, New York, Waldorf Astoria.
SCORE: vs ([n.p.], 1898; LCCN: 84-84548).

Pickwick, opera in three acts by Albert Coates; libretto (Eng) by the composer, after Charles Dickens's *Pickwick Papers*. First performance November 20, 1936, London, Covent Garden.

Also set by C. Wood, as *A Scene from Pickwick** (1922); E. Solomon (1889); and N. S. Burnand (1956, Eureka Springs, Ark.).

Picnic, The, opera in two acts by Richard Cumming; libretto (Eng) by Henry Butler. First performance (one scene) July 29, 1979, Central City, Colorado, Central City Opera.

The story takes place in Virginia in the past. A picnic is attended by a varied bunch, the beautiful Rebecca, who has been blinded in an accident, and Shaun, her husband; Anna, a young cousin and Shaun's ward; Inah Ames, mother of Rebecca; Dr. Martin, a family friend; and Carl and Mylo, two young, mischievous brothers. The apparent calm of the affair is disturbed when the brothers flirt with Rebecca but harass Anna. In the end the true story emerges about Rebecca's blindness: instead of being thrown from a horse that Shaun had struck, Rebecca fell down the stairs after she hit Shaun during a fight. Shaun and Anna, who are attracted to each other, realize that Rebecca will never let him go.

Major roles: Anna Ferris (sop), Rebecca Ferris (mezzo), Shaun Ferris (bar), Inah Ames (alto), Dr. Andrew Martin (bass), Mylo (ten), and Carl (ten).

For a detailed description, see Eaton/*OP* II, 181.

Picture, The, or, The Cuckold in Conceit, ballad opera by Thomas Augustine Arne; libretto by Rev. James Miller, after Molière's *Sganarelle, ou, Le cocu imaginaire*. First performance February 11, 1745, London, Drury Lane Theatre.

See *Sganarelle* and *Signor Deluso* for other settings.

LIBRETTO: English (London: J. Watts, 1745).

Picture of Dorian Gray, The, opera in two acts by Lowell Liebermann; libretto (Eng) by the composer, after Oscar Wilde's story. First performance May 8, 1996, Monte Carlo, L'Opéra de Monte Carlo, Salle Garnier, with Jeffrey Lentz (Dorian Gray), John Hancock (Lord Henry Wotten), Gregory Reinhart (Basil Hallward), and Korliss Uecker (Sibyl Vane); conducted by Steuart Bedford; directed by John Cox.

The plot begins with Basil Hallward's completing the portrait of Dorian Gray. It continues with Dorian's obsession with Lord Henry Wotten, his unhappy affair with Sibyl Vane, an actress, and his disintegration, highlighted by his murder of the artist and stabbing of the portrait.

The work, composed in a neoclassical style, contains no recitative. It is based on a twelve-note row employed tonally rather than serially, and it consists of twelve consecutive scenes in the keys of the row's consecutive pitches.

Other settings include F. Mannino's *Il ritratto di Dorian Gray* (1982, Catania, Italy) and H. Deutsch's *Dorian** (1995).

BIBLIOGRAPHY: Joel Kasow, "Monaco," *ON* LXI (Nov. 1996), 52–53 [on premiere]; Alan Riding, "Making New Opera Unstylishly Melodic," *NYT* (May 22, 1996), C, 13, 23.

Piece of String, A, opera in three acts by Seymour Barab; libretto (Eng) by the composer, after Guy de Maupassant's tale. First performance May 23, 1985, Greeley, Colorado, University of North Colorado Opera Theater.

When the leading citizen of a town in France loses his wallet, a peasant is accused of having found the money and kept it for himself, despite his claims of innocence. He disintegrates because his claims of doing no wrong are never accepted.

Pied Piper, The, opera for children in two acts by Elizabeth Swados; libretto (Eng), after Browning. First performance January 1989, Orlando, Florida, Orlando Opera.

Pied Piper of Hamelin, The, opera in three acts by Joseph W. Clokey; libretto (Eng) by Anna J. Beiswenger, after Robert Browning's poem (1842). First performance May 14, 1920, Miami, University of Miami, Music Department; conducted by the composer.

In the familiar tale, the Pied Piper, after ridding the town of Hamelin of its rats, lures the children of the town to follow him after the townspeople refuse to pay him. The only child left is a little lame boy.

After several months the Pied Piper returns and chides the people for their greed and stupidity. He rejects their offer of riches until the little lame boy moves him with his tales of loneliness and pleas for the safe return of the children.

SCORE: vs (Boston: C. C. Birchard & Co., 1923).

LIBRETTO: English, the same.

Pied Piper of Hamelin, The, masque in one act by James Wilson; libretto (Eng), after Browning. First performance October 25, 1969, Wexford, White's Hotel.

Pied Piper of Hamelin, The, opera in one act by Nicolas Flagello; libretto (Eng) by the composer, after Browning. First performance, as *The Piper of Hamelin*, April 18, 1970, New York, Manhattan School of Music.

Pierrette, comic opera in one act by Fritz Hart; libretto (Eng) by the composer. First performance August 3, 1914, Sydney, Repertory Theatre.

Pierrot and Pierrette, "lyrical music drama" in two scenes by Joseph Holbrooke; libretto (Eng) by Walter E. Grogan. First performance November 11, 1909, London, His Majesty's. Revised as *The Stranger*, October 1924, Liverpool.

The Faustian story covers the strong love of Pierrot and Pierrette in the face of the temptation of worldly pleasures that the Stranger offers to Pierrot and the Stranger's attempt to seduce Pierrette, aided by the evil Nurse.

Roles: Pierrot (bar), the Stranger (ten), Pierrette (sop), and the Nurse (alto).

Pierrot of the Minute, opera in one act by Lehman Engel; libretto (Eng) by the composer, after Ernest Dowson. First performance April 3, 1929, Cincinnati, Cincinnati College of Music.

The pastoral work shows contemporary French musical influences.

Piers Plowman, opera-cantata in two acts by Gerard Schurmann; libretto (Eng) by the composer, after William Langland. First performance August 22, 1980, Gloucester, Gloucester Cathedral.

In this allegorical tale, Lady Meed complains about the troubles caused by love. She is ordered by the King to marry Conscience. Piers is a shepherd who shields his flock from the storm. The dreamer Will imagines that he challenges the Devil to a jousting contest.

Pietro's Petard, chamber opera in one act by Hall Overton; libretto (Eng) by Robert DeMaria. First performance June 1963, New York, After Dinner Opera Company.

Pilate, ballet-opera in one act by Alan Hovhaness; libretto (Eng) by the composer. First performance June 26, 1966, Los Angeles, Pepperdine College.

The work concerns Pilate, who washes his hands after his judgment of Christ. Pilate wants to kill himself on the summit of Mount Pilatus near Lucerne. As he comes to the mountain, Silent Wings dances. He hears the cries of the mob, which wants to "slay poverty and free the murderer," and decides to throw himself to his death on the rocks below.

For a detailed description, see Eaton/*OP* II, 314.

Roles: Pilate (bass); Silent Wings (alto); chorus (bass); Sacred Poverty (vision of a Saint, dancer); and murderer (vision of a murderer, dancer).

SCORE: miniature score (New York: C. F. Peters, 1964).

Pilgrim Fathers, The, opera-cantata in two acts by George F. Root; libretto (Eng) by Fanny J. Crosby. Composed ca. 1854.
SCORE: vs (Boston: Oliver Ditson Co., [1854]).
LIBRETTO: English (New York: Mason Brothers, 1854).

Pilgrim's Progress, The, "morality with music" in four acts by Ralph Vaughan Williams; libretto (Eng) by the composer, after the allegory of Paul Bunyan, part 1 (1674–1679) and part 2 (1684). First performance April 26, 1951, London, Covent Garden, with Arnold Matters (the Pilgrim), Inia Te Wiata (Paul Bunyan), and Norman Walker (the Evangelist); conducted by Leonard Hancock.

The work, introduced by John Bunyan, shows the travels of the Pilgrim toward the Heavenly City in a succession of scenes that depict his best-known encounters, for example his battle with Apollyon.

Included also is the *Shepherds of the Delectable Mountains*,* set originally by the composer as a one-act pastoral episode (1922); in the opera it comprises the second scene of act 4.

For detailed descriptions, see K/*KOB*, 1123–26; K/*NKOB*, 848–50.

Major roles: John Bunyan (bass-bar), the Pilgrim (bar), and Apollyon (bass).
BIBLIOGRAPHY: Stephen Williams, "New Opera on Bunyan," *NYT* (May 6, 1951), 7.
DISCOGRAPHY: D. Jones, E. Kendal, C. Groves, R. Leggate, BBC Northern Sym. Orch.; cond. V. Handley, IMP 5691662 ("BBC" Radio Classics series).

Pillow-Song, The, opera in one act by Paul Barker; libretto (Eng) by the composer. First performance June 1, 1988, London, Modern Music Theatre Troupe, with Christine Barker.

A Japanese woman living 1,000 years ago recounts her experiences as one of the emperor's concubines.
BIBLIOGRAPHY: Arthur Jacobs, review, *Opera* XXXIX (Aug. 1988), 1008–9 [on premiere].

Pincushion, The, farce by Thomas Arne; libretto (Eng) by John Gay. First performance March 17, 1756, Dublin, Smock Alley Theatre.

Pink Lady, The, operetta by Ivan Caryll; libretto (Eng) by C. M. S. McLellan, after the French play *Le satyre* by Georges Berr and Marcel Guillemaud. First performance March 13, 1911, New York, New Amsterdam Theatre, with Hazel Dawn (Claudine, the Pink Lady). First British performance April 11, 1912, London, Globe Theatre.

An antiques dealer, Dondidier, is accused of being a satyr who embraces ladies in the Forest of Compiègne. His friend Lucien, who is to be wed, meets Claudine, an old flame.

The New York run of 316 performances far surpassed that of the London show.

Pipe of Desire, The, opera in one act by Frederick Converse; libretto (Eng) by George Edward Barton. First performance January 31, 1906, Boston, Jordan Hall, Opera School of the New England Conservatory of Music, with George Dean (Iolan), Bertha Cushing Child (Naoia), Stephen Townsend (Old One), Mabel Stanaway (Undine), and Ralph Osborne (gnome); conducted by Wallace Goodrich; March 18, 1910, New York, Metropolitan Opera, with Louise Homer (Naoia), Riccardo Martin (Iolan), Clarence Whitehill (Old One), Lenora Sparkes (Sylph), Lilla Snelling (Undine), Glenn Hall (Salamander), and Herbert Witherspoon (gnome); conducted by Alfred Hertz; directed by Kurt Stern.

Iolan employs the Elf King's pipe for his own needs, resulting in catastrophe for him and Naoia, his lover, and death for the King.

Major roles: Naoia (mezzo), Iolan (ten), Old One (bar), Sylph (sop), Undine (mezzo), Salamander (ten), and gnome (bass).

Pippa's Holiday, monologue in one scene by John Parsons Beach; libretto (Eng), after Robert Browning's *Pippa Passes* (1841). First performance 1915, Paris, Théâtre Réjane.

The protagonist is a poor girl who works in an Italian silk factory every day except for one, New Year's Day, her "holiday."

The piece is set for mezzo and orchestra.

Pirate, The, musical play by William Michael Rooke; libretto (Eng) by William Dimond, after Sir Walter Scott. First performance January 15, 1822, London, Drury Lane Theatre.

Pirate Moon, The, opera in one act by Gillian Whitehead; libretto (Eng) by Anna Maria dell'Oso. First performance August 1986, Auckland, New Zealand, University Music Theatre.

Pirates, The, opera in three acts, with music partially adapted by Stephen Storace; libretto (Eng) by James Cobb. First performance November 21, 1792, London, Little Theatre in the Haymarket, with Mr. Kelly (Don Altador), Mrs. Crouch (Donna Aurora), Mr. Bannister (Blazio), Miss Storace (Fabulina), and Mrs. Bland (Fidelia).

The setting of this rescue opera is in and around Naples. As the story opens, the Spanish Don Altador has had to leave his beloved, Donna Aurora, in the care of Don Gaspero, a pirate living near Naples, because of one of Altador's duels. Don Gaspero, meanwhile, wants Aurora to wed Guillermo, his nephew. Gaspero learns of the situation when he arrives in Naples from Fabulina, Aurora's faithful maid. Blazio, Altador's servant, then falls in love with Fabulina. When Gaspero finds Altador attempting to enter the house, he chases him away and leaves Sotillo, an old pirate, as a guard. Sotillo is lulled to sleep by Fabulina's singing.

The lovers plan their escape, but they are interrupted by Gaspero's early return. Gaspero pretends to let the lovers have their way, but he secretly plots to take Aurora and Fabulina away to his pirate hideout, after he cleverly gets Blazio to reveal his master's plans. Despite the efforts of Blazio and Altador, Gaspero's men manage to take Aurora away, leaving Fabulina behind. Aided by the disguised Fidelia, an old friend of Aurora, Altador and Blazio gain entrance to Gaspero's castle in the guise of a troupe of Savoyards, and during the entertainment they secretly admit a group of the king's soldiers. After a scuffle, the pirates and Gasparo are defeated, and the lovers are reunited.

For a detailed description, see Fiske/*ETM*, 514–19, 610.

Revised as *Isidore de Merida** (1827, London).

The work includes sections from Storace's *Gli equivoci* (1786, Vienna), a quintet from Guglielmi's *La bella pescatrice* (1789, Naples), and airs by Anfossi and Bianchi (the numbers from these three other composers are not in the printed score).

SCORE: vs (London: J. Dale, 1792?).

LIBRETTO: English (London: E. Cox, 1792).
BIBLIOGRAPHY: Jane Girdham, *English Opera in Late Eighteenth-Century London* (Oxford: Clarendon Press, 1997), 153–70.

Pirates of Penzance, The, or, The Slave of Duty, comic opera in two acts by Arthur S. Sullivan; libretto (Eng) by William S. Gilbert. First performance December 31, 1879, New York, Fifth Avenue Theatre, with Signor Brocolini (Samuel), Hugh Talbot (Frederic), J. H. Ryley (Major-General Stanley), Mr. F. Clifton (Edward), Blanche Roosevelt (Mabel), Miss R. Brandram (Kate), Jessie Bond (Edith), Miss Barlow (Isabel), and Alice Barnett (Ruth); produced by Richard D'Oyly Carte. First British performance April 3, 1880, London, Opéra Comique, with George Grossmith (Major-General Stanley), Richard Temple (Pirate King), G. Temple (Samuel), George Power (Frederic), Rutland Barrington (Sergeant of Police), Marion Hood (Mabel), Julia Gwynne (Edith), Lillian La Rue (Kate), Neva Bond (Isabel), and Emily Cross (Ruth). Among the many revivals is the highly successful one in summer 1980, New York, Delacorte Theatre, with Linda Ronstadt (Mabel), Kevin Kline (Pirate King), Rex Smith (Frederic), Patricia Routledge (Isabel), and George Rose (Major-General Stanley); directed by Wilford Leach; reorchestrated by William Elliott; the production was transferred to the Uris Theatre (Jan. 8, 1981), where it ran for 772 performances.

The setting is a rocky shore on the coast of Cornwall. Because of a mistake made at birth by his hard-of-hearing nurse, Ruth, Frederic has been apprenticed to a band of pirates, rather than the intended group, pilots, until he becomes twenty-one. To his horror Frederic discovers that he was born on February 29, in a leap year, which increases his terms of apprenticeship astronomically. The pirates surrender him, however, when their patriotism is appealed to, since they are in reality, as Ruth explains, "all noblemen who have gone wrong," and he weds the beautiful Mabel, ward of the pompous Major-General Stanley.

Major roles: Major-General Stanley (bar); the Pirate King (bar); Samuel, his lieutenant (bar); Frederic, the pirate apprentice (ten); Ruth, a pirate maid of all work (alto); and Mabel (sop), Edith (mezzo), Kate (mezzo), and Isabel (mezzo), General Stanley's wards.

For detailed discussions, see Stedman/*WGS*, 174–79; and Traubner/*O*, 160–63.

Among the musical highlights is Major-General Stanley's famous patter song, "I Am the Very Model of a Modern Major-General," Mabel's "Poor Wand'ring One," and the pirates' song "With Cat-Like Tread," which, given new lyrics, became well known as "Hail, Hail, the Gang's All Here." The work includes parodies of Gounod and Verdi.

It received its first performance in New York, with the London premiere coming three months later.
SCORE: vs (New York: G. Schirmer, [1940?]).
LIBRETTO: English (Philadelphia: J. M. Stoddart & Co., [1880]).
DISCOGRAPHY: V. Masterson, P. Potter, J. Reed, D'Oyly Carte, London PIR6OC (2 CDs).

Pit, The, dramatic scene by Elisabeth Lutyens; libretto (Eng) by William Robert Rodgers. First performance (concert) May 18, 1947, London, Wigmore Hall. First performance (stage) April 24, 1949, Palermo, Italy, Massimo Theater.

The work concerns the plight of miners who are trapped underground.

Pizza con funghi, La (Mushroom Pie), bel canto opera in one act by Seymour Barab; libretto (Eng) by the composer. First performance November 6, 1989, New York, After Dinner Opera.

In order to rid herself of her aging husband, Count Formaggio, and marry Scorpio, her lover, the young Voluptua tries to poison Formaggio. When Phobia, Voluptua's maid, attempts to warn the Count, unforeseen complications ensue.

Pizza del destino, La, opera buffa in one scene by Steve Cohen; libretto (Eng) by Joseph Renard. Composed 1979.
   The setting is Joe's Pizzeria at lunchtime.
   Roles: soprano, alto/tenor in drag, bass-baritone.
SCORE: ms vs (New York: American Music Center, 1979).

Pizzaro, pastiche by Michael Kelly; libretto (Eng) by Richard Sheridan, after Kotzebue's *Die Spanier in Peru.* First performance April 29, 1799, London, Drury Lane Theatre, with Mrs. Jordan (Cora), John and Charles Kemble, and Mrs. Siddons. First U.S. performance May 19, 1800, Philadelphia.
   The score includes a march by Gluck and choruses by A. Sacchini and L. Cherubini.
   Also incidental music settings by Rayner Taylor, as *Pizzaro* (1800, New York); James Hewitt, as *Pizzaro in Peru, or, The Death of Rolla* (1800, New York).
SCORE: vs (London, 1799); repr. ed. Stoddard Lincoln (New York: Da Capo Press, 1979).

Place to Call Home, A, opera by Edward Barnes; libretto (Eng). First performance March 2, 1992, Los Angeles, Los Angeles Opera's Resident Artists, various high schools (from March 2 to March 20).
   The work is concerned with the immigrant experience.
BIBLIOGRAPHY: Kikmi Lani Iwata, "Immigrant Theme in Opera for Teens," *Los Angeles Times* (Mar. 2, 1992), F, 10.

Plantation, The, grand opera in three acts by Harry Lawrence Freeman; libretto (Eng) by the composer. Composed 1914. First performance 1930, New York.

Playing Away, opera in two acts by Benedict Mason; libretto (Eng) by Howard Brenton. First performance May 19, 1994, Munich, Munich Biennale, Opera North.
   The setting is Munich, at the finals of the European soccer league. The central character of the opera is an English soccer star, Terry Bond, who made a Faustian agreement ten years ago in order for him to reach his current status. The upcoming game represents the pinnacle of his career, but he also has to make good on his devilish bargain.
BIBLIOGRAPHY: John Warnaby, review, *Tempo*, No. 190 (Sept. 1994), 31–32 [on premiere].

Play of Mother Courage, The, opera in two acts by John McCabe; libretto (Eng) by Monica Smith, after Grimmelshausen's play *Trutz Simplex* (1669). First performance October 3, 1974, Middlesbrough, England.
   The setting is Germany during the time of the Thirty Years War (1618–1648). Mother Courage, now old, recalls her younger years, during which she survived through prostitution and, looking for valuables after a bloody battle, met and combined forces with another woman, her "mother," who had been a nurse. Becoming well-to-do again through prostitution, she earned a degree of respectability, only to lose everything by attempting to marry.

Plot, The, ballad opera in one act; libretto (Eng) by John Kelly. First performance January 22, 1735, London, Drury Lane Theatre.
LIBRETTO: English (London, 1735); repr. ed. Rubsamen/*BO*, vol. 4, *The Medical and Legal Professions* (1974).

Plots!, or, The North Tower, melodramatic opera by Matthew King; libretto (Eng) by Samuel J. Arnold. First performance September 3, 1810, London, English Opera at the Lyceum.
LIBRETTO: English (London: Lowndes and Hobbs, [1810?]).

Plough and the Stars, The, opera in three acts by Elie Siegmeister; libretto (Eng) by Edward Mabley, after Sean O'Casey's play. First performed as *The Dublin Song*, May 15, 1963, St. Louis, Washington University. First performance as *The Plough and the Stars*, March 16, 1969, Louisiana State University; conducted by Peter Paul Fuchs. Revived October 19, 1979, New York, Symphony Space, with Elizabeth Kirkpatrick (Nora), Ronald Madden (John), Molly Stark (Mrs. Gogan), Barbara Nowicki (Mollser), Ryan Allen (Fluther Good), and Nadine Asher (Bessie Burgess); conducted by the composer.

The story concerns a cross-section of a slum tenement in Dublin during the 1916 Irish rebellion against the British. Nora, a resident of the slum, hides a letter with a commission for her husband John to join the Irish Citizens' Army, and when her uncle, Peter Flynn, tries to interfere, she burns the missive. A group of residents meet in the street, including Fluther, the carpenter, Peter and Mrs. Gogan, who have a sickly child, Mollser, and Bessie Burgess, the only Protestant in the neighborhood. The group moves to the pub, where John sings about "The Plough and the Stars," the flag that represents the Irish revolution. He joins the fighting after Captain Brennan finds out that his letter was destroyed.

During Easter Nora, who is pregnant, looks for John at the barricades; he eventually returns, together with Lieutenant James Langdon, who has been wounded, and Captain Brennan, who forces John back to the fighting. When the fighting increases, Nora goes into labor prematurely, and Mollser dies, as does Nora's baby, causing Nora to slip into madness; she is attended by Bessie. When Bessie tries to prevent Nora from going out into the street during the fighting, she is shot by Corporal Stoddard, who had thought Bessie was a sniper. James, still in his uniform, runs down the street and is also shot by Stoddard, who then joins Sergeant Tinley to drink the tea that Nora had set out.

For a detailed description, see Eaton/*OP* II, 184–85.

Major roles: Nora Clitheroe (sop), John Clitheroe (bar), Bessie Burgess (mezzo), Lieutenant James Langdon (ten), Mrs. Cogan (mezzo), Mollser (sop), Fluther Good (bass-bar), the covey (bass-bar), Peter Flynn (ten), Captain Brennan (bass), Corporal Stoddard (bar), and Sergeant Tinley (bar).

The neo-Romantic score contains a number of set pieces.
SCORE: vs ([n.p.], 1961–1963; LCCN: 66-43751).
BIBLIOGRAPHY: E. Siegmeister, "A Long, Long Road," *ON* XXXIV (Mar. 14, 1970), 27–29.

Plumber's Gift, The, opera in two acts by David Blake; libretto (Eng) by John Birtwhistle. First performance May 25, 1989, London, Coliseum.

The setting is a guest house on the southern coast of England. Among the guests are a couple who believe that their relation should be based on sincerity, while another think! that reserve and courtesy are the main elements of a good relationship.

The work includes a long bucolic interlude between the acts.

Plymouth in an Uproar, musical farce in two acts by Charles Dibdin; libretto (Eng) by Edward Neville. First performance October 20, 1779, London, Covent Garden.
LIBRETTO: English (London: G. Kearsley, 1779).

Poet's Dilemma, The, opera in one act by Dai-Keong Lee; libretto (Eng). First performance April 12, 1940, New York, Juilliard School.

Withdrawn by the composer.

Poison, opera in one act by Frederic Hart; libretto (Eng) by Marion Farquhar, after a story by Katherine Mansfield. First performance February 3, 1984, Brooklyn, New York, Brooklyn College Conservatory of Music.

The setting is a villa in the south of France, 1913. The young Larry, an Englishman, comes back to his villa after being away from it for ten years. When his friend Adrian asks to buy the villa for his wife, Larry hesitates, recalling ten years earlier, when he wanted to marry Beatrice but saw their relationship become poisoned.

For a description, see Summers/*OOA*, 142–43.

Major roles: Larry (bar), Beatrice (sop), and Adrian (bass-bar/bar).

Poisoned Kiss, The, or The Empress and the Necromancer, romantic extravaganza in three acts by Ralph Vaughan Williams; libretto (Eng) by Evelyn Sharp, following Richard Garnett's tale *The Poison Maid,* part of the collection *The Twilight of the Gods* (1888) and Nathaniel Hawthorne's *Rappaccini's Daughter* (1844). First performance May 12, 1936, Cambridge, with Margaret Field-Hyde, Margaret Ritchie, and Parry Jones; conducted by Cyril Rootham. First U.S. performance April 21, 1937, New York, Juilliard School, with Annamary Dickey (Angelica), Gean Greenwell (Dipsacus), Albert Gifford (Amaryllus), Alice George (Tormentilla), William Fletcher Smith (Gallanthus), and Mary Frances Lehnerts (Persicaria); conducted by Albert Stoessel.

The fantasy story concerns the bitter rivalry of an empress, Persicaria, and a sorcerer, Dipsacus. Dipsacus has raised his daughter Tormentilla on poison, so that when she meets Amaryllus, son of Persicaria, her kiss will kill him. When Tormentilla and Amaryllus finally meet, they fall deeply in love, which negates the poison, and Persicaria and Dipsacus are reconciled.

For detailed descriptions, see Eaton/*OP* I, 115–16; K/*NKOB*, 846–47.

Major roles: Dipsacus (bass); Tormentilla (sop); Empress Persicaria (alto); Amaryllus (ten); Gallanthus, his attendant (bar); and Angelica, Tormentilla's companion (mezzo). SCORE: vs (London and New York: Oxford University Press, 1936). DISCOGRAPHY: serenade, Northern Sinfonia of England; cond. R. Hickox, Angel DS-38129 (Hollywood, Calif., 1984; 1 LP).

Policeman's Serenade, The, comic opera in one act by Alfred Reynolds; libretto (Eng) by Alan Patrick Herbert. First performance April 10, 1926, Hammersmith, England, Lyric Theatre. Played together with Thomas Arne's *Thomas and Sally** (1760), to form a portion of the revue entitled *Riverside Nights.*

Politics of Harmony, masque in one act by Charles Wuorinen; libretto (Eng) by Richard Monaco, after an ancient Chinese story of Ssu-ma-Ch'ien. First performance October 28, 1968, New York, Columbia University; also July 26, 1974, Wheatleigh, Massachusetts.

The story concerns a visiting ruler, who plays a bewitching tune for his host. Despite warnings from the host's music master, the ruler urges the tune to be played several times, after which a great storm descends and destroys the host. His guests escape unscathed.

The serial work is composed for bass, alto, and instrumentalists.

For an analysis, see William Hibbard, "Charles Wuorinen: *The Politics of Harmony,*" *Perspectives of New Music* VII (Spring-Summer 1969), 155–70.

Politics of Quiet, The, music theater piece by Meredith Monk; text (Eng). First performance June 24, 1996, Copenhagen. First U.S. performance October 10, 1996, Brooklyn, New York, Brooklyn Academy of Music, Next Wave Festival, with Thomas Bogdan, Katie Geissinger, Ching Gonzalez, Dina Emerson, Stephen Kalm, Carlos Arevalo, Randall Wong, Theo Bleckmann, Janis Brenner, and Allison Easter; Harry Huff and Allison Sniffin, musicians.

The work, which uses almost no dialogue or narrative, is a stylized view of the psychological and technological debris of the twentieth century, presented in minimalist terms.
BIBLIOGRAPHY: Neil Strauss, "A New Look at 'Less Is More,'" *NYT* (Oct. 14, 1996), C, 15 [on premiere].

Poll Booth, The, musical entertainment in one act by James Hook; libretto (Eng). First performance June 29, 1784, London, Vauxhall Gardens.

The poll signifies a vote to determine the favorite singer.

The work was scored for four singers.

Polly, "an Opera, being the second part of the Beggar's Opera" (ballad opera); libretto (Eng) by John Gay. The preface of the libretto carries the date of March 15, 1729, and the text and songs were published in the same year.

The work's premiere was canceled because of the interference of the Lord Chamberlain, who probably bowed to pressure from Walpole, the target of ridicule in Gay's *Beggar's Opera** of 1728, but the libretto, available by subscription, sold extremely well. The work was finally performed in 1777 (see below).

The setting is the West Indies, where Macheath has been put to work on a plantation. He escapes in the guise of a black and calls himself "Morano." Jenny Diver passes herself off as his wife, and he leads a band of pirates. Polly comes in search of Macheath but, robbed of all her possessions, is bought as a slave by Ducat, a letch, who quickly changes his mind and lets her go when she tells him about Macheath. Polly, now disguised as a boy, is seized by Macheath and his gang, who do not recognize her. When she rebuffs Jenny Diver's advances, Jenny accuses the "boy" of having attacked her. Macheath throws the still-disguised Polly into a cell with Cawwawkee, son of the Indian king. They are freed during a battle between the pirates and the Indians, and Macheath, in his disguise as Morano, is executed. Polly, appreciating Cawwawkee's morality, agrees to marry him.

For a detailed description, see Fiske/*ETM*, 108–9.

Revised version in three acts, with music arranged by John Pepusch, with textual changes by George Colman Sr. and six new airs by Samuel Arnold. First performance June 19, 1777, London, Little Theatre in the Haymarket. Modern revivals include Sir Nigel Playfair's version, based on the 1777 one, 1922, London, Hammersmith, Lyric Theatre; and March 21, 1963, London, Guildhall School of Music and Drama; version (cut) by Allen Percival and Eric Capon. First U.S. performance October 10, 1925, New York, Cherry Lane Playhouse.
SCORE: vs, arr. Alexander Laszlo, as *The Pirate's Opera* (Hollywood: Guild Publications of California, 1966).
LIBRETTO: English (London: author, 1729); repr. ed. Rubsamen/*BO*, vol. 1, *The Beggar's Opera, Imitated and Parodied* (1974).
BIBLIOGRAPHY: Stanley Sadie, review, *Opera* 14 (May 1963), 355 [on 1963 revival].

Ponder Heart, The, comic opera in two acts by Alice Parker; libretto (Eng) by the composer, after Eudora Welty's novel (1954). First performance September 10, 1982, Jackson, Mississippi, New Stage Theater.

The story concerns life in a small Mississippi town.

Pond in a Bowl, opera in one act by David Macbride; libretto (Eng), after Chinese poems. First performance March 24, 1983, New York.

Poorest Suitor, The, children's opera in one act by Leslie Kondorossy; libretto (Eng) by Shawn Hall, after a tale of the Blackfoot Indians. First performance May 24, 1967, Cleveland.

Poor Old Drury!!!, afterpiece opera in one act by Stephen Storace; libretto (Eng) by James Cobb. First performance September 22, 1791, London, King's Theatre in the Haymarket.

The story concerns the disarray caused by the move of the Drury Lane company to the King's Theatre in September 1791. The piece received sixteen performances during the 1791–1792 season.

Poor Sailor, The, or, Little Ben and Little Bob, musical drama in two acts by Thomas Attwood; libretto (Eng) by John Bernard. First performance May 29, 1795, London, Covent Garden. First U.S. performance, as *Little Bob and Little Ben,* April 11, 1810, Boston.

Possibly the same librettist as "Mr. Bernard" for Boyton's *The British Sailor** (1789, London).

SCORE: vs (London: Longman & Broderip, [1795]).

Poor Soldier, The, opera in two acts by William Shield; libretto (Eng) by John O'Keeffe. First performance November 4, 1783, London, Covent Garden, with Mrs. Kennedy (Patrick), Mr. Johnstone (Dermott), Mr. Edwin (Darby), Mr. Bannister (Captain Fitzroy), Mr. Wilson (Father Luke), Mrs. Martyr (Kathleen), and Mrs. Bannister (Norah). First U.S. performance December 2, 1785, New York, John Street Theatre.

Norah has accepted the attentions of Captain Fitzroy after turning away Patrick, who joined the army and went to America. When Patrick returns and proves to be the man who once saved Fitzroy, Fitzroy renounces his claim to Norah.

For a detailed description, see Fiske/*ETM*, 459–60; also 611–12 for the provenance of the numbers.

The role of Patrick is a trouser part.

This is a new version of *The Shamrock.** *Love in a Camp, or, Patrick in Prussia** (1786) is its sequel. See also *Darby's Return,** billed as another sequel.

SCORES: fs ed. William Brasmer and William Osborne, *Recent Researches in American Music,* vol. 6 (Madison, Wisc.: A-R Editions, 1978); vs (London: J. Bland, etc. [1783]).

LIBRETTO: English (London, 1784); repr. Rubsamen/*BO,* vol. 23, *Irish Ballad Operas and Burlesques II* (1974); (New York: D. Longworth, 1804).

Poor Vulcan, comic opera in one act by Charles Dibdin, with one air by Samuel Arnold; libretto (Eng) by Charles Dibdin, after Motteux. First performance February 4, 1778, London, Covent Garden. First U.S. performance February 22, 1793, Charleston, South Carolina, Charleston Theatre.

Vulcan and Venus have been tossed out of Olympus for their behavior and find themselves the owners of a pub in an English village. They are the object of ridicule by the other gods, who come to the town in the guise of humans, taking on English names such as Stud (Jupiter), the local squire, and Pike (Mars), the sergeant.

For a detailed description, see Fiske/*ETM*, 422–23.

LIBRETTOS: English (London: G. Kearsley et al., 1778; London: John Johnston and W. Randall, [1778]; Dublin: Booksellers, 1789).

Poor Vulcan, burletta/extravaganza in two acts by Henry Rowley Bishop; libretto (Eng) by Charles Dibdin Jr., after Dibdin's burletta (see preceding entry). First performance February 3, 1813, London, Covent Garden.

Among the numbers are the duet "The Moon-Beam Plays on Yonder Grove" and the air "A Shepherd Become."

SCORE: ms fs, duet (1813, British Library, Add. MS. 36962/3).

Porgy and Bess, folk opera in three acts by George Gershwin; libretto (Eng) by Du Bose Heyward and Ira Gershwin, after Du Bose and Dorothy Heyward's drama *Porgy* (1925). First performance September 30, 1935, Boston, Colonial Theater, with Ann Wiggins Brown (Bess), Abbie Mitchell (Clara), Helen Dowdy (Lily), Ruby Elzy (Serena), Georgette Harvey (Maria), Todd Duncan (Porgy), Eddie Matthews (Jake), Warren Coleman (Crown), and John W. Bubbles (Sportin' Life); conducted by Alexander Smallens; produced and directed by Rouben Mamoulian. First New York performance October 10, 1935, Alvin Theatre, with the same cast. First British performance October 9, 1952, London, Stoll Theatre, with Leontyne Price (Bess), William Warfield (Porgy), Helen Colbert (Clara), Helen Dowdy (Lily), Cab Calloway (Sportin' Life), and John McCurry (Crown); conducted by Alexander Smallens; performed 1953, New York, Ziegfield Theater, with the same cast. Performed as an opera in its original, full version July 30, 1976, Houston Grand Opera, with Clamma Dale (Bess), Donnie Ray Albert (Porgy), Betty Lane (Clara), Wilma Shakesnider (Serena), Carol Brice (Maria), Henry Davis (Robbins), Henry Andrew Smith (Crown), and Larry Marshall (Sportin' Life); conducted by John DeMain. First Metropolitan Opera performance February 6, 1985, with Grace Bumbry (Bess), Simon Estes (Porgy), Myra Merritt (Clara), Florence Quivar (Serena), Charles Williams (Sportin' Life), and Gregg Baker (Crown); conducted by James Levine; designed by Robert O'Hearn; directed by Nathaniel Merrill.

The setting is in and around Charleston, South Carolina, "the recent past" (the 1920s). The work opens on Catfish Row, a black neighborhood near the waterfront, on a hot summer day. It revolves around the crippled Porgy, who vies for the love of Bess with the stevedore Crown. Following a dice game, Crown kills Robbins, a local inhabitant, and is forced to flee. The anguish of Serena, Robbins's wife, is expressed in "My Man's Gone Now" (act 1, scene 2), and Porgy sums up his own situation in "I Got Plenty o' Nuttin'," sung by Porgy to a banjo and orchestra accompaniment (act 2, scene 1). In Crown's absence, Bess turns to Porgy, who has long loved her; their feelings are expressed in the duet "Bess, You Is My Woman Now" (act 2, scene 1). He convinces her to go on a picnic to Kittiwah Island, where she again meets Crown, who has been hiding there, and spends the night with him. Sportin' Life, a drug dealer, also appears and presents his sardonic view of life during the picnic, in "It Ain't Necessarily So" (act 2, scene 2).

Bess returns to Catfish Row and to Porgy, who takes her back. Crown returns also and, after mocking Porgy about his disability, goes to help rescue the Catfish Row fisherman, who have been caught by the storm; Clara leaves also to search for her husband, Jake. When Crown comes back to reclaim Bess, Porgy stabs him in a fight. Porgy is arrested by the police and led off to jail. In his absence, Sportin' Life convinces Bess to go with him to New York, in "Listen: There's a Boat Dat's Leavin' Soon for New York" (act 3, scene 2), telling her that Porgy will not be freed. Porgy is, however, let go after a few days because of lack of evidence. Maria and Serena break the news to him that Bess has left with Sportin' Life. Porgy, still in love with Bess, sets out after her, concluding with the hope-filled "Oh Lawd, I'm on My Way" (act 3, scene 3).

Major roles: Porgy, a crippled beggar (bar); Bess (sop); Crown, a stevedore (bass); Serena, wife of Robbins (sop); Robbins (ten); Clara, Jake's wife (sop); Maria, keeper of the cook shop (alto); Jake, a fisherman (bar); and Sportin' Life (ten).

For a detailed plot synopsis, see K/KOB, 1330–36; K/NKOB, 243–47.

The work uses the operatic devices of aria, recitative, and reminiscence themes. Its many musical highlights, often performed separately, include the numbers cited above, as well as the perennial favorite "Summertime," a lullaby sung by Clara to her crying child, followed by Jake's "A Woman Is a Sometime Thing" (act 1, scene 1).

Its subject matter, almost all-black cast, and Gershwin's reputation as a composer of popular music prevented the work from being given on an operatic stage in its first decades of existence. As Bordman notes (AMT, p. 494), it turned up on Broadway because "it had no place else to go," and its initial Broadway run was in a greatly cut version. This was remedied only in 1976, when it was presented in its original version, uncut, in Houston. Its first performance in Charleston took place in 1970.

The 1959 film, directed by Otto Preminger, featured Sidney Poitier, Dorothy Dandridge, Pearl Bailey, Sammy Davis Jr., Brock Peters, and Diahann Carroll. Gershwin's music was arranged by André Previn and Ken Darby, both of whom received Oscars.

SCORES: vs (New York: Gershwin Publishing Corp., [1935]); condensed score (New York: Chappell, 1959).

LIBRETTO: English (Winona, Minn.: Chappell/Intersong Music Group-USA. 1935 [1988?]).

BIBLIOGRAPHY: Hollis Alpert, The Life and Times of Porgy and Bess, The Story of an American Classic (New York: Alfred Knopf, 1990); Shirley Flatow, "Premiere Porgy," ON XLIX (Mar. 16, 1983), 34–35, 43; E. F. M., "Gershwin's Opera Makes Boston Hit," NYT (Oct. 1, 1935), 27 [on premiere]; Harper MacKay, "Porgy in Hollywood," ON LIV (Jan. 20, 1990), 8-12, 46; Ethan Mordden, "A Long Pull," ON XLIX (Mar. 16, 1983), 30–33, 46.

DISCOGRAPHY: Dale, Shakesnider, Lane, Brice, Bash, Albert, Smith, Marshall, Wallace; cond. DeMain, RCA ARL 3-2109 (3 LPs); rev. John W. Freeman, "Records," ON XLII (Dec. 10, 1977), 37; Haymon, Clarey, Blackwell, Simpson, White, Baker, Hubbard, Evans, Worthy, Coleman, Glyndebourne Chorus, London Philharmonic; cond. S. Rattle, EMI CD7-495682 (3 CDs); highlights: Price, Warfield, Bubbles, Boatwright, Victory Chorus and Orch.; cond. Henderson, RCA 5234-2RG; both rev. John W. Freeman, "Recordings," ON LIV (Sept. 1989), 50; Mitchell, Quivar, Hendricks, Floyd, Conrad, White, Boatwright, Clemmons, Pickens, Hagan, Cleveland Orch. and Chorus; cond. L. Maazel, London OSA-13116 (3 CDs).

VIDEO: W. White, C. Haymon, G. Baker D. Evans, S. Simpson, Glyndebourne Chorus, London Phil.; cond. S. Rattle, dir. T. Nunn, EMI VHS MVB4 91131-3 (1992, BBC-TV).

Portrait, The, burletta (all-sung afterpiece) in three acts by Samuel Arnold; libretto by George Colman Sr. (Eng), after Louis Anseaume's Le tableau parlant, set by Grétry (1769, Paris). First performance November 22, 1770, London, with Miss Catley (Isabella), Mr. Reinhold (Leader), Mrs. Thompson (Colombine), and Mr. Shuter (Pantaloon).

The aging and portly Pantaloon is in love with Isabella, his ward. In order to keep an eye on her, he cuts holes into his portrait on the dining room wall and peeks through them. To his dismay he sees her carrying on with the young Leander.

SCORE: vs (London: Joseph Welcker, [1770]).

LIBRETTO: English (London: T. Becket and Co., 1770).

Portrait, The, burletta in two parts by François Hippolyte Barthelemon; anonymous libretto (Eng). First performance ca. 1771, Dublin, Rotunda.

LIBRETTO: English (Dublin: S. Powell, 1772).

Portrait in Brownstone, opera in two acts by Paul Reif; libretto by Henry Butler, after Louis Auchincloss's novel (1962). First performance (excerpts) May 15, 1966, New York, Central Opera Service Conference.

The story concerns a society woman in New York City.

Port Town, comedy-drama in one act by Jan Meyerowitz; libretto (Eng) by Langston Hughes. First performance August 4, 1960, Lenox, Massachusetts, Tanglewood, Berkshire Music Center; conducted by Boris Goldovsky.

Positive Man, The, musical farce in two acts by Samuel Arnold and Michael Arne; libretto (Eng) by John O'Keeffe, after his comedy *The She Gallants,* itself based on George Granville. First performance March 16, 1782, London, Covent Garden, with Mr. Quick (Sir Toby Tacit), Mr. Edwin (Rupee), Mr. Whitfield (Captain Bellcamp), Mr. Booth (Lake), Mr. Lee Lewis (Grog), Mr. Mahon (Maurice), Mr. Fearon (Sterne), Mrs. Webb (Lady Tacit), Mrs. Martyr (Cornelia), and Mrs. Inchbald (Florimel). First U.S. performance May 10, 1802, New York, Park Theatre.
LIBRETTO: English (London: T. N. Longman and O. Rees, 1800).

Postcard from Morocco, opera in one act by Dominick Argento; libretto (Eng) by John Donahue. First performance October 14, 1971, Minneapolis, Cedar Village Theater, Center Opera, with Barbara Brandt (lad with a hat box), Janis Hardy (a foreign singer), Sarita Roche (lady with a hand mirror), Barry Busse (shoe salesman), Edward Foreman (man with a cornet case), Yale Marshall (man with old luggage), and Vern Sutton (Owen); conducted by Philip Brunelle.

Seven travelers are assembled in a gloomy waiting room, somewhere in Morocco, in 1914; each is trying to discover what is in the other's luggage. The only traveler with a name, Mr. Owen, is found to have an empty paint box.

For detailed plot descriptions, see Eaton/*OP* II, 185–86; K/*NKOB*, 11.

Major roles: Mr. Owen (ten), lady with hand mirror (col sop), lady with cake box (sop), foreign singer (mezzo), puppet no. 1/old luggage man (lyr ten), puppet no. 2/ shoe salesman (bar), and man with a cornet case/puppet maker (bass).

The eclectic score combines serial techniques, elements of Viennese operetta, Baroque counterpoint, and 1920s jazz.
SCORE: vs: (New York: Boosey & Hawkes, [1971]).
BIBLIOGRAPHY: Leslie Hollister, "U.S.," *ON* XXXV (Dec. 11, 1971), 28 [on premiere].
DISCOGRAPHY: S. Roche, B. Brandt, J. Hardy, Y. Marshall, V. Sutton, B. Busse, M. [E.] Foreman, Minnesota Opera; cond. P. Brunelle, Desto DC-7137/8 (1972, 2 LPs), reissued as Composers Recordings CRI 614 (1992, 2 CDs).

Postilion!, comic opera in three acts, an arrangement by George Frederick Stansbury of Adam's *Le postillon de Longjumeau* (1836, Paris); libretto (Eng) by Gilbert A. A'Beckett, after the text by A. de Leuven and L. L. Brunswick. First performance March 13, 1837, London, St. James's Theatre.

Postman Always Rings Twice, The, opera in two acts by Stephen Paulus; libretto (Eng) by Colin Graham, after the novel by J. M. Cain (1934). First performance June 19, 1982, St. Louis, Opera Theatre of St. Louis, with David Parsons (Frank), Kathryn Bouleyn (Cora), Michael Myers (Nick), and Carroll Freeman (Katz); conducted by C. William Harwood; directed by Colin Graham. Revised version March 1, 1985, Fort Worth, Texas, Fort Worth Opera; conducted by Mark Flint.

The story centers around a love triangle: the handsome and muscular vagrant Frank and the wild Cora plot to murder Nick Papadakis, her husband and owner of a roadside joint. Frank tells the story in flashbacks from his jail cell. He has been arrested for ostensibly murdering the pregnant Cora, who, in reality, died in a car accident in which he was at the wheel.

Major roles: Frank Chambers (bar); Nick Papadakis (ten); Cora, his wife (sop); Sackett, the D.A. (bass); and Katz, the lawyer (ten).

SCORE: vs (Valley Forge, Pa: European American Music, 1982).

LIBRETTO: the same.

BIBLIOGRAPHY: Harold Blumenfeld, "America: 'Postman' Premiere," *Opera* XXXIII (1982), 1030–52; Michael Fleming, "Fort Worth," *ON* (June 1985), 36–37 [on rev. version]; Andrew Porter, "American Verismo," *NY* LVIII (Aug. 2, 1982), 80–82 [on premiere].

Pot of Broth, A, opera in one act by Herbert Haufrecht; libretto (Eng) by the composer, after W. B. Yeats's play. First performance 1964, New York, WNYC radio, After Dinner Opera.

Roles: Mezzo, tenor, and baritone.

SCORE: fs, facsimile (New York: American Composers Alliance, 1965).

Pot of Fat, The, opera in one act (six scenes) by Theodore Chanler; libretto (Eng) by Hester Pickman, after a Grimm fairy tale, *The Cat and the Mouse in Partnership.* First performance May 9, 1955, Cambridge, Massachusetts, Longy School of Music, Harvard University, Sanders Theatre, with Ramon Gilbert (the cat), Virginia Murray (the mouse), and Paul Matthen (the narrator); conducted by Kalman Novak.

In this satire the narrator is skeptical when a cat and mouse marry for love. In fact, the cat is secretly eating a pot of fat that he and his wife have stored for the winter. When the mouse discovers this deception, the mouse becomes her husband's dinner.

For a detailed description, see Eaton/*OP* I, 210–11.

Roles: the narrator (bass-bar/ten), the cat (bass-bar), and the mouse (sop).

BIBLIOGRAPHY: Arthur Berger, review, *NYT* (May 15, 1955, II, 7 [on premiere].

Potter Thompson, children's opera in one act by Gordon Crosse; libretto (Eng) by Alan Garner. First performance January 9, 1975, London, Highgate School, Finchley Children's Music Group, with John Winfield (Potter Thompson); conducted by John Andrewes; produced by Michael Elliot; designed by Anne Sinclair.

The story concerns the reclusive Potter Thompson, brokenhearted as a young man who lost his beloved. He finds the Sleeping Hero under the Hill and begins to awaken him but stops at the last moment, having realized that the Hero's promise is of the future, not the present.

SCORE: vs (Oxford: Oxford University Press, 1985).

Powder Her Face, opera in eight scenes by Thomas Adès; libretto (Eng) by Philip Hensher. First performance July 5, 1995, London, Almeida Theatre, with Jill Gomez (the Duchess), Valdine Anderson (her maid), Niall Morris (an electrician), and Roger Bryson (judge); directed by Jonathan Reekie. First U.S. performance (concert) July 23, 1997, Berkeley, California, Berkeley Symphony; conducted by Kent Nagano. First U.S. stage performance July 25, 1997, Aspen, Colorado, Aspen Music Festival, with Maire O'Brien (the Duchess), Allen Schott (the Duke), and Heather Buck (the maid); conducted by the composer; directed by Edward Berkeley.

The opera concerns the decline into sordid affairs and poverty by the once very wealthy and sexually obsessive Margaret, Duchess of Argyll. The story unfolds in a series of tableaux that begins in 1934, when the Duchess is in her prime, and ends with her ultimate decline in 1990. At its American stage premiere in Aspen, signs were posted in the opera house warning that the work contained "explicit language and adult situations."

For a detailed plot description, see K/*NKOB*, 7–8.

Among the musical devices the composer employs to portray the milieu is the tango, supported by a dance band. The score also contains Sprechstimme and arias and includes dissonant and tonal passages. In addition, it uses quotations from Stravinsky's *Rake's Progress** in the trial scene.

BIBLIOGRAPHY: Jeffrey Joseph, review, *MT* (Sept. 1995), 511–12 [on premiere]; Paul Griffiths, review, *TLS*, no. 4814 (July 7, 1995), 20 [on premiere]; Pierre Ruhe, "A Suite in Opera's Heartbreak Hotel," *Washington Post* (Aug. 3, 1997), G, 4 [on U.S. stage premiere]; David Patrick Stearns, review, *USA Today* (July 31, 1997), D, 8 [on U.S. stage premiere].

Power Failure, music theater/opera in two acts by Paul Dresher; libretto (Eng) by Rinde Eckert. First performance May 4, 1989, Iowa City, University of Iowa, American Music Theatre Festival.

The story centers on the unscrupulous entrepreneur Charles Smithson, owner of a large chemical firm. Charles is suffering from an incurable illness and hires a talented young biochemist, Ruth Lehman, to find a cure, which he intends to keep secret from the public. When a power failure puts Charles in peril, his demise is watched by Merle, a security guard, whose own daughter's medical needs were sacrificed for Charles's benefit.

For a description, see Kornick/*RAO*, 83–84.

The eclectic score combines elements of jazz, rock, and minimalism.

Prankster, The, comic opera in one act by Robert Wykes; libretto (Eng) by the composer. First performance January 12, 1952, Bowling Green, Ohio.

Preciosa, opera in four acts, an adaptation by William Hawes of Weber's opera (1821, Berlin); libretto (Eng) probably by George Soane, after P. A. Wolff's text, itself after Cervantes's *La gitanella*. First performance April 28, 1825, London, Covent Garden.

A beautiful gypsy girl is loved by an aristocrat. She turns out to be from a noble family, having been kidnapped as a child. Her background thus makes her suitable for her admirer.

Preciosa, or, The Spanish Student, opera by Eleanor Everest Freer; libretto (Eng) by the composer, after Henry Wadsworth Longfellow. Composed 1928.

Predators, comic opera in one act by Seymour Barab; libretto (Eng) by the composer. First performance (concert) May 12, 1985, New York, After Dinner Opera, with Jocelyn Wilkes and Bill Bonecutter; Conrad Strasser, piano. Presented together with *Out the Window** under the designation "Tour de Farce."

Set in present-day New York, the story concerns a desperate Jewish mother who is trying to get her unmarried daughter together with a suitable mate. The mother's choice, unfortunately, turns out to be a disguised Count Dracula.

BIBLIOGRAPHY: Bernard Holland, review, *NYT* (May 16, 1985), C, 26 [on premiere].

Prelude and Fugue, opera in one act by Arnold Franchetti; libretto (Eng) by Clifford Bax after his play. First performance April 21, 1959, Hartford, Connecticut, Hartt College of Music.

Prelude to Einstein on the Fritz, "undiscovered opera" by "P. D. Q. Bach" (Peter Schickele); libretto (Eng) by the composer. First performance 1989, New York, Carnegie Hall.

A takeoff on Philip Glass's *Einstein on the Beach.**

'Prentice Pillar, The, romantic opera in one act by Reginald Somerville; libretto (Eng) by Guy Eden. First performance 1897, London.
LIBRETTO: English (London: J. MacQueen, 1897).

President Lincoln, opera in four acts and nine scenes by Sam Raphling; libretto (Eng) by the composer. Composed 1976.
SCORE: vs ([Hastings-on-Hudson, N.Y.]): General Music Pub. Co., [1976]).

Press Gang, The (The Enraged Apprentice), children's opera by Alan Bush; libretto (Eng) by Nancy Bush. First performance March 7, 1947, Letchworth, England, St. Christopher School.

Pride of the Regiment, The, or, Cashiered for His Country, light opera by Walter Leigh; libretto (Eng) by Clinton-Baddeley. First performance September 19, 1931, Midhurst, England.
SCORE: vs (London: Boosey & Co., Ltd., [1932]).

Prima Donna, opera in a prologue and one act by Arthur Benjamin; libretto (Eng) by Cedric Cliffe. First performance February 23, 1949, London, Fortune Theatre.

In order to entertain his rich old uncle, Count Rinaldo, Florindo, on the advice of his friend Alcino, borrows money to pay for a rich feast. Rinaldo requests that the opera star Filomela appear, but Florindo instead brings Olimpia, his current lover, while Alcino brings his lady love, Fiammetta. The count is thereby entertained by two "Filomelas" but is convinced that he is hearing double because of his drunkenness. The two ladies, disgusted by having to sing against each other, refuse to perform anymore, but their part is taken over by Bellina, while the young men are faced with calming their own girlfriends.

For a detailed description, see Eaton/*OP* I, 212.

Major roles: Florindo (bar), Alcino (ten), Count Rinaldo (bass-bar), and Olimpia and Fiammetta (col sop).
SCORE: vs (London: Boosey, [1935]).

Primal Void, opera in one act by John Vincent; libretto (Eng) by the composer and H. Reese. Composed 1969. First performance May 14, 1973, Vienna.

A well-to-do art lover, Magnus Taylor, comes to the gallery of Armen Xykl. Taylor considers that a good piece of art can be judged by its price. Seeking to make a fast sale, Armen presents a painting by "Anonymous Bosh," which consists of an empty frame, and sells it to Taylor for two million dollars. Taylor leaves without the frame, since he has a good one at home.

For a description, see Summers/*OOA*, 300–1.

Roles: Magnus Taylor (bar), Armen Xykl (bass-bar), and Mrs. Taylor (speaking).

Prince Ferelon, or, The Princess's Suitors, "a musical extravaganza" in one act by Nicholas Gatty; libretto (Eng) by the composer. First performance November 27, 1919, London, Florence Ettlinger Opera School. First professional performance May 21, 1921, London, Old Vic.

Prince of Coxcombs, The, comic opera in three acts by Inglis Gundry; libretto (Eng) by the composer, after John Vanbrugh's *The Relapse* (1696). First performance February 3, 1965, London, Morley College.

Loveless, once a libertine, lives happily with his wife until he returns to London alone and falls into his former ways.

Princess, The, opera in one act by Arnold Franchetti; libretto (Eng) by M. Franchetti. First performance March 16, 1952, Hartford, Connecticut, Hartt College of Music.

Part 1 of a trilogy that consists also of *The Maypole** and *The Game of Cards.**

Princess and the Pea, The, fairy tale in one act by Ernst Toch; libretto (Eng) by Marion J. Farquhar, after the original German text by Benno Elkan, based on Hans Christian Andersen's fairy tale. First performance July 27, 1954, Lenox, Massachusetts, Tanglewood Festival, with John Hornor, Emelina de Vita, Robert Simpson, and Evelyn Lear; conducted by Paul Vermel. Revision of the composer's *Die Prinzessin auf der Erbse* (1927, Baden-Baden).

In this children's tale, no suitable wife can be found for the prince until a young woman, tested by sleeping on many mattresses covering a pea, awakes with bruises from the vegetable.

Roles: the king (bass), the queen (sop), the prince (ten), the chancellor (bar), the minister (ten), the nurse (sop), and the princess (sop).

Once upon a Mattress by Mary Rogers (1959, New York) is a musical-comedy version of the tale.

SCORE: vs, German version (Mainz: B. Schott's Söhne, 1927); vs, English version (n.p., Schott, n.d.).
BIBLIOGRAPHY: Olin Downes, "3 Operas Staged at Berkshire Fete," *NYT* (July 28, 1954), 27 [on English-version premiere].

Princess and the Vagabond, The, folk opera in four scenes by Isadore Freed; libretto (Eng) by Ruth Sawyer. First performance May 18, 1948, Hartford, Connecticut, Main Auditorium.

Princess Ida, or, Castle Adamant, comic opera in three acts by Arthur S. Sullivan; libretto (Eng) by William S. Gilbert, after Tennyson's poem *The Princess*. First performance January 5, 1884, London, Savoy Theatre, with Rutland Barrington (King Hildebrand), Henry Bracey (Hilarion), George Grossmith (King Gama), Leonora Braham (Princess Ida), Rosina Brandram (Lady Blanche), Kate Chard (Lady Psyche), and Jessie Bond (Melissa). First U.S. performance February 11, 1884, New York, Fifth Avenue Theatre, with J. H. Ryley (King Gama), Cora S. Tanner (Princess Ida), Wallace Macreery (Hilarion), W. S. Rising (Cyril), Charles F. Lang (Florian), Signor Brocolini (King Hildebrand), and Genevieve Reynolds (Lady Blanche); staged by Frank Thornton.

The action takes place in the pavilion, gardens, and courtyard of Castle Adamant. The ruler, King Adamant, is waiting for King Gama, a neighboring sovereign, who is bringing his daughter Ida to wed Adamant's son, Prince Hilarion, thus fulfilling an engagement arranged twenty years ago.

To everyone's disappointment, the party arrives without Ida, who has gone off to head a university that excludes men. Threatened with hanging, Gama has his sons fight Hilarion and two of his friends. When the sons are wounded, Ida surrenders and accepts her betrothal.

For detailed discussions, see Stedman/*WSG*, 202–6; Traubner/*O*, 168–69.

Major roles: King Hildebrand (bass-bar); Hilarion, his son (ten); King Gama (bar); Princess Ida, Gama's daughter (sop); Lady Blanche, professor of abstract science (alto); Lady Psyche, professor of humanities (sop); and Melissa, Lady Blanche's daughter (mezzo).

The musical highlights include the quartet "The World Is But a Broken Toy" (act 1); the duet of Melissa and Lady Blanche, "Now Wouldn't You Like to Rule the Roost" (act 1); Ida's "O, Goddess Wise" (act 2); and the operatic finale to act 2.

SCORE: vs (Boston: Ditson, 1884; London: Chappell, [19??]).

LIBRETTO: English (London: Chappell, [1884]; [Boston: O. Ditson], 1884).

DISCOGRAPHY: D'Oyly Carte Opera Company and Chorus, Philharmonic Orch.; cond. M. Sargent, London 436 810-2 London (1966, 2 LPs), rereleased London 436810 (1993, 2 CDs).

Princess Maleen, opera in two acts by Ruth Schonthal; libretto (Eng) by the composer and Wallis Wood, after the Brothers Grimm. First performance May 20, 1989, White Plains, Westchester Conservatory of Music Chorus and Orchestra.

SCORE: ms score, holograph (1988, photocopy, NYPL).

Princess Toto, comic opera in three acts by Frederic Clay; libretto (Eng) by William S. Gilbert. First performance June 26, 1876, Nottingham, Theatre Royal, with Kate Santley (Princess Toto). First U.S. performance December 13, 1879, New York, Standard Theatre, with Leonora Braham (Princess Toto).

In the story Princess Toto has a very bad memory, which results in her marrying two husbands in quick succession. She is "rescued" by her father and two ministers disguised as American Indians.

SCORE: vs (London: Metzler & Co., [n.d.])

LIBRETTO: English (London: Metzler, [1876]).

Prisoner, The, musical romance in three acts by Thomas Attwood, including music by W. A. Mozart; libretto (Eng) by John Rose. First performance October 18, 1792, London, Haymarket Theatre, with Thomas Sedgwick (Pasquil). Revised as *The Castle of Sorrento** (1799). First U.S. performance May 29, 1795, Philadelphia, Chestnut Street Theatre.

The work, a rescue opera, is set in South America. It includes "Non più andrai" from Mozart's *Le nozze di Figaro,* with the title "Where the Banners of Glory Are Streaming."

SCORE: vs (London: Longman & Broderip, [1792]).

LIBRETTO: English (London: C. Lowndes, 1792).

Prisoner, The, opera in two acts by John Joubert; libretto (Eng) by Stephen Tunnicliffe, after Tolstoy's short story *Too Dear!* First performance March 14, 1973, London.

The setting is an Eastern European state around 1900. The well-respected and generous master Sergei has been wrongly accused and imprisoned of a crime he did not commit.

Prisoner Paul, The, chamber opera in two acts by Inglis Gundry; libretto (Eng) by the composer. First performance October 16, 1970, London, St. Paul's, Covent Garden.

Prisoner's Opera, The, all-sung ballad opera in one act; libretto (Eng) possibly by Edward Ward. First performance summer 1730, London, Sadler's Wells.

For a description of the music, see Fiske/*ETM*, 119–20.

LIBRETTO: English (British Library, Add. MS. 27831).

Prisoner's Play, The, children's opera by John Rea; libretto (Eng) by Paul Woodruff. First performance May 12, 1973, Toronto, University of Toronto, MacMillan Theatre.

The work concerns the sorceress Circe.

Private, television opera by Felix Werder; libretto (Eng) by Peter Rorke. First performance 1969, ABC television.

Privilege and Privation, satire in one act by John Becker; libretto (Eng) by Alfred Kreymborg. Composed 1939. First performance June 22, 1982, Amsterdam.

The work features seven male voices and a male quartet.

Prize, The, or, 2, 5, 3, 6, "a new musical farce" in two acts by Stephen Storace; libretto (Eng) by Prince Hoare. First performance March 11, 1793, London, Theatre Royal, Drury Lane, with Mr. Bannister (Lenitive), Miss Storace (Caroline), and Mrs. Bland (Juba). First U.S. performance May 26, 1795, Philadelphia, Chestnut Street Theatre.

Lenitive is a country apothecary, and he is attended by his black slave, Juba. When the chemist gets the news that he has won the lottery, he tries to make himself into a gentleman in order to impress Caroline, whom he is courting. Only at the end does Lenitive learn that there was a mistake, and the lottery was really won by somebody else.

Among the numbers is "Beaux yeux," from Storace's *La cameriera astuta* (1788, London). SCORE: vs (London: J. Dale, 1793; repr. Redcroft, Huntington: King's Music, [1989?]). LIBRETTOS: English (Dublin: F. Farquhar, 1793; New York: D. Longworth, 1805).

Prodigal Son, A, or, Gleaners of Life, "a new and original opera" in two acts by Frederick Nicholls; libretto (Eng) by Ernest Willett. First performance 1896, Liverpool? LIBRETTO: English (Liverpool: Lee and Nightingale, 1896?).

Prodigal Son, The, opera in three acts by Frederick Jacobi; libretto (Eng) by Herman Voaden, after four early American prints. First performance August 1944 (excerpts) Palo Alto, California, Stanford University. First complete performance April 10, 1951, London, Central Music Library.

The work is set in nineteenth-century America and involves the family of Robert: his father; Ruth, an adopted daughter; John; and Nancy. During a celebration of the father's birthday Robert says that he is going away and asks for his inheritance. He falls into bad company and loses all of his money, eventually finding his way back home. There he is welcomed by his father, Ruth, and Nancy, but his brother John is hostile, since he wanted to marry Ruth. John defers to Robert in the end when he realizes that Ruth is still in love with the prodigal son.

Major roles: Robert (ten), father (bar), John (bass-bar), Nancy (sop), and Ruth (mezzo).

For a detailed description, see Eaton/*OP* II, 186–87.

Prodigal Son, The, third parable for church performance by Benjamin Britten; libretto (Eng) by William Plomer from the New Testament (Luke XV, 11–32). First performance June 10, 1968, Aldeburgh Festival, Orford Church, with Peter Pears (the Tempter/ Abbot), Robert Tear (the Younger Son), John Shirley-Quirk (the Father), and Bryan Drake (the Elder Son); conducted by the composer. First U.S. performance June 29, 1969, Katonah, New York, Caramoor Festival, with John Lankston, Andrea Velis, David Clatworthy, and William Metcalf; conducted by Julius Rudel.

The story concerns the Father, his Elder Son, and his Younger Son. The latter is lured away from working in the fields by the Tempter. Going to the city, the Younger Son is robbed by Parasites. He finally returns to his family, who forgive him.

For detailed descriptions, see K/*KOB*, 1230–32; K/*NKOB*, 134–35.

Major roles: the Father (bass-bar), the Elder Son (bar), the Younger Son (ten), and the Tempter (ten). Like Britten's *Billy Budd,** this work contains no female roles.

Other settings of the tale include A. Ponchielli's *Il figliuol prodigo* (1880, Milan); and C. Debussy's cantata *L'enfant prodigue* (1884, Paris).
SCORE: vs, fs (London: Faber, 1971).
LIBRETTO: English (London: Faber, 1971).
BIBLIOGRAPHY: Peter Heyworth, "Birtwistle: Better Than Britten?" *NYT* (June 23, 1968), D, 17, 26 [on premiere].

Professor Lookalike and the Children, opera in one act for children by Leonard Kastle; libretto (Eng) by the composer. First performance 1988, Albany.

Professor Tattle, comic opera by Joseph Carl Breil; libretto (Eng) by the composer. First performance 1913, New York.

Project 1521, science fiction satire in three acts by Robert Gross; libretto (Eng) by the composer. First performance November 1974, Los Angeles, Occidental College.

When the brilliant Dr. Verano, who has developed a diet to produce worms that are intellectually advanced, leaves his research and body to Ur University, the Dean and President Cumak decide to liquefy his brain and use it to produce a vitamin formula to enhance the intellect of humans. They name their experiment "Project 1521," the time of the Diet of Worms. Their unknowing subjects are the football team, who get the vitamin and proceed to do remarkably well in their academic work.

But the formula starts to run out, and so the Dean and President hold a banquet for the most respected and brilliant retired members of the faculty. They also plan an explosion, which convinces the Board of Trustees to give the university new labs and also, by eliminating some of the faculty at the banquet, provides raw material for more of the intellect-engendering potion.

For a detailed description, see Kornick/*RAO*, 129–30.

Prometheus, opera in two acts by Meyer Kupferman; libretto (Eng-Germ) by the composer, after Goethe. First performance (excerpts) 1978, New York, Manhattan School of Music.

Prometheus Bound, opera in three acts by Halim El-Dabh; libretto (Eng) by the composer, after Robert Lowell. First performance 1969, Washington, D.C., Hawthorne School.

Promise, The, biblical opera by Jill Townsend; libretto (Eng) by the composer, after the Gospel of St. Luke and the Acts of the Apostles. First performance March 17, 1997, London, Queen Elizabeth Hall, Opera Brava, with Bronek Pomorski (Luke/narrator), David Ashmore-Turner (Jesus), Christopher Parke (John the Baptist), Iwona Januszajtis (Gabriel), Amanda Buckland (Mary), and Judy Slater (Mary Magdalene); conducted by Keith Willis.

A treatment of the life of Jesus and the crucifixion.

The music includes the use of the augmented second to suggest local color.
BIBLIOGRAPHY: John Allison, review, *Opera* XLVIII (June 1997), 728–29 [on premiere].

Promised Valley, The, music drama by Crawford M. Gates; libretto (Eng) by Arnold Sundgaard. Composed ca. 1961.
SCORE: vs ([Provo, Utah: Pacific Publications, 1961?]).

Prophecy, The, grand opera in one act by Harry Lawrence Freeman; libretto (Eng) by the composer. First performance 1912, New York.

Prophet, The, comic opera in three acts by William Shield; libretto (Eng) by Richard Bentley. First performance December 13, 1788, London, Covent Garden, with Elizabeth Billington. Revised as afterpiece in two acts, February 4, 1789, London, with an overture by Antonio Salieri.

Both versions were failures.

SCORE: vs (London: Longman & Broderip, [1788]).

Prophetess, The, or, The History of Dioclesian (Purcell). See **Dioclesian**.

Prophetess, The, or, The History of Dioclesian, opera with spoken dialogue by John Pepusch; libretto (Eng) by Thomas Betterton and John Dryden, after *The Prophetess* (1622) by John Fletcher and Massinger. First performance November 28, 1724, London, Lincoln's Inn Fields.

The music is lost.

Purcell's *Dioclesian** (1629, London) is an earlier setting.

Proposal, The, opera in one act by Gerald Humel; libretto (Eng) by Roger Brucker. First performance 1958, Winfield, Kansas, Southwestern College.

The setting is an American home, the present. Anxious to get their daughter married off, the parents of a young woman coach her before her suitor, Jeremy, appears at the house and continue to offer her advice from their hiding place when he speaks to her. The daughter, completely confused, is unable to accept Jeremy's proposal until she explains that her parents, hovering nearby, are causing her problems. Jeremy quickly proposes, and the parents think they are responsible for his declaration.

For a description, see Summers/*OOA*, 159.

Roles: the father (bass-bar), the mother (alto), the daughter (sop), and Jeremy (ten).

SCORE: vs (n.p., n.d.; LCCN: 84-70826).

Proposal, The, operatic jest in one act by James Walker; libretto (Eng) by Elisabeth Fen and Simon Carter, a translation and adaptation of Anton Chekhov's play *Betrothed* (1903). Composed 1974.

Lomov visits his neighbor Choobukov to ask permission to wed Choobukov's daughter Natalyia. When the daughter returns, she does not know of Lomov's proposal and gets into a fight with him. Lomov, upset by the unforeseen turn of events, leaves. Natalyia, learning the reason for Lomov's visit, faints and then clamors for Lomov to return. When he does, another argument erupts, but the father intervenes and agrees to the union.

Proscenium: . . . on the Demise of Gertrude, chamber opera in one act by Meyer Kupferman; libretto (Eng) by the composer. First performance November 3, 1991, New York, Columbia University, Miller Theatre.

Prude, The, comic ballad opera; libretto (Eng) by Elizabeth Ryves. First performance 1765, London.

The setting is a village in a remote part of England, with the Earl of Lewington disguised as a peasant and in love with Clementina, whose father, Don Pedro de Mendoza, has decided she is to become a nun. Lewington's friend, Sir William Sandby, also disguised as a peasant, is in love with Jenny, as is the villager Roger.

LIBRETTO: English, in *Poems on Several Occasions* (London, 1777); repr. ed. Rubsamen/ *BO*, vol. 2, *Historical and Patriotic Subjects* (1974).

Prunella, intermezzo in four scenes, with music from Thomas Clayton's *Arsinoe* (1705), Bononcini's *Camilla* (1696), and Clayton's *Thomyris* (1707); text (Eng) by Richard Estcourt. First performed at a revival of George Villiers's *The Rehearsal*, between the acts, February 12, 1708, London, Drury Lane Theatre.

The heroine is the daughter of Racina, a grocer.

Psyche, tragedy in a prologue, five acts, and epilogue by Matthew Locke; libretto (Eng) by Thomas Shadwell, after the French tragédie-ballet of Molière, Corneille, and Quinault (1671, Paris). First performance March 9, 1675, London, Dorset Gardens. SCORE: vs (London: T. Ratcliff and N. Thompson, 1675).

Psychles, "opera of groupings and juxtapositions" by Augusta Read Thomas; libretto (Eng) by Andrew Saul Barron. First performance 1987, Chicago, Chicago Opera Theater. SCORE: ms score, holograph (1986, photocopy, NYPL).

Psycho Red, opera in two acts by Charles Wilson; libretto (Eng) by Eugene Benson. First performance May 16, 1978, Guelph, Canada, Spring Festival.

The work concerns a psychiatrist.

Ptahmose and the Magic Spell, trilogy by Halim El-Dabh, which includes *Aton, the Ankh, and the Word** (1972, Washington, D.C.), *The Osiris Ritual** (1972, Washington, D.C.), and *The Twelve Hours Trip** (1972–1973, not perf.).

Pumpkin, The, comic opera in one act by Leslie Kondorossy; libretto (Eng) by the composer and Shawn Hall (Elizabeth Davis), after Bela Pasztor's comedy; translated by C. E. Kulin and J. Klavins. First performance (concert) May 15, 1954, Cleveland, Severance Hall. First stage performance June 1954, Cleveland, American New Opera.

The setting is an American farm. Two old friends, Helen and Rosemary, almost come to blows when Helen's daughter, Shirley, notices that their pumpkin plant has taken root in Rosemary's garden and produced an immense pumpkin. Johnnie, Shirley's fiancé and Rosemary's son, solves the problem by dividing the pumpkin in half and giving the old friends one half each.

For a description of the plot, see Summers/*OOA*, 184–85.

Roles: Shirley (sop), Helen (mezzo), Rosemary (mezzo), and Johnnie (ten/bar). SCORE: vs, holograph (1953, photocopy, NYPL).

Punch and Judy, "tragical comedy or comical tragedy" in one act by Harrison Birtwistle; libretto (Eng) by Stephen Pruslin. First performance June 8, 1968, Aldeburgh Festival, with Jenny Hill, Maureen Morelle (Judy), John Winfield, John Cameron, Geoffrey Chard, and Wyndham Parfitt; conducted by David Atherton. First U.S. performance January 1970, Minnesota, Center Opera Company, Tyrone Guthrie Theater, with Barbara Brandt (Judy), Vern Sutton (Punch), Dan Merriman (Choregos), Sarita Roche (Pretty Polly), Walter Cherwien (the Lawyer), and LeRoy Lehr (the Doctor); conducted by Philip Brunelle; directed by H. Wesley Balk.

Taking the traditional story of Punch and Judy, the author gives Punch a double life. He is violent on the one hand, tossing a baby into the fire, stabbing Judy to death, and killing the Doctor and Lawyer. With the other part of his nature he searches for the ideal woman, Pretty Polly, and eventually succeeds in winning her affections.

For detailed descriptions, see K/*KOB*, 1245–48; K/*NKOB*, 65–67.

Roles: Pretty Polly/Witch (sop), Judy/Fortune Teller (mezzo), Lawyer (ten), Doctor (low bass), Punch (bar), Choregos (bar), and Jack Ketch (low bar).

SCORE: vs ([London]: Universal Edition, [1968]).
LIBRETTO: English (London: Universal Edition, 1968).
BIBLIOGRAPHY: Peter Heyworth, "Birtwistle: Better Than Britten?" *NYT* (June 23, 1068), II, 17 [on premiere]; Harold C. Schonberg, "Opera: 'Punch and Judy,'" *NYT* (Feb. 1, 1970), I, 70 [on U.S. premiere]
DISCOGRAPHY: Bryn-Julson, DeGaetani, Langridge, Roberts, et al., London Sinfonietta; cond. Atherton, Etcetera KTC 2014 (1 CD).

Purgatory, dramatic opera in one act by Hugo Weisgall; libretto (Eng), a setting of the play by William Butler Yeats. First performance February 17, 1961, Washington, D.C., Library of Congress, with Loren Driscoll.
     See the following entry for the plot.
     Roles: Old Man (bass) and Boy (high ten/bar).
SCORE: miniature score, facsimile of ms (Bryn Mawr, Pa.: Merion Music, 1959).

Purgatory, opera in one act by Gordon Crosse; libretto (Eng) by the composer, after Yeats. First performance July 7, 1966, Cheltenham Festival, with Raimund Herincx (the Old Man) and Bernard Dickenson (the Boy); conducted by Leon Lovett; produced by Vladek Sheybal; designed by Cyrile Fradan.
     The story is a line-for-line setting of the text. The Old Man and the Young Boy arrive at a ruined house that once belonged to the Old Man's mother. The mother fell in love with a stable hand, and they married. When she died in childbirth, the father burned down the house during a drunken stupor, after which the son killed him. The Old Man imagines his parents' bridal night and kills the Young Man, his son, with the same knife he used to kill his father, whereupon the bridal scene returns.
     Roles: Old Man (bass) and Young Boy (ten).
BIBLIOGRAPHY: Gordon Crosse, "A Setting of W. B. Yeats," *Opera* XVII (1966), 534–37; John Warrack, "World Reports," *MT* CVII (1966), 588–90 [on premiere].
DISCOGRAPHY: Modenham, Hargreaves, Orch. and Chorus of the Royal Northern College of Music; cond. Lakester, Argo ZRG 810 (CD).

Puritania, or, The Earl and the Maid of Salem, opera in two acts by Edgar Stillman Kelley; libretto (Eng) by C. M. S. McLellan. First performance June 6, 1892, Boston, Tremont Theatre, Prentice Hall Opera Company.
     The setting is near Salem, an English palace, and Whitehall.
     Roles: Vivian Smith (sop); George Trevelyan, Earl of Barrenland, a witch-finder general (bar); Jonathan Blaze, Chief Justice of Salem (bass); Charles II, King of England (bar); Killsin Burgess, a conspirator (bar); Chief Chamberlain (ten); Elizabeth, a maid of Salem (sop); and Abigail, a woman hater (alto).
SCORE: vs (Cincinnati: John Church Co., 1892).

Puritan's Daughter, The, opera in three acts by Michael Balfe; libretto (Eng) by John Vipon Bridgeman. First performance November 30, 1861, London, Covent Garden.
LIBRETTO: English (London: [Royal English Opera] Theatre, [1861?]; New York: Season Print, 1869).

Purse, The, or, The Benevolent Tar, musical drama in one act by William Reeve; libretto (Eng) by James C. Cross. First performance February 8, 1794, London, Little Theatre. First U.S. performance January 7, 1795, Philadelphia, Chestnut Street Theatre.
     Roles: Baron; Will Steady, Theodore, Edmund, Page, and Sally.

Revived as *The Purse, or, American Tar*, 1796, Boston, and *The American Tar Returned from Tripoli*, 1804, Charleston, as a bow to current events.
SCORE: vs (London, ca. 1794).
LIBRETTOS: English (London: William Lane, [1794?]; Boston: W. Pelham, 1797).

Pygmalion, grand opera in one act by Henry Houseley; libretto (Eng) by S. Frances Houseley. First performance January 30, 1912, Denver, El Jebel Temple.

In this treatment of the Greek myth, Narcissus ignores the nymph Echo, who is desperately in love with him, and she wastes away until only her voice is left. As punishment Nemesis gets Narcissus to drink from and gaze into a fountain, in which he sees his own reflection and falls hopelessly in love with an image that, of course, does not return his love, which leads to his death.

Also burlesque, with music by Frank Musgrave, text by William Brough (1867, London).

Pyramus and Thisbe, comic masque by Richard Leveridge; libretto (Eng) by the composer, after the last act of Shakespeare's *A Midsummer Night's Dream*. First performance April 11, 1716, London, Drury Lane Theatre, with Leveridge (Pyramus) and George Pack (Thisbe).

The work is a parody of Italian opera.
LIBRETTO: English (London: W. Mears, 1716).

Pyramus and Thisbe, "mock opera" in one act by Frederic Lampe; libretto (Eng) probably by the composer, after the version by Richard Leveridge (see previous entry). First performance January 25, 1745, London, Covent Garden.

The work includes an introduction that presents Mr. Semibreve, composer of the pretend opera, which is all-sung. The "opera" itself is constantly interrupted by rude interjections by the Master and the Prompter (not unlike, perhaps, Richard Strauss's *Ariadne auf Naxos*.

In keeping with the practice that an opera could not have an unhappy conclusion, a "happy ending" is added, whereby the couple is revived, and they sing the Epilogue.

For a detailed description, see Fiske/*ETM*, 157–59.

Also melodrama, with music by Baudron (1783, Paris).
SCORE: vs (London: J. Walsh, n.d.).

Pyramus and Thisbe, chamber opera in one scene by Neely Bruce; libretto (Eng) by the composer, after Shakespeare. First performance spring 1965, Tuscaloosa, University of Alabama.

Pyramus and Thisbe, opera in two scenes by Robert Convery; libretto (Eng) by the composer, after Shakespeare. First performance Waterford, Connecticut, 1982. Also October 18, 1985, New York, Juilliard School.

Pyrrus and Demetrius, opera in three acts by Nicola Haym, after A. Scarlatti's *Pirro e Demetrio* (1694, Naples) and *Gli equivoci nel sembiante* (1690, Rome); libretto (Eng), a translation by Owen Swiney and Armstrong of A. Morselli's original text. First performance December 14, 1708, London, Queen's Theatre, Haymarket, with the castrato Nicolini (i.e., Nicolo Grimaldi) and Mrs. Tofts.

The first bilingual opera, the work was sung in English and Italian. Twenty-one of the airs were by Haym, fourteen by Scarlatti, and nineteen by other composers.
SCORE: vs ([London: Walsh, Randall & Hare, 1709]).

Q

Quaker, The, comic opera in two acts by Charles Dibdin; libretto (Eng) by the composer, after Charles Shadwell. First performance May 3, 1775, London, Drury Lane Theatre, with Mr. Bannister (the Quaker), Mr. Dibdin (Lubin), and Miss Wilde (Gillian).

The hero, Steady, is a middle-aged Quaker beloved by the entire town. He hopes to wed Gillian, the daughter of Easy, his steward. The young Lubin, who has been away, returns and also wants to wed Gillian. Playing on Steady's good nature, Lubin asks the Quaker for his advice on how Lubin can get his beloved to marry him (but without the Quaker's knowing the identities of those involved). When Steady writes a letter to support Lubin in his quest, Gillian accepts his proposal. But Steady has not been fooled at all. His generosity has allowed him to give way to his rival.

For a detailed description, see Fiske/*ETM*, 373–77.
LIBRETTO: English (London: J. Bell, 1777; New York: D. Longworth, 1806).

Quaker's Opera, The, ballad opera in three acts; libretto (Eng) by Thomas Walker. First performance September 24, 1728, London, Bartholemew Fair; October 31, 1728, London, Little Theatre in the Haymarket.

The work is set in and around Newgate Prison, London. Its hero is Jack Shepherd, and many of the characters are robbers and prostitutes.

Major roles: Rust, an old Quaker, and Jack Shepherd, a new Quaker.
LIBRETTO: English, with airs (1728, London); repr. ed. Rubsamen/*BO*, vol. 2, *Historical and Patriotic Subjects* (1974).

Quarry, The, opera in one act for young players by John Joubert; libretto (Eng) by David Holbrook. First performance May 26, 1965, Wembley, England.

The setting is near an old quarry on the property of John Blunt, near Ware, Hertfordshire, and is concerned with the destruction of the earth's natural resources.
SCORE: vs (London: Novello; New York: Mills Music, [1967]).
LIBRETTO: English (London: Novello, [1966]).

Quarry, opera by Meredith Monk. Composed 1976.

The work is scored for thirty-eight voices, two pump organs, two soprano recorders, and tape.

Quartette, The, or, Interrupted Harmony, opera in one act by Charles Edward Horn; libretto (Eng). First performance April 29, 1829, New York, Bowery Theatre.

Quasimodo, or, The Gipsy Girl of Notre Dame, operatic romance by George Rodwell; libretto (Eng) by Edward Fitzball, after Victor Hugo's novel *Notre-Dame de Paris* (1831). First performance February 2, 1836, London, Covent Garden, with Miss Vincent (Esmeralda).

A telling of the story of Quasimodo, the hunchback of Notre Dame, and Esmeralda, the gypsy girl whom he saves from the evil Friar Frollo.

W. Fry's *Notre-Dame of Paris** (1864, Philadelphia) is another setting.

Queen Christina, opera by Beth Anderson; libretto (Eng). First performance December 1, 1973, Oakland, California, Mills College.

Queenie Pie, "street opera buffa" by Edward ("Duke") Ellington; completed by Maurice Peress and Barrie Lee Hall; libretto (Eng) by Ellington and George C. Wolfe; lyrics by George David Weiss. First performance September 20, 1986, Philadelphia, with Teresa Burrell (Queenie Pie), Patty Holley (Cafe Olay), and Larry Marshall (Lil Daddy); conducted by Mercer Ellington.

The plot concerns an annual beauty contest for hairdressers. The vain and proud Queenie Pie is about to win the contest for the thirteenth straight year when she is challenged by the long-legged Cafe Olay, a visitor from New Orleans. The challenge makes Queenie examine her empty life, and although she wins the title, she surrenders her crown and accepts the enamored Lil Daddy's offer to go away with him.

Among the musical highlights are the opening "Harlem Seat," the flapper dance "The Hairdo Hop," and the rousing finale.

The work was incomplete when Ellington died in 1974; Peress, supervised by Mercer Ellington, redid the score, Wolfe retooled the libretto, and Weiss put new words to the tunes.
BIBLIOGRAPHY: Michael Walsh, "Sounding a Joyous Jubilee," *Time* (Sept. 29, 1986), 70 [on premiere].

Queen of a Day, The, comic opera in two acts by Edward Fitzwilliam, after Adam's *La reine d'un jour*; libretto (Eng) by John Thomas Haines (1841) and John B. Buckstone (1851), after Scribe and Vernoy de Saint-Georges. First performance June 14, 1841, London, Surrey Theatre; August 13, 1851, London, Theatre Royal, Haymarket.
LIBRETTO: English, Buckstone version (Boston: J. H. Eastburn, 1855).

Queen of Cornwall, The, music drama in two acts by Rutland Boughton; libretto (Eng) by the composer, after Thomas Hardy's drama (1923). First performance August 21, 1924, Glastonbury, Assembly Rooms.

A setting of the story of King Mark, Queen Iseult, and Tristram. Unlike Wagner's *Tristan und Isolde*, there are two Iseults in this version; Tristram's wife, Iseult, lyingly tells him that Queen Iseult will not meet him. Nonetheless, Tristram goes to Cornwall in disguise, followed by the suspicious Mark and Iseult. When King Mark finds Queen Iseult and Tristram together, he kills Tristram, whereupon the queen stabs Mark and leaps to her death over a precipice.

Also unfinished opera by John Becker (begun 1956).
SCORE: overture, vs (London: Joseph Williams, 1926).

Queen of Spain, The, or, Farinelli in Madrid, musical entertainment by John Frederick Lampe; libretto (Eng) probably by James Ayres. First performance April 16, 1744, London, Little Theatre in the Haymarket, with Isabella Lampe and Gustavus Waltz.

Queen of the May, The, musical entertainment in one act by James Hook. First performance May 22, 1787, London, Vauxhall Gardens.

Queen of the Thames, The, or, The Anglers, operetta in one act by John Liptrot Hatton; libretto (Eng) by Edward Fitzball. First performance February 25, 1842, London, Drury Lane Theatre, with Emma Romer.

LIBRETTO: English (London: G. Berger, 1843).

Queerest Courtship, The, comic operetta in one act by Alfred B. Sedgwick, after Jacques Offenbach's *La princesse de Trébizonde* (1869, Baden-Baden); libretto (Eng) by the composer. First performance ca. 1875, Chicago?

The story concerns Peter, whose dishonest physician plots to cheat him out of his intended wife's substantial dowry by turning Peter into a hypochondriac. Peter and the young woman meet accidentally, and all ends well for the young couple.

Roles: Mary, a young lady; and Peter Popper, a hypochondriac.
SCORE AND LIBRETTO: vs (Chicago: Dramatic Publishing Company, 1911?); repr. ed. Michael Meckna, *NAMT*, vol. 7 (1994).

Quentin Durward, "new grand opera" in three acts by Henry R. Laurent; libretto (Eng) by Edward Fitzball, after Sir Walter Scott's novel (1823). First performance December 6, 1848, London, Covent Garden.

The hero of the title is a young member of the French king's guards. He seeks to wed Isabella; his request gains momentum when he saves the king's life during a boar hunt.
LIBRETTO: English (London: J. K. Chapman, 1848).

Quentin Durward, opera in three acts by Alick Maclean; libretto (Eng) by Sheridan Ross, after Sir Walter Scott's novel (1823). Composed 1893. First performance January 13, 1920, Newcastle-upon-Tyne, Carl Rosa Opera Company.

Also set by F. A. Gevaert (1858, Paris).
SCORE: vs (London: E. Ascherberg; New York: E. Schuberth, 1894).

Question of Love, A, monodrama by Patricia Gilbert; libretto (Eng) by the composer. First performance November 7, 1985, London, Conway Hall, with Gilbert (Barbara).

The work concerns a woman, Barbara, who fears that her husband is unfaithful. She attempts to find out the truth by making a series of telephone calls.
BIBLIOGRAPHY: Richard Fairman, review, *Opera* XXXVI (June 1985), 112 [on premiere].

Question of Taste, A, opera in one act by William Schuman; libretto (Eng) by J. D. McClatchy, based on Roald Dahl's story *Taste*. First performance June 24, 1989, Cooperstown, New York, Glimmerglass Opera, with Risa Renae Harman (Louise) and Michael Rees Davis (Tom); conducted by Stewart Robertson. Also December 12, 1990, New York, Juilliard School.

The setting is New York at the turn of the twentieth century. In the story, a rich businessman, Mr. Schofield, is willing to offer his daughter Louise's hand in marriage to the winner of a blind wine-tasting test, convinced that Phillisto Pratt, a wine connoisseur, will be unable to do so and thereby forfeit a large sum to serve as Louise's dowry. Tom, Louise's boyfriend, becomes increasingly dismayed as Pratt seems to be succeeding and passes the test. The tables are turned when Mrs. Hudson, the housekeeper, enters with Mr. Pratt's reading glasses, which she discovered in the wine cabinet. The disgraced Pratt leaves, and Tom and Louise prepare for a future sweetened by Pratt's hefty check.

For a description, see Summers/*OOA*, 269–70.
Major roles: Louise (sop), Mr. Schofield (bar), Phillisto Pratt (bass-bar), Tom (ten), and Mrs. Judson (mezzo).

SCORE: vs (Bryn Mawr, Pa.: Merion Music, 1990).
BIBLIOGRAPHY: Bernard Holland, "'Casey,' New Schuman Work," *NYT* (June 26, 1989), C, 14 [on premiere]; Leslie Kandell, "Cooperstown," *MA* CIX (Nov. 1989), 36 [on premiere]. DISCOGRAPHY: Juilliard Orch., Juilliard Opera soloists; cond. Schwarz, Delos DE 1030.

Quiet Game of Cribble, A, opera in one act by Martin Kalmanoff; libretto (Eng) by the composer. First performance (radio) June 8, 1954, New York, WNYC, Greenwich House Workshop.

A husband and wife become consumed by a new word game called Cribble, during which they turn down tickets to the opera and almost come to blows because of the game.

For a description, see Summers/*OOA*, 170–71.

Roles: wife (sop) and husband (bar).
BIBLIOGRAPHY: review, *NYT* (June 9, 1954), 38 [on radio premiere].

Quiet Place, A, opera in one act by Leonard Bernstein; libretto (Eng) by Stephen Wadsworth; sequel to *Trouble in Tahiti*.* First performance June 17, 1983, Houston, Houston Grand Opera, with Timothy Nolen (Junior), Chester Ludgin (Sam), Peter Kazaras (François), Sheri Greenawald (Dede), Theodor Uppman (Bill), Dana Krueger (Susie), Carolyne James (Mrs. Doc), Peter Harrower (Doc), and Douglas Perry (the analyst); conducted by John DeMain; directed by Peter Mark Schifter. Revised version, in three acts, June 19, 1984, Milan, Teatro alla Scala, with the same cast, except for Robert Galbraith (Junior) and Sheila Nadler (Mrs. Doc); conducted by John Mauceri; directed by Stephen Wadsworth.

The story, with its autobiographical references to the composer and his family, resumes thirty years after *Trouble in Tahiti* ends. The unhappy family has disintegrated, with the unhappy wife, Dinah, dying while in a drunken haze at the wheel of her car. At her funeral, her husband, Sam, full of guilt and hurt, faces his unhappy and mixed-up children: his homosexual and psychotic son Junior and daughter Dede, who has wed François, her brother's former lover; the three live together.

As the opera progresses, the protagonists come to accept their loss and, after bitter squabbling, are able to reconcile, with the help of advice left in Dinah's suicide note.

For a detailed plot synopsis, see K/*NKOB*, 61–62.

Roles (orig. version): Sam (bass), Dede (sop), François (ten), Junior (bar), Susie (mezzo), Mrs. Doc (alto), Bill (bar), and analyst (ten).

In the revised version, *Trouble in Tahiti* forms the second act and is presented as a reverie of Sam.

SCORE: vs (New York: Jalni, 1988).
BIBLIOGRAPHY: Donal Henahan, "Opera: Bernstein's 'Quiet Place' Opens in Houston," *NYT* (June 20, 1983), III, 13; Scott F. Heumann, "Our Critics Abroad: America. The New Bernstein," *Opera* XXXIV (1983), 1117–20 [on premiere]; Robert Jacobson, "Reports: U.S.," *ON* XLVIII (Sept. 1983), 52–53 [on premiere].
DISCOGRAPHY: White, Morgan, Kraft, James, Brandstetter, Kazaras, Ludgin, Uppman, Kuether, Austrian Radio; cond. Bernstein, DG 419761 (2 CDs); rev. John W. Freeman, "Recordings," *ON* LII (Mar. 26, 1988), 43.

Quiros, television opera by Peter Sculthorpe; libretto (Eng) by Brian Bell. First performance July 1, 1982, Australian Broadcasting Company; conducted by Myer Fredman.

The story revolves around a seventeenth-century Portuguese sea captain who searches in vain for *Terra Australis*, the promised land; the captain's quest is mirrored by his parallel emotional search.

R

Rab the Rhymer, ballad opera in three acts, with songs arranged by Isobel Dunlop and Hans Oppenheim; libretto (Eng) by Eric Crozier. First performance July 3, 1953, Aberdeen, Scotland, Haddo House.

Rachel, opera in two acts by Kenton Coe; libretto (Eng) by Anne Howard Bailey. First performance April 9, 1989, Knoxville, Tennessee, Knoxville Opera.
The plot is based on the love story of Andrew Jackson and his wife, Rachel.

Raft, The, musical drama in one act by William Reeve; libretto (Eng) by James C. Cross. First performance March 31, 1798, London, Covent Garden.
LIBRETTO: English (London: J. Barker, 1798).

Ragged Uproar, The, or, The Oxford Roratory, "a new dramatic satire in many scenes, and one very long act"; libretto (Eng) by Joan Plotwell (pseud.). First performance 1754, London.
The characters include witches, gypsies, politicians, and fortune tellers.
LIBRETTO: English (London: Printed for G. Pote . . . [1754]); repr. ed. Rubsamen/*BO*, vol. 6, *Satire, Burlesque, Protest, and Ridicule,* II (1974).

Rajah of Shivapore, "comic opera of the East" in two acts by Alfred Hill; libretto (Eng) by David H. Souter. First performance December 15, 1917, Sydney, Australia.
The setting is India, and the story involves a gullible rajah, an unscrupulous temple keeper, and the latter's daughter, with whom the rajah falls in love.

Rajah's Diamond, The, television opera in one act by Alun Hoddinott; libretto (Eng) by Myfanwy Piper, after Robert Louis Stevenson. First performance November 24, 1979, London, BBC.

Rajah's Ruby, The, opera in one act by Seymour Barab; libretto (Eng) by the composer. First performance April 29, 1958, New York, Sullivan Street Playhouse, with Ronald Bush and Arthur Komar providing the piano accompaniment.
In the story a bored couple tries to create excitement by means of having a mystery enacted in their living room.
BIBLIOGRAPHY: Ross Parmenter, review, *NYT* (April 30, 1958), 29 [on premiere].

Rake's Progress, The, opera by John Whitaker; libretto (Eng) by Charles Dibdin Jr. First performance July 10, 1826, London, Surrey Theatre.

Rake's Progress, The, opera in three acts and an epilogue by Igor Stravinsky; libretto (Eng) by W. H. Auden and Chester Kallman, after Hogarth's eight engravings (1735). First performance September 11, 1951, Venice, Teatro La Fenice, with Elisabeth Schwarzkopf (Anne Trulove), Jennie Tourel (Baba the Turk), Robert Rounseville (Tom Rakewell), Otakar Kraus (Nick Shadow), and Hughes Cuénod (Sellem); conducted by the composer. First U.S. performance February 14, 1953, New York, Metropolitan Opera, with Hilde Gueden (Anne), Blanche Thebom (Baba), Eugene Conley (Tom), and Mack

Harrell (Shadow); conducted by Fritz Reiner; directed by Horace Armistead; produced by George Balanchine. First British performance August 25, 1953, Edinburgh, Glyndebourne Company, with Elsie Morison (Anne), Nan Merriman (Baba), Richard Lewis (Tom), and Jerome Hines (Nick Shadow); conducted by Alfred Wallenstein. Revived, in a version updated to 1920s London, November 20, 1997, New York, Metropolitan Opera, with Dawn Upshaw (Anne), Denyce Graves (Baba), Jerry Hadley (Tom), David Pittsinger (Trulove), and Samuel Ramey (Nick Shadow); conducted by James Levine; directed by Jonathan Miller; designed by Peter Davison.

The setting is eighteenth-century England. In the garden of Trulove's country home, Anne Trulove and her suitor, the poor Tom Rakewell, sing of their love in "The Woods Are Green." But when Anne's father offers Tom a job as an accountant, he refuses it, whereupon Trulove warns that he will not let his daughter marry a wastrel. The Truloves leave Tom to his thoughts, which he utters in the recitative and aria "Here I Stand"/ "Since It Is Not by Merit" and wishes aloud that he had money. Suddenly, he is approached by the mysterious Nick Shadow. Anne and his father return, and Shadow declares that Tom has come into a great deal of money following the death of "an uncle," in the aria "Fair Lady, Gracious Gentlemen." Shadow arranges to serve Tom for a year and a day, after which Shadow will name his fee. Following the quartet "I Wished but Once," Shadow and Tom head off to London. As the first scene ends, Shadow turns to the audience and declares, ominously, "The Progress of a Rake Begins."

The second scene takes place in Mother Goose's brothel in London. The group of Whores and Roaring Boys offer the lusty chorus "A Toast to Our Commanders," and Shadow and Mother Goose begin their tutelage of Tom for a life of debauchery, urged on by the chorus. Scene 3 is set back in Trulove's garden. Anne, in an extended scena, agonizes over Tom's absence. As the act concludes, she sings the coloratura aria/ cabaletta "Quietly, Night"/ "I Go, I Go to Him."

The second act opens in the morning room of Tom's town house. He is bored, and Shadow uses Tom's state to convince him to defy convention and marry the bearded Baba the Turk, in the aria "In Youth the Panting Slave." The scene closes with Tom and Shadow's duet "My Tale Shall Be Told"/"Come Master Prepare." The next scene is set before Tom's house. Anne has come in search of her beloved, and she voices her unease in the recitative and arioso "How Strange!"/"O Heart Be Stronger." Her fears are confirmed when Tom arrives and admits to her that he has married another; Baba, his new bride, is sitting in his carriage and voicing her unhappiness about the delay that his discussion with Anne has caused. The scene closes with the trio "Could It Then Have Been Known"/"It Is Done, It Is Done"/ "Why This Delay?" and Tom's telling the curious Baba that Anne is "only a milk-maid." Scene 3 is set in Tom's morning room, now cluttered with outlandish acquisitions. Baba tries to arouse Tom's interest with "Come, Sweet, Come," but he ignores her. Shadow arrives and convinces Tom to invest his money in an "excellent machine" that seems to turn stones into bread; their duet "Thanks to This Excellent Device"/"A Word to All My Friends" ends the act, during which Shadow tells the audience that his master is a fool.

As the third act begins, Tom, of course, has lost everything because of Shadow's scheme. Sellem is conducting an auction in Tom's morning room, with Baba being the final "object" offered. She takes exception to this in the aria "Sold! Annoyed!" Anne comes in, looking for Tom, who has disappeared, and Baba urges her to go after him, since he still loves her, in the recitative and duet "You Love Him, Seek to Set Him

Right," accompanied by chorus and Sellem. The scene closes with Anne's "I Go to Him" and Baba's "The Next Time You See Baba." Rakewell and Shadow sing a ballad offstage. The second scene is set in a graveyard, on the 366th day of Shadow's service. Tom is filled with foreboding when he sees a newly dug grave and sings "How Dark and Dreadful Is This Place," accompanied by a harpsichord. Shadow reveals himself to be the Devil and tries to claim Tom's soul as payment for his services. As the clock begins to strike the midnight hour, Shadow offers Rakewell his freedom if he can name each of three cards Shadow pulls out. Tom thinks of Anne and guesses, correctly, the Queen of Hearts. Seeing the gravedigger's spade, Tom guesses "the deuce," which is also correct. Thinking he can fool Tom, Shadow pulls out the Queen of Hearts again, which Tom guesses when he hears Anne singing a part of her act 2 aria. Shadow, defeated, intones "I Burn! I Freeze!" and descends into the grave meant for Tom. But Tom is not free—Shadow has taken Tom's sanity. The final scene is set in Bedlam, an asylum. Tom believes himself to be Adonis, who longs for Venus (Anne). The accompanying chorus, now asylum inmates, mock his delusions. Anne comes to visit Tom one last time, and they offer the touching duet "In a Foolish Dream"/"What Should I Forgive?" She sings him to sleep with a lullaby and leaves, at the urging of her father, who has accompanied her. Tom awakes; not seeing Anne, he sings the plaintive "Where Art Thou, Venus?" and dies, his heart broken. The chorus grieves with "Mourn for Adonis."

The Epilogue, in vaudeville style, is sung by the five principals, Anne, Baba, Trulove, Tom, and Shadow; the men are without their wigs, and Baba is minus her beard. The quintet concludes with the moral of the tale: "For idle ears/And hands and minds/ The Devil finds/A work to do."

For more detailed descriptions, see *COH*, ed. Paul Griffiths (1982); K/*KOB*, 1064–69; K/*NKOB*, 797–801; *ENOG* 43 (1991), 45–74.

Major roles: Tom Rakewell (ten); Anne Trulove (sop); Nick Shadow (bar); Baba the Turk (mezzo); Sellem, the auctioneer (ten); Trulove, Anne's father (bass); and Keeper of the Madhouse (bass).

The work epitomizes Stravinsky's neoclassic style, and various recitatives are accompanied by a harpsichord, for example, in the graveyard scene. The sinister Shadow has as his counterpart such figures as Mephistopheles in Gounod's *Faust* (1859) and the evil foursome in Offenbach's *Les contes d'Hoffmann* (1882). Despite the brilliance of the work, it has rarely been revived, retuning to the Met in 1997 after a forty-four-year absence (see above).

SCORE: miniature score (London: Boosey & Hawkes, 1951).

LIBRETTO: English (London and New York: Boosey & Hawkes, 1951).

BIBLIOGRAPHY: Shirley Fleming, "A Sweeping 'Rake': We Met Again," *New York Post* (Nov. 23, 1997), 35 [on Met revival]; Andrew Porter, "Musical Events: A Rake among Scholars," *NY* LVIII (Nov. 22, 1988), 181–82 [on 1988 revival, Ann Arbor, Mich.].

DISCOGRAPHY: Metropolitan Opera; cond. F. Reiner (1953), CBS.

VIDEO: N. Willis, F. Lott, R. Elias, L. Goeke, T. Lawlor, J. Fryatt, R. Van Allan, S. Ramey; cond. B. Haitink, Glyndebourne Opera (1977), Historical Recording Enterprises 543; F. Lott, R. Elias, L. Goeke, S. Ramey, Glyndebourne Chorus, London Philharmonic Orch.; cond. B. Haitink, cond. Heather, Pickwick VHS SL 2008 (1985, 2 VHS).

Raleigh's Dream, opera in a prologue and eight scenes by Iain Hamilton; libretto (Eng) by the composer. First performance June 3, 1984, Durham, North Carolina, Duke University, with Roger Roloff (Raleigh), and Janice Harsanyi (Elizabeth I); conducted by the composer; directed by J. Bennett Smith.

In the prologue, set in 1618, Sir Walter Raleigh, about to be executed for defying the orders of James I, relives the important events of his life. The following scenes examine his relationship with Queen Elizabeth I and his sponsorship of the ill-fated colony in Roanoke, Virginia. The work concludes with the discovery of the disappearance of the colony at Roanoke in 1591.

Composed to celebrate the 400th anniversary of Raleigh's Roanoke expedition.
BIBLIOGRAPHY: Tim Page, "Opera: Raleigh's Story," *NYT* (June 5, 1984), III, 24 [on premiere].

Ralph and the Stalking Bear, children's opera in one act by Martin Kalmanoff; libretto (Eng). First performance July 8, 1979, Monticello, New York.

Ramah Droog, or, Wine Does Wonders, comic opera in three acts by William Reeve and Joseph Mazzinghi; libretto (Eng) by James Cobb. First performance November 12, 1798, London, Covent Garden. First U.S. performance March 18, 1803, Philadelphia, Chestnut Street Theatre.

The title comes from the name of a hilltop fort in India. A contingent of British troops is taken prisoner during a skirmish with the rajah, but they are freed when one of them pretends to be a doctor and cures the ailing ruler. A second group attacks the fortress and restores the princess to her rightful throne.
SCORE: vs (London, ca. 1798).
LIBRETTO: English (London: T. N. Longman and O. Rees, 1800; New York: D. Longworth, 1809).

Ramuntcho, opera in three acts by Deems Taylor; libretto (Eng) by the composer, after the novel (1897) by Pierre Loti. First performance February 7, 1942, Philadelphia, Academy of Music.

The work takes place in the Basque village of Etchézar, near the Spanish border, at the end of the nineteenth century.

Major roles: Ramuntcho, a young smuggler (ten); Arrochkoa, his best friend (bar); Gracieuse, Arrochkoa's sister (sop); Pantchika, his sweetheart (sop); Dolores (alto); Gorosteguy, head smuggler (bass); Haramburu, retired champion (bass); and Vicar of Etchézar (bar).
SCORE: vs (New York: J. Fischer & Bro., 1942).

Ransom of Red Chief, The, opera in one act by Robert Xavier Rodríguez; libretto (Eng) by Daniel Dibbern, after O. Henry. First performance October 10, 1986, Mesquite, Texas, Lyric Opera of Dallas.

The setting is a small town on the plains of west Texas in the mid-1890s. Two minor criminals from the North, Sam and Bill, have taken refuge outside a town after kidnapping Johnny, the only child of the widowed town banker. The child is having a good time, including playing the part of "Red Chief" and carrying out several raids. Sam and Bill have had their fill of the situation and want to get rid of their eager captive. They receive a ransom note *from* the banker, who offers to take the boy back if his kidnappers will pay $250. Accepting the banker's demands, Bill and Sam, despite Johnny's best efforts to disrupt his return, give Johnny back and beat a hasty retreat.

Major roles: Sam (ten), Bill (bass-bar), and Johnny (boy sop).

Rape of Europa by Jupiter, The, masque in one act, with music by John Eccles; libretto (Eng) by Peter Anthony Motteux. First performance, with a revival of John Wilmot's *Valentinian*, October 1694, London, Dorset Garden, with Mr. Bowman (Jupiter), Mrs. Bracegirdle (Europa), and Mr. Magnus (Mercury).

Jupiter, in the guise of a bull, abducts and woos Europa, daughter of King Agenor.

LIBRETTO: English (London: M. Bennet, 1694); repr. ed. introd. Lucyle Hook, Augustan Reprint Society, no. 208 (Los Angeles: Clark Memorial Library, University of California, 1981).

Rape of Helen, The, "a mock opera" (ballad opera); libretto (Eng) by John Breval. First performance 1737, London, Covent Garden, with Mr. Laguerre (Mercury), Mr. Hippisley (Menelaus), Thomas Salway (Paris), Mrs. Cantrell (Juno), Mrs. Egleton (Minerva), Miss Norsa (Venus), and Miss Binks (Helen).

The setting is Mycenae.

LIBRETTO: English (London: J. Wilford, 1737); repr. ed. Rubsamen/*BO*, vol. 7, *Classical Subjects I: Satire and Burlesque* (1974).

Rape of Lucretia, The, opera in a prologue, two acts, and epilogue by Benjamin Britten; libretto (Eng) by Ronald Duncan, after André Obey's play *Le viol de Lucrèce* (1931), itself based on Shakespeare's poem *The Rape of Lucrece* (1594). First performance July 12, 1946, Glyndebourne, Opera House, with Joan Cross (female chorus), Kathleen Ferrier (Lucretia), Peter Pears (male chorus), Otakar Kraus (Tarquinius), Edmund Donlevy (Junius), Anna Pollak (Bianca), and Margaret Ritchie (Lucia); conducted by Ernest Ansermet; designed by John Piper. First U.S. performance June 1, 1947, Chicago, with Regina Resnik (Lucretia); conducted by Paul Breisach.

The story concerns the proud, self-destructive Tarquinius, who, learning of the infidelity of the Roman wives, tries to seduce the lone exception, Lucretia, wife of Collatinus, one of his comrades. When she refuses Tarquinius's advances, he rapes her. Crushed by her shame, she kills herself before the return of her husband.

For a detailed plot synopsis see K/*KOB*, 1169–74; K/*KNOB*, 105–7.

A male (ten) and female (sop) chorus comment on the unfolding events and offer a moral on the tragedy.

Major roles: Tarquinius, Prince of Rome (bar); Lucretia (mezzo); Collatinus, her husband (bass); Lucia, her attendant (sop); Bianca, her nurse (alto); and Junius, a Roman general (bar).

Among the musical highlights is Lucretia's pensive arioso of act 1, scene 1, "How Cruel Men Are to Teach Us Love!" Britten's first opera for chamber ensemble, it is also unusual in his output in having a female voice as the central character.

SCORE: vs (London and New York: Boosey & Hawkes, [1947]).

LIBRETTO: English (London: Faber and Faber, [1953]).

BIBLIOGRAPHY: *The Rape of Lucretia: A Symposium* (London: Bodley Head, 1948).

DISCOGRAPHY: H. Harper, J. Baker, P. Pears, B. Drake, B. Luxon, J. Shirley-Quirk, English Chamber Orch.; cond. Britten, London 2-42566-2 (2 CDs).

VIDEO: K. Harries, C. Pope, J. Rigby, A. M. Owens, A. R. Johnson, R. Smythe, A. Opie, R. Van Allan, English National Orch., cond. L. Friend, Virgin VHS VVD 617.

Rappaccini's Daughter, opera in three acts by Margaret Garwood; libretto (Eng) by the composer, after Nathaniel Hawthorne's tale (1844). First performance November 23, 1980, Philadelphia (concert); first performance (stage) May 6, 1983, Philadelphia, Trocadero Theater, with Jean Bradel (Beata), Michael Ballam (Giovanni), Barry Ellison (Baglione), Ralph Bassett (Rappaccini), and Jeanne Haughan (the landlady); conducted by Barbara Silverstein; produced by Maggie Harrer.

Ignoring warnings from his friend Baglione, Giovanni courts Beata, the daughter of the scientist Rappaccini. Soon Giovanni finds himself in love with the girl, despite the fact that he realizes that her touch means illness and death. Baglione intervenes and gives his friend, now ill, medicine he says will counteract the poisons in Beata's garden and cure the girl as well. Beata takes the antidote, although she knows it will kill her. As Rappaccini returns, Beata dies.

Major roles: Beata (sop), Giovanni (ten), Baglione (bar), Rappaccini (bass-bar), and the landlady (mezzo).

For a detailed description, see Kornick/*RAO*, 109–10.

SCORE: ms score, holograph (photocopy, 1993?, NYPL).

BIBLIOGRAPHY: William Ashbrook, "Philadelphia," *Opera* XXXIV (1983), 1122–23 [on stage premiere]; Max de Schauensee, review, *Opera* XXXII (Feb. 1981), 163 [on premiere].

Rappaccini's Daughter, opera in one act by Dennis Riley; libretto by the composer and Joseph Pazillo, after Hawthorne. Composed 1981–1984.

SCORE: vs (New York: American Music Center, 1984).

Rappaccini's Daughter, chamber opera in one act by Sam Dennison; libretto (Eng) by Karen Campbell, after Hawthorne. First performance 1984, Philadelphia. Revised version March 22, 1985, Washington, D.C.

SCORE: vs, rev. ed. Georgia Marshall (Miami: E. F. Kalmus, 1985).

Rappaccini's Daughter, opera in one act by Ellen Bender; libretto (Eng) by Robert DiDomenica, after Hawthorne. First performance October 28, 1992, Boston, New England Conservatory of Music.

For solo voices (sop, mezzo, ten, bass-bar, bass) and orchestra.

Other settings include C. Cadman's *The Garden of Mystery** (1915, New York); D. Catán's *La hija de Rappaccini* (1991, Mexico City); and R. Vaughan Williams's *The Poisoned Kiss** (1936, Cambridge).

SCORE: holograph, signed (photocopy, 1990, NYPL).

Rapunzel, opera in three acts by Tom Hammond; libretto (Eng) by the composer, after the Brothers Grimm. First performance March 5, 1953, Colchester, Essex, Cooperative Hall.

In this fairy-tale setting, Rapunzel is locked in a tower and saved by the prince.

Rapunzel, opera in one act by Lou Harrison, "a psychological reinterpretation of the old fairy tale"; libretto (Eng) by William Morris, after his poem (1883). First performance May 14, 1959, New York, YMHA, Kaufmann Concert Hall, with Marianne Weltmann (Rapunzel), David Smith (Prince Sebald), and Ruth Conway (the witch); conducted by Newell Jenkins; produced by James Price; designed by Robert Mitchell.

The music is based on a tone row.

SCORE: vs, "My Mother Taught Me Many Prayers," for voice, flute, string trio, harp, piano (New York: Peer International, [1966]).

BIBLIOGRAPHY: Howard Taubman, "Opera: Two Premieres," *NYT* (May 15, 1959), 25.

DISCOGRAPHY: Maginnis, McMurty, Duykers, Ensemble Parallèle; cond. Paiement, New Albion Records, NAR CD 093 (1997, San Francisco); rev. Patrick J. Smith, "Recordings," *ON* LXII (Aug. 1997), 33.

Rapunzel, opera in one act by Richard Brooks; libretto (Eng) by Harold Mason, after the Brothers Grimm. First performance January 22, 1971, Binghamton, New York.

In this version of the fairy tale, Rapunzel is imprisoned in a tower by the Witch and guarded by the Strawman. When the Prince comes to rescue Rapunzel, he is stopped by the Witch, who blinds him and escapes with the maiden. The Prince is aided by the Minstrel to find his beloved, the Witch's power is destroyed, and the opera ends happily.

For a detailed description, see Eaton/*OP* II, 317–18.

Major roles: Rapunzel (sop), the Prince (ten), the Minstrel (bar), and the Witch (mezzo).

RareArea, music theater piece by Marc Ream; libretto (Eng) by George Coates. First performance 1985, Brussels. First U.S. performance June 22, 1985, Berkeley, George Coates Performance Works, with John Duykers and Kathryn Neale.

The work has no story per se but protests against nationalism.

The music is composed in a minimalist, tonal style.

BIBLIOGRAPHY: Stephanie von Buchau, review, *ON* L (Sept. 1985), 53 [on U.S. premiere].

Rasputin, opera in two acts by Jay Reise; libretto (Eng) by the composer and Frank Corsaro. First performance (excerpts, concert) March 13, 1988, New York, Solomon R. Guggenheim Museum, with Margaret Cusack, Mark S. Doss, Jon Garrison, and John Lankston; John Beeson (piano). First full performance September 17, 1988, New York, City Opera, with Cusack, Garrison, and John Cheek; conducted by Christopher Keene.

The story focuses on the megalomaniacal Rasputin and Yusupov, the immoral Russian aristocrat who has his own view of the country's future. In order to break Rasputin's hold over Tsar Nicholas and Alexandra, his wife, Yusupov and his henchmen are finally able to kill the resilient Rasputin. Chaos results, and the work ends with the gunfire that kills the royal family.

Major roles: Rasputin (bass-bar); Alexandra (sop); Prince Felix Yusupov, the Tsar's cousin (ten); and Tsar Nicholas II (ten).

Other operas on Rasputin are K. A. Hartmann's *The Life and Death of the Holy Devil* (comp. 1928; perf. 1988, Munich); and N. Nabokov's *The Holy Devil** (1959, Louisville, Ky.).

SCORE: vs, holograph ([1988], photocopy, NYPL).

BIBLIOGRAPHY: Mark Gevisser, "Holy Devil," *ON* LIII (Sept. 1988), 14–16, 18 [on Hartmann and Reise versions]; Mark S. Laporta, "Reise Meets Rasputin," *ON* LIII (Sept. 1988), 10–11, 13.

Ray and the Gospel Singer, opera in one act by Elizabeth Gould; libretto (Eng) by Eugene J. Hochman. First performance September 3, 1967, Toledo, Ohio, Toledo Zoo Amphitheater.

The setting is an urban American community, the present. While waiting to see the doctor, Ray's father and Fay's mother complain about their children's generation. The young Ray, fearing for his future, calls on the Devil, who appears in the guise of Gus, and offers his soul for the promise of peace and the security of old age. Ray is granted his requests in the person of Fay, a folk singer. The couple, now aged, regret that they have led a boring life and have no worthwhile memories. The Devil, now old himself, comes to collect Ray's soul but is outsmarted by Fay. Fay and Ray become young again and prepare to begin adulthood.

For a description, see Summers/*OOA*, 135–36.

Major roles: Ray (ten), Fay (sop), and Gus (bar).

Raymond and Agnes, grand opera in three acts by Edward J. Loder; libretto (Eng) by Edward Fitzball, after M. G. Lewis's novel *The Monk* (1796). First performance August 14, 1855, Manchester, Theatre Royal; 1859, London, with George Perren (Raymond), Hamilton Braham (Baron of Lindenberg), Charles Lyall (Theodore), J. H. Leffler (Francesco), J. T. Haines (Antoni), G. C. Rowland (Roberto), E. Connell (landlord of the Golden Wolf), Madame Rudersdorff (Agnes), Susan Pyne (Madelina), and Madame Louise (Ravella). The work was revived in May 1966 in Cambridge, Massachusetts, Arts Theatre, using the Temperley edition (see below).

The family of Inigo, Baron of Lindenberg, lives under the shadow of a curse uttered by St. Agnes, a nun who stabbed herself when she was attacked by one of Inigo's forebears. In order to rid himself of the curse, Inigo has to wed the last survivor of St. Agnes's line, Lady Agnes, his ward, who unhappily consents to marry him, even though she loves Don Raymond, a Spanish nobleman. Raymond follows Agnes to Bavaria, where the marriage is to take place, and when he discovers that the Baron killed Raymond's father, a duel results. Inigo is victorious and, pretending to release Raymond, has his man Antoni shoot at Raymond. The appearance of St. Agnes's ghost startles Antoni, who misfires and kills Inigo instead.

Major roles: Inigo, Baron of Lindenberg (bass-bar); Lady Agnes (sop); Don Raymond (ten); and Antoni (bar).

Also pantomime by William Reeve (1797, London).

SCORES: vs (London, 1859), rev. ed. Nicholas Temperley, rev. text Max Miradin (Cambridge, Mass.: E. & E. Plumridge, 1966).

LIBRETTO: English (London: Charles Jefferys, 1859).

Realitillusion, opera in one act by Michel-Georges Brégent; libretto (Eng and Fr) by the composer. First performance May 11, 1988, Toronto, Canadian Opera Company.

Seven historical figures, among them Rosa Luxemburg, Virginia Woolf, Jack London, and Vincent van Gogh, discuss their artistic and personal travails.

Rebecca, opera in three acts by Wilfred Josephs; libretto (Eng) by Edward Marsh, after Daphne du Maurier's novel. First performance October 15, 1983, Leeds.

The story of a servant girl, unnamed in this work, who falls in love with the handsome Maxim de Winter. She leaves her employer to marry de Winter and live at his estate at Manderley. The new wife keeps on resurrecting the memory of de Winter's dead first wife, Rebecca, for reasons he cannot understand. It turns out that the second wife has been manipulated by the jealous and evil housekeeper, Mrs. Danvers, who aided Rebecca in her unfaithfulness. The housekeeper burns Manderley to the ground and dies, thus erasing any memory of Rebecca.

Major roles: the Girl (sop), Maxim de Winter (bar), and Mrs. Danvers (mezzo).

SCORE: vs (London: Novello, 1986).

Rebel, The, television opera in one act by Thomas Eastwood; libretto (Eng) by Ronald Duncan. First performance April 4, 1969, BBC.

Rebel Maid, The, light opera in three acts by Montague Phillips; libretto (Eng) by A. M. Thompson; lyrics by Gerald Dodson. First performance March 12, 1921, London, Empire Theatre.

The musical highlights include "Sail My Ships" and "The Fishermen of England."

SCORE: vs (London: Chappell & Co., 1921).

Reconciliation, The, or, The Triumph of Nature, comic ballad opera in two acts; libretto (Eng) by Peter Markoe, after Salomon Gessner's *Erastus*. Composed 1790 for Philadelphia, Southwark Theatre. Not performed (see below).

Wilson, after incurring the wrath of his wealthy father by marrying Amelia, is forced to lead a poverty-stricken existence until his servant, Simon, meets the father and, not knowing who he is, forces him to surrender half his money. When Wilson discovers that the money Simon gives to him has come from a man he robbed, not from an unknown friend, he forces Simon to seek out the stranger. As Simon is about to depart, the father enters, and father and son are reconciled.

Roles: the men: Wilson senior; Wilson; William, his son; Simon, a servant; and the women: Amelia, Wilson's wife; and Deborah, a servant.

For a detailed description, see Sonneck/*SIMG* 451–56; Virga/*AO*, 205–10.

The libretto was printed on May 24, 1790 (making this work the first American opera to be printed), but there was no performance (see Porter/*WAD*, 8). The music contains seven ballad airs.

LIBRETTO: English (Philadelphia: Prichard & Hall, 1790); repr. Rubsamen/*BO*, vol. 28, *American Ballad Operas* (1974).

Recruiting Sergeant, The, all-sung afterpiece in one act by Charles Dibdin; libretto (Eng) by Isaac Bickerstaffe. First performance July 20, 1770, London, Ranelagh Gardens. First U.S. performance March 15, 1799, Boston, Federal Street Theatre.

The young wife of the countryman pleads in vain when the recruiting sergeant comes to take her husband away to war.

For a description, see Fiske/*ETM*, 357–58.

Roles: sergeant, countryman, mother, wife.

LIBRETTOS: English (London: W. Griffin, 1770; Philadelphia, 1850; London: J. Dicks, n.d.; New York: Samuel French & Son, n.d.).

Red Carnations, opera in one act by Robert Baksa; libretto by the composer, after the play by Glenn Hughes. First performance October 24, 1974, New York, St. Luke's Chapel, Metropolitan Opera Studio.

Roles: sop, ten, and bar.

SCORES: vs (New York: A. Broude, 1969; New York: Composers Library Editions, 1981).

Red-Cross Knights, The, play in five acts, with music by Thomas Attwood; libretto (Eng) by Joseph G. Holman, an "avowed alteration" of F. Schiller's *Die Räuber* (1781). First performance August 21, 1799, London, Haymarket Theatre, with Mr. Aickin (Count de Ladesma), Mr. C. Kemble (Ferdinand), Mr. Barrymore (Roderic de Froila), Mr. Caulfield (Bertram), Mrs. Bland (Rosa), and Miss De Camp (Eugenia). First U.S. performance July 12, 1802, Philadelphia, Southwark Theatre.

The noble Ferdinand is alienated from his father, Count de Ladesma, through the machinations of Roderic and Bertram. The hero is ultimately reconciled with his father and allowed to wed Eugenia, his beloved.

The work includes a setting of Pamina and Papageno's duet "Bei Männern" from Mozart's *Die Zauberflöte,* and music by John W. Calcott and Samuel Arnold.

Other settings by S. Mercadante, as *I briganti* (1836, Paris); Verdi, as *I masnadieri* (1847, London); and G. Klebe, as *Die Räuber* (1957, Düsseldorf).

SCORE: vs (London: Goulding, Phipps, & D'Almaine, [1799]).

LIBRETTO: English (London: Geo. Cawthorn, 1799).

Red Feather, The, comic opera in two acts by Reginald De Koven; libretto (Eng) by Charles Klein; lyrics by C. E. Cook. First performance November 9, 1903, New York, Lyric Theatre, with George Tallman (Capt. Trevor), Grace Van Studdiford (Countess Hilda Von Draga), and Thomas Q. Seabrooke (Baron Bulverstrauss).

Capt. Trevor, a member of the Romancian army, is unaware that his beloved, Countess Hilda, leads a double life and passes herself off as the feared "Red Feather" bandit, whom he has been ordered to apprehend. The plot is similar to Sousa's *El Capitan,** but with the male lead having two identities. Klein was the librettist for both works.

SCORE: vs (New York: J. B. Stern, 1903).

Red-Headed League, The, opera in one act by Judith Dvorkin; libretto (Eng) by the composer, after Arthur Conan Doyle's story. Composed 1992.
SCORE: ms score, holograph (1992; photocopy, NYPL).

Red Mask, The, or, The Council of Three, adaptation by Thomas S. Cooke, of M. A. Marliani's *Il bravo* (1834, Paris); libretto (Eng) by James R. Planché, after A. Berrettoni's text. First performance November 15, 1834, London, Drury Lane Theatre.

Red Rose and the Briar, The, folk opera by Irving Mopper; libretto (Eng) by Irwin Stahl. First performance May 5, 1951, Syracuse, New York, Syracuse University; directed by Sawyer Falk.
BIBLIOGRAPHY: Meg Hale, review, *NYT* (May 6, 1951), II, 7 [on premiere].

Red Sea, The, opera in one act by Malcolm Williamson; libretto (Eng) by the composer. First performance April 14, 1972, Devon, England, Dartington College of the Arts.
SCORE: vs (London: J. Weinberger, [1973]).

Red Spider, The, romantic comic opera in three acts by Learmont Drysdale; libretto (Eng), by Sabine Baring-Gould, after her novel. First performance July 25, 1898, Lowestoft, Scotland, Marina.
    The story is built on themes from Devon folklore.
    The work was very popular on tour and received some 100 performances.
LIBRETTO: English (London: J. Tamblyn, 1898).

Red Tide. See **Three Visitations.**

Reform'd in Time, comic opera in two acts by Thomas Attwood; libretto (Eng) by Henry Heartwell. First performance May 23, 1798, London, Covent Garden.

Regina, opera in three acts by Marc Blitzstein; libretto (Eng) by the composer, after the play *The Little Foxes* by Lillian Hellman. First performance as musical play in a prologue and two acts October 31, 1949, New York, Broadway Theatre, with Jane Pickens (Regina), Brenda Lewis (Birdie), Priscilla Gillette (Alexandra), William Warfield (Cal), and William Wilderman (Horace). First performance as an opera 1953, New York, City Center, with Lewis (Regina), Ellen Faull (Birdie), Lucretia West (Addie), and Wilderman (Horace); conducted by Julius Rudel. Revived October 1977, Detroit, Michigan Opera Theatre, with Joan Diener-Marre (Regina), Barbara Hocher (Birdie), Sarah Rice (Alexandra), George Gaynes (Horace), and Joseph Kolinski (Leo); May 4, 1980, Houston, Grand Opera, with Maralin Niska (Regina), Elizabeth Carron (Birdie), Rodney Stenborg (Oscar), Carroll Freeman (Leo), Giorgio Tozzi (Ben), Don Garrad (Horace), Jennifer Jones (Addie), and Jennifer Ringo (Alexandra); conducted by John DeMain. First British performance May 17, 1991, Glasgow, Scottish Opera, with Katherine Terrell (Regina); conducted by John Mauceri.
    The setting is Bowden, Alabama, in the spring of 1900. William Marshall of Chicago comes to visit the Giddens family to arrange a financial deal with them, unaware of the scheming and greedy nature of Regina Giddens and her two brothers, Ben and Oscar Hubbard. Marshall needs the consent of the gentle Horace, Regina's banker husband, who has taken ill and is in Baltimore. To seal the bargain Regina sends their daughter Alexandra (Zan) to get him, while Birdie, Oscar's well-bred wife, discovers that plans are afoot to have her worthless son Leo marry the girl.
    Sure of the success of her plans, Regina arranges a ball for her husband's return. When he comes back, Horace refuses to go along with the agreement, so that Leo, dispatched by

the brothers, steals Horace's bonds from the bank to secure the deal with Marshall. Not understanding her husband's refusal to cooperate, Regina argues with him, whereupon he changes his will and leaves the bonds solely to his wife, since he knows that they have been stolen. Under taunting from Regina Horace suffers a fatal heart attack. She threatens to sue her brothers unless they give her three quarters of the profits of their joint venture. In disgust, Alexandra departs, leaving her mother with a hollow victory.

For a detailed plot synopsis, see K/*KOB*, 1336–40; K/*NKOB*, 85–88.

Major roles: Regina Giddens (sop); Alexandra Giddens, her daughter, called Zan (sop); Horace Giddens, Regina's husband (bass); Benjamin Hubbard, Regina's elder brother (bar); Oscar Hubbard, Regina's younger brother (bar); Birdie Hubbard, Oscar's wife (alto); Leo Hubbard, their son (ten); and William Marshall, a businessman from the North (ten).

Among the musical highlights are Addie's comforting lullaby in act 2 for Birdie, "Night Could Be Time to Sleep"; the stunning Rain Quartet that opens the third act, with Birdie, Zan, Addie, and Horace, which includes Horace's solo "Consider the Rain" and, at the end, gospel singing from another part of the house as a counterpart, "Have You Got Good Religion"; and Birdie's reminiscence or confession aria that follows. The work combines traditional operatic genres such as arias with elements from more popular-music styles such as blues, Dixieland, and salon music, a variant of the last used to portray the nasty members of the story.

SCORE: vs (New York: Chappell, [1954]).

LIBRETTO: English (New York: Chappell, 1953).

BIBLIOGRAPHY: Carl Cunningham, review, *MA* XXX (Sept. 1980), 22 [on Houston revival]; Scott F. Heumann, review, *ON* XLV (Aug. 1980), 28 [on Houston revival]; "Musical Events: The Right Subjects," *NY* LIII (Oct. 24, 1977), 162–63 [on Detroit revival]; Patrick O'Connor, "Chinkypin Music," *TLS* (May 24, 1991), 18 [on British premiere].

DISCOGRAPHY: B. Lewis, E. Carron, C. Brice, J. Hecht, New York City Opera Orch.; cond. S. Krachmalnick, Columbia 03L-260 (3 LPs); K. Ciesinski, A. Réalix, S. Greenawald, S. Ramey; cond. J. Mauceri, Scottish Opera Orch. and Chorus, London 2-4331812-2 LLH2 (1992, London, 2 CDs).

Rehearsal, The, "pastoral interlude" in two acts by William Boyce; libretto (Eng) by Kitty Clive. First performance March 1, 1750, London, Drury Lane Theatre, with Mrs. Clive (Mrs. Hazard).

This spoof of Italian opera concerns Mrs. Hazard, who has composed a burletta and is waiting for the dress rehearsal to start. The work concerns one Marcella, who has been rejected by Corydon. She is approached by a mysterious young woman who wants a part in the Italian burletta, despite her very obvious Cockney accent.

For a detailed description, see Fiske/*ETM*, 216.

LIBRETTO: English (London: R. Dodsley, 1753).

Rehearsal, The, opera in one act by Thomas Benjamin; libretto (Eng) by Cynthia MacDonald. First performance March 1, 1981, New York, Golden Fleece; conducted by John Klingberg; directed by Lou Rodgers.

The plot concerns romantic involvements of a cast giving Mozart's *The Impresario*.

SCORE: vs (New York: American Music Center, 1978).

BIBLIOGRAPHY: Peter G. Davis, review, *NYT* (Mar. 2, 1981), C, 18 [on premiere].

Rehearsal Call, opera in three acts by Vittorio Giannini; libretto (Eng) by Francis Swann and Robert A. Simon, after Swann's play *Out of the Frying Pan*. First performance February 15, 1962, New York, Juilliard School, with Meredith Zara, Lorna

Haywood, Paul Ukena, Marylin Zschau, Enrico di Giuseppe, Ronald Freed, David Bender, George Pollock, and James Justice; conducted by Frederic Waldman; produced by Frederic Cohen.

A comic treatment of struggling young actors trying to succeed in New York.

BIBLIOGRAPHY: Harold C. Schonberg, review, *NYT* (Feb. 16, 1962), 36 [on premiere].

Reilly and the 400, musical drama by David Braham; text (Eng) by Ned Harrigan. First performance December 29, 1891, New York, Harrigan's, with Ned Harrigan (Wiley Reilly), Harry Davenport (Ned Reilly), Isabelle Archer (Emeline), James Radcliffe (Commodore Toby Tow), and Harry Fisher (Herman Smeltz).

The story focuses on an Irish pawnbroker, Reilly, who deceives the "400," a group of high-society people, in order to help his son Ned marry Emeline, niece of the Commodore. Reilly turns the table on his victims by revealing that Herman Smeltz, a sausage tycoon and one of the 400, was once a ship's butcher who was fired for stealing.

The musical highlights include "The Jolly Commodore," "Annie Laurie," and "The Great 400."

TEXT AND LIBRETTO: typed libretto (NYPL, contemporary sheet music, score and parts); repr. ed. Katherine K. Preston, *NAMT*, vol. 10 (1994).

Rencontre, The, or, Love Will Find the Way Out, operatic comedy in two acts by Henry Rowley Bishop; libretto (Eng) by James R. Planché. First performance July 12, 1827, London, Little Theatre in the Haymarket, with George Alexander Lee.

Roles: Justine, the Colonel, Pierre, the landlord, the Baron, St. Leon, and the servant.

SCORE: fs, autograph (1827, British Library, MS. Add. 27721).

Rendezvous, The, opera in two acts by Gerard Victory; libretto (Eng) by the composer, after M. Renard. First performance November 2, 1989, Dublin, St. Stephen's Church; conducted by Colman Pearce.

Rent, "rock-opera" in two acts by Jonathan Larson; book and lyrics (Eng) by the composer, with contributions by Lynn Thomson, inspired by Henry Murger's serial novel *Scènes de la vie de bohème* (1847–1849). First performance February 13, 1996, New York, New York Theater Workshop, with Anthony Rapp (Mark Cohen), Adam Pascal (Roger Davis), Daphne Rubin-Vega (Mimi Marquez), Idina Menzel (Maureen Johnson), Jessie L. Martin (Tom Collins), Fredi Walker (Joanne Jefferson), Wilson Jermaine Heredia (Angel Shunard), and Taye Diggs (Benjamin Coffin 3d); directed by Michael Greif; conducted by Tim Weil.

Concerned with a group of struggling artists, the story is an updating of Puccini's *La bohème* (1896), with the setting moved from Paris to the East Village in New York. Rodolfo has become Roger, a songwriter, Marcello is Mark, a video artist and roommate of Roger; Maureen is a contemporary Musetta, who has left Mark for a woman lawyer, Joanne; Mimi Marquez, the updated Mimi, is a dancer at a sex club and is HIV-positive, as are Roger, Tom Collins (Colline in the Puccini), and Angel Shunard (originally Schaunard), a transvestite sculptor and friend of Roger; Benoit, the Parisian landlord, is Benjamin Coffin 3d, who owns the building in which Mark and Roger live.

The show, a combination of rock music and Broadway effects, made a particularly spectacular impression, aside from its intrinsic merits, because of Larson's sudden death just before the premiere, at the age of thirty-five (Thomson was later given title-page credit as dramaturge after a legal battle). *Rent* was so successful that it was moved to the Nederlander Theater on Broadway and won a Tony as best musical. Its highlights include

Roger's "One Song Glory"; "Light My Candle," by Roger and Mimi; and the ensemble "La Vie Boheme" (act 1); and the ensemble "Seasons of Love," which opens act 2.
BIBLIOGRAPHY: Clive Barnes, "Puccini Meets the E. Village," *New York Post* (Feb. 14, 1996), 40 [on premiere]; Ben Brantley, "Rock Opera à la 'Bohème' and 'Hair,'" *NYT* (Feb. 14, 1996), C, 11, 18 [on premiere]; Jesse McKinley, "Family of 'Rent' Creator Settles Suit over Authorship: Dramaturge Gets Money and Playbill Credit," *NYT* (Sept. 10, 1998), B, 3.

Requiem for a Rich Young Man, opera in one act by Normand Lockwood; libretto (Eng) by Donald Sutherland. First performance November 24, 1964, Denver.

The setting is a living room, the present. The work opens after the funeral of Hubert. His widow, Gladys, and his brother, Terence, gather at the house and find that they are attracted to each other. Gladys's sister Olivia arrives, along with her husband, William, and the group discusses the deceased and whether the four of them could pair up differently. When no practical solution is forthcoming, Gladys resolves to devote herself to her husband's memory and to the cultivation of his fortune, which he has left to her.

For a description, see Summers/*OOA*, 204–5.

Roles: Gladys (sop), Olivia (alto), Terence (ten), and William (bass).

Rescue, The, chamber opera in one act by Alan Ridout; libretto (Eng) by David J. Holbrook. First performance 1963, Hastings, England.

Research, The, comic opera in one act by Walter Kaufmann; libretto (Eng). First performance 1953, Tallahassee, Florida State University.

Restauration of King Charles II, The, "an histori-tragi-comic ballad opera"; libretto (Eng) by Walter Ashton (Aston). First performance 1732, London.

Roles: the men: King Charles II; Lesly, General of the Scot's forces; Col. Carlos; General Monk; Trusty Dick; Oliver Cromwell; Ireton; Lambert; Corporal Cudden; and Grimbald, a bosom friend of Cromwell's; the women: Britannia, Genius of the Isle; Miss Jane Lane, a loyal girl; Lady Claypool, daughter of Cromwell; and Dame Sarah, a treacherous virago.
LIBRETTO: English (London: R. Walker, 1732); repr. ed. Rubsamen/*BO*, vol. 2, *Historical and Patriotic Subjects* (1974).

Resurrection, "black comic opera" in one act and a prologue by Peter Maxwell Davies; libretto (Eng) by the composer. First performance September 8, 1988, Darmstadt, Staatstheater, in German. First British performance May 14, 1997, Glasgow, Theatre Royal, with Ines Carsauw, Jan Lund, Wilfried van den Brande, Roland Purcell, Jeremy Pick, Conor Biggs, and Paul Zachariades; conducted by Peter Benjamin.

In this biting parody the hero, Dummy, appropriately a silent role, is the son of a "traditional" family from the north of England. He is subjected to a series of operations to correct his "faults": the first for his moral and intellectual ones, the second for his emotional and religious ones, and the third for his sexual "defects." The result is that he is resurrected as the Antichrist.

The work combines vocal soloists, a chamber orchestra, and rock band.
SCORE: fs (London: Chester Music, 1994).
LIBRETTO: English (London: Chester Music, [1994?]).
BIBLIOGRAPHY: John Allison, review, *Opera* XLVIII (Aug. 1997), 970–71 [on British premiere]; Paul Griffiths, review, *ON* LIII (Dec. 10, 1988), 46 [on premiere].
DISCOGRAPHY: Jones, Robson, Hill, Jenkins, Herford, Finley, Best, Blaze, rock band, Carewe, vocals, BBC Philharmonic; cond. Davis, Collins Classics 7034 (1995, 2 CDs).

Return of Odysseus, The, opera in three acts by Inglis Gundry; libretto (Eng) by the composer, after Homer. First performance (act 1) May 25, 1940, London, Royal College of Music.

Return of Odysseus, The, children's opera in one act by David Bedford; libretto (Eng) by the composer, after Homer. First performance 1988, London.

Revelation in the Courthouse Park, dramatic work by Harry Partch; text (Eng) by the composer, after Euripides' *Bacchae*. First performance April 11, 1962, Urbana, Illinois; conducted by John Garvey. Revived October 8, 1987, Philadelphia, American Music Theater Festival, with Obba Babatune (Dion/Dionysus), Christopher Durham (Pentheus/Sonny), and Suzanne Costallos (Mom/Agave).

The plot switches between present-day America and ancient Greece. It involves Dionysus, who becomes Dion, a rock star.
DISCOGRAPHY: cond. D. Mitchell, Tomato 269655 (1989, Philadelphia, 2 CDs).

Revenge, The, burletta sometimes attributed to Samuel Arnold; libretto (Eng) by Thomas Chatterton. First performance 1770, London, Marylebone Gardens, with Mrs. Thompson, Mr. Reinhold (Jupiter), Mr. Bannister (Bacchus), and Master Cheney (Cupid).

In order to get even with Jupiter and Bacchus, Cupid tells Juno that her husband (Jupiter) has his eye on Maia and, at the same time, talks Bacchus into trying to seduce Maia in the guise of Jupiter. Juno interrupts the proceedings and believes that her husband is carrying on with the young woman.
LIBRETTO: English (London: T. King, H. Chapman, and J. Egerton, 1795).

Revenge of Athridates, The, "a new English Opera" by Ferdinando Tenducci; anonymous libretto (Eng), after Thomas Hull, perhaps based on that of *Pharnaces.** First performance December 12, 1766, Dublin, with Clementina Cremonini (Aspasia).

The work includes J. C. Bach's "Oh! Turn, Behold My Streaming Eyes," from act 1, scene 2, sung by Aspasia. It comes from J. C. Bach's *Adriano in Siria* (No. 20).
SCORES: vs, *The Favorite Songs in the Opera of Athridates* (London: John Johnston, [1766]); one Bach number repr. in *The Collected Works of J. C. Bach*, vol. 25, *Works with English Texts*, ed. Ernest Warburton (New York: Garland, 1990).

Reverend Everyman, television opera in two acts by Salvador Brotons; libretto (Eng) by Gary Corsari, after Hugo von Hofmannsthal's play *Jedermann* (1911). First performance summer 1990, Tallahassee, Florida, WFSU-TV, Florida State University.

Reverend Jim, grand opera in three acts by John Eaton; libretto (Eng) by James Reston Jr. Composed 1989.

About the Reverend Jim Jones and the mass suicide of more than 900 of his followers in Guyana in 1978.

Review, The, or, The Wags of Windsor, comic opera in two acts by Samuel Arnold; libretto (Eng) by George Colman Jr., after Henry Lee's *Caleb Quotem,** set by Arnold (1809). First performance September 1, 1800, London, Little Theatre in the Haymarket. First U.S. performance March 19, 1802, Philadelphia, Chestnut Street Theatre.
SCORE: vs (London: J. & H. Caulfield, n.d.).
LIBRETTO: English (London: J. & H. Caulfield, [1800?]; New York: D. Longworth, 1804).

Revoke, The, opera in one act by Gustav Holst; libretto (Eng) by Fritz B. Hart. Composed 1895. Not performed publicly.

Rich and Poor, comic opera in three acts by Charles Edward Horn; libretto (Eng) by Matthew G. Lewis, after his comedy *The East Indian* (1800). First performance July 22, 1812, London, Lyceum Theatre. First U.S. performance November 23, 1812, Boston, Federal Street Theatre.
LIBRETTO: English ([London]: W. Oxberry, Somerstown, 1812).

Richard Coeur de Lion, comic opera in three acts by William Shield; libretto (Eng) Leonard MacNally, after Sedaine's *Richard Coeur-de-lion*, set by Grétry (1784, Paris). First performance October 16, 1786, London, Covent Garden, with Mr. Inchbald (Richard), Mrs. Martyr (Lauretta), and Mrs. Billington (Berengaria).

King Richard is being held prisoner in a castle, and his would-be rescuers include Blondel, his minstrel. In order for the plan to succeed, the governor of the castle, who is in love with Lauretta, a Welsh girl, is persuaded to go visit her. When he does, he is seized, and Richard is freed by Berengaria, Richard's wife.

The work was changed into an afterpiece after the first four performances. See next entry for Linley's version. Both settings are discussed in Fiske/*ETM,* 466–67.
LIBRETTO: English (London: T. Cadell, 1786).

Richard Coeur de Lion, historical afterpiece, an adaptation by Thomas Linley Sr., of *Richard Coeur-de-lion,* set by Grétry (1784, Paris); libretto (Eng) by General John Burgoyne, after Sedaine's text. First performance October 24, 1786, London, Drury Lane Theatre, with Charles Kemble (Richard), Mrs. Crouch (Lauretta), and Mrs. Jordan (Matilda). First U.S. performance January 23, 1797, Boston.

The plot is similar to the Shield setting, but here Richard is rescued by Matilda, his mistress.
SCORE: vs (London: Harrison, Cluse [1802?]).
LIBRETTO: English (London: J. Debrett, 1786; New York: R. Hobbs, 1831).

Richard III, opera in four acts by Paul Turok; libretto (Eng), after Shakespeare's play (1594). Composed 1975. First performance (concert) April 28, 1980, Philadelphia.

Other settings include G. Salvayre, as *Riccardo III* (1883, St. Petersburg); J. Van Durme, as *König Richard der Dritte* (comp. 1961); I. Kuljerić (1987, Zagreb); and F. Testi, as *Riccardo III* (1987, Milan).

Richest Girl in the World Finds Happiness, The, celebratory opera in one act by Gregory Sandow; libretto (Eng) by Robert Patrick. First performance December 1, 1975, New York, Theater at Noon.

Geraldine, who is the Richest Girl in the World, gets a proposal of marriage from the Handsomest Movie Star in The World. They leave to get married, after which Madalayna, the maid, opens the mail to see that her employer has been named Miss America, which would be invalidated by the wedding. The maid tracks down Geraldine in Egypt, and Geraldine figures that she can cross the international dateline and still be eligible for the award. Overwhelmed by her happiness, Geraldine bestows her wealth on the poor children of the world, who return it to her as a wedding present. A singer leads the cast in a paean to happiness.

For a fuller description, see Summers/*OOA,* 265–66.

Roles: Geraldine, the Richest Girl in the World (sop); Madalayna (sop/mezzo); Geoffrey, the Handsomest Movie Star in the World (ten); and a singer (ten).
SCORE: ms vs, holograph (photocopy, NYPL).

Rich Man, Poor Man, Beggar Man, Saint, opera for young people in two acts by Antony Hopkins; libretto (Eng) by G. David Nixon. First performance October 18, 1969, Stroud, England, Trinity Church.

Riders to the Sea, opera in one act by Fritz Hart; libretto (Eng), after J. M. Synge. Composed 1915.
    See next entry for the story.

Riders to the Sea, opera in one act by Ralph Vaughan Williams; libretto (Eng) by J. M. Synge, after his play. First performance (private) December 1, 1937, London, Royal College of Music. First performance (public) February 22, 1938, Cambridge, Cambridge Arts Theatre, with Janet Smith-Miller, Margaret Field-Hyde, Olive Hall, and Marcus Dods. First U.S. performance June 21, 1950, New York, After Dinner Opera, Master Theatre, with Beatrice Krebs, James Beni, Sylvia Stahlman, Anita Jordan, and Eleanor Wold; conducted by Georgette Palmer.
    The old Maurya, living in a village by the sea, has already lost her husband and four of her six sons to drowning. Another son, Michael, is missing. Maurya's two daughters, Cathleen and Nora, try to hide Michael's wet clothing, which has been pulled from the sea, from their mother. Her last son, Bartley, rides off without his mother's blessing. He is thrown into the sea by his horse, leaving the hopeless Maurya without any sons.
    For detailed descriptions, see K/*KOB*, 1121–23; K/*NKOB*, 847–48.
    Major roles: Maurya, an old woman (alto); Bartley, her son (bar); Cathleen, her daughter (sop); and Nora, her younger daughter (sop).
SCORE: octavo score (London: Oxford University Press, 1972).
BIBLIOGRAPHY: H. C. S., review, *NYT* (June 22, 1950), 33 [on U.S. premiere].

Rime of the Ancient Mariner, The, opera for young people in one act by David Bedford; libretto (Eng) by the composer, after the words of Samuel Taylor Coleridge. Composed 1975–1976. First performance 1979, London.
    A seaman, as punishment for shooting an albatross, is forced to tell his story indefinitely, his audience being a man on his way to a wedding.
    Roles: the Ancient Mariner (sop/ten); the Wedding Guest (alto/bar); first and second Spirits (2 sop/2 ten); Life-in-Death (speaking); Death (silent); Hermit (silent); and Pilor (any voice).
SCORE: vs (New York: Universal Edition, [1979]).

Rimshot, chamber opera in six scenes by Russell Currie; libretto (Eng) by the composer, after Scott Speed's play *Best.* First performance May 10, 1990, New York, Pace University, Downtown Theatre.
    The story concerns a famed rock drummer who, after a downward slide, becomes successful once again.

Rinaldo and Armida, semi-opera by John Eccles; libretto (Eng) by John Dennis, after Tasso's *Gerusalemme liberata* (1580–81). First performance November 1698, London, Lincoln's Inn Fields.
    The setting is the sorceress Armida's magic island, and the work ends with her demise.
    The many operatic treatments of the legend include those by Lully, as *Armide* (1686. Paris); G. M. Ruggieri, as *Armida abbandonata* (1707, Venice); Handel (1711); P. Winter, as *Reinhold und Armida* (1793, Vienna); and G. Andreozzi, as *Armida e Rinaldo* (1802, Naples).

LIBRETTO: English (London: Jacob Tonson, 1699).

Ring, The, opera in one act by Stephen Oliver; libretto (Eng) by the composer, after the British television serial *Coronation Street*. First performance May 31, 1984, Manchester, Free Trade Hall.

Rip Van Winkle, grand romantic opera in three acts by George F. Bristow; libretto (Eng) by Jonathan Howard Wainwright, after Washington Irving's tale. First performance September 27, 1855, New York, Niblo's Garden, with Louisa Pyne (Dame Van Winkle), William Harrison (Edward Gardinier), Mrs. Hood (Anna), Mr. Setchell (Derrick Van Bummel), Miss Gourley (Alice Van Winkle), and George Stratton (Rip Van Winkle); conducted by the composer.

The work is set from 1763 to 1783. The first and third acts take place in the Catskills (spelled Kaatskills by Irving and Bristow). The second, the librettist's invention (a departure from Irving), takes place during Rip's long sleep and covers events in the American Revolution. It features the only love interest of the work, between the heroic Captain Edward Gardinier and Alice Van Winkle, Rip's daughter (unlike the other settings). When Rip awakes in act 3, he finds that most of his contemporaries have passed away.

Roles: act 1, autumn 1763: Rip Van Winkle, a Kaatskills farmer (bass); Nicholas Vedder, landlord of the Inn (bass); Derrick Van Bummel, schoolmaster (ten); Diedrich Van Slaus, burgomaster (bar); Herman, his son (bar); Dame Van Winkle, Rip's wife (sop); spirit of Hendrick Hudson (bar); act 2, autumn 1777: Edward Gardinier, captain in the Continental Army (ten); Herman Van Slaus and Rip Van Winkle Jr. (ten); Dame Van Winkle and Alice Van Winkle, Rip's daughter (sop); act 3, 1783; Rip Van Winkle; Judge Knickerbocker; Herman Van Slaus; Alice Van Winkle, and Rip Van Winkle Jr.
SCORE: vs (New York: G. Schirmer, 1882); ed. Steven Ledbetter, libretto reconstr. J. W. Shannon; repr. New York: Da Capo, 1991).
LIBRETTO: English (New York: W. Corbyn, 1855).

Rip Van Winkle, romantic comic opera in three acts by Jules Jordan; libretto (Eng) by the composer, after Irving. First performance May 25, 1897, Providence, Rhode Island, Opera House; conducted by the composer.
SCORE: vs (Boston: Oliver Ditson Co., 1898).

Rip Van Winkle, opera in three acts by Reginald De Koven; libretto (Eng) by Percy W. Mackaye, after Irving. First performance January 2, 1920, Chicago, Chicago Opera, with Evelyn Herbert (Peterkee Vedder), George Baklanoff (Rip Van Winkle), Hector Dufranne (Hendrick Hudson), Edouard Cotreuil (Dirck Spuytenduyvil), Gustave Huberdeau (Nicholas Vedder), Edna Darch (Katrina Vedder), Constantin Nicolay (Derrick Van Bummel), and Edmond Warnery (Jan Van Bummel); conducted by Alexander Smallens.

The setting is the Catskill Mountains in New York in the eighteenth century. Rip Van Winkle is in love with Peterkee Vedder. Her father, Nicholas Vedder, wants his daughter Katrina to wed Jan, the foolish son of Derrick Van Bummel. In order to escape the father's will, Rip Van Winkle and Peterkee journey high into the Catskills, where they meet Hendrick Hudson and his ghostly crew. Peterkee is able to escape, but Hudson puts Rip to sleep. He wakes twenty years later, as an old man. Peterkee has waited for him and gives him Hudson's flask, which restores Rip and Peterkee to youth.

Roles: Rip Van Winkle (bar), Hendrick Hudson (bass-bar), Dirck Spuytenduyvil (bass), Nicholas Vedder (bass), Derrick Van Bummel (ten), Peterkee Vedder (sop), and Katrina Vedder (sop).

SCORE: vs (New York: G. Schirmer, 1919).
LIBRETTO: English (New York: Alfred A. Knopf, 1919).

Rip Van Winkle, opera in three acts by Edward Manning; libretto (Eng) by the composer, after Irving. First performance February 12, 1932, New York, Town Hall, Charlotte Lund Opera Company, with H. Wellington-Smith (Rip Van Winkle).

Rip Van Winkle, opera by Jeffrey Rockwell; libretto (Eng) by J. Sherwood Montgomery, after Irving. First performance October 18, 1989, San Diego.

Rip Van Winkle, children's opera in one act by Gregg Smith; libretto (Eng), after Irving. First performance May 3, 1991, Syracuse, New York.
   Other settings include the musical farce *Rip Van Winkle, or, Some Nambulistic Knickerbockers* by John Strachan Jr. and Henry Davis (1866); Robert Panquette's operetta (1882, London); F. Leoni (1897); and Walter Kaufmann's children's opera (comp. 1966).

Rising of the Moon, The, opera in three acts by Nicholas Maw; libretto (Eng) by Beverley Cross. First performance July 19, 1970, Glyndebourne, with Alexander Oliver (Brother Timothy), Anne Howells (Cathleen Sweeney), John Gibbs (Donal O'Dowd), Richard Van Allan (Colonel Lord Jowler), John Fryatt (Captain Lillywhite), Peter Gottlieb (Major Max von Zastrow), Rae Woodland (Lady Eugenie Jowler), Kerstin Meyer (Frau Elizabeth von Zastrow), Annon Lee Silver (Miss Atalanta Lillywhite), John Wakefield (Cornet John Stephen Beaumont), and Anne Howells (Cathleen Sweeney); conducted by Raymond Leppard; produced by Colin Graham.
   The story takes place in 1875 in the town of Ballinvourney in the Plains of Mayo, Ireland. Beaumont, a young officer, has to prove his manhood to his superior officers by being able to seduce three women in one night. The Irish villagers "help" the young man by arranging to have him win the affections of Lady Eugenie Jowler, wife of his commanding officer, Colonel Lord Jowler, and Elizabeth von Zastrow, wife of a Prussian officer. Cathleen Sweeney, daughter of the innkeeper, willingly takes the place of the third would-be conquest, Atalanta Lillywhite, daughter of Captain Lillywhite. Beaumont's actions necessitate the exit of his regiment from the area, bringing joy to the villagers and sadness to Cathleen. Brother Timothy, whose monastery has become the officers' mess, contemplates the events in the prologue and epilogue.
   Major roles: Brother Timothy (high ten), Cathleen Sweeney (sop), Lady Eugenie Jowler (sop), Frau Elizabeth von Zastrow (mezzo), Miss Atalanta Lillywhite (sop), Colonel Lord Jowler (bar), and Cornet John Stephen Beaumont (ten).
SCORE: vs (London and New York: Boosey & Hawkes, 1971).
LIBRETTO: English (London and New York: Boosey & Hawkes, 1970, 1971).
BIBLIOGRAPHY: Frank Granville Barker, "Glyndebourne," *ON* XXXV (Sept. 19, 1970), 23 [on premiere]; Winton Dean, "Glyndebourne," *MT* CXII (1971), 688–89 [on premiere]; Anthony Payne, review, *Tempo* XCIV (Aug. 1970), 26ff. [on premiere].

Rites of Passage, theater piece with five "Rites" alternating with five "Chorales" by Peter Sculthorpe; libretto (Eng) by the composer, after texts from the Australian aboriginal "Aranda" poems (the "Rites") and *The Consolation of Philosophy* by Boethius (the "Chorales"). First performance September 27, 1974, Sydney, Australia, Opera House.
   The music of the work, which the composer has revised, shows Asian influences in its tonality and rhythm. It has no real plot but consists of the contrasting "Rites" and "Chorales" sections; the former includes "Preparing the Ground," "Ordeal," "Interlude," and "Death" and is written for mixed chorus and a small instrumental group;

"Chorales" are based on Boethius's work cited earlier and are for mixed chorus and a larger group of instruments.

Rival Candidates, The, comic opera in two acts by Thomas Carter; libretto (Eng) by Henry Bate. First performance February 1, 1775, London, Drury Lane Theatre. First U.S. performance March 1, 1787, New York, John Street Theatre
LIBRETTO: English (London: T. Becket et al., 1775).

Rival Captains, The, or, The Imposter Unmasked, ballad opera; libretto (Eng) by Thomas Phillips. First performance May 26, 1736, London, Little Theatre in the Haymarket.

Rival Clans, The, ballad opera by Henry Deval; libretto (Eng) by the composer. First performance January 27, 1847, Newcastle upon Tyne, Theatre Royal.

Rival Milliners, The, "tragi-comi-operatic-pastoral farce"; libretto (Eng) by Robert Drury. First performance January 19, 1736, London, Little Theatre in the Haymarket, with Mr. Talbot (Pleadwell), Mr. Freeman (Goosequill), Mr. Blastock (Fieri Facias), Mr. Jones (Hunks), Mr. Yates (Trim), Mr. Richards (Staytape), Mrs. Egerton (Mrs. Plainstich), Miss Atherton (Sukey Ogle), and Miss Burgess (Molly Wheedle).
     The setting is Covent Garden.
LIBRETTO: English (London: G. Spavan, 1737).

Rival Queens, The, or, The Death of Alexander the Great, tragic semi-opera by Gottfried Finger and Daniel Purcell; libretto (Eng), after Nathaniel Lee. First performance February 1701, London, Drury Lane Theatre.
     The queens in question are Roxana and Statira, Alexander the Great's two wives. The work ends with Roxana's stabbing Statira and with Alexander's death, too.
SCORE: ms fs (Fitzwilliam Museum, Cambridge, 23.H.12).

Rival Soldiers, The, musical entertainment in one act by William Shield; libretto (Eng) by John O'Keeffe. First performance May 17, 1797, London.
     A revision of *Sprigs of Laurel.**

River, The, radio opera in one act by Wells Hively; libretto (Eng). Composed 1938.
SCORE: fs, facsimile (New York: American Composers Alliance, 1938).

River-Sprite, The, comic opera in one act by Frank Mori; libretto (Eng) by George Linley. First performance February 9, 1865, London.
     A treatment of the Undine story.
SCORE: vs (London: Cramer, [1865]).

Robbers, The, melodrama in one act by Ned Rorem; libretto (Eng) by the composer, after Chaucer's *The Pardoner's Tale.* First performance April 14, 1958, New York, 92nd Street Y, Kaufmann Concert Hall, Mannes [College] Opera Workshop, with Daniel Caruso, Robert Schmorr, and Harold Sien; conducted by Carl Bamberger; produced by Ralph Herbert.
     The setting is a squalid upstairs room in a fourteenth-century inn. After three thieves kill a man for his gold, the young man, part of the trio, tries to repent, but the leader and his companion threaten to kill him also. The older men divide the gold into two parts, while the young man fetches them some wine. They stab him, but they die also when they drink the wine, which has been poisoned.
     For a detailed description, see Eaton/*OP* I, 215.
     Roles: the leader (bass-bar), his companion (ten), and the young novice (lyr bar).

Robber's Bride, The, grand opera in three acts by William Hawes, an adaptation of F. Ries's *Die Räuberbraut* (1828, Frankfurt); libretto (Eng) by Edward Fitzball, after G. Döring's text. First performance July 15, 1829, London, Lyceum. A competing translation by Isaac Pocock was given on October 22, 1829, London, Covent Garden. SCORE: vs (London: Hawes, [1829]).

Robert the Devil, Duke of Normandy, musical romance in two acts by John Barnett; libretto (Eng) by Richard J. Raymond. First performance February 2, 1830, London, Covent Garden, with G. Bennet (Robert, Duke of Normandy), Mr. Duruset (Count Lindor), Miss Lacy (Countess de Rosambert), and Miss Hughes (Blanche).

According to the libretto, "Mr. Raymond has kept in view the celebrated opera of Don Giovanni and is indebted little or nothing to the original story." LIBRETTOS: English (London: T. Richardson, [1830?]; London: John Cumberland, [1830?]).

Robert the Devil, or, The Nun, the Dun, and the Son of a Gun, pastiche by "Kettenus," after Meyerbeer's *Robert le diable* (1831, Paris); libretto (Eng) by William S. Gilbert. First performance December 21, 1868, London, Gaiety Theatre, with Nellie Farren (Robert), Anna Bossi (Lady Abbess), and Richard Barker (Bertram); directed by John Hollingshead.

The devilish Bertram, reduced here to a "Town trav'ller to the Gentleman below," accompanied by his valet, Gobetto, tries to gain control of the soul of Robert (a travesty role) by getting him to sign a contract binding him to Bertram. They come to Madame Tussaud's Chamber of Horrors (a ruined convent in the original) to find a policeman's nightstick (formerly a mystic cypress branch), which is supposed to allow Robert to gain access to Isabella, his beloved. Bertram's plans are foiled when Robert is diverted from signing the contract by a dancing Lady Abbess and her attendant nuns until after midnight strikes, at which time Bertram's power is nullified, and he becomes a wax figure himself.

The score includes, in addition to Meyerbeer's music, melodies by Bellini, Hervé, Offenbach, and Hérold; and a ghostly ballet inspired by John Martin's painting of Pandemonium.

For a detailed description, see Stedman/*WSG*, 58–62.

See also *The Fiend-Father* and *The Demon.*

LIBRETTO: English (London: Phillips, [1868?]).

Robin Goodfellow, or, The Frolics of Puck, ballad opera arranged by Edward J. Loder; libretto (Eng) by the composer. First performance December 6, 1848, London, Princess's Theatre.

Robin Hood, ballad opera; anonymous libretto (Eng). First performance August 22, 1730, London, Bartholemew Fair.

A setting of the Robin Hood legend, but without Maid Marian. It includes a tune from Purcell's *The Indian Queen.**

Major roles: King Edward; Earl of Huntington, alias Robin Hood; the Earl of Pembrook; Darnel, friend to Huntington, alias Little John; Pindar of Wakefield; Matilda, the princess; and Marina, in love with Darnel.

LIBRETTO: English, with music (London: J. Watts, 1730); repr. ed. Rubsamen/*BO*, vol. 2, *Historical and Patriotic Subjects* (1974).

Robin Hood, burletta in two acts by Charles Burney; libretto (Eng) by Moses Mendez. First performance December 13, 1750, London, Drury Lane Theatre, with John Beard (Robin Hood), Miss Norris (Clarinda), and Master Mattocks (Leander). Revived January 11, 1985, Boston, Museum of Fine Arts, Boston's Friends of Dr. Burney; conducted by Charlotte Kaufman; directed by Craig Wich.

In this treatment of the story Robin, in disguise, saves Clarinda from marrying the man picked out by her father and makes it possible for her to marry Leander, her beloved.
LIBRETTO: English (London: M. Cooper, 1750).
BIBLIOGRAPHY: Tim Page, review, *NYT* (Jan. 14, 1985), C, 14 [on 1985 revival].

Robin Hood, or, Sherwood Forest, opera in three acts by William Shield; libretto (Eng) by Leonard MacNally and E. Lysaght, after popular ballads and Oliver Goldsmith's *The Vicar of Wakefield.* First performance April 17, 1784, London, Covent Garden, with Mrs. Bannister and Mr. Parke. Revised into two acts, with additions by Alexander Reinagle and James Hewitt; text revised by John Hodgkinson. First U.S. performance February 16, 1793, Charleston, South Carolina, Charleston Theatre.

The overture is from Karl Friedrich Baumgarten's *William and Nanny** (1779).
For a detailed description see Fiske/*ETM*, 462–63.
SCORE: vs (London: John Bland, [1784?]).
LIBRETTO: English (London: Cadell, 1784).

Robin Hood, opera in three acts by George Macfarren; libretto (Eng) by John Oxenford. First performance October 11, 1860, London, Her Majesty's Theatre, with Helen Lemmens-Sherrington, Sims Reeves, and Charles Santley.

The opera contains a recurrent theme, the melody "True Love" of Maid Marian.
For a detailed musical description, see Biddlecombe/*EO*, 156–57.

Robin Hood, comic opera in three acts by Reginald De Koven; libretto (Eng) by Harry B. Smith. First performance June 9, 1890, Chicago; September 28, 1891, New York, Standard Theatre, with Tom Karl (Robin), Henry Clay Barnabee (Sheriff of Nottingham, Caroline Hamilton (Maid Marian), Peter Lang (Guy of Gisborne), Lea Van Dyke (Annabel), George B. Frothingham (Friar Tuck), W. H. MacDonald (Little John), and Jessie Bartlett Davis (Alan a Dale). First British performance September 20, 1890, London, Camden Town Park Hall.

In this version of the story, which keeps to the standard tale, the Sheriff of Nottingham takes away the lands of Robert, Earl of Huntington, forcing him to become Robin Hood, and favors his own man, Guy of Gisborne, promising him Maid Marian in marriage. Robin is betrayed by one of his band and forced to watch the wedding of Marian to Guy and of Annabel, the beloved of Alan a Dale, to the Sheriff, before Robin's scheduled execution. Before the marriages can be completed, however, Friar Tuck and Little John lead members of Robin's band to the rescue, complete with a pardon from King Richard, who has returned from the Crusades.

For a detailed description, see Gänzl/*BBM*, 18–23.
Roles: Robert of Huntington (Robin Hood) (ten); the Sheriff of Nottingham (bar); Sir Guy of Gisborne (ten); Little John (bar); Will Scarlet (bass); Friar Tuck (bass); Alan a Dale (alto); Lady Marian Fitzwalter (Maid Marian) (sop); Dame Durden (mezzo); and Annabel, her daughter (sop).

The work included the soon-to-be-famous number "O Promise Me," sung by Alan a Dale, a travesty role; it was added as a showcase number for Jessie Bartlett Davis at the premiere. The opera's sequel was *Maid Marian** (1901, Philadelphia).

LIBRETTO: English (Chicago: S. Thompson, 1890).
SCORE: vs (New York: G. Schirmer, 1891; repr. ed. by Martha Furman Schleifer, *American Opera and Music for the Stage*, vol. 5 ([Boston]: G. K. Hall, 1990).

Robin Hood, folk-song opera in two acts by Michael Tippett; libretto (Eng) by the composer, David Ayerst, and Ruth Pennyman. First performance 1934, Boosbeck, England.
   The story concerns Marret, who is in love with Alan-a-Dale but courted by Lord Lamkin, the warden of Sherwood Forest. Robin Hood, in disguise, arranges to have Friar Tuck marry Marret and Alan-a-Dale while Lamkin is otherwise occupied.
   For a detailed description, see Kemp/*Tippett*, 26–27, 80–83.
   The work is for voices and chamber ensemble. Two of the numbers were used in the composer's *Suite for the Birthday of Prince Charles* (1948).
   Other modern treatments of the Robin Hood legend include Glenn Paxton's *Friar Tuck* (ca. 1983); and the Stephen Oliver-Tim Rice musical *Blondel* (1983, Bath, Engl.).

Rob of the Fens, or, The Daughter's Vow, adaptation by Frank Romer of H. Marschner's *Des Falkners Braut* (1832, Leipzig); libretto (Eng) by Mark Lemon, a translation of Wohlbrück's text. First performance July 7, 1838, London, Lyceum Theatre.
LIBRETTO: printed vs, ms orch. parts (British Library, MS. Add. 33806–33809).

Rob Roy, or, The Thistle and the Rose, romantic comic opera in three acts by Reginald De Koven; libretto (Eng) by Harry B. Smith, after Sir Walter Scott's novel (1818). First performance October 29, 1894, New York, Herald Square Theatre, with William Pruette (Rob Roy), Richard F. Carroll (the mayor of Perth), Juliette Corden (Janet), Lizzie MacNichol (Flora MacDonald), Barron Berthald (Prince Charles), and William McLaughlin (Lochiel); conducted by Antonio DeNovellis.
   Joining Scott's hero Rob Roy in the action of this opera is the comic villain mayor of Perth, Douglas MacWheeble. The mayor's daughter, Janet, in reality the wife of Rob Roy, is married off by her father first to a Scotsman and then to an Englishman. A parallel romantic interest is that of Prince Charles and Flora MacDonald, an heiress. Flora protects her lover from capture by putting on his clothes and being imprisoned in his place. Rob Roy, Lochiel, and the other Highlanders eventually help Flora and the prince make their way to France.
SCORE: vs (New York: G. Schirmer, 1894).
LIBRETTO: English ([Chicago]: Stone and Kimball, 1894).

Rob Roy Macgregor, or, Auld Lang Syne, musical drama in three acts by John Davy; libretto (Eng) by Isaac Pocock, after Scott. First performance March 12, 1818, London.
   Rob Roy saves Francis Osbaldistone, who is then able to marry his beloved, Diana Vernon.
LIBRETTO: English (London: J. Miller; New York: D. Longworth, 1818).

Rocket, The, opera in one act by Edward M. Goldman; libretto (Eng) by the composer, after Ray Bradbury's story of the same name. Composed 1960.
SCORE: ms fs, holograph (1960, photocopy, NYPL).

Rocking Stone, The, opera in two acts by David Selwyn; libretto (Eng) by the composer. First performance February 23, 1980, Bristol, England, Bristol Grammar School.

Rock Justice, rock opera by Marty Balin; libretto (Eng) by Robert Heyman. First performance December 1979, San Francisco.

Roland for an Oliver, A, musical farce in two acts by Henry Rowley Bishop; libretto by Thomas Morton (Eng). First performance April 29, 1819, London, Covent Garden, with Mrs. Selbourne.
SCORE: ms score (1819, British Library, MS. Add. 27711).

Romance, or, Bold Dick Turpin, opera by Henry Leslie; libretto (Eng) by J. Palgrave Simpson. First performance 1857, London.
LIBRETTO: English (London: Published and Sold in the Theatre, [186?]).

Romance of a Day, The, "operatic drama" in two acts by Henry Rowley Bishop; libretto (Eng) by James R. Planché. First performance February 3, 1831, London, Covent Garden.
SCORE: ms fs (British Library, Add. MS. 36959).

Roman Fever, opera in one act by Robert Ward; libretto (Eng) by Roger Brunyate, after the short story by Edith Wharton (1934). First performance June 9, 1993, Durham, North Carolina, Triangle Opera Theater, Duke University, with Katherine Kulas (Alida Slade), Monica Reinagel (Grace Ansley), Paul Gibson (Eduardo), Karie Brown (Barbara Ansley), and Melody Morrison (Jenny Slade); conducted by Scott Tilley; directed by Charles St. Clair.

The setting is the terrace restaurant of a Roman hotel at the edge of Capitoline Hill in the middle of the 1920s. Two American widows in their forties, together with their daughters, are vacationing in Rome. While their daughters are going on dates with eligible Italian men, the mothers, Grace Ansley and Alida Slade, reminisce about their own experiences in Rome when they were young. Alida recalls how she became violently ill with a fever, while Grace went to meet Delphin Slade, Alida's eventual husband, because of a forged note to Grace, supposedly from Delphin, that Alida had written herself. The women become angry with each other, and when Alida points out that Grace got nothing from her encounter with Delphin, Grace turns around and reveals: "Nothing? I had Barbara!"

Roles: Alida Slade (sop); Jenny Slade, her daughter (lyr sop); Grace Ansley (mezzo); Barbara Ansley, her daughter (mezzo); and Eduardo, a waiter (bar).

Among the musical highlights is Eduardo's "Ballad of Roman Fever."

Also set by Philip Hagemann (1989, Santa Fe).
SCORE: vs (Boston: Vireo Press, n.d.).
BIBLIOGRAPHY: Carl J. Halperin, "Durham," *ON* LVIII (Nov. 1993), 51–52 [on premiere].

Romeo and Juliet, lyric drama in three acts by Harry Rowe Shelley; libretto (Eng) by the composer, after Shakespeare's play (1594–1595). Composed 1901.

A setting of the tragic love story.

Roles: Juliet (sop), Lady Capulet (mezzo), nurse (alto), Romeo (ten), Capulet (bar), Tybalt (bar), Mercutio (bass), Benvolio (bar), the prince (bass), Peter (ten), Paris (nonspeaking), and Friar Lawrence (nonspeaking).
SCORE: vs, English-German (New York and London: Edw. Schuberth, 1901).

Romeo and Juliet, opera in four acts by George W. L. Marshall-Hall; libretto (Eng) by the composer, after Shakespeare. First performance (one scene), December 14, 1912, Melbourne, Australia, Her Majesty's Theatre.
SCORE: vs (London: Enoch & Sons, 1914).

Romeo and Juliet, opera in four acts by John Edmund Barkworth; libretto (Eng) by the composer, after Shakespeare's play. First performance January 7, 1916, Middlesbrough, England.

Among the many other operatic treatments of the Shakespeare play are G. Benda's *Romeo und Julie* (1776, Gotha); V. Bellini's *I Capuleti e i Montecchi* (1830, Venice); C. Gounod's *Roméo et Juliette* (1867, Paris); F. Delius's *A Village Romeo and Juliet** (1907, Berlin); R. Zandonai's *Giuletta e Romeo* (1922, Rome); H. Sutermeister's *Romeo und Julia* (1940, Dresden); B. Blacher's *Romeo und Julia* (1947, Berlin-Zehlendorf); and L. Bernstein's musical *West Side Story** (1957, New York).

Romp, The, or, A Cure for the Spleen, musical entertainment in two acts by Charles Dibdin; libretto (Eng) by John Lloyd, after Bickerstaffe's *Love in the City** (1767, London). First performance January 23, 1771, Dublin, Capel Street, with Dorothy Jordan. First U.S. performance August 5, 1791, Fredericksburg, Virginia, West-Bignall Company; October 1792, Philadelphia, Southwark Theatre, Old American Company.

See Fiske/*ETM*, 337–39, for a description.

LIBRETTO: English (London: W. Lowndes [etc.], 1786; Philadelphia: Mathew Carey, 1792).

Romulus Hunt, children's opera by Carly Simon; libretto (Eng) by the composer and Jacob Brackman; orchestrated by Matthias Gohl; arranged by Gohl and Greg Pliska. First performance February 22, 1993, New York, John Jay Theater, with Andrew Harrison Leeds (Romulus), Luretta Bybee (Mom), Greer Grimsley (Dad), Wendy Hill (Mica), and Jeff Hairston (Zoogy); conducted by Jeff Halpern; directed by Francesca Zambello.

A twelve-year-old boy living in New York attempts to bring his divorced parents back together again. He is comforted by Zoogy, his imaginary friend.

SCORE: vs (Milwaukee: H. Leonard, 1995).

BIBLIOGRAPHY: Brian Kellow, "Mother of Reinvention," *ON* LVII (Feb. 13, 1993), 36–37, 45; Robert Sandla, "New York," *ON* LVII (June 1993), 46 [on premiere].

DISCOGRAPHY: K. Ollman, A. Leeds, J. Hairston, L. Bybee, W. Hill; cond. J. Halpern, Angel CDQ 0777 7 54915 24 (1993, 1 CD).

Room No. 12, opera in one act by Ernest Kanitz; libretto (Eng) by Richard Thompson. First performance February 26, 1958, Los Angeles, UCLA Workshop.

A young man tries to kill himself in Room No. 12 of a rooming house, but his neighbor, smelling gas, calls the police. The young man, as he regains consciousness, sees visions from his past and present. To escape from this nightmare, he breaks through the window and falls to his death.

Major roles: the young man (ten), Myrtle (mezzo), the mother (alto), the father (bass), Beth (sop), Mae (sop), Joe (bar), and George (bar).

For a detailed description see Eaton/*OP* II, 319.

Rope, The, opera in one act by Louis Mennini; libretto (Eng) by the composer, after the play by Eugene O'Neill. First performance August 8, 1955, Lenox, Massachusetts, Tanglewood, with Holly McLennan, Sarana Maidich, Robert Kerns, Stephen Harbachick, and Peyton Higgison; conducted by Boris Goldovsky.

Abraham Bentley, infuriated that Luke, his son from a second marriage, has abandoned him, spends his days cursing the missing boy and making the lives of his daughter, Annie, her husband, Pat, and their child, Mary, unbearable. The old man has hung a rope in the old barn with which to hang his son should he return. Pat discovers that Abraham has left the farm to Luke in his will and also hidden $1,000 of gold pieces somewhere on the property. When Luke shows up suddenly, he gives Mary a silver dollar, which he tells her to skip off the cliff into the sea. Pat then makes plans with

Luke to get Abraham to reveal where he has hidden the gold; they will use force if necessary. Mary, alone in the barn, swings on the rope, which breaks and deposits the girl on an old bag full of shiny gold pieces. She takes them one by one and skips them into the sea, as her uncle has shown her with the silver piece.

For a detailed description, see Eaton/*OP* I, 215–16.

Roles: Abraham Bentley (bass), Annie (mezzo), Pat Sweeney (ten), Luke Bentley (bar), and Mary (speaking).

BIBLIOGRAPHY: Winthrop Sargeant, review, *NY* XXXI (Aug. 20, 1955), 78ff. [on premiere].

Rosalinda, musical drama in one act by John Christopher Smith; libretto (Eng) by John Lockman. First performance January 4, 1740, London, Hickford's Rooms, Apollo Society, with Cecilia Young (Rosalinda) and John Beard (Garcia).

Believing that her lover, Garcia, has been killed, Rosalinda goes into seclusion. He turns up quite alive, however.

LIBRETTO: English (London: Printed by W. Strahan for the author, 1740).

Rosamond, opera in three acts by Thomas Clayton; libretto (Eng) by John Addison, after Thomas May's poem *The Death of Rosamond*. First performance March 4, 1707, London, Drury Lane Theatre, with Mr. Hughes (King Henry), Mrs. Tofts (Queen Eleanor), Mr. Leveridge (Sir Trusty), Miss Gallia (Rosamond), and Miss Lindsey (Grideline).

The story concerns Rosamond, the mistress of King Henry II. Although the Queen, jealous of her rival, poisons Rosamond, all ends happily as Henry repents, promising to remain faithful, and Rosamond recovers from the poison, whose effect was only temporary. The happy ending, required by the newly emerging operatic convention, is contrary to the fate of Rosamond in May's poem.

For a detailed description, see Fiske/*ETM*, 45–48.

Major roles: Rosamond (sop); King Henry (counterten); Sir Trusty, his aide (bass); and Grideline, his wife (alto).

The work, trumpeted as the first all-sung English opera, was a miserable failure, because of both the turgid libretto and insipid music.

Rosamond, opera in three acts by Thomas A. Arne; libretto (Eng) by John Addison. First performance March 7, 1733, London, Haymarket. Revived as an afterpiece March 8, 1740, London, Drury Lane Theatre.

LIBRETTO: English (Dublin: Ebenezer Rider et al., 1743).

Rosamond, all-sung afterpiece in one act by Samuel Arnold; libretto (Eng) by John Addison, first set by Clayton and Arne (see preceding entries). First performance April 21, 1767, London, Covent Garden, with Miss Poitier.

LIBRETTO: English (London: L. Davis and C. Reymers, 1767).

Rose, The, comic opera in two acts by Thomas Augustine Arne; libretto (Eng) probably by the composer. First performance December 2, 1772, London, Drury Lane Theatre.

Following his father's will, Lord Gainlove invites all eligible young women to his coming-out party displaying a "Rose which Time can ne'r decay," that is, their virtue.

SCORE: overture, parts ([London]: John Johnson, Longman, Lukey & Co., n.d.).

LIBRETTO: English (London: E. & C. Dilly and W. Griffin, 1773).

Rose, The, or, Love's Ransom, grand opera in three acts by John Liptrot Hatton; libretto (Eng) by Henry Sutherland Edwards. First performance November 26, 1864, London, Covent Garden, with George Perren (Stephen), Henry Corri (Blancbec), Mr.

Weiss (Jacques), Aynsley Cook (Captain), Mr. Dussek (sergeant), Mr. Jones (corporal), Madame Weiss (Georgette), and Miss Poole (Theresa).

The work was a failure.

LIBRETTO: English (London: Boosey and Co., [1864?]).

Rose Affair, The, opera in one act by Norman Kay; libretto (Eng), after Alun Owen's play. First performance May 19, 1968, London, BBC.

Rose and Colin, comic opera in one act by Charles Dibdin; libretto (Eng) by the composer, after Sedaine. First performance September 18, 1778, London, Covent Garden. LIBRETTO: English (London: G. Kearsly, 1778).

Rose and the Ring, The, opera in three acts by Ethel Leginska; libretto (Eng) by E. E. Ohlson, after Thackeray's fairy tale (1854). Composed 1932. First performance February 23, 1957, Los Angeles, Wiltshire Ebell Theater.

A magic rose and a magic ring make their possessors seem to be good-looking and lovable. Prince Giglio and Princess Rosalba lose their magic amulets and thereby the position they grant; now humbled, Giglio and Rosalba acquire their rightful places once again with the help of Fairy Blackstick.

Rose and the Ring, The, chamber opera by Betsy Warren; libretto (Eng) by the composer, after Thackeray. Composed 1980. SCORE: vs, ed. John Blood (London and Boston: Wicasset Music, 1983).

Rose Garden, The, theater piece in one act by Anne Boyd; libretto (Eng) by Robin Hamilton. Composed 1972.

The symbolic story presents humankind's desire to reach an ideal, here, the Rose, which the Searcher must get after surmounting many obstacles in the Rose Garden.

The work, which contains electronic passages, is scored for dramatic soprano, three mimed roles, chorus, and chamber ensemble. SCORE: vs ([London]: Faber Music, 1973).

Rose-Marie, operetta by Rudolf Friml, with Herbert Stothart; libretto (Eng) by Otto Harbach and Oscar Hammerstein II. First performance September 2, 1924, New York, Imperial Theatre, with Mary Ellis (Rose-Marie) and Dennis King (Jim Kenyon). First British performance March 20, 1925, London, Drury Lane Theatre, with Edith Day (Rose-Marie) and Derek Oldham (Jim).

The setting is the Canadian Rockies. Rose-Marie, a part-Indian singer, is in love with Jim Kenyon, who is falsely accused of murdering his neighbor, Black Eagle, by Jim's rival, Ed Hawley. Ultimately, Jim is cleared, and the lovers are reunited.

Among the memorable numbers of the highly successful work, which was immortalized by the movie with Jeanette MacDonald and Nelson Eddy (1936), are "Indian Love Call" and the title song. SCORE: vs (New York: Harms, 1925).

Rose of Aragon, The, or, The Vigil of St. Mark, "melo-drama" in two acts by Rayner Taylor; libretto (Eng) by Samuel B. H. Judah. First performance 1822, New York. LIBRETTO: English (New York: S. King, 1822).

Rose of Castille, The, opera in three acts by Michael Balfe; libretto (Eng) by Augustus G. Harris and Edmund Falconer, after d'Ennery and Clairville's text for A. Adam's *Le muletier de Tolède* (1854, Paris). First performance October 29, 1857, London, Lyceum.

Major roles: Pablo, Elvira, Carmen, Manuel, Don Sallust, Don Cesar, Don Pedro, and Beatrix.
SCORES: ms fs, chiefly autograph (1857, British Library, MS. Add. 29352, 29353); vs (London and New York: Boosey & Co., [n.d.]; with libretto).
LIBRETTO: English (London: Cramer, Beale, and Wood, [1857]).

Rose of Destiny, The, opera in a prelude and three acts by Céleste de Longpré Heckscher; libretto (Eng) by the composer. First performance May 2, 1918, Philadelphia, Metropolitan House.

In the allegorical story, Time and Fate live in the Abode of Destiny. Fate brings news that two Mortals have stolen the "Rose of Destiny," which will bring reprisals on the Man and the Woman. Time, after Fate leaves, vows to help the Mortals. In the second act, set in the Garden of Mortals, Fate pursues the Mortals, helped by Misfortune and Jealousy. Time intervenes to save the pair, and, in the third act, gives them the mystical flower.

Rose of Persia, The, or The Story-Teller and the Slave, comic opera in two acts by Arthur S. Sullivan; libretto (Eng) by Basil Hood. First performance November 29, 1899, London, Savoy Theatre, with Robert Evett (Jussuf), Henry Lytton (Sultan Mahmoud), Walter Passmore (Hassan), Ellen Beach Yaw (the Sultana), and Rosina Brandram (Zubeydeh). First U.S. performance September 6, 1900, New York, Daly's Theatre.

The story concerns the rich Hassan. Bored by his numerous wives, he arranges nightly entertainments, one of which includes a dancer who is really the Sultana, and her husband, the Sultan, disguised as a dervish.

Among the musical highlights are the drinking song "I Care Not if the Cup I Hold," sung by Jussuf. The work received 213 performances during its first London run. It was Sullivan's final success.
SCORE: vs (London: Chappell, Hopwood & Crew; New York: Boosey, 1900).

Rosina, comic opera in two acts by William Shield; libretto (Eng) by Frances Brooke, after Charles Favart's *Les moissoneurs*, set by E. Duni (1768, Paris). First performance December 31, 1782, London, Covent Garden, with Mr. Bannister (Captain Belville), Mr. Johnstone (Captain Belville), Mrs. Kennedy (William), Miss Harper (Rosina), Mrs. Pitt (Dorcas), and Mrs. Martyr (Phoebe). First U.S. performance April 19, 1786, New York. Revived May 1983, London, Regent's Park, Open Air Theatre, with Laureen Livingstone and Martyn Hill; conducted by Howard Williams.

Two supposed sisters, Rosina and Phoebe, live in the cottage of Dorcas, their mother. The beautiful Rosina is desired by the villainous Captain Belville. After she refuses a purse of money from him, he has her abducted by his servants. His brother, a decent chap, learns from Dorcas that Rosina is really of noble birth. She is rescued by Irish laborers, and Captain Belville repents. Rosina weds Mr. Belville, and Phoebe marries William, an attentive farm hand.

For a detailed description, see Fiske/*ETM*, 456–58.

Six of the eighteen numbers are based on ballad tunes. The musical highlights include Belville's "Her Mouth, Which a Smile" and "Sweet Transports." The work also has an Irish tune.
SCORES: vs (London and New York: Boosey & Co., [18??]); ss (London: J. Dale, ca. 1791).
LIBRETTO: English (12th ed., London: T. Cadell, 1788).
DISCOGRAPHY: E. Harwood, M. Sinclair, R. Tear, K. MacDonald, Ambrosian Singers, London Symphony Orch.; cond. R. Bonynge, Decca LXT 6254 (LP); rev. Arthur Jacobs, *Opera* XVIII (Jan. 1967), 51.

Rosina, opera by Hiram Titus; libretto (Eng) by Barbara Field. First performance April 26, 1980, Minneapolis, Minnesota Opera, with Sharon Daniels (Rosina), Evan Bortnick (Cherubino), Evelyn Petros (Amparo), and Robert Orth (the Count); conducted by Philip Brunelle.

The opera's story continues the tale begun in Rossini's *Barber of Seville* and Mozart's *Marriage of Figaro*. Unlike Beaumarchais's own sequel, *La mère coupable* (1792), Field's plot contains a live Cherubino (Beaumarchais killed him off before the 1792 story begins), who has deserted the army and run off to Madrid with Rosina, where the couple are struggling in poverty and awaiting the birth of their child. When Count Almaviva arrives, in disguise, with another young woman, Amparo, he asks Rosina to return with him. She does in the end, leaving Cherubino to try his luck with Amparo.
BIBLIOGRAPHY: Michael Anthony, "Minnesota Opera: Titus Premiere," *MA* XXX (Sept. 1980), 22–23; M. A. Feldman, "Minneapolis," *ON* XLV (Aug. 1980), 28–29 [on premiere].

Roswell Incident, The, opera in two acts by John Hardy; libretto (Eng) by Heledd Wyn. First performance May 9, 1997, Bury St. Edmunds, England, Theatre Royal, with Sian Winstanley (child/alien), Gareth Lloyd, and Gwion Thomas (officer); conducted by Michael Rafferty; produced by Michael McCarthy; designed by Simon Banham.

The plot is set against the backdrop of the Roswell Incident, in which, in 1947, residents in the New Mexico town saw what they thought was a UFO and alien bodies; the official explanation was that the United States Air Force was testing a new type of alloy, and the alien bodies were dummies used in the testing. In the opera, a neurotic American intelligence officer relates the events and the subsequent cover-up and ends with a warning that the earth's inhabitants should treat each other better.
BIBLIOGRAPHY: Rodney Milnes, review, *Opera* XLVIII (Aug. 1997), 990 [on premiere].

Round Robin, afterpiece in one act by Charles Dibdin; libretto (Eng) by Charles Isaac Mungo Dibdin. First performance June 21, 1811, London, Little Theatre in the Haymarket.

Dibdin's last stage work.
SCORE: ms, songs (British Library, Add. MS. 30952–3).

Round Table, The, music drama in a prologue and three acts by Rutland Boughton; libretto (Eng) by R. Buckley and the composer. First performance August 14, 1916, Glastonbury.

Part of the Arthurian cycle, which also includes *The Birth of Arthur** (1920), *The Lily Maid** (1934), *Galahad** (comp. 1944, not perf.), and *Avalon** (1945, not perf).

Royal Auction, opera in one act by Ernest Kanitz; libretto (Eng) by Sidney Shrager and Alexander Chorney. First performance (with *Room No. 12**) February 26, 1958, Los Angeles, UCLA Workshop.

The pretender to the throne of the mythical Microtania, Count Michael Massarotti, is in love with Sally Jones, an American schoolteacher, but his aide, General de Luro, wants him to marry either Iris Stoner or Kitty De Vries, both wealthy women. When the three women meet, the Count tells them that the revolution to restore him to the throne has failed. Although this is a lie, the two wealthy women quickly leave him, with only Sally, his real love, staying by his side as he declares his intention to become plain "Mike Massarotti."

For a detailed description, see Eaton/*OP* II, 320–21.

Major roles: Sally (sop), Michael (bar), Iris (sop), and Kitty (sop).

Royal Garland, The, all-sung afterpiece in one act by Samuel Arnold; libretto (Eng) by Isaac Bickerstaffe. First performance October 10, 1768, London, Covent Garden.

Composed for the visit of the young king of Denmark.

LIBRETTO: (London: T. Becket and P. A. De Hondt, 1768).

Royal Hunt of the Sun, opera in two acts by Iain Hamilton; libretto (Eng) by the composer, after Peter Shaffer's play (1965). First performance February 2, 1977, London, Coliseum, English National Opera, with Harry Coghill (Martin Ruiz), Geoffrey Chard (Francisco Pizarro), Emile Belcourt (Hernando de Soto), Dennis Wicks (Fray Vincente de Valverde), Alan Woodrow (young Martin), Tom McDonnell (Atahuallpa), Stuart Kale (Miguel de Estete), and David Bartleet (Rodas); conducted by David Lloyd-Jones; produced by Colin Graham; designed by David Collis.

The story takes place first in Spain, Panama, and Peru. Martin Ruiz, page of Pizarro and now an old man, reminisces about his past. The story moves to the Spanish conquest of Peru and the Incas. Pizarro, the Spanish commander, promises to set Atahuallpa, the Incas's king, free, once he has filled the Sun-chamber with gold. Pizarro goes back on his promise when the Spanish soldiers kill the Incas and their rulers.

Major roles: Francisco Pizarro, commander of the expedition (bar); Atahuallpa, sovereign Inca of Peru (bar); Hernando de Soto, second in command (ten); Miguel de Estete, royal veedor (ten); Martin Ruiz, Pizarro's page, as an old man (bass-bar); and Fray Vincente de Valverde, chaplain to the expedition (bass).

SCORE: vs (Bryn Mawr, Pa.: Theodore Presser, 1971).

Royal Merchant, The, comic opera by Thomas Linley Sr.; libretto (Eng) by Thomas Hull, after Beaumont and Fletcher's *The Royal Merchant, or, The Beggar's Bush* (1761). First performance December 14, 1767, London, Covent Garden.

The work is set in Flanders.

SCORE: vs (London: Welcker, [1768]).

LIBRETTO: English (London: W. Griffin, 1768).

Royal Oak, The, musical "drama" by Michael Kelly; libretto (Eng) by William Dimond. First performance June 10, 1811, London, Theatre Royal, Haymarket, with Mr. Elliston (Charles II), Mr. Eyre (Colonel Wyndham), Mrs. Glover (Lady Matilda Wyndham), and Mrs. Barnes (Elinor).

Set in the middle of the seventeenth century, the work concerns Charles II of England.

LIBRETTO: English (London: J. Barker, 1811).

Royal Pastoral, The, all-sung afterpiece by James Nares; libretto (Eng) by Daniel Bellamy. First performance 1769, Windsor Castle.

The work centers on the shepherds Damon and Delia, who represent George III and his wife.

SCORE: vs (London: Welcker, [1770?]).

Royal Shepherd, The, opera in three acts by George Rush; libretto (Eng) by Richard Rolt, an English version of *Il re pastore* by Pietro Metastasio. First performance February 24, 1764, London, Drury Lane Theatre, with Mr. Vernon (Amintas), Miss Young (Thamiris), Miss Cremonini (Eliza), and Mrs. Dorman (Agenor).

The plot centers on the love affair of the shepherd Amintas (in reality the heir to the throne of Sidon), who is in love with Eliza. Alexander the Great, who has deposed the king of Sidon, wants Amintas to wed Thamiris, the former king's daughter; she herself is in love with another.

Roles: Alexander, King of Macedon; Amintas, a shepherd; Eliza, in love with Amintas; Thamiris, fugitive princess, in love with Agenor; Camilla, confidante to Eliza; and Agenor.

*Amintas** (1769, London) is an adaptation of the libretto. Metastasio's text was first set by G. Bonno in 1751 (Vienna), as *Il rè pastore*. Other settings include that by Mozart (1775, Salzburg).

SCORE: vs (London: Welcker, [1764]).
LIBRETTO: English (2d ed., London: W. Owen, 176?).

Royal Vagrants, The, "a story of conscientious objection," comic opera in two acts by Harry Waldo Warner; libretto (Eng) by Cyril Hurst. First performance October 27, 1899, London, Forest Gate, Earlham Hall.
LIBRETTO: English (London: H. J. Drane, 1901).

Royal Word, The, comic opera in one act by Isidore de Lara; libretto (Eng) by Henry Hersee. First performance April 17, 1883, London, Gaiety Theatre, with de Lara (Charles II), W. S. Rising (Frank Trevallyan), and Mathilde Wadman (Katherine).

Rubios, Los, opera in three acts by Mary Moore; libretto (Eng) by Neeta Marquis. First performance September 10, 1931, Los Angeles, Greek Theater, with Harold Hodge (Don Miguel Rubio), Dorothy Newman Smith (Ramoncita), and William Wheatley (Henry Durley); conducted by Glenn Tindall.

Ramoncita, daughter of Don Miguel Rubio, is in love with Mark McGregor, a county surveyor. The unscrupulous Sheriff Henry Durley plans to seize the land of the Rubio family and marry Ramoncita, but he is foiled by McGregor.

Among the musical highlights is the American square dance series in act 3, which is based on the dance tune "Sir Roger de Coverly."
SCORE: ms vs (1931, LC, LCCN: 84-68861).

Ruby, The, lyric drama in one act by Norman Dello Joio; libretto (Eng) by William Mass, after Lord Dunsany's *A Night at an Inn*. First performance May 13, 1955, Bloomington, Indiana, University of Indiana, with Millicent McConochy (Laura), Ticho Parley (Scott), Eugene Bayliss (Albert), Brandt Curtis (Sniggers), and James Serviss (Bull); conducted by Ernst Hoffman; produced by Hans Busch.

Scott, an English gentleman who has turned to crime, is the leader of a group of criminals who stole a great ruby from the eye of a statue in an Eastern temple. He and the other thugs have sought refuge from the three Indian priests who have pursued them to their English hideout, Scott's hunting lodge. Scott has his men, the ruthless Albert, Sniggers, and Bull, kill the priests, and, to the horror of his wife, Laura, Scott kills his cohorts also. But Scott is doomed as well, as the statue with the missing eye has come to life and hunted down the thieves.

Major roles: Laura (sop), Scott (bar), Albert (ten), Sniggers (ten), and Bull (bass), three Indian priests (silent, preferably dancers).

For a detailed description, see Eaton/*OP* I, 217.
BIBLIOGRAPHY: review, "Dello Joio Work Bows," *NYT* (May 15, 1955), 77 [on premiere].

Ruddigore (orig. **Ruddygore**), **or, The Witch's Curse**, comic opera in one act by Arthur S. Sullivan; libretto (Eng) by William S. Gilbert, after his text for Clay's *Ages Ago.** First performance January 22, 1887, London, Savoy Theatre, with George Grossmith (Robin Oakapple), Durward Lely (Richard Dauntless), Richard Temple (Sir Roderic Murgatroyd), Rutland Barrington (Sir Despard Murgatroyd), Rudolph Lewis (Old Adam Goodheart), Leonora Braham (Rose Maybud), Jessie Bond (Mad Margaret), Rosina Brandram (Dame Hannah), Jessie Bond (Mad Margaret), and Miss Lindsay (Ruth). First U.S. performance February 21, 1887, New York, Fifth Avenue Theatre, with Courtice Pounds, George Thorne, Geraldine Ulmar, Kate Foster, and Fred Billington.

In the satirical story, the Murgatroyd family is cursed by having to commit a grave crime every day or die in agony. The curse has been put on the family by one of the victims of Sir Rupert Murgatroyd, first baronet of the family. The newest baronet, Robin, finds a way to get rid of the curse and also marry his beloved, Rose Maybud, while Sir Despard Murgatroyd, now free of having to commit crimes daily, weds Mad Margaret.

For a detailed discussion, see Stedman/*WSG*, 239–44.

Major roles: Sir Ruthven Murgatroyd, disguised as Robin Oakapple, a young farmer (bar); Richard Dauntless, his foster brother (ten); Sir Despard Murgatroyd, a wicked baronet (bar); Mad Margaret (mezzo); Old Adam Goodheart, Robin's faithful servant (bass); Rose Maybud, a village maiden (sop); Dame Hannah, Rose's aunt (alto); Zorah (sop) and Ruth (mezzo), professional bridesmaids; and Sir Roderic Murgatroyd, the twenty-first baronet (bass).

The character of Mad Margaret is a spoof on the various mad heroines of nineteenth-century Italian opera. Among the highlights is the finale of act 1, which includes the madrigal-like "When the Buds Are Blossoming," and the Ghost Scene of act 2.
SCORE: vs, arr. G. L. Tracy (New York: W. A. Pond, 1887).
LIBRETTO: English (London: Chappell, [1887?]; New York: Pond, 1887).

Ruined Maid, The, comic opera in one act by Seymour Barab; libretto (Eng) by the composer, after a poem by Thomas Hardy. First performance June 3, 1981, New York, Abraham Goodman Hall, with Carolyn Marcell and Brionna McMahon; Michael Fardink, piano.

An innocent scullery maid is blamed for other people's mistakes and subsequently fired. She becomes a successful courtesan, and when she meets her onetime employer, she finds that her former mistress has fallen on hard times. Each woman, however, envies the other.
BIBLIOGRAPHY: review, *NYT* (June 7, 1981).

Rule Britannia, afterpiece pastiche by Samuel Arnold; libretto (Eng) by J. Roberts. First performance August 18, 1794, London, Little Theatre in the Haymarket.
Also masque by Thomas Arne (*Britannia,** 1755).

Ruling Passion, The, comic opera by Philip Cogan; libretto (Eng) by Leonard MacNally. First performance February 24, 1778, Dublin, Capel Street Theatre.

Rumpelstiltskin, opera in two acts by Joseph Barber; libretto (Eng) by John Gardner, after the Brothers Grimm. First performance December 26, 1978, Philadelphia.

Rural Felicity, comic opera in two acts, partly adapted, by Henry Rowley Bishop; libretto (Eng) by John B. Buckstone. First performance June 9, 1834, London, Little Theatre in the Haymarket.
Roles: Layton, Cecilia, and Harriet.
SCORE: ms fs, autograph (1834, British Library, Add. MS. 27728).
LIBRETTO: English (London: W. Strange, 1834).

Russian Imposter, The, or, The Siege of Smolensko, opera by John Addison; libretto (Eng) by Henry Siddons and Samuel J. Arnold. First performance July 22, 1809, London, Lyceum.
LIBRETTO: English, songs, duets, choruses, finales (London: J. & E. Boyle, 1809).

Ruth, opera in one act by Lennox Berkeley; libretto (Eng) by Eric Crozier. First performance October 2, 1956, London, Scala Theatre, with Una Hale (Naomi), April Cantelo (Orpah), Anna Pollak (Ruth), Peter Pears (Boaz), and Thomas Hemsley (the head reaper); conducted by Charles Mackerras; produced by Peter Potter.

In a telling of the biblical story, Naomi, after her son dies, comes back to Bethlehem accompanied by Ruth, her daughter-in-law, who has pledged to remain with her, while another daughter-in-law, Orpah, returns to Moab. Although the reapers are hostile toward Ruth, since she is a foreigner, their mood changes when Boaz, their master and Naomi's wealthy kinsman, appears. In the end he agrees to marry Ruth.

Major roles: Naomi, an elderly widow; Ruth and Orpah (sop), her daughters-in-law; and Boaz, master of the reapers (ten).

The work consists of seven musical numbers in each scene, with the third connected by recitative, accompanied by piano. Among the numbers are Orpah's aria "Ah, Must I Leave Thee" and the duet "Ah, Let Not Anger Fill Your Voice" for Ruth and Boaz.
SCORE: vs (London: J. & W. Chester, [1960]).
BIBLIOGRAPHY: A. P., "Reports. London," *Opera* VII (1956), 701–2 [on premiere].

Ruth and Naomi, opera in seven scenes by Fritz Hart; libretto (Eng) by the composer, after the Bible. First performance July 7, 1917, Melbourne, Australia, Playhouse.

Ruth and Naomi, church opera in one act by Leslie Kondorossy; libretto (Eng) by Shawn Hall (Elizabeth Davis) and R. Glass, after the Bible. First performance April 28, 1974, Cleveland, Church of the Master.

Ruy Blas, grand opera in four acts by William Howard Glover; libretto (Eng) by the composer, after Victor Hugo's drama (1838). First performance October 24, 1861, London, Covent Garden, with Charles Santley (Don Sallust de Bazan), Charles Lyall (Don Caesar de Bazan), F. Payne (Don Diego), Aynsley Cook (Don Gomez), W. Harrison (Ruy Blas), Laura Baxter (Oscar), Susan Pyne (Duchess d'Alberquerque), Miss Thirlwall (Casilda), and Louisa Pyne (Anne of Neuberg).

Don Caesar de Bazan, who has frittered away his fortune, disappears, joining a group of bandits, with only Don Sallust de Bazan, one of his relatives, knowing where he is. Ruy Blas, Don Sallust's valet, is secretly in love with the Queen, the Don's enemy. When Don Sallust discovers Ruy Blas's secret, he forces the valet to help him humiliate the ruler by pretending to be Don Caesar and setting up a rendezvous with her. When the real Don Caesar arrives and nearly upsets the plan, Don Sallust gets him out of the way. Ruy Blas, unable to help the Queen escape, kills Don Sallust and takes poison.

Other operatic settings of the story include one by F. Marchetti (1869, Milan). Among the comic versions are William S. Gilbert's *Ruy Blas,* a parody subtitled "a preposterous piece of nonsense for private representation" (1866); Robert Reece's burlesque *Ruy Blas Righted, or, The Love, the Lover, and the Lackey* (1874); and Meyer Lutz's burlesque *Ruy Blas, or, The Blasé Roué* (1889, Birmingham).
LIBRETTO: English (London: Boosey and Sons, [1861?]).

S

Sacco and Vanzetti, unfinished opera in three acts by Marc Blitzstein; libretto (Eng) by the composer. Composed 1959–1964.

The work is about the trial of the two Italian anarchists who were convicted of murdering a paymaster and a guard at a shoe factory in Massachusetts in 1920. The defendants, who claimed they were innocent, were executed in 1927.

Blitzstein envisioned that act one would center on the title characters and their guilt or innocence. The second act would cover the trial, and the third the denial of appeals and the execution itself.

For a description and compositional history of the work, see Gordon/*MM*, 471–83, 498–501, and passim.

The work was commissioned by the Ford Foundation and initially set for a premiere at the Metropolitan Opera in January 1963.

Sack of Calabasas, The, opera in three acts by Grant Fletcher; libretto (Eng) by John Meyers. First performance (excerpts) April 6, 1964, Phoenix, Arizona, Musicians Club.

The setting is Calabasas, southern Arizona, 1882. The town of Calabasas, awash in sin, has started to boom because it is to become a stop on the new railroad. Abimelach, who says he is a preacher, arrives and gives a sermon about playing cards. The suspicious Sedalia Sue and Longhorn Charlie try to get him inebriated in order to learn the truth, but their plan fails. Slim Parr, the sheriff from a neighboring town, reveals Abimelach's true identity; he is a con man. When the townspeople go after Abimelach, they meet Ah Chin Honk, who gives them a letter from the pretend preacher that reveals that, according to a railway engineer, the railroad will not come through Calabasas. The crowd, angered, get drunk and torch the town.

Major roles: Abimelach Jones (dram bar), Deuces Wild (bass), Sedalia Sue (spinto sop), Longhorn Charlie (ten), Slim Parr (bar), and Ah Chin Honk (ten).

For a detailed description, see Eaton/*OP* II, 203–4.

Sacrapant, the Sorcerer, opera in one act for children by Peter Aston; libretto (Eng) by Paul Morgan. Composed 1967.
LIBRETTO: English (London: Novello, [1968]).

Sacrifice, The, opera in three acts by Frederick Converse; libretto (Eng) by the composer; lyrics by John A. Macy. First performance March 3, 1911, Boston, Boston Opera Company, with Alice Nielson (Chonita), Florencio Constantino (Bernal), Roman Bianchart (Burton), Maria Claessene (Tomasa), C. Stroesco (Pablo), Bernice Fisher (Magdalena), Grace Fisher (Marianna), Hedwig Berger (Señora Anaya), Carl Gantvoort (Padre Gabriel), and Howard White (Corporal Tom Flynn); conducted by Wallace Goodrich.

The setting is southwest California in 1846. The beautiful Chonita, a Mexican, is at the cottage of her aunt, Señora Anaya. While Chonita is waiting for the arrival of Bernal, a suitor, she learns that Captain Burton, an American, is also expected. He appears and asks for her hand in marriage, which Bernal, who is outside, overhears. He is enraged, but Chonita begs him to understand that she needs Burton's protection. He leaves.

Corporal Tom tells Chonita, who is praying at a ruined church, that Bernal has been killed in the fighting between the Americans and the Mexicans. She is left alone, and Bernal, who has merely been wounded, finds her there. He hides when Burton comes in with his soldiers. When they depart, Bernal emerges and begins to duel with Burton; Chonita steps between the two and is badly wounded. Filled with remorse and seeing that Chonita loves Bernal, Burton lets himself be killed by a Mexican soldier.

For a detailed description, see Hipsher/*AO*, 135–38.

Sadak and Kalasrade, or, The Waters of Oblivion, opera in two acts by Charles Packer; libretto (Eng) by Mary Russell Mitford, after Charles Morell's *Tales of the Genii*. First performance April 20, 1835, London, English Opera House, with Emma Romer, Henry Phillips, Charles Bland, and John Wilson.

An "oriental" tale along the lines of Weber's *Abu Hassan* (1811, Munich); G. Meyerbeer's *Wirth und Gast* (1813, Stuttgart); E. Loder's *Nourjahad** (1834); and P. Cornelius's *Der Barbier von Bagdad* (1858, Weimar).

Also set as a pantomime by Thomas J. Dibdin (1796, London) and as a musical by H. R. Bishop (1814, London).

SCORE: ms fs (1835, British Library, Add. MS. 36575–36577).
LIBRETTO: English (London: Printed for the proprietor by S. G. Fairbrother, [1835]).

Sadie Thompson, opera by Richard Owen; libretto (Eng) by the composer, after Somerset Maugham's short story *Rain* (1921). First performance November 1997, New York, Musical Theater Works, with Lynn Owen (Sadie) and Richard Holmes (Rev. Alfred Davidson).

The story deals with the fateful meeting of a prostitute, Sadie Thompson, and a missionary, the Reverend Alfred Davidson, on American Samoa, during the rainy season. After he converts Sadie, the missionary seduces the girl, whereupon she goes back to her old ways. Filled with guilt, Davidson kills himself.

Safe and Sound, comic opera in three acts by James Hook; libretto (Eng) by Theodore Edward Hook. First performance 1809, London, Lyceum Theatre.
LIBRETTOS: English (London: S. Tipper, 1809; New York: D. Longworth, 1810).

Safié, opera in one act by Henry Hadley; libretto (Eng) by Edward Oxenford. First performance, in a German translation by Otto Neitzel, April 4, 1909, Mainz, Stadttheater, with Marguerite Lemon (Safié), Konrad Röszner (Ahmed), Fritz Kupp (Alasman), Karl Bara (Zehu), and Jean Emsing (Mahud Khan); conducted by the composer.

Major roles: Safié, a Persian princess; Ahmed; Alasman, a magician; Zehu, his son; and Mahud Khan, a Persian noble and uncle of Safié.

Saga, folk opera by Kelly Hamilton; libretto (Eng) by the composer. First performance April 24, 1979, New York, Wonderhorse Theater, Lyric Theater of New York.

The work concerns Hoppin' Joe's trek across the United States in the nineteenth century. Three "Weavers of Legend" narrate much of the action.
LIBRETTO: English (New York: Broadway Play Publishers, 1983).
BIBLIOGRAPHY: Allen Hughes, "Opera: 'Saga,' Folk Work, at Lyric," *NYT* (Apr. 26, 1979), C, 21 [on premiere].

Sagegrass, folk opera by Shirl Jae Atwell; libretto (Eng) by Delmas W. Abbott. First performance (excerpts) January 13, 1986, New York.

Sailing of the Nancy Belle, The, opera in one act by Allan Davis; libretto (Eng) by the composer. Composed 1948. First performance August 3, 1955, Duxbury, Massachusetts, Plymouth Rock Center of Music and Art.

Roles: mezzo, ten/bar, bar.

SCORE: ms vs, holograph (photocopy, NYPL; New York: Boosey & Hawkes, 1948).

Saint of Bleecker Street, The, musical drama in three acts by Gian Carlo Menotti; libretto (Eng) by the composer. First performance December 27, 1954, New York, Broadway Theater, with Virginia Copeland (Annina), Maria Di Gerlando (Carmela), Leon Lishner (Don Marco), David Poleri (Michele), and Gloria Lane (Desideria); conducted by Thomas Schippers. First British performance October 4, 1956, BBC television, with Copeland (Annina), Raymond Nilsson (Michele), June Bronhill (Carmela), Jess Walters (Don Marco), and Rosalind Elias (Desideria); conducted by Schippers. First British stage performance July 27, 1962, with Mary Wells (Annina), Malcolm Robertson (Michele), and Moyna Cope (Desideria); conducted by Audrey Langford.

The setting is Little Italy in New York. The sickly Annina, called the "Saint of Bleecker Street" because of the stigmata on her hands, wants to take the veil before she dies. Michele, her nonbelieving brother, tries to keep her from taking part in religious rites. When he refuses to acknowledge his girlfriend, Desideria, the insulted woman accuses him of having an unnatural love for his sister. Enraged by the accusation, Michele stabs Desideria to death. Annina goes through with the religious ceremony to become Sister Angela, as her brother's attempts fail to stop her, and she dies.

For a detailed plot summary see K/*KOB*, 1353–56; K/*NKOB*, 462–63.

Major roles: Annina (sop); Carmela (sop); Don Marco, a priest (bass); Michele (ten); and Desideria (mezzo).

This verismo opera is one of several of the composer's works that stress his religious upbringing. It was tremendously successful in its Broadway run and drew a full house for 100 consecutive evenings. It also won the Pulitzer Prize in music in 1955.

SCORE: vs (New York: G. Schirmer, 1954).

LIBRETTO: English (New York: G. Schirmer, 1954).

BIBLIOGRAPHY: Lionel Dunlop, "Kentish Opera Group Season," *Opera* XIII (Sept. 1962), 634–35 [on British stage premiere]; James Hinton Jr., review, *Opera America* II (1955–1956), 113–40; John Warrack, review, *Opera* VII (1956), 703–4 [on British premiere].

Salem Witch, The, "an American comic opera" in three acts by Richard Stahl; libretto (Eng) by George Russell Jackson. First performance 1883, Boston?

LIBRETTO: English (Boston: W. A. Evans, 1883).

Salesgirl, The, opera in one act by Charles Hamm; libretto (Eng) by the composer. First performance March 1, 1955, Bristol, Virginia, Virginia Intermont College.

Sam Slick, chamber opera by Kelsey Jones; libretto (Eng), after Thomas Chandler Haliburton's *The Clockmaker* (1837). First performance September 5, 1967, Halifax.

About the fictional nineteenth-century Yankee clock peddler who plies his trade in Nova Scotia.

Samuel Pepys, comic opera in one act by Albert Coates; libretto (Eng) by William Price Drury and Richard Pryce; translated into German by Max Meyerfeld. First performance (in German) December 21, 1929, Munich, Staatstheater.

SCORE: ms vs, in German (n.p., n.d., LCCN: 85-69851).

BIBLIOGRAPHY: "Albert Coates's 'Pepys,'" *NYT* (Feb. 9, 1930), VII, 6 [on premiere].

Sancho at Court, or, The Mock-Governor, "an opera-comedy" (ballad opera); libretto (Eng) by James Ayres. First performance 1742, London, Drury Lane Theatre.

Major roles: Sancho, governor of Barataria; Antonio, a courtier in love with Lucinda; Alonzo, secretary; Rezio, state physician; Teresa Sancho, the governor's lady; Mary, Sancho's daughter; and Lucinda, beloved by Antonio.

LIBRETTO: English (London: J. Torbuck, 1742); repr. ed. Rubsamen/*BO*, vol. 6, *Satire, Burlesque, Protest, and Ridicule,* II (1974).

Sandhog, folk opera in three acts by Earl Robinson; libretto (Eng) by Waldo Salt, after the short story *St. Columba and the Stream* by Theodore Dreiser. First performance November 23, 1954, New York, Phoenix River Theatre, with Jack Cassidy (Johnny O'Sullivan), Betty Oakes (Katie O'Sullivan), David Brooks (Tim Cavanaugh), Alice Ghostley (Sheela Cavanaugh), Gordon Dilworth (Sharkey), Mordecai Bauman (Henderson), and Paul Ukena (Fred Burger).

The story centers on Johnny O'Sullivan, a New York City tunnel worker in the 1880s.

Roles: Johnny O'Sullivan (ten), Katie O'Sullivan (sop), Tim Cavanaugh (bar), Sheela Cavanaugh (alto), Sharkey (bar), Henderson (bass-bar), and Fred Burger (ten).

SCORE: vs (New York: Chappell [1956]).

DISCOGRAPHY: excerpts, Robinson, Salt, Vanguard VRS-9001 (1955, 1 LP).

Santa Claus, opera in five scenes by Leland Smith; libretto (Eng) by E. E. Cummings, after his morality play (1946). First performance December 9, 1955, Chicago.

San Toy, or, The Emperor's Own, "Chinese musical comedy" in two acts by Sidney Jones; libretto (Eng) by Edward Morton, Harry Greenbank, and Adrian Ross. First performance October 21, 1899, London, Daly's, with Marie Tempest (San Toy), Rutland Barrington (the Mandarin), Lionel Mackinder (Captain Bobbie Preston), Huntley Wright, and Gracie Leigh. First U.S. performance October 1, 1900, New York, with Marie Celeste (San Toy) and James T. Powers (Captain Bobbie Preston).

Like Jones's *The Geisha,** the work is set in Asia. Act 1 takes place in the make-believe Chinese town of Pynka Pong, and act 2 in the hall of the Emperor's palace in Peking.

Roles: San Toy, daughter of Yen How; Captain Bobbie Preston; Yen How, a mandarin; Sir Bingo Preston, the British Consul at Pynka Pong; Poppy, Bingo's daughter; Dudley, her maid; and Chu, a widow.

SCORE: vs (London: Keith Prowse; Cincinnati: J. Church, 1899).

LIBRETTO: English (London: Keith Prowse, 1899).

Sapphire Necklace, The (The False Heiress), opera in four acts by Arthur Sullivan; libretto (Eng) by Henry F. Chorley. First performance (excerpts) April 13, 1867, London, Crystal Palace.

Most of the music is lost. Two arias and the overture were performed in 1867.

DISCOGRAPHY: overture, RTE Concert Orch., Dublin; cond. A. Penny, Marco Polo Records 8-223461 (1992, 1 CD).

Sappho, opera in three acts by Peggy Glanville-Hicks; libretto (Eng) by Lawrence Durrell, after his play (1958). Composed 1963. Not performed.

The setting is the island of Lesbos, ca. 650. The elderly Kreon is married to Sappho, and he sends Phaon, brother of General Pittakos, to find out the truth about Sappho's birth, since she was found in the ruins of an earthquake. Sappho and Phaon fall in love, and Sappho rebuffs the advances of Pittakos, who has returned after a great victory.

Sappho is, in fact, an Oracle, which is known only by the poet Diomedes, whose son Pittakos has killed because of jealousy. She prepares to take over the duties of the Oracle, but Kreon finds, to his horror, that Sappho is in fact his own daughter. As punishment he and Sappho lose their possessions and are forced into exile. Their children are kept as hostages by Pittakos when she refuses to be his spy.

For a detailed description, see Eaton/*OP* II, 205–6.

Major roles: Sappho (mezzo), Diomedes (bar), Minos (bass-bar), Phaon (lyr ten), Pittakos (dram ten), and Kreon (bass).

Sarah, television opera in one act by Ezra Laderman; libretto (Eng) by Clair Roskam, after the Bible. First performance November 30, 1958, New York, CBS television, with Patricia Neway (Sarah).

A telling of the biblical story of Sarah and her love for her husband, Abraham.

BIBLIOGRAPHY: A. Hughes, "Sacred Triangle," *ON* XXIII (Dec. 29, 1958), 27 [on premiere].

Sarajevo, music theater piece in three parts by Nigel Osborne; libretto (Eng). First performance August 23, 1994, London, Queen Elizabeth Hall, Opera Factory.

The work focuses on the present-day conflict and killing in Bosnia and includes an abridged version of Don Taylor's translation of Euripides' *Trojan Women*; an operatic section, based on contemporary writings such as diaries; and an oratorio-like coda with a text by Craig Raine.

BIBLIOGRAPHY: Rodney Milnes, review, *Opera* XLV (Oct. 1994), 1223 [on premiere].

Sarrona, or, The Indian Slave, opera in a prologue and one act by William Legrand Howland; original libretto (Eng) by the composer; translated into Italian by R. P. G. First performance August 3, 1903, Bruges. First U.S. performance February 8, 1910, New York, Amsterdam Theater (in English).

The setting is the Ganges, India. The treacherous King Accaro, having brought about the ruin of his country and infatuated by a Greek dancer, is overheard by Queen Sarrona plotting further evils. When she tries to stab her husband, she is stopped by a slave. The rulers, however, admit that they are still in love with each other, which causes the slave to stab himself.

Sasha, opera in three acts by Stephen Oliver; libretto (Eng) by the composer, after A. N. Ostrovsky's *Artists and Admirers*. First performance April 7, 1983, Banff, Alberta.

When James, an Englishman, travels to Russia without his fiancée, he meets the singer Sasha, who is being dismissed from her post because she has refused the Prince's advances. In order to help her, James buys all of the tickets for a benefit performance. The attraction that Sasha and James have for each other is ruined when Nina, James's landlady, reminds him of his fiancée back at home, and Sasha gets an offer of a job from an impresario in St. Petersburg.

Satanella, or The Power of Love, opera in four acts by Michael Balfe; libretto (Eng) by A. G. Harris and Edmund Falconer, after Lesage's *Le diable boîteux*. First performance December 20, 1858, London, Covent Garden, with Louisa Pyne (Satanella). First U.S. performance February 23, 1863, New York, Park Theatre.

The setting is in the castle and palaces of Count Rupert, at the seashore at Tunis, and in the dominion of Arimanes. Count Rupert, losing his fortune by gambling on the evening of his wedding to Princess Stella, has taken up residence in the Castle of Brockenberg. According to legend, he has sold his soul to the devil in order to reclaim his fortune.

When Rupert finds an old book of magic, he utters one of the commands, upon which the devilish Arimanes appears, accompanied by Satanella, a female demon. Angered at having been summoned by a mere mortal, Arimanes has Satanella take the disguise of a pageboy to trap Rupert. Satanella meanwhile falls in love with Rupert, while he, amassing great wealth, proposes to his foster sister, Lelia, although he still loves Stella.

Satanella, upset by Rupert's attentions to Lelia, has her kidnapped and takes her place at the wedding, but Rupert notices the substitution and learns that his real bride has been seized. Arimanes demands that Satanella carry out her order and get Rupert's soul. Rupert has gone to the slave market in Tunis to save Lelia. Satanella offers to help him if he agrees to sign a contract giving her his soul. Rupert agrees, and Satanella obtains Lelia's release. Rupert and Lelia return to the castle and, after thirty days, Satanella comes to claim Rupert's soul. Lelia wants to share her husband's fate and prepares herself, at which point Satanella destroys the contract and becomes the victim herself. Lelia gives her a holy rosary, and when Arimanes and the furies arrive to drag her away, the relic repulses the demons, and she is saved by the power of her unselfish love.

For a detailed description, see Biddlecombe/*EO*, 119–22.

Major roles: Stella (mezzo), Satanella (sop), Rupert (ten), Lelia (mezzo), and Arimanes (bass).

SCORES: ms fs, autograph (1858, British Library, Add. MS. 29354, 29355); vs (Boosey & Co., n.d.).

LIBRETTOS: English (London: Theatre, [1858?]; [New York]: Wm. C. Bryant & Co., 1871).

DISCOGRAPHY: E. Falconer, A. G. Harris, S. Debret, B. Galloway, Opera Integra, Addison Orch., Rare Recorded Editions SRRE 173-174.

Satan's Trap, opera in three acts by Frederick Piket; libretto (Eng) by Charles S. Levy, after Gottfried Keller's short story *Romeo und Julia auf dem Dorfe*, from his collection *Leute von Seldwyla* (part 1, 1856; part 2, 1874). First performance November 26, 1960, New York, Clark Center, with Naomi Ornest, Arne Markussen, Keith Cota, and Ben Plotkin; conducted by Kurt Saffir; produced by Maurice Edwards.

Two children from warring families, encouraged by a stranger to leave their homes, go off together and drown in a river.

Another setting is Delius's *A Village Romeo and Juliet** (1907, Berlin).

Satyagraha, opera in three acts by Philip Glass; libretto (Eng, Sanskrit) by the composer and Constance DeJong, based on texts from the *Bhaghavad-Ghita*. First performance September 5, 1980, Rotterdam, Netherlands Opera, with Douglas Perry (Gandhi), Beverly Morgan (Kasturbai, his wife), Claudia Cummings (Miss Schlesen), and Bruce Hall (Mr. Kallenbach); conducted by Bruce Ferden; directed by David Pountney. First U.S. performance November 6, 1982, New York, Brooklyn Academy of Music, with Douglas Perry (Gandhi).

The work examines the early career of Gandhi in South Africa from 1893 to 1910. During this time Gandhi introduced his idea of "satyagraha," that is, truth force, which came to be known as "passive resistance."

The three acts, which are not chronological and are independent plotwise, are each observed by a historical figure (silent role) that inspired Gandhi: the first by Leo Tolstoy, representing the past; the second by the Indian poet Rabindranath Tagore, representing the present; and the third by Martin Luther King Jr., representing the future. In the first act, which opens with a mythological battle on the Kuru Field of Justice, Gandhi leads his fellow Indians in South Africa to form a self-sustaining collective, the

Tolstoy farm, in 1904. In the second, the newspaper *Indian Opinion* is started, and Gandhi rallies his followers to oppose the harsh "Black Act." In the third, the women of the collective, tutored by Gandhi in passive resistance, join the striking Newcastle miners.

The text is chanted, and the acts are connected by musical devices.

For a description, see Kornick/*RAO*, 124–27.

Major roles: Gandhi (ten); Miss Schlesen, his secretary (sop); Mrs. Naidoo, an Indian coworker (sop); Kasturbai, Gandhi's wife (mezzo); and Mr. Kallenbach, a European coworker (bar).

This is the second of Glass's series of "portrait" operas; the others are *Einstein on the Beach** (1976) and *Akhnaten** (1984).

LIBRETTOS: English and Sanskrit (Bryn Mawr, Pa.: Theodore Presser Co., 1980; New York: Standard Editions, 1980).

BIBLIOGRAPHY: Michael Altmann, *Sakrales Musiktheater im 20. Jahrhundert* (Regensburg: S. Roderer, 1993); Menno Feenstra, "Rotterdam," *ON* XLV (Jan. 17, 1981), 38–39 [on premiere]; Robert T. Jones, "The Sound of Glass," *ON* XLVI (July 1981), 17–18; Patrick J. Smith, "Glass Divides Opinions," *Opera* XXXIII (1982), 153–54 [on U.S. premiere].

Sāvitri, opera da camera in one act by Gustav Holst; libretto (Eng) by the composer, after an episode in the *Mahābhārata*. First performance December 5, 1916, London, Wellington Hall; conducted by Hermann Grunebaum. First public performance June 23, 1921, London, Lyric Theatre, with Dorothy Silk, Steuart Wilson, and Clive Carey; conducted by Arthur Bliss. First U.S. performance January 23, 1934, Chicago, Palmer House; conducted by Krueger. Modern revivals include one on November 15, 1978, Glasgow, Theatre Royal, with Janet Baker, Philip Langridge, and John Shirley-Quirk; conducted by Charles Mackerras.

Satyavān, a woodman, returns home to his wife, Sāvitri, and finds that Death has come to claim him. Moved by Sāvitri's welcome, Death promises her life in all its fullness and thereby is forced to surrender his claim on her husband.

For detailed descriptions, see K/*KOB*, 1127–28; K/*NKOB*, 367–68.

Roles: Satyavān (ten), Sāvitri (sop), and Death (bass).

The work has no overture, and the music contains rhythms patterned after speech and has a simple harmonic structure. The orchestra is small, and a wordless female chorus sings offstage.

The story was also set by H. Zumpe (unfinished, 1903, completed by Rössler, 1907).

SCORES: vs, fs, facsimile ed. (London: Curwen, [19??]); min. score (rev. ed. London: E. Eulenburg; New York: Edition Eulenburg, 1973, [1976]).

BIBLIOGRAPHY: J. B. Trend, "An Opera from the Sanskrit," *ML* II (Oct. 1921), 345–50.

DISCOGRAPHY: Palmer, Langridge, Varcoe, Hickox Singers, City of London Sinfonia; cond. Hickox, Hyperion A-66099 (Harmonia Mundi); rev. John W. Freeman, "Records," *ON* XLVIII (Apr. 14, 1984), 45.

Savonarola, opera in a prologue and three acts by Charles Villiers Stanford; original English libretto (Eng) by Gilbert A. A'Beckett; translated into German by Ernst Frank. First performance, in German, April 18, 1884, Hamburg, with Rosa Sucher (Clarice) and Ernst Frank (Savonarola); conducted by Josef Sucher. First British performance (in German) July 9, 1884, London, Covent Garden, with Miss Schaernack (Clarice), Mr. Stritt (Savonarola), and Karl Scheidemantel (Rucello); conducted by Hans Richter.

In the story the young Savonarola, a poor student, is in love with Clarice, who comes from a wealthy home. She is promised to Rucello, a Florentine noble. In despair Savonarola takes holy orders.

Savoyard, The, or, The Repentant Seducer, musical farce in two acts by Alexander Reinagle; libretto (Eng). First performance July 12, 1797, Philadelphia, New Theatre, with Mr. Moreton (Jacques), Mr. Fox (Belton), Mr. Harwood (Front), Mr. Warren (Simond), Mr. L'Estrange (Father Bertrand), Mrs. Francis (Countess), Mrs. Oldmixon (Nanette), and Mrs. Warrell (Claudine).

Saw-Mill, The, or, A Yankee Trick, ballad opera in two acts by Micah Hawkins; libretto (Eng) by the composer. First performance 1824, New York.

Considered the first opera by an American-born composer on an American subject.
LIBRETTO: English (New York : J. & J. Harper, 1824).
BIBLIOGRAPHY: Oscar Wegelin, *Micah Hawkins* (New York: author, 1917).

Scandal at Mulford Inn, The, opera by William Clifton Byrd; libretto (Eng). First performance May 20, 1954, Cincinnati, College of Music, Odeon; conducted by the composer.

Scarecrow, The, opera fantasy in two acts by Normand Lockwood; libretto (Eng) by Dorothy Lockwood, after Percy MacKaye's work (1908), itself based on Hawthorne's *Feathertop*. First performance May 19, 1945, New York, Columbia University.

The setting is early New England. The esteemed justice Gilead Merton has deserted Bess Rigby and their child. When the woman survives, the townspeople think she is a witch. Bess gives Rachel, the niece of Merton, a magic mirror that will show the truth to the viewer and makes a scarecrow with the help of Dickson, a Yankee devil. The scarecrow becomes alive via a corncob pipe, and Bess sends her creation, disguised as Lord Ravensbane, to win the affections of Rachel, who is engaged to Squire Richard Talbot. Although Talbot, using the mirror, shows Rachel that her new beloved is really a scarecrow, Rachel vows to stand by Ravensbane, and her love allows him to become human. He dies when the pipe is broken, but the townspeople, who have come to hang the scarecrow and Bess, are astounded by what they find.

Major roles: Bess Rigby (mezzo), Dickson (ten), Rachel Merton (sop), Richard Talbot (ten), Justice Gilead Merton (bass), and Scarecrow/Lord Ravensbane (ten).

For a detailed description, see Eaton/*OP* II, 206–7.

See *Feathertop* for other settings.

Scarf, The, opera in one act by Lee Hoiby; libretto (Eng) by Harry Duncan, after Anton Chekhov's short story *The Witch* (1886). First performance June 20, 1958, Spoleto, Italy, Teatro Caio Melisso, Festival of Two Worlds, with Patricia Neway (Miriam), John McCollum (Reuel), and Richard Cross (postman); conducted by Reinhard Peters; produced by Richard Evans. First U.S. performance April 5, 1959, New York, City Opera, City Center, with John Druary (Reuel), Neway (Miriam), and Cross (postman); conducted by Kirk Browning.

The story opens in an isolated farmhouse. The young, unhappy Miriam is married to the old Reuel. When he calls her to bed, she refuses. A postman, lost in the storm, arrives and is given refuge in the house. He and Miriam are attracted to each other, and when he leaves, in the company of Reuel, Miriam gives him a scarf to wrap around his neck. Alone, Miriam conjures up evil spirits to bring the postman back to her, with the help of the scarf. Reuel returns, the scarf around his neck. When he approaches Miriam, she chokes him with the scarf and summons the postman to return.

Roles: Miriam (sop); Reuel, her husband (ten); and the postman (bar).

For a detailed description, see Eaton/*OP* I, 219.

SCORE: vs (New York: G. Schirmer, 1959).
LIBRETTO: English (New York: G. Schirmer, 1959).
BIBLIOGRAPHY: Howard Taubman, review, *NYT* (Apr. 6, 1959), 33 [on U.S. premiere].

Scarlet Letter, The, grand opera in three acts by Walter Damrosch; libretto (Eng) by George Parsons Lathrop, after Nathaniel Hawthorne's novel (1850). First stage performance February 10, 1896, Boston, with Johanna Gadski (Hester Prynne), Wilhelm Mertens (Roger Chillingworth), and Baron Berthald (Arthur Dimmesdale).

The story is set in the seventeenth century in Puritan Boston. It sticks closely to the original, in which Hester Prynne is forced to wear a scarlet A on her breast for her adultery, but Hester's illegitimate child, Pearl, is left out. The plot centers on Hester; her secret lover, Reverend Arthur Dimmesdale; and Hester's evil husband, who has been away, returns and disguises himself as Chillingworth in an effort to discover his wife's lover. In the end the tormented Dimmesdale confesses publicly that he is Hester's lover and dies in Hester's arms.

Major roles: Hester Prynne (sop), Roger Chillingworth (bar), and Arthur Dimmesdale (ten).

The librettist was the son-in-law of Hawthorne.

SCORE: vs (Leipzig: Breitkopf & Härtel, 1896); repr. ed. Elise K. Kirk, *NAMT*, vol. 16 (1994).
LIBRETTO: English (Boston?: G. P. Lathrop, 1894); repr. ed. as above.

Scarlet Letter, The, opera in two acts by Vittorio Giannini; libretto (Eng) by Karl Flaster, after Hawthorne. First performance June 2, 1938, Hamburg, Staatsoper, with Dusolina Giannini (Hester Prynne), Ferdinand Frantz, Hans Hotter, and Joachim Sattler; conducted by Eugen Jochum.

Scarlet Letter, The, opera in three acts by Walter Kaufmann; libretto (Eng) by the composer, after Hawthorne. First performance May 6, 1961, Bloomington, Indiana, Indiana University Opera Theater.

Scarlet Letter, The, opera by Donald Lybbert; libretto (Eng), after Hawthorne. Composed 1964–1967.

Scarlet Letter; The, opera in four acts by Frederic Kroll; libretto (Eng) from the novel of the same name by Nathaniel Hawthorne. Composed 1965.
SCORE: vs (n.p., 1965; LCCN: 85-67020).

Scarlet Letter, The, opera by Robert W. Mann; libretto (Eng), after Hawthorne. Composed 1970.

The work was awarded the Italian Copyright Society gold medal.

BIBLIOGRAPHY: "Unpublished Opera Wins a Music Prize," *NYT* (Oct. 14, 1970), 42.

Scarlet Letter, The, opera in three acts by Robert DiDomenica; libretto (Eng) by E. H. Elgin, after Hawthorne. Composed 1986.
SCORE: vs (Newton Centre, Mass.: Margun Music, [198?]).

Scarlet Letter, The, opera in two acts by Martin Herman; libretto (Eng) by Tom F. Curley, after Hawthorne. First performance April 1, 1992, Berkeley, Julia Morgan Theater, Berkeley Contemporary Opera, with Linda Jaqua (Hester Prynne), Frank Farris (Rev. Arthur Dimmesdale), and Richard Cohan (Roger Chillingworth); conducted by Marc Lowenstein.

Also set by A. L. Iverson (n.d.); Michael Gehlen (comp. 19??); musical by Nathan Birnbaum (1997, Los Angeles). See also *Hester Prynne*.

SCORE: ms fs (1992, NYPL).
BIBLIOGRAPHY: Stephanie von Buchau, "Berkeley," *ON* LVII (Oct. 1992), 50 [on premiere].

Scarlet Mill, The, opera in two acts by Eugene Zador; libretto (Eng) by George Jellinek, after Ferenc Molnár's play *Vörös Malum.* First performance October 26, 1968, Brooklyn, New York, with John Hyer (the professor), Gayna Sauler (Ilonka), Diana Tramontini (Mara), and Kerry McDevitt (János); conducted and directed by Károly Köpe.

The story concerns a devilish professor who has created a mill that can turn any virtuous individual into a scoundrel. The latest victim is a young man, János, who leaves his devoted wife, Ilonka, and their baby after he is captured. János is seduced by Mara, under the control of the professor. The young man's overwhelming goodness, however, allows him to free himself from his demonic possession and dispatch the devilish characters.
BIBLIOGRAPHY: Allen Hughes, "College Theater Unveils an Opera," *NYT* (Oct. 28, 1968), 54; Patrick Mahoney, "The Scarlet Mill by Eugene Zador," *OJ* VII (1974), 25–27.

Scena, "opera for broadcasting" in one act by Antony Hopkins; libretto (Eng) by Patric Dickinson. First performance May 1, 1953, London, BBC radio.

Scene: Domestic, chamber opera in one act by Paul Turok; libretto (Eng). First performance August 2, 1973, Aspen, Colorado.

Scene from Pickwick, A, chamber opera in one act by Charles Wood; libretto (Eng), after Charles Dickens's *Pickwick Papers,* Chapter 18. First performance June 20, 1922, London, Royal College of Music.

The work concerns conversation between Mr. and Mrs. Port and Mr. Winkle.

Another setting is A. Coates's *Pickwick** (1936, London).
BIBLIOGRAPHY: Ian Copley, "Two Dickensian Chamber Operas," *Dickensian* LXIX (May 1973), 102–4.

Scene Machine, "entertainment" in one act for young people by Anthony Gilbert; libretto (Eng) by George MacBeth; German translation, as *Frank Lord Faust,* by Lutz and Irene Liebelt. First performance, in German, April 1, 1971, Kassel, Kassel State Theater. First performance in English (and first British performance), March 1, 1972, London, Sadler's Wells, New Opera Company.

Frank, a folk singer, is exploited by big business, personified by a woman. As his art becomes corrupted because of his connections, Frank is vilified by his onetime fans, who bring about his ruin in their attempt to defeat the system that changed his art.

Roles: Frank, a young pop singer (bar); narrator/reporter (ten); and woman (mezzo).

Frank is represented by a theme that changes throughout the opera as he does.
BIBLIOGRAPHY: S. Walsh, interview with the composer, *MT* CXIII (1972), 137–39.

Scent of Sarsaparilla, A, opera in one act by Charles Hamm; libretto (Eng) by the composer. First performance September 5, 1954, San Francisco.

School for Fathers, The. See **Lionel and Clarissa.**

School for Wives, The, opera in one act by Rolf Liebermann; libretto (Eng) by Elizabeth Montague, after Molière's *L'école des femmes* (1663). First performance December 3, 1955, Louisville, Kentucky, Louisville Philharmonic Society, with Audrey Nossmann, Monas Harlan, William Pickett, and Robert Fischer; conducted and produced by Moritz Bomhard. Expanded to three acts with a libretto (Ger) by Heinrich Strobel, as *Die Schule der Frauen.* First performance of this version October 14, 1957,

Salzburg, with Walter Berry (Poquelin), Kurt Böhme (Arnolphe), Anneliese Rothenberger (Agnes), Alois Pernerstorfer (Oronte), Nicolai Gedda (Horace), and Christa Ludwig (Georgette); conducted by George Szell.

The old cynic Arnolphe tries to win the hand of the young Agnes; competing for her affections is the young love-struck Horace. Arnolphe's plan fails when Heinrich, played by the commentator Poquelin, intercedes.

Major roles: Arnolphe (bar); Agnes (lyr sop); Horace (lyr ten); Heinrich/Poquelin (bar); and Georgette, Arnolphe's servant (alto).

For a detailed description, see Eaton/*OP* I, 221.

Also set by V. Mortari, as *La scuola delle moglie* (1959, Milan); and by Bruce Montgomery, as the musical comedy *The Amorous Flea* (1974, Delaware, Ohio).
SCORES: fs, vs, English version; fs, German version (Vienna: Universal Edition, 1955; 1957).
LIBRETTO: German (Vienna: Universal Edition, 1957).

Scipio's Dream, short television opera by Judith Weir, after Mozart's *Il sogno di Scipione* (1772, Salzburg); libretto (Eng) by the composer, after Metastasio. First performance, as a television film in the Not Mozart Series, November 1991, BBC 2. First stage performance March 14, 1992, London, Purcell Room, Vocem Opera Company, with Francis Lynch (Fortune), Josephine McNally (Constancy), and Gwion Thomas (Scipio).

In this updating of the story, Scipio is an office worker who is bored by his chores until two of his coworkers are changed into the goddesses Fortune and Constancy. When he is forced to choose between them, he ultimately decides on Constancy, enraging Fortune. He is returned to the present-day world with a jolt.
BIBLIOGRAPHY: B. H., review, *MO* CLV (May 1992), 214 [on stage premiere].

Seabird Island, children's opera in two acts by Derek Healey; libretto (Eng) by Norman Newton, after a story by the Tsimshian Indians of British Columbia. First performance May 7, 1977, Guelph, Ontario, Guelph Spring Festival.

The setting is Tsimshian, on the northern coast of British Columbia, in mythical times. A princess, scorning the love of a prince, is carried away by a mysterious lover, a shaman disguised as a young man, and the attempts by the prince and the maid to rescue her are thwarted by the sorcerer. When the princess discovers who her lover really is, she is repulsed by him. In revenge he leaves her on an island to be consumed by the birds. Instead, she hides from them and, when the shaman returns, escapes in his canoe, leaving him to the fate he had planned for her. As punishment she is forced to wear the mask of an old woman and take over the role of the shaman.

For a description, see Kornick/*RAO*, 137–38.

Major roles: the princess (sop), the shaman (ten), the maid (sop), and the prince (bass-bar).
SCORE: vs, holograph (1976, photocopy, NYPL).
BIBLIOGRAPHY: F. B. St. Clair, "Canada: An Indian Legend," *Opera* XXIX (Oct. 1978), 1008 [on premiere].

Seagull, The, opera in three acts by Thomas Pasatieri; libretto (Eng) by Kenward Elmslie, after Anton Chekhov's play (1896). First performance March 5, 1974, Houston, Grand Opera, with Frederica von Stade (Nina), Evelyn Lear (Irina), Patricia Wells (Masha), Richard Stilwell (Constantine), and John Reardon (Trigorin); conducted by Charles Rosekrans; designed by Allen Charles Klein; directed by Frank Corsaro.

In the story, set at an estate in the 1890s, the young playwright Constantine is attracted to Nina, who is to perform in his play. Nina becomes drawn to another guest,

Trigorin, a famous writer, who is currently the lover of the famous actress Arkadina, Constantine's mother. At the same time Masha reveals to Dr. Dorn that she loves Constantine. During a picnic Constantine, angered by Nina's interest in Trigorin, places a dead seagull at her feet and recounts the story of a young girl brought to grief by her lover. Constantine fails in a suicide attempt, and Masha decides to wed the schoolteacher Medvedenko.

Two years pass, and as Constantine has predicted, Trigorin has abandoned Nina. She returns to the estate, revealing that she still loves Trigorin. When she leaves, Constantine destroys his manuscripts and succeeds in killing himself.

Major roles: Irina Arkadina (sop), Constantine (bar), Nina (mezzo), Masha (sop), and Trigorin (bar).

SCORE: vs ([Melville, N.Y.]: Belwin-Mills, 1975).

BIBLIOGRAPHY: Robert Jacobson, "Reports. U.S.," *ON* XXXVIII (Apr. 20–27, 1974), 30 [on premiere]; Arthur Schoep, review, *OJ* VII (1974), 29–33 [on premiere].

Sea King, The, romantic opera-comique by Richard Stahl; libretto (Eng). First performance June 23, 1889, New York, Casino Theater.

About a wandering Dutch sea captain who finds his true love.

SCORE: vs, selections (New York: T. B. Harms & Co., 1900).

Seal-Woman, The, "Celtic folk-opera" in two acts by Granville Bantock; libretto (Eng) by Marjory Kennedy-Fraser, after her collection *Songs of the Hebrides*. First performance September 27, 1924, Birmingham, England, Repertory Theatre.

In this Celtic setting the title character is a daughter of the King of Lochlann and has been transformed into a nonhuman form. Like her sisters, who are in the same state, she is able to take human form only three times a year. During one of these occasions she is observed by an Isleman, who falls in love with her and hides her sea robe, thus forcing her to remain human. The two wed and she gives birth to a child, but after seven years, unable to fight the lure of the sea, she gets hold of her sea robe and returns to her watery habitat.

The music is based on Celtic folk songs.

Major roles: Seal-Woman (mezzo); Isleman (ten); and Cailleach, an old crone (alto).

Sea-Side Story, The, operatic drama in two acts by Thomas Attwood; libretto (Eng) by William Dimond. First performance May 12, 1801, London, Covent Garden. First U.S. performance April 1, 1809, Philadelphia.

LIBRETTO: English, 2d ed. (London: Barker, 1801).

Seasons, The, serenade opera in two acts by John Christopher Smith; libretto (Eng) by John Lockman. Composed 1740. Not performed.

Seasons in Hell, the Lives of Arthur Rimbaud, opera in two acts by Harold Blumenfeld; libretto (Eng) by Charles Kondek, with paraphrases of Rimbaud. First performance February 8, 1996, Cincinnati, with Michael Kavelhuna (Younger Rimbaud), Timothy Swain (Verlaine), Craig Philips (Older Rimbaud), and Mary Elizabeth Kures (voice of Rimbaud); conducted by Gerhard Samuel.

An examination of the life of the poet Arthur Rimbaud, focusing on his affair with the poet Paul Verlaine. It covers aspects from the early and later stages of Rimbaud's life and emphasizes Rimbaud at the age of nineteen.

SCORE: fs ([St. Louis]: MMB Music, 1994).

LIBRETTO: English (St. Louis: MMB Music, ca. 1996).

BIBLIOGRAPHY: Charles H. Parsons, review *ON* LX (Apr. 13, 1996), 58–59 [on premiere].

Second Hurricane, The, "play-opera for high school performance" in two acts by Aaron Copland; libretto (Eng) by Edwin Denby. First performance April 21, 1937, New York, Neighborhood Playhouse, with choral forces from the Music School of the Henry Street Settlement, Professional Children's School, and Seward Park High School, with Clifford Mack, Joe Cotton, and Charles Pettinger (adult speaking roles), Vivienne Block, Estelle Levy, Arthur Anderson, Buddy Mangan, John Doepper, Harry Olive, and Carl Crawford (singing roles); conducted by Lehman Engel; directed by Orson Welles. Revived April 1960 (selections, concert), Carnegie Hall, High School of Music and Art Senior Choral ensemble, New York Philharmonic, with Steven Wertheimer, Julian Liss, John Richardson, Lawrence Willis, Omega Milbourne, Julie Makis, and Marion Cowings; conducted by Leonard Bernstein. First British performance June 8, 1990, Aldeburgh, the libretto shortened and adapted by Lynne Schey, with Michael Grandage (the narrator); conducted by Lukas Foss.

The setting is a Midwestern high school in the 1930s. A group of high school students, desiring to be heroes, attempt to help victims of a hurricane and flood; instead, they are marooned when their plane is forced down because of bad weather. At first afraid and bickering, the youngsters, faced by a second hurricane, work together to survive the encounter with nature's fury.

Major roles: Butch, class president (ten); Fat, center tackle (bass); Gyp, his younger brother (bar); Lowrie, "wears glasses" (ten); Gwen, "resolute" (alto); Queenie, "pretty" (sop); and Jeff, a farm boy (sop).

Among the musical highlights are the first-act choral overture (No. 1), "Have You Ever Had an Adventure?," Gyp's Song (No. 4), "Look at the River Over There," and, in the second act, Queenie's Song (No. 9c), "I Never Knew I Could Feel."

SCORE: vs (New York: Boosey & Hawkes, 1938).

BIBLIOGRAPHY: Noël Goodwin, "Aldeburgh," *ON* LV (Jan. 5, 1991), 41 [on British premiere]; N. S., "'Second Hurricane' in World Premiere," *NYT* (April 22, 1937), 18.

DISCOGRAPHY: soloists and chorus of the High School of Music and Art, New York Philharmonic, narrated and cond. L. Bernstein, Columbia MS 6181 (1 LP).

Second Mrs. Kong, The, opera in two acts by Harrison Birtwistle; libretto (Eng) by Russell Hoban. First performance October 24, 1994, Glyndebourne, with Philip Langridge (Kong) and Michael Chance (Head of Orpheus).

The slim plot centers around the movie character King Kong. The first act is set in "the world of shadows where the dead live" and has King Kong hearing Pearl, the model for Vermeer's painting *Girl with a Pearl Earring* as she sings to a mirror. The two characters eventually meet but are told by the mirror that they cannot remain together.

For a detailed plot description, see K/NKOB, 74–75.

Major roles: Anubis (bass-bar); Swami Zumzum (ten); Mr. Dollarama (bar); Inanna, his wife (mezzo); Eurydice (sop); Head of Orpheus (counterten); Vermeer (bar); Pearl (sop); Kong (ten); Death of Kong (bass-bar); and Joe Shady (bass).

BIBLIOGRAPHY: "On-Line with King Kong," *NY* LXXI (July 10, 1995), 81–82 [on premiere]; Alex Ross, "The Opera in England: Vigorous but Spiky," *NYT* (June 24, 1995), C, 11, 12.

Second Thought Is Best, opera in two acts by William Bates; libretto (Eng) by John Hough. First performance March 30, 1778, London, Covent Garden.

LIBRETTO: English ([London]: Mr. Murray [etc.], 1788 [1778?]).

Secret, The, opera in one act by Val Patacchi; libretto (Eng) by William Ashbrook, after Honoré Balzac's *La grande Bretèche*. First performance December 5, 1955, Columbia, Missouri, Stephens College Workshop, with Patacchi, Jolene Abboud, and Lou Anderson; conducted by Edward Murphy.

For other settings, see *La grande Bretèche* and *The Fatal Oath.*

Secret Garden, The, opera by Greg Pliska; libretto (Eng) by David Ives, after the children's book by Frances Hodgson Burnett. First performance February 22, 1991, Philadelphia, Haverford School, Pennsylvania Opera Theater, with Darynn Zimmer (Mary) and Peter Gillis (Colin); conducted by Barbara Silverstein.

A treatment of the story about the spoiled orphan Mary, who discovers an abandoned garden. While working to revive it, she meets her sickly cousin Colin. He joins her in restoring the garden and becomes healthy once again, while Mary finds true happiness.

Also musicals by Sharon Burgett (1986, London); Lucy Simon (1991, New York).

BIBLIOGRAPHY: Robert Baxter, "Philadelphia," *ON* LVI (Sept. 1991), 52 [on premiere].

Secret Life of Walter Mitty, The, opera in one act by Charles Hamm; libretto (Eng) by the composer, after James Thurber's short story (1939). First performance July 30, 1953, Athens, Ohio, Ohio University.

A mild-mannered and timid man dreams that he is a dashing hero.

BIBLIOGRAPHY: L. J. Johnen, review, *Musical Courier* CXLIX (Apr. 15, 1954), 29 [on premiere].

Secret Mine, The, "grand melo-dramatic spectacle" in two acts by Henry Rowley Bishop and Henry Condell; libretto (Eng) by John Fawcett. First performance 1813, Dublin.

LIBRETTO: English (Dublin: Tyrrell, 1813).

Secret of the Mirror, The, comic opera in one act by Dennis Busch; libretto (Eng) by the composer. Composed 1983.

Doctor Iodine asks his friend Lord Powderly, a justice of the peace, to help prevent the marriage of Iodine's daughter, Joanne, and Count Bradford by throwing a stone at a large mirror. He hopes that the couple, seeing the shattered mirror, will take it as a bad omen and call off the wedding. The couple arrives, but Powderly fails to throw the stone. Iodine takes this as a good sign and gives his blessing to the marriage.

For a fuller description, see Summers/*OOA*, 68–69.

Roles: Joanne (sop), Lord Powderly (bar), Doctor Iodine (bass), and Count Bradford (ten).

SCORE: ms score, holograph (1983, photocopy, NYPL).

Secular Masque, The, masque in one act by Daniel Purcell; libretto (Eng) by John Dryden. First performance March 25, 1700, London, Drury Lane Theatre.

Performed along with John Vanbrugh's comedy *The Pilgrim.* See the following entry for another setting.

Secular Masque, The, masque in one act by William Boyce; libretto (Eng) by John Dryden (1700). First performance July 1749, London, Drury Lane Theatre.

Dryden wrote the work to commemorate the end of the century, and in Boyce's treatment among the characters are Chronos and Diana.

For a detailed description, see Fiske/*ETM*, 210–12.

Sedain Chair, The, operetta in one act by Henry Rowley Bishop; libretto (Eng) by Edward Fitzball. First performance August 27, 1822, London, Vauxhall Gardens.

Seduction of a Lady, The, opera in one act by Richard Wargo; libretto (Eng) by the composer, after Neil Simon's play *The Good Doctor*, itself based on Anton Chekhov. First performance August 20, 1985, Glens Falls, New York, with Pamela South (Irina), Joseph Evans (Nicky), and David Barron (Peter Semyonych); conducted by Paulette Haupt-Nolan; directed by Dorothy Danner.

The philanderer Peter tries to seduce Irina, wife of Nicky, by telling the husband of his desires and plans for a mysterious woman. Nicky repeats the tale to Irina, who understands that she is the object of Peter's desires. When Irina meets Peter secretly, he understands that his seduction will destroy a happy marriage. He vows to give up his ways until his eye is caught by another attractive lady visiting the park with her husband.

Major roles: Peter Semyonych (ten), Nicky (bar), and Irina (sop).

The first part of *A Chekhov Trilogy.**

BIBLIOGRAPHY: John Rockwell, review, *NYT* (Aug. 22, 1985), C, 24 [on premiere].

See-See, comic opera in two acts by Sidney Jones and Frank E. Tours; libretto (Eng) by Charles H. Brookfield and Adrian Ross, after Fred de Grésac and Paul Ferrier's *La troisième lune*. First performance June 20, 1906, London, Prince of Wales Theatre, with Denise Orme and Maurice Farkoa.

As with the composer's *San Toy** and *The Geisha,** the work is set in the East, specifically, Peking.

LIBRETTO: English (London: Keith, Prowse & Co. Ltd., [etc.] 1906).

Selfish Giant, The, "fable for television" in two acts by Raymond Wilding-White; libretto (Eng) by the composer, after Oscar Wilde. Composed 1952. First performance November 30, 1965, Cleveland, Karamu House.

The work is for narrator, ten solo voices, and accompaniment.

SCORE: ms vs ([1952], photocopy, NYPL).

Selfish Giant, The, opera-ballet in two acts by Julia Perry; libretto (Eng) by the composer, after Wilde, Composed 1964.

SCORE: ms vs (New York: American Music Center, 1964).

Selfish Giant, The, opera in one act by Mervyn Burtch; libretto (Eng), after Wilde. First performance December 25, 1969, BBC Television, Wales.

Selfish Giant, The, opera for young people by Francis Shaw; libretto (Eng) by Michael Ffinch, after Wilde. Composed 1973.

SCORE: vs (London: J. & W. Curwen, [1973]).

Selfish Giant, The, children's opera by Charles Wilson; libretto (Eng), after Wilde. First performance December 21, 1973, Toronto, St. Lawrence Centre.

Also set by David Barlow (comp. 1974–1975).

Selfish Giant, The, chamber opera in one act by Alan Ridout; libretto by J. Platt, after Wilde. First performance 1977, Kent, Wye Church.

Selfish Giant, The, opera in one act by Stanley Hollingsworth; libretto (English) by the composer and Herbert Moulton, after Wilde. First performance May 24, 1981, Charleston, Spoleto Festival.

When the children enter the giant's garden to play, he angrily chases them away, whereupon the flowers and birds disappear. The giant, now lonely, welcomes a little boy when he tries to climb a tree in the enclave, and life comes back to the garden.

For a description, see Kornick/*RAO*, 151–52.

Major roles: the giant (bass-bar) and the little boy (boy sop).

Selfish Giant, The, opera in one act by Michael Easton; libretto (Eng) by the composer and Michael Atkinson, after Wilde. Composed 1994.

In this updating of the story, a businessman interested only in profits is the giant. He abandons his ruinous plans after a mystical conversion and tries to be successful in ways that are safe for the earth.

Selima and Azor, Persian tale in two acts by Thomas Linley Sr.; libretto (Eng) by George Collier, after *Zémire et Azor* by Marmontel; set by Grétry (1771, Fontainebleau). First performance December 5, 1776, London, Drury Lane Theatre, with Mr. Dodd (Ali), Mr. Bannister (Scander), Mr. Vernon (Azor), Mrs. Baddeley (Selima), Miss Collett (Fatima), and Mrs. Scott (Lesbia). Revised by Henry Rowley Bishop and Thomas Cooke, October 5, 1812, London, Covent Garden. First U.S. performance June 1, 1787, New York, John Street Theatre.

A treatment of the Beauty and the Beast story, with Selima as Beauty and Azor as the Beast. The father of Selima is called Scander, and his servant, Ali.

SCORE: vs (London: Charles Samuel Thompson, [1776]).

LIBRETTO: English (London: J. Bell, 1784).

Semele, serious opera in three acts by John Eccles; libretto (Eng) by William Congreve, after Ovid's *Metamorphoses*, iii. Completed ca. December 1706 but not performed until June 4, 1964, Oxford, Holywell Music Room; April 22, 1972, London, St. John's.

Major roles: Jupiter (bass), Juno (sop), Somnus (bass), and Semele (sop).

The through-composed work, which was written for the opening of the Queen's Theatre in the Haymarket, tries to combine the contemporary Italian and English operatic styles. It was pushed aside by the Italianate *Thomyris,** as arranged by John Pepusch.

Semele, masque in three acts by George Frideric Handel; libretto (Eng) by William Congreve, after Ovid's *Metamorphosis,* iii. First performance February 10, 1744, London, Covent Garden, with Elizabeth Duparc (Semele), John Beard (Jupiter), Esther Young (Ino/Juno), and Henry Reinhold (Cadmus/High Priest/Somnus). First stage performance February 10, 1925, Cambridge, in the version by Dennis Arundell. First U.S. performance January 1959, Evanston, Illinois, Northwestern University; conducted by Thor Johnson. First U.S. stage performance 1980, Washington, D.C.

In this version of the Greek myth, the lovely Semele, daughter of Cadmus, is betrothed to Athamas. Unhappy about her impending marriage, Semele calls on the disguised Jupiter, her lover, for assistance. He obliges, thereby raising the ire of Juno, his wife. Alerted to Jupiter's infidelity by Iris, her messenger, Juno summons Somnus, the god of sleep, to help her. Masquerading as Ino, Semele's sister, Juno tricks Semele into forcing Jupiter to reveal himself. When he appears as a thunderbolt, Semele dies in the resulting flames. Ino recounts Semele's end to Cadmus and the priests; she and Athamas marry, and Apollo predicts that Bacchus will ascend from Semele's remains.

For a comparison of the Eccles and Handel versions, see Fiske/*ETM*, 35–39.

Major roles: Cadmus (bass), Semele (sop), Ino (alto), Athamas (counterten), Jupiter (ten), Juno (alto), Apollo (ten), and Somnus (bass).

Among the numbers are Semele's "Oh Sleep, Why Dost Thou Leave Me" (act 2), the duet "Obey My Will" of Jupiter and Juno (act 3), and the concluding chorus "Happy Shall We Be."

Semper virens, music drama by Henry Hadley; libretto (Eng) by Joseph Redding. First performance 1923, San Francisco, Bohemian Club.
LIBRETTO: English (San Francisco: Bohemian Club, [1923?]).

Sensation Novel, A, comic opera in one act by Thomas German Reed; libretto (Eng) by William S. Gilbert. First performance January 30, 1871, London, Gallery of Illustration. Rescored by "Florian Pascal" (Joseph Benjamin Williams) for a performance in 1912.
    For a detailed analysis, see Stedman/*GBS*, 34–39.
LIBRETTO: English, 1912 version (London: J. Williams, 1912).

Sequel to the Opera of Flora, A, ballad opera in one act; libretto (Eng) by John Hippisley. First performance March 20, 1732, London, Lincoln's Inn Fields.
LIBRETTO: English, with ballad airs (London: A. Bettesworth and C. Hitch . . . , 1732).

Seraglio, The, comic opera in two acts by Charles Dibdin (four nos. by Samuel Arnold); libretto (Eng) by Dibdin. First performance November 14, 1776, London, Covent Garden. First U.S. performance May 19, 1794, Philadelphia.
    In this harem tale, the heroine, Lydia, beloved of Frederick, has been captured and put in the seraglio of Abdallah Chiquan. Frederick tries to rescue Lydia but is, not surprisingly, apprehended by Abdallah's followers (this is similar to Belmonte's fate in Mozart's *Die Entführung aus dem Serail* of 1782). At the last moment, however, Abdallah shows himself to be a "generous Turk" and releases the pair of Europeans in the name of true love, along with another European captive, Polly, and Tom Reef, the sailor lover who has come to save her. The opera thus concludes with a joyful quartet and chorus.
    In addition to the three characters just mentioned, the opera includes the Osmin-like figure Muli Alouf Hali Hassan, head of the seraglio.
    Some of the airs were written by Samuel Arnold and some by J. A. Fisher.
SCORE: vs (London: John Johnston, [1776]).
LIBRETTO: English (London: T. Evans, 1776).

Seraphic Vision, The, dramatic scene by Rutland Boughton; libretto (Eng) by Laurence Housman, after his religious play. First performance August 20, 1924, Glastonbury, Assembly Rooms.

Serenade at Noon, opera in one act by Peter Paul Fuchs; libretto (Eng) by the composer. First performance March 22, 1965, Baton Rouge, Louisiana State University.

Serf, The, opera in three acts by George Lloyd; libretto (Eng) by William Lloyd. First performance October 20, 1938, London, Covent Garden.
SCORE: vs (London: W. and G. Lloyd, 1938).

Servant Mistress, The, afterpiece by Samuel Arnold, an arrangement of Pergolesi's *La serva padrona*; anonymous libretto (Eng). First performance June 16, 1770, London, Marylebone Garden. Revised version, with text by John O'Keeffe, February 14, 1783, London, Covent Garden.
    A servant girl tricks her master into marrying her.

Servant of Two Masters, The, comic opera in two acts by Vittorio Giannini; libretto (Eng) by Bernard Stambler, after Carlo Goldoni. First performance (posthumous) March 9, 1967, New York, State Theater, New York City Opera, with Michael Devlin (Pantalone), Donna Jeffrey (Clarissa), David Smith (Lombardi), Charles Hindsley (Silvio), Eileen Schauler (Beatrice), Frank Porretta (Florindo), Nico Castel (Brighella), Patricia

Brooks (Smeraldina), and Raymond Myers (Truffaldino); conducted by Julius Rudel; directed by Tito Capobianco; designed by Robert Fletcher.

In this farce, the blunders of Truffaldino, a servant, cause everything to turn out well.
LIBRETTO: English (New York: Franco Colombo, 1967).
BIBLIOGRAPHY: Harold C. Schonberg, review, *NYT* (Mar. 10, 1967), 28 [on premiere].

Servants, The, opera in three acts by William Mathias; libretto (Eng) by Iris Murdoch, after her play *The Servants and the Snow*. First performance September 15, 1980, Cardiff, New Theatre, Welsh National Opera, with Nigel Douglas (Basil), Eiddwen Harrhy (Oriane), Claire Powell (Marina), Henry Newman (Peter Jack), Phillip Joll (General Klein); conducted by Anthony Hose; produced by Adrian Slack; designed by Patrick Robertson and Rosemary Vercoe.

The work takes place around 1900 in Central Europe. Basil, a well-to-do landowner, returns to his ancestral estate upon the death of his father and declares to the servants that they are now his equal and should forget the past. Despite his sentiments, Basil plans to continue his father's brutality of the *droit du seigneur*, the practice of which resulted in the killing of Marina's first husband, Alexander. On the day of her wedding to Peter Jack, her son kills Basil and Peter, and General Klein, brother of Oriane, Basil's wife, takes control of the estate by force and once again suppresses the servants.

The work uses a group of some 200 singers for the servants' chorus, which functions as a sort of Greek chorus and remarks on and responds to the action that is unfolding. The musical highlights include Basil's "This Is a New Day" and Marina's "Learn from Me."
SCORE: vs (London: Oxford University Press, 1980).
BIBLIOGRAPHY: Jane Birkhead, "Music Reviews," *Notes* XXXVIII (Sept. 1982), 221–22.

Seven Deadly Sins, The, opera in two acts by Colin Brumby; libretto (Eng) by Thomas Shapcott. First performance September 12, 1970, Brisbane, Australia, Queensland Opera Company.
LIBRETTO: English, with 2 LPs (Ipswich, Queensland: T. W. Shapcott and Queensland Opera Company, 1970).

Seven Maids of Munich, The, or, The Ghost's Tower, musical drama by George Rodwell; libretto (Eng) by the composer. First performance December 19, 1846, London, Princess's Theatre.
SCORE: vs (London, 1846).

Seventh Chord, The, comic opera in four acts by Joseph Carl Breil; libretto (Eng) by the composer and A. Miller. First performance 1913, Chicago.

Sexton of Cologne, The, or, The Burgomaster's Daughter, operatic romance by George Rodwell; libretto (Eng) by Edward Fitzball. First performance June 13, 1836, London.

Sganarelle, comic opera in one act by Walter Kaufmann; libretto (Eng) by the composer, after Molière. First performance August 28, 1958, Vancouver, University of British Columbia; conducted by George Schick; produced by Robert Gill.

Sganarelle, comic opera in one act by Violet Archer; libretto (Eng) by Samuel A. Eliot Jr., after Molière. First performance February 5, 1974, Edmonton, Alberta, University of Alberta.

Sganarelle, opera in one act by Martin Kalmanoff; libretto (Eng), after Molière. First performance May 18, 1974, New York, Manhattan School of Music.

Sganarelle finds a miniature of a man he believes, wrongly, to be his wife's lover. *The Picture** and *Signor Deluso** are other settings.

Shadow on the Wall, The, musical play by John Thomson; libretto (Eng) by Thomas J. Serle. First performance April 20, 1835, London, Lyceum.
SCORE: vs (London, 1835).

Shadowplay, music theater in two acts by Alexander Goehr; libretto (Eng) by Kenneth Cavander, after Plato's *Republic*, Book VII. First performance July 8, 1970, London. First U.S. performance December 11, 1991, New York, Manhattan School of Music.

The work is set around the cave allegory. A prisoner, confined to a cave, views only shadows and thinks they are real. When he is released, he cannot explain the shadows to the world.

Scored for actor, tenor, alto flute, alto saxophone, horn, violoncello, and piano.

Part 2 of the composer's *Triptych*, consisting also of *Naboth's Vineyard** (1968) and *Sonata about Jerusalem** (1971).
SCORE: fs, English-German (London: Schott; New York: Schott Music Corp., [1976]).
BIBLIOGRAPHY: Philip Kennicott, "Composer's Page," *ON* LVI (Dec. 7, 1991), 48, 70.

Shadows among Us, opera in two acts by Ezra Laderman; libretto (Eng) by Norman Rosten. Composed 1968. First performance December 1, 1979, Philadelphia.

The story concerns a group of refugees in a camp who have been forced to flee their homeland because of war and political upheavals. They are haunted by memories of the past, and their desire to leave the camp and find a better life in another land is overwhelmed by their realization that things would be no better anywhere else.

Shala Fears for the Poor, opera in three acts by Anthony Braxton; libretto (Eng) by the composer, after short stories of William Saroyan. First performance October 25, 1996, New York, John Jay Theater, with Lisa Bielawa (Shala); conducted by the composer; directed by Paul Germaine-Brown.

The plot, with twelve archetypal characters, consists of various manifestations of evil in contemporary society and the failure of liberalism to overcome the wrongdoing.

The opera is the third of the composer's twelve three-act works scheduled to contain the same twelve characters. Braxton explains the philosophy of the opera in his book *Tri-Axlum Writings*.

The music is performed by a group of jazz improvisers and classical musicians.
BIBLIOGRAPHY: Ben Ratliff, review, *NYT* (Oct. 30, 1996), C, 18 [on premiere].

Shaman, opera by Alice Shields; libretto (Eng) by the composer. Composed 1978. First performance (one scene) March 25, 1983, Seattle. First complete performance May 8, 1987, New York, American Chamber Opera Company.

Sham Conjuror, The, comic masque by Frederick Lampe; libretto (Eng). First performance April 18, 1741, London, Covent Garden, with Richard Leveridge (the conjurer).

Dingle and Dangle are after the hand of a young woman with the help of a conjurer.

Shamrock, The, or, The Anniversary of St. Patrick, "a pastoral romance" in two acts by William Shield; libretto (Eng) by John O'Keeffe. First performance April 15, 1777, Dublin, Crow Street Theatre; April 7, 1783, London, Covent Garden.

Revived November 4, 1783, London, in a new version, as *The Poor Soldier.**
LIBRETTO: English, ms (Huntington Library, San Marino, Calif., Larpent 620).

Shamus O'Brien, "a story of Ireland a hundred years ago" in two acts by Charles Stanford; libretto (Eng) by G. H. Jessop. First performance March 2, 1896, London, Opera Comique, with Louise Kirkby Lunn (Nora).

Shanewis, or, The Robin Woman, "Indianist opera" in two acts by Charles Wakefield Cadman; libretto (Eng) by Nelle Richmond Eberhart, after a sketch of Tsianina Redfeather. First performance March 23, 1918, New York, Metropolitan Opera, with Sophie Braslau (Shanewis), Marie Sundelius (Amy), Kathleen Howard (Mrs. Everton), Thomas Chalmers (Philip), and Paul Althouse (Lionel); conducted by Roberto Moranzoni; designed by James Fox; directed by Richard Ordynski. Revived December 5, 1924, Denver, with Princess Tsianina Redfeather in the title role; conducted by the composer; and on June 24, 1926, Los Angeles. Revived again July 1979, Central City, Colorado, with Stephanie Friede (Shanewis).

The title character is a "native forest bird" who has been captured by Mrs. J. A. Everton, a prominent Californian. She gives a musicale, at which Shanewis sings a strange song that captures the attention of the young architect Lionel Rhodes, who is the fiancé of Amy, Mrs. Everton's daughter. Lionel and Shanewis flee to an Indian reservation, pursued in act 2 by Mrs. Everton and Amy. When Shanewis learns of the engagement, she surrenders Lionel, but Philip Harjo, Shanewis's foster brother, shoots Lionel with a poisoned arrow.

Major roles: Shanewis (mezzo), Amy Everton (sop), Mrs. Everton (alto), Philip Harjo (bar), and Lionel Rhodes (ten).

The Puccini-like score contains the title character's aria "For Half a Thousand Years/ Your Race Has Cheated Mine."
SCORE: vs, as *The Robin Woman* (Boston: White-Smith, 1918).
LIBRETTO: English (New York: Rullman, 1918).
BIBLIOGRAPHY: Andrew Porter, review, *NY* LV (Aug. 27, 1979), 82–83 [on 1979 revival].

Sharp and Flat, operatic farce in two acts by James Hook; libretto (Eng) by Dennis Lawler. First performance August 4, 1813, London, Lyceum.
LIBRETTO: English (London: Chapple, 1813).

Sheep Shearing, The, or, Florizel and Perdita, "pastoral comedy" in two acts by Thomas Arne; libretto (Eng) by Macnamara Morgan, after Shakespeare's *A Winter's Tale*, acts 4 and 5. First performance March 25, 1754, London, Covent Garden.
LIBRETTO: English (London: J. Truman, 1762; 1771, London); repr. ed. (London: Cornmarket P., 1969).

Sheep Shearing, The, afterpiece pastiche in three acts by Samuel Arnold; libretto (Eng) by George Colman Sr., after Shakespeare's *A Winter's Tale*. First performance July 18, 1777, London, Little Theatre in the Haymarket.

Includes music by Thomas Arne (see preceding entry) and two airs by Arnold.
LIBRETTO: English (London: Printed for G. Kearsly, 1777).

Shephardes Playe, The, pageant opera by John La Montaine; libretto (Eng) by the composer, after four medieval Corpus Christi plays. First performance December 1, 1967, Washington, D.C.

Part of the composer's Christmas trilogy; see also *Novellis, Novellis* (1961) and *Erode the Great* (1969).
SCORE: fs (Hollywood: P. J. Sifler, 1967).

Shepherdess and the Chimneysweep, The, Christmas opera in one act by Julia Smith; libretto (Eng) by Constance D'Arcy Mackay, after Hans Christian Andersen. First performance December 28, 1966, Fort Worth, Texas.

The setting is a mantelpiece in a London home, 1860. At midnight on Christmas Eve the city bells strike and bring the porcelain figurines to life. The beautiful Shepherdess is courted by the simple Chimneysweep and the haughty Mandarin. When the supernatural Christmas tree wights sing to the Chimneysweep and the Shepherdess, the Mandarin becomes infuriated and challenges his rival to a duel. The Chimneysweep inadvertently strikes the Mandarin's bag of gunpowder, which blows the latter to bits, leaving the Chimneysweep and the Shepherdess to rejoice. The London bells strike one, and the figurines resume their lifeless forms.

For a description, see Summers/*OOA*, 282–83.

Roles: the Shepherdess (sop), the Chimneysweep (ten), and the Mandarin (bass-bar).
SCORE: vs (New York: Mowbray Music, [1978]).

Shepherdess of the Alps, The, comic opera in three acts by Charles Dibdin; libretto (Eng) by the composer, after Marmontel's *La bergère des Alpes*, from his *Contes moraux*. First performance January 18, 1780, London, Covent Garden.

The work, set in the Swiss mountains, was a failure.
LIBRETTO: English (London: G. Kearsly, 1780).

Shepherd of Derwent Vale, The, or, The Innocent Culprit, musical drama in two acts by Charles Edward Horn; libretto (Eng) by Joseph Lunn. First performance February 12, 1825, London, Drury Lane Theatre.
LIBRETTO: English (London: J. Cumberland, n.d.).

Shepherd's Artifice, The, all-sung dramatic pastoral by Charles Dibdin; libretto (Eng) by the composer. First performance May 21, 1764, London, Covent Garden, with the composer as the shepherd.
LIBRETTO: English (London: T. Becket and P. A. De Hondt, 1765).

Shepherds' Christmas, The, chamber opera in one act by William Russo; libretto (Eng) by Jon Swan, after the medieval *Second Shepherds' Play*. First performance December 1979, Chicago. First New York performance December 10, 1988.

In the story a couple's attempts to seize a lamb from three shepherds is thwarted.
SCORE: vs (New York: Southern Music Publishing; and Hamburg: Peer Musikverlag, 1991).
BIBLIOGRAPHY: Will Crutchfield, review, *NYT* (Dec. 16, 1988), C, 7.

Shepherd's Lottery, The, musical entertainment by William Boyce; libretto (Eng) by Moses Mendez. First performance November 19, 1751, London, Drury Lane Theatre, with Miss Norris (Phyllis), John Beard (Colin), Joseph Vernon (Thyrsis), and Mrs. Clive (Daphne).

The lottery of the title refers to the custom on May Day of having the shepherds select their wives by picking names from an urn. Phyllis is afraid that her beloved, Thyrsis, will fail to pick her name during the lottery, while Daphne does not care whom she marries, and Colin, also not caring, refuses to enter the lottery. Thyrsis is successful and draws his beloved's name.
SCORES: fs (London: John Walsh [1745]: repr. intro. Robert J. Bruce, *Music for London Entertainment 1660–1800* (London: Stainer & Bell, 1990); also has early libretto.
LIBRETTO: English (London: M. Cowper, 1751).

Shepherds of the Delectable Mountains, The, "pastoral episode" in one act by Ralph Vaughan Williams; libretto (Eng) by the composer, after Bunyan's *The Pilgrim's*

Progress. First performance July 11, 1922, London, Royal College of Music; the work was incorporated into *The Pilgrim's Progress.**

A pilgrim, searching for immortality, comes into the company of three shepherds in the Delectable Mountains. A celestial messenger then takes him to the master, who plunges an arrow sharpened with love into the pilgrim's heart. The shepherds then anoint him in preparation for his crossing the river. The pilgrim is able to ford the river and is welcomed into heaven. The shepherds rejoice.

For a detailed description, see Eaton/*OP* I, 223.

Roles: pilgrim (ten), celestial messenger (sop/ten), three shepherds (2 ten, bass), and voice of a bird (sop).

She Stoops to Conquer, comic opera in three acts by George Macfarren; libretto by Edward Fitzball, after Oliver Goldsmith's play of the same name (1773). First performance February 11, 1864, London, Covent Garden, with Mr. Weiss (Squire Hardcastle), Henry Corri (Tony Lumpkin), George Perren (George Hastings), W. Harrison (Charles Marlow), Anna Hiles (Miss Constance Neville), and Louisa Pyne (Miss Kate Hardcastle).

The shy Charles Marlow, nervous in the presence of Miss Kate Hardcastle, whom he wants to wed, is at ease only with working-class girls. She tricks him into thinking that she is a barmaid at the village inn, which in reality is her father's house, and all ends happily when Marlow's father arrives and explains all to his baffled son.

For a musical description, see Biddlecombe/*EO*, 158–59.

LIBRETTO: English (London: Cramer, Wood & Co., [1861?]).

She Stoops to Conquer, opera in four acts by Denis ApIvor; libretto (Eng) by the composer, after Oliver Goldsmith's play. Composed 1943–1947; revised 1976–1977.

Also musical by David Leroy Smith (comp. 1958).

Shining Brow, opera in two acts and a prologue by Daron Hagen; libretto (Eng) by Paul Muldoon. First performance April 4, 1992, Oscar Mayer Theatre, Madison, Wisconsin, Madison Opera and Symphony Orchestra, with Michael Sokol (Wright), Carolann Page (Mamah), Barry Busse (Sullivan), Kitt Reuter-Foss (Catherine Wright), and Bradley Garvin (Edwin Cheney); conducted by Roland Johnson; Stephen Wadsworth, stage director. Reduced version July 25, 1997, Chicago, Chicago Opera Theater, with Robert Orth (Wright), Brenda Harris (Mamah), Busse (Sullivan), Garvin (Edwin Cheney), and Reuter-Foss (Catherine Wright); conducted by Lawrence Rapchak.

The story concerns the legendary architect Frank Lloyd Wright in the years between 1903 and 1914, which include his break with Louis Sullivan, his mentor, the burning of his home, Taliesin, and his disastrous affair with Mamah Cheney, the wife of a wealthy client, which ends when she is murdered.

The title of the opera comes from the English translation of Taliesin, Wright's Welsh designation for the home he designed for himself in Wisconsin.

Musical interludes connect the scenes, a choral interlude is used to represent Wright's love for Mamah, and a brass choir underscores Wright's break with Sullivan. The work also uses hymns, a barber shop quartet sung by reporters, and Broadway-style pieces. The librettist employs brief text phrases as verbal motifs to represent various characters and situations.

Major roles: lyric baritone, soprano, mezzo soprano, tenor, and bass.

SCORE: vs (Boston: E. C. Schirmer, 1995).

LIBRETTO: English (London and Boston: Faber and Faber, 1993).

BIBLIOGRAPHY: Paul Griffiths, "Musical Events," NY LXIX (May 17, 1993), 98–100 [on premiere]; John Koopman, review, ON LVIII (Nov. 1993), 48–49; John Van Rhein, "Chicago," ON LXII (Nov. 1997), 56 [on rev. version].

Shining Chalice, The, opera in one act by Isaac Van Grove; libretto (Eng) by Janice Lovoos, after her play. First performance July 30, 1964, Eureka Springs, Arkansas.

The young Timothy, son of the poor Simon and Mary, is a gifted, but unappreciated, maker of pottery. He is approached by Sir Guy, troubadour of the blind Sad King, who wishes to have the boy make a beautiful chalice. When the King feels the beauty of the work, he smiles for the first time since he lost his sight and his son. The opera ends as the chalice, possessed of an inner light, shines in the darkness.

For a detailed description, see Eaton/OP II, 321.

Major roles: Simon, a poor carpenter (bar); Mary, his wife (mezzo); Timothy, their son (sop); and the Sad King (bass).

Ship of Heaven, The, musical fantasy in three acts by Alfred Hill; text (Eng) by Hugh McCrae. First performance (excerpts, private) 1923, Sydney, Australia. First full stage performance October 7, 1933, Sydney, Savoy Theatre.

The plotless text consists of verses on fanciful themes.

SCORE: vs (Sydney: Angus and Robertson, [1951]).

Shipwreck, The, comic opera in two acts by Samuel Arnold; libretto (Eng) by the composer. First performance December 10, 1796, London, Drury Lane Theatre. First U.S. performance March 2, 1783, Philadelphia.

The plot centers around Angelica, the heroine, who is disguised as a boy, and Harry Hawser, the hero.

SCORE: vs (London: Longman & Broderip, n.d.).

LIBRETTO: English (London: Longman & Broderip, [1796?]).

Shivaree, The, chamber opera in two acts by John Beckwith; libretto (Eng) by James Reaney. First performance April 3, 1982, Toronto, St. Lawrence Centre.

Shizuka's Dance, children's opera in one act by Leslie Kondorossy; libretto (Eng) by Shawn Hall (Elizabeth Davis), after a tale by Prince Bantam. First performance April 22, 1969, Cleveland.

Shloyme Gorgl, an arrangement by Mark Slobin of the musical drama (1890s, New York; see below); libretto (Eng), translated by Judith Slobin, Norval Slobin, and Mark Slobin, of the text (Yiddish), probably written by Joseph Lateiner. First performance 1978, Middletown, Connecticut, Wesleyan University.

The story, set in Galicia, Poland, revolves around a cantor who is down on his luck. He discovers that his daughter, Hadassah, has unjustly been accused of the murder of her infant daughter, Shifra, who was in fact switched with a dead child and is now a grown woman with a family of her own.

Major roles: Shloyme Gorgl, once a famous cantor, now a street musician; Hadassah, his daughter; Shifra, her long-lost daughter; Mesholem, her husband; Gitele, his mother; and the Judge.

The reconstructed (abridged) version includes a cantorial solo, a dance by Sigmund Mogulesco, a duet between Shifra and Solomon using music by Abraham Goldfaden; Joseph M. Rumshinsky's "Up Stairs-Down Stairs"; and "Raisins and Almonds," featured prominently in Goldfaden's opera Shulamis (ca. 1898).

TEXT AND SCORE: sheet music (New York, 1905–1920); Yiddish text (Warsaw, 1907); repr. ed. Mark Slobin, Yiddish-English, *NAMT*, vol. 11.

Shoemaker's Holiday, The, ballad opera in two parts by Dominick Argento; libretto (Eng) by John Olon-Scrymgeour, after Thomas Dekker's play (1600). First performance June 1, 1967, Minneapolis, Tyrone Guthrie Theatre, with Douglas Campbell (Simon Eyre), Helen Carey (Rose), and Nick Savian (Sir Roger Oteley); conducted by Herbert Pilhofer; directed by Douglas Campbell and Olon-Scrymgeour.

The setting is London and its surroundings in the seventeenth century. Simon Eyre tells the story of two young lovers, Rowland Lacy and Rose, who are separated by the actions of both their families. Lacy is sent off to war, and Rose, daughter of the Lord Mayor of London, is taken away by her father. Lacy leaves his regiment and returns to Simon Eyre's house in the dress of Hans, a Dutch shoemaker. He and his beloved are saved when Eyre becomes Lord Mayor and permits the two to marry.

Major roles: Simon Eyre (bar), Rowland Lacy (ten), Rose (sop), and Sir Hugh Lacy (bar).

For a detailed description, see Eaton/*OP* II, 209.

SCORE: vs (New York: Broude, 1967).

Show Boat, musical play in two acts with music by Jerome Kern; book and lyrics (Eng) by Oscar Hammerstein II, after Edna Ferber's novel; orchestrations by Robert Russell Bennett. First performance December 27, 1927, New York, Ziegfeld Theater, with Charles Winninger (Cap'n Andy), Helen Morgan (Julie La Verne), Edna May Oliver (Parthy Ann), Norma Terris (Magnolia), Howard Marsh (Gaylord Ravenal), Jules Bledsoe (Joe), and Charles Ellis (Steve); designed by Joseph Urban. It ran for a triumphant 572 performances on Broadway. First British performance May 3, 1928, London, Drury Lane Theatre, with Cedric Hardwicke (Cap'n Andy), Marie Burke (Julie), Edith Day (Magnolia), Howett Worster (Gaylord), and Paul Robeson (Joe), who was supposed to have appeared in the United States (he did, however, have the role in the film version of 1936). The London production ran for 350 nights. It was given at the New York City Opera in 1954 and enjoyed great success at its revivals in Toronto in autumn 1993 and in New York in 1995, directed by Harold Prince.

The action starts on the *Cotton Blossom*, a traveling showboat that has docked in Natchez, Tennessee. Cap'n Andy, with his wife Parthy Ann and Magnolia, their young daughter, try to attract people to the show by telling them about the main attraction, the singer Julie. Left alone, Magnolia meets Gaylord Ravenal, a handsome riverboat gambler, and they are immediately attracted to each other, an attraction they experience in "Make Believe." The sheriff comes and orders Ravenal off the ship. Magnolia tries to learn more about her newfound love from Joe, a black work hand, but he is unwilling to tell her anything; he then sings the famous "Ol' Man River."

Julie has her own romantic problems with Steve, as she reveals in "Can't Help Lovin' Dat Man," but Magnolia ignores her warnings to be careful. The sheriff returns and reveals that Julie is part black (a fact told to him by one of Julie's spurned suitors), which means that she and Steve have broken the laws of miscegenation; Steve cuts Julie's finger and mixes her blood with his own in order to make himself part black. The two leave the ship, allowing Magnolia to assume Julie's part and Gaylord, who has sneaked back on the ship, to take Steve's.

Gaylord and Magnolia fall deeply in love and leave for Chicago, where they are married. But Gaylord's continued gambling takes its toll on his finances and marriage, and he deserts his wife and their young daughter, Kim, thinking it is for their own good. Magnolia, desperate for work, learns that the Trocadero needs a new singer; their own star, Julie, now a drunk, has become unreliable. When Magnolia appears for an audition, the star, Julie, recognizes her young friend, who, however, fails to realize who the singer is. The good-hearted Julie quits so that Magnolia can fill her position. After a shaky beginning, Magnolia overwhelms the crowd with the famous "After the Ball" (by Charles Harris). She soon gives up the uncertainty of the performing life and rejoins her family on the *Cotton Blossom*.

Years later, when Kim Ravenal has grown to adulthood, a tired old man comes to the showboat. Magnolia does not recognize him at first, but when he sings "You Are Love," which they had sung to each other before they ran off to be married, Magnolia realizes that he is Ravenal, and the couple, reunited, go back to the showboat together.

For a detailed plot description, see Bordman/*AO*, 434–35; Gänzl/*BBM*, 74–79.

One of the most famous numbers, Julie's "Bill" (with words by P. G. Wodehouse), had been eliminated from a musical written by Kern for the Princess Theater a decade earlier, *Oh Lady! Lady!!* (February 1, 1917). Another number, "Mis'ry's Comin' Aroun'," was cut from the original production because it was deemed too unhappy. The popularity of the Kern work was evidenced by the fact that three film versions were made of it, in 1929, 1936, and 1951.

Many consider *Show Boat* a masterpiece; Richard Traubner calls it "the greatest of all American operettas" (*Operetta*, 393), and Gerald Bordman describes it as "one of the masterpieces of our lyric stage" (*AMT*, 434). Considered daring in its time for its frank look at white racism, it was the first major work to treat black-white relations and predated another major American stage work about African Americans, *Porgy and Bess*, by eight years. It was the first musical incorporated into the repertory of an opera company (1954, New York City Opera).

The work is frequently revived today. When it was staged in 1993 in Toronto, Hal Prince, its producer, eliminated "any inadvertent stereotype in the original material" to counter charges of "Uncle Tom" caricatures by some members of the African-American community. The run in Toronto was extremely successful, as was the New York revival, which began in 1995.

BIBLIOGRAPHY: Miles Kreuger, *Show Boat: The Story of a Classic American Musical* (New York: Oxford University Press, 1977).

DISCOGRAPHY: T. Stratas, F. von Stade, J. Hadley; cond. J. McGlinn (with orig. Bennett orch. and 45 minutes of music cut from first production), Angel A23-49108 (3 CDs); excerpts: Morgan, Albani, Melton, Robeson, Munn, Young, CBS mono A-55 (CD); both rev. John F. Freeman, "Recordings," *ON* LIV (Mar. 3, 1990), 31, 43.

Shylock, opera by Wesley La Violette; libretto (Eng) by the composer, after Shakespeare's *The Merchant of Venice*. First performance (excerpts) February 9, 1930, Chicago, Casino Club, with John Charles Thomas (Shylock).

Sibyl, The: Parable XX, opera in one act by Vincent Persichetti; libretto (Eng) by the composer, after the tale of Chicken Little. Composed in 1976. First performance April 13, 1985, Philadelphia, Pennsylvania Opera Theater; conducted by Barbara Silverstein.

The parable on modern life, in which predictions of doom are ignored, places the story in the era of the Depression.

The music of the work is atonal.

BIBLIOGRAPHY: Will Crutchfield, "Opera," *NYT* (Apr. 21, 1985), 62 [on premiere].

Sicilian Bride, The, opera in four acts by Michael Balfe; libretto (Eng) by Alfred Bunn. First performance March 6, 1852, London, Drury Lane Theatre.

Among the characters are Sirena, Pietro, Bianca, Rodolfo, Andreozzi, and San Gennaro. SCORE: ms fs, chiefly autograph (British Library, Add. MS. 28350, 29351).

Sicilian Limes, opera in one act by Dominick Argento; libretto (Eng) by John Olon-Scrymgeour. First performance spring 1954, Baltimore, Peabody Conservatory; October 1, 1954, New York.

Sicilian Romance, The, "musical dramatic tale" in two acts by William Reeve; libretto (Eng) by Henry Siddons, after Horace Walpole's romance *The Castle of Otranto.* First performance May 28, 1794, London. First U.S. performance, with new music by Victor Pelissier and Alexander Reinagle, May 6, 1795, Philadelphia.

Manfred, the tyrannical ruler of Otranto, arranges to have his son, Conrad, marry Isabella of Vincenza. When Conrad is killed by an immense helmet that falls from the statue of the old prince, Alfonso the Good, Theodore, a young man in the crowd, is imprisoned on suspicion of having brought about Conrad's death. Theodore escapes and helps Isabella to avoid Manfred, who wants to wed Isabella himself. Theodore turns out to be the grandson of Alfonso, whom Manfred poisoned, and Theodore, the true prince, weds Isabella.

LIBRETTO: English (London: J. Barker, 1794; Philadelphia, Thomas Bradford, 1794).

Sid the Serpent Who Wanted to Sing, children's opera in five scenes by Malcolm Fox; libretto (Eng) by Susan and Jim Vilé. First performance May 1977, Adelaide, State Opera of South Australia Schools Company.

Sid, a circus snake who wants to learn how to sing, tries various styles of singing, including opera and rock, until he finds that his own style is best. SCORE: vs (New York: G. Schirmer, 1985).

Siege of Belgrade, The, opera in three acts, with music partially by Stephen Storace and adaptations from Vincente Martín y Soler's opera *Una cosa rara* (1786, Vienna); libretto (Eng) by James Cobb. First performance January 1, 1791, London, Drury Lane Theatre, with Signora Storace (Lilla), Mr. Bannister (Leopold), Mr. Kelly (the Seraskier), Mr. Dignum (Peter), Mrs. Bland (Ghita), Mrs. Crouch (Catherine), Mr. Palmer (Colonel Cohenberg), Mr. Suett (Yuseph), and Mr. Fox (Ismael). First U.S. performance December 30, 1796, New York.

The story concerns one of the Austrian forays to wrest control of Belgrade from the Turks, in 1456. Included are the attempted rescue of the European girl Catherine, the wife of Colonel Cohenberg, from Turkish captivity, and the amorous designs of the Turkish Seraskier Mahamed Aboubeker Ben Abdallah Ben Ali on her and Lilla, another European captive, who is allowed to wed Leopold, her intended. The Europeans' plan to flee is, to be sure, unmasked, but the lovers are saved when Lilla escapes, and the Austrians are victorious. Cohenberg then spares the Seraskier, who has been captured.

Major roles: the Seraskier (ten), Lilla (sop), Leopold (bar), Colonel Cohenberg (speaking), Leopold (bar), and Catherine (sop).

The music includes borrowings from Mozart's *rondo alla turca* (from K. 331) in the overture, used to promote an "exotic" effect. Mozart's music is the model for the opening chorus of the opera, "Wave Our Prophet's Fam'd Standard of Glory and High" and for the dance of the Turkish soldiers and women, which modulates into another

key, the minor and major sections of the rondo. The opera concludes with a triumphant chorus of the Austrians, "Loud Let the Song of Triumph Rise," from *Una cosa rara.*
SCORES: selections (London: J. Jarvis, 1791); vs (London: J. Dale, 1791?); repr. (Melville, N.Y.: Belwin Mills, 19??).
LIBRETTOS: English (London: J. Jarvis, 1791; Dublin: Booksellers, [1792]).

Siege of Corinth, The, opera in three acts, an adaptation by Thomas S. Cooke of Rossini's *Le siège de Corinthe* (1826, Paris); libretto (Eng) by James R. Planché, after G. L. Balocchi and L. A. Soumet. First performance November 8, 1836, London, Drury Lane Theatre.

The Turks, led by Mahomet II, lay siege to the Greek city of Corinth and ultimately are successful. When Mahomet comes to claim Pamira, daughter of the governor, he finds that she and the other women have killed themselves.

Siege of Curzola, The, comic opera in three acts by Samuel Arnold; libretto (Eng) by John O'Keeffe. First performance August 12, 1786, London, Little Theatre in the Haymarket, with Signora Sestini (Baba) and Mr. Edwin (Cricola).

The plot is based on the historical event of the Turkish siege of 1588 against the island in Dalmatia. In the opera, the heroine is Baba, who leads the female defenders against the invaders.

The work includes an aria by Cherubini.
SCORE: vs (London: Longman & Broderip, [1786]).

Siege of Gibraltar, The, musical farce in two acts by William Shield; libretto (Eng) by Frederick Pilon. First performance April 25, 1780, London, Covent Garden.

Set during the siege from 1780 to 1783, the plot concerns the English hero, in love with an Arab girl called Zayde, who, pretending to be a drunk Arab, "saves" her from marrying a Jew in Africa.
LIBRETTO: English (London: G. Kearsly, 1780).

Siege of Rhodes, The, part 1, opera in five entries (acts) by Henry Lawes (one and five), Henry Cooke (two and three), and Matthew Locke (four); libretto (Eng) by William Davenant. First performance (private) September 1656, London, Rutland House, with Cooke (Solyman), Locke (Admiral of Rhodes), Henry Purcell (uncle of the composer) (Mustapha), and Mrs. Edward Coleman (Ianthe). Part 2, with music (lost) by, perhaps, the same composers, appeared on June 29 (?), 1661, London, Lincoln's Inn Fields.

The opera is concerned with the emperor Solyman, who, like his counterpart in Mozart's *Die Entführung aus dem Serail* (1782, Vienna), is portrayed as a magnanimous ruler. Ianthe, wife of Duke Alphonso of Sicily, leaves the besieged Rhodes to find reinforcements but is captured by Solyman. Touched by her courage, he sets her free.

It was the first of many English operas dealing in a serious or comic way with exotic themes and set in, or concerning, the Ottoman Empire (e.g., *The Captive,** *The Sultan,** and *The Fall of Algiers**).

The instrumental music was composed by Charles Coleman and George Hudson.

This work is often considered the first English opera, although Flecknoe's *Ariadne* (1654, not perf.) predates it. The music itself is lost. Its performance marked perhaps the first appearance of a woman on an English stage.
LIBRETTO: English (1656; repr. 1659, 1663, 1670); second part (1661).

Siege of Rochelle, The, opera in two acts by Michael Balfe; libretto (Eng) by Edward Fitzball, after Mme. de Genlis's novel *Le siège de La Rochelle.* First performance October 29, 1835, London, Drury Lane Theatre. First U.S. performance April 9, 1838, New York.

Clara, the daughter of Count Rosenberg, has been raised by the evil Montalban, causing her to believe that she is Montalban's child. When she desires to wed the Marquis de Valmour, a widower, Montalban kills the Marquis's young son in order to seize the inheritance. Clara discovers this terrible deed but, unwilling to betray the man she thinks is her father, remains silent when she is accused of the killing. Count Rosenberg lays siege to Rochelle, during which Clara learns of her true parentage and declares Montalban's guilt. The French forces succeed, and Valmour and Clara are wed.

Major roles: Clara (sop), Count Rosenberg (bass), Montalban (bass), and Marquis de Valmour (ten).

The first opera of Balfe set to an English text.

The story was also set by L. Ricci as *Chiara di Rosembergh* (1831, Milan).

SCORES: ms fs, partially autograph (1836, British Library, Add. MS. 29325, 29326); vs (London: Cramer, Addison & Heale, [ca. 1835]).

Signa, opera in three acts by Frederick Cowen; libretto (Eng) by Gilbert A. A'Beckett, H. A. Rudall, and F. E. Weatherly, after Ouida's novel. First performance (in an Italian version by G. A. Mazzucato) November 12, 1893, Milan, Teatro dal Verne. First British performance (in Italian, cut to two acts) June 30, 1894, London, Covent Garden.

SCORE: vs, Italian-English (London: Ascherberg; New York: Schubert, 1894).

Signor Deluso, opera buffa in one act by Thomas Pasatieri; libretto (Eng) by the composer, after Molière's *Sganarelle, ou, Le cocu imaginaire* (1660). First performance July 27, 1974, Greenway, Virginia, Madeira School, Wolf Trap Company, with Alise Veloze (Célie), Stanley Wexler (Gorgibus), Judith Christin (Rosine), Raeder Anderson (Signor Deluso), Linda Lane Smith (Clara), Modesto Crisci (Léon), and J. Scott Brumit (town magistrate); conducted by John Moriarty; produced by David Bartholomew.

The title character believes that the portrait he has found is of his wife Clara's lover, when, in fact, it is of the young Célie's amour, Léon.

Roles: Célie (sop); Signor Deluso (bar); Clara (sop); Rosine, her maid (mezzo); Gorgibus, her father (bass-bar); town magistrate (bass-bar); and Léon (ten).

The work is composed for voices and chamber ensemble.

SCORE: vs (New York: Belwin-Mills, 1974; Bryn Mawr, Pa.: T. Presser, 1990).

Silas Marner, opera in three acts by John Joubert; libretto (Eng) by Rachel Trickett, after the novel by George Eliot. First performance May 20, 1961, University of Cape Town, Cape Town, South Africa, with Noreen Hastings (Nancy), Gudrun Barrella (Eppie), Albie Loew (Silas), and Robert Garcia (Squire Cass); conducted by Erik Chisholm; produced by Gregorio Fiasconaro.

The title character, a weaver who has been disgraced because of his friend's thievery, which includes taking Silas's beloved, lives alone in a cottage. After his fortune of gold is stolen, he finds and raises an abandoned baby girl, whom he calls Eppie. The gold is found, together with the remains of Dunstan, the wild son of Squire Cass. The girl turns out to be the daughter of Godfrey, Squire Cass's other son. She refuses her father's offer to come live with him and instead stays with her adoptive father and marries a boy from the village.

BIBLIOGRAPHY: Marcel Sénéchaud, review, *Opera* XII (Oct. 1961), 662 [on premiere].

Silent Shepherd, The, opera in one act by Robert Marek; libretto (Eng). Composed ca. 1968.

For baritone, bass, and speaking role.

Silver Fox, The, children's opera in one act by Libby Larsen; libretto (Eng) by John Oliver. First performance May 11, 1979, St. Paul.

The setting is a remote part of Louisiana during the nineteenth century.

Roles: two sopranos, mezzo-soprano, two tenors, bass-baritone.

Scored for chamber ensemble.

SCORE: holograph photocopy ms score (1978, NYPL).

Silverlake, opera in three acts by Kurt Weill, adapted from *Der Silbersee* (1933, Leipzig) by Lys Symonette; libretto (Eng) by Hugh Wheeler, after the original German version of Georg Kaiser. First performance March 20, 1980, New York, City Opera, with William Neill (Severin), Joel Grey (Olim), Elizabeth Hynes (Fennimore), and Elaine Bonazzi (Frau von Luber); conducted by Julius Rudel. First British performance of this version March 30, 1987, London, Camden Festival; conducted by Antony Shelley; directed by John Eaton.

Set in a mythical country, but meant to be Germany, the work concerns Severin, the leader of a group of out-of-work young men. Leading his gang in a robbery attempt, he is shot by a policeman named Olim, who later regrets his actions. After Severin recovers, Olim uses the money he has won in a lottery to buy a castle for himself and Severin. Frau von Luber, the embittered and once-noble housekeeper, plots with Baron Laur to cheat Olim and Severin. Desperate, the two rush into the lake to drown themselves. They find that the lake is frozen, and, encouraged by the voice of Fennimore, the housekeeper's idealistic niece, they decide to go on living.

Major roles: Severin (ten), Olim (bar), Baron Laur (ten), Fennimore (sop), and Frau von Luber (mezzo).

Among the musical highlights are "Fennimore's Song," which the niece sings at the beginning of the second act, and her "Ballad of Caesar's Death," which she sings to her employers; it describes the demise of tyrants. The controversial nature of the material and the increasing successes of the Nazis caused the work to be closed down shortly after it opened in 1933.

The English version, which is a slight abridgment of the original, uses music from other Weill works, such as the 1927 incidental music to Strindberg's play *Gustavus III.* It was only moderately successful.

SCORE: vs (Vienna: Universal Edition, 1933).

BIBLIOGRAPHY: Robert Jacobson, "North America," *ON* XLIV (June 1980), 30 [on English-version premiere]; Robert Jones, review, *HiFi/MA* XXX (July 1980), 30; Nicholas Kenyon, "Musical Events," *NY* LVI (Apr. 14, 1980), 115–18 [on English-version premiere]. DISCOGRAPHY: Hynes, Bonazzi, Grey, Neill, New York City Opera, cond. Rudel, Nonesuch DB-79003 (2 LPs) (Eng); rev. John W. Freeman, "Records," *ON* XLV (Dec. 20, 1980), 52; David Hamilton, "*Silverlake: Der Silbersee* It's Not!" *HiFi* XXXI (Feb. 1981), 57–58; reissued as Nonesuch/Elektra 79003-2 (1 CD).

Silver River, The, chamber opera in one act by Bright Sheng; libretto (Eng) by David Henry Hwang, after a Chinese legend. First performance July 27, 1997, Santa Fe, Santa Fe Chamber Music Festival, with Wu Man (Goddess Weaver), Jamie Guan (Jade Emperor), Arye Gross (Golden Buffalo), and Michael Chioldi (Buffalo).

The setting is "long ago." Conflict arises when the Western Cowherd and the Eastern Goddess Weaver fall in love. This convinces the Jade Emperor, the ruler of heaven, to send the Golden Buffalo to separate the lovers, which causes even the heavens to cry, thereby flooding the earth. To allay these problems, the couple is allowed to spend one day a year with each other as the stars Vega and Altair in the Silver River (Milky Way).

The work has four contrasting characters: the Golden Buffalo, composed for a traditional Western actor; the poor Cowherd, for a Western opera singer; the Jade Emperor, for a singer in the style of the Peking Opera; and the Goddess Weaver, for a nonsinging musician who plays the pipa.
BIBLIOGRAPHY: Mark Swed, review, *Los Angeles Times* (July 29, 1997), F, 3 [on premiere].

Silver Tankard, The, or, The Point at Portsmouth, afterpiece pastiche in two acts by Samuel Arnold; libretto (Eng) by Lady Craven. First performance July 18, 1781, London, Little Theatre in the Haymarket.
LIBRETTO: English, ms (incomplete) (Huntington Library, San Marino, Calif., Larpent 564).

Silvia, or, The Country Burial, "an opera"; libretto (Eng) by George Lillo. First performance November 10, 1731, London, Lincoln's Inn Fields.
LIBRETTO: English, with ballad airs (London: J. Watts, 1731); repr. Rubsamen/*BO*, vol. 17, *Country Operas III: Sentimental and Moral Comedies* (1974).

Sima, opera in two acts by Leonard Lehrman; libretto (Eng) by the composer, after D. Aizman's *The Krasovitsky Couple*. First performance August 6, 1976, Ithaca, New York, Cornell University.
About an orphaned Jewish girl in Russia who has lost her family during a pogrom and is adopted by a Christian couple.
SCORE: ms score (19??, photocopy, NYPL).

Simón Bolívar, opera in two acts by Thea Musgrave; libretto (Eng) by the composer. First performance January 20, 1995, Norfolk, Virginia, Virginia Opera, with Stephen Guggenheim (Bolívar), Amy Johnson (Manuela Sáenz de Thorne), Douglas Nagel (Santander), Russell Cusick (Páez), Michael Lynn Galanter (Sucre), and Richard Lewis (Rodríguez); conducted by Peter Mark. First British performance (concert, excerpts of act 2) August 26, 1995, London, BBC Promenade Concerts, soloists from premiere, BBC Scottish Symphony; conducted by Mark.
The opera focuses on the Venezuelan hero who freed five countries in South America from Spanish rule but failed to unify them under one banner. It begins with Bolívar's childhood, when he is influenced by his tutor, Rodríguez, who tells him about the French Revolution and is arrested on charges of subversion. It includes his meeting of Manuela Sáenz in 1821, who becomes his mistress, the revolution, and his final days, when he is bitter and disillusioned.
Major roles: Bolívar, "El Libertador" (ten); Bolívar's generals: José Antonio Páez (bass), Antonio José Sucre (ten), Francisco de Paula Santander (bar); Manuela Sáenz de Thorne, Bolívar's mistress (sop); and Rodríguez, Bolívar's tutor (bar).
The musical highlights include the hymn to the sun, which contains elements of folk music, and the lyrical love scene of Bolívar and Manuela.
BIBLIOGRAPHY: Janice Hamer, "Liberator," *ON* LIX (Jan. 7, 1995), 20–23 [preview]; Sorab Modi, "Richmond, Virginia," *ON* LIX (May 1995), 52–53 [on premiere].

Simoon, melodrama in one act by Jan Meyerowitz; libretto (Eng) by Peter John Stephens, after August Strindberg. First performance August 2, 1950, Lenox, Massachusetts, Tanglewood Music Festival.

Simoon, opera in one act by Erik Chisholm; libretto (Eng) by the composer, after Strindberg. First performance July 6, 1954, New York, Cherry Lane Theater.
Part 3 of the *Murder in Three Keys* * trilogy, with *Dark Sonnet* *and *Black Roses.**

Simple Decision, A, opera in one act by Dennis Busch; libretto (Eng) by the composer. Composed 1982.

The setting is Salem, Massachusetts, in colonial times. Lord Haines is an opera impresario, and his daughter, Susanna, desires the lead role in a new opera. The father wants the young Dicky Doo to supply his work, while Susanna pushes for that of Sir Alexander, an established composer. When it is revealed that Dicky's opera is really a plagiarism of Pergolesi's *La serva padrona,* the choice is made simple.

For a detailed description, see Summers/*OOA,* 70–71.

Major roles: Lord Haines (bar), Susanna (sop/mezzo), Sir Alexander (ten/bar), and Dicky Doo (ten).

SCORE: ms score, holograph (photocopy, 1982; NYPL)

Singing Child, The, opera in one act by Gian Carlo Menotti; libretto (Eng) by the composer. First performance May 31, 1993, Charleston, South Carolina, Spoleto Festival U.S.A., Gailliard Municipal Auditorium, with William Cole (Jeremy), Harold Haughton (the playmate), and Maria Fenty (the baby-sitter); conducted by the composer.

Jeremy, an eight-year-old child, is often left in the care of a baby-sitter he dislikes, because his parents are very career-oriented. The lonely boy conjures up a playmate, a singing child who chants, but never speaks, a mode that Jeremy also adopts. The parents become concerned when they witness their child communicating with his unseen friend, and they finally realize that they have ignored their offspring too long, to the detriment of the whole family.

BIBLIOGRAPHY: Alex Ross, review, *NYT* (June 9, 1993), C, 16 [on premiere].

Single Married Man, A, "parlor opera" (comic operetta) by Alfred B. Sedgwick, adapted from J. Offenbach's opéra-bouffe *Madame l'archiduc* (1874, Paris); libretto (Eng) by the composer, after Millaud, Meilhac, and L. Halévy. First performance 1883, New York?

In this story the married, but unfaithful, Mr. Arden Leslie's philandering is brought to an end when he is discovered pursuing Grace, who is secretly married to Leslie's servant Sam.

Major roles: Mr. Arden Leslie, newly married; Sam Double, his confidential servant; Emily, Leslie's wife; and Grace, the village belle.

SCORE/TEXT: vs (New York: De Witt, 1883); repr. ed. Michael Meckna, *NAMT,* vol. 7 (1994).

Sire de Maledroit, The, opera in one act by John Duke; libretto (Eng) by Dorothy Duke, after Robert Louis Stevenson's *Sire de Malétroit's Door.* First performance August 15, 1958, Schroon Lake, New York, Oscar Seagle Music Colony.

I. Mopper's *The Door** and S. Barab's *The Maletroit Door** are other settings.

Siren Song, opera in one act by Jonathan Dove; libretto (Eng) by Nick Dear, after a novel by Gordon Honeycombe. First performance July 15, 1994, London, Almeida Opera.

Sir Gawain and the Green Knight, opera by Andrew Wilson-Dickson; libretto (Eng). First performance 1977, Leicester, England, Leicester University.

BIBLIOGRAPHY: Jim Samson, review, *Tempo* CXXIV (Mar. 1978), 29–30 [on premiere].

Sir John in Love, opera in four acts by Ralph Vaughan Williams; libretto (Eng) selected by the composer from the texts of Shakespeare's *The Merry Wives of Windsor, Love's Labours Lost,* and *Much Ado about Nothing,* and the works of such authors as Thomas Middleton, Ben Jonson, Thomas Campion, and Christopher Marlowe. First performance March 21, 1929, London, Royal College of Music; conducted by Malcolm Sargent. First U.S. performance January 20, 1949, New York, Columbia University. More recent U.S. revivals include May 1978, New York, Hunter College Playhouse, Bronx Opera; conducted by Michael Spierman; January 9, 1988, Bronx, New York, Lehman College Theatre, Bronx Opera; conducted by Spierman.

The story concerns the doings of the wives, their problems with Falstaff, and their revenge against him. Ten characters who play minor roles in Nicolai's *Die lustigen Weiber von Windsor* (1849, Berlin) and Verdi's *Falstaff* (1893, Milan) have larger roles here, including Shallow, Slender, Sir Hugh, Dr. Caius, Simple, Nym, and Rugby.

For a detailed description, see Eaton/*OP* I, 133–34.

Major roles: Sir Hugh Evans (bar), Slender (ten), Page (bar), Sir John Falstaff (bar), Nym (bar), Pistol (bass), Anne Page (sop), Mrs. Page (sop), Mrs. Ford (mezzo), Fenton (ten), Dr. Caius (bar), Mrs. Quickly (mezzo/alto), and Ford (bass).

The score includes ten folk songs, for example, the famous "Greensleeves," sung by Mrs. Ford in act 3 (the orchestral introduction of which the composer turned into his *Fantasia on Greensleeves*). Another highlight is Falstaff's "O That Joy So Soon Should Waste" in act 2. Three of the choruses became the cantata *In Windsor Forest* (1931).

Other settings of the Shakespeare are, in addition to the Nicolai and Verdi, those by P. Ritter, *Die lustigen Weiber von Windsor* (1794, Mannheim); Dittersdorf, *Die lustigen Weiber von Windsor* (1796, Oels); A. Salieri, *Falstaff* (1799, Vienna); C. E. Horn et al., *The Merry Wives of Windsor* (1824, London); M. Balfe, *Falstaff* (1838, London, in Italian); A. Adam, *Falstaff* (1856, Paris), C. F. Swier, *When the Cat's Away* (1941, Philadelphia); and A. Rea, *Falstaff in and out of Love* (1982, Fresno, Calif.).

SCORE: vs (London: Oxford University Press, 1930, 1970).

BIBLIOGRAPHY: Andrew Porter, review, *NY* LIV (May 29, 1978), 87–89 [on 1978 revival].

Sisters, The, opera in one act by Nicolas Flagello; libretto (Eng) by the composer. First performance February 22, 1961, New York, Manhattan School of Music, with Shirley Chester, Helen Klimek, Martha Husser Konyos, Johanna Heier, Lucille Perret, Marilyn Turner, James Cosenza, Stanley Kolk, and William Weiler; conducted by the composer; produced by John Brownlee.

The setting is a Massachusetts farmhouse on the coast in the early 1800s. Three sisters live with their severe father, Caleb. The oldest, Martha, is very bitter and hates the youngest, Maryanna, who is in love with Paul, a French sailor, with whom she wants to run away. Martha is particularly anxious to prevent the elopement since Paul once rejected her. Maryanna manages to flee, leaving Hester, the third sister and a peacemaker, to live out her days with Martha.

For a detailed description, see Eaton/*OP* II, 322.

Roles: Maryanna (lyr sop); Hester (dram sop); Martha (alto); Paul (ten); and Caleb, the father (bar).

Sita, opera in three acts by Gustav Holst; libretto (Eng) by the composer, after Valmiki's *Ramayana*. Composed 1899–1906. Not performed.

Six Characters in Search of an Author, opera in three acts by Hugo Weisgall; libretto (Eng) by Denis Johnston, after Luigi Pirandello's play (1921). First performance April 26, 1959, New York, City Center, with Beverly Sills (the coloratura), Adelaide Bishop (the stepdaughter), Patricia Neway (the mother), Ernest McChesney (the director), Craig Timberlake (the accompanist), Paul Ukena (the father), Robert Trehy (the son), Marc Sullivan (the boy), Barbara Becker (the girl), and Ruth Robart (Madame Pace); conducted by Sylvan Levin; directed by William Ball; designed by Gary Smith. Revived June 14, 1990, Chicago, Lyric Opera, with Robert Orth (the father), Elizabeth Byrne (the stepdaughter), Gary Lehman (the son), Kevin Anderson (the director), and Elizabeth Futral (the coloratura); conducted by Lee Schaenen.

The work opens on a director and cast rehearsing a new opera, whereupon six characters come on the scene: a father, mother, two small children, a son, and a stepdaughter. The family convinces the original group that they are also a group and that they are searching for an author to finish this play. When the substitution is made, it is soon clear that the family has many problems—the son hates his father, and the other children are illegitimate.

In the second act the original company object to the idea that the six characters play themselves, and they are supported by the director. Suddenly, Madame Pace appears and performs for the group. She leaves, insulted, and the stepdaughter is thwarted in her attempt to take off her dress. The disruptions continue in the third act, during which the mother and son argue and he slaps her. The two young children are missing, and the son finds the girl, whom the boy has drowned in a fountain. The boy in turn shoots himself. There is a blackout on the stage, and when the lights go back on, none of the six characters is to be seen.

Members of the chorus suggest that the characters where figments of the director's imagination, which angers him. Suddenly, the six characters reappear upstage. The director hears but does not see them, and when he asks who is there, there is no answer. The stage is empty, and the story is over.

For a detailed description, see Eaton/*OP* I, 134–35.

Roles: real people: the director, Burt Betts (ten); tenore buffo, Terrence O'Flaherty (ten); the coloratura, Lili Klein (sop); the accompanist, Sam Stein (bar); the basso cantante, Pasquale Subito (bass); the stage manager, Mike Pampanickli (bass); the prompter, Gertrude Glubb (sop); the mezzo, Gwen Thomas (alto); the wardrobe mistress (alto); the characters: the father (bar); the stepdaughter (sop); the mother (mezzo); the son (bar); the stepdaughter (sop); Madame Pace, owner of a dress shop (alto); the boy (silent); and the girl (silent).

SCORE: vs (Bryn Mawr, Pa.: Merion Music, 1960).

LIBRETTO: English (Bryn Mawr, Pa.: Merion Music, Theodore Presser, 1957).

BIBLIOGRAPHY: John Von Rhein, "Chicago," *ON* LV (Dec. 8, 1990), 62 [on Chicago revival]; review, *NYT* (Apr. 27, 1959), 22 [on premiere].

DISCOGRAPHY: E. Byrne, E. Foster, Futral, King, LoVerne, Maultsby, Prichett, K. Anderson, B. Fowler, Lehman, R. Orth, Schroeder, Wadsworth, Zawissa, Lyric Opera Center; cond. Schaenen; New World 80454–2 (2); rev. Anthony Tommasini, *ON* LIX (Jan. 7, 1995), 36.

Sixty-Third Letter, The, musical farce in two acts by Samuel Arnold; libretto (Eng) by Walley Chamberlain Oulton. First performance July 18, 1802, London, Little Theatre in the Haymarket. First U.S. performance January 21, 1803, Philadelphia, Chestnut Street Theatre.

LIBRETTO: English (London: Barker, 1802).

Skeleton Lover, The, romantic musical drama by George Rodwell; anonymous libretto (Eng). First performance July 16, 1830, London, Adelphi Theatre, English Opera House Company.

Slave, The, musical drama in three acts by Henry Rowley Bishop; libretto (Eng) by Thomas Morton. First performance November 12, 1816, London, Covent Garden.

In the story, set in Surinam, the slave in question is Zelinda, who is owned by Colonel Lindenburg. Captain Clifton, who has fallen in love with Zelinda, attempts to free her. He leads his troops in a successful foray against a rebellion and as a reward is offered the chance to free a slave. He is forced to choose freedom for Gambia, since the latter had saved his life during the fighting. When Lindenburg arrives and attempts to seize Zelinda, Gambia discovers that Lindenburg has been branded a thief, and Zelinda is reunited with the faithful Clifton.

Bishop wrote the overture and some of the music and adapted the rest, including music by Boieldieu.

SCORE: ms fs (British Library, Add. MS. 36947).

LIBRETTOS: English, with songs (London: John Miller, 1816; New York: D. Longworth, 1817).

Sleeper Awakened, The, serenata in four scenes by George Alexander Macfarren; libretto (Eng) by John Oxenford, after the *Thousand and One Nights*. First performance November 15, 1850, London, Her Majesty's Theatre.

LIBRETTO: English (London: J. K. Chapman, [1850?]).

Sleeping Beauty, children's opera in three scenes by Beryl Rubinstein; libretto (Eng) by John Erskine, after Charles Perrault. First performance January 19, 1938, New York, Juilliard School.

In this fairy tale the prince awakens the princess from her long slumber with a kiss.

Sleeping Children, The, opera in three acts by Brian Easdale; libretto (Eng) by Tyrone Guthrie. First performance July 9, 1951, Cheltenham, England, Opera House, English Opera Group.

BIBLIOGRAPHY: P. Hamburger, "Cheltenham," *Opera* II (Sept. 1951), 504–8 [on premiere]; A. Jacobs, "Cheltenham Festival Gives New Easdale Opera," *MA* LXXI (Aug. 1951), 13.

Sleeping Queen, The, comic opera in one act by Michael Balfe; libretto (Eng) by Henry Brougham Farnie. First performance September 8, 1864, London, Royal Gallery of Illustration. Revised into two acts 1868.

The characters include Agnes, the Queen, and Philippe d'Aguilar.

SCORE: ms score (mostly autograph, 1865, British Museum, MS. Add. 37265); vs, two-act version (London: Cramer & Co., [1860?]).

Sleepy Hollow, or, The Headless Horseman, pastoral opera in three acts by Max Maretzek; libretto (Eng) by Charles Gayler, after Washington Irving's *The Legend of Sleepy Hollow*. First performance September 25, 1879, New York, Academy of Music.

See also *The Headless Horseman* and *The Legend of Sleepy Hollow*.

LIBRETTO: English (New York: Theatre Ticket Office, 1879).

Slippery Soules, Christmas drama in four parts by Stephen Oliver; libretto (Eng) by the composer. First performance December 1969, Oxford, Wychwood School. Revised 1976. Revised version performed December 12, 1988, London, St. Paul's Girls' School.

The work involves a retelling of the Christmas story, with the emphasis on the reactions of the three kings and the shepherds.

Slow Dusk, opera in one act by Carlisle Floyd; libretto (Eng) by the composer. First performance May 2, 1949, Syracuse, Syracuse University.

Despite the objections of her Aunt Sue and brother Jess, the young farm girl Sadie wants to marry Micah, a member of a religious sect at war with her own sect. After

Micah agrees to marry Sadie, she tells her aunt, who reacts angrily. Sadie leaves the house in a fury but returns later, only to learn that her beloved Micah has drowned.
Roles: Aunt Sue (mezzo), Jess (bar), Sadie (sop), and Micah (ten).
SCORE: ([New York?]: Boosey & Hawkes, [1957]).

Small Jewel Box, The, chamber opera by Paul Griffiths after the music of Mozart; libretto (Eng) by the composer. First performance June 22, 1995, New York, John Jay Theater, American Opera/Musical Theater Company, with Mary Paul (the Singer), Wren Marie Harrington, Neal Harrelson, Lars Woodul, John Koch, and Mary Ellen Phillips; conducted by Yuri Krasnapolsky. A shortened version of *The Jewel Box** (1991).
In the work the commedia dell'arte characters Columbina, Pedrolino, and Pantalone are changed to Pamina, Tamino, and Papageno.
BIBLIOGRAPHY: Edward Rothstein, "Opera about Opera, Tersely," *NYT* (June 24, 1995), I, 13 [on premiere].

Smart Aleck and the Talking Wire, children's opera in one act by Martin Kalmanoff; libretto (Eng) by the composer. First performance 1976, New York, tour of Producers' Association.

Smoky Mountain, American folk opera in two acts by Eusebia Simpson Hunkins, after folk music from the Appalachian Mountains; libretto (Eng) by the composer. First performance February 1954, Monmouth, Illinois, Monmouth College.
The work, which is based on folk music of the Appalachians, focuses on George and Ben, who love Jess. Jess likes George but does not know if he is reliable.
Roles: George (bar), Andy (bass), Ben (ten), Jess (dram sop), Arabella (lyric sop), Grandpa (ten/bar), and Aunt Sary (mezzo).
Included are versions of "Comin' 'Round the Mountain" and "Turkey in the Straw."
SCORE: vs (Boston: C. Fischer, 1950).

Smugglers, The, musical drama in two acts by Thomas Attwood; libretto (Eng) by Samuel Birch. First performance April 13, 1796, London, Drury Lane Theatre. First U.S. performance May 13, 1799, Boston, Haymarket Theatre.
SCORE: vs (London: Longman & Broderip, 1796?).
LIBRETTO: English (London: C. Dilly, 1796).

Snatched by the Gods, opera in one act by Param Vir; libretto (Eng) by William Radice, after Rabindranath Tagore. First performance May 11, 1992, Amsterdam. First British performance July 11, 1996, London, Almeida Opera, London Sinfonietta; conducted by Markus Stenz. Performed together with *Broken Strings*.*
When a rich Brahmin, Maitra, assembles a group of pilgrims to go to the mouth of the Ganges, Moksada, a young widow, begs him to take her along, saying that she can leave her son Rahkal with Ananda, her sister. While she goes to fetch the boy, Rahkal is found hidden on the boat. The boatman declares that there are too many on the vessel but lets the boy remain anyway. When Moksada returns, she unknowingly curses her son. Maitra then blames Moksada when a huge storm threatens, which causes the passengers to toss Rahkal overboard. Overwhelmed by guilt, Maitra throws himself into the water also.
For a detailed plot description, see *KINKOB*, 916–17.
Major roles: Maitra (bar), Moksada (sop), Ananda (mezzo), and Rahkal (treble).

Snowbird, lyric opera in one act by Theodore Stearns; libretto (Eng) by the composer. First performance January 13, 1923, Chicago, Civic Opera, with Mary McCormick

(Snowbird), Charles Marshall (the hermit), Edouard Cotreuil (first chieftain), Milo Luka (second chieftain), and Jose Mojica (the archer); conducted by Giorgio Polacco.

The setting is the Siberian coast, around 900 A.D. A Tartar prince who has stolen an amulet from his father is now living as a hermit. He saves a young Tartar girl, whom he dubs his snowbird, and she convinces him to give her his charm.

Three Tartar chieftains and an archer appear; they are searching for the missing prince and the charm and declare that the possessor of the amulet will be punished. When the moonlight falls on the talisman, which the young girl is wearing, the archer shoots her. The prince asks the chieftains to kill him also, saying that the dying snowbird is his daughter.

Snow Leopard, opera in one act by William Harper; libretto (Eng) by Roger Nieboer. First performance November 9, 1989, St. Paul; revised version November 1991, St. Paul, Minnesota, New Music-Theater Ensemble, St. Paul's Seventh Place Theater, with Dan Dressen (Man); conducted by Jerry Rubino; staged by Ben Krywosz.

An American military officer, Man, is secretly helping the Chinese to build a dam in Tibet. When the endeavor fails, he is blamed and, left without any support, suffers a nervous breakdown. He becomes reborn via Buddhist spirits and abandons his old, technology-obsessed life.

The electronic score incorporates elements of popular music.

BIBLIOGRAPHY: Michael Anthony, "St. Paul," *ON* LVI (Feb. 1, 1992), 41 [on 1991 revival].

Snow Queen, The, fairy music drama by Abbie Gerrish Jones; libretto (Eng) by Gerda Wismer Hofmann, after Hans Christian Andersen. First performance February 9, 1917, San Francisco, with Margaret Wismer Nicholls (Snow Queen).

After a birthday party attended by Gerda and her best friend, Kay, a boy, the Snow Queen takes Kay back to the North. The heartbroken Gerda, taking the red rose that Kay gave her, starts out to find her friend. Her great love shields her from the power of the witch. When she finds Kay, he has become a frozen shadow of himself. She sings "The Flower of Love," which brings him back to life and forces the Snow Queen to retreat.

Snow Queen, The, fairy-tale opera in one act by Kenneth Gaburo; libretto (Eng) by Marjorie Wilson, after Andersen. First performance May 5, 1952, Lake Charles, Louisiana.

Snow Queen, The, children's opera by Grahame Dudley; libretto (Eng) by Nick Enright, after Andersen. First performance May 13, 1985, Adelaide, Australia, Opera Theatre.

Also set by Michael Easton (comp. 1986).

Snow Storm, The, ballad opera by James Hewitt; libretto (Eng). First performance 1823, Atlanta.

Snow Wolf, The, "cassation for audience and piano" by Malcolm Williamson in one act; libretto (Eng) by the composer. First performance April 30, 1968, Brighton.

Soap Opera, comic opera in one act by Arnold Franchetti; libretto (Eng) by Kathleen Lombardo. First performance 1973, Hartford, Connecticut, University of Hartford.

For two sopranos, baritone, instruments, and loudspeaker.

SCORE: ms vs, holograph (1973, photocopy, NYPL).

Sofa, The, comic opera in one act by Elizabeth Maconchy; libretto (Eng) by Ursula Vaughan Williams, after Crébillon's novel *Le sofa*. First performance December 13, 1959, London, Sadler's Wells, New Opera Workshop, with Anne Abbott, Anne Pashley, Jack Irons, and Delme Bryn Jones; conducted by Keith Darlington; directed by Michael Geliot.

The setting is Paris in the nineteenth century, in a ballroom. A man inexplicably turns into a sofa!

SCORE: fs (London: Chester, ca. 1987).

So How Does Your Garden Grow, opera in one act by Robert Russell; libretto (Eng) by the composer. First performance 1966, New York, Carnegie Hall.

The setting is a kitchen and dining room, "in the beginning." Adam complains to Eve that he is too limited in what he can do, especially in the garden. God explains the reasons for the restrictions, whereupon Adam proceeds to complain that Eve is too bossy. God tells Adam to try once more, and Eve serves a new dessert, which she calls "apple pie."

For a description, see Summers/*OOA*, 264–65.

Roles: Eve (sop), Adam, (ten), and God (bass-bar).

Sojourner, opera in one act by Valerie Capers; libretto (Eng). First performance February 24, 1985, New York, Opera Ebony, All City Concert Choir, with Loretta Holkmann (Sojourner), Harry L. Burney III (slave auctioneer/the Lord); conducted by John Robinson.

A musical biography of the nineteenth-century freed slave Sojourner Truth, who preached about emancipation and the rights of women.

The score includes extensive jazz and gospel elements.

BIBLIOGRAPHY: Tim Page, "Opera Ebony, 2 New Works," *NYT* (Feb. 25, 1985), III, 12.

Sojourner and Mollie Sinclair, The, comic opera in one act by Carlisle Floyd; libretto by the composer. First performance December 2, 1963, Raleigh, North Carolina, East Carolina College, with Patricia Neway (Mollie) and Norman Treigle (Sojourner).

The story concerns Scottish settlers in the Carolinas in the mid-1700s, led by the conservative Sojourner, who must contend with the independent-minded Mollie Sinclair.

SCORE: vs (London: Boosey & Hawkes, 1968).

Sold Again and Got the Money, comic operetta in one act by Alfred B. Sedgwick; libretto (Eng) by the composer. First performance 1876, New York?

The hardworking and honest carpenter Jack Hammer is aided in his wooing Louisa, daughter of the quack Dr. Pompous, by an itinerant book peddler, Jabez Bookstaver. Jabez uses the father's vanity to help the lovers, who are united in the end.

Roles: Louisa (sop), Jack Hammer (ten), Jabez Bookstaver (bar), and Dr. Pompous (bass).

SCORE: vs (New York: R. M. De Witt, 1876); repr. ed. Michael Meckna, *NAMT*, vol. 7 (1994).

Soldier, The, opera in one act by Lehman Engel; libretto (Eng) by Lewis Allan, after a story by Roald Dahl. First performance (concert) November 25, 1956, New York, Carnegie Hall.

Coming back from war, Robert is beset by disturbing memories, including mistreatment by the doctor and nurse, and he withdraws to his own world, thinking himself a child again. He then remembers his happiness with his wife, Edna, but his sense of loss drives him into madness, and he threatens his spouse with a knife. She calls the doctor and asks for her husband to be taken away.

For a detailed description, see Eaton/*OP* I, 224.

Major roles: Robert (bar); Edna (speaking); their friends: He (ten), She (mezzo); doctor (bar); and nurse (speaking).

The music combines stretches of dissonance and diatonic, Broadway-inspired passages to represent the soldier's flashbacks.

LIBRETTO: English (New York: Chappell, [1956]).

Soldier Boy, Soldier, opera by T[homas] J[efferson] Anderson Jr.; libretto (Eng) by Leon Forrest. First performance October 23, 1982, Bloomington, Indiana; conducted by Robert Porco; directed by Alan Brody.

The work concerns Clarence Cratwell, a private returning from the Vietnam War, and the difficulty of his adjustment to civilian life in the United States, complicated by a jealous former mistress who threatens his recent marriage.

BIBLIOGRAPHY: Andrew Porter, review, *NY* LVIII (Dec. 13, 1982), 181–82 [on premiere].

Soldier's Legacy, The, opera di camera in two acts by George Macfarren; libretto (Eng) by John Oxenford. First performance February 11, 1864, London, Royal Gallery of Illustration.

The work is set in 1814 Staffordshire. The hero, a young soldier, has promised his dying fellow soldier that he would care for the man's child. The child turns out to be the woman with whom the young soldier has fallen in love, and the opera ends happily.

For a detailed plot and musical description, see Biddlecombe/*EO*, 157–58.

SCORE: vs ("London: Ewer & Co., [1865?]").

Soldier's Return, The, or, What Can Beauty Do?, comic opera in two acts by James Hook; libretto (Eng) by Theodore Edward Hook. First performance April 23, 1805, London, Drury Lane Theatre, with Mrs. Bland. First U.S. performance November 23, 1807, Baltimore.

Among the numbers is "Down in the Valley."

LIBRETTO: English (London: Longman, Hurst, Rees and Orme, 1805).

Soldier's Widow, The, or, The Ruins of the Mill, musical drama in two acts by John Barnett; libretto (Eng) by Edward Fitzball. First performance May 4, 1833, London, Adelphi Theatre.

LIBRETTO: English (London: Duncombe and Moon, [183?]).

Solomon and Balkis (The Butterfly That Stamped), comic opera in one act by Randall Thompson; libretto (Eng) by the composer, after Rudyard Kipling's *Just So Stories*. First performance (concert) March 29, 1942, CBS radio. First performance (stage) April 14, 1952, Cambridge, Massachusetts.

In order to restore order to the feuding wives of Solomon, Balkis, his favorite wife, arranges a cautionary display. She has them see the Butterfly, who is fighting with his wife. He claims he can destroy the royal palace by merely stamping his foot. When she laughs at his claim, Solomon arranges for djinns to carry out his threat. The Butterfly stamps his foot, and the palace disappears (because of the djinns). The Butterfly's wife and the wives of Solomon are filled with respect and fear, the Butterfly stamps his foot to make the palace reappear, and peace is restored.

For a detailed description, see Eaton/*OP* I, 224–25.

Major roles: King Solomon (bar); Balkis, Queen of Sheba (mezzo); the Butterfly (ten); Butterfly's wife (sop); and Egyptian queen (sop).

Solomon and Sheba, improvisational opera by Sam Rivers; libretto (Eng), after the Bible. First performance June 23, 1973, New York, Harlem Opera Society.

BIBLIOGRAPHY: Peter Davis, review, *NYT* (June 25, 1973), 49 [on premiere].

Some Pig, children's opera in one act by Libby Larsen; libretto (Eng) by the composer, after *Charlotte's Web* by E. B. White. First performance June 6, 1973, Minneapolis, University of Minnesota.

Some Place of Darkness, television opera in one act by Christopher Whelen; libretto (Eng) by John Hopkins. First performance January 23, 1967, London, BBC television, with Robin Fairhurst (Jerry), Margaret Neville (girlfriend), and Raymond Hayter; conducted by Leon Lovett; directed by Bill Hays.

The story concerns a young man, Jerry, who drifts into thuggery and murder.
BIBLIOGRAPHY: Arthur Jacobs, review, *Opera* XVIII (March 1967), 261–62 [on premiere].

Something New for the Zoo, opera buffa in one act by Lee Hoiby; libretto (Eng) by Dudley Huppler. First performance May 17, 1982, Cheverly, Maryland.

The setting is Vienna after World War II, during the Soviet occupation. Emma Leintraub, star of the Staatsoper, has in her possession a magic potion that can turn men into animals, which she has done with several Soviet commanders, sending the "animals" to the Vienna Zoo. Her next victim is supposed to be General Vorchiekleff, but her servant Heinrich accidentally drinks some of the potion himself and turns into a gorilla. Emma says that she will restore Heinrich to his human form but in the meantime lines up her next victim, General Malinoff.
SCORE: vs (New York: G. Schirmer, 1989).

Something's Gonna Happen, children's opera in one act by Michael Colgrass; libretto (Eng) by the composer. First performance May 1978, Toronto, Huron Elementary School.

A contemporary version of the tale of Jack and the Beanstalk.

Sonata about Jerusalem, cantata-music theater by Alexander Goehr; text (Eng) by the composer and Recha Freier, after Obadiah the Proselyte's *Autobiography* and Samuel ben Yahya ben al Maghribi's *Chronicle*. First performance 1971, Jerusalem. First U.S. performance December 11, 1991, New York, Manhattan School of Music.

The work is a dramatization of the tale of Obadiah the Proselyte, a Christian who became a Jew in the twelfth century. It includes the simple melodic chorus refrain "The sun shall turn into darkness and the moon into blood before the great and terrible day of the Lord."

Sonata is scored for bass solo, soprano solo, boy's voice (speaking), women's chorus, and instrumental ensemble.

It is part 3 of the composer's *Triptych,** which consists also of *Naboth's Vineyard** (1968) and *Shadowplay** (1970).
SCORE: fs, English-German (London: Schott; New York: Schott Music Corp., [1976]).
BIBLIOGRAPHY: Philip Kennicott, "Composer's Page," *ON* LVI (Dec. 7, 1991), 48, 70.

Song of David, The, biblical opera in two acts by Ira Arnstein; libretto (Eng). First performance (concert) May 17, 1925, New York, Aeolian Hall; conducted by the composer.

Roles: David (ten), Saul (bass), Ruth (sop), and the Witch of Endor (alto).
The work includes a short ballet with jazz elements.

Song of Insanity, opera in one act by Harold Seletsky; libretto (Eng) by the composer. First performance June 14, 1987, New York, Golden Fleece Ltd., with Lucy Sorlucco (Amy), Roldan Rene (doctor), Mark Amspoker (Amy's father), and Ruth Stoner, Cynthia Steward, and Laura Campbell (Amy's alter egos); conducted by Jerome Shannon.

Described as a "schizophrenic journey," the story concerns Amy, a mental patient with three alter egos.

The mostly dissonant score includes a short jazzy section.
BIBLIOGRAPHY: Michael Kimmelman, review, *NYT* (June 18, 1987), C, 17 [on premiere].

Song of Majnun, The, chamber opera in one act by Bright Sheng; libretto (Eng) by Andrew Porter, after the twelfth-century Islamic epic poem *Layla and Majnun* by Nizami. First performance April 9, 1992, Chicago, Civic Theater, Lyric Center for American Artists, with Rodrick Dixon (Majnun), Yan Wan Yang (Layla), and Beverly Thiele and Julia Bentley (gossips); conducted by Richard Buckley.

The Romeo-and-Juliet type of story has the Persian lovers Majnun and Layla kept apart until death. Although Majnun is consumed with love for Layla, her parents keep them apart and force her to marry a man of their own choosing. When Majnun returns after a pilgrimage to save himself from madness, he finds that Layla has died of grief. He sings a parting love song during her funeral.

BIBLIOGRAPHY: Andrew Porter, "Desire in the Desert," *ON* LVI (Mar. 28, 1992), 30–31; Thomas C. Willis, "Chicago," *ON* LVII (Oct. 1992), 48–49 [on premiere].

DISCOGRAPHY: A. M. Martinez, J. Grove, M. Petro, J. Lattimore, R. Very, G. Youngblood, P. Blackwell, Houston Grand Opera; cond. W. Holmquist, Delos DE 3211 (1995, 1 CD).

Song of Pegasus, opera in two acts, with ballet, by Ron McFarland; libretto (Eng) by Maria Woodward. First performance June 28, 1985, Forest Meadows, California, with Lee Velta (Noah) and Vicki Shaghoian (serpent); choreographed by Carlos Carvajal.

About the mythical horse Pegasus and how it causes problems on Noah's ark.

The eclectic score includes several popular songs, such as "Deep River."

BIBLIOGRAPHY: Stephanie von Buchau, review, *ON* L (Sept. 1985), 53 [on premiere].

Song of the Maypole, The, children's opera in one act by George Dreyfus; libretto (Eng) by Frank Kellaway. First performance 1967, Canberra, Australia.

Son-in-Law, The, comic opera in two acts by Samuel Arnold; libretto (Eng) by John O'Keeffe. First performance August 14, 1779, London, Little Theatre in the Haymarket, with Charles Bannister (Signor Arionelli). First U.S. performance March 8, 1793, Charleston, South Carolina, Charleston Theatre.

The story involves a merchant who, in order to win the hand of Cecilia, passes himself off as a gentleman in the West End. Cecilia's father, however, thinks that her suitor is the old Italian castrato Signor Arionelli, who declines to marry her.

For a detailed description, see Fiske/*ETM*, 436–37.

SCORE: vs (London, J. Preston, [1779?]).

LIBRETTO: English (Dublin: Booksellers, 1783).

Sonnambula, La, opera in two acts by Henry Rowley Bishop, an adaptation of Bellini's work (1831, Paris); libretto (Eng) translated by Samuel Beazley from Romani's text, based on Scribe and Aumer's vaudeville (1816). First performance May 1, 1833, London, Drury Lane Theatre, with Maria Malibran. First U.S. performance October 3, 1836, New York.

See *Love's Dream* (1821, London) for an earlier version in English.

LIBRETTOS: English (London: n.p., [1833]); New York: J. Perry, London: T. H. Lacy, [18??].

Sopranos Only, opera in one act by Tom Johnson; libretto (Eng) by the composer. First performance, in French, as *Réservé aux sopranes*, March 1984, Paris, American Center. First performance in English, October 1, 1990, Oneonta, New York.

Sorcerer, The, comic opera in two acts by Arthur Sullivan; libretto (Eng) by William S. Gilbert. First performance November 17, 1877, London, Opera-Comique, with Richard Temple (Sir Marmaduke Pointdextre), George Bentham (Alexis), Rutland Barrington (Dr. Daly), Frederick Clifton (a notary), George Grossmith (John Wellington

Wells), Isabella Paul (Lady Sangazure), Alice May (Aline), Harriet Everard (Mrs. Partlet), and Giulia Warwick (Constance). First U.S. performance February 21, 1879, New York, Broadway Theatre.

The townsfolk are celebrating the betrothal of Alexis, son of the elderly Sir Marmaduke Pointdextre, to Aline, the daughter of Lady Sangazure. Pointdextre and Lady Sangazure are secretly in love but are unable to declare their affection openly. Alexis buys a love potion from Mr. Wells to help the parents, but his plan backfires when the entire village drinks it, including Lady Sangazure, who proceeds to fall in love with Dr. Daly, the vicar. The only way to break the spell is by having Alexis or Wells depart. The people vote for Mr. Wells to leave, and the power of the potion is broken.

For a detailed description, see Stedman/*WSG*, 152–55.

Major roles: Sir Marmaduke Pointdextre, an elderly baronet (bass-bar); Alexis, his son, a member of the Grenadier Guards (ten); Dr. Daly, vicar of Ploveridge (bar); a notary (bass); John Wellington Wells, of J. W. Wells & Co., family sorcerers (bar); Lady Sangazure, a lady of ancient lineage (alto); Aline, her daughter, fiancée of Alexis (sop); Mrs. Partlet, a pew-opener (alto); and Constance, her daughter (sop).

SCORE: vs (Boston: O. Ditson, [188?]; Melville, N.Y.: Belwin Mills, [1979?]).
LIBRETTO: English (London: Chappell, [1884?]).
DISCOGRAPHY: Soloists and chorus, D'Oyly Carte Company, Royal Philharmonic Orchestra; cond. I. Godfrey and R. Nash, London 436 807-2 (1993?, London, CD; reissue of 1967 recording).
VIDEO: D. Adams, N. Christie, N. Willis, J. Martin, Ambrosian Opera Chorus; cond. McCarthy; London Symphony Orchestra; cond. A. Faris; dir. S. Pimlott, Goldcrest Films International, Opera World, VHS SOR-10V (1982 perf.); rev. F. Paul Driscoll, *ON* LXII (Oct. 1997), 65.

Sorceress, The, opera in two acts by Ferdinand Ries; libretto (Eng) by Edward Fitzball, after the English translation (1827) of C. F. van der Velde's story *Arwed Gyllenstjerna* (1822). First performance August 4, 1831, London, Adelphi Theatre.

Sorry, Wrong Number, opera in one act by Jerome Moross; libretto (Eng), after Lucille Fletcher's radio play. First performance August 7, 1980, Lake George, New York.

Sorry, Wrong Number, conversational chamber opera in one act by Jack Beeson; libretto (Eng) by the composer, after Fletcher. Composed 1996. Premiere scheduled for May 25, 1999, New York, Kaye Playhouse, Center for Contemporary Opera; conducted and directed by Richard Marshall.

A faulty connection allows an invalid, Mrs. Guglielmo Stevenson, to overhear a telephone conversation in which, she realizes too late, her own murder is being planned.

Sot, The, burletta by Thomas Arne; libretto (Eng) by the composer, after his comic opera *Squire Badger** (1772). First performance February 16, 1775, London, King's Theatre, Haymarket.

Sotoba Komachi, opera in one scene by Marvin David Levy; libretto (Eng) by Sam Houston Brock, a translation of the Noh play by Kan'ami Kigotsugu. First performance April 7, 1957, New York, Music in Our Time.

Komachi, once beautiful and heartless, is now a withered old woman. She reveals her identity to priests, who try to make her reform. The chorus tells of her story, how she made Captain Shii No Shosho, who was desperately in love with her, come to her for 100 nights before she would see him. Just before the 100 days were up, he died, and his love and anger took possession of Komachi's soul, leading her to her wretched state.

For a detailed description, see Eaton/*OP* I, 225–26.

Roles: first priest (bass-bar); second priest (ten); Komachi (sop); chorus (mezzo); young Komachi (female dancer); and Shii No Shosho, the captain (male dancer).

Sourwood Mountain, opera in one act by Arthur Kreutz; libretto (Eng) by Zoë Lund Schiller. First performance January 8, 1959, Clinton, Mississippi.

The Romeo-and-Juliet-type story is set in the Appalachian Mountains. The feuding families are the Porters and the Lowells, and trouble arises when Danny Lowell falls in love with Lucy Porter, this coming after Nancy Porter was betrayed by Robert Lowell. This time, when Lucy and Danny run off, the women from both sides want peace to prevail. After Ben Porter shoots Lucy because she is wearing Danny's cap, he sees the madness of the situation, the families reconcile, and Lucy and Danny are allowed to marry.

Major roles: the judge (bar), Danny Lowell (bar/ten), Lucy Porter (sop), Ida Porter (sop), and Ben Porter (bar/bass).

SCORE: vs (New York: Franco Colombo, 1963).

Soyazhe, opera in one act by Garland Anderson; libretto (Eng) by Jamie Leo Cooper. First performance July 29, 1979, Central City, Colorado, Central City Opera.

As Witch Slayer lies dying, he is surrounded by members of his tribe, including Stands Alone, husband of the slain witch Soyazhe. Soyazhe's spirit enters, and Witch Slayer berates Stands Alone for failing to kill Soyazhe when ordered. Soyazhe, believing that her husband has indeed killed her, stabs him, but it is revealed that Ruins, her father, killed Soyazhe on Witch Slayer's orders, because she had witnessed Witch Slayer rifling the graves of the tribe. The revelation of the truth causes the spirit of Stands Alone to enter, and he joins his wife's spirit.

For a detailed description, see Kornick/*RAO*, 14–16.

Major roles: Soyazhe (mezzo); Ruins, her father (ten); Stands Alone (ten); and Witch Slayer (bar).

BIBLIOGRAPHY: Andrew Porter, review, *NY* LV (Aug. 27, 1979), 85 [on premiere].

Spanish Barber, The, or, Fruitless Precaution, comic opera in three acts by Samuel Arnold; libretto (Eng) by George Colman Sr., after Beaumarchais's *Le barbier de Séville* (1776). First performance August 30, 1777, London, Little Theatre in the Haymarket, with John Edwin (Lazarillo), Elizabeth Farren (Rosina/Rosara), and John Palmer (the Count). First U.S. performance July 7, 1794, Philadelphia, Chestnut Street Theatre.

An early setting of the Barber of Seville story. Figaro is here called Lazarillo, and Rosina is on occasion called Rosara. The Count has no singing numbers. Bartolo shares a trio with two of his servants.

For a detailed description, see Fiske/*ETM*, 434–35.

The more famous settings of Beaumarchais's text were Paisiello's 's *Il barbiere di Siviglia* (1782, St. Petersburg); and Rossini's *Il barbiere di Siviglia* (1816, Rome).

SCORE: vs (London: Harrison, Cluse, [1799?]).

LIBRETTO: English (London: T. Cadell, 1784).

Spanish Bond, A, opera in one act by Thomas German Reed; libretto (Eng) by Gilbert A. A' Beckett. First performance November 1, 1875, London, St. George's Hall.

Spanish Castle, The, or, The Knight of Guadalquivir, comic opera by James Hewitt; libretto (Eng) by William Dunlop. First performance December 5, 1800, New York, with Mr. Fennel (Montalvan), Mr. Hallam (Sebastian), Mr. Martin (Algiziras), Mr.

Hodgkinson (O'Tipple), Mrs. Hodgkinson (Olivia), Miss Brett (Henerica), and Miss Harding (Lisetta).

Spanish Dollars! or, The Priest of the Parish, operatic sketch in one act by John Davy; libretto (Eng) by Andrew Cherry. First performance May 9, 1806, London, Covent Garden. First U.S. performance March 4, 1807, Philadelphia.

The work includes the song "The Bay of Biscay."
LIBRETTO: English (London: Barker, 1806).

Spanish Lady, The, "a musical entertainment" (ballad opera); libretto (Eng) by Thomas Hull. First performance May 2, 1765, London, Covent Garden, with George Mattocks (Worthy), Mr. Perry (Major Hearty), Mr. Dunstall (lieutenant), Mr. R. Smith (ensign), Isabella Mattocks (Elvira), Miss Valois (Anna), and Mrs. White (a duenna).

Roles: Worthy, a noble English officer; Major Hearty; a sea lieutenant; an ensign; Elvira, the lady; Anna, her younger sister; and a duenna.
LIBRETTO: English (London: L. Cooper [1769]); repr. ed. Rubsamen/*BO*, vol. 2, *Historical and Patriotic Subjects* (1974).

Spanish Lady, The, opera in two acts by Edward Elgar; libretto (Eng) by Barry Jackson, after Ben Jonson's play *The Devil Is an Ass*. Composed 1929–1933. Performing version reconstructed by Percy Young. Young version performed May 15, 1986, London, St. John's Smith Square. First stage performance of complete reconstruction November 26, 1994, Cambridge, England, West Road Concert Hall, Cambridge University Opera Society, with Rowan Wright (Frances) and Christopher Genz (Wittipol); conducted by William Lacey; directed by Adrian Osmond; choreographed by Darren Royston.

The work is set in Jacobean London. The shady Meercraft enlists the socialite Lady Tailbush in his plan to make a lot of money, a prospect she relishes and a ploy by Meercraft to defraud the wealthy Fitzdottrel. Frances, a young lady, is the ward of the greedy Fitzdottrel, who wants to make her his wife. Wittipol, Frances's lover, has other ideas. He gains entrance to a party given by Lady Tailbush in the disguise of a "Spanish Lady." His costume allows Wittipol to usher Frances out of the party, and he gets a nearby clergyman to perform a quick wedding ceremony.

Major roles: Fitzdottrel (bass), Meercraft (bar), Wittipol (ten), Manly (ten), Frances (sop), Lady Tailbush (mezzo), and Lady Eitherside (col sop).

Elgar worked on the opera from 1929 to 1933, whereupon he abandoned it, leaving an annotated text and manuscript sketches.
SCORE: vs, ed., arr., orch. by Percy Young (London: Novello, 1994).
BIBLIOGRAPHY: Robert Anderson, review, *MT* CXXXVI (Jan. 1995), 53 [on 1994 revival].

Spanish Patriots, The, or, Royal Restoration, musical entertainment by Charles Gilfert; libretto (Eng) by Edward Riley. First performance January 4, 1809, New York, Park Theatre.

Spanish Patriots a Thousand Years Ago, The, opera in three acts by John Stevenson; libretto by H. B. Code. First performance September 22, 1812, London, Lyceum Theatre, Drury Lane Company.

The work includes the "celebrated boat glee" "See Our Oars with Feather'd Spray."
LIBRETTO: English (London: J. Walker, 1812).

Spanish Rivals, The, musical farce in two acts by Thomas Linley Sr.; libretto (Eng) by Mark Lonsdale. First performance November 4, 1784, London, Drury Lane Theatre, with Mr. Parsons (Don Narcisso), Mr. Dodd (Peter), Mr. Barrymore (Don Ferdinand), and Miss Philips (Roxella).

The setting is Spain and concerns a rich aging gentleman, Don Narcisso de Medicis, whose English servant, Peter, is a former naval man from Cumberland.

SCORE: vs (London: S. A. & P. Thompson, 1784?); repr. ed. Redcroft (Huntingdon, Cambs., England: King's Music, [1989?]).

LIBRETTO: English (London: Almon, 1784).

Spark Plugs, comic opera in one act by Milton Granger; libretto (Eng) by the composer. Composed 1987.

The plot concerns Walter, who writes for an ad agency, and Donovan, an artist, who work together to create ads for spark plugs. Walter would really like to be a novelist, but his manuscript is turned down, while Donovan gets a grant to study full-time. He then becomes defensive about working for an advertising business and says that Donovan is a snob. Despite the fact that the two love each other, Donovan departs, and Walter resumes his humdrum existence.

Speakeasy, opera by Dai-Keong Lee; libretto (Eng) by Robert Healey. First performance February 8, 1957, New York, Cooper Union.

Revised as *The Ballad of Kitty the Barkeep.**

Specialist, The, opera in one act by Lou Rodgers; libretto (Eng) by Stuart Michaels. First performance April 1, 1978, New York, Golden Fleece Ltd.

The setting is Brooklyn Heights at the turn of the twentieth century. Andre, a skilled seducer, sets his sights on Nora, wife of Edward. Andre's method is to use her husband to relay his seemingly innocent feelings, including that he is sick and needs her attentions. Nora answers that, although she finds Andre attractive, she knows that an affair would end her marriage. Feeling that she is indeed sincere, Andre determines to use his skills on single women in the future.

For a description, see Summers/*OOA*, 252–53.

Roles: Edward (ten), Nora (sop), Annabelle, a maid (sop); and Andre (bar).

SCORE: ms score, holograph (1980, photocopy, NYPL).

BIBLIOGRAPHY: Peter G. Davis, "Golden Fleece," *NYT* (Apr. 3, 1978), C, 22 [on premiere].

Speed the Plough, or, The Return of Peace, musical play by John Moorehead; libretto by Charles Dibdin. First performance May 1, 1802, London, Sadler's Wells.

Spirit of the Avalanche, chamber opera in one act by Alan Hovhaness; libretto (Eng) by the composer. First performance February 15, 1963, Tokyo.

Roles: mountain climber (bar), priest (bar), and mad bird (col sop).

SCORE: miniature score (New York: C. F. Peters, 1962).

Spirit of the Bell, The, comic opera in two acts by George Rodwell; libretto (Eng) by James Kenney. First performance June 8, 1835, London, Lyceum Theatre.

Sprigs of Laurel, comic opera in two acts by William Shield; libretto (Eng) by John O'Keeffe. First performance May 11, 1793, London, Covent Garden. Revived 1829, London, Covent Garden, with Mr. Powell (Captain Cruizer), Mr. Gattie (Serjeant-Major Tactic), Mr. Horn (Lenox), Mr. Sinclair (Sinclair), G. Smith (George Streamer), Mr. Yarnold (Corporal Squib), Mr. Mathews (Nipperkin), and Miss Paton (Mary). Revised as *The Rival Soldiers** (1797).

The story concerns a contingent of British guards, under the command of the Duke of York, who leave for Holland, undergoing military and amorous exploits.

The work uses folk songs and music by Handel and Anfossi.

Roles: Cruizer, a captain; Tactic, a "serjeant-major"; Lenox; Sinclair; George Streamer; Squib, a corporal; Nipperkin; and Mary.
SCORE: vs (London: Longman & Broderip, n.d.).
LIBRETTO: English (London: John Cumberland, [1829?]).

Spring Lock, The, operatic romance in two acts by George Rodwell; libretto (Eng) by Richard Brinsley Peake. First performance August 18, 1829, London, Lyceum Theatre.
LIBRETTO: English (London: Chapman and Hall, [1839]).

Spur of the Moment, The, opera in one act by Guy Halahan; libretto (Eng) by Joe Mendoza. First performance June 17, 1959, BBC television.

Squire Badger, comic opera in two acts by Thomas Arne; libretto (Eng) by the composer, after H. Fielding's *Don Quixote in England*. First performance March 16, 1772, London, Little Theatre in the Haymarket. Revised as *The Sot** (1775).

Stable Home, A, opera in one act by Stephen Oliver; libretto (Eng) by the composer. First performance December 1977, Canada.

Stanley and the Monkey King, chamber opera in two acts by John White; libretto (Eng) by Robin Barson, after Kafka's *Der Prozess*. First performance March 27, 1975, London, Drama Centre.

Starbird, The, opera in one act by Henry Mollicone; libretto (Eng) by Kate Pogue. First performance May 17, 1979, Houston, Grand Opera, with Neal Nease (the Dog), Lynn Yakes (the Cat), Ray Jacobs (the Donkey), and Kathryn Wright (the Starbird); conducted by Louis Saleno.

In this parable three animals, the Dog, the Cat, and the Donkey, are fighting among themselves after losing their jobs. They are abducted by robots, who take them to their spaceship, wanting to use them for their experiments. The Starbird, from the planet Arcturus, who had warned the animals about the robots, intervenes and helps them overpower their captors. She guides the spaceship back to earth when she realizes that the animals have learned their lesson and have begun to appreciate each other.

For a detailed description, see Kornick/*RAO*, 200–2.

Major roles: Starbird (sop), the Cat (mezzo), the Dog (ten), the Donkey (bass-bar), Robot 1 (ten), and Robot 2 (bass).

Stations, space opera in three acts by James Penberthy; libretto (Eng) by Gwen Harwood. Composed 1975.

The action is set in a space time warp.

Statue for the Mayor, A, children's opera in three acts by Hugo Cole; libretto (Eng) by the composer. First performance July 17, 1952, London, Wimbledon High School.

The conceited and strong-willed mayor of a town decides that the marketplace needs a statue of his likeness, a move dreaded by the market women. He therefore announces a competition for the best design, a competition he will judge. The winner turns out to be a stranger who, unknown to the mayor, is a friend of the market ladies.
BIBLIOGRAPHY: review, *Notes* XII (Dec. 1954), 152.

Statues on a Lawn, opera in one act by Thomas J. Flanagan; libretto (Eng) by Matthew Calhoun, after his own short story. First performance March 24, 1983, New York, Golden Fleece, Ltd.

Stauf, opera in two acts by Michael Sahl and Eric Salzman; libretto (Eng) by the composers. First performance May 25, 1976, New York, Cubiculo. Also September 20, 1987, Philadelphia, American Musical Theatre Festival.

In this treatment of the Faust story, the setting is a modern American city. It concerns the young inventor Henry Stauf, who is devoted to Dr. Jove. Jove is part of the Goodco Corporation, which specializes in nuclear power, and when the Karen Silkwood-like Margarita, Stauf's girlfriend, joins forces against the company's trouble-plagued power plant, Stauf is forced to stop her to avoid a scandal.

BIBLIOGRAPHY: Robert Baxter, "Philadelphia," *ON* LII (Jan. 30, 1988), 34 [on revival].

St. Carmen of the Main, opera in two acts by Sydney Hodkinson; libretto (Eng) by Lee Devin, including "a pop song fantasia" from the English translation of the play by Michel Tremblay. First performance May 19, 1988, Guelph, Ontario, Guelph Spring Festival.

The story centers on Carmen, a singer of country and western music, employed in a club in the Main, a tenderloin district of Montreal. Her manager, Maurice, has booked her into the Club Rodeo, but she is hesitant to sing if Toothpick, his partner, attends, since he once assaulted her. Maurice convinces her to go on anyway, since he has been involved with Toothpick in a crime. Carmen gives a triumphant performance, but Toothpick ambushes her after the show and kills her, making it look as if somebody else killed her. He has already picked her replacement, the faded singer Gloria.

St. David's Day, comic opera in two acts by Thomas Attwood; libretto (Eng) by Thomas Dibdin. First performance March 25, 1800, London, Covent Garden.

An honest Welshman finds a purse with £100, which he returns to its rightful owner twenty years later.

SCORE: vs (London: Goulding, Phipps & D'Almaine, [1800]).
LIBRETTO: English (London: J. Cumberland, [n.d.]).

Stella, opera in one act by George W. L. Marshall-Hall; libretto (Eng) by the composer. First performance May 4, 1912, Melbourne, Her Majesty's Theatre. First British performance (abridged) June 8, 1914, London, Palladium, advertised as the first Australian opera performed in England.

Set to an Australian subject.

SCORE: fs (Parkville, [Australia]: Centre for Studies in Australian Music, 1992.

Sterlingman, or, Generosity Rewarded, opera in one act by Klaus Roy; libretto (Eng) by the composer, translated from a short story by Arkady Averchenko. First performance (concert) April 18, 1957, Boston, WBGH. First performance (stage) May 26, 1960, Cleveland, Case Western Reserve University.

The setting is a small town, November 10, the night before St. Martin's Day. The custom is to prepare a goose for the saint, who visits in the guise of a beggar. An older couple are visited on St. Martin's Eve by a stranger, who has a tempting proposition. Their efforts to take advantage of the offer create numerous difficulties.

For a detailed description, see Eaton/OP II, 324.

Roles: Jonathan, an old man (buffo ten); Jacqueline, an old woman (mezzo/sop); a stranger (bar); and a beggar (bass).

SCORE: suite, Op. 30a (Bryn Mawr, Pa.: T. Presser, [1969]).

Sterne's Maria, or, The Vintage, comic opera in two acts by Victor Pelissier; libretto (Eng) by William Dunlap, after Laurence Sterne's *Sentimental Journey*. First performance January 14, 1799, New York, with Mr. Cooper (Yorick) and Miss E. Westray (Mary).

The work concerns the travels of Parson Yorick and his encounter with mad Maria.

St. Francis of Assisi, opera in one act by Fritz Hart; libretto (Eng) by the composer. Composed 1937.

St. George and the Dragon, opera in one act by Fritz Hart; libretto (Eng), after the Cornish mummers' play. First performance July 10, 1931, Melbourne, Australia, St. Kevin's Hall.

Stoned Guest, The, satirical comedy, "a half-act opera" by "P. D. Q. Bach" (Peter Schickele); libretto (Eng) by the composer. First performance December 1967, New York, Carnegie Hall; November 1975, Ogden, Utah, Weber State College.

A parody of Mozart's *Don Giovanni*, with a little *Carmen* thrown in, the work involves Donna Ribalda, who has been kidnapped; having escaped, she finds herself alone in a forest. She meets Carmen Ghia, who helps her disguise herself as a man. Don Octave comes on the scene, and Donna Ribalda realizes that he is the man who carried her off and is also her brother. Carmen now makes a play for Don Octave, until the three realize that they all have to be rescued. A St. Bernard appears, with an empty cask around its neck. Jealous over Don Octave's attentions to Carmen, Donna Ribalda strangles her, and when Don Octave tries to stab his sister, he stabs himself instead. Il Commendatoreador, who enjoyed the contents of the St. Bernard's cask, enters and shoots Ribalda. He himself falls down dead drunk. A happy finale is provided when the cast is revived miraculously.

For a detailed description, see Kornick/*RAO*, 274–75.

Roles: Donna Ribalda ("mezzanine soprano" [mezzo]); Carmen Ghia ("off-coloratura" [sop]); Don Octave ("bargain counter tenor" [ten]); Il Commendatoreador ("basso blotto" [bass]); and Dog ("houndentenor" [ten]).

The score (p. 3) points out that an important aspect of the work "is its large canine part (known in the 18th Century as a barcarolle, which exceeds in virtuosity even the famous 'Woofenpoof Song' from FIDO AND AENEAS." Among the thirteen numbers is the "Don Octave" quartet (No. 12).

SCORE: vs (Bryn Mawr, Pa.: T. Presser Co., 1968).
DISCOGRAPHY: M. Kleinman, L. Haywood, J. Ferrante, P. Schickele, Orch. of the University of Southern North Dakota, Hoople Heavy Opera Co.; cond. J. Nelson, Vanguard VSD 6536 ([1970], 1 LP).

Stone Man, The, opera by Daniel Dutton; libretto (Eng) by the composer. First performance January 6, 1990, Louisville, Kentucky, Kentucky Opera, with Fred Love (the Dreamer), Kenneth Shaw, Anne Nispel, Elizabeth Huling, and Dean Anthony; conducted by David Berger; directed by John Hoomes.

The main character, the Dreamer, journeys between the real and fantasy worlds in his search for love.

BIBLIOGRAPHY: William Mootz, "Louisville," *ON* LIV (March 17, 1990), 42 [on premiere].

Stone Soup, operatic fable in one act by Daniel Dorff; libretto (Eng) by the composer. First performance 1982, Philadelphia, Young Audiences of Greater Philadelphia Opera Workshop.

For four soloists, optional chorus, and piano accompaniment or chamber orchestra.

Stone Wall, The, "cassation for audience and orchestra" in one act by Malcolm Williamson; libretto (Eng) by the composer. First performance September 18, 1971, London, Royal Albert Hall.

Stormy Interlude, opera in one act by Max Brand; libretto (Eng) by the composer. Composed 1955.

Story of Mary O'Neill, The, radio opera in three acts by Nicola LeFanu; libretto (Eng) by Sally McInerney. First performance January 4, 1989, BBC.

The work concerns a woman dealing with the pull of European and Indian cultures in South America.

Story of Vasco, The, opera in three acts by Gordon Crosse; libretto (Eng) by Ted Hughes, after Georges Schehadé's *L'histoire de Vasco.* First performance March 13, 1974, London, Sadler's Wells Opera, Coliseum, with John Brecknock (Vasco), Tom McDonnell (Lieutenant September), John Fryatt (Caesar), Neil Howlett (the Mirador), Josephine Barstow (Marguerite), Brian Burrows (Rondo), Harry Coghill (Troppo), and Harold Blackburn (Monsieur Corfan).

The story takes place in the nineteenth century during an unnamed war. Vasco is a simple village barber, who becomes a hero on the battlefield, while Marguerite, daughter of the scholar Caesar, imagines that she is Vasco's fiancée.

Major roles: Vasco (ten), Caesar (high ten), and Marguerite (sop).

St. Patrick, church opera in two acts by Raymond Warren; libretto (Eng) by David Selwyn. First performance May 3, 1979, Liverpool, Anglican Cathedral.

Stranger of Manzano, The, opera in one act by Julia Smith; libretto (Eng) by J. W. Rogers. First performance May 1, 1946, Denton, Texas, North Texas State University.

Strangers at Home, The, comic opera in three acts by Thomas Linley Sr.; libretto (Eng) by James Cobb. First performance December 8, 1785, London, Drury Lane Theatre, with Mrs. Jordan (Viola), John Bannister, and Charles Dignum. Revived as *The Algerine Slaves,* March 17, 1792, London, King's Theatre.

The setting is Florence and concerns Viola, who is freed from slavery in North Africa by a brother she does not recognize.

SCORE: vs (London: Longman & Broderip, n.d.).

Strange Life of Ivan Osokin, The, opera by Peter Gordon; libretto (Eng) by Constance Congdon, after P. D. Ouspensky's novel. First performance April 1994, New York, River Arts Repertory and Arts, La Mama E.T.C., with Tamara Walker (Zinaida) and Jeff Reynolds (Osokin); directed by Lawrence Sacharow.

A young good-for-nothing is given another chance to relive twelve years of his wasted years and reform. Given this chance, he does no better than the first time around.

The score combines elements of jazz and minimalism.

BIBLIOGRAPHY: James R. Oestreich, review, *NYT* (April 20, 1994), C, 26 [on premiere].

Street Scene, "dramatic musical" ("Broadway opera") in two acts by Kurt Weill; libretto (Eng) by Elmer Rice, after his play of the same name; lyrics (Eng) by Langston Hughes. First performance December 16, 1946, Philadelphia, Shubert Theatre, with Polyna Stoska (Anna Maurrant), Anne Jeffreys (Rose Maurrant), and Brian Sullivan (Sam Kaplan); conducted by Maurice Abravanel. Repeated January 9, 1947, New York, Adelphi Theatre, with the same cast. Revived November 5, 1978, New York, City

Opera, with Sharon Daniels (Rose), Alan Kays (Sam Kaplan), and William Chapman (Frank Maurrant). Also October 12, 1989, London, English National Opera.

The setting is a New York City tenement. The love-starved Anna Maurrant, married to the brutish Frank, has an affair with Steve Sankey. Simultaneously, her daughter, Rose, is in love with the college student Sam Kaplan, who wants to forego his studies in order to marry her. Frank, who has been out of town, comes home early and finds his wife together with Sankey, whereupon he shoots them both. He is arrested by the police, and Rose sends Sam off, certain that an early marriage would ruin his life. Rose and her young brother, Willie, leave to search for a new life somewhere else. After their departure a couple comes to look at the now empty apartment, and the neighbors continue their usual gossiping, with life returning to "normal."

For a detailed plot description, see K/NKOB, 969–72.

Major roles: Anna Maurrant (sop); Frank Maurrant (bass-bar); Willie Maurrant (boy sop); Rose Maurrant (lyric sop); Sam Kaplan, a poet (ten); Henry Davis, a janitor (bar); and Steve Sankey, a milk driver (speaking).

Weil made the work continuous in order to avoid the "Broadway musical" designation. *Street Scene*, nevertheless, blends elements of the Broadway musical with European operatic traits, such as musical references to Puccini and Wagner. He first dubbed the work a "dramatic musical" and then changed the description to "Broadway opera." The vocal score carries the description "American opera."

The work begins with an orchestral prelude that contains two motives that appear throughout, the melody of Sam Kaplan's plaintive arioso "Lonely House" (act 1) and the syncopations representing New York. Highlights of the first act include the blues song "I Got a Marble and a Star," sung by Henry Davis, the janitor, Anna's aria "Somehow I Never Could Believe," her brutal husband Frank's "Let Things Be Like They Always Was," and Sam Kaplan's number. "Moon-Faced, Starry-Eyed" is sung and danced by Mae Jones and Dick McGann. The act concludes with the beautiful love duet of Rose and Sam, "Remember That I Care."

The second act includes the trio between Maurrant, Anna Maurrant, and Rose, "There'll Be Trouble." An orchestral interlude, a reprise of Anna's lullaby "A Boy Like You," which she sings to her young son, ends the first scene of the second act. Rose and Sam sing their wistful "Do You Remember" in the concluding scene.

Street Scene ran for 148 performances, a modest success for a work on Broadway, with only its "Moon-Faced, Starry-Eyed" drawing attention initially. It soon became part of the repertory of the New York City Opera.
SCORE: vs (New York: Chappell, 1948).
BIBLIOGRAPHY: Brooks Atkinson, review, *NYT* (Jan. 10, 1947), 17 [on New York premiere]; John Rockwell, review, *NYT* (Nov. 12, 1978), 85 [on New York revival].
DISCOGRAPHY: J. Barstow, S. Ramey, A. Réaux, J. Hadley; cond. J. Mauceri, London 433 371-2 (2 CDs).

String Quartet, The, radio opera in one act by Leslie Kondorossy; libretto (Eng) by the composer. First performance May 8, 1955, Cleveland, WSRS.

Strolling Clerk from Paradise, The, chamber opera by Charles Wilson; libretto (Eng), after Hans Sachs. Composed ca. 1952.

Stronger, The, opera in one act by Hugo Weisgall; libretto (Eng) by Richard Hart, after the play by August Strindberg. First performances (concert) August 9, 1952, Lutherville, Maryland, Hilltop Opera Company of Baltimore; Dominick Argento, piano; and August

16, 1952, Westport, Connecticut, White Barn Theatre. First performance (stage) January 1955, New York, Composers' Forum, Columbia University, with Adelaide Bishop (Estelle); conducted by Siegfried Landau. First British performance June 4, 1963, London, Park Lane Opera Group, St. Pancras Town Hall, with Josephine Nendick (Estelle).

Estelle, married to Harold, meets her friend Lisa for a drink. She berates Lisa for trying to steal her husband. Estelle calms down and leaves, after which Lisa turns to the audience with a mysterious smile on her face.

Roles: Estelle (sop) and Lisa (silent role).

SCORE: vs (Bryn Mawr, Pa.: Merion Music, 1956).

BIBLIOGRAPHY: review, *MA* LXXII (Oct. 1952), 32 [on Westport performance]; Harold Rosenthal, review, *Opera* XIV (Aug. 1963), 567 [on British premiere].

DISCOGRAPHY: Bishop, Columbia Chamber Orch.; cond. Alfredo, Columbia, ML 1506 (1956, 1 LP); J. Meier, Composer Recordings CRI 757 (1997, 1 CD, reissue of 1972 LP).

Student from Salamanca, The, comic opera in one act by Jan Bach; libretto (Eng) by the composer, after Cervantes. First performance October 9, 1980, New York, New York City Opera, with Beverly Evans (Cristina); conducted by Judith Somogi.

The setting is a drawing room of an elegant home in Spain, early seventeenth century. The plot involves an old man, Craccio, and his young and beautiful wife, Mariana. While he is away Cristina, the maid, arranges a party and invites Gonzalo and Nicolas, friends of Craccio. Stephano, a poor student, appears seeking lodging and attracts the interest of Cristina. As they depart, Craccio suddenly reappears; his carriage has lost a wheel, and he has been thrown into a ditch. Craccio hears noises and demands to know who is visiting. Cristina produces Stephano, who, she says, is a skilled magician. Demonstrating his powers, Stephano sets some gunpowder on fire and, when the smoke lifts, Gonzalo and Nicolas are seen holding piles of food. Craccio, unaware of the party, is impressed and requests that Stephano stay on.

For a fuller description, see Summers/*OOA*, 20–21.

Roles: Mariana (sop), Craccio (ten), Cristina (mezzo), Gonzalo (ten), Nicolas (bass-bar/bar), and Stephano (bar).

BIBLIOGRAPHY: Robert Jacobson, review, *ON* XLV (Dec. 20, 1980), 42 [on premiere].

Student Prince, The, operetta in four acts by Sigmund Romberg; libretto (Eng) by Dorothy Donnelly, after Wilhelm Meyer-Förster's *Alt-Heidelberg*. First performance December 2, 1924, New York, Jolson Theatre, with Howard Marsh (Karl Franz) and Ilse Marvenga (Kathie). First British performance February 3, 1926, London, His Majesty's Theatre.

In the bittersweet story, Prince Karl Franz comes to Heidelberg as a simple student to study at the university. He falls in love with Kathie, a local barmaid, but is forced to give her up and marry another when he succeeds his grandfather as ruler.

Among the best-known numbers are the Drinking Song; the Serenade, "Overhead the Moon Is Beaming"; and the love duet "Deep in My Heart, Dear."

SCORE: vs (New York: Harms, 1932).

BIBLIOGRAPHY: William A. Everett, "Golden Days in Old Heidelberg: The First-Act Finale of Sigmund Romberg's *The Student Prince*," *AM* XII (1994), 255–82.

Sublime and the Beautiful, The, opera by George Alexander Lee; libretto (Eng). First performance 1828, London, Covent Garden.

Sugar Reapers, The, opera in two acts by Alan Bush; libretto (Eng) by Nancy Bush, translated into German by Hans Michael Richter and Reinhard Geilert, as *Guyana Johnny*. First performance, in German, December 11, 1966, Leipzig, Opera House.

SCORE: vs, German-English (Oxford: Blackwell's Music Shop, [1978?]).
BIBLIOGRAPHY: T. Armstrong, review, *Opera* XVIII (Feb. 1967), 113–15 [on premiere].

Sultan, The, or, A Peep into the Seraglio, afterpiece in two acts by Charles Dibdin; libretto (Eng) by Isaac Bickerstaffe, after Marmontel's *Soliman II*, from his *Contes moraux*. First performance December 12, 1775, London, Drury Lane Theatre, with Mr. Claremont (Solyman), Mr. Blanchard (Osmyn), Mrs. Dibdin (Elmira), Mrs. Margeram (Ismena), and Mrs. Glover (Roxalana). First U.S. performance March 3, 1794, New York.

In this tale concerning Solyman II, the ruler is in love with Elmira, a Georgian member of his harem. Her rivals are the Englishwoman Roxalana and Ismena. As in Mozart's later *Die Entführung aus dem Serail*, Osmyn is the overseer of the seraglio. Roxalana eventually wins the heart of Solyman and becomes queen.

Thomas Arne's masque *The Sultan* appeared on January 3, 1759, at Covent Garden. Both the music and text are lost.

Roles: Solyman the Great, emperor of the Turks; Osmyn, chief of the eunuchs; Elmira; Ismena; and Roxalana, an English slave.
LIBRETTO: English (London: Longman, Hurst, Rees, and Orme, 1809).

Sultan of Mocha, The, comic opera in three acts by Alfred Cellier; libretto (Eng) by A. Jarrett. First performance October 16, 1874, Manchester, Prince's Theatre. First U.S. performance September 14, 1880, New York, Union Square Theater, with Leonora Braham (Dolly), Harry Allen (Captain Flint), William Hamilton (the sultan), and Eugene Clarke (the sailor). Revised, with a new text by W[illiam] Lestocq, September 21, 1887, London, Strand Theatre.

The exotic setting has the greedy Captain Flint selling his ward, Dolly, to the sultan. As in *Die Entführung*, she is rescued by her lover, here a sailor, and, when she is captured again, she is once more freed by her beloved, passing himself off as a pilgrim.
SCORE: vs (London, ca. 1880).

Sumidagawa, opera in one act by Nicholas Scarim; libretto (Eng) by the composer, after the Japanese Noh play by Jūro Motomasa. First performance July 27, 1979, New London, Connecticut, Eugene O'Neill Theater Center.
SCORE: ms score (1979, photocopy, NYPL).

Sumida River, The, opera in one act by Clarence Raybould; libretto (Eng) by Marie Stopes, after the Japanese Noh play. First performance August 15, 1916, Glastonbury.
See B. Britten's *Curlew River* (1964) for another version.

Summer Amusement, or, An Adventure at Margate, pastiche by Samuel Arnold; libretto (Eng) by Miles Peter Andrews and W. A. Miles. First performance July 1, 1779, London, Little Theatre in the Haymarket.

Arnold composed much of the music. Among the borrowings were a number from C. Dibdin's *The Seraglio** and one from T. A. Arne's *Thomas and Sally.**
SCORE: vs (London: Samuel, Anne and Peter Thompson, [1779?]).
LIBRETTO: English (London: T. Cadell, 1781).

Summer and Smoke, opera in two acts by Lee Hoiby; libretto (Eng) by Lanford Wilson, after Tennessee Williams's play. First performance June 19, 1971, St. Paul, Minnesota, O'Shaughnessy Auditorium, St. Paul Opera Association, with Mary Beth Peil (Alma Winemiller), Mary Cross Leuders (Rosa Gonzales), James Christiansen (Reverend Winemiller), Leroy Peterson (Dr. Buchanan), Zoya Leporska (Mrs. Winemiller), Sondra Harnes (Nellie Ewell), Clifton Ware (Roger Doremus), and John Reardon (John

Buchanan); conducted by Igor Buketoff; directed by Frank Corsaro. Revised 1989, with the addition of a scene in act I from Williams's *Three Women* (1988).

The tale, set in a small Mississippi town, concerns Alma Winemiller, the repressed spinster daughter of a Southern minister and disturbed mother. She loves John Buchanan, a young doctor, but is unable to communicate her love to him. He turns his attentions to the charming Rosa Gonzales, but when their upcoming marriage is celebrated during the absence of John's father, Alma secretly phones the elder Buchanan, who breaks onto the joyous scene and is killed by Rosa's father. Holding Alma responsible for his father's death, John leaves. When he returns, she makes her feelings for him plain, but her actions are too late; he has become betrothed to Nellie, a young piano student of Alma.

For a detailed description, see Eaton/*OP* II, 214–15.

Major roles: Alma Winemiller (sop); John Buchanan (bar); Rosa Gonzales (mezzo); Reverend Winemiller (bass-bar); Mrs. Winemiller (speaking); Nellie Ewell (lyric sop); Roger Doremus, Alma's friend (ten); Dr. Buchanan (bass-bar); Papa Gonzales (speaking). SCORE: vs (New York: Belwin-Mills, 1989). BIBLIOGRAPHY: Raymond Ericson, review, *NYT* (June 25, 1971), 16 [on premiere].

Summer Carol, opera in one act by Colin Brumby; libretto (Eng) by Thomas Shapcott. First performance August 10, 1991, Canberra, Australia, Llewellyn Hall.

Summer of the Seventeenth Doll, The, opera in two acts by Richard Mills; libretto (Eng) by Peter Goldsworthy, after the play of the same name (1953) by Ray Lawler. First performance October 19, 1996, Melbourne, Australia, Victoria State Opera, with Gillian Sullivan (Olive), Gary Rowley (Roo), Elizabeth Campbell (Pearl), Eileen Hannan (Emma), Natalie Jones, and Nicholas Todorovic; conducted by the composer.

A group of cane-cutters must spend seven months of the year in a remote subtropical area of Queensland at their work, and the other five in Melbourne during the rainy season. In Melbourne each worker has a part-time "wife." The main male character, Roo, gives his "wife," Olive, a "doll" or toy each year that they are together. When he proposes marriage after seventeen years of this arrangement, Olive refuses, having preferred the original setup. BIBLIOGRAPHY: John Cargher, "Melbourne," *ON* LXI (Jan. 25, 1997), 50–51 [on premiere].

Summer's Night, A, opera in one act by George H. Clutsam; libretto (Eng) by the composer, after a story from the *Heptameron*. First performance July 23, 1910, London, His Majesty's.

Summer's Tale, The, pastiche opera in three acts, arranged by Samuel Arnold (6 nos.); libretto (Eng) by Richard Cumberland. First performance December 6, 1765, London, Covent Garden, with Charlotte Brent (Maria) and John Beard. Revised as *Amelia*.*

According to the 1765 score (see below), the music was composed by Abel, Arne, Arnold, Boyce, Bach, Cocchi, Ciampi, C. St. Germain, Giardini, Hasse, Howard, Lampe, Lampugnani, Richter, Russell, and Stanley.

It includes three numbers by J. C. Bach. The first is the newly composed "So Profound an Impression I Bear" in act 2, scene, 3, sung by Frederick. The two others were adaptations: the duet "Yes 'Tis Plain," sung by Bellafont and Maria in act 3, scene 2, is from *Alessandro nell'Indie* (1762, London); the second (which follows), "Nature, When She Gave Us Pleasure," sung by Maria, comes from *Zanaida* (1763, London). SCORE: vs (London: I. Walsh [1765]); 3 Bach nos. reprinted in *The Collected Works of J. C. Bach*, vol. 25, *Works with English Texts*, ed. Ernest Warburton (New York: Garland, 1990). LIBRETTO: English (London: J. Dodsley [etc.], 1765).

Summoning of Everyman, The, church opera in one act by Charles Wilson; libretto (Eng) by Eugene Benson, after the morality play *Everyman* (ca. 1500). First performance April 6, 1973, Halifax, Nova Scotia, Dalhousie University, Arts Center.

Sun and the Wind, The, musical fable in three scenes by Edith Borroff; libretto (Eng) by the composer, after Aesop. First performance April 29, 1977, Binghamton, State University of New York.

Sun-Bride, The, opera in one act by Charles Sanford Skilton; libretto (Eng). First performance April 17, 1930, NBC radio; conducted by Cesare Sodero.
    The work is based on a Native American story.
LIBRETTO: English, typewritten (Denver, Colo., [1930], LCCN: 84-157359).

Suncatcher, The, opera in one act by Arnold Franchetti; libretto (Eng) by Barbara Sargeant. First performance February 8, 1973, Hartford, Connecticut, University of Hartford.

Sun Dance, The, "romantic American Indian opera" in five acts by William F. Hanson; libretto (Eng) by Gertrude Bonnin (Zitkala-Sa). First performance February 20, 1913, Vernal, Utah, Sioux reservation, with Beulah Bondi. Repeated April 27, 1938, New York, Light Opera Guild, with Erika Zaranova and Chief Yowalche; conducted by John Hand.
    The romance of Ohiya, a Sioux brave, and Winona, daughter of a Sioux chieftain, is set against the traditional Sun Dance of the Sioux Indians.
    For a description, see Hipsher/*AO*, 246–47.
SCORE: ms (n.p., [1912]; LCCN: 84-77470).

Sunday Costs Five Pesos, Mexican folk opera in one act by Charles Haubiel (Pratt); libretto (Eng) by Josephina Niggli, after her play (1937). First performance November 6, 1950, Charlotte, North Carolina, Charlotte Symphony. Concert revival May 24, 1956, New York, Mannes College of Music, with Henry Bannon, Esperanza de Thomas, Harriet Franklin, Anne Polen, and Linda MacNaughton; directed by Patricia Neway; Paul Berl and Otto Guth, pianists.
BIBLIOGRAPHY: "Opera in Premiere," *NYT* (Nov. 7, 1950), 33; review, *NYT* (May 25, 1956), 28 [on Mannes revival].

Sunday Excursion, curtain-raiser in one scene by Alec Wilder; libretto (Eng) by Arnold Sundgaard. First performance April 17, 1953, New York.
    The time is around 1910. The story involves two boys and two girls who are coming back on the train after a trip to New York. They become friends during their discussion and are so engrossed in their conversation that the candy seller has to warn them to get off the train—they have reached their destination.
    For a detailed description, see Eaton/*OP* I, 226.
    Roles: Alice (sop); Veronica (alto); Hillary (ten); Marvin (bar); and Tim, the candy seller (bass-bar).
SCORE: vs (New York: G. Schirmer, [1953]).

Sunken Bell, The, unfinished opera by Carl Ruggles; libretto (Eng) by C. H. Melzer, after Gerhard Hauptmann's *Die versunkene Glocke*. Composed 1912–1923.
BIBLIOGRAPHY: Robert Y. McMahan, "A Brief History," *AM* XI (Summer 1993), 131–57.

Sunset Trail, A, operatic cantata by Charles Wakefield Cadman; libretto (Eng) by Gilbert Moyle. First performance December 5, 1922, Denver, Municipal Auditorium, Denver Music Week Association. Revived November 13, 1926, Rochester, New York, Kilbourn Hall; conducted by Howard Hanson.

The plot concerns a love affair between Red Feather and Wild Flower, set against the resettling of their tribe to a reservation.

Sun-Up, opera in one act by Tadeusz Kassern; libretto (Eng) by the composer, after Lula Vollmer's play (1923). First performance November 10, 1954, New York, Provincetown Playhouse, Opera Players, with Ethel Erdos (Widow Cagle), Ruth Willis (Emmy), George Ritner (Stranger), and Fred Patrick (sheriff); conducted by Paul Aron.

The story centers on the bitter Widow Cagle, as she broods over the loss of her son on the battlefield.

The bulk of the music is composed in parlando style. An intermezzo divides the work's two scenes. It concludes with a folk-like ballad by Widow Cagle.

BIBLIOGRAPHY: Olin Downes, review, *NYT* (Nov. 11, 1954), 43 [on premiere].

Suor Isabella, opera in one act by Robert Xavier Rodríguez; libretto (Eng) by Daniel Dibbern, after the second story of the ninth day from Giovanni Boccaccio's *Decameron*. First performance July 7, 1982, Dallas, Texas, University of Texas.

The setting is a medieval convent in Italy. Isabella, a postulant, finds it difficult to repress her earthy desires with her chosen avocation. The sisters enjoy watching her bedroom activities via a keyhole until it turns out that the Abbess suffers from similar desires.

Major roles: Sister Isabella (sop), Abbess Usimbalda (mezzo), Sister Ficcanaso (sop), Sister Sgridaretta (mezzo), and Isabella's lover (nonsinging).

SCORE: ms vs, holograph (1982, photocopy, NYPL).

Suppose a Wedding, opera in one act by Leonard Lehrman; libretto (Eng) by the composer, after Bernard Malamud's story (1963). First performance (concert) September 2, 1996, Commack, New York, International Jewish Arts Festival of Long Island. First stage performance June 1, 1997, New York, Hebrew Union College.

The story concerns a family with an unmarried daughter.

Surrender of Calais, The, comic opera in three acts by Samuel Arnold; libretto (Eng) by George Colman Jr. First performance July 30, 1791, London, Little Theatre in the Haymarket, with John Johnstone. First U.S. performance April 29, 1793, Charleston.

The work includes an extended chorus for a group of English soldiers.

SCORE: vs (London: Preston & Son, [1791]).

LIBRETTO: English (Dublin: P. Byrne, 1792).

Survival of St. Joan, The, "medieval rock opera" by Hank and Gary Ruffin; libretto (Eng) by James Lineberger, after Shaw's *St. Joan*. First performance February 28, 1971, New York, Anderson Theater, with Gretchen Corbett (Joan), F. Murray Abraham, Jenny Baker, and Ronald Bishop; conducted by Stephen Schwartz; directed by Chuck Ghys; musical pieces performed by Smoke Rise.

The story concentrates on what would have happened if St. Joan had not been burned at the stake. Another girl is burned in her stead, and Joan meets the victims of the wars she brought about and those who suffered because of her supposed execution. Joan cannot hold her tongue in the face of all that is happening around her, and she is condemned once more and burned.

In this work the singers, a rock group, are separated from the actors.

BIBLIOGRAPHY: Clive Barnes, review, *NYT* (Mar. 1, 1971), 25 [on premiere].

Susanna and the Elders, opera in two acts by Myron Fink; libretto (Eng) by Donald Moreland, after the biblical story. First performance 1955, Vienna.

Also set by Jerome Moross (comp. 1940; perf. 1961, Augusta, Ga.).

Susannah, opera in two acts by Carlisle Floyd; libretto (Eng) by the composer, after the biblical story. First (student) performance February 24, 1955, Florida State University, with Phyllis Curtin (Susannah Polk), Walter James (Sam Polk), and Mack Harrell (Olin Blitch); conducted by Karl Kuersteiner; directed by Lynn Orr. First professional performance September 27, 1956, New York, City Center, with Phyllis Curtin (Susannah Polk) and Norman Treigle (Olin Blitch); conducted by Erich Leinsdorf; produced by Leo Kerz. Often revived, the work's Metropolitan Opera debut was scheduled for March 1999.

The setting is New Hope Valley, in the Tennessee mountains. The attractive Susannah Polk is the envy of the other women of the town, since she appeals to all of the men, including the preacher Olin Blitch. On the advice of her brother, Sam, she attends one of Blitch's prayer meetings. Blitch comes to her home and seduces her. Upon hearing about the seduction, Sam shoots the preacher as he is baptizing congregants. The crowd tries to storm Susannah's house, but she scares them off with Sam's gun, and, after inviting the attention of the slow Little Bat, son of Elder McLean, she beats him. Embittered, she is left alone.

For detailed descriptions, see Eaton/*OP* I, 136–37; K/*NKOB*, 235–36.

Major roles: Susannah Polk (sop), Sam Polk (ten), Olin Blitch (bass-bar), and Little Bat McLean (ten/speaking).

The score uses elements of Appalachian folk songs, a square dance, and revival hymns. Its highlights include Susannah's "Ain't It a Pretty Night?" (act 1), Blitch's fervent "I'm Fixin' to Tell" (act 2), and Susannah's subsequent "The Trees on the Mountain."
SCORE: vs, ed. Ross Reimueller (New York: Boosey & Hawkes, 1967).
BIBLIOGRAPHY: Howard Taubman, review *NYT* (Oct. 7, 1956), II, 106 [on premiere].
DISCOGRAPHY: P. Curtin, R. Cassilly, N. Treigle, K. Kaldenberg, New Orleans Opera Orch. and Chorus; cond. Andersson, VAI Audio 1115-2; C. Studer, S. Ramey, J. Hadley, Lyons Opera Chorus and Orch.; cond. K. Nagano, Virgin Classics VCD 5 45039 (1994, 2 CDs), rev. John Rockwell, *NYT* (Oct. 30, 1994), II, 40.

Swans, The, opera in three acts by Alva Henderson; libretto (Eng) by Janet Lewis, after the story by the Brothers Grimm. Composed 1986.
SCORE: vs (Santa Barbara, Calif.: J. Daniel, 1986).

Sweeney Agonistes, melodrama for voices and jazz band by John Dankworth; text (Eng) by T. S. Eliot, after Aristophanes. First performance June 1965, London.

Sweeney Todd, the Demon Barber of Fleet Street, musical thriller in two acts by Stephen Sondheim; orchestrated by Jonathan Tunick; book (Eng) by Hugh Wheeler, after the drama by Christopher Bond (1973), based on George Dibdin Pitt's melodrama *The String of Pearls* (1847); lyrics by the composer. First performance March 1, 1979, New York, Uris Theatre, with Victor Garber (Anthony Hope), Len Cariou (Sweeney Todd), Merle Louise (beggar woman), Angela Lansbury (Mrs. Lovett), Edmund Lyndeck (Judge Turpin), Jack Eric Williams (the Beadle), Sarah Rice (Johanna), Ken Jennings (Tobias Ragg), Joaquin Romaguera (Pirelli), and Robert Ousley (Jonas Fogg); conducted by Paul Gemignani; directed by Harold Prince. First performance in an opera house June 14, 1984, Houston, Houston Grand Opera, with Timothy Nolen (Sweeney Todd), Joyce Castle (Mrs. Lovett), Will Roy (Turpin), and Cris Groenendaal (Anthony Hope); conducted by John DeMain.

The work is set in nineteenth-century London, in Fleet Street and its surroundings. "The Ballad of Sweeney Todd" is a prelude to the action. The bitter Sweeney Todd, imprisoned for a crime he did not commit, returns to London and attempts to reconstruct his life. He becomes a barber once again and is driven to murder some of the customers who have come for a shave in his barber shop. Among those he kills are Judge Turpin, who sent him away unjustly to be able to seduce Sweeney's wife and has become the guardian of Johanna, Sweeney's daughter. He also unwittingly kills his wife, whom he does not recognize in her present dissolute state. Learning what he has done, Sweeney kills Mrs. Lovett, his accomplice, who had used Sweeney's butchered customers for ingredients in her meat pies and hidden the fact from Sweeney that his wife was still alive. He in turn is killed by a young boy whom Mrs. Lovett had taken under her wing. The innocent Johanna is left to be comforted by the young sailor Anthony Hope, who had come to town with Sweeney.

For more detailed descriptions, see Gänzl/*BBM*, 337–43; K/*NKOB*, 744–46.

Major roles: Sweeney Todd (bar), Mrs. Lovett (mezzo), Johanna (sop), Judge Turpin (bass-bar), and Anthony Hope (ten).

The work musically has many operatic moments, especially Johanna's "Green Finch and Linnet Bird" and the duet of the young lovers, "Kiss Me." More than three-quarters of the drama is set to music, and the work is united musically by the recurring theme of the "Ballad of Sweeney Todd."

Although quite successful, it was criticized for its savage plot and brutal, sometimes profane, lyrics. It has been performed by several opera companies, the first being the Houston Grand Opera.

SCORE: vs (New York: Revelation Music Publishing and Rilting Music, 1981).

BIBLIOGRAPHY: Alfred Mollin, "Mayhem and Morality in Sweeney Todd," *AM* IX (1992), 405–17.

DISCOGRAPHY: Cariou, Garber, Louise, Lansbury, Rice, Jennings, Romaguera, Williams, Lyndeck; cond. Gemignani, RCA CBL2-3370 (1979, New York, 2 LPs), reissued as RCD 3379-2-RC (2 CDs).

Sweeney Todd the Barber, Victorian melodrama by Carey Blyton; libretto (Eng) by the composer. Composed 1980.

Set for narrator and unison voices, accompanied by small ensemble to replicate a "musical hall" sound.

SCORE: vs (Borough Green, Kent: Novello, 1981).

Sweet Betsy from Pike, "horse opera extravagantly based on the folk opera" in one act by Mark Bucci; libretto (Eng) by the composer. First performance December 8, 1953, New York. Revived November 17, 1967, Fredonia, New York, Opera Theatre, State University.

Roles: narrator (sop/mezzo), Betsy (col/dram sop), Ike (bar), and Dan (any voice).

SCORE: vs (New York: Frank Music, 1953).

BIBLIOGRAPHY: review, *MA* LXXIV (Jan. 1, 1954), 14 [on premiere].

Sweet Bye and Bye, The, opera in three acts by Jack Beeson; libretto (Eng) by Kenward Elmslie. First performance November 22, 1957, New York, Juilliard School, with Shirlee Emmons (Sister Rose), Ruth Kobart (Mother Rainey), and William McGrath (Billy Wilcox); conducted by Frederic Waldman; produced by Frederic Cohen.

While followers of Sister Rose Ora Easter believe that she drowned while swimming in the sea near Atlantic City, Mother Rainey, who brought her up, thinks that she has in fact run away with Billy Wilcox, with the both of them planning to travel to the Holy Land on money from the Lifeshine Gospel, the organization Rose founded.

Mother Rainey and Sister Gladys, Rose Ora's good friend, pick up the couple's trail at a New York hotel, and they are able to convince her to return to her followers. Rose Ora tells the congregation how she was kidnapped, but in the middle of her story she admits that she took her vows as a child and now, having found love, has decided to give up her former life. Billy, who has also shown up, is about to leave with Rose Ora when Mother Rainey draws a gun. She shoots Billy and justifies her actions by having "saved" Rose Ora and getting back the Gospel's money. Billy dies, and Mother Rainey receives the devotion of the congregation. Rose is now alone and free, but without the man she loves.

For a detailed description, see Eaton/*OP* I, 137–38.

Major roles: Sister Rose Ora Easter (sop); Sister Gladys (col sop); Mother Rainey (mezzo); Billy Wilcox (ten); Sister Rees, the Sister Elect (sop); and Brother Smiley (bass).

SCORE: vs (New York: Boosey & Hawkes, 1966).

DISCOGRAPHY: Patterson, Kansas City Lyric Theater, Desto DC-7179/80 (2 LPs).

Sweethearts and Wives, comic opera in two acts by Isaac Nathan, Thomas S. Cooke, John Whitaker, and George Frederick Perry; libretto (Eng) by James Kenney. First performance July 7, 1823, London, Haymarket Theatre.

LIBRETTO: English (London: T. H. Lacy, [1823?]).

Sweetwater Affair, The, opera in two acts by Robert Beadell; libretto (Eng) by Bruce Nicoll. First performance February 8, 1961, Lincoln, Nebraska, University of Nebraska.

The plot, about a lynching in Wyoming in 1889, is based on a true story.

The George Hufsmith-Eleanor Hufsmith *The Sweetwater Lynching* (1976, Laramie, Wyo.) is another setting.

Swineherd, the Toad and the Princess, The, opera in five acts by Fritz Hart; libretto (Eng) by the composer. Composed 1944.

Swing, The, dramatic opera in one act by Leonard Kastle; libretto (Eng) by the composer. First performance June 11, 1954, NBC television.

Sylvana, opera in three acts, an adaptation by Jonathan Blewitt, of Weber's *Silvana* (1810, Frankfurt); libretto by Charles A. Somerset, after F. X. Hiemer's text. First performance September 2, 1828, London, Surrey Theatre.

A knight, Rudolph, falls in love with the mysterious Silvana, whom he finds in the forest. He is allowed to wed her when she turns out to be the noble Ottile, who had been kidnapped as a child to prevent her from marrying Rudolph.

LIBRETTO: English (London: J. Cumberland, 1828?).

Sylvia, "legendary grand opera" in three acts by Joseph Parry; libretto (Eng) by Mendelssohn Parry. First performance August 12, 1895, Cardiff.

System, The, opera in one act by Jan Bach; libretto (Eng) by the composer, after a story by Edgar Allan Poe, *The System of Doctor Tarr.* First performance March 5, 1974, New York, Mannes College of Music.

Edgar Allen seeks shelter on a rainy night and finds it at a mansion that seems to be an insane asylum. The warden, McCoy, tells Allen of the "system" he uses to help his patients, letting them act out their delusions. It turns out, however, that the "staff" of the institution are really the inmates, and the wardens are the unwilling "patients." Order is restored as the opera ends.

For a detailed description, see Kornick/*RAO*, 38–39.

Major roles: Hiram McCoy, the "warden" (bass); Edgar Allen, a young author (ten); Mrs. Henry, head nurse (sop); Madame Chauvenet, dietician (mezzo); Mr. Brayer, hospital orderly (ten); and Dr. Green (bass-bar).

T

Tabasco, burlesque opera in two acts by George W. Chadwick; libretto (Eng) by R. A. Barnet. First performance January 29, 1894, Boston.

The work, which concerns a Tunisian bey with a passion for the condiment of the title, uses music from Chadwick's operetta *The Peer and the Pauper* (comp. 1884).
SCORE: vs (Boston and Leipzig: The B. F. Wood Music Co., [etc.], 1894).

Tables Meet, opera in one act by Stephen Oliver; libretto (Eng) by the composer. First performance May 20, 1990, London, Royal Festival Hall, Review Restaurant.

Tailor of Gloucester, The, opera in two acts by Douglas Young; libretto (Eng) by the composer and John Michael Phillips after the original story by Beatrix Potter; translated into Italian by Robert Mann. Composed 1991.
SCORE: vs, English-Italian (Milan: Ricordi, 1991).

Táin, The, monodrama in one act by James Wilson; libretto (Eng) by Ian Fox, after *The Book of Leinster.* First performance June 29, 1972, Dublin, Trinity College.

The work is scored for soprano, piano, and percussion.

Takeover, The, school opera in one act by George Dreyfus; libretto (Eng) by Frank Kellaway. First performance October 6, 1969, Canberra, Australia.

The work focuses on land rights of the Aboriginals.

Tale for a Deaf Ear, The, opera in one act by Mark Bucci; libretto (Eng) by the composer, with one aria in Italian and one in German, after a story by Elizabeth Enright, *The Moment of the Rain.* First performance August 5, 1957, Tanglewood, Lenox, Massachusetts, with Jean Kraft (Laura Gates) and John Hornor (Tracy Gates); conducted by James Billings; produced by Boris Goldovsky.

Laura and Tracy Gates fight furiously, after which Tracy succumbs to a heart attack. The remorseful Laura wishes that her husband could come back to life; her wish comes at the exact time of death of an ancient mariner, Hypraemius, whose goodness has permitted him to have four miracles. Three have already been granted, and three people have been brought back to life through the ages. Tracy is restored as the last wish is used, but he is as argumentative as ever and fails to heed Laura's pleas. He again has a heart attack and dies, and this time he cannot be brought back to life.

For a detailed description, see Eaton/*OP* I, 228–29.

Major roles: Laura Gates (sop/mezzo) and Tracy Gates (bar).
SCORE: vs (New York: Frank Music, 1957).

Tale from Chaucer, A, opera in one act by Philip Gordon; libretto (Eng) by Marie C. Scanlon, after Chaucer's *The Nun's Priest's Tale* from the *Canterbury Tales.* Composed 1959. First performance May 1966, Trenton, New Jersey, Trenton State College.

Roles: soprano, tenor, baritone, bass.

See *Chanticleer* and *The Nun's Priest's Tale* for other settings.
SCORE: vs, holograph (1959; LCCN: 84-93063).

Tale of the Sun Goddess Going into the Stone House, The, chamber opera by Alan Hovhaness; libretto (Eng) by the composer. First performance 1978, Salinas, California. Revised 1990.

Tale of Two Cities, A, melodrama in a prologue and three acts by Arthur Benjamin; libretto (Eng) by Cedric Cliffe, after the novel (1859) by Charles Dickens. First performance July 23, 1957, London, Sadler's Wells, with Heather Harper (Lucie Manette), Ruth Packer (Madame Defarge), John Kentish (Charles Darnay), Heddle Nash (Dr. Manette), John Cameron (Sydney Carton), and Leyland White (Mr. Lorry); conducted by Leon Lovett; produced by Anthony Besch.

An abridgement of the Dickens tale, it opens in the wine shop of Defarge, where Lucie Manette brings her just-released father. Madame Defarge, who tries to bring about Charles Darnay's execution, is the main focus of the work.

Major roles: Lucie Manette (sop), Dr. Manette (ten), Charles Darnay (ten), Sydney Carton (bar), and Madame Defarge (dram sop).
SCORE: vs (London and New York: Hawkes, 1954).

Tales of Malamud, two one-act operas, consisting of Marc Blitzstein's *Idiots First** (completed by Leonard Lehrman) and Lehrman's *Karla.** First performance (concert) March 7, 1976, Bloomington, Indiana. First orchestral performance of the two (semi-staged) March 19, 1992, New York, Center for Contemporary Opera; *Idiots First*: James (Mendel) and Mark Tobias (Itzak); *Karla*: Rodney Miller (Clem), Lori Ann Phillips (Karla), Ronald Edwards (Max), and Helene Williams (secretary); conducted by Richard Marshall.
BIBLIOGRAPHY: Arlo McKinnon, "New York City," *ON* LVI (June 1992), 52–53 [on stage premiere].

Talisman, The, opera by Henry Rowley Bishop; libretto (Eng) by Samuel Beazley, after Sir Walter Scott. First performance 1825, London.
LIBRETTO: English (London: J. Cumberland, 1826).

Talisman, The, or, The Genii of the Elements, romantic opera in three acts by Jonathan Blewitt; libretto (Eng) by George Macfarren. First performance April 7, 1828, Surrey.

Another setting, in Italian, is by Michael Balfe, as *Il talismano* (1874, London), and, in English, as *The Knight of the Leopard** (1891, London).
LIBRETTO: English (London: S. G. Fairbrother, 1828).

Tamar and Judah, opera by Marc Lavry; libretto (Eng) by the composer, after Rabbi Newman's play *Woman on the Wall*. Composed 1958. First performance (concert, posth.) March 22, 1970, New York, Temple Rodeph Sholom.

The plot is based on the story from Genesis of Tamar, a daughter of King David, and Judah.

The work consists of a series of cantillations, accompanied homophonically.
SCORE: vs, copy of holograph ([Jerusalem], 1959; LCCN: 84-86845).
LIBRETTO: English ([n.p.], 1959; LCCN: 84-15673).
BIBLIOGRAPHY: Theodore Strongin, review, *NYT* (Mar. 23, 1970), 48 [on premiere].

Tambourlaine, lyric drama for radio in twenty-four scenes by Iain Hamilton; libretto (Eng) by the composer, after Christopher Marlowe's drama *Tamburlaine the Great* (ca. 1587). First performance (concert) March 14, 1977, BBC.

A treatment of the life of the fierce Mongol conqueror of the fourteenth century.

Hamilton also wrote a two-act version for stage performance.
BIBLIOGRAPHY: review, *Opera* XXVIII (May 1977), 511–12 [on radio premiere].

Tamburlaine, opera by Elaine Murdoch; libretto (Eng) by John Murdoch, after Marlowe. First performance September 9, 1971, Liverpool, Stanley Theatre, with Eric Stannard (Tamburlaine); conducted by Clive Timms.

Another setting about the Mongol ruler is Handel's *Tamerlano* (1724, London).

Taming of the Shrew, The, operatic farce, with music by John Braham and Thomas S. Cooke; libretto (Eng) by Frederick Reynolds, after Shakespeare's play (ca. 1594) and David Garrick's *Catherine and Petruccio* (1756). First performance May 14, 1828, London, Drury Lane Theatre.

The score includes pieces by Rossini, Mercadante, and John Stevenson.

Taming of the Shrew, The, opera in three acts by Vittorio Giannini; libretto (Eng) by the composer and Dorothy Fee, after Shakespeare's play, with additions from *Romeo and Juliet* and the sonnets. First performance (concert) January 31, 1953, Cincinnati, Music Hall, Symphony Orchestra, with Walter Eyer (Baptista), Dorothy Short (Katharina), Patricia Forquer (Bianca), Robert Kircher (Petruchio), Hal Dieffenwierth (Lucentio), and Eugene Hines (Hortensio); conducted by Thor Johnson; directed by Eva Parnell. Television broadcast March 13, 1954, NBC Opera Theater. First stage performance April 13, 1958, New York, City Center. Revived August 11, 1979, Vienna, Virginia, with Julian Patrick (Petruchio), Anna Moffo (Katharina), Elizabeth Knighton (Bianca), Barry McCauley, Spiro Malas, Robert Orth, and William Eichorn.

The story follows the Shakespeare version. Baptista has decided that his daughter Bianca, who is courted by Hortensio, Gremio, and Lucentio, cannot wed the man of her choice, Lucentio, until her older sister, the sharp-tongued Katharina, has a husband. Katharina's spouse turns out to be Petruchio, who tames her to win her love.

For a detailed description, see Eaton/*OP* I, 138.

Major roles: Baptista (bass), Bianca (sop), Lucentio (ten), Hortensio (bar), Gremio (ten), Katharina (sop), and Petruchio (bar).

The work, in the style of Italian verismo, features leitmotifs connected with the main characters.

The many other treatments of the plot include J. Worsdale, *A Cure for a Scold** (1735, London); H. Goetz, *Der Widerspenstigen Zähmung* (1874); S. Samara, *La furia domata* (1895, Milan); A. Maclean, *Petruccio** (1895, London); F. Le Rey, *La mérgère apprivoisée* (1895, Rouen); C. Silver, *La mérgère apprivoisée* (1922, Paris); R. Bossi, *Volpino* (1925, Milan); E. Wolf-Ferrari, *Sly* (1927, Milan); M. Persico, *La bisbetica domata* (1931, Rome); P. G. Clapp (1948); H. Groth, *Petruchio* (1954, Conway, Alaska); V. Shebalin (1957); T. Eastwood, *Christopher Sly** (1962, Pforzheim); and D. Argento, *Christopher Sly** (1963, Minneapolis). Cole Porter's musical *Kiss Me, Kate* (1948, New York) presents the Shakespeare work as a play-within-a-play.

SCORE: vs (New York: Ricordi, 1953).
BIBLIOGRAPHY: Richard Hundley, "Cincinnati Premiere," *ON* XVII (Mar. 2, 1953), 10.
DISCOGRAPHY: Jennings, Christensen, Harris, McGowen, Hook, Davis, Kansas City Lyric Theater; cond. Patterson. CRI SD-272 (1972, 2 LPs).

Täm-Män'-Näcŭp', opera by William F. Hanson; libretto (Eng) by the composer. First performance May 3, 1928, Provo, Utah; conducted by the composer.

The opera centers on the "Bear Dance" celebration of the Ute Indians.

Major roles: Täm-män' (Spring) (sop); Täva-moŭ-i'-scie (Sun Comes) (ten); Cŭtchî' (No Good) (bar); and Medicine Man, father of Täm-män' (bass).

Tammany, or, The Indian Chief, opera in three acts by James Hewitt; libretto (Eng) by Ann Julia Hatton. First performance March 3, 1794, New York, John Street Theatre, with Mr. Hodgkinson (Tammany), Mr. Hallam (Columbus), Mr. King (Perez), Mr. Martin (Ferdinand), Mr. Prigmore (Wegaw), Mrs. Hodgkinson (Manana), and Mrs. Hamilton (Zulla). Performed in a two-act reduced version under the title *America Rediscovered*, March 13, 1795, New York. The music, and all but the lyrics of the text are lost.

The work supported the anti-Federalists and their approval of the French Revolution.

For a detailed description, see Sonneck/*SIMG*, 459–64.

LIBRETTO: English, *The Songs of T-a-m-m-a-n-y* ([New York]; 1794; repr. [Tarrytown, N.Y.]: W. Abbott, 1931]).

Tamu-Tamu (The Guests), chamber opera in two acts by Gian Carlo Menotti; libretto (Eng and Indonesian) by the composer. First performance September 6, 1972, Chicago, Studebaker Theatre, with Robert J. Manzari (husband), Sylvia Davis (wife), Sung Sook Lee (Radna), Theresa Teng Chen (Nenek), Sung Kil Kim (Anonto), Sumiko Murashima (Indra), Ferlina Newyanti Darmodihardjo (Salema), and Douglas Perry (doctor); conducted by Christopher Keene. Revived May 1987, New York, Juilliard American Opera Center.

The opera concerns a comfortable, but quarrelsome, American couple whose apartment is invaded by seven wounded and poor Indonesian refugees. Ultimately, soldiers force their way into the apartment, drag the refugees out, and shoot them. The husband and wife return to the way they were before the intrusions.

The refugees are represented by seven silent roles.

Major roles: husband (high bar), wife (sop), Radna (sop), Nenek (mezzo), Anonto (bar), Indra (sop), Solema (child sop), and doctor (ten).

BIBLIOGRAPHY: Peter G. Davis, *New York* XX (May 11, 1987), 64ff. [on revival]; Robert Finn, "Menotti Opera Hits Deep Chord," *Cleveland Plain Dealer* (Mar. 18, 1974) [on Oberlin performance].

Tango, opera in one act by Robert Xavier Rodríguez; libretto (Eng) by the composer, after news clippings of 1913–1914. First performance January 29, 1986, Dallas, Southern Methodist University, Voices of Change, with Paul Sperry.

The work consists of three scenes performed without interruption, concerning news stories about the worldwide craze for the tango. The performer plays a tango dancer, a journalist writing about the tango craze, and a clergyman who disapproves of the dance.

Roles: tango dancer/radio newscaster/cardinal (ten).

The music incorporates tango rhythms, quotations from several composers, including Bach and Beethoven, and the sounds of a typewriter.

BIBLIOGRAPHY: Wayne Lee Gay, review, *MA* XXXVI (June 1986), 40–41 [on premiere].

Tania, opera in one act by Anthony Davis; libretto (Eng) by Michael John LaChiusa. First performance June 17, 1992, Philadelphia, American Music Theater Festival, Plays & Players Theater, with Cynthia Aaronson (Patty/Tania), John Daniecki (husband), Lynnen Yakes (Mom/Betty Ford), John Duykers (Dad/Fidel), and Mark Doss (Cinque); conducted by William McGlaughlin; directed by Christopher Alden.

A treatment, taking liberties with the details, of the kidnapping of the newspaper heiress Patricia Hearst in 1974 in California by the Symbionese Liberation Army. It starts with Patty being married and leading a conventional and consumeristic American life. After she is abducted, Patty becomes Tania, a revolutionary. The work contrasts the world of the American bourgeoisie and the character of Patty with the hidden world of the terrorists, led by Cinque.

The score, for chamber orchestra, includes jazz-influenced parts for tenor saxophone and percussion.

BIBLIOGRAPHY: Edward Rothstein, "Tania, Cinque and the Super Bowl," *NYT* (July 19, 1992), C, 3 [on premiere]; Gene Santoro, review, *The Nation* CCLV (July 13, 1992), 65–66 [on premiere]; Patrick J. Smith, "Philadelphia," *ON* LVII (Nov. 1992), 53–54 [on premiere].

Tantivy Towers, comic opera in three acts by Thomas Dunhill; libretto (Eng) by Alan Patrick Herbert. First performance January 16, 1931, Hammersmith, London, Lyric Theatre.

LIBRETTO: English (London, Methuen & Co., Ltd. [1931]).

Tapu, or, The Tale of a Maori Pah, romantic opera in two acts by Alfred Hill; libretto (Eng) by Arthur Adams, revised by J. C. Williamson. First performance February 16, 1903, Wellington, New Zealand, Opera House, Pollard Opera Company.

The plot involves the unbelievable experiences of an Australian politician who becomes a prisoner of the Maori.

It toured successfully via the New Zealand Opera Tour.

Tarquin, drama with music in two parts by Ernst Krenek; libretto (Eng) by Emmet Lavery; German text by M.-C. Schultze-Strathaus and P. Funk. First performance (reading) May 13, 1941, Poughkeepsie, New York. First stage performance July 16, 1950, in German, Cologne, Kammerspiele.

Major roles: Marius (bar), Corinna (sop), Cleon (ten), the Archbishop (bass), and the chancellor (ten).

SCORE: vs (n.p., n.d., LCCN: 84-86851).

Tars from Tripoli, The, ballad opera in two acts by James Hewitt, after John Moorehead's *The Naval Pillar** (1799); libretto (Eng) by H. Charnock, after Thomas Dibdin's text. First performance February 24, 1806, New York, Park Theatre.

Tartuffe, opera in two acts and an epilogue by Arthur Benjamin; libretto (Eng) by J. C. Cliffe, after Molière. First performance (posthumous; orchestration completed by Alan Boustead) November 30, 1964, London, Sadler's Wells, with Anna Pollak (Mme. Pernelle), Jeannette Sinclair (Dorine), Bettina Jonic (Elmire), Morag Noble (Mariane), Eric Garrett (Orgon), Gwyn Griffiths (Tartuffe), and David Hillman (Valère); conducted by Alan Boustead; produced by Peter Ebert.

Tartuffe, a troublemaker, manages to bring on total confusion in the household of the rich Orgon before his true nature is uncovered.

Major roles: Orgon (bass-bar), Tartuffe (bar), Mariane (sop), and Valère (ten).

Tartuffe, comic opera in three acts by Kirke Mechem; libretto (Eng) by Thomas Phillip Martin, after Molière. First performance May 27, 1980, San Francisco, San Francisco Opera, with Susan Quittmeyer (Elmire), Rebecca Cook (Mariane), Evelyn de la Rosa (Dorine), John Del Carlo (Tartuffe), Edward Huls (Damis), Thomas Hammons (Orgon), and Robert Tate (Valère); conducted by David Agler.

The hypocritical Tartuffe gains entry into Orgon's house in an attempt to marry Orgon's daughter. Orgon's wife, Elmire, however, is not fooled by Tartuffe and, in order to reveal his deceit, Elmire lets him seduce her. Tartuffe seizes the upper hand, however, and takes control of the house, and only the intervention of the king saves the family.

The text is full of wordplays and internal rhymes, and the tonal score contains a number of parodies and direct quotations, such as the famed opening chords of Beethoven's Fifth Symphony, which precede the line "It sounds like fate, knocking at the door."

Major roles: Tartuffe, a hypocrite (bar); Orgon, Elmire's husband (bass); Elmire, Orgon's wife (mezzo); Damis, Orgon's son and Elmire's stepson (high bar); Mariane, Orgon's daughter, Elmire's stepdaughter, in love with Valère (sop); Valère, in love with Mariane (ten); and Dorine, Mariane's maid (sop).
SCORE: vs (New York: G. Schirmer, 1980).
BIBLIOGRAPHY: Stephanie von Buchau, "Reports: U.S.," *ON* XLV (Sept. 1980), 56 [on premiere].

Taverner, opera in two acts by Peter Maxwell Davies; libretto (Eng) by the composer, after sixteenth-century documents. First performance July 12, 1972, London, Covent Garden, with Ragnar Ulfung (Taverner), Gwynne Howell (Richard Taverner), John Lanigan (the Cardinal), Noel Mangin (the King), Benjamin Luxon (the Jester), Raimund Herincx (the White Abbot), James Bowman (the Priest-Confessor), Robert Bowman (the Antichrist), John Dobson (the Archangel Gabriel), Dennis Wicks (the Archangel Michael), and Gillian Knight (Rose Parrowe); conducted by Edward Downes; produced by Michael Geliot. First U.S. performance March 13, 1986, Boston, Opera Company, with John Moulson (John Taverner), Raimund Herincx (the White Abbot), Rose-Marie Freni (Rose Parrowe), and Jeffrey Gall (Priest-Confessor); conducted by Sarah Caldwell.

The work is based on the sixteenth-century English composer John Taverner (1495–1545). It opens with the composer's being tried for heresy before the Reformation, during which Taverner, although convicted by the White Abbot, is saved by the Cardinal. In the second act, which takes place during the Reformation, Taverner is in control, but his forced decision to abandon his musical past signifies the end of his own creative life, as the White Abbot is executed.

For a detailed plot description, see K/*NKOB*, 179–80.

Major roles: John Taverner (ten); Richard Taverner, his father, later St. John (bar); the Cardinal, later Archbishop (ten); the King (bass); the Jester, later Death and Joking Jesus (bar); the White Abbot (bar); the Priest-Confessor, later God the Father (counter-ten); the Antichrist (ten, speaking); the Archangels Gabriel and Michael (high ten, deep bass); and Rose Parrowe, Taverner's mother, later Virgin Mary (mezzo).

Much of the music is based on Taverner's *In nomine* and on Maxwell Davies's two Fantasias.
SCORE: vs (London: Boosey & Hawkes, 1972).
BIBLIOGRAPHY: Shirley Fleming, review, *MA* XXXVI (July 1986), 22–23 [on U.S. premiere]; John Rockwell, "The Opera: "Taverner,' by Davies, in Boston," *NYT* (Mar. 14, 1986) [on U.S. premiere].

Tea Party, opera in one act by Jack Gottlieb; libretto (Eng) by Horace Everett. First performance August 4, 1957, Athens, Ohio. First New York performance (concert) April 18, 1964, Donnell Library, Composers' Forum, with Barbara Miller, Jean Kraft, Robert White, and Ramon Gilbert.

The story concerns a wealthy woman who schemes to get her nephew interested in a pretty chorus girl. After the predictable setbacks, the aunt is successful and gets to marry the gambler father after his horse comes in.

The work was booed at its first New York performance in 1964 because of its lyric tonality! (See Klein review.)

BIBLIOGRAPHY: Howard Klein, "Cheers and Jeers Greet Opera by Gottlieb at Forum Concert," *NYT* (Apr. 20, 1964), 36 [on first New York performance].

Tears and Triumphs of Parnassus, The, masque by John Stanley; libretto (Eng) by Robert Lloyd and Arthur Murphy. First performance November 17, 1760, London, Drury Lane Theatre.

Written to commemorate the death of George II and the accession of George III.

LIBRETTO: English (London: P. Vaillant, 1760).

Tea Symphony, A, or, The Perils of Clara, "kitsch-opera in 9 drinks" by Gabriel Charpentier; libretto (Eng) by the composer. First performance May 6, 1972, Banff, Ontario.

Teddy the Tiler, farce in one act by George Rodwell; libretto (Eng) by the composer, after Pierre le Couvreur. First performance February 8, 1830, London, Covent Garden.

LIBRETTOS: English (London: J. Cumberland, [1830?]; New York: E. B. Clayton, 1830).

Tekeli, or, The Siege of Montgatz, melodrama in three acts by James Hook; libretto (Eng) by Theodore Edward Hook, after Pixérécourt's *Tékéli, ou, Le siège de Montgatz.* First performance November 24, 1806, London, Drury Lane Theatre. First U.S. performance December 21, 1807, New York, Park Theatre.

LIBRETTOS: English (London: C. and R. Baldwin, 1806; New York: D. Longworth, 1807).

Telemachus, masque in two acts by Philip Hayes; libretto, after the Rev. George Graham's masque *Telemachus* (1763). First performance (act 1, private, concert) May 10, 1763, Oxford Music School; complete work (concert) February 14, 1765, London.

The story is similar to that of *Calypso and Telemachus.**

The piece is Hayes's only dramatic composition. There is no record of a staged performance.

Major roles: Telemachus (ten), Calypso (sop), Parthenope (sop), Eucharis (sop), Leucothea (sop), and Mentor (bass).

LIBRETTO: English (London: Messrs. Curtis [etc.], 1765).

BIBLIOGRAPHY: Simon Heighes, *The Lives and Works of William and Philip Hayes* (New York: Garland, 1995), 236–45.

Telemachus, ballad opera in two acts by Henry Rowley Bishop; libretto (Eng) by George Graham. First performance June 7, 1815, London, Covent Garden.

The music was partly adapted.

LIBRETTO: English, with airs and duets (London: E. Macleish, 1815).

Telephone, The, or, L'Amour à Trois, opera buffa in one act by Gian Carlo Menotti; libretto (Eng) by the composer. First performance February 18, 1947, New York, Heckscher Theatre, with Marilyn Cotlow (Lucy) and Paul Kwartin (Ben); conducted by Leon Barzin. First British performance April 29, 1948, London, Aldwych Theatre, with Marilyn Cotlow (Lucy) and Frank Rogier (Ben); conducted by Emmanuel Balaban.

The story, set in Lucy's apartment, concerns Ben, who tries in vain to ask Lucy, a telephone addict, to marry him. When he calls her on the telephone, he is successful.

For detailed plot synopses, see K/*KOB*, 1345–46; K/*NKOB*, 457–58.

Roles: Lucy (sop) and Ben (bar).

The musical highlights include Lucy's aria.

SCORES: vs, fs (New York: G. Schirmer, [1947]).

BIBLIOGRAPHY: Olin Downes, "Opera by Menotti Has Its Premiere," *NYT* (Feb. 19, 1947), 32.

DISCOGRAPHY: Louisville Orch., LS 767 (1979, 1 LP).

VIDEO: C. Farley, R. Smythe, Scottish Chamber Orch.; cond. J. Serebrier; designed D. Beeton, Decca/BBC Scotland 071 243-1 London (1992, London, 1 videodisc).

Telephone Show, The, opera by Stephen Wadsworth; libretto (Eng) by the composer. First performance October 25, 1989, Milwaukee, Skylight Opera Theatre.

The story is similar to Menotti's *The Telephone*.* Two opera singers attempt to further their love affair and at the same time carry on their professional careers.

Tell Me on a Sunday, mini-television opera by Andrew Lloyd Webber; libretto (Eng) by Don Black. First performance 1980, BBC, London.

The story concerns an English girl who lives in New York.

Tell-Tale Heart, The, opera in one act by Bruce Adolphe; libretto (Eng) by the composer, after the story by Edgar Allan Poe. First performance January 22, 1982, Boston, Opera Theater of Boston and the New England Conservatory; conducted and directed by John Moriarity.

The sensitive poet Andrew List becomes obsessed with the sightless eyes of Mason, owner of the house in which Andrew lives. Sensing Andrew's increasing agitation, the poet's girlfriend, Helen, tries to turn his attention to other matters but fails. Andrew kills Mason and hides the body under the floorboards. When two policemen come to investigate after neighbors complain of hearing a scream, Andrew says that Mason is away, only to be driven to confess after hearing the beating of a heart growing louder and louder.

For a description, see Summers/*OOA*, 4–5.

Major roles: Andrew List (ten), Helen (sop), and Mason (bass).

SCORE: vs (New York: Galaxy Highgate Press, 1982).

Tempest, The, dramatic opera in five acts by John Bannister et al.; libretto (Eng) by Thomas Shadwell, after the adaptation by William Davenant and John Dryden (1667) of Shakespeare's play. First performance April 30 (?), 1674, London, Duke's, Dorset Garden.

The instrumental music was by Matthew Locke. Other music was provided by Giovanni Battista Draghi, Pelham Humfrey, and Pietro Reggio.

Tempest, The, semi-opera, with music probably by John Weldon; libretto (Eng) by William Davenant, John Dryden, and Thomas Shadwell, after William Shakespeare's play (1612). First performance ca. January 7, 1712, London, Theatre Royal, Drury Lane.

The work was long thought to be by Henry Purcell, until M. Laurie advanced the case for Weldon as its composer (see Bibliography).

Among its revisions are those by Thomas Arne, William Boyce, Thomas Linley, and J. C. Smith.

LIBRETTO: English [ascribed to Purcell], a performing script from Shakespeare's play and the 1674 adaptation (Sevenoaks, Kent: Novello, 1974).

BIBLIOGRAPHY: M. Laurie, "Did Purcell Set '*The Tempest*'?" *PRMA* (1963–64), 43–57.

Tempest, The, masque by Thomas Augustine Arne, after Weldon's version; libretto (Eng) by David Garrick, after Shakespeare. First performance January 1746, London, Drury Lane Theatre.

Arne added three songs for Ariel.

Tempest, The, or, The Enchanted Isle, opera in three acts by John Christopher Smith; libretto (Eng) by David Garrick, after Shakespeare. First performance February 11, 1756, London, Drury Lane Theatre, with John Beard (Prospero and Trinculo), Rosa Curioni (Ferdinand), and Mrs. Vernon (Ariel, Miranda).

The work includes the overture of *Il Ciro riconosciuto* and texts by John Dryden.

See Fiske/*ETM*, 244–46, for a detailed description.

SCORE: vs/libretto; introduction by George Robert Guffey (New York: AMS Press, 1992).
LIBRETTO: English (London, J. and R. Tonson, 1756; facsimile of 1756 copy in Shakespeare Library, Birmingham, England (London: Cornmarket Press, 1969).

Tempest, The, masque by William Boyce; libretto (Eng) by David Garrick, after Shakespeare. First performance October 20, 1757, London, Drury Lane Theatre.

Tempest, The, opera in three acts by Nicholas Gatty; libretto (Eng) by Reginald Gatty, after Shakespeare. First performance April 17, 1920, London, Surrey.

Tempest, The, opera in three acts by John Eaton; libretto (Eng) by Andrew Porter, after Shakespeare. First performance July 28, 1985, Santa Fe, New Mexico, Santa Fe Opera, with Timothy Noble (Prospero), Sally Wolf (Miranda), Colenton Freeman (Ferdinand), Kevin Langan (Gonzalo), Susan Quittmeyer (Ariel), Ann Howard (Caliban), David Parsons (Alonzo), John Stewart (Sebastian), and Joseph Frank (Antonio); conducted by Richard Bradshaw.

The magician Prospero, the rightful Duke of Milan, rules over an enchanted isle, helped by his daughter, Miranda. He creates a tempest, which causes the boat carrying his enemies, Alonzo and Antonio, to wash ashore. Alonzo's son, Ferdinand, comes ashore alone and finds Miranda, with whom he falls immediately in love. When Alonzo learns that his son has also survived the shipwreck, he gives his blessing to the union of Miranda and Ferdinand, and returns the kingdom to Prospero.

Major roles: Prospero (bar), Miranda (sop), Ariel (mezzo), and Ferdinand (ten).

In this version the libretto has been condensed to one-third of the original, with some modernization of the language and rearrangement of scenes.

The score includes electronic music and a combination of musical styles, for example, jazz elements in the music accompanying Caliban and a Renaissance instrumental group for Ariel.

LIBRETTO: English (New York: G. Schirmer, 198?).
BIBLIOGRAPHY: John Rockwell, "Opera: World Premiere of Eaton's 'Tempest,'" *NYT* (July 30, 1985), III, 14.

Tempest, The, opera in three acts by Lee Hoiby; libretto (Eng) by Mark Shulgasser, after Shakespeare. First performance June 21, 1986, Indianola, Iowa, Des Moines Metro Opera, with Constance Hauman (Ariel), Jacque Trussel (Caliban), Peter Van Derick (Prospero), and Carol Sparrow (Miranda); conducted by Robert L. Larsen. Revived November 1996, Dallas, Dallas Opera, with Julian Patrick (Prospero), Joan Gibbons (Miranda), Gary Martin (Ferdinand), Jacques Trussel (Caliban), Kevin Langan (King of Naples), Constance Hauman (Ariel), and Jonathan Green (Gonzalo); conducted by Patrick Summers; produced by Colin Graham.

The Duke of Milan, Prospero, together with his baby daughter Miranda, has been exiled to a deserted island because of the deceit of his brother Antonio, aided by the King of Milan. The spirit Ariel has aided him on the island, and when his enemies approach by ship, Prospero has the chance to gain revenge. He opts, however, for forgiveness and blesses the wedding of his daughter, now grown, and Ferdinand, son of the King of Naples.

Major roles: Ariel (sop), Prospero (bass-bar), Caliban (ten), and Ferdinand (bar).

The score, set in a late-Romantic style, features difficult coloratura arias for Ariel, especially her second-act piece, and includes Caliban's lyrical aria "Be Not Afeard." The text uses all of the characters and major speeches, with some rearranging of the action to fit the music.

SCORE: vs (New York: G. Schirmer, 1986).
BIBLIOGRAPHY: M. A. Feldman, "In Review," *ON* LI (Nov. 1986), 56–57 [on premiere]; John Rockwell, "Opera: Hoiby's 'Tempest' in Iowa," *NYT* (July 12, 1986), I, 12 [on premiere].

Tempest, The, opera in three acts by Peter Westergaard; libretto (Eng) by the composer, a shortened version of Shakespeare's text. First performance July 8, 1994, Lawrenceville, New Jersey, Opera Festival, with William Parcher (Prospero), Michael Wilson (Antonio), Maria Tegzes (Ariel), Frank Kelly (Ferdinand), and Martha Elliott (Miranda); conducted by Christopher Mattaliano.

The text is a reduction of Shakespeare's play, with most of the characters and subplots left intact.

Major roles: Prospero, Ariel, Antonio, Miranda, and Ferdinand.

Other English settings include T. Linley Sr., incidental music (1777, London); H. R. Bishop, incidental music, with text by F. Reynolds (1821, London); A. S. Sullivan, incidental music (1862, London); A. Farwell, music for the pageant *Caliban* (1916, New York); A. M. Hale (1917, London); J. Kresky, secular cantata (comp. 1971); A. Henderson (comp. 1975); and M. Nyman, *Noises, Sounds & Sweet Airs** (1994, Tokyo).
BIBLIOGRAPHY: Robert Baxter, "Lawrenceville, N.J.," *ON* LIX (Oct. 1994), 54 [on premiere]; Bernard Holland, "New Musical 'Tempest,' Servant of Shakespeare," *NYT* (July 18, 1994), C, 12 [on premiere].

Temple Dancer, The, opera in one act by John Adam Hugo; libretto (Eng) by Jutta Bell-Ranske. First performance March 12, 1919, New York, Metropolitan Opera, with Florence Easton (temple dancer), Morgan Kingston (guard), and Karl Schlegel (Yoga); conducted by Roberto Moranzoni. Revived February 19, 1925, Honolulu.

The setting is the Mahadeo Temple in India. A dancer of the temple falls in love with a man of a different religion. When her prayers for help in her situation are not answered, the dancer plans to steal the temple's jewels. She poisons the guard who had tried to seduce her and stop her theft. Cursing the gods and the temple, the dancer is killed by lightning when she touches the jewels.

Major roles: temple dancer (sop), guard (ten), and Yoga (bar).
SCORE: vs (Bridgeport, Conn.: John Adams Hugo, 1918).

Temple of Dullness, The, comic opera in two acts by Thomas Arne; libretto (Eng) by Colley Cibber, after Lewis Theobald's interludes for J. Galliard's *The Happy Captive** (1741). First performance January 17, 1745, London, Drury Lane Theatre, with Mrs. Arne.

The work satirizes Italian opera and has characters such as Waltz, described as an opera director, and a female role as a virtuosa. *Capocchio and Dorinna** (1745) is an adaptation.

LIBRETTO: English (London: J. Watts, 1745).

Temple of Love, The, pastoral in a prologue, three acts, and an epilogue by Giuseppe Fedelli (Saggione); libretto (Eng) by Peter Anthony Motteux, "English'd from the Italian." First performance March 7, 1706, London, Queen's Theatre, with Maria Galia, Marcellus Laroon, Anne Bracegirdle, Mr. Lawrence, and Mr. Cook.

The work includes among its highlights an instrumental bird-song imitation in the coloratura aria "Warbling the Birds Enjoying."

Also masque, with anonymous music and text by Davenant (1635, Whitehall).

LIBRETTO: English (London: J. Tonson, 1706).

Temple of Peace, The, masque by Nicolo Pasquali; libretto (Eng). First performance February 9, 1749, Dublin, Smock Alley.

The work was composed to commemorate the Peace of Aix-la Chapelle. It includes many borrowed numbers, such as "Your Hay It Is Mown," from *King Arthur** of Purcell, and "O Peace," from *Alfred** by T. A. Arne, as well as numbers from Handel and Boyce.

SCORE: overture, fs, ed. Adam Carse (London: Augener, [1951]).

Tender Land, The, opera in two acts by Aaron Copland; libretto (Eng) by Edwin Denby, after James Agee's book *Let Us Now Praise Famous Men* (1941). First performance April 1, 1954, New York, City Center, City Opera, with Rosemary Carlos (Laurie Moss), Jon Crain (Martin), Andrew Gainey (Top), Jean Handzlik (Ma Moss), and Norman Treigle (Grandpa Moss); conducted by Thomas Schippers; directed by Jerome Robbins. Enlarged to three acts and first performed in this version May 20, 1955, Oberlin, Ohio, Oberlin College Opera Workshop. First British performance February 26, 1962, Cambridge, Cambridge Arts Theatre, Cambridge University Opera Group, with Mary Wells (Laurie), Joan Westwood (Ma Moss), and John Ford (Martin). First professional British performance June 9, 1990, Aldeburgh, with Vern Sutton (the postman), Dan Dressen (Martin), James Bohn (Top), Elizabeth Comteaux (Laurie Moss), Janis Hardy (Ma Moss), and LeRoy Lehr (Grandpa Moss); conducted by Philip Brunelle.

Laurie Moss, who lives with her overprotective Ma and Grandpa, is about to be graduated from high school. She meets two drifters, Martin and Top, who come looking for work on Grandpa Moss's farm. Laurie is taken with Martin, and the two plan to elope right after Laurie's graduation. Top, however, convinces Martin that Laurie is not suited for their type of life, and the men disappear before dawn breaks. Laurie, despite her disappointment, resolves to leave home anyway and seek her own life, and her mother prepares to transfer her attentions to Laurie's younger sister.

For a detailed description, see Eaton/*OP* I, 140.

Major roles: Laurie Moss (sop), Martin (ten), Ma Moss (alto), Top (bar), and Grandpa Moss (bass).

The work, composed in an almost completely diatonic vein, includes a number of folk songs. Among its highlights are "The Promise of Living," "Laurie's Song," "Stomp Your Feet," the "Tender Land" duet of Laurie and Martin, and the concluding quintet.

BIBLIOGRAPHY: Noël Goodwin, "Aldeburgh," *ON* LV (Jan. 5, 1991), 41 [on professional British premiere]; Andrew Porter, "Student and Amateur Performances," *Opera* XIII (May 1962), 345–46 [on British premiere].

DISCOGRAPHY: Comeaux, Hardy, Lehr, Dressen, Bohn, Chorus and Orch. of the Plymouth Music Series; cond. P. Brunelle, Virgin Classics VCD 7 9111302 (2 CDs); rev. John W. Freeman, "Recordings," *ON* LV (Aug. 1990), 40; Harris Goldsmith, "Recordings: The Soul of Copland," *Classical* II (Nov. 1990), 54–56.

Tennessee's Partner. See **The Argonauts.**

Ten Nights in a Bar-Room, temperance play in five acts with assorted music; script by William W. Pratt, after Timothy Shay Arthur's novel *Ten Nights in a Bar-Room, and What I Saw There* (1854). First recorded performance August 23, 1858, New York, National Chatham Theatre.

The work, which deals with the problem of drunkenness, focuses on Joe Morgan, an alcoholic, and his unfortunate family, including his daughter Mary.

Although only moderately successful at the beginning, the work was revived in 1866 to much greater interest, and in the 1870s it was a regular part of American stage offerings. The advent of Prohibition in 1919 revived its popularity, and four film versions were made (1913, 1921, 1926, 1930).

The music includes Mary's "Come Home, Father" (1864), Henry Clay Work's famed temperance song.

TEXT AND MUSIC: script, various (New York: Fitzgerald, 1890); repr. ed. Dale Cockrell, *NAMT,* vol. 8 (1994).

Ten O'Clock Call, opera in one act by Antony Hopkins; libretto (Eng) by Winifred Radford. First performance July 11, 1956, Cheltenham, England, Opera House, Intimate Opera Company, with Stephen Manton (the director), Elisabeth Wade (the soprano), and Eric Shilling (the baritone).

The opera is a satire on the preparation of a new opera for a "Festival of Indeterminate Tonalities." When an eager director arrives for a rehearsal, he finds that all are ready to go to the bar for refreshment.

BIBLIOGRAPHY: Arthur Jacobs, "Cheltenham," *Opera* VII (Sept. 1956), 527 [on premiere]; June P. Austen, "Opera across England," *ON* XXI (Nov. 5, 1956), 26 [on premiere].

Tenor, The, opera in one act by Hugo Weisgall; libretto (Eng) by Karl Shapiro and Ernst Lert, after Frank Wedekind's *Der Kammersänger* (1899). First performance (concert) February 11, 1952, Baltimore, Peabody Conservatory of Music, conducted by the composer.

Gerardo, a haughty and cynical tenor, is pursued by hordes of female admirers. Resting in his dressing room, he is approached by a young girl, who has hidden herself until he is alone. Eventually, Maurice, his manager, gets rid of the girl and threatens to hire a replacement for Gerardo if he does not behave. The singer agrees to reform, but when Helen, a married woman with whom he is having a dalliance, appears, he loses his resolve after she tells him she has left her husband for him. He agrees to marry her, despite the fact that his contract forbids his marrying. A phone call from Maurice breaks the lovers' spell, and Gerardo decides to leave. In despair Helen shoots herself. Stunned, he extricates himself from the room.

For a detailed description, see Eaton/*OP* I, 229–30.

Major roles: Gerardo (ten), Maurice (bass-bar), and Helen (sop).

SCORE: vs (Bryn Mawr, Pa.: Merion Music, 1956).

BIBLIOGRAPHY: Henry Cowell, "Current Chronicle," *MQ* XXXVIII (Apr. 1952), 285–87.

DISCOGRAPHY: R. Cassilly, Vienna State Opera; cond. H. Grossman, CRI 757 (1 CD).

Teora, or, The Enchanted Flute, grand opera in one act by Alfred Hill; libretto (Eng) by the composer. First performance March 23, 1929, Sydney, Australia, Turret Theatre; conducted by Joseph Post.

Teraminta, opera in three acts by John Christopher Smith; libretto (Eng) by Henry Carey. First performance November 20, 1732, London, Lincoln's Inn Fields, with Mrs. Barbier (Xarino) and Miss Jones (Cratander).

The pastoral plot, set in Cuba (!), concerns Prince Xarino, who passes himself off as a shepherd in order to win the hand of the shepherdess Teraminta, despite the complication of his friend Cratander, who also falls in love with the shepherdess and tries to turn Xarino and Teraminta against each other. His scheme is foiled by Ardelia, to whom the repentant Cratander turns his attentions. Xarino is able to rescue Gonzanes, his imprisoned father, who realizes that Teraminta is really the daughter of the deposed king, and he gives his blessings to the union of his son and Teraminta and his throne to his offspring. The opera ends with the marriage of the pair and that of Cratander and Ardelia.

See Fiske/*ETM*, 135–37, for a detailed description and, especially, the problem of the identity of the actual composer of the extant score, once thought to be by Smith; it was probably composed in the 1750s by John Stanley (see p. 135 and articles by Sands, Gillespie, and Williams). Smith's music is lost. See next entry for Stanley's version.
LIBRETTO: English (London: J. Watts, 1732).
BIBLIOGRAPHY: Norman Gillespie, "The Text of Stanley's 'Teraminta,'" *ML* LIV (July-Oct. 1983), 218–24; Mollie Sands, "The Problem of 'Teraminta,'" *ML* XXXIII (1952), 217–22; A. Glyn Williams, "Stanley, Smith and 'Teraminta,'" *ML* LX (July 1979), 312–15.

Teraminta, opera in three acts by John Stanley; libretto (Eng) by Henry Carey. Composed ca. 1754, unperformed. First performance early 1950s, London, BBC.

Major roles: Prince Xarino (counterten), Teraminta (sop), Cratander (ten), Ardelia (sop), and Gonzanes (bass).

See the previous entry for the provenance of the existing score, which is composed in the style of Handel, and the plot.
SCORE: ms fs, probably in Stanley's hand (London, Royal College of Music, 1020).

Terra Incognita, opera by Roberto Sierra; libretto (Eng) by Maria Irene Fornes. First performance April 10, 1997, New York, Intar Theater, Intar Hispanic Arts Center, with Lawrence Craig (Cristobal), John Muriello (Bartolome), Jennifer Alagna, Candace Rodgers-O'Connor, and Matthew Perri; Stephen Gosling (piano).

The work opens with three American tourists visiting a cafe in Palos, Spain, the port of departure for Christopher Columbus. The tourists encounter Cristobal, a disheveled native who rambles on about oppression, accompanied by the monk Bartolome, who recites excerpts from the writings of Friar Bartolome de Las Casas about the mistreatment of the native Indians by the Spanish colonists.
BIBLIOGRAPHY: Anthony Tommasini, "Taking on a Few Legends," *NYT* (April 12, 1997), 20 [on premiere].

Terrible Mouth, opera in one act by Nigel Osborne; libretto (Eng) by Howard Baker. First performance July 10, 1992, London, Almeida Theatre.

The work concerns the life and achievements of the painter Francisco Goya and is set in a war hospital.
LIBRETTO: English (London: Universal, 1992).
BIBLIOGRAPHY: D. Murray, review, *Opera* XLIII (Sept. 1992), 1034–37 [on premiere].

Thais and Talmaae, opera in one act by Colin Macleod Campbell; libretto (Eng) by C. H. Bourne, after Anatole France's novel (1890). First performance September 13, 1921, Manchester.

The setting is fourth-century Egypt. A young monk convinces Thais, a courtesan, to undertake a more pious life and enter a convent. Unable to shake off his memories of her, he returns to the convent to find her dying. She blesses him for having saved her soul, but he is anguished by not having been able to go beyond the physical love he feels for her.

Also set by J. Massenet, as *Thaïs* (1894, Paris).

Thalaba the Destroyer, or, The Burning Sword, operatic romance in three acts by George Rodwell; libretto by Edward Fitzball, after the poem (1801) by Robert Southey. First performance 1836, London.

The young hero Thalaba is aided by his faithful wife to destroy the sorceress Kawala and her evil assistant Abdala, who had tried to kill him.

LIBRETTO: English (London: J. Cumberland, [183?]).

Thanksgiving, opera in one act by Paul Alan Levi; libretto (Eng) by Toni Mergentime Levi. First performance November 2, 1977, New York, Juilliard School, Opera Training Program.

A seemingly loving family gives vent to its suppressed hostility at an annual Thanksgiving dinner. The family finally remembers what the holiday is about and resumes its outer air of decorum.

For a description, see Summers/*OOA*, 198–99.

Major roles: Stanley (ten); Mildred, his wife (sop); Marian, their daughter (alto); Leonard, their son (bar); Susan (mezzo); Harry, her husband (bass-bar); Charlie and Arnie, their sons (bar, bass-bar); Charlie's wife (mezzo); Sam (ten); Ethel, his wife (sop); and Grandma (mezzo).

SCORE: ms vs, holograph (1976, photocopy, NYPL).

That Morning Thing, stage opera by Robert Ashley; libretto (Eng) by the composer. First performance February 8, 1968, Ann Arbor, Michigan.

Theatrical Candidates, The, "musical prelude" in one act by William Bates; libretto by David Garrick. First performance September 23, 1775, London, Drury Lane Theatre. First U.S. performance October 14, 1801, Philadelphia, Chestnut Street Theatre.

The candidates of the title are Tragedy, Comedy, and Pantomime, the last one personified by Harlequin.

Thérèse, opera in one act by John Taverner; libretto (Eng) by Gerard McLarnon. First performance October 1, 1979, London, Covent Garden, with Vivien Townley (Thérèse), Robert Tear (Rimbaud), Keith Lewis (Christ/Father), and Joseph Rouleau (Pranzini); conducted by Edward Downes.

The story is based on the life of Thérèse Martin, the daughter of a Normandy watchmaker; she spat up blood on Good Friday in 1896 and took it as a summons from Christ. In 1925 she was canonized as St. Thérèse of Lisieux. In the opera she encounters the poet Rimbaud, who takes her through purgatory and hell, the murderer Pranzini, and the horrors of the Flanders trenches and concentration camps of the twentieth century, all of which serve to fortify her faith.

Major roles: Thérèse (sop), Rimbaud (ten), Pranzini (bass), and Christ (high ten).

Taverner opens his work with the Good Friday summons and concludes with Thérèse's duet with Christ, who calls to her "Veni speciosa mea," to which she replies.
SCORE: vs (London: Chester, 1977).
BIBLIOGRAPHY: Frank Granville Barker, "Reports," *ON* XLIV (Dec. 29, 1979), 28 [on premiere]; Andrew Porter, "Musical Events," *NY* LV (Oct. 15, 1979), 188–90 [on premiere].

Thérèse Raquin, opera in two acts by Richard Stoker; libretto (Eng) by Terence Hawkes, after Emile Zola. Composed 1975.

Thérèse Raquin and her lover, Laurent, kill Camille, her husband, and then get married. But their overwhelming guilt over their deed drives them to murder-suicide.

Thérèse Raquin, chamber opera by Michael Finnissy; libretto (Eng) by the composer, after Zola. First stage performance October 16, 1993, London, French Institute, with Heather Lorimer (Thérèse), Richard Jackson (Laurent), and Andrew Watts (Camille).
BIBLIOGRAPHY: A. Pritchard, review, *Tempo*, No. 187 (Dec. 1993), 34–35 [on premiere].

Thespis, or, The Gods Grown Old, "an entirely original grotesque opera" in two acts by Arthur S. Sullivan; libretto (Eng) by William S. Gilbert. First performance December 26, 1871, London, Gaiety, with Nellie Farren (Mercury), J. L. Toole (Thespis), Miss Clary (Sparkeion), and Fred Sullivan (Apollo).

A group of actors, managed by Thespis, climb to the top of Mount Olympus and change places with the gods, who are tired of their divine existence.

Roles: Jupiter, Apollo, Mars, and Diana, aged deities; Thespis, Sillimon, Timidon, Tipseion, Preposteros, Stupidas, Sparkeion, Nicemis, Pretteia, Daphne, and Cymon, all thespians.

The only surviving music is Sparkeion's "Little Maid of Arcadee," and the choral "Climbing over Rock and Mountain," used later in *The Pirates of Penzance** (1879). The original work consisted of an overture, fifteen numbers, and a ballet, employed earlier in Sullivan's ballet *L'île enchantée* (1864).

For a detailed description of the work's beginnings and fate, see Jacobs/*AS*, 72–73, 417–18.
SCORE: vs, "Little Maid" (London: Cramer, 1872).

Thief and the Hangman, The, opera in one act by Abraham Ellstein; libretto (Eng) by Morton Wishengrad. First performance January 17, 1959, Athens, Ohio, University of Ohio.

Thief of Love, The, allegorical opera by Sheila Silver; libretto (Eng) by the composer, after a seventeenth-century Bengali tale. First performance June 1985, New York, National Music Theater Network.

Things That Gain by Being Painted, music-theater piece by Gerald Barry, text (Eng) from Sei Shonagon's *Pillow Book* (1929). First performance February 24, 1980, London, Institute of Contemporary Arts. First U.S. performance June 1988, New York, New Music Ensemble, with Carmen Pelton (Lady Murasaki), Allen Kennedy (speaker), Chris Finckel (cello), and Cameron Grant (piano).

The work presents a singer conversing with a hidden narrator.
BIBLIOGRAPHY: Andrew Porter, review, *NY* LXIV (June 27, 1988), 81 [on U.S. premiere].

Thirty Thousand, or, Who's the Richest?, comic opera in one act by William Reeve, John Davy, and John Braham; libretto (Eng) by Thomas Dibdin, after Maria Edgeworth's tale *The Will*. First performance December 10, 1804, London, Covent Garden. First U.S. performance February 15, 1806, Philadelphia, Chestnut Street Theatre.

The work includes the aria "Beneath the Willow Tree."

Reeve also composed a pantomime with the same name (April 18, 1808, London, Sadler's Wells).

SCORE: vs (London: Dale, [180?]).

LIBRETTO: English (London: Barker, 1804).

This Is the Rill Speaking, opera in one act by Lee Hoiby; libretto (Eng) after Lanford Wilson's play (1965). First performance November 11, 1994, New York, Fashion Institute, American Chamber Opera Company, with Rosemary George, Joseph Marchese, Lisa Pierce, Elaine Valby, Mark Victor Smith, and Allan Roberts; conducted by Douglas Anderson.

A presentation of the memories of six players from the Ozarks.

BIBLIOGRAPHY: Bernard Holland, "2 Operas Make Contrast of the Pastoral and Shrieks," *NYT* (Nov. 14, 1994), C, 18 [on premiere].

Thomas and Sally, or, The Sailor's Return, pastoral in two acts by Thomas Arne; libretto (Eng) by Isaac Bickerstaffe. First performance November 28, 1760, London, Covent Garden, with Mr. Mattocks (the squire), Mr. Dubellamy (Thomas), Mrs. Pinto (Sally), and Mrs. Thompson (Dorcas). First American performance November 14, 1766, Philadelphia, Southwark Theatre. Revised with new finale by Samuel Arnold, February 24, 1794, London, Little Theatre. Modern revivals include May 1983, London, Regent's Park, Open Air Theatre, with Lesley Garrett (Sally), and Richard Berkeley-Squire (Thomas); conducted by Howard Williams.

The setting is the country. Sally, the object of the evil squire's attention, is rescued when her beloved Thomas, a sailor, reappears.

For a detailed description, see Fiske/*ETM*, 302–5.

The work was the first to use clarinets in the orchestra in England.

Roles: the squire, Thomas, Sally, and Dorcas.

SCORE: vs (London: author, J. Phillips, 1761).

LIBRETTO: English (Edinburgh: C. Eliot, 1782).

Thomas and Susan, musical entertainment by William Reeve; libretto (Eng). First performance 1787, London, Royalty Theatre.

Thomyris, Queen of Scythia, pastiche opera in three acts by John Pepusch, with airs by A. Scarlatti, Giovanni Bononcini, Steffani, Gasparini, and Albinoni; libretto (Eng) by Peter A. Motteux; Pepusch adapted and arranged the music and composed the recitatives; April 1, 1707, London, Drury Lane Theatre, with Margherita de L'Epine (Thomyris), Mrs. Tofts (Cleora), and Valentino Urbani (Orontes).

The story centers around Orontes, son of Thomyris.

The work was sung in English except for the arias performed by Urbani, a castrato, who sang the role of Orontes in Italian.

The work displaced Eccles's *Semele*,* scheduled for performance at Drury Lane Theatre.

Thorgrim, opera in four acts by Frederick Cowen; libretto (Eng) by Joseph Bennett, after the Icelandic romance *Viglund the Fair*. First performance April 22, 1890, London, Drury Lane Theatre.

Thorn of Avalon, The, opera in three acts by Martin Shaw; libretto (Eng) by Barclay Baron. First performance June 6, 1931, London, Crystal Palace.
SCORE: vs (London: Oxford University Press, [1931]).

Thorwald, opera by William Dinsmore; libretto (Eng) by Marion Hazard. First performance (excerpts) March 17, 1940, New York, Carnegie Hall, New York Philharmonic Symphony Orchestra, conducted by Josef Blant.
The story concerns the Vikings.
SCORE: ms score (n.p., n.d.; LCCN: 84-87459).
BIBLIOGRAPHY: Olin Downes, "Opera 'Premieres' at Carnegie Hall," *NYT* (Mar. 18, 1940), 12.

Thousand Names to Come, A, opera in one act by Jerome P. Kitzke; libretto (Eng) by James Hazard. First performance September 18, 1981, Milwaukee, Wisconsin, Alverno College.
A woman, after much inner searching, discovers that her given name does not reveal her real self, and that she should be called by a thousand or more names to represent her exact essence.
For a description, see Summers/*OOA*, 180–81.
Roles: a woman (sop) and a reader (speaking).

Three and the Deuce, The, comic opera in three acts by Stephen Storace; libretto (Eng) by Prince Hoare, after Antonio Mattiuzzi's comedy *Les trois jumeaux venitiens* and the Spanish comedy *Los tres mellizos*. First performance September 2, 1795, London, Little Theatre in the Haymarket, with Jack Bannister. First U.S. performance May 26, 1797, Boston, Haymarket Theatre.
The story revolves around triplets who are staying, unknown to each other, at a Cheltenham inn. The three parts were performed at the premiere by Bannister.
The overture is based on no. 4 of Storace's *Six Easy and Progressive Sonatinas* (1791).
LIBRETTO: English (London: Barker and Son, 1806; Philadelphia: T. H. Palmer, 1821).

Three Blind Mice, comic opera in one act by John Verrall; libretto (Eng) by Glenn Hughes. First performance May 22, 1955, Seattle.
LIBRETTO: Seattle: University of Washington, School of Drama, [n.d.]).

Three Hermits, church opera in one act by Stephen Paulus; libretto (Eng) by Michael Dennis Browne, after Leo Tolstoy. First performance April 29, 1997, St. Paul, Minnesota.
A bishop receives a lesson in spirituality from three simple hermits.
The music includes the closing pilgrims' hymn, based on a Russian liturgical text.
DISCOGRAPHY: Heidemann, Johnson, Langsjoen, Lannigham, Bitterman, Harney, Jorgenson, McKeel, Showalter, Welch, Wintle, St. Paul Sinfonietta, House of Hope Presbyterian Church Motet Choir; cond. T. Lancaster, d'Note Classics DND 1025 (1 CD).

Three Instant Operas, operas for children by Stephen Oliver; libretto (Eng) by the composer. First performance 1973, London.
I. **Paid Off**. Concerns the failure of the magicians to seduce the wives of the soldiers and steal their gold.
II. **Time Flies**. About the fate of a group of flies and spiders.
III. **Old Haunts**. The wine merchants are chased out of their lodgings by the drunk ghosts.

Three Mimes, opera in one act by Robert B. Cantrick; libretto (Eng). Composed 1969. First stage performance November 11, 1994, New York, Fashion Institute, American Chamber Opera Company, with John Uehlein (singing mime) and Margaret Lancaster (flute).

The work, scored for male singer and flutist, concerns love and personal travail.
BIBLIOGRAPHY: Bernard Holland, "2 Operas Make Contrast of the Pastoral and Shrieks," *NYT* (Nov. 14, 1994), C, 18 [on stage premiere].

Threepenny Opera, The, opera in a prologue and three acts, an adaptation, with new English translation and revised lyrics, by Marc Blitzstein, of *Die Dreigroschenoper* by Kurt Weill (1928, Berlin; see below for the U.S. premiere of 1933); libretto (Ger) by Bertolt Brecht, after Elisabeth Hauptmann's translation of John Gay's *The Beggar's Opera** (1728, London). Preliminary version June 14, 1952, Waltham, Massachusetts, Brandeis University; conducted by Leonard Bernstein. First performance March 10, 1954, New York, Theatre de Lys (96 performances), with Lotte Lenya (Jenny), Martin Wolfson (Peachum), Charlotte Rae (Mrs. Peachum), Jo Sullivan (Polly Peachum), Scott Merrill (Mack the Knife), Beatrice Arthur (Lucy Brown), Gerald Price (Street Singer), and George Tyne (Tiger Brown); conducted by Samuel Matlowsky; directed by Carmen Capalbo. Reopened there on September 20, 1955 (2,611 performances). First British performance of the Blitzstein version February 9, 1956, London, Royal Court Theatre, with Daphne Anderson (Polly), Bill Owen (Mack), Georgia Brown (Lucy), Eric Pohlmann (Peachum), and Maria Remusat (Jenny); conducted by Berthold Goldschmidt.

The work is set in 1837 London (1870s New York in the Brandeis version), just before the coronation of Queen Victoria. Polly, daughter of Peachum, head of the Beggar's Guild, weds her robber lover Macheath (also called Mack the Knife, Mackie Messer in the Brecht). Polly's parents are furious that she has married a thief and threaten to inform on him. When Polly tells Macheath of the danger, he hides in a brothel.

He is arrested, having been betrayed by his old friend Jenny, head of the brothel, who has been bribed by Mrs. Peachum. Polly visits Macheath in Newgate Prison and meets Lucy, daughter of the police chief, Tiger Brown (Lockit in the Gay version), a former lover who has assisted the thief. After the ladies quarrel, Mrs. Peachum removes Polly, and Lucy helps Macheath escape. But, betrayed again by Jenny, Macheath's freedom is short-lived; he is recaptured and sentenced to be hanged. Just before he is to be executed, he is saved by a pardon from the Queen herself, who grants him a castle and a pension and makes him a Knight of the Garter (!). The crowd offers thanks in the closing chorale.

Major roles: Jenny (mezzo), Polly Peachum (sop), Macheath/Mack (ten), Mr. Peachum (bass-bar), Mrs. Peachum (alto), Lucy Brown (mezzo), Street Singer (ten/high bar), and Tiger Brown (bar).

The original Weill-Brecht version was a failure at its 1933 U.S. premiere (April 13, New York, Empire Theater), in an English translation by Gifford Cochran and Jerold Krimsky. It folded after twelve performances.

The work includes the famous "Ballad of Mack the Knife" ("Die Moritat von Mackie Messer" in the German), which launched the career of the pop singer Bobby Darin, who revived it in 1959. The song was also a favorite vehicle for Louis Armstrong. The "Barbara Song" is sung in the Blitzstein version by Lucy (by Polly in the original).

The score mixes classical writing with blues and Tin Pan Alley styles.
SCORE: vs ([New York?]: Weill-Brecht-Harms Co./Warner Bros., 1984).
BIBLIOGRAPHY: Brooks Atkinson, review, *NYT* (Mar. 21, 1954), II, 1; Gordon/*MM*, 360–61, 374–77; Howard Taubman, preview, *NYT* (Mar. 7, 1954), II, 3.
DISCOGRAPHY: orig. Theatre de Lys cast, Polydor 820 260 (2 CDs, reissue of 1954 perf.).

Three Scenes from Aboriginal Life, children's opera by Larry Sitsky; libretto (Eng) by Gwen Harwood. First performance October 1991, Canberra, Australia, School of Music.

The work, which uses children's voices, consists of three brief pieces for music theater.

Three's Company, "improbable opera" in one act by Antony Hopkins; libretto (Eng) by Michael Flanders. First performance November 10, 1953, Crewe, England, Cheshire County Training College.

The setting is in an office. The young Mr. Love has taken over his father's thriving business, but since he is inexperienced, he is aided by the efficient Mr. Three. They hire a new secretary, the attractive Miss Honey, with whom Mr. Love falls promptly in love. Mr. Three steps in and whisks her off for a week together, leaving Mr. Love alone, in despair. During Mr. Three's absence, however, profits double, and when he returns, Mr. Love claims seniority over him, and Miss Honey returns to him.

Roles: Mr. Three (bar), Mr. Love (ten), and Miss Honey (sop).
SCORE: vs (London: J. &. W. Chester, [1955]).

Three Sisters, opera in two acts by Thomas Pasatieri; libretto (Eng) by Kenward Elmslie, after the play by Anton Chekhov. First performance March 13, 1986, Columbus, Ohio, Opera Columbus, with Marvellee Cariaga (Olga), Patricia Wells (Masha), Maryanne Telese (Irina), Marilyn Brustadt (Natasha), Stephen Dickson (Andrei), Louis Otley (Vershinin), Stephen Alexus Williams (Solyony), and Will Roy (Chemtkin); conducted by Cal Stewart Kellogg.

Three sisters, Olga, Masha, and Irina, endure a drab existence in a garrison town. Andrei, their brother, is unhappily married to Natasha. The sisters seek happiness in love affairs and marriage, but in the end they are left alone, as they were at the start.

Roles: Natasha (sop), Olga (mezzo), Masha (sop), Irina (mezzo), the baron (ten), Fyodor (ten), Vladimir (ten), Yakov (ten), Andrei (bar), Vershinin (bar), Solyony (bass), and Chemtkin (bass).

Among the compositional devices used is continuous recitative.
SCORE: vs (New York: Seesaw Music, 1979).
LIBRETTO: English (Calais, Vt.: Z Press, 1986).
BIBLIOGRAPHY: Barbara Zuck, "Columbus," *ON* L (June 1986), 34 [on premiere].
DISCOGRAPHY: P. Wells, M. Telese, M. Cariaga; cond. C. S. Kellogg, Battery Records Battery PS-1333 (2 LPs); rev. John W. Freeman, "Recordings," *ON* LI (May 1987), 59.

Three Sisters Who Are Not Sisters, opera in three acts by David Ahlstrom; libretto (Eng), a setting of Gertrude Stein's play (1946). First performance March 1, 1953, Cincinnati. Revived September 17, 1982, San Francisco.
SCORE: vs (New York: Seesaw Music Corp., 1979).

Three Sisters Who Are Not Sisters, opera in three scenes by Ned Rorem; libretto (Eng), a setting of Stein's play. First performance July 24, 1971, Philadelphia, Temple University, Student Opera Workshop; directed by Henry Butler. Revived April 1, 1978, New York, Golden Fleece.

The story concerns a group of siblings, three sisters and two brothers, who are playing a game of murder, taking the parts of the killers and victims alike. At the end only Jenny is left, but since she realizes that life is worthless if one is alone, she drinks poison. The siblings leave their imaginary world and, since nobody has really died, they all go to bed.

For a description, see Eaton/*OP* II, 325.

Roles: Jenny (sop), Helen (sop), Ellen (mezzo), Samuel/policeman/Apache (ten), and Sylvester (bar).

SCORE: vs (New York: Boosey & Hawkes, [1974]).

BIBLIOGRAPHY: Peter Davis, "Golden Fleece in Three Operas," *NYT* (Apr. 3, 1978), C, 22 [on 1978 revival].

Three Sisters Who Are Not Sisters, opera by William Hellerman; libretto (Eng), after Stein. First performance November 5, 1983, New York, Medicine Show. Revised version April 7, 1988, New York.

Set for five actors/musicians.

Three Strangers, The, opera in one act by Elizabeth Maconchy; libretto (Eng) by the composer, after Thomas Hardy. First performance June 5, 1968, London, Bishop's Stortford College.

Three strangers invade a party being held in a shepherd's cottage.

Three Tenants, The, opera in one act by Thomas German Reed; libretto (Eng) by Gilbert A. A' Beckett. First performance December 16, 1874, London, St. George's Hall.

LIBRETTO: English (London: Joseph Williams, 1897).

Three Visitations, trilogy of theater pieces by Kim D. Sherman; text (Eng) by Paul Selig. First performance June 13, 1996, Minneapolis, Southern Theater.

Red Tide, with Peter Vitale (Lutece). First performed separately March 8, 1987, Minneapolis, Minnesota Opera.

The plot concerns an anxious teenager, Lutece, who awaits salvation at the hands of the lifeguard who rescued him ten years earlier. The work ends with the boy's walking toward the blinding light of the water, after scorning the advice of his friend Worm.

Lamentations

The plot centers on an assemblage of shadows on the wall of a New York apartment. They are viewed by Milo, who has just lost his father, possibly because of the boy's mother.

Long Island Dreamer, with Norah Long (Amana Del Ray). First performed separately April 9, 1987, St. Paul, Minnesota Opera.

Amana Del Ray is a fading singer who is in a sound studio trying to record one last hit. During the proceedings she remembers how she was assaulted by an intruder at a motel in which she was staying.

BIBLIOGRAPHY: Michael Anthony, "Minneapolis/St. Paul," *ON* LXI (Nov. 1996), 48–49 [on premiere].

Three Wise Men, The, opera in one act by Inglis Gundry; libretto (Eng) by the composer. First performance January 7, 1967, Kings Langley.

Through the Looking Glass, opera by Wilfred Josephs; libretto (Eng) by the composer, after Lewis Carroll. Composed 1977–1978.

Major role: Alice (sop).

See also *Alice in Wonderland* for other settings of the story.

Throw Physic to the Dogs!, musical farce in two acts by Samuel Arnold; libretto (Eng) by Henry Lee. First performance July 8, 1798, London, Little Theatre in the Haymarket.

Revised into three acts as *Caleb Quotem and His Wife, or, Paint, Poetry, and Putty!* (1809, London), with Mr. Fawcett in the title role.
LIBRETTO: English, as *Caleb Quotem* (London: J. Roach, [1809]).

Tibetan Dreams, opera in two acts by Stephen Dickman; libretto (Eng) by Gary Glickman, after Alexandra David-Neel's novella *La puissance du néant.* First performance October 20, 1990, New York, Merce Cunningham Studio, with Frank Ream (Munpa), David Anchel (Lobsang), and Lisa Asher (Pasagma).

The story plots the lives of two monastic novices, Munpa and Lobsang, the first honest and idealistic, the second unbelieving and worldly. When Lobsang accidentally kills his master when trying to steal a reliquary with a valuable gem inside, he flees with his lover, Pasagma, and is pursued by Munpa. After a lengthy chase Munpa learns that the novice-turned-thief has died, after discovering that the object he stole did not contain the valuable turquoise he coveted.

Major roles: Munpa (ten), Lobsang (bass), and Pasagma (sop).

The composer, in order to achieve an Eastern flavor, uses modal scales and personifies the two protagonists by giving Munpa lyrical music and Lobsang angular vocal lines.
BIBLIOGRAPHY: Allan Kozinn, review, *NYT* (Oct. 22, 1990), C, 14 [on premiere].

Tickets, Please, opera in one act by Robert Nelson; libretto (Eng) by Sidney L. Berger, after D. H. Lawrence's story. First performance June 1985, Houston, Texas, Texas Opera Theater.

The setting is an English tram depot, early 1900s. A group of female tram operators gather and compare notes about a male colleague, John Thomas, who has seduced almost all of them. They determine to teach him a lesson, and when he comes into the room in which they have gathered, they lock the door, give the key to Annie, an unwilling participant, and demand that he choose one of them to take home with him. When he hesitates, they attack him verbally and physically. The women finally let Annie unlock the door so that he can leave, departing themselves, except for Annie, who wistfully retrieves the key he has tossed to the floor.

For a plot description, see Summers/*OOA*, 229–30.

Roles: Annie (sop/mezzo), Cissy (alto), Emmy (alto), Nora (sop), Laura (mezzo), Polly (mezzo/alto), and John Thomas (high bar/ten).
SCORE: ms vs, holograph (1985, photocopy, NYPL).

Tigers, The, burlesque opera in a prologue and three acts by Havergal Brian; libretto (Eng) by the composer. Composed 1916–1919; orchestrated 1928–1929. The score, thought to be lost, was found in 1977. First performance (concert) 1976, London, St. John's, Smith Square. Also May 3, 1983, London, BBC radio; conducted by Lionel Friend.

In this fantasy, set at a carnival on Hampstead Heath, the activities of the participants are interrupted by the declaration of war. The Tigers are the name of a hopeless band of infantry recruits led by the aging colonel Sir John Stout, who, in the course of the opera, plays host to a number of ghosts of great generals of the past and, at the same time, is pursued by the well-meaning Mrs. Pamela Freebody.

The music includes references to themes from works by Wagner and Richard Strauss.
SCORE: vs (London: Cranz, [1932]).
LIBRETTO: English (Aberdeen: Aberdeen Branch of the Havergal Brian Society, 1976).

Tight-Rope, opera in nine uninterrupted scenes by Chester Biscardi; libretto (Eng) by Henry Butler. First performance October 5, 1986, Madison, Wisconsin, University of

Wisconsin, with John Reardon (Luther Dane), Marcus Haddock (the actor), and Adria Firestone (Kathryn).

When a film is being made about the supposedly dead poet and hero Luther Dane, the actor in the role has trouble creating his part. Suddenly, Dane appears, quite alive, and shows him how to speak the lines, especially the "memory scenes" in which the poet revisits a love from his past, Kathryn.

BIBLIOGRAPHY: James Chute, review, *MA* XXXVI (Jan. 1986), 16–17 [on premiere]; Andrew Porter, "Musical Events," *NY* LXII (July 14, 1986), 62 [on premiere].

Time Flies. See **Three Instant Operas.**

Time for Growing, A, opera in three acts by Antony Hopkins; libretto (Eng) by Nesta Pain. First performance June 5, 1967, Norwich, St. Andrew's Hall.

This is a pageant opera for children and a short examination of human evolution and the attempt to find meaning in existence.

Time Off? Not a Ghost of a Chance!, charade in four scenes and three interruptions by Elisabeth Lutyens; libretto (Eng) by the composer. First performance March 1, 1972, London, Sadler's Wells, the New Opera Company.

The work concerns the nature of time and consists of various puns, riddles, and quotations. The music is in serial style.

SCORE: fs, facsimile (London: Olivan Press, [1968]).
BIBLIOGRAPHY: Winton Dean, review, *MT* CXIII (Apr. 1972), 376 [on premiere]; S. Walsh, "'Time Off' and 'The Scene Machine,'" *MT* CXIII (1972), 137–39.

Time Rocker, pop rock opera, with songs and lyrics by Lou (Lewis) Reed; text (Eng-Ger) by Darryl Pinckney, loosely inspired by H. G. Wells's *Time Machine*. First performance June 1996, Hamburg, Thalia Theater; directed by Robert Wilson. First U.S. performance November 12, 1997, Brooklyn, New York, Brooklyn Academy of Music, Next Wave Festival, with Stefan Kurt (Nick) and Annette Paulmann (Priscilla); directed by Wilson.

The work concerns a young couple, Nick and Priscilla, who work for the elusive Dr. Procopius. After Dr. Procopius disappears into another time zone, they are accused of his murder and use as their mode of travel a "big fish" (akin to Wells's time machine) to search both in the future and in the past for their employer.

Among the musical highlights is "Turning Time Around," which concludes the first act. The spoken dialogue is in German, while the songs are sung to English words.

Part one of Robert Wilson's pop-rock opera trilogy. See also *The Black Rider* (1992, Hamburg) and *Alice* (1990, Hamburg).

BIBLIOGRAPHY: Clive Barnes, review, *New York Post* (Nov. 14, 1997), 47, 57 [on U.S. premiere]; Alan Riding, review, *NYT* (Jan. 15, 1997), C, 11 [on Paris premiere].

Timon in Love, or, The Innocent Theft, comic ballad opera; libretto (Eng) by John Kelly, after L. F. Delisle's *Thimon misanthrope* (1722). First performance December 5, 1733, London, Drury Lane Theatre.
LIBRETTO: English (London: J. Watts, 1733).

Timon of Athens, opera in two acts by Stephen Oliver; libretto (Eng) by the composer, a direct adaptation of Shakespeare's play. First performance May 17, 1991, London, English National Opera, Coliseum, with Monte Jaffe (Timon) and Gregory Jurisch (Alcibiades); conducted by Graeme Jenkins; staged by Graham Vick.

In this setting of the Shakespeare, Alcibiades kills Timon after Timon fails to commit suicide. Musically, the work is expressionist in style, and the score includes exotic instrumentation.

Also masque, with incidental music by Henry Purcell, text by Thomas Shadwell (comp. 1694).

SCORE: vs (London: Novello, 1992).

BIBLIOGRAPHY: Antony Bye, "Live Performance," *MT* CXXXII (July 1991), 353 [on premiere]; Matthew Rye, "Oliver's *Timon of Athens*," *MT* CXXXII (May 1991), 228, 230.

Tinners of Cornwall, The, opera in three acts by Inglis Gundry; libretto (Eng) by the composer. First performance September 30, 1953, London, Rudolf Steiner Hall.

Tin Pan Alley, opera in one act by Sam Raphling; libretto (Eng) by the composer. First performance June 6, 1954, New York, WNYC Festival, with Rawn Spearman (Johnny), Daisy Spearman (Rosey), George Goodman (Mr. Day), Betty Allen and Jeanette Scavotti (the girls), and Frances Hester (the tap dancer).

The work is set in the office of a publisher of popular songs. Johnny, the hero, has been unable to write hit tunes since Rosey, his girlfriend, left him. When she calls him to say she loves him, Johnny's inspiration returns, and his boss, Mr. Day, hires Rosey as Johnny's "assistant" to make sure that his composing inspiration stays put.

Among the highlights are "Love Is Nothing but a Bunch of Sighs."

BIBLIOGRAPHY: R. P., "Premiere of Sam Raphling's 'Tin Pan Alley' Begins Week-Long Opera Fete on WNYC," *NYT* (June 7, 1954), 20.

Tit for Tat, or, The Tables Turned, adaptation by William Hawes of Mozart's *Così fan tutte* (1790, Vienna); libretto (Eng) possibly by S. J. Arnold, after da Ponte. First performance July 29, 1828, London, Lyceum.

To Arms, or, The British Recruit, musical interlude in one act by William Shield; libretto (Eng) by Thomas Hurlstone. First performance May 3, 1793, London, Covent Garden. Revived there as *The British Recruit*, or, *Who's Afraid*," March 16, 1795.

Includes music by T. Giordani and Dr. Stevenson.

LIBRETTO: English (London: J. Debrett, 1793).

Tobias and the Angel, television opera in two acts by Arthur Bliss; libretto (Eng) by Christopher Hassall, after the Apocryphal Book of Tobit. First performance May 19, 1960, BBC, with Elaine Malbin, Janet Howe, Ronald Lewis, Jess Walters, Trevor Anthony, and John Ford; conducted by Norman Del Mar; directed by Rudolph Cartier.

The work is scored for ten characters and mixed chorus.

Tod's Gal, opera in five scenes by Robert Kelly; libretto (Eng) by the composer. Composed 1951. First performance January 8, 1971, Norfolk, Virginia, Old Dominion University Opera Workshop.

The story is set in a secluded cabin in the southern Appalachian mountains at the end of the Second World War. It centers around a hardworking mother, burdened by an extremely lazy husband and son. Her first son, Tod, returns with an English bride, Ginny, but this does not stop Lula Belle, an old flame, from making a play for Tod. Faced by the uneasy situation at his boyhood home, Tod and his wife leave.

BIBLIOGRAPHY: Harold G. Hawn, "Tod's Gal," *OJ* IV (1971), 27–28 [on premiere].

To Let the Captive Go, chamber opera in one act by Frank Stewart; libretto (Eng) by John Hubsky. First performance March 3, 1974, New York, Mannes College.

Tom and Lily, comic opera in one act by Elliott Carter; libretto (Eng). Composed 1934.

The work is scored for four solo voices, small mixed chorus, and chamber orchestra. It was destroyed by the composer.

BIBLIOGRAPHY: David Schiff, *The Music of Elliott Carter* (London: Eulenburg, 1980), 328, passim.

Tom Jones, pastiche opera in three acts by Samuel Arnold and Michael Arne; libretto (Eng) by Joseph Reed, partly based on A. H. Poisonet's text for Philidor (1765, Paris), itself based on Fielding's novel. First performance January 14, 1769, London, Covent Garden, with Mrs. Pinto (formerly Miss Charlotte Brent, as Sophia), Mrs. Baker (Nancy), and Mr. Du Bellamy (Nightingale).

The story is a sanitized version of the Fielding novel via the French text, with Parson Supple changed to a country squire and the character of Western made less coarse.

Six numbers by Arnold, eight by Arne, and three by J. C. Bach: Sophia's "Thirst of Wealth Too Oft Bewitches" (from the first collection of Vauxhall Songs); the second, in act 2, Nancy's "Blest with Thee, My Soul's Dear Treasure" (from *Carattaco*, No. 24); the third, in act 3, sung by Nightingale, "Ah Why Shou'd Love with Tyrant Sway" (from the first Vauxhall Songs). The overture was from a Piccinni opera, and the finale from Corelli's Concerto Grosso No. 2 in F.

Other settings include those by E. German (1907, London) and S. Oliver (1976, Newcastle upon Tyne) (see following entries); and Philidor (1765, Paris).

SCORE: vs (London: Welcker, [1769]); three Bach numbers repr. in *The Collected Works of J. C. Bach*, vol. 25, *Works with English Texts*, ed. Ernest Warburton (New York: Garland, 1990).

LIBRETTO: English (Dublin: W. and W. Smith, G. Faulkner, P. and W. Wilson [etc.], 1769).

Tom Jones, comic opera in three acts by Edward German; libretto (Eng) by A. M. Thompson and Robert Courtneidge, after Henry Fielding's novel of the same name; lyrics by Charles H. Taylor. First performance April 18, 1907, London, Apollo, with Hayden Coffin (Tom Jones) and Ruth Vincent (Sophia). First U.S. performance November 11, 1907, New York, Astor Theater.

A subdued version of the Fielding original. Tom eventually marries Sophia, daughter of Squire Western.

Tom Jones, opera in three acts by Stephen Oliver; libretto (Eng) by the composer, after Henry Fielding. First performance April 6, 1976, Newcastle upon Tyne.

The main action centers on Tom's journey to London.

LIBRETTO: English (Borough Green, [Engl.]: Novello, [1976]).

Tommy, "rock opera" by Pete Townshend; libretto (Eng) by the composer; adapted for the stage by Townshend and Des McAnuff. First performance October 20, 1968, New York, with The Who (Townshend, Roger Daltry, and Keith Moon). Revived (concert) 1969, New York; June 7, 1970, New York, Metropolitan Opera.

The story concerns a boy, Tommy, who is rendered deaf, mute, and blind when he sees his mother's lover killed. After becoming a successful pinball player, Tommy develops a following and is cured of his disabilities, acquiring an image as a young messiah. Put off by his noisy fans, he finds a way for them to reject him.

TOM SAWYER

According to the vocal score, the work "has combined the classical form of the opera with the musical form of contemporary rock." Among the musical numbers is the hero's "Pinball Wizard."
SCORE: vs (Miami Beach: C. Hansen, [1969]).
LIBRETTO: English (New York: Pantheon Books, 1993).
BIBLIOGRAPHY: review, *NYT* (Oct. 21, 1968), 41 [on premiere]; Mike Jahn, "The Who Brings Rock Opera Here," *NYT* (June 8, 1970), 42 [on revival].
DISCOGRAPHY: The Who, Decca DSXW 75126-75127 (1969); reissued as MCA MCAD2-10005 (1984, 2 CDs).

Tomorrow, Tomorrow, monodrama in one act by Timothy Sullivan; libretto (Eng) by the composer. First performance March 28, 1987, New York, with Suzan Hanson.
    The work examines a woman's life, culminating in her suicide.

Tom Sawyer, musical play in one act by Jonathan Elkus; libretto (Eng) by the composer, after Mark Twain's novel. First performance May 22, 1953, San Francisco; February 20, 1954, New York, New York College of Music Opera Workshop, Carl Fischer Hall; conducted by Siegfried Landau.
SCORE: vs (London: Novello, [1956]).
LIBRETTO: English (London: Novello, [1956]).
BIBLIOGRAPHY: R. P., "Operas for Amateurs," *NYT* (Feb. 21, 1956), 36 [on premiere].

Tom Sawyer, children's opera in one act by Richard Owen; libretto (Eng) by the composer, after Mark Twain's novel. First performance April 9, 1989, New York, Manhattan School of Music, Children's Opera Theatre.
    Roger Miller's *Big River* is a musical on the same subject (1985, New York).
SCORE: vs, holograph (1989, NYPL, photocopy).

Tom Thumb, burlesque opera in two acts by J. Markordt; libretto (Eng) by Kane O'Hara, after Henry Fielding's novel. First performance October 3, 1780, London, Covent Garden, with Miss Catley. First U.S. performance October 7, 1790, New York, City Tavern.
    In this satire the diminutive Tom Thumb stands taller than his so-called betters.
    The characters include King Arthur, Lord Grizzle, Tom Thumb, Merlin, Noodle, Doodle, Queen Dollallolla, Princess Huncamunca, Glumdalca, Frizaletta, and Plumante.
    See *Opera of Operas* by Lampe and Arne for earlier settings of the story.
LIBRETTO: English (London: Longman, Hurst, Rees, and Orme, 1809).

Tom-Tom, opera in three acts by Shirley Graham; libretto (Eng) by the composer. First performance July 3, 1933, Cleveland, Cleveland Stadium, with Jules Bledsoe (voodoo man), Charlotte Murray (mother), Luther King (boy), Lillian Cowan (the girl), Hazel M. Walker (leader), and Augustus Grist (preacher/captain); conducted by Clifford Barnes.
    The work, which has three settings and times, opens in an African jungle village, before 1619 (act 1); the South, before the Civil War (act 2); and Harlem, the present [i.e., 1933] (act 3). The main characters are a boy and girl, pursued by a voodoo man throughout the work. In the first act, the boy and girl are about to be sacrificed by their village for the elephant hunt, signalled by the tom-tom. They escape their fate when slave hunters arrive and disperse the villagers.
    In the second act, the boy and girl are now slaves in the antebellum South. They are about to be separated by the sale of the girl to another plantation, when the Union army is heard in the distance. In the last act, set in Harlem, the voodoo man has initiated a "back to Africa" movement, which is opposed by the boy, who has become a

young preacher. The girl, now a queen of the blues, is about to be carried away on a ship with the voodoo man when an explosion occurs. The crowd blames him for the destruction, and a young cabaret dancer stabs the voodoo man to death.

For a detailed description, see Hipsher/*AO*, 219–20.

Tonkin, opera in three acts by Conrad Cummings; libretto (Eng) by Thomas Bird and Robert T. Jones. First performance November 27, 1993, Wilmington, Delaware, OperaDelaware, with Peggy Kriha, Matthew Lord, and Perry Ward (Ho Chi Minh); conducted by David Lawton; produced by Harry Silverstein

A stylized treatment of the Vietnam War, the work centers on a fictional Vietnamese girl and an American, and the figure of Ho Chi Minh.

The music is written in a minimalist style.
BIBLIOGRAPHY: Patrick J. Smith, "Wilmington, Delaware," *ON* LVIII (March 5, 1994), 46 [on premiere].

Tony Beaver, folk opera in one act by Josef Marais; libretto (Eng) by Max Berton. First performance August 1, 1953, Idyllwild, California, Idyllwild School.

Tony Beaver encounters characters from the world of folklore, including Paul Bunyan, Pecos Bill, and Davy Crockett, and although he is slowed by many obstacles, he triumphs in the end.

One of several stage works by the famed South African-born folk singer, author of *Songs from the Veld* (1942).
SCORE: vs (n.p., n.d.; LCCN: 84-128292).
BIBLIOGRAPHY: D. S. Wheelwright, review, *Music News* XLIV (Oct. 1952), 15.

Too Civil by Half, farce by James Hook; libretto (Eng) by John Dent. First performance November 4, 1782, London, Drury Lane Theatre, with Miss Anna Phillips.

In order to get the attention of Sir Toby Treacle, who is obsessed by ships, his daughter's lover dresses as a sea captain. The young man is hindered, however, by his ignorance of nautical matters and his prospective father-in-law's thinking that the suitor is talking about a ship when in reality he is discussing the young lady.

Among the six songs is the imitation Scottish song "In Youth When a Lover We Meet."
SCORE: vs (London: S. A. and P. Thompson, etc. [1783]).
LIBRETTO: English (London: J. Stockdale, 1783).

Too Many Cooks, musical farce in two acts by Matthew King; libretto (Eng) by James Kenney. First performance February 12, 1805, London, Covent Garden. First U.S. performance October 25, 1805, Boston, Federal Street Theatre.

Tornrak, opera in two acts by John Metcalf; libretto (Eng) by Michael Wilcox. First performance May 19, 1990, Cardiff, New Theatre, with David Owen (Arthur) and Penelope Walker (Milak); conducted by Richard Armstrong.

Set in the nineteenth century, the work examines the clash between cultures. Milak, an Inuit woman, rescues the shipwrecked Arthur. The pair go to England, where they are separated. The mistreated Milak is ultimately executed for killing sheep.

The composer employs Inuit throat-singing techniques in the score.
BIBLIOGRAPHY: Antony Bye, review, *MT* CXXXI (Aug. 1990), 435–36 [on premiere].

Torquil, a Scandinavian Dramatic Legend, opera by Charles Harriss; libretto (Eng) by Edward Oxenford. First performance May 22, 1900, Toronto.

Touchstone, The, or, Harlequin Traveller, "operatical" (speaking) pantomime by Charles Dibdin; libretto (Eng) by the composer. First performance January 4, 1779, London, with Lee Lewis (Harlequin), Miss Brown (Columbine), John Mahon (Watchman), and Charles Frederick Reinhold (Pierrot). First U.S. performance September 1, 1785, New York, John Street Theatre.

For a description, see Fiske/*ETM*, 424.

The work, unique for a pantomime because it has spoken dialogue, features a chorus of spirits, Celestial March, and "Music for the Battle." The overture includes a "fuga."
SCORE: vs (London: S. and A. Thompson, [1779]).

Toussaint, or, The Aristocracy of the Skin, grand opera in twenty-two scenes (three acts) by David Blake; libretto (Eng) by Anthony Ward, after C. L. R. James's biography *The Black Jacobins*. First performance September 28, 1977, London, English National Opera, with Neil Howlett (Toussaint), Geoffrey Chard (Dessalines), Emile Belcourt (Mars Plaisir), Sarah Walker (Suzanne), and Teresa Cahill (Pauline); conducted by Mark Elder; directed by David Pountney.

The story of Toussaint L'Ouverture and the creation of an independent state in Haiti. The tolerant Toussaint, who supports a multiracial society, is opposed by Dessalines, whose policy advocates the death of the whites. The story ends in 1803, after Haiti is freed from French rule, Toussaint dies in prison, and Dessalines declares himself emperor.

For a detailed description, see K/*NKOB*, 84–85.

Major roles: Toussaint (bar); Suzanne, his wife (mezzo); Mars Plaisir (ten); Pauline, Napoleon's sister (sop); and Dessalines (bar).

Most of the scenes are linked by the spoken commentary of Mars Plaisir, the mulatto valet of Toussaint. The music includes voodoo chant and drumming, neoclassicism, and echoes of Schoenberg and Hindemith.

Another opera concerning this period, which concentrates on Dessalines, is William Grant Still's *Troubled Island** (1938, perf. 1949, New York).
SCORE: vs (Borough Green, Kent: Novello, [1977]).
BIBLIOGRAPHY: Frank Granville Barker, "Reports: U.S.," *ON* XLII (Dec. 10, 1977), 34–35 [on premiere]; Andrew Porter, review, *NY* LIII (Oct. 24, 1977), 165–67 [on premiere].

Tower, The, opera in one act by Marvin David Levy; libretto (Eng) by Townsend Brewster. First performance August 2, 1957, Santa Fe, New Mexico, with Carol Bergey, Peter Binder, William McGrath, and Robert Rue; conducted by Robert Baustian; produced by the composer.

In order to prevent the scholar Reuel's prophecy that Solomon's daughter, Achlamah, will wed the poorest man in his kingdom, the King orders that a tower be built within which she can be held and kept from meeting such a man. The poor Joash, sleeping in the skeleton of an ox, finds himself in the tower when the remains are brought to the roof. He is welcomed by Tabitha, nurse to the princess, because she believes in the prophecy. Joash and Achlamah fall in love, and, when the old scholar Nabarias keeps all of the ink for writing to himself, the young couple sign the marriage contract with Joash's blood. Solomon reluctantly gives in to the prophecy.

For a detailed description, see Eaton/*OP* I, 230–31.

Roles: Reuel (bass-bar); King Solomon (ten); Princess Achlamah (sop); Tabitha (mezzo); Nabarias (bass); Abigail, Achlamah's maid (sop); and Joash (bar).

Tower of London, comic opera in three acts by Alfred Cellier; libretto (Eng). First performance October 4, 1875, Manchester, Prince's Theatre. Revised as *Doris** (1889, London).

Toy-Maker, The, opera by George Linley, an adaptation of Adam's *La poupée de Nuremberg* (1852, Paris); libretto (Eng) by the composer, after the text of A. de Leuven and L. L. Brunswick. First performance November 19, 1861, London, Covent Garden.

Toy Shop, The, opera in one act for a young audience by Seymour Barab; libretto (Eng) by the composer. First performance June 3, 1978, New York, City Opera Theatre.

Set in a toy shop, the story involves two lifelike dolls created by the toy maker and thought of by him as his children, Pauline and Paul. When a magician, Aaron Blunder, hears of these creations, he tries to steal them but is stopped by the dolls themselves.

Major roles: Pauline (sop), Paul (ten), toy maker (bar), and Aaron Blunder (bass).

For a detailed description, see Kornick/*RAO*, 42–43.

BIBLIOGRAPHY: Raymond Ericson, review, *NYT* (June 11, 1978), 60, 63 [on premiere].

Tragicall History of Christopher Marlowe, The, opera in four acts and two interludes by Wilfrid Mellers; libretto (Eng) by R. J. White. Composed 1950–1952.

Transatlantic—The People's Choice, opera in three acts by George Antheil; libretto (Eng) by the composer. First performance May 25, 1930, Frankfurt, in a German translation (as *Transatlantik*) by Rudolf Stephan Hoffmann. First U.S. performance (abridged), in English, October 2, 1981, Trenton, New Jersey, Encompass Music Theatre; reorchestrated by F. Johnson. First fully staged, complete performance in English April 18, 1998, Minneapolis, Minnesota Opera; conducted by David Agler.

The satirical story, whose main characters bear names from Greek mythology and literature, begins on a ship headed from Europe to New York. Helen and Hector, fellow passengers, fall in love. The millionaire industrialist Ajax is pushing Hector to become president, and since Helen works for Ajax, Ajax's plan to control Hector after Hector has become president seems to be working. Once in New York, Hector and Leo, his campaign manager, pay a visit to Jason, whereupon Hector discovers, to his dismay, that Helen is Jason's wife, the marriage having been orchestrated by Ajax to unsettle Hector. Leo falls for Helen, also, and gives her an extravagant diamond ring, using money that he has stolen from the campaign fund. Hector is upset further when he barely escapes a police raid at a nightclub, another event arranged by Ajax.

Although Hector no longer cares for Helen, she thinks she is in love with him and sends him a letter detailing Ajax's deeds and plans to control him. Hector discards the missive without reading it, but Leo finds it and, needing money to cover his purchase of the ring, gives Ajax the letter in the expectation of a generous payment. Instead, Ajax becomes infuriated and throws his support to Hector's opponent. On election night, when Leo admits to Hector that he stole money and let Ajax have Helen's damning letter, Hector strikes Leo, who then pulls out his gun and shoots himself, ending up in the hospital.

A confused Hector retreats to his hotel room, and when Helen finds him and declares her love, he attacks her also. She then says that she is leaving for Paris but in fact tries to kill herself by jumping off the Brooklyn Bridge, which he, having followed her, prevents. He then learns that he has been elected president. Ajax, who has come to congratulate Hector, is arrested for his evil deeds, and all rejoice.

Major roles: Helen (sop), Hector (bar), Ajax (bass), Jason (ten), and Leo (ten).

The score uses jazz rhythms among its musical devices. The work was the first American opera to have its premiere in Europe, where it was acclaimed wildly, but the initial enthusiasm did not cross the Atlantic during the composer's lifetime.

SCORE: vs, English-German ([Vienna]: Universal-Edition, 1929).

Transformations, "entertainment" in two acts by Conrad Susa; libretto (Eng), a modern interpretation of ten fairy tales of the Brothers Grimm, "transformed" by Anne Sexton. First performance May 5, 1973, Minneapolis, Minnesota Opera. First fully staged performance June 26, 1996, New York, Kaye Playhouse, Center for Contemporary Opera, with Janna Baty (Anne Sexton), Elizabeth Weigle (Snow White), and Mary Sophia Nessinger; conducted by Richard Marshall.

The tales are told through the eyes of the narrator, Anne Sexton, with the emphasis on the psychological revelations they represent. The stories examined include "Snow White and the Seven Dwarfs," "Rumpelstiltskin," "Hansel and Gretel," and "Sleeping Beauty."

Roles: eight singers playing various roles.

For a detailed description, see Kornick/*RAO*, 307–9.

The composer employs many styles of music, including cabaret, blues, and tango.

SCORE: vs (Boston: E. C. Schirmer Music Co., [1976]).

BIBLIOGRAPHY: Shirley Fleming, "Sexton's Grimm Take on Susa," *New York Post* (June 28, 1996), 53 [on 1996 performance]; A. Hughes, *NYT* (May 28, 1976), II, 14 [on N.Y. premiere]; Robert Jacobson, "Reports: U.S.," *ON* XLV (Sept. 1980), 50; Alfred Frankenstein, "Opera Everywhere," *MA* XXX (Sept. 1980), 25–26.

Transit through Fire, radio opera in one act by Healey Willan; libretto (Eng) by John Coulter. First performance March 8, 1942, CBC. First stage performance February 18, 1943, Toronto, University of Toronto.

The sentimental story, which concerns a young soldier on leave, was tailored for a wartime audience.

For a detailed description, see Clarke/*HW*, 118–24.

LIBRETTO: English ([Toronto] Macmillan Co. of Canada Ltd., [1942]).

Transposed Heads, The, opera in two acts by Peggy Glanville-Hicks; libretto (Eng) by the composer, after a novel by Thomas Mann, translated into English by H. T. Lowe-Porter. First performance April 4, 1954, Louisville, Kentucky, Louisville Philharmonic Society, with Audrey Nossaman (Sita), Monas Harlan (Shridaman), and William Pickett (Nanda); conducted by Moritz Bomhard. Performed February 10, 1958, New York, Phoenix Theatre, with Loren Driscoll (Shridaman), Peter Binder (Nanda), Maria Ferriero (Sita), and Peggy Wood (Kali); conducted by Carlos Surinach.

In this love triangle, set in India, Sita married Shridaman and then falls in love with his friend Nanda. Shridaman cuts off his rival's head, and in turn Sita beheads her husband. When she places the heads back on the bodies, she finds that she has mixed them up. In the end all three die so that they can be reunited in the afterworld.

For a detailed description, see Eaton/*OP* II, 325–26.

Roles: Sita (sop); Shridaman (ten); Nanda (bar); Goddess Kali (speaking); and Kamadamana, a guru (speaking).

The opera includes a number of tunes and rhythms from Hindu folk and classical music.

SCORE: vs (New York: Associated Music Publishers, [1958]).

BIBLIOGRAPHY: Douglas A. Mackinnon, "New York," *ON* XXII (Mar. 1958), 26 [on New York premiere].

DISCOGRAPHY: Louisville, Ky.: Louisville Philharmonic Society, LOU-545-6 (1955).

Travellers, The, or, Music's Fascination, "an operatic drama" in five acts by Domenico Corri; libretto (Eng) by Andrew Cherry. First performance January 22, 1806,

London, Drury Lane Theatre. First U.S. performance April 20, 1807, Philadelphia, Chestnut Street Theatre.

The work deals with the music of various cultures.

LIBRETTO: English (London: E. Phillips, 1806).

Travellers, The, chamber opera in one scene by Alan Hovhaness; libretto (Eng) by the composer. First performance April 22, 1967, San Francisco, Foothill College.

In this surrealistic setting, an old couple sit in a train compartment. A newlywed couple come in, the elderly occupants rise, open the window, and disappear, with the young couple taking their seats. The couple talk until nightfall, when there is a knock at the door. A couple that is younger still enter, the present occupants rise, open the window, and vanish.

For a plot description, see Summers/*OOA*, 157–58.

Major roles: man (bass) and woman (alto).

SCORE: vs (New York: C. F. Peters Corp., [1965]).

Travellers in Switzerland, The, comic opera in three acts by William Shield; libretto (Eng) by Bate Dudley. First performance February 22, 1794, London, Covent Garden, with John Johnstone (Dorimond), Mrs. Mattocks (Lady Philippa Sidney), Mrs. Clendining (Julia), Joseph Munden (Lord Sidney), John Fawcett (Count Friponi), Miss Poole (Miss Somerville), and Charles Incledon (Dalton).

In order to be near his beloved, Julia, Dorimond follows her and her mother, Lady Philippa Sidney, to Switzerland, where he dons the disguise of a Swiss servant. Lady Philippa's husband, meanwhile, becomes a Swiss guide to see if she is having an affair with Count Friponi, who is really interested in Julia. In a subplot, Miss Somerville buys a Swiss castle to get away from Dalton, who, she thinks, wants her money.

For a detailed description, see Fiske/*ETM*, 552.

LIBRETTO: English (London: J. Debrett, 1794).

Travelling Companion, The, opera in four acts by Charles Stanford; libretto (Eng) by Henry Newbolt, after Hans Christian Andersen's fairy tale. Composed 1919. First performance April 30, 1925, Liverpool.

Travelling Man, The, opera in one act by Fritz Hart; libretto (Eng), after Lady Gregory's miracle play (1910). Composed 1920.

Travels, opera by Victoria Bond; libretto (Eng) by Ann Goethe, after Jonathan Swift's *Gulliver's Travels*. First performance May 18, 1995, Roanoke, Virginia, with Nicholas Loren (Gull).

A modernization of the satirical story, in which the hero, Gull, goes on a voyage of self-discovery.

BIBLIOGRAPHY: Priscilla Richardson, "Roanoke," *ON* LX (Sept. 1995), 65 [on premiere].

Treemonisha, opera in three acts by Scott Joplin; libretto (Eng) by the composer. Composed 1908–1911. First performance (concert) 1915, New York? First stage performance January 28, 1972, Atlanta, Symphony Hall, with Carmen Balthrop (Treemonisha), Betty Allen (Monisha), Curtis Rayam (Remus), Ben Harney (Zodzetrick), and Willard White (Ned); orchestrated by T. J. Anderson.

The setting is an abandoned Arkansas plantation, 1884. A baby girl, found under a tree and called Treemonisha, has been raised by Ned and Monisha and given a good education. As a grown woman, she clashes with the local conjurer, Zodzetrick, and his companion, Luddud, who feed upon the superstitions of the people; to keep her from interfering, they kidnap her. She is saved by Remus, a friend, and returned to her family. Refusing to punish her captors when they are caught, she requests that they be given a stiff lecture instead; for her foresight she is hailed as the leader of the people, and the work concludes with the dance "A Real Slow Drag."

Major roles: Ned (bass), Monisha (mezzo), Treemonisha (sop), Remus (ten), Zodzetrick (ten), and Luddud (bar).

Joplin's own 1915 orchestration is lost. Among the musical highlights, in addition to the concluding number, is the quartet "We Will Rest Awhile." The work combines elements of ragtime and light opera.

SCORES: vs (New York: Scott Joplin, 1911); fs, ed. Gunther Schuller (Chicago: Dramatic Pub. Co., 1976).

DISCOGRAPHY: excerpts: "An Evening with Scott Joplin," W. Bolcom, M. L. Williams, J. Rifkin, pno; soloists, chorus; dir. J. Motley, New York Public Library (Oct. 22, 1971); G. Schuller, Houston Grand Opera Orch. and Chorus, DGG 2-435700-2 (1975, 2 CDs); R. Zimmerman, pno arr., Olympic OL 8139 (1975, 1 LP).

Tree on the Plains, A, opera in one act by Ernst Bacon; libretto (Eng) by Paul Horgan. First performance May 2, 1942, Spartanburg, South Carolina, Converse College Opera Workshop.

The setting is a house on the plains. The work opens at the funeral of Mom's father during a long drought. Corrie Mae, the daughter, longs to go to the city, to the dismay of the cowboy Lou, who hopes she will marry him. He argues with Buddy, Corrie's college-student brother. Just then a storm breaks, and the rain revives the dying little elm tree in the yard. The tension of the house breaks also. Lou comes for Corrie, and they sneak off to be married by the Reverend. When they return the next morning, they are welcomed by Corrie's parents. Buddy goes back to the city.

For a detailed description, see Eaton/*OP* I, 144.

Roles: Lou (bar), Pop (bass), Corrie Mae (sop), Mom (alto), Buddy (ten/high bar), neighbors (ten, ten/sop), little Shirley (tap dancer), and the Reverend (speaking).

SCORE: vs ([n.p.], 1942; LCCN: 45-30338).

LIBRETTO: English (New York: A. L. Williams, [1942?]).

Tree That Was Christmas, The, opera by George Kleinsinger; libretto (Eng) by Joe Darion, after the story by Christopher Morley. First performance December 17, 1955, New York, Hunter College, with Ruth Kobart, Lee Cass, and Frank Rogier; conducted by Thomas Schermann.

Trevallion, opera in three acts by Roy Phillips; libretto (Eng) by Malcolm Morley and Philip Phillips. First performance March 21, 1956, London, Palace Theatre, with Janet Hamilton-Smith, Jean Carol, Edmond Donlevy, and Dennis Noble; conducted by Charles Brill; produced by Malcolm Morley.

Trial at Rouen, The, television opera in two acts by Norman Dello Joio; libretto (Eng) by Joseph Machlis. First performance April 8, 1956, New York, NBC television, with Elaine Malbin (Joan), Hugh Thompson (Pierre Cauchon), Chester Watson, and Paul Ukena; conducted by Peter Herman Adler; produced by Kirk Browning.

A revision of *The Triumph of (Saint) Joan.**

Trial by Jury, comic opera in one act by Arthur S. Sullivan; libretto (Eng) by William S. Gilbert. First performance March 25, 1875, London, Royalty Theatre, with Fred Sullivan (the Learned Judge). First U.S. performance November 15, 1875, New York, Eagle Theatre.

The setting is a courtroom. Edwin is on trial for breach of promise to Angelina because he is enamored of someone else. The spurned lady appears in court and dazzles the judge and jury with her beauty. Edwin offers to wed Angelina today and her rival tomorrow. His solution is rejected, but the judge decides to marry Angelina himself. All parties are satisfied, and the trial comes to an end.

Major roles: the Learned Judge (bar), the Plaintiff (sop), the Defendant (ten), and Counsel for the Plaintiff (bar).

Set in the style of an opera buffa, the work contains recitatives, arias, and ensembles; there is no spoken dialogue. Among the highlights are the Judge's explanation of how he was able, as a person of lowly origin, to achieve his prominent rank, "When I, Good Friends, Was Called to the Bar," and the Bellini-like bel canto number "A Nice Dilemma We Have Here," set in the middle of the court proceedings.

SCORE: fs, *W. S. Gilbert-Arthur Sullivan, the Operas, a Critical Edition*, vol. 1, ed. Steven Ledbetter (Williamstown, Mass.: Broude Brothers, 1994).

VIDEO: K. Flowers, F. Howerd, R. Davies, Ambrosian Opera Chorus; cond. McCarthy; London Sym. Orch.; cond. A. Faris; dir. W. Toye, Goldcrest Films International, Opera World, VHS TRI-10V (1982 performance); rev. F. Paul Driscoll, *ON* LXII (Oct. 1997), 65.

Trial of Lucullus, The, opera in one act by Roger Sessions; libretto (Eng), after a radio play by Bertolt Brecht. First performance April 18, 1947, Berkeley, California.

The opera begins with the funeral of the Roman general Lucullus, who is judged by a ghostly tribunal for his actions during his lifetime.

Another setting of the text is P. Dessau's *Das Verhör des Lukullus* (1951, East Berlin).

BIBLIOGRAPHY: review, *NYT* (May 20, 1966), 42.

Trial of Mary Lincoln, The, opera in one act by Thomas Pasatieri; libretto (Eng) by Anne Howard Bailey. First performance February 14, 1972, NET opera, with Elaine Bonazzi (Mrs. Lincoln), Robert Wayne Turnage (her son), Carol Bogarde (Elizabeth, her sister), Julian Patrick (Lincoln's clerk), and Alan Titus (Mary's confederate nephew); conducted by Peter Herman Adler; directed by Kirk Browning.

The story begins in the Cook County Courthouse, scene of Mrs. Lincoln's insanity hearing. It includes flashbacks that show her courtship by Lincoln, her troubled marriage and loss of a son, and the assassination. In the end she is found insane and committed to an institution.

BIBLIOGRAPHY: Speight Jenkins, review, *ON* XXXVI (Feb. 26, 1972), 32 ([on premiere].

Trial of the Gipsy, The, children's opera ("dramatic cantata for boys' choir") by Gian Carlo Menotti; libretto (Eng) by the composer. First performance May 24, 1978, New York, Alice Tully Hall, Newark Boys Chorus.

A young gypsy boy is on trial for stealing and other crimes. He is appearing before three judges, while the chorus provides background information, support, and comments. The audience serves as the jury.

The work is scored for four soloists and boys' choir, accompanied by a piano. It was written for the Newark Boys Chorus.

BIBLIOGRAPHY: Andrew Porter, review, *NY* LIV (June 12, 1978), 103 [on premiere].

Trials of Psyche, The, opera in one act by Neely Bruce; libretto (Eng) by J. Orr, after an episode in *The Golden Ass* by Lucius Apuleius. First performance 1971, Urbana-Champaign, University of Illinois.

A telling of the love story of Psyche and Cupid.

Triangle, The, opera in two acts by Gerald Humel; libretto (Eng) by Roger Brucker. First performance November 14, 1958, Oberlin, Ohio.

Triboulet, or, The King's Jester, musical drama by Isaac Nathan; libretto (Eng) by John G. Millingen. First performance 1840, London, Sadler's Wells; April 21, 1846, Sydney, Australia, Victoria Theatre.

The music is lost.

Trick for Trick, ballad opera in two acts; libretto (Eng) by R. Fabian. First performance May 10, 1735, London, Drury Lane Theatre, with William Hallam (Guzman), Mr. Berry (Don Lopes), Mr. Salway (Don Fernand), Mr. Shepherd (Don Garcia), Mr. Mecklin (Sancho), Mr. Turbut (Don Diego), Mrs. Chantrel (Elvira), and Mrs. Pritchard (Eugenia).

Major roles: Don Lopes, governor of Sevil [sic]; Don Fernand, son of the Duke of Medina Sidonia, in love with Elvira; Don Garcia, Elvira's father; Guzman, Don Lopes's servant; Sancho, Don Fernand's servant; Don Diego, Medina Sidonia's steward; Elvira; and Eugenia, her confidante.

LIBRETTO: English (London, 1735); repr. Rubsamen/*BO*, vol. 12, *Farce: Amorous Intrigue and Deception I* (1974).

Tricks upon Travellers, comic opera in three acts by Charles Edward Horn and William Reeve; libretto (Eng) by James Bland Burges. First performance July 9, 1810, London, Lyceum Theatre. First U.S. performance March 18, 1811, New York, Park Theatre.

The story is set in Spain.

LIBRETTO: English, selections (London: W. H. Wyatt, 1810).

Trilby, opera in one act by Frederick Piket; libretto (Eng). First performance May 15, 1967, New York.

Triple Sec, opera-farce in one act by Marc Blitzstein; libretto (Eng) by Ronald Jeans. First performance May 6, 1929, Philadelphia, Bellevue-Stratford Ballroom, with Ruth Montague (the hostess) and Albert Mahler (Lord Silverside); conducted by Alexander Smallens. Revived May 1966, New York, New School.

The work makes fun of the drawing-room melodrama through the device of using two or more singers for each character and thereby promoting the piece's central "thesis," the triple vision of a drinker. It was written during Prohibition.

SCORE: fs, holograph, 1928, and two typescript librettos, English-German (NYPL).

LIBRETTO: English, typescript, ca. 1928 (Madison, Wisc., Wisconsin State Historical Society; photocopy NYPL).

BIBLIOGRAPHY: review, *NYT* (May 29, 1966), 42 [on revival].

Trip to Portsmouth, The, comic sketch in one act by Charles Dibdin; libretto (Eng) by George Alexander Stevens. First performance August 11, 1773, London, Little Theatre in the Haymarket.

The work includes T. A. Arne's overture for *The Rose** (1772, London).

LIBRETTO: English (London: T. Waller, [1773]).

Triptych, three music theater pieces by Alexander Goehr: *Naboth's Vineyard,* Shadowplay,** and *Sonata about Jerusalem.** First performance of complete work June 10, 1990, Aldeburgh; conducted by Richard Bernas. First U.S. performance December 11, 1991, New York, Manhattan School of Music; conducted by David Gilbert.
BIBLIOGRAPHY: Noël Goodwin, "Aldeburgh," *ON* LV (Jan. 5, 1991), 41 [on British premiere]; Philip Kennicott, "Composer's Page," *ON* LVI (Dec. 7, 1991), 48, 70; Andrew Porter, "Musical Events," *NY* LXVII (Dec. 30, 1991), 76ff. [on U.S. premiere].

Tristan and Iseult, chamber opera in one act by Gillian Whitehead; libretto (Eng) by Malcolm Crowthers and Michael Hill. First performance May 1978, Auckland, New Zealand, Auckland Festival.
    The work is scored for singers, mimes, puppets, and instrumental ensemble.
SCORE: vs (Wellington, New Zealand: Price Milburn Music, 1977).

Tristan and Iseult, opera by Joel Cohen; libretto (Eng) by the composer, after the medieval song. First performance February 1988, New York, Boston Camerata.

Tristram Shandy, opera in two acts; libretto (Eng) by Leonard MacNally, after Laurence Sterne's novel. First performance April 26, 1783, London, Covent Garden. Two songs by Michael Arne.
LIBRETTO: English (London: S. Bladon, 1783).

Triumph of Beauty, The, musical entertainment by James Hook; libretto (Eng) by Mrs. James Hook (Harriet Horncastle). First performance 1786, London, Vauxhall Gardens, with Charles Incledon, Miss Leary, Mrs. Martyr, and Mrs. Elizabeth Wrighten.
SCORE: vs (London: Longman and Broderip, [1786]).

Triumph of Beauty and Deceit, The, opera by Gerald Barry; libretto (Eng) by Meredith Oakes, after Benedetto Pamphili's libretto for Handel's masque *The Triumph of Time and Truth.* First performance (television) March 5, 1995, London, Channel 4, with Stephen Richardson and Denis Lakey.
    Described as an "allegorical tale set in a bizarre world," the work is scored for two countertenors.
BIBLIOGRAPHY: Jeffrey Joseph, "The Little Picture Show," *MT* CXXXVI (May 1995), 254–55 [on premiere].

Triumph of Columbus, The, opera in five acts by Silas Gamaliel Pratt; libretto (Eng). First performance October 12, 1892, New York.
    Written to commemorate the 400th anniversary of Columbus's discovery of America.

Triumph of Peace, The, masque in five scenes by William Lawes, Simon Ives, and Davis Mell; text (Eng) by James Shirley. First performance February 3, 1634, London, Whitehall, Banqueting House.
SCORE: fs, ed. Murray Lefkowitz (Paris: Editions du Centre National de la Recherche Scientifique, 1970).
LIBRETTO: English (London: William Cooke, 1633).

Triumph of Peace, The, "a masque . . . on the occasion of the general peace, concluded at Aix-la-Chapelle, October 7th, 1748," by Thomas Arne; libretto (Eng) by Robert Dodsley. First performance February 21, 1749, London, Theatre Royal, Drury Lane.
LIBRETTO: English (London: R. Dodsley, 1749).

Triumph of Punch, The, comic opera in one act by Ashley Vernon; libretto (Eng) by Greta Hartwig. First performance January 25, 1969, Brooklyn, New York, Brooklyn Academy of Music, Youth Music Festival.
BIBLIOGRAPHY: review, *NYT* (June 27, 1969), 25 [on premiere].

Triumph of (Saint) Joan, The, opera in three acts by Norman Dello Joio; libretto (Eng) by Joseph Machlis and the composer. First performance (with piano accompaniment) May 9, 1950, Bronxville, New York, Sarah Lawrence College, with Gisela Fischer (Joan), John Druary (the Dauphin), Jerome Swinford (Pierre Cauchon), and Robert Goss (the sentry); conducted by Hugh Ross; the composer, Helen Ahola, pianos. Revised as *The Trial at Rouen** (1956) and, reduced to one act, as *The Triumph of Saint Joan*; this version was first performed on April 16, 1959, New York, City Center, with Lee Venora, Mack Harrell, Frank Porretta, and Chester Walson; conducted by Herbert Grossman; produced by José Quintero.

The story concerns Joan of Arc; the first act opens in her prison cell at Rouen. The succeeding scenes of the act are flashbacks and cover her victories and the coronation of Charles VII. In the second act, Joan is put on trial at Rouen and, refusing to recant, is condemned to be burned at the stake.

Among the highlights are Joan's soliloquy in act 2, scene 1; the sentry's solo, act 2, scene 2; and Joan's duet with the Dauphin, act 2, scene 3. The score includes Gregorian chant, spoken passages, and dance episodes.

The one-act version concentrates on Joan's imprisonment, trial, and condemnation.
SCORE: vs, as *The Triumph of Saint Joan* (New York: G. Ricordi, [1959]).
BIBLIOGRAPHY: Olin Downes, "Dello Joio's New Lyric Drama a Notable Attempt in Sequence and Integration," *NYT* (May 14, 1950), II, 7 [on premiere]; Robert Sabin, "New Dello Joio Opera Staged at Sarah Lawrence College," *MA* LXX (May 1950), 70 [on premiere]; review, *NYT* (Apr. 17, 1959), 21 [on rev. version].

Triumphs of Hibernia, The, all-sung masque by Nicolo Pasquali; libretto (Eng). First performance November 4, 1748, Dublin, Smock Alley.
The overture was published in 1751.

Triumphs of the Prince d'Amour, The, masque by Henry and William Lawes; text (Eng) by William Davenant. First performance February 24, 1636, London, Middle Temple.
The work is through-composed, and there is no recitative.
SCORE: ms (Bodleian, Mus. Sch. B2); one song, by W. Lawes, in *Select Ayres and Dialogues* (London: John Playford, 1669).

Troilus and Cressida, opera in three acts by William Walton; libretto (Eng) by Christopher Hassall, after Chaucer. First performance December 3, 1954, London, Covent Garden, with Magda László (Cressida), Monica Sinclair (Evadne), Richard Lewis (Troilus), Peter Pears (Pandarus), Otakar Kraus (Diomede), Geraint Evans (Antenor), Frederick Dalberg (Calkas), and Forbes Robinson (Horaste); conducted by Malcolm Sargent; produced by George Devine. First U.S. performance 1955, New York, City Opera. Revised by the composer in 1963; performed April 1963, London, Covent Garden, with Marie Collier (Cressida). Revised by the composer in 1976; performed November 12, 1976, London, Royal Opera House, with Janet Baker (Cressida) and Richard Cassilly (Troilus); conducted by Lawrence Foster. Revised by Stuart Hutchinson, performed January 14, 1995, Leeds, Opera North, with Judith Howarth (Cressida) and Arthur Davies (Troilus); conducted by Richard Hickox.

The story focuses on the ill-fated lovers Troilus and Cressida in Troy at the time of the Trojan War. Thinking herself abandoned, after her servant Evadne destroys letters from Troilus, Cressida accepts the attentions of the Greek warrior Diomede. In the end Troilus is killed in a fight with Diomede, and Cressida takes her own life.

For detailed descriptions, see K/*KOB*, 1131–1134; K/*NKOB*, 953–55.

Major roles: Calkas, high priest of Pallas (bass); Antenor, Captain of Trojan spears (bar); Troilus, Prince of Troy (ten); Pandarus, brother of Calkas (ten buffo); Cressida, daughter of Calkas (sop); Evadne, her servant (mezzo); Horaste, friend of Pandarus (bar); and Diomede, Prince of Argos (bar).

Among the musical highlights are a sextet with chorus and Cressida's lament "As the Haunted End of Day."

W. Zillig set the Shakespeare version (1951, Düsseldorf).

SCORE: vs, rev. ed. (Oxford: University Press, 1980), rev. Corey Field, "Music Reviews," *MLA Notes* XXXIX (Sept. 1982), 222–24.

LIBRETTO: English (London: Oxford University Press, [1955]).

BIBLIOGRAPHY: Stuart Hutchinson, "'Troilus'—Forty Years On," *Opera* XLVI (Jan. 1995), 16–23 [on various versions].

DISCOGRAPHY: Baker, Bainbridge, Cassilly, Luxon, Van Allan, Royal Opera; cond. Foster, EMI SLS-997 (3); rev. John W. Freeman, *ON* XLIV (Apr. 19, 1980), 28.

Trojan Women, The, opera in one act by Margaret Garwood; libretto (Eng) by Howard Wiley, after Euripides. First performance October 22, 1967, Chester, Pennsylvania, Suburban Opera. Revised 1979.

SCORE: ms vs, holograph (photocopy, 1967, NYPL).

LIBRETTO: English, typescript (photocopy, 1967, NYPL).

Troubled Island, The, opera in three acts by William Grant Still; libretto (Eng) by Langston Hughes. Composed 1938. First performance March 31, 1949, New York, City Center, with Robert Weede (Dessalines), Marie Powers (Azelia), Helena Bliss (Claire), and Richard Charles (Vuval); conducted by Laszlo Halasz; directed by Eugene S. Bryden; choreographed by George Balanchine and Jean-Leon Destine.

The action concentrates on Dessalines, successor of Toussaint L'Ouverture in Haiti. Dessalines becomes Haiti's new emperor and abandons his faithful wife, Azelia, in favor of his new mistress, Claire, a beautiful mulatto, whom he makes empress. Dessalines ignores the warnings of Azelia that his mistress, along with others, including her lover, Vuval, are planning a coup. Another warning is provided by the clamor of voodoo drums that interrupt a fancy state banquet. Dessalines begins to deal with the uprising and enters a duel with Stenio, a traitorous general. Just as Dessalines is about to defeat Stenio, Vuval shoots the emperor in the back. Only Azelia is left to weep over his body.

Major roles: Dessalines (bar) and Azelia (mezzo).

See *Toussaint* for another story about Haiti.

Trouble in Tahiti, opera in one act by Leonard Bernstein; libretto (Eng) by the composer. First performance June 12, 1952, Waltham, Massachusetts, Festival of the Creative Arts, Brandeis University. First British performance November 11, 1985, Cambridge, One Off Productions at the ADC Theatre, with Richard Craddock (Sam), Vickie Jaffee (Dinah), and Peter Crockford (piano accompaniment).

Based on the clichés of modern life, this short work concerns a couple, Dinah and Sam, who are drifting apart and fantasize what life would be like on Tahiti, which they know only through television.

For a detailed description see Eaton/*OP* I, 231–32.

Major roles: Dinah (mezzo) and Sam (bass-bar).

Among the numbers is Dinah's "Island Magic" and a jazz trio.

A Quiet Place* is the sequel to *Trouble in Tahiti.*

SCORE: vs (New York: Jalni, 1988).

LIBRETTO: English (New York: G. Schirmer, 1953).

BIBLIOGRAPHY: William Davies, review, *Opera* XXXV (1984), 211 [on British premiere]; Cecil Smith, "Brandeis Festival," *MA* LXXII (July 1952), 7, 33 [on premiere].

DISCOGRAPHY: Wolff, Atkinson; cond. Winograd, Heliodor H-25020 (reissue of MGM E3646), on Polydor 827845-2 (CD, mono), 827845-4 (cassette, mono).

VIDEO: N. Williams, J. Patrick, A. Burler, M. Clark, M. Brown, London Sym. Wind Band; cond. L. Bernstein, dir. B. Hays, Kultur (1992, 1 VHS).

True Friends, musical farce in two acts by Thomas Attwood; libretto (Eng) by Thomas Dibdin. First performance February 19, 1800, London, Covent Garden.

Trumpet Major, The, opera in three acts by Alun Hoddinott; libretto (Eng) by Myfanwy Piper, after Thomas Hardy. First performance April 1, 1981, Manchester, Royal Northern College of Music.

The story concerns a soldier fighting in the Napoleonic Wars.

Truth about Windmills, The, opera in one act by Alec Wilder; libretto (Eng) by Arnold Sundgaard. First performance October 12, 1973, Rochester, New York.

DISCOGRAPHY: McFadden, Redmon, Thomsen, Lau, Eastman Chamber Ensemble; cond. D. Neuen, CA-PFN Pantheon (1971, cassette).

Tryst, The, opera in one act by Harry Lawrence Freeman; libretto (Eng) by the composer. First performance May 1911, New York, Crescent Theater, Freeman Operatic Duo, with Carlotta Freeman (Wampum) and Hugo Williams (Lone Star).

The setting is a forest in southern Michigan at the time of the pioneers. Lone Star, a young Indian, is looking for Wampum, his beloved. He has eluded his white pursuers. When he hears a commotion in the brush, he hurls his knife and discovers, to his horror, that his target was Wampum, now dead.

Tumble-Down Dick, or, Phaeton in the Suds, ballad opera; libretto (Eng) by Henry Fielding. First performance April 1736, London, Little Theatre in the Haymarket.

A sequel to Fielding's play *Pasquin.* The story includes Mr. Machine, author of the pantomime that is rehearsed. The work also makes fun of *The Fall of Phaeton*, a pantomime by Thomas Arne, with a text by Pritchard (1734, London).

LIBRETTO: English (London: J. Watts, 1736); repr. Rubsamen/*BO*, vol. 9, *The Influence of Pantomime and Harlequinade* (1974).

Tumbledown Dick, or, The Tastes of Time, opera in two acts by Libby Larsen; libretto (Eng) by Vern Sutton, after Fielding. First performance May 16, 1980, Minneapolis.

Tunnel, The, opera in three acts by Hugo Cole; libretto (Eng) by the composer. First performance October 24, 1960, London, John Lewis Auditorium.

Turk and No Turk, comic opera in three acts by Samuel Arnold; libretto (Eng) by George Colman Jr. First performance July 9, 1785, London, Little Theatre in the Haymarket, with Miss George (Emily).

The impoverished Young Ramble disguises himself as a Turk to improve his fortunes, but his deception is discovered. Nonetheless, he finally makes peace with his father.

For a detailed musical description, see Fiske/*ETM*, 475–76.
SCORE: vs (London: Thos. Killern, 1785).

Turkish Lovers, The, comic opera by Michael Rophino Lacy, an adaptation of Rossini's *Il Turco in Italia* (1814, Milan); libretto (Eng), after F. Romani's text. First performance May 1, 1827, London, Drury Lane Theatre.

In the story Zaida has left Turkey for Italy because Selim has not returned her love. Selim shows up and is attracted to the flirtatious Fiorilla, married to Geronio. In the end things are sorted out, and Selim and Zaida return to their homeland.

Turn of the Screw, The, opera in a prologue and two acts by Benjamin Britten; libretto (Eng) by Myfanwy Piper, after the story by Henry James. First performance September 14, 1954, Venice, La Fenice, with Joan Cross (Mrs. Grose), Olive Dyer (Flora), Arda Mandikian (Miss Jessel), Jennifer Vyvyan (the Governess), Peter Pears (Peter Quint), and David Hemmings (Miles); conducted by the composer; produced by Basil Coleman. First U.S. performance March 20, 1958, New York, New York College of Music, 92nd Street Y, Kaufman Concert Hall, with John King (Quint), Irene Sherrock (Miss Jessel), Carolyn Christman (the Governess), Douglas Ahlstedt (Miles), Roxanne Brandt (Flora), Helen Waller (the housekeeper), and Donato Bracco (singer of the prologue); conducted by Siegfried Landau. First professional U.S. performance January 1961, Boston, with Patricia Neway (the Governess), Ruth Kobart (Mrs. Grose), Naomi Farr (Miss Jessel), and Richard Cassilly (Quint); conducted by Julius Rudel; designed by Jac Venza.

In this setting of the James tale, the Governess controls the lives of the orphaned Miles and Flora, who live on an English country estate, Bly. Mrs. Grose, the housekeeper, cannot dispel her sense that there is a mystery about the whole situation. The seemingly innocent children turn out to be haunted by the ghosts of Peter Quint, the former caretaker, and Miss Jessel, the erstwhile governess, and the evil pair are trying to win the children's souls. As the situation worsens, the Governess sends Flora, with Mrs. Grose, to the guardian, but her attempt to have Miles exorcised of the ghost by saying his name kills him.

For detailed descriptions, see *COH*, ed. Patricia Howard (1985); K/*KOB*, 1201–12; K/*NKOB*, 122–27.

Major roles: Governess (sop), Mrs. Grose (sop), Miss Jessel (sop), Peter Quint (ten), Miles (boy sop), and Flora (sop).

Britten uses certain tonalities to represent characters and themes. Each interlude between the scenes contains a variation of the "turning" 12-note theme delineating the opera's title (act 1, scene 1 is entitled "Theme," and the fifteen subsequent scenes are designated "Variation").

BIBLIOGRAPHY: A. E. F. Dickinson, "Britten's New Opera," *MQ* LX (July 1974), 470–78; R. P., "Britten's 'Turn of the Screw' Introduced," *NYT* (Mar. 20, 1958), 34 [on U.S. premiere]; E. Stein, "'The Turn of the Screw' and Its Musical Idiom," *Tempo* XXXIV (1955), 6–14; William Allin Storrer, "'The Turn of the Screw' in Boston," *Opera* XII (Oct. 1961), 648 [on professional U.S. premiere].
DISCOGRAPHY: O. Dyer, J. Vyvyan, A. Mandikian, D. Hemmings, G. Cross, P. Pears, English Opera Group Orch.; cond. B. Britten, London 425672-2 (2 CDs, mono); H. Donath, H. Harper, C. Watson, R. Tear, R. Langridge, Royal Opera (Covent Garden); cond. C. Davis, Philips 410426-1 (2 CDs), 410426-4 (tape); rev. John W. Freeman, "Records," *ON* XLVIII (June 1984), 52.
VIDEO: Donath, Harper, June, Langridge, Tear; cond. Davis, Philips VHS 070 400-3 (1982).

Turn Out!, musical farce in two acts by Matthew King; libretto (Eng) by James Kenney. First performance March 7, 1812, London, Drury Lane Theatre. First U.S. performance December 8, 1813, New York.

Turnpike Gate, The, comic opera in two acts by William Reeve and Joseph Mazzinghi; libretto (Eng) by Thomas Knight. First performance November 14, 1799, London, Covent Garden. First U.S. performance January 5, 1801, Boston, Federal Street Theatre.
SCORE: vs (London, ca. 1799).
LIBRETTO: English (London: Longman, Hurst, Rees, and Orme, 1809).

Twelfth Night, opera in two acts by David Amram; libretto (Eng) by Joseph Papp, after Shakespeare's play. First performance August 1, 1968, Glens Falls, New York, Lake George Opera Festival.

In this story of mistaken identities, Olivia falls in love with Viola, disguised as Cesario; Olivia finally settles for Sebastian, Viola's brother. Viola, meanwhile, loves Orsino, who, in turn, is pursuing Olivia. The situations are further muddled by the interference of Sir Andrew Aguecheek, Sir Toby Belch, and Malvolio, Olivia's steward.

Major roles: Orsino (bar); Feste, the Fool (ten); Viola (mezzo); Sir Toby Belch (bass); Maria (mezzo); Sir Andrew Aguecheek (ten); Olivia (sop); and Malvolio (bar).

For a detailed description, see Eaton/*OP* II, 228–29.

Also incidental music by Henry Rowley Bishop, text revised by Frederick Reynolds, after Shakespeare (1820, London, Covent Garden).
SCORE: vs (New York: C. F. Peters, 1968).
BIBLIOGRAPHY: Shirley Fleming, "David Amram's 'Twelfth Night,'" *HiFi/MA* XVIII (Oct. 1968), 24ff. [on premiere]; review, *NYT* (Aug. 5, 1968), 47 [on premiere].

Twelfth Night, opera in three acts by James Wilson; libretto (Eng) by H. Moulton, after Shakespeare's play. First performance November 1, 1969, Wexford, Wexford Festival; conducted by Hans Waldemar Rosen.

Twelve Hours Trip, The, opera by Halim El-Dabh; libretto (Eng) by the composer. Composed 1972–1973. Not performed.

Part of the trilogy *Ptahmose and the Magic Spell,* which includes *Aton, the Ankh, and the Word** and *The Osiris Ritual.**

Twice in a Blue Moon, opera in one act by Phyllis Tate; libretto (Eng) by Christopher Hassall. First performance May 12, 1969, Farnham, England.

The plot centers on an incident in the life of the landscape painter John Crome (1768–1829). It opens with the poor John and his wife, Pheby, lamenting that they have nothing of value that they can sell at the Norwich Fair. Pheby comes up with the idea to split one of his paintings in two and sell each half as a separate work, a plan he agrees to very reluctantly. The scene moves to the present; a guide is explaining the unusual history of the Crome painting, now restored to its original form and hanging in the National Gallery of Art. When the guide mentions the great monetary worth of the painting, there is a crash, and the painting falls and breaks into two parts. The scene shifts back to the Crome residence in the nineteenth century; the Cromes are preparing to leave for the Norwich Fair but are now very secure financially.

For a description, see Summers/*OOA*, 289–90.

Roles: John Crome (bar), Pheby (mezzo), and museum guide (speaking).

Twice through the Heart, dramatic scena by Mark-Anthony Turnage; libretto (Eng) after poems of Jackie Kay. First performance June 13, 1997, Aldeburgh, Snape Maltings Hall, with Sally Burgess.

The work presents the reminiscences of a woman imprisoned after stabbing her brutal husband to death.

Composed for mezzo-soprano, it consists of a series of flashbacks, which are separated by brief instrumental pieces that comment on the action.

BIBLIOGRAPHY: Andrew Clements, review, *Guardian* (June 16, 1997), 1 [on premiere].

Twin Sisters, The, comic operetta in one act by Alfred B. Sedgwick, after Lecocq's *Giroflé Giroflá* (1874, Brussels); libretto (Eng) by the composer. First performance 1876, New York?

The successful lawyer Frank Duryea turns his attentions to his wife's sister, Lucy, his first love. Marion Duryea, the wronged wife, is able to win back her husband's affections by a plan in which she disguises herself as her sister and acts obnoxiously, thus repulsing Frank. This action is paralleled by the romance of the couple's maid, Nelly, and Peter Gamut, a variety show performer.

Roles: Marion Duryea (sop); Nelly, a servant (mezzo/alto); Peter Gamut, a variety performer (ten); and Frank Duryea, "an eminent lawyer residing on 5th Avenue" (bass).

SCORE: vs (New York: De Witt, 1876); repr. ed. Michael Meckna, *NAMT*, vol. 7 (1994).

Twist of Treason, opera by Julian Livingston; libretto (Eng) by the composer. First performance spring 1979, Freehold, New Jersey, Battleground Arts Center, with Ralph Brown.

The work treats Benedict Arnold's change into a traitor during the Revolution.

Two Cadis, The, comic opera in one act by Julius Eichberg; libretto (Eng) by the composer, with additional lyrics by Dexter Smith. First performance March 5, 1868, Boston, Chickering Hall, with Allen A. Brown (Hassan).

The story, set in Iraq, concerns two cadis who fleece travelers to their region. They are foiled by Hassan, son of the grand vizier, who disguises himself as a servant.

For a detailed description, see Root/*APSM*, 145–48.

SCORE: vs (Boston: Oliver Ditson, 1868).

Two Faces under a Hood, comic opera in three acts by William Shield; libretto (Eng) by Thomas Dibdin. First performance November 17, 1807, London, Covent Garden. First U.S. performance February 22, 1809, Boston, Federal State Theatre.

SCORE: vs (London: Clementi et al., [1807]).

Two Fiddlers, The, opera in two acts "for young people to play and sing" by Peter Maxwell Davies; libretto (Eng) by the composer, after Mackay Brown. First performance June 16, 1978, Kirkwall, Scotland. First U.S. performance April 21, 1979, New York.

Two fiddlers are granted one wish by a group of trolls, with unexpected results.

SCORE: vs (London and New York: Boosey & Hawkes, [1978]).

BIBLIOGRAPHY: Gerard McBurney, review, *Tempo* CXXVI (Sept. 1978), 33–35.

Two Gentlemen of Verona, comic opera in one act by John Laurence Seymour; libretto (Eng) by the composer and H. C. Tracy, after Shakespeare's play (1595). Composed 1937.

Other English settings are by Bishop (incidental music, 1821, London); G. MacDermot (1971, New York); F. Fonesca (1985, Miami); and P. Taylor (1987, Edinburgh).

Two Houses of Granada, The, comic opera by Joseph Wade; libretto (Eng) by the composer. First performance October 31, 1826, London, Drury Lane Theatre.

The work includes the once popular ballad "Meet Me by Moonlight Alone."

Two Imposters, The, opera in one act by Leslie Kondorossy; libretto (Eng) by the composer. First performance (concert) April 10, 1955, Cleveland, WSRS. First performance (stage) October 21, 1956, Cleveland.

The music contains sections in a jazz-like style.

Two in the Bush, opera buffa in one act by Peter Wishart; libretto (Eng) by Don Roberts. First performance June 23, 1959, Birmingham, England, Barber Institute.

A young woman's attempts to prevent her two lovers from meeting fails, with predictable results.

The work is scored for three voices and piano. It includes quotes of various musical styles and cultures. Revised version for orchestra 1962.
BIBLIOGRAPHY: C. Acton, "Belfast," *MT* CIII (June 1962), 410 [on rev. version].

Two Knickerbocker Tales, two one-act operas by Dai-Keong Lee; libretto (Eng) by Robert Healey and the composer. Composed 1957.

Two Misers, The, pastiche comic opera in two acts by Charles Dibdin; libretto (Eng) by Kane O'Hara, after F. de Falbaire's text for Grétry's *Les deux avares* (1770, Fontainebleau). First performance January 21, 1775, London, Covent Garden. First U.S. performance March 14, 1783, Baltimore.

Set in Smyrna, it concerns young lovers, Harriet and Lively; they are abused by their miserly relatives, who have fled their homeland because of their shady dealings. When the misers, Hunks and Gripes, plan to rob the grave of a Mufti because they are sure it contains a considerable amount of treasure, Harriet's faithful servant, Jenny, gives Harriot a key to her uncle Gripe's safe that contains Harriet's jewels.

Also set by G. von Baumgarten (1778, Breslau) and J. A. Hiller (1779, Leipzig?), as *Das Grab des Mufti, oder, Die zwey Geizigen.*
SCORE: vs (London: John Johnston, [1775]).
LIBRETTO: English (London: Whittingham and Arliss, 1816).

Two Sisters, The, opera in three acts by Cyril Rootham; libretto (Eng) by Marjorie Fausset, after the ballad *The Twa Sisters o'Binnorie.* First performance February 14, 1922, Cambridge, New Theatre.

Two Tickets to Omaha, or, Perfidy Compounded, comic opera in one act by Roger Hannay; libretto (Eng) by Jerome Lamb. First performance July 21, 1960, Moorhead, Minnesota, Concordia College Opera Theater.

Two to One, comic opera in three acts by Samuel Arnold; libretto (Eng) by George Colman Jr. First performance June 19, 1784, London, Little Theatre in the Haymarket.

One of the work's numbers is the famed "Yankee Doodle."

For a detailed musical description, see Fiske/*ETM*, 474.
LIBRETTO: English (London: Harrison & Co., 1784).

Tyrolese Peasant, The, domestic opera in two acts by Henry Rowley Bishop; libretto (Eng) by John Howard Payne. First performance May 8, 1832, London, Drury Lane Theatre.

Tzigaine, "Russian" comic opera by Reginald De Koven; libretto (Eng) by Harry B. Smith. First performance May 16, 1895, New York, Abbey's Theatre, with Lillian Russell.

About the enduring love between a Russian gypsy, Vera, and a wellborn officer.

U

Ubu, opera by Andrew Toovey; libretto (Eng) by Michael Finnissy and the composer, after Alfred Jarry's *Ubu roi* (1896). First performance September 23, 1992, Cardiff, Music Theatre Wales, with Richard Morris (Pa Ubu) and Gale Otley (Ma Ubu); conducted by Michael Rafferty. First London performance October 5, 1992, Queen Elizabeth Hall.

About the abuses of authority by a pompous bourgeois character, Pa Ubu, who, urged on by his wife, Ma Ubu, kills the king and brings ruin to the country.

BIBLIOGRAPHY: Andrew Clements, review, *Opera* XLIII (Oct. 1992), 1362–63 [on premiere]; Gavin Thomas, "Opera Nasty," *MT* CXXXIII (Dec. 1992), 656 [on London premiere].

Ubu Roi, "opera pataphysica" in three acts by Denis ApIvor; libretto (Eng) by the composer, after Jarry. Composed 1966–1967.

Also set by F. Hummel, as *König Ubü* (1984, Salzburg); K. Penderecki, as *Ubu Rex* (1991, Munich).

Ulysses, opera in three acts by John Christopher Smith; libretto (Eng) by Samuel Humphreys, after Homer's *Odyssey*, Books 16–24. First performance April 16, 1733, London, Lincoln's Inn Fields. Revived 1963, London; directed by Charles Farncombe.

A setting of the familiar story, in which Ulysses comes back home suddenly and confides in his son, Telemachus, that he will hide in order to see if his wife is faithful. He steps forward in the third act and dispatches Penelope's suitors.

For a detailed musical description, see Fiske/*ETM*, 138–42.

Roles: Antinous, Antiope, Penelope, Telemachus, and Ulysses.

Among the work's numbers are Penelope's siciliano "O God of Sleep" (act 1) and her "Say I to His Commands Resign" (act 3). It was performed but once during the composer's lifetime.

SCORE: ms. score of overture, recitative, aria (Hamburg, Staats- und Universitätsbibliothek Carl Von Ossietzky, M A/279).

Uncle Remus, unfinished opera by Henry F. Gilbert; libretto (Eng) by Charles Johnson, after Joel Chandler Harris's story. Composed 1905–1907.

The work uses themes from spirituals, slave songs, and tunes from the West Indies.

BIBLIOGRAPHY: Katherine and Rey M. Longyear, "Henry F. Gilbert's Unfinished 'Uncle Remus' Opera," *Yearbook of Inter-American Musical Research* X (1974), 50–67.

Uncle Tom's Cabin, domestic drama in six acts, with music by George Howard; text (Eng) a dramatization by George L. Aiken, after Harriet Beecher Stowe's novel (1852). First performance September 27, 1852, Troy, New York, with G. C. Germon (Uncle Tom), Caroline Fox Howard (Topsy), Cordelia Howard (Eva), and George Howard (St. Clare).

The work followed Stowe's novel about the cruelties of slavery quite closely, but Aiken added two comic characters common to the period, a Yankee and a Quaker.

Among the musical tunes are those specific to the story and the well-known "Old Folks at Home." Its "St. Clare to Little Eva in Heaven" is quite like the Italian opera numbers in currency at the time.

SCORE AND TEXT: vs, English (New York and London: Samuel French, [1852]); repr. ed. Thomas Riis, *NAMT*, vol. 5 (1994).

Uncle Tom's Cabin, opera by Caryl Florio; libretto (Eng) by H. Wayne Ellis, after Stowe. First performance 1882, Philadelphia.
LIBRETTO: English ([New York: Brentano Bros.], ca. 1882).

Uncle Tom's Cabin, opera in three acts by Leslie Grossmith; libretto (Eng) by A. M. Stephen, after Stowe. Composed 1928.

Uncle Tom's Cabin, opera by Avery Claflin; libretto (Eng) by Dorothea Claflin, after Stowe. First performance 1964, New York, Metropolitan Opera Studio.

Also a musical, as *Topsy and Eva*, with songs composed and performed by the Duncan Sisters (1924, New York).

Undertaker, The, opera in one act by John Purser; libretto (Eng) by the composer. First performance September 1, 1969, Edinburgh, Edinburgh Festival, Gateway Theatre.

An undertaker's shop doubles as a wine cellar, with unexpected results.
BIBLIOGRAPHY: Conrad Wilson, *Scottish Opera* (London: Collins, 1972), 125–27, 162.

Under the Arbor, opera by Robert Greenleaf; libretto (Eng) by the composer and Marian Motley Carache, after her short story. First performance October 16, 1992, Birmingham, Alabama, Birmingham Civic Center, Auburn and Alabama Symphony, with Sunny Joy Langton, Mark Calkins, Ruby Hinds, Claudia Cummings, Carmen Balthrop, and Bruce Hall; conducted by Paul Polivnick.

The opera takes place in the small southern town of Chattahoochee. It involves a pair of teenager cousins who are attracted to each other. They are freed from the guilt that their first kiss engenders by the black fortune-teller Madame Queen.
BIBLIOGRAPHY: Thomas C. Willis, review, *ON* LVII (Jan. 30, 1993), 41 [on premiere].

Under the Double Moon, opera in two acts by Anthony Davis; libretto (Eng) by Deborah Atherton. First performance July 15, 1989, St. Louis, Opera Theatre, with Cynthia Clarey (Kanaxa), Jake Gardner (Gaxulta), John Duykers (Krillig), Thomas Young (the Inspector), Ai-Lan Zhu (Xola), and Eugene Perry (Tarj); conducted by William McGlaughlin.

The science fiction plot concerns the mythical watery planet Undine. The fisherman Krillig and his wife, the fortune-telling Kanaxa, have twins, Xola and Tarj, who are telepathic. The children meet Gaxulta, a man who has been transformed into an amphibious creature and who says that he, not Krillig, is their real father. When the Inspector, sent by the Empress, tries to kidnap the children so that their youthful powers can keep the Empress from dying, he is swept away by the sea.

For a detailed description, see Kornick/*RAO*, 78–79.

Major roles: Kanaxa (mezzo), Xola (sop), Tarj (bar), the Inspector (ten), and Gaxulta (bar).
SCORE: vs (New York: E. Schuberth, 1897).
BIBLIOGRAPHY: Tim Page, "A Change of Pace," *ON* LIII (June 1989), 24, 26, 28–29; William Weaver, "In Review," *ON* LIV (Sept. 1989), 53 [on premiere].

Under the Oak, or, The London Shepherdess, vaudeville opera in one act by Henry Rowley Bishop; libretto (Eng) by Edward Fitzball, after John Burgoyne's *The Maid of the Oaks*,* set by Barthelemon (1774, London). First performance June 25, 1830, London, Vauxhall Gardens.

Under Western Eyes, opera in three acts by John Joubert; libretto (Eng) by Cedric Cliffe, after the novel by Joseph Conrad. First performance May 29, 1969, London, St. Pancras Town Hall.

After a revolutionary student is disloyal to a colleague, his conscience leads him to confess to a wrongdoing and be punished for it.

SCORE: vs (London: Novello, [1968]).

Undine, lyric tone poem in one scene by Harriet Ware; libretto (Eng) by Edwin Markham, after de La Motte Fouqué's tale (1811). First performance May 19, 1923, Baltimore, Peabody Conservatory.

When the sea nymph Undine chooses human companionship with Prince Hildebrand in order to win a soul, she endures unhappiness and suffering.

For women's voices, soprano and tenor solo, with accompaniment of orchestra and piano solo.

Among the many settings of the tale are F. Kauer, as *Das Donauweibchen* (1798, Vienna); E. T. A. Hoffmann (1816, Berlin); K. F. Girschner (Berlin, 1830); A. Lortzing (1845, Magdeburg); A. Dargomyzhsky, as *Rusalka* (1856, St. Petersburg); F. Mori, as *The River-Sprite** (1865, London); A. Dvořák, as *Rusalka* (1901, Prague); W. Fortner (1969, Ober Hambach, Ger.); and S. Barab, as *Ondine** (1995, New York).

SCORE: vs (Cincinnati: J. Church, [1915]).

Undivine Comedy, chamber opera in two acts by Michael Finnissy; libretto (Eng) by the composer, after Zygmunt Krasinski's drama *Nieboska komedia* (1835), Friedrich Hölderlin, and the Marquis De Sade. First performance May 1988, Paris. First British performance July 3, 1988, London, Almeida Opera, with Richard Jackson (Count), Nigel Robson (Leader), and Mary King (Muse).

The work concerns the struggle between art and revolution.

It is scored for five singers and nine instrumentalists.

BIBLIOGRAPHY: Andrew Clements, review, *MT* CXXIX (1988), 330–32 [on premiere]; Noël Goodwin, review, *ON* LIII (Mar. 18, 1989), 37 [on British premiere].

Unexpected Visitor, The, opera in one act by Leslie Kondorossy; libretto (Eng) by Julia Kemeny, the composer, and Shawn Hall (Elizabeth Davis), after a short story by Julia Kemeny. First performance October 21, 1956, Cleveland.

Unicorn in the Garden, The, opera in one act by Russell Smith; libretto (Eng), after James Thurber's *Fables for Our Time.* First performance May 1, 1957, Hartford, Connecticut, Julius Hartt College.

A husband wakes up, goes into the kitchen, and sees a unicorn in the garden. He is unable to convince his wife of what he has seen. Believing her husband has become crazy, she calls a policeman and a psychiatrist. When they arrive, the wife recounts the story; as a result, however, she is put into a straitjacket and led away, the husband declaring that he knows that unicorns do not exist.

For a plot description, see Summers/*OOA*, 283–84.

Roles: the husband (bar), the wife (col sop), the policeman (bar), and the psychiatrist (mezzo).

Unicorn, the Gorgon, and the Manticore, The, or, The Three Sundays of a Poet, madrigal fable in one act by Gian Carlo Menotti for chorus, ten dancers, and nine instrumentalists; libretto (Eng) by the composer. First performance (concert) October 21, 1956, Washington, D.C., Coolidge Auditorium, with Talley Beatty (the unicorn), Loren Hightower (the Count), and Gemze De Lappe (the Countess); conducted by Paul Callaway; choreographed by John Butler; produced by the composer.

In this symbolic tale, the Man in the Castle, who has no use for society, creates a scandal when he shows up on a Sunday with a white unicorn. Disparagement by the community soon turns to approval, with the lead taken by the Count and Countess, who get their own unicorn, as do other townspeople. The Man is soon bored, however, and repeats the process using first a gorgon and then a manticore, with the Count and Countess and the others following the same pattern. Since the animals have disappeared, the townspeople suspect the Man of having done them in and rush toward the castle in indignation. There they find the Man on his deathbed, being attended to by the three loving creatures.

SCORE: vs (New York: G. Ricordi & Co., 1956).

BIBLIOGRAPHY: Constance Mellers, "Beastes among the Books," *ON* XXI (Dec. 3, 1956), 14 [on premiere].

DISCOGRAPHY: Paul Hill Chorale, Golden Crest CRS 4180 (1978, 1 LP); Boston Cecilia, Newport Classics 85621 (1997, Newport, R.I., 1 CD).

United States: Parts I–IV, multimedia work by Laurie Anderson. First performance February 3–4, 5–6, 7–8, 9–10, 1982, Brooklyn, New York, Academy of Music, Next Wave Festival.

The collage follows the themes of politics, money, travel, and love.

The work includes the song "Difficult Listening Hour," which has a reference to William S. Burroughs, and "Language Is a Virus."

DISCOGRAPHY: Warner Bros 25192-1 (5 LPs).

University Greys, The, opera by Arthur Kreutz; libretto (Eng) by Zoë Schiller, after the historical account by Maud Morrow Brown. First performance March 15, 1954, Clinton, Mississippi.

The work is set at an army camp at the University of Mississippi during the Civil War.

Roles: Margaret Meadows and Dora McCrea, the mothers (sop, mezzo); Boone McCrea (bar); Laura Meadows (sop); and Lochvinar, Professor of Astronomy and Classical Languages (bar).

Unknown Guest, The, "opera" by Michael Kelly; libretto (Eng) by Samuel J. Arnold. First performance March 29, 1815, London, Drury Lane Theatre.

Unmusical Impresario, The, musical comedy in one act by Katherine Davis; libretto (Eng) by the composer and Heddie Root Kent. First performed as *The Disappointed Impresario*, July 15, 1955, Duxbury, Massachusetts, Plymouth Rock Center of Music and Art.

The action concerns the doings at the studio of Madame's School of Opera.

SCORE: vs (New York: G. Schirmer, [1956]).

Unto These Hills, opera by Jack Kilpatrick; libretto (Eng) by the composer, after Kermit Hunter's drama (1950). First performance July 1, 1950, Cherokee, North Carolina.

About the Cherokees in North Carolina.

Up All Night, or, The Smuggler's Cave, comic opera in three acts by Matthew King; libretto (Eng) by Samuel J. Arnold. First performance June 26, 1809, London, English Opera at the Lyceum, with Charles E. Horn.

Up from Paradise, musical play in two acts by Stanley Silverman; libretto (Eng), after Arthur Miller's play *The Creation of the World and Other Business* (1972). First performance summer 1974, Ann Arbor, Michigan. Revivals include 1977, Washington, D.C., Kennedy Center; 1983, New York, Jewish Repertory Theater.

A seriocomical treatment of the Book of Genesis.

Up to Town, comic opera in three acts by William Reeve, Henry Condell, Thomas Welsh, and John Whitaker; libretto (Eng) by Thomas Dibdin. First performance November 6, 1811, London, Convent Garden.

LIBRETTO: English (London: J. Barker, [1811?]).

Utopia Limited, or, The Flowers of Progress, comic opera in two acts by Arthur S. Sullivan; libretto (Eng) by William S. Gilbert. First performance October 7, 1893, London, Savoy Theatre, with Rutland Barrington (King Paramount), Scott Russell (Lord Dramaleigh), Charles Kenningham (Captain Fitzbattleaxe), Lawrence Grindley (Captain Sir Edward Corcoran), Scott Fische (Mr. Goldbury), Herbert Ralland (Mr. Blushington), Nancy McIntosh (Princess Zara), Emmie Owen (Princess Nekaya), Florence Perry (Princess Kalyba), and Rosina Brandram (Lady Sophy). First U.S. performance May 26, 1894, New York., with Mr. Peterkin (Captain Corcoran), J. J. Dallas, Kate Talby, and Clinton Elder.

The title refers to an island in the South Pacific that is ruled by the kindly Paramount the First. He sends his daughter Zara to England to be educated, and her sisters take as their model the actions of Lady Sophy, an English governess in residence on the island. When Zara returns, with six British "flowers of progress" in tow, including Captain Corcoran, her ideas for reform lead to chaos until she suggests that Utopia become a limited monarchy. Everyone is then satisfied.

For a detailed description, see Stedman/*WSG*, 288–97; Jacobs/*AS*, 352–56.

Major roles: King Paramount; Princess Zara; Princess Nekaya; Princess Kalyba; Lady Sophy; and six "flowers of progress": Lord Dramaleigh, a British Lord Chamberlain; Captain Fitzbattleaxe, of the First Life Guards; Captain Sir Edward Corcoran; Mr. Goldbury; Sir Bailey Barre; and Mr. Blushington.

Ut Pictora Poesis! or, The Enraged Musician, all-sung afterpiece by Samuel Arnold; libretto (Eng) by George Colman Sr., after Hogarth's print. First performance May 18, 1789, London, Little Theatre in the Haymarket, with Mrs. Bannister (Castruccina), and Mrs. Plomer (Piccolina). First U.S. performance, as *The Enraged Musician*, March 14, 1803, Philadelphia, Chestnut Street Theatre.

Castruccio, an Italian singing teacher, becomes enraged by the noise from the street outside his window, which disrupts his music lessons with Castruccina and Piccolina.

For a description, see Fiske/*ETM*, 558.

The work includes a quote from F. Bertoni's *Demofoonte* (1778, London), sung in falsetto by the singing teacher.

Uzziah, grand opera by Harry Lawrence Freeman; libretto (Eng) by the composer. Composed 1931.

V

Vagabond Queen, The, musical tale in one act by Edward Barnes; libretto (Eng) by the composer. First performance April 22, 1989, Los Angeles, McPherson College. SCORE: ms score (1988, NYPL).

Valdo, grand opera in one act and intermezzo by Harry Lawrence Freeman; libretto (Eng) by the composer. First performance May 1906, Cleveland, Weisgerber's Hall, Grand Opera Company, with Katherine Skeene Mitchel (Dulcinea), Dazalia Underwood (Axella), Walter Revels (Valdo), and Walter Randolph (Xerifa); conducted by the composer.

The setting is Mexico. Valdo, an intelligent young man who was kidnapped as an infant, is now a welcome guest at the home of the beautiful Dulcinea. He runs afoul of Xerifa, a shadowy mariner who is Dulcinea's fiance. Before the two men duel, Valdo gives Dulcinea an unusual locket, which she is to keep in the event of his death. When Dulcinea opens the locket and reads the enclosed message, she calls out Valdo's first name. He turns and, caught off guard, is stabbed fatally by Xerifa. Axella, Dulcinea's confidante, cries out that Xerifa has, in fact, murdered Dulcinea's lost-long brother.

VALIS (Vast Active Living Intelligent System), opera in two parts by Tod Machover; libretto (Eng) by the composer, Catherine Ikam, and Bill Raymond, after Philip K. Dick's novel. First performance December 1, 1987, Paris, Pompidou Center (in French). First U.S. performance (in English) February 1988 (concert), Cambridge, Massachusetts, MIT Experimental Media Facility.

In this psychological drama, the events are explained by the narrator, Philip K. Dick, whose split personality is personified by Horselover Fat, plagued by mystical visions. They include his despair over the suicide of his friend Gloria, his interpretation of a rock song by Eric and Linda Lampton, called "VALIS," and his conjuring up of the ethereal Sophia, perhaps another version of Gloria. In the end Sophia disappears, and Fat is left with his visions, while Phil is more at peace with himself, having heard a wonderful song (based on the music of Gloria in part one) that seems to be Sophia's good-bye to him.

For a detailed description, see Kornick/*RAO*, 180–82.

Major roles: Horselover Fat/Philip K. Dick, narrator (bar); Gloria (mezzo); Dr. Stone (bass); Linda Lampton (sop); Eric Lampton (bar); and Sophia (sop).

Vanessa, opera in four acts by Samuel Barber; libretto (Eng) by Gian Carlo Menotti. First performance January 15, 1958, New York, Metropolitan Opera, with Eleanor Steber (Vanessa), Rosalind Elias (Erika), Regina Resnik (the Baroness), Nicolai Gedda (Anatol), Giorgio Tozzi (the Doctor), George Cehanovsky (Nicholas), and Robert Nagy (a footman); conducted by Dimitri Mitropoulos; staged by Menotti; designed by Cecil Beaton. Revised as three acts in 1964 (with acts 1 and 2 combined); first performance March 13, 1965, New York, Metropolitan Opera; conducted by William Steinberg. It was revived on May 27, 1979, at the Spoleto Festival U.S.A. in Charleston, South Carolina, and broadcast over WNET on January 31, 1979, with Johanna Meier (Vanessa),

Katherine Ciesinski (Erika), Henry Price (Anatol), Alice Garrott (the Baroness), William Bender (Nicholas), and Irwin Densen (the Doctor); conducted by Christopher Keene.

The opera opens at Vanessa's country estate "in a northern country about 1905." Vanessa, an aging beauty living with her disapproving mother, the Baroness, has waited for twenty years for her lover to return. The young Anatol arrives and discloses that he is her lover's son, and that his father, also called Anatol, has died. Vanessa becomes drawn to Anatol, as does her niece, Erika.

Erika tells the Baroness, her grandmother, that she has become pregnant by Anatol, but she refuses his offer of marriage, since he cannot say he will always love her. Anatol weds the lovestruck Vanessa instead. They go off to Paris, leaving Erika alone to wait for her true love, much as had Vanessa before her.

For a detailed plot description, see K/*NKOB*, 19–20.

Major roles: Vanessa, a lady of great beauty in her late thirties (sop); Anatol, a handsome young man in his early twenties (ten); Erika, her niece, a young girl of twenty (mezzo); the old Baroness, Vanessa's mother (alto); the old Doctor (bar); and Nicholas, the major domo (bass).

Among the musical highlights of the work are Erika's ballad "Must the Winter Come So Soon," Vanessa's aria "Do Not Utter a Word," and the canonic quintet of the last act, "To Leave, to Break, to Find, to Keep," sung by Vanessa, Anatol, Erika, the Doctor, and the Baroness. The orchestral interlude between the first two acts is performed on occasion as a concert piece.

Barber received the Pulitzer Prize for the work in 1958, and it was the first American opera to be performed at the Salzburg Festival (1958).

SCORE: vs (New York: G. Schirmer, [1958]).

LIBRETTO: English (New York: G. Schirmer, [1957]).

BIBLIOGRAPHY: Raymond Ericson, "'Vanessa'—The New Samuel Barber Opera," *Opera America* V (1958), 116–27; Hans Heinsheimer, "Vanessa Revisited," *ON* XLII (May 1978), 23–25; Harriet Johnson, "'Vanessa' on TV; Splendid," *New York Post* (Jan. 31, 1979). DISCOGRAPHY: cast of premiere, Metropolitan Opera; cond. D. Mitropoulos, RCA ARL2-2094 (2 LPs), rereleased as RCA Gold Seal 7899-2-RG (2 CDs).

Van Gogh Video Opera, multimedia opera by Michael Gordon; libretto (Eng), after the letters of Vincent Van Gogh. Video by Elliot Caplan. First performance July 1991, New York, Bang on a Can.

The work examines the inner life of the famous artist via his letters to his brother Theo.

BIBLIOGRAPHY: Kyle Gann, *Village Voice*, review (July 9, 1991), 36 [on premiere].

Van Hunks and the Devil, opera by Albert Coates; libretto (Eng). First performance 1952, Cape Town.

Vanishing Bridegroom, The, opera in three acts by Judith Weir; libretto (Eng) by the composer, after *Popular Tales of the West Highlands* (1890) and *Carmina Gadelica*. First performance October 17, 1990, Glasgow, Scotland, Scottish Opera, with Virginia Kerr (bride/wife/ mother), Peter Snipp (bridegroom/husband/father), and Robert Poulton (the stranger); conducted by Alan Hacker. First U.S. performance June 2, 1992, St. Louis, Opera Theatre, with Lauren Flanigan (bride/wife/mother), John Brandstetter (bridegroom/husband/father), Brad Cresswell (bride's lover/husband's friend/preacher), Andrew Wentzel (the stranger), and Julie Parks (the daughter); conducted by Scott Bergeson; directed by Francesca Zambello.

The stories deal with greed, abandonment, lust, and escape. They center around a young bride and the acts of generosity, propriety, and evil that follow her pledge to her beloved.

In the first part, "The Inheritance," the bride is treated harshly by both her husband and her lover. In the second, "The Disappearance," she has a baby and is abandoned by her husband, who goes off to the world of the evil fairies. In the third, "The Stranger," the child has become a young woman, and the stranger (devil) tries to become her bridegroom; she is warned by a preacher and finds safety in a holy spot.

BIBLIOGRAPHY: Rodney Milnes, review, *Opera* XLI (1990), 1496–1500 [on premiere]; Edward Rothstein, "A Scottish Opera Has U.S. Premiere in St. Louis," *NYT* (June 4, 1992), C, 13, 17; Patrick J. Smith, "St. Louis," *ON* LVII (Nov. 1992), 52 [on U.S. premiere].

Veil, The, opera in one act by Bernard Rogers; libretto (Eng) by Robert Lawrence. First performance May 18, 1950, Bloomington, Indiana, Indiana University, with Juliana Larson, Pete Smith, and Lee Fiser; conducted by Ernst Hoffman; directed by Hans Busch.

In the story, which takes place in nineteenth-century London, Lucinda has been put into a madhouse by her brother, who hopes thereby to cheat her out of her inheritance. The young Dr. Keane saves her from thinking she is insane, but she is hounded by Dr. Betts, director of the institution, who has fallen in love with her and tries to make her marry him in a grotesque ceremony. Dr. Betts then strangles her with the veil that was to be part of her bridal outfit.

For a detailed description, see Eaton/*OP* I, 232.

Major roles: Lucinda (sop), Mrs. Frohn (alto), Dr. Betts (bar), and Dr. Keane (ten).

BIBLIOGRAPHY: Paul Nettl, review, *MA* LXX (June 1950), 11 [on premiere].

Veiled Prophet of Khorassan, The, romantic opera in three acts by Charles Stanford; original (Eng) libretto (Eng) by W. Barclay Squire, after Moore's *Lalla Rookh*, translated into German and performed as *Der verschleierte Profet* by Ernst Frank. First performance February 6, 1881, Hanover, Germany, with Miss Börs (Zelica) and Mr. Nollett (Mocanna). First British performance (in an Italian translation by G. A. Mazzucato) July 26, 1893, London, Covent Garden, with Lillian Nordica (Zelica), Mario Ancona (Mocanna), Francesco Vigna (Azim), and Lucille Hill (Fatima).

In the tale the prophet, Mocanna, wears a veil to hide his ugliness.

SCORE: vs (London: Boosey, [1893?]).

BIBLIOGRAPHY: [J. A. Fuller-Maitland], review, *MT* (Mar. 1881) [on premiere].

Vendetta, grand opera in three acts by Harry Lawrence Freeman; libretto (Eng) by the composer. First performance November 12, 1923, New York, Lafayette Theater, Negro Grand Opera Company, with Carlotta Freeman (Donna Carlotta), Cecil de Silva (Zanita), Louise Mallory (Maria), Marie Woodby (Inez), E. Taylor Gordon (Alonzo), and Valdo Freeman (Don Castro); conducted by the composer.

Set in Mexico, the story concerns Alonzo, a famous toreador, who is vying, with the overlord Don Castro, for the hand of Donna Carlotta. When Don Castro accuses Alonzo of being the son of a lowly herder, Alonzo wounds his accuser and escapes. When he returns to take Donna Carlotta with him, Alonzo is killed by the lurking Abdullah, Don Castro's Arab attendant.

SCORE: vs, with libretto (English) (New York?: Negro Grand Opera Co., 1923).

Vengeance of Faery, The, opera in three acts by Fritz Hart; libretto (Eng) by the composer. Composed 1947.

Venus, "one-act jungle opera," by Jacques Van Rhijn, to the libretto of John Blow's masque (see next entry). First performance October 4, 1997, London.
BIBLIOGRAPHY: David Blewitt, review, *Opera* XLVIII (Dec. 1997), 1512–13 [on premiere].

Venus and Adonis, opera in a prologue and three acts by John Blow; anonymous librettist (Eng). First performance ca. 1683 (see Bibliography), London or Windsor Court, with Mary Davies (Venus) and Lady Mary Tudor (Cupid). Revived April 17, 1684, Chelsea.
    A telling of the Venus and Adonis myth, in which the human Adonis is killed by a boar while on a hunt. The work is through-composed and has no spoken dialogue, and it ends with the striking chorus in G minor, "Mourn for Thy Servant." The work is considered the earliest extant English opera.
SCORE: ms score (British Museum, MS Add. 22100); fs ed. G. E. P. Arkwright, Old English Edition, vol. 25 (London: J. Williams, 1902); fs ed. Anthony Lewis (Paris: Editions de L'Oiseau Lyre, 1939; Monaco, 1949); fs score ed. Clifford Bartlett (Redcroft, Engl.: King's Music, 1984).
BIBLIOGRAPHY: Richard Luckett, "A New Source for *Venus and Adonis,*" *MT* CXXX (Feb. 1989), 76–79.
DISCOGRAPHY: Ritchie, Field-Hyde, Cooper, Ellis, Clinton, Frost, Cynfelin, Ensemble Orchestral de L'Oiseau-Lyre, London 50004 (LP); Argenta, Dawson, Varcoe, London Baroque Ensemble; cond. Medlam, Harmonia Mundi HMC-90.1276 (CD).

Venus and Adonis, all-sung masque by John Pepusch; libretto (Eng) by Colley Cibber. First performance March 12, 1715, London, Drury Lane Theatre, with Mrs. Barbier (Venus) and Margherita L'Epine (Adonis). Revived September 17, 1980, Nottingham, Holme Pierrepont Hall.
    Major roles: Venus (sop), Adonis (sop), and Mars (ten/bass).
    The music has a definite Italian flavoring, complete with an Italian overture and fourteen of the fifteen arias in da capo form. The musical highlight is Adonis' parting solo, "O Welcome Gentle Death."
    For a detailed musical description, see Fiske/*ETM*, 56–58.
    Story also set by H. W. Henze as *Venus und Adonis* (1997, Berlin).
LIBRETTO: English (London: B. Lintott, 1715).

Venus, Cupid, and Hymen, masque by Seedo; libretto (Eng). First performance May 21, 1733, London, Drury Lane Theatre, with Mrs. Seedo (Maria Manina).

Venus in Africa, operatic fantasy in three scenes by George Antheil; libretto (Eng) by Michael Dyne. First performance May 24, 1957, Denver, University Theatre. Revived October 1970, St. Paul, with Alexandra Hunt (Venus), Sondra Harnes (Yvonne), and Harrison Somers (Charles); conducted by Raymond Cutting.
    The story follows a pair of lovers, Charles and Yvonne, who go to Tunisia, fight, leave each other, and get back together again because of the efforts of the goddess of love.
BIBLIOGRAPHY: Philip Gainsley, review, *ON* XXXV (Dec. 12, 1970), 31 [on 1970 revival].

Vera of Las Vegas, "nightmare cabaret" in one act by Daron Hagen; libretto (Eng) by Paul Muldoon. First performance March 8, 1996, Las Vegas, Nevada, Artemus Ham Concert Hall, University of Nevada Opera Theatre; conducted by Donna Plotz; directed by the composer.
    In the surreal story, two illegal aliens, Taco and Dumdum, stop in Las Vegas on their way to Los Angeles. They are set up by Doll, a former blackjack dealer, who now is a rogue INS agent, and her friend Vera, a transvestite lap dancer.
    Major roles: Taco (ten), Dumdum (bar), Doll (sop), and Vera (counterten).

Vercingétorix, or, Love and Patriotism, lyric drama in three acts by Henri Kowalski; libretto (Eng) by Joshua Lake. First performance April 1, 1881, Sydney, in a French version by M. Mainiel; September 24, 1881, Melbourne, Town Hall, in the English version.

About the title character, who led the revolt against Caesar's armies in Gaul in 52 B.C.
LIBRETTO: English (Melbourne: W. H. Williams, 1881).

Vercingetorix, opera in one act by Michael Smolanoff; libretto (Eng) by Frank McQuilkin. Composed 1973.
SCORE: vs (New York: Seesaw Music, 1973).

Vertumnus and Pomona, opera by Michael Arne; libretto (Eng) by Matthew Feilde. First performance February 21, 1782, London, Covent Garden.

Vessel, opera epic by Meredith Monk. First performance (part 3) October 1971, New York, Wooster Street parking lot, with members of The House
The work is scored for seventy-five voices, electronic organ, dulcimer, and accordion.
DISCOGRAPHY: M. Monk, R. Een, ECM new series 78118-21482-2 (1992, CD).

Veteran Soldier, The, or, The Farmer's Sons, comic opera in three acts by Thomas S. Cooke, John Whitaker, and J. Perry; libretto (Eng) by Edward P. Knight. First performance February 23, 1822, London, Drury Lane Theatre.

Veteran Tar, The, comic opera in two acts by Samuel Arnold, after Gaveaux's *Le petit matelot* (1796, Paris); libretto (Eng) by the composer, after Pigault-Lebrun's text. First performance January 29, 1801, London, Drury Lane Theatre. First U.S. performance November 24, 1802, New York, Park Theatre.
LIBRETTO: English (London: J. Barker, 1801).

Vicar of Bray, The, operetta by Edward Solomon; libretto (Eng) by William S. Gilbert. First performance July 22, 1882, London, Globe Theatre. Revised version, with a new libretto by Sydney Grundy, January 28, 1892, London, with Rutland Barrington (Rev. William Barlow). First U.S. performance of the original October 1882, New York, Fifth Avenue Theatre.

A vicar is blackmailed into letting his daughter choose the husband she desires.

Viceroy, The, comic opera in three acts by Victor Herbert; libretto (Eng) by Harry B. Smith. First performance February 12, 1900, San Francisco, Columbia Theatre; repeated April 30, 1900, New York, Knickerbocker Theatre, with Henry Clay Barnabee (the viceroy), Helen Bertram (Tivolini), Grace Cameron (Beatrice), Frank Rushworth (Luigi), and Marcia Van Dresser (Fioretta).

The setting is sixteenth-century Venice. The viceroy holds his position under false pretenses after stealing the throne from his cousin, the pirate chief Tivolini. Tivolini eventually regains his throne and his beloved, Beatrice, and generously agrees to share his rule with his dishonest cousin.

For a detailed description, see Waters/*VH*, 162–64.

The musical highlights include Tivolini's serenade "Hear Me"; the love song "Just for Today," which the fisherman Luigi sings to Fioretta, daughter of the viceroy; and Beatrice's serious "The Robin and the Rose."
SCORE: vs (New York: Witmark, 1900).

Vicious Square, The, opera-masque in two acts by Felix Werder; libretto (Eng) by Peter Rorke. Composed 1971. Not performed.

Victorian, opera in four acts by Julian Edwards; libretto (Eng) by J. F. R. Anderson, after Longfellow's *The Spanish Student*. First performance March 6, 1883, London.
SCORE: vs (London: Hutchings & Romer, [n.d.]).

Victorine, opera in three acts by Alfred Mellon; libretto (Eng) by Edmund Falconer. First performance December 19, 1859, London, Covent Garden, with Charles Santley (Julien) and Euphrosyne Parepa (Victorine).
LIBRETTO: English ([Royal English Opera] Theatre, [1859]).

Victory, opera in three acts by Richard Rodney Bennett; libretto (Eng) by Beverley Cross, after the novel by Joseph Conrad. First performance April 13, 1970, London, Covent Garden, with Donald McIntyre (Heyst), Anne Howells (Lena), John Lanigan (Mr. Jones), Inia Te Wiata (Schomberg), and Ava June (Frau Schomberg); conducted by Edward Downes; produced by Colin Graham.

In the story, the noble and generous Axel Heyst has been exiled to the South Seas. He assists the troubled Lena, who is pursued by the lecherous Schomberg, manager of the hotel where she worked. When Schomberg tells the unscrupulous Jones that Heyst has hidden a treasure on his island, Jones leads a marauding band who kill Lena, who is trying to save herself and her beloved. Their love and the new directions they have taken represent the victory of the title.
BIBLIOGRAPHY: review, *NYT* (Apr. 26, 1970), II, 19 [on premiere].

Victory at Masada, The, opera in one act by Martin Kalmanoff; libretto (Eng) by the composer. First performance November 10, 1968, Detroit, Detroit Symphony and Opera.

The setting is in Masada, in southern Israel, in 1967 and in A.D. 73. During the war of 1967 in the Middle East, Rachel, Jacob, Aaron, and Rabbi Eleazar recall the events of Masada during Roman control in the first century, during which the entire populace of Masada killed themselves rather than submit to the Romans. The tale is told to the young Israelis by Flavius Joseph, who went over to the Roman side because he was a coward.

For a detailed description, see Eaton/*OP* II, 329.

Major roles: Rachel (sop), Jacob (ten/bar), Aaron (ten), Flavius Joseph (bar), and Rabbi Eleazar (speaking).

Videomania, "musical something or other" by Martin Kalmanoff; libretto (Eng) by the composer. First performance February 18, 1965, Granville, Ohio, Denison University Opera Workshop.

The work is a satire on television quiz shows and America's obsession with the medium. Joe Info, Jr. has entered a game show and stands to win a lot of money. His wife urges him to gamble for the top prize, while his father wants him to be cautious and keep the earnings he already has. Joe has other ideas, however, and deliberately loses, finishing with a nationally broadcast verbal attack on television shows, particularly game shows.

For a detailed plot description, see Summers/*OOA*, 171–72.

Roles: Mr. M. C. Charmboy (bar); Mr. Joe Info., Jr., a beetle expert (ten/high bar); Mrs. Joe Info, Jr. (sop); and Mr. Joe Info, Sr., his idealistic father (bass-bar).
SCORE: vs ([New York]: Operation Opera, 1957).

View from the Bridge, A, opera by Hayward Morris; libretto (Eng) by Stone Widney, after Arthur Miller's play (1955). First performance January 1981, Washington, D.C., Opera America Showcase.

About illegal Italian immigrants who work as longshoremen in New York.

Also set by R. Rossellini, as *Un sguardo del ponte* (1961, Rome); version by William Bolcom, with a libretto by Arnold Weinstein, planned for October 1999, Chicago.

Village, The, opera by Joel Mandelbaum; libretto (Eng) by Susan Fox. First performance March 1995, Queens, Queens College; directed by Susan Einhorn.

The work takes place during the Holocaust and involves French villagers, who must decide whether to hide a Jewish child or betray him and save themselves.
BIBLIOGRAPHY: David Gonzalez, "A Tale of Moral Courage Finds Its Voice in Opera," *NYT* (March 25, 1995), I, 7 [on premiere].

Village Coquettes, The, operatic burletta in two acts by John Hullah; libretto (Eng) by Charles Dickens. First performance December 6, 1836, London, St. James's Theatre, with John Braham (Squire Norton) and Elizabeth Rainforth (Lucy Benson).

The setting is an English village in 1729.

Village Opera, The, ballad opera in three acts; libretto (Eng) by Charles Johnson. First performance February 6, 1729, London, Drury Lane Theatre. Realization by Michael Tippett 1927–1928, for voices and nine instruments. Performed in this version 1928, Oxted, England, Barn Theatre.

The story concerns a young man who passes himself off as a gardener and a young lady who pretends she is a lady's maid, both in an effort to advance their romantic affairs.

Revised version as *Love in a Village** (1762, London).

Village Romeo and Juliet, A, opera in a prologue and three acts by Frederick Delius; libretto (Eng) by the composer, after a story by Gottfried Keller from his collection *Leute von Seldwyla* (part 1, 1856; part 2, 1874), *Romeo und Julia auf dem Dorfe*, translated into German for the premiere by Jelka Delius. First performance, in German, as *Romeo und Julia auf dem Dorfe*, February 21, 1907, Berlin, Königliches Opernhaus, with Lola Artôt de Padilla (Vreli), Willi Merkel (Sali), and Desider Zádor (Dark Fiddler); conducted by Fritz Cassirer. First performance in English February 22, 1910, London, Covent Garden, with Walter Hyde, Ruth Vincent, and Robert Maitland; conducted by Thomas Beecham. First U.S. performance April 26, 1972, Washington, D.C., Kennedy Center, with John Stewart, Patricia Wells, and John Reardon; conducted by Paul Callaway.

The story is set in Seldwyla, Switzerland, in the middle of the nineteenth century. It stresses the love between two children, offspring of quarreling farmers. Sali, son of Manz, loves Vreli, daughter of Marti; they leave their homes after they are encouraged to flee by the Dark Fiddler. After visiting the fair in the Paradise Garden, they reach the river and, realizing they cannot find happiness on earth, perish together by sinking the barge on which they are traveling.

For detailed descriptions, see *K/KOB*, 1116–18; *K/NKOB*, 188–89.

Major roles: Sali (treble, then ten), Vreli (girl sop, then sop), Manz (bar), Marti (bar), and the Dark Fiddler (bar).

Delius uses a number of leitmotifs in the work and brings them together in "The Walk to the Garden," which connects the two last scenes. The interlude was composed five years after the rest of the opera.

Another setting is F. Piket's *Satan's Trap** (1956, New York).
VIDEO: H. Field, A. Davies, T. Hampson, A. Schoenberg Choir and ORTF Sym. Orch; cond. C. Mackerras, dir. P. Weigl, Decca VHS 071 134-3 (1989).

Village Singer, The, opera in one act by Stephen Paulus; libretto (Eng) by Michael Dennis Browne, after a story by Mary Wilkins Freeman. First performance June 9, 1979, St. Louis, Opera Theatre, with Pauline Tinsley (Candace).

After many years of devoted service in a church choir, the aging Candace Whitcomb is suddenly replaced by Alma Way, fiancée of Wilson Ford, Candace's nephew. Hurt by her abrupt dismissal, Candace disrupts the church service by singing loudly from her nearby home. She does so again during the next service, despite the pleas from Rev. Pollard. When Wilson comes to chastise her, she threatens to cut him out of her will. She becomes ill and takes to her bed. William Emmons, director of the choir, comes to see Candace, and he apologizes for his actions, and she does for hers. Candace assures Wilson that she has not changed her will, and she dies peacefully.

For a detailed description, see Kornick/*RAO*, 235–37.

Major roles: Candace Whitcomb (sop), Alma Way (sop), Wilson Ford (ten), Rev. Pollard (ten), and William Emmons (bar).

SCORE: vs (Valley Forge, Pa.: European American Music, 1979).

BIBLIOGRAPHY: Robert Jacobson, review, *ON* XLIV (Sept. 1979), 50 [on premiere].

Vintagers, The, musical romance in two acts by Henry Rowley Bishop; libretto (Eng) by Edmund John Eyre. First performance August 1, 1809, London, Haymarket Theatre, with Mr. Jones (Henry), Mrs. Liston (Nannette), Mr. Grove (Baptiste), Mr. Lister (Duval), Mr. Taylor (Jaques), Mr. Treby (Montval), and Mrs. Eyre (Adelaide). First U.S. performance March 10, 1814, Philadelphia, Theatrical Commonwealth, Olympic Theatre.

SCORE: ms (ca. 1809, British Library, Add. 27702).

LIBRETTO: English (London: J. Barker, 1809; New York: D. Longworth, 1809).

Violins of St. Jacques, The, opera in a prologue and three acts by Malcolm Williamson; libretto (Eng) by William Chappell, after P. L. Fermor's novel. First performance November 29, 1966, London, Sadler's Wells, with April Cantelo (Berthe), David Hillman (Sosthène), Patricia Kern (Josephine), and David Bowman (Marcel); conducted by Vilem Tausky; produced by William Chappell; designed by Peter Rice.

The setting is the small Caribbean island of St. Jacques, which lies in the shadow of a volcano. Two feuding families host carnival night festivities in order to smooth over their differences. Marcel, from one family, tries to get Josephine, a member of the other family, to elope with him. Berthe, who is Josephine's cousin and is loved by Sosthène, Josephine's brother, distrusts Marcel. Her suspicions prove to be correct, when Marcel turns out to be married. In the midst of these events the volcano erupts, killing all of the inhabitants but Berthe, who has rowed out to sea to prevent Marcel from escaping with Josephine.

Major roles: Marcel (bar), Josephine (mezzo), Berthe (sop), and Sosthène (ten).

BIBLIOGRAPHY: Harold Rosenthal, review, *Opera* XVIII (Jan. 1967), 73–75 [on premiere].

Virgil's Dream, satiric fantasy for musical chamber theater in one act by Michael Colgrass; libretto (Eng) by the composer. First performance April 1967, Brighton.

A child prodigy who wants to be a concert pianist is offered an insurance policy to protect his future.

Roles: alto, two tenors, and baritone.

SCORE: vs (New York: C. Fischer, 1976).

Virgin and the Fawn, The, opera in one act by Eugene Zador; libretto (Eng) by L. Zilahy. First performance October 24, 1964, Los Angeles.

Virginia, opera in three acts by Samuel Arnold; libretto (Eng) by Mrs. Frances Plowden. First performance October 30, 1800, London, Drury Lane Theatre.
LIBRETTO: English (London: J. Barker, 1800).

Virgin of the Sun, The, grand operatic drama in three acts by Victor Pelissier; libretto (Eng) by William Dunlop, after Anne Plumptre's translation of A. von Kotzebue's *Die Spanier in Peru* (1797). First performance March 12, 1800, New York, Park Theatre.
LIBRETTO: English (New York: Charles Smith and S. Stephens, 1800).

Virgin of the Sun, The, operatic drama in three acts by Henry Rowley Bishop; libretto (Eng) by Frederick Reynolds, after Kotzebue's play and Marmontel's *Les Incas.* First performance January 31, 1812, London, Covent Garden, with Miss Smith (Cora), Mr. Huntley (Don Alonzo), Mr. Barrymore (Ataliba), and Mr. Young (Rolla). First U.S. performance November 15, 1813, New York, Park Theatre.

The title character is Cora, a Peruvian priestess, who runs off with Don Alonzo, a Spaniard, and they are wed. Since she has broken her vows of chastity, Cora is sentenced to death, along with Alonzo. Both are pardoned by Ataliba, the Inca ruler, when Cora halts a rebellion begun by Rolla, Cora's onetime lover. The work ends with a chorus praising "our happy land and king."
SCORE: vs selections (London, 1812).
LIBRETTO: English (London: C. Chapple, 1812).

Virgin of the Sun, The, grand operatic drama in three acts by Charles Gilfert; libretto (Eng) by William Dunlop?, after Plumptre's translation of Kotzebue. First performance 1823, Philadelphia.

Virgin Prophetess, The, or, The Fate of Troy, semi-opera in five acts by Gottfried Finger; libretto (Eng) by Elkanah Settle. First performance May 2, 1701, London, Drury Lane Theatre.

The virgin is Cassandra, and the work ends with Troy ablaze and Helen jumping into the flames.

Vision, A, monodrama in nine scenes by Alan Ridout; libretto (Eng) by the composer, after Richard Jefferies's *Story of My Heart.* First performance 1974, Manchester.

Vision of Ariel, The, opera-ballet in one act by Lazare Saminsky; libretto (Eng) by the composer. Composed 1915. First performance May 9, 1954, Chicago, University of Chicago.

The setting is Flanders, late sixteenth century, during the Spanish occupation. Ariel and a group of Jews secretly celebrate the holiday of Purim in a hidden synagogue. They try to help Ariel escape the Spanish soldiers, but he takes out a concealed sword and dies in the fighting.
SCORE: vs (New York: Block, 1950).

Visions of Midnight, opera-cantata by Ernest Kanitz; libretto (Eng). First performance February 26, 1964, Los Angeles.

Visitation, The, opera in three acts by Gunther Schuller; libretto (Eng) by the composer, after a theme by Franz Kafka. First performance, in German, as *Die Heimsuchung,* October 11, 1966, Hamburg, Hamburg State Opera; conducted by the composer; directed by Günther Rennert. First U.S. performance June 1967, New York, Lincoln Center.

Three men and an inspector harass Carter Jones, a black student, and accuse him of wrongdoing. Although he is innocent, he is pursued by the law and ridiculed by his friends and neighbors. He is also ignored by the Legal Aid Society, his uncle, and even the preacher to whom he turns in desperation. Wandering hopelessly through the streets, Jones is pursued to his death. After the funeral a procession of humanity expresses its guilt.

Major roles: Carter Jones (bar), the inspector (bass-bar), the presiding officer (bar), Uncle Albert (bass), and a deacon (bass).

The work, using elements of jazz and serialism, is written in a style the composer calls "third stream."

SCORE: vs (New York: Associated Music Publishers, Mainz: B. Schott's Söhne, 1967).

BIBLIOGRAPHY: review, *NYT* (June 30, 1967), 28 [on U.S. premiere].

Visitors, The, opera in three acts by Carlos Chávez; libretto (Eng) by Chester Kallman. First performance May 9, 1957, New York, Columbia University, Brander Matthews Theater, as *Panfilo and Lauretta*, with Sylvia Stahlman (Lauretta), Mary McMurray (Elissa), Frank Porretta (Panfilo), Thomas Stewart (Dioneo), Craig Timberlake (a monk), and Michael Kermoyan (a physician); conducted by Howard Shanet; produced by Bill Butler. It was revised and produced in a Spanish version under the title *El amor propiciado*, October 28, 1959, Mexico City. It was then renamed *The Visitors*.

The story is set in a villa in the Tuscan hills in the fifteenth century. Four people attempting to escape the plague that is decimating the populace of the city flee to a villa, where they pass the time presenting plays. The director is the poet Dioneo. Lauretta refuses Panfilo's love, while Elissa is desperate for his attentions. Tensions are raised by a play about Cupid and Psyche, which seems to mirror the real relationships among the performers. When a monk enters, he stages a play to show the four that they cannot stay apart from the tragedy unfolding in the city. He lets in the crowd, and Dioneo and Lauretta catch the plague. Lauretta survives and is changed by her illness—she accepts Panfilo. The dying Dioneo convinces Elissa to abandon her unrequited love. His last request is honored, to resume the performance of the play.

BIBLIOGRAPHY: review, *ON* XXII (Nov. 11, 1957), 16 [on premiere]; Howard Taubman, "Opera: First by Chavez," *NYT* (May 10, 1957), 21 [on premiere].

Visitors, The, chamber opera in three acts by John Gardner; libretto (Eng) by John Ormerod Greenwood. First performance June 7, 1972, Aldeburgh, Jubilee Hall, English Opera Group.

The work concerns the affairs of an everyday family.

Visit to the Country, A, opera in one act by Richard Wargo; libretto (Eng) by the composer, after several Anton Chekhov stories. First performance July 28, 1990, Chautauqua, New York, with Donna Ames (Tania), Deborah Golembiski (Nadia), and Steve Simmons (Misha); conducted by Gary Magby.

The landowner Tania, desperate to save her estate, tries to have her sister Nadia marry the wealthy Misha, a lawyer from Moscow.

Major roles: Tania (sop); Nadia, her sister (sop); and Misha (ten).

Part of *A Chekhov Trilogy.**

Vivandiere, The, operetta in three acts by John Hill Hewitt; libretto (Eng) by J. A. Signaigo, after Donizetti's *La fille du régiment* (1840, Paris). First performance March 17, 1863, Augusta, Georgia, Concert Hall.

In the original setting the work takes place during the Civil War in Louisiana. Hewitt revised the work and set it in Prussia during the Austro-Prussian War of 1867. It was performed in this version in 1868 in Stanton, Virginia.

Among its highlights are the patriotic "I Love the Rolling of the Drum" and "The Valiant Conscript."

SCORE: vs (1879); repr. ed. N. Lee Orr and Lynn Wood Bertrand, *NAMT*, vol. 6 (1994).
LIBRETTO: English (1869); repr. ed. N. Lee Orr and Lynn Wood Bertrand, the same.

Vivandière, La, or, True to the Corps, "operatic extravaganza" by Ferdinand Wallerstein, a burlesque of Donizetti's *La fille du régiment* (1840, Paris); libretto (Eng) by William S. Gilbert. First performance June 15, 1867, Liverpool, with Harriet Everard (the Marchioness); January 22, 1868, London, New Holborn Theatre, with Lionel Brough (Roberto), Harriet Everard (the Marchioness), Pauline Markham (Tonio), and Henrietta Hodson (the daughter).

This work parodies Byron's *Manfred* and badly behaved British tourists on the Continent. The subtitle is a reference to Angiolo Robson Slous's melodrama *True to the Core, a Story of the Armada* (1866). Included from the Donizetti original is the Marchioness of Birkenfeldt who, at the age of twenty-one, in typical Gilbert logic, meets her long-lost daughter, who is nineteen!

LIBRETTO: English (Liverpool: Matthews Brothers, 1867, and Montague, 1868).

Voice, The, opera fantasy in one act by Leslie Kondorossy; libretto (Eng) by Stephen N. Linek and Shawn Hall. First performance May 15, 1954, Cleveland, American New Opera Theater Society.

The setting is New York City.

Roles: soprano and alto.

SCORE: vs (Cleveland: American New Opera Theater Society, 1953).

Voice of Ariadne, The, chamber opera in three acts by Thea Musgrave; libretto (Eng) by Amalia Elguera, after Henry James's *The Last of the Valerii*. First performance June 11, 1974, Aldeburgh, with Thomas Allen (the Count), Jill Gomez (the Countess), Elizabeth Bainbridge (Mrs. Tracy), Anne Wilkens (Marchesa Bianca Bianchi), and Bernard Dickerson (Baldovino); conducted by the composer. First U.S. performance September 30, 1977, New York, City Opera, with David Holloway (the Count), Cynthia Clarey (the Countess), Sandra Walker (Marchesa Bianca Bianchi), Frances Bible (Mrs. Tracy), and David Griffith (Baldovino); conducted by the composer.

The setting is Rome in the 1870s. Count Marco Valerio is obsessed with the voice of Ariadne, which he hears from the pedestal of her statue. His increasing preoccupation drives him from his American wife, Martha. Marchesa Bianca Bianchi, enamored of the Count, tries to convince Martha that her husband is in love with someone else, while Mr. Lamb tries to comfort her. In the end Ariadne and the Count's wife are joined, as he realizes it is his wife he desires most of all. In a subplot, Baldovino tries to seduce the nosy Mrs. Tracy.

Roles: Count Marco Valerio (bar); Martha, the Countess (sop); Mr. Lamb (bass-bar); Marchesa Bianca Bianchi (mezzo); Mrs. Tracy (alto); Baldovino (ten); Gualtiero, a servant (bass); Giovanni (ten); and the statue (prerecorded voice [of Joan Davies]).

The work is divided into three acts, one for the Count, one for the Countess, and one for the two together.

SCORE: vs (Borough Green, Kent: Novello, [1977]).
BIBLIOGRAPHY: Robert Jacobson, "U.S.," *ON* XLII (Dec. 3, 1977), 46 [on U.S. premiere]; Peter Mark, "Musgrave's 'Ariadne,'" *Opera* XXV (June 1974), 476ff. [on premiere]; Andrew Porter, "Musical Events," *NY* (Sept. 1977), 163–64 [on U.S. premiere]; Brigitte Schiffer, "'The Voice of Ariadne,'" *Tempo* CX (Sept. 1974), 43–44 [on premiere]; Harold C. Schonberg, "Thea Musgrave, at City Opera, Introduces 'Voice of Ariadne,'" *NYT* (Oct. 2, 1977), 67.

Voice of Nature, The, drama with music in three acts by Victor Pelissier; libretto (Eng) by William Dunlap, a translation and adaptation of L. C. Caignez's *Le jugement de Salomon* (1802, Paris). First performance July 31, 1802, London, Little Theatre in the Haymarket. First U.S. performance February 4, 1803, New York, Park Theatre, with Mrs. Johnson (Alzaira).

The story, inspired by the Judgment of Solomon, concerns Lilla, whose illegitimate child, son of King Alfonso's brother, is stolen by Alzaira, who substitutes her own dead offspring in its place. When Lilla recognizes a birthmark on the child, the king is forced to make a judgment.
SCORE: music reconstructed by Karl Kroeger from parts in the New York Public Library, *NAMT*, vol. 2 (1994).
LIBRETTO: English (New York: D. Longworth, 1807), repr. ed. *NAMT*, vol. 2 (1994).

Voices for a Mirror, fantasy opera in one act by Meyer Kupferman; libretto (Eng) by Alastair Reid. First performance June 5, 1957, New York, the Master Theatre Institute, with Ellen Faull (Christina), Ruth Kobart (mother), and Francis Monachino (father).

The tragic story is set in New England.

Roles: the mother (mezzo); the father (bass-bar); Christina, their daughter (dram sop); and the dumb girl (lyr sop).
SCORE: ms (Sept. 1954, NYPL).
BIBLIOGRAPHY: Ross Parmenter, review, *NYT* (June 6, 1957), 34 [on premiere].

Voices in Limbo, radio opera by Larry Sitsky; libretto (Eng) by Gwen Harwood. Composed 1977. First performance August 12, 1981, Australian Broadcasting Corporation.

The voices are filtered and changed by electronic devices.

Volpone, opera in three acts by Louis Gruenberg; libretto (Eng) by the composer, after Ben Jonson. Composed 1948–1958. Not performed.

The setting is sixteenth-century Venice. See the next entry for the plot.
SCORES: ms, vs (University of California, Berkeley, 198?).

Volpone, opera in three acts by George Antheil; libretto (Eng) by Alfred Perry, after the play by Ben Jonson. First performance January 9, 1953, Los Angeles, University of California, Bovard Auditorium, with Paul Keast (Volpone) and Caesar Curzi (Mosca); May 3, 1954, Rochester, Eastman School of Music.

The story, set in modern times in this version, concerns the greedy Volpone, who pretends to be mortally ill in order to get gifts from his would-be heirs. Since Volpone faces execution if he does not indeed die, he sneaks away, and his servant Mosca, who has aided him in his deception, ends up inheriting everything from a bogus will.
BIBLIOGRAPHY: Juliette Laine, review, *ON* XVII (Feb. 16, 1953), 11–12 [on premiere]; review, *NYT* (May 4, 1954), 36 [on Eastman performance].

Volpone, opera in three acts by John Coombs; libretto (Eng) by the composer, after Jonson. First performance May 2, 1957, London, Toynbee Hall, with Eugenie Weiner,

Donald Gowing, and William Hoare; conducted by Alec Dempster; produced by Ambrose Winship.

Volpone, opera in four acts by Francis Burt; libretto (Eng) by the composer, after Ben Jonson. First performance June 2, 1960, Stuttgart, Staatsoper. First British performance April 24, 1961, London, Sadler's Wells, New Opera Company.
SCORE: vs (New York: Boosey & Hawkes, 1962?).

Voodoo, grand opera in three acts by Harry Lawrence Freeman; libretto (Eng) by the composer. First performance September 10, 1928, New York, 52nd Street Theater, with Carlotta Freeman (Lolo, the Voodoo Queen), Doris Trotman (Cleota), and Ray Yates (Mando); conducted by the composer.

When Lolo, the Voodoo Queen, discovers that her beloved, Mando, is in love with Cleota, Lolo vows to get revenge by using her voodoo powers. She crushes one of Mando's charms and, after Cleota is saved from being a sacrifice to the voodoo snake god, attempts another spell; before she can succeed, Lolo is shot by Mando.
LIBRETTO: English, typewritten copy (n.p., n.d.: LCCN: 85-61401).

Voss, opera in two acts by Richard Meale; libretto (Eng) by David Malouf, after Patrick White's novel of the same name. First performance (one scene) 1982, Adelaide Festival; first full performance March 1, 1986, Adelaide, Australia, Adelaide Festival Centre, with Geoffrey Chard (Voss), Marilyn Richardson (Laura), John Pringle (Palfreyman), Robert Eddie (Judd), and Anne-Maree McDonald (Belle); conducted by Stuart Challender; produced by Jim Sharman.

The story, loosely based on the doomed expedition of Ludwig Leichhardt, follows the travels of the German explorer Johann Ulrich Voss. He sets out in 1845 with a small group, including the religious naturalist Palfreyman, to attempt the first crossing of the Australian continent. The expedition ends in disaster, with Judd, an ex-convict, as the only survivor.

The tale is framed by the spiritual communication of Voss and Laura Trevelyan, his beloved, whom he leaves back in Sydney; she is the niece of Bonner, his wealthy sponsor.

For a detailed plot description, see K/NKOB, 453–54.

Major roles: Voss (bar); Laura Trevelyan, Bonner's niece (sop); Belle, Bonner's daughter (sop); Edward Bonner, a rich merchant (bass); and Mercy, Laura's adopted child (sop).
SCORE: ms fs ([Sydney]: Australian Music Centre, [198?]).
BIBLIOGRAPHY: John Carmody, "Australia: Meale Premiere," *Opera* XXXVII (May 1986), 531–32.
DISCOGRAPHY: Richardson, McDonald, Chard, Eddie, Gard, Pringle, Tomlinson; Australian Opera Chorus, Sydney Sym.; cond. Challender, Philips 42028-2 (1987, 2 CDs); rev. John W. Freeman, "Recordings," *ON* LIV (Mar. 17, 1990), 36.

Voyage, The, opera in a prologue, two acts, and an epilogue by Philip Glass; libretto (Eng) by David Henry Hwang; story by Philip Glass. First performance October 12, 1992, New York, Metropolitan Opera, with Douglas Perry (Scientist/First Mate), Patricia Schuman (Commander), Kaaren Erickson (Ship's Doctor/Space Twin #1), Julien Robbins (Second Mate/Space Twin #2), Tatiana Troyanos (Isabella), Timothy Noble (Columbus), Jane Shaulis (Earth Twin #1), and Jan Opalach (Earth Twin #2); conducted by Bruce Ferden.

The opera centers on the voyage of Christopher Columbus to the New World and exploration in general. It opens, in the prologue, with a Steven Hawking-like figure, called the Scientist, who is confined to a wheelchair, examining the idea of exploration. In act 1 aliens land their spaceship on earth 15,000 years ago; they each take a crystal, the combination of two crystals being necessary to find their way home, and they blend in with the earthlings. The second act opens in 1492 in Granada. Christopher Columbus is bid farewell by Queen Isabella and her court. He then sails to the New World and is beset by nightmare views of sea creatures and the brutality of his fellow beings.

In act 3, set in 2092, the Space Twins are in a space station and are scanning the universe, looking for signs of life. On Earth, the Earth Twins have found the crystals left by the Ice Age space travelers. When they combine the crystals, the station picks up their signal. The space travelers from the "home" planet prepare again for a voyage. In the epilogue they give way to Columbus, seen on his deathbed in 1506. He resists the temptations of the ghost of Isabella, and he is transported to the stars.

Roles: the Scientist/First Mate (ten), the Commander (sop), the Ship's Doctor/Space Twin #1 (sop), the Second Mate/Space Twin #2 (bass), Isabella (mezzo), Columbus (bass-bar), Earth Twin #1 (mezzo), and Earth Twin #2 (bass).

LIBRETTO: English (New York: Metropolitan Opera Guild, 1992).
BIBLIOGRAPHY: *ON* LVII (Oct. 1992): K. Robert Schwarz, "Glass Plus," 10–12; Robert Marx, "Hwang's World," 14, 16–17; Michael Kennedy, "Outer Limits," 28, 30; Philip Kennicott, "The Columbus Conundrum," 32–36.

Voyage of Edgar Allan Poe, The, opera in two acts by Dominick Argento; libretto (Eng) by Charles Nolte. First performance April 24, 1976, St. Paul, Minnesota Opera Company, with George Livings (Poe), Karen Hunt (Virginia Poe), Barbara Brandt (Mrs. Poe), Vern Sutton (the doctor), Kathryn Asman (Mrs. Clemm), Rose Taylor (Mrs. Allan), and Peter Strummer (theater director); conducted by Philip Brunelle.

The setting is 1849 at a dock in Richmond, Virginia, and on a ship. The dying Poe, wishing to sail to Baltimore, comes to the dock, informed by Griswold, his literary executor, that a ship will sail that night. Poe begins to hallucinate and sees events from his life; his fictional detective Dupin brings Poe to trial for causing the death of Virginia, Poe's wife; Griswold becomes the judge and, ultimately, Poe's soul. When dawn breaks, Poe's doctor finds him lifeless on the dock, with Griswold standing over the dead man and swearing that no vessel has left the dock during the night.

For a detailed description, see Kornick/*RAO*, 28–31.

Major roles: the doctor (ten); Edgar Allan Poe (ten); Griswold (bar); Poe's mother (sop); Mrs. Clemm (mezzo); Mrs. Allan (alto); theater director (bass-bar); and Virginia, Poe's wife (sop).

SCORE: vs (New York: Boosey & Hawkes, 1979).
LIBRETTO: English (Baltimore: The Center, 1977).
BIBLIOGRAPHY: Raymond Erickson, review, *NYT* (Apr. 26, 1976), 38.

Voyage of Marco Polo, The. See **Marco Polo**.

Voyage of St. Brendan, The, music drama by John Paynter; libretto (Eng) by Elizabeth Paynter. First performance 1979, Norwich, England.

The work concerns Saint Brendan the Voyager (ca. 483–577).

It is scored for bass-baritone, actors, dancers, choruses, and orchestra.

SCORE: vs (London: Universal Edition, 1984).

W

Wager, The, opera in one act by Buxton Orr; libretto (Eng) by Hamilton Johnston. First performance December 16, 1962, London, Sadler's Wells, New Opera Company.

The story concerns two cheats who ruin the lives of a blind beggar and his daughter.
BIBLIOGRAPHY: Edmund Tracy, "London Diary," *MT* CIV (Feb. 1963), 118 [on premiere].

Waiter's Revenge, The, "an absurd fable" by Stephen Oliver; libretto (Eng) by the composer. First performance June 15, 1976, Nottingham, England.

Waiting, opera in one act by Stephen Oliver; libretto (Eng) by the composer. First performance June 1987, Buxton; also June 1, 1988, London, Modern Music Theatre Troupe, with Penelope Mackay.

The work is a monologue presenting three women: a landlady waiting for her lodger; a young girl who has met a soldier; and Penelope awaiting Ulysses's return.
BIBLIOGRAPHY: Arthur Jacobs, review, *Opera* XXXIX (Aug. 1988), 1008–9 [on London premiere].

Waituhi, opera in four acts by Ross Harris; libretto (Eng) by Witi Ihimaera. First performance September 8, 1984, Christchurch, New Zealand.

The work, concerned with the conflicts faced by Maori youth who leave their villages for life in the city, includes traditional operatic pieces and Maori songs.

Wake Up, It's Time to Go to Bed!, opera-music theater by Carson Kievman; libretto (Eng) by the composer. First performance August 9, 1978, Lenox, Massachusetts, Tanglewood Festival of Contemporary Music.

About a man, Orpheus, who is abandoned by Eurydice, his girlfriend.

For actor, singers, chamber ensemble, and tape.
SCORE: ms score, facsimile (New York: Associated Music Publishers, 1983).

Waltz on a Merry-Go-Round, opera in three acts by Bruce Taub; libretto (Eng) by Edward F. Gallardo, after his play. Composed 1979.

Wanderer: A Ballad for Today, The, folk opera by Paul and Martha Boesing; libretto (Eng) from *I Ching*. First performance March 1970, Minneapolis, Center Opera Company. Same production July 31, 1970, Houston, Miller Theatre, with Isabelle Lipschutz (Mother/Young Woman), Paul Clark (Father/Young Man), and Barbara Brandt (Birdwoman); conducted by Yale Marshall.

The focus of the work is the passage of universal man through various stages, from youth to old age, and from celebration to war. Its source, *I Ching*, is the Chinese book of changes.
BIBLIOGRAPHY: Ann Holmes, "Houston," *ON* XXXV (Oct. 10, 1970), 22–23 [on premiere].

Wandering Boys, The, or, The Castle of Olival, romantic drama in two acts by Henry Rowley Bishop; libretto (Eng) by Isaac Pocock, after *Le pèlerin blanc* of Pixérécourt. First performance February 24, 1814, London, Covent Garden.

Wandering Scholar, The, opera in one act by W. H. Bell; libretto (Eng) by Clifford Bax. First performance October 28, 1935, Cape Town.

Wandering Scholar, The, chamber opera in one act by Gustav Holst; libretto (Eng) by Clifford Bax, after an incident in *The Wandering Scholars* (1928) by Helen Waddell. First performance January 31, 1934, Liverpool, David Lewis Theatre, with Irene Eastwood (Alison); conducted by J. E. Wallace; produced by Frederick Wilkinson. Revised by Benjamin Britten (1951) and Britten and Imogen Holst (1968). Revived March 25, 1966, Toronto, Royal Conservatory of Music. First U.S. performance August 1, 1968, Potsdam, New York, State University of New York.

The story is set in a thirteenth-century farmhouse in France. While the farmer, Louis, is absent, his wife, Alison, is flirting with Father Philippe, the lusty parish priest. A poor scholar, Pierre, begs for a meal but is rudely turned away. He returns later with the farmer and by his quick wit catches the guilty pair. For this he is rewarded with a meal.

Major roles: Louis (bar), Alison (sop), Father Philippe (bar), and Pierre (ten).
SCORES: octavo, ed. Imogen Holst and Benjamin Britten (London: Faber, 1971).

Warchild, opera by Richard Taylor; libretto (Eng) by Wendy Cook. First performance April 19, 1997, London, Peterborough Cathedral, National Youth Music Theatre, with Michael Kerry, Kathryn Smith, and Mica Penniman; conducted by Jonathan Gill.

The text comes from diaries, letters, and poems preserved from the Warsaw Ghetto.
BIBLIOGRAPHY: J. Allison, "'Warchild,'" *Opera* XLVIII (July 1997), 865–66 [on premiere].

Ward of the Castle, The, comic opera in two acts by Tommaso Giordani; libretto (Eng) by Mrs. Burke. First performance October 24, 1793, London, Covent Garden.
LIBRETTO: English, ms (Huntington Library, San Marino, Calif., Larpent 992).

Warrior, The, opera in one act by Bernard Rogers; libretto (Eng) by Norman Corwin, after the Book of Judges. First performance January 11, 1947, New York, Metropolitan Opera, with Regina Resnik (Delilah) and Mack Harrell (Samson); conducted by Max Rudolf; directed by Herbert Graf.

A setting of the story of Samson and Delilah, beginning with Samson's capture and ending with the destruction of the temple.

Other settings include Handel's oratorio *Samson* (1743, London); and Saint-Saëns's *Samson et Delilah* (1877, Weimar).
LIBRETTO: English (New York: F. Rullman, 1946).

Washington Square, opera in three acts by Thomas Pasatieri; libretto (Eng) by Kenward Elmslie, after Henry James's novel of the same name. First performance October 1, 1976, Detroit, Michigan Opera Theatre, with Catherine Malfitano (Catherine Sloper), Brent Ellis (Morris Townsend), Richard Cross (Dr. Sloper), Elaine Bonazzi (Lavinia Davenport), and Sheri Greenawald (Marian Harrington); conducted by Henry Holt; produced by Nikos Psacharopoulos; designed by Santo Loquasto; also October 13, 1977, New York, New York Lyric Opera Company, with Sheri Greenawald (Catherine), Stephen Dickson (Morris), Judith Christin (Lavinia), and Marc Embree (Dr. Sloper).

Morris Townsend, a charming, but penniless, young man, sets out to woo the wealthy, but not attractive, Catherine Sloper; he is aided by Lavinia Davenport, Catherine's silly aunt. Catherine's stern father, Dr. Austin Sloper, opposes the union, and when he confronts Morris's sister, he gets her to admit that Morris is not the marrying kind.

Major roles: Catherine (sop), Dr. Sloper (bass-bar), Morris (bar), and Lavinia (mezzo).

The score includes the simple ballad "First Love" of Morris, a trio, and a quartet sung by Catherine, her father, Aunt Lavinia, and Morris.

SCORE: vs (Melville, N.Y.: Belwin-Mills, 1977).

LIBRETTO: English (Melville, N.Y.: Belwin-Mills, 1976).

BIBLIOGRAPHY: Benjamin Ivry, "Portrait of an Author," *ON* LIII (Nov. 1988), 20, 22; Hubert Saal, "James as Opera," *Newsweek* (Nov. 7, 1977), 103 [on premiere].

Water Bird Talk, A, monodrama in one act by Dominick Argento; libretto (Eng) by the composer, after Anton Chekhov's play *On the Harmfulness of Smoking Tobacco* (1903) and J. J. Audubon's *The Birds of America* (1838). First performance May 19, 1977, Brooklyn, New York, Brooklyn Academy, Orpheus Chamber Ensemble, with Vern Sutton (the lecturer); conducted by Philip Brunelle.

The work is set in a lecture room at a Maryland or Virginia club in the second half of the nineteenth century. A middle-aged lecturer speaks to a group of provincial ladies about various birds, and his images mirror his own dismal life as a henpecked husband.

For a detailed description, see Kornick/*RAO*, 31–32.

Role: the lecturer (low ten/bar).

The serial score includes lyrical passages for the vocalist and taped birdsongs. The wife's presence is signaled offstage by coughs, the slamming of doors, and crow-like chastisements.

SCORE: vs (New York: Boosey & Hawkes, 1980).

BIBLIOGRAPHY: Robert Jackson, review, *ON* XLII (Aug. 1977), 40 [on premiere]; Andrew Porter, "A Lecture and a Parable," *NY* (June 6, 1977), 108, 111, 113 [on premiere].

DISCOGRAPHY: Sutton, Manhattan Chamber Orch.; cond. Clark, Newport Classic 85602; rev. Patrick J. Smith, *ON* LXI (Feb. 8, 1997), 40.

Waterloo Leave, ballad opera in two acts by Martin Shaw; libretto (Eng) by Clifford Bax. First performance November 12, 1928, Norwich, England, Maddermarket.

Waterman, The, or, The First of August, ballad opera in two acts partly composed and partly compiled by Charles Dibdin; libretto (Eng) by the composer. First performance August 8, 1774, London, Haymarket, with Charles Bannister (Tom).

The story centers on the attempts of the well-lettered Robin and Tom Tug, the waterman, to win the hand of Wilhelmina Bundle. Robin is favored by Mrs. Bundle, while the working-class Tom has the support of Mr. Bundle.

Wilhelmina declares that she will wed the man who does something deserving of her hand. Tom enters the rowing race at Chelsea and, of course, wins the race and her love.

For a detailed description, see Fiske/*ETM*, 371–73 .

The piece includes borrowings from *Damon and Phillida** (1729), ballad collections, and *The Ephesian Matron** (1769).

SCORE: vs (London: John Johnston, n.d.).

LIBRETTO: English (London: Longman, Hurst, Rees, and Orme, 1809).

Wat Tyler, opera in a prologue and six scenes by Alan Bush; libretto (Eng) by Nancy Bush. First performance September 6, 1953, Leipzig, in German, Städtische Theater.

The story is that of Wat Tyler, leader of Tyler's Rebellion of 1381 in Kent and Essex, in which the peasants demanded the end to serfdom and various other matters. Wat Tyler, after meeting with Richard II and demanding more concessions than the monarch is willing to make, is provoked by Bampton, the tax commissioner, and stabbed in the back by Walworth, the mayor of London. Richard then declares that serfdom will never be abolished.

Major roles: Wat Tyler (bar); Bampton, the royal tax commissioner (bass-bar); Richard II (ten); and Walworth (bass-bar).

Also an "operatic extravaganza," *Wat Tyler, M.P.*, with text by G. A. Sala (ca. 1869). SCORE: vs, German-English (London: Novello, [1959]).

Waverley, or, Sixty Years Since, melodramatic burletta in three acts by George Rodwell; libretto (Eng) by Edward Fitzball, after the novel by Sir Walter Scott (1814). First performance March 1, 1824, London, Adelphi Theatre.

The setting is Scotland in the middle of the seventeenth century. The hero, Captain Edward Waverley, is dismissed from the army because he is suspected of having Jacobite sympathies. When he saves Colonel Talbot from death, Waverley is pardoned and allowed to wed the faithful Rose Bradwardine.

LIBRETTO: English (London: L. Lowndes, [1824]).

Wayfarers, The, opera in two acts for young people by John Joubert; libretto (Eng) by Stephen Tunnicliffe, after Chaucer's *The Pardoner's Tale*. First performance April 4, 1984, Huntingdon, England.

In this loose adaptation of Chaucer, set in medieval England, three friends, Oswald, Malkyn, and Aleyn, vow to punish Death because of the ravages of the Black Plague. They end up killing each other because of their greed over a pot of gold.

See *The Pardoner's Tale* for other settings.

BIBLIOGRAPHY: Kenneth Birken, "The Wayfarers: Joubert's New School Opera," *MT* CXXVI (May 1985), 281–83.

Way of How, The, music theater by Paul Dresher; libretto (Eng) by George Coates. First performance August 8, 1980, Seattle, Cornish Institute.

The music ranges from synthesizer passages to arias from Leoncavallo's *Pagliacci*. BIBLIOGRAPHY: Samuel G. Freedman, "Well-Traveled 'Way of How' Arrives in Brooklyn," *NYT* (Oct. 14, 1983), C, 3 [on 1983 performance].

Weathercock, The, afterpiece pastiche, with overture by Samuel Arnold; libretto (Eng) by Theodosius Forrest. First performance October 17, 1775, London, Covent Garden. LIBRETTO: English (London: T. Evans, 1775).

Weathercock, The, comic opera in two acts by Matthew King; libretto (Eng) by John T. Allingham. First performance November 18, 1805, London, Drury Lane Theatre. First U.S. performance 1806, New York.

LIBRETTO: English (New York: David Longworth, 1806).

We Come to the River, "actions for music" by Hans Werner Henze; libretto (Eng) by Edward Bond. First performance July 12, 1976, London, Covent Garden, with Norman Welsby (the General), Josephine Veasey (the Emperor), Josephine Barstow (the Young Woman), Anne Wilkens (the Old Woman), Robert Tear (the Deserter), and Michael Langdon (the Doctor); conducted by David Atherton; produced by the composer and David Pountney; designed by Jürgen Henze. First U.S. performance August 10, 1984, Santa Fe, Santa Fe Opera, with Victor Braun (the General), David Kuebler (the Deserter), Greg Ryerson (the Doctor), Nancy Shade (the Young Woman), Carolyne James (the Old Woman), and Susan Quittmeyer (the Emperor); conducted by Dennis Russell Davies.

The main character is the brutal General, who, after he discovers he is becoming blind, becomes more softhearted and for this is sent to a madhouse. Here he is ultimately killed by the inmates.

Major roles: the General (bar), the Deserter (ten), the Emperor (lyric sop), the Governor (bar), the Doctor (bass-bar), the Young Woman (dram sop), and the Old Woman (dram mezzo).

This experimental piece includes the presentation of three scenes simultaneously and the use of three acting areas, each with its own orchestra. The 59 singers in this work have 112 roles among them. The role of the Emperor is a travesty part, written for soprano.

SCORE: vs, German-English (Mainz: B. Schott's Söhne; New York: Schott, 1976).

BIBLIOGRAPHY: Frank Granville Barker, "Reports: Foreign," *ON* XLI (Oct. 1976), 51–52 [on premiere]; Robert Jacobson, "Santa Fe," *ON* XLIX (Nov. 1984), 45 [on U.S. premiere].

Wedding, The, "tragi-comi-pastoral-farcical" ballad opera, with the overture and twenty-three airs arranged by John Pepusch; libretto (Eng) by Essex Hawker. First performance May 6, 1729, London, Lincoln's Inn Fields, with Mr. Clarke (first brideman), Mr. Salway (Peartree), Mr. Wilcox (Razoir), and Mrs. Cantrel (Margery).

The work concerns Margery, a fruit gatherer, in love with the gardener Peartree and pursued by Razoir, a French barber.

The overture is by Pepusch.

LIBRETTO: English (London: W. Mears, 1729); repr. Rubsamen/*BO*, vol. 16, *Country Operas II: Farcical Humor and Stratagem* (1974).

Wedding, The, opera in three acts by A. J. Potter; libretto (Eng) by the composer. First performance June 8, 1981, Dublin, Abbey Theatre.

Wedding, The, comic opera in two acts by Gian Carlo Menotti; libretto (Eng) by the composer. First performance September 16, 1988, Seoul, Korea.

Wedding Day, The, burletta in two parts by François Hippolyte Barthelemon; libretto (Eng). First performance July 15, 1773, London. Marylebone Gardens.

Wedding Day, The, comic opera in three acts by Julian Edwards; libretto (Eng) by Stanislaus Stangé. First performance April 8, 1897, New York.

SCORE: vs (Cincinnati: J. Church, 1897).

Wedding Eve, The, comic opera in three acts by Ernest Ford, with Frédéric Toulmouche and "Yvolde"; libretto (Eng) by William Yardley, after the French text *Vielles des noces* of A. Bisson and Bureau-Jattiot (1888, Paris); lyrics adapted by Frank Latimer. First performance September 10, 1892, London, Trafalgar Square.

SCORE: vs (London: Hopwood & Crew, [ca. 1890]).

Wedding Knell, The, dramatic opera in one act by John Verrall; libretto (Eng), after Nathaniel Hawthorne. First performance December 5, 1955, Seattle.

Wedding Night, The, afterpiece in one act by Samuel Arnold; libretto (Eng) by James Cobb. First performance August 12, 1780, London, Little Theatre in the Haymarket.

Wedding Present, The, comic opera in three acts by Charles E. Horn; libretto (Eng) by James Kenney. First performance October 28, 1825, London, Drury Lane Theatre.

Wedding Ring, The, comic opera in two acts, an adaptation by Charles Dibdin of Galuppi's *Il filosofo di campagna* (1754, Venice); libretto (Eng) by Dibdin, after Goldoni's text. First performance February 1, 1773, London, Drury Lane Theatre, with Mr. Bannister (Pandolfo), Mr. Vernon (Zerbino), Mr. Davies (Henrico), Mr. Vernon (Zerbino), Mrs. Wrighten (Felicia), and Mrs. Smith (Lissetta).

The story concerns a father, Pandolfo, and his daughter, Felicia, who is aided by her wily companion, Lissetta, to discourage her would-be husband and wed the man she loves.
SCORE: vs (London: John Johnston, Longman, Lukey & Co., [1773]).
LIBRETTO: English (London: T. Becket, 1773).

Wedding Trip, The, opera bouffe in three acts by Reginald De Koven; book and lyrics (Eng) by Fred De Gresac and Harry B. Smith. First performance December 25, 1911, New York, Knickerbocker Theater, with Christine Nielson (Fritzi), John McCloskey (Felix), and Dorothy Jardon (Aza).

Just after Fritzi marries Felix, the bridegroom is forced to take the place of François, his twin brother, who has deserted the army. Despite temptations from the girlfriends of François, Felix remains true to his wedding vows, but he is condemned to death when he reveals that he has taken his brother's place. His death is prevented by the gypsy dancer Aza, whose kiss changes the mind of Felix's hard-hearted commanding officer.

The work was not a success.
SCORE: vs (New York and Detroit: Jerome H. Remick & Co., 1911).

Weep Torn Land, opera in seven scenes by Ross Lee Finney; libretto (Eng) by the composer. Composed 1983–1985.

The work concerns three areas of strife: that of the whites and Native Americans, culminating in the Sand Creek Massacre of 1864, during which 500 Cheyennes were killed; the fighting between the North and the South during the Civil War; and the conflict between the five children of William Bent and his wife, the daughter of a Cheyenne chief—two joined the Union Army, two the Confederate, and one took part in the Sand Creek Massacre.
BIBLIOGRAPHY: Ross Lee Finney, *Profile of a Lifetime* (New York: C. F. Peters), passim; Kenneth Peacock, "Ross Lee Finney at Eighty-Five: *Weep Torn Land,*" AM 9/1 (Spring 1991), 1–19.

Well, The, opera by Louis Mennini; libretto (Eng) by the composer. First performance May 8, 1951, Rochester, New York, Eastman School of Music.

Welsh Opera, The, or, The Grey Mare the Better Horse, ballad opera; libretto (Eng) by "Scriblerus Secundus" (Henry Fielding). First performance April 22, 1731, London, Haymarket, with Mr. Furnival (Squire ap Shinken), Mr. Davenport (Master Owen), Mr. Reynolds (Parson Puzzle-Text), Mr. Mullart (Robin), Mr. Hallam (John), Mr. Jones (William), Mr. Dove (Thomas), Mrs. Jones (Madam ap Shinken), Miss Price (Molly), Mrs. Clark (Goody Scratch), Mrs. Nokes (Sweetissa), Mrs. Mullart (Susan), Mrs. Lacy (Margery), and Mrs. Furnival (Betty). Revised as *The Grub-Street Opera** (1731).

Roles: Squire ap Shinken; Master Owen, his son, in love with Molly; Robin, the butler, in love with Sweetissa; John, the coachman, his friend, in love with Betty; William, the groom, Robin's enemy, in love with Susan; Thomas, the gardiner [sic], his friend, in love with Margery; Madam ap Shinken; Molly, in love with Master Owen; Goody Scratch, a witch, secretly in love with the pastor; Sweetissa, in love with Robin; Susan, in love with William; Margery, in love with Thomas; and Betty, in love with John.
LIBRETTO: English (London, H. Cook, [1731]); repr. Rubsamen/*BO*, vol. 20, *Political Operas II* (1974).

Wenceslas, church opera in two acts by Alan Ridout; libretto (Eng) by Patric Dickinson. First performance 1978, Bournemouth, England.

We're Back, opera in one act by Eugene Armour; libretto (Eng) by Richard P. Schmidt. First performance May 2, 1981, New York, Golden Fleece Ltd.; with Matthew Ward, pianist.

The story has Gertrude Stein and Alice B. Toklas in their apartment in Paris as they remember Ohio, which they just left.

Among the numbers is the amusing "What Is Paris after Dinner in Columbus."
BIBLIOGRAPHY: Bernard Holland, review, *NYT* (May 7, 1981), C, 15 [on premiere].

We're Not Robots, You Know, puppet opera in one act for stage or television by Eric Stokes; libretto (Eng) by Keith Gunderson. First performance autumn 1986, Minneapolis, Institute of Art, Synergenesis Corporation. First performance (stage) May 15, 1988, Chicago.

A suburban marionette family become the owners of two robots that are able to perform all kinds of household chores.

West of Washington Square, opera in two parts by Alva Henderson; libretto (Eng) by the composer (part one) and Janet Lewis (part two), after O. Henry's *The Last Leaf* and *Room across the Hall*. First performance November 26, 1988, San Jose, California, Opera San Jose.

West Side Story, musical in two acts by Leonard Bernstein; libretto (Eng) by Arthur Laurents, after Shakespeare's *Romeo and Juliet* (1595); lyrics by Stephen Sondheim; conceived, directed, and choreographed by Jerome Robbins. First performance (previews) August 19, 1957, Washington, D.C., National Theater; September 26, 1957, New York, Winter Garden, with Carol Lawrence (Maria), Larry Kert (Tony), Chita Rivera (Anita), Ken Le Roy (Bernardo), Mickey Calin (Riff), and Jamie Sanchez (Chino); conducted by the composer. First British performance December 12, 1958, London, Her Majesty's Theatre.

In this updating of the Romeo and Juliet story, here set in New York, the feuding families are replaced by warring gangs, the native-born Jets and the Puerto Rican Sharks. In the middle of the hostilities comes Maria, just arrived from the Island. She is the sister of Bernardo, leader of the Sharks, who wants her to wed his friend Chino. Tony, just returned to the neighborhood, is a former leader of the Jets who is trying to make a new life for himself. Tony and Maria meet at a dance arranged to defuse tensions between the two groups and fall immediately in love, Tony rhapsodizing in "Maria." The two have a secret rendezvous after the dance and promise to love each other in the tender "Tonight" (the original balcony scene), which is played out on a tenement fire escape.

When the rival gangs confront one another at the drugstore to plan a "rumble," or fight, their scheme is interrupted momentarily by the local policeman, Officer Krupke. Tony meets Maria in the bridal shop in which she works, and they sing again of their love in "Tonight," which becomes a quintet, with Anita planning to meet Bernardo, her boyfriend, and Bernardo and Riff getting ready, separately, for the rumble. The gangs assemble under a deserted part of the highway, and Tony tries to prevent his friend Riff from fighting, only to see Riff stabbed by Bernardo. Enraged and grief-stricken, Tony kills Bernardo with Riff's knife.

Maria, unaware of what has transpired, awaits Tony's arrival and sings "I Feel Pretty." Her joy is destroyed by the arrival of Chino, who tells her the terrible news and leaves to avenge Bernardo's death. The desperate Tony comes to Maria, and they fantasize about a better life together, away from all the hatred, as the ballet "Somewhere" unfolds. When Tony leaves, Maria convinces the grieving Anita to warn Tony of Chino's intentions. Anita's attempts to deliver the message are met with cruel taunts from the Jets, and so she tells them instead that Chino has killed Maria. When Tony hears the devastating lie, he wanders through the streets, only to be shot and killed by Chino just as he finally finds Maria. Realizing that their actions have led to the deaths of their friends, members of both gangs emerge and carry Tony's body away.

For a more detailed description, see Gänzl/*BBM*, 179–83.

Major roles: Tony (ten), Maria (sop), Anita (mezzo), Riff (bar), and Bernardo (bar).

The work, one of the seminal compositions for the American musical stage, ran for 734 performances in New York after its Washington, D.C., previews. It was revived again on April 27, 1960, at the Winter Garden, and ran for another 249 performances. Its music continues to be popular; various numbers are concert favorites, as are the Symphonic Dances, which include the ballet "Somewhere" and the "Dance at the Gym." It has been recorded by opera singers (see Discography), and it is occasionally performed by opera companies. The 1961 film starred Natalie Wood and Richard Beymer (whose singing voices were dubbed by Marni Nixon and Jim Bryant).

SCORE: vs (New York: G. Schirmer, 1957?).

BIBLIOGRAPHY: Brooks Atkinson, "Theatre: 'West Side Story,' The Jungles of the City," *NYT* (Sept. 27, 1957), 14 [on New York premiere]; Keith Garebian, *The Making of West Side Story* (Toronto: ECW Press, 1995).

DISCOGRAPHY: original cast (Lawrence, Kert, Rivera, Smith), Columbia CK32603 (1 CD, remastering of original); K. Te Kanawa, T. Troyanos, J. Carreras, K. Ollmann; cond. L. Bernstein, DG 2-415253-4 GH2 (tapes); 415253-2 GH2 (2 CDs).

Westward Ho!, opera in three acts by Philip Napier Miles; libretto (Eng) by E. F. Benson, after Charles Kingsley's novel (1855). First performance December 4, 1913, London, Lyceum Theatre.

Set in the period of Elizabeth I, the story involves a British seaman, Amyas Leigh, who fights against the Spanish Armada and a Spanish captain, Don Guzman, who is competing for the hand of Leigh's beloved.

What a Blunder, comic opera in three acts by John Davy; libretto (Eng) by Joseph Holman. First performance August 14, 1800, London, Little Theatre in the Haymarket, with John Fawcett (Dashington).

The setting is Spain, and the heroine of the work is Leonora and the hero is Dashington. The title refers to a love triangle and mixed-up identities.

For a detailed musical description, see Fiske/*ETM*, 583–84.

LIBRETTO: English (London: W. Miller, 1800; New York: David Longworth, 1814).

What D'Ye Call It, The, comic opera in one act by Phyllis Tate; libretto (Eng) by V. C. Clinton-Baddeley after John Gay's "tragi-comi-pastoral farce." First performance July 7, 1966, Cheltenham, England, Everyman Theatre, New Opera Company

BIBLIOGRAPHY: John Warrack, review, *MT* CVII (Sept. 3, 1966), 792–93 [on premiere].

What Happened, chamber opera in five acts by Charles Shere; libretto (Eng) after Gertrude Stein's play. Composed 1991.

Part 3 of a trilogy set to plays by Stein; see also *I Like It to Be A Play* and *Ladies Voices*.

What Price Confidence, comic opera in one act by Ernst Krenek; libretto (Eng) by the composer. Composed 1945. First performance, in German, as *Vertrauenssache*, May 25, 1962, Saarbrücken. First performance in English (and first U.S. performance), August 2, 1968, Hanover, New Hampshire, Dartmouth College.

The work takes place in London around 1900. To make up for his lack of self-confidence and his jealousy, Edwin promises Gloria that he will put his trust in the first person who asks for his trust. Gloria meets Richard, her admirer, and agrees to run away with him if he can get Edwin to have some self-confidence. Richard gets Edwin to accept a bad check to pay for a gambling debt and then takes the jewels of his wife, Vivian, to pawn in order to cover the check. When Edwin finds out about the deception, he wants to throw himself off Waterloo Bridge, but Vivian intervenes and asks him to come to tea. Vivian manages to obtain the pawn ticket from Richard, gives it to Edwin, and arranges to meet him in Paris. The new couple hail "confidence," while the other couple sadly ask at what price it is achieved.

For a detailed description, see Eaton/*OP* II, 332–33.

Roles: Edwin (bar), Gloria (sop), Richard (ten), and Vivian (mezzo).

What the Old Man Does Is Always Right, children's opera in one act by Alun Hoddinott; libretto (Eng) by Myfanwy Piper, after a story by Hans Christian Andersen. First performance July 27, 1977, Fishguard Festival, Wales, with Geraint Evans (the old man) and Eiddwen Harrhy (the old woman).

An old couple decide to sell their horse, and the husband goes to the fair. On the way he undertakes a series of exchanges, each worse than the last, and he is scolded and mocked by the village children for his foolishness. He meets two rich young Travellers, who bet that his wife will be furious with him for his folly, despite the husband's assurances that she will be satisfied. When he returns home, he proves to be right, and the Travellers get a lesson in life.

Major roles: the Old Man (bass bar), the Old Woman (sop), first Traveller (ten), and second Traveller (ten).

SCORE: vs (London: Oxford University Press, 1980).

Wheel of the World, The, "entertainment" in one act by Gordon Crosse; libretto (Eng) by D. Cowan, after Chaucer's *The Knight's Tale*, *The Nun's Priest's Tale*, and *The Pardoner's Tale*. First performance June 5, 1972, Aldeburgh Festival.

When Opportunity Knocks, opera by Robert Ashley; libretto (Eng) by the composer. Composed 1984–1985.

Where's Dick, opera in three acts by Stewart Wallace; libretto (Eng) by Michael Korie. First performance (staged preview) September 26, 1987, Omaha, Nebraska, Opera/Omaha, Strauss Performing Arts Center, with Henry Stram (Junior), Consuela Hill (Chief Blowhard), and Lauren Flanigan (Mrs. Heimlich); conducted by Jeff Halpern. First regular performance June 1, 1989, Houston, Houston Grand Opera.

A satirical and comedic treatment of corruption and the fruitless search by the inept hero, Junior, for the all-American hero, Dick, as in Dick Tracy, the comic-strip character.

SCORE: vs, ms (1986–1987, holograph, photocopy, NYPL).

LIBRETTO: English (1987, typescript, photocopy, NYPL).

BIBLIOGRAPHY: Robert G. Ruetz, "Omaha," *ON* LII (Jan. 16, 1988), 39–40 [on Omaha preview].

Where the Wild Things Are, fantasy opera in nine scenes by Oliver Knussen; libretto (Eng) by Maurice Sendak and the composer. First performance November 28, 1980 (incomplete version), Brussels, Théâtre de la Monnaie, with Jane Mannings (Max). First British performance (concert) May 1982, London, Elizabeth Hall, London Sinfonietta, with Rosemary Hardy (Max). First British performance (revised version, staged) January 9 and 10, 1984, London, Glyndebourne at the National Theatre, with Karen Beardsley/ Rosemary Hardy (Max), Mary King (Mama/Tzippy), Hugh Hetherington (Moishe/Goat), Jeremy Munro (Bruno), Stephen Rhys-Williams (Emile), and Andrew Gallacher (Bernard); conducted by the composer/Jane Glover. First U.S. performance June 1984, New York, Horizons, with Karen Beardsley (Max); conducted by Zubin Mehta.

The naughty child Max, deprived of his supper for his antics, takes a voyage to the land of the kind Wild Things, who make him their king. During one of the wild rumpuses a Wild Thing loses its head, which makes Max realize the harm his bad behavior can cause.

For a detailed plot synopsis, see K/*KOB*, 1254–57; K/*NKOB*, 399–400.

Major roles: Max, a small boy (sop); Mama (mezzo); Tzippy, a female Wild Thing (mezzo); Moishe, a Wild Thing with beard (ten); Bruno, a Wild Thing with horns (bar); Emile, a rooster (bass-bar); Bernard, a bull (bass); and goat (dance mime).

The libretto includes, in Sendak's words, "pidgin Yiddish."

LIBRETTO: English (London: Faber, 19??).

BIBLIOGRAPHY: Dominic Gill, "Théâtre de la Monnaie, Brussels," *Financial Times* (Dec. 1980); Max Loppert, review, *Opera* XXXV (1984), 328–31 [on British stage premiere]; Andrew Porter, "Musical Events," *NY* LX (July 2, 1984), 98 [on U.S. premiere].

DISCOGRAPHY: R. Hardy, M. King, London Sinfonietta; cond. O. Knussen, Arabesque Z 6535 (1984, Morden, Surrey, 1 CD).

VIDEO: Beardsley, Glyndebourne Festival, NVC/BBC.

Whim, The, or, The Miser's Retreat, ballad opera in one act; libretto (Eng), after *La maison rustique*. First performance 1734, London, Goodman's Fields.

LIBRETTO: English, with ballad airs (London, 1734); repr. Rubsamen/*BO*, vol. 16, *Country Operas II: Farcical Humor and Stratagem* (1974).

Whipping Boy, The, comic opera by Alfred Hill; libretto (Eng) by Arthur Adams. First performance (excerpts) 1896, Wellington, New Zealand.

The work mocks stuffy official receptions and includes the song "My Fairest Child."

Whirligig, opera in one act by Heskel Brisman; libretto (Eng) by Jerome Greenfield, after a short story by O. Henry. First performance October 25, 1977, Muncie, Indiana, Ball State University.

The setting is hillbilly country. Ariela and Rance Hilbo come to the office of the local justice of the peace, Benja Widdup, to ask for a divorce. Widdup agrees to dissolve the marriage for the fee of five dollars, the sum total of Rance's assets. Ariela then demands alimony, which Widdup sets at five dollars; Rance has no more money to pay alimony but must raise the sum in order not to be in contempt of court. He disguises himself as a robber and relieves Widdup of the money. Appearing before Widdup the next day, Ariela and Rance report that they have reconsidered and do not want to get divorced. Widdup says that this is impossible, since the divorce has already been finalized. To get married, the couple needs five dollars, which Ariela produces, and Widdup proceeds.

For a description, see Kornick/*RAO*, 71–72.

Roles: Benja Widdup (bar), Rance Hilbo (ten), and Ariela Hilbo (sop).

White Agony, The, opera by Peter Paul Fuchs; libretto (Eng) by the composer, after Karel Čapek's *The White Plague* (1937). First performance, in German, as *Die weisse Krankheit*, June 12, 1989, East Berlin, Komische Oper. First U. S. performance (in English) March 27, 1992, Greensboro, North Carolina, Greensboro Opera, with John Pierce (Dr. Gomez), Harold Glenn Mackintosh (Marshal), William Stevens (Baron Krondorf), Frances Hurcherson Bailey (Mrs. Stransky), and William Beck (Mr. Stransky); conducted by the composer; directed by Elissa Minet Fuchs; designed by Daniel A. Seaman.

The setting is a war-torn European country in the future, in which disease is killing off the populace. When Dr. Gomez develops a cure, he offers it to the now-stricken dictator, Marshal, only if the latter will agree to end the fighting. On his way to treat the ruler, Gomez is killed by an enraged male mob, whose fury the peace-loving women had tried unsuccessfully to diffuse. Thus the cure for the disease and the chance for peace are destroyed.
BIBLIOGRAPHY: Carl J. Halperin, review, *ON* LVII (Oct. 1992), 52 [on U.S. premiere].

White Bird, The, opera in one act by Ernest Carter; libretto (Eng) by Brian Hooker. First performance (concert) May 23, 1922, New York, Carnegie Chamber Music Hall. First performance (stage) March 6, 1924, Chicago, Studebaker Theater, with Ward Pound (Reginald Warren), Hazel Eden (Elinor), Bryce Talbot (Basil), and Haydn Thomas (John Wardwell); conducted by Leroy N. Wetzel.

The setting is the Adirondacks in the early nineteenth century. A forester, Basil, falls in love with Elinor, the wife of Reginald Warren, his employer. He is fooled into shooting her when he thinks her white scarf is a gull that had been hovering around the camp. When Basil learns that Warren had arranged the deception with the help of the steward John Wardwell, Basil strangles Warren.
LIBRETTO: English (New Haven, Conn.: Yale University Press, 1924).

White Butterfly, The, opera by Alan Leichtling; libretto (Eng) by Gabriela Roepke, after her drama. First performance February 18, 1971, New York, Juilliard School.

White Chrysanthemum, The, lyrical comedy in three acts by Howard Talbot; libretto (Eng) by Arthur Anderson and Leedham Bantock. First performance August 31, 1905, London, Criterion, with Rutland Barrington (Reginald), Isabel Jay (O San), and Henry Lytton.

In this variation on the "Oriental" plots of *The Geisha** and *San Toy,** a British lieutenant, Reginald, falls in love with a native Japanese girl, O San, who turns out to be Sybil, a British girl running away from an arranged marriage.

White Doe, The, church opera in two acts by Alan Ridout; libretto (Eng) by Allan Wicks, after William Wordsworth. First performance 1987, Ripon, North Yorkshire, England, Ripon Cathedral.

White Lady, The, adaptation by Thomas S. Cooke of Boieldieu's *La dame blanche* (1825, Paris); libretto (Eng) by Samuel Beazley, after the French text by Scribe, after Scott's *Guy Mannering* and *The Monastery*. First performance October 9, 1826, London, Drury Lane Theatre.

The setting is eighteenth-century Scotland. A former English officer, George Brown, stays with Dickson, a Scottish farmer, and Jenny, his wife, who tells him the tale of the "white lady" said to haunt the neighboring castle. At the castle George meets Anna, ward of the steward. Left alone, he falls asleep; when he awakes, he sees the apparition, which is, in fact, Anna in disguise, who remembers having cared for George when he was wounded.

At the auction of the castle the next day, Anna, saying she has instructions from the "white lady," urges George to outbid the other parties interested in buying the property. When he is successful, she shows him a treasure hidden in the base of the statue of the "white lady." It turns out that he is the rightful heir to the estate. Anna then reveals her true identity to George, and the two embrace.

White Plume, The, or, The Border Chieftains, "musical-romantick drama" in three acts by William Reeve; libretto (Eng) by Thomas Dibdin, after Scott's *Lay of the Last Minstrel* (1805). First performance April 10, 1806, London, Covent Garden.

The love of Lady Margaret, a widow, and Baron Henry of Cranstoun is threatened by their feuding families. When Henry defeats an enemy of Margaret's family in battle and saves her son, the feud is ended, and the pair are wed.
LIBRETTO: English (London: Barker, 1806).

White Wings, chamber fantasy opera in two acts by Douglas Moore; libretto (Eng) by Philip Barry, after his play (1927). First performance February 9, 1949, Hartford, Connecticut, Hartt Auditorium.

Whitsunday, chamber opera in three acts by Brian Howard; libretto (Eng) by Louis Nowra. First performance September 2, 1988, Sydney, Opera House, Drama Theatre.

A wealthy family and their maid are drawn into a surreal world on a strange island.
BIBLIOGRAPHY: M. Prerauer, review, *Opera* XXXIX (Dec. 1988), 1439–40 [on premiere].

Who Pays the Reckoning?, afterpiece by Samuel Arnold; libretto (Eng) by the composer. First performance July 16, 1795, London, Little Theatre in the Haymarket.

Who's the Composer?, farce in one act by Thomas German Reed; libretto (Eng) by J. M. Morton. First performance October 28, 1845, London, Haymarket Theatre.

Who's to Have Her?, short opera by William Reeve and John Whitaker; libretto (Eng) by Thomas Dibdin. First performance November 22, 1813, London, Drury Lane Theatre.
SCORE: vs (London, ca. 1813).

Who Stole the American Crown Jewels?, "Singspiel" by Norman Siegel; libretto (Eng) by Jean Reavey. First performance May 5, 1971, New York, Cubiculo Theater, with Alice Dutcher (Loretta Mermaid); conducted by Mimi Stern-Wolfe.

The surreal story includes a child king and queen, a mermaid, and a Mrs. Woman, who kills her son; he comes back to life as a soldier.

The music is eclectic in style and mixes Gilbert and Sullivan, Menotti, and Baroque elements in the score.
BIBLIOGRAPHY: Raymond Ericson, review, *NYT* (May 9, 1971), 61 [on premiere].

Who Wants a Wife? or, The Law of the Land, musical drama in three acts by Henry Rowley Bishop; libretto (Eng) by Isaac Pocock. First performance April 16, 1816, London, Covent Garden.

The work includes the designation "Arabian tale."
SCORE: ms fs (British Library, Add. MS. 36946); vs, selections (London: Goulding, D'Almaine, and Potter, ca. 1816).

Who Wins, comic opera in two acts by Henry Condell; libretto (Eng) by John Till Allingham. First performance February 25, 1808, London. First U.S. performance March 3, 1810, Philadelphia.

Wicked Duke, The, opera in one act by Thomas German Reed; libretto (Eng) by Gilbert A'Beckett. First performance June 9, 1876, London, St. George's Hall.

Wicklow Mountains, afterpiece in two acts by William Shield; libretto (Eng) by John O'Keeffe. First performance October 7, 1796, London. Originally entitled *The Wicklow Gold Mines.*
     A revision of *The Lad of the Hills.**
     The finale of act 2 is supposedly by William T. Parke.
LIBRETTO: English (Dublin: John Whitworth, 1797).

Wicklow Rose, The, opera by George Benjamin Allen; libretto (Eng). First performance 1882, Manchester.

Widow, The, comic opera in three acts by Calixa Lavallée; libretto (Eng) by Frank H. Nelson. First performance March 25, 1882, Springfield, Illinois, Chatterton's Theatre, C. D. Hess Acme Opera Company. First New York performance May 8, 1882, New York, Standard Theatre.
     A duke who at first attempts to bar his niece's wedding is convinced to allow it to proceed and himself weds the widow who brought about the match.
LIBRETTO: English (Boston: J. M. Russell, 1881).
DISCOGRAPHY: excerpts; cond. R. Armenian, CBC Records SMCD 5126.

Widow of Delphi, The, or, The Descent of the Deities, music drama in five acts by Thomas Butler; libretto (Eng) by Richard Cumberland. First performance February 2, 1780, London, Covent Garden.
     An all-sung dialogue opera.
LIBRETTO: English, songs (London: G. Kearsly . . . , 1780).

Widow of Ephesus, The, chamber opera in one act by Michael Hurd; libretto (Eng) by David Hughes and the composer. First performance October 23, 1971, Stroud, England.
     When a young and attractive woman is widowed, she decides to follow her husband and moves in, with her maidservant, to her husband's expansive tomb. While there, she meets a young soldier, who changes her mind about leaving the land of the living.
     Roles: the widow (alto), the maid (sop), and the soldier (bar).

Wife of Bath's Tale, The, "moralistic fairy-tale" in one act by James Legg; libretto (Eng) by the composer and Melvin Freedman, after Chaucer. First performance summer 1986 (workshop), Aspen, Colorado, Aspen Music Festival.
     A knight caught romancing the daughter of the king is condemned to death unless he can answer the riddle posed by the queen: "What is it that women desire most?" He has a year and a day to come up with the answer. An old woman provides it on the last day of his quest in exchange for the knight's granting her one wish. When the knight offers the correct answer to the court, the old woman steps forth and makes her demand, that the knight marry her. He tries to refuse, but the king compels him to wed her. When they are alone, she tells him of the worth of virtue and chivalry. Moved by her explanation, he kisses her and discovers that she is really the princess he has desired all along.
     For a plot description, see Summers/*OOA*, 194–95.

Major roles: the princess/old woman (sop), the knight (bar), the king (bass-bar), and the queen (mezzo).

SCORE: ms vs, holograph (1986, photocopy, NYPL).

Wife of Martin Guerre, The, opera in three acts by William Bergsma; libretto (Eng) by Janet Lewis, after her play. First performance February 15, 1956, New York, Juilliard School, with Mary Judd (Bertrande), Guy Baker (Father Antoine), and Stephen Harbachick (Martin Guerre); conducted by Frederic Waldman; produced by Frederic Cohen.

A young peasant, Martin Guerre, leaves his home in southern France in 1548 because his father is angry over a minor theft. Eight years pass, during which time his family has no news about his whereabouts. He then returns and takes over his dead father's farm. His wife, Bertrande, becomes pregnant, whereupon she believes that the man who has returned is not really her husband. She is then racked with guilt, because she realizes that she loves this man more than she did her husband, and she has him brought to trial, claiming that he tricked her into committing adultery. When her real husband returns, she is relieved, only to be told by him that she had accepted the stranger because of "willful blindness" and that she alone is responsible for his dishonor.

Major roles: Bertrande (sop); Martin Guerre, the impostor (bar); and Father Antoine (ten).

For a detailed description, see Eaton/*OP* I, 153–54.

Among the other settings are three musicals, two entitled *Martin Guerre*, by Roger Ames, with a text by Laura Harrington (1989, New York); and by Claude-Michel Schonberg, with a text by Alain Boublil (1996, London); and *The House of Martin Guerre*, with music and lyrics by Leslie Arden (1996, Chicago).

LIBRETTO: English (Denver: A. Swallow, [1958]).

BIBLIOGRAPHY: Abraham Skulsky, "The Music of William Bergsma," *Juilliard Review* III (Spring 1956), 20–22, 32.

Wife of Two Husbands, The, musical drama in three acts by Joseph Mazzinghi; libretto (Eng) by James Cobb, after Pixérécourt's *La femme à deux maris*. First performance November 1, 1803, London, Drury Lane Theatre.

SCORE: vs (London: Goulding, Phipps & D'Almaine, [1803]).

LIBRETTO: English (London: Longman et al., 1811).

Wild Boy, The, opera in one act by Solomon Epstein; libretto (Eng) by the composer. First performance 1986, Philadelphia.

The story is based on an actual case and is set in the Institute for Special Education in Paris, 1800. It concerns Dr. Jean-Marc Itard and his attempts to educate Victor, the nonverbal wild boy discovered living in the forest. While Dr. Itard agonizes over whether he did the right thing by taking the boy out of his environment, Victor remembers what his life was like before he was captured. Dr. Itard leaves the room to prepare the day's lessons and returns just as Victor leaps out of the second-story window to rejoin his bird friends.

For a plot description, see Summers/*OOA*, 110–11.

Major roles: Dr. Jean-Marc Itard (bar), Victor I (actor and mime), and Victor II (dancer).

SCORE: vs, holograph (photocopy, NYPL).

Wild Goose Chase, The, comic opera in three acts by James Hewitt; libretto (Eng) by William Dunlap, after August Kotzebue's *Der Wildfang*. First performance January 24, 1800, New York, with Mr. Hodgkinson (the baron). Revised as two acts.

For a description, see Sonneck/*SIMG*, 484–85.

Wildman, The, opera in two acts by Nicola LeFanu; libretto (Eng) by Kevin Crossley-Holland. First performance June 21, 1995, Aldeburgh, with Gwion Thomas (Wildman).

The setting is the East Anglia Coast. A wildman, the male equivalent of a mermaid, is captured by the villagers and learns to talk. Not bound by human restraints, he helps a local family overcome its problems.

LIBRETTO: English (Woodbridge, Engl.: Boydell Press, 1995).

BIBLIOGRAPHY: Alex Ross, "The Opera in England: Vigorous but Spiky," *NYT* (June 24, 1995), C, 11 [on premiere].

Wild Swans, The, fairy-tale opera in one act by Susan Hulsman Bingham; libretto (Eng) by the composer, after the story by Hans Christian Andersen. First performance April 25, 1988, at the Worthington Hooker Elementary School, New Haven, Connecticut.

Scored for narrator, adult soloists, children's chorus, and adult chorus.

SCORE: fs (New Haven, Conn.: Chancel Opera Co., 1987).

William and Nanny, or, The Cottagers, comic opera in two acts by Karl Baumgarten; libretto (Eng) by Richard Goodenough. First performance November 12, 1779, London, Covent Garden, with Mr. Wilson (Hearty), Mr. Moody (Murtagh Mulrooney), Mrs. Webb (Dame Hearty), and Miss Brown (Nanny).

The setting is an English village. The librettist admits that the story bears a certain resemblance to *Il filosofo di campagna* (Goldoni's text set by Galuppi in 1754, Venice; see p. vii of the 1779 edition).

The overture was used in William Shield's *Robin Hood.**

LIBRETTO: English (London: J. Kearby, 1779).

William Derrincourt, entertainment in twelve scenes by Roger Smalley; text by the composer, after William Derrincourt's memoirs. First performance August 1977, Perth, Australia.

William Derrincourt, an Englishman, is sentenced in 1839, at the age of twenty, to ten years of transportation to Australia for attempting to steal a waistcoat. The work is built around the most striking moments of his life, as per his memoirs.

William Penn, opera in three acts by Romeo Cascarino; libretto (Eng) by Peggy Oppenlander. First performance October 24, 1982, Philadelphia, Academy of Music, with John Cheek (William Penn) and Dolores Ferraro (Gulielma); conducted by Cristofer Macatsoris.

The work covers events in Penn's life, including his signing of a treaty with the Delaware Indians in 1683, led by Chief Taminent (historically, Tamanend or Tammany).

Major roles: William Penn, Chief Taminent, and Gulielma, Penn's wife.

BIBLIOGRAPHY: William Ashbrook, "Philadelphia," *Opera* XXXIV (1983), 303 [on premiere].

Willie Stark, "musical drama" by Carlisle Floyd; libretto (Eng) by the composer, after Robert Penn Warren's novel *All the King's Men.* First performance May 1, 1981, Houston, Grand Opera, with Timothy Nolen (Willie Stark), Jan Curtis (Sadie Burke), Alan Kays (Jack Burden), Julia Conwell (Anne Stanton), Don Garrard (Judge Burden), Robert Moulson (Sugarboy), David Vosburg (Tiny Duffy), and Lowell Thomas (radio announcer); conducted by John DeMain; directed by Harold Prince.

The story concerns a Southern political demagogue, Willie Stark, whose rise and fall from power is narrated by the young Jack Burden.

BIBLIOGRAPHY: Scott Heumann, "The Trial of Willie Stark," *ON* XLV (Apr. 11, 1981), 11–14, and "Reports: U.S.," *ON* XLVI (Aug. 1981), 30 [on premiere].

Will of Her Own, A, comic chamber opera in four scenes by Inglis Gundry; libretto (Eng) by the composer, after Gerald Findler's *Legends of the Lake Counties* (1967). Composed 1971–1973. First performance May 31, 1985, London, Essex Hall.

Willow Tree, The, radio opera in one act by Charles Cadman; libretto (Eng) by Nelle R. Eberhardt. First performance October 3, 1933, NBC.

Will You Marry Me?, opera in one act by Hugo Weisgall; libretto (Eng) by Charles Kondek, after Alfred Sutro's play *A Marriage Has Been Arranged.* First performance March 8, 1989, New York, Opera Ensemble.

Two people meet at a party, with the girl's parents expecting her to wed the young man. Put off by his boorish behavior, the girl tells him of her beloved, a lieutenant too poor to make her his wife. The man tells the woman that he will help the poor lieutenant financially, to enable the soldier to wed. The woman is touched by the man's good character, and the two accept each other's proposal of marriage.

For a detailed description, see Kornick/*RAO*, 332–33.

Roles: She (sop) and He (bar).

SCORE: vs, holograph (1987, photocopy, NYPL).

Wilmore Castle, comic opera in two acts by James Hook; libretto (Eng) by Robert Houlton. First performance October 1, 1800, London, Drury Lane Theatre.

LIBRETTO: English (London: R. H. Westley, 1800).

Wind Drum, dance-opera by Alan Hovhaness; libretto (Eng) by the composer. First performance 1962, Honolulu, University of Hawaii; May 23, 1964, Gatlinburg, Tennessee, Union College.

SCORE: miniature score (New York: C. F. Peters, 1962).

Wind in the Willows, The, children's opera by John Rutter; lyrics by David Grant, after Kenneth Grahame's book (1908). Composed 1981 for voices and orchestra. Revised for stage performance March 8, 1997, Wilmington, Delaware, OperaDelaware, with a revised libretto (Eng) by Evelyn Swensson, with Ed Emmi (Mr. Mole), Rob Hull (Mr. Rat), Alan Wagner (Mr. Badger), and Ray Murphy (Mr. Toad); conducted by Lee Kimball.

The children's story concerns the lives of Mr. Rat, Mr. Mole, Mr. Badger, and Mr. Toad, who live near the river.

SCORE: vs (Oxford: Oxford University Press, 1986).

BIBLIOGRAPHY: Frank Lewin, review, *ON* LXI (June 1997), 57 [on stage version].

Wind Remains, The, zarzuela in one act by Paul Bowles; libretto (Eng) by the composer after García Lorca's *Asi que pasen cinco anos.* First performance March 30, 1943, New York, Museum of Modern Art; conducted by Leonard Bernstein.

DISCOGRAPHY: Eos Ensemble; cond. J. Sheffer, Catalyst 099-26-684092 (1995, 2 CDs).

Windsor Castle, or, The Fair Maid of Kent, opera-ballet; libretto (Eng) by William Pearce. First performance April 6, 1795, London, Covent Garden.

The work, written for the marriage of the Prince of Wales to Caroline, Princess of Brunswick, concerns the Black Prince's marriage to the Fair Maid.

For a detailed musical description, see Fiske/*ETM*, 554–55.

Windsor Castle, or, The Prisoner-King, operetta in two acts by John Henry Gries-bach; libretto (Eng) probably by Thomas James Serle. First performance 1838, London.
LIBRETTO: English (London: Johnson, 1838).

Windsor Castle, opera-burlesque by Frank Musgrave; libretto (Eng) by Francis C. Burnand. First performance 1865, London.
LIBRETTO: English (London: T. H. Lacy, 1865?).

Wings of the Dove, The, opera in six scenes by Douglas Moore; libretto (Eng) by Ethan Ayer, after the novel by Henry James. First performance October 12, 1961, New York, with Regina Sarfaty (Kate Croy), Paul Ukena (Homer Croy), Martha Lipton (Aunt Maud Lowder), John Reardon (Miles Dunster), and Dorothy Coulter (Milly Theale); conducted by Julius Rudel; directed by Christopher West; choreographed by Robert Joffrey; designed by Donald Oenslager.

The story opens in London in 1900. The penniless Kate Croy cannot wed the young journalist Miles Dunster because of her poverty and the disapproval of her aunt, Maud Lowder. Instead, Miles marries the rich and frail Milly Theale, whose wealth he hopes to inherit upon her death. Milly learns of Miles's unscrupulousness but forgives him before she dies. Miles then offers to marry Kate if she will renounce his newly acquired wealth. When she refuses, the two part for good.

For a detailed description, see Eaton/*OP* II, 241–42.

Major roles: Kate Croy (mezzo); Homer Croy, her father (bar); Aunt Maud Lowder, her aunt (alto); Miles Dunster, a young journalist (bar); and Milly Theale, an American heiress (sop).
SCORE: vs (New York: G. Schirmer, 1961).
LIBRETTO: English (New York: G. Schirmer, 1961).
BIBLIOGRAPHY: Richard Repass, "America," *Opera* XII (Dec. 1961), 786–87 [on premiere].

Win Her and Wear Her, comic opera in three acts by John Barnett; libretto (Eng) by Samuel Beazley, after *A Bold Stroke for a Wife* (1718) by Susanna Centlivre. First performance December 18, 1832, London, Drury Lane Theatre.

In order to get a Quaker guardian to consent to his marrying the man's charge, a colonel impersonates a Quaker preacher, only to have the fellow himself turn up.

Winona, opera in three acts by Alberto Bimboni; libretto (Eng) by Perry Williams. First performance November 11, 1926, Portland, Oregon; repeated 1928, Minneapolis, American Grand Opera Company, with Minna Pelz (Winona), Alice Price Moore (Weeko), J. McMillan Muir (Chatonska), A. K. Houghton (Matosapa), and William Fraser Robertson (Wabashaw); conducted by the composer.

Winona is in love with Chatonska, a young brave, who breaks the tribal law by abandoning the hunting trail in order to meet with her in secret. He is branded on the forehead as a coward, and when Wabashaw, Winona's guardian, tries to make Winona marry Matosapa, chief of the Dakota village at Lake Pepin, Winona throws herself into the lake.

For a detailed description, see Hipsher/*AO*, 75–76.

The score includes Chippewa melodies.

Winter's Tale, A, opera in two acts by John Harbison; libretto (Eng) by the composer, after Shakespeare's play (1611). First performance August 20, 1979, San Francisco,

San Francisco Opera, with Susan Quittmeyer (Hermione), David Arnold (Leontes), Ellen Kerrigan (Perdita), David Koch (Polixenes), Tonio Di Paolo (Florizel); conducted by David Agler.

Leontes, King of Sicilia, develops an overriding jealousy of Hermione, his wife, and his friend Polixenes, causing him to imprison her and leave his infant daughter, whom he believes to be illegitimate, on a deserted shore. The daughter, Perdita, is found and brought up by a shepherd. She meets Florizel, son of Polixenes, and they are attracted to each other, but Polixenes prevents them from marrying, thinking Perdita is a commoner. When Perdita flees with Florizel to her homeland, she is recognized and accepted by her father. Still mourning for the wife he wrongfully condemned and believes is dead, Leontes declares his love for her, whereupon her statue, which Perdita had been viewing, comes to life as Hermione.

Major roles: Leontes, King of Sicilia (bass-bar); Hermione, his wife (sop); Perdita, their daughter (sop); Polixenes, King of Bohemia (bar); and Florizel, his son (ten).

The libretto is a condensation of Shakespeare's play and compresses a span of sixteen years using a dumb show, to represent the daughter's banishment and return.

Among other settings of the Shakespeare are a parody by William Brough, *Perdita, or, The Royal Milkmaid*, set to popular and borrowed airs (1856); C. E. Di Barbieri, *Perdita, oder, Ein Wintermärchen* (1865, Prague); Max Bruch, *Hermione* (1872, Berlin); J. Nesvera, *Perdita* (1897, Prague); K. Goldmark, *Ein Wintermärchen* (1908, Vienna); Field (1975); D. Douglas, *The Winter's Tale* (1984, Burbank, Calif); and S. Shaffer (not perf.).
BIBLIOGRAPHY: "America Opera Project: Harbison's 'A Winter's Tale,'" *MA* XXIX (Dec. 1979), 20–21 [on premiere].

Wise and Foolish, The, operatic fantasy in one act by Kurt List; libretto (Eng) by the composer, after the Brothers Grimm. First performance June 2, 1951, New York, 92nd Street Y, with Connie Dose (the musician) and Ralph Magelssen (the woodcutter); conducted by Franz Bibo; produced by Muriel Sharon.

The story centers on a musician's attempts to be understood.

The music is atonal, and the action is presented as a play within a play that includes a stage audience who interrupt the proceedings with comments.
BIBLIOGRAPHY: C H., "List's First Opera," *NYT* (June 4, 1951), 31.

Wish, The, opera in one act by George Antheil; libretto (Eng) by the composer. First performance April 2, 1955, Louisville, Kentucky, Louisville Philharmonic Society; conducted by Moritz Bomhard.

Witch Boy, The. See **Conjur Moon**.

Witches' Well, The, opera in a prologue and one act by Adeline Appleton; libretto (Eng) by the composer and Percy Davis. First performance May 1928, Tacoma, Washington.

Set in Salem in 1692, the plot concerns Paul, who has found the beautiful Zara near a well and brought her to the house of the Puritan woman Ellen. Zara's beauty raises such passion that she is accused of witchcraft and thrown into a well. Although she is rescued by Paul, Zara dies, and Paul, in despair, kills himself. The villagers, incensed, prepare to hang the women in the jail who have been condemned as witches, but they are stopped by Zara's spirit, which rises from the well.
SCORE: ms vs (1928; LCCN: 84–185430).

Witch of Salem, A, grand opera in two acts by Charles Wakefield Cadman; libretto (Eng) by Nelle R. Eberhardt. First performance December 8, 1926, Chicago, with Charles Hackett (Arnold Talbot), Howard Preston (Nathaniel Willoughby), Irene Pavloska (Sheila Meloy), Eidé Norena (Clarise Willoughby), and Augusta Lenska (Tibuda); conducted by Henry G. Weber. Revived March 29, 1951 (concert), New York, Greenwich Mews Playhouse, Frantz Opera Players; conducted by Arthur Frantz; Esther Hoffmann and Kenneth Zimmerli, pianists.

The story is set in Salem, in 1692. Sheila Meloy loves Arnold Talbot, who himself is in love with Clarise Willoughby, Sheila's cousin. In revenge Sheila, aided by Tibuda, a black servant from Barbados, gets Clarise accused of witchcraft. Just as Clarise is to be hanged as a witch, Sheila confesses her deception, on the condition that Arnold give her one kiss. She dies happily, having made Arnold kiss her, even if only once.

For a description, see Hipsher/*AO*, 108–10.

R. Ward's *The Crucible** (1961) also concerns witchcraft trials in Salem.

SCORE: vs (Boston: O. Ditson, [1926]).

LIBRETTO: English (Boston: Ditson, 1928).

BIBLIOGRAPHY: Harold C. Schonberg, "New Opera Group Gives Double Bill," *NYT* (Mar. 30, 1951), 27 [on 1951 revival].

Without Memorial Banners, jazz opera in two acts by Herbert Six; libretto (Eng) by Dan Jaffe. First performance March 24, 1966, Kansas City, Coffee Concerts.

Composed in memory of jazz great Charlie Parker.

BIBLIOGRAPHY: preview, *Variety* (Mar. 23, 1966), 242.

Wittikind and His Brothers, or, The Seven Swan Princes and the Fair Melusine, "original fairy tale" (musical) in two acts; libretto (Eng) by Tom Taylor. First performance ca. 1852, London.

LIBRETTO: English (London: T. H. Lacy, 1852).

Wives Avenged, The, comic opera in one act by Charles Dibdin; libretto (Eng) by the composer, after Sedaine's *Les femmes vengées*, set by Philidor (1775, Paris). First performance September 18, 1778, London, Covent Garden.

Wizard, The, or, The Brown Man of the Moor, melodramatic romance by Charles Edward Horn; libretto (Eng) by Samuel J. Arnold, after Scott's *The Black Dwarf* (1817). First performance July 26, 1817, London, Lyceum.

Wizard of the Nile, The, comic opera by Victor Herbert; libretto (Eng) by Harry B. Smith. First regular performance November 4, 1895, New York, Casino Theater, with Frank Daniels (Kibosh), Walter Allen (the king), Dorothy Morton (Cleopatra), and Edwin Isham (Ptarmigan).

The plot is set in Egypt at the time of Cleopatra and centers on Kibosh, a traveling fakir, whose promise to bring rain to the drought-plagued land works too well. The rains will not cease, so that the king has Kibosh sealed in a tomb. When the monarch finds himself entombed as well, he pardons Kibosh when he is rescued. The plot also involves a romance between Cleopatra and Ptarmigan, a musician.

For a detailed description, see Waters/*VH*, 108–14.

The score contains the waltz "Star Light, Star Bright," which remained popular for some time after the opera's premiere. Its sequel was *The Idol's Eye** (1897).

LIBRETTO: English, typescript ([1895], NYPL).

Wizards of Balizar, The, children's opera in two acts by Normand Lockwood; libretto (Eng) by Russell Porter. First performance August 1, 1962, Denver.

The setting is Balizar in the distant past. Abdullah narrates the tale of Ismad, a tailor, who is urged by his wife to become a wizard, which he does by studying a book. The King's treasurer asks for Ismad's help in locating a lost ruby. Ismad is unsuccessful and goes to the palace to attempt to find the stone himself, while Maki, his nephew, keeps on trying through magic and makes the treasurer's wife appear at his door. She turns out to be the thief, and she gives him the stone. When Ismad is discovered in the palace, he is arrested, but Maki saves him by bringing out the ruby. Ismad gets a reward, his wife promises to wear only simple clothes, and Ismad and Maki promise to use their magic only for amusement.

Roles: Abdullah, a singer (bar); Ismad (ten); Maki (unchanged boy's voice); Ismad's wife (mezzo); Kamal, the King's treasurer (speaking); and Lady, his wife (sop).

W. of Babylon, The, "baroque burlesque" in two acts by Charles Wuorinen; libretto (Eng) by Charles Bruce. First performance (excerpts) December 15, 1975, New York, Manhattan School of Music, with Catherine Rowe (the Marquise), Richard Frisch (Count Roberto), Kenneth Bell (Albertine), Judith Bettina (Sucrette), and Merja Sargon (Wu Tse T'ien), narrated by Coburn Britton; conducted by Daniel Schulman. First complete performance (concert) January 2, 1989, San Francisco, San Francisco Symphony's New and Unusual Music Series, Herbst Theater, with Miriam Abramowitsch (the Marquise), Thomas Manguem (Count Roberto), Judy Hubbell (Sucrette), and John Duykers (Albertine).

The story, set in 1685, concerns the lascivious Marquise de Babylon and Count Roberto, her cousin, who attempt to seduce the servant lovers Albertine and Sucrette. Among the other characters are a "pretty boy" and Wu Tse T'ien, a Chinese princess.

Major roles: the Marquise (sop), Count Roberto (bar), Albertine (bass), Sucrette (sop), and Wu Tse T'ien (sop).

The work is scored for eight soloists and narrator. It includes a duet by Purcell.
BIBLIOGRAPHY: Stephanie von Buchau, "San Francisco," *ON* LIII (Apr. 1989), 33–34 [on San Francisco premiere]; Donal Henahan, "Opera: 'W. of Babylon,'" *NYT* (Dec. 17, 1975), 38 [on 1975 performance].

Woman at the Otowi Crossing, The, opera by Stephen Paulus; libretto (Eng) by Joan Vail Thorne. First performance June 17, 1995, St. Louis, Opera Theatre of St. Louis, with Sheri Greenawald (Helen Chalmers), Kimm Julian (Jack Turner), Christine Abraham (Emily Chalmers), and Andrew Wentzel (Tilano); conducted by Richard Buckley; directed by Colin Graham.

The work, set in New Mexico, has as its background the Manhattan Project and the development of the atomic bomb. It centers on Helen Chalmers, who believes in the "Oneness and All." She reveals her philosophy in the closing number, "Journal Aria." The story also involves Helen's estrangement from her daughter Emily and the redemption of Tilano, a young Pueblo Indian who has turned to drink.

Major roles: Helen Chalmers (sop); Emily Chalmers (mezzo); Jack Turner, Helen's lover (bar); and Tilano (bass-bar).
BIBLIOGRAPHY: Charles Morton, "St. Louis," *ON* LX (Oct. 1995), 54–55 [on premiere]; review, *NYT* (June 20, 1995), C, 15.

Woman in the Garden, The, chamber opera in one act by Vivian Fine; libretto (Eng) by the composer, after writings by Emily Dickinson, Isadora Duncan, Gertrude Stein, and

Virginia Woolf. First performance December 2, 1978, San Francisco, Opera Center, Porta Costa Players. Revised version March 24, 1984, Syracuse, Society for New Music, with Karen Holohan (Isadora Duncan), JoElyn Wakefield-Wright (Emily Dickinson), Jean Loftus (Gertrude Stein), and Neva Pilgrim (Virginia Woolf); conducted by Rhonda Kess.

The opera centers on four women artists of the past two centuries, Emily Dickinson, Isadora Duncan, Gertrude Stein, and Virginia Woolf, who meet and bond emotionally.

The work includes elements of jazz and quotes from Chopin's *Funeral March* and Erik Satie's *Véritables préludes flasques, pour un chien.*
BIBLIOGRAPHY: William D. West, review, *ON* XLIX (Aug. 1984), 46 [on premiere].

Woman's Will, a Riddle, "operatic drama" in three acts by John Davy; libretto (Eng) by Edmund L. Swift, after Chaucer's *Wife of Bath's Tale.* First performance July 20, 1820, London, Drury Lane Theatre.
SCORE: vs, selections (London: Clementi, 182?).
LIBRETTO: English (London: J. J. Stockdale, 1820).

Woman Who Dared, The, or, A Fine Agitation, opera in one act by Zelman Bokser; libretto (Eng) by Cynthia Fuller on the trial of Susan B. Anthony. First performance November 18, 1984, Rochester, New York, with Gwendolyn Lentz (Susan B. Anthony); conducted by Benton Hess; directed by Ruth Rosenberg.

A dramatization of the period from 1872 to 1873, when Susan B. Anthony was put on trial for supporting a woman's right to vote. The subtitle is taken from Anthony's description of the judicial proceedings.

The music includes quasi-Gregorian chant underlying the pronouncements of the judge at the trial.
BIBLIOGRAPHY: "Rochester," *ON* XLIX (Feb. 16, 1985), 39–40 [on premiere].

Woman Who Laughed at Faery, The, opera in one act by Fritz Hart; libretto (Eng) by the composer. First performance September 25, 1929, Melbourne, Australia, Playhouse.

Women, The, chamber opera in one act by Thomas Pasatieri; libretto (Eng) by the composer. First performance August 20, 1965, Aspen, Colorado, Aspen Music Festival, with Vicky Bond (the mother), Pamela Kucenic (the wife), and James Everett (the man); conducted by Leonard Slatkin; produced by Madeleine Milhaud and the composer.

The story concerns the struggle among a man, his wife, and his mother, a conflict that is eternal in nature.

Roles: the mother (sop), the wife (mezzo), and the man (bar).

The first work of the composer's triptych. The others are *La divina** and *Padrevia.**
SCORE: vs (Ger-Eng) (Bryn Mawr, Pa.: T. Presser Co., [1970]).

Wonderful Water Cure, The, operetta by Thomas German Reed, an adaptation of Grisar's *L'eau merveilleuse* (1839, Paris); libretto (Eng) by Benjamin N. Webster, after T. M. F. Sauvage's French text. First performance July 15, 1846, London, Haymarket Theatre.

Wonders in the Sun, or, The Kingdom of the Birds, masque; libretto (Eng) by Thomas D'Urfey, a sequel to Bishop Godwin's *The Man in the Moone* (1638). First performance April 5, 1706, London, Queen's Theatre.

The hero Gonzales, a Spaniard, is accompanied by Diego, his servant. They have come to the sun via a special machine drawn by birdlike animals called ganzas. According to Socrates, in Gonzales's service, everything on the sun is the exact opposite of situations on Earth. Therefore, the undeserving acquire wealth, and being beaten is a sign of friendliness. Confused by all around him, Gonzales and Diego return to Earth.

The dances were composed by John Smith, a violinist; the work, with an all-sung prologue, includes music by some fifteen composers and adaptations of popular airs.

For a detailed description, see Fiske/*ETM*, 41–46.

Wood Daemon, The, or, "The Clock Has Struck," "romantic drama" in two acts by Michael Kelly; libretto (Eng) by Matthew G. Lewis. First performance April 1, 1807, London, Drury Lane Theatre. First U. S. performance March 18, 1808, Boston, with additional music by James Hewitt; arranged by Victor Pelissier.

One O'Clock, or, The Knight and the Wood Daemon* (1811, London) is the sequel.

Woodlanders, The, romantic tragedy in three acts by Stephen Paulus; libretto (Eng) by Colin Graham, after the novel by Thomas Hardy (1887). First performance June 13, 1985, St. Louis, with Carol Gale (Grace Melbury), Lisbeth Lloyd (Mrs. Charmond), Cory Miller (Marty South), Joanna Levy (Grammer Oliver), Mark Thomsen (Edred Fitzpiers), and James McGuire (Giles Winterbourne); conducted by Richard Buckley.

The setting is in the woods of Dorset. Giles Winterbourne, a woodlander, is engaged to Grace Melbury, the daughter of a successful timber merchant, George Melbury. When she returns after finishing school, she has become too polished for Giles; this, added to Giles's loss of income, makes her father cancel the engagement. Grace's father has picked out another husband for his daughter, the handsome young doctor Edred Fitzpiers. But Fitzpiers turns his attention to Felice Charmond, a wealthy widow who has moved into the area.

Grace seeks comfort from Giles in his forest cottage, but, fearing impropriety in their presence together, he goes into the woods, although he is ill, and dies shortly thereafter. The faithful Marty, who has long loved Giles, tends to his grave, and Grace is brought together with Fitzpiers after Mrs. Charmond dies.

Major roles: Grace Melbury (sop); Felice Charmond (sop); Marty South (mezzo-sop); Suke Damson (mezzo); Grammer Oliver (alto); Edred Fitzpiers, doctor (ten); John South (ten); Giles Winterbourne (bar); and George Melbury (bass-bar).

SCORE: vs (Valley Forge, Pa.: European American Music, [1985]).
LIBRETTO: English (Valley Forge, Pa.: European American Music, [1985]).
BIBLIOGRAPHY: Andrew Porter, review, *NY* LXI (July 1, 1985), 88ff. [on premiere]; James Wierzbicki, review, *HiFi/MA* XXXV (Nov. 1985), MA32.

Woodman, The, comic opera in three acts by William Shield; libretto (Eng) by Henry Bate. First performance February 26, 1791, London, Covent Garden, with Madame Pieltain (Emily) and Charles Incledon (Sir Walter). First U.S. performance 1794, Philadelphia.

The work centers on female archery, with the heroine Emily the first to hit the bull's-eye. The hero is Sir Walter, accompanied by his cousin, Di Clacket. The two get drenched when they are fooled into going off on a fake rendezvous with their lovers.

For a detailed musical description, see Fiske/*ETM*, 543.
LIBRETTO: English (London: Longman & Broderip, n.d.).

Woodman's Hut, The, "melo-dramatic romance" in three acts by Charles Edward Horn; libretto (Eng) by W. H. Arnold or Samuel J. Arnold. First performance April 12, 1814, London, Drury Lane Theatre.
LIBRETTO: English (London: J. Miller, 1814).

Word to Wives, A, or, The Cryer's Sequel, musical entertainment in one act by James Hook; libretto (Eng). First performance May 19, 1785, London, Vauxhall Gardens. SCORE: vs (London: T. Skillern, [1785?]).

World in the Moon, The, semi-opera by Daniel Purcell and Jeremiah Clarke; libretto (Eng) by Settle. First performance June 1697, London, Dorset Gardens.

Two young London men, Frank Wildblood and Palmerin Worthy, are interested in obtaining girlfriends, but Palmerin is more genteel in his pursuit of Jacintha, whose father wants her to marry a rich old man.

Wreckers, The, opera in three acts by Ethel Smyth; libretto (Fr) by Harry Brewster, as *Les naufrageurs,* after a Cornish drama; translated into German by H. Decker and John Bernhoff, as *Strandrecht.* First performance, in German, November 11, 1906, Leipzig. First British performance (concert, in German) May 30, 1908, London, Queen's Hall; conducted by Artur Nikisch. First British performance, as *The Wreckers,* translated by the composer and Alma Strettell, June 22, 1909, London, His Majesty's Theatre, with Mme. de Vere Sapio (Thirza), Elizabeth Amsden (Avis), John Coates (Mark), and Arthur Winckworth (Pascoe); conducted by Thomas Beecham. Revived August 3, 1972, Newport Festival.

The story is set in an eighteenth-century Cornish village, where the townspeople's livelihood depends on shipwrecks. The young Thirza, married to Pascoe, the preacher and head of the village, is in love with Mark; furthermore, Avis, daughter of the lighthouse keeper, is in love with Mark. Thirza and Mark light a fire to warn ships away from the treacherous coast. When Pascoe is discovered near the fire and accused of setting it, Mark admits that he started it. He and Thirza then drown themselves.

For a detailed plot description, see K/*NKOB,* 740–41.

Major roles: Thirza (mezzo), Pascoe (bass-bar), Mark (ten), and Avis (sop).

The musical highlights include a depiction of the sea at the beginning of the second act, in "On the Cliffs of Cornwall."

SCORE: vs (London: Universal, 1916).

DISCOGRAPHY: J. Howarth, A. Sand, A.-M. Owens, P. Sidhom, D. Wilson-Jones, B. Bannatyne-Scott, Huddersfield Choral Society, BBC Phil.; cond. O. de la Martinez, Conifer Records/BGM Music, Conifer 51250-2 (1994, 2 CDs).

Wreck of the Pinafore, music by Luscombe Searelle; libretto (Eng) by Horace Lingard. First performance May 27, 1882, London, Opera Comique; a sequel to Arthur S. Sullivan's *H.M.S. Pinafore** (1878, London).

In this sequel affections change, with Josephine becoming interested in Sir Joseph.

Wrestler, The, sacred opera in one act by Samuel Adler; libretto (Eng) by Judith Stampfer, after the Bible. First performance June 22, 1972, Dallas.

The plot concerns the biblical story of Jacob.

Wrinkle in Time, A, children's opera by Libby Larsen; libretto (Eng) by Walter Green, after Madeleine L'Engle's book. First performance March 27, 1992, Wilmington, Delaware, Playhouse Theatre, with Andrea Brown (Meg Murry), Debra Fields (the mother), Andrew Rumbaugh (Calvin), Alan Wagner (Mr. Jenkins/Man with the Red Eyes), and David Price (Dr. Murry); conducted by Evelyn Swensson; directed by Leland Kimball.

The story, which unfolds in outer space, concerns the age-old battle of good versus evil. Meg Murry, together with her friends, runs into alien creatures while searching for her father, Dr. Murry, who has vanished while carrying on secret work for the government.

BIBLIOGRAPHY: Frank Lewin, "Wilmington, Del.," *ON* LVII (July 1992), 40 [on premiere].

Wuthering Heights, opera in four acts by Bernard Hermann; libretto (Eng) by Lucille Fletcher, after the novel by Emily Brontë. Composed 1943. First performance November 6, 1982, Portland, Oregon, Portland Opera, with Victor Braun (Heathcliff), Barrie Smith (Cathy), Geraldine Decker (Nelly), John Walker (Edgar Linton), Alyce Rogers (Isabella), Chester Ludgin (Hindley), and Michael Gallup (Joseph); conducted by Stefan Minde.

The work, set in the moor country of northern England in 1835 (prologue) and 1817 to 1821 (acts 1–4), is based on the first part of Brontë's novel but includes some of the author's poems and some of the poetic speeches from the second part of the novel. See following entry for a plot description.

Major roles: Cathy Earnshaw (sop), Heathcliff (bar), Nelly Dean (mezzo), Edgar Linton (ten), Isabella Linton (mezzo), and Hindley Earnshaw (bar).

SCORE: vs (London: Novello, [1965]).

LIBRETTO: English-German (London: Novello, [1965]).

BIBLIOGRAPHY: Frank Kinkaid, "Scaling the Heights," *ON* XLVII (Nov. 1982), 16, 17; the same, "Reports: U.S.," *ON* XLVII (Jan. 15, 1983), 43 [on premiere].

Wuthering Heights, opera in a prologue and four acts by Carlisle Floyd; libretto (Eng) by the composer, after the novel by Emily Brontë. First performance July 16, 1958, Santa Fe, with Phyllis Curtin (Cathy), Regina Sarfaty (Nelly Dean), Robert Trehy (Heathcliff), Davis Cunningham (Hindley Earnshaw), Loren Driscoll (Edgar Linton), John Macurdy (Mr. Earnshaw), and Mildred Allen (Isabella); conducted by John Crosby; produced by Irving Gutman; designed by Patton Campbell. Revised into three acts 1959.

The opera opens with a prologue, in which Lockwood, a tenant at Thrushcross Grange, is granted refuge from a storm by the sullen Heathcliff, who now owns the Earnshaws' former estate. At night Lockwood sees the ghost of Cathy, once a resident at the estate and Heathcliff's lover. The opera then presents a series of flashbacks. Earnshaw, who has lost his wife, has left the rearing of his children, Cathy and Hindley, along with the mysterious Heathcliff, a gypsy boy, to the servant Nelly. When Earnshaw dies suddenly, after arguing with his son because the father treats Heathcliff as one of his own, Hindley relegates Heathcliff to a subservient position, although the boy still meets Cathy in secret.

At one of their meetings Cathy sprains her ankle and is offered hospitality by the Lintons, who live nearby with their children, Edgar and Isabella. After Cathy becomes angry with Heathcliff, she accepts Edgar's offer of marriage. Distraught, Heathcliff runs off and returns, several years later, having become a man of some means. Although Cathy still loves him, she refuses to leave with him, and so he marries Isabella in spite. Cathy, pregnant with Edgar's child, becomes seriously ill. Heathcliff returns once more and grants her last request, to take her into the air and light. Her death haunts Heathcliff and drives his wife to madness.

For a detailed description, see Eaton/*OP* I, 156–57.

Major roles: Cathy Earnshaw (sop), Heathcliff (bar), Nelly Dean (mezzo), Edgar Linton (ten), Isabella Linton (sop), Mr. Earnshaw (bass), and Hindley Earnshaw (bar).

SCORE: vs ([n.p.]: Boosey & Hawkes, 1961).

LIBRETTO: English (New York: Boosey & Hawkes, 1958; rev. 1959).

Wyf of Bathes Tale, The. See **The Canterbury Tales** (Chisholm).

X

X (**The Life and Times of Malcolm X**), opera in three acts by Anthony Davis; libretto (Eng) by Thulani Davis, story by Christopher Davis. First performance October 1985, Philadelphia, American Music Theatre Festival, with Avery Brooks (Malcolm) and Thomas Young (Street/Elijah Muhammad); conducted by Peter Aaronson. Revised version September 28, 1986, New York, City Opera, New York State Theater, with Ben Holt (Malcolm), Thomas Young (Street/Elijah Muhammad), Priscilla Baskerville, and Marietta Simpson.

Set in various U.S. cities and Mecca in the 1950s and 1960s, the opera traces the life of Malcolm X from his childhood in Lansing, Michigan, and his brushes with the law, to his conversion to the teachings of Muhammad through the Nation of Islam, led by Elijah Muhammad. It also deals with his ministry, his break with Elijah, his pilgrimage to Mecca, a trip that results in his conversion to orthodox Islam, and his assassination in New York in 1965.

For a detailed description, see Kornick/*RAO*, 80–82.

Major roles: Malcolm X (bar); Elijah (ten); Reginald (bar); Ella, Malcolm's sister (mezzo); and Louise, Malcolm's mother/Muslim woman/Betty Shabazz, Malcolm's wife (sop).

The work combines traditional operatic conventions with elements of rap, jazz, and swing.

SCORE: vs, holograph score (New York: Episteme Music, 1985).

BIBLIOGRAPHY: Andrew Porter, reviews, *NY* LXI (Oct. 28, 1985), 83–87 [on premiere] and *NY* LXII (Oct. 27, 1986), 118ff. [on New York premiere]; John Rockwell, "Malcolm X—Hero to Some, Racist to Others—Is Now the Stuff of Opera," *NYT* (Sept. 28, 1986), II, 1.

DISCOGRAPHY: E. Perry, T. Young; cond. W. H. Curry, Gramavision (CD); rev. Patrick J. Smith, "Recordings," *ON* LVII (Dec. 5, 1992), 50.

Y

Yan Tan Tethera, opera by Harrison Birtwistle; libretto (Eng) by Tony Harrison. First performance August 5, 1986, London, Queen Elizabeth Hall, Opera Factory, with Omar Ebrahim (Alan), Helen Charnock (Hannah), and Richard Stuart (Caleb); conducted by Elgar Howarth.

The work examines the clash of good and evil as personified by two shepherds.

For a detailed description, see K/*NKOB*, 71–72.

Major roles: Alan, a northern shepherd (bar); Caleb Raven, a scheming shepherd (bar); and Hannah (sop).

SCORE: vs (London: Universal Edition, 1986).

BIBLIOGRAPHY: Andrew Clements, "Birtwistle Counts Sheep," *MT* CXXVII (1986), 428–30; Anthony Marks, "'Yan Tan Tethera,'" *MT* LXXVII (1986), 570 [on premiere].

Yehu, a Christmas Legend, opera in one act by Eugene Zador; libretto (Eng) by Anna Együd, after the Bible. First performance December 21, 1974, Los Angeles, Bureau of Music, with Janet Smith (Rachel), Patricia Smith (the cousin), Octavio Orochena (Yehu), and Ralph Bassett (the father); accompanied by Paul Pitman on piano.

The opera in set in Bethlehem at the time of the first Christmas. Rachel is awaiting the return of her son, Yehu, one of Herod's soldiers. When Rachel answers a knock at the door, she finds a poor couple, with the wife about to give birth. Rachel and Simon, her husband, offer to accommodate the couple in their stable. Sharah brings news of Herod's orders to kill all the newborn children in Bethlehem. When Yehu arrives, he is drunk and suffering from leprosy. He ignores his mother and Zura, his cousin, and, hearing that a child has been born in the family's stable, rushes to complete Herod's orders. Yehu comes back, however, without having harmed the infant, and he decides to give his life for that of the newborn child. He then realizes that the leprosy has disappeared. Zura, formerly mute, now sings a hymn of praise.

For a detailed description, see Kornick/*RAO*, 338–40.

Major roles: Yehu (ten), Rachel (alto), Simon (bass), and Sharah (sop).

SCORE: vs (New York: C. Fischer, 1975).

BIBLIOGRAPHY: Henry Reese, *"Yehu,"* *OJ* VIII (1975), 19–20 [on premiere].

Yellow Wallpaper, The, chamber opera in two acts by Ronald Perera; libretto (Eng) by Constance Congdon, after Charlotte Perkins Gilman's novella of the same name (1986). First performance May 17, 1989, Northampton, Massachusetts. Performed December 9, 1992, New York, Manhattan School of Music, with Peggy Kriha (Charlotte), Kyle Pfortmiller (John), and Charles Bressler (Dr. Mitchell); conducted by David Gilbert; directed by Mark Harrison.

Inspired by the life of Charlotte Perkins Gilman, a nineteenth-century feminist, the work concerns the severely depressed Charlotte. She is forced to undergo a "cure" developed by Dr. Mitchell for depressed women, which involves confining her to a room (decorated by yellow wallpaper) and allowing her to leave it for only one hour a day.

The work includes a lament in act 2 by John, Charlotte's husband, who remembers the happy times before his wife became ill.

BIBLIOGRAPHY: Allan Kozinn, review, *NYT* (Dec. 11, 1992), C, 19 [on New York premiere]; Arlo McKinnon Jr., review, *ON* LVII (Mar. 13, 1993), 38–39 [on New York premiere].

Yelva, or, The Orphan of Russia, musical drama in two acts by Henry Rowley Bishop; libretto (Eng) by the composer, after a French text by Scribe, Villeneuve, and Desvergers (1828). First performance February 5, 1829, London, Covent Garden.

Major roles: Vincent, Baptiste, Mina, Lovinsky, Alfred, Koli, Fedora, and Poleska.
SCORE: ms fs (1828–1829, British Library, Add. MS. 27723).
LIBRETTO: English (London: Goulding & D'Almaine, [n.d.]).

Yeomen of the Guard, The, or, The Merryman and His Maid; opera in two acts by Arthur S. Sullivan; libretto (Eng) by William S. Gilbert. First performance October 3, 1888, London, Savoy Theatre, with Courtice Pounds (Colonel Fairfax), Richard Temple (Sergeant Meryll), George Grossmith (Jack Point), Geraldine Ulmar (Elsie Maynard), Jessie Bond (Phoebe Meryll), Rosina Brandram (Dame Carruthers), and Rose Hervey (Kate). First U.S. performance October 17, 1888, New York, Casino Theater, with J. H. Ryley (Jack Point), Henry Hallam (Colonel Fairfax), George Olmi (Sergeant Meryll), Fred Solomon (Wilfred Shadbolt), Bertha Ricci (Elsie Maynard), Sylvia Gerrish (Phoebe Meryll), Isabelle Urquhart (Dame Carruthers), and Kate Uart (Kate).

The story is set in the sixteenth century on the Tower of London Green. Colonel Fairfax, who has been unjustly accused of wrongdoing and sentenced to death, must wed in order to prevent an unscrupulous relative from inheriting Fairfax's fortune. Elsie, a singer, agrees to marry the condemned man. In the meantime Fairfax escapes with the help of Sergeant Meryll and Phoebe, his daughter. Fairfax woos Elsie in disguise in order to find out whether she really loves him. She refuses the advances of the stranger, since she is already wed, and when Fairfax is cleared of all charges, the lovers are reunited. Dame Carruthers, housekeeper of the Tower, finds romance with Sergeant Meryll. The real loser is the jester Jack Point, who had hoped to have Elsie for himself. As the ensemble sings joyously to end the work, he falls dead ("insensible at their feet," says the text) on hearing the news of Fairfax's good fortune.

For a detailed description, see Jacobs/*AS*, 274–81.

Major roles: Colonel Fairfax, sentenced to death (ten); Sergeant Meryll, of the Yeomen of the Guard (bass-bar); Leonard Meryll, his son (ten); Jack Point, a strolling jester (bar); Wilfred Shadbolt, head jailer (bass-bar); Elise Maynard, a strolling singer (sop); Phoebe Meryll, daughter of Sergeant Meryll (mezzo); Dame Carruthers, housekeeper of the Tower (alto); and Kate, her niece (sop).

Unlike other Sullivan works, which begin with choruses, *Yeoman* opens with a solo, Phoebe's "When a Maiden Loves." Among the other musical highlights are the introductory duet of Jack Point and Elsie, "I Have a Song to Sing, O!" (act 1), which is reprised at the end as Point dies; Point's "Oh a Private Buffoon" (act 2), in which he laments his lot and suggests his desire to do more serious drama; and the famous quartet of Elsie, Phoebe, Fairfax, and Point (act 2), "When a Wooer Goes a-Wooing."

This is the only one of the Gilbert and Sullivan collaborations with a major character coming to a sad end. On the question of whether Jack Point really dies or simply faints upon hearing of Fairfax's reprieve, see Stedman/*WSG*, 252. The story has been likened to Wallace's *Maritana** (1845, London)
SCORE: vs (London: Chappell; New York: William A. Pond, n.d.).
LIBRETTO: English (London: G. Bell, 1912).
BIBLIOGRAPHY: Nigel Burton, "'Yeomen of the Guard': Apogee of a Style," *MT* CXXIX (Dec. 1988), 656–59.

DISCOGRAPHY: D'Oyly Carte Opera Orch., Chorus; cond. I. Godfrey, London 417358-2 (1950, 2 LPs); the same, cond. J. O. Edwards, Sony Classical S2K 58901 (1993, 2 CDs). VIDEO: J. Grey, A. Marks, Ambrosian Opera Chorus, London Sym. Orch.; cond. Faris, Goldcrest/Opera World YEO-10V.

Yerma, opera by Paul Bowles; libretto (Eng) by the composer after García Lorca's play. First performance July 29, 1958, Denver, University of Denver, with Libby Holman.

Yerma, opera in three acts by Denis ApIvor; libretto (Eng) by Montagu Slater, after García Lorca. First performance December 17, 1961, BBC.

Yerma, opera by Raymond Wilding-White; libretto (Eng) by the composer, after García Lorca. Composed 1962.
    The work is scored for eight solo voices, choruses, guitarist, and orchestra.
    Also set by H. Villa-Lobos (comp. 1956, perf. 1971, Santa Fe).
SCORE: ms vocal score (1962, photocopy; NYPL).

Yolanda of Cyprus, opera in three acts by Clarence Loomis; libretto (Eng) by Cale Young Rice, after his play. First performance September 25, 1929, London, Ontario, American Opera Company, with John Moncrieff (Renier Lusignan), Edith Piper (Queen Berengere), Charles Kullman (Amaury), Clifford Newdall (Camarin), and Natalie Hall (Yolanda); conducted by Isaac Van Grove; directed by Vladimir Rosing. First U.S. performance, with the same cast, January 8, 1930, New York, Casino Theatre.
    The setting is sixteenth-century Venice. Yolanda is in love with Amaury, but when Queen Berengere has an affair with Camarin, Yolanda saves the Queen's honor by telling Renier Lusignan, the Queen's husband, that she, Yolanda, has been indiscreet. Yolanda, now rejected by Amaury, is forced to wed Camarin. Just after the ceremony the Queen, rising from her deathbed, admits that she was the guilty party. Camarin is then killed in a duel with Renier, the Queen dies, and Yolanda and Amaury are united.
BIBLIOGRAPHY: Olin Downes, review, *NYT* (Jan. 9, 1930), 22 [on U.S. premiere].

You'll Never Get It Off the Ground, children's opera in one act by Martin Kalmanoff; libretto (Eng) by the composer and A. Drake. Composed 1980.

You Never Know, comic opera in one act by Boris Koutzen; libretto (Eng) by the composer. Composed 1962.
    The work is set in a family's comfortable living room.
    Roles: Mary (sop), Fred (ten), and Mary's father (bar).
SCORE: vs (New York: General Music, 1960).

Young Caesar, puppet opera by Lou Harrison; libretto (Eng) by Robert Gorden. First performance August 21, 1971, Aptos, California. First professional performance November 5, 1971, Pasadena, Ramo Auditorium, Cal Tech.
    The story treats Caesar's life beginning with his ceremony of manhood to the end of his liaison with the King of Bithynia.
    The work is scored for five singers and various instruments.
BIBLIOGRAPHY: "San Francisco," *ON* XXXVI (Jan. 15, 1972), 30 [on prof. premiere]).

Young Goodman Brown, opera in one act by Ludwig Lenel; libretto (Eng) by Jane Lenel, after Nathaniel Hawthorne's story. First performance April 25, 1963, Allentown, Pennsylvania, Muhlenberg College Opera Workshop.
    The setting is New England at the time of the Puritans. The young Goodman Brown tells his wife, Faith, that he is going to see the devil and ignores her pleas not to do so.

Drawn into the forest by the devil, in the guise of the man with a staff, he witnesses a witches' sabbath in which many of his friends and neighbors are taking part. His final disillusionment occurs when he discovers that his wife is one of the participants.

For a description, see Summers/*OOA*, 197–98.

Major roles: Goodman Brown (ten/high bar), Faith Brown (sop), and the man with a staff (bass/bass-bar).

Young Goodman Brown, opera in one act by Henry Mollicone; libretto (Eng), after Hawthorne. First performance summer 1970, Glens Falls, New York.

Also music-theater work by Philip Johnston; text by Richard Foreman (New York, 1995). *Goodman Brown** is another setting.

Young Hussar, The, or, Love and Mercy, "operatic piece" in two acts by Michael Kelly; libretto (Eng) by William Dimond. First performance March 12, 1807, London, Drury Lane Theatre, with Mr. Eyre (Bertrand de Valencourt), Mr. Elliston (Florian), Mrs. Harlowe (Madame Larole), Mrs. Mountain (Caroline), and Mrs. Bland (Ninette).

The story is based on an incident in the French Revolution and takes place in Nancy, France. The title character is Florian, son of Bertrand de Valencourt.

LIBRETTO: English (London: Barker and Son, 1807).

Young Kabbarli, The, chamber opera in one act by Margaret Sutherland; libretto (Eng) by Maie Casey. First performance August 19, 1965, Hobart, Australia.

The story is based on an episode in the life of Daisey Bates (1861–1951), who devoted her efforts to aiding the aborigines in western and south Australia at the end of the nineteenth and beginning of the twentieth century. She earned the designation "Kabbarli," or "grandmother."

The music combines various elements, including those of Irish folk melody and aboriginal song.

SCORE; fs, limited ed. ([Sydney, Austral.: J. Albert, 1972]).

DISCOGRAPHY: G. Stevens, D. Patterson, J. McKenzie, T. Patrick, His Master's Voice Q40ASD-7569 (1973, 1 LP).

Young Lincoln, "American folk opera" in one act by Eusebia Simpson Hunkins; libretto (Eng). First performance October 1959, Galesburg, Illinois, Knox College.

SCORE: vs ([n.p., 1960]; LCCN: 84-180963.

Young Thomas Edison, children's opera in one act by Martin Kalmanoff; libretto (Eng) by Robert K. Adams. First performance April 1963, New York, Greenwich Mews.

Youth, Love, and Folly, comic opera by Michael Kelly; libretto (Eng) by William Dimond. First performance May 24, 1805, London, Drury Lane Theatre.

The text was used again for Diamond's melodrama *Adrian and Orilla* (1806, London), with songs by Attwood and Kelly

LIBRETTO: English (London: Barker and Son, 1805).

Youth's Choice, The, musical idyll in one act by Gustav Holst; libretto (Eng) by the composer. Composed 1902. Not performed.

The work is infused with Wagnerian touches.

Yo, Yea, or, The Friendly Tars, dialogue opera by Charles Dibdin; libretto (Eng) by the composer. First performance August 18, 1777, London, Sadler's Wells.

Z

Zaida, or, The Pearl of Granada, comic opera by Meyer Lutz; libretto (Eng) by Oliver Summers, after a German text by Dr. Franks. First performance February 14, 1859, Liverpool, Amphitheatre.

Zapata!, opera in two acts by Leonardo Balada; libretto (Eng) by Tito Capobianco and Gabriela Roepke. First performance 1985, Pittsburgh.
   The plot centers on the revolutionary Mexican leader (ca. 1897–1919).

Zaporogues, The, opera in one act by John D. Davis; libretto (Eng). First performance May 7, 1895, Birmingham, England.
SCORE: ms vs (n.p., n.d.; LCCN: 84-140952).

Zenobia, Queen of Palmyra, lyric opera in four acts by Silas Gamaliel Pratt; libretto (Eng) by the composer. First performance (concert) June 15, 1882, New York; conducted by the composer. First stage performance March 26, 1883, Chicago, McVickers Theater, with Annie Louise Cary (Zenobia).
   Zenobia, ruler of Palmyra, defies Rome's authority. When her armies are defeated, she tries to escape through a secret passage in her palace but is betrayed by Sindarina and Zabdas, who were both rebuffed in their efforts to marry the queen's daughter, Julia. Zenobia is finally spared execution by Aurelian, the emperor of Rome, who weds Julia himself and frees the loyal Longinus also.
   The story, which is set in A.D. 263, is based on historical characters but combines the traits of the heroic Zabdas with the treacherous Antichius.
   Roles: Zenobia (alto); Julia, her daughter (sop); Sindarina, her slave, once princess of Egypt (sop); Zabdas, Zenobia's general (bar); Longinus, high priest (bass); Aurelian, emperor of Rome (ten); Probus, Roman ruler (bar); and ghost of Odentus (bass).
   The Earl of Mount Edgcumbe's *Zenobia* was composed to Metastasio's Italian text (1800, London), set previously some twenty times. An earlier treatment is Albinoni's *Zenobia, regina de' Palmireni* (1694, Venice). The story was also set by the American composer Louis Coerne to a German text (1905, Bremen).
SCORE: vs (Boston: Oliver Ditson & Co., 1881).
LIBRETTO: English (Chicago: author, [1882]).

Zingara, La, or, The Gipsey, burletta in two parts by François Hippolyte Barthelemon; libretto (Eng). First performance August 25, 1773, London, Marylebone Gardens.

Zoo, The, "musical folly" in one act by Arthur S. Sullivan; libretto (Eng) by Bolton Rowe (Benjamin Charles Stephenson). First performance June 5, 1875, London, St. James's Theatre.
   The work, set in the Zoological Gardens of London, concerns two sets of lovers, the apothecary Aesculapius Carboy and Laetitia; and Thomas Brown, a stuttering public speaker who is in fact a duke, and Eliza.

SCORE: vs (London: J. B. Cramer, [1975]).
DISCOGRAPHY: Soloists and chorus, D'Oyly Carte Opera Company, Royal Philharmonic Orch.; cond. R. Nash, London 436-807-2 (1993?, London, 2 CDs; reissue of 1977 recording).

Zoraida, tragedy by Thomas Linley Sr.; libretto (Eng) by William Hodson. First performance December 13, 1779, London, Drury Lane Theatre.

In another treatment of the "generous Turk" theme (as in Dibdin's *The Sultan,** 1775, London), Sultan Selim releases Almaimon and Zoraida from captivity after he learns that Zoraida is really his sister.
LIBRETTO: English (London: W. Richardson, 1780).

Zorinski, opera by Samuel Arnold; libretto (Eng) by Thomas Morton, after Henry Brooke's *Gustavus Vasa.* First performance June 20, 1795, London, Little Theatre in the Haymarket, with John Johnstone and Mrs. Bland.

As Zorinski is too good a person to kill King Casimir, who is ruining the country, his disgust drives him to live in a salt mine. The plot is based on the historical King Stanislaus of Poland.
SCORE: vs (London: Preston & Son, n.d.).
LIBRETTO: English (London: T. N. Longman, 1795).

Zuluki, grand opera in three acts by Harry Lawrence Freeman; libretto (Eng) by the composer. First performance 1898 (concert), Cleveland.

A revision of *Nada.**

Zululand, trilogy of music dramas by Harry Lawrence Freeman, composed 1934–1947; libretto (Eng) by the composer, after H. Rider Haggard:
Nada and the Lily (1941–1944)
Allah (1947)
The Zulu King (1934)

Zuma, or, The Tree of Health, comic opera in three acts by Henry Rowley Bishop and John Braham; libretto (Eng) by Thomas Dibdin, after Stephanie F. Genlis's *Zuma, ou, La découverte du quinquina.* First performance February 21, 1818, London, Covent Garden, with Mr. Abbott (Carlo di Cinchona), Mr. Fawcett (Doctor Bonoro), Mr. Liston (Picquillo), Braham (Mirvan), Miss Boden (Zamorin), Miss Healy (Zoro), and Miss Stephens (Zuma).

The setting is Peru. Zuma attempts to save her ill mistress, wife of the kindly Spanish viceroy, by obtaining the forbidden quinine, which is derived from the "tree of life." Zuma and her husband are condemned to death by their countrymen but are spared when the queen intervenes.
SCORE: ms fs (British Library, Add. MS. 36948).
LIBRETTO: English (London: John Miller, 1818).

Composers

Each entry includes short title and year and city of premiere. *Year of composition (no performance information available). +Libretto by composer. See pp. 735–36 for adaptations and arrangements; Index of Names, pp. 931–78, for composers of other English settings.

A' BECKETT, MARY
b. London, 1817; d. there, Dec. 11, 1863
Agnes Sorel 1835 London
+Little Red Riding
Hood 1842 London

ADAMS, JOHN
b. Worcester, Mass., Feb. 15, 1947
Death of Klinghoffer 1991 Brussels
I Was Looking at
the Ceiling 1995 Berkeley
Nixon in China 1987 Houston

ADAMS, LESLIE
b. Cleveland, Dec, 30, 1932
Blake 1985 Oberlin, Ohio

ADASKIN, MURRAY
b. Toronto, Mar. 28, 1906
Grant, Warden of
the Plains 1967 Winnipeg, Manit.

ADDISON, JOHN
b. London, ca. 1766; d. there, Jan. 30, 1844
False Alarms 1807 London
(with Braham, King)
Free and Easy 1816 London
My Aunt 1815 London
My Uncle 1817 London
Russian Imposter 1809 London

ADÈS, THOMAS
b. London, 1971
Powder Her Face 1995 London

ADLER, SAMUEL
b. Mannheim, Ger., Mar. 4, 1928
Lodge of Shadows 1988 Fort Worth, Tex.
Outcasts of Poker Flat 1962 Denton, Tex.
Wrestler, The 1972 Dallas

ADOLPHE, BRUCE
b. New York, May 31, 1955
Amazing Adventure
of Alvin Allegretto 1995 New York
False Messiah 1983 New York
Marita and Her
Heart's Desire 1995 New York
Mikhoels the Wise 1982 New York
+Tell-Tale Heart 1982 Boston

AHLIN, LEE
Charlotte's Web 1988 St. Petersburg, Fla.

AHLSTROM, DAVID
b. Lancaster, N.Y., Feb. 22, 1927; d. San
Francisco, Aug. 23, 1992
+Aesop's Fables 1986 San Francisco
America, I Love You 1981 New Orleans
Birds, The 1990 San Francisco
Bishop's Horse 1984 San Francisco
Charlie's Uncle 1954 Columbus, Ohio
+Doctor Faustus 1982 San Francisco
+Fourth Day 1961*
+My Heart's in the
Highlands 1955*
+Open Window 1953 Cincinnati
Three Sisters Who
Are Not Sisters 1953 Cincinnati

AIN, NOA
b. Brooklyn, N.Y., 1941
+Outcast, The 1994 Houston

AITKEN, HUGH
b. New York, Sept. 7, 1924
+Fables 1975 Washington, D.C.
+Felipe 1981*
(lib. with L. Tapia)

ALBÉNIZ, ISAAC
b. Camprodín, Spain, May 29, 1860; d.
Cambô-les-Bains (Pyrénées), May 18, 1909
Magic Opal 1893 London

ALBRIGHT, LOIS
b. U.S., 1904
Hopitu 1955 New York

ALEXANDER, WILLIAM P.
b. Lompoc, Calif., Nov. 8, 1927
+Monkey's Paw 1972 Edinboro, Pa.

ALLANBROOK, DOUGLAS
b. Melrose, Mass., Apr. 1, 1921
Ethan Frome 1952*
Nightmare Abbey 1960*

ALLEN, GEORGE BENJAMIN
b. Engl., 1822; d. 1897
Castle Agrazant 1865 London
Fayette 1892 Brisbane, Austral.?
Wicklow Rose 1882 Manchester

ALLEN, JUDITH. SEE SHATIN, JUDITH

ALWYN, WILLIAM
b. Northampton, Engl., Nov. 7, 1905; d.
Southwold, Sept. 11, 1985

Libertine, The 1969*
+Miss Julie 1979 London

AMES, ROGER
b. Cooperstown, N.Y., Dec. 2, 1944
Amarantha 1980 New London
Angel Face 1988 St. Paul, Minn.
Hearts on Fire 1995 Minneapolis

AMRAM, DAVID
b. Philadelphia, Nov. 17, 1930
Final Ingredient 1965 New York
Twelfth Night 1968 Glens Falls, N.Y.

ANDERSON, BETH
b. Lexington, Ky., Jan. 3, 1950
Queen Christina 1973 Oakland, Calif.

ANDERSON, GARLAND
b. Union City, Iowa, June 10, 1933
Soyazhe 1979 Central City, Colo.

ANDERSON, LAURIE
b. Chicago, June 5, 1947
Empty Places 1989 Charleston, S.C.
United States 1982 Brooklyn, N.Y.

ANDERSON JR., T[HOMAS] J[EFFERSON]
b. Coatesville, Pa., Aug. 17, 1928
Soldier Boy, Soldier 1982 Bloomington, Ind.

ANTHEIL, GEORGE
b. Trenton, N.J., July 8, 1900; d. New York,
Feb. 12, 1959
+Brothers, The 1954 Denver
Helen Retires 1934 New York
+Transatlantic 1930 Frankfurt
Venus in Africa 1957 Denver
Volpone 1953 Los Angeles
Wish, The 1955 Louisville, Ky.

ANTILL, JOHN HENRY
b. Sydney, Austral., Apr. 8, 1904; d. there,
Dec. 29, 1986
+Endymion 1924*
1953 Sydney, Austral.
First Christmas 1969 Sydney, Austral.
+Music Critic 1953 Sydney, Austral.

APIVOR, DENIS
b. Collinstown, West Meath, Ire.; Apr.
14, 1916
**+Bouvard and
Pécuchet** 1971–74*
**+She Stoops to
Conquer** 1943–47*
+Ubu Roi 1966–67*
Yerma 1961 BBC

APPLEBAUM, EDWARD
b. Los Angeles, Sept. 28, 1937
Frieze of Life 1983 Newport Beach,
Calif.

APPLETON, ADELINE
b. Waverly, Iowa, Nov. 29, 1886
+Witches' Well 1928 Tacoma, Wash.
(lib. with P. Davis)

APPLETON, JON
b. Los Angeles, Jan. 4, 1939
+Lament of Kamuela 1983 Hanover, N.H.

ARCHER, VIOLET
b. Montreal, Apr. 24, 1913
Meal, The 1985 Edmonton, Alta.
Sganarelle 1974 Edmonton, Alta.

ARGENTO, DOMINICK
b. York, Pa., Oct. 27, 1927
+Aspern Papers 1988 Dallas
Boor, The 1957 Rochester, N.Y.
**+Casanova's
Homecoming** 1985 St. Paul, Minn.
Christopher Sly 1963 Minneapolis
**Colonel Jonathan
the Saint** 1961 Denver
Dream of Valentino 1994 Washington, D.C.
Masque of Angels 1964 Minneapolis
Miss Havisham's Fire 1979 New York
**Miss Havisham's
Wedding Night** 1981 Minneapolis
**Postcard from
Morocco** 1971 Minneapolis
Shoemaker's Holiday 1967 Minneapolis
Sicilian Limes 1954 Baltimore
**Voyage of Edgar
Allan Poe** 1976 St. Paul, Minn.
Water Bird Talk 1977 Brooklyn, N.Y.

ARIA, PIETRO
b. ca. 1897, Italy
Jericho Road 1968 Philadelphia

ARLAN, DENNIS
b. 1945; d. 1979
**Ballad of the Bremen
Band** 1977 Katonah, N.Y.
**Daughter of the Double
Duke of Dingle** 1978 Katonah, N.Y.
**Meanwhile, Back
at Cinderella's** 1976 New York

ARLINGTON, DONALD
I Love My Voice 1978 New York

ARMOUR, EUGENE
b. 1929
We're Back 1981 New York

ARNE, MICHAEL
b. London, ca. 1740; d. there, Jan. 14, 1786
Almena 1764 London
(with J. Battishill)
Artifice, The 1780 London
Cymon 1767 London

Edgar and Emmeline	1761	London
Elfrida	1772	London
Emperor of the Moon	1777	London
Fairy Tale	1777	London
Hymen	1764	London
Linco's Travels	1767	London
(with J. Vernon)		
Maid of the Vale	1775	London
Positive Man	1782	London
(with S. Arnold)		
Tom Jones	1769	London
Tristram Shandy	1783	London
Vertumnus and		
Pomona	1782	London

ARNE, THOMAS AUGUSTINE
b. London, Mar. 12, 1710; d. there,
Mar. 5, 1778

Achilles in Petticoats	1773	London
Alfred	1740	London
Arcadian Nuptials	1764	London
+Artaxerxes	1762	London
Birth of Hercules	1763*	
Blind Beggar	1741	London
Britannia (Love		
and Glory)	1734	London
Britannia	1755	London
Caractacus	1776	London
Comus	1738	London
Cooper, The	1772	London
(lib. prob. by comp.)		
Dido and Aeneas	1734	London
Don Saverio	1750	London
(lib. prob. by comp.)		
Eliza	1754	London
Fairy Prince	1771	London
Guardian Outwitted		
(lib. prob. by comp.)	1764	London
Henry and Emma	1749	London
Hospital for Fools	1739	London
Judgment of Paris	1742	London
King Pepin's		
Campaign	1745	London
Lethe	1749	London
Love Finds the Way	1777	London
(with Sacchini, Fisher)		
Love in a Village	1762	London
May Day	1775	London
Miss Lucy in Town	1742	London
Opera of Operas	1733	London
Phoebe at Court	1776	London
(lib. prob. by comp.)		
Picture, The	1745	London
Pincushion, The	1756	Dublin
Rosamond	1733	London
Rose, The	1772	London
(lib prob. by comp.)		
Sheep Shearing	1754	London

+Sot, The	1775	London
+Squire Badger	1772	London
Tempest, The	1746	London
Temple of Dullness	1745	London
Thomas and Sally	1760	London
Triumph of Peace	1748	London

ARNELL, RICHARD
b. London, Sept. 15, 1917

Combat Zone	1969	Hempstead, N.Y.
Love in Transit	1958	London
+Moon Flowers	1959	Kent, Engl.
Petrified Princess	1959	London

ARNOLD, MALCOLM
b. Northampton, Engl., Oct. 21, 1921

Dancing Master	1962	London
Open Window	1956	BBC

ARNOLD, MAURICE
b. St. Louis, Jan. 19, 1865; d. New York, Oct.
23, 1937

Merry Benedicts	1896	Brooklyn, N.Y.

ARNOLD, SAMUEL
b. London, Aug. 10, 1740; d. there Oct. 22, 1802

Agreeable Surprise	1781	London
Amintas	1769	London
(with Guglielmi et al.)		
April Day	1777	London
Auld Robin Gray	1794	London
Banditti, The	1781	London
Bannian Day	1796	London
Baron Kinkverkankotsdors-		
sprakingatchdern	1781	London
Basket Maker	1790	London
Battle of Hexham	1789	London
Birth-Day, The	1783	London
Britain's Glory	1794	London
Cambro-Britons	1798	London
Castle of Andalusia	1782	London
Children in the Wood	1793	London
Daphne and Amintor	1765	London
Dead Alive	1781	London
Death of Captain		
Faulkner	1795	London
Don Quixote	1774	London
Enchanted Wood	1792	London
Fairies' Revels	1802	London
False and True	1798	London
Fire and Water	1780	London
Gipsies, The	1778	London
Gretna Green	1783	London
Hovel, The	1797	London
How to Be Happy	1794	London
Hunt for the Slipper	1784	London
Inkle and Yarico	1787	London
Irish Legacy	1797	London
Lilliput	1777	London

Love and Madness	1795	London
Love and Money	1795	London
Madman, The	1770	London
Magnet, The	1771	London
Maid of the Mill	1765	London
Mountaineers, The	1793	London
New Spain	1790	London
None So Blind	1782	London
Peeping Tom	1784	London
Portrait, The	1770	London
Positive Man	1782	London
(with M. Arne)		
Revenge, The	1770	London
Review, The	1800	London
Rosamond	1767	London
Royal Garland	1768	London
Rule Britannia	1794	London
Servant Mistress	1770	London
Sheep Shearing	1777	London
Shipwreck, The	1796	London
Siege of Curzola	1786	London
Silver Tankard	1781	London
Sixty-Third Letter	1802	London
Son-in-Law	1779	London
Spanish Barber	1777	London
Summer Amusement	1779	London
Summer's Tale	1765	London
Surrender of Calais	1791	London
Throw Physic to the		
Dogs!	1798	London
Tom Jones	1769	London
Turk and No Turk	1785	London
Two to One	1784	London
Ut Pictora Poesis!	1789	London
Veteran Tar	1801	London
Virginia	1800	London
Weathercock, The	1775	London
Wedding Night	1780	London
Who Pays the		
Reckoning?	1795	London
Zorinski	1795	London

ARNSTEIN, IRA B.

Song of David	1925	New York

ASCHAFFENBURG, WALTER
b. Essen, Ger., May 20, 1927

Bartleby	1964	Oberlin, Ohio

ASHLEY, ROBERT
b. Ann Arbor, Mich., Mar. 28, 1930

+Atalanta	1982	Paris
+Atalanta Strategy	1985	Montreal
Balseros	1997	Miami Beach
+eL/Aficionado	1988	Marseilles
+In Memoriam	1964	Ann Arbor, Mich.
Lessons, The	1981	New York
Music with Roots	1976	Paris

+My Brother Called	1988	Chicago
+Now Eleanor's Idea, tetralogy:		
Improvement	1986*	1991 New York
Foreign Experiences	1987*	1991 New York
Now Eleanor's Idea	1988*	1991 New York
+Perfect Lives	1978	New York
+That Morning Thing	1968	Ann Arbor, Mich.
+When Opportunity		
Knocks	1984–85*	

ASHMAN, MIKE [VINCENT CROCKER]
b. London, Apr. 16, 1950

José's Carmen	1984	London

ASTON, PETER
b. Birmingham, Engl., Oct. 3, 1948

+Sacrapant Sorcerer	1967*	

ATTWOOD, THOMAS
b. London, Nov. 23, 1765; d. there, Mar. 24, 1838

Adopted Child	1795	London
Albert and Adelaide	1798	London
(with D. Steibelt)		
Bondocani, Il	1800	London
(with J. Moorehead)		
Britain's Brave Tars!!	1797	London
Caernarvon Castle	1793	London
Castle of Sorrento	1799	London
David Rizzio	1820	London
(with Braham et al.)		
Day at Rome	1798	London
Devil of a Lover	1798	London
Elphi Bey	1817	London
Escapes, The	1801	London
Fairy Festival	1797	London
Fast Asleep	1797	London
Guy Mannering	1816	London
(with H. R. Bishop)		
Hermione	1800	London
Irish Tar	1797	London
Mouth of the Nile	1798	London
Old Cloathsman	1799	London
Osmyn and Daraxa	1793	London
Packet Boat	1794	London
Poor Sailor	1795	London
Prisoner, The	1792	London
Red-Cross Knights	1799	London
Reform'd in Time	1798	London
Sea-Side Story	1801	London
Smugglers, The	1796	London
St. David's Day	1800	London
True Friends	1800	London

ATWELL, SHIRL JAE

Sagegrass	1986	New York

AUSTIN, JOHN
b. Mt. Vernon, N.Y., June 8, 1954

+Orpheus	1967	Chicago

BACH, JAN
  b. Forrest, Ill., Dec. 11, 1937
  +Student from
  Salamanca   1980 New York
  System, The   1974 New York

BACH, JOHANN CHRISTIAN
  b. Leipzig, Sept. 5, 1735; d. London, Jan. 1,
  1782
  Fairy Favour   1767 London
  Manaclas   1764 Salisbury

BACH, LEONHARD EMIL
  b. Posen, Mar. 11, 1849; d. London, Feb.
  15, 1902
  Irmengarda   1892 London
  Lady of Longeford 1896 London

BACON, ERNST
  b. Chicago, May 26, 1898; d. Orinda, Calif.,
  Mar. 16, 1990
  Drumlin Legend   1949 New York
  Tree on the Plains 1942 Spartanburg, S.C.

BAINTON, EDGAR LESLIE
  b. London, Feb. 14, 1880; d. Sydney, Austral.,
  Dec. 8, 1956
  Crier by Night   1919 *1942 ABC
  Oithona   1915 Glastonbury, Engl.
  Pearl Tree   1927* 1944 Sydney

BAKER, LARRY
  b. Ft. Smith, Ark., Sept. 7, 1948
  Haydn's Head   1987 Cleveland

BAKSA, ROBERT
  b. New York, February 7, 1938
  +Aria da Capo   1968 New York
  +Red Carnations   1974 New York

BALADA, LEONARDO
  b. Barcelona, Sept, 22, 1933
  +Hangman,
  Hangman!   1982 Barcelona
  Zapata!   1985 Pittsburgh

BALFE, MICHAEL
  b. Dublin, May 15, 1808; d. Rowney Abbey,
  Hertfordshire, Engl., Oct. 20, 1870
  Armourer of Nantes 1863 London
  Bianca   1860 London
  Blanche de Nevers 1863 London
  Bohemian Girl   1843 London
  Bondman, The   1846 London
  Castle of Aymon   1844 London
  Catherine Grey   1837 London
  Daughter of St. Mark 1844 London
  Devil's in It   1852 London
  Diadesté   1838 London
  Enchantress, The   1845 London
  Geraldine   1843 Dublin
  Joan of Arc   1837 London

Keolanthe   1841 London
Knight of the Leopard 1891 Liverpool
Letty   1871 London
Maid of Artois   1836 London
Maid of Honour   1847 London
Moro   1882 London
Puritan's Daughter 1861 London
Rose of Castille   1857 London
Satanella   1860 London
Sicilian Bride   1852 London
Siege of Rochelle 1835 London
Sleeping Queen   1864 London

BALIN, MARTY [MARTYN JEREL BUCHWALD]
  b. Cincinnati, Jan. 30, 1942
  Rock Justice   1979 San Francisco

BALK, H. WESLEY
  Newest Opera in the
  World   1974 Minneapolis

BALKIN, ALFRED [ALAN BLAKE]
  b. Boston, Aug. 12, 1931
  +Musicians of
  Bremen   1972*

BALL, MICHAEL
  b. Manchester, Engl., Nov. 10, 1946
  Belly Bag   1992*

BANFIELD, RAFFAELLO DE
  b. 1922
  Alissa   1965 Geneva
  Lord Byron's Love
  Letter   1955 New Orleans

BANNISTER, JOHN
  b. ca. 1630, London; d. there, Oct. 3, 1679
  Circe   1677 London
  Tempest, The   1674 London
  (Bannister et al.)

BANTOCK, GRANVILLE
  b. London, Aug. 7, 1868; d. there, Oct. 16,
  1946
  Caedmar   1892 London
  Eugene Aram   1892*
  Pearl of Iran   1894*
  Seal-Woman   1924 Birmingham

BARAB, SEYMOUR
  b. Chicago, Jan. 9, 1921
  +At Last I've Found
  You   1984 Charlotte, S.C.
  Chanticleer   1956 Aspen, Colo.
  +Fair Means or Foul 1983*
  +Father of the Child 1985 Bayside, N.Y.
  +Fortune's Favorites 1982 New York
  Game of Chance   1957 Rock Island, Ill.
  +I Can't Stand
  Wagner   1986 New York

+Little Red Riding
  Hood   1958 San Francisco
+Little Stories   1979 New York
Maletroit Door   1960 New York
+Not a Spanish Kiss   1977 New York
+Ondine   1995 New York
+Only a Miracle   1985*
+Out the Window   1985 New York
+Philip Marshall   1974 Chautauqau, N.Y.
+Piece of String   1985 Greeley, Colo.
+Pizza con funghi   1989 New York
+Predators   1985 New York
+Rajah's Ruby   1958 New York
+Ruined Maid   1981 New York
+Toy Shop   1978 New York

BARATI, GEORGE
  b. Győr, Hungary, Apr. 3, 1913; d. Los
  Gatos, Calif., June 22, 1996
Feather Cloak   1970*
Noelani   1968*

BARBER, JOSEPH
Rumpelstiltskin   1978 Philadelphia

BARBER, SAMUEL
  b. West Chester, Pa., Mar. 9, 1910; d. New
  York, Jan. 23, 1981
Antony and Cleopatra 1966 New York
Hand of Bridge   1959 New York
Vanessa   1958 New York

BARKER, PAUL ALAN
  b. 1956
Albergo Empedocle   1990 London
+Marriages between
  Zones 3, 4, and 5   1985 London
+Pillow-Song   1985 London

BARKIN, ELAINE R.
  b. Bronx, New York, Dec. 15, 1932
+De Amore   1982 Oberlin, Ohio

BARKWORTH, JOHN EDMUND
  b. Beverley, Engl., May 20, 1898; d. Geneva,
  Nov. 18, 1929
+Romeo and Juliet   1916 Middlesbrough

BARLOW, DAVID
  b. Rothwell, May 20, 1927; d. Newcastle upon
  Tyne, June 9, 1975
David and Bathsheba 1969 Newcastle u. Tyne

BARNARD, FRANCIS
Glory Coach   1982 New York

BARNES, EDWARD
  b. Gettysburg, Pa., Dec. 16, 1957
Feathertop   1980 New York
+Muskrat Lullaby   1989 Los Angeles
Place to Call Home   1992 Los Angeles
+Vagabond Queen   1989 Los Angeles

BARNETT, DAVID
  b. New York, Dec. 1, 1907; d. Weston, Conn.,
  Dec. 7, 1985
Inner Voices   1972 New York

BARNETT, JOHN
  b. Bedford, Engl., July 15, 1802; d.
  Leckhampton, Apr. 17, 1890
Before Breakfast   1828 London
Fair Rosamond   1837 London
Farinelli   1839 London
Mountain Sylph   1834 London
Robert the Devil   1830 London
Soldier's Widow   1833 London
Win Her   1832 London

BARON, MAURICE
  b. Lille, France, Jan. 1, 1889; d. Oyster Bay,
  N.Y., Sept. 5, 1964
François Villon   1940 New York
Gay Musketeers   1925*

BARRY, GERALD
  b. County Clare, Apr. 28, 1952
Intelligence Park   1990 London
Things That Gain   1980 London
Triumph of Beauty
  and Deceit   1994 London

BARTHELEMON [BARTHÉLEMON], FRANÇOIS
  HIPPOLYTE
  b. Bordeaux, France, July 27, 1741; d. Christ
  Church, Surrey, July 20, 1808
Belphegor   1778 London
Election, The   1774 London
Magic Girdle   1770 London
Maid of the Oaks   1774 London
Noble Pedlar   1770 London
Oithona   1768 London
Orpheus   1767 London
Portrait, The   ca. 1771 London
Zingara, La   1773 London

BARTHELSON, JOYCE [HELEN JOYCE
  HOLLOWAY]
  b. Yakima, Wash., May 18, 1900; d. 1986
+Chanticleer   1967 New York
+Devil's Disciple   1977 White Plains
+Feathertop   1968 New York
King's Breakfast   1973 Atlantic City
Lysistrata   1981 New York

BATES, WILLIAM
  fl. ca. 1750–1780
Flora   1770 London
Jovial Crew   1760 London
Ladies Frolick   1770 London
Marriage-Office   1777 London
Pharnaces   1765 London
Second Thought Is
  Best   1778 London

Theatrical Candidates 1775 London

BATH, HUBERT
  b. Barnstaple, Engl., Nov. 6, 1883; d.
  Harefield, Apr. 24, 1945
  Bubbles 1923 Belfast

BATTISHILL, JONATHAN
  b. London, May 1738; d. Islington, Dec. 10,
  1801
  Almena (with M. Arne) 1764 London

BAULD, ALISON
  b. Sydney, May 7, 1944
  +Nell 1988 London

BAUMAN, JON WARD
  b. Big Rapids, Mich., June 7, 1939
  Dialogues 1987 Frostburg, Md.

BAUMGARTEN, KARL
  b. Lübeck, Ger., ca. 1740; d. London, 1824
  William and Nanny 1779 London

BAYLOR, MURRAY
  b. What Cheer, Iowa, Apr. 8, 1913
  By Gemini 1949 Galesburg, Ill.

BEACH, AMY
  b. Henniker, N.H., Sept. 5, 1867; d. New
  York, Dec. 27, 1944
  Cabildo 1932* 1995 New York

BEACH, JOHN PARSONS
  b. Gloversville, N.Y., Oct. 11, 1877; d.
  Pasadena, Calif., Nov. 6, 1953
  Pippa's Holiday 1915 Paris

BEADELL, ROBERT
  b. Chicago, June 18, 1925
  Sweetwater Affair 1961 Lincoln, Neb.

BEALL, JOHN
  b. Belton, Tex., 1942
  Ethan Frome 1997 Morgantown,
  W. Va.

BEALL, MARK
  Going, The 1987 Cincinnati

BECK, JEREMY
  b. Painesville, Ohio, Jan. 15, 1960
  +Anne Boleyn 1984 New York

BECKER, JOHN J.
  b. Henderson, Ky., Jan. 22, 1886; d. Wilmette,
  Ill., Jan. 21, 1961
  Deirdre of the
    Sorrows 1945* 1956 Chicago
  Faust 1951* 1965 Los Angeles
  Privilege and
    Privation 1939* 1982 Amsterdam

BECKFORD, WILLIAM
  b. 1760; d. 1844

Arcadian Pastoral 1782 London

BECKLER, STANWORTH R.
  b. Escondido, Calif., Dec. 26, 1923
  Outcasts of Poker Flat 1960 Stockton, Calif.

BECKLEY, CONNIE
  Funeral of Jan Palach 1990 New York

BECKWITH, JOHN
  b. Victoria, B.C., Mar. 9, 1927
  Crazy to Kill 1989 Guelph, Ont.
  Night Blooming
    Cereus 1959 Toronto
  Shivaree 1982 Toronto

BEDFORD, DAVID
  b. London, Aug. 4, 1937
  Death of Baldur 1980 Elgin, Scot.
  Fridholf's Saga 1981 Elgin, Scot.
  +Return of Odysseus 1988 London
  +Rime of the Ancient
    Mariner 1976–76*

BEECHAM, ADRIAN WELLES
  +Merchant of Venice 1922 Brighton, Engl.

BEECROFT, NORMA
  b. Oshawa, Ont., Apr. 11, 1934
  Dissipation of Purely
    Sound 1988 Toronto

BEESON, JACK HAMILTON
  b. Muncie, Ind., July 15, 1921
  Captain Jinks 1975 Kansas City
  Cyrano 1994 Hagen, Ger.
  Dr. Heidegger's
    Fountain of Youth 1978 New York
  +Hello Out There 1954 New York
  +Jonah 1950*
  Lizzie Borden 1965 New York
  +My Heart's in the
    Highlands 1970 New York, NET
  +Sorry, Wrong
    Number 1996*
  Sweet Bye and Bye 1957 New York

BELL, W[ILLIAM] H[ENRY]
  b. St. Albans, Engl., Aug. 20, 1973; d.
  Gordon's Bay, Cape Province, Apr. 13, 1946
  Wandering Scholar 1935 Cape Town

BENDER, ELLEN
  b. 1949
  Rappaccini's Daughter 1992 Boston

BENEDICT, JULIUS
  b. Stuttgart, Nov. 27, 1804; d. London, June 5,
  1885
  Bride of Song 1864 London
  Brides of Venice 1844 London
  Crusaders, The 1846 London
  Gipsy's Warning 1838 London

Lily of Killarney   1862 London

BENJAMIN, ARTHUR
  b. Sydney, Sept. 18, 1893; d. London, Apr. 9,
  1960
Devil Take Her   1931 London
Mañana   1956 London, BBC
Prima Donna   1949 London
Tale of Two Cities   1957 London
Tartuffe   1964 London (posth.)

BENJAMIN, THOMAS
  b. Bennington, Vt., Feb. 17, 1940
Chicken Little   1985 Houston
Rehearsal, The   1981 New York

BENNETT, RICHARD RODNEY
  b. Broadstairs, Kent, Mar. 29, 1936
All the King's Men   1969 Coventry
Ledge, The   1961 London
Mines of Sulphur   1965 London
Penny for a Song   1967 London
Victory   1970 London

BENNETT, ROBERT RUSSELL
  b. Kansas City, Mo., June 15, 1894; d. New
  York, Aug. 17, 1981
Carmen Jones   1943 New York
Enchanted Kiss   1945 New York
Endymion   1927*1935 Rochester
Maria Malibran   1935 New York

BEREZOWSKY, NICOLAI
  b. St. Petersburg, May 17, 1900; d. New York,
  Aug. 27, 1953
Babar the Elephant   1953 New York

BERGERSEN, BALDWIN
  b. Vienna, Feb. 20, 1914
Far Harbour   1948 New York

BERGSMA, WILLIAM
  b. Oakland, Apr. 1, 1921; d. Seattle, Mar. 18,
  1994
+Murder of Comrad   1973*
Sharik   1986 Brooklyn, N.Y.
Wife of Martin Guerre   1956 New York

BERKELEY, LENNOX
  b. Boar's Hill, near Oxford, May 12, 1903; d.
  London, Dec. 26, 1989
Castaway   1967 Aldeburgh
Dinner Engagement   1954 Aldeburgh
Nelson   1954 London
Ruth   1956 London

BERKELEY, MICHAEL
  b. London, May 29, 1948
Baa Baa Black Sheep   1993 Cheltenham, Engl.

BERKOWITZ, SOL
  b. Warren, Ohio, Apr. 27, 1922
Fat Tuesday   1956 Tamiment, Pa.

BERNARDO, JOSÉ RAOUL
  b. Havana, Oct. 3, 1938
Child, The   1974 Albany, N.Y.

BERNSTEIN, LEONARD
  b. Lawrence, Mass., Aug. 25, 1918; d. New
  York, Oct. 14, 1990
Candide   1956 Boston
Quiet Place   1983 Houston
+Trouble in Tahiti   1952 Waltham, Mass.
West Side Story   1957 New York

BERRY, WALLACE
  b. La Crosse, Wis., Jan. 10, 1928; d.
  Vancouver, Nov. 16, 1991
Admirable Bashville   1954*

BEVERIDGE, THOMAS
  b. New York, Apr. 6, 1938
Dido and Aeneas   1958 Boston

BEVERSDORF, THOMAS
  b. Yoakum, Tex., Aug. 8, 1924; d. Bloomington, Ind., Feb. 15, 1981
Hooligan, The   1969*

BEZANSON, PHILIP
  b. Athol, Mass., Jan. 6, 1916; d. Hadley,
  Mass., Mar. 11, 1975
Golden Child   1959 Iowa City

BIALES, ALBERT
+Belisa   1989 St. Paul, Minn.

BIELAWA, HERBERT
  b. Chicago, Feb. 3, 1930
Bird in the Bush   1962 Los Angeles

BIMBONI, ALBERTO
  b. Florence, Aug. 24, 1882; d. New York, June
  18, 1960
In the Name of Culture 1949 Rochester, N.Y.
Winona   1926 Portland, Oreg.

BINDER, ABRAHAM WOLFE
  b. New York, Jan. 13, 1895; d. there, Oct. 10, 1966
Goat in Chelm   1960 New York

BINGHAM, SUSAN ADAMS HULSMAN
  b. May 31, 1944, Waltham, Mass.
Alice Meets the Mock
Turtle   1988 New York
Emperor and the
Nightingale   1982 New Haven
+Fisherman and His
Wife   1987*
+Gift of the Magi   1984 New Haven
Wild Swans   1988 New Haven

BIRD, ARTHUR
  b. Belmont, Mass., July 23, 1856; d. Berlin,
  Dec. 22, 1923
Daphne   1895 New York

BIRTWISTLE, HARRISON
b. Accrington, Lancashire, Engl., July 15, 1934

Bow Down	1977	London
Down by the		
Greenwood Side	1969	Brighton
Gawain	1991	London
Mask of Orpheus	1986	London
Punch and Judy	1968	Aldeburgh
Second Mrs. Kong	1994	Glyndebourne
Yan Tan Tethera	1986	London

BISCARDI, CHESTER
b. Oct. 19, 1948, Kenosha, Wisc.

| Tight-Rope | 1986 | Madison, Wisc. |

BISHOP, HENRY ROWLEY
b. London, Nov. 18, 1786; d. there, Apr. 30, 1855

Adelaide	1830	London
Aethiop, The	1812	London
Aladdin	1826	London
Alchymist, The	1832	London
Angelina	1804	London
(with L. Gesualdo?)		
Antiquary	1820	London
Barber of Seville	1818	London
Battle of Bothwell		
Brigg	1820	London
Bottle of Champagne	1832	London
Brazen Bust	1813	London
Burgomaster of		
Saardam	1818	London
Circassian Bride	1809	London
Clari	1823	London
Comedy of Errors	1819	London
Comus	1815	London
Cortez	1823	London
Cymon (with M. Arne)	1815	London
December and May	1818	London
Demon, The	1832	London
Don John	1821	London
Doom-Kiss	1832	London
Duke of Savoy	1817	London
Englishmen in India	1827	London
Fall of Algiers	1825	London
Farmer's Wife	1814	London
(with Davy et al.)		
Faustus	1825	London
For England, Ho!	1813	London
Fortunate Isles	1840	London
Freischütz, Der	1824	London
Guillaume Tell	1838	London
Guy Mannering	1816	London
Haroun Alraschid	1813	London
Harry le Roi	1813	London
Heart of Midlothian	1849	London
Heir of Vernoni	1817	London

Henri Quatre	1820	London
Hofer	1830	London
Home Sweet Home	1829	London
Humorous Lieutenant	1817	London
John of Paris	1814	London
Knight of Snowdoun	1811	London
Knights of the Cross	1826	London
Law of Java	1822	London
Libertine, The	1817	London
Love Charm	1831	London
Magpie or Maid	1815	London
Maid Marian	1822	London
Maid of the Mill	1814	London
Maniac, The	1810	London
Marriage of Figaro	1819	London
Masaniello	1829	London
Miller and His Men	1813	London
Montrose	1822	London
Magic Fan	1832	London
Midsummer Night's		
Dream	1816	London
Native Land	1824	London
Night before the		
Wedding	1829	London
Ninetta	1830	London
Noble Outlaw	1815	London
Poor Vulcan	1813	London
Rencontre, The	1827	London
Roland for an Oliver	1819	London
Romance of a Day	1831	London
Rural Felicity	1834	London
Secret Mine	1813	Dublin
Sedain Chair	1822	London
Slave, The	1816	London
Sonnambula, La	1833	London
Talisman, The	1825	London
Telemachus	1815	London
Tyrolese Peasant	1832	London
Under the Oak	1830	London
Vintagers, The	1809	London
Virgin of the Sun	1812	London
Wandering Boys	1814	London
Who Wants a Wife?	1816	London
Yelva	1829	London
Zuma (with Braham)	1818	London

BLAKE, DAVID
b. London, Sept. 2, 1936

| Plumber's Gift | 1989 | London |
| Toussaint | 1977 | London |

BLAKESLEE, S. EARLE
b. Oberlin, Ohio, Nov. 2, 1883; d. San Luis Obispo, Calif. Mar. 9, 1972

| Legend of Wiwaste | 1926 | Ontario, Calif. |

BLANK, ALLAN
b. New York, Dec. 27, 1925

| Aria da Capo | 1958–60* | |

Excitement at the
Circus   1969 Paterson, N.J.
+Magic Bonbons   1983*

BLEWITT, JONATHAN
  b. London, July 19, 1782; d. there, Sept. 4, 1853
Auld Robin Gray   1828 Surrey
My Old Woman   1829 London
Talisman, The   1828 Surrey

BLISS, ARTHUR
  b. London, Aug. 2, 1891; d. there, Mar. 27, 1975
Olympians, The   1949 London
Tobias and the Angel 1960 London, BBC

BLITZSTEIN, MARC
  b. Philadelphia, Mar. 2, 1905; d. Fort-de-
  France, Martinique, Jan. 22, 1964
+Condemned, The   1932*
+Cradle Will Rock   1937 New York
+Harpies, The   1931*
+Idiots First   1962–64*
  (compl. L. Lehrman)   1976 Bloomington
+Magic Barrel   1962–64*
+No for an Answer   1941 New York
Parabola and Circula 1929*
Regina   1949 New York
Sacco and Vanzetti   1959–64*
Triple Sec   1929 Philadelphia

BLOW, JOHN
  b. Newark-on-Trent, bapt. Feb. 23, 1649; d.
  Westminster, Oct. 1, 1708
Venus and Adonis ca. 1683 London/Windsor

BLUMENFELD, HAROLD
  b. Seattle, Oct. 15, 1923
+Amphitryon 4   1962*
Breakfast Waltzes   1991* 1997 Des Moines
Four-Score   1984* 1989 Cincinnati
Fritzi   1979* 1988 Chicago
Seasons in Hell   1996 Cincinnati

BLYTON, CAREY
  b. Beckenham, Kent, Mar. 14, 1932
+Dracula   1983*
+Frankenstein   1987*
+Sweeney Todd   1980*

BOESING, MARTHA/BOESING, PAUL
Wanderer, The   1970 Minneapolis

BOHMLER, CRAIG
Harlot and the Monk 1985 Atlanta

BOHRNSTEDT, WAYNE
  b. Onalaska, Wisc., Jan. 19, 1923
Necklace, The   1956 Redlands, Calif.

BOKSER, ZELMAN
Woman Who Dared   1984 Rochester, N.Y.

BOLCOLM, WILLIAM
  b. Seattle, May 26, 1938

Casino Paradise   1989 Philadelphia
Dynamite Tonite   1963 New York
Greatshot   1969 New Haven
McTeague   1992 Chicago

BOND, VICTORIA
  b. Los Angeles, May 6, 1945
Gulliver   1988 Louisville, Ky.
Travels   1995 Roanoke, Va.

BOOTH, THOMAS
+Gentlemen in Waiting 1967 New York?

BOREN, MURRAY
Dead, The   1993 New York
Emma   1984 Provo, Utah

BORROFF, EDITH
  b. New York, Aug. 2, 1925
+Sun and the Wind   1977 Binghamton, N.Y.

BOSWELL, WILLIAM
  b. Cynthiana, Ky., June 18, 1948
Frog-Hopping   1982 Brooklyn, N.Y.

BOUGHTON, RUTLAND
  b. Aylesbury, Engl., Jan. 23, 1878; d. London,
  Jan. 24, 1960
+Agincourt   1924 Glastonbury, Engl.
Alkestis   1922 Glastonbury, Engl.
+Avalon   1944–45*
+Bethlehem   1915 Street, Engl.
Birth of Arthur   1909*
                         1920 Glastonbury, Engl.
+Chapel in Lyonesse 1914 Glastonbury, Engl.
+Ever Young   1929* 1935 Bath, Engl.
+Galahad   1943–44*
Immortal Hour   1914 Glastonbury, Engl.
+Lily Maid   1934 Stroud, Engl.
Moon Maiden   1918 Glastonbury, Engl.
+Queen of Cornwall   1924 Glastonbury, Engl.
Round Table   1916 Glastonbury, Engl.
Seraphic Vision   1924 Glastonbury, Engl.

BOWLES, ANTHONY
Grub Street Opera   1986 New York

BOWLES, PAUL
  b. Jamaica, N.Y., Dec. 30, 1910
Denmark Vesey   1937 New York
+Wind Remains   1943 New York
+Yerma   1958 Denver

BOYCE, WILLIAM
  b. London, bapt. Sept. 11, 1711; d.
  Kensington, Feb. 7, 1779
Chaplet, The   1749 London
Florizel and Perdita 1756 London
Peleus and Thetis ca. 1740 London
Rehearsal, The   1750 London
Secular Masque   ca. 1746 London
Shepherd's Lottery   1751 London
Tempest, The   1757 London

BOYD, ANNE
b. Sydney, Austral., Apr. 10, 1946
Beginning of the Day 1980*
Little Mermaid 1978* 1986 Sydney
Rose Garden 1972*

BOYTON, WILLIAM
b. ca. 1750; d. ca. 1818
British Sailor 1789 London

BRAHAM, DAVID
b. London, 1834; d. New York, 1905
Mulligan Guard Ball 1879 New York
Reilly and the 400 1891 New York

BRAHAM, JOHN
b. London, Mar. 20, 1774; d. there, Feb. 17, 1856
David Rizzio 1820 London
(with Attwood et al.)
English Fleet 1803 London
False Alarms 1807 London
(with King et al.)
Family Quarrels 1802 London
Isidore de Merida 1792 London
Paragraph, The 1804 London
Taming of the Shrew
(with Cooke) 1828 London
Zuma (with Bishop) 1818 London

BRAND, MAX
b. Lemberg (now Lvov), Apr. 26, 1896; d. Langenzersdorf, near Vienna, Apr. 5, 1980
+Gate, The 1944 New York
+Stormy Interlude 1955*

BRANDT, WILLIAM EDWARD
b. Butte, Mont., Jan. 14, 1920
+No Neutral Ground 1961 Pullman, Wash.

BRAXTON, ANTHONY
b. Chicago, June 4, 1945
+Shala Fears for the
Poor 1996 New York

BRAY, JOHN
b. Engl., June 19, 1782; d. Leeds, June 19, 1822
Alberto Albertini 1811 New York
Hamlet Travestie 1811 London
Indian Princess 1808 Philadelphia

BRÉGENT, MICHEL-GEORGES
+Realitillusion 1988 Toronto

BREIL, JOSEPH
b. Pittsburgh, June 29, 1870; d. Los Angeles, Jan. 23, 1926
Legend, The 1919 New York
+Love Laughs at
Locksmiths 1910 Portsmouth, Me.
+Professor Tattle 1913 New York

+Seventh Chord 1913 Chicago

BRENT-SMITH, ALEXANDER
b. 1889; d. 1950
Captain's Parrot ca.1950*

BRETTINGHAM SMITH, JOLYON
b. Southampton, Engl., 1949
Death of Cuchulain 1973*

BRIAN, HAVERGAL
b. Dresden, Staffordshire, Jan. 29, 1876; d. Shoreham-by-the-Sea, Sussex, Nov. 28, 1972
+Agamemnon 1957* 1971 London
Cenci, The 1951–52* 1997 London
+Tigers, The 1916–19* 1976 London

BRIDGE, FRANK
b. Brighton, Engl., Feb. 26, 1879; d. Eastbourne, Jan. 10, 1941
Christmas Rose 1919–29* 1931 London

BRISMAN, HESKEL
b. New York, Mar. 12, 1923
Whirligig 1977 Muncie, Ind.

BRISTOW, GEORGE F.
b. Brooklyn, N.Y., Dec. 19, 1825; d. New York, Dec. 13, 1898
Rip Van Winkle 1855 New York

BRITTEN, BENJAMIN
b. Lowestoft, Suffolk, Nov. 22, 1913; d. Aldeburgh, Dec. 4, 1976
Albert Herring 1947 Glyndebourne
Billy Budd 1951 London
Burning Fiery
Furnace 1966 Aldeburgh
Curlew River 1964 Aldeburgh
Death in Venice 1973 Aldeburgh
Gloriana 1953 London
Golden Vanity 1967 Aldeburgh
Let's Make an Opera!/
Little Sweep 1949 St. Louis
+Midsummer Night's
Dream 1960 Aldeburgh
Noyes Fludde 1958 Aldeburgh
Owen Wingrave 1971 London, BBC
Paul Bunyan 1941 New York
Peter Grimes 1945 London
Prodigal Son 1968 Aldeburgh
Rape of Lucretia 1946 Glyndebourne
Turn of the Screw 1954 Venice

BROADSTOCK, BENTON
b. Melbourne, Dec. 12, 1952
Fahrenheit 451 1992*

BROEKMAN, DAVID
b. Leiden, May 13, 1899; d. New York, Apr. 1, 1958
Barbara Allen 1954 New York

BROOKS, RICHARD
b. Syracuse, Dec. 26, 1942
+Moby Dick   1987*
Rapunzel   1971 Binghamton, N.Y.

BROTONS, SALVADOR
b. Barcelona, July 17, 1959
Reverend Everyman 1990 Tallahassee, Fla.

BROWN, RICHARD
b. Gloversville, N.Y., Feb. 21, 1947
Gift of the Magi   1985*

BRUCE, NEELY
b. Memphis, Tenn., Jan. 21, 1944
Americana   1980 Middletown,
                             Conn.
+Pyramus and Thisbe 1965 Tuscaloosa, Ala.
Trials of Psyche   1971 Urbana-
                             Champaign, Ill.

BRUMBY, COLIN JAMES
b. Melbourne, Austral., June 18, 1933
Donna, La   1988 Sydney
+Fire on the Wind   1991 Brisbane
+Lorenzaccio   1986 Sydney
+Marriage Machine   1972 Sydney
Seven Deadly Sins   1970 Brisbane
Summer Carol   1991 Canberra

BRYARS, GAVIN
b. Yorkshire, Engl., 1943
Doctor Ox's
  Experiment   1988 London
Medea   1984 Lyons

BRYSON, ERNEST
Leper's Flute   1926 Glasgow

BUCCI, MARK
b. New York, Feb. 26, 1924
Boor, The   1949 New York
+Dress, The   1953 New York
+Hero, The   1965 New York
+Sweet Betsy from
  Pike   1953 New York
+Tale for a Deaf Ear 1957 Lenox, Mass.

BUCHAROFF [BUCHHALTER], SIMON
b. Berdichev, Russia, Apr. 20, 1881; d.
  Chicago, Nov. 24, 1955
Lover's Knot   1916 Chicago

BUCK, DUDLEY
b. Hartford, Conn., Mar. 10, 1839; d. West
  Orange, N.J., Oct. 6, 1909
Deseret   1880 New York

BUGG, G. WILLIAM
b. Memphis, Tenn., Oct. 27, 1943
Bartolo   1986 Birmingham, Ala.

BUHR, GLENN
Heavenfields   1995 Victoria, B.C.

BULLER, JOHN
b. London, Feb. 7, 1927
+Bacchae, The   1992 London

BURGESS, HENRY
fl. ca. 1738 to 1781
Coffee House   1738 London
(with H. Carey)

BURGHERSH, LORD JOHN FANE
b. London, Feb. 3, 1784; d. Wansford,
  Northamptonshire, Oct. 16, 1859
Catherine   1830 London

BURGON, GEOFFREY
b. Hambledon, Engl., July 16, 1941
+Hard Times   1991*
Joan of Arc   1970*
Orpheus   1982 Wells, Somerset

BURNEY, CHARLES
b. Shrewsbury, Apr. 7, 1762; d. Chelsea, Apr.
  12, 1814
+Cunning Man   1766 London
Midsummer Night's
  Dream   1763 London
Robin Hood   1750 London

BURRELL, DIANA
b. 1948, Norwich, England
+Albatross, The   1997 London

BURNHAM, CARDON
b. Kewanee, Ill., Feb. 25, 1927
Aria da Capo   1955 New Orleans

BURT, FRANCIS
b. London, Apr. 28, 1926
Barnstable   1969 Kassel, Ger.
+Volpone   1960 Stuttgart, Ger.

BURTCH, MERVYN
Selfish Giant   1969 BBC, Wales

BURTON, STEPHEN DOUGLAS
b. Whittier, Calif., Feb. 24, 1943
+American Triptych: 1975* 1989 Alexandria,
  Maggie   Va.
  Dr. Heidegger's Experiment
  Benito Cereno
Duchess of Malfi   1978 Vienna, Va.

BUSCH, DENNIS
b. 1947
+Alchemist of
  Trenton   1982*
+Idle Rumor   1986*
+Secret of the Mirror 1983*
+Simple Decision   1982*

Bush, Alan
b. Dulwich, Engl., Dec. 22, 1900; d. Watford, Engl., Oct. 31, 1995
Ferryman's Daughter 1964 Letchworth, Engl.
Joe Hill 1970 Berlin (East)
Men of Blackmoor 1956 Weimar
Press Gang 1947 Letchworth, Engl.
Sugar Reapers 1966 Leipzig
Wat Tyler 1953 Leipzig

Bush, Geoffrey
b. London, Mar. 23, 1920
Blind Beggar's Daughter 1954 Farnham, Engl.
Cat Who Went to Heaven 1976 Croydon
+Equation, The 1968 London
+If the Cap Fits 1956 Cheltenham, Engl.
+Lord Arthur Savile's Crime 1972 London
+Love's Labour's Lost 1988*

Buskirk, Carl van
Land between the Rivers 1956 Bloomington, Ind.

Butler, O'Brien (Whitwell)
b. Cahersiveen, Ireland, ca. 1870; d. May 7, 1915 (on *Lusitania*)
Muirgheís 1903 Dublin

Butler, Thomas Hamly
b. 1762; d. 1823
Calypso 1779 Dublin
Widow of Delphi 1780 London

Byrd, William Clifton
Lyneia 1949 Cincinnati
Scandal at Mulford Inn 1954 Cincinnati

Byrne, David
b. Dumbarton, Scot., May 14, 1952
Forest, The 1988 Berlin (West)
Knee Plays 1984 Minneapolis

Cadman, Charles Wakefield
b. Johnstown, Pa., Dec. 24, 1881; d. Los Angeles Dec. 30, 1946
Garden of Mystery 1925 New York
Land of the Misty Water 1909–12*
Shanewis 1918 New York
Sunset Trail 1922 Denver
Witch of Salem 1926 Chicago
Willow Tree 1933*

Cage, John
b. Los Angeles, Sept. 5, 1912; d. New York, Aug. 12, 1992
Europeras 1 & 2 1987 Frankfurt
Europeras 3 & 4 1990 London
Europera 5 1991 Buffalo

Cain, Thomas
+Jack and Roberta 1981 Riverside, Md.

Caldwell, Mary Elizabeth
b. Tacoma, Wash., Aug. 1, 1909
+Gift of Song 1961 Pasadena, Calif.
Pepito's Golden Flower 1955 Pasadena, Calif.

Callcott, John W.
b. London, Nov. 20, 1766; d. Bristol, May 15, 1821
Mistakes of a Day 1787 Norwich, Engl.

Camilleri, Charles
b. Humrum, Malta, Sept. 7, 1931
Melita 1968 Belfast

Campbell, Colin Macleod
b. London, Mar. 12, 1890; d. Surrey, June 24, 1953
Thais and Talmane 1921 Manchester

Canning, Thomas
b. 1911
Beyond Belief 1956 Rochester, N.Y.

Cannon, Philip
b. Paris, Dec. 21, 1929
Man from Venus 1967 Waltham Abbey, Essex, Engl.
Morvoren 1964 London

Cantrick, Robert B.
b. Adrian, Mich., Dec. 8, 1917
Three Mimes 1969* 1994 New York

Capers, Valerie
b. 1935
Paul Laurence Dunbar 1988 New York
Sojourner 1995 New York

Carbon, John
b. Chicago, 1951
Benjamin 1987 Lancaster, Pa.

Carey, Clive
b. Essex, Engl., May 30, 1883; d. London, Apr. 30, 1968
All Fool's Day 1921 Glastonbury, Engl.

Carey, Henry
b. Yorkshire?, 1687; d. London, Oct. 4, 1743
Britannia 1734 London
Chrononhotonthologos 1734 London
Coffee House 1738 London
(with Burgess)
+Contrivances, The 1729 London
+Happy Nuptials 1733 London
+Honest Yorkshireman 1735 London
+Nancy 1739 London

CARLSEN, PHILIP
+Implications of
  Melissa   1982 Brooklyn, N.Y.

CARLSON, DAVID
  Dreamkeepers   1996 Salt Lake City
  Midnight Angel   1993 St. Louis

CARMINES, AL (ALVIN)
  b. Hampton, Va., 1938
  +**Duel, The**   1974 Brooklyn, N.Y.
  +**Joan**   1971 New York

CARR, BENJAMIN
  b. London, Sept. 12, 1768; d. Philadelphia,
  May 24, 1831
  American in London   1798 Philadelphia
  Archers, The   1796 New York
  Bourville Castle   1797 New York
  Philander and Silvia   1792 London

CARR, F[RANK] OSMOND
  b. 1858; d. 1916
  His Excellency   1894 London

CARTER, ELLIOTT
  b. New York, Dec. 11, 1908
  Tom and Lily   1934*

CARTER, ERNEST
  b. Orange, N.J., Sept. 3, 1866; d. Stamford,
  Conn., June 21, 1953
  +**Blonde, Donna**   1931 Brooklyn, N.Y.
  White Bird   1922 New York

CARTER, THOMAS
  b. ca. 1704; d. 1804
  Birthday   1787 London
  Constant Maid   1788 London
  Fair Americans   1782 London
  Just in Time   1792 London
  Milesian, The   1777 London
  Rival Candidates   1775 London

CARYLL, IVAN [FÉLIX TILKINS]
  b. Liège, May 12, 1861; d. New York, Nov.
  29, 1921
  Duchess of Dantzic   1903 London
  Lucky Star   1899 London
  Pink Lady   1911 New York

CASCARINO, ROMEO
  b. Philadelphia, Sept. 28, 1922
  William Penn   1982 Philadelphia

CASKEN, JOHN
  b. Barnsley, Engl., July 15, 1949
  +**Golem** (lib. with Audi) 1989 London

CAVE, MICHAEL
  b. Springfield, Mo., May 17, 1944
  +**Pandora's Box**   1971 Los Angeles

CELLIER, ALFRED
  b. London, Dec. 1, 1844; d. there, Dec. 28, 1891
  Charity Begins at Home 1872 London
  Doris   1889 London
  Dorothy   1886 London
  Masque of Pandora   1881 Boston
  Mountebanks   1892 London
  Nell Gwynne   1878 Manchester
  Sultan of Mocha   1874 Manchester
  Tower of London   1875 Manchester

CESARINI, CARLO FRANCESCO
  b. San Martino, Italy, 1666; d. after 1741
  Love's Triumph   1708 London
  (with Violone, Gasparini)

CHADWICK, GEORGE W.
  b. Lowell, Mass., Nov. 13, 1854; d. Boston,
  Apr. 4, 1931
  Judith   1901 Worcester, Mass.
  Love's Sacrifice   1923 Chicago
  Padrone, The   1912* 1995 Waterbury, Conn.
  Tabasco   1894 Boston

CHANLER, THEODORE WARD
  b. Newport, R.I., Apr. 29, 1902; d. Boston,
  July 27, 1961
  Pot of Fat   1955 Cambridge, Mass.

CHAPIN, TOM
  b. 1945
  Magic Fishbone   1988 New York

CHARPENTIER, GABRIEL
  b. Richmond, Quebec, Sept. 13, 1925
  +**Orpheus II**   1972 Stratford, Ont.
  +**Tea Symphony**   1972 Banff, Albta

CHAULS, ROBERT
  b. Port Chester, N.Y., July 18, 1942
  +**Alice in Wonderland**   1976 Van Nuys, Calif.

CHÁVEZ, CARLOS
  b. Calzada de Tacube (near Mexico City),
  June 13, 1899; d. Mexico City, Aug. 2, 1978
  Visitors, The   1957 New York

CHEN, EVAN
  Bok Choy Variations   1995 St. Paul, Minn.

CHESLOCK, LOUIS
  b. London, Sept. 25, 1899; d. 1981
  Jewel Merchants   1940 Baltimore

CHILD, FRANCIS JAMES
  b. 1825; d. 1896
  Pesceballo, Il   1862 Boston

CHING, MICHAEL
  Buoso's Ghost   1997 Memphis
  Cue 67   1992 Richmond, Va.
  King of the Clouds   1993 Dayton, Ohio
  (with Moffat)

CHISHOLM, ERIK
  b. Glasgow, Jan. 4, 1904; d. Cape Town, June
  8, 1965
  +Canterbury Tales, trilogy, 1961–62*:
  Wyf of Bathes Tale 1962*
  Pardoner's Tale   1961 Cape Town
  Nonnes Preestes
  Tale   1961*
  +Dark Sonnet   1952 Cape Town
  +Feast of Samhain   1941*
  +Importance of Being
  Earnest   1963*
  +Inland Woman   1953 Cape Town
  +Murder in Three
  Keys, trilogy:
  Black Roses   1954 New York
  Dark Sonnet   1952 Cape Town
  Simoon   1954 New York

CHLARSON, LINDER
  b. 1936
  Love and Psyche   1978*
  Montezuma's Death   1982 New York

CHUDACOFF, EDWARD
  b. 1925
  Circus, The   1953 Interlochen, Mich.

CLAFLIN, AVERY
  b. Keene, N.H., June 21, 1898; d. Greenwich,
  Conn., Jan. 9, 1979
  +Fall of the House of
  Usher   1921*
  Grand Bretèche, La   1957 New York
  Hester Prynne   1934 Hartford
  Uncle Tom's Cabin   1964 New York

CLARKE, HENRY LELAND
  b. Dover, N.H., Mar. 9, 1907
  Loafer and the Loaf 1956 Los Angeles

CLAY, FREDERIC
  b. Paris, Aug. 3, 1838; d. Great Marlow, Engl.,
  Nov. 29, 1889
  Ages Ago   1869 London
  Black Crook   1872 London
  (with Jacob)
  Cattarina   1874 Manchester
  Constance   1865 London
  Court and Cottage   1862 London
  Don Quixote   1876 London
  Gentleman in Black   1870 London
  Golden Ring   1883 London
  Happy Arcadia   1872 London
  In Possession   1871 London
  Merry Duchess   1883 London
  On the March   1896 Sheffield, Engl.
  Oriana   1873 London
  Out of Sight   1860 London
  Princess Toto   1876 Nottingham, Engl.

CLAYTON, THOMAS
  b. London, bapt. Oct. 28, 1673; d. there, buried
  Sept. 23, 1725
  Arsinoe   1705 London
  (with G. Bononcini)
  Prunella   1708 London
  Rosamond   1707 London

CLEEVE, V. DE
  Bird Catcher   1799 London

CLOKEY, JOSEPH WADDEL
  b. New Albany, Ind., Aug. 28, 1890; d.
  Covina, Calif., Sept. 14, 1960
  Nightingale, The   1925 Miami
  Pied Piper of Hamelin 1920 Miami

CLUTSAM, GEORGE H.
  b. Sydney, Sept. 26, 1866; d. London, Nov. 17,
  1951
  +Summer's Night   1910 London

COATES, ALBERT
  b. St. Petersburg, Apr. 1882; d. Milnerton,
  South Africa, Dec. 11, 1953
  Gainsborough   1941 Los Angeles
  Pickwick   1936 London
  Samuel Pepys   1929 Munich
  Van Hunks   1952 Cape Town

COCKSHOTT, GERALD WILFRED
  b. Bristol, Nov. 15, 1915; d. London, Feb. 3,
  1979
  +Apollo and
  Persephone   1954 Kirkwall, Scot.
  +Faun in the Forest 1959 Westport, Conn.

COE, KENTON
  b. Nov. 12, 1932, Tenn.
  Rachel   1989 Knoxville, Tenn.

COFFEY, CHARLES
  d. London, May 13, 1745
  +Female Parson   1730 London

COGAN, PHILIP
  b. Cork?, 1748; d. Dublin, Feb. 3, 1833
  Contract, The   1782 Dublin
  Love in a Blaze   1799 Dublin
  Ruling Passion   1778 Dublin

COHEN, JOEL
  b. Providence, R.I., May 23, 1942
  +Tristan and Iseult 1988 New York

COHEN, STEVE
  b. New York, Sept. 3, 1954
  Cop and the Anthem   1982 New York
  Pizza del destino   1980 Lake George, N.Y.

COHN, JAMES
  b. Newark, N.J., Feb. 12, 1928
  Fall of the City   1955 Athens, Ohio

COKE, ROGER SACHEVERELL
  b. Derbyshire, Engl., Oct. 20, 1912
  +Cenci, The   1959 London

COLD, MARSHALL
  Bundle Man   1993 New York

COLE, HUGO
  b. London, July 6, 1917; d. there, Mar. 2, 1995
  +Asses' Ears   1950 Los Angeles
  +Fair Traders   1971 Wokingham, Engl.
  Falcon, The   1968 Bath
  Flax into Gold   1966 Oxford
  +Jonah   1967*
  +Persephone   1955 London
  +Statue for the Mayor   1952 London
  +Tunnel, The   1960 London

COLEMAN, EDWIN
  Christmas Carol   1962 London, BBC

COLGRASS, MICHAEL
  b. Chicago, Apr. 22, 1932
  +Nightingale, Inc.   1975 Urbana, Ill.
  +Something's Gonna
    Happen   1978 Toronto
  +Virgil's Dream   1976*

COLLINGWOOD, LAWRANCE ARTHUR
  b. London, Mar. 14, 1887; d. Killin,
    Perthshire, Engl., Dec. 19, 1982
  Death of Tintagiles   1950 London
  +Macbeth   1934 London

COLLINS, ANTHONY
  b. Hastings, Engl., Sept. 3, 1893; d. Los
    Angeles, Dec. 11, 1963
  Catherine Parr   1949 New York

CONDELL, HENRY
  b. 1757; d. 1824
  Bridal Ring   1810 London
  (with Pelissier)
  Up to Town   1811 London
  (with Reeve et al.)
  Who Wins?   1810 New York

CONTE, DAVID
  b. Denver, Dec. 20, 1955
  Dreamers, The   1996 Sonoma, Calif.

CONVERSE, FREDERICK
  b. Newton, Mass., Jan. 5, 1871; d. Westwood,
    Mass., June 8, 1940
  Immigrants, The ca. 1914*
  Pipe of Desire   1906 Boston
  +Sacrifice, The   1911 Boston

CONVERY, ROBERT
  b. 1954
  +Pyramus and Thisbe 1982 Waterford, Conn.

CONYGHAM, BARRY
  b. Sydney, Austral., Aug. 27, 1944
  **Apology of Bony
    Anderson**   1978 Melbourne
  Bennelong   1988 Groningen, Neth.
  Edward John Eyre   1971 Sydney
  Fly   1984 Melbourne
  Oath of Bad Brown Bill 1985 Melbourne

COOK, WILL MARION
  b. Washington, D.C., Jan 27, 1869; d. New
    York, July 19, 1944
  Abyssinia   1906 New York
  (with B. Williams)
  In Dahomey   1903 New York

COOKE, HENRY
  b. Litchfield?, Engl., ca. 1615; d. Hampton
    Court, Engl., July 13, 1672
  Siege of Rhodes   1656 London
  (with H. Lawes, M. Locke)

COOKE, THOMAS S. (TOM)
  b. Dublin, 1782; d. London, Feb. 26, 1848
  Abou Hassan   1825 London
  Actors al fresco   1823*
  (with Blewitt, Horn)
  Amoroso   1818 London
  Boy of Santillane   1827 London
  (with Blewitt)
  Challenge, The   1834 London
  Child of the Wreck   1837 London
  David Rizzio   1820 London
  (with Braham et al.)
  Frederick the Great   1814 London
  Gustavus III   1833 London
  Jewess, The   1835 London
  King's Proxy   1815 London
  Lestocq   1835 London
  Oberon   1826 London
  Red Mask   1834 London
  Selima and Azor   1813 London
  (with Bishop, Walsh)
  Siege of Corinth   1836 London
  **Sweethearts and
    Wives** (with Nathan)   1823 London
  Taming of the Shrew   1828 London
  (with Braham)
  Veteran Soldier   1822 London
  (with Whitaker, Perry)
  White Lady   1826 London

COOMBS, JOHN
  +Volpone   1957 London

COOPER, SETH
  **Echoes of the Shining
    Prince**   1985 New York

COPELAND, STEWART
  b. 1953
  Cask of Amontillado   1993*
  **Holy Blood and
    Crescent Moon**   1989 Cleveland

COPLAND, AARON
  b. Brooklyn, N.Y., Nov. 14, 1900; d. North
  Tarrytown, N.Y., Dec. 2, 1990
Second Hurricane   1937 New York
Tender Land   1954 New York

CORBETT, WILLIAM
  d. ca. 1747
British Enchanters   1706 London

CORDER, FREDERICK
  b. London, Jan. 26, 1852; d. there, Aug. 20, 1932
Nordisa   1887 Liverpool

CORIGLIANO, JOHN
  b. New York, Feb. 16, 1938
Ghosts of Versailles   1987 New York
Naked Carmen   1970*
  (with Hess)

CORRI, DOMENICO
  b. Rome, Oct. 4, 1744; d. London, May 22,
  1825
Travellers, The   1806 London

COTEL, MORRIS
  b. Baltimore, Md., Feb. 20, 1943
Dreyfus   1985 Brooklyn, N.Y.
Jest of Hahalabra   1961*

COWARD, NOËL
  b. Teddington, Middlesex, Engl., Dec. 16,
  1899; d. Port Maria, Jamaica, Mar. 25, 1973
+Bitter-Sweet   1929 London

COWELL, HENRY
  b. Menlo Park, Calif., Mar. 11, 1897; d.
  Shady, N.Y., Dec. 10, 1965
Building of Bamba   1917 Halcyon, Calif.
Commission, The   1954*
                 1992 Woodstock, N.Y.

COWEN, FREDERIC[K] HYMEN
  b. Kingston, Jan. 29, 1852; d. London, Oct.
  6, 1935
Garibaldi   1860 London
Harold   1895 London
One Too Many   1874 London
Pauline   1876 London
Signa   1893 Milan
Thorgrim   1890 London

COWIE, EDWARD
  b. Birmingham, Engl., Aug. 17, 1943
+Commedia   1979 Kassel

CRAWFORD, JOHN C.
  b. Philadelphia, Jan. 19, 1931
+Don Cristóbal   1970 Wellesley, Mass.

CROSSE, GORDON
  b. Bury, Engl., Dec. 1, 1937
Grace of Todd   1969 Aldeburgh

Holly from the Bongs   1974 Manchester
Potter Thompson   1975 London
+Purgatory   1966 Cheltenham, Engl.
Story of Vasco   1974 London
Wheel of the World   1972 Aldeburgh

CUMMING, RICHARD
  b. Shanghai, June 9, 1928
Picnic, The   1979 Central City, Colo.

CUMMINGS, CONRAD
  b. San Francisco, Feb. 10, 1948
+Eros and Psyche   1983 Oberlin, Ohio
Photo-Op   1990 New York
Tonkin   1993 Wilmington, Del.

CURRIE, RUSSELL
  b. North Arlington, N.J., Apr. 3, 1954
Cask of Amontillado   1982 New York
Dream within a Dream   1984 Bronx, N.Y.
Ligeia   1987 Riverdale, N.J.
+Rimshot   1990 New York

DAIKEN, MELANIE
  b. London, July 27, 1945
Mayakovsky and
  the Sun   1971 Edinburgh

DAMROSCH, WALTER
  b. Breslau (now Wrocław), Jan. 30, 1862; d.
  New York, Dec. 22, 1950
Cyrano   1913 New York
Dove of Peace   1912 Philadelphia
Man without a
  Country   1937 New York
Opera Cloak   1942 New York
Scarlet Letter   1896 Boston

DANKWORTH, JOHN
  b. London, Sept. 20, 1927
Sweeney Agonistes   1965 London

DARLEY, FRANCIS T. S.
Fortunio   1883 Philadelphia

DAUGHERTY, MICHAEL
  b. 1954
Jackie O   1997 Houston

DAVIES, JOHN
  fl. 1819–1826
Forest Rose   1825 New York

DAVIES, PETER MAXWELL
  b. Manchester, Sept. 8, 1934
+Blind Man's Bluff   1972 London
+Cinderella   1980 Kirkwall, Scot.
Doctor of Myddfai   1996 Kirkwall, Scot.
Eight Songs for a
  Mad King   1969 London
+Jongleur de Notre
  Dame   1978 Kirkwall, Scot.

+**Lighthouse, The**   1980 Edinburgh
+**Martyrdom of St.**
  Magnus   1977 Kirkwall, Scot.
+**Medium, The**   1981 Kirkwall, Scot.
Miss Donnithorne's
  Maggot   1974 Adelaide
+**No. 11 Bus**   1984 London
+**Notre Dame des**
  Fleurs   1973 London
+**Rainbow, The**   1981 Kirkwall, Scot.
+**Resurrection**   1988 Darmstadt
+**Taverner**   1972 London
Two Fiddlers   1978 Kirkwall, Scot.

DAVIS, ALLAN
  b. Watertown, N.Y., Aug. 29, 1922
+**Departure, The**   1975 Montevallo, Ala.
+**Ordeal of Osbert**   1949 Duxbury, Mass.
+**Otherwise Engaged**   1958 New York
+**Sailing of the Nancy**   1948*
  Belle   1955 Duxbury, Mass.

DAVIS, ANTHONY
  b. Paterson, N.J., Feb. 20, 1951
Amistad   1997 Chicago
Tania   1992 Philadelphia
Under the Double
  Moon   1989 St. Louis
X   1985 Philadelphia

DAVIS, CARL
Arrangement, The   1965 London, BBC

DAVIS, JOHN
  b. Birmingham, Engl., Oct. 22, 1867; d.
  Estoril, Portugal, Nov. 20, 1942
Zaporoges   1895 Birmingham

DAVIS, JOHN S.
  b. Evanston, Ill., Oct. 1, 1935
Pardoner's Tale   1967 Tucson, Ariz.

DAVIS, KATHERINE
  b. St. Joseph, Mo., June 25, 1892; d. Littleton,
  Mass., Apr. 20, 1980
+**Unmusical**
  Impresario   1955 Duxbury, Mass.
  (lib. with H. R. Kent)

DAVIS, MARY
Columbine   1973 Boulder, Colo.

DAVY, JOHN
  b. Upton Hellions, Engl., Dec. 23, 1763; d.
  London, Feb. 22, 1824
Caffres, The   1802 London
Rob Roy Macgregor   1818 London
Spanish Dollars!   1806 London
What a Blunder   1800 London
Woman's Will   1820 London

DAWES, WILLIAM
Court Masque   1833 London

DE KENESSEY, STEFANIA MARIA
  b. Budapest, 1956
Monster Bed   1990 New York
Other Wise Man   1996 New York

DE KOVEN [DE KOVEN], REGINALD
  b. Middletown, Conn., Apr. 3, 1859; d.
  Chicago, Jan. 16, 1920
Algerian, The   1893 Philadelphia
Begum, The   1887 New York
Canterbury Pilgrims   1917 New York
Don Quixote   1889 Boston
Fencing Master   1892 New York
Foxy Quiller   1900 New York
Girls of Holland   1907 New York
Golden Butterfly   1908 New York
Highwayman, The   1897 New York
Knickerbockers, The   1893 New York
Maid Marian   1902 New York
Mandarin, The   1896 New York
Paris Doll   1897 Hartford, Conn.
Red Feather   1903 New York
Rip Van Winkle   1920 Chicago
Robin Hood   1891 New York
Rob Roy   1894 New York
Tzigaine   1895 New York
Wedding Trip   1911 New York

DE LARA, ISIDORE
  b. London, Aug. 9, 1858; d. Paris, Sept. 2, 1935
Amy Robsart   1893 London
Light of Asia   1892 London
Minna   1866 London
Royal Word   1883 London

DELIUS, FREDERICK
  b. Bradford, Jan. 19, 1862; d. Grez-sur-Loing,
  France, June 10, 1934
+**Fennimore and**
  Gerda   1919 Frankfurt
+**Irmelin**   1890–92* 1953 Oxford
+**Koanga**   1895–97*
  (lib. with C. F. Keary)   1899 London
+**Magic Fountain**   1893–95* 1977 London
+**Village Romeo and**
  Juliet   1907 Berlin

DELLO JOIO, NORMAN
  b. New York, Jan. 24, 1913
Blood Moon   1961 San Francisco
Nativity   1987 Midland, Mich.
Ruby, The   1955 Bloomington, Ind.
Trial at Rouen   1956 New York
Triumph of Joan   1950 Bronxville, N.Y.

DEL TREDICI, DAVID
  b. Cloverdale, Calif., Mar. 16, 1937
Final Alice   1976 Chicago

DEMBO, ROYCE
b. Troy, N.Y., 1933
Audience, The 1982 New York

DENNISON, SAM
b. 1926
**Rappaccini's
Daughter** 1984 Philadelphia

DE SIMONE, ROBERTO
+Cat Cinderella 1988 Edinburgh

DEUTSCH, HERBERT ARNOLD
b. Baldwin, N.Y., Feb. 9, 1932
Dorian 1995 Garden City, N.Y.

DEVAL, HENRY
+Rival Clans 1847 Newcastle u. Tyne

DIBDIN, CHARLES
b. Southampton, bapt. Mar. 15, 1745; d.
London, July 25, 1814
Amelia 1771 London
+Annette and Lubin 1778 London
+Benevolent Tar 1785 London
Blackamoor, The 1776 London
Brickdust Man 1772 London
+Broken Gold 1806 London
Captive, The 1769 London
+Chelsea Pensioner 1779 London
Christmas Tale 1773 London
+Cobler, The 1774 London
Damon and Phillida 1768 London
Deserter, The 1773 London
Ephesian Matron 1769 London
+Graces, The 1782 London
Grenadier, The 1773 London
+Hannah Hewitt 1798 London
+Harvest Home 1787 London
**Institution of the
Garter** 1771 London
+Islanders, The 1780 London
Jubilee, The 1769 London
+Jupiter and Alcmena 1781 London
+Ladle, The 1773 London
+Liberty Hall 1785 London
**+Life, Death, of
Tom Thumb** 1785 London
Lionel and Clarissa 1768 London
+Long Odds 1783 London
+Marriage Act 1781 London
Match for a Widow 1788 London
Metamorphoses, The 1776 London
+Mischance, The 1773 London
Old Woman of Eighty 1797 London
Padlock, The 1768 London
Palace of Mirth 1772 London
Plymouth in an Uproar 1779 London
+Poor Vulcan 1778 London
+Quaker, The 1775 London

Recruiting Sergeant 1770 London
Romp, The 1771 Dublin
+Rose and Colin 1778 London
Round Robin 1811 London
+Seraglio, The 1776 London
+Shepherd's Artifice 1764 London
**+Shepherdess of the
Alps** 1780 London
Sultan, The 1775 London
+Touchstone, The 1779 London
Trip to Portsmouth 1773 London
Two Misers 1775 London
Wedding Ring 1773 London
+Wives Revenged 1778 London
Yo, Yea (Dibdin et al.) 1777 London
Waterman, The 1774 London

DICKINSON, PETER
b. Lytham St. Annes, Lancashire, Engl., Nov.
15, 1934
Judas Tree 1965 London

DICKMAN, STEPHEN
b. Chicago, Mar. 2, 1943
Tibetan Dreams 1990 New York

DIDOMENICA, ROBERT
b. New York, Mar. 4, 1927
+Balcony, The 1975 Boston
Scarlet Letter 1986*

DIGIACOMO, FRANK
Beauty and the Beast 1974 Syracuse
+Dybbuk, The 1978 New York

DIJULIO, MAX
b. Philadelphia, Oct. 10, 1919
Baby Doe 1952 Denver

DINSMORE, WILLIAM
Thorwald 1940 New York

DOELLNER, ROBERT
Escape from Liberty 1948 Hartford, Conn.

DORAN, MATT
b. Covington, Ky., Sept, 1, 1921
Committee, The 1958 New York
Fee First ca. 1970*
Marriage Counselor 1977 Los Angeles

DORFF, DANIEL
b. New Rochelle, N.Y., Mar. 7, 1956
+Stone Soup 1982 Philadelphia

DORMAN, JOSEPH
d. 1754
Female Rake 1736 London

DOUGHERTY, CELIUS
b. Glenwood, Minn., May 27, 1902; d. Effort,
Pa., Dec. 22, 1986
+Many Moons 1962 Poughkeepsie, N.Y.

DOVE, JONATHAN
  b. 1959
  Siren Song   1994 London
DRATTELL, DEBORAH
  Lilith   1997*
                                    1998 Cooperstown, N.Y.
DRESHER, PAUL
  b. Los Angeles, Jan. 8, 1951
  Power Failure   1989 Iowa City, Iowa
  Way of How   1980 Seattle
DREYFUS, GEORGE
  b. Wuppertal, Ger., July 22, 1928
  Garni Sands   1965* 1972 Sydney
  Gilt-Edged Kid   1976 Melbourne
  Lamentable Reign
    of Charles   1976 Adelaide
  Song of the Maypole   1967 Canberra
  Takeover, The   1969 Canberra
DROBNY, CHRISTOPHER
  Lucy's Lapses   1987 New York
DRURY, ROBERT
  Fancy'd Queen   1733 London
DRYSDALE, LEARMONT
  b. Edinburgh, Oct. 3, 1866; d. there, June 18, 1909
  Fionn and Terra   1909*
  Red Spider   1898 Lowenstoft, Scot.
DUDLEY, GRAHAME
  b. Sydney, Austral., Aug. 4, 1942
  Snow Queen   1985 Adelaide
DUFFY, JOHN
  b. New York, June 23, 1928
  Black Water   1997 Philadelphia
  Eve of Adam   1955 Interlaken, Mass.
DUKE, JOHN
  b. Cumberland, Md., July 30, 1869; d.
    Northampton, Mass., Oct. 26, 1984
  +Captain Lovelock   1953 Hudson Falls, N.Y.
  Sire de Maledroit   1958 Schroon Lake, N.Y.
DUKE, VERNON [VLADIMIR DUKELSKY]
  b. Parfianovka, Russia, Oct. 1903; d. Santa
    Monica, Jan. 16, 1969
  Cabin in the Sky   1940 New York
  +Mistress into Maid   1958 Santa Barbara
DUNHILL, THOMAS
  b. London, Feb. 1, 1877; d. Scunthorpe,
    Lincolnshire, Mar. 13, 1946
  +Enchanted Garden   1928 London
  Happy Families   1933 London
  Tantivy Towers   1931 London
DUNLOP, ISOBEL
  b. Edinburgh, Mar. 4, 1901; d. there, May 12,
    1975

Rab the Rhymer   1953 Aberdeen
  (with H. Oppenheim)
DUSSEK, JOHN
  b. Tschaslau, Bohemia, Feb. 12, 1760; d. St.
    Germain-en-Laye, France, Mar. 20, 1812
  Captive of Spilburg   1798 London
  (with Kelly)
DUTTON, DANIEL
  +Stone Man   1990 Louisville, Ky.
DVORKIN, JUDITH
  b. New York, 1930
  +Blue Star   1983 New York
  Crescent Eyebrows   1956 New York
  +Emperor's New
    Clothes   1989 New York
  +Red-Headed League 1991*
  +Three Musketeers   1992 New York
EAKIN, CHARLES G.
  b. Pittsburgh, Feb. 24, 1927
  +Box, The   1968 New York
EARLS, PAUL
  b. Springfield, Mo., June 9, 1934
  Death of King Philip   1976 Brookline, Mass.
  Grimm Duo   1976 Boston
  Icarus   1982 Linz, Austria
EARNEST, JOHN DAVID
  b. 1940
  Howard   1987 New York
EASDALE, BRIAN
  b. Manchester, Engl., Aug. 10, 1909;
    d. Oct. 30, 1995
  Corn King   1950 London
  Sleeping Children   1951 Cheltenham, Engl.
EASTON, MICHAEL
  b. Hertfordshire, Engl., 1954
  Beauty and the Beast 1989 Melbourne
  Cinderella   1989*
  Little Redinka   1991 Melbourne
  Obelisk, The   1984*
  +Petrov   1992 Melbourne
  +Selfish Giant   1994*
EASTWOOD, THOMAS
  b. 1922
  Christopher Sly   1960 London
  Rebel, The   1969 BBC
EATON, JOHN
  b. Bryn Mawr, Pa., Mar. 30, 1935
  Cry of Clytaemnestra 1980 Bloomington, Ind.
  Danton and
    Robespierre   1978 Bloomington
  Heracles   1972 Bloomington
  Lion and Androcles   1974 Indianapolis
  Ma Barker   1957*

Myshkin	1973	PBS
Reverend Jim	1989*	
Tempest, The	1985	Santa Fe, N.M.

ECCLES, JOHN
b. London?, ca. 1668; d. Hampton Wick,
Jan. 12, 1735

Acis and Galatea	1701	London
Judgment of Paris	1701	London
Loves of Mars and		
Venus (with Finger)	1696	London
Macbeth	1696	London
Rape of Europa	1694	London
Rinaldo and Armida	1698	London
Semele	ca. 1706*	

EDWARDS, JULIAN
b. Manchester, Engl., Dec. 11, 1855; d.
Yonkers, N.Y., Sept, 5, 1910

Brian Boru	1896	New York
Dolly Varden	1901	London
Friend Fritz	1893	New York
Goddess of Truth	1896	New York
Jupiter	1892	New York
King Rene's Daughter	1893	New York
Madeleine	1894	New York
Patriot, The	1908	New York
Victorian	1883	London
Wedding Day	1897	New York

EDWARDS, LEO
b. Cincinnati, Jan. 31, 1937

Harriet Tubman	1986	New York

EDWARDS, ROSS
b. Sydney, Dec. 23, 1943

Christina's World	1983	Sydney

EFFINGER, CECIL
b. Colorado Springs, July 22, 1914; d.
Boulder, Colo., Dec. 22, 1990

Cyrano de Bergerac	1968	Boulder, Colo.
Pandora's Box	1962*	

EICHBERG, JULIUS
b. Düsseldorf, June 13, 1824; d. Boston, Jan.
19, 1893

Doctor of Alcantara	1862	Boston
Two Cadis	1868	Boston

EL-DABH, HALIM
b. Cairo, Mar. 4, 1921

+Birds, The	1988*	
+Black Epic	1968*	
+Drink of Eternity	1981	Washington, D.C.
+Eye of Horus	1967	Boston
+Opera Flies	1971	Washington, D.C.
+Prometheus Bound	1969	Washington, D.C.
+Ptahmose and the		
Magic Spell, trilogy:		
Aton, the Ankh, and		
the Word	1972	Washington, D.C.

Osiris Ritual	1972	Washington, D.C.
Twelve Hours Trip	1972–73*	

ELGAR, EDWARD
b. Broadheath, Engl., June 2, 1857; d.
Worcester, Feb. 23, 1934

Spanish Lady	1929–33*	1986 London

ELKUS, JONATHAN
b. San Francisco, Aug. 8, 1931

Helen in Egypt	1970	Milwaukee
Mandarin, The	1967	New York
Medea	1970	Milwaukee
+Tom Sawyer	1953	San Francisco

ELLINGTON, DUKE (EDWARD)
b. Washington, D.C., Apr. 29, 1899; d. New
York, May 24, 1974

Queenie Pie	1986	Philadelphia

ELLIOTT, LIONEL. SEE WILLIAMS, JOSEPH
BENJAMIN.

ELLSTEIN, ABRAHAM
b. New York, July 9, 1907; d. there, Mar. 22,
1963

+Golem, The	1962	New York
Thief and the		
Hangman	1959	Athens, Ohio

ELMORE, ROBERT
b. Ramapatnam, India, Jan. 2, 1913; d.
Ardmore, Pa., Sept. 22, 1985

It Began at Breakfast	1941	Philadelphia

EMILE, ANDERS

King Harald	1948	New York

ENEBACH, FREDERIC
b. Des Moines, Iowa, Dec. 1, 1945

Crimson Bird	1979	Crawfordsville, Iowa

ENGEL, LEHMAN
b. Jackson, Miss., Sept. 14, 1910; d. New
York, Aug. 29, 1982

Brother Joe	1953	Cleveland
Malady of Love	1954	New York
+Pierrot of the		
Minute	1929	Cincinnati
Soldier, The	1956	New York

ENNA, EMIL
b. 1877; d. 1951

Dawn of the West	1915	Portland, Oreg.

EPSTEIN, SOLOMON
b. 1939

+Moby Dick	1989*	
+Wild Boy	1986	Philadelphia

EWART, FLORENCE MAUD
b. London, Nov. 1864; d. Melbourne, Austral.,
Nov. 1949

+Courtship of Miles
   Standish   1931 Melbourne
+Ekkehard   1923 Melbourne

EYERLY, SCOTT
   b. Lake Forest, Ill., 1958
+On Blue Mountain   1986 New York

FARBERMAN, HAROLD
   b. New York, Nov. 2, 1929
Losers, The   1971 New York

FARMER, JOHN
   b. Nottingham, Aug. 16, 1836; d. Oxford,
   July 17, 1901
Cinderella   1883 Harrow, Engl.

FEDELLI, GIUSEPPE (SAGGIONE)
   fl. 1680–1733
Temple of Love   1706 London

FELDMAN, JAMES
Intruder, The   1984 Berea, Ohio

FELDMAN, MORTON
   b. New York, Jan. 12, 1926; d. Buffalo,
   Sept. 3, 1987
Neither   1977 Rome

FENNIMORE, JOSEPH
   b. New York, Apr. 16, 1940
+Apache Dance   1975 New York
+Don't Call Me by
   My Right Name 1975 New York

FINE, VIVIAN
   b. Chicago, Sept. 28, 1913
Guide to Life Expectancy
   of a Rose   1959 New York
Woman in the Garden 1978 San Francisco

FINGER, GOTTFRIED
   b. Olomouc?, Moravia, ca. 1660; d.
   Mannheim, buried Aug. 31, 1730
Judgment of Paris   1701 London
Loves of Mars and
   Venus (with Eccles) 1696 London
Rival Queens   1701 London
   (with D. Purcell)
Virgin Prophetess   1701 London

FINK, HAROLD
Goodman Brown   1968 Painesville, Ohio

FINK, MYRON
   b. Chicago, Apr. 19, 1932
Boor, The   1955 St. Louis
Chinchilla   1986 Binghamton, N.Y.
Conquistador, The   1997 San Diego
Island of Tomorrow 1986 New York
Jeremiah   1962 Binghamton, N.Y.
Judith and Holofernes 1978 Purchase, N.Y.

Susanna and the
   Elders   1955 Vienna

FINK, ROBERT
Lysistrata & the War 1967 Detroit

FINNEY, ROSS LEE
   b. Wells, Minn., Dec. 23, 1906; d. Feb. 4,
   1997, Carmel, Calif.
+Computer Marriage 1989*
+Nun's Priest's Tale 1965 Hanover, N.H.
+Weep Torn Land   1984*

FINNISSY, MICHAEL
   b. London, Mar. 17, 1946
+Thérèse Raquin   1993 London
+Undivine Comedy 1988 Paris

FIRSOVA, ELENA
   b. Leningrad (now St. Petersburg), Mar. 21, 1950
Nightingale and
   the Rose   1994 London

FIRST, DAVID
Manhattan Book
   of the Dead   1995 New York

FISHER, JOHN ABRAHAM
   b. Dunstable/London, 1744; d. Dublin/
   London, May/June 1806
Court of Alexander 1770 London
Golden Pippen   1773 London
Love Finds the Way 1777 London
   (with T. Arne, Sacchini)

FITZWILLIAM, EDWARD
   b. Deal, Aug. 1, 1824; d. London, Jan. 20, 1857
+Love's Alarms   1853 London
Queen of a Day   1841 London

FLAGELLO, NICOLAS
   b. New York, Mar. 15, 1928; d. New Rochelle,
   N.Y., Mar. 16, 1994
Judgment of St.
   Francis   1966 New York
+Pied Piper   1970 New York
+Sisters, The   1961 New York

FLANAGAN, THOMAS J.
   b. New Haven, Nov. 30, 1927
I Rise in Flame   1980 New York
Statues on a Lawn   1983 New York

FLANAGAN, WILLIAM
   b. Detroit, Aug. 14, 1923; d. New York, Aug.
   31, 1969
Bartleby   1961 New York

FLECKNOE, RICHARD
   d. ca. 1676
+Ariadne Deserted
   by Theseus   ca. 1654*
+Marriage of Oceanus
   and Brittania   ca. 1659*

FLETCHER, GRANT
b. Hartsburg, Ill., Oct. 25, 1913
Carrion Crow 1953 Bloomington, Ill.
Sack of Calabasas 1964 Phoenix

FLORIO, CARYL [WILLIAM JAMES ROBJOHN]
b. Tavistock, Devon, Engl., Nov. 3, 1843; d.
Morganton, N.C., Nov. 21, 1920
Uncle Tom's Cabin 1882 Philadelphia
Undine ca. 1920 Philadelphia

FLORIO, CHARLES
Egyptian Festival 1800 London

FLOYD, CARLISLE
b. Latta, S.C., June 11, 1926
+Bilby Doll 1976 Houston
+Flower and Hawk 1972 Jacksonville, Fla.
+Fugitives 1951 Tallahassee, Fla.
+Markheim 1966 New Orleans
+Of Mice and Men 1970 Seattle
+Passion of Jonathan
Wade 1962 New York
+Slow Dusk 1949 Syracuse, N.Y.
+Sojourner and
Mollie Sinclair 1963 Raleigh, N.C.
+Susannah 1955 Tallahassee, Fla.
+Willie Stark 1981 Houston
+Wuthering Heights 1958 Santa Fe, N.M.

FORBES, HENRY
b. London, 1804; d. there Nov. 24, 1859
Fairy Oak 1845 London

FORD, ERNEST
b. Warminster, Feb. 17, 1858; d. London,
June 2, 1919
Jane Annie 1893 London
Joan 1890 London
Wedding Eve 1892 London
(with Toulmouche, "Yvolde")

FORE, BURDETTE
Aria da Capo 1951 Stockton, Calif.

FORREST, HAMILTON
b. Chicago, Jan. 8, 1901; d. London, Dec. 26, 1963
+Camille 1930 Chicago
+Daelia 1954 Interlochen, Mich.
+Don Fortunato 1952 Interlochen, Mich.
+Matinee Idyll 1954 Interlochen, Mich.

FORSTER, ARNOLD
Lord Bateman 1958 London

FOSS, LUKAS
b. Berlin, Aug. 15, 1922
Griffelkin 1955 NBC
Introductions and
Good-Byes 1960 New York
Jumping Frog of
Calaveras Country 1950 Bloomington, Ind.

FOX, MALCOLM
b. Windsor, Engl., Oct. 13, 1946
Iron Man 1987 Adelaide, Austral.
Sid the Serpent 1977 Adelaide, Austral.

FRAGALE, FRANK D.
b. 1894
Dr. Jekyll and Mr.
Hyde 1953 Berkeley, Calif.

FRANCHETTI, ALDO
b. Mantua, Italy, 1883
+Namiko-San 1925 Chicago

FRANCHETTI, ARNOLD
b. Lucca, Italy, 1909; d. Cromwell, Conn.,
Mar. 7, 1993
Anachronism 1956 Hartford, Conn.
Dowser, The 1956*
+Dracula 1979*
Game of Cards 1955 Hartford, Conn.
+Lion, The 1950 New London, Conn.
Married Men Go to
Hell 1975*
Maypole 1952 Westport, Conn.
Notturno in La 1966 Hartford, Conn.
Prelude and Fugue 1959 Hartford, Conn.
Princess, The 1952 Hartford, Conn.
Soap Opera 1973 Hartford, Conn.
Suncatcher 1973 Hartford, Conn.

FRANCIS, WILLIAM
Lady of the Lake 1811 Edinburgh

FREED, ISADORE
b. Brest-Litovsk, Russia, Mar. 26, 1900; d.
Rockville Centre, N.Y., Nov. 10, 1960
Princess and the
Vagabond 1948 Hartford, Conn.

FREEMAN, HARRY LAWRENCE
b. Cleveland, Oct. 9, 1869; d. New York,
Mar. 21, 1954
+African Kraal 1903 Chicago
+American Romance 1927*
+Athalia 1916*
+Ephelia 1893 Denver
+Flapper, The 1929*
+Leah Kleschna 1930*
+Martyr, The 1893 Denver
+Nada 1900 Cleveland
+Octoroon, The 1904*
+Plantation, The 1914*
+Prophecy, The 1912 New York
+Tryst, The 1911 New York
+Uzziah 1931*
+Valdo 1960 Cleveland
+Vendetta, The 1923 New York
+Voodoo 1928 New York
+Zululand, triology: 1934–47*
Allah 1947*

Nada and the Lily 1941–44*
Zulu King 1934*

FREER, ELEANOR EVEREST
b. Philadelphia, May 14, 1864; d. Chicago, Dec. 13, 1942
Brownings Go to Italy 1938 Chicago
Chilkoot Maiden 1927 Skagway, Ala.
+Christmas Tale 1929 Houston
Frithiof 1929 Chicago
+Joan of Arc 1929 Chicago
+Legend of Spain 1931 Milwaukee
Legend of the Piper 1925 South Bend, Ind.
+Little Women 1934 Chicago
+Masque of Pandora 1935 Chicago
Massimilliano 1926 Lincoln, Neb.
+Preciosa 1928*

FRIML, RUDOLF
b. Prague, Dec. 2, 1879; d. Los Angeles, Nov. 12, 1972
Rose-Marie 1924 Los Angeles
(with H. Stothart)

FRY, WILLIAM
b. Philadelphia, Aug. 19, 1813; d. Santa Cruz, Virgin Islands, Dec. 21, 1864
Leonora 1845 Philadelphia
Notre-Dame of Paris 1864 Philadelphia

FUCHS, PETER PAUL
b. Vienna, Oct. 30, 1916
+Serenade at Noon 1965 Baton Rouge, La.
+White Agony 1989 Berlin

FUSSELL, CHARLES
b. Feb. 14, 1938, Winston-Salem, N.C.
Julian 1972 Winston-Salem, N.C.

GABRIEL, VIRGINIA (MARY ANN)
b. Banstead, Surrey, Feb. 7, 1825; d. London, Aug. 7, 1877
Follies of a Night ca. 1870 London

GABURO, KENNETH
b. Somerville, N.J., July 5, 1926; d. Iowa City, Iowa, Jan. 26, 1993
Snow Queen 1952 Lake Charles, La.

GALLIARD, JOHN
b. Celle, Ger., ca. 1687; d. London, 1749
Calypso and Telemachus 1712 London
Circe 1719 London
Decius and Paulina 1718 London
Happy Captive 1741 London
Pan and Syrinx 1718 London

GALLOWAY, JAMES
Pastoral 1988 Albuquerque, N.M.

GARDNER, JOHN
b. Manchester, Engl., Mar. 2, 1917
Moon and Sixpence 1957 London

GARWOOD, MARGARET
b. Haddonfield, N.J., Mar. 22, 1927
+Joringel 1987 Roxborough, Pa.
+Nightingale and the Rose 1973 Chester, Pa.
+Rappaccini's Daughter 1980 Philadelphia
Trojan Women 1967 Chester, Pa.

GASPARINI, FRANCISCO
b. Camaiore, near Lucca, Italy, Mar. 5, 1668; d. Rome, Mar. 22, 1727
Love's Triumph 1708 London
(with Violone, Cesarini)

GATES, CRAWFORD M.
b. 1921
Promised Valley 1961*

GATTY, NICHOLAS
b. Bradfield, Engl., Sept. 13, 1874; d. London, Nov. 10, 1946
Duke or Devil 1909 Manchester
Greysteel 1906 Sheffield, Engl.
King Alfred and the Cakes 1930 London
+Prince Ferelon 1919 London
Tempest, The 1920 London

GERHARD, ROBERTO
b. Valls, Catalonia, Sept. 25, 1896; d. Cambridge, Engl, Jan. 5, 1970
+Duenna, The 1951 Wiesbaden, Ger.

GERMAN, EDWARD
b. Whitchurch, Shropshire, Feb. 17, 1862; d. London, Nov. 11, 1936
Fallen Fairies 1909 London
Merrie England 1902 London
Tom Jones 1907 London

GERSHWIN, GEORGE
b. Brooklyn, N.Y., Sept. 26, 1898; d. Hollywood, Calif., July 11, 1937
Blue Monday 1922 New York
Porgy and Bess 1935 Boston

GESSNER, JOHN
Faust Counter Faust 1971 Minneapolis

GIANNINI, VITTORIO
b. Philadelphia, Oct. 19, 1903; d. New York, Nov. 28, 1966
Beauty and the Beast 1938 CBS Radio
Blennerhasset 1939 CBS Radio
+Harvest, The 1961 Chicago
Rehearsal Call 1962 New York
Scarlet Letter 1938 Hamburg

Servant of Two
  Masters 1967 New York
+Taming of the Shrew 1953 Cincinnati

GIBBONS, CHRISTOPHER
  b. Westminster, bapt. Aug. 22, 1615; d. there,
  Oct. 20, 1676
Cupid and Death 1653 London
(with M. Locke)

GIBBS, CECIL ARMSTRONG
  b. Great Bradow, near Chelmsford, Engl.,
  Aug. 10, 1889; d. Chelmsford, May 12, 1960
Blue Peter 1923 London
Midsummer Madness 1924 London

GIDEON, MIRIAM
  b. Greeley, Colo., Oct. 23, 1906; d. New
  York, June 18, 1996
Fortunato 1954–56*

GILBERT, ANTHONY
  b. London, July 26, 1934
+Chakravaka-Bird 1982 London, BBC
Scene Machine 1971 Kassel

GILBERT, HENRY F.
  b. Somerville, Mass., Sept. 26, 1868; d.
  Cambridge, Mass., May 19, 1928
Fantasy in Delft 1919*
Uncle Remus 1905–7*

GILBERT, PATRICIA
+Question of Love 1985 London

GILFERT, CHARLES
  b. Prague?, 1787; d. New York, July 30, 1829
Spanish Patriots 1809 New York
Virgin of the Sun 1823 Philadelphia

GIORDANI, TOMMASO
  b. Naples, ca. 1730; d. Dublin, Feb. 1806
Calypso 1785 Dublin
Cottage Festival 1796 Dublin
Distressed Knight 1791 Dublin
Don Fulimone 1765 Dublin
Enchantress, The 1783 Dublin
Gibraltar 1783 Dublin
Happy Disguise 1784 Dublin
Haunted Castle 1783 Dublin
Love in Disguise 1766 Dublin
Maid of the Mill 1765 Dublin
Phillis at Court 1767 Dublin
Ward of the Castle 1793 London

GLANVILLE-HICKS, PEGGY
  b. Melbourne, Austral., Dec. 29, 1912; d.
  Sydney, Austral., June 15, 1990
Glittering Gate 1959 New York
Nausicaa 1961 Athens
Sappho 1963*
+Transposed Heads 1954 Louisville, Ky.

GLASS, PHILIP
  b. Baltimore, Jan. 31, 1937
+Akhnaten 1984 Stuttgart
CIVIL warS, Act V 1984 Rome
Einstein on the Beach 1976 Avignon
Fall of the House
  of Usher 1988 Louisville, Ky.
Hydrogen Jukebox 1990 Charleston, S.C.
Juniper Tree 1985 Cambridge, Mass.
Madrigal Opera 1980 Amsterdam
Making of the
  Representative 1988 Houston
Marriages between
  Zones 3, 4, and 5 1995 New York
1000 Airplanes 1988 Vienna
+Photographer, The 1982 Amsterdam
(text with R. Malasch)
+Satyagraha 1981 Rotterdam
(text with De Jong)
Voyage, The 1992 New York

GLEASON, FREDERICK G.
  b. Middletown, Conn., Dec. 18, 1848; d.
  Chicago, Dec. 6, 1903
+Otho Visconti 1907 Chicago

GLOVER, JOHN WILLIAM
  b. Dublin, June 19, 1815; d. there, Dec. 18, 1899
Deserted Village 1880 London

GLOVER, (WILLIAM) HOWARD
  b. 1819; d. 1875
+Ruy Blas 1861 London

GODFREY, PAUL
+Once in a While 1990 London

GOEHR, ALEXANDER
  b. Berlin, Aug. 10, 1932
Arden Must Die 1967 Hamburg
+Behold the Sun 1985 Duisburg, Ger.
Naboth's Vineyard 1968 London
Shadowplay 1970 London
+Sonata about
  Jerusalem 1971 Jerusalem
Triptych 1990 Aldeburgh

GOLDMAN, EDWARD MERRILL
  b. Manchester, Conn., July 2, 1917
+David 1967*
+Macbeth 1961*
+Rocket, The 1960*

GOLDSCHMIDT, BERTHOLD
  b. Hamburg, Jan. 18, 1903; d. London, Oct.
  17, 1996
Beatrice Cenci 1952 BBC

GOLDSTAUB, PAUL
  b. 1947
Marriage Proposal 1978 Mankato, Minn.
+Rocket, The 1960*

GOLDSTEIN, LEE
  d. Chicago, Jan. 12, 1990
  Fan, The   1989 Chicago

GOODMAN, ALFRED
  b. Berlin, Mar. 1, 1920
  Audition, The   1954 Athens, Ohio

GOOSSENS, EUGENE
  b. London, May 26, 1893; d. Hillingdon,
    Middlesex, June 13, 1962
  Don Juan de Mañara 1937 London
  Judith   1929 London

GORDON, MICHAEL
  b. 1956
  Chaos   1994*
  Van Gogh Video
  Opera   1991*

GORDON, PETER
  b. 1946
  Birth of the Poet   1985 Brooklyn, N.Y.
  Strange Life of
  Ivan Osokin   1994 New York

GORDON, PHILIP
  Tale from Chaucer   1959* 1966 Trenton, N.J.

GOTHAM, NIC
  Nigredo Hotel   1992 Stratford, Ont.

GOTTLIEB, JACK
  b. New Rochelle, N.Y., Oct. 12, 1930
  +Death of a Ghost   1988 New York
  +Movie Opera   1986 New York
  Tea Party   1957 Athens, Ohio

GOUGH, ORLANDO
  Hotel   1997 London

GOULD, ELIZABETH
  b. 1904
  Ray and the
  Gospel Singer   1967 Toledo, Ohio

GRABU, LOUIS
  b. Catalonia; d. after 1693
  Albion and Albanius 1685 London

GRAHAM, JACK [HARRY JEROME]
  b. Mishawaka, Ind., Sept. 14, 1896
  Lord Byron   1926 South Bend, Ind.

GRAHAM, SHIRLEY
  b. Indianapolis, Nov. 11, 1904
  +Tom-Tom   1933 Cleveland

GRANGER, MILTON
  +Spark Plugs   1987*

GRANT, JULIAN
  Family Affair   1993 London

GRANT, ROBIN
  I Am in Search   1994 London

GRANTHAM, DONALD
  b. 1947
  Boor, The   1989 Austin, Tex.

GREENE, MAURICE
  b. London, Aug. 12, 1696; d. there, Dec. 1, 1755
  Florimel   1734 Winchester, Engl.
  Judgment of
  Hercules   before 1740*
  Phoebe   1747* 1755 London

GREENLEAF, ROBERT
  +Under the Arbor   1992 Birmingham, Ala.

GRIESBACH, JOHN HENRY
  b. Windsor, June 20, 1798; d. London, Jan. 9,
    1875
  Belshazzar's Feast   1835*
  Windsor Castle   ca. 1838*

GRIFFITHS, PAUL
  b. 1947
  +Jewel Box   1991 Nottingham, Engl.
  +Small Jewel Box   1995 New York

GROSS, ERIC
  b. Vienna, Sept. 16, 1926
  Amorous Judge   1965 Sydney

GROSS, ROBERT
  b. Colorado Springs, Colo., Mar. 23, 1914; d.
    Los Angeles, Nov. 6, 1983
  +Project 1521   1974 Los Angeles

GROSSMITH, GEORGE
  b. London, Dec. 9, 1847; d. Folkestone,
    Mar. 1, 1912
  Haste to the Wedding 1892 London

GROSSMITH, LESLIE
  b. Birmingham, Engl., May 19, 1870
  Uncle Tom's Cabin   1928*

GRUENBERG, LOUIS
  b. near Brest-Litovsk, Aug. 3, 1884; d. Beverly
    Hills, Calif., June 10, 1964
  +Antony and
  Cleopatra   1955*
  +Delicate King   1955*
  +Dumb Wife   1922–23*
  Emperor Jones   1933 New York
  Green Mansions   1937 CBS
  Helena's Husband   1938*
  Jack and the
  Beanstalk   1931 New York
  Miracle of Flanders   1954*
  +One Night of
  Cleopatra   1954*
  Volpone   1948–58

GUNDRY, INGLIS
b. London, May 8, 1905

+Avon	1949	London
+Logan Rock	1956	Porthcurno, Engl.
+Partisans, The	1946	London
+Prince of Coxcombs	1965	London
+Prisoner Paul	1970	London
+Return of Odysseus	1940	London
+Three Wise Men	1967	Kings Langley
+Tinners of Cornwall	1953	London
+Will of Her Own	1970*1985	London

GUSTAFSON, DWIGHT
b. Seattle, Apr. 20, 1930

Hunted, The	1960	Greenville, S.C.
Jailer, The	1954	Greenville, S.C.

HADLEY, HENRY
b. Somerville, Mass., Dec. 20, 1871; d. New York, Sept. 7, 1937

Atonement of Pan	1912	Philadelphia
Azora	1917	Chicago
Bianca	1918	New York
Cleopatra's Night	1920	New York
Nancy Brown	1903	New York
Night in Old Paris	1924	New York
Safié	1909	Mainz, Ger.

HAGEMAN, RICHARD
b. Leeuwarden, Neth., July 9, 1882; d. Beverly Hills, Calif., Mar. 6, 1966

Caponsacchi	1937	New York
Crucible, The	1943	Los Angeles

HAGEMANN, PHILIP
b. Mt. Vernon, Ind., Dec. 21, 1932

Aspern Papers	1980	Bloomington, Ind.
King Who Saved Himself	1987	Chico, Calif.

HAGEN, DARON
b. Milwaukee, Nov. 4, 1961

Bandanna	1997*	
+Elephant's Child	1994*	
+Madness and Sorrow	1997	Tacoma, Wash.
Shining Brow	1992	Madison, Wisc.
Vera of Las Vegas	1996	Las Vegas

HALAHAN, GUY

+Elanda and Eclipse	1957	London
Spur of the Moment	1959	BBC

HALPERN, SIDNEY

+Macbeth	1965	New York
+Monkey's Paw	1965	New York

HAMILTON, IAIN
b. Glasgow, June 6, 1922

+Agamemnon	1967–69*	
+Anna Karenina	1982	London
+Catiline Conspiracy	1974	Stirling, Scot.

+Lancelot	1985	Arundel Castle
+Pharsalia	1969	Edinburgh
+Raleigh's Dream	1984	Durham, N.C.
+Royal Hunt of the Sun	1977	London
+Tambourlaine	1977*	

HAMM, CHARLES
b. Charlottesville, Va., Apr. 21, 1925

+Box, The	1961	New Orleans
+Cask of Amontillado	1953	Cincinnati
+Monkey's Paw	1952	Cincinnati
+Salesgirl, The	1955	Bristol, Va.
+Scent of Sarsaparilla	1959	San Francisco
+Secret Life of Walter Mitty	1953	Athens, Ohio

HAMMOND, TOM

+Rapunzel	1953	Colchester, Engl.

HAND, COLIN

King of the Golden River	1969*	

HANDEL, GEORGE FRIDERIC
b. Halle, Ger., Feb. 23, 1685; d. London, Apr. 14, 1759

Acis and Galatea	1718	Cannons
Alceste	1749*	
Hercules	1745	London
Semele	1744	London

HANNAY, ROGER
b. Plattsburgh, N.Y., Sept. 22, 1930

Fortune of Saint Macabre	1964	Moorhead, Minn.
Journey of Edith Wharton	1988	Chapel Hill, N.C.
Two Tickets to Omaha	1960	Moorhead, Minn.

HANSON, HOWARD
b. Wahoo, Neb., Oct. 28, 1896; d. Rochester, N.Y., Feb. 26, 1981

Merry Mount	1933	Ann Arbor, Mich.

HANSON, WILLIAM F.
b. Vernal, Utah, Oct. 23, 1887

+Bleeding Heart of Timpanogas	1939	Provo, Utah
Sun Dance	1913	Vernal, Utah
+Täm-Män'-Näcŭp'	1928	Provo, Utah

HARBISON, JOHN
b. Orange, N.J., Dec. 20, 1938

+Full Moon in March	1979	Boston
Winter's Tale	1979	San Francisco

HARDY, JOHN
b. Wales, 1957

Flowers	1994	Cardiff
Roswell Incident	1997	Bury St. Edmunds, Engl.

HARLING, WILLIAM FRANKE
  b. London, Jan. 18, 1887; d. Sierra Madre,
  Calif., Nov. 22, 1958
  Deep River   1926 New York
  Light from St. Agnes   1925 Chicago

HARNICK, SHELDON
  b. Chicago, Apr. 30, 1924
  +Frustration   1968 Washington, D.C.

HARPER, EDWARD
  b. Taunton, Engl., Mar. 17, 1941
  +Fanny Robin   1975 Edinburgh
  +Hedda Gabler   1985 Glasgow
  Mellstock Quire   1988 Edinburgh

HARPER, WILLIAM
  El Greco   1993 New York
  Snow Leopard   1989 St. Paul, Minn.

HARRIS, ROSS
  b. Amberley, North Canterbury, N.Z., Aug. 1, 1945
  Waituhi   1984 Chirstchurch, N.Z.

HARRISON, LOU
  b. Portland, Ore., May 14, 1917
  Rapunzel   1959 New York
  Young Caesar   1971 Aptos, Calif.

HARRISS, CHARLES
  b. London, Dec. 16–17 (midnight) 1862; d.
  Ottawa, July 31, 1929
  Torquil   1900 Toronto

HARROWAY, JOHN
  b. 1810; d. 1857
  Arcadia   1841 London

HART, FREDERIC
  b. Aberdeen, Wash., Sept. 5, 1894
  Farewell Supper   1984 Brooklyn, N.Y.
  Poison   1984 Brooklyn, N.Y.

HART, FRITZ B.
  b. Greenwich, Engl., Feb. 11, 1874; d.
  Honolulu, July 9, 1949
  +Deirdre in Exile   1926 Melbourne
  Deirdre of the
    Sorrows   1916*
  +Esther   1923*
  +Even unto Bethlehem   1943 Honolulu
  Fantastics, The   1918*
  Forced Marriage   1928*
  Isolt of the White
    Hands   1933*
  +King, The   1921*
  Land of Heart's Desire 1914*
  Malvolio   1919 Melbourne
  Nativity, The   1931*
  +Pierrette   1914 Sydney
  Riders to the Sea   1915*
  +Ruth and Naomi   1917 Melbourne

+St. Francis of Assisi   1937*
St. George and the
  Dragon   1930 Melbourne
+Swineherd and
  the Princess   1944*
Travelling Man   1920*
+Vengeance of Faery   1947*
Woman Who Laughed
  at Faery   1924 Melbourne

HARVEY, EVA NOEL
  Esther   1974*

HARVEY, JONATHAN
  b. Sutton Coldfield, Warwickshire, Engl.,
  May 3, 1939
  +Inquest Love   1992 London
  Passion and
    Resurrection   1981 Winchester, Engl.

HASKINS, ROBERT JAMES
  b. 1937
  Bell Tower   1976*
  Legend of Sleepy
    Hollow   1976*

HATTON, JOHN LIPTROT
  b. Liverpool, Oct. 12, 1809; d. Margate, Sept.
  20, 1886
  Pasqual Bruno   1844 Vienna
  Queen of the Thames   1842 London
  Rose, The   1864 London

HAUBIEL, CHARLES TROWBRIDGE (PRATT)
  b. Delta, Ohio, Jan. 30, 1892; d. Los Angeles,
  Aug. 26, 1978
  Sunday Costs Five
    Pesos   1950 Charlotte, N.C.

HAUFRECHT, HERBERT
  b. New York, 1909; d. Albany, June 23, 1998
  +Boney Quillen   1951 Chichester, N.Y.
  +Pot of Broth   1965*

HAWES, WILLIAM
  b. London, June 21, 1785; d. there, Feb. 18, 1846
  Broken Promises   1825 London
  Climbing Boy   ca. 1834*
  Freebooters, The   1827 London
  Gay Deceivers   1804 London
  (with M. Kelly)
  Not for Me   1828 London
  Oracle, The   1826 London
  Robber's Bride   1829 London
  Rob Roy MacGregor   1818 London
  Tit for Tat   1828 London

HAWKINS, MICAH
  b. Head of the Harbor, near Stony Brook, N.Y.,
  Jan. 1, 1777; d. New York, July 29, 1825
  Saw-Mill   1824 New York

HAYES, PHILIP
  b. Oxford, bapt. Apr. 17, 1738; d. London,
    Mar. 19, 1797
Telemachus 1763 Oxford

HAYES, WILLIAM
  b. Gloucester, Engl., bapt. Jan. 26, 1708; d.
    Oxford, July 27, 1777
Circe 1742* 1749 Aston, Engl.
Peleus and Thetis ca. 1749

HAYM, NICOLA FRANCESCO
  b. Rome, July 6, 1678; d. London, Aug. 11, 1729
Pyrrus and Demetrius 1708 London

HEAD, MICHAEL
  b. Eastbourne, Engl., Jan. 28, 1900; d. Cape
    Town, Aug. 24, 1976
After the Wedding 1972 London
Day Return 1970 London
Key Money 1970 London

HEALEY, DEREK
  b. Wargrave, Engl., May 2, 1936
Seabird Island 1977 Guelph, Ont.

HEALEY, PETER
Jane Heir 1989 New York

HECKSCHER, CELESTE DE LONGPRE
  b. Philadelphia, Feb. 23, 1860; d. there, Feb.
    18, 1928
+Rose of Destiny 1918 Philadelphia

HEIDEN, BERNHARD
  b. Frankfurt, Aug. 24, 1910
Darkened City 1963 Bloomington

HEINRICH, ANTHONY PHILIP
  b. Schönbüchel, Bohemia, Mar. 11, 1781;
    d. New York, May 3, 1861
Child of the Mountain 1821 Philadelphia

HELLERMANN, WILLIAM
  b. Milwaukee, July 15, 1939
Three Sisters Who Are
Not Sisters 1983 New York

HENDERSON, ALVA
  b. San Luis, Obispo, Calif., Apr. 8, 1940
+Last Leaf 1979 Saratoga, Calif.
Last of the Mohicans 1976 Wilmington, Del.
+Medea 1972 San Diego
Swans, The 1986*
West of Washington
Square 1988 San Jose, Calif.

HENZE, HANS WERNER
  b. Gütersloh, Ger., July 1, 1926
Bassarids, The 1966 Salzburg
Cimarrón, El 1970 Aldeburgh
Cubana, La 1974 New York
Elegy for Young
Lovers 1961 Schwetzingen

English Cat 1983 Schwetzingen
Moralities 1968 Cincinnati
We Come to the River 1976 London

HERBERT, VICTOR
  b. Dublin, Feb. 1, 1859; d. New York, May
    26, 1924
Ameer, The 1899 Scranton, Pa.
Cyrano de Bergerac 1899 Montreal
Fortune Teller 1898 Toronto
Idols' Eye 1897 Troy, N.Y.
Madeleine 1914 New York
Natoma 1911 Philadelphia
Naughty Marietta 1910 Syracuse
Viceroy, The 1900 San Francisco
Wizard of the Nile 1895 New York

HERMAN, MARTIN
  b. 1953
Scarlet Letter 1992 Berkeley

HERMANN, BERNARD
  b. New York, June 29, 1911; d. Los Angeles,
    Dec. 24, 1975
Christmas Carol 1954 CBS
Wuthering Heights 1943* 1982 Portland, Ore.

HESS, DAVID
Naked Carmen 1970*
(with Corigliano)

HEWITT, JAMES
  b. Dartmoor?, June 4, 1770; d. Boston, Aug. 2, 1827
Cottagers, The 1801 New York
Don Raphael 1804 New York
Flash in the Pan 1798 New York
Honey Moon 1805 London
(with Kelly)
Snow Storm 1823 Atlanta
Spanish Castle 1800 New York
Tammany 1794 New York
Wild Goose Chase 1800 New York

HEWITT, JOHN HILL
  b. New York, July 12, 1801; d. Baltimore, Oct.
    7, 1890
Vivandiere, The 1863 Augusta, Ga.

HEWITT, MARK
Lamentations of Doctor
Faustus 1994 London

HEWITT, THOMAS J.
  b. 1880
Don Quixote 1909 London

HILL, ALFRED
  b. Melbourne, Nov. 16, 1870; d. Sydney, Oct.
    30, 1960
Auster 1922 Sydney
Don Quixote 1904*
Giovanni 1914 Sydney
Lady Dolly 1900 Sydney

Moorish Maid   1905 Auckland, N.Z.
Rajah of Shivapore   1917 Sydney
Ship of Heaven   1923 Sydney
Tapu   1903 Wellington, N.Z.
+Teora   1928 Sydney
Whipping Boy   1896 Wellington, N.Z.

HINDEMITH, PAUL
  b. Hanau, Ger., Nov. 16, 1895; d. Frankfurt,
  Ger., Dec. 28, 1963
+Long Christmas
Dinner   1961 Mannheim, Ger.

HINES, JEROME
  b. Hollywood, Nov. 8, 1921
I Am the Way   1959 South Orange, N.J.

HIVELY, WELLS
  b. 1902; d. 1969
+Junípero Serra   1953 Palma de Mallorca
River, The   1938*

HODDINOTT, ALUN
  b. Bargoed, Wales, Aug. 11, 1929
Beach of Falesá   1974 Cardiff
Magician, The   1976 Welsh radio
Rajah's Diamond   1979 London
Trumpet Major   1981 Manchester
What the Old Man   1977 Fishguard
Does   Festival, Wales

HODKINSON, SYDNEY
  b. Winnepeg, Jan. 17, 1934
St. Carmen of the
Main   1988 Guelph, Ont.

HOIBY, LEE
  b. Madison, Wisc., Feb. 17, 1926
Beatrice   1959 Louisville, Ky.
Bon Appétit!   1989 Washington, D.C.
Christmas Carol   1987 San Francisco
Italian Lesson   1982 Newport, R.I.
Natalia Petrovna   1964 New York
Scarf, The   1958 Spoleto, Italy
Something New   1982 Cheverley, Md.
Summer and Smoke   1971 St. Paul, Minn.
Tempest, The   1986 Indianola, Iowa
This Is the Rill   1994 New York

HOLBROOKE, JOSEPH
  b. Croydon, July 5, 1878; d. London, Aug. 5,
  1958
Cauldron of Annwn, trilogy:
  Children of Don   1912 London
  Dylan   1914 London
  Bronwen   1929 Huddersfield
Enchanter, The   1915 Chicago
Pierrot and Pierrette 1909 London

HOLLINGSWORTH, STANLEY
  b. Berkeley, Calif., Aug. 27, 1924
Grand Bretèche, La   1957 New York

Harrison Loved His
** Umbrella**   1981 Charleston, S.C.
+Mother, The   1954 Philadelphia
+Selfish Giant   1981 Charleston, S.C

HOLLOWAY, ROBIN
  b. Leamington Spa, Engl., Oct. 19, 1943
+Clarissa   1990 London

HOLST, GUSTAV
  b. Cheltenham, Engl., Sept. 21, 1874; d.
  London, May 25, 1934
+At the Boar's Head   1925 Manchester
Idea, The   ca. 1896*
Landsdown Castle   1893 Cheltenham, Engl.
Magic Mirror   1896*
+Perfect Fool   1923 London
Revoke, The   1895*
+Sāvitri   1916 London
+Sita   1899–1906*
Wandering Scholar   1934 Liverpool
Youth's Choice   1902*

HOOK, JAMES
  b. Norwich, June 1746; d. Boulogne, 1827
Apollo and Daphne   1773 London
Catch Him Who Can   1806 London
Cupid's Revenge   1772 London
Diamond Cut
** Diamond**   1797 London
Dido and Aeneas   1771 London
Dilettante, Il   1772 London
Divorce, The   1771 London
Double Disguise   1784 London
Fair Peruvian   1786 London
Fortress, The   1807 London
Invisible Girl   1806 London
Jack of Newbury   1795 London
Killing No Murder   1809 London
Lady of the Manor   1778 London
Music Mad   1807 London
Poll Booth   1784 London
Queen of the May   1787 London
Safe and Sound   1809 London
Sharp and Flat   1813 London
Soldier's Return   1805 London
Tekeli   1806 London
Too Civil by Half   1782 London
Triumph of Beauty   1786 London
Wilmore Castle   1800 London
Word to Wives   1785 London

HOPKINS, ANTONY
  b. London, Mar. 21, 1921
+Dr. Musikus   1969 London
Hands across the Sky 1959 Cheltenham, Engl.
+Lady Rohesia   1948 London
Man from Tuscany   1951 Canterbury, Engl.
Rich Man, Poor Man   1969 Stroud, Engl.

Scena 1953 London, BBC
Ten O'Clock Call 1956 Cheltenham, Engl.
Three's Company 1953 Crewe, Engl.
Time for Growing 1967 Norwich, Engl.

HORN, CHARLES EDWARD
b. London, June 21, 1786; d. Boston, Oct. 21, 1849
Ahmad al Ramel 1840 New York
+Annette 1822 Dublin
Bee-Hive 1811 London
Boarding House 1811 London
Dead Fetch 1826 London
Devil's Bridge 1812 London
(with Braham, Corri)
Dido 1829 New York
Dirce 1821 London
Election, The 1817 London
Justice 1820 London
Honest Frauds 1830 London
Lallah Rookh 1818 Dublin
Love Spell 1831 London
Magic Flute 1833 New York
Maid of Saxony 1842 New York
Merry Wives of
Windsor 1824 London
M.P. (with T. Moore) 1811 London
Narensky 1814 London
(with Braham, Reeve)
Ninth Statue 1814 London
Pay to My Order 1827 London
Persian Hunters 1817 London
(with G. Perry)
Peveril of the Peak 1826 London
Philandering
(with Braham) 1824 London
Quartette, The 1829 New York
Rich and Poor 1812 London
Shepherd of Derwent
Vale 1825 London
Tricks upon Travellers
(with Reeve) 1810 London
Wedding Present 1825 London
Wizard, The 1817 London
Woodman's Hut 1814 London

HOROVITZ, JOSEPH
b. Vienna, May 26, 1926
Dumb Wife 1953 Lowestoft, Engl.
Gentleman's Island 1958 London

HORTON, AUSTIN ASADATA DAFORA
b. Freetown, Sierra Leone, Aug. 4, 1890; d. New York, Mar. 4, 1965
Kykuntor 1934 New York

HOUSELEY, HENRY
b. Sutton in Ashfield, Nottinghamshire, Engl., Sept. 20, 1852; d. Denver, Mar. 13, 1925
+Pygmalion 1912 Denver

HOUSTON, MARK
Hazel Kirke 1987 Glens Falls, N.Y.

HOVEY, SERGE
b. New York, Mar. 10, 1920; d. Los Angeles, May 3, 1989
+Dreams in Spades 1949 Philadelphia

HOVHANESS, ALAN
b. Somerville, Mass., Mar. 8, 1911
+Blue Flame 1959 San Antonio
+Burning House 1964 Gatlinburg, Tenn.
+Frog Man 1987*
+Lady of Light 1974 Montana
+Leper King 1969 Chicago
+Pericles 1975*
1979 Shippensburg, Pa.
+Pilate 1966 Los Angeles
+Spirit of the
Avalanche 1963 Tokyo
+Tale of the Sun
Goddess 1978 Salinas, Calif.
+Travellers 1967 San Francisco
+Wind Drum 1964 Gatlinburg, Tenn.

HOWARD, BRIAN
b. Sydney, Jan. 3, 1941
Inner Voices 1985 London
Whitsunday 1988 Sydney

HOWARD, GEORGE
Uncle Tom's Cabin 1852 Troy, N.Y.

HOWLAND, WILLIAM LEGRAND
b. Asbury Park, N.J., 1873; d. Long Island, N.Y., July 26, 1915
+Sarrona 1903 Bruges, Belgium

HUGHES, ARWEL
b. Rhosllanerchrugog, Wales, Aug. 25, 1909; d. Cardiff, Sept. 23, 1988
Menna 1953 Cardiff

HUGO, JOHN ADAM
b. Bridgeport, Conn., Jan. 5, 1874; d. there, Dec. 29, 1945
Temple Dancer 1919 New York

HULLAH, JOHN
b. Berlin, Sept. 6, 1855; d. there, Apr. 24, 1928
Barbers of Bassora 1837 London
Outpost, The 1838 London
Village Coquettes 1836 London

HUMEL, GERALD
b. Cleveland, Nov. 7, 1931
Proposal, The 1958 Winfield, Kan.
Triangle, The 1958 Oberlin, Ohio

HUMPHREYS, HENRY RAUSCHER (SIGURD)
b. Vienna, Nov. 27, 1909
+Mayerling 1957 Cincinnati

HUNKINS, EUSEBIA SIMPSON
b. Troy, Ohio, June 20, 1902; d. Sept. 9, 1980
Magic Laurel Tree 1974 Cleveland
+Smoky Mountain 1954 Monmouth, Ill.
Young Lincoln 1959 Galesburg, Ill.

HURD, MICHAEL
b. Gloucester, Engl., Dec. 19, 1928
+Little Billy 1964 Stroud, Engl.
+Mr. Punch 1970 Gothenburg
+Widow of Ephesus 1971 Stroud, Engl.

IMBRIE, ANDREW
b. New York, Apr. 6, 1921
Angle of Repose 1976 San Francisco

ISAACS, GREGORY SULLIVAN
+Death of Tintagiles 1973 Indianola, Ind.
+Henry Faust 1993 Forest Park, Ill.

ITO, GENJI
Ghosts 1993 New York

IVES, SIMON
b. Earl's Colne, Essex, ca. 1626; d. before 1662
Triumph of Peace 1634 London
(with Lawes, Mell)

JACKSON, WILLIAM
b. Exeter, May 29, 1730; d. there, July 5, 1803
Lord of the Manor 1780 London
+Lycidas 1767 London
+Metamorphosis 1783 London

JACOBI, FREDERICK
b. San Francisco, May 4, 1891; d. New York,
Oct. 24, 1952
Prodigal Son 1944 Palo Alto, Calif.

JACOBI, GEORGE
b. Berlin, Feb. 13, 1840; d. London, Sept. 13, 1906
Don Quixote 1894 London

JARRETT, JACK
+Cinderella 1956 Gainesville, Fla.
Cyrano de Bergerac 1972 Greensboro, N.C.

JENKINS, LEROY
b. Chicago, Mar. 11, 1932
Mother of Three Sons 1990 Munich

JOHN, ALAN
+Eighth Wonder 1995 Adelaide
(lib. with D. Watkins)
Frankie 1987 Sydney

JOHNSON, LOCKREM
b. Davenport, Iowa, Mar. 15, 1924; d. Seattle,
Mar. 5, 1977
+Letter to Emily 1951 Seattle

JOHNSON, ROBERT
Macbeth (with Locke) 1673 London

JOHNSON, SAMUEL
b. 1691; d. 1773
+Hurlothrumbo 1729 London

JOHNSON, TOM
b. Greeley, Colo., Nov. 18, 1939
Five Shaggy-Dog
Operas 1978 New York
+Four Note Opera 1972 New York
+Masque of the
Clouds 1975 New York
Sopranos Only 1984 Paris

JONES, ABBIE GERRISH
b. Vallejo, Calif., Sept. 10, 1863; d. 1929
Snow Queen 1918 San Francisco

JONES, DANIEL
b. Pembroke, Wales, Dec.7, 1912; d. Swansea,
Engl., Apr. 23, 1993
Knife, The 1963 London

JONES, GEORGE THADDEUS
Cage, The 1959 Washington, D.C.

JONES, JOHN
Enchanted Horse 1844 New York

JONES, JEREMY PAYTON
Menaced Assassin 1989 London

JONES, KELSEY
b. South Norwalk, Conn., June 17, 1922
Sam Slick 1967 Halifax

JONES, SIDNEY
b. London, June 17, 1861; d. there, Jan. 29, 1946
Geisha, The 1896 London
King of Cadonia 1908 London
My Lady Molly 1903 London
San Toy 1899 London
See-See (with F. Tours) 1906 London

JOPLIN, SCOTT
b. prob. near Marshall, Tex., Nov. 24, 1868; d.
New York, Apr. 1, 1917
+Guest of Honor 1903 St. Louis
+Treemonisha 1915 New York

JORDAN, JULES
b. Willimantic, Conn., Nov. 10, 1850; d.
Providence, R.I., Mar. 5, 1927
+Rip Van Winkle 1897 Providence, R.I.

JOSEPHS, WILFRED
b. Newcastle upon Tyne, July 24, 1927
+Alice in Wonderland 1985–88*
Appointment, The 1966 BBC
Pathelin 1963*
Prisoner, The 1973 London
Rebecca 1983 Leeds
+Through the Looking
Glass 1977–78*

JOUBERT, JOHN
  b. Cape Town, Mar. 20, 1927
  Antigone   1954 London, BBC
  In the Drought   1956 Johannesburg
  Quarry   1965 Wembley
  Silas Marner   1961 Cape Town
  Under Western Eyes 1969 London
  Wayfarers, The   1984 Huntington

KAGEN, SERGIUS
  b. St. Petersburg, Aug. 22, 1909; d. New
  York, Mar. 1, 1964
  Hamlet   1962 Baltimore

KALMANOFF, MARTIN
  b. Brooklyn, May 24, 1920
  +Aesop   1969 Camp
                                Pemiquewasset, N.H.
  Audition, The   1968 Pittsburgh
  (lib. with S. Spaeth)
  Bald Prima Donna   1963 New York
  Brandy Is My True
    Love's Name   1953 New York
  Canterville Ghost   1967 New York
  +Christopher
    Columbus   1976*
  +Delinquents, The   1955 Philadelphia
  Empty Bottle   1966 New York
  Fit for a King   1949 New York
  Give Me Liberty   1975 New York
  Godiva   1953 New York
  +Great Stone Face   1968 Muncie, Ind.
  Half Magic in King 1963 Walding River,
    Arthur's Court   N.Y.
  Harmfulness of
    Tobacco   1979 New York
  +Hipopera   1977 Boise, Idaho
  Insect Comedy   1977* 1993 New York
  Legends Three   1969 New York
  +Lizzie Strotter   1958 Des Moines
  Magic Beanstalk   1976 Monticello, N.Y.
  +Magic Land of
    Opera   1972 New York
  Mr. Scrooge   1966 New York
  Noah and the
    Stowaway   1951 New York
  +Opera, Opera   1956 New York
  +Photograph—1920   1971 Lake Placid, N.Y.
  +Quiet Game of
    Cribble   1954 New York
  Ralph and the
    Stalking Bear   1979 Monticello, N.Y.
  Sganarelle   1974 New York
  +Smart Aleck and the
    Talking Wire   1976 New York
  +Victory at Masada 1968 Detroit
  +Videomania   1965 Granville, Ohio
  You'll Never Get It
    Off the Ground   1980*

Young Thomas Edison   1963 New York

KANITZ, ERNEST
  b. Vienna, Apr. 9, 1894; d. Menlo Park,
  Calif., Apr. 7, 1978
  Kumana   1953*
  Lucky Dollar   1958 Los Angeles
  Perpetual   1961 Los Angeles
  Room No. 12   1958 Los Angeles
  Royal Auction   1958 Los Angeles
  Visions of Midnight 1964 Los Angeles

KAPILOW, ROBERT
  Many Moons   1997 Princeton, N.J.

KASSERN, TADEUSZ
  b. Lemberg (now Lvov), Mar. 19, 1904; d.
  New York, May 2, 1957
  Sun-Up   1954 New York

KASTLE, LEONARD
  b. New York, Feb. 11, 1929
  +Calling of Mother
    Ann   1985 Albany
  Deseret   1961 New York
  +Journey of Mother
    Ann   1987 Postdam
  +Pariahs   1966* 1985 Albany
  +Professor Lookalike 1988 Albany
  +Swing, The   1954*

KAUFMAN, W. G.
  Don Quixote   1903 New York

KAUFMANN, WALTER
  b. Karlsbad, Apr. 1, 1907; d. Bloomington,
  Ind., Sept. 9, 1984
  +Hoosier Tale   1966 Bloomington, Ind.
  +Parfait for Irene 1952 Bloomington, Ind.
  Research, The   1953 Tallahassee, Fla.
  +Scarlet Letter   1961 Bloomington, Ind.
  +Sganarelle   1958 Vancouver

KAY, DON HENRY
  b. Smithton, Tasmania, Austral., Jan. 23, 1933
  Golden Krane   1985*

KAY, NORMAN
  Rose Affair   1968 London, BBC

KAY, ULYSSES
  b. Tucson, Jan. 7, 1917; d. Englewood, N.J.,
  May 20, 1995
  +Boor, The   1968 Lexington, Ky.
  Capitoline Venus   1971 Quincy, Ill.
  Frederick Douglass 1991 Newark, N.J.
  Jubilee   1976 Jackson, Miss.
  Juggler of Our Lady 1962 New Orleans

KECHLEY, GERALD
  b. Seattle, Mar. 18, 1919
  Beckoning Fair One 1954 Seattle
  Golden Lion   1959 Seattle

KELLEY, EDGAR STILLMAN
  b. Sparta, Wisc., Apr. 14, 1857; d. New York,
  Nov. 12, 1944
  Puritania   1892 Boston

KELLY, BRYAN
  b. Oxford, Jan. 30, 1934
  Herod, Do Your Worst 1968*

KELLY, MICHAEL
  b. Dublin, Dec. 25, 1762; d. Margate, Oct. 9,
  1826
  Benyowsky   1826 London
  Blue-Beard   1798 London
  Captive of Spilburg   1798 London
  Feudal Times   1799 London
  Forty Thieves   1806 London
  Foundling of the
    Forest   1809 London
  Friend in Need   1797 London
  Gipsey Prince   1801 London
  Hero of the North   1803 London
  Honey Moon   1805 London, New
  (with J. Hewitt)   York
  House to Be Sold   1802 London
  Hunter of the Alps   1804 London
  Illusion, The   1813 London
  Lady and the Devil   1820 London
  Love Laughs at
    Locksmiths   1803 London
  Of Age Tomorrow   1800 London
  Peasant Boy   1811 London
  Pizzaro   1799 London
  Royal Oak   1811 London
  Unknown Guest   1815 London
  Wood Daemon   1807 London
  Young Hussar   1807 London
  Youth, Love, and Folly   1805 London

KELLY, ROBERT
  b. Clarksburg, W. Va., Sept. 26, 1916
  +Tod's Gal   1951*
                                  1971 Norfolk, Va.

KERN, JEROME
  b. New York, Jan. 27, 1885; d. there, Nov. 11,
  1945
  Show Boat   1927 New York

KESSELMAN, WENDY
  +Juniper Tree   1982 Lenox, Mass.

"KETTENUS"
  Robert the Devil   1868 London

KIESERLING, RICHARD
  Fairies' Revelry   1924*

KIEVMAN, CARSON
  b. Dec. 27, 1949, Los Angeles
  California Mystery
    Park   1993 New York

Intelligent Systems   1984 Baden-Baden, Ger.
Ladies Voices   1973–74*
Wake Up! It's Time   1978 Lenox, Mass.

KILPATRICK, JACK
  b. Stillwater, Okla., Sept. 23, 1915; d.
  Muskogee, Okla., Feb. 22, 1967
  +Blessed Wilderness   1959 Dallas
  Golden Crucible   1959 Pittsburgh
  +Unto These Hills   1950 Cherokee, N.C.

KIMPER, PAULA M.
  Patience and Sarah   1996 New York

KING, MATTHEW PETER
  b. London, ca. 1773; d. there, Jan. 1823
  Americans, The   1811 London
  (with J. Braham)
  Benyowsky   1826 London
  (with T. Cooke et al.)
  False Alarms   1807 London
  Matrimony   1804 London
  Oh, This Love   1810 London
  One O'Clock   1811 London
  (with M. Kelly)
  Plots, The   1810 London
  Too Many Cooks   1805 London
  Turn Out!   1812 London
  Up All Night   1809 London
  Weathercock, The   1805 London

KIRCHNER, LEON
  b. Brooklyn, N.Y., Jan. 24, 1919
  +Lily   1977 New York

KIRKPATRICK, HOWARD
  b. Tiskilwa, Ill., Feb. 26, 1873
  +Olaf   1912 Lincoln, Neb.

KIRSCHNER, BOB
  Bohemians, The   1990 New York

KITZKE, JEROME P.
  b. Milwaukee, Feb. 5, 1955
  Thousand Names   1981 Milwaukee

KLEINSINGER, GEORGE
  b. San Bernardino, Calif., Feb. 13, 1914; d.
  New York, July 28, 1982
  archy and mehitabel   1954 New York
  Tree That Was
    Christmas   1955 New York

KNOLLER, JACOB
  b. 1887, Ger.?
  +Esther   ca. 1941* 1950 New York

KNOPF, PAUL
  Letter from an
    Astrologer   1976 New York

KNOWLTON, E. BRUCE
  b. Hillsboro, Wisc., June 25, 1895; d. 1941
  +Monk of Toledo   1926 Portland

KNUSSEN, OLIVER
  b. Glasgow, June 12, 1952
  +Higglety Pigglety   1984 Glyndebourne
  Pop! (lib. with Sendak)
  Where the Wild
    Things Are   1980 Brussels

KOEHNE, GRAEME
  b. Aug. 3, 1956, Adelaide, Austral.
  Love Burns   1992 Adelaide

KOHS, ELLIS B.
  b. Chicago, May 12, 1916
  +America   1970 Los Angeles

KONDOROSSY, LESLIE
  b. Pressburg, June 25, 1915
  Fox, The   1961 Cleveland
  Kalamona   1971 Cleveland
  Midnight Duel   1955 Cleveland
  +Mystic Fortress   1955 Cleveland
  Nathan the Wise   1969 Cleveland
  +Night in the Puszta   1953 Cleveland
  Poorest Suitor   1967 Cleveland
  Pumpkin, The   1954 Cleveland
  Ruth and Naomi   1974 Cleveland
  Shizuka's Dance   1969 Cleveland
  +String Quartet   1955 Cleveland
  +Two Imposters   1955 Cleveland
  Unexpected Visitor   1956 Cleveland
  Voice, The   1954 Cleveland

KOUTZEN, BORIS
  b. Uman, near Kiev, Apr. 1, 1901; d. Mount
    Kisco, N.Y., Dec. 10, 1966
  +Fatal Oath   1955 New York
  You Never Know   1962*

KOWALSKI, HENRI
  b. Paris, 1841; d. Bordeaux, France, July 8, 1916
  Moustique   1883 Brussels
  Vercingétorix   1881 Sydney

KRAFT, LEO
  b. New York, July 24, 1922
  Caliph's Clock   1951 New York

KRANE, SHERMAN
  Giant's Garden   1960 Norfolk, Va.

KRENEK, ERNST
  b. Vienna, Aug. 23, 1900; d. Palm Springs,
    Calif., Dec. 23, 1991
  +Bell Tower   1957 Urbana, Ill.
  +Dark Waters   1951 Los Angeles
  Tarquin   1941 Poughkeepsie, N.Y.
  +What Price   1945*
    Confidence   1962 Saarbrücken, Ger.

KREUTZ, ARTHUR
  b. La Crosse, Wisc., July 25, 1906; d. Oxford,
    Miss., Mar. 11, 1991
  Acres of Sky   1951 Fayetteville, Ark.
  Sourwood Mountain   1959 Oxford, Miss.
  University Greys   1954 Clinton, Miss.

KROLL, FREDERIC
  Scarlet Letter   1965*

KROLL, LOUIS
  Belle, Le   1935 New York

KUBIK, GAIL
  b. South Coffeyville, Okla., Sept. 5, 1914; d.
    Covina, Calif., July 20, 1984
  +Boston Baked Beans   1952 New York
  Mirror for the Sky   1939 Eugene, Oreg.

KUPFERMAN, MEYER
  b. New York, July 3, 1926
  Antigonae   1973 Stockbridge, Mass.
  Curious Fern   1957 New York
  +Doctor Faustus   1953 Bronxville, N.Y.
  +Draagenfut Girl   1958 Bronxville, N.Y.
  In a Garden   1949 New York
  Judgment, The   1966*
  +Prometheus   1978 New York
  +Proscenium   1991 New York
  Voices for a Mirror   1957 New York

KURKA, ROBERT
  b. Cicero, Ill., Dec. 22, 1921; d. New York,
    Dec. 12, 1957
  Good Soldier Schweik   1958 New York

LACY, MICHAEL ROPHINO
  b. Bilbao, July 19, 1795; d. London, Sept. 20,
    1867
  Casket, The   1829 London
  +Cinderella   1830 London
  (lib. with G. Pons)
  Coiners, The   1833 London
  +Fiend-Father   1821 London
  +Fra Diavolo   1831 London
  Israelites in Egypt   1833 London
  Love in Wrinkles   1828 London
  +Maid of Judah   1829 London
  Turkish Loves   1827 London

LADERMAN, EZRA
  b. Brooklyn, N.Y., June 29, 1924
  And David Wept   1980 New York
  Galileo Galilei   1979 New York
  Goodbye to the Clown   1960 New York
  Hunting of the Snark   1961 New York
  Jacob and the Indians 1957 Woodstock, N.Y.
  Marilyn   1993 New York
  Sarah   1958 New York
  Shadows among Us   1968* 1979 Philadelphia

LA MONTAINE, JOHN
b. Chicago, Mar. 17, 1920
+Be Glad Then   1976 University Park,
  America   Pa.
+Erode the Great   1969 Washington, D.C.
+Magi, The   1967 Washington, D.C.
+Novellis, Novellis   1961 Washington, D.C.
+Shepardes Playe   1967 Washington, D.C.

LAMPE, JOHN FREDERICK
b. Saxony, ca. 1703; d. Edinburgh, July 25, 1751
Amelia   1732 London
Britannia   1732 London
Dione   1733 London
Dragon of Wantley   1737 London
Margery   1738 London
Orpheus and Eurydice   1740 London
Pyramus and Thisbe   1745 London
(lib. prob. by comp.)
Queen of Spain   1744 London
Sham Conjuror   1741 London

LANG, DAVID
b. Los Angeles, 1957
Modern Painters   1995 Santa Fe, N.M.

LARSEN, LIBBY [ELIZABETH BROWN]
b. Wilmington, Del., Dec. 24, 1950
Christina Romana   1988 Minneapolis
Clair de Lune   1985 Little Rock, Ark.
Emperor's New
  Clothes   1979 Minneapolis
+Frankenstein   1990 St. Paul, Minn.
Mrs. Dalloway   1993 Cleveland
Silver Fox   1979 St. Paul, Minn.
+Some Pig   1973 Minneapolis
Tumbledown Dick   1980 Minneapolis
Wrinkle in Time   1992 Wilmington, Del.

LARSON, JONATHAN
b. White Plains, N.Y., Feb. 4, 1960; d. New
  York, Jan. 25, 1996
+Rent   1996 New York
(lib. with L. Thomson)

LATHAM, WILLIAM
b. Shreveport, La., Jan. 4, 1917
Orpheus in Pecan
  Springs   1980 Denton, Tex.

LAUFER, BEATRICE
b. New York, Apr. 27, 1923
Ile   1957 New York

LAURENT, HENRI R.
fl. 1848–1867
Quentin Durward   1848 London

LAVALLÉE, CALIXA
b. Ste. Théodosie de Verchères, Quebec, Dec.
  28, 1842; d. Boston, Jan. 21, 1891
Widow, The   1882 Springfield, Ill.

LAVENU, LOUIS
Loretta   1846 London

LA VIOLETTE, WESLEY
b. St. James, Minn., Jan. 4, 1894; d.
  Escondido, Calif., July 29, 1978
+Shylock   1930 Chicago

LAVRY, MARC
b. Riga, Dec. 22, 1903; d. Haifa, Mar. 24, 1967
+Tamar and Judah   1958* 1970 New York

LAWES, HENRY
b. Dinton, Wiltshire, Jan. 5, 1596; d. London,
  Oct. 21, 1662
Comus   1634 Ludlow
Siege of Rhodes   1656 London
(with H. Cooke, M. Locke)
Triumphs of the Prince
  d'Amour   1636 London
(with W. Lawes)

LAWES, WILLIAM
b. Salisbury, Engl., bapt. May 1, 1602; d.
  Chester, Engl., Sept. 24, 1645
Britannia triumphans   1638 London
Triumph of Peace   1634 London
(with Ives, Mell)
Triumphs of the Prince
  d'Amour   1636 London
(with H. Lawes)

LEAVITT, BURTON E.
Charter Oak   ca. 1885
Frogs of Windham   ca. 1891*

LEBARON, ANNE
b. May 30, 1953, Baton Rouge, La.
E. & O. Line   1996 Annandale, Va.

LEE, DAI-KEONG
b. Honolulu, Sept. 2, 1915
+Ballad of Kitty   1979*
Jenny Lind   1981*
Open the Gates   1951 New York
Phineas and the
  Nightingale   1952*
Poet's Dilemma   1940 New York
Speakeasy   1957 New York
Two Knickerbocker
  Tales   1957*

LEE, GEORGE ALEXANDER
b. London, 1802; d. there, Oct. 8, 1851
Afrancesado   1837 London
Devil's Brother   1831 London
Dragon, The   1834 London
Fairy Lake   1839 London
Invincibles, The   1828 London
Magic Horn   1846 London
Malvina   1826 London
Nothing Superfluous   1829 London

Nymph of the Grotto 1829 London
Sublime and the
  Beautiful 1828 London

LEE, THOMAS OBOE
  b. Peking [now Beijing], Sept. 5, 1945
Photograph, 1920 1978*

LEES, BENJAMIN
  b. Harbin, China, Jan. 8, 1924
Gilded Cage 1964 New York
+Medea in Corinth 1971 London
+Oracle, The 1955*

LEFANU, NICOLA
  b. Wickham Bishops, Essex, Engl., Apr. 28, 1947
Blood Wedding 1992 London
+Dawnpath 1997 London
Story of Mary O'Neill 1989 London, BBC
Wildman, The 1995 Aldeburgh

LEGG, JAMES
  b. 1962
Wife of Bath's Tale 1986 Aspen, Colo.

LEGINSKA [LIGGINS], ETHEL
  b. Hull, Apr. 13, 1886; d. Los Angeles, Feb.
  26, 1970
Gale 1935 Chicago
Rose and the Ring 1932* 1957 Los Angeles

LEHRMAN, LEONARD J.
  b. Ft. Riley, Kans., Aug. 20, 1949
+Birthday of the Bank 1988 Glens Falls, N.Y.
+Family Man 1984 New York
+Hannah 1980 Mannheim-
(lib. with O. Odinov)   Seckenheim, Ger.
+Karla 1974 Ithaca, N.Y.
+New World 1991 New York
+Sima 1976 Ithaca, N.Y.
+Suppose a Wedding 1996 Commack, N.Y.

LEICHTLING, ALAN
White Butterfly 1971 New York

LEIGH, WALTER
  b. London, June 22, 1905; d. near Tobruk,
  Libya, June 12, 1942
Jolly Roger 1933 Manchester
Pride of the Regiment 1931 Midhurst, Engl.

LEIGHTON, KENNETH
  b. Wakefield, Yorkshire, Oct. 2, 1929; d.
  Edinburgh, Aug. 24, 1988
Columba 1981 Glasgow

LENEL, LUDWIG
  b. 1914
Young Goodman
  Brown 1963 Allentown, Pa.

LEONI, FRANCO
  b. Milan, Oct. 24, 1864; d. London, Feb. 8, 1949
Ib and Little Christina 1901 London

LEPAGE, ROBERT
Letters, Riddles 1991 London, BBC
(with M. Nyman)

LEPS, WASSILI
  b. St. Petersburg, Russia, May 12, 1870; d.
  Toronto, Dec. 22, 1942
Hoshi-San 1909 Philadelphia

LESLIE, HENRY
Ida 1865 London
Romance, The 1857 London

LESSNER, GEORGE
  b. Budapest, 1905; d. New Rochelle, N.Y.,
  May 12, 1997
Nightingale and the
  Rose 1942 NBC radio

LESTER, WILLIAM
+Everyman 1927 Chicago

LEVERIDGE, RICHARD
  b. London?, ca. 1670; d. London, Mar. 22, 1758
Macbeth 1702 London
+Pyramus and Thisbe 1716 London

LEVI, PAUL ALAN
  b. 1941
Thanksgiving 1977 New York

LEVISTER, ALONZO
Blues in the Subway 1958 New York

LEVY, MARVIN DAVID
  b. Passaic, N.J., Aug. 2, 1932
+Escorial, The 1958 New York
(lib. with L. Abel)
Mourning Becomes
  Electra 1967 New York
Sotoba Komachi 1957 New York
Tower, The 1957 Santa Fe, N.M.

LEWIN, FRANK
+Burning Bright 1993 New Haven

LIEBERMANN, LOWELL
  b. Feb. 22, 1961, New York
+Picture of Dorian
  Gray 1996 Monte Carlo

LIEBERMANN, ROLF
  b. Zurich, Sept. 14, 1910
School for Wives 1955 Louisville, Ky.

LIEBERSON, PETER
  b. New York, Oct. 25, 1946
Ashoka's Dream 1997 Santa Fe

LINDSEY, EDWIN S.
Elizabeth and
  Leicester 1936 Chattanooga, Tenn.

LINLEY, GEORGE
  b. Leeds, 1798; d. London, Sept. 10, 1865

Law versus Love 1862 London
+Toy-Maker 1861 London

LINLEY, THOMAS, JR.
b. Bath, Engl., May 5, 1756; d. Grimsthorpe, Aug. 5, 1778
Cadi of Bagdad 1778 London
Duenna, The 1775 London
(with Linley Sr.)

LINLEY, THOMAS, SR.
b. Badminton, Engl., Jan. 17, 1733; d. London, Nov. 19, 1795
Camp, The 1778 London
Carnival of Venice 1781 London
Duenna, The 1775 London
(with Linley Jr.)
Gentle Shepherd 1781 London
Love in the East 1788 London
Richard Coeur de
 Lion 1786 London
Royal Merchant 1767 London
Selima and Azor 1776 London
+Spanish Rivals 1784 London
Strangers at Home 1785 London
Zoraida 1779 London

LINLEY, WILLIAM
b. Bath, Engl., Feb. 1772; d. London, May 6, 1835
+Honey Moon 1797 London
+Pavilion, The 1799 London

LIST, KURT
b. Vienna, June 21, 1913; d. Milan, Nov. 16, 1970
+Wise and Foolish 1951 New York

LIVINGSTON, JULIAN
b. Spencer, Ind., Aug. 25, 1932
+Twist of Treason 1979 Freehold, N.J.

LIVIUS, BARHAM
d. 1865
Benyowsky 1826 London
(with Cooke et al.)

LLOYD, ALAN
Letter for Queen
 Victoria 1974 Spoleto, Italy

LLOYD, GEORGE
b. St. Ives, Cornwall, June 28, 1913; d. London, July 3, 1998
Iernin 1934 Penzance, Engl.
John Socman 1951 Bristol
Serf, The 1938 London

LLOYD, TIMOTHY CAMERON
Conjur Moon 1979 Houston

LLOYD WEBBER, ANDREW
b. London, Mar. 22, 1948
Evita 1978 London

Jesus Christ
 Superstar 1971 New York
+Phantom of the Opera
(lib. with Stilgoe) 1986 London
Tell Me on a Sunday 1980 London

LOCKE, MATTHEW
b. Devon, ca. 1622; d. London, Aug. 1677
Macbeth 1673 London
(with R. Johnson)
Orpheus and Euridice 1673 London
Psyche 1675 London
Siege of Rhodes 1656 London
(with H. Cooke, H. Lawes)

LOCKLAIR, DAN
b. Charlotte, N.C., Aug. 7, 1949
Good Tidings from
 the Holy Beast 1978 Lincoln, Neb.

LOCKWOOD, NORMAND
b. New York, Mar. 19, 1906
Early Dawn 1961 Denver
Hanging Judge 1964 Denver
Requiem for a Rich
 Young Man 1964 Denver
Scarecrow 1945 New York
Wizards of Balizar 1962 Denver

LODER, EDWARD
b. Bath, 1813; d. London, Apr. 5, 1865
Covenanters, The 1835 London
Deer Stalker 1841 London
Dice of Death 1835 London
Foresters, The 1838 London
Francis the First 1838 London
Heart of Midlothian 1849 London
Marie 1849 London
Night Dancers 1846 London
Nourjahad 1834 London
Raymond and Agnes 1855 Manchester
Robin Goodfellow 1848 London

LOESSER, FRANK
b. New York, June 29, 1910; d. there, July 26, 1969
+Most Happy Fella 1956 New York

LONDON, EDWIN
b. Philadelphia, Mar. 16, 1929
Death of Lincoln 1976* 1988 Cleveland

LOOMIS, CLARENCE
b. Sioux City, S.D., Dec. 13, 1889; d. Aptos, Calif., July 3, 1965
Fall of the House of
 Usher 1941 Indianapolis
Yolanda of Cyprus 1929 London, Ont.

LOVER, SAMUEL
b. Dublin, Feb. 24, 1797; d. St. Helier, Jersey, July 6, 1868

Gran Uile	1832	Dublin
+Paddy Whack	1841	London

LOW, JAMES
Moby Dick	1955	Idylwild, Calif.

LUBIN, ERNEST
b. New York, May 2, 1916
Pardoner's Tale	1966	Denver

LUENING, OTTO
b. Milwaukee, June 15, 1900; d. New York,
Sept. 2, 1996
+Evangeline	1948	New York

LUKE, RAY
b. Fort Worth, Texas, May 30, 1926
Medea	1979	Boston

LUNN, JOHN
Misper	1997	Glyndebourne

LUTYENS, ELISABETH
b. London, July 9, 1906; d. there, Apr. 14, 1983
Infidelio	1973	London
+Isis and Osiris	1976	London
+Like a Window	1977	London
+Linnet from the Leaf	1979	London
Numbered, The	1965–67*	
+One and the Same	1976	York, Engl.
Pit, The	1947	London
+Time Off?	1972	London

LUTZ, MEYER
b. Männerstadt, Ger., 1822; d. London,
Jan. 31, 1903
Felix	1865	London
Mephistopheles	1855	Surrey
Zaida	1859	Liverpoool

LYBBERT, DONALD
b. Cresco, Iowa, Feb. 19, 1923; d. Norwalk,
Conn., July 26, 1981
Scarlet Letter	1964–67*	

LYFORD, RALPH
b. Worcester, Mass., Feb. 22, 1882; d.
Cincinnati, Sept. 3, 1927
Castle Agrazant	1926	Cincinnati

MACALPIN, COLIN
Cross and the Crescent	1903	London

MACBRIDE, DAVID
b. Oakland, Calif., Oct. 3, 1951
Pond in a Bowl	1983	New York

MACCUNN, HAMISH
b. Greenock, Mar. 22, 1868; d. London, Aug.
2, 1916
Diarmid	1897	London
Jeanie Deans	1894	Edinburgh

Masque of War and Peace	1900	London
Pageant of Darkness and Light	1908*	

MACFARREN, GEORGE A.
b. London, Mar. 2, 1813; d. there, Oct. 31, 1887
Adventure of Don Quixote	1846	London
Devil's Opera	1838	London
Genevieve	1834	London
Helvellyn	1864	London
Jessy Lea	1863	London
King Charles II	1849	London
Robin Hood	1860	London
She Stoops to Conquer	1864	London
Sleeper Awakened	1850	London
Soldier's Legacy	1864	London

MACHOVER, TOD
b. New York, Nov. 24, 1953
Brain Opera	1996	New York
+VALIS	1987	Paris

MACKENZIE, ALEXANDER
b. Edinburgh, Aug. 22, 1847; d. London, Apr.
28, 1935
Colomba	1883	London
Cricket on the Hearth	1914	London
Eve of St. John	1924	Liverpool
Guillem	1886	London
His Majesty	1897	London

MACLEAN, ALICK
b. Eton, July 20, 1872; d. London, May 18, 1936
King's Price	1904	London
Petruccio	1895	London
Quentin Durward	1893*	
	1920	Newcastle u. Tyne

MACMILLAN, JAMES
b. Kilwinning, Scot., 1959
+Inés de Castro	1996	Edinburgh

MACONCHY, ELIZABETH
b. Broxbourne, Hertfordshire, Mar. 19, 1907;
d. Norwich, Engl., Nov. 11, 1994
+Birds, The	1968	London
Departure, The	1962	London
Jessie Tree	1970	Dorchester, Engl.
+Johnny and the Mohawks	1970	London
King of the Golden River	1975	Oxford
Sofa, The	1959	London
+Three Strangers	1968	London

MACSEMS, WILLIAM
Outcasts of Poker Flat	1972*	

MAGANINI, QUINTO
  b. Fairield, Calif., Nov. 30, 1897; d. Greenwich, Conn., Mar. 10, 1974
  Argonauts, The   ca. 1937* 1942 WOR radio

MAGNEY, RUTH TAYLOR
  +Gift of the Magi   1964 Minneapolis

MAILMAN, MARTIN
  b. New York, June 30, 1932
  +Hunted, The   1959 Rochester, N.Y.

MALLETT, CHARLES
  Governess, The   1954 London

MANDELBAUM, JOEL
  b. New York, Oct. 12, 1932
  +Dybbuk, The   1972 New York
  Village, The   1995 Queens, N.Y.

MANN, ROBERT W.
  Scarlet Letter   1970*

MANNING, EDWARD
  +Rip Van Winkle   1932 New York

MANSCHINGER, KURT. SEE ASHLEY, VERNON

MARAIS, JOSEF
  b. Sir Lowry Pass, South Africa, Nov. 17,
  1905; d. Los Angeles, Apr. 27, 1978
  African Heartbeat   1953 Idyllwild, Calif.
  Tony Beaver   1953 Idyllwild, Calif.

MAREK, ROBERT
  Arabesque   1967 Vermillion, S.D.
  Silent Shepherd   ca. 1968*

MARETZEK, MAX
  b. Brünn (now Brno), June 28, 1821; d.
  Staten Island, N.Y., May 14, 1897
  Sleepy Hollow   1879 New York

MARKORDT, J.
  Tom Thumb   1780 London

MARSHALL, PAUL
  +Mink Stockings   1961 Columbus, Ohio

MARSHALL-HALL, GEORGE W. K.
  b. London, Mar. 28, 1862; d. Melbourne,
  Austral., July 18, 1915
  Alcestis   1898 Melbourne
  Harold   1888 London
  +Romeo and Juliet   1912 Melbourne
  Stella   1914 Melbourne

MARTÍN, JORGE
  b. Santiago de Cuba, Mar. 21, 1959
  Beast and Superbeast 1996 Bethesda, Md.

MARTIN, VERNON
  b. Guthrie, Okla, Dec. 15, 1924
  Ladies Voices   1956 Norman, Okla.

MARTINŮ, BOHUSLAV
  b. Policka, Czech., Dec. 8, 1890; d. Liestal,
  Switz., Aug. 28, 1959
  +Greek Passion   1961 Zurich

MASLAND, WILLIAM
  b. 1954
  Happy Hypocrite   1978*

MASON, BENEDICT
  b. 1954
  ChaplinOperas   1988* 1992 Strasbourg
  Playing Away   1994 Munich

MATHIAS, WILLIAM
  b. Whitland, Nov. 1, 1934; d. Menai Bridge,
  Gwynedd, Wales, July 29, 1992
  Servants, The   1980 Cardiff

MASON, WILTON
  Kingdom Come   1953 Boone, N.C.

MATSHIKIZA, TODD
  d. 1968
  King Kong   1961*

MAURY, LOWNDES
  b. Butte, Mont., July 7, 1911; d. Encino, Calif.,
  Dec. 11, 1975
  Celebration, The   1955*

MAW, NICHOLAS
  b. Grantham, Engl., Nov. 5, 1935
  One Man Show   1964 London
  Rising of the Moon   1970 Glyndebourne

MAXWELL DAVIES, PETER. SEE DAVIES,
  PETER MAXWELL.

MAYER, CHARLES
  Conspiracy of Pontiac 1887 Detroit

MAYER, WILLIAM
  b. New York, Nov. 18, 1925
  Brief Candle   1967 New York
  +Death in the Family 1983 Minneapolis
  +One Christmas
  Long Ago   1962 Muncie, Ind.

MAZZINGHI, JOSEPH
  b. London, Dec. 25, 1765; d. Downside, near
  Bath, Jan. 15, 1844
  Exile, The   1809 London
  Free Knights   1810 London
  Magician No
  Conjuror   1792 London
  Wife of Two Husbands 1803 London

MCCABE, JOHN
  b. Huyton, Engl., Apr. 21, 1939
  Lion, the Witch   1969 Manchester
  Play of Mother   1974 Middlesbrough,
  Courage   Engl.

MCCLURE, LEE
Mother and Child 1990 New York

MCCOY, WILLIAM J.
b. Crestline, Ohio, Mar. 15, 1848; d.
Oakland, Calif., Oct. 15, 1926
+Egypt 1921 Berkeley, Calif.

MCFARLAND, RON
Song of Pegasus 1985 Murphys, Calif.

MCINTYRE, DAVID
Architect, The 1994 Vancouver

MCQUEEN, IAN
East and West 1995 London
Line of Terror 1993 London

MEACHEM, MARGARET
b. Brooklyn, N.Y., Jan. 1, 1922
+Alice in Wonderland 1982*

MEALE, RICHARD
b. Sydney, Austral., Aug. 23, 1932
Mer de Glace 1991 Sydney
Voss 1986 Adelaide

MECHEM, KIRKE
b. Wichita, Kans., Aug. 16, 1925
+John Brown 1989*
Tartuffe 1980 San Francisco

MELL, DAVIS
b. Wilton, near Salisbury, Engl., Nov. 15,
1604; d. London, Apr. 4, 1662
Triumph of Peace 1634 London
(with W. Lawes, S. Ives)

MELLERS, WILFRED
b. Leamington, Warwickshire, Apr. 26, 1914
Borderline, The 1959 London
Tragicall History of
Marlowe 1950–52*

MELLON, ALFRED
b. 1820; d. 1867
Victorine 1859 London

MENNINI, LOUIS
b. Erie, Pa., Nov. 18, 1920
+Rope, The 1955 Lenox, Mass.
Well, The 1951 Rochester, N.Y.

MENOTTI, GIAN CARLO
b. Cadegliano, Italy, July 7, 1911
+Amahl and the
Night Visitors 1951 New York, NBC
+Amelia Goes to the
Ball 1937 Philadelphia
+Boy Who Grew
Too Fast 1982 Wilmington, Del.
+Bride from Pluto 1982 Washington, D.C.
+Chip and His Dog 1979 Guelph, Ont.
+Consul, The 1950 Philadelphia

+Egg, The 1976 Washington, D.C.
Goya 1986 Washington, D.C.
+Help, Help, the
Globolinks! 1968 Hamburg
+Hero, The 1976 Philadelphia
+Island God 1942 New York
+Labyrinth, The 1963 NBC
+Last Savage 1963 Paris
+Loca, La 1979 San Diego
+Maria Golovin 1958 Brussels
+Martin's Lie 1964 Bath, Engl.
+Medium, The 1946 New York
+Most Important Man 1971 New York
+Old Maid and the
Thief 1939 NBC radio
+Saint of Bleecker
Street 1954 New York
+Singing Child 1993 Charleston, S.C.
+Tamu-Tamu 1972 Chicago
+Telephone, The 1947 New York
+Trial of the Gipsy 1978 New York
+Unicorn and the
Manticore 1956 Washington, D.C.
+Wedding, The 1988 Seoul

METCALF, JOHN
b. Swansea, Engl., Aug. 13, 1946
+Crossing, The 1984 Cardiff
Journey, The 1981 Cardiff
Kafka's Chimp 1996 Banff, Albta
Tornrak 1990 Cardiff

MEYEROWITZ, JAN
b. Breslau (now Wrocław), Apr. 23, 1913; d.
Colmar, France, Dec. 15, 1998
+Bad Boys in School 1953 Lenox, Mass.
Barrier, The 1950 New York
Eastward in Eden 1951 Detroit
Esther 1957 Urbana, Ill.
Godfather Death 1961 New York
Port Town 1960 Lenox, Mass.

MIDDLETON, ROBERT
b. Diamond, Ohio, Nov. 18, 1920
Command 1961 Poughkeepsie,
Performance N.Y.
+Life Goes to a Party 1947 Lenox, Mass.

MIKI, MINORU
b. Tokushima, Japan, Mar. 16, 1930; d. 1996
Actor's Revenge 1979 London
Jōruri 1985 St. Louis

MILANO, ROBERTO
b. Brooklyn, N.Y., Nov. 18, 1936
Hired Hand 1959 New York

MILES, PHILIP NAPIER
b. Shirehampton, Engl., Jan. 21, 1865; d.
King's Weston, July 19, 1935

+**Markheim**   1923 London
Westward Ho!   1913 London

MILLER, ROBERT
Cat in the Box   1993 New York

MILLS, RICHARD
  b. Toowoomba, Queensland, Nov. 14, 1949
Summer of the
  Seventeenth Doll   1996 Melbourne

MOBBS, KENNETH
Engaged   1962 Bristol, Engl.
(with Rowell, after Sullivan)

MOFFAT, HUGH
King of the Clouds   1993 Dayton, Ohio
(with M. Ching)

MOHAUPT, RICHARD
  b. Breslau (now Wrocław), Sept. 14, 1904; d.
  Reichenau, Austria, July 3, 1957
Double Trouble   1954 Louisville, Ky.

MOLLICONE, HENRY
  b. Providence, R.I., Mar. 20, 1946
Dream Child   1975*
Emperor Norton   1981 San Francisco
Face on the Barroom
  Floor   1978 Central City, Colo.
Hotel Eden   1989 San Jose
Mask of Evil   1982 Minneapolis
Starbird, The   1979 Houston
Young Goodman
  Brown   1970 Glen Falls, N.Y.

MONK, MEREDITH
  b. Lima, Peru, Nov. 20, 1942
+**Atlas**   1991 New York
+**Education of the**
  Girlchild   1973 New York
Politics of Quiet   1996 Copenhagen
Quarry   1976* 1985 New York

MONTGOMERY, BRUCE
  b. Philadelphia, June 20, 1927
John Barleycorn   1962*

MOORE, DOROTHY RUDD
  b. New Castle, Del., June 4, 1940
Frederick Douglass   1985 New York

MOORE, DOUGLAS
  b. Cutchogue, N.Y., Aug. 10, 1893; d.
  Greenport, N.Y., July 25, 1969
Ballad of Baby Doe   1956 Central City, Colo.
Carry Nation   1966 Lawrence, Kan.
Devil and Daniel
  Webster   1939 New York
Emperor's New
  Clothes   1949 New York
Gallantry   1958 New York
Giants in the Earth   1951 New York

Headless Horseman   1937 Bronxville, N.Y.
White Wings   1949 Hartford
Wings of the Dove   1961 New York

MOORE, HOMER
  b. near Chattauqua, N.Y., Apr. 29, 1863
+**Columbus**   1903 St. Louis
+**Louis XIV**   1917 St. Louis

MOORE, MARY CARR
  b. Memphis, Aug. 6, 1873; d. Inglewood,
  Calif., Jan. 9, 1957
David Rizzio   1932 Los Angeles
Flaming Arrow   1922 San Francisco
Légende Provençale   1929–39*
Leper, The   1912*
Narcissa   1912 Seattle
Rubios, Los   1931 Los Angeles

MOORE, THOMAS
  b. Dublin, May 28, 1779; d. near Calne,
  Wiltshire, Feb. 25, 1852
M.P. (with Horn)   1811 London

MOOREHEAD, JOHN
  b. Ireland, ca. 1760; d. near Deal, Mar. 1804
+**Birds of a Feather**   1796 London
(with J. Calcott)
Bondocani, Il   1800 London
(with T. Attwood)
Cabinet, The   1802 London
(with Moorehead et al.)
Family, The   1802 London
(with J. Braham, W. Reeve)
Family Quarrels   1802 London
(with W. Reed)
Naval Pillar
(with Moorehead et al.) 1799 London
Old Fools   1800 London
Speed the Plough   1802 London

MOPPER, IRVING
  b. Savannah, Ga., Dec. 1, 1914
Door, The   1956 Newark, N.J.
Red Rose and the
  Briar   1951 Syracuse, N.Y.

MORAN, JOHN
  b. 1966
Jack Benny Show   1988 New York
+**Manson Family**   1990 New York

MORAN, ROBERT
  b. Denver, Jan. 8, 1937
Desert of Roses   1992 Houston
Divertissement No. 3 1971 London
Dracula Diary   1994 Houston
From the Towers
  of the Moon   1992 St. Paul, Minn.
Let's Build a Nut
  House   1969 San Jose, Calif.

Mathew in the
School of Life 1994 New York
Metamenagerie 1974*
Night Passage 1997 Seattle

MORE, MARGARET
Mermaid, The 1951 Birmingham, Engl.

MORGENSTERN, SAM
d. New York, Dec. 22, 1989
Big Black Box 1968 New York
Haircut 1969 New York

MORI, FRANK
b. London, Mar. 21, 1820; d. Chaumont,
France, Aug. 2, 1873
River-Sprite 1865 London

MOROSS, JEROME
b. Brooklyn, Aug. 1, 1913; d. Miami, July 25, 1983
Gentlemen, Be Seated! 1963 New York
Golden Apple 1954 New York
Sorry, Wrong Number 1980 Lake George, N.Y.

MORRIS, RICHARD
Agamemnon 1969 Oxford

MORROW, CHARLIE
Light Opera 1983 New York

MOSS, LAWRENCE
b. Los Angeles, Nov. 18, 1927
Brute, The 1961 New Haven

MOSS, M.
Love's Dream 1821 London

MULLER, GERALD FRANK
Chronicles 1977 Rockville, Md.
+Mary Surratt 1989 Ft. Washington,
Md.

MURRAY, BAIN
b. Evanston, Ill., Dec. 26, 1926
Legend, The 1987 Cleveland

MURDOCH, ELAINE
Tamburlaine 1971 Liverpool

MURRAY, JEREMIAH
+Beauty and the Beast 1974 New York
+Marriage Proposal 1973 New York

MUSGRAVE, FRANK
b. 1834; d. 1888
Caliph of Bagdad 1867 London
Windsor Castle 1865 London

MUSGRAVE, THEA
b. Barnton, Midlothian, Scot., May 27, 1928
Abbot of Drimock 1962 London
+Christmas Carol 1979 Norfolk, Va.
Decision, The 1967 London
Harriet, a Woman
Called Moses 1985 Norfolk, Va.

+Marko the Miser 1963 Farnham, Engl.
Mary, Queen of Scots 1977 Edinburgh
+Occurrence at Owl
Creek Bridge 1982 London, BBC
+Simón Bolívar 1995 Norfolk, Va.
Voice of Ariadne 1974 Aldeburgh

NABOKOV, NICOLAS
b. near Lubcha, Minsk, Apr. 17, 1903; d. New
York, Apr. 6, 1978
+Holy Devil 1958 Louisville, Ky.
(lib. with S. Spender)
Love's Labour's Lost 1973 Brussels

NAGEL, CHARLES
b. Engl., 1806; d. Liverpool, New South Wales,
1870
Mock Catalani 1842 Sydney, Austral.

NARES, JAMES
b. 1715; d. 1783
Royal Pastoral 1769 Windsor Castle

NATHAN, ISAAC
b. Canterbury, 1790; d. Sydney, Jan. 15, 1864
Alcaid, The 1824 London
Don John of Austria 1847 Sydney
Illustrious Stranger 1827 London
Merry Freaks 1843 Sydney
Sweethearts and Wives 1823 London
(with Cooke et al.)
Triboulet 1840 London

NAYLOR, EDWARD
b. Cambridge, Engl., Nov. 22, 1907; d.
Keswick, Cumbria, Engl., May 20, 1986
Angelus, The 1909 London

NEIL, WILLIAM
+Guilt of Lillian Sloan 1986 Chicago

NELHYBEL, VACLAV
b. Polanka nad Odrou, Czech., Sept. 24, 1919
Everyman 1974 Memphis

NELSON, ROBERT
b. 1941
Man Who Corrupted
Hadleyville 1986*
Tickets Please 1985 Houston

NELSON, RONALD
b. Joliet, Ill., Dec. 14, 1929
+Birthday of the
Infanta 1956 Rochester, N.Y.

NEUENDORF, ADOLF
b. Hamburg, June 13, 1843; d. New York, Dec.
4, 1897
Don Quixote 1881 New York

NEVIN, ARTHUR
b. Edgeworth, Pa., Apr. 27, 1871; d. Sewickley,
Pa., July 10, 1943

Daughter of the Forest 1918 Chicago

NEWBERN, KENNETH
  Armor of Life   1957 New York

NICHOLLS, FREDERICK C.
  b. 1871
  Prodigal Son   1896 Liverpool?

NIXON, ROGER
  b. Tulare, Calif., Aug. 8, 1921
  Bride Comes to
   Yellow Sky   1968 Charleston, Ill.

NOBLE, HAROLD
  Lake of Menteith   1967 London

NOVAK, LIONEL
  b. Cleveland, Sept. 25, 1911
  Clarkstown Witch   1959 Piermont, N.Y.

NOYES-GREENE, EDITH
  b. Cambridge, Mass., Mar. 26, 1875
  Osseo   1917 Brookline, Mass.

NYMAN, MICHAEL
  b. London, Mar. 23, 1944
  Kiss, The   1984 London
  Letters, Riddles   1991 London, BBC
  (with R. Lepage)
  Man Who Mistook
   His Wife   1986 London
  Noises, Sounds   1994 Tokyo

O'CONNELL, KEVIN
  My Love   1997 Belfast

OLENICK, ELMER
  +Diet, The   1979*

OLIVER, HAROLD
  b. Easton, Md., Sept. 15, 1942
  King of Cats   1976*

OLIVER, JOHN
  Guacamayo's Old
   Song and Dance   1991 Toronto

OLIVER, STEPHEN
  b. Chester, Engl., Mar. 10, 1950; d. London,
   Apr. 29, 1992
  +All the Tea in China 1969 Oxford
  +Bad Times   1975 London
  +Ba-Ta-Clan   1988*
  +Beauty and the
   Beast   1985 London
  Britannia Preserv'd 1984 Hampton Court
  +Cinderella   1991*
  +Dissolute Punished, tetralogy:
   Dialogue between
    Jupiter and Cupid
   Blind, The
   Fall of Miss Moss
   Dissoluto punito   1972 Edinburgh

Donkey, The   1973 Stirling
+Duchess of Malfi   1971 Oxford
+Exposition of a
 Picture   1986 London
+Garden, The   1977 Batigniano, Italy
+Girl and the Unicorn 1978 London
+Great McPorridge
 Disaster   1976 Bath
+Man of Feeling   1980 London
+Mario and the
 Magician   1989 Milwaukee
+Past Tense:
 Come and Go
 Old Times   1974 Huddersfield
Phoenix Too Frequent 1970 Oxford
+Ring, The   1984 Manchester
+Sasha   1983 Banff, Alberta
+Slippery Soules   1969 Oxford
+Stable Home   1977 Canada
+Tables Meet   1990 London
+Three Instant Operas:
 Paid Off
 Time Flies
 Old Haunts   1973 London
+Timon of Athens   1991 London
+Tom Jones   1976 Newcastle
+Waiter's Revenge   1976 Nottingham
+Waiting   1987 Buxton

O'NEAL, BARRY
  b. New York, June 9, 1942
  Dr. Jekyll and Mr.
   Hyde   1980*

OPPENHEIM, HANS
  Rab the Rhymer   1953 Aberdeen
  (with I. Dunlop)

ORR, BUXTON
  Wager, The   1962 London

ORR, ROBIN [ROBERT KEMSLEY]
  b. Brechin, Scot., June 2, 1909
  Full Circle   1968 Perth
  Hermiston   1975 Edinburgh
  +On the Razzle   1988 Glasgow

OSBORNE, NIGEL
  b. Manchester, June 23, 1948
  Electrification of the Soviet
   Union   1987 Glyndebourne
  Hells' Angels   1986 London
  Sarajevo   1994 London
  Terrible Mouth   1992 London

OSBORNE, WILLIAM
  Alice   1985 Jerusalem

OVERTON, HALL
  b. Bangor, Mich., Feb. 23, 1920; d. New
   York, Nov. 24, 1972

Enchanted Pear Tree 1950 New York
+Huckleberry Finn 1971 New York
Pietro's Petard 1963 New York

OWEN, RICHARD
b. Dec. 11, 1922, New York
+Abigail Adams 1987 New York
Death of the Virgin 1981 New York
Dismissed with
Prejudice 1956*
+Fisherman Called
Peter 1965 Carmel, N.Y.
+Mary Dyer 1976 Suffern, N.Y.
Moment of War 1958*
1964 Buenos Aires
+Sadie Thompson 1997 New York
+Tom Sawyer 1989 New York

PACKER, CHARLES
Sadak and Kasalrade 1835 London

PAINE, JOHN KNOWLES
b. Portland, Maine, Jan. 9, 1939; d. Cambridge, Mass., Apr. 25, 1906
+Azara 1883–98*

PAINTAL, PRITI
Biko 1992 Birmingham

PANNELL, RAYMOND
b. London, Ont., Jan. 25, 1935
Luck of Ginger Coffey 1967 Toronto

PARKE, WILLIAM THOMAS
Nina (with W. Shield) 1787 London

PARKER, ALICE
b. Boston, Dec. 16, 1925
+Ponder Heart 1982 Jackson, Miss.

PARKER, HORATIO
b. Auburndale, Mass., Sept. 15, 1863; d. Cedarhurst, N.Y., Dec. 18, 1919
Fairyland 1915 Los Angeles
Mona 1912 New York

PARRY, JOHN
b. Denbigh, Wales, Feb. 18, 1776; d. London, Apr. 8, 1851
Ivanhoe 1820 London
Oberon's Oath 1816 London

PARRY, JOSEPH
b. Merthyr Tydfil, Wales, May 21, 1841; d. Penarth, Feb. 17, 1903
Blodwen 1878 Swansea, Wales
Sylvia 1895 Cardiff

PARTCH, HARRY
b. Oakland, Calif., June 24, 1901; d. San Diego, Sept. 3, 1974
Oedipus 1952 Oakland, Calif.

Revelation in the
Courthouse Park 1962 Urbana, Ill.

PASATIERI, THOMAS
b. New York, Oct. 20, 1945
Before Breakfast 1980 New York
+Black Widow 1972 Seattle
Calvary 1971 Seattle
+Divina, La 1966 New York
+Goose Girl 1981 Fort Worth, Tex.
Ines de Castro 1976 Baltimore
+Maria Elena 1983 Tucson, Ariz.
+Padrevia 1967 Brooklyn, N.Y.
Penitentes, The 1974 Aspen, Colo.
Seagull, The 1974 Houston
+Signor Deluso 1974 Greenway, Va.
Three Sisters 1986 Columbus, Ohio
Trial of Mary Lincoln 1972 NET
Washington Square 1976 Detroit
Women, The 1965 Aspen, Colo.

PASCAL, FLORIAN. SEE WILLIAMS, JOSEPH
BENJAMIN

PASQUALI, NICOLO
d. 1757
Temple of Peace 1749 Dublin
Triumphs of Hibernia 1748 Dublin

PATACCHI, VAL
Bandit, The 1958 Columbia, Mo.
Secret, The 1955 Columbia, Mo.

PATTERSON, FRANKLIN PEALE
b. Philadelphia, Jan. 5, 1871; d. New Rochelle, N.Y., July 6, 1966
+Beggar's Love 1929 New York
+Echo, The 1926 Portland, Oreg.
+Mountain Blood 1926*

PAULUS, STEPHEN
b. Summit, N.J., Aug. 24, 1949
Harmoonia 1991 Muscatine, La.
Postman Always Rings
Twice 1982 St. Louis
Three Hermits 1997 St. Paul
Village Singer 1979 St. Louis
Woman at the
Otowi Crossing 1995 St. Louis
Woodlanders, The 1895 St. Louis

PAYNTER, JOHN
Voyage of the St.
Brendan 1979 Norwich, Engl.

PELISSIER, VICTOR
b. Paris?, ca. 1740–50; d. ?, New Jersey, ca. 1820
Ariadne Abandoned
by Theseus 1797 New York
Bridal Ring 1810 London
(with H. Condell)

Edwin and Angelina   1796 New York
Fourth of July   1799 New York
Merry Gardner   1801 New York
Sterne's Maria   1799 New York
Voice of Nature   1802 New York

PENBERTHY, JAMES
  b. Melbourne, Austral., May 3, 1917
Creation of the World 1990*
Dalgerie   1959 Perth, Austral.
+Earth Mother   1957–59*
+Miracle, The   1964 Perth, Austral.
+Ophelia   1965 Tasmania, Austral.
Stations   1975*

PENDERECKI, KRZYSTOF
  b. Debica, Poland, Nov. 23, 1933
Paradise Lost   1978 Chicago

PENTLAND, BARBARA
  b. Winnipeg, Jan. 2, 1912
Lake, The   1954 Vancouver

PEPUSCH, JOHN (JOHANN CHRISTOPH)
  b. Berlin, 1667; d. London, July 20, 1752
Apollo and Daphne   1716 London
Beggar's Opera   1728 London
Death of Dido   1716 London
Myrtillo   1715 London
Orestes   1731 London
Prophetess, The   1724 London
Thomyris   1707 London
Venus and Adonis   1715 London
Wedding, The   1729 London

PERERA, RONALD
  b. Boston, Dec. 25, 1941
Yellow Wallpaper   1989 Northampton, Mass.

PERL, PAUL
Judgment Day   1951 New York

PERRY, GEORGE FREDERICK
  b. 1793; d. 1862
Family Jars   1822 London
Morning, Noon,
  and Night   1822 London
Sweethearts and   1823 London
Wives (with Nathan et al.)
Veteran Soldier   1822 London
(with Whitaker, Cooke)

PERRY, JULIA
  b. Lexington, Ky., Mar. 25, 1924; d. Akron,
  Ohio, Apr. 24, 1979
+Cask of Amontillado
  (lib. with V. Card)   1954 New York
+Selfish Giant   1964*

PERSICHETTI, VINCENT
  b. Philadelphia, June 6, 1915; d. there, Aug.
  13, 1987

+Sibyl, The   1985 Philadelphia

PETERS, RANDOLPH
Nosferatu   1993 Toronto

PETERSON, HANNIBAL [MARVIN CHARLES]
  b. Smithville, Tex., Nov. 11, 1948
Diary of an African-
  American   1991 New York

PHILLIPS, BURRILL
  b. Omaha, Neb., Nov. 9, 1907; d. Berkeley,
  Calif., June 22, 1988
Don't We All?   1949 Rochester, N.Y.

PHILLIPS, EDWARD
  fl. 1730–1740
Chamber-Maid   1730 London

PHILLIPS, MONTAGUE
  b. London, Nov. 13, 1885; d. Esher, Engl., Jan.
  4, 1969
Rebel Maid   1921 London

PHILLIPS, ROY
Trevallion   1956 London

PHILPOT, STEPHEN ROWLAND
Dante and Beatrice   1889 London

PICKER, TOBIAS
  b. New York, July 18, 1954
Emmeline   1996 Santa Fe

PIKET, FREDERICK
  b. Constantinople, Jan 6, 1903; d. Long Island
  City, N.Y., Feb. 28, 1974
Isaac Levi   1956 White Plains, N.Y.
Satan's Trap   1950 New York
Trilby   1967 New York

PINKHAM, DANIEL
  b. Lynn, Mass., June 5, 1923
Garden of Artemis   1948 Cambridge, Mass.

PITTMAN, EVELYN LaRUE
  b. McAlester, Okla., Jan. 6, 1910
+Esther and Cousin
  Mordecai   1957 Paris

PLISKA, GREG
Secret Garden   1991 Philadelphia

POKRASS, SAMUEL D.
Cyrano de Bergerac   1932*

POTTER, ARCHIBALD JAMES
  b. Belfast, Sept. 22, 1918; d. Greystones, July
  5, 1980
Patrick   1965 Dublin
+Wedding, The   1981 Dublin

PRATT, SILAS GAMALIEL
  b. Addison, Vt., Aug. 4, 1846; d. Pittsburgh,
  Oct. 30, 1916

Lucille	1887	Chicago
Triumph of Columbus	1892	New York
Zenobia	1882	New York

PRELLEUR, PETER
  b. 1705?; d. 1741

Baucis and Philemon	1740	London

PROVENZANO, ALDO
  b. Philadelphia, May 3, 1930

Cask of Amontillado	1968	Rochester, N.Y.

PURCELL, DANIEL
  b. London, ca. 1660; d. there, Dec. 12, 1717

Brutus of Alba	1696	London
(with Playford, Scott)		
Grove, The	1700	London
Island Princess	1699	London
(with Leveridge, Clark)		
Judgment of Paris	1701	London
Rival Queens	1701	London
(with G. Finger)		
Secular Masque	1700	London
World in the Moon	1697	London
(with J. Clarke)		

PURCELL, HENRY
  b. London, 1658/1659; d. there, Nov. 21, 1695

Dido and Aeneas	1689	London
Dioclesian	1690	London
Fairy Queen	1692	London
Indian Queen	1695	London
King Arthur	1691	London

PURSER, JOHN
  b. Glasgow, 1942

Bell, The	1972	BBC, Scotland
Undertaker, The	1969	Edinburgh

PUTSCHÉ, THOMAS
  b. Scarsdale, N.Y., June 29, 1929

+Cat and the Moon	1960	Hartford

QUILTER, ROGER
  b. 1877; d. 1953

Julia	1936	London

RAMSIER, PAUL
  b. 1927, Louisville, Ky.

Man on a Bearskin Rug	1969	Aberdeen, S.D.

RAN, SHULAMITH
  b. Tel Aviv, Oct. 21, 1949

Between Two Worlds	1997	Chicago

RANKL, KARL
  b. Gaaden, Austria, Oct. 1, 1898; d. Salzburg, Sept. 6, 1968

Deirdre of the Sorrows	1951*	

RAPCHAK, LAWRENCE

Lifework of Juan Diaz	1990	Chicago

RAPHLING, SAM
  b. Fort Worth, Tex., Mar. 19, 1910; d. New York, Jan. 8, 1988

Dr. Heidegger's Experiment	1956	New York
Liar, Liar	1972*	
+President Lincoln	1976*	
Tin Pan Alley	1954	New York

RAYBOULD, CLARENCE
  b. Birmingham, Engl., June 28, 1886; d. Bideford, Mar. 27, 1972

Sumida River	1916	Glastonbury, Engl.

REA, ALAN
  b. 1933

Fête at Coqueville	1976	Fresno, Calif.
Old Pipes and the Dryad	1980	Fresno, Calif.

REA, JOHN
  b. Toronto, Jan. 14, 1944

Prisoner's Play	1973	Toronto

REAM, MARC

RareArea	1985	Brussels

REDDING, JOSEPH DEIGHN
  b. Sacramento, Sept. 13, 1859; d. San Francisco, Nov. 21, 1932

Land of Happiness	1917	San Francisco

REED, HERBERT OWEN
  b. Odessa, Mo., June 17, 1910

Butterfly Girl	1985	Brooklyn, N.Y.
+Earth-Trapped	1962	East Lansing, Mich.
Living Solid Face	1962	East Lansing, Mich.
Peter Homan's Dream	1955	East Lansing, Mich.

REED, LOU (LEWIS)
  b. Brooklyn, N.Y., Mar. 2, 1947

Time Rocker	1996	Hamburg

REED, THOMAS GERMAN
  b. Bristol, June 27, 1817; d. Upper East Sheen, Mar. 21, 1888

Ancient Britons	1875	London
Drama at Home	1844	London
Eyes and No Eyes	1875	London
Golden Fleece	1845	London
He's Coming	1874	London
Indian Puzzle	1876	London
Matched and Mated	1876	London
Mildred's Well	1873	London
Night's Surprise	1877	London
No. 204	1877	London

Our Island Home 1870 London
Sensation Novel 1871 London
Spanish Bond 1875 London
Three Tenants 1874 London
Who's the Composer? 1845 London
Wicked Duke 1876 London
Wonderful Water Cure 1846 London

REEVE, GEORGE W.
Frozen Lake 1824 London

REEVE, WILLIAM
b. London, 1757; d. there, June 22, 1815
Apparition, The 1794 London
Bannian Day 1796 London
Bantry Bay 1797 London
Blind Girl 1801 London
(with J. Mazzinghi)
British Fortitude 1794 London
(with H. R. Bishop)
Brother and Sister 1815 London
Caravan, The 1803 London
Chains of the Heart 1801 London
(with J. Mazzinghi)
Charity Boy 1796 London
Council of Ten 1811 London
David Rizzio 1820 London
(with Braham et al.)
Embarkation, The 1799 London
Family Quarrels 1802 London
(with J. Moorehead)
Hero and Leander 1787 London
Jamie and Anna ca. 1801*
Kais (with J. Braham) 1808 London
Magic Minstrel 1808 London
Out of Place 1805 London
(with J. Braham)
Paul and Virginia 1800 London
(with J. Mazzinghi)
Purse, The 1794 London
Raft, The 1798 London
Ramah Droog 1798 London
(with J. Mazzinghi)
Sicilian Romance 1794 London
Thirty Thousand 1804 London
(with Davy, Braham)
Thomas and Susan 1787 London
Turnpike Gate 1799 London
(with J. Mazzinghi)
Up to Town 1811 London
(with Condell et al.)
White Plume 1806 London
Who's to Have Her? 1813 London
(with J. Whitaker)

REICH, STEVE
b. New York, Oct. 3, 1936
Cave, The 1993 Vienna
Hindenburg 1997 Bonn

REID, BOB
Africa Is Calling Me 1976 New York
REID, MIKE
Different Fields 1996 New York
REIF, PAUL
b. Prague, Mar. 23, 1910; d. New York, July 7,
1978
**+Curse of Mauvais-
Air** 1974 New York
Mad Hamlet 1965*
**Portrait in
Brownstone** 1966 New York
REINAGLE, ALEXANDER
b. Portsmouth, Engl., bapt. Apr. 23, 1756; d.
Baltimore, Sept. 21, 1809
Columbus 1797 Philadephia
Savoyard, The 1795 Philadelphia
REISE, JAY
b. New York, Feb. 9, 1950
+Rasputin 1988 New York
REYNOLDS, ALBERT
b. 1884
Derby Day 1932 Hammersmith,
London
+Fountain of Youth 1931*
Policeman's Serenade 1926 London
RICE, EDWARD EVERETT
b. Brighton, Mass, Dec. 21, 1848; d. New
York, Nov. 16, 1924
Evangeline 1874 New York
RIDOUT, ALAN
b. West Wickham, Engl., Dec. 9, 1934; d. Mar.
20, 1996
Angelo 1971 Canterbury
**Boy from the
Catacombs** 1965 Canterbury
Cat, The 1971 Canterbury
Children's Crusade 1968 Canterbury
Creation, The 1973 Ely, Engl.
Gift, The 1971 Canterbury
Greek Kalends 1956 Tunbridge Wells
Pardoner's Tale 1971 Canterbury
Phaeton 1974 London, BBC
Rescue, The 1963 Hastings
+Vision, The 1974 Manchester
Wenceslas 1978 Bournemouth
White Doe 1987 Ripon, Engl.
RIDOUT, GODFREY
b. Toronto, May 6, 1918; d. there, Nov. 24, 1984
Lost Child 1975 CBS
RIES, FERDINAND
b. Bonn, bapt. Nov. 28, 1784; d. Frankfurt,
Jan. 13, 1838

Sorceress, The   1831 London

RIETI, VITTORIO
  b. Alexandria, Egypt, Jan. 28, 1898; d. Feb.
  19, 1994, New York
Clock, The   1960*
+Don Perlimplin   1952 Urbana, Ill.
Pet Shop   1958 New York

RILEY, DENNIS
  b. Los Angeles, May 28, 1943; d. New York,
  May 5, 1999
Cats' Corner   1983*
+Rappaccini's Daughter
  (lib. with J. Pazillo) 1981–84*

RIVERS, SAM
  b. El Reno, Okla., Sept. 25, 1930
Solomon and Sheba   1973 New York

RIVINGTON, HILL
Mr. Bellamy Comes
  Home   1950 London

ROBERTS, EDWIN
Hunting of the Snark 1971 New York

ROBINSON, EARL
  b. Seattle, July 2, 1910; d. there, July 20, 1991
Sandhog   1954 New York

ROCHBERG, GEORGE
  b. Paterson, N.J., July 5, 1918
+Confidence Man   1982 Santa Fe, N.M.

ROCKWELL, JEFFREY
Rip Van Winkle   1989 San Diego

RODGERS, LOU
  b. 1936
+Nights of Annabel
  Lee   1996 New York
Specialist, The   1978 New York

RODRÍGUEZ, ROBERT XAVIER
  b. San Antonio, June 28, 1946
Diable amoureux   1979 Dallas
Frida   1991 Philadelphia
+Monkey See   1987 Dallas
Old Majestic   1988 San Antonio
Ransom of Red Chief 1986 Mesquite, Tex.
Suor Isabella   1982 Dallas
+Tango   1986 Dallas

RODWELL, GEORGE
  b. London, Nov. 15, 1800; d. there, Jan. 22,
  1852
Black Vulture   1830 London
Bottle Imp   1828 London
Bronze Horse   1835 London
Cornish Miners   1827 London
Devil's Elixir   1829 London
Don Quixote   1840 London
Earthquake   1828 London

Evil Eye   1831 London
Flying Dutchman   1827 London
Jack Sheppard   1839 London
Last Days of Pompeii 1834 London
Lord of the Isles   1834 London
Mason of Buda   1828 London
+My Own Lover   1832 London
New Don Juan!   1828 London
Paul Clifford   1835 London
Phantom Ship   1827 London
Quasimodo   1836 London
+Seven Maids of
  Munich   1846 London
Sexton of Cologne   1836 London
Skeleton Lover   1830 London
Spirit of the Bell   1835 London
Spring Lock   1829 London
+Teddy the Tiler   1830 London
+Thalaba the
  Destroyer   1836 London
Waverley   1824 London

ROE, BETTY
  b. London, July 30, 1930
Canterbury Tale   1986 Oakham, Engl.

ROGERS, BERNARD
  b. New York, Feb. 4, 1893; d. Rochester, N.Y.,
  May 24, 1968
Marriage of Aude   1931 New York
+Nightingale, The   1955 New York
Veil, The   1950 Bloomington, Ind.
Warrior, The   1947 New York

ROLFE, FOURNESS
+Minstrel's Return 1855 Newcastle u. Tyne

ROMBERG, SIGMUND
  b. Nagykanizsa, Hung., July 29, 1887; d. New
  York, Nov. 9, 1951
Student Prince   1924 New York

ROMER, FRANK (FRANCIS)
  b. 1810; d. 1889
Fridolin   1840 London
Pacha's Bridal   1836 London
Rob of the Fens   1838 London

ROOKE (O'ROURKE), WILLIAM MICHAEL
  b. Dublin, Sept. 29, 1794; d. London, Oct. 14,
  1847
Amilie   1818*1837 London
Henrique   1839 London
Pirate, The   1822 London

ROOSEVELT, WILLARD
  b. Madrid, Jan. 16, 1918
And the Walls   1976 New York

ROOT, GEORGE F.
  b. Sheffield, Mass., Aug. 30, 1820; d. Bailey's
  Island, Maine, Aug. 6, 1895

Belshazzar's Feast ca. 1853
Flower Queen   1853 New York
+Haymakers, The   1860 Chicago
Pilgrim Fathers ca. 1854*

ROOTHAM, CYRIL
 b. Bristol, Engl., Oct. 5, 1875; d. Cambridge,
 Engl., Mar. 18, 1938
Two Sisters   1922 Cambridge

ROREM, NED
 b. Richmond, Ind., Oct. 23, 1923
Anniversary, The ca. 1961*
Bertha   1973 New York
Cain and Abel   ca. 1946*
Childhood Miracle   1955 New York
Fables   1971 Martin, Tenn.
Hearing   1977 New York
Last Day   1967 New York
+Robbers, The   1958 New York
Three Sisters Who
 Are Not Sisters   1971 Philadelphia

ROUSE, MIKEL [MICHAEL JOSEPH]
 b. St. Louis, Jan. 26, 1957
+Dennis Cleveland   1996 New York
+Failing Kansas   1995 New York

ROWELL, GEORGE
+Engaged   1962 Bristol, Engl.
 (with K. Mobbs, after Sullivan)

ROY, KLAUS GEORGE
 b. Vienna, Jan. 24, 1924
+Sterlingman   1957 Boston

RÔZE, RAYMOND
 b. London, 1875; d. there, Mar. 31, 1920
+Joan of Arc   1913 London

RUBINSTEIN, BERYL
 b. Athens, Ga., Oct. 26, 1908; d. Cleveland,
 Dec. 22, 1952
Sleeping Beauty   1938 New York

RUFFIN, GARY/HANK RUFFIN
Survival of St. Joan 1971 New York

RUGER, MORRIS HUTCHINS
 b. Superior, Wisc., Dec. 2, 1902
Fall of the House
 of Usher   1953 Los Angeles
Gettysburg   1938 Los Angeles

RUGGLES, CARL
 b. Marion, Mass., Mar. 11, 1876; d.
 Bennington, Vt., Oct. 24, 1971
Sunken Bell   1912–27*

RUSH, GEORGE
 fl. London, ca. 1760–1780
Capricious Lovers   1764 London
Royal Shepherd   1764 London

RUSSELL, ROBERT
 b. 1933
So How Does Your
 Garden Grow   1966 New York

RUSSO, WILLIAM
 b. Chicago, June 25, 1928
Cabaret Opera   1970 New York
Isabella's Fortune   1974 New York
John Hooten   1967 London
Pedrolino's Revenge   1974 New York

RUTTER, JOHN
 b. London, Sept. 24, 1945
Bang!   1976*
Wind in the Willows   1997 Wilmington, Dela.

SACCHINI, ANTONIO M. G.
 b. Florence, June 14, 1730; d. Paris, Oct. 6, 1786
Love Finds the Way   1777 London
 (with T. Arne, Fisher)

SAHL, MICHAEL
 b. Boston, Sept. 2, 1934
+Boxes   1981–82 New York radio
+Civilization & Its
 Discontents   1977 New York
+Conjurer, The   1975 New York
Dream Beach   1988 New York
+Noah   1978 Brooklyn, N.Y.
+Passion of Simple
 Simon   1979 New York
+Stauf   1976 New York
 (all but **Dream Beach** with E. Salzman)

SALZMAN, ERIC
 b. New York, Sept. 8, 1933
+Civilization & Its
 Discontents   1977 New York
+Conjurer, The   1975 New York
+Noah   1978 Brooklyn, N.Y.
+Passion of Simple
 Simon   1979 New York
+Stauf   1976 New York
 (all with M. Sahl)

SAMINSKY, LAZARE
 b. Valegotsulova, near Odessa, Nov. 8, 1882; d.
 Port Chester, N.Y., June 30, 1959
+Gagliarda of a
 Merry Plague   1925 New York
+Julian, the Apostate
 Caeser   1933–38*
+Vision of Ariel   1915* 1954 Chicago

SANDOW, GREGORY
 b. New York, June 3, 1943
+Christmas Carol   1977 Norfolk, Va.
Fall of the House
 of Usher   1979 New York
Frankenstein   1980 Glens Falls, N.Y.

Richest Girl in the
World 1975 New York

SAUNDERS, MAX
b. 1903
Little Beggars 1958 London, BBC

SAWYER, DAVID
Panic, The 1991 London

SAXON, ROBERT
b. London, Oct. 8, 1953
Caritas 1991 Wakefield, Engl.

SAYLOR, BRUCE
b. Philadelphia, Apr. 24, 1946
My Kinsman,
Major Molineux 1976 Pittsburgh
Orpheus Descending 1994 Chicago

SCARIM, NICHOLAS
Sumidagawa 1979 New London,
Conn.

SCHAFER, R. MURRAY
b. Sarnia, Ont., July 18, 1933
+Loving/Toi 1966 CBC, Montreal
+Patria, cyle, 1966–83*:
Patria, Prologue 1981 Heart Lake, Ont.
Patria, no. 1 1974 Toronto
Patria, no. 2 1972 Stratford, Ont.
Patria, no. 3 1987 Petersborough,
Ont.
Patria, no. 4 1989 Liège
Patria, no. 5 1992 Toronto

SCHAT, PETER
b. Utrecht, Holland, June 5, 1935
Houdini 1979 Aspen, Colo.

SCHICKELE, PETER ("P. D. Q. BACH")
b. Ames, Iowa, July 17, 1935
+Abduction of Figaro 1984 Minneapolis
+Hansel & Gretel
& Ted & Alice 1972 Dallas
+Little Nightmare
Music 1982 New York
+Oedipus Tex 1988 Minneapolis
+Prelude to Einstein
on the Fritz 1989 New York
+Stoned Guest 1975 Ogden, Utah

SCHMIDT, KARL
b. Schwerin, Ger., Sept. 24, 1864; d. 1950
Lady of the Lake 1931 Chicago

SCHONTHAL, RUTH
b. Hamburg, June 27, 1924
Courtship of Camilla 1980*
Jocasta 1996 New York
Princess Maleen 1989 White Plains, N.Y.

SCHUBERT, PETER
New York, Apr. 1, 1946
Bus to Stockport 1986 New York
(with E. Valinsky)

SCHULLER, GUNTHER
b. New York, Nov. 22, 1925
Fisherman and
His Wife 1970 Boston
+Visitation, The 1966 Hamburg

SCHUMAN, WILLIAM
b. New York, Aug. 4, 1910; d. there, Feb. 16,
1992
Mighty Casey 1951 Hartford, Conn.
Question of Taste 1989 Cooperstown, N.Y.

SCHURMANN, GERARD
b. Kertosono, Dutch East Indies, Jan. 19, 1924
+Piers Plowman 1980 Gloucester, Engl.

SCHWARTZ, PAUL
b. Vienna, July 27, 1907
+Experiment, The 1956 Gambier, Ohio

SCOTT, CYRIL
b. Oxton, England, Sept. 27, 1879; d.
Eastbourne, Dec. 31, 1970
+Alchemist, The 1925 Essen, Ger.
+Maureen O'Mara 1946*

SCOTT, TOM
b. Campbellsburg, Ky., May 28, 1912; d. New
York, Aug. 12, 1961
Fisherman, The 1956*

SCULTHORPE, PETER
b. Launceston, Tasmania, Apr. 29, 1929
Quiros 1982 Austral. television
+Rites of Passage 1974 Sydney

SEARELLE, LUSCOMBE
b. Devon, Engl., 1853; d. 1907
Wreck of the Pinafore 1882 London

SEARLE, HUMPHREY
b. Oxford, Aug. 26, 1915; d. London, May 12,
1982
+Diary of a Madman 1958 Berlin
+Hamlet 1968 Hamburg
+Photo of the Colonel 1964 London, BBC

SEDGWICK, ALFRED B.
Africanus Blue Beard 1874 Gloucester, Mass.
+Circumstances
Alter Cases 1876 New York?
Estranged 1876 New York?
Gambrinus 1876 Jackson, Mich.
Leap Year 1875 New York
My Walking
Photograph 1876 Chicago?

+Queerest
  Courtship   1875 Chicago?
+Single Married
  Man   1883 New York?
+Sold Again and
  Got the Money   1876 New York?
+Twin Sisters   1876 New York?

SEEDO, MR.
  b. ca. 1700; d. Prussia?, ca. 1754
Lottery, The   1732 London
Venus, Cupid   1733 London

SELETSKY, HAROLD
Song of Insanity   1987 New York

SELWYN, DAVID
  b. Nov. 21, 1951, Bristol, Engl.
+Rocking Stone   1980 Bristol, Engl.

SESSIONS, ROGER
  b. Brooklyn, N.Y., Dec. 28, 1896; d.
  Princeton, N.J., Mar. 16, 1985
Emperor's New
  Clothes   1984*
Fall of the House of
  Usher   1925*
Montezuma   1964 Berlin (West)
Trial of Lucullus   1947 Berkeley, Calif.

SEYMOUR, JOHN LAURENCE
  b. Los Angeles, Jan. 18, 1893; d. San
  Francisco, Feb. 1, 1986
In the Pasha's Garden   1935 New York
+Two Gentlemen of
  Verona   1937*
  (lib. with H. C. Tracy)

SHADLE, CHARLES
Friends and Dinosaurs   1989 Needham, Mass.

SHATIN (ALLEN), JUDITH
  b. Boston, Nov. 21, 1949
Follies and Fancies   1987 New York

SHAUGHNESSY, ROBERT
Enchanted Garden   1972*

SHAW, FRANCIS RICHARD
  b. June 23, 1942, Maidenhead, Berkshire, Engl.
Selfish Giant   1973*

SHAW, GEOFFREY
  b. 1879; d. 1943
All at Sea   1952 London

SHAW, MARTIN
  b. London, Mar. 9, 1875; d. Southwold, Oct.
  24, 1958
Master Valiant   1936 London
Mr. Pepys   1926 London
Thorn of Avalon   1931 London
Waterloo Leave   1928 Norwich, Engl.

SHAW, THOMAS
  b. ca. 1760; d. ca. 1830
Island of St.
  Marguerite   1789 London

SHEFFER, JONATHAN B.
  b. 1953
Mistake, The   1981 Denver

SHELDON, ROBERT
Fifth for Bridge   1961 San Francisco

SHELLEY, HARRY ROWE
  b. New Haven, June 2, 1858; d. Short Beach,
  Conn., Sept. 12, 1947
Old Black Joe   1911 New York
+Romeo and Juliet   1901*

SHENG, BRIGHT
  b. Shanghai, Dec. 6, 1955
Silver River   1997 Santa Fe
Song of Majnun   1992 Chicago

SHERE, CHARLES EVERETT
  b. Berkeley, Calif., Aug. 20, 1935
Bride Stripped Bare   1984 Oakland, Calif.
I Like It to Be a Play   1989 San Francisco
Ladies Voices   1987 Berkeley, Calif.
What Happened   1991*

SHERMAN, KIM D.
  b. Elgin, Ill., Aug. 6, 1954
Three Visitations: 1996 Minneapolis
  Red Tide   1989 Minneapolis
  Lamentations
  Long Island
  Dreamer   1987 Minneapolis

SHIELD, WILLIAM
  b. Swalwell, Engl., Mar. 5, 1748; d. London,
  Jan. 25, 1829
Abroad and at Home   1796 London
Arrived at Portsmouth   1794 London
Campaign, The   1785 Dublin
Choleric Fathers   1785 London
Cobler of Castlebury   1778 London
Crisis, The   1778 London
Crusade, The   1790 London
Czar, The   1790 London
Farmer, The   1787 London
Flitch of Bacon   1778 London
Fontainbleau   1784 London
Hartford Bridge   1792 London
Highland Reel   1788 London
Irish Mimic   1795 London
Italian Villagers   1797 London
Lad of the Hills   1796 London
Lock and Key   1796 London
Love and War   1787 London
Love in a Camp   1786 London
Marian   1788 London

Midnight Wanderers	1793	London
Mysteries of the Castle	1795	London
Netly Abbey	1794	London
(with W. T. Parke)	1787	London
Noble Peasant	1784	London
Nunnery, The	1785	London
Poor Soldier	1783	London
Prophet, The	1788	London
Richard Coeur de		
Lion	1786	London
Rival Soldiers	1797	London
Robin Hood	1784	London
Rosina	1782	London
Shamrock, The	1777	Dublin
Siege of Gibraltar	1780	London
Sprigs of Laurel	1793	London
To Arms	1793	London
Travellers in		
Switzerland	1794	London
Two Faces under		
a Hood	1807	London
Wicklow Mountains	1796	London
Woodman, The	1791	London

SHIELDS, ALICE
b. New York, Feb. 18, 1943

+Odyssey	1975	Glens Falls, N.Y.
+Shaman	1978* 1987	New York

SIEGEL, NORMAN

Who Stole the American		
Crown Jewels?	1971	New York

SIEGMEISTER, ELIE
b. New York, Jan. 15, 1909; d. Manhasset, N.Y., Mar. 10, 1991

Angel Levine	1985	New York
Darling Corie	1954	Hempstead, N.Y.
Lady of the Lake	1985	New York
Marquesa of O	1982*	
Mermaid in Lock No. 7	1958	Pittsburgh
Miranda	1956	Hartford, Conn.
Night of the Moonspell	1976	Shreveport, La.
Plough and the Stars	1963	St. Louis

SIERRA, ROBERTO
b. Vega Baja, Puerto Rico, Oct. 9, 1953

Terra Incognita	1997	New York

SILSBEE, ANN
b. Cambridge, Mass., Aug. 21, 1930

Nightingale's		
Apprentice	1984	Ithaca, N.Y.

SILVER, SHEILA
b. Seattle, Wash., Oct. 3, 1946

+Thief of Love	1985	New York

SILVERMAN, FAYE-ELLEN
b. New York, Oct. 2, 1947

+Miracle of Nemirov	1974*	

SILVERMAN, STANEY J.
b. New York, July 5, 1938

Africanus Instructus	1986	New York
Columbine String Quartet		
Tonight!	1981	Lenox, Mass.
Dr. Selavy's Magic	1972	Stockbridge,
Theatre		Mass.
Elephant Steps	1968	Lenox, Mass.
Hotel for Criminals	1974	Lenox, Mass.
Madame Adare	1980	New York
Up from Paradise	1974	Ann Arbor, Mich.

SILVESTER, BARRET [J. G. NOE]

Don Quixote	1873	New York

SIMON, CARLY
b. New York, 1945

+Romulus Hunt	1993	New York
(lib. with J. Brackman)		

SITSKY, LARRY
b. Tientsin, China, Sept. 10, 1934

De Profundis	1982	Canberra, Austral.
Fall of the House		
of Usher	1965	Hobart, Austral.
Fiery Tales	1976	Adelaide
Golem, The	1980* 1993	Sydney
Lenz	1974	Sydney
Three Scenes	1991	Canberra, Austral.
Voices in Limbo	1977*	
	1981	Austral. radio

SIX, HERBERT

All Cats Turn Gray	1971	New York
Without Memorial		
Banners	1966	Kansas City, Mo.

SKILLING, ROBERT P.

David	1951	New York

SKILTON, CHARLES SANFORD
b. Northampton, Mass., Aug. 16, 1868; d. Lawrence, Kans., Mar. 12, 1941

Sun-Bride	1930	NBC radio

SLATES, PHILIP
b. Canton, Ohio, Sept. 24, 1924; d. Indianapolis, 1966

+Bargain, The	1956	Athens, Ohio
+Candle, The	1956	Athens, Ohio

SLAUGHTER, WALTER

Alice in Wonderland	1906*	
French Maid	1896	London
Gentleman Joe	1895*	

SMALLEY, ROGER
b. Swinton, Manchester, Engl., July 26, 1943

William Derrincourt	1977	Perth, Austral.

SMART, HENRY
b. London, Oct. 26, 1838; d. there, July 6, 1879

Berta	1854	London

STANFORD, CHARLES VILLIERS
  b. Dublin, Sept. 30, 1852; d. London, Mar. 29,
  1924
Canterbury Pilgrims 1884 London
Critic, The   1916 London
**Much Ado about
  Nothing**   1901 London
Savonarola   1884 Hamburg
Shamus O'Brien   1896 London
Travelling   1919*
  Companion   1925 Liverpool
**Veiled Prophet of
  Khorassan**   1881 Hanover, Ger.

STANLEY, JOHN
  b. London, Jan. 17, 1712; d. there, May 19,
  1786
Arcadia   1761 London
**Tears and Triumphs
  of Parnassus**   1760 London

STANSBURY, GEORGE FREDERICK
Postilion!   1837 London

STARER, ROBERT
  b. Vienna, Jan. 8, 1924
**Anna Marguerita's
  Will**   1981 New York
Apollonia   1979 St. Paul, Minn.
Intruder, The   1956 New York
Last Lover   1975 Katonah, N.Y.
Mystic Trumpeter   1983 Brooklyn, N.Y.
+Pantagleize   1973 Brooklyn, N.Y.

STEARNS, THEODORE
  b. Berea, Ohio, June 10, 1880; d. Los
  Angeles, Nov. 1, 1935
+Snowbird, The   1923 Chicago

STEIBELT, DANIEL
  b. Berlin, Oct. 22, 1765; d. St. Petersburg, ca.
  Oct. 1823
Albert and Adelaide 1798 London
  (with T. Attwood)

STEIN, LEON
  b. Chicago, Sept. 18, 1910
Deirdre   1957 Chicago
Fisherman's Wife   1955 St. Joseph, Mich.

STEVENS, NOEL
Enchanted Canary   1961 Bemidji, Minn.

STEVENSON, JOHN
  b. Dublin, Nov. 1761; d. Kells, Sept. 14, 1833
Bedouins, The   1801 Dublin
Benyowsky   1826 London
Cavern, The   1825 Dublin
Contract, The   1782 Dublin
Love in a Blaze   1799 Dublin
  (with P. Cogan)
Spanish Patriots   1812 London

STEWART, FRANK
  b. La Junta, Colo., Dec. 12, 1920
To Let the Captive Go 1974 New York

STEWART, HUMPHREY JOHN
  b. London, May 22, 1856; d. San Diego, Dec.
  28, 1932
Hound of Heaven   1924 San Francisco
King Hal   1906*
                         1911 San Francisco

STILL, WILLIAM GRANT
  b. Woodville, Miss., May 11, 1895; d. Los
  Angeles, Dec. 3, 1978
Bayou Legend   1941*
                         1974 Jackson, Miss.
Costaso   1954*
                         1989 Flagstaff, Ariz.
Highway 1, U.S.A.   1963 Miami
Minette Fontaine   1984 Baton Rouge, La.
Troubled Island   1938* 1949 New York

STODDARD, MARLA
+Hansel and Gretel   1986 Arcata, Calif.

STOESSEL, ALBERT
  b. St. Louis, Oct. 11, 1894; d. New York, May
  12, 1943
Garrick   1937 New York

STOKER, RICHARD
  b. Castleford, Yorkshire, Nov. 8, 1938
**Birthday of the
  Infanta**   1963 London
+Chinese Canticle   1991 London
Johnson Preserv'd   1967 London
**+Make Me a Willow
  Cabin**   1973 London
Thérèse Raquin   1975*

STOKES, ERIC
  b. Haddon Heights, N.J., July 14, 1930
Further Voyages   1984*
+HAPP   1977 Minneapolis
Horspfal   1969 Minneapolis
Jealous Cellist   1979 Minneapolis
We're Not Robots   1986 Minneapolis

STORACE, STEPHEN
  b. London, Apr. 4, 1762; d. there, Mar. 15–16,
  1796
Algonah (with Kelly) 1802 London
Cave of Trophonius   1791 London
Cherokee, The   1794 London
Dido   1792 London
**Doctor and the
  Apothecary**   1788 London
Glorious First of June 1794 London
Haunted Tower   1789 London
Iron Chest   1796 London
Lodoiska   1794 London

Mahmoud	1796	London
My Grandmother	1793	London
No Song, No Supper	1790	London
Pirates, The	1792	London
Poor Old Drury!!!	1791	London
Prize, The	1793	London
Siege of Belgrade	1791	London
Three and the Deuce	1795	London

STOTHART, HERBERT
b. 1885; d. 1949

Rose-Marie	1924	Los Angeles

(with R. Friml)

STRASSBURG, ROBERT
b. New York, Aug. 30, 1915

Chelm	1956	White Plains, N.Y.

STRAVINSKY, IGOR
b. Oranienbaum, near St. Petersburg, June 17, 1882; d. New York, Apr. 6, 1971

Flood, The	1962	CBS
Rake's Progress	1951	Venice

STRILKO, ANTHONY
b. New York, 1931

Last Puppet	1963	New York

STROUSE, CHARLES
b. New York, June 7, 1928

Charlotte's Web	1989	Wilmington, Dela.
+Nightingale	1982	Vienna, Va.

SUBOTNICK, MORTON
b. Los Angeles, Apr. 14, 1933

Intimate Immensity	1997	New York
Jacob's Room	1987	St. Paul, Minn.

SULLIVAN, ARTHUR S.
b. London, May 13, 1842; d. there, Nov. 22, 1900

Beauty Stone	1898	London
Chieftain, The	1894	London
Contrabandista	1867	London
Cox and Box	1867	London
Emerald Isle	1901	London

(compl. E. German)

Gondoliers, The	1889	London
Grand Duke	1896	London
Haddon Hall	1892	London
H.M.S. Pinafore	1878	London
Iolanthe	1882	London
Ivanhoe	1891	London
Mikado, The	1885	London
Patience	1881	London
Pirates of Penzance	1879	New York
Princess Ida	1884	London
Rose of Persia	1899	London
Ruddigore	1887	London
Sapphire Necklace	1867	London
Sorcerer, The	1877	London

Thespis	1871	London
Trial by Jury	1875	London
Utopia Limited	1893	London
Yeomen of the Guard	1888	London
Zoo, The	1875	London

SULLIVAN, TIMOTHY
b. Ottawa, Dec. 16, 1954

+Dream Play	1988	Toronto
+Tomorrow, Tomorrow	1987	New York

SUSA, CONRAD
b. Springdale, Pa., Apr. 26, 1935

+Black River	1975	St. Paul, Minn.

(lib. with R. Street)

Dangerous Liaisons	1994	San Francisco
+Love of Don Perlimplin	1984	Purchase, N.Y.
Transformations	1973	Minneapolis

SUTHERLAND, MARGARET
b. Adelaide, Austral., Nov. 20, 1897; d. Melbourne, Aug. 12, 1984

Young Kabbarli	1965	Hobart, Austral.

SWADOS, ELIZABETH
b. Buffalo, N.Y., Feb. 5, 1951

+Esther	1988	New York

(lib. with E. Wiesel)

Pied Piper	1989	Orlando, Fla.

TALBOT, HOWARD (MUNKITTRICK)
b. Yonkers, N.Y., Mar. 9, 1865; d. Reigate, Engl., Sept. 12, 1928

White Chrysanthemum	1906	London

TALMA, LOUISE
b. Arcachon, France, Oct. 31, 1906; d. Macdowell Colony, Vt., Aug. 13, 1996

Alcestiad, The	1962	Frankfurt
+Have You Heard	1981	New York

TAMKIN, DAVID
b. Aug. 28, 1906, Chernigov, Russia; d. Los Angeles, June 21, 1975

+Dybbuk, The	1951	New York

TAN DUN
b. China, 1957

Marco Polo	1996	Munich

TARHOUDIN, PETER

+Heloise and Abelard	1991*

TATE, PHYLLIS
b. Gerards Cross, Buckinghamshire, Engl., Apr. 6, 1911; d. London, May 27, 1987

Dark Pilgrimage	1962	London, BBC
Lodger, The	1960	London
Twice in a Blue Moon	1969	Farnham, Engl.
What D'Ye Call It	1966	Cheltenham, Engl.

TAUB, BRUCE
b. New York, Feb. 6, 1948
+Passion, Poison   1976   New York
Waltz on a Merry-Go-
Round   1979*

TAVERNER, JOHN
b. London, Jan. 28, 1944
Cappemakers, The   1964   Sussex, Engl.
Gentle Spirit   1977   Bath, Engl.
Mary of Egypt   1992   Aldeburgh
Thérèse   1979   London

TAYLOR, CLIFFORD
b. Avalon, Pa., Oct. 23, 1923; d. Abington,
Pa., Sept. 19, 1987
Freak Show   1975*

TAYLOR, DEEMS
b. New York, Dec. 22, 1885; d. there, July 3, 1966
+Dragon, The   1958   New York
King's Henchman   1927   New York
+Peter Ibbetson   1931   New York
+Ramuntcho   1942   Philadelphia

TAYLOR, RAYNER
b. London, 1747; d. Philadelphia, Aug. 17,
1825
Aethiop, The   1814   Philadelphia
Buxom Joan   1778   London
Capocchio and
Dorinna   1793   Annapolis, Md.
Pizzaro   1800*
Rose of Aragon   1822   New York

TAYLOR, RICHARD
Warchild   1997   London

TCHEREPNIN, ALEXANDER
b. St. Petersburg, Jan. 21, 1899; d. Paris, Sept.
29, 1977
Farmer and the
Nymph   1952   Aspen, Colo.

TELGMANN, OSCAR F.
b. Mengeringhausen, Ger., ca. 1855; d.
Toronto, Mar. 30, 1946
Leo, the Royal Cadet   1889   Kingston, Ont.

TENDUCCI, FERDINANDO
b. Siena, ca. 1735; d. Genoa, Jan. 25, 1790
Revenge of Athridates   1766   Dublin

THOMAS, ARTHUR GORING
b. Ratton Park, Engl., Nov. 20, 1850; d.
London, Mar. 20, 1892
Esmerelda   1883   London
Golden Web   1893   Liverpool
(compl. S. P. Waddington)
Light of the Harem   1897   London
Nadeshda   1885   London

THOMAS, AUGUSTA READ
b. Glen Cove, N.Y., Apr. 24, 1964
Ligeia   1994   Baltimore
Psychles   1987   Chicago

THOMAS, EDWARD
b. Chisholm, Minn., Oct. 1, 1924
Desire under the Elms   1978   New London

THOMPSON, RANDALL
b. New York, Apr. 21, 1899; d. Boston,
July 9, 1984
Nativity according to
St. Luke, The   1961   Cambridge, Mass.
+Solomon and Balkis   1942   Cambridge, Mass.

THOMSON, JOHN
b. Sprouston, Roxburgh, Scot., Oct. 28, 1805;
d. Edinburgh, May 6, 1841
Hermann   1834   London
Shadow on the Wall   1835   London

THOMSON, VIRGIL
b. Kansas City, Mo., Nov. 25, 1896; d. New
York, Sept. 30, 1989
Four Saints in Three
Acts   1933   Ann Arbor, Mich.
Lord Byron   1972   New York
Mother of Us All   1947   New York

THORNE, FRANCIS
b. Bay Shore, Long Island, June 23, 1922
Mario and the
Magician   1994   Brooklyn, N.Y.

THORNE, T. PEARSALL
Maid of Plymouth   1893   New York

TIPPETT, MICHAEL
b. London, Jan. 2, 1905; d. there, Jan. 8, 1998
+Ice Break   1977   London
+King Priam   1962   London
+Knot Garden   1970   London
+Midsummer
Marriage   1955   London
+New Year   1989   Houston
+Robin Hood   1934   Boosbeck, Engl.
(text with Ayerst, Pennyman)

TITUS, HIRAM
b. Minneapolis, Jan. 28, 1947
Rosina   1980   Minneapolis

TOCH, ERNST
b. Vienna, Dec. 7, 1887; d. Santa Monica, Oct.
1, 1964
+Edgar and Emily   1965   New York
Princess and the Pea   1954   Lenox, Mass.

TONNING, GERARD
b. Stavanger, Norway, May 25, 1860; d. New
York, June 10, 1940
All in a Garden Fair   1913   Seattle

Blue Wing	1917 Seattle

TOOVEY, ANDREW
  b. 1962, London

Juniper Tree	1993 Broomhill, Kent
+Ubu	1992 Cardiff

  (lib. with M. Finnissy)

TORKE, MICHAEL
  b. Milwaukee, Sept. 22, 1961

Directions, The	1986 Iraklion, Crete
King of Hearts	1996 Aspen, Colo.

TOULMOUCHE, FRÉDÉRIC
  b. Nantes, France, Aug. 3, 1850; d. Paris, Feb. 20, 1909

Wedding Eve	1892 London

  (with E. Ford)

TOVEY, SIR DONALD
  b. Elton, Engl., July 17, 1875; d. Edinburgh, July 10, 1940

Bride of Dionysus	1929 Edinburgh

TOWNSEND, DOUGLAS
  b. New York, Nov. 8, 1921

Lima Beans	1956 New York

TOWNSEND, JILL

+Promise, The	1997 London

TOWNSHEND, PETE(R) [DENNIS BLANDFORD]
  b. Chiswick, Engl., May 19, 1945

Tommy	1968 New York

TRANCHELL, PETER
  b. Cuddalore, India, July 14, 1922

| +Mayor of
Casterbridge	1951 Cambridge, Engl.

TRAVIS, ROY
  b. New York, June 24, 1922

+Passion of Oedipus	1968 Los Angeles

TREFOUSSE, ROGER

+Found Objects	1991 New York
Monkey Opera	1982 Brooklyn, N.Y.

TRIMBLE, JOAN
  b. Enniskillen, N. Ire., June 18, 1915

Blind Raferty	1957 BBC, London

TRIMBLE, LESTER
  b. Bangor, Wisc., Aug. 28, 1920; d. New York, Dec. 31, 1986

| Boccaccio's
Nightingale	1962*

TULLY, JAMES H.

Bluebeard Repaired	1866 London

TURNAGE, MARK-ANTHONY
  b. Essex, Engl., June 10, 1960

Country of the Blind	1997 Aldeburgh
+Greek	1988 Munich

| Twice through the
Heart	1997 Aldeburgh

TURNER, ROBERT
  b. Montreal, June 6, 1920

Brideship, The	1967 Vancouver

TURNER, TOM

| Four-Thousand
Dollars	1969 Iowa City

TUROK, PAUL
  b. New York, Dec. 3, 1929

Richard III	1975 Philadelphia
Scene: Domestic	1955* 1973 Aspen, Colo.

VALINSKY, ERIC

Bus to Stockport	1986 New York

  (with P. Schubert)

Freshwater	1984 New York

VALINSKY, KEN

Embrace the Monster	1993 New York

VAN ETTEN, JANE
  b. St. Paul, Minn., ca. 1875

Guido Ferranti	1914 Chicago

VAN GROVE, ISAAC
  b. Philadelphia, Sept. 5, 1892; d. 1979

Music Lover	1926 Cincinnati
+Other Wise Man	1959 Bentonville, Ark.
Shining Chalice	1964 Eureka Springs, Ark.

VAN RIHJN, JACQUES

Venus	1997 London

VAUGHAN WILLIAMS, RALPH
  b. Down Ampney, England, Oct. 12, 1872; d. London, Aug. 26, 1958

Hugh the Drover	1924 London
+Pilgrim's Progress	1951 London
Poisoned Kiss	1936 Cambridge, Engl.
Riders to the Sea	1937 London
+Shepherds of the Delectable
Mountains	1922 London
+Sir John in Love	1929 London

VERNON, ASHLEY [KURT MANSCHINGER]
  b. Zeil-Wieselburg, Austria, July 25, 1902; d. New York, Feb. 23, 1968

Barber of New York	1953 New York
Cupid and Psyche	1956 Woodstock, N.Y.
Grand Slam	1955 Stamford, Conn.
Triumph of Punch	1969 Brooklyn, N.Y.

VERRALL, JOHN
  b. Britt, Iowa, June 17, 1908

| Cowherd and the Sky
Maiden	1952 Seattle
Three Blind Mice	1955 Seattle
Wedding Knell	1955 Seattle

VICTORY, GERARD
b. Dublin, Dec. 24, 1921; d. there, Mar. 14, 1995

+Chatterton	1971	Paris, ORTF
+Circe	1972	Dublin, RTE
Eloise and Abelard	1973	Dublin, RTE
+Evening for Three	1976	Dublin, RTE
Magic Trumpet	1974	Dublin, RTE
+Music Hath Mischief	1967	Dublin
Once upon a Moon	1950	Dublin
+Rendezvous	1989	Dublin

VINATIERI, FELIX (FELICE VILLIET)
b. Turin, Italy, 1834; d. Yankton, S.D., Dec. 9, 1891

+American Volunteer	1891* 1961	Yanktor, S.D.

VINCENT, JOHN
b. Birmingham, Ala., May 17, 1902; d. Santa Monica, Calif., Jan. 21, 1977

Primal Void	1969*	

VIOLONE, GIOVANNI DEL

Love's Triumph	1708	London

(with Gasparini, Cesarini)

VIR, PARAM
b. Delhi, India, Feb. 6, 1952

Broken Strings	1992	Amsterdam
Snatched by the Gods	1991	Amsterdam

VOLANS, KEVIN
b. 1949

Man with Footsoles of Wind	1993	London

WADE, JAMES
b. Granite, Ill., Jan. 5, 1930

+Martyred, The	1970	Seoul

WADE, JOSEPH AUGUSTINE
b. Dublin, ca. 1801; d. London, July 15, 1845

+Two Houses of Grenada	1826	London

WADSWORTH, STEPHEN
b. Mt. Kisco, N.Y., Apr. 3, 1953

+Telephone Show	1989	Milwaukee

WAITS, TOM
b. Pomona, Calif., Dec. 7, 1949

Alice	1992	Hamburg
Black Rider	1990	Hamburg

WALKER, JAMES
b. 1929

Proposal, The	1974*	

WALKER, RAYMOND

Cinderella in Salerno	1976*	

WALLACE, STEWART
b. 1960

Harvey Milk	1995	Houston
Hopper's Wife	1997	Long Beach, Calif.
Kabballah, The	1989	Brooklyn, N.Y.
Where's Dick	1987	Omaha, Nebr.

WALLACE, VINCENT
b. Waterford, Ire., Mar. 11, 1812; d. Château de Haget, Haute-Garonne, France, Oct. 12, 1865

Amber Witch	1861	London
Desert Flower	1863	London
Love's Triumph	1862	London
Lurline	1860	London
Maritania	1845	London
Matilda of Hungary	1847	London

WALLACH, JOELLE
b. New York, June 29, 1946

King's Twelve Moons	1989	New York

WALLERSTEIN, FERDINAND

Viandière, La	1867	Liverpool

WALTON, WILLIAM
b. Oldham, Mar. 29, 1902; d. Ischia, Mar. 8, 1983

+Bear, The	1967	Aldeburgh
Troilus and Cressida	1954	London

WARD, ROBERT
b. Cleveland, Sept. 13, 1917

Abelard and Heloise	1982	Charlotte, N.C.
Claudia Legare	1978	Minneapolis
Crucible, The	1961	New York
He Who Gets Slapped	1956	New York
Lady from Colorado	1964	Central City, Colo.
Lady Kate	1994	Wooster, Ohio
+Minutes till Midnight	1982	Miami
Roman Fever	1993	Durham, N.C.

WARE, HARRIET
b. Aug. 27, 1877, Waupun, Wisc.; d. New York, Feb. 9, 1962

Undine	1923	Baltimore

WARE, WILLIAM HENRY

Mother Goose	1806	London

WARGO, RICHARD

+Chekhov Trilogy	1990	Chautauqua, N.Y.
+Music Shop	1985	St. Paul, Minn.
+Seduction of a Lady	1985	Glens Falls, N.Y.
+Visit to the Country	1990	Chautauqua, N.Y.

WARNER, CAPTAIN

Armo[u]rer, The	1793	London

WARNER, HARRY WALDO
b. Northampton, Engl., Jan. 4, 1874; d. London, June 1, 1945

Royal Vagrants	1899	London

WARREN, BETSY
b. Boston, 19??

WESTBROOK, MIKE
Coming through
Slaughter 1994 London
Good Friday 1663 1995 London, Channel 4
(with K. Westbrook)

WESTERGAARD, PETER
b. Champaign, Ill., May 28, 1931
+Charivari 1953 Cambridge, Mass.
+Mr. and Mrs.
Discobbolos 1966 New York
+Tempest, The 1994 Lawrenceville, N.J.

WHELEN, CHRISTOPHER
b. London, Apr. 17, 1927
Cancelling Dark 1965 London, BBC
+Findings 1972 London, BBC
+Incident at Owl
Creek 1969 London, BBC
Some Place of
Darkness 1967 London, BBC

WHITAKER (WHITTAKER), JOHN
b. 1776; d. 1847
Rake's Progress 1826 London
Sweethearts and
Wives 1823 London
(with Nathan et al.)
Up to Town 1811 London
(with Reeve et al.)
Veteran Soldier 1822 London
(with Cooke, Perry)

WHITE, CLARENCE CAMERON
b. Clarksville, Tenn., Aug., 10, 1880; d. New
York, June 30, 1960
Ouanga 1932 Chicago

WHITE, CLAUDE
Love, Death, and
High Notes 1988 St. Louis

WHITE, JOHN
b. Berlin, Apr. 5, 1936
Orpheus 1976 London
Stanley and the
Monkey King 1975 London

WHITE, MICHAEL
b. Chicago, Mar. 6, 1931
Metamorphosis 1968 Philadelphia

WHITEHEAD, GILLIAN
b. Hamilton, N.Z., Apr. 23, 1941
Bride of Fortune 1991 Perth
Eleanor of Aquitaine 1967 Sydney
King of the Other
Country 1984 Sydney
Pirate Moon 1986 Auckland, N.Z.
Tristan and Iseult 1978 Auckland, N.Z.

WHITON, PETER
Bottle Imp 1958 Wilton, Conn.

WIDDOES, LAWRENCE
How to Make Love 1994 New York

WILDER, ALEC
b. Rochester, N.Y., Feb. 16, 1907; d.
Gainesville, Fla., Dec. 24, 1980
Cumberland Fair 1953 Montclair, N.J.
Ellen 1955*
Impossible Forest 1958 Westport, Conn.
Long Way 1955 Nyack, N.Y.
Lowland Sea 1952 Montclair, N.J.
Miss Chicken Little 1954 New York
Opening, The 1969 Boston
Sunday Excursion 1953 New York
Truth about
Windmills 1973 Rochester, N.Y.

WILDING-WHITE, RAYMOND
b. Caterham, Surrey, Engl., Oct. 9, 1922
Selfish Giant 1952* 1965 Cleveland
+Yerma 1962*

WILLAN, HEALEY
b. Balham, Engl., Oct. 12, 1880; d. Toronto,
Feb. 16, 1968
Deirdre 1946 CBC radio
Order of Good Cheer 1928 Quebec
Transit through Fire 1942 CBC radio

WILLIAMS, BURT (EGBERT)
b. Antigua, prob. Nov. 12, 1874; d. 1922
Abyssinia (with Cook) 1906 New York

WILLIAMS, D. M.
Florence Nightingale 1943 New York

WILLIAMS, GRACE
b. Barry, Glamorganshire, Wales, Feb. 19,
1906; d. there, Feb. 10, 1977
+Parlour, The 1966 Cardiff

WILLIAMS, JACK ERIC
Mrs. Farmer's
Daughter 1983 Purchase, N.Y.

WILLIAMS, JOSEPH BENJAMIN [A.K.A.
FLORIAN PASCAL/LIONEL ELLIOTT]
b. London, 1847; d. 1923
Cymbia 1883 London
No Cards 1869 London

WILLIAMSON, MALCOLM
b. Sydney, Nov. 21, 1931
Dunstan and the Devil 1967 Cookham
English Eccentrics 1964 Aldeburgh
+Genesis 1973 London
+Growing Castle 1968 Dynevor Castle,
Wales
+Happy Prince 1965 Farnham, Engl.
Julius Caesar Jones 1966 London

Lucky-Peter's 1968 Dynevor Castle,
Journey Wales
Moonrakers, The 1967 Brighton, Engl.
Our Man in Havana 1963 Aldeburgh
+Red Sea 1972 Darrington
College, Engl.
+Snow Wolf 1968 Brighton, Engl.
Stone Wall 1971 London
Violins of St. Jacques 1966 London

WILSON, CHARLES
b. Toronto, May 8, 1931
+Kamouraska 1979 Toronto
Phrases from Orpheus 1971 Guelph, Canada
Psycho Red 1978 Guelph, Canada
Selfish Giant 1973 Toronto
Strolling Clerk ca. 1952*
Summoning of
Everyman 1973 Halifax

WILSON, JAMES
b. London, Sept. 27, 1922
+Fand 1975 Kilkenny
Grinning at the Devil 1989 Copenhagen
Hunting of the Snark 1965 Dublin
+Letters to Leo 1984 Dublin
Passionate Man 1995 Dublin
Pied Piper 1969 Wexford
Táin, The 1972 Dublin
Twelfth Night 1969 Wexford

WILSON, THOMAS
b. Trinidad, Colo., Oct. 10, 1927
Charcoal Burner 1969 BBC, Scotland
Confessions of a
Justified Sinner 1976 York

WILSON-DICKSON, ANDREW
Errors 1980 Leicester, Engl.
Sir Gawain 1977 Leicester, Engl.

WISHART, PETER
b. Crowborough, Engl., June 25, 1921; d.
Frome, Aug. 14, 1984
Captive, The 1960 Birmingham
Clandestine
Marriage 1971 Cambridge
Clytemnestra 1974 London
Lady of the Inn 1983 Reading, Engl.
Two in the Bush 1959 Birmingham

WOLFE, JACQUES
b. Botoshan, Apr. 29, 1896; d. Bradenton, Fla.,
June 22, 1973
Mississippi Legend 1951 New York

WOLFE, NEIL
Birth/Day 1993 Dallas

WOOD, CHARLES
b. Armagh, Ire., June 15, 1866; d. Cambridge,
Engl., July 12, 1926

Family Papers 1924 London
Scene from Pickwick 1922 London

WOOD, JOSEPH
b. Pittsburgh, May 12, 1915
Mother, The 1942 New York

WOOLLEN, RUSSELL
d. Charlottesville, Va., Mar. 16, 1994
Decorator, The 1959 Washington, D.C.

WOOLRICH, JOHN
b. 1954, Cirencester, England
In the House of
Crossed Desires 1996 Cheltenham, Engl.

WUORINEN, CHARLES
b. New York, June 9, 1938
Politics of Harmony 1968 New York
W. of Babylon 1975 New York

WYKES, ROBERT
b. Aliquippa, Pa., May 19, 1926
+Prankster, The 1952 Bowling Green,
Ohio

YARMOLINSKY, BEN
Blind Witness News 1990 New York

YATES, WILLIAM
Choice of Apollo 1765 London

YAVELOW, CHRISTOPHER
b. Cambridge, Mass., June 15, 1950
Countdown 1987 Boston
+Passion of Vincent
Van Gogh 1984 Dallas

YOUNG, DOUGLAS
b. London, July 18, 1947
+Tailor of Gloucester 1991*
(lib. with J. M. Phillips)

ZADOR, EUGENE
b. Bátaszék, Hung., Nov. 5, 1894; d.
Hollywood, Calif., Apr. 4, 1977
+Inspector General 1928* 1971 Torrance,
Calif.
Magic Chair 1966 Baton Rouge, La.
Scarlet Mill 1968 Brooklyn, N.Y.
Virgin and the Fawn 1964 Los Angeles
Yehu 1974 Los Angeles

ZAIMONT, JUDITH LANG
b. Memphis, Tenn., Nov. 8, 1945
Goldilocks 1996 Chappaqua, N.Y.

ZIMBALIST, EFREM
b. Rostov-on-the-Don, Apr. 21, 1889; d. Reno,
Nev., Feb. 22, 1985
Landara 1956 Phildadelphia

ADAPTATIONS AND ARRANGEMENTS

(excluding ballad operas; see also Appendix 2; ** = ballad opera/anon. composer)

ADAM, ADOLPHE CHARLES (1803–1856)
Reine d'un Jour, La (1839, Paris)
Queen of a Day Fitzwilliam,
        E.   1841 London

ARNE, THOMAS AUGUSTINE (1710–1778)
Cymon (1767, London)
Cymon Bishop, H. R. 1815 London

AUBER, D.-F.-E. (1782–1871)
Cheval de bronze (1835, Paris)
Bronze Horse Rodwell, G. 1835 London
Fra Diavolo (1830, Paris)
Devil's Brother Lee, A.   1831 London
Gustave III (1833, Paris)
Gustavus III Cooke, T. S. 1833 London
Lestocq (1834, Paris)
Lestocq Cooke, T. S. 1835 London
Muette de Portici, La (1828, Paris)
Masaniello Cooke, T. S. 1829 London
Philtre, Le (1831, Paris)
Love Charm Bishop, H. R. 1831 London
Serment, Le (1832, Paris)
Coiners, The Lacy, M. R. 1833 London

BELLINI, VINCENZO (1801–1835)
Sonnambula, La (1831, Milan)
Sonnambula, La Bishop, H. R. 1833 London

BISHOP, HENRY ROWLEY (1786–1855)
Aethiop, The (1812, London)
Aethiop, The Taylor, R.   1814 Philadelphia

BIZET, GEORGES (1838–1875)
Carmen (1875, Paris)
Carmen Jones Bennett, R. 1947 New York
José's Carmen Ashman, M. 1984 London
Naked Carmen Corigliano/
    Hess   1970*

BOIELDIEU, FRANÇOIS ADRIEN (1775–1834)
Dame blanche, La (1825, Paris)
White Lady Cooke, T. S. 1826 London
Deux nuits, Les (1829, Paris)
Night before the
  Wedding Bishop, H. R. 1829 London
Jean de Paris (1812, Paris)
John of Paris Bishop, H. R. 1814 London

CARAFA, MICHELE (1787–1872)
Prison d'Edimbourg, La (1833, Paris)
Heart of
  Midlothian Loder, E.   1849 London

DALAYRAC, NICOLAS-MARIE (1753–1809)
Adolphe et Clara (1799, Paris)

Matrimony Hewitt, J.   1804 London
Camille (Paris, 1791)
Captive of
  Spilburg Dussek/Kelly 1798 London

DEBUSSY, CLAUDE (1862–1918)
Pelléas et Mélisande (1902, Paris)
Frustration Harnick, S. 1973 Washington,
                              D.C.

DITTERSDORF, CARL DITTERS VON (1739–1799)
Doktor und Apotheker (1786, Vienna)
Doctor and
  Apothecary Storace, S. 1788 London

DONIZETTI, GAETANO (1797–1848)
Fille du régiment, La (1840, Paris)
Vivandiere, The Hewitt, J.   1863 Augusta, Ga.
Vivandière, La Wallerstein 1867 Liverpool

FÉTIS, FRANÇOIS-JOSEPH (1784–1871)
Vieille, La (1826, Paris)
Love in Wrinkles Lacy, M. R. 1826 London

FRANCESCHINI, G. B. (1662/63–1732)
Arsinoe (1676, Bologna)
Arsinoe Clayton, T. 1705 London

GALUPPI, BALDASSARE (1706–1785)
Filosofo di campagna, Il (1754, Venice)
Wedding Ring Dibdin, C. 1773 London

GAVEAUX, PIERRE (1761–1825)
Petit matelot, Le (1786, Paris)
Veteran Tar Arnold, S. 1801 London

GRÉTRY, A.-E.-M. (1741–1813)
Deux avares, Les (1770, Fontainebleau)
Two Misers Dibdin, C. 1775 London
Evénements imprévus, Les (1799, Versailles)
Gay Deceivers Kelly, M. 1804 London

GRISAR, ALBERT (1808–1869)
Eau merveilleuse, L' (1839, Paris)
Wonderful Water
  Cure Reed. T.   1846 London

HALÉVY, FROMENTAL (1799–1862)
Juive, La (1835, Paris)
Jewess, The Cooke, T. S. 1835 London

HÉROLD, FERDINAND (1791–1833)
Pré aux clercs, Le (1832, Paris)
Court Masque Dawes, W. 1833 London

LECOCQ, CHARLES (1832–1918)
Giroflé Giroflá (1874, Brussels)

Twin Sisters   Sedgwick, A. 1876 New York?

MARLIANI, MARCO AURELIO (1805–1849)
Bravo, Il (1834, Paris)
Red Mask   Cooke, T. S. 1834 London

MARSCHNER, HEINRICH (1796–1861)
Des Falkners Braut (1832, Leipzig)
Rob of the Fens Romer, F.   1838 London

MEYERBEER, GIACOMO (1791–1864)
Robert le diable (1831, Paris)
Demon, The   Bishop, H. R. 1832 London
Fiend-Father   Lacy, M. R. 1832 London
Robert the Devil pastiche   1868 London

MOGULESCO, SIGMUND (1858–1914)
Dovid's fiedele (1897, New York)
David's Violin arr. M. Slobin 1976 Middle-
town, Conn.

MOZART, WOLFGANG AMADEUS (1756–1791)
Così fan tutte (1790, Vienna)
Tit for Tat   Hawes, W.   1828 London
Don Giovanni (1787, Prague)
Giovanni in
   London   **   1817 London
Libertine, The Bishop, H. R. 1817 London
Idomeneo (1781, Munich)
Casket, The   Lacy, M. R. 1829 London
Nozze di Figaro, Le (1786, Vienna)
Marriage of
   Figaro   Bishop, H. R. 1819 London
Sogno di Scipione, Il (1772, Salzburg)
Scipio's Dream Weir, J.   1991*
various
Jewel Box   Griffiths, P. 1991 New York
Letters, Riddles Nyman/   1991 London,
   Lepage   BBC
Small Jewel Box Griffiths, P. 1995 New York

OFFENBACH, JACQUES (1819–1880)
Ba-Ta-Clan (1855, Paris)
Ba-Ta-Clan   Oliver, S.   1988*

PEPUSCH, JOHN (1667–1752)
Beggar's Opera (1728, London)
Bow-Street Opera **   1773 London

PUCCINI, GIACOMO (1858–1924)
Bohème, La (1896, Turin)
Bohemians, The Kirschner, B. 1990 New York
Rent   Larson, J.   1996 New York
Gianni Schicchi (1918, New York)
Buoso's Ghost Ching, M. 1997 Memphis

RIES, FERDINAND (1784–1838)
Raüberbraut, Die (1828, Frankfurt)

Robber's Bride Hawes, W.   1892 London

ROSSINI, GIOACCHINO (1792–1868)
Barbiere di Siviglia, Il (1816, Rome)
Barber of Seville Bishop, H. R. 1818 London
Cenerentola, La (1817, Rome)
Cinderella   Lacy/Pons 1830 London
Gazza ladra, La (1817, Milan)
Magpie and
   Maid   Bishop, H. R. 1815 London
Ninetta   Bishop, H. R. 1830 London
Guillaume Tell (1829, Paris)
Guillaume Tell Bishop, H. R. 1838 London
Hofer   Bishop, H. R. 1830 London
Siège de Corinthe, Le (1826, Paris)
Siege of Corinth Cooke, T. S. 1836 London
Tancredi (1813, Venice)
Native Land   Bishop, H. R. 1824 London
Turco in Italia, Il (1814, Milan)
Turkish Lovers Lacy, M. R. 1827 London

SPOHR, LUDWIG (1784–1859)
Alchemist, Der (1830, Kassel)
Alchemyst, Der Bishop, H. R. 1832 London

STORACE, STEPHEN (1762–1796)
Pirates, The (1792, London)
Isadore de
   Merida   Cooke, T. S. 1827 London

SULLIVAN, ARTHUR S. (1842–1900)
various
Engaged   Rowell/   1962 Bristol,
   Mobbs   Engl.

VERDI, GIUSEPPE (1813–1901)
Trovatore, Il (1853, Rome)
Estranged   Sedgwick, A. 1876 New York?

WEBER, CARL MARIA VON (1786–1826)
Abu Hassan (1811, Munich)
Abou Hassan Cooke, T. S. 1825 London
Freischütz, Der (1821, Berlin)
Black Rider   Waits, T.   1990 Hamburg
Freischütz, Der parody   1824 Edinburgh
Freischütz, Der Bishop, H. R. 1824 London

WEIL, KURT (1900–1950)
Dreigroschenoper, Die (1928, Berlin)
Threepenny
   Opera   arr. M. Blitzstein 1954 New York
Happy End (1929, Berlin)
Happy End arr. M. Feingold 1972 New Haven
Silbersee, Der (1933, Leipzig)
Silverlake arr. L. Symonette 1980 New York

WINTER, PETER VON (1754–1825)
Unterbrochene Opferfest, Das (1796, Vienna)
Oracle, The   Hawes, W.   1826 London

Librettists

Entries include dates of librettist (where known), short title, composer, and year of premiere; * = year of composition; ** = anon. composer/ballad opera. For composers who wrote their own librettos, see Appendix 1. See pp. 778–80 for adaptations and arrangements.

ABARBANEL, JAMES
Pedrolino's Revenge	Russo, W.	1974

ABBOTT, DELMAS W.
Sagegrass	Atwell, S. J.	1986

A' BECKET, GILBERT A. (1811–1856)
Agnes Sorel	A'Beckett, M.	1835
Ancient Britons	Reed, T.	1875
Canterbury Pilgrims	Stanford, C.	1884
Castle of Aymon	Balfe, M.	1844
Geraldine	Balfe, M.	1843
Indian Puzzle	Reed, T.	1876
Postilion!	Stansbury, G.	1837
Savonarola	Stanford, C.	1884
Signa	Cowen, F.	1893
Spanish Bond	Reed, T.	1875
Three Tenants	Reed, T.	1874

ABEL, LIONEL
Escorial, The	Levy, M.	1958
(with comp.)		

ABRASHKIN, RAYMOND (1911–1960)
Emperor's New Clothes	Moore, D.	1949

ACKER, KATHY (B. 1948)
Birth of the Poet	Gordon, P.	1985

ADAMS, ARTHUR
Tapu	Hill, A.	1903
Whipping Boy	Hill, A.	1896

ADAMS, R. K.
Give Me Liberty	Kalmanoff, M.	1975

ADCOCK, FLEUR
Eleanor of Aquitaine	Whitehead, G.	1967
King of the Other		
Country	Whitehead, G.	1984

ADDISON, JOSEPH (1672–1719)
Rosamond	Arne, T. A.	1733
Rosamond	Arnold, S.	1767
Rosamond	Clayton, T.	1707

ADLER, JOYCE
Moby Dick (with comp.)	Solomon, E.	1989*

AIKEN, GEORGE L. (1830–1876)
Uncle Tom's Cabin	Howard, G.	1852

ALAN, CHARLES
Eternal Road	Weill, K.	1937
(with L. Lewissohn)		

ALBERY, JAMES (1838–1889)
Oriana	Clay, F.	1873

ALDRICH, ELIZABETH (B. 1947)
Echoes of the Shining		
Prince	Cooper, S.	1985

ALEXANDER, HARTLEY
Butterfly Girl	Reed, H. O.	1985
Living Solid Face	Reed, H. O.	1962
(both with F. W. Coggan)		

ALLAN, LEWIS [ABEL MEEROPOL] (1903–1986)
Darling Corie	Siegmeister, E.	1954
Good Soldier Schweik	Kurka, R.	1958
Insect Comedy	Kalmanoff, M.	1977
Malady of Love	Engel, L.	1954
Soldier, The	Engel, L.	1956

ALLEN, MR.
Hymen	Arne, M.	1764

ALLINGHAM, JOHN TILL (FL. 1799–1810)
Weathercock, The	King, M.	1805
Who Wins	Condell, H.	1808

ANDERSON, MAXWELL (1888–1959)
Christmas Carol	Hermann, B.	1954
Lost in the Stars	Weill, K.	1949

ANDERSON, ROD (B. 1935)
Mario and the		
Magician	Somers, H.	1992

ANDREWS, MILES PETER (D. 1814)
Belphegor	Barthelemon, F.	1778
Election, The	Barthelemon, F.	1774
Fire and Water	Arnold, S.	1780
Mysteries of the Castle	Shield, W.	1795
(poss. with F. Reynolds)		
Summer Amusement	Arnold, S.	1779
(with W. A. Miles)		

ARCHIBALD, WILLIAM
Far Harbour	Bergersen, B.	1948

ARGYLL, JOHN, DUKE OF (1845–1914)
Diarmid	MacCunn, H.	1897
Fionn and Terra	Drysdale, L.	1909

ARKELL, REGINALD (1882–1959)
Kingdom for a Cow	Weill, K.	1935
(with D. Carter)		

ARLUCK, ELLIOT (B. 1916)
Audition, The   Goodman, A.   1954

ARMSTRONG, W[ILLIAM] H[ENRY]
Pay to My Order   Horn, C. E.   1827
(with J. R. Planché)

ARNOLD, BRUCE (B. 1936)
Passionate Man   Wilson, J.   1995

ARNOLD, SAMUEL JAMES (1774–1852)
Americans, The   King, M.   1811
Auld Robin Gray   Arnold, S.   1794
Baron Kinkverkankotsdor-
  sprakingatchdern   Arnold, S.   1781
Broken Promises   Hawes, W.   1825
Devil's Bridge   Horn, C. H.   1812
Election, The   Horn, C. H.   1817
Frederick the Great Cooke, T. S.   1814
Free and Easy   Addison, J.   1816
Hovel, The   Arnold,S.   1797
Illusion, The   Kelly, M.   1813
Irish Legacy   Arnold, S.   1797
King's Proxy   Cooke, T.   1815
Maniac, The   Bishop, H. R. 1810
My Aunt   Addison, J.   1815
Nourjahad   Loder, E.   1834
Plots, The   King, M.   1810
Russian Imposter   Addison, J.   1809
(with H. Siddons)
Shipwreck, The   Arnold, S.   1796
Tit for Tat   Hawes, W.   1828
Unknown Guest   Kelly, M.   1815
Up All Night   King, M.   1809
Veteran Tar   Arnold, S.   1801
Wizard, The   Horn, C. E.   1817

ARONSON, BILLY
Monster Bed   de Kenessey, S. 1990

ARTHUR, JOHN (1708?–1772)
Lucky Discovery   **   1738

ARVEY, VERNA (B. 1910)
Bayou Legend   Still, W. G.   1941
Costaso   Still, W. G.   1954*
Highway 1, U.S.A.   Still, W. G.   1963
Minette Fontaine   Still, W. G.   1984

ASHBROOK, WILLIAM (B. 1922)
Bandit, The   Patacchi, V.   1958
Secret, The   Patacchi, V.   1955

ASTON, ANTHONY (FL. 1682–1747)
Fool's Opera   **   1731

ASTON, WALTER (1660–1748)
Restauration of King
  Charles II   **   1732

ATHERTON, DEBORAH
Under the Double Moon Davis, A.   1989

ATKINSON, JOSEPH (1743–1818)
Love in a Blaze   Stevenson, J. 1799
Match for a Widow   Dibdin, C.   1788

ATKINSON, M.
Selfish Giant   Easton, M.   1994
(with comp.)

AUDEN, W. H. (1907–1973)
Bassarids, The   Henze, H. W.   1966
(with C. Kallman)
Elegy for Young
  Lovers   Henze, H. W.   1961
(with C. Kallman)
Love's Labour's Lost Nabokov, N.   1973
(with C. Kallman)
Moralities   Henze, H. W.   1968
Paul Bunyan   Britten, B.   1941
Rake's Progress   Stravinsky, I. 1951

AUDI, PIERRE
Golem   Casken, J.   1989
(with comp.)

AULICINO, ARMAND
Judgment of St.
  Francis   Flagello, N.   1966

AUSTIN, SYDNEY
Amorous Judge   Gross, E.   1965
(with L. McGlashan)

AYERST, DAVID
Robin Hood   Tippett, M.   1934
(with comp., Pennyman)

AYRES, JAMES (FL. 1742)
Queen of Spain   Lampe, J. F.   1744
Sancho at Court   **   1742

BAER, ATRA
Brandy Is My True
  Love's Name   Kalmanoff, M. 1953
Empty Bottle   Kalmanoff, M. 1966
Fit for a King   Kalmanoff, M. 1949
Godiva   Kalmanoff, M. 1953
Noah and the
  Stowaway   Kalmanoff, M. 1951

BAGG, TERRY
Death of Baldur   Bedford, D.   1980
(with M. Needham)

BAILEY, ANNE HOWARD
Deseret   Kastle, L.   1961
Penitentes, The   Pasatieri, T. 1974
Rachel   Coe, K.   1989
Trial of Mary Lincoln Pasatieri, T. 1972

BAKER, HOWARD
Terrible Mouth   Osborne, N.   1992

BAKER, ROBERT (FL. 1737)
Mad House   **   1737

BALIS, ANDREA
Lady of the Castle   Spektor, M.   1982

BALK, H. WESLEY
Faust Counter Faust   Gessner, J.   1971

BALL, WILLIAM G.
Natalia Petrovna   Hoiby, L.   1964

BAMBERGER, DAVID
Cask of Amontillado   Copeland, S.   1993*

BARER, MARSHALL (D. 1998)
Impossible Forest   Wilder, A.   1958

BARETTI, T. M.
All Fool's Day   Carey, C.   1921

BARING-GOULD, SABINE (1834–1924)
Red Spider   Drysdale, L.   1898

BARKER, JAMES NELSON (1784–1858)
Indian Princess   Bray, J.   1808

BARNET, R[OBERT] A[YRES] (1850?–1933)
Tabasco   Chadwick, G. W. 1894

BARNETT, C[HARLES] Z[ACHARY]
Fair Rosamond   Barnett, J.   1837
Farinelli   Barnett, J.   1839

BARNETT, JOSEPHINE
Inner Voices   Barnett, D.   1972

BARON, BARCLAY
Master Valiant   Shaw, M.   1936
Thorn of Avalon   Shaw, M.   1931

BARON-WILSON, MARGARET (1797–1846)
Genevieve   Macfarren, G.   1834

BARR, ISABEL HARRISS
Jericho Road   Aria, P.   1969

BARRAS, CHARLES M. (1826–1873)
Black Crook   **   1866

BARRETT, WILLIAM A. (1836–1891)
Moro   Balfe, M.   1882

BARRIE, JAMES M. (1860–1937)
Jane Annie (with Doyle) Ford, E.   1893

BARRON, ANDREW SAUL
Psychles   Thomas, A. R.   1987

BARRY, N.
Campaign, The   Shield, W.   1784
(with R. Jephson)

BARSON, ROBIN
Orpheus   White, J.   1976
Stanley and the
   Monkey King   White, J.   1975

BARTON, ANDREW [PSEUD., PROB. OF
   THOMAS FORREST] (1747–1825)
Disappointment, The   **   1767

BARTON, GEORGE EDWARD
Pipe of Desire   Converse, F.   1906

BARTON, HAL
Love in Transit   Arnell, R.   1958

BASSMAN, GEORGE (B. 1914)
Blue Monday   Gershwin, G.   1922
(with B. De Sylva)

BATE, HENRY (DUDLEY) (1745–1824)
Blackamoor, The   Dibdin, C.   1776
Cobler of Castlebury   Shield, W.   1778
Flitch of Bacon   Shield, W.   1778
Rival Candidates   Carter, T.   1775
Travellers in
   Switzerland   Shield, W.   1794

BATES, WILLIAM (D. 1813?)
Jovial Crew   **   1760

BATHURST, SHEILA
Blind Beggar's
   Daughter (with comp.) Bush, G.   1954

BAX, CLIFFORD (1886–1962)
Midsummer Madness Gibbs, C. A.   1924
Mr. Pepys   Shaw, M.   1926
Prelude and Fugue   Franchetti, A.   1959
Waterloo Leave   Shaw, M.   1928

BAYLEY, THOMAS HAYNES (1797–1839)
Alchymist, The   Bishop, H. R.
(with E. Fitzball)

BEACH, LAZARUS (1760–1816)
Jonathan Postfree   **   1807

BEATTIE, W.
Don Quixote   Hill, A.   1904*

BEATTY-KINGSTON, WILLIAM (1837–1900)
Irmengarda   Bach, L. E.   1892
Light of Asia   Bach, L. E.   1892

BEAUMONT, WILLIAM
Cinderella in Salerno Walker, R.   1976*

BEAZLEY, SAMUEL (1786–1851)
Boarding House   Horn, C. E.   1811
Ivanhoe   Parry, J.   1820
Love's Dream   Moss, M.   1821
My Uncle   Addison, J.   1817
Philandering   Horn, C. E.   1824
Sonnambula, La   Bishop, H. R.   1833
White Lady   Cooke, T. S.   1826

BECKETT, SAMUEL (1906–1997)
Neither   Feldman, M.   1977

BLACKBURN, THOMAS (B. 1916)
Judas Tree   Dickinson, P.   1965

BLANCHARD, EDWARD (1820–1889)
Arcadia   Harroway, J.   1841

BLECHER, HILARY
Frida (with M. Cruz) Rodríguez, R.   1991
Many Moons   Kapilow, R.   1997

BLITZSTEIN, MARC (1905–1964)
Threepenny Opera   Weill-Blitzstein 1954

BLOOM, HARRY
King Kong   Matshikiza, T.   1961*
(with P. Williams)

BOADEN, JAMES (1762–1839)
Cambro-Britons   Arnold, S.   1798
Osmyn and Daraxa   Attwood, T.   1793

BOERLAGE, FRANS
Diable amoureux   Rodríguez, R.   1978*

BOND, EDWARD
English Cat   Henze, H. W.   1983

BONNIN, GERTRUDE (ZITKALA-SA) (1876–
1938)
Sun Dance   Hanson, W. F.   1913

BOOTH, BARTON (1681–1733)
Death of Dido   Pepusch, J.   1716
Dido and Aeneas   Arne, T. A.   1734

BORGESE, GIUSEPPE ANTONIO (1882–1952)
Montezuma   Sessions, R.   1964

BOTTOMLEY, GORDON (B. 1874)
Crier by Night   Bainton, E. L.   1919

BOUCICAULT, DION (1820–1890)
Lily of Killarney   Benedict, J.   1862
(with J. Oxenford)

BOURJAILY, VANCE
Four-Thousand Dollars Turner, T.   1969

BOURNE, C. H.
Thais and Talmane   Campbell, C. M.   1921

BOWMAN, JOHN S.
Emperor Norton   Mollicone, H.   1981
**Face on the Barroom
Floor**   Mollicone, H.   1978

BOYD, ELIZABETH (FL. 1730–1744)
Don Sancho   **   1739

BRACKMAN, JACOB
Romulus Hunt   Simon, C.   1993
(with comp.)

BRADBURY, RAY (B. 1920)
Fahrenheit 451   Broadstock, B.   1992

BRADFORD, JOSEPH (1843–1886)
Out of Bondage   **   1876

BRADY, LEO (B. 1917)
Cage, The   Jones, G. T.   1959

BRAGG, TERRY
Fridiof's Saga   Bedford, D.   1981

BRAHMS, CARYL (B. 1901)
Little Beggars   Saunders, M.   1958
(with N. Sherrin)
Mañana (with G. Foa) Benjamin, A.   1956

BRENTON, HOWARD (B. 1942)
Playing Away   Mason, B.   1994

BREVAL, JOHN (1680?–1738)
Rape of Helen   **   1737

BREWER, GEORGE (B. 1766)
Bannian Day   Arnold, S.   1796
How to Be Happy   Arnold, S.   1794

BREWSTER, HENRY (1850–1908)
Forest, The (with comp.) Smyth, E.   1902

BREWSTER, TOWNSEND
Tower, The   Levy, M. D.   1957

BRIDGEMAN, JOHN VIPON (1819–1889)
Armourer of Nantes   Balfe, M.   1863
Puritan's Daughter   Balfe, M.   1861

BRIDGES, THOMAS (FL. 1759–1775)
Dido and Aeneas   Hook, J.   1771

BROADHURST, GEORGE (1866–1952)
Nancy Brown   Hadley, H.   1903
(with F. Ranken)

BROCK, SAM HOUSTON
Sotoba Komachi   Levy, M. D.   1957

BROOKE, FRANCES (1724?–1789)
Marian   Shield, W.   1788
Rosina   Shield, W.   1782

BROOKFIELD, CHARLES H. (1857–1913)
See-See (with A. Ross) Jones, S.   1906

BROUGH, WILLIAM (1826–1870)
Caliph of Bagdad   Musgrave, F.   1867

BROUGHAM, JOHN (1810–1890)
Blanche de Nevers   Balfe, M.   1863

BROUGHTON, THOMAS (1704–1774)
Hercules   Handel, G. F.   1745

BROVSKY, LINDA
**Love, Death, and
High Notes**   White, C.   1988

BROWN, CHARLES ARMITAGE (1786–1842)
Narensky   Horn, C. E.   1814

BROWN, DIANE
| **Bohemians, The** | Kirschner, B. | 1990 |
(with L. Olesker)

BROWNE, EMANUEL
| **David Rizzio** | Moore, M. | 1932 |

BROWNE, MARGERY
| **Lady Dolly** | Hill, A. | 1900 |

BROWNE, MICHAEL DENNIS
Harmoonia	Paulus, S.	1991
Three Hermits	Paulus, S.	1997
Village Singer	Paulus, S.	1979

BRUCKER, ROGER
| **Proposal, The** | Humel, G. | 1958 |
| **Triangle, The** | Humel, G. | 1958 |

BRUNELLE, PHILIP (B. 1943)
| **Newest Opera** | Balk, H. W. | 1974 |

BRUNYATE, ROGER
| **Roman Fever** | Ward, R. | 1993 |

BRYDEN, BILL (B. 1942)
| **Hermiston** | Orr, R. | 1975 |

BUCKLEY, REGINALD R. (B. 1882)
| **Birth of Arthur** | Boughton, R. | 1909 |
| **Round Table** | Boughton, R. | 1916 |
(with comp.)

BUCKSTONE, JOHN BALDWIN (1802–1879)
| **Dead Fetch** | Horn, C. E. | 1826 |
| **Demon, The** | Bishop, H. R. | 1832 |
(with E. Fitzball)
Don Quixote	Rodwell, G.	1840
Jack Sheppard	Rodwell, G.	1839
Last Days of Pompeii	Rodwell, G.	1834
New Don Juan	Rodwell, G.	1828
Queen of a Day	Fitzwilliam, E.	1851
Rural Felicity	Bishop, H. R.	1834

BUNN, ALFRED (1796–1860)
Bohemian Girl	Balfe, M.	1843
Bondman, The	Balfe, M.	1846
Brides of Venice	Benedict, J.	1844
Crusaders, The	Benedict, J.	1846
Daughter of St. Mark	Balfe, M.	1844
Devil's in It	Balfe, M.	1852
Enchantress, The	Balfe, M.	1845
Guillaume Tell	Bishop, H. R.	1838
Loretta	Lavenu, L.	1846
Maid of Artois	Balfe, M.	1836
Matilda of Hungary	Wallace, V.	1847
Sicilian Bride	Balfe, M.	1852

BURCH, JOHN YOULIN
| **Moorish Maid** | Hill, A. | 1905 |

BURGES, JAMES BLAND (1752–1824)
| **Tricks upon Travellers** | Horn, C. E. | 1810 |

BURGOYNE, JOHN (GENERAL) (1722–1792)
Lord of the Manor	Jackson, W.	1780
Maid of the Oaks	Barthelemon, F.	1774
Richard Coeur de Lion	Linley, T.	1786

BURNAND, F[RANCIS] C[OWLEY] (1836–1917)
Chieftain, The	Sullivan, A. S.	1894
Contrabandista, The	Sullivan, A. S.	1867
Cox and Box	Sullivan, A. S.	1867
He's Coming	Reed, T. G.	1874
His Majesty	Mackenzie, A.	1897
Matched and Mated	Reed, T. G.	1876
Mildred's Well	Reed, T. G.	1873
No. 204	Reed, T. G.	1877
One Too Many	Cowen, F.	1874

BURROUGHS, WILLIAM (B. 1914)
| **Black Rider** | Waits, T. | 1990 |

BURROWS, DUDLEY
| **Leper, The** | Moore, M. | 1912* |

BURTON, HAL (B. 1908)
| **Love in Transit** | Arnell, R. | 1958 |

BUSH, NANCY
After the Wedding	Head, M.	1972
Day Return	Head, M.	1970
Ferryman's Daughter	Bush, A.	1964
Key Money	Head, M.	1970
Men of Blackmoor	Bush, A.	1956
Sugar Reapers	Bush, A.	1966

BUTLER, HENRY (1919–1998)
Mourning Becomes Electra	Levy, M. D.	1967
Picnic, The	Cumming, R.	1979
Portrait in Brownstone	Reif, P.	1966
Tight-Rope	Biscardi, C.	1986

BYRNE, JACQUES
| **Legend, The** | Breil, J. C. | 1919 |

CAHALAN, JAMES
| **Magic Beanstalk** | Kalmanoff, M. | 1976 |

CALHOUN, MATTHEW
| **Statues on a Lawn** | Flanagan, T. J. | 1983 |

CALLAN, HARRIET
| **Giovanni, the Sculptor** | Hill, A. | 1914 |

CAMERON, GEORGE FREDERICK (1854–1885)
| **Leo, the Royal Cadet** | Telgmann, O. F. | 1889 |

CAMERON, MELISSA
| **Guacamayo's Old Song** | Oliver, J. | 1991 |

CAMPBELL, KAREN
| **Rappaccini's Daughter** | Dennison, S. | 1984 |

CAPOBIANCO, TITO
| **Zapata** (with Roepke) | Balada, L. | 1985 |

CARACHE, MARIAN MOTLEY
Under the Arbor Greenleaf, R. 1992
(with comp.)

CARD, VIRGINIA
Cask of Amontillado Perry, J. 1954
(with comp.)

CARDELLI, GIOVANNI
**Farmer and the
Nymph** Tcherepnin, A. 1952

CAREY, GEORGE SAVILLE (1743–1807)
Cottagers, The Shield, W. 1766
Magic Girdle Barthelemon, F. 1770
Noble Pedlar Barthelemon, F. 1770

CAREY, HENRY (1687–1743)
Amelia Lampe, J. F. 1732
Dragon of Wantley Lampe, J. F. 1737
Margery Lampe, J. F. 1738
Teraminta Smith, J. C. 1732
Teraminta Stanley, J. 1754

CARR, J. COMYNS (1849–1916)
Beauty Stone (lyrics) Sullivan, A. S. 1898

CARR, SARAH PRATT (B. 1850)
Flaming Arrow Moore, M. 1922
Narcissa Moore, M. 1912

CARRILLO, LEO
Chipita Rodríguez Weiner, L. 1982
(with J. Wilson)

CARTER, DESMOND
Kingdom for a Cow Weill, K. 1935
(with R. Arkell)

CARTER, SIMON
Proposal, The Walker, J. 1974
(with E. Fen)

CARUS, HELENA
Drumlin Legend Bacon, E. 1949

CASEY, MAIE
Young Kabbarli Sutherland, M. 1965

CASSADAY, JAMES LEWIS
Lord Byron Graham, J. 1926
(with N. Engels)

CAVANAGH, MICHAEL
City Workers Weisensel, N. 1995

CAVANDER, KENNETH
Shadowplay Goehr, A. 1970

CAVE, JUDYTH WALKER
Pandora's Box Cave, M. 1971

CHAPPELL, WILLIAM EVELYN (B. 1908)
Violins of St. Jacques Williamson, M. 1966
(with comp.)

CHATTERTON, THOMAS (1752–1770)
Revenge, The Arnold, S. 1770

CHERRY, ANDREW (1763–1824)
Spanish Dollars Davy, J. 1806
Travellers, The Corri, D. 1806

CHESSON, NORA (1871–1906)
Muirgheís Butler, O'B. 1903
(with T. O'Donoghue)

CHETWOOD, WILLIAM R.
Generous Free-Mason ** 1730
Lover's Opera ** 1729

CHILD, HAROLD (1869–1945)
Hugh the Drover Vaughan
Williams, R. 1924

CHORLEY, HENRY FOTHERGILL (1808–1872)
Amber Witch Wallace, V. 1861
Sapphire Necklace Sullivan, A. S. 1867

CHORNEY, ALEXANDER
Royal Auction Kanitz, E 1958
(with S. Shrager)

CHRISTOPHER, TRAY
Howard Earnest, J. D. 1987

CHURCHILL, CARYL
Hotel Gough, O. 1997

CIBBER, COLLEY (1671–1757)
Damon and Phillida ** 1729
Love in a Riddle ** 1729
Myrtillo Pepusch, J. 1715
Temple of Dullness Arne, T. A. 1745
Venus and Adonis Pepusch, J. 1715

CIBBER, THEOPHOLUS (1703–1758)
Patie and Peggy ** 1730

CLAFLIN, DOROTHEA
Hester Prynne Claflin, A. 1934
Uncle Tom's Cabin Claflin, A. 1964

CLARK, BARRETT HARPER (1890–1953)
Christmas Tale Freer, E. E. 1929

CLARKE, HENRY SAVILE (1841–1893)
Alice in Wonderland Slaughter, W. 1906

CLARKE, MARCUS
Moustique Kowalski, H. 1889

CLARKE, ROGER
Man with Footsoles Volans, K. 1993

CLAY, C.
On the March Clay, F. 1896
(with Yardley, Stephenson)

CLIFFE, CEDRIC
Blind Raferty Trimble, J. 1957

Devil Take Her (lyrics) Benjamin, A. 1931
Prima Donna Benjamin, A. 1949
Tale of Two Cities Benjamin, A. 1957
Tartuffe Benjamin, A. 1964
Under Western Eyes Joubert, J. 1969

CLINTON-BADDELEY, VICTOR C. (1900–1970)
Jolly Roger Leigh, W. 1933
(with S. Mackenzie)
Pride of the Regiment Leigh, W. 1931
What D'Ye Call It Tate, P. 1966

CLIVE, KITTY (CATHERINE) (1711–1785)
Rehearsal, The Boyce, W. 1750

COATES, GEORGE
RareArea Ream, M. 1985
Way of How Dresher, P. 1980

COBB, JAMES (1756–1818)
Algonah Storace, S. 1802
Catherine Burghers, L. 1830
Cherokee Storace, S. 1794
Doctor and the Apothecary Storace, S. 1788
Glorious First of June (Cobb et al.) Storace, S. 1794
Haunted Tower Storace, S. 1789
House to Be Sold Kelly, M. 1802
Love in the East Linley Sr., T. 1788
Paul and Virginia Reeve, W. 1800
Pirates, The Storace, S. 1792
Poor Old Drury!!! Storace, S. 1791
Ramah Droog Reeve, W. 1798
Siege of Belgrade Storace, S. 1791
Strangers at Home Linley Sr., T. 1785
Wife of Two Husbands Mazzinghi, J. 1803

CODE, H[ENRY] B[RERETON]
Spanish Patriots Stevenson, J. 1812

COFFEY, CHARLES (D. 1745)
Beggar's Wedding ** 1729
Boarding School ** 1733
Devil to Pay ** 1731
(with J. Mottley)
Devil upon Two Sticks ** 1729
Merry Cobler ** 1735

COHEN, DAVID STEVEN (B. 1943)
Lilith Drattell, D. 1997*

COLLARD, ALAN
Devil Take Her Benjamin, A. 1931
(with J. C. Gordon)

COLLIER, CONSTANCE
Peter Ibbetson Taylor, D. 1931
(with comp.)

COLLIER, GEORGE (1738–1795)
Selima and Azor Linley Sr., T. 1776

COLLS, P. H.
Mistakes of a Day Callcott, J. W. 1787

COLMAN, GEORGE, JR. (1762–1836)
Battle of Hexham Arnold, S. 1789
Blue-Beard Kelly, M. 1798
Feudal Times Kelly, M. 1799
Forty Thieves Kelly, M. 1806
Inkle and Yarico Arnold, S. 1787
Iron Chest Storace, S. 1796
Law of Java Bishop, H. R. 1822
Love Laughs at Locksmiths Kelly, M. 1803
Mountaineers, The Arnold, S. 1793
Review, The Arnold, S. 1800
Surrender of Calais Arnold, S. 1791
Turk and No Turk Arnold, S. 1785
Two to One Arnold, S. 1784

COLMAN, GEORGE, SR. (1732–1794)
Achilles in Petticoats Arne, T. A. 1773
Caractacus Arne, T. A. 1776
Elfrida Arne, T. A. 1772
Fairy Prince Arne, T. A. 1771
Fairy Tale Arne, M. 1777
Gay Deceivers Hawes, W. 1804
Midsummer Night's Dream (with Garrick) Burney, C. 1763
Portrait, The Arnold, S. 1770
Sheep Shearing Arnold, S. 1877
Spanish Barber Arnold, S. 1777
Ut Pictora Poesis! Arnold, S. 1789

COLVIN, IAN DUNCAN
Leper's Flute Bryson, E. 1926

CONE, TOM
Architect, The McIntyre, D. 1994

CONGDON, CONSTANCE
Strange Life of Ivan Osokin Gordon, P. 1994
Yellow Wallpaper Perera, R. 1989

CONGREVE, WILLIAM (1670–1729)
Judgment of Paris Arne, T. A. 1742
Judgment of Paris Eccles, J. 1701
Judgment of Paris Finger, G. 1701
Judgment of Paris Purcell, D. 1701
Semele Eccles, J. ca. 1706*
Semele Handel, G. F. 1744

CONNOR, TONY
Americana Bruce, N. 1980

CONWAY, JAMES
My Love O'Connell, K. 1997

COOK, C. E.
Red Feather   De Koven, R.   1903

COOK, WENDY
Warchild, The   Taylor, R.   1997

COOKE, THOMAS
Love and Revenge   **   1729
Penelope   **   1728

COOPER, JAMIE LEE
Soyazhe   Anderson, G.   1979

COPE, HENRY C.
Fairy Oak   Forbes, H.   1845
(with E. Fitzball)

COPLAND, MURRAY
Apology of Bony
Anderson   Conyngham, B. 1978
Bennelong   Conyngham, B. 1988
Fly   Conyngham, B. 1984
Oath of Bad Brown
Bill   Conyngham, B. 1985

CORCORAN, ROBERT
Mad Hamlet   Reif, P.   1965*

CORDER, FREDERICK (1852–1932)
Golden Web   Thomas, A. G.   1893
(with B. C. Stephenson)
Nordisa   Corder, F.   1887

CORSARI, GARY
Reverend Everyman   Brotons, S.   1990

CORSARO, FRANK
Before Breakfast   Pasatieri, T.   1980
Rasputin (with comp.) Reise, J.   1988

CORWIN, NORMAN (B. 1910)
Blennerhasset   Giannini, V.   1939
(with P. Roll)

COTTERRELL, CONSTANCE
Christmas Rose   Bridge, F.   1919–
(with M. Kemp-Welch)   29*

COULTER, JOHN
Deirdre of the Sorrows Willan, H.   1946
Transit through Fire Willan, H.   1942

COWEN, ROSALIND
Garibaldi   Cowen, F.   1860

CRAFT, ROBERT
Flood, The   Stravinsky, I. 1962

CRAVEN, ELIZABETH (LADY) (1750–1828)
Arcadian Pastoral   Beckford, W.   1782
Silver Tankard   Arnold, S.   1781

CREAGH, PATRICK
Cry of Clytaemnestra Eaton, J.   1980

Danton and
Robespierre   Eaton, J.   1978
Myshkin   Eaton, J.   1973

CROCKER, CHARLES TEMPLETON
Land of Happiness   Redding, J.   1917

CROFFUT, WILLIAM AUGUSTUS (1835–1915)
Deseret   Buck, D.   1880

CROMER, WEST (A. LAW)
Night's Surprise   Reed, T. G.   1877

CROSBY, FANNY (1820–1915)
Flower Queen   Root, G. F.   1852
Pilgrim Fathers   Root, G. F. ca. 1854*

CROSS, BEVERLEY (B. 1931)
All the King's Men   Bennett, R. R. 1969
Mines of Sulphur   Bennett, R. R. 1965
Rising of the Moon   Maw, N.   1970
Victory   Bennett, R. R. 1970

CROSS, JAMES C. (D. 1810)
Apparation, The   Reeve, W.   1794
British Fortitude   Reeve, W.   1794
Charity Boy   Reeve, W.   1796
Purse, The   Reeve, W.   1794
Raft, The   Reeve, W.   1798

CROSSLEY-HOLLAND, KEVIN
Wildman   LeFanu, N.   1995

CROWTHERS, MALCOLM
Tristan and Iseult   Whitehead, G.   1978
(with M. Hill)

CROZIER, ERIC (B. 1914)
Albert Herring   Britten, B.   1947
Billy Budd   Britten, B.   1951
(with E. M. Forster)
Little Sweep   Britten, B.   1949
Rab the Rhymer   Dunlop/
                         Oppenheim   1953
Ruth   Berkeley, L.   1956

CUMBERLAND, RICHARD (1732–1811)
Armourer, The   Warner, Capt.   1793
Calypso   Butler, T. H.   1779
Eros and Psyche   Cummings, C.   1983
Summer's Tale   Arnold, S.   1765

CUMMINGS, E [DWARD] E[STLIN] (1894–1962)
Santa Claus   Smith, L.   1955

CUNNINGHAM, A. C.
Landsdown Castle   Holst, G.   1893

CURLEY, TOM F.
Scarlet Letter   Herman, M.   1992

CURREY, CLAUDINE
Mermaid, The   More, M.   1951

CURRIE, JOHN
Confessions of a
    Justified Sinner   Wilson, T.   1976

DALTON, JOHN (1709–1763)
Comus   Arne, T. A.   1738
Comus   Bishop, H. R.   1815

DANCE, CHARLES (1794–1863)
Magic Horn   Lee, G. A.   1846
Nautch Girl   Solomon, E.   1891

DARION, JOE (B. 1917)
And David Wept   Laderman, E.   1971
archy and mehitabel   Kleinsinger, G.   1954
(with M. Brooks)
Galileo Galilei   Laderman, E.   1979
Tree That Was
    Christmas   Kleinsinger, G.   1955

DAVENANT, CHARLES (1656–1714)
Circe   Bannister, J.   1677

DAVENANT (D'AVENANT), WILLIAM (1606–
1668)
Britannia triumphans   Lawes, W.   1638
Circe   Galliard, J. E.   1719
Macbeth   Locke/Johnson   1673
Macbeth   Eccles, J.   1696
Macbeth   Leveridge, R.   1702
Siege of Rhodes   Lawes, H.   1656
Tempest, The   Weldon, J.   ca. 1712
Triumphs of the   Lawes, H./W.   1636
    Prince   Lawes

DAVIS, THULANI
Amistad   Davis, A.   1997
E. & O. Line   LeBaron, A.   1996

DAWSON-SCOTT, CATHERINE A. (1865–
1934)
Gale (with Lowry)   Leginska, E.   1935

DEANE, VINCENT
Intelligence Park   Barry, G.   1990

DEAR, NICK
Family Affair   Grant, J.   1993
Siren Song   Dove, J.   1994

DEBNEY, PATRICIA
Juniper Tree   Watkins, R.   1997

DECLUE, DENISE
Pay Off   Russo, W.   1984

DE GRESAC, FRED
Wedding Trip   De Koven, R.   1911
(with H. B. Smith)

DEHN, PAUL (1912–1976)
Bear, The (with comp.)   Walton, W.   1967

Castaway   Berkeley, L.   1967
Dinner Engagement   Berkeley, L.   1954

DE JAFFA, KATHLEEN
Emperor Jones   Gruenberg, L.   1933

DEJONG, CONSTANCE
Satyagraha
(with comp.)   Glass, P.   1981

DELAMERE, MARGARET
All at Sea (with comp.)   Shaw, G.   1952

DELYNN, JANE
Monkey Opera   Trefousse, R.   1982

DEMARIA, ROBERT
Pietro's Petard   Overton, H.   1963

DENBY, EDWIN (B. 1903)
Second Hurricane   Copland, A.   1937
Tender Land   Copland, A.   1954

DENNIS, JOHN (1657–1734)
Rinaldo and Armida   Eccles, J.   1698

DENT, JOHN (FL. 1782–1795)
Too Civil by Half   Hook, J.   1782

DE SYLVA, BUDDY (1896–1950)
Blue Monday   Gershwin, G.   1922
(with G. Bassman)

DEVIN, LEE
St. Carmen of the
    Main   Hodkinson, S.   1988

DIBBERN, DANIEL
Ransom of Red Chief   Rodríguez, R.   1986
Suor Isabella   Rodríguez, R.   1982

DIBDIN, CHARLES (1745–1814)
Gipsies, The   Arnold, S.   1778
None So Blind   Arnold, S.   1782
Old Fools   Moorehead, J.   1800
Speed the Plough   Moorehead, J.   1802

DIBDIN, CHARLES, JR. (1768–1833)
Council of Ten   Reeve, W.   1811
Farmer's Wife   Bishop, H. R.   1814
Magic Minstrel   Reeve, W.   1808
Poor Vulcan   Bishop, H. R.   1813
Rake's Progress   Whitaker, J.   1826
Round Robin   Dibdin, C.   1811

DIBDIN, THOMAS (1771–1841)
Bondoncani, Il   Attwood, T.   1800
Cabinet, The   Reeve, W., et al.   1802
Covenanters, The   Loder, E. J.   1835
Family Quarrels   Reeve, W.   1802
Hermione   Attwood, T.   1800
Morning, Noon   Perry, G.   1822
Mother Goose   Ware, W. H.   1806
Mouth of the Nile   Attwood, T.   1798

Naval Pillar	Moorehead, J.	1799
Of Age Tomorrow	Kelly, M.	1800
St. David's Day	Attwood, T.	1800
Thirty Thousand	Reeve, W.	1804
True Friends	Attwood, T.	1800
Two Faces under a Hood	Shield, W.	1807
Up to Town	Reeve, W. et al.	1811
White Plume	Reeves, W.	1806
Zuma	Bishop, H. R.	1818

DICKENS, CHARLES (1812–1870)

Village Coquettes	Hullah, J.	1836

DICKINSON, PATRIC (B. 1914)

Creation, The	Ridout, A.	1973
Phaeton	Ridout, A.	1974
Scena	Hopkins, A.	1953
Wenceslas	Ridout, A.	1978

DIDOMENICA, ROBERT (B. 1927)

Rappaccini's Daughter	Bender, E.	1992

DIMOND, WILLIAM (FL. 1800–1830)

Abou Hassan	Cooke, T. S.	1825
Aethiop, The	Bishop, H. R.	1812
Brother and Sister	Reeve, W.	1815
December and May	Bishop, H. R.	1818
Englishmen in India	Bishop, H. R.	1827
Foundling of the Forest	Kelly, M.	1809
Haroun Alraschid	Bishop, H. R.	1813
Hero of the North	Kelly, M.	1803
Hunter of the Alps	Kelly, M.	1804
Lady and the Devil	Kelly, M.	1820
Native Land	Bishop, H. R.	1824
Nymph of the Grotto	Lee, G. A.	1829
Peasant Boy	Kelly, M.	1811
Pirate, The	Rooke, W. M.	1822
Sea-Side Story	Attwood, T.	1801
Young Hussar	Kelly, M.	1807
Youth, Love	Kelly, M.	1805

DISCH, THOMAS M.

Fall of the House of Usher	Sandow, G.	1979
Frankenstein	Sandow, G.	1980

DOBRIN, BETTINA MAE

Committee, The	Doran, M.	1958

DODD, LEE WILSON (1879–1933)

Merrymount	Smith, D. S.	1913*

DODSLEY, ROBERT (1703–1764)

Blind Beggar	Arne, T. A.	1741
Triumph of Peace	Arne, T. A.	1748

DODSON, GERALD (1884–1966)

Rebel Maid (with A. Thompson)	Phillips, M.	1921

DONAHUE, JOHN

Postcard from Morocco	Argento, D.	1971

DONNELLY, DOROTHY

Student Prince	Romberg, S.	1924

DORMAN, JOSEPH (D. 1754)

Female Rake	**	1736

DORR, DONALD

Frederick Douglass	Kay, U.	1991
Jubilee	Kay, U.	1976

DOYLE, ARTHUR CONAN (1859–1930)

Jane Annie (with Barrie)	Ford, E.	1893

DRAPER, EVELYN MANACHER

Game of Chance	Barab, S.	1957

DRAYTON, HENRI (1822–1872)

Mephistopheles	Lutz, M.	1855

DRURY, ROBERT (FL. 1732–1735)

Devil of a Duke	**	1732
Fancy'd Queen	**	1733
Mad Captain	**	1733
Rival Milliners	**	1736

DRURY, WILLIAM PRICE (B. 1861)

Samuel Pepys (with R. Pryce)	Coates, A.	1929

DRYDEN, JOHN (1631–1700)

Albion and Albanius	Grabu, L.	1685
Indian Queen (with R. Howard)	Purcell, H.	1695
Secular Masque	Purcell, D.	1700

DUBOIS, LADY DOROTHY (1728–1774)

Divorce, The	Hook, J.	1771
Magnet, The	Arnold, S.	1771

DUCKWORTH, COLIN

Beauty and the Beast	Easton, M.	1989
Cinderella	Easton, M.	1989

DUDLEY, HENRY BATE. SEE BATE, HENRY

DUFFIELD, BRAINERD

Moby Dick	Low, J.	1955

DUKE, DOROTHY

Sire de Maletroit	Duke, J.	1958

DUMONT, FRANK

Africanus Blue Beard	Sedgwick, A. B.	1874
Gambrinus	Sedgwick, A. B.	1876

DUNBAR, PAUL L. (1872–1906)

In Dahomey (with J. A. Shipp)	Cook, W. M.	1903

DUNCAN, HARRY

Last Puppet	Strilko, A.	1963
Scarf, The	Hoiby, L.	1958

ENGLE, PAUL (B. 1908)
Golden Child   Bezanson, P.   1959

ENGVICK, WILLIAM
Ellen   Wilder, A.   1955*
Miss Chicken Little Wilder, A.   1953

ENRIGHT, NICK
Snow Queen   Dudley, G.   1985

ERICH, W.
**Dr. Jekyll and
  Mr. Hyde**   Fragale, F. D.   1953

ERSKINE, JOHN (1879–1951)
Helen Retires   Antheil, G.   1934
**Jack and the
  Beanstalk**   Gruenberg, L.   1931
Sleeping Beauty   Bernstein, B.   1938

ESSLIN, MARTIN
Beatrice Cenci   Goldschmidt, B. 1952

ESTCOURT, RICHARD (1668–1712)
Prunella   Clayton, T.   1708

EVERETT, HORACE
Tea Party   Gottlieb, J.   1957

EVERETT, LEOLYN LOUISE (B. 1888)
Magnifica, La   Spelman, T.   1920*

EYRE, EDMUND JOHN (1787–1816)
Caffres, The   Davy, J.   1802
Lady of the Lake   Francis, W.   1811
Vintagers, The   Bishop, H. R.   1809

FABIAN, R.
Trick for Trick   **   1735

FAIRCLOUGH, MARY
John Barleycorn   Montgomery, B. 1962

FALCONER, EDMUND (1814–1879)
Deserted Village   Glover, S.   1880
Rose of Castille   Balfe, M.   1857
(with A. G. Harris)
Satanella (with Harris) Balfe, M.   1860
Victorine   Mellon, A.   1859

FANDEL, JOHN (B. 1924)
Mother, The   Hollingsworth,
(with comp.)   S.   1954

FARJEON, ELEANOR (1881–1965)
Eve of St. John   Mackenzie, A.   1924

FARLEY, CHARLES (1771–1859)
**Battle of Bothwell
  Brigg**   Bishop, H. R.   1820

FARNIE, HENRY B. (1836–1889)
Bride of Song   Benedict, J.   1864
Nell Gwynne   Cellier, A.   1878

Sleeping Queen   Balfe, M.   1864

FARQUAR, MARION
Poison   Hart, F.   1984
Princess and the Pea Toch, E.   1954

FAUCIT, J. S.
Justice   Horne, C. E.   1820

FAUSSET, MARJORIE
Two Sisters   Rootham, C.   1922

FAWCETT, JOHN (1768–1837)
Barber of Seville   Bishop, H. R.   1818
(with D. Terry)
Fairies' Revels   Arnold, S.   1802
Marriage of Figaro Bishop, H. R.   1819
Secret Mine   Bishop/Condell   1813

FAWKES, RICHARD (B. 1944)
Biko   Paintal, P.   1992

FEE, DOROTHY
Taming of the Shrew Giannini, V.   1953
(with comp.)

FEILDE, MATTHEW
**Vertumnus and
  Pomona**   Arne, M.   1782

FEIN, JUDITH
Hotel Eden   Mollicone, H.   1989

FEINGOLD, MICHAEL
Happy End   Weill-Feingold. 1972

FEIST, MILTON
Brief Candle   Mayer, W.   1967

FEN, ELIZABETH
Proposal, The   Walker, J.   1974
(with S. Carter)

FFINCH, MICHAEL
Selfish Giant   Shaw, F.   1973

FIELD, BARBARA
Rosina   Titus, H.   1980

FIELDING, HENRY (1707–1754)
Author's Farce   **   1730
**Don Quixote in
  England**   **   1734
Eurydice   **   1743?
Fathers, The   **   1778
Grub-Street Opera   **   1731
**Intriguing
  Chambermaid**   **   1734
Lottery, The   Seedo, Mr.   1732
Miss Lucy in Town   Arne, T. A.   1742
Mock Doctor   **   1732
**Old Man Taught
  Wisdom**   **   1735

| Tumble-Down Dick | ** | 1736 |
| Welsh Opera | ** | 1731 |

FINE, MORTON
| Hunted, The | Mailman, M. | 1959 |
| (with D. Friedkin) | | |

FINK, BONNIE
| Boor, The | Fink, M. | 1955 |

FINLETTER, GRETCHEN DAMROSCH
(D.1969)
| Opera Cloak | Damrosch, W. | 1942 |

FINN, H[ENRY] J[AMES] (1787–1840)
| Ahmad al Ramel | Horn, C. E. | 1840 |

FINNISSY, MICHAEL (B. 1946)
| Ubu (with comp.) | Toovey, A. | 1992 |

FISKE, MINNIE MADDERN (1865–1932)
| Light from St. Agnes | Harling, W. F. | 1925 |

FITZBALL, EDWARD (1792–1873)
Adelaide	Bishop, H. R.	1830
Alchymist, The	Bishop, H. R.	1832
(with T. H. Bayly)		
Berta	Smart, H.	1854
Black Vulture	Rodwell, G.	1830
Bottle of Champagne	Bishop, H. R.	1832
Bronze Horse	Rodwell, G.	1835
Demon, The	Bishop, H. R.	1832
(with J. B. Buckstone)		
Devil's Elixir	Rodwell, G.	1829
Diadesté	Balfe, M.	1838
Earthquake, The	Rodwell, G.	1828
Fairy Oak (with Cope)	Forbes, H.	1845
Flying Dutchman	Rodwell, G.	1827
Joan of Arc	Balfe, M.	1837
Keolanthe	Balfe, M.	1841
Lord of the Isles	Rodwell, G.	1834
Lurline	Wallace, V.	1860
Magic Fan	Bishop, H. R.	1832
Maid of Honour	Balfe, M.	1847
Maritania	Wallace, V.	1845
Night Before the Wedding	Bishop, H. R.	1829
Ninetta	Bishop, H. R.	1830
Pasqual Bruno	Hatton, J. L.	1844
Paul Clifford	Rodwell, G.	1835
Quasimodo	Rodwell, G.	1836
Queen of the Thames	Hatton, J. L.	1842
Raymond and Agnes	Loder, E. J.	1855
Robber's Bride	Hawes, W.	1829
Sedain Chair	Bishop, H. R.	1822
Sexton of Cologne	Rodwell, G.	1836
She Stoops to Conquer	Macfarren, G.	1864
Siege of Rochelle	Balfe, M.	1835
Soldier's Widow	Barnett, J.	1833
Sorceress, The	Ries, F.	1831

Thalaba	Rodwell, G.	1836
Under the Oak	Bishop, H. R.	1830
Waverly	Rodwell, G.	1824

FLAIG, ELEANOR (1902–1954)
| Légende Provençale | Moore, M. | 1929–35* |

FLANDERS, MICHAEL
| Three's Company | Hopkins, A. | 1953 |

FLASTER, KARL (1905–1965)
| Scarlet Letter | Giannini, V. | 1938 |

FLETCHER, LUCILLE
| Wuthering Heights | Hermann, B. | 1943* |

FLOWERS, PAT
| First Christmas | Antill, J. H. | 1969 |

FORD, CHARLES-HENRY
| Denmark Vesey | Bowles, P. | 1937 |

FOREMAN, RICHARD (B. 1937)
Africanus Instructus	Silverman, S.	1986
Columbine String Quartet Tonight!	Silverman, S.	1981
Dr. Selavy's Magic Theatre (with Hendry)	Silverman, S.	1972
Elephant Steps	Silverman, S.	1968
Hotel for Criminals	Silverman, S.	1974
Madame Adare	Silverman, S.	1980
Young Goodman Brown	Johnston, P.	1995

FORNES, MARIA IRENA
| Balseros | Ashley, R. | 1997 |
| Terra Incognita | Sierra, R. | 1997 |

FORREST, EBENEZER
| Momus | ** | 1729 |

FORREST, LEON
| Soldier Boy, Soldier | Anderson, T. | 1982 |

FORREST, THEODOSIUS (1728–1784)
| Weathercock, The | Arnold, S. | 1775 |

FORSTER, E. M. (1879–1970)
| Billy Budd | Britten, B. | 1951 |
| (with E. Crozier) | | |

FORTUNE, JAN (B. 1892)
| Cynthia Parker | Smith, J. | 1939 |

FOX, IAN
| Táin, The | Wilson, J. | 1972 |

FOX, SUSAN (B. 1943)
| Village, The | Mandelbaum, J. | 1995 |

FRAM, MICHAEL
| Fool, The | Somers, H. | 1956 |

FRANCHETTI, MARIE
| Princess, The | Franchetti, A. | 1952 |

FRANKLIN, ANDREW (D. 1845)

Egyptian Festival	Florio, C.	1800
Embarkation, The	Reeve, W.	1799

FRANKLIN, DAVID

Dark Pilgrimage	Tate, P.	1962
Lodger, The	Tate, P.	1960

FREEDMAN, MELVIN

Wife of Bath's Tale	Legg, J.	1986
(with comp.)		

FREEMAN, DAVID (B. 1945)

Hell's Angels	Osborne, N.	1986

FREEMAN, P.

Judgment, The	Kupferman, M.	1966

FREIER, RECHA

Sonata about		
Jerusalem (with comp.)	Goehr, A.	1971

FRIED, BARBARA

Losers, The	Farberman, H.	1971

FRIED, MICHAEL

Heracles	Eaton, J.	1972

FRIEDKIN, DAVID

Hunted, The	Mailman, M.	1959
(with M. Fine)		

FROST, TOM

Capitan, El	Sousa, J. P.	1896
(with C. Klein)		

FRY, CHRISTOPHER (B. 1907)

Paradise Lost	Penderecki, K.	1978
Phoenix Too Far	Oliver, S.	1970

FRY, JOSEPH REESE

Leonora	Fry, W.	1845
Notre-Dame of Paris	Fry, W.	1864

FULLER, JOHN

Herod, Do Your Worst	Kelly, B.	1968

FYLEMAN, ROSE (1877–1957)

Happy Families	Dunhill, T.	1931

GALATI, FRANK

Guilt of Lillian Sloan	Neil, W.	1986
(with comp.)		

GARDNER, DOROTHY

Eastward in Eden	Meyerowitz, J.	1951

GARDNER, JOHN

Rumpelstiltskin	Barber, J.	1978

GARNER, ALAN

Belly Bag	Ball, M.	1992
Holly from the Bongs	Crosse, G.	1974
Potter Thompson	Crosse, G.	1975

GARRICK, DAVID (1717–1779)

Christmas Tale	Dibdin, C.	1773
Cymon	Arne, M.	1767
Cymon	Bishop, H. R.	1815
Enchanter, The	Smith, J. C.	1760
Fairies, The	Smith, J. C.	1755
Florizel and Perdita	Boyce, W.	1756
Grenadier, The	Dibdin, C.	1773
Institution of the		
Garter	Dibdin, C.	1771
Lethe	Arne, T. A.	1749
Lilliput	Arnold, S.	1777
Linco's Travels	Arne, M.	1767
May Day	Arne, T. A.	1775
Midsummer Night's		
Dream (with Colman)	Burney, C.	1763
Orpheus	Barthelemon, F.	1767
Quentin Durward	Laurent, H. R.	1848
Tempest, The	Arne, T. A.	1746
Tempest, The	Smith, J. C.	1756
Tempest, The	Boyce, W.	1757
Theatrical Candidates	Bates, W.	1775

GARZA, JULIA

Frieze of Life	Applebaum, E.	1983

GATAKER, THOMAS (FL. 1730)

Jealous Clown	**	1730

GATTY, I.

Duke or Devil	Gatty, N.	1909

GATTY, REGINALD

Greysteel	Gatty, N.	1906
King Alfred	Gatty, N.	1930
Tempest, The	Gatty, N.	1920

GAY, JOHN (1685–1732)

Achilles	**	1733
Acis and Galatea	Handel, G. F.	1718
Beggar's Opera	Pepusch, J.	1728
Pincushion, The	Arne, T. A.	1756
Polly	**	1729

GAYLER, CHARLES (1821–1897)

Sleepy Hollow	Maretzek, M.	1879

GENTLEMAN, FRANCIS (1728–1784)

Cupid's Revenge	Hook, J.	1772

GEOGHEGAN, EDWARD (B. CA. 1812)

Currency Lass	1844	Sydney

GERDINE, ELAINE

Chicken Little	Benjamin, T.	1985

GERSHWIN, IRA (1896–1983)

Porgy and Bess	Gershwin, G.	1935
(with D. Heyward)		
Lady in the Dark	Weill, K.	1941
(with M. Hart)		

GERSUNY, CARL
Diet, The (with comp.) Olenick, E.   1979*

GETLEIN, P.
Decorator, The Woolen, R.   1959

GIBSON, WILLIAM
Nativity Dello Joio, N.   1987

GIKOW, LOUISE
Marita Adolphe, B.   1995

GILBERT, ILSA
Bundle Man Cold, M.   1993

GILBERT, WILLIAM S. (1836–1911)
Ages Ago Clay, F.   1869
Dulcamara ** 1866
Eyes and No Eyes Pascal, F.   1875
Fallen Fairies German, E.   1909
Gentleman in Black Clay, F.   1870
Gondoliers, The Sullivan, A. S.   1889
Grand Duke Sullivan, A. S.   1896
Haste to the Wedding Grossmith, G.   1892
His Excellency Carr, F. O.   1894
H.M.S. Pinafore Sullivan, A. S.   1878
Iolanthe Sullivan, A. S.   1882
Mikado, The Sullivan, A. S.   1885
Mountebanks, The Cellier, A.   1892
No Cards "Elliott, L."   1869
Our Island Home Reed, T.   1870
Patience Sullivan, A. S.   1881
Pirates of Penzance Sullivan, A. S.   1879
Princess Ida Sullivan, A. S.   1884
Princess Toto Clay, F.   1876
Robert the Devil "Kettenus"   1868
Ruddigore Sullivan, A. S.   1887
Sensation Novel Reed, T. G.   1871
Sorcerer, The Sullivan, A. S.   1877
Thespis Sullivan, A. S.   1871
Trial by Jury Sullivan, A. S.   1875
Utopia Limited Sullivan, A. S.   1893
Vicar of Bray Solomon, E.   1882
Vivandière, La Wallerstein, F.   1867
Yeomen of the Guard Sullivan, A. S.   1888

GILLIAT, SIDNEY
Open Window Arnold, M.   1956
Our Man in Havana Williamson, M.   1963

GINSBERG, ALLEN (1926–1997)
Hydrogen Jukebox Glass, P.   1990

GLICKMAN, GARY (B. 1959)
Tibetan Dreams Dickman, S.   1990

"GLOBUS, SEPTIMUS"
Freischütz, Der ** 1824

GODDARD, DAVID
Donna, La Brumby, C.   1988

GODFREY, PAUL
Panic, The Sawyer, D.   1991

GODWIN, GAIL
**Anna Marguerita's
Will** Starer, R.   1981
Apollonia Starer, R.   1979
Last Lover Starer, R.   1975

GOETHE, ANN
Travels Bond, V.   1995

GOLD, ARTHUR
Ma Barker Eaton, J.   1957

GOLDBERG, MILTON
Metamorphosis White, M.   1968

GOLDBERG, MOSES
Gulliver Bond, V.   1988

GOLDMAN, RICHARD FRANKO
Athaliah Weisgall, H.   1964
Mandarin, The Elkus, J.   1967

GOLDSMITH, M.
Angelina Bishop, H. R.   1804

GOLDSWORTHY, PETER
**Summer of the
Seventeenth Doll** Mills, R.   1996

GOODALL, WILLIAM (FL. 1740)
**False Guardians
Outwitted** ** 1740

GOODMAN, ALICE
Death of Klinghoffer Adams, J.   1991
Nixon in China Adams, J.   1987

GOODMAN, PAUL
Cain and Abel Rorem, N.   ca. 1946*

GOODRICH, ARTHUR (1878–1941)
Caponsacchi Hageman, R.   1937

GOODWIN, JOHN CHEEVER
Evangeline Rice, E. E.   1874
Merry Monarch Sousa, J. P.   1890
(with W. Morse)

GORDON, MEL
False Messiah Adolphe, B.   1983
Mikhoels the Wise Adolphe, B.   1982

GRACE, BONNIE
Mrs. Dalloway Larsen, L.   1993

GRAHAM, COLIN (B. 1931)
Golden Vanity Britten, B.   1967
Jōruri Miki, M.   1985
Penny for a Song Bennett, R. R.   1967
**Postman Always Rings
Twice** Paulus, S.   1982

GRAHAM, GEORGE (1728?–1767)

Telemachus	Bishop, H. R.	1815

GRANT, DAVID

Bang!	Rutter, J.	1976*
Wind in the Willows	Rutter, J.	1997

GRANVILLE, GEORGE (LORD GRANVILLE/ LANDSDOWNE) (1667–1735)

British Enchanters	Corbett, W.	1706
Peleus and Thetis	Boyce, W.	ca. 1740
Peleus and Thetis	Hayes, W.	ca. 1749

GRAVES, ROBERT (1895–1985)

Nausicaa	Glanville-Hicks	1961

GRAY, TYNDALL

Beggar's Love (with comp.)	Patterson, F.	1929

GREEN, WALTER

Wrinkle in Time	Larsen, L.	1992

GREENBANK, HARRY

Geisha, The (with Hall)	Jones, S.	1896
San Toy (with Ross, Morton)	Jones, S.	1899

GREENBANK, PERCY

My Lady Molly (with Jessop, Taylor)	Jones, S.	1903

GREENBERG, ALVIN

Further Voyages	Stokes, E.	1984
Horspfal	Stokes, E.	1969
Jealous Cellist	Stokes, E.	1979

GREENE, ANN T.

Mother of Three Sons	Jenkins, L.	1990

GREENE, CLAY M. (1850–1933)

Maid of Plymouth	Thorne, T. P.	1893
Old Black Joe	Shelley, H. R.	1911

GREENFIELD, JEROME

Whirligig	Brisman, H.	1977

GREENWOOD, JOHN ORMEROD

Visitors, The	Gardner, J.	1972

GRESS, ELSA (B. 1919)

Grinning at the Devil	Wilson, J.	1989

GRIFFITH, WYN

Menna	Hughes, A.	1953

GRIFFITHS, PAUL (B. 1947)

Marco Polo	Tan Dun	1996

GROBE, NANCY

Gift of the Magi	Brown, R.	1985

GROGAN, WALTER E.

Pierrot and Pierrette	Holbrooke, J.	1909

GRUNDY, CECIL REGINALD (1870–1944)

Gainsborough	Coates, A.	1941

GRUNDY, SYDNEY (1848–1914)

Haddon Hall	Sullivan, A. S.	1892

GUINESS, BRYAN

Petrified Princess	1959	London

GUITERMAN, ARTHUR (1871–1943)

Man without a Country	Damrosch, W.	1937

GUNDERSON, KEITH

We're Not Robots	Stokes, E.	1986

GURY, JEREMY

Mighty Casey	Schuman, W.	1951

GUTHRIE, TYRONE (1900–1971)

Sleeping Children	Easdale, B.	1951

HAINES, JOHN THOMAS (1799?–1843)

Amilie	Rooke, W. M.	1818
Henrique	Rooke, W. M.	1839
Queen of a Day	Fitzwilliam, E.	1841

HALL, OAKLEY

Angle of Repose	Imbrie, A.	1976

HALL, OWEN [JIMMY DAVIS] (1853–1907)

Geisha, The (with H. Greenback)	Jones, S.	1896

HALL, SHAWN [ELIZABETH DAVIS]

Kalamona (with comp.)	Kondorossy, L.	1971
Midnight Duel	Kondorossy, L.	1955
Nathan the Wise	Kondorossy, L.	1969
Ruth and Naomi	Kondorossy, L.	1974
Poorest Suitor	Kondorossy, L.	1967
Pumpkin, The (with comp.)	Kondorossy, L.	1954
Shizuka's Dance	Kondorossy, L.	1969
Unexpected Visitor (with Kemeny, comp.)	Kondorossy, L.	1956
Voice, The (with S. N. Linek)	Kondorossy, L.	1954

HAMBLETON, RONALD

Luck of Ginger Coffey	Pannell, R.	1967

HAMILTON, HENRY (1853–1918)

Duchess of Dantzic	Caryll, I.	1903

HAMILTON, RALPH

David Rizzio	Braham, J., et al.	1820
Elphi Bey	Attwood, T.	1817

HAMILTON, ROBIN

Rose Garden	Boyd, A.	1972

HAMMERSTEIN II, OSCAR (1895–1960)

Carmen Jones	Bizet-Bennett	1943

HATTON, ANN JULIA (1764–1838)
| Tammany | Hewitt, J. | 1794 |

HAUN, EUGENE
| Boor, The | Bucci, M. | 1949 |

HAWKES, TERENCE
| Thérèse Raquin | Stoker, R. | 1975* |

HAWKESWORTH, JOHN (1715–1773)
| Edgar and Emmeline | Arne, M. | 1761 |

HAWKINS-AMBLER, G. A.
| Brownings Go to Italy | Freer, E. E. | 1938 |
| Chilkoot Maiden | Freer, E. E. | 1927 |

HAWLEY, EARLENE
| Jeremiah | Fink, M. | 1962 |

HAYWOOD, ELIZA (1693–1756)
| Opera of Operas | Arne, T. A. | 1733 |
| (with W. Hatchett) | | |

HAZARD, JAMES (B. 1935)
| Thousand Names | Kitzke, J. | 1981 |

HAZARD, MARION
| Thorwald | Dinsmore, W. | 1940 |

HEALEY, ROBERT
Ballad of Kitty the		
Barkeep (with comp.)	Lee, D.-K.	1979
Phineas and the		
Nightingale	Lee, D.-K.	1952
Speakeasy	Lee, D.-K.	1957
Two Knickerbocker		
Tales	Lee, D.-K.	1957

HEARTWELL, HENRY
| Castle of Sorrento | Attwood, T. | 1799 |
| Reform'd in Time | Attwood, T. | 1798 |

HELD, JACK
| Ethan Frome | Beall, J. | 1997 |

HELLMAN, LILLIAN (1905–1984)
| Candide (with Wilbur) | Bernstein, L. | 1956 |

HENDERSON, WILLIAM J. (1855–1937)
| Cyrano | Damrosch, W. | 1913 |

HENDRY, TOM
Dr. Selavy's Magic		
Theatre	Silverman, S.	1972
(with R. Foreman)		

HENRY, JAN
| Haircut | Morgenstern, S. | 1969 |

HENSHER, PHILIP
| Powder Her Face | Adès, T. | 1995 |

HERBERT, ALAN PATRICK (1890–1971)
| Blue Peter | Gibbs, C. A. | 1923 |
| Derby Day | Reynolds, A. | 1932 |

| Tantivy Towers | Dunhill, T. | 1931 |

HERSEE, HENRY (1820–1896)
| Pauline | Cowen, F. | 1876 |
| Royal Word | de Lara, I. | 1883 |

HEWETT, DOROTHY
| Christina's World | Edwards, R. | 1983 |

HEYMAN, ROBERT
| Rock Justice | Balin, M. | 1979 |

HEYWARD, DOROTHY HARTZELL (1890–1961)
| Babar the Elephant | Berezowsky, N. | 1953 |
| (with J. Randal) | | |

HEYWARD, DU BOSE (1885–1940)
| Porgy and Bess | Gershwin, G. | 1935 |
| (with I. Gershwin) | | |

HILL, MICHAEL
| Tristan and Iseult | Whitehead, G. | 1978 |
| (with M. Crowthers) | | |

HILL, SUSAN
| Joan of Arc | Burgon, G. | 1970 |

HILLYER, ROBERT (1895–1961)
| Garden of Artemis | Pinkham, D. | 1948 |

HINTON, JAMES, JR.
| Bartleby | Flanagan, W. | 1961 |

HIPPISLEY, JOHN (D. 1748)
| Flora | ** | 1729 |
| Sequel to Flora | ** | 1732 |

HITCHCOCK
| Fifth for Bridge | Sheldon, R. | 1961 |

HOADLEY, JOHN (1711–1776)
Florimel	Greene, M.	1734
Judgment of Hercules	Greene, M.	1740
(prob. by Hoadley)		
Phoebe	Greene, M.	1747

HOARE, PRINCE (1755–1834)
Captive of Spilburg	Dussek, J.	1798
Cave of Trophonius	Storace, S.	1791
Chains of the Heart	Reeve, W.	1801
Dido	Storace, S.	1792
Friend in Need	Kelly, M.	1797
Italian Villagers	Shield, W.	1797
Lock and Key	Shield, W.	1796
Mahmoud	Storace, S.	1796
My Grandmother	Storace, S.	1793
No Song, No Supper	Storace, S.	1790
Paragraph	Braham, J.	1804
Prize, The	Storace, S.	1793
Three and the Deuce	Storace, S.	1795

HOBAN, RUSSELL
| Second Mrs. Kong | Birtwistle, H. | 1994 |

HOCHMAN, EUGENE J.
Ray and the Gospel
　Singer　　　　　　Gould, E.　　　1967

HOELTERHOFF, MANUELA
　Modern Painters　Lang, D.　　　1995

HOFFMAN, GALE
　Blood Moon　　　Dello Joio, N.　1961

HOFFMAN, WILIAM M. (B. 1939)
　Ghosts of Versailles　Corigliano, J.　1991

HOFMANN, GERDA WISMER
　Snow Queen　　　Jones, A. G.　　1917

HOLBROOK, DAVID J.
　Borderline, The　　Mellers, W.　　1959
　Children's Crusade　Ridout, A.　　1968
　Quarry, The　　　Joubert, J.　　1965
　Rescue, The　　　Ridout, A.　　1963

HOLCROFT, THOMAS (1745–1809)
　Choleric Fathers　Shield, W.　　1785
　Crisis, The　　　Shield, W.　　1778
　Escapes, The　　Attwood, T.　　1801
　Maid of the Vale　Arne, M.　　　1775
　Noble Peasant　　Shield, W.　　1784
　Old Cloathsman　Attwood, T.　　1799

HOLDEN, ANTHONY
　Agamemnon　　　Moris, R.　　　1969

HOLLANDER, JOHN
　Jenny　　　　　Weisgall, H.　　1976

HOLLIDAY, THOMAS
Orpheus in Pecan
　Springs　　　　Latham, W.　　1980

HOLMAN, DAVID
　Frankie　　　　John, A.　　　1987

HOLMAN, JOSEPH GEORGE (1764–1817)
　Abroad and at Home　Shield, W.　　1796
　Red-Cross Knights　Attwood, T.　　1799

HOLMES, JAMES
　Hearing　　　　Rorem, N.　　1977

HOLMES, MARTIN R.
Mr. Bellamy Comes
　Home　　　　Rivington, H.　1950

HOLT, STEPHEN
　I Love My Voice　Arlington, D.　1978

HOOD, BASIL (1864–1917)
　Emerald Isle　　Sullivan, A. S.　1901
　French Maid　　Slaughter, W.　1896
　Gentleman Joe　Slaughter, W.　1895
　Ib and Little Christina　Leoni, F.　　1901
　Merrie England　German, E.　　1902
　Rose of Persia　Sullivan, A. S.　1899

HOOK, JAMES, JR. (1772?–1828)
Diamond Cut
　Diamond　　　Hook, J.　　　1797
　Jack of Newbury　Hook, J.　　　1795

HOOK, MRS. JAMES. SEE HORNCASTLE, HARRIET.

HOOK, THEODORE EDWARD (1788–1841)
　Catch Him Who Can　Hook, J.　　　1806
　Fortress, The　　Hook, J.　　　1807
　Invisible Girl　　Hook, J.　　　1806
　Music Mad　　　Hook, J.　　　1807
　Safe and Sound　Hook, J.　　　1809
　Soldier's Return　Hook, J.　　　1805
　Tekeli　　　　Hook, J.　　　1806

HOOKER, BRIAN (1880–1946)
　Fairyland　　　Parker, H.　　1915
　Mona　　　　Parker, H.　　1912

HOPGOOD, ALAN
　Little Redinka　Easton, M.　　1991
　Petrov (with comp.)　Easton, M.　　1992

HOPKINS, JOHN
Some Place of
　Darkness　　　Whelen, C.　　1967

HOPKINS, PAULINE ELIZABETH
　Peculiar Sam　　**	****　　　　1879

HOPPWOOD, AUBREY (B. 1863)
　Lucky Star　　　Caryll, I.　　　1899
　(with A. Ross)

HORDYK, MARGARET
　Door, The　　　Mopper, I.　　1956

HORGAN, PAUL
　Tree on the Plains　Bacon, E.　　1942

HORNCASTLE (HOOK), HARRIET (D. 1795)
　Double Disguise　Hook, J.　　　1784
　Triumph of Beauty　Hook, J.　　　1786

HOUGH, JOHN (FL. 1778)
Second Thought Is
　Best　　　　Bates, W.　　1778

HOULTON, ROBERT (B. 1739)
　Calypso　　　Giordani, T.　1785
　Contract, The　Stevenson, J.　1782
　Gibraltar　　　Giordani, T.　1783
　Pharnaces　　******　　　　1783

HOUSMAN, LAURENCE (1865–1959)
　Seraphic Vision　Boughton, R.　1924

HOUSTON, ROXANNE
　Governess, The　Mallett, C.　　1954

HOWARD, ROBERT (1626–1698)
　Indian Queen　　Purcell, H.　　1695
　(with J. Dryden)

HOWE, T.
Columbine String Quartet
Tonight!   Silverman, S.   1981

HOWLEY, JAMES
Harlot and the Monk   Bohmler, C.   1985

HUBBARD, ALISON
Cop and the Anthem   Cohen, S.   1982

HUBSKY, JOHN
To Let the Captive Go Stewart, F.   1974

HUEFFER, FRANCIS (1843–1889)
Colomba   Mackenzie, A.   1883
Guillem   Mackenzie, A.   1886

HUFF, KEITH
Bok Choy Variations   Chen, E.   1995
(with Servoss, Simonson)

HUGHES, DAVID (B. 1930)
Widow of Ephesus   Hurd, M.
(with comp.)

HUGHES, GLENN
Three Blind Mice   Verrall, J.   1955

HUGHES, JOHN
Apollo and Daphne   Pepusch, J.   1716
Apollo and Daphne   Hook, J.   1773
Telemachus   Galliard, J. E.   1712

HUGHES, LANGSTON (1902–1967)
Barrier, The   Meyerowitz, J.   1950
Esther   Meyerowitz, J.   1957
Street Scene
(with Rice)   Weill, K.   1946
Port Town   Meyerowitz, J.   1960
Troubled Island   Still, W. G.   1938

HUGHES, TED (B. 1930)
Story of Vasco   Crosse, G.   1974

HUGHES, WALLACE TAYLOR
Lady of the Lake   Schmidt, K.   1931

HULL, THOMAS (1728–1808)
Fairy Favour   Bach, J. C.   1767
Love Finds the Way   Arne, T. A., et al. 1777
Pharnaces   Bates, W.   1765
Royal Merchant   Linley Sr, T.   1767
Spanish Lady   **   1765

HUMPHREYS, SAMUEL (1698–1738)
Ulysses   Smith, J. C.   1733

HUNT, JOHN CLINTON (B. 1925)
Ethan Frome   Allanbrook, D.   1952

HUPPLER, DUDLEY
Something New   Hoiby, L.   1982

HURLSTONE, THOMAS (FL. 1792–1794)
Just in Time   Carter, T.   1792

To Arms   Shield, W.   1793

HURST, CYRIL
Royal Vagrants   Warner, H. W.   1899

HWANG, DAVID HENRY (B. 1957)
One Thousand
Airplanes   Glass, P.   1988
Silver River   Sheng, B.   1997

IKAM, CATHERINE
VALIS   Machover, T.   1987
(with comp., B. Raymond)

IOCAVETTI, BETTY
Fête at Coqueville   Rea, A.   1976
Old Pipes and the
Dryad   Rea, A.   1980

IRWIN, EYLES (1751?–1817)
Bedouins, The   Stevenson, J.   1801

IRWIN, WALLACE (1876–1959)
Dove of Peace   Damrosch, W.   1912

ISDELL, SARAH
Cavern, The   Stevenson, J.   1825

IVES, DAVID
Secret Garden   Pliska, G.   1991

JACKMAN, ISAAC (FL. 1776–1795)
Hero and Leander   Reeve, W.   1787
Milesian, The   Carter, T.   1777

JACKSON, BARRY (B. 1879)
Spanish Lady   Elgar, E.   1933*

JACKSON, GEORGE RUSSELL
Salem Witch   Stahl, R.   ca. 1883*

JACKSON, ISAAC (FL. 1776–1795)
Hero and Leander   Reeve, W.   1787

JACOBS, ARTHUR (B. 1922)
One Man Show   Maw, N.   1964

JACOBS, W[ILLIAM] W[YMARK] (1863–1943)
Captain's Parrot   Brent-Smith ca. 1950

JAFFE, DAN
All Cats Turn Gray   Six, H.   1971
Without Memorial
Banners   Six, H.   1966

JAMES, LEWIS CAIRNS
Critic, The   Stanford, C.   1916

JARRETT, A.
Sultan of Mocha   Cellier, A.   1874

JAYME, WILLIAM NORTH
Carry Nation   Moore, D.   1966

Turn Out!	King, M.	1812
Wedding Present	Horn, C. E.	1825

KENYON, BERNICE (B. 1897)
Landara	Zimbalist, E.	1956

KESSLER, JASCHA
Anniversary, The	Rorem, N.	ca. 1961*

KINCH, M.
Death of Enkidu	Somers, H.	1977

KING, ALEXANDER
Juggler of Our Lady	Kay, U.	1962

KING, THOMAS (1730–1805)
Love at First Sight	**	1763

KINOY, ERNEST
Goodbye to the Clown	Laderman, E.	1960
Jacob and the Indians	Laderman, E.	1957

KIRKUP, JAMES (B. 1918)
Actor's Revenge	Miki, M.	1979

KLASDER, KARL
Harvest, The	Giannini, V.	1961
(with comp.)		

KLEIN, CHARLES (1867–1915)
Capitan, El	Sousa, J. P.	1896
(with Frost)		
Charlatan, The	Sousa, J. P.	1898
Red Feather	De Koven, R.	1903

KLIEWER, WARREN (B. 1931)
Bird in the Bush	Bielawa, H.	1962

KNAPP, HENRY RYDER
Hunt the Slipper	Arnold, S.	1784

KNIGHT, EDWARD P. (1774–1826)
Veteran Soldier	Cooke, T., et al.	1822

KNIGHT, JERE
Helen in Egypt	Elkus, J.	1970

KNIGHT, THOMAS (D. 1820)
Turnpike Gate	Reeve, W.	1799

KNUTSON, WAYNE
Arabesque	Marek, R.	1967

KOCH, KENNETH (B. 1925)
Bertha	Rorem, N.	1973

KOESTENBAUM, WAYNE
Jackie O	Daughterty, M.	1997

KONDEK, CHARLES
Between Two Worlds	Ran, S.	1997
Breakfast Waltzes	Blumenfeld, H.	1988
Esther	Weisgall, H.	1993
Fan, The	Goldstein, L.	1989
Four-Score	Blumenfeld, H.	1984
Fritzi	Blumenfeld, H.	1979

Seasons in Hell	Blumenfeld, H.	1996

KOPPENHAVER, ALLEN JOHN (B. 1931)
Bell Tower	Haskins, R.	1976*
Legend of Sleepy Hollow	Haskins, R.	1976*

KOPS, BERNARD (B. 1926)
Appointment, The	Josephs, W.	1966

KORIE, MICHAEL
Harvey Milk	Wallace, S.	1995
Hopper's Wife	Wallace, S.	1997
Kabballah	Wallace, S.	1989
Where's Dick	Wallace, S.	1987

KORNFELD, ROBERT
Dream within a Dream	Currie, R.	1984
Ligeia	Currie, R.	1987

KOSLOFF, DORIS L.
Goldilocks	Zaimont, J. L.	1986

KREYMBORG, ALFRED (1883–1966)
Privilege and Privation	Becker, J.	1939

LAANES, CARL
Cask of Amontillado	Currie, R.	1982

LaCHIUSA, MICHAEL JOHN
Desert of Roses	Moran, R.	1992
From the Towers	Moran, R.	1992
Tania	Davis, A.	1992

LAIDLAW, JACQUELINE
Man from Venus	Cannon, P.	1966

LAKE, J.
Vercingétorix	Kowalski, H.	1881

LAMB, JEROME
Two Tickets to Omaha	Hannay, R.	1960

LAMBOURNE, JEFFREY
Julia	Quilter, R.	1936

LANG, DANIEL (B. 1935)
Minutes till Midnight	Ward, R.	1982
(with comp.)		

LANGDON, WILLIAM C.
Judith	Chadwick, G.	1901

LANGFORD, ABRAHAM (1711–1774)
Lover His Own Rival	**	1736

LARNER, GERALD
Lion, the Witch	McCabe, J.	1969

LARSON, JACK
Lord Byron	Thomson, V.	1972

LA SHELLE, KIRKE
Ameer, The	Herbert, V.	1899
(with F. Ranken)		

LATHROP, GEORGE PARSONS
Scarlet Letter   Damrosch, W.   1896

LATOUCHE, JOHN (1917–1956)
Ballad of Baby Doe   Moore, D.   1956
Cabin in the Sky   Duke, V.   1940
(with L. Root)
Golden Apple   Moross, J.   1954

LAVERY, EMMET (B. 1902)
Tarquin   Krenek, E.   1941

LAW, ARTHUR (1844–1913)
Magic Opal   Albéniz, I.   1893

LAWLER, DENNIS
Sharp and Flat   Hook, J.   1813

LAWRENCE, ROBERT
Veil, The   Rogers, B.   1950

LEAVITT, NASON W.
Charter Oak   Leavitt, B. E. ca. 1885*
Frogs of Windham   Leavitt, B. E. ca. 1891*

LEBOWITZ, G.
Mr. Scrooge   Kalmanoff, M.   1966

LEDIARD, THOMAS
Britannia   Lampe, J. F.   1732

LEE, HENRY (1765–1836)
**Throw Physic to
the Dogs!**   Arnold, S.   1798

LEE, ROBIN
Little Mermaid   Boyd, A.   1978

LEHMAN, LEO
Arrangement, The   Davis, C.   1965

LEIGH, HENRY S. (1837–1883)
Cinderella   Farmer, J.   1883

LEITNER, IRVING
**Excitement at the
Circus**   Blank, A.   1969

LEMON, MARK (1809–1870)
Deer Stalker   Loder, E. J.   1841
Fridolin   Romer, F.   1840
Pacha's Bridal   Romer, F.   1836
Rob of the Fens   Romer, F.   1838

LENEL, JANE
**Young Goodman
Brown**   Lenel, L.   1963

LERNER, ALAN JAY (1918–1986)
Love Life   Weill, K.   1948

LERT, ERNST
Tenor, The   Weisgall, H.   1952
(with K. Shapiro)

LESSING, DORIS (B. 1919)
**Making of the
Representative**   Glass, P.   1988
**Marriage between Zones
3, 4, and 5**   Glass, P.   1997

LESTOCQ, W[ILLIAM] (D. 1920)
Sultan of Mocha   Cellier, A.   1874

LEVI, TONI MERGENTIME
Thanksgiving   Levi, P. A.   1977

LEVINE, RHODA
**Harrison Loved His
Umbrella**   Hollingsworth   1981

LEVY, CHARLES S.
Satan's Trap   Piket, F.   1960

LEVY, DEBORAH
Blood Wedding   LeFanu, N.   1992

LEWIS, JANET
Last of the Mohicans   Henderson, A.   1976
Legend, The   Murray, B.   1987
Swans, The   Henderson, A.   1986

LEWIS, MATTHEW GREGORY (1775–1818)
One O'Clock   King, M.   1811
Rich and Poor   Horn, C. E.   1812

LEWISOHN, LUDWIG (B. 1882)
Eternal Road   Weill, K.   1937
(with C. Alan)

LEYDEN, JAY
Bartleby   Aschaffenburg, W. 1964

LILLO, GEORGE (1693–1739)
Britannia   Carey, H.   1734
Silvia   **   1731

LIND, EDWARD
Freak Show   Taylor, C.   1975*

LINDSAY, MAURICE
Abbot of Drimock   Musgrave, T.   1962
Decision, The   Musgrave, T.   1967

LINEBERGER, JAMES
Survival of St. Joan   Ruffin, G./H.
                            Ruffin   1971

LINEK, STEPHEN N.
Voice, The   Kondorossy, L. 1954
(with S. Hall)

LINLEY, GEORGE (1798–1865)
Catherine Grey   Balfe, M.   1837
Gipsy's Warning   Benedict, J.   1838
(with R. B. Peake)

LINN, JOHN BLAIR (1777–1804)
Bourville Castle   Carr, B.   1797

MACKAYE, PERCY W. (B. 1875)
Canterbury Pilgrims	De Koven, R.	1917
Immigrants, The	Converse, F.	1914
Rip Van Winkle	De Koven, R.	1920

MACKENZIE, ELIZABETH
Incognita	Wellesz, E.	1951

MACKENZIE, SCOBIE (B. 1906)
Jolly Roger	Leigh, W.	1933
(with Clinton-Baddely)		

MACLEOD, FIONA [WILLIAM SHARP]
Immortal Hour	Boughton, R.	1914

MACNALLY, LEONARD (1752–1820)
Cottage Festival	Giordani, T.	1796
Critic upon Critic	**	ca. 1792
Richard Coeur de Lion	Shield, W.	1786
Robin Hood	Shield, W.	1784
(with E. Lysaght)		
Ruling Passion	Cogan, P.	1778
Tristram Shandy	**	1783

MACY, JOHN ALBERT (1877–1932)
Sacrifice, The	Converse, F.	1911
(with comp.)		

MAGUIRE, MATTHEW
Chaos	Gordon, M.	1994

MALAMUD, BERNARD (1914–1986)
Magic Barrel	Blitzstein, M.	1963*

MALASCH, ROB
Photographer, The	Glass, P.	1982
(with comp.)		

MALET, EDWARD (1837–1908)
Harold	Cowen, F.	1895

MALLETT, DAVID (1705?–1765)
Alfred (with Thomson)	Arne, T. A.	1740
Britannia	Arne, T. A.	1755

MALLOCH, DOUGLAS (1877–1938)
Enchanter, The	Holbrooke, J.	1915

MALOUF, DAVID (B. 1934)
Baa Baa Black Sheep	Berkeley, M.	1993
Voss	Meale, R.	1982

MALTBY, A.
Don Quixote	Clay, F.	1876
(with H. Paulton)		

MANDEL, MEL
Cubana, La	Henze, H. W.	1974

MANLOVE, JOHN
Christopher Sly	Argento, D.	1963

MARCH, GEORGE (1834–1922)
Follies of a Night	Gabriel, V.	187?

MARCH, LUCILE
Necklace, The	Bohrnstedt, W.	1956

MAREN, ROGER
Double Trouble	Mohaupt, R.	1954

MARK, MICHAEL
Magic Fishbone	Chapin, T.	1988
(lyrics)		

MARKHAM, EDWIN
Undine	Ware, H.	1923

MARKOE, PETER (1752–1792)
Reconciliation, The	**	1790

MARQUIS, NITA
Rubios, Los	Moore, M.	1931

MARSH, EDWARD
Pathelin	Josephs, W.	1963
Rebecca	Josephs, W.	1983

MARSHALL, JANE
Kumana	Kanitz, E.	1953

MARTIN, R.
Joan	Ford, E.	1890

MARTIN, THOMAS PHILIP
Tartuffe	Mechem, K.	1980

MARZIALS, T. J. H.
Esmerelda	Thomas, A. G.	1883
(with A. Randegger)		

MASON, HAROLD
Rapunzel	Brooks, R.	1971

MASON, JOHN HOPE
Journey, The	Metcalf, J.	1981

MASON, TIMOTHY
Emperor's New Clothes	Larsen, L.	1979

MASS, WILLIAM
Ruby, The	Dello Joio, N.	1955

MASTEROFF, JOSEPH
Desire under the Elms	Thomas, E.	1978

MATHEUS, JOHN FREDERICK
Ouanga	White, C. C.	1932

MAURA, SISTER (B. 1916)
Dialogues	Bauman, J.	1987

MAYERS, DANIEL
Blake	Adams, L.	1985

McCLATCHY, J. D.
Emmeline	Picker, T.	1996
Mario and the Magician	Thorne, F.	1994
Question of Taste	Schuman, W.	1989

McCORD, DAVID
Gift of the Magi   Warren, B.   1985

McCRAE, HUGH (B. 1876)
Ship of Heaven   Hill, A.   1923

McDONAGH, DONAGH
Patrick   Potter, A. J.   1965

McGLASHAN, LEN
Amorous Judge   Gross, E.   1965
(with S. Austin)

McGRATH, JOHN (B. 1935)
Behold the Sun   Goehr, A.   1985
(with comp.)

McINERNEY, SALLY (B. 1946)
Story of Mary O'Neill   LeFanu, N.   1989

McKINLAN
Francis the First   Loder, E. J.   1838

McLARNON, GERARD
Gentle Spirit   Taverner, J.   1977
Thérèse   Taverner, J.   1979

McLELLAN, C[HARLES] M[ORTON]
S[TEWART] (1865–1916)
Pink Lady   Caryll, I.   1911
Puritania   Kelley, E. S.   1892

McNALLY, LEONARD (1752–1820)
Tristram Shandy   Arne, M.   1783

McNEIL, JANET
Finn and the Black
Hag   Warren R.   1959
Graduation Ode   Warren, R.   1963

McPHEE, COLIN
Commission, The   Cowell, H.   1954

MEDLEY, MAT. SEE ASTON, WALTER.

MEGROTH, EDWARD J.
Goodman Brown   Fink, H.   1968

MELTZER, C. H.
Sunken Bell   Ruggles, C.   1912–23*

MENDEZ, MOSES (D. 1758)
Chaplet, The   Boyce, W.   1749
Double Disappointment **   1746
Robin Hood   Burney, C.   1750
Shepherd's Lottery   Boyce, W.   1751

MENDOZA, JOE
Dancing Master   Arnold, M.   1962
Spur of the Moment   Halahan, G.   1959

MENOTTI, GIAN CARLO (B. 1911)
Hand of Bridge   Barber, S.   1959
Introductions and
Good-Byes   Foss, L.   1960
Vanessa   Barber, S.   1958

MEREDITH, WILLIAM
Bottle Imp   Whiton, P.   1958

MERINGTON, MARGUERITE (1857–1951)
Daphne   Bird, A.   1895

MERRY, ROBERT (1755–1798)
Magician No Conjuror   Mazzinghi, J.   1792

MEYERS, JOHN
Sack of Calabasas   Fletcher, G.   1964
(with comp.)

MICHAELS, STUART
Specialist, The   Rodgers, L.   1978

MILES, WILLIAM AUGUSTUS (1753–1817)
Artifice, The   Arne, M.   1780
Summer Amusement   Arnold, S.   1779
(with M. P. Andrews)

MILLAY, EDNA ST. VINCENT (1892–1950)
King's Henchman   Taylor, D.   1927

MILLER, GLEN
Audience, The   Dembo, R.   1981*

MILLER, JAMES (1706–1744)
Coffee House   Carey, H.   1738
Hospital for Fools   Arne, T. A.   1739
Picture, The   Arne, T. A.   1745

MILLER, W. J.
Dante and Beatrice   Philpot, S. R.   1889

MILLIET, PAUL (B. 1858)
Amy Robsart   de Lara, I.   1893
(with A. Harris)

MILLINGEN, JOHN G. (1782–1862)
Bee-Hive, The   Horn, C. H.   1811
Illustrious Stranger   Nathan, I.   1827
(with J. Kenney)
Triboulet   Nathan, I.   1840

MILLINGTON, FRANCIS
Fall of the House of
Usher   Rugar, M. H.   1953

MILLS, E. R.
Anachronism, The   Franchetti, A.   1956
Dowser, The   Franchetti, A.   1956
Maypole, The   Franchetti, A.   1952

MILLS, ROSWELL GEORGE
Grande Bretèche, La   Claflin, A.   1957

MILNER, HENRY M.
Challenge, The   Cooke, T. S.   1834

MILNS, WILLIAM (1761–1801)
Flash in the Pan   Hewitt, J.   1798

MILTON, JOHN (1608–1674)
Comus   Lawes, H.   1634

MIRRIAM, LILLIE FULLER
| Osseo | Noyes-Greene, E. | 1917 |

MITCHELL, ADRIAN (B. 1932)
| Houdini | Schat, P. | 1979 |
| Ledge, The | Bennett, R. R. | 1961 |

MITCHELL, JOSEPH
| Highland Fair | ** | 1731 |

MITCHELL, LOFTON
| And the Walls | Roosevelt, W. | 1976 |

MITCHISON, NAOMI (B. 1897)
| Corn King | Easdale, B. | 1950 |

MITFORD, MARY RUSSELL (1786–1855)
| Sadak and Kalasrade | Packer, C. | 1835 |

MOELLER, PHILIP
| Helena's Husband | Gruenberg, L. | 1938 |

MONACO, RICHARD
| Politics of Harmony | Wuorinen, C. | 1968 |

MONSOUR, SALLY
| Pandora's Box | Effinger, C. | 1962 |

MONTAGUE, ELIZABETH
| School for Wives | Liebermann, R. | 1955 |

MONTCRIEFF, WILLIAM T. (1794–1857)
| Actors al fresco | Cooke, T. S. | 1823 |
| Giovanni in London | ** | 1817 |

MONTEFIORE, JACOB L.
| Don John of Austria | Nathan, I. | 1847 |

MONTGOMERY, J. SHERWOOD
| Rip Van Winkle | Rockwell, J. | 1989 |

MOORE, JONATHAN
| East and West | McQueen, I. | 1995 |

MOORE, MARIANNE
| Fables | Rorem, N. | 1971 |

MOORE, MAVOR
| Louis Riel | Somers, H. | 1967 |
| (with J. Languirand) | | |

MOORE, THOMAS
| Gipsey Prince | Kelly, M. | 1801 |
| M.P. | King, M. P. | 1811 |

MOOREHEAD, JOHN
| Birds of a Feather | Moorehead/ Calcott | 1796 |

MORELAND, DONALD
Chinchilla	Fink, M.	1986
Conquistador, The	Fink, M.	1997
Susanna and the Elders	Fink, M.	1955

MORGAN, EDWIN
| Charcoal Burner | Wilson, T. | 1969 |
| Columba | Leighton, K. | 1981 |

MORGAN, JOHN
| Magician, The | Hoddinott, A. | 1976 |

MORGAN, MACNAMARA (D. 1762)
| Sheep Shearing | Arne, T. A. | 1754 |

MORGAN, PETER
| Sacrapant | Aston, P. | 1967 |

MORLEY, MALCOLM
| Trevallion | Phillips, R. | 1956 |
| (with P. Phillips) | | |

MORRIS, GEORGE P.
| Maid of Saxony | Horn, C. E. | 1842 |

MORRIS, WILLIAM
| Rapunzel | Harrison, L. | 1959 |

MORRISON, BLAKE
| Doctor Ox's Experiment | Bryars, G. | 1988 |

MORSE, WOOLSON
| Merry Monarch | Sousa, J. P. | 1890 |
| (with J. C. Goodwin) | | |

MORTON, EDWARD
| San Toy | Jones, S. | 1899 |
| (with Greenbank, Ross) | | |

MORTON, JOHN M.
| Barbers of Bassora | Hullah, J. | 1837 |
| Dragon, The | Lee, G. A. | 1834 |

MORTON, THOMAS
Blind Girl	Reeve, W.	1801
Children in the Wood	Arnold, S.	1793
Columbus	Reinagle, A.	1797
Henri Quatre	Bishop, H. R.	1820
Invincibles, The	Lee, G. A.	1828
Knight of Snowdoun	Bishop, H. R.	1811
Roland for an Oliver	Bishop, H. R.	1819
Slave, The	Bishop, H. R.	1816

MOSS, J.
| Good Life | Silverman, S. | 1986 |

MOTTEUX, PETER ANTHONY (1663–1718)
Acis and Galatea	Eccles, J.	1701
Arsinoe	Clayton, T.	1705
Island Princess	Purcell, D.	1699
Loves of Mars and Venus	Eccles, J./ Finger, G.	1696
Rape of Europa	Eccles, J.	1694
Temple of Love	Fedelli, G.	1706
Thomyris	Pepusch, J.	1707

MOTTLEY, JOHN (1692–1750)
| Craftsman, The | ** | 1728 |

MOUBRAY, GEORGE
Devil of a Lover | Attwood, T. | 1798

MOULTON, HERBERT
Selfish Giant | Hollingsworth, | 1981
(with comp.) | S.
Twelfth Night | Wilson, J. | 1969

MOULTRIE, GEORGE (FL. 1790–1800)
False and True | Arnold, S. | 1798

MOYLE, GILBERT
Sunset Trail | Cadman, C. W. | 1922

MULDOON, PAUL (B. 1951)
Shining Brow | Hagen, D. | 1992
Vera of Las Vegas | Hagen, D. | 1996

MÜLLER, HEINER (B. 1929)
Forest, The | Byrne, D. | 1988
(with D. Pinckney)

MURDOCH, IRIS (B. 1919)
Servants, The | Mathias, W. | 1980

MURDOCH, JOHN
Tamburlaine | Murdoch, E. | 1971

MURPHY, ARTHUR (1727–1805)
Tears and Triumphs of
Parnassus (with Lloyd) Stanley, J. | 1760

MURRAY, GILBERT (1866–1957)
Alkestis | Boughton, R. | 1922
Hippolytus | Drysdale, L. | 1905

MURRAY, JOHN
Order of Good Cheer | Willan, H. | 1928

NAGEL, CHARLES
Merry Freaks | Nathan, I. | 1843
Mock Catalani | Nagel, C. | 1842

NAPIER, HAMPDEN
Freebooters, The | Hawes, W. | 1827
Not for Me | Hawes, W. | 1828
Oracle, The | Hawes, W. | 1826

NARDI, MARCIA
Beatrice | Hoiby, L. | 1959

NEEDHAM, MARIAN
Death of Baldur | Bedford, D. | 1980
(with T. Bagg)

NELSON, FRANK H.
Widow, The | Lavallée, C. | 1882

NELSON, GLEN
Dead, The | Boren, M. | 1993

NEVILLE, EDWARD
Plymouth in an
Uproar | Dibdin, C. | 1779

NEWBOLDT, HENRY
Travelling Companion Stanford, C. | 1919

NEWMAN, MORDECAI
Dreyfus | Cotel, M. | 1985

NEWSOM, JEREMY
Letters, Riddles | Nyman, M. | 1991

NEWTON, NORMAN
Seabird Island | Healey, D. | 1977

NICHOLAS, CLAIRE
Clock, The | Rieti, V. | 1960
Pet Shop | Rieti, V. | 1958

NICOLL, BRUCE (B. 1912)
Sweetwater Affair | Beadell, R. | 1961

NIEBOER, ROGER
Snow Leopard | Harper, W. | 1989

NIGGLI, JOSEPHINA
Sunday Costs Five
Pesos | Haubiel, C. | 1950

NISCEMI, MAITA DI
CIVIL warS | Glass, P. | 1984
(with R. Wilson)
Naked Revolution | Soldier, D. | 1997

NIXON, G. DAVID
Rich Man, Poor Man | Hopkins, A. | 1969

NOBLE, THOMAS
Persian Hunters | Horn, C. E. | 1817

NOLTE, CHARLES
Dream of Valentino | Argento, D. | 1994

NOWRA, LOUIS (B. 1950)
Inner Voices | Howard, B. | 1977
Whitsunday | Howard, B. | 1988

NYMAN, MICHAEL (B. 1944)
Down by the Greenwood
Side | Birtwistle, H. | 1969

OAKES, MEREDITH
Edward John Eyre | Conyngham, B. | 1971
Triumph of Beauty
and Deceit | Barry, G. | ca. 1990*

OATES, JOYCE
Black Water | Duffy, J. | 1997

ODELL, THOMAS
Patron, The | ** | 1729

ODINGSELLS, GABRIEL (1690–1734)
Bays's Opera | ** | 1730

ODINOV, OREL
Hannah (with comp.) | Lehrman, L. | 1980

OERKE, ANDREW
Enchanted Canary | Stevens, N. | 1961

O'HARA, KANE (1714–1782)

April Day	Arnold, S.	1777
Golden Pippen	Fischer, J. A.	1773
Midas	**	1762
Tom Thumb	Markordt, J.	1780
Two Misers	Dibdin, C.	1775

OHLSON, E. E.

| Rose and the Ring | Leginska, E. | 1932* |

O'KEEFFE, JOHN (1747–1833)

Agreeable Surprise	Arnold, S.	1781
Banditti, The	Arnold, S.	1781
Basket Maker	Arnold, S.	1790
Birth-Day, The	Arnold, S.	1783
Britain's Brave Tars!!	Attwood, T.	1797
Castle of Andalusia	Arnold, S.	1782
Constant Maid	Carter, T.	1788
Czar, The	Shield, W.	1790
Dead Alive	Arnold, S.	1781
Farmer, The	Shield, W.	1787
Fontainbleau	Shield, W.	1784
Gretna Green (with C. Stuart)	Arnold, S.	1783
Highland Reel	Shield, W.	1788
Irish Mimic	Shield, W.	1795
Lad of the Hills	Shield, W.	1796
Love and War	Shield, W.	1787
Love in a Camp	Shield, W.	1786
Peeping Tom	Arnold, S.	1784
Poor Soldier	Shield, W.	1783
Positive Man	Arnold, S.	1782
Rival Soldiers	Shield, W.	1797
Shamrock, The	Shield, W.	1777
Siege of Curzola	Arnold, S.	1786
Son-in-Law	Arnold, S.	1779
Sprigs of Laurel	Shield, W.	1793
Wicklow Mountains	Shield, W.	1796

OLDHAM, J. H.

| Greek Kalends | Ridout, A. | 1956 |

OLDMIXON, JOHN

| Grove, The | Purcell, D. | 1700 |

OLESKER, LIZZIE

| Bohemians, The (with D. Brown) | Kirschner, B. | 1990 |

OLIVE, JOHN

| Silver Fox | Larsen, L. | 1979 |

OLON-SCRYMGEOUR, JOHN

Boor, The	Argento, D.	1957
Colonel Jonathan the Saint	Argento, D.	1961
Gardens of Artemis	Weisgall, H.	1959*
Masque of Angels	Argento, D.	1964
Miss Havisham's Fire	Argento, D.	1979
Miss Havisham's Wedding Night	Argento, D.	1981

| Shoemaker's Holiday | Argento, D. | 1967 |
| Sicilian Limes | Argento, D. | 1954 |

OPIE, MRS. [AMELIA ALDERSON] (1769–1853)

| Noble Outlaw | Bishop, H. R. | 1815 |

ORR, J.

| Trials of Psyche | Bruce, N. | 1971 |

OSO, ANNA MARIA DELL'

| Bride of Fortune | Whitehead, G. | 1991 |
| Pirate Moon | Whitehead, G. | 1986 |

OSTERHAUS, CARVETH

| Medea | Luke, R. | 1979 |

OTT, SUSAN

| Hello, World! | Mayer, W. | 1956 |

OULTON, WALLY CHAMBERLAIN

Happy Disguise	Giordani, T.	1784
Haunted Castle	Giordani, T.	1783
Irish Tar	Attwood, T.	1797
Sixty-Third Letter	Arnold, S.	1802

OXENFORD, EDWARD

| Safié | Hadley, H. | 1909 |
| Torquil | Harriss, C. | 1900 |

OXENFORD, JOHN

Dice of Death	Loder, E.	1835
Felix	Lutz, M.	1865
Helvellyn	Macfarren, G. A.	1864
Jessy Lea	Macfarren, G. A.	1863
Lily of Killarney (with D. Boucicault)	Benedict, J.	1862
Robin Hood	Macfarren, G. A.	1860
Sleeper Awakened	Macfarren, G. A.	1850
Soldier's Legacy	Macfarren, G. A.	1864

OXENHAM, JOHN

| Pageant of Darkness and Light | MacCunn, H. | 1908* |

PAIN, NESTA (B. 1905)

| Time for Growing | Hopkins, A. | 1967 |

PAPP, JOSEPH (1921–1991)

| Twelfth Night | Amram, D. | 1968 |

PARKER, LOUIS NAPOLEON (1852–1944)

| Masque of War and Peace | MacCunn, H. | 1900 |

PARRY, MENDELSSOHN

| Sylvia | Parry, J. | 1895 |

PASCAL, FLORIAN [JOSEPH BENJAMIN WILLIAMS] (1847–1923)

| No Cards (with W. S. Gilbert) | "Elliott, L." | 1869 |

PATRICK, ROBERT (B. 1937)
Richest Girl	Sandow, G.	1975

PAULTON, HARRY (1842–1917)
Black Crook	Clay, F.	1872
(with J. Paulton)		
Cymbia	Pascal, F.	1883
Don Quixote	Clay, F.	1876
(with A. Maltby)		

PAULTON, JOSEPH
Black Crook	Clay, F.	1872
(with H. Paulton)		

PAYNE, JOHN HOWARD (1791–1852)
Clari	Bishop, H. R.	1823
Tyrolese Peasant	Bishop, H. R.	1832

PAYNE, R.
Open the Gates	Lee, D.-K.	1951

PAYNTER, ELIZABETH
Voyage to St. Brendan	Paynter, J.	1979

PAZILLO, JOSEPH
Cats' Corner	Riley, D.	1983*
Rappaccini's Daughter	Riley, D.	1981–84*

PEABODY, JOSEPHINE PRESTON (1874–1922)
Legend of the Piper	Freer, E E.	1925

PEAKE, RICHARD BRINSLEY (1792–1847)
Before Breakfast	Barnett, J.	1826
Bottle Imp	Rodwell, G.	1828
Climbing Boy	Hawes, W.	ca. 1834*
Cornish Miners	Rodwell, G.	1827
Evil Eye	Rodwell, G.	1831
Gipsy's Warning	Benedict, J.	1838
(with G. Linley)		
Spring Lock	Rodwell, G.	1829

PEARCE, JON (B. 1937)
Outcasts of Poker Flat	Beckler, S. R.	1960

PEARCE, WILLIAM
Arrived at Portsmouth	Shield, W.	1794
Death of Captain Faulkner	Arnold, S.	1795
Hartford Bridge	Shield, W.	1792
Midnight Wanderers	Shield, W.	1793
Netly Abbey	Shield, W.	1794
Nunnery, The	Shield, W.	1785
Windsor Castle	**	1795

PEATTIE, ELIA W.
Massimilliano	Freer, E. E.	1926

PENICK, DOUGLAS (B. 1944)
Ashoka's Dream	Lieberson, P.	1997

PENNYMAN, RUTH
Robin Hood	Tippett, M.	1934
(with Ayerst, comp.)		

PERRY, ALFRED
Volpone	Antheil, G.	1953

PERSONS, WENDE
Patience and Sarah	Kimper, P.	1996

PETERSON, WILLIAM M.
Enchanted Garden	Shaughnessy, R.	1972*

PFLANZER, HOWARD
Dream Beach	Sahl, M.	1988

PHILLIPS, ALBERTA
Don't We All?	Phillips, B.	1949

PHILLIPS, EDWARD
Britons, Strike Home	**	1739
Chamber-Maid, The	**	1730
Livery Rake	**	1733
Mock Lawyer	**	1733

PHILLIPS, JOHN MICHAEL
Tailor of Gloucester	Young, D.	1991*
(with comp.)		

PHILLIPS, PHILIP
Trevallion	Phillips, R.	1956
(with M. Morley)		

PHILLIPS, THOMAS
Britannia	Arne, T. A.	1734
Rival Captains	**	1736

PICKMAN, HESTER
Pot of Fat	Chanler, T.	1955

PIGUENIT, D. G.
Don Quixote	Arnold, S.	1774

PILON, FREDERICK (1750–1788)
Fair American	Carter, T.	1782
Siege of Gibraltar	Shield, W.	1780

PINCKNEY, DARRYL (B. 1935)
Forest, The	Byrne, D.	1988
(with H. Müller)		
Time Rocker	Reed, L.	1997

PINERO, ARTHUR WING (1855–1934)
Beauty Stone	Sullivan, A. S.	1898

PIPER, MYFANWY (1911–1996)
Death in Venice	Britten, B.	1973
Owen Wingrave	Britten, B.	1971
Rajah's Diamond	Hoddinott, A.	1979
Trumpet Major	Hoddinott, A.	1981
Turn of the Screw	Britten, B.	1954

PLAICE, STEPHEN
Misper	Lunn, J.	1997

PLANCHÉ, JAMES ROBINSON (1796–1880)
Amoroso	Cooke, T. S.	1818
Cortez	Bishop, H. R.	1823
Court Masque	Dawes, W.	1833

Drama at Home	Reed, T. G.	1844
Fortunate Isles	Bishop, H. R.	1840
Frozen Lake	Reeve, G. W.	1824
Golden Fleece	Reed, T. G.	1845
Graciosa and Percinet	**	1845
Hofer	Bishop, H. R.	1830
Jewess, The	Cooke, T.	1835
Law versus Love	Linley, G.	1862
Lilla	**	1825
Love Charm	Bishop, H. R.	1831
Love's Triumph	Wallace, V.	1862
Maid Marian	Bishop, H. R.	1822
Mason of Buda	Rodwell, G.	1828
Oberon	Weber, C. M. von	1826
Pay to My Order	Horn, C. E.	1827
(with W. H. Armstrong)		
Red Mask	Cooke, T. S.	1834
Rencontre, The	Bishop, H. R.	1827
Romance of a Day	Bishop, H. R.	1831
Siege of Corinth	Cooke, T. S.	1836

PLATT, J.

Angelo	Ridout, A.	1971
Cat, The (with N. Platt)	Ridout, A.	1971
Selfish Giant	Ridout, A.	1977

PLATT, NORMAN (B. 1920)

Cat, The (with J. Platt)	Ridout, A.	1971
Falcon, The	Cole, H.	1968
Pardoner's Tale	Ridout, A.	1971

PLOMER WILLIAM (1913–1976)

Burning Fiery		
Furnace	Britten, B.	1966
Curlew River	Britten, B.	1964
Gloriana	Britten, B.	1953
Prodigal Son	Britten, B.	1968

PLOTKIN, CARY

My Kinsman	Saylor, B.	1976

PLOTWELL, JOAN (PSEUD.)

Ragged Uproar	**	1754

PLOWDEN, FRANCES (D. 1827)

Virginia	Arnold, S.	1800

POCOCK, ISAAC (1782–1835)

Antiquary, The	Bishop, H. R.	1820
(with D. Terry)		
Doom-Kiss, The	Bishop, H. R.	1832
For England, Ho!	Bishop, H. R.	1813
Harry le Roi	Bishop, H. R.	1813
Heir of Vironi	Bishop, H. R.	1817
Home Sweet Home	Bishop, H. R.	1829
John of Paris	Bishop, H. R.	1814
Libertine, The	Bishop, H. R.	1817
Magpie or Maid	Bishop, H. R.	1815
Miller and His Men	Bishop, H. R.	1813
Montrose	Bishop, H. R.	1822
Peveril of the Peak	Horn, C. E.	1826

Rob Roy MacGregor	Davy, J.	1818

POGUE, KATE

Man Who Corrupted		
Hadleyville	Nelson, R.	1986*
Mask of Evil	Mollicone, H.	1982
Starbird, The	Mollicone, H.	1979

POLLOCK, ALICE L.

Cleopatra's Night	Hadley, H.	1920

POLLON, MICHAEL

Judgment Day	Perl, P.	1951

PONS, G.

Cinderella	Lacy, M. R.	1830

POOLE, JOHN (1786?–1872)

Hamlet Travestie	Bray, J.	1811

PORTAL, ABRAHAM

Cadi of Bagdad	Linley Jr., T.	1778

PORTER, ANDREW (B. 1928)

Emperor's New		
Clothes	Sessions, R.	1978–84*
Song of Majnun	Sheng, B.	1992
Tempest, The	Eaton, J.	1985

PORTER, PETER

Orpheus	Burgon, G.	1982

PORTER, RUSSELL

Early Dawn	Lockwood, N.	1961
Hanging Judge	Lockwood, N.	1964

POTTER, HENRY

Decoy, The	**	1733

POTTER, JOHN (FL. 1754–1804)

Choice of Apollo	Yates, W.	1765

POUNTNEY, DAVID

Doctor of Myddfai	Davies, P. M.	1996
Donkey, The	Oliver, S.	1973

POWELL, GEORGE (1658?–1714)

Brutus of Alba	Purcell, D.	1696
(prob. librettist, with J. Verbruggen)		

POWELL, MRS. H. W.

All in a Garden Fair	Tonning, G.	1913

POWELL, MARILYN

Nosferatu	Peters, R.	1993

POWERS, DENNIS

Christmas Carol	Hoiby, L.	1987
(with L. Williamson)		

PRATT, WILLIAM W. (1821–1864)

Ten Nights in a		
Bar-Room	**	1858

PRIESTLY, JOHN BOYNTON

Olympians, The	Bliss, A.	1949

PRUSLIN, STEPHEN
Punch and Judy Birtwistle, H. 1968

PRYCE, RICHARD (1864–1942)
Samuel Pepys Coates, A. 1929
(with W. P. Drury)

PRYCE-JONES, ALAN
Nelson Berkeley, L. 1954

PRYOR, MARY ANNE
Intruder, The Starer, R. 1956

PURSER, J. W. R.
Bell, The Purser, J. 1972

QUILKIN, FRANK
Vercingetorix Smolanoff, M. 1973*

RADFORD, MAISIE
Morvoren Cannon, P. 1964

RADFORD, WINIFRED
Ten O'Clock Call Hopkins, A. 1956

RADIC, LEONARD
Affair, The Werder, F. 1974
Bellyful Werder, F. 1975
General, The Werder, F. 1966

RADICE, WILLIAM
Snatched by the Gods Vir, P. 1992

RAFTER, CAPTAIN
Heart of Midlothian ** 1849

RAINE, CRAIG
Electrification of the Soviet
Union Osborne, N. 1987
Sarajevo Osborne, N. 1994

RALPH, JAMES
Fashionable Lady ** 1730

RAMSAY, ALLAN (1686–1758)
Gentle Shepherd ** 1729

RAMSEY, JAROLD
Lodge of Shadows Adler, S. 1988

RANDAL, JUDITH
Babar the Elephant Berezowsky, N. 1953
(with D. H. Heyward)

RANDALL, JOHN (FL. 1732)
Disappointment, The ** 1732

RANDEGGER, ALBERTO (1832–1911)
Esmerelda Thomas, A. G. 1883
(with Marzials)

RANKEN, FREDERIC
Ameer, The Herbert, V. 1899
(with K. La Shelle)

Nancy Brown Hadley, H. 1903
(with G. Broadhurst)

RATNER, CARL J.
Lifework of Juan Diaz Rapchak, L. 1990

RAWLENCE, CHRISTOPHER
Man Who Mistook
His Wife Nyman, M. 1986

RAYMOND, BILL
VALIS Machover, T. 1987
(with C. Ikam, comp.)

RAYMOND, RICHARD J.
Robert the Devil Barnett, J. 1830

REANEY, JAMES (B. 1952)
Crazy to Kill Beckwith, J. 1989
Night Blooming
Cereus Beckwith, J. 1959
Shivaree Beckwith, J. 1982

REAVEY, JEAN
Who Stole the American
Crown Jewels? Siegel, N. 1971

REDDING, JOSEPH D. (1859–1924)
Atonement of Pan Hadley, H. 1912
Natoma Herbert, V. 1911
Semper virens Hadley, H. 1923

REECE, ROBERT (1838–1891)
Cattarina Clay, F. 1874
In Possession Clay, F. 1871

REED, JOSEPH (1723–1787)
Tom Jones Arnold, S. 1769

REED, STUART
Cyrano de Bergerac Herbert, V. 1899

REESE, H.
Primal Void Vincent, J. 1969*
(with comp.)

REGAN, SYLVIA
Golem, The Ellstein, A. 1962
(with comp.)

REID, ALASTAIR
Curious Fern Kupferman, M. 1957
Gilded Cage Lees, B. 1964
Griffelkin Foss, L. 1955
Voices for a Mirror Kupferman, M. 1957

REID, JOHN
Lost Child Ridout, G. 1975

REITER, SEYMOUR
Cask of Amontillado Provenzano, A. 1968

RENARD, JOSEPH
Pizza del destino Cohen, S. 1979*

RESTON, JAMES, JR.
Reverend Jim   Eaton, J.   1989

REYNOLDS, FREDERICK (1764–1841)
Bridal Ring   Condell/Pelissier 1812
**Burgomaster of
  Saardam**   Bishop, H. R.   1818
Caravan   Reeve, W.   1803
Comedy of Errors   Bishop, H. R.   1819
Crusade, The   Shield, W.   1790
Don John   Bishop, H. R.   1821
Duke of Savoy   Bishop, H. R.   1817
Exile, The   Mazzanghi, J.   1809
Free Knights   Mazzinghi, J.   1810
Humorous Lieutenant Bishop, H. R.   1817
Illustrious Traveller **   1818
**Merry Wives of
  Windsor**   Horn, C. E., et al. 1824
**Midsummer Night's
  Dream**   Bishop, H. R.   1816
Taming of the Shrew Braham/Cooke   1828
Virgin of the Sun   Bishop, H. R.   1812

REYNOLDS, G. N.
Bantry Bay   Reeve, W.   1797

REYNOLDS-ANDERSON, J. F.
Victorian   Edwards, J.   1883

RICE, CALE YOUNG (1872–1942)
Yolanda of Cyprus   Loomis, C.   1929

RICE, ELMER (1892–1967)
Street Scene   Weill, K.   1946
  (with L. Hughes)

RICE, TIM
Evita   Lloyd Webber   1978
**Jesus Christ
  Superstar**   Lloyd Webber   1971

RICHARDS, MR.
Marriage-Office   Bates, W.   1777

RICHARDS, M. C.
Chanticleer   Barab, S.   1956

RICHARDSON, HOWARD
Dream Child   Mollicone, H.   1975

RIDER, SUE
Iron Man (with J. Vilé) Fox, M.   1987

RIDLER, ANNE
Departure, The   Maconchy, E.   1962
Jessie Tree   Maconchy, E.   1970

RILEY, EDWARD (1769–1829)
Spanish Patriots   Gilfert, C.   1809

ROACH, B.
Once upon a Moon   Victory, G.   1950

ROBERTS, DON
Captive, The   Wishart, P.   1960
Clandestine Marriage   Wishart, P.   1971
Clytemnestra   Wishart, P.   1974
Lady of the Inn   Wishart, P.   1983
Two in the Bush   Wishart, P.   1959

ROBERTS, J.
Rule Britannia   Arnold, S.   1794

ROBERTSON, T.
Constance   Clay, F.   1865

ROBERTSON, TIM
Lamentable Reign   Dreyfus, G.   1976

ROBINETTE, JOSEPH
Charlotte's Web   Strouse, C.   1989

ROBINSON, E. A.
**Isolt of the White
  Hands**   Hart, F.   1933

ROBINSON, JAMES
Child of the Wreck   Cooke, T. S.   1837

ROBINSON, THOMAS P.
Fantasy in Delft   Gilbert, H. F.   1919

RODDA, CHARLES
Marriage of Aude   Rogers, B.   1931

RODGERS, LOU
Island of Tomorrow   Fink, M.   1986

RODGERS, WILLIAM ROBERT (1909–1969)
Pit, The   Lutyens, E.   1947

ROEPKE, GABRIELA
White Butterfly   Leichtling, A.   1971
Zapata   Balada, L.   1985
  (with T. Capobianco)

ROGERS, ALEX
Abyssinia (with Shipp) Cook/Williams   1906

ROGERS, J. W.
Stranger of Manzano   Smith, J.   1946

ROLL, PHILIP
Blennerhasset   Giannini, V.   1939
  (with N. Corwin)

ROLT, RICHARD (1725?–1770)
Almena   Arne, M.   1764
Amintas   Arnold, S.   1769
  (with F. Tenducci)
Eliza   Arne, T. A.   1754
Royal Shepherd   Rush, G.   1764

ROOME, EDWARD (D. 1729)
Jovial Crew   **   1731

ROOT, LYNN (B. 1905)
Cabin in the Sky   Duke, V.   1940
  (with J. Latouche)

RORKE, PETER
Private, The — Werder, F. — 1969
Vicious Square — Werder, F. — 1971

ROSE, JOHN
Caernarvon Castle — Attwood, T. — 1793
Fairy Festival — Attwood, T. — 1797
Prisoner, The — Attwood, T. — 1792

ROSEN, ROSLYN
Fisherman's Wife — Stein, L. — 1955

ROSKAM, CLAIR
Sarah — Laderman, E. — 1958

ROSS, ADEN
Dreamkeepers — Carlson, D. — 1996

ROSS, ADRIAN (1859–1933)
Lucky Star — Caryll, I. — 1899
(with A. Hoppwood)
San Toy — Jones, S. — 1899
(with Morton, Greenbank)

ROSS, GEORGE M.
Boccaccio's
Nightingale — Trimble, L. — 1958

ROSS, SHERIDAN
Quentin Durward — Maclean, A. — 1893

ROSTEN, NORMAN (B. 1914)
Marilyn — Laderman, E. — 1993
Marquesa of O — Siegmeister, E. — 1982
Shadows among Us — Laderman, E. — 1968

ROWLANDS, DAVID
Blodwen — Parry, J. — 1878

ROYLE, J[OHN] F[ORBES] (1799–1858)
Gooseherd and the
Goblin — Smith, J. — 1947

RUDKIN, DAVID (B. 1936)
Broken Strings — Vir, P. — 1992
Grace of Todd — Crosse, G. — 1969
Inquest of Love — Harvey, J. — 1993
(with comp.)

RUSSO, GLORIA
Follies and Fancies — Allen, J. S. — 1987

RYAN, LACY (1694?–1760)
Cobler's Opera — ** — 1728

RYVES, ELIZABETH (1750–1797)
Prude, The — ** — 1765

SALOMON, ROBERT
Frog-Hopping — Boswell, W. — 1982

SALT, WALDO
Sandhog — Robinson, E. — 1954

SAMSON, F.
Marko the Miser — Musgrave, T. — 1963
(with comp.)

SAMPSON, JOANNA
Columbine — Davis, M. — 1973

SAMUELSEN, ERIC
Emma — Boren, M. — 1984

SANDERSON, RUTH HOWARD
Lion, The (with comp.) Franchetti, A. — 1950

SARGEANT, B.
Suncatcher, The — Franchetti, A. — 1973

SAUNDERS, JAMES (B. 1925)
Barnstable — Burt, F. — 1969

SAVAGE, R.
Mellstock Quire — Harper, E. — 1988

SAWYER, RUTH (1880–1970)
Princess and the
Vagabond — Freed, I. — 1948

SCANLON, MARIE C.
Tale from Chaucer — Gordon, P. — 1959

SCANNELL, VERNON
Cancelling Dark — Whelen, C. — 1965

SCAWEN, JOHN (FL. 1733–1790)
New Spain — Arnold, S. — 1790–83*

SCHILLER, ZOË LUND
Acres of Sky — Kreutz, A. — 1951
Sourwood Mountain — Kreutz, A. — 1959
University Greys — Kreutz, A. — 1954

SCHLESINGER, SARAH MARIE
Amazing Adventure — Adolphe, B. — 1995
Different Fields — Reid, M. — 1996

SCHMIDT, PAUL (B. 1934)
Alice — Waits, T. — 1992
Black Sea Follies — Silverman, S. — 1986

SCHMIDT, RICHARD P.
We're Back — Armour, E. — 1981

SCRYMGEOUR, JOHN OLON. SEE OLON-
SCRYMGEOUR, JOHN.

SELIG, PAUL
Three Visitations — Sherman, K. D. — 1996

SELWYN, DAVID
St. Patrick — Warren, R. — 1979

SENDAK, MAURICE (B. 1928)
Higglety Pigglety Pop! Knussen, O. — 1984
(with comp.)

SERLE, THOMAS JAMES (1798–1889)
Afrancesado — Lee, G. A. — 1837

Foresters, The	Loder, E.	1838
Shadow on the Wall	Thomson, J.	1835

SERVOSS, FIFI
Bok Choy Variations	Chen, E.	1995
(with Huff, Simonson)		

SETTLE, ELKANAH (1648–1724)
Fairy Queen (possib.)	Purcell, H.	1692
Lady's Triumph	**	1718
Orpheus and Euridice	Locke, M.	1673
Virgin Prophetess	Finger, G.	1701

SEXTON, ANNE (D. 1974)
Transformations	Susa, C.	1973

SHADWELL, THOMAS (1642–1692)
Psyche	Locke, M.	1675
Tempest, The	Bannister et al.	1674

SHAFFER, PETER (B. 1926)
Dumb Wife	Horovitz, J.	1953

SHANKS, EDWARD (1892–1953)
Fête Galante	Smyth, E.	1923

SHAPCOTT, THOMAS
Seven Deadly Sins	Brumby, C.	1970
Summer Carol	Brumby, C.	1991

SHAPIRO, DAVID
Funeral of Jan Palach	Beckley, C.	1990

SHAPIRO, KARL
Tenor, The (with Lert)	Weisgall, H.	1952

SHARP, EVELYN (1869–1955)
Loafer and the Loaf	Clarke, H. L.	1956
Poisoned Kiss	Vaughan Williams, R.	1936

SHARP, JAN
Lord Bateman	Forster, A.	1958

SHAW, CLEMENT B.
Frithiof	Freer, E. E.	1929

SHAW, SEBASTIAN
All at Sea	Shaw, G.	1952
(with M. Delamere)		

SHEPHERD, ESTHER (B. 1899)
Cowherd and the Sky Maiden	Verrall, J.	1952

SHERIDAN, RICHARD BRINSLEY (1751–1816)
Duenna, The	Linley Jr./ Linley Sr.	1775
Pizzaro	Kelly, M.	1799

SHERRIN, NEAL
Little Beggars	Saunders, M.	1958
(with C. Brahms)		

SHIPP, JESSE A. (1859–1934)
Abyssinia	Cook, W. M.	1906
(with A. Rogers)		
In Dahomey	Cook, W. M.	1903
(with P. L. Dunbar)		

SHIRLEY, JAMES
Cupid and Death	Gibbons, C.	1653
Triumph of Peace	Lawes, W., et al.	1634

SHIRLEY, WILLIAM (FL. 1739–1780)
Birth of Hercules	Arne, T. A.	1763

SHIRWEN, SUSAN
Holy Blood and Crescent Moon	Copeland, S.	1989

SHRAGER, SIDNEY
Royal Auction	Kanitz, E	1958
(with A. Chorney)		

SHULGASSER, MARK
Bon Appétit!	Hoiby, L.	1989
Italian Lesson	Hoiby, L.	1982
Tempest, The	Hoiby, L.	1986

SIDDONS, HENRY (1774–1815)
Russian Imposter	Addison, J.	1809

SIENA, JAMES
Photo-Op	Cummings, C.	1990

SIGNAIGO, JOHN AUGUSTINE
Vivandiere, The	Hewitt, J. H.	1863

SIMON, ROBERT A.
Beauty and the Beast	Giannini, V.	1938
Enchanted Kiss	Bennett, R. R.	1945
Endymion	Bennett, R. R.	1927
Garrick	Stoessel, A.	1937
Maria Malibran	Bennett, R. R.	1935
Rehearsal Call	Giannini, V.	1962
(with F. Swann)		

SIMONSON, ERICK
Bok Choy Variations	Chen, E.	1995
(with Servoss, Huff)		

SIMPSON, HELEN
Good Friday 1663	Westbrook, M./ Westbrook, K.	1995

SIMPSON, JOHN PALGRAVE (1807–1887)
Bianca	Balfe, M.	1860
Ida	Leslie, H.	1865
Letty	Balfe, M.	1871
Romance, The	Leslie, H.	1857

SIMS, G[EORGE] R[OBERT] (1847–1922)
Golden Ring	Clay, F.	1883
Merry Duchess	Clay, F.	1883

SKOFIELD, JAMES
Dracula Diary	Moran, R.	1994

SKELTON, GEOFFREY (B. 1916)
Arden Must Die   Goehr, A.   1967
(with E. Fried)

SLATER, MONTAGU (1902–1956)
Peter Grimes   Britten, B.   1945
Yerma   ApIvor, D.   1961

SLOBIN, MARK, TRANS., ARR.
David's Violin   Mogulesco, S.   1976
Shloyme Gorgl   **   1978
(with J., N. Slobin)

SMITH, CHARLES (1749?–1824)
Day at Rome   Attwood, T.   1798

SMITH, ELIHU HUBBARD (1771–1798)
Edwin and Angelina Pelissier, V.   1796

SMITH, HAROLD WENDELL (B. 1922)
**Command
Performance**   Middleton, R.   1961

SMITH, HARRY BACHE (1860–1936)
Begum, The   De Koven, R.   1887
Cyrano de Bergerac Herbert, V.   1899
Don Quixote   De Koven, R.   1889
Fortune Teller   Herbert, V.   1898
Foxy Quiller   De Koven, R.   1900
Free Lance   Sousa, J. P.   1905
Golden Butterfly   De Koven, R.   1908
Highwayman, The   De Koven, R.   1897
Idols' Eye   Herbert, V.   1897
Jupiter   Edwards, J.   1892
Maid Marian   De Koven, R.   1902
Mandarin, The   De Koven, R.   1896
Paris Doll   De Koven, R.   1897
Robin Hood   De Koven, R.   1891
Rob Roy   De Koven, R.   1894
Tzigaine   De Koven, R.   1895
Viceroy, The   Herbert, V.   1900
Wedding Trip   De Koven, R.   1911
(with F. De Gresac)

SMITH, MONICA
**Play of Mother
Courage**   McCabe, J.   1974

SMITH, SYDNEY GOODSIR (1915–1975)
Full Circle   Orr, R.   1968

SMOLIN, PAULINE
Judith   Smith, D.   1982

SMOLLETT, TOBIAS (1721–1771)
Alceste   Handel, G. F.   1749

SMOLOVER, RAYMOND
Golem, The   Weiner, L.   1957
Isaac Levy   Piket, F.   1956

SNELL, GORDON
Gentleman's Island Horovitz, J.   1959

Hands across the Sky Hopkins, A.   1959

SOANE, GEORGE (1790–1860)
Aladdin   Bishop, H. R.   1826
Faustus   Bishop, H. R.   1825
Freischütz, Der   Bishop, H. R.   1824
Masaniello   Bishop, H. R.   1825
Night Dancers   Loder, E. J.   1846

SOLANO, BERNARDO
El Greco   Harper, W.   1993

SOUTER, DAVID H. (1862–1935)
Rajah of Shivapore Hill, A.   1917

SPAETH, SIGMUND (1885–1965)
Audition, The   Kalmanoff, M.   1968

SPENDER, STEPHEN (1909–1995)
Holy Devil   Nabokov, N.   1958
(with comp.)

SQUIRE, WILLIAM BARCLAY (1855–1927)
Veiled Prophet   Stanford, C.   1881

STAFFORD, ANN
Lucky Dollar   Kanitz, E.   1958

STAHL, IRWIN
**Red Rose and the
Briar**   Mopper, I.   1951

STALLINGS, LAURENCE
Deep River   Harling, W. F.   1926

STAMBLER, BERNARD (1910–1994)
Claudia Legare   Ward, R.   1978
Crucible, The   Ward, R.   1961
He Who Gets Slapped Ward, R.   1956
Ines de Castro   Pasatieri, T.   1976
Lady from Colorado Ward, R.   1964
Lady Kate   Ward, R.   1994
**Servant of Two
Masters**   Giannini, V.   1967

STAMPFER, JUDITH
Huckleberry Finn   Overton, H.   1971
(with comp.)

STANGÉ, STANISLAUS (D. 1917)
Brian Boru   Edwards, J.   1896
Dolly Varden   Edwards, J.   1901
Girls of Holland   De Koven, R.   1907
Goddess of Truth   Edwards, J.   1896
Madeleine   Edwards, J.   1894
Patriot, The   Edwards, J.   1908

STAVIS, BARRIE
Joe Hill   Bush, A.   1970

STEEGMULLER, FRANCIS
Big Black Box   Morgenstern, S. 1968

STEIN, ELLIOTT
Childhood Miracle   Rorem, N.   1955

STEIN, GERTRUDE (1874–1946)
Four Saints in Three
Acts   Thomson, V.   1933
Mother of Us All   Thomson, V.   1947

STEPHENS, HENRY P.
Lord Bateman   Solomon, E.   1882

STEPHENS, JAMES BRUNTON (1822–1897)
Fayette   Allen, G.   1892

STEPHENS, JOHN P.
Godfather Death   Meyerowitz, J.   1961
Simoon   Meyerowitz, J.   1950

STEPHENS, NAN BAGBY
Cabildo   Beach, A.   1932

STEPHENSON, B[ENJAMIN] C[HARLES]
(D. 1906)
Charity Begins at
Home   Cellier, A.   1872
Doris   Cellier, A.   1889
Dorothy   Cellier, A.   1886
Golden Web   Thomas, A. G.   1893
(with F. Corder)
Masque of Pandora   Cellier, A.   1881
Out of Sight   Clay, F.   1860

STEVENS, DAVID K. (1860–1946)
Azora   Hadley, H.   1917
Love's Sacrifice   Chadwick, G.   1923

STEVENS, GEORGE ALEXANDER (1710–1784)
Court of Alexander   Fisher, J. A.   1770
Trip to Portsmouth   Dibdin, C.   1773

STEVENS, K.
Padrone, The   Chadwick, G.   1912*

STEWART, GRANT (1871–1937)
Bianca   Hadley, H.   1918
Madeleine   Herbert, V.   1914

STILGOE, RICHARD
Phantom of the Opera Lloyd Weber, A. 1986
(with comp.)

STOKES, RICHARD L. (1882–1957)
Merry Mount   Hanson, H.   1933
Music Robber   Van Grove, I.   1926

STOLZENBACH, NORMA F.
In the Name of
Culture   Bimboni, A.   1949

STOPES, MARIE (1880–1958)
Moon Maiden   Boughton, R.   1918
Sumida River   Raybould, C.   1916

STORR, CATHERINE
Flax into Gold   Cole, H.   1966

STOTCALS, GARY
Intruder, The   Feldman, J.   1984

STOW, RANDOLPH (B. 1935)
Eight Songs for a
Mad King   Davies, P. M.   1969
Miss Donnithorne's
Maggot   Davies, P. M.   1974

STRAHAN, LYNNE (B. 1938)
Gilt-Edged Kid   Dreyfus, G.   1976

STRAIGHT, MICHAEL
Death of the Virgin   Owen, R.   1981

STRASFOGEL, IAN
Icarus   Earls, P.   1982

STRAWN, RICHARD
Crimson Bird   Enebach, F.   1979

STREET, RICHARD
Black River
(with comp.)   Susa, C.   1975
Love of Don
Perlimplin (with comp.) Susa, C.   1984

STUART, CHARLES (FL. 1777–1791)
Gretna Green   Arnold, S.   1783
(with J. O'Keeffe)

STUART, D.
Earth Mother   Penberthy, J.   1957–
(with comp.)   59*

STURGIS, JULIAN R. (1848–1904)
Cricket on the Heart Mackenzie, A.   1914
Ivanhoe   Sullivan, A. S. 1891
Much Ado about
Nothing   Stanford, C.   1901
Nadeshda   Thomas, A. G.   1885

SULLIVAN, ARTHUR S. (1842–1900)
Happy Arcadia   Clay, F.   1872

SULLIVAN, M. J.
Lallah Rookh   Horn, C. E.   1818

SUMMERS, OLIVER
Zaida   Lutz, M.   1859

SUNDGAARD, ARNOLD (B. 1909)
Cumberland Fair   Wilder, A.   1953
Down in the Valley   Weill, K.   1948
Gallantry   Moore, D.   1958
Giants in the Earth   Moore, D.   1951
Long Way   Wilder, A.   1955
Lowland Sea   Wilder, A.   1952
Opening, The   Wilder, A.   1969
Promised Valley   Gates, C. M. ca. 1961*
Sunday Excursion   Wilder, A.   1953
Truth about
Windmills   Wilder, A.   1973

SUTHERLAND, DONALD
Cyrano de Bergerac Effinger, C. 1968
Requiem for a Rich
Young Man Lockwood, N. 1964

SUTTON, VERN
Christina Romana Larsen, L. 1988
Tumbledown Dick Larsen, L. 1980

SUTRO, ALFRED
Death of Tintagiles Collingwood, L. 1950

SWAN, JON
Aesop's Fables Russo, W. 1972
Shepherds' Christmas Russo, W. 1979

SWANN, FRANCIS
Rehearsal Call Giannini, V. 1962
(with R. A. Simon)

SWENSSON, EVELYN
Wind in the Willows Ritter, J. 1997

SWIFT, EDMUND LENTHAL (1777–1875)
Woman's Will Davy, J. 1820

SWINEY, OWEN (CA. 1675–1754)
Pyrrus and Demetrius Haym, N. 1708

SYNGE, J[OHN] M[ILLINGTON] (1871–1909)
Riders to the Sea Vaughan
Williams, R. 1937

TABER, EDWARD
Désirée Sousa, J. P. 1884

TATE, NAHUM (1652–1715)
Dido and Aeneas Purcell, H. ca. 1689

TAYLOR, BAYARD (1825–1878)
Faust Becker, J. J. 1951

TAYLOR, CHARLES H.
My Lady Molly Jones, S. 1903
(with Jessop, Greenbank)

TAYLOR, FREDERICK
Court and Cottage Clay, F. 1862

TAYLOR, TOM (1817–1880)
Wittikind and His
Brothers ** ca. 1852*

TCHKIRIDES, BILL
Hunting of the Snark Roberts, E. 1971

TENDUCCI, FERDINANDO (CA. 1735–1790)
Amintas (with R. Rolt) Arnold, S. 1769

TERRY, DANIEL
Antiquary, The Bishop, H. R. 1820
(with I. Pocock)
Barber of Seville Bishop, H. R. 1818
(with J. Fawcett)

Guy Mannering Attwood, T. 1816
Heart of Midlothian Bishop, H. R. 1819

TERRY, ELLEN
Perpetual Kanitz, E. 1961

TERRY, PATRICK
Moon and Sixpence Gardner, J. 1957

THACKERAY, THOMAS JAMES
Mountain Sylph Barnett, J. 1834

THEKLA, MOTHER (B. 1918)
Mary of Egypt Taverner, J. 1992

THEOBALD, LEWIS (1688–1744)
Decius and Paulina Galliard, J. 1718
Happy Captive Galliard, J. 1741
Orpheus and Eurydice Lampe, J. F. 1740
Orestes Pepusch, J. 1731
Pan and Syrinx Galliard, J. 1718

THOMSON, LYNN
Rent (with comp.) Larson, J. 1996

THOMPSON, A. M.
Rebel Maid Phillips, M. 1921
(with G. Dodson)
Tom Jones German, E. 1907

THOMPSON, BENJAMIN (1776–1816)
Oberon's Oath Parry, J. 1816

THOMPSON, C. PELHAM
Nothing Superfluous Lee, G. A. 1829

THOMPSON, FRANCIS (1859–1907)
Hound of Heaven Stewart, H. 1924

THOMPSON, JOHN
Enchanted Pear Tree Overton, H. 1950

THOMPSON, RICHARD
Room No. 12 Kanitz, E. 1958

THOMSON, JAMES (1700–1748)
Alfred (with D. Mallett) Arne, T. A. 1740

THOMSON, LYNN
Rent (with comp.) Larson, J. 1996

THORNLEY, WILFRID (1879–1926)
Angelus, The Naylor, E. 1909

TICKELL, RICHARD (1751–1793)
Camp, The Linley Sr., T. 1778
Carnival of Venice Linely Sr., T. 1781
Gentle Shepherd Linely Sr., T. 1781
Metamorphosis Jackson, W. 1783
(with comp.)

TILL, NICHOLAS
Albergo Empedocle Barker, P. 1990

TOBIN, JOHN (1770–1804)
Honey Moon Hewitt/Kelly 1805

TRACY, E.
Lucky-Peter's
Journey Williamson, M. 1968

TRACY, HENRY C.
In the Pasha's
Garden Seymour, J. 1935

TREVELYAN, ROBERT C.
Bride of Dionysus Tovey, D. 1929
Pearl Tree Bainton, E. L. 1944

TRICKETT, RACHEL
Antigone Joubert, J. 1954
Silas Marner Joubert, J. 1961

TROUTMAN, RON
Birth/Day Wolfe, N. 1993

TRUESDELL, FREDERICK
Night in Old Paris Hadley, H. 1924

TUNNICLIFFE, STEPHEN
Prisoner, The Joubert, J. 1973

TURPIN, ALLAN (?)
Box, The Hamm, C. 1961

TYLER, ROYALL (1757–1826)
May Day in Town 1787 New York

UPDIKE, JOHN (B. 1932)
Fisherman and His
Wife Schuller, G. 1970

USSACHEVSKY, VLADIMIR (1911–1990)
Boor, The (with comp.) Kay, U. 1968

VALENCY, MAURICE (B. 1903)
Feathertop Barnes, E. 1980

VARIAN, JOHN O.
Building of Bamba Cowell, H. 1917

VAUGHAN WILLIAMS, URSULA
David and Bathsheba Barlow, D. 1969
Melita Camilleri, C. 1968
Sofa, The Maconchy, E. 1959

VENABLES, CLARE
Country of the Blind Turnage, M.-A. 1997

VERBRUGGEN, JOHN (FL. 1688–1707?)
Brutus of Alba Purcell, D. 1696
(prob. librettist, with G. Powell)

VILÉ, JIM
Iron Man (with Rider) Fox, M. 1987
Sid the Serpent Fox, M. 1977
(with S. Vilé)

VILÉ, SUSAN
Sid the Serpent Fox, M. 1977
(with J. Vilé)

VINCENT, S.
Birthday of the Infanta Stoker, R. 1963

VOADEN, HERMAN (B. 1903)
Prodigal Son Jacobi, F. 1944

VOLKONAKIS, M.
Numbered, The Lutyens, E. 1965–67*

VORASSI, JOHN
Diva, The Ferris, W. 1987

WADSWORTH, MICHAEL
Passion and
Resurrection Harvey, J. 1981

WADSWORTH, STEPHEN (B. 1929)
Mistake, The Sheffer, J. B. 1981
Quiet Place Bernstein, L. 1983

WAINRIGHT, JONATHAN HOWARD
Rip Van Winkle Bristow, G. F. 1855

WALDRON, DANIEL GORDON (B. 1925)
Circus, The Chudacoff, E. 1953

WALDRON, FRANCIS
Love and Madness Arnold, S. 1795

WALKER, THOMAS (1698–1744)
Quaker's Opera ** 1728

WALLACE, PETER
Other Wise Man de Kenessey, S. 1996

WALTER, C. E.
Fall of Algiers Bishop, H. R. 1825

WALTER, E.
Lion and Androcles Eaton, J. 1974
(with D. Anderson)

WARD, ANTHONY
Toussaint Blake, D. 1977

WARD, CHARLES
Circassian Bride Bishop, H. R. 1809

WARD, EDWARD
Prisoner's Opera ** 1730
(prob. librettist)

WARD, HENRY
Happy Lovers ** 1736

WARNER, MARINA
In the House of Crossed
Desires Woolrich, J. 1996

WARREN, ROGER
Errors Wilson-Dickson 1980

WATKINS, DENNIS
Eighth Wonder John, A. 1995
(with comp.)

WATSON, DONALD
Bald Prima Donna   Kalmanoff, M.   1963

WATT, JILL
Johnson Preserv'd   Stoker, R.   1967

WEATHERLEY, F. E.
Lady of Longeford   Bach, L. E.   1896
(with A. G. Harris)

WEBER, MAX
Game of Cards   Franchetti, A.   1955

WEINSTEIN, ARNOLD
Casino Paradise   Bolcolm, W.   1989
Dynamite Tonite   Bolcom, W.   1963
Final Ingredient   Amram, D.   1965
Greatshot   Bolcom, W.   1969
McTeague   Bolcom, W.   1992
(with R. Altman)

WEISS, GEORGE DAVID
Queenie Pie   Ellington, E.   1986

WELLS, FRANCES
Carrion Crow   Fletcher, G.   1953

WESKER, ARNOLD
Caritas   Saxon, R.   1991

WEST, JESSAMYN (1907–1984)
Mirror for the Sky   Kubik, G.   1939

WEST, RAY B. JR. (B. 1908)
**Bride Comes to Yellow
   Sky**   Nixon, R.   1968

WHEELER, HUGH (B. 1912)
Silverlake   Weill, K.   1980
Sweeney Todd   Sondheim, S.   1979
(with comp.)

WHITE, EDGAR NKOSI (B. 1947)
Ghosts   Ito, G.   1993

WHITE, PAUL DAVID
Cathedral, The   Spivack, L.   1986

WHITE, R. J.
Tragicall History   Mellers, W.   1950–52*

WHITE, SARAH
Benjamin   Carbon, J.   1987

WHITSETT, GEORGE (B. 1889)
Parabola and Circula Blitzstein, M.   1929*

WHYTE, RON (1942–1989)
Mother and Child   McClure, L.   1990

WICKS, ALLAN
Gift, The   Ridout, A.   1971
White Doe   Ridout, A.   1987

WIDDOES, C. C.
How to Make Love   Widdoes, L.   1994

WIESEL, ELIE (B. 1928)
Esther (with comp.)   Swados, E.   1988

WILBOR, ELSIE M.
Guido Ferranti   Van Etten, J.   1914

WILBUR, RICHARD (B. 1921)
Candide   Bernstein, L.   1956
(with L. Hellman)

WILCOX, MICHAEL
Tornrak   Metcalf, J.   1990

WILDER, THORNTON (1897–1975)
Alcestiad, The   Talma, L.   1962

WILKINSON, F. H.
**Boy from the
   Catacombs**   Ridout, A.   1965

WILEY, HOWARD A.
Trojan Women   Garwood, M.   1967

WILLET, THOMAS (FL. 1778)
Buxom Joan   Taylor, R.   1778

WILLETT, ERNEST NODDALL
Prodigal Son   Nicholls, F.   1896

WILLHEIM, EMANUEL
**Married Men
   Go to Hell**   Franchetti, A.   1975

WILLIAMS, ALBERT
Isabella's Fortune   Russo, W.   1974

WILLIAMS, PAT
King Kong   Matshikiza, T.   1961*
(with H. Bloom)

WILLIAMS, TENNESSEE (1911–1983)
**Lord Byron's Love
   Letter**   Banfield, R. de   1955

WILLIAMS, THOMAS JOHN (1824–1874)
Desert Flower   Wallace, V.   1863
(with A. G. Harris)

WILLIAMSON, LAIRD
Christmas Carol   Hoiby, L.   1987
(with D. Powers)

WILSON, A. N. (B. 1950)
Britannia Preserv'd   Oliver, S.   1984

WILSON, JAMES
Chipita Rodríguez   Weiner, L.   1982
(with L. Carrillo)

WILSON, LANFORD (B. 1937)
Summer and Smoke   Hoiby, L.   1971

WILSON, ROBERT (B. 1928)
CIVIL warS   Glass, P.   1984
(with M. di Niscemi)
Einstein on the Beach Glass, P.   1976

Letter for Queen
Victoria   Lloyd, A.   1974
Medea   Bryars, G.   1984

WILSON, ROWLAND HOLT
Meal, The   Archer, V.   1985

WISHENGRAD, MORTON (1913–1963)
Thief and the
Hangman   Ellstein, A.   1961

WOLCOTT, JOHN [PETER PINDAR] (1738–1819)
Nina   Shield, W.   1787

WOLFE, GEORGE C.
Queenie Pie   Ellington, E.   1986

WOOD, ADOLPH
In the Drought   Joubert, J.   1956

WOOD, WALLIS
Princess Maleen   Schonthal, R.   1989
(with comp.)

WOODRUFF, PAUL (B. 1943)
Della's Gift   Welcher, D.   1987
Prisoner's Play   Rea, J.   1973

WOODWARD, MARIA
Song of Pegasus   McFarland, R.   1985

WOODWORTH, SAMUEL (1784–1842)
Deed of Gift   **   1822
Forest Rose   Davies, J.   1825

WOOLF, BENJAMIN E.
Doctor of Alcantara Eichberg, J.   1862

WORSDALE, JAMES (1692–1767)
Cure for a Scold   **   1735
Gasconado the Great **   1759?

WYN(-HARDY), HELEDD
Flowers   Hardy, J.   1994
Roswell Incident   Hardy, J.   1997

YARDLEY, WILLIAM (1849–1900)
Wedding Eve   Ford, E., et al. 1892

YARROW, JOSEPH
Love at First Sight **   1742

YAVELOW, MONIQUE
Passion of Vincent van
Gogh   Yavelow, C.   1984

YORINKS, ARTHUR
Fall of the House of
Usher   Glass, P.   1988
Juniper Tree   Glass, P.   1985

YOUNG, RIDA JOHNSON (B. 1895)
Naughty Marietta   Herbert, V.   1910

ZEFFIRELLI, FRANCO (B. 1923)
Antony and Cleopatra Barber, S.   1966

ZILAHY, LAJOS (1891–1974)
Virgin and the Fawn Zador, E.   1964

ZINOVIEFF, PETER
Mask of Orpheus   Birtwistle, H.   1986

ADAPTATIONS AND ARRANGEMENTS

AUDINOT, NICOLAS-MÉDARD (1732–1801)
Tonnelier, Le, with Quétant (F.-J. Gossec, 1765)
Cooper, The   Arne, T. A.   1772

AUMER, PIERRE (1774–1833)
Sonambule, La, with E. Scribe (1816)
Love's Dream   arr. M. Moss   1821
Sonnambula, La   Bishop, H. R.   1833

BERRETTONI, ARCANGELO
Bravo, Il (M. A. Marliani, 1834)
Red Mask   Cooke, T. S.   1834

BICKERSTAFFE, ISAAC (1733–1808)
Love in the City (C. Dibdin et al., 1767)
Romp, The   Dibdin, C.   1771

BRECHT, BERTOLT (1898–1956)
Dreigroschenoper, Die (K. Weill, 1928)
Threepenny Opera   Weill-Blitzstein 1954

Happy End, with E. Hauptmann (K. Weill, 1929)
Happy End   Weill-Feingold   1972

BRUNSWICK, LÉON LÉVY
Poupée de Nuremberg, La, with A. de Leuven (A. Adam, 1852)
Toy-Maker   Linley, G.   1861
Quatre fils Aymon, Les, with A. de Leuven (M. Balfe, 1844)
Castle of Aymon   Balfe, M.   1844

COBB, JAMES (1756–1818)
Pirates, The (S. Storace, 1792)
Isadore de Merida   Cooke, T. S.   1827

DA PONTE, LORENZO (1749–1838)
Così fan tutte (W. A. Mozart, 1790)
Tit for Tat   Hawes, W.   1828
Don Giovanni (W. A. Mozart, 1787)

Libertine, The Bishop, H. R. 1817
Nozze di Figaro, Le (W. A. Mozart, 1786)
Marriage of Figaro Bishop, H. R. 1819

DELAVIGNE, GERMAIN (1782–1871)
Muette de Portici, with Scribe (D. F. E. Auber, 1828)
Masaniello Cooke, Livius 1829
Vieille, La, with Scribe (F.-J. Fétis, 1826)
Love in Wrinkles Lacy, M. R. 1826

DESVERGERS [ARMAND CHAPEAU]
Yelva, with Scribe, Villeneuve (vaudeville, 1828)
Yelva Bishop, H. R. 1829

DIMOND, WILLIAM (FL. 1800–1830)
Aethiop, The (H. R. Bishop, 1812)
Aethiop, The Taylor, R. 1814

DÖRING, GEORG
Räuberbraut, Die (F. Ries, 1828)
Robber's Bride Hawes, W. 1829

FAVART, CHARLES-SIMON (1710–1792)
Annette et Lubin, with M. Favart, Lourdet de Santerre (A. Blaise, 1762)
Annette and Lubin Dibin, C. 1778
Caprice amoureux, Le (E. Duni et al., 1755)
Capricious Lovers Rush, G. 1764

GAY, JOHN (1695–1732)
Achilles (**, 1733)
Achilles in Petticoats Arne, T. A. 1773
Beggar's Opera, The (J. Pepusch, 1728)
Bow-Street Opera Pepusch, J. 1773
Fool's Opera ** 1731
Macheath in the Shades ** 1735
Macheath Turn'd Pyrate ** 1737
Threepenny Opera Weill-Blitzstein 1954

GHERADINI, GIOVANNI (1778–1861)
Gazza ladra, La (G. Rossini, 1817)
Ninetta Bishop, H. R. 1830

GIACOSA, GIUSEPPE (1847–1906)
Bohème, La, with L. Illica (G. Puccini, 1896)
Bohemians, The Kirschner, B. 1990
Rent Larson, J. 1996

GOLDONI, CARLO (1707–1793)
Buona figliuola, La (N. Piccini, 1760)
Maid of the Vale Arne, M. 1775

HALÉVY, LUDOVIC (1833–1908)
Ba-Ta-Clan (J. Offenbach, 1855)
Ba-Ta-Clan Oliver, S. 1988*

Madame l'archiduc, with Millaud, Meilhac (J. Offenbach, 1874)
Single Married Man Sedgwick, A. 1883*

HAUPTMANN, ELISABETH
Happy End, with B. Brecht (K. Weill, 1929)
Happy End Weill-Feingold 1972

HÈLE, THOMAS D' (1740–1780)
Evénéments imprévus, Les (Grétry, 1799)
Gay Deceivers Kelly, M. 1804

HIEMER, FRANZ KARL (1768–1822)
Abu Hassan (C. M. von Weber, 1811)
Abou Hassan Cooke, T. S. 1825
Freischütz, Der (C. M. von Weber, 1821)
Black Rider Waits, T. 1990
Freischütz, Der ** 1824

HUBER, FRANZ XAVER (1755–1814)
Unterbrochene Opferfest, Das (P. Winter, 1796)
Oracle, The Hawes, W. 1826

ILLICA, LUIGI (1857–1919)
Bohème, La, with G. Giacosa (G. Puccini, 1896)
Bohemians, The Kirschner, B. 1990
Rent Larson, J. 1996

KAISER, GEORG (1878–1945)
Silbersee, Der (K. Weill, 1933)
Silverlake Weill-Symonette 1980

LATEINER, JOSEPH (1853–1935)
Dovid's fiedele (S. Mogulesco, 1897)
David's Violin arr. M. Slobin 1976
Shloyme Gorgl (**, ca. 1890)
Shloyme Gorgl arr. M. Slobin 1978

LEUVEN, ADOLPHE DE (1800–1884)
Jaguarita l'Indienne, with Vernoy de St.-Georges (F. Halévy, 1855)
Desert Flower Wallace, V. 1863
Poupée de Nuremberg, La, with L. L. Brunswick (A. Adam, 1852)
Toy-Maker Linley, G. 1861
Quatre fils Aymon, Les, with L. L. Brunswick (M. Balfe, 1844)
Castle of Aymon Balfe, M. 1844

MARSOLLIER, BENOÎT JOSEPH (1750–1817)
Adolphe et Clara (N. Dalayrac, 1799)
Matrimony Hewitt, J. 1804
Camille (N.-M. Dalayrac, 1791)
Captive of Spilburg Dussek/Kelly 1798

MEILHAC, HENRI (1831–1897)
Carmen, with L. Halévy (G. Bizet, 1875)
Carmen Jones Bennett, R. R. 1947

José's Carmen   Ashman, M.   1984
Madame l'archiduc, with Millaud, Halévy
(J. Offenbach, 1874)
Single Married Man   Sedgwick, A.   1883*

METASTASIO, PIETRO (1698–1782)
Demofoonte (A. Caldara, 1733)
Dirce   Horne, C. E.   1821
Didone abbandonata (D. Sarro, 1724)
Dido   Storace, S.   1792

MILLAUD, ALBERT (1844–1892)
Madame l'archiduc, with H. Meilhac, L.
Halévy (J. Offenbach, 1874)
Single Married Man   Sedgwick, A.   1883*

MORSELLI, ADRIANO (17TH CENT.)
Pirro e Demetrio (A. Scarlatti, 1694)
Pyrrus and Demetrius Haym, N.   1708

PLANARD, F. A. E. DE (1783–1855)
Pré aux clercs, La (F. Hérold, 1832)
Challenge, The   Cooke, T. S.   1834
Court Masque   Dawes, W.   1833
Prison d'Edimbourg, Le, with E. Scribe
(M. Carafa, 1833)
Heart of Midlothian Loder, E.   1849

QUÉTANT, ANTOINE-FRANÇOIS (1733–1823)
Tonnelier, Le, with Audinot (F.-J. Gossec,
1765)
Cooper, The   Arne, T. A.   1772

ROMANI, FELICE (1788–1865)
Elisir d'amore, L' (G. Donizetti, 1832)
Dulcamara   **   1866

ROSSI, GAETANO (1774–1855)
Tancredi (G. Rossini, 1813)
Native Land   Bishop, H. R. 1824

SAINT-GEORGES, JULES-HENRI VERNOY DE
(1801?–1875)
Jaguarita l'Indienne, with de Leuven
(F. Halévy, 1855)
Desert Flower   Wallace, V.   1863

SAINT-HILAIRE, AMABLE VILAIN DE
Diadesté (J. J. Godefroid, 1836)
Diadesté   Balfe, M.   1838

SCRIBE, EUGÈNE (1791–1861)
Cheval de bronze, Le (D. F. E. Auber,
1835)
Bronze Horse   Rodwell, G.   1835
Deux nuits, Les (A. Boieldieu, 1829)
Night before the
Wedding   Bishop, H. R. 1829
Fra Diavolo (D. F. E. Auber, 1830)
Devil's Brother   Lee, G. A.   1831

Juive, La (F. Halévy, 1835)
Jewess, The   Cooke, T. S.   1835
Muette de Portici, La, with Delavigne
(D. F. E. Auber, 1828)
Masaniello   Cooke/Livius   1829
Prison d'Edimbourg, Le, with Planard
(M. Carafa, 1833)
Heart of Midlothian Loder, E.   1849
Robert le diable (G. Meyerbeer, 1831)
Demon, The   Bishop, H. R. 1832
Fiend-Father   Lacy, M. R.   1832
Robert the Devil   Barnett, J.   1830
Robert the Devil   "Kettenus"   1868
Vieille, La, with Delavigne (F.-J. Fétis,
1826)
Love in Wrinkles   Lacy, M. R.   1826
Sonambule, La, with P. Aumer (1816)
Love's Dream   arr. M. Moss   1821
Sonnambula, La   Bishop, H. R. 1833
Yelva, with Villeneuve, Desvergers (**,
1828)
Yelva   Bishop, H. R. 1829

SEDAINE, MICHEL-JEAN (1719–1797)
Femmes vengées, Les (F. A. D. Philidor,
1775)
Wives Avenged   Dibdin, C.   1778
Richard Coeur-de-lion (A. E. M. Grétry,
1784)
Richard Coeur de
Lion   Linley Sr., T. 1786
Richard Coeur de
Lion   Shield, W.   1786

STANZANI, TOMASO (FL. 1677–1684)
Arsinoe (G. B. Franceschini, 1676)
Arsinoe   Clayton, T.   1705

STEPHANIE, GOTTLIEB JR. (1741–1800)
Doktor und Apotheker (K. D. von Ditters-
dorf, 1786)
Doctor and Apothecary Storace, S.   1788

STERBINI, CESARE (1783–1851)
Barbiere di Siviglia, Il (G. Rossini, 1816)
Barber of Seville   Bishop, H. R. 1818

THEOBALD, LEWIS (1688–1744)
Happy Captive, The (J. Galliard, 1741)
Temple of Dullness   Arne, T. A.   1745

VILLENEUVE, F. V. DE (1799–1858)
Yelva, with E. Scribe and Desvergers
(**, 1828)
Yelva   Bishop, H. R. 1829

WOHLBRÜCK, J. G. (1770–1822)
Des Falkners Braut (H. Marschner, 1832)
Rob of the Fens   Romer, F.   1838

Authors and Sources

Opera entries include short title, composer, and year of premiere; * = year of composition; ** = anon. composer/ballad opera. Dates of authors given where known. See pp. 808–16 for alphabetical listing of titles of sources.

Part I: Authors and Anonymous Titles

ADAMS, ABIGAIL (1744–1818)
letters:

Abigail Adams	Owen, R.	1987

AESCHYLUS (525–456 B.C.)
Agamemnon

Agamemnon	Brian, H.	1957*
Agamemnon	Hamilton, I.	1967*
Agamemnon	Morris, R.	1969
Agamemnon	Werder, F.	1967
Cry of Clytaemnestra	Eaton, J.	1980

AESOP (LEGENDARY, CA. 6TH CENT. B.C.)
Aesop's Fables

Cat, The	Ridout, A.	1971
Moralities	Henze, H. W.	1968

AFANASYEV, ALEXANDR NIKOLAEVICH
  (1826–1871)
tales:

Marko the Miser	Musgrave, T.	1963

AGEE, JAMES (1909–1955)
Death in the Family, A (1957, posth.)

Death in the Family	Mayer, W.	1983

AINSWORTH, WILLIAM HARRISON (1805–
  1882)
Jack Sheppard (1839)

Jack Sheppard	Rodwell, G.	1839

AIZIMAN, DAVID
Krasovitsky Couple, The

Sima	Lehrman, L.	1976

ALCOTT, LOUISA MAY (1832–1888)
Little Women (1868–69)

Little Women	Freer, E. E.	1934

ALDEN, RAYMOND MACDONALD (1873–
  1924)
Why the Chimes Rang

One Christmas Long Ago	Mayer, W.	1962

ALEICHEM, SHOLEM (1859–1916)
tales:

Chelm	Strassburg, R.	1955
Goat from Chelm	Binder, A.	1960

ALEXANDER, HARTLEY (1873–1939)
Manito Masks

Earth-Trapped	Reed, H. O.	1962

ANDERSEN, HANS CHRISTIAN (1805–1875)
Cat and the Mouse in Partnership, The

Pot of Fat	Chandler, T.	1955

Emperor's New Clothes, The

Emperor's New Clothes	Dvorkin, J.	1989
Emperor's New Clothes	Larsen, L.	1979
Emperor's New Clothes	Moore, D.	1949
Eyes and No Eyes	Reed, T. G.	1875
Fit for a King	Kalmanoff, M.	1949

Ib

Ib and Little Christina	Leoni, F.	1901

Little Mermaid, The

Little Mermaid	Boyd, A.	1978
Mermaid, The	More, M.	1951

Mother, The

Mother, The	Hollingsworth, S.	1954
Mother, The	Wood, J.	1942

Nightingale, The

Emperor and the Nightingale	Bingham, S.	1982
Nightingale, The	Clokey, J.	1925
Nightingale, The	Rogers, B.	1955
Nightingale	Strouse, C.	1982

Shepherdess and the Sweep, The

Shepherdess and the Chimneysweep	Smith, J.	1966

Snow Queen, The

Snow Queen	Dudley, G.	1985
Snow Queen	Jones, A. G.	1917

What the Old Man Does Is Always Right

What the Old Man Does	Hoddinott, A.	1977

Wild Swans, The

Wild Swans	Bingham, S.	1988

ANDREYEV, LEONID (1871–1919)
He Who Gets Slapped (1922)

He Who Gets Slapped	Ward, R.	1956

ANICET-BOURGEOIS, AUGUSTE (1806–1871)
Charlot (with Lockroy, Vanderburch)

Follies of a Night	Gabriel, V.	ca. 1870

ANSKY (AN-SKI), S. (1863–1920)
Dybbuk, The

Between Two Worlds	Ran, S.	1997
Dybbuk, The	DiGiacomo, F.	1978
Dybbuk, The	Mandelbaum, J.	1972
Dybbuk, The	Tamkin, D.	1951

APOTHICAIRE DE MURCIA, L' (FR., ANON.)
Doctor and the
  Apothecary   Storace, S.   1788
APULEIUS, LUCIUS (2ND CENT.)
Golden Ass, The
Trials of Psyche   Bruce, N.   1971
ARANDA POEMS (AUSTRALIAN ABORIGINAL)
Rites of Passage   Sculthorpe, P.   1974
ARDEN OF FAVERSHAM (1592, ANON.)
Arden Must Die   Goehr, A.   1967
ARISTOPHANES (CA. 450–CA. 388 B.C.)
general:
Sweeney Agonistes   Dankworth, J.   1965
Birds, The
Birds, The   Ahlstrom, D.   1990
Birds, The   El-Dabh, H.   1988*
Birds, The   Maconchy, E.   1968
Lysistrata
Lizzie Strotter   Kalmanoff, M.   1958
Lysistrata   Barthelson, J.   1981
Lysistrata & the War   Fink, R.   1967
ARNOLD, SIR EDWIN (1832–1904)
Light of Asia, The (1879)
Light of Asia   Lara, I. de   1892
ARTHUR, TIMOTHY SHAY (1809–1885)
Ten Nights in a Bar-Room (1854)
Ten Nights in a
  Bar-Room   **   1858
ASCH, SHOLEM (1880–1957)
Night (1921)
Night   Weisgall, H.   1932
AUBIGNEY, T. BADOUIN D'
Pie voleuse, La (1815, with Caigniez)
Magpie or the Maid   Bishop, H. R.   1815
Ninetta   Bishop, H. R.   1830
AUCASSIN ET NICOLLETE (13TH CENT., ANON.)
Azara   Paine, J. K.   1883*
AUCHINCLOSS, LOUIS
Portrait in Brownstone (1962)
Portrait in Brownstone Reif, P.   1966
AUDUBON, JOHN JAMES (1785–1851)
Birds of America, The
Water Bird Talk   Argento, D.   1977
AULNOY, COUNTESS MARIE-CATHERINE D'
  (1650–1705)
Contes (1698)
Belle Belle
Fortunio   Darley, F.   1883
Gracieuse et Percinet
Graciosa and Percinet   **   1845
AVERCHENKO, ARKADY (1881–1925)
tales:

Sterlingman   Roy, K.   1957
AXELSEN, STEPHEN
Oath of Bad Brown Bill, The
Oath of Bad Brown Bill Conygham, B.   1985
BAILLIE, JOANNA (1762–1851)
Election, The (1802)
Election, The   Horn, C.   1811
BALLAD OF THE CRUEL MOTHER, THE
Down by the Greenwood
  Side   Birtwistle, H.   1969
BALZAC, HONORÉ DE (1799–1850)
general:
Miracle of Flanders   Gruenberg, L.   1954
Grande Bretèche, La
Fatal Oath   Koutzen, B.   1955
Grande Bretèche, La   Claflin, A.   1957
Grande Bretèche, La   Hollingsworth, S. 1957
Secret, The   Patacchi, V.   1955
BANCROFT, CAROLINE
Silver Queen (1950)
Baby Doe   DiJulio, M.   1952
BANTAM, PRINCE
tales:
Shizuka's Dance   Kondorossy, L.   1969
BARHAM, RICHARD HARRIS (1788–1845)
Ingoldsby Legends (ca. 1840)
Lady Rohesia   Hopkins, A.   1948
BARING, MAURICE (1874–1945)
short story:
Fête Galante   Smyth, E.   1923
BARNET, MIGUEL (B. 1940)
Canción de Rachel, La
Cubana, La   Henze, H. W.   1974
BARNUM, P. T. (1810–1891)
Recollections (1878)
Jenny Lind   Lee, D.-K.   1981
BARRY, PHILIP (1896–1949)
White Wings (P. Barry)
White Wings   Moore, D.   1949
BASILE, GIAMBATTISTA (CA. 1575–1632)
Cinderella (1636)
Cat Cinderella   De Simone, R.   1988
Cinderella   Easton, M.   1989*
Cinderella   Farmer, J.   1883
Cinderella   Jarrett, J.   1956
Cinderella   Lacy, M. R.   1830
Cinderella   Oliver, S.   1991*
Cinderella in Salerno   Walker, R.   1976*
Draagenfut Girl   Kupferman, M.   1958
BAUM, L. FRANK (1856–1919)
stories:
Magic Bonbons   Blank, A.   1983*

BEAUMARCHAIS, P. A. C. DE (1732–1799)
Barbier de Seville, Le (1775)
Barber of Seville Bishop, H. R. 1818
Spanish Barber Arnold, S. 1777
Mère coupable, La
Ghosts of Versailles Corigliano, J. 1991

BEAUMONT, FRANCIS (1584–1616)
Chances, The (possibly with J. Fletcher)
Don John Bishop, H. R. 1821
Humorous Lieutenant, The (with J. Fletcher)
Humorous Lieutenant Bishop, H. R. 1817
Royal Merchant, The (1761, with J. Fletcher)
Royal Merchant Linley Sr., T., 1767

BECKETT, SAMUEL (1906–1989)
general:
Past Tense Oliver, S. 1974
Neither
Neither Feldman, M. 1977

BEERBOHM, MAX (1872–1956)
Happy Hypocrite, The
Happy Hypocrite Masland, W. 1978*

BEHN, APHRA (1610–1689)
Emperor of the Moon, The (1688)
Emperor of the Moon Arne, M. 1777

BELLOW, SAUL (B. 1915)
Henderson the Rain King
Lily Kirchner, L. 1977

BENÉT, STEPHEN VINCENT (1898–1943)
Devil and Daniel Webster, The (1937)
Devil and Daniel Webster Moore, D. 1939
Jacob and the Indians (ca. 1940)
Jacob and the Indians Laderman, E. 1957
King of Cats, The
King of Cats Oliver, H. 1976*

BERKOFF, STEVEN (B. 1937)
Greek (1979)
Greek Turnage, M.-A. 1988

BERR, GEORGES (1867–1942)
Satyr, Le (with M. Guillemaud)
Pink Lady Caryll, I. 1911

BHAGHAVAD-GHITA
Satyagraha Glass, P. 1981

BIBLE, THE, APOCRYPHA:
Hannah Lehrman, L. 1980
Judith Chadwick, G.W. 1901
Judith Goossens, E. 1929
Judith Smith, D. 1982
Judith and Holofernes Fink, M. 1978
Line of Terror McQueen, I. 1993
Susanna and the Elders Fink, M. 1955
Susannah Floyd, C. 1955
Tobias and the Angel Bliss, A. 1960

BIBLE, THE, NEW TESTAMENT:
Amahl Menotti, G. C. 1951

Calvary Pasatieri, T. 1971
Dialogues Bauman, J. 1987
Erode the Great La Montaine, J. 1969
Jericho Road Aria, P. 1968
Jesus Christ Superstar Lloyd Webber 1971
Judas Tree Dickinson, P. 1965
Nativity Dello Joio, N. 1987
Nativity, The Hart, F. 1931*
Nativity, The Thompson, R. 1961
Novellis, Novellis La Montaine, J. 1961
Prodigal Son Britten, B. 1968
Promise, The Townshend, J. 1997
Wenceslas Ridout, A. 1978
Yehu Zador, E. 1974

BIBLE, THE, OLD TESTAMENT:
Akhnaten Glass, P. 1984
Belshazzar's Feast Griesbach, J. H. 1835*
Belshazzar's Feast Root, G. F. ca. 1853*
Bellyful Werder, F. 1975*
Burning Fiery Furnace Britten, B. 1966
Creation, The Ridout, A. 1973
David Goldman, E. 1967*
David and Bathsheba Barlow, D. 1969
Esther Hart, F. 1923
Esther Harvey, E. N. 1974
Esther Knoller, J. ca. 1941
Esther Swados, E. 1988
Esther Meyerowitz, J. 1957
Esther Weisgall, H. 1993
Esther and Cousin
  Mordecai Pittman, E. 1957
Flood, The Stravinsky, I. 1962
In the Beginning Warren, R. 1982
Jonah Cole, H. 1967
Naboth's Vineyard Goehr, A. 1968
Noye's Flood Stravinsky, I. 1958
Outcast, The Ain, N. 1995
Ruth Berkeley, L. 1956
Ruth and Naomi Hart, F. 1917
Ruth and Naomi Kondorossy, L. 1974
Sarah Laderman, E. 1958
Solomon and Sheba Rivers, S. 1973
Warrior, The Rogers, B. 1947

BIERCE, AMBROSE (1842–1914)
Tales of Soldiers and Civilians (1891):
  Occurence at Owl Creek Bridge
Incident at Owl Creek Whelen, C. 1969
Occurrence at Owl
  Creek Bridge Musgrave, T. 1982

BLACKIE, JOHN STUART (1809–1895)
Lyrical Dramas of Aeschylus (1906)
Agamemnon Brian, H. 1957*

BLAKE, QUENTIN (B. 1931)
Angelo (1970)
Angelo Ridout, A. 1971

BOCCACCIO, GIOVANNI (1313–1375)
Decameron, The (1351–53)
Boccaccio's Nightingale Trimble, L.   1962*
Enchanted Pear Tree Overton, H.   1950
Falcon, The Cole, H.   1968
Fiery Tales Sitsky, L.   1976
Fourth Day Ahlstrom, D.   1961*
Padrevia Pasatieri, T.   1967

BOETHIUS (D. 524)
Consolation of Philosophy, The (ca. 524)
Rites of Passage Sculthorpe, P.   1974

BOND, CHRISTOPHER (B. 1945)
Sweeney Todd (1973)
Sweeney Todd Blyton, C.   1980*
Sweeney Todd Sondheim, S.   1979

BOOK OF LEINSTER (CA. 950)
Táin, The Wilson, J.   1972

BOSCH, HIERONYMOUS (D. 1516)
Adoration of the Magi, The
Amahl Menotti, G. C.   1951

BOSWELL, JAMES (1710–1795)
verses:
Johnson Preserv'd Stoker, R.   1967

BOTTRELL, WILLIAM (1816–1881)
Traditions and Hearthside Stories (1870)
Logan Rock Gundry, I.   1956

BOUCHOR, MAURICE (1855–1929)
Conte de Noël (1895)
Christmas Tale Freer, E. E.   1929

BOUCICAULT, DION (1822?–1890)
Colleen Bawn
Lily of Killarney Benedict, J.   1862

BRADBURY, RAY (B. 1920)
general:
Lifework of Juan Diaz Rapchak, L.   1990
Rocket, The Goldman, M.   1960*
Fahrenheit 451 (1953)
Fahrenheit 451 Broadstock, B.   1992

BRADDON, M[ARY] E[LIZABETH] (1837–1915)
Octoroon, The
Octoroon, The Freeman, H. L.   1904

BRAHMS, CARYL (B. 1901)
Under the Juniper Tree
Mañana Benjamin, A.   1956

BRECHT, BERTOLT (1898–1956)
Kinderkreuzzug
Children's Crusade Ridout, A.   1968
Verhör des Lukullus, Das
Trial of Lucullus Sessions, R.   1947

BROD, MAX (1884–1968)
Amerika
America Kohs, E. B.   1970

BROME, RICHARD (D. 1652?)
Jovial Crew (1641)
Jovial Crew **   1731

BRONTË, EMILY (1818–1848)
Jane Eyre (1847)
Jane Heir Healey, P.   1989
Wuthering Heights
Wuthering Heights Floyd, C.   1958
Wuthering Heights Hermann, B.   1943*

BROOKE, HENRY (1703?–1783)
Gustavus Vasa (1739)
Hero of the North Kelly, M.   1803
Zorinski Arnold, S.   1795

BROUGHAM, JOHN (1810–1880)
Duke's Motto, The
Blanche de Nevers Balfe, M.   1863

BROWN, GEORGE MACKAY
Magnus (1973)
Martyrdom of St.
Magnus Davies, P. M.   1977

BROWN, MAUD MORROW
University Greys, The (1940)
University Greys Kreutz, A.   1954

BROWNING, ROBERT (1812–1889)
Pied Piper of Hamelin, The (1842)
Pied Piper of Hamelin Clokey, J. W.   1920
Pied Piper of Hamelin Wilson, J.   1969
Pippa Passes (1841)
Pippa's Holiday Beach, J. P.   1915
Ring and the Book, The (1868–69)
Caponsacchi Hageman, R.   1937

BÜCHNER, GEORG (1813–1837)
Lenz (1838)
Lenz Sitsky, L.   1974
Leonce und Lena (1836)
Blind Man's Bluff Davis, P. M.   1972

BULGAKOV, M. A. (1891–1940)
Heart of a Dog (1925)
Murder of Comrad
Sharik Bergsma, W.   1973

BULWER-LYTTON, EDWARD (1803–1873)
Eugene Aram (1832)
Eugene Aram Bantock, G.   1892*
Lady of Lyons, The (1838)
Leonora Fry, W.   1845
Paul Clifford Rodwell, G.   1835
Pauline Cowen, F.   1876
Last Days of Pompeii, The (1834)
Last Days of Pompeii Rodwell, G.   1834

BUNYAN, JOHN (1628–1688)
Pilgrim's Progress, The
Shepherds of the Delectable
Mountains Vaughan Williams   1922

BURNETT, FRANCES HODGSON (1849–1924)
Secret Garden, The (1911)
Secret Garden   Pliska, G.   1991
BYRON, GEORGE GORDON (1788–1824)
Don Juan (1824)
New Don Juan   Rodwell, G.   1828
poems:
Lord Byron   Graham, J.   1926

CABLE, GEORGE W. (1844–1925)
Grandissimes, The (1880)
Koanga   Delius, F.   1895*
CAGE, JOHN (1912–1992)
Silence, Year from Monday (1961, 1967)
But to Stockport   Schubert/Valinsky   1986
CAIGNIEZ, LOUIS-CHARLES (1762–1842)
Jugement de Salomon, Le (1802)
Voice of Nature   Pelessier, V.   1802
Pie voleuse, La (1815, with d'Aubigny)
Magpie or the Maid   Bishop, H. R.   1815
Ninetta   Bishop, H. R.   1830

CALHOUN, MATTHEW
Statues on a Lawn
Statues on a Lawn   Flanagan, T. J.   1983

CAMPBELL, JOHN FRANCIS, COMP., TRANS.
(1822–1885)
Popular Tales of the West Highlands (1890)
Vanishing Bridegroom   Weir, J.   1992

CANETTI, ELIAS
Befristeten, Die (1964)
Numbered, The   Lutyens, E.   1965–67*

ČAPEK, JOSEF (1887–1945)
Insect Life (1923, with K. Čapek)
Insect Comedy   Kalmanoff, M.   1977*

ČAPEK, KAREL (1890–1938)
White Plague (1937)
White Agony   Fuchs, P. P.   1989
Insect Life (1923, with J. Čapek)
Insect Comedy   Kalmanoff, M.   1977*

CAPELLANUS, ANDREAS (A. LE CHAPELAIN)
De amore et amoris remedio
De Amore   Barkin, E.   1982

CAPOTE, TRUMAN (1924–1984)
In Cold Blood (1969)
Failing Kansas   Rouse, M.   1995

CARAVAGGIO, POLIDORO CALDARA DA
(CA. 1495–CA. 1543)
Death of the Virgin
Death of the Virgin   Owen, R.   1981

CARDWELL, ANN [JEAN MAKINS PAWLEY]
Crazy to Kill (1941)
Crazy to Kill   Beckwith, J.   1989

CARMICHAEL, ALEXANDER, COMP. (1832–1912)
Carmina gadelica
Vanishing Bridegroom   Weir, J.   1990
CARROLL, LEWIS [CHARLES DODGSON]
(1832–1898)
Alice's Adventures in Wonderland (1865)
Alice   Osborne, W.   1985
Alice   Waits, T.   1992
Alice in Wonderland   Chauls, R.   1976
Alice in Wonderland   Josephs, W.   1985*
Alice in Wonderland   Meachem, M.   1982*
Alice in Wonderland   Slaughter, W.   1906*
Alice Meets the
Mock Turtle   Bingham, S.   1988
Final Alice   Del Tredici, D.   1976
Hunting of the Snark, The (1876)
Hunting of the Snark   Laderman, E.   1961
Hunting of the Snark   Roberts, E.   1971
Hunting of the Snark   Wilson, J.   1965
Through the Looking Glass (1872)
Through the Looking
Glass   Josephs, W.   1977*

CASANOVA, GIOVANNI GIACOMO (1725–1798)
Histoire de ma vie, L'
Casanova's
Homecoming   Argento, D.   1985
CAZOTTE, JACQUES DE (1719–1792)
Diable amoureux, Le (1776)
Diable amoureux, Le   Rodriguez, F.   1978*
CENTLIVRE, SUSANNA (1667–1723)
Bold Stroke for a Wife, A (1718)
Win Her   Barnett, J.   1832
CERVANTES, MIGUEL DE (1547–1616)
general:
Happy Captive   Galliard, J.   1741
Don Quixote
Adventure of Don
Quixote   Macfarren, G.   1846
Don Quixote   Arnold, S.   1774
Don Quixote   Clay, F.   1876
Don Quixote   De Koven, R.   1889
Don Quixote   Hewitt, T. J.   1909
Don Quixote   Hill, A.   1904*
Don Quixote   Rodwell, G.   1840
Don Quixote in England **   1734
Mountaineers, The   Arnold, S.   1793
Novelas exemplares (1613):
Celoso extremeño, El
Felipe   Aitken, H.   1981
Padlock, The   Dibdin, C.   1768
Gitanella, La (ca. 1614)
Bohemian Girl   Balfe, M.   1843
CHAO FAMILY ORPHAN, THE (13TH CENT. TALE)
Night at the Chinese
Opera   Weir, J.   1987

CHATRIAN, ALEXANDRE (1826–1890)
Ami Fritz (1846, with E. Erckmann)
Friend Fritz Edwards, J. 1893
CHATWIN, BRUCE (1940–1989)
Songlines, The
Man with Footsoles Volans, K. 1993
CHAUCER, GEOFFREY (D. 1400)
Canterbury Tales (ca. 1387–1400)
general:
Canterbury Tale Roe, B. 1986
Fiery Tales Sitsky, L. 1976
Cock and the Fox, The
Tales from Chaucer Gordon, P. 1959*
Franklin's Tale, The
Franklin's Tale Sokoloff, N. 1961
Nun's Priest's Tale, The
Chanticleer Barab, S. 1956*
Chanticleer Barthelson, J. 1967
Nun's Priest's Tale Finney, R. L. 1965
Tale from Chaucer Gordon, P. 1959*
Wheel of the World Crosse, G. 1972
Pardoner's Tale, The
Pardoner's Tale Chisholm, E. 1961
Pardoner's Tale Davis, J. S. 1967
Pardoner's Tale Lubin, E. 1966
Pardoner's Tale Rorem, N. 1958
Pardoner's Tale Ridout, A. 1970
Wayfarers, The Joubert, J. 1984
Troilus and Cressida
Troilus and Cressida Walton, W. 1954
Wife of Bath's Tale, The
Wife of Bath's Tale Legg, J. 1986
Woman's Will Davy, J. 1820
CHEKHOV, ANTON (1860–1904)
Bear, The (1888)
Bear, The Walton, W. 1967
Boor, The Argento, D. 1957
Boor, The Bucci, M. 1949
Boor, The Fink, M. 1955
Boor, The Grantham, D. 1989
Boor, The Kay, U. 1968
Brute, The Moss, L. 1961
Box, The
Box, The Eakin, C. G. 1968
Box, The Hamm, C. 1961
Forgot
Music Shop Wargo, R. 1985
Good Doctor, The
Seduction of a Lady Wargo, R. 1985
Jubilee (1891)
Birthday of the Bank Lehrman, L. 1988
On the Harmfulness of Smoking Tobacco (1903)
Harmfulness of Tobacco Kalmanoff, M. 1979
Water Bird Talk Argento, D. 1977
Proposal, The (1889)
Marriage Proposal Goldstaub, P. 1978

Marriage Proposal Murray, J. 1973
Proposal, The Humel, G. 1958
Seagull, The (1896)
Seagull, The Pasatieri, T. 1974
Three Sisters, The (1901)
Three Sisters Pasatieri, T. 1986
Visit to the Country, A
Visit to the Country Wargo, R. 1990
Witch, The (1886)
Scarf, The Hoiby, L. 1958
CHESTER MIRACLE PLAY
Good Tidings Locklair, D. 1978
Noyes Fludde Britten, B. 1958
CHICKEN LITTLE
Sibyl, The Persichetti, V. 1985
CHIKAMATSU, MONZAEMON (1653–1724)
puppet plays:
Jōruri Miki, M. 1985
CHILD, JULIA (B. 1912)
general:
Bon Appétit! Hoiby, L. 1989
CLARE, JOHN (1793–1864)
general:
I Am in Search Grant, R. 1994
CLEMENTS, COLIN (1894–1948)
All on a Summer Day (with F. Reyerson)
Game of Chance Barab, S. 1957
CLIFFORD, JOHN (B. 1950)
Inés de Castro
Inés de Castro MacMillan, J. 1996
COATSWORTH, ELIZABETH (B. 1893)
Cat Who Went to Heaven (1930)
**Cat Who Went to
  Heaven** Bush, G. 1976
COFFEY, CHARLES (D. 1745)
Devil to Pay, The
Devil's in It Balfe, M. 1852
COGNIARD, THÉODORE (1806–1872)
Biche au bois, La
Black Crook Clay, F. 1872
COLERIDGE, TAYLOR, SAMUEL (1772–1834)
Rime of the Ancient Mariner, The (1798)
**Rime of the Ancient
  Mariner** Bedford, D. 1975–76*
COLMAN, GEORGE, SR.
Clandestine Marriage, The (1766, with Garrick)
Clandestine Marriage Wishart, P. 1971
Elfrida
Elfrida Arne, T. A. 1772
COLVIN, IAN DUNCAN (1877–1938)
Leper's Flute, The
Leper's Flute Bryson, E. 1926

Maid of Saxony	Horn, C. E.	1842
Will, The		
Thirty Thousand	Reeve, W., et al.	1804
ELGUERA, AMALIA		
Moray		
Mary, Queen of Scots	Musgrave, T.	1977

ELIOT, GEORGE (1819–1880)
Silas Marner (1861)

Silas Marner	Joubert, J.	1961

ELIOT, THOMAS STEARNS (1888–1965)
general:

Black Roses	Chisholm, E.	1954
Sweeney Agonistes (1932)		
Sweeney Agonistes	Dankworth, J.	1965

ENNERY, ADOLPHE D' (1811–1899)
Don César de Bazan (1844, with M. Dumanoir)

Maritania	Wallace, V.	1845

ENRIGHT, ELIZABETH (1909–1968)
Moment of Rain, The

Tale for a Deaf Ear	Bucci, M.	1957

ERCKMANN, EMILE (1822–1899)
Ami Fritz, with P.-A. Chatrian (1846)

Friend Fritz	Edwards, J.	1893

ERSKINE, JOHN (1879–1951)
Private Life of Helen of Troy, The (1925)

Helen Retires	Antheil, G.	1934

EURIPIDES (CA. 484–CA. 406 B.C.)
Alkestis (438 B.C.)

Alceste	Handel, G. F.	1749*
Alcestiad, The	Talma, L.	1962
Alkestis	Boughton, R.	1922
Bacchae, The		
Bacchae, The	Buller, J.	1992
Bassarids, The	Henze, H. W.	1966
Revelation in the		
Courthouse Park	Partch, H.	1962
Hippolytus		
Hippolytus	Drysdale, L.	1905
Medea		
Medea	Bryars, G.	1984
Medea	Elkus, J.	1970
Medea	Henderson, A.	1972
Medea	Werder, F.	1985
Trojan Women, The		
Sarajevo	Osborne, N.	1958
Trojan Women	Garwood, M.	1967

EVERYMAN (CA. 1500)

Everyman	Lester, W.	1927
Reverend Everyman	Brotons, S.	1990
Summoning of		
Everyman	Wilson, C.	1973

EYRE, EDWARD JOHN (1815–1901)
Journals of Expeditions of Discovery (1845)

Edward John Eyre	Conyngham, B.	1971

FAVART, CHARLES (1710–1792)
Bohémienne, La

Gipsies, The	Arnold, S.	1778

FÉNELON DE LA MOTHE (1651–1715)
Télémaque (1699)

Calypso and Telemachus	Galliard, J. E.	1712

FERBER, EDNA (1887–1968)
Show Boat (1926)

Show Boat	Kern, J.	1927

FERMOR, PATRICK LEIGH
Violins of Saint-Jacques, The

Violins of St. Jacques	Williamson, M.	1966

FÉVAL, PAUL (1817–1887)
Bossu, Le (1858)

Blanche de Nevers	Balfe, M.	1863

FIELDING, HENRY (1707–1754)
general:

Grub Street Opera	Bowles, A.	1986
Don Quixote in England		
Sot, The	Arne, T. A.	1775
Squire Badger	Arne, T. A.	1772
Tom Jones (1749)		
Tom Jones	Arnold/Arne	1769
Tom Jones	German, E.	1907
Tom Jones	Oliver, S.	1976
Tragedy of Tragedies, The, or, The Life and Death of Tom Thumb the Great (1730)		
Life, Death, of		
Tom Thumb	Dibdin, C.	1785
Opera of Operas	Arne, T. A.	1733
Tom Thumb	Markordt, J.	1780
Tumbledown Dick		
Tumbledown Dick	Larsen, L.	1980

FINDLER, GERALD
Legends of the Lake Counties (1967)

Will of Her Own	Gundry, I.	1971–73*

FITCH, CLYDE
Captain Jinks (1902)

Captain Jinks	Beeson, J.	1975

FLAUBERT, GUSTAVE (1821–1880)
Bouvard et Pécuchet (1881)

Bouvard and Pecuchet	ApIvor, D.	1971–74*
Julian		
Julian	Fussell, C.	1972

FLETCHER, JOHN (1579–1625)
Chances, The (possibly with F. Beaumont)

Don John	Bishop, H. R.	1821
Humorous Lieutenant, The (with F. Beaumont)		
Humorous Lieutenant	Bishop, H. R.	1817
Island Princess, The		
Island Princess	Purcell, D.	1698
Pilgrim, The		
Noble Outlaw	Bishop, H. R.	1815
Prophetess, The (with P. Massinger)		

Dioclesian   Purcell, H.   1690
Royal Merchant, The (1761, with Beaumont)
Royal Merchant   Linley, T., Sr.   1767
Two Noble Kinsmen (1612–13, prob. with Shakespeare)
Love and Madness   Arnold, S.   1795
FLETCHER, LUCILLE
Sorry, Wrong Number
Sorry, Wrong Number   Beeson, J.   1996*
Sorry, Wrong Number   Moross, J.   1980
FONTENELLE, BERNARD LE BOVIER (1657–1757)
Endymion
Endymion   Bennett, R. R.   1927*
FORBES, ESTHER
Mirror for Witches, A (1928)
Bilby's Doll   Floyd, C.   1976
FORSCHER, J.
general:
Christopher Columbus Kalmanoff, M.   1976
FORSTER, E[DWARD] M[ORGAN] (1879–1970)
Albergo Empedocle
Albergo Empedocle   Barker, P.   1990
Obelisk, The   Eaton, M.   1984
FOUQUÉ, F. H. K., BARON DE LA MOTTE (1777–1843)
Undine (1811)
Ondine   Barab, S.   1995
Undine   Ware, H.   1923
FRANCE, ANATOLE (1844–1924)
Celui qui épousa une femme muette
Dumb Wife   Gruenberg, L. 1922– 23*
Thais (1890)
Thais and Talmaae   Campbell, C.   1921
FREEMAN, MARY WILKINS (1852–1930)
Village Singer
Village Singer   Paulus, S.   1979

GAGE, NICHOLAS
Eleni (1983)
Jacob's Room   Subotnick, M.   1993
GARCÍA LORCA, FEDERICO (1898–1936)
Amor de Don Perlimplín con Belisa en su jardín (1931)
Belisa   Biales, A.   1989
Don Perlimplin   Rieti, V.   1952
Love of Don Perlimplin Susa, C.   1984
Asi que pasen cinco anos
Wind Remains   Bowles, P.   1943
Bodas de sangre (1933)
Blood Wedding   LeFanu, N.   1992
Blood Wedding   Smith, H.   1953
Retablillo de Don Cristóbal
Don Cristóbal   Crawford, J.   1970

Yerma (1934)
Yerma   ApIvor, D.   1961
Yerma   Bowles, P.   1958
Yerma   Wilding-White   1962*
GARDNER, DOROTHY
Eastward in Eden
Eastward in Eden   Meyerowitz, J. 1951
GARRICK, DAVID (1717–1779)
general:
Garrick   Stoessel, A.   1937
Jubilee   Dibdin, C.   1769
Catherine and Petruccio (1756)
Taming of the Shrew   Braham/Cooke 1828
Clandestine Marriage, The, with Colman Sr. (1766)
Clandestine Marriage Wishart, P.   1971
GAUTIER, THÉOPHILE (1811–1872)
Nuit de Cléopâtre, Une
Cleopatra's Night   Hadley, H.   1920
One Night of Cleopatra Gruenberg, L.   1954
GAWAIN (LATE 14TH CENT.)
Gawain   Birtwistle, H.   1991
GAY, JOHN (1695–1732)
What D'Ye Call It, The (ca. 1715)
What D'YE Call It   Tate, P.   1966
GENET, JEAN (1910–1986)
Balcon, Le (1956)
Balcony, The   DiDomenica, R.1975
GENLIS, S. F., COMTESSE DE (1746–1830)
Adèle et Théodore
Captive of Spilburg   Dussek/Kelly   1798
Siège de La Rochelle, La
Siege of Rochelle   Balfe, M.   1835
Zuma, ou, La découverte du quinquina
Zuma   Bishop/Braham 1818
GHELDERODE, MICHEL DE (1898–1962)
Escuriale (1928)
Escorial, The   Levy, M.   1958
Pantagleize   Starer, R.   1973
GIBSON, WILLIAM (B. 1914)
Father of the Child
Father of the Child   Barab, S.   1985
GILBERT, WILLIAM S. (1836–1911)
Engaged ! (1877)
Engaged   Rowell/Mobbs 1962
Etiquette
Gentleman's Island   Horovitz, J.   1958
GILGAMESH, EPIC OF (CA. 2000 B.C., BABYLONIAN)
Death of Enkidu   Somers, H.   1977
Forest, The   Byrne, D.   1988
GILHAM, GEOFF
Crossing, The
Crossing, The   Metcalf, J.   1984

GILMAN, CHARLOTTE PERKINS
Yellow Wallpaper, The (1986)
Yellow Wallpaper   Perera, R.   1989

GILROY, FRANK D. (B. 1925)
Far Rockaway
Hero, The   Bucci, M.   1965

GIRAUDOUX, JEAN (1882–1944)
Judith (1931)
Judith and Holofernes   Fink, M.   1978
Ondine (1939)
Ondine   Barab, S.   1995

GODWIN, FRANCIS (BISHOP) (1562–1633)
Man in the Moon, The
Wonders in the Sun   **   1706

GODWIN, WILLIAM
Things As They Are, or, The Adventures of
   Caleb Williams (1794)
Iron Chest   Storace, S.   1796

GOETHE, JOHANN WOLFGANG VON (1749–
1832)
Faust (1832)
Faust   Becker, J. J.   1951
Faust Counter Faust   Gessner, J.   1971
Faustus   Bishop, H. R.   1825
Henry Faust   Isaacs, G.   1993
Lamentations of Doctor
   Faustus   Hewitt, M.   1994
Mephistopheles   Lutz, M.   1855

GOGOL, NIKOLAI VASIL'EVICH (1809–1852)
Diary of a Madman, The (1835)
Diary of a Madman   Searle, H.   1958
Inspector General, The (1836)
Inspector General   Zador, E.   1928

GOLDBERG, LEA
Lady of the Castle
Lady of the Castle   Spektor, M.   1982

GOLDONI, CARLO (1707–1793)
Locandiera, La (1753)
Bianca   Hadley, H.   1918
Servitore di due padroni (1753)
Servant of Two Masters Giannini, V.   1967
Ventaglio, Il
Fan, The   Goldstein, L.   1989

GOLDSMITH, OLIVER (1730–1774)
Deserted Village, The (1770)
Deserted Village   Glover, J.   1880
Edwin and Angelina (1764)
Edwin and Angelina   Pelissier, V.   1796
She Stoops to Conquer (1864)
She Stoops to Conquer ApIvor, D.   1943–47*
She Stoops to Conquer Macfarren, G.   1864
Vicar of Wakefield, The
Robin Hood   Shield, W.   1784

GOODMAN, PAUL
Jonah
Jonah   Beeson, J.   1948–50*

GOTTHELF, JEREMIAS
Schwarze Spinne, Die (1842)
Black Spider   Weir, J.   1985

GRAHAME, KENNETH (1859–1932)
Wind in the Willows, The (1908)
Wind in the Willows   Rutter, J.   1981*

GRANVILLE, GEORGE [LANDSDOWNE, GEORGE
   GRANVILLE, BARON] (1667–1735)
Poems (1712)
Peleus and Thetis   Boyce, W.   ca. 1740
Peleus and Thetis   Hayes, W.   ca. 1749

GRAVES, ROBERT (1895–1985)
general:
Journey of Edith
   Wharton   Hannay, R.   1988
Homer's Daughter (1955)
Nausicaa   Glanville-Hicks 1961

GREENE, GRAHAM (1904–1991)
Our Man in Havana
Our Man in Havana   Williamson, M. 1963

GREGORY, ISABELLA AUGUSTA (1852–1932)
Dragon, The
Dragon, The   Taylor, D.   1958
Spreading the News (1904)
Bubbles   Bath, H.   1923

GRIMM, JACOB LUDWIG CARL (1785–1863)/
   GRIMM, WILHELM CARL (1786–1859)
fairy tales, various:
Golden Bird   Russo, W.   1984*
Juniper Tree   Glass, P.   1985
Juniper Tree   Kesselman, W. 1982
Juniper Tree   Toovey, A.   1993
Juniper Tree   Watkins, R.   1997
Princess Maleen   Schonthal, R.   1989
Transformations   Susa, C.   1973
Wise and Foolish   List, K.   1951
Brementown Musicians, The
Ballad of the Bremen
   Band   Arlen, D.   1977
Grimm Duo   Earls, P.   1976
Musicians of Bremen   Balkin, A.   1972
Fisherman and His Wife, The
Fisherman and His Wife Bingham, S.   1987
Fisherman and His Wife Schuller, G.   1970
Fisherman's Wife   Stein, L.   1955
Goose Girl, The
Goose Girl   Pasatieri, T.   1981
Hansel and Gretel
Hansel & Gretel   Schickele, P.   1972
Little Red Riding Hood
Little Redinka   Eaton, M.   1991

Little Red Riding Hood	A'Becket, M.	1842
Rapunzel		
Rapunzel	Hammond, T.	1953
Rapunzel	Harrison, L.	1959
Rapunzel	Brooks, R.	1971
Rumpelstiltskin		
Rumpelstiltskin	Barber, K.	1978

GRIMMELSHAUSEN, J. J. C. VON (1622–1676)
Trutz Simplex (1669)

Play of Mother Courage	McCabe, J.	1974*

GUERDON, DAVID
Buanderie, La

Dream Child	Mollicone, H.	1975
Golden Bull, The		
Cabinet, The	Reeve, W., et al.	1802

GUTTIL JATTAK (BUDDHIST TALE)

Broken Strings	Vir, P.	1992

HALE, EDWARD EVERETT (1822–1909)
Man without a Country

Man without a Country	Damrosch, W.	1937

HARDY, THOMAS (1840–1928)
Mayor of Casterbridge, The (1874)

Mayor of Casterbridge	Tranchell, P.	1951
Ruined Maid	Barab, S.	1981
Three Strangers, The		
Three Strangers	Maconchy, E.	1968
Trumpet Major, The (1879)		
Trumpet Major	Hoddinott, A.	1981
Under the Greenwood Tree (1872)		
Mellstock Quire	Harper, E.	1988
Woodlanders, The (1887)		
Woodlanders, The	Paulus, S.	1985

HARRIS, ED
Flowers of the Dead Red Sea (1991)

Flowers	Hardy, J.	1994

HARRIS, JOEL CHANDLER (1848–1908)
Uncle Remus (1880)

Uncle Remus	Johnson, C.	1905–7*

HARTE, BRETT (1836–1902)
Outcasts of Poker Flat, The

Outcasts of Poker Flat	Adler, S.	1962
Outcasts of Poker Flat	Beckler, S. R.	1960
Outcasts of Poker Flat	MacSems, W.	1972*

HAŠEK, JAROSLAV (1883–1923)
Good Soldier Schweik, The (1930)

Good Soldier Schweik	Kurka, R.	1958

HAUPTMANN, GERHARD (1862–1946)
Versunkene Glocke, Die (1896)

Sunken Bell	Ruggles, C.	1912–23*

HAWTHORNE, NATHANIEL (1804–1864)
general:

My Kinsman	Saylor, B.	1976
Wedding Knell	Verrall, J.	1955

Dr. Heidegger's Experiment (1837)

Dr. Heidegger's Experiment	Raphling, S.	1956
Dr. Heidegger's Fountain of Youth	Beeson, J.	1978
Experiment, The	Schwartz, P.	1956

Feathertop (1846)

Clarkstown Witch	Novak, L.	1959
Feathertop	Barnes, E.	1980
Feathertop	Barthelson, J.	1968
Scarecrow, The	Lockwood, N.	1945

Great Stone Face, The (1851)

Great Stone Face	Kalmanoff, M.	1968

Maypole of Merry Mount (1836)

Merry Mount	Hanson, H.	1933
Merry Mount	Smith, D. S.	1912–13*

Rappaccini's Daughter (1844)

Garden of Mystery	Cadman, C. W.	1925
Poisoned Kiss	Vaughan Williams, R.	1936
Rappaccini's Daughter	Bender, E.	1992
Rappaccini's Daughter	Dennison, S.	1984
Rappaccini's Daughter	Garwood, M.	1980
Rappaccini's Daughter	Riley, D.	1981–84*

Scarlet Letter, The (1850)

Hester Prynne	Claflin, A.	1934
Scarlet Letter	Damrosch, W.	1896
Scarlet Letter	DiDomenica, R.	1972*
Scarlet Letter	Giannini, V.	1938
Scarlet Letter	Herman, M.	1992
Scarlet Letter	Kaufmann, W.	1961
Scarlet Letter	Kroll, F.	1965*
Scarlett Letter	Lybbert, D.	1964–67*
Scarlet Letter	Mann, R. W.	1970*

The Snow Image (1851)

Childhood Miracle	Rorem, N.	1955

Young Goodman Brown (1835)

Goodman Brown	Fink, H.	1968
Young Goodman Brown	Lenel, L.	1963

HEINE, HEINRICH (1797–1856)
Belsazer

Belsazer	Werder, F.	1988

HELLMAN, LILLIAN (1905–1984)
Little Foxes, The (1939)

Regina	Blitzstein, M.	1949

HENRY, O. [WILLIAM SYDNEY PORTER] (1862–1910)
general:

Cop and the Anthem	Cohen, S.	1982

Gift of the Magi, The (1906)

Della's Gift	Welcher, D.	1987
Enchanted Kiss	Bennett, R. R.	1945
Gift of the Magi	Bingham, S.	1984
Gift of the Magi	Brown, R.	1985
Gift of the Magi	Magney, R. T.	1964

Last Leaf, The

Last Leaf	Henderson, A.	1979

INGRISCH, LOTTE
general:
Evening for Three   Victory, G.   1976
IONESCO, EUGÈNE (1912–1997)
Cantatrice chauve, La (1948)
Bald Prima Donna   Kalmanoff, M.   1963
Jacques, ou, La soumission (1953)
Jack and Roberta   Cain, T.   1981
Tueur sans gages (1958)
Photo of the Colonel   Searle, H.   1964
IRVING, WASHINGTON (1783–1859)
Alhambra (1832)
Ahmad al Ramel   Horn, C. E.   1840
Legend of Sleepy Hollow, The (1820)
Headless Horseman   Moore, D.   1937
Legend of SleepyHollow   Haskins, R.   1976*
Sleepy Hollow   Maretzek, M.   1879
Rip Van Winkle (1819–20)
Rip Van Winkle   Bristow, G. F.   1855
Rip Van Winkle   De Koven, R.   1920
Rip Van Winkle   Jordan, J.   1897
Rip Van Winkle   Manning, E.   1932
Rip Van Winkle   Rockwell, R. W.   1989
Rip Van Winkle   Smith, G.   1991
Student of Salamanca, The
Alchymist, The   Bishop, H. R.   1832

JACOBS, WILLIAM WYMARK (1863–1943)
Captains All
Boatswain's Mate   Smyth, E.   1916
Monkey's Paw, The
Monkey's Paw   Alexander, W.   1972
Monkey's Paw   Halpern, S.   1965
Monkey's Paw   Hamm, C.   1952
JACOBSEN, JENS PETER (1847–1885)
Niels Lyhne (1880)
Fennimore and Gerda   Delius, F.   1919
JAMES, C. L. R. (B. 1901)
Black Jacobins, The
Toussaint   Blake, D.   1977
JAMES, HENRY (1843–1916)
Aspern Papers, The (1888)
Aspern Papers   Argento, D.   1988
Last of the Valerii, The
Voice of Ariadne   Musgrave, T.   1974
Owen Wingrave (1892)
Owen Wingrave   Britten, B.   1971
Turn of the Screw, The (1898)
Turn of the Screw   Britten, B.   1954
Washington Square (1881)
Washington Square   Pasatieri, T.   1976
Wings of the Dove (1902)
Wings of the Dove   Moore, D.   1961
JARRY, ALFRED (1873–1907)
Ubu roi (1896)
Ubu   Toovey, A.   1992

Ubu Roi   ApIvor, D.   1966–67*
JEFFERIES, RICHARD (1848–1887)
Story of My Heart
Vision, A   Ridout, A.   1974
JEFFERS, ROBINSON (1872–1962)
Medea (1946)
Medea in Corinth   Lees, B.   1971
JEVON, THOMAS (1652–1688)
Devil of a Wife (1686, possib. with T. Shadwell)
Devil to Pay   **   1731
JOHNSON, CHARLES (1679–1748)
Country Lasses (1715)
Lady of the Manor   Hook, J.   1778
JONSON, BEN (1573–1637)
Alchemist, The (1612)
Alchemist, The   Scott, C.   1925
Catiline Conspiracy (1611)
Catiline Conspiracy   Hamilton, I.   1974
Devil Is an Ass, The
Spanish Lady   Elgar, E.   1929–33*
Oberon, the Fairy Prince (1611)
Fairy Prince   Arne, T. A.   1771
Volpone (1606)
Volpone   Antheil, G.   1953
Volpone   Burt, F.   1960
Volpone   Coombs, J.   1957
Volpone   Gruenberg   1948–58*
JOYCE, JAMES (1882–1941)
poems:
Dead, The   Boren, M.   1993

KAFKA, FRANZ (1883–1924)
Amerika (Der Verschollene, pub. 1927)
America   Kohs, E. B.   1970
Visitation, The   Schuller, G.   1967
Prozess, Der (pub. 1925)
**Stanley and the Monkey
  King**   White, J.   1975
Verwandlung, Die (1915)
Metamorphosis   Howard, B.   1983
Metamorphosis   White, M.   1968
KAGUYAHME LEGEND
**From the Towers of
  the Moon**   Moran, R.   1992
KARINTHY, FERENC
tales:
Magic Chair   Zador, E.   1966
KAY, JACKIE
poems:
Twice through the Heart Turnage, M.-A. 1997
KAZANTZAKIS, NIKOS (1883–1957)
Christ Recrucified (1951)
Greek Passion   Martinů, B.   1961

KEATS, JOHN (1795–1821)
Endymion (1817)
Endymion   Antill, J. H.   1953

KELLER, GOTTFRIED (1819–1890)
Leute von Seldwyla, Die (pts. 1 and 2, 1856, 1874): *Romeo und Julia auf dem Dorfe*
Satan's Trap   Piket, F.   1960
Village Romeo and
Juiliet   Delius, F.   1907

KEMENY, JULIA
tales:
Unexpected Visitor Kondorossy, L. 1956

KENNEDY-FRASER, MARJORY
Songs of the Hebrides
Seal-Woman   Bantock, G.   1924

KIM, RICHARD E. (B. 1932)
Martyred, The (1964)
Martyred, The   Wade, J.   1970

KIM KI-PAL (B. 1937)
Martyred, The
Martyred, The   Wade, J.   1970

KING KONG (1933)
Second Mrs. Kong   Birtwistle, H.   1994

KINGSLY, CHARLES (1819–1875)
Westward Ho! (1855)
Westward Ho!   Miles, P. N.   1913

KIPLING, RUDYARD (1865–1936)
general:
Elephant's Child   Hagen, D.   1994*
Jungle Book, The (1894)
Baa Baa Black Sheep Berkeley, M.   1993
Just So Stories
Solomon and Balkis Thompson, R.   1942

KLEIST, HEINRICH VON (1777–1811)
Marquise von O, Die (1808)
Marquesa of O   Siegmeister, E. 1982
Zerbrochene Krug, Der (1811)
Amorous Judge   Gross, E.   1965

KOCH, KENNETH (B. 1925)
Bertha
Bertha   Rorem, N.   1973
poems:
Hearing   Rorem, N.   1977

KOTZEBUE, AUGUST VON (1761–1819)
Spanier von Peru, Die (1797)
Virgin of the Sun Bishop, H. R.   1812
Virgin of the Sun Gilfert, C.   1823
Virgin of the Sun Pelissier, V.   1800
Wildfang, Der
Of Age Tomorrow   Kelly, M.   1800

KRASINSKI, ZYGMUNT (1812–1859)
Nie-boska komedia (1835)
Undivine Comedy   Finnissy, M.   1988

KREYMBORG, ALFRED (1883–1966)
Lima Beans
Lima Beans   Townsend, D.   1956

LABICHE, EUGÈNE (1815–1888)
Chapeau de paille d'Italie, Un (1851)
Haste to the Wedding Grossmith, G. 1892

LACLOS, PIERRE CHODERLOS DE (1741–1803)
Liaisons dangereuses, Les (1782)
Dangerous Liaisons Susa, C.   1994

LACY, JOHN (D. 1681)
Sauny the Scot, or, The Taming of the Shrew
Cure for a Scold   **   1735

LA FLESCHE, FRANCIS (D. 1932)
short stories:
Land of the Misty Water Cadman, C. 1909–12*

LA FONTAINE, JEAN DE (1621–1695)
Fables (1668–94)
Fables   Aitken, H.   1975
Fables   Rorem, N.   1971

LANCASTER, CHARLES SEARS
Advice to Husbands
Estranged   Sedgwick, A. B. 1876

LARDNER, RING (1885–1933)
Haircut, The
Haircut   Morgenstern, S. 1969

LAVIN, MARY (B. 1912)
stories:
Inland Woman   Chisholm, E.   1953

LAWLER, RAY
Summer of the Seventeenth Doll, The (1953)
Summer of the Seventeenth
Doll   Mills, R.   1996

LAWRENCE, D. H. (1885–1930)
Tickets, Please
Tickets, Please   Nelson, R.   1985

LEAR, EDWARD (1812–1888)
Mr. and Mrs. Discobbolos
Mr. and Mrs.
Discobbolos   Westergaard, P. 1966

LEE, NATHANIEL (1653?–1692)
Rival Queens, The (1677)
Rival Queens   Gottfried/Purcell 1701

LEIVICK, HALPER (1888–1962)
Goylem
Golem   Casken, J.   1989
Golem, The   Ellstein, A.   1962
Golem, The   Sitsky, L.   1980*
Golem, The   Weiner, L.   1957

LEPRINCE DE BEAUMONT, MME. (JEANNE-MARIE) (1711–1780)
Belle et la bête, La

Beauty and the Beast   DiGiacomo, F. 1974
Beauty and the Beast   Easton, M. 1989
Beauty and the Beast   Giannini, V. 1938
Beauty and the Beast   Murray, J. 1974
Beauty and the Beast   Oliver, S. 1984
Beauty and the Beast   Schafer, R. 1938

LEROUX, GASTON (1868–1927)
Fantôme de l'Opéra, Le (1911)
Phantom of the Opera   Lloyd Webber, A. 1986

LESAGE, ALAIN RENÉ (1668–1747)
Diable boîteux, Le
Satanella   Balfe, M. 1860
Histoire de Gil Blas de Santillane
Boy of Santillane   Cooke/Blewitt 1827

LESSING, DORIS (B. 1919)
Canopus in Argos: Archives (1979–83)
Making of the
  Representative   Glass, P. 1988
Marriages between
  Zones   Glass, P. 1995

LESSING, GOTTHOLD EPHRAIM (1729–1781)
Nathan der Weise (1779)
Nathan the Wise   Kondorossy, L. 1969

LESY, MICHAEL (B. 1945)
Wisconsin Death Trip (1973)
Black River   Susa, C. 1975

LEVINE, RHODA
Harrison Loved His Umbrella
Harrison Loved His
  Umbrella   Hollingsworth, S. 1981

LEWIS, C. S. (1898–1963)
Lion, the Witch, and the Wardrobe, The
Lion, the Witch   McCabe, J. 1990

LEWIS, JANET (B. 1899)
Invasion, The (1932)
Legend, The   Murray, B. 1987
Wife of Martin Guerre, The (1941)
Wife of Martin Guerre   Bergsma, W. 1956

LEWIS, MATTHEW G. (1775–1818)
East Indian, The (1800)
Rich and Poor   Horn, C. E. 1812
Monk, The (1796)
Raymond and Agnes   Loder, E. J. 1855
Rugantino, or, The Bravo of Venice
Bianca   Balfe, M. 1860
Wood Daemon, The (1811)
One O'Clock   King, M. 1811

LEYA, LEON
Portrait vivant, Le (1842, with Mélesville)
Love's Triumph   Wallace, V. 1862

LIADOV, ANTOL C. (1855–1914)
Soeur Béatrice
Beatrice   Hoiby, L. 1959

LINNEY, ROMULUS (B. 1930)
Death of King Philip, The
Death of King Philip   Earls, P. 1976

LOCKROY, JOSEPH PHILIPPE (1803–1891)
Charlot (with Anicet-Brougeois, Vanderburch)
Follies of a Night   Gabriel, V. ca. 1870

LONGFELLOW, HENRY WADSWORTH (1807–1882)
Courtship of Miles Standish, The (1858)
Courtship of Miles
  Standish   Ewart, F. 1931
Courtship of Miles
  Standish   Spelman, T. 1941
Evangeline (1847)
Evangeline   Luening, O. 1948
Evangeline   Rice, E. E. 1874
Masque of Pandora, The (1875)
Masque of Pandora   Cellier, A. 1881
Masque of Pandora   Freer, E. E. 1933
Spanish Student, The (1843)
Victorian   Edwards, J. 1883

LOOVIS, JANICE
Shining Chalice, The
Shining Chalice   Van Grove, I. 1964

LOTI, PIERRE (L. M. J. VIAUD, 1850–1923)
Madame Chrysathème (1887)
Geisha, The   Jones, S. 1896
Ramuntcho (1897)
Ramuntcho   Taylor, D. 1942

LOWNDES BELLOC, MARIE (1868–1947)
Lodger, The (1913)
Lodger, The   Tate, P. 1960

MABINOGION, THE (MEDIEVAL WESLH)
Cauldron of Annwn, triology:
  Bronwen   Holbrooke, J. 1929
  Children of Don   Holbrooke, J. 1912
  Dylan   Holbrooke, J. 1914

MACDONALD, GEORGE (1824–1905)
Phantastes
Magic Mirror   Holst, G. 1896

MACDONOUGH, GLEN (1870–1924)
Night in Old Paris, A
Night in Old Paris   Hadley, H. 1924

MACHIAVELLI, NICCOLÒ (1469–1527)
general:
Married Men Go to Hell   Franchetti, A. 1975

MACKAYE, PERCY (1875–1956)
Scarecrow, The (1917)
Scarecrow, The   Lockwood, N. 1945

MACKAYE, STEELE (1842–1894)
Hazel Kirke (1880)
Hazel Kirke   Houston, M. 1987

MacLeish, Archibald (1892–1982)
Fall of the City, The (1937)
Fall of the City   Cohn, J.   1955

Macpherson, James (1736–1796)
Poems of Ossian: Son of Fingal, The
Oithona   Barthelemon, F. 1768

Maeterlinck, Maurice (1862–1949)
Aveugles, Les (1890)
Blind, The   Oliver, S.   1972
Intruse, L' (1890)
Intruder, The   Feldman, J.   1984
Mort de Tintagiles, La (1894)
Death of Tintagiles   Collingwood, L. 1950
Death of Tintagiles   Isaacs, G.   1973

MAHABHARATA (ANCIENT INDIAN)
Sāvitri   Holst, G.   1916

Mahadevi (B. 1946)
poems, trans. A. K. Ramanujan
Chakravaka-Bird   Gilbert, A.   1982

Malamud, Bernard (1914–1986)
Angel Levine
Angel Levine   Siegmeister, E. 1985
Idiots First (1963)
Idiots First   Blitzstein, M.   1976
Lady of the Lake   Siegmeister, E. 1985
Magic Barrel, The (1958)
Magic Barrel   Blitzstein, M.   1964*
Notes from a Lady at a Dinner Party
Karla   Lehrman, L.   1974
Suppose a Wedding
Suppose a Wedding   Lehrman, L.   1996

Mann, Thomas (1875–1955)
Tod in Venedig, Der (1913)
Death in Venice   Britten, B.   1973
Mario und der Zauberer (1929)
Mario and the Magician Oliver, S.   1988
Mario and the Magician Somers, H.   1992
Mario and the Magician Thorne, F.   1994
Vertauschten Köpfe, Die (1940)
Transposed Heads   Glanville-Hicks 1954

Mansfield, Katherine (1888–1923)
short stories:
Fall of Miss Moss   Oliver, S.   1972
Poison
Poison   Hart, F.   1984

Marie de France (13th cent.)
Lai de Freine
Crimson Bird   Enebach, F.   1979

Marlowe, Christopher (1564–1593)
Tambourlaine the Great (ca. 1587)
Tambourlaine   Hamilton, I.   1977
Tamburlaine   Murdoch, E.   1971

Marmontel, Jean François (1723–1799)
Bergère des Alpes, La (from *Contes moraux*)
Shepherdess of the Alps Dibdin, C.   1780
Incas, Les
Columbus   Reinecke, A.   1797
Laurette
Clari   Bishop, H. R.   1823

Martí, José (1853–1895)
Niña, La
Child, The   Bernardo, J. R. 1974

Mason, William (1725–1797)
Caractacus (1759)
Caractacus   Arne, T. A.   1776

Massinger, Philip (1583–1640)
Prophetess, The (with J. Fletcher)
Dioclesian   Purcell, H.   1690

Mattiuzzi, Antonio (1717?–1778)
Tres mellizo and *Trois jumeaux venitiens*
Three and the Deuce   Storace, S.   1795

Maugham, W. Somerset (1874–1965)
Moon and Sixpence, The (1919)
Moon and Sixpence   Gardner, J.   1957
Rain (1921)
Sadie Thompson   Owen, R.   1997

Maupassant, Guy de (1850–1893)
En famille
Parlour, The   Williams, G.   1966
Rosier de Madonne Husson, Le (1828)
Albert Herring   Britten, B.   1947

May, Thomas (1595–1650)
Death of Rosamond, The
Rosamond   Arne, T. A.   1740
Rosamond   Arnold, S.   1767
Rosamond   Clayton, T.   1707

Mayakovsky, Vladimir (1893–1930)
general:
Mayakovsky and the Sun Daiken, M.   1971

McGahern, John (B. 1934)
short stories:
My Love   O'Connell, K.   1997

McLellan, Charles (1865–1916)
Leah Kleschna (1920)
Leah Kleschna   Freeman, H. L.   1930

Meinhold, Wilhelm (1797–1851)
Maria Schweidler (1843)
Amber Witch   Wallace, V.   1861

Mélésville [A.-H.-J. Duveyrier] (1787–1865)
Chevalier de Saint-Georges, Le (1840)
Bondman, The   Balfe, M.   1846
Portrait vivant, Le (1842, with L. Leya)
Love's Triumph   Wallace, V.   1862

MELVILLE, HERMAN (1819–1891)
Bartleby the Scrivener (1853)
Bartleby   Aschaffenburg   1964
Bartleby   Flanagan, W.   1961
Bell Tower, The (1856)
Bell Tower   Haskins, R.   1976*
Bell Tower   Krenek, E.   1957
Billy Budd (1891, pub. 1924)
Billy Budd   Britten, B.   1951
Confidence Man, The
Confidence Man   Rochberg, G.   1982
Moby Dick
Moby Dick   Brooks, R.   1987*
Moby Dick   Epstein, S.   1989*
Moby Dick   Low, J.   1955

MÉRIMÉE, PROSPER (1803–1870)
Colomba (1841)
Colomba   Mackenzie, A.   1883

MEYER-FÖRSTER, WILHELM (1862–1934)
Alt-Heidelberg (1902)
Student Prince   Romberg, S.   1924

MIDRASH, THE
Lilith   Drattel, D.   1997*

MIKAMI, OTOKICHI (1891–1944)
Yokinojo Henge
Actor's Revenge   Miki, M.   1979

MIKSZATH, KALMAN (1847–1910)
stories:
Fox, The   Kondorossy, L. 1961

MILLAY, EDNA ST. VINCENT
Aria da Capo (1920)
Aria da Capo   Baksa, R.   1968
Aria da Capo   Blank, A.   1958–60*
Aria da Capo   Burnham, C.   1955
Aria da Capo   Fore, B.   1951

MILLER, ARTHUR (B. 1915)
Creation of the World, The (1973)
Up from Paradise   Silverman, S.   1983
Crucible, The (1953)
Crucible, The   Ward, R.   1961

MILLER, ISABEL (B. 1924)
Place for Us (1969)
Patience and Sarah   Kimper, P.   1996

MILNER, HENRY M.
Masaniello (1824)
Masaniello   Bishop, H. R.   1825

MILNE, A. A. (1882–1956)
Ugly Duckling, The
Courtship of Camilla   Schonthal, R.   1980*

MILTON, JOHN (1608–1674)
Comus (1634)
Comus   Arne, T. A.   1738
Comus   Bishop, H. R.   1815
Paradise Lost (1667)
In the Beginning   Warren, R.   1982
Paradise Lost   Penderecki, K. 1978

MITCHISON, NAOMI (B. 1897)
Corn King and the Spring Queen, The
Corn King   Easdale, B.   1950

MOLIÈRE (1622–1673)
Amphitryon (1668)
Amphitryon 4   Blumenthal, H. 1962*
Ecole des femmes, Les (1662)
School for Wives   Liebermann, R. 1955
George Dandin (1668)
Metamorphoses, The   Dibdin, C.   1776
Mariage forcé, Le (1664)
Forced Marriage   Hart, F.   1928
Précieuses ridicules, Les (1659)
If the Cap Fits   Bush, G.   1956
Sicilien, Le (1667)
Metamorphoses   Dibdin, C.   1776
Sganarelle (1660)
Picture, The   Arne, T. A.   1745
Sganarelle   Archer, V.   1974
Sganarelle   Kalmanoff, M.   1974
Sganarelle   Kaufmann, W.   1958
Signor Deluso   Pasatieri, T.   1974
Tartuffe (1664)
Tartuffe   Benjamin, A.   1964
Tartuffe   Mechem, K.   1980

MOLNÁR, FERENC (1878–1952)
Witch, The
Breakfast Waltzes   Blumenfeld, H. 1988
Fritzi   Blumenfeld, H. 1979
Vörös Malum
Scarlet Mill   Zador, E.   1968

MONCRIEFF, W. T. (1794–1857)
Rochester
Nell Gwynne   Cellier, A.   1878

MONTEJO, ESTEBAN (1860–1973)
Autobiography of a Runaway Slave, The
Cimarrón, El   Henze, H. W.   1970

MONTIGNY, LOUVIGNY DE
Ordre du bon temps, L'
Order of Good Cheer   Willan, H.   1928

MOORE, BRIAN (B. 1921)
Luck of Ginger Coffey, The
Luck of Ginger Coffey   Pannell, R.   1967

MOORE, THOMAS (1779–1852)
general:
Light of the Harem   Thomas, A. G.   1879
Lallah Rookh (1817)
Lallah Rookh   Horn, C. E.   1818
Veiled Prophet of
  Khorassan   Sanford, C.   1881

Ring, The
Fairies' Revels Arnold, S. 1802

MOREAU, EMILE (1852–1922)
Madame Sans-Gêne (with V. Sardou)
Duchess of Dantzic Caryll, I. 1903

MORELL, CHARLES, SIR (1736–1765)
Tales of the Genii, The (1797)
Sadak and Kalasrade Packer, C. 1835

MORGENSTERN, CHRISTIAN (1871–1914)
Egon und Emilie
Edgar and Emily Toch, E. 1965

MORLEY, CHRISTOPHER (1890–1957)
Tree That Didn't Get Trimmed, The (1942)
Tree That Was
Christmas Kleinsinger, G. 1955

MORLEY, JAMES
Pastoral Galloway, J. 1988

MORTE D'ARTHUR, LE (1470)
Lancelot Hamilton, I. 1985

MORTON, JOHN MADISON (1811–1891)
Box and Cox (1848)
Cox and Box Sullivan, A. S. 1867
Our Wife (1856)
Désirée Sousa, J. P. 1884

MORTON, THOMAS (1764?–1838)
Columbus (1792)
Columbus Reinagle, A. 1797

MOSEL, TAD
All the Way Home (1961)
Death in the Family Mayer, W. 1983

MOSENTHAL, SALOMON (1821–1877)
Sonnenwendhof, Der
Helvellyn Macfarren, G. 1864

MOTOMASA, JÜRO (1395–1432)
Sumidagawa
Curlew River Britten, B. 1964
Sumidagawa Scarem, N. 1979
Sumida River Raybould, C. 1916

MUNCH, EDVARD (1864–1944)
paintings:
Frieze of Life Applebaum, E. 1983

MUNRO, H. H. SEE SAKI.

MURASAKI SHIKIBU (978?–1015?)
Genji monogatari hyoshaku (Tale of Genji)
Echoes of the Shining
Prince Cooper, S. 1985

MURDOCH, IRIS (B. 1919)
Servants and the Snow, The
Servants, The Matthias, W. 1980

MURGER, HENRY (HENRI) (1822–1861)
Scènes de la vie de bohème (1847–49)

Bohemians, The Kirschner, B. 1990
Rent Larson, J. 1996

MURPHY, ARTHUR (1727–1805)
School for Guardians, The (1767)
Love Finds the Way Arne, T., et al. 1777

MUSSET, ALFRED DE (1810–1857)
Notre-Dame
Notre-Dame of Paris Fry, W. 1864

NAGGLI, JOSEPHINA (B. 1910)
Sunday Costs Five Pesos (1937)
Sunday Costs Five
Pesos Haubiel, C. 1950

NAUFRAGEURS, LES (CORNISH DRAMA)
Wreckers, The Smyth, E. 1906

NAZIMI, GANJAVI (1141?–1203?)
Layla and Majnun
Song of Majnun Sheng, B. 1992

NESTROY, JOHANN (1801–1862)
Einen Jux will er sich machen
On the Razzle Orr, R. 1988
Haus der Temperamente, Das (1837)
Four-Score Blumenfeld, H. 1984
Schlimmen Buben in der Schule, Die (1847)
Bad Boys in School Meyerowitz, J. 1953

NEWMAN, RABBI LOUIS (B. 1893)
Woman on the Wall
Tamar and Judah Lavry, M. 1970

NILES, JOHN JACOB (1892–1980)
Carrion Crow Fletcher, G. 1953

NORRIS, FRANK (1870–1902)
McTeague (1900)
McTeague Bolcom, W. 1992

OATES, JOYCE (B. 1938)
Black Water
Black Water Duffy, J. 1997

OBADIAH THE PROSELYTE
Autobiography
Sonata about Jerusalem Goehr, A. 1971

OBEY, ANDRÉ (1892–1975)
Viol de Lucrèce, Le (1931)
Rape of Lucretia Britten, B. 1946

O'NEILL, EUGENE (1888–1953)
Before Breakfast (1913)
Before Breakfast Pasatieri, T. 1980
Dark Sonnet Chisholm, E. 1952
Desire Under the Elms (1924)
Desire Under the Elms Thomas, E. 1978
Emperor Jones (1920)
Emperor Jones Gruenberg, L. 1933
Ile (1917)
Ile Laufer, B. 1957

Mourning Becomes Electra (1931)
**Mourning Becomes
 Electra**   Levy, M. D.   1967
Rope, The
Rope, The   Mennini, L.   1955
OSTROVSKY, A. N. (1823–1886)
Artists and Admirers
Sasha   Oliver, S.   1983
Family Affair
Family Affair   Grant, J.   1994
OUIDA [MARIE LOUISE DE LA RAMÉEE]
 (1839–1908)
Signa
Signa   Cowen, F.   1893
OUSPENSKY, P. D. (1878–1947)
Strange Life of Ivan Osokin, The
**Strange Life of Ivan
 Osokin**   Gordon, P.   1994
OVID (43 B.C.–?A.D. 17)
Metamorphoses, iii
Semele   Eccles, J.   1706*
Semele   Handel, G. F.   1744
Metamorphoses, xiii, 750–897
Acis and Galatea   Handel, G. F.   1718
Hercules   Handel, G. F.   1745
OWEN, ALUN (B. 1926)
Rose Affair, The
Rose Affair   Kay, N.   1968

PARKMAN, FRANCIS (1823–1893)
Conspiracy of Pontiac, The (1870)
Conspiracy of Pontiac   Mayer, C.   1887
PASTERNAK, BORIS (1890–1960)
Last Summer, The and *Spectorsky*
**Electrification of the Soviet
 Union**   Osborne, N.   1987
PATON, ALAN (1903–1988)
Cry the Beloved Country (1948)
Lost in the Stars   Weill, K.   1949
PATRAT, JOSEPH (1732–1801)
Heureuse erreur, L' (1783)
Brother and Sister   Bishop, H. R.   1815
Match for a Widow   Dibdin, C.   1788
PAYNE, JOHN HOWARD (1791–1852)
Clari, the Maid of Milan (1823)
Clari   Bishop, H. R.   1823
Fall of Algiers   Bishop, H. R.   1825
PEABODY, JOSEPHINE PRESTON (1874–1922)
Piper, The (1921)
Legend of the Piper   Freer, E. E.   1925
PEACOCK, THOMAS L. (1785–1866)
Maid Marian (1822)
Maid Marian   Bishop, H. R.   1822

Nightmare Abbey (1818)
Nightmare Abbey   Allanbrook, D.   1960*
PERRAULT, CHARLES (1628–1703)
Contes de ma mère l'Oye (1697):
Barbe bleue
Blue-Beard   Kelly, M.   1798
Belle au bois dormant, La
Sleeping Beauty   Rubinstein, B.   1938
Cendrillon
Cinderella   Lacy, M. R.   1830
PETRONIUS, GAIUS (D. A.D. 66)
Satyricon, The
Ephesian Matron   Dibdin, C.   1769
PIGAULT-LEBRUN (1753–1835)
Rivaux d'eux mêmes, Les
Bee-Hive, The   Horn, C. E.   1811
PIRANDELLO, LUIGI (1867–1936)
Six Characters in Search of an Author (1921)
**Six Characters in Search
 of an Author**   Weisgall, H.   1959
PITT, CHARLES DIBDIN
String of Pearls, The (1847)
Sweeney Todd   Blyton, C.   1980*
Sweeney Todd   Sondheim, S.   1979
PIXÉRÉCOURT, R. C. G. DE (1773–1844)
Femme à deux maris, La
Wife of Two Husbands   Mazzinghi, J.   1803
Fortresse du Danube, La (1805)
Fortress, The   Hook, J.   1807
Pèlerin blanc, Le
Wandering Boys   Bishop, H. R.   1814
Tékéli, ou, Le siège de Montgatz (1803)
Tekeli   Hook, J.   1806
PLANCHÉ, JAMES ROBINSON (1796–1880)
Fortunio (1843)
Fortunio   Darley, F.   1883
PLATO (CA. 428–348 B.C.)
general:
Jacob's Room   Subotnick, M.   1993
Republic, The, Book VII
Shadowplay   Goehr, A.   1970
PLAUTUS, TITUS MACCIUS (CA. 254–184 B.C.)
Menaechmi
Double Trouble   Mohaupt, R.   1954
PLUTARCH (CA. A.D. 46–CA. 120)
general:
Isis and Osiris   Lutyens, E.   1976
POE, EDGAR ALLAN (1809–1849)
Cask of Amontillado, The (1846)
Cask of Amontillado   Copeland, S.   1993*
Cask of Amontillado   Currie, R.   1982
Cask of Amontillado   Hamm, C.   1953
Cask of Amontillado   Provenzano, A.   1968

Menaced Assassin	Jones, J. P.	1989

Fall of the House of Usher, The (1839)

Dream within a Dream	Currie, R.	1984
Fall of the House of Usher	Claflin, A.	1921*
Fall of the House of Usher	Glass, P.	1988
Fall of the House of Usher	Loomis, C.	1941
Fall of the House of Usher	Ruger, M. H.	1953
Fall of the House of Usher	Sandow, G.	1979
Fall of the House of Usher	Sitsky, L.	1965

Ligeia (1838)

Ligeia	Currie, R.	1987
Ligeia	Thomas, A. R.	1994

Masque of the Red Death, The (1842)

Gagliarda of a Merry Plague	Saminsky, L.	1925

System of Doctor Tarr, The (1845)

System, The	Bach, J.	1974

Tell-Tale Heart, The (1843)

Tell-Tale Heart	Adolphe, B.	1982

POTTER, BEATRIX (1866–1943)
Tailor of Gloucester, The

Tailor of Gloucester	Young, D.	1991*

POWELL, JAMES
Narcotic, The (1787)

Fast Asleep	Attwood, T.	1797

PRESCOTT, WILLIAM HICKLING
History of the Conquest of Mexico, The

Cortez	Bishop, H. R.	1823

PRIOR, MATTHEW (1664–1721)
Ladle, The

Ladle, The	Dibdin, C.	1773

Nut-Brown Maid, The

Henry and Emma	Arne, T. A.	1749

PURDY, JAMES (B. 1923)
Apache Dance

Apache Dance	Fennimore, J.	1975

Don't Call Me by My Right Name

Don't Call Me	Fennimore, J.	1975

PUSHKIN, ALEKSANDR (1799–1837)
Tales of Belkin, The

Mistress into Maid	Duke, V.	1958

QUEIROZ, JOSÉ MARIA EÇA DE (1845–1900)
Mandarim, O

Mandarin, The	Elkus, J.	1967

RABELAIS, FRANÇOIS (CA. 1490–1553?)
Femme muette, La

Dumb Wife	Horovitz, J.	1972
Dumb Wife	Gruenberg, L.	1922– 23*

RABINOFF, MAX (1877–1966)

Enchanter, The	Holbrooke, J.	1915

RACINE, JEAN (1639–1699)
Athalie (1691)

Athaliah	Weisgall, H.	1964

Esther (1689)

Esther	Meyerowitz, J.	1957

RADCLIFFE, ANN WARD (1764–1823)
Sicilian Romance, The (1790)

Apparition, The	Reeve, W.	1794

REGNARD, JEAN-FRANÇOIS (1655–1709)
Retour imprévu

Intriguing Chambermaid	**	1734

RENARD, M.

Rendezvous, The	Victory, G.	1989

REYERSON, FLORENCE
All on a Summer's Day (with C. Clements)

Game of Chance	Barab, S.	1957

RICE, CALE YOUNG (1872–1943)
Yolanda of Cyprus

Yolanda of Cyprus	Loomis, C.	1929

RICE, ELMER (1892–1967)
Street Scene (1929)

Street Scene	Weill, K.	1946

RICHARDSON, HOWARD
Dark of the Moon

Conjur Moon	Lloyd, T. C.	1979

RICHARDSON, SAMUEL (1689–1761)
Clarissa Harlowe (1747–48)

Clarissa	Holloway, R.	1990

Pamela (1740)

Maid of the Mill	Arnold, S.	1765
Maid of the Mill	Bishop, H. R.	1814
Maid of the Mill	Giordani, T.	1765
Maid of the Vale	Arne, M.	1775

RIMBAUD, ARTHUR (1854–1891)
general:

Seasons of Hell	Blumenfeld, H.	1996

ROBERTS, E. L.
Bleeding Heart, The

Bleeding Heart of Timpanogas	Hanson, W. F.	1928

ROBERTSON, T. W. (1829–1871)
David Garrick (1800)

David Garrick	Somerville, R.	1920

ROBIN HOOD BALLAD

Robin Hood	Ashton, W.	1730
Robin Hood	Burney, C.	1750
Robin Hood	De Koven, R.	1891
Robin Hood	Hewitt, J.	1800
Robin Hood	Macfarren, G.	1860

Robin Hood	Shield, W.	1784
Robin Hood	Tippett, M.	1934*

RÖLVAAG, OLE E. (1876–1931)
Giants in the Earth (1927)

Giants in the Earth	Moore, D.	1951

ROSE, REGINALD (B. 1920)
Final Ingredient, The (1959)

Final Ingredient	Amram, D.	1965

ROSSETTI, CHRISTINA GEORGINA (1830–1894)
Goblin Market (1893)

Gift, The	Ridout, A.	1971

poems:

Nightingale and the Rose	Firsova, E.	1994

ROSSNER, JUDITH
Emmeline (1980)

Emmeline	Picker, T.	1996

ROSTAND, EDMOND (1868–1918)
general:

Fantastics, The	Hart, F.	1918

Cyrano de Bergerac

Cyrano	Beeson, J.	1994
Cyrano	Damrosch, W.	1913
Cyrano de Bergerac	Effinger, C.	1968
Cyrano de Bergerac	Herbert, V.	1899
Cyrano de Bergerac	Jarrett, J.	1972
Cyrano de Bergerac	Pokrass, S. D.	1932

Trois Mousquetaires, Les (1844)

Three Musketeers	Dvorkin, J.	1991

ROSTEN, NORMAN (B. 1914)
Marilyn: The Untold Story

Marilyn	Laderman, E.	1993

ROUSSEAU, JEAN-JACQUES (1712–1778)
Café, Le

Coffee House	Carey, H.	1738

Devin du village, Le (1752)

Cunning Man	Burney, C.	1766
Magic Girdle	Barthelemon, F.	1770

RUTHENBURG, GRACE
Hans Bulow's Last Puppet (1930)

Last Puppet	Strilko, A.	1963

RYERSON, FLORENCE (B. 1894)
All on a Summer's Day

Game of Chance	Barab, S.	1957

SACHS, HANS (1494–1576)
general:

Strolling Clerk from Paradise	Wilson, C.	ca. 1952*

SACKS, OLIVER
Man Who Mistook His Wife for a Hat and Other Clinical Tales, The (1985)

Man Who Mistook His Wife for a Hat	Nyman, M.	1986

SADE, MARQUIS DE (1705–1778)
general:

Undivine Comedy	Finnissy, M.	1988

SAINT-FOIX [GERMAIN-FRANÇOIS POULLAIN] (1698–1776)
Isle sauvage, L' (1760)

Islanders, The	Dibdin, C.	1780

Oracle, L'

Daphne and Amintor	Arnold, S.	1765

SAKI [H. H. MUNRO] (1870–1916)
Background, The

One Man Show	Maw, N.	1964

Baker's Dozen

Fortune's Favorites	Barab, S.	1982

Beasts and Superbeasts (1914)

Beast and Superbeast	Martín, J.	1996

Open Window

Open Window	Arnold, M.	1956

SAMUEL BEN YAHYA BEN AL MAGHRIBI (12TH CENT.)
Chronicle

Sonata about Jerusalem	Goehr, A.	1971

SARDOU, VICTORIEN (1831–1908)
Madame Sans-Gêne (with E. Moreau)

Duchess of Dantzic	Caryll, I.	1903

SAROYAN, WILLIAM (1908–1981)
general:

Opera, Opera	Kalmanoff, M.	1956

Hello Out There (1941)

Hello Out There	Beeson, J.	1954

My Heart's in the Highlands (1939)

My Heart's in the Highlands	Ahlstrom, D.	1955*
My Heart's in the Highlands	Beeson, J.	1970

short stories:

Shala Fears for the Poor	Braxton, A.	1996

SAUNDERS, JAMES (B. 1925)
Barnstable (1961)

Barnstable	Burt, F.	1969

SCHEFFEL, JOSEPH VIKTOR VON (1826–1886)
Ekkehard (1857)

Ekkehard	Ewart, F.	1923

SCHEHADÉ, GEORGES
Histoire de Vasco, L' (1956)

Story of Vasco	Crosse, G.	1974

SCHILLER, FRIEDRICH (1759–1805)
Räuber, Die (1782)

Red Cross Knights	Attwood, T.	1799

Wilhelm Tell (1804)

Archers, The	Carr, B.	1796
Helvetic Liberty	**	1792

SCHNITZLER, ARTHUR (1862–1931)
Abschiedssouper

Farewell Supper	Hart, F.	1984

Empfindsame, Der

Man of Feeling	Oliver, S.	1980

SCOTT, (SIR) WALTER (1771–1832)
general:

Lord of the Isles	Rodwell, G.	1834
White Plume	Reeve, W.	1806

Antiquary, The (1826)

Antiquary, The	Bishop, H. R.	1820

Black Dwarf, The (1817)

Wizard, The	Horn, C. E.	1817

Guy Mannering (1815)

Guy Mannering	Attwood, T.	1816
White Lady	Cooke, T. S.	1826

Heart of Midlothian (1818)

Heart of Midlothian	Bishop, H. R.	1819
Heart of Midlothian	**	1849
Jeanie Deans	MacCunn, H.	1894

Ivanhoe (1819)

Ivanhoe	Parry, J.	1820
Ivanhoe	Sullivan, A. S.	1891

Kenilworth (1821)

Amy Robsart	Lara, I. de	1893

Lady of the Lake, The (1810)

Knight of Snowdoun	Bishop, H. R.	1811
Lady of the Lake	Francis, W.	1811
Lady of the Lake	Schmidt, K.	1931*

Legend of Montrose, The (1820)

Montrose	Bishop, H. R.	1822

Monastery, The

White Lady	Cooke, T. S.	1826

Old Morality (1817)

Battle of Bothwell Brigg	Bishop, H. R.	1820

Quentin Durward (1823)

Quentin Durward	Laurent, H. R.	1848
Quentin Durward	Maclean, A.	1893*

Rob Roy (1811)

Rob Roy	De Koven, R.	1894
Rob Roy Macgregor	Davy, J.	1818

Talisman, The (1825)

Talisman, The	Bishop, H. R.	1825

Waverley (1814)

Waverley	Rodwell, G.	1824

SEI SHONAGON (B. CA. 967)
Pillow Book, The (ca. 1002)

Pillow Book	Barry, G.	1980

SENECA (4 B.C.–A.D. 65)
Hercules Oetaeus

Heracles	Eaton, J.	1972

SHAFFER, PETER (B. 1926)
Amadeus (1980)

Little Nightmare Music	Schickele, P.	1982

Royal Hunt of the Sun, The (1965)

Royal Hunt of the Sun	Hamilton, I.	1977

SHAKESEPARE, WILLIAM (1564–1616)
general:

Make Me a Willow		
Cabin	Stoker, R.	1973

Anthony and Cleopatra (1607)

Antony and Cleopatra	Gruenberg, L.	1955*
Antony and Cleopatra	Barber, S.	1966

Comedy of Errors, The (1592–93)

Comedy of Errors	Bishop, H. R.	1819
Errors	Wilson-Dickson	1980

Hamlet (1600–1)

Hamlet	Kagen, S.	1962
Hamlet	Searle, H.	1968
Hamlet Travestie	Bray, J.	1811

Henry V (1599)

Agincourt	Boughton, R.	1924
At the Boar's Head	Holst, G.	1925

Love's Labour's Lost (1594–95)

Love's Labour's Lost	Bush, G.	1988
Love's Labour's Lost	Nabokov, N.	1973

Macbeth (1605–6)

Macbeth	Collingwood, A.	1934
Macbeth	Eccles, J.	1696
Macbeth	Goldman, E.	1961*
Macbeth	Halpern, S.	1965
Macbeth	Leveridge, R.	1702
Macbeth	Locke/Johnson	1673

Merchant of Venice, The (1596)

Merchant of Venice	Beecham, A. B.	1922
Shylock	La Violette, W.	1930

Merry Wives of Windsor, The (1600–1)

Merry Wives of		
Windsor	Horn et al.	1824
Sir John in Love	Vaughan Williams	1929

Midsummer Night's Dream, A (1596)

Fairies, The	Smith, J. C.	1755
Fairy Queen	Purcell, H.	1692
Midsummer Night's		
Dream	Bishop, H. R.	1816
Midsummer Night's		
Dream	Britten, B.	1960
Midsummer Night's		
Dream	Burney, C.	1763
Pyramus and Thisbe	Bruce, N.	1965
Pyramus and Thisbe	Converly R.	1982

Much Ado about Nothing (1598–99)

Much Ado about		
Nothing	Stanford, C.	1901
Sir John in Love	Vaughan Williams	1929

Othello (1604)

John Hooten	Russo, W.	1963

Pericles (1608–9)

Night of the Moonspell	Siegmeister, E.	1976
Pericles	Hovhaness, A.	1975

Rape of Lucrece, The (1594)

Rape of Lucretia	Britten, B.	1946

Richard III (1592–93)

STEELE, RICHARD (1672–1729)
essay:
Inkle and Yariko Arnold, S. 1787
STEELE, WILBUR D. (1886–1970)
How Beautiful with Shoes
Amarantha Ames, R. 1980
STEGNER, WALLACE (B. 1909)
Angle of Repose (1971)
Angle of Repose Imbrie, A. 1976
STEIN, GERTRUDE (1874–1946)
First Reader
In a Garden Kupferman, M. 1949
Woman in the Garden Fine, V. 1978
Three Plays
Doctor Faustus Ahlstrom, D. 1982
Doctor Faustus Kupferman, M. 1953
I Like It to be a Play Shere, C. 1989
Ladies Voices Kievman, C. 1973–74*
Ladies Voices Martin, V. 1956
Ladies Voices Shere, C. 1987
What Happened Shere, C. 1991*
Three Sisters Who Are Not Sisters (1946)
Three Sisters Who Are
 Not Sisters Ahlstrom, D. 1953
Three Sisters Who Are
 Not Sisters Hellerman, W. 1983
Three Sisters Who Are
 Not Sisters Rorem, N. 1971
STEINBECK, JOHN (1902–1968)
Burning Bright (1950)
Burning Bright Lewin, F. 1993
Of Mice and Men (1937)
Of Mice and Men Floyd, C. 1970
STEPHEN, JAMES
Isle of Youth, The
Feast of Samhain Chisholm, E. 1941
STERNE, LAURENCE (1713–1768)
Sentimental Journey (1768)
Sterne's Maria Pelissier, V. 1799
Tristram Shandy (1759–67)
Tristram Shandy McNally, L. 1783
STEVENSON, ROBERT LOUIS (1850–1894)
Beach of Falesá, The (1897)
Beach of Falesá Hoddinott, A. 1974
Bottle Imp, The
Bottle Imp Whiton, P. 1958
Markheim
Markheim Floyd, C. 1966
Markheim Miles, P. N. 1923
Rajah's Diamond, The
Rajah's Diamond Hill, A. 1979
Sire de Malétroit's Door, The
Door, The Mopper, I. 1956
Maletroit Door Barab, S. 1959
Sire de Maletroit Duke, J. 1958

Strange Case Dr. Jekyll and Mr. Hyde, The
(1886)
Dr. Jekyll and Mr. Hyde Fragale, F. D. 1953
Dr. Jekyll and Mr. Hyde O'Neal, B. 1980*
Weir of Hermiston, The (1896)
Hermiston Orr, R. 1975
ST. GEORGE AND THE DRAGON (MUMMER'S PLAY)
St. George and the
 Dragon Hart, F. 1931
STOCKTON, FRANK R. (1834–1902)
Old Pipes and the Dryad
Old Pipes and the
 Dryad Rea, A. 1980
STOKER, BRAM (1847–1912)
Dracula (1897)
Dracula Blyton, C. 1983
Dracula Franchetti, A. 1979
STOWE, HARRIET BEECHER (1811–1896)
Uncle Tom's Cabin (1852)
Uncle Tom's Cabin Florio, C. 1882
Uncle Tom's Cabin Grossmith, L. 1928*
Uncle Tom's Cabin Howard, G. 1852
STRACHEY, LYTTON (1880–1932)
Elizabeth and Essex (1928)
Gloriana Britten, B. 1953
STRINDBERG, AUGUST (1849–1912)
Dream Play (1902)
Dream Play Sullivan, T. 1988
Growing Castle Williamson, M. 1968
Lucky Peter's Travels (1882)
Lucky-Peter's Journey Williamson, M. 1968
Miss Julie (1888)
Miss Julie Alwyn, W. 1983
Miss Julie Rorem, N. 1965
Simoon (1905)
Simoon Chisholm, E. 1954
Simoon Meyerowitz, J. 1950
SUTRO, ALFRED (1863–1933)
Marriage Has Been Arranged, A
Will You Marry Me? Weisgall, H. 1989
SWANN, FRANCIS
Out of the Frying Pan
Rehearsal Call Giannini, V. 1962
SWIFT, JONATHAN (1667–1745)
Gulliver's Travels (1726)
Gulliver Bond, V. 1988
Lilliput Arnold, S. 1777
Travels Bond, V. 1995
SYLVIUS, AENEAS [PIUS II] (1405–1464)
works:
Lion and Androcles Eaton, J. 1974
SYNGE, JOHN M. (1871–1909)
Deirdre of the Sorrows

VOLTAIRE [F. M. AROUET] (1694–1778)
Anecdote sur l'homme au masque de fer (1764)
Island of St. Marguerite Shaw, T. 1789
Candide (1759)
Candide Bernstein, L. 1956

WADDELL, HELEN (1889–1965)
Wandering Scholars, The (1928)
Wandering Scholar Holst, G. 1934

WADSWORTH, WILLIAM (1821–1893)
White Doe of Rylstone, The
White Doe Ridout, A. 1987

WAKEFIELD MASTER (FL. 1400)
Wakefield Mystery Plays
Glory Coach Barnard, F. 1982

WALKER, MARGARET
Jubilee (1966)
Jubilee Kay, U. 1976

WALKER, GEORGE (1772–1847)
Don Raphael (1803)
Don Raphael Hewitt, J. 1804

WALPOLE, HORACE (1717–1797)
Castle of Otranto, The (1764)
Sicilian Romance Reeve, W. 1794

WARREN, MERCY (MRS.) (1728–1814)
Blockheads, The
Blockheads, The ** 1782?

WARREN, ROBERT PENN (1905–1989)
All the King's Men (R. P. Warren)
Willie Stark Floyd, C. 1981
Ballad of Billie Potts, The
Land between the
Rivers Buskirk, C. van 1956

WEBSTER, JOHN (CA. 1580–1625)
Duchess of Malfi, The (ca. 1613)
Duchess of Malfi Burton, S. D. 1978
Duchess of Malfi Oliver, S. 1971

WEDEKIND, FRANK (1864–1918)
general:
Conversion, The Werder, F. 1973
Kammersänger, Der (1899)
Tenor, The Weisgall, H. 1952

WELLS, H. G. (1866–1946)
Country of the Blind (1911)
Country of the Blind Turnage, M.-A. 1997
Time Machine, The (1895)
Time Rocker Reed, L. 1997

WERFEL, FRANZ (1890–1945)
Weg der Verheissung, Der (1935)
Eternal Road Weill, K. 1937

WESKER, ARNOLD (B. 1932)
Caritas (1981)
Caritas Saxon, R. 1991

WEST, GILBERT (1703–1756)
Institution of the Order of the Garter, The
Institution of the Garter Dibdin, C. 1771

WHARTON, EDITH (1862–1937)
Ethan Frome (1911)
Ethan Frome Allanbrook, D. 1952
Ethan Frome Beall, J. 1997
Roman Fever
Roman Fever Ward, R. 1993

WHITE, E[LWYN] B[ROOKS] (B. 1899)
Charlotte's Web
Charlotte's Web Ahlin, L. 1988
Some Pig Larsen, L. 1973

WHITE, PATRICK (B. 1912)
Voss (1957)
Voss Meale, R. 1982

WHITING, JOHN ROBERT (1917–1963)
Penny for a Song
Penny for a Song Bennett, R. R. 1967

WHITMAN, WALT (1819–1892)
Mystic Trumpeter, The
Mystic Trumpeter Starer, R. 1983

WIELAND, CHRISTOPH MARTIN (1733–1813)
Oberon (1780)
Oberon Cooke, T. S. 1826
Oberon Weber, C. M. v. 1826

WIESEL, ELIE (B. 1928)
Night (1958)
Jacob's Room Subotnick, M. 1987

WILDE, OSCAR (1854–1900)
Birthday of the Infanta, The (1889)
Birthday of the Infanta Nelson, R. 1956
Birthday of the Infanta Stoker, R. 1963
Canterville Ghost, The (1887)
Canterville Ghost Kalmanoff, M. 1967
Death of a Ghost Gottlieb, J. 1988
De Profundis (1905)
De Profundis Sitsky, L. 1982
Duchess of Padua, The (1891)
Guido Ferranti Van Etten, J. 1914
Happy Prince, The (1888)
Happy Prince Williamson, M. 1965
Lord Arthur Savile's Crime (1891)
Lord Arthur Savile's
Crime Bush, G. 1972
Nightingale and the Rose, The (1888)
Nightingale and the Rose Firsova, E. 1994
Nightingale and the Rose Garwood, M. 1973
Nightingale and the Rose Lessner, G. 1942
Picture of Dorian Gray, The (1891)
Dorian Deutsch, H. A. 1995
Picture of Dorian Gray Liebermann, L. 1996
Selfish Giant, The (1888)
Giant's Garden Krane, S. 1960

Selfish Giant	Burtch, M.	1969
Selfish Giant	Easton, M.	1994*
Selfish Giant	Hollingsworth, S.	1981
Selfish Giant	Perry, J.	1964*
Selfish Giant	Ridout, A.	1977
Selfish Giant	Shaw, F.	1973*
Selfish Giant	Wilding-White	1955
Selfish Giant	Wilson, C.	1973

WILDER, THORNTON (1897–1975)
Life in the Sun, A (1955)
| Alcestiad, The | Talma, L. | 1962 |
Long Christmas Dinner, The (1931)
| Long Christmas Dinner | Hindemith, P. | 1961 |

WILLIS, JEANNE
Monster Bed, The
| Monster Bed | de Kenessey, S. | 1990 |

WILLIAMS, TENNESSEE (1911–1983)
I Rise in Flame, Cried the Phoenix (1951)
| I Rise in Flame | Flanagan, T. J. | 1980 |

WILSON, CHARLES MORROW
Acres of Sky (1930)
| Acres of Sky | Kreutz, A. | 1951 |

WILSON, JOHN MACKAY (1804–1835)
Tales of the Borders
| Abbot of Drimock | Musgrave, T. | 1962 |

WILSON, LANFORD (B. 1937)
This Is the Rill Speaking (1965)
| This Is the Rill Speaking | Hoiby, L. | 1994 |

WODEHOUSE, P. G. (1881–1975)
Mr. Mulliner Speaks
| Ordeal of Osbert | Davis, A. | 1949 |

WOOLF, VIRGINIA (1882–1941)
Jacob's Room (1922)
| Jacob's Room | Subotnick, M. | 1993 |
Mrs. Dalloway (1925)
| Mrs. Dalloway | Larsen, L. | 1995 |

writings:
| Woman in the Garden | Fine, V. | 1978 |

WORDSWORTH, WILLIAM (1770–1850)
White Doe of Rylstone, The
| White Doe | Ridout, A. | 1987 |

WYCHERLY, WILLIAM (1610?–1716)
Gentleman Dancing Master, The (1673)
| Dancing Master | Arnold, M. | 1962 |

YAMAGUCHI, TOHR
Golden Crane
| Golden Crane | Kay, D. H. | 1985* |

YEATS, WILLIAM BUTLER (1865–1939)
Cat and the Moon, The
| Cat and the Moon | Putsché, T. | 1960 |
Calvary
| Calvary | Pasatieri, T. | 1971 |
Death of Cuchulain, The
| Death of Cuchulain | Brettingham Smith, J. | 1973* |
Deirdre (1907)
| Deirdre | Stein, L. | 1957 |
Land of Heart's Desire, The (1904)
| Land of Heart's Desire | Hart, F. | 1914 |
Full Moon in March (1935)
| Full Moon in March | Harbison, J. | 1979 |
Pot of Broth, A (1929)
| Pot of Broth | Haufrecht, H. | 1965* |

YORK MYSTERY PLAYS (EARLY 14TH CENTURY)
| Cappemakers, The | Taverner, J. | 1964 |

ZOLA, EMILE (1840–1902)
Fête à Coqueville, La (1883)
| Fête at Coqueville | Rea, A. | 1976 |
Thérèse Raquin (1868)
| Thérèse Raquin | Finnissy, M. | 1993 |
| Thérèse Raquin | Stoker, R. | 1975* |

Part II: Titles Cited in Part I

ABSCHIEDSSOUPER (A. SCHNITZLER)
ACRES OF SKY (C. M. WILSON)
ADÈLE ET THÉODORE (S. F. GENLIS)
ADMIRABLE BASHVILLE, THE (G. B. SHAW)
ADORATION OF THE MAGI, THE (H. BOSCH)
ADVICE TO HUSBANDS (C. S. LANCASTER)
AGAMEMNON (AESCHYLUS)
ALBERGO EMPEDOCLE (E. M. FORSTER)
ALCHEMIST, THE (B. JONSON)
ALHAMBRA (W. IRVING)
ALICE'S ADVENTURES IN WONDERLAND
  (L. CARROLL)

ALKESTIS (EURIPIDES)
ALL ON A SUMMER'S DAY (RYERSON/CLEMENTS)
ALL THE KING'S MEN (R. P. WARREN)
ALL THE WAY HOME (T. MOSEL)
ALT-HEIDELBERG (W. MEYER-FÖRSTER)
AMADEUS (P. SHAFFER)
AMERIKA (*DER VERSCHOLLENE*, F. KAFKA)
AMI FRITZ (ERCKMANN-CHATRIAN)
AMOR DE DON PERLIMPLÍN CON BELISA EN SU JARDÍN (F. GARCÍA LORCA)
AMPHITRYON (J. DRYDEN)
AMPHITRYON (MOLIÈRE)

CHANGED BRIDEGROOM, THE (L. HOLBERG)
CHAO FAMILY ORPHAN, THE
CHAPEAU DE PAILLE D'ITALIE, UN (LABICHE)
CHARLOT (J. P. LOCKROY ET AL.)
CHARLOTTE'S WEB (E. B. WHITE)
CHATTERTON (A. DE VIGNY)
CHEVALIER DE SAINT-GEORGES, LE (MÉLÉSVILLE)
CHICKEN LITTLE
CHRISTMAS CAROL, A (C. DICKENS)
CHRIST RECRUCIFIED (N. KAZANTZAKIS)
CINDERELLA (G. BASILE)
CLANDESTINE MARRIAGE, THE (GARRICK/
    COLMAN SR.)
CLARISSA HARLOWE (S. RICHARDSON)
COCK AND THE FOX, THE (SEE*THE CANTERBURY
    TALES*)
COLLEEN BAWN (D. BOUCICAULT)
COLOMBA (P. MÉRIMÉE)
COLUMBUS (T. MORTON)
COMEDY OF ERRORS, THE (W. SHAKESPEARE)
COMUS (J. MILTON)
CONFIDENCE MAN, THE (H. MELVILLE)
CONSIDER THE LILIES (R. HUPTON)
CONSOLATION OF PHILOSOPHY, THE (BOETHIUS)
CONTES DE MA MÈRE L'OYE (C. PERRAULT)
CORN KING AND THE SPRING QUEEN, THE
    (N. MITCHISON)
CORONATION STREET
CORPUS CHRISTI PLAYS
COUNTRY LASSES (C. JOHNSON)
COUNTRY OF THE BLIND (H. G. WELLS)
COUNTRY-WAKE, THE (T. DOGGET)
COURTSHIP OF MILES STANDISH, THE
    (H. W. LONGFELLOW)
CRAZY TO KILL (A. CARDWELL)
CREATION OF THE WORLD, THE (A. MILLER)
CRICKET ON THE HEARTH, THE (C. DICKENS)
CRITIC, THE (R. SHERIDAN)
CROSS AND THE CRESCENT, THE (J. DAVIDSON)
CROSSING, THE (G. GILHAM)
CRUCIBLE, THE (A. MILLER)
CRY THE BELOVED COUNTRY (A. PATON)
CYMON AND IPHIGENIA (J. DRYDEN)
CYRANO DE BERGERAC (E. ROSTAND)

DAME AUX CAMÉLIAS, LA (A. DUMAS)
DARK OF THE MOON (H. RICHARDSON)
DAVID GARRICK (T. W. ROBERTSON)

DAYMIO, THE (L. DURAN)
DEATH OF CUCHULAIN, THE (W. B. YEATS)
DEATH OF ROSAMOND, THE (T. MAY)
DEATH OF THE VIRGIN (CARAVAGGIO)
DECAMERON, THE (G. BOCCACCIO)
DECISION, THE (K. TAYLOR)
DEIRDRE (W. B. YEATS)
DEIRDRE OF THE SORROWS (J. M. SYNGE)
DE PROFUNDIS (O. WILDE)
DESERTED VILLAGE, THE (O. GOLDSMITH)
DESIRE UNDER THE ELMS (E. O'NEILL)
DEVIL AND DANIEL WEBSTER, THE (S. V. BENÉT)
DEVIL IS AN ASS, THE (B. JONSON)
DEVIL OF A WIFE (T. JEVON)
DEVIL TO PAY, THE (C. COFFEY)
DEVIL'S DISCIPLE, THE (G. B. SHAW)
DEVIN DU VILLAGE, LE (J.-J. ROUSSEAU)
DIABLE AMOUREUX, LE (J. DE CAZOTTE)
DIARY OF A MADMAN, THE (N. GOGOL)
DON CÉSAR DE BAZAN (D. ENNERY)
DON JUAN (BYRON)
DON QUIXOTE (CERVANTES)
DON QUIXOTE IN ENGLAND (H. FIELDING)
DON RAPHAEL (G. WALKER)
DON'T CALL ME BY MY RIGHT NAME (J. PURDY)
DOS MADRES (M. DE UNAMUNO)
DRACULA (B. STOKER)
DRAGON, THE (LADY GREGORY)
DREAM OF EUGENE ARAM, THE (T. HOOD)
DREAM PLAY (A. STRINDBERG)
DR. HEIDEGGER'S EXPERIMENT (N. HAWTHORNE)
DR. OX'S EXPERIMENT (J. VERNE)
DUCHESS OF MALFI, THE (J. WEBSTER)
DUCHESS OF PADUA, THE (O. WILDE)
DUENNA, THE (R. B. SHERIDAN)
DUKE AND NO DUKE, A (N. TATE)
DUKE'S MOTTO, THE (J. BROUGHAM)
DYBBUK, THE (S. ANSKY)

EAST INDIAN, THE (M. G. LEWIS)
EASTWARD IN EDEN (D. GARDNER)
EGON UND EMILIE (C. MORGENSTERN)
EINEM JUX WILL ER SICH MACHEN (J. NESTROY)
EKKEHARD (J. V. VON SCHEFFEL)
ELECTION, THE (J. BAILLIE)
ELENI (N. GAGE)
ELFRIDA (G. COLMAN SR.)

ELISABETH, OU, LES EXILÉS DE SIBÉRIE (S. COTTIN)
ELIXIERE DES TEUFELS, DIE (E. T. A. HOFFMANN)
ELIZABETH AND ESSEX (L. STRACHEY)
EMMELINE (J. ROSSNER)
EMPEROR JONES (E. O'NEILL)
EMPEROR OF THE MOON, THE (A. BEHN)
EMPEROR'S NEW CLOTHES, THE (H. C. ANDERSEN)
EMPFINDSAME, DER (A. SCHNITZLER)
ENDYMION (FONTENELLE)
ENDYMION (J. KEATS)
EN FAMILLE (G. DE MAUPASSANT)
ENGAGED! (W. S. GILBERT)
ENGLISH ECCENTRICS, THE (E. SITWELL)
ESCURIAL, THE (GHELDERODE)
ETHAN FROME (E. WHARTON)
ETIQUETTE (W. S. GILBERT)
EUGENE ARAM (E. BULWER-LYTTON)
EVANGELINE (H. W. LONGFELLOW)
EVERYMAN

FABLES (J. DE LA FONTAINE)
FABLES FOR OUR TIME (J. THURBER)
FACE UPON THE FLOOR, THE (H. A. D'ARCY)
FAHRENHEIT 451 (R. BRADBURY)
FALL OF THE CITY, THE (A. MACLEISH)
FALL OF THE HOUSE OF USHER, THE (E. A. POE)
FANTÔME DE L'OPÉRA, LE (LEROUX)
FAR FROM THE MADDING CROWD (T. HARDY)
FAR ROCKAWAY (F. D. GILROY)
FATHER OF THE CHILD (W. GIBSON)
FAUST (G. W. VON GOETHE)
FEATHERTOP (N. HAWTHORNE)
FEMME À DEUX MARIS, LA (PIXÉRÉCOURT)
FEMME MUETTE, LA (F. RABELAIS)
FÊTE À COQUEVILLE, LA (E. ZOLA)
FISHERMAN AND HIS WIFE, THE (BROTHERS GRIMM)
FLOYD AND THE EUMENIDES (E. E. SMITH)
FORGOT (A. CHEKHOV)
FORTRESSE DU DANUBE, LA (PIXÉRECOURT)
FORTUNIO (J. R. PLANCHÉ)
FRANKENSTEIN (M. SHELLEY)
FRANKLIN'S TALE, THE (SEE *THE CANTERBURY TALES*)
FRITHIOFS SAGA (E. TEGNÉR)
FULL MOON IN MARCH (W. B. YEATS)

GAWAIN
GENTLE CREATURE, A (F. DOSTOYEVSKY)

GENTLEMAN DANCING MASTER, THE (W. WYCHERLY)
GEORGE DANDIN (MOLIÈRE)
GERUSALEMME LIBERATA (TASSO)
GIANTS IN THE EARTH (O. E. RÖLVAAG)
GIFT OF THE MAGI, THE (O. HENRY)
GILGAMESH, EPIC OF
GISLI, THE SOURSOP (TRANS. G. W. DASENT)
GITANELLA, LA (M. CERVANTES)
GOBLIN MARKET (C. ROSSETTI)
GOLDEN ASS, THE (L. APUELEIUS)
GOLDEN CRANE (T. YAMAGUCHI)
GOOD SOLDIER SCHWEIK, THE (J. HAŠEK)
GOOSE GIRL, THE (BROTHERS GRIMM)
GORDON, LADY DUFF, TRANS.
GOYLEM (H. LEIVICK)
GRACIEUSE ET PERCINET (M.-C. D'AULNOY)
GRANDE BRETÈCHE, LA (H. BALZAC)
GRANDISSIMES, THE (G. W. CABLE)
GREAT EXPECTATIONS (C. DICKENS)
GREAT STONE FACE, THE (N. HAWTHORNE)
GREEK (S. BERKOFF)
GREY PARROT, THE (W. W. JACOBS)
GULLIVER'S TRAVELS (J. SWIFT)
GUSTAVUS VASA (H. BROOKE)
GUTTIL JATTAK (BUDDHIST TALE)
GUY MANNERING (W. SCOTT)

HAIRCUT, THE (R. LARDNER)
HAMLET (W. SHAKESPEARE)
HÄNSEL UND GRETEL (BROTHERS GRIMM)
HAPPY HYPOCRITE, THE (M. BEERBOHM)
HAPPY PRINCE, THE (O. WILDE)
HARD TIMES (C. DICKENS)
HARRISON LOVED HIS UMBRELLA (R. LEVINE)
HAUNTING, THE (C. A. DAWSON-SCOTT)
HAUS DER TEMPERAMENTE, DAS (J. NESTROY)
HAZEL KIRKE (S. MACKAYE)
HEART OF A DOG (M. BULGAKOV)
HEART OF MIDLOTHIAN, THE (W. SCOTT)
HEDDA GABLER (H. IBSEN)
HELLO OUT THERE (W. SAROYAN)
HENDERSON THE RAIN KING (S. BELLOW)
HENRY V (W. SHAKESEPARE)
HERCULES OETAEUS (SENECA)
HEUREUSE ERREUR, L' (J. PATRAT)
HIPPOLYTUS (EURIPIDES)
HISTOIRE DE GIL BLAS DE SANTILLANE (LE SAGE)

Histoire de ma vie, L' (J. Casanova)
Histoire de Vasco, L' (G. Schehadé)
History of Nourjahad, The (Mrs. Sheridan)
History of the Conquest of Mexico, The
 (W. H. Prescott)
Homer's Daughter (R. Graves)
How Beautiful with Shoes (W. D. Steele)
Huckleberry Finn (M. Twain)
Hunting of the Snark, The (L. Carroll)
Huon de Bordeaux

Ib (H. C. Andersen)
I Ching
Idiot, The (F. Dostoyevsky)
Ile (E. O'Neill)
Iliad, The (Homer)
Incas, Les (J. F. Marmontel)
Incognita (W. Congreve)
In Cold Blood (T. Capote)
Indian Emperor, The (J. Dryden)
Inés de Castro (J. Clifford)
Ingoldsby Legends (R. H. Barham)
Insect Life (K. Čapek, J.Čapek)
Inspector General, The (N. Gogol)
In the Pasha's Garden (H. G. Dwight)
Intruse, L' (M. Maeterlinck)
Invasion, The (J. Lewis)
I Rise in Flame, Cried the Phoenix (T. Williams)
Island God, An (G. S. Mumford)
Island Princess, The (J. Fletcher)
Italian Lesson, The (R. Draper)
Ivanhoe (W. Scott)

Jacob's Room (W. Woolf)
Jacques, ou, La soumission (E. Ionesco)
Jane Eyre (C. Brontë)
Jedermann (H. von Hofmannsthal)
Je dîne chez ma mère (Decourcelle/Thiboust)
Journals of Expeditions of Discovery (E. J. Eyre)
Jovial Crew, The (R. Brome)
Jubilee (A. Chekhov)
Jubilee (M. Walker)
Jugement de Salomon, Le (L.-C. Caignez)
Julian (G. Flaubert)
Jungle Book, The (R. Kipling)
Just So Stories (R. Kipling)

Kaguyahme legend
Kammersänger, Der (F. Wedekind)

Kamouraska (A. Hébert)
Keep Him My Country (M. Durack)
Kenilworth (W. Scott)
Kinderkreuzzug (B. Brecht)
King and the Miller of Mansfield, The (R.
 Dodsley)
King Kong
King of Cats, The (S. V. Benét)
Kong Renes Datter (H. Hertz)
Krasovitsky Couple, The (D. Aizman)

Lady of the Castle (L. Goldberg)
Lady of Lyons (E. Bulwer-Lytton)
Lady of the Lake, The (W. Scott)
Lai de Freine (Marie de France)
Lallah Rookh (T. Moore)
Land of Happiness, The (C. T. Crocker)
Last Days of Pompei, The (E. Bulwer-Lytton)
Last Leaf, The (O. Henry)
Last of the Mohicans, The (J. F. Cooper)
Last of the Valerii, The (H. James)
Last Summer, The (B. Pasternak)
Laurette (J.-F. Marmontel)
Layla and Majnun (G. Nizami)
Leah Kleschna (C. McLellan)
Legend of Montrose, The (W. Scott)
Legend of Sleepy Hollow, The (W. Irving)
Legends of the Lake (G. Findler)
Lenz (G. Büchner)
Leonce und Lena (G. Büchner)
Leper's Flute, The (I. D. Colvin)
Leute von Seldwyla, Die (G. Keller)
Liaisons dangereuses, Les (P. C. de Laclos)
Life in the Sun, A (T. Wilder)
Lima Beans (A. Kreymborg)
Lion, the Witch, and the Wardrobe (C. S. Lewis)
Little Billy (W. Thackeray)
Little Foxes, The (L. Hellman)
Little Mermaid, The (H. C. Andersen)
Little Red Riding Hood (Brothers Grimm)
Little Women (L. M. Alcott)
Locandiera, La (C. Goldoni)
Lodger, The (Mrs. Belloc Lowndes)
Long Christmas Dinner, The (T. Wilder)
Love for Love (W. Congreve)
Love for Money (T. D'Urfey)
Love's Labour's Lost (W. Shakespeare)

Love's Revenge (J. Hoadly)
Luck of Ginger Coffey, The (B. Moore)
Lucky Peter's Travels (A. Strindberg)
Lysistrata (Aristophanes)

Mabinogion, The
Macbeth (W. Shakespeare)
Madame Chrysathème (P. Lot)
Madame Sans-Gêne (V. Sardou)
Magic Barrel, The (B. Malamud)
Mahabharata
Maid Marian (T. L. Peacock)
Maison rustique, La
Mama Don't Allow (T. Hurd)
Man in the Moon, The (F. Godwin)
Manito Masks (H. Alexander)
Man Who Never Died, The (B. Stavis)
Man without a Country, The (E. E. Hale)
Many Moons (J. Thurber)
Mariage forcé, Le (Molière)
Maria Schweidler (W. Meinhold)
Marie Tudor (V. Hugo)
Marilyn: The Untold Story (N. Rosten)
Mario und der Zauberer (T. Mann)
Markheim (R. L. Stevenson)
Marquise von O, Die (H. von Keist)
Marriage Has Been Arranged, A (A. Sutro)
Martin Chuzzlewit (C. Dickens)
Masaniello (H. M. Milner)
Masque of Pandora, The (Longfellow)
Masque of the Red Death, The (E. A. Poe)
Mayor of Casterbridge, The (T. Hardy)
Maypole of Merry Mount (N. Hawthorne)
McTeague (F. Norris)
Medea (Euripides)
Menaechmi (Plautus)
Merchant of Venice, The (W. Shakespeare)
Mère coupable, La (Beaumarchais)
Merry Wives of Windsor, The (W. Shakespeare)
Metamorphoses, III (Ovid)
Metamorphoses, XIII, 750–897 (Ovid)
Midrash, The
Midsummer Night's Dream, A (W. Shakespeare)
Mirror for Witches, A (E. Forbes)
Miss Julie (A. Strindberg)
Moby Dick (H. Melville)
Moment of Rain, The (E. Enright)

Monastery, The (Scott)
Monk, The (M. G. Lewis)
Monkey's Paw, The (W. W. Jacobs)
Monster Bed, The (J. Willis)
Month in the Country, A (I. S. Turgenev)
Moon and Sixpence, The (S. Maugham)
Moray (A. Elguera)
Mort de Tintagiles, La (M. Maeterlinck)
Morte d'Arthur, Le
Mother, The (H. C. Andersen)
Mountain Blood (J. Hergesheimer)
Mourning Becomes Electra (E. O'Neill)
Mr. and Mrs. Discobbolos (E. Lear)
Mr. Mulliner Speakes (P. G. Wodehouse)
Mrs. Dalloway (V. Woolf)
Much Ado about Nothing (W. Shakespeare)
Mulatto, The (L. Hughes)
My Heart's in the Highlands (W. Saroyan)
Mystic Trumpeter, The (W. Whitman)

Narcotic, The (J. Powell)
Nathan der Weise (G. E. Lessing)
Neither (S. Beckett)
Nie-boska komedia (Z. Krasinski)
Niels Lyhne (J. P. Jacobsen)
Night (S. Asch)
Night (E. Wiesel)
Night at an Inn, A (Lord Dusany)
Nightingale, The (H. C. Andersen)
Nightingale and the Rose, The (O.Wilde)
Night in Old Paris, A (G. McDonough)
Nightmare Abbey (T. Peacock)
Niña, La (J. Martí)
Notes from a Lady (B. Malamud)
Notre-Dame de Paris (V. Hugo)
Novelas exemplares (M. Cervantes)
Nuit de Cléopâtre, Une (T. Gautier)
Nut-Brown Maid, The (M. Prior)

Oath of Bad Brown Bill, The (S. Axelson)
Oberon (C. M. Wieland)
Oberon, the Fairy Prince (B. Jonson)
Occurence at Owl Creek Bridge, An
   (A. Bierce)
Octoroon, The (M. E. Braddon)
Odyssey, The (Homer)
Oedipus Rex (Sophocles)
Of Mice and Men (J. Steinbeck)

OLAF (L. COX)
OLD MORALITY (W. SCOTT)
O MANDARIM (EÇA DE QUEIROZ)
ONDINE (F. DE LA MOTTE-FOUQUÉ)
ONDINE (J. GIRAUDOUX)
1001 NIGHTS. SEE *THE THOUSAND AND ONE NIGHTS.*
ON THE HARMFULNESS OF SMOKING TOBACCO (A. CHEKHOV)
OPEN WINDOW, THE (SAKI)
ORACLE, L' (SAINT-FOIX)
ORDRE DU BON TEMPS, L' (L. DE MONTIGNY)
OTHELLO (W. SHAKESPEARE)
OTHER WISE MAN, THE (H. VAN DYKE)
OUR MAN IN HAVANA (G. GREENE)
OUR WIFE (J. M. MORTON)
OUTCASTS OF POKER FLAT, THE (B. HARTE)
OUT OF THE FRYING PAN (F. SWANN)
OWEN WINGRAVE (H. JAMES)

PAMELA (S. RICHARDSON)
PARADISE LOST (J. MILTON)
PARDONER'S TALE, THE (SEE *THE CANTERBURY TALES*)
PASQUAL BRUNO (A. DUMAS)
PEINES DE COEUER (H. BALZAC)
PELERIN BLANC, LE (PIXÉRÉCOURT)
PENNY FOR A SONG (J. WHITING)
PERICLES (W. SHAKESPEARE)
PHANTASTES (G. MACDONALD)
PICKWICK PAPERS (C. DICKENS)
PICTURE OF DORIAN GRAY, THE (O. WILDE)
PIED PIPER OF HAMELIN, THE (R. BROWNING)
PIERROT OF THE MINUTE (E. DOWSON)
PIERS PLOWMAN (W. LANGLAND)
PIE VOLEUSE, LA (D'AUBIGNY/CAIGNIEZ)
PILGRIM, THE (FLETCHER)
PILGRIM'S PROGRESS, THE (J. BUNYAN)
PILLOW BOOK, THE (SEI SHONAGON)
PIPER, THE (J. P. PEABODY)
PIPPA PASSES (R. BROWNING)
PLACE FOR US (I. MILLER)
POEMS OF OSSIAN (J. MACPHERSON)
POISON (K. MANSFIELD)
POPULAR TALES OF THE WEST HIGHLANDS (J. F. CAMPBELL)
PORTRAIT IN BROWNSTONE (L. AUCHINCLOSS)
PORTRAIT VIVANT, LE (MÉLESVILLE/LAYA)

POT OF BROTH, A (YEATS)
POUR LA COURONNE (F. COPPÉE)
PRÉCIEUSES RIDICULES, LES (MOLIÈRE)
PRINCESS MONA (E. CONGEAU)
PRIVATE LIFE OF HELEN OF TROY, THE (J. ERSKINE)
PRIVATE MEMOIRS AND CONFESSIONS OF A JUSTIFIED SINNER, THE (J. HOGG)
PROPHETESS, THE (J. FLETCHER/P. MASSINGER)
PROPOSAL, THE (A. CHEKHOV)
PROZESS, DER (F. KAFKA)
PUISSANCE DU NÉANT, LA (A. DAVID-NEEL)

QUENTIN DURWARD (W. SCOTT)

RAIN (S. MAUGHAM)
RAJAH'S DIAMOND, THE (R. L. STEVENSON)
RAMAYANA (VALMIKI)
RAMUNTCHO (P. LOTI)
RANSOM OF RED CHIEF, THE (O. HENRY)
RAPE OF LUCRECE, THE (W. SHAKESPEARE)
RAPPACCINI'S DAUGHTER (N. HAWTHORNE)
RAPUNZEL (BROTHERS GRIMM)
RÄUBER, DIE (F. SCHILLER)
REBECCA (D. DU MAURIER)
RECOLLECTIONS (P. T. BARNUM)
RECORDS OF THE HISTORIAN (S. CHIEN)
RED CARNATIONS, THE (G. HUGHES)
RED-HEADED LEAGUE, THE (A. C. DOYLE)
REINE DE CHYPRE, LA (J. H. VERNOY DE SAINT-GEORGES)
RELAPSE, THE (J. VANBRUGH)
REPUBLIC, THE, BOOK VII (PLATO)
RETABLILLO DE DON CRISTÓBAL (F. GARCÍA LORCA)
RETOUR IMPRÉVU, LE (J.-F. REGNARD)
RICHARD III (W. SHAKESPEARE)
RIDERS TO THE SEA (J. M. SYNGE)
RIME OF THE ANCIENT MARINER, THE (S. T. COLERIDGE)
RING, THE (T. MOORE)
RING AND THE BOOK, THE (R. BROWNING)
RIP VAN WINKLE (W. IRVING)
RIVAUX D'EUX MÊMES, LES (PIGAULT-LEBRUN)
ROBIN HOOD
ROB ROY (W. SCOTT)
ROCHESTER (MONCRIEFF)
ROMAN FEVER (E. WHARTON)
ROMEO AND JULIET (W. SHAKESPEARE)
ROOM ACROSS THE HALL (O. HENRY)

ROPE, THE (E. O'NEILL)

ROSE AFFAIR, THE (A. OWEN)

ROSE AND THE RING, THE (W. P. THACKERAY)

ROSIER DE MADONNE HUSSON, LE (G. DE MAUPASSANT)

ROYAL HUNT OF THE SUN, THE (P. SHAFFER)

ROYAL MERCHANT, THE (BEAUMONT/ FLETCHER)

RUGANTINO (M. LEWIS)

RUY BLAS (V. HUGO)

SAINTE-CARMEN DE LA MAIN (M. TREMBLAY)

SANDMANN, DER (E. T. A. HOFFMANN)

SANTA CLAUS (E. E. CUMMINGS)

SATYRICON (PETRONIUS)

SAUNY THE SCOT (J. LACY)

SCARECROW, THE (P. MACKAYE)

SCARLET LETTER, THE (N. HAWTHORNE)

SCÈNES DE LA VIE DE BOHÈME (H. MURGER)

SCHLIMMEN BUBEN IN DER SCHULE, DIE (J. NESTROY)

SCHOOL FOR GUARDIANS, THE (A. MURPHY)

SCHWARZE SPINNE, DIE (J. GOTTHELF)

SEAGULL, THE (A. CHEKHOV)

SECRET GARDEN, THE (F. J. BURNETT)

SECULAR MASQUE, THE (J. DRYDEN)

SELFISH GIANT, THE (O. WILDE)

SENTIMENTAL JOURNEY (L. STERNE)

SERVANTS AND THE SNOW, THE (I. MURDOCH)

SERVITORE DI DUE PADRONI (C. GOLDONI)

SGANARELLE (MOLIÈRE)

SHE STOOPS TO CONQUER (O. GOLDSMITH)

SHOEMAKER'S HOLIDAY, THE (T. DEKKER)

SHOW BOAT (E. FERBER)

SICILIAN ROMANCE, THE (A. W. RADCLIFFE)

SICILIEN, LE (MOLIÈRE)

SIÈGE DE LA ROCHELLE, LA (MADAME DE GENLIS)

SIGNA (OUIDA)

SILAS MARNER (G. ELIOT)

SILVER QUEEN (C. BANCROFT)

SIMOON (A. STRINDBERG)

SIRE DE MALÉTROIT'S DOOR, THE (R. L. STEVENSON)

SIX CHARACTERS IN SEARCH OF AN AUTHOR (L. PIRANDLLO)

SNOW IMAGE, THE (N. HAWTHORNE)

SNOW QUEEN, THE (H. C. ANDERSEN)

SOEUR BÉATRICE (A. C. LIADOV)

SOFA, LE (CRÉBILLON)

SONGLINES, THE (B. CHATWIN)

SONG OF ROLAND, THE

SONNENWENDHOF, DER (S. MOSENTHAL)

SORRY, WRONG NUMBER (L. FLETCHER)

SOTOBA KOMACHI

SPANISH STUDENT, THE (W. W. LONGFELLOW)

SPECTORSKY (B. PASTERNAK)

SPREADING THE NEWS (LADY GREGORY)

STAMBOUL NIGHTS (H. G. DWIGHT)

ST. COLUMBA AND THE STREAM (T. DREISER)

ST. GEORGE AND THE DRAGON

STORY OF MY HEART, THE (R. JEFFERIES)

STORY OF THE OTHER WISE MAN (H. VAN DYKE)

STRANGE CASE OF DR. JEKYLL AND MR. HYDE, THE (R. L. STEVENSON)

STRANGE LIFE OF IVAN OSOKIN, THE (P. D. OUSPENSKY)

STRING OF PEARLS, THE (G. D. PITT)

STUDENT OF SALAMANCA, THE (W. IRVING)

SUMIDA-GAWA (J. MONTOMASA)

SUMMER OF THE SEVENTEENTH DOLL, THE (R. LAWLER)

SUMMER'S TALE, THE (R. CUMBERLAND)

SUNDAY COSTS FIVE PESOS (J. NIGGLI)

SUPPOSE A WEDDING (B. MALAMUD)

SWEENEY AGONISTES (T. S. ELIOTT)

SWEENEY TODD (C. BOND)

SYSTEM OF DOCTOR TARR, THE (E. A. POE)

TAILOR OF GLOUCESTER, THE (B. POTTER)

TALE FOR CHRISTMAS, A (LADY CRAVEN)

TALE OF GENJI, THE (MURASAKI SHIKIBA)

TALE OF TWO CITIES, A (C. DICKENS)

TALES OF BELKIN (PUSHKIN)

TALES OF SOLDIERS AND CIVILIANS (A. BIERCE)

TALES OF THE BORDER (J. M. WILSON)

TALES OF THE GENII, THE (C. MORELL)

TALISMAN, THE (W. SCOTT)

TAMBOURLAINE THE GREAT (C. MARLOWE)

TAMING OF THE SHREW, THE (W. SHAKESPEARE)

TARTUFFE (MOLIÈRE)

TEKELI (PIXÉRECOURT)

TÉLÉMAQUE (FÉNELON)

TELL-TALE HEART, THE (E. A. POE)

TEMPEST, THE (W. SHAKESPEARE)

TEN NIGHTS IN A BAR-ROOM (T. S. ARTHUR)

THAIS (A. FRANCE)

THÉRÈSE RAQUIN (E. ZOLA)

THEY KNEW WHAT THEY WANTED (S. HOWARD)
THIEF OF LOVE, THE
THIMON LE MISANTHROPE (L. F. DELISLE)
THINGS AS THEY ARE (W. GODWIN)
THIS IS THE RILL SPEAKING (L. WILSON)
THOUSAND AND ONE NIGHTS, THE
THREE SISTERS, THE (A. CHEKHOV)
THREE SISTERS WHO ARE NOT SISTERS (G. STEIN)
THREE STRANGERS, THE (T. HARDY)
THROUGH THE LOOKING GLASS (L. CARROLL)
TICKETS, PLEASE (D. H. LAWRENCE)
TIME MACHINE (H. G. WELLS)
TIMON OF ATHENS (W. SHAKESPEARE)
TOD IN VENEDIG, DER (T. MANN)
TOM JONES (H. FIELDING)
TOM SAWYER (M. TWAIN)
TOM THUMB (H. FIELDING)
TONNELIER, LE (A. F. QUÉTANT)
TRACHIMIAE (SOPHOCLES)
TRAGEDY OF TRAGEDIES, THE (H. FIELDING)
TRAVELLING COMPANIONS (H. JAMES)
TREE THAT DIDN'T GET TRIMMED, THE (C. MORLEY)
TRES MELLIZO (A. MATTIUZZI)
TRISTAN AND ISEULT
TRISTRAM SHANDY (L. STERNE)
TROILUS AND CRESSIDA (G. CHAUCER)
TROIS JUMEAUX VENITIENS, LES (A. MATTIUZZI)
TROISIÈME LUNE, LA (F. DE GRÉSAC, P. FERRIER)
TROIS MOUSQUETAIRES, LES (E. ROSTAND)
TRUMPET MAJOR, THE (T. HARDY)
TRUTZ SIMPLEX (GRIMMELSHAUSEN)
TUEUR SANS GAGES (E. IONESCO)
TUMBLEDOWN DICK (H. FIELDING)
TURN OF THE SCREW, THE (H. JAMES)
TWA SISTERS O'BINNORIE, THE
TWELFTH NIGHT (W. SHAKESPEARE)
TWO GENTLEMEN OF VERONA (W. SHAKESPEARE)
TWO NOBLE KINGS (SHAKESPEARE/FLETCHER)
TWO SISTERS, THE

UBU ROI (A. JARRY)
UGLY DUCKLING, THE (A. A. MILNE)
UNCLE REMUS (J. H. HARRIS)
UNCLE TOM'S CABIN (H. B. STOWE)
UNDER THE GREENWOOD TREE (T. HARDY)
UNDER THE JUNIPER TREE (C. BRAHMS)
UNDINE (DE LA MOTTE FOUQUÉ)

UNIVERSITY GREYS, THE (M. BROWN)
UNTO THESE HILLS (K. HUNTER)

VERWANDLUNG, DIE (F. KAFKA)
VISIT TO THE COUNTRY, A (A. CHEKHOV)
VOLPONE (B. JONSON)
VÖRÖS MALUM (F. MOLNÁR)
VOSS (P. WHITE)

WAKEFIELD MYSTERY PLAYS (WAKEFIELD MASTER)
WANDERING SCHOLARS, THE (H. WADDELL)
WASHINGTON SQUARE (H. JAMES)
WAVERLEY (W. SCOTT)
WEG DER VERHEISSUNG (F. WERFEL)
WEIR OF HERMISTON (R. L.STEVENSON)
WESTWARD HO! (C. KINGSLEY)
WHAT D'YE CALL IT, THE (J. GAY)
WHITE DOE OF RYLSTONE, THE (W. WORDSWORTH)
WHITE PLAGUE (K. ČAPEK)
WHITE WINGS (P. BARRY)
WHY THE CHIMES RANG (R. M. ALDEN)
WIFE OF MARTIN GUERRE, THE (J. LEWIS)
WILDFANG, DIE (A. VON KOTZEBUE)
WILD SWANS, THE (H. C. ANDERSEN)
WILHELM TELL (F. SCHILLER)
WILL, THE (M . EDGEWORTH)
WIND IN THE WILLOWS, THE (K. GRAHAME)
WINGS OF THE DOVE (H. JAMES)
WINTER'S TALE, THE (W. SHAKESPEARE)
WISCONSIN DEATH TRIP (M. LESY)
WITCH, THE (A. CHEKHOV)
WITCH, THE (F. MOLNÁR)
WOMAN ON THE WALL (RABBI NEWMAN)
WOMEN OF TRACHIS (SOPHOCLES)
WOOD DAEMON, THE (M. G. LEWIS)
WOODLANDERS, THE (T. HARDY)
WUTHERING HEIGHTS (E. BRONTË)

X=0 (J. DRINKWATER)

YELLOW WALLPAPER, THE (C. P. GILMAN)
YERMA (F. GARCÍA LORCA)
YOKINOJO HENGE (O. MIKAMI)
YOLANDA OF CYPRUS (C. Y. RICE)
YORK MYSTERY PLAYS
YOUNG GOODMAN BROWN (N. HAWTHORNE)

ZERBROCHENE KRUG, DER (H. VON KLEIST)
ZUMA (S. F. GENLIS)

Chronology

Dates given are of premiere; * year of composition where year of premiere unknown; ? = month/city of premiere unknown; ** = ballad opera/anon. composer. Hyphenated composer names = adaptations.

AA = Ann Arbor, Mich; Al = Aldeburgh; Ams = Amsterdam; Bal = Baltimore; Bel = Belfast; Berk = Berkeley, Calif; Bin = Binghamton, NY; Bir = Birmingham; Bklyn = Brooklyn, NY; Bl = Bloomington, Ind; Bos = Boston; BR = Baton Rouge, La; Cam = Cambridge; Can = Canterbury; Car = Cardiff; CC = Central City, Colo; Ch = Chicago; Chel = Cheltenham; Cin = Cincinnati; Cl = Cleveland; CT = Cape Town; D = Dublin; Dal = Dallas; Den = Denver; Det = Detroit; E = Edinburgh; Gl = Glyndebourne; Gla = Glasgow; Glast = Glastonbury; Gue = Guelph, Ont; Hart = Hartford, Conn; Hou = Houston; Inter = Interlochen, Mich; L = London; LA = Los Angeles; Len = Lenox, Mass; Lin = Lincoln, Neb; Liv = Liverpool; Lou = Louisville, Ky; Man = Manchester; Mel = Melbourne; Mil = Milwaukee; Min = Minneapolis; New = Newcastle upon Tyne; NH = New Haven; NO = New Orleans; Nor = Norfolk, Va; NY = New York; O = Oxford; Ph = Philadelphia; Pitt = Pittsburgh; Port = Portland, Oreg; Roch = Rochester, NY; San D = San Diego; Sea = Seattle; SF = San Francisco; S Fe = Santa Fe; SL = St. Louis; SP = St. Paul; Stock = Stockbridge, Mass; Syd = Sydney; Syr = Syracuse, NY; Tor = Toronto; Urb = Urbana, Ill; Van = Vancouver; Wa = Washington, DC; WP = White Plains, NY

Date	Title (Short)/City	Composer	Date	Title (Short)/City	Composer
1634			**1690**		
Feb. 3	**Triumph of Peace** L	Lawes, W.	June	**Dioclesian** L	Purcell, H.
Sept. 29	**Comus** Ludlow	Lawes, H.	**1691**		
1636			May	**King Arthur** L	Purcell, H.
Feb. 24	**Triumphs of the Prince d'Amour** L	Lawes, H./W.	**1692**		
			May 2	**Fairy Queen** L	Purcell, H.
1638			**1694**		
Jan. 7	**Britannia triumphans** L	Lawes, W.	Oct.	**Rape of Europa** L	Eccles, J.
1653			**1695**		
Mar. 26	**Cupid and Death** L	Gibbons, C.	autumn	**Indian Queen** L	Purcell, H.
1654			**1696**		
* (ca.)	**Ariadne Deserted by Theseus**	Flecknoe, R.	Oct.	**Brutus of Alba** L	Purcell, D.
			Nov.	**Loves of Mars and Venus** L	Eccles, J.
1656					
Sept.	**Siege of Rhodes** L	Lawes, H.	?	**Macbeth** L	Eccles, J.
1659			**1697**		
* (ca.)	**Marriage of Oceanus**	Flecknoe, R.	June	**World in the Moon** L	Purcell, D.
1673			**1698**		
July 3?	**Orpheus and Euridice** L	Locke, M.	Nov.	**Rinaldo and Armida** L	Eccles, J.
1674			**1699**		
Apr. 30?	**Tempest, The** L	Bannister et al.	Jan.	**Island Princess** L	Purcell, D.
1675			**1700**		
			Feb. 19	**Grove, The** L	Purcell, D.
Feb. 18?	**Macbeth** L	Locke, M.	Mar. 25	**Secular Masque** L	Purcell, D.
Feb. 27	**Psyche** L	Locke, M.	**1701**		
1683			Feb.	**Rival Queens** L	Finger, G.
(ca.)	**Venus and Adonis** L	Blow, J.	Mar. 21	**Judgment of Paris** L	Eccles, J.
1685			Mar. 28	**Judgment of Paris** L	Finger, G.
June 3	**Albion and Albanius** L	Grabu, L.	Apr. 11	**Judgment of Paris** L	Purcell, D.
1689			May?	**Acis and Galatea** L	Eccles, J.
ca. Dec.	**Dido and Aeneas** L	Purcell, H.	May 2	**Virgin Prophetess** L	Finger, G.

Date	Title	Composer
1702		
Nov. 21	**Macbeth** L	Leveridge, R.
1705		
Jan. 16	**Arsinoe** L	Clayton, T.
1706		
Feb. 21	**British Enchanters** L	Corbett, W.
Mar. 7	**Temple of Love** L	Fedelli, G.
Apr. 5	**Wonders in the Sun** L	**
*	**Semele** (prem. 1964 O)	Eccles, J.
1707		
Mar. 4	**Rosamond** L	Clayton, T.
Apr. 1	**Thomyris** L	Pepusch, J.
1708		
Feb. 12	**Prunella** L	Clayton, T.
Feb. 26	**Love's Triumph** L	Cesarini et al.
Dec. 14	**Pyrrus and Demetrius** L	Haym, N.
1712?		
Jan. 7	**Tempest** L	Weldon, J.
1712		
May 14	**Calypso and Telemachus** L	Galliard, J.
1715		
Mar. 12	**Venus and Adonis** L	Pepusch, J.
Nov. 5	**Myrtillo** L	Pepusch, J.
1716		
Jan. 12	**Apollo and Daphne** L	Pepusch, J.
Apr. 4	**Death of Dido** L	Pepusch, J.
Apr. 11	**Pyramus and Thisbe** L	Leveridge, R.
1718		
Jan. 14	**Pan and Syrinx** L	Galliard, J.
Mar. 22	**Decius and Paulina** L	Galliard, J.
Mar. 22	**Lady's Triumph** L	**
summer	**Acis and Galatea** Cannons	Handel, G. F.
1719		
Apr. 11	**Circe** L	Galliard, J.
1724		
Nov. 28	**Prophetess, The** L	Pepusch, J.
1728		
Jan. 29	**Beggar's Opera** L	Pepusch, J.
Apr. 26	**Cobler's Opera** L	**
May 8	**Penelope** L	**
Sept. 24	**Quaker's Opera** L	**
Oct. 15	**Craftsman, The** L	**
*	**Polly** (prem. 1777 L)	**
1729		
Jan. 7	**Love in a Riddle** L	**
Jan. 29	**Gentle Shepherd** E	**
Feb. 6	**Village Opera** L	**
Mar. 13	**Beggar's Wedding** D	**
Mar. 29	**Hurlothrumbo** L	Johnson, S.
Apr. 16	**Devil upon Two Sticks** L	**
Apr. 18	**Flora** L	**
May 6	**Wedding, The** L	Pepusch, J.
May 7	**Patron, The** L	**
May 14	**Lover's Opera** L	**
June 20	**Contrivances, The** L	Carey, H.
Aug. 16	**Damon and Phillida** L	**
Dec. 3	**Momus Turn'd Fabulist** L	**
?	**Love and Revenge** L?	**
1730		
Feb. 10	**Chamber-Maid** L	**
Mar. 11	**Metamorphosis of the Beggar's Opera** L	**
Mar. 30	**Author's Farce** L	**
Mar. 30	**Bays's Opera** L	**
Apr. 2	**Fashionable Lady** L	**
Apr. 27	**Female Parson** L	Coffey, C.
May 1	**Patie and Peggy** L	**
summer	**Prisoner's Opera** L	**
Aug. 20	**Generous Free-Mason** L	**
Aug. 22	**Robin Hood** L	**
Dec. 16	**Jealous Clown** L	**
1731		
Feb. 8	**Jovial Crew** L	**
Mar. ?	**Fool's Opera** O	**
Mar. 20	**Highland Fair** L	**
Apr. 3	**Orestes** L	Pepusch, J.
Apr. 22	**Welsh Opera** L	**
May 4	**Judgment of Paris** L	**
Aug. 6	**Devil to Pay** L	
Nov. 10	**Silvia** L	**
?	**Grub-Street Opera**	**
1732		
Jan. 1	**Lottery** L	Seedo, Mr.
Mar. 13	**Amelia** L	Lampe, J. F.
Mar. 20	**Sequel to Flora** L	**
June 26	**Mock Doctor** L	**
Aug. 17	**Devil of a Duke** L	**
Nov. 16	**Britannia** L	Lampe, J. F.
Nov. 20	**Teraminta** L	Smith, J. C.
?	**Disappointment, The** L	**
?	**Restauration of King Charles II** L	**
1733		
Jan. 29	**Boarding School** L	**
Feb. 5	**Decoy, The** L	**
Feb. 10	**Achilles** L	**
Feb. 23	**Dione** L	Lampe, F.
Mar. 5	**Mad Captain** L	**
Mar. 7	**Rosamond** L	Arne, T. A.
Apr. 16	**Ulysses** L	Smith, J. C.
Apr. 27	**Mock Lawyer** L	**
May 5	**Livery Rake** L	**
May 21	**Venus, Cupid** L	Seedo, Mr.

May 31	**Opera of Operas** L	Lampe, J. F.
summer?	**Oxford Act** O	**
Aug. 14	**Fancy'd Queen** L	**
Nov. 7	**Opera of Operas** L	Arne, T. A.
Nov. 24	**Happy Nuptials** L	Carey, H.
Dec. 5	**Timon in Love** L	**
1734		
Jan. 12	**Dido and Aeneas** L	Arne, T. A.
Feb. 22	**Chrononhotonthologos** L	Carey, H.
Feb.?	**Britannia** L	Carey, H.
Mar. 21	**Britannia** L	Arne, T. A.
Apr. 5	**Don Quixote in England** L	**
?	**Florimel** Winchester	Greene, M.
?	**Intriguing Chambermaid** L	**
?	**Whim, The** L	**
1735		
Jan. 6	**Old Man Taught Wisdom** L	**
Jan. 22	**Plot, The** L	**
Feb. 25	**Cure for a Scold** L	**
May 6	**Merry Cobler** L	**
May 10	**Trick for Trick** L	**
July 15	**Honest Yorkshireman** L	Carey, H.
?	**Macheath in the Shades** L	**
1736		
Feb. 10	**Lover His Own Rival** L	**
Apr.	**Tumble-Down Dick** L	**
Apr. 26	**Female Rake** L	**
May 26	**Rival Captains** L	**
?	**Happy Lovers** L	**
1737		
May 16	**Dragon of Wantley** L	Lampe, J. F.
May 30	**Macheath Turn'd Pyrate** L	**
?	**Mad House** L	**
?	**Rape of Helen** L	**
1738		
Jan. 26	**Coffee House** L	Carey, H.
Mar. 4	**Comus** L	Arne, T. A.
Dec. 9	**Margery** L	Lampe, J. F.
?	**Lucky Discovery** L	**
1739		
Nov. 15	**Hospital for Fools** L	Arne, T. A.
Dec. 1	**Nancy** L	Carey, H.
Dec. 31	**Britons, Strike Home** L	**
?	**Don Sancho** L	**
1740		
Jan. 4	**Rosalinda** L	Smith, J. C.
Feb. 12	**Orpheus and Eurydice** L	Lampe, J. F.

Apr. 7	**Baucis and Philemon** L	Prelleur, P.
Aug. 1	**Alfred** L	Arne, T. A.
?	**False Guardians Outwitted** L	**
?	**Judgment of Hercules** L?	Greene, M.
*	**Seasons, The**	Smith, J. C.
1741		
Apr. 3	**Blind Beggar** L	Arne, T. A.
Apr. 16	**Happy Captive** L	Galliard, J.
Apr. 18	**Sham Conjuror** L	Lampe, F.
1742		
Mar. 12	**Judgment of Paris** L	Arne, T. A.
May 6	**Miss Lucy in Town** L	Arne, T. A.
?	**Love at First Sight** L	**
?	**Sancho at Court** L	**
*	**Circe**	Hayes, W.
1743		
*	**Eurydice**	**
1744		
Feb. 10	**Semele** L	Handel
Apr. 16	**Queen of Spain** L	Lampe, J. F.
1745		
Jan. 5	**Hercules** L	Handel, G. F.
Jan. 17	**Temple of Dullness** L	Arne, T. A.
Jan. 25	**Pyramus and Thisbe** L	Lampe, F.
Feb. 11	**Picture, The** L	Arne, T. A.
Apr. 15	**King Pepin's Campaign** L	Arne, T. A.
1746		
Jan.	**Tempest, The** L	Arne, T. A.
Mar. 18	**Double Disappointment** L	**
1747		
Apr. 29	**Peleus and Thetis** L	Boyce, W.
*	**Phoebe** (prem. 1755 L)	Greene, M.
1748		
Feb. 21	**Triumph of Peace** L	Arne, T. A.
Nov. 4	**Triumphs of Hibernia** D	Pasquali, N.
1749		
Jan. 18	**Lethe** L	Arne, T. A.
Feb. 9	**Temple of Peace** L	Pasquali, N.
Mar. 31	**Henry and Emma** L	Arne, T. A.
July	**Secular Masque** L	Boyce, W.
Dec. 2	**Chaplet, The** L	Boyce, W.
*	**Alceste**	Handel, G. F.
*	**Peleus and Thetis**	Hayes, W.
1750		
Feb. 15	**Don Saverio** L	Arne, T. A.
Mar. 1	**Rehearsal, The** L	Boyce, W.
Dec. 13	**Robin Hood** L	Burney, C.
1751		
Nov. 19	**Shepherd's Lottery** L	Boyce, W.
1754		
Mar. 25	**Sheep Shearing** L	Arne, T. A.

Date	Title	Composer
May 29	Eliza L	Arne, T. A.
?	Ragged Uproar L	**
*	Teraminta L	Stanley, J.
1755		
Feb. 3	Fairies, The L	Smith, J. C.
May 9	Britannia L	Arne, T. A.
1756		
Jan. 21	Florizel and Perdita L	Boyce, W.
Feb. 11	Tempest, The L	Smith, J. C.
Mar. 17	Pincushion, The D	Arne, T. A.
1757		
Oct. 20	Tempest, The L	Boyce, W.
1759?		
?	Gasconado the Great L	**
1760		
Feb. 14	Jovial Crew L	**
Nov. 17	Tears and Triumphs of Parnassus L	Stanley, J.
Nov. 28	Thomas and Sally L	Arne, T. A.
Dec. 13	Enchanter, The L	Smith, J. C.
1761		
Jan. 31	Edgar and Emmeline L	Arne, M.
Oct. 26	Arcadia L	Stanley, J.
1762		
Jan. 22	Midas D	**
Feb. 2	Artaxerxes L	Arne, T. A.
Dec. 8	Love in a Village L	Arne, T. A.
1763		
May 10	Telemachus O	Hayes, P.
Oct. 17	Love at First Sight L	**
Nov. 23	Midsummer Night's Dream L	Burney, C.
*	Birth of Hercules L	Arne, T. A.
1764		
Jan. 20	Arcadian Nuptials L	Arne, T. A.
Jan. 23	Hymen L	Arne, M.
Feb. 24	Royal Shepherd L	Rush, G.
May 21	Shepherd's Artifice L	Dibdin, C.
Aug.	Manaclas Salisbury	Bach, J. C.
Nov. 2	Almena L	Arne, M.
Nov. 28	Capricious Lovers L	Rush, G.
Dec. 12	Guardian Outwitted L	Arne, T. A.
1765		
Jan. 7	Don Fulimone D	Giordani, T.
Jan. 31	Maid of the Mill L	Arnold, S.
Feb. 15	Pharnaces L	Bates, W.
Mar. 11	Choice of Apollo L	Yates, W.
Mar. 26	Maid of the Mill L	Giordani, T.
May 2	Spanish Lady L	**
Oct. 8	Daphne and Amintor L	Arnold, S.
Dec. 6	Summer's Tale L	Arnold, S.
?	Prude, The L	**
1766		
Apr. 24	Love in Disguise	Giordani, T.
Nov. 21	Cunning Man	Burney, C.
Dec. 12	Revenge of Athridates D	Tenducci, F.
?	Cottagers, The L	Shield, W.?
1767		
Jan. 2	Cymon L	Arne, M.
Jan. 31	Fairy Favour L	Bach, J. C.
Feb. 21	Love in the City L	Dibdin, C.
Feb. 25	Phillis at Court D	Giordani, T.
Apr. 6	Linco's Travels L	Arne, M.
Apr. 20	Disappointment, The Ph	Barton, A.
Apr. 21	Rosamond L	Arnold, S.
Oct. 23	Orpheus L	Barthelemon
Nov. 4	Lycidas L	Jackson, W.
Dec. 14	Royal Merchant L	Linley Sr.
1768		
Feb. 25	Lionel and Clarissa L	Dibdin, C.
Mar. 3	Oithona L	Barthelemon
Aug. 16	Damon and Phillida L	**
Oct. 3	Padlock, The L	Dibdin, C.
Oct. 10	Royal Garland L	Arnold, S.
Dec. 21	Damon and Phillida L	Dibdin, C.
1769		
Jan. 14	Tom Jones L	Arnold, S.
May 12	Ephesian Matron L	Dibdin, C.
June 21	Captive, The L	Dibdin et al.
Oct. 14	Jubilee L	Dibdin, C.
Dec. 15	Amintas L	Arnold, S.
?	Royal Pastoral Windsor Castle	Nares, J.
1770		
Jan. 5	Court of Alexander L	Fisher, J. A.
Apr. 25	Flora L	Bates, W.
May 7	Ladies Frolick L	Bates, W.
June 16	Servant Mistress L	Arnold, S.
July 17	Magic Girdle L	Barthelemon
July 20	Recruiting Sergeant L	Dibdin, C.
Aug. 21	Noble Pedlar L	Barthelemon
Aug. 28	Madman, The L	Arnold, S.
Nov. 22	Portrait, The L	Arnold, S.
?	Revenge, The L	Arnold, S.
1771		
Jan. 23	Romp, The D	Dibdin, C.
June 27	Magnet, The L	Arnold, S.
July 24	Dido and Aeneas L	Hook, J.
Oct. 28	Institution of the Garter L	Dibdin, C.
Nov. 12	Fairy Prince L	Arne, T. A.
Dec. 14	Amelia L	Dibdin, C.
?	Divorce, The L	Hook, J.
?	Portrait, The D	Barthelemon
1772		
Mar. 16	Squire Badger L	Arne, T. A.
June 10	Cooper, The L	Arne, T. A.

Date	Title	Author
July 27	Cupid's Revenge L	Hook, J.
Aug. 22	Dilettante, Il L	Hook, J.
Nov. 21	Elfrida L	Arne, T. A.
Dec. 2	Rose, The L	Arne, T. A.
?	Brickdust Man L	Dibdin, C.
?	Palace of Mirth L	Dibdin, C.
1773		
Feb. 1	Wedding Ring L	Dibdin, C.
Feb. 6	Golden Pippen L	Fischer, J. A.
Apr. 14	Ladle, The L	Dibdin, C.
Apr. 19	Grenadier, The L	Dibdin, C.
July 12	Mischance, The L	Dibdin, C.
July 15	Wedding Day L	Barthelemon
Aug. 11	Trip to Portsmouth L	Dibdin, C.
Aug. 25	Zingara, La L	Barthelemon
Sept. 27	Apollo and Daphne L	Hook, J.
Nov. 2	Deserter, The L	Dibdin, C.
Dec. 16	Achilles in Petticoats L	Arne, T. A.
Dec. 27	Christmas Tale L	Dibdin, C.
?	Bow-Street Opera L	Pepusch, J.
1774		
June 30	Don Quixote L	Arnold, S.
Aug. 8	Waterman, The L	Dibdin, C.
Oct. 19	Election, The L	Barthelemon
Nov. 5	Maid of the Oaks L	Barthelemon
Dec. 9	Cobler, The L	Dibdin, C.
1775		
Jan. 21	Two Misers L	Dibdin, C.
Feb. 1	Rival Candidates L	Carter, T.
Feb. 15	Maid of the Vale L	Arne, M.
Feb. 16	Sot, The L	Arne, T. A.
May 3	Quaker, The L	Dibdin, C.
Sept. 23	Theatrical Candidates L	Bates, W.
Oct. 17	Weathercock, The L	Arnold, S.
Oct. 28	May Day L	Arne, T. A.
Nov. 21	Duenna, The L	Linley Jr./ Linley Sr.
Dec. 12	Sultan, The L	Dibdin, C.
1776		
Feb. 1	Blackamoor, The L	Dibdin, C.
Aug. 26	Metamorphoses L	Dibdin, C.
Nov. 14	Seraglio, The L	Dibdin, C.
Dec. 5	Selima and Azor L	Linley Sr.
Dec. 7	Caractacus L	Arne, T. A.
?	Phoebe at Court L	Arne, T. A.
1777		
Mar. 20	Milesian, The L	Carter, T.
Mar. 22	Emperor of the Moon L	Arne, M.
Apr. 15	Shamrock, The D	Shield, W.
May 5	Marriage-Office L	Bates, W.
May 15	Lilliput L	Arnold, S.
July 18	Fairy Tale L	Arne, M.
July 18	Sheep Shearing L	Arnold, S.
Aug. 18	Yo, Yea L	Dibdin, C.
Aug. 22	April Day L	Arnold, S.
Aug. 30	Spanish Barber L	Arnold, S.
Nov. 18	Love Finds the Way L	Arne et al.
?	Old Woman of Eighty L	Dibdin, C.
1778		
Feb. 4	Poor Vulcan L	Dibdin, C.
Feb. 19	Cadi of Bagdad L	Linley Jr.
Feb. 24	Ruling Passion D	Cogan, P.
Mar. 16	Belphegor L	Barthelemon
Mar. 30	Second Thought Is Best L	Bates, W.
May 1	Crisis, The L	Shield, W.
June 26	Buxom Joan L	Taylor, R.
Aug. 3	Gipsies, The L	Arnold, S.
Aug. 17	Cobler of Castlebury L	Shield, W.
Aug. 17	Flitch of Bacon L	Shield, W.
Sept. 18	Rose and Colin L	Dibdin, C.
Sept. 18	Wives Avenged L	Dibdin, C.
Oct. 2	Annette and Lubin L	Dibdin, C.
Oct. 15	Camp, The L	Linley Sr.
Nov. 23	Lady of the Manor L	Hook, J.
Nov. 30	Fathers, The L	**
1779		
Apr.	Calypso D	Butler, T. H.
May 6	Chelsea Pensioner L	Dibdin, C.
July 1	Summer Amusement L	Arnold, S.
Aug. 14	Son-in-Law L	Arnold, S.
Oct. 20	Plymouth in an Uproar L	Dibdin, C.
Nov. 12	William and Nanny L	Baumgarten
Dec. 13	Zoraida L	Linley, T.
?	Touchstone, The L	Dibdin, C.
1780		
Jan. 18	Shepherdess of the Alps L	Dibdin, C.
Feb. 2	Widow of Delphi L	Butler, T.
Apr. 14	Artifice, The L	Arne, M.
Apr. 25	Siege of Gibraltar L	Shield, W.
July 8	Fire and Water L	Arnold, S.
Aug. 12	Wedding Night L	Arnold, S.
Oct. 3	Tom Thumb L	Markordt, J.
Nov. 25	Islanders, The L	Dibdin, C.
Dec. 27	Lord of the Manor L	Jackson, W.
1781		
June 16	Dead Alive L	Arnold, S.
July 9	Baron Kinkverkankots-dorsprakingatchdern L	Arnold, S.
July 18	Silver Tankard L	Arnold, S.
Sept. 4	Agreeable Surprise L	Arnold, S.
Sept. 17	Marriage Act L	Dibdin, C.
Oct. 27	Jupiter and Alcmena L	Dibdin, C.
Oct. 29	Gentle Shepherd L	Linley, T.
Nov. 28	Banditti, The L	Arnold, S.
Dec. 13	Carnival of Venice L	Linely Sr.
1782		
Feb. 21	Vertumnus and Pomona L	Arne, M.
Mar. 16	Positive Man L	Arnold, S.
Apr. 13	Arcadian Pastoral L	Beckford

Date	Title	Composer
May 14	Contract, The D	Stevenson
May 18	Fair American L	Carter, T.
July 2	None So Blind L	Arnold, S.
Nov. 2	Castle of Andalusia L	Arnold, S.
Nov. 4	Too Civil by Half L	Hook, J.
Dec. 31	Rosina L	Shield, W.
?	Blockheads, The NY	**
?	Graces, The L	Dibdin, C.
1783		
Apr. 26	Tristram Shandy L	Arne, M.
May 8	Pharnaces L	**
Aug. 12	Birth-Day, The L	Arnold, S.
Aug. 28	Gretna Green L	Arnold, S.
Nov. 4	Poor Soldier L	Shield, W.
Nov. 13	Long Odds L	Dibdin, C.
Dec. 5	Metamorphosis L	Jackson, W.
Dec. 18	Gibralter D	Giordani, T.
Dec. 18	Haunted Castle D	Giordani, T.
Dec. 31	Enchantress, The D	Giordani, T.
1784		
Jan. 7	Happy Disguise D	Giordani, T.
Jan. 30	Campaign, The D	Shield, W.
Mar. 8	Double Disguise L	Hook, J.
Apr. 2	Noble Peasant L	Shield, W.
Apr. 17	Robin Hood L	Shield, W.
June 19	Two to One L	Arnold, S.
June 29	Poll Booth L	Hook, J.
Aug. 21	Hunt the Slipper L	Arnold, S.
Sept. 6	Peeping Tom of Coventry L	Arnold, S.
Nov. 4	Spanish Rivals L	Linley Sr.
Nov. 16	Fontainbleau L	Shield, W.
1785		
Feb. 8	Liberty Hall L	Dibdin, C.
Mar. 28	Life of Tom Thumb L	Dibdin, C.
Apr. ?	Calypso D	Giordani, T.
Apr. 12	Nunnery, The L	Shield, W.
May 19	Word to Wives L	Hook, J.
July 9	Turk and No Turk L	Arnold, S.
Nov. 10	Choleric Fathers L	Shield, W.
Dec.	Strangers at Home L	Linley, Sr.
?	Benevolent Tar L	Dibdin, C.
1786		
Feb. 17	Love in a Camp L	Shield, W.
Mar. 18	Fair Peruvian L	Hook, J.
Aug. 12	Siege of Curzola L	Arnold, S.
Oct. 16	Richard, Coeur de Lion L	Shield, W.
Oct. 24	Richard, Coeur de Lion L	Linley Sr.
?	Triumph of Beauty L	Hook, J.
1787		
Mar. 12	Love and War L	Shield, W.
Apr. 24	Nina L	Shield, W.
May 16	Harvest Home L	Dibdin, C.
May 19	May Day in Town NY?	Tyler, R.
May 22	Queen of the May L	Hook, J.

Date	Title	Composer
Aug. 4	Inkle and Yarico L	Arnold, S.
Oct. 31	Farmer, The L	Shield, W.
?	Birthday, The L	Carter, T.
?	Hero and Leander L	Reeve, W.
?	Mistakes of a Day Norwich, Engl	Callcott, J.
?	Thomas and Susan L	Reeve, W.
1788		
Jan. 16	Constant Maid L	Carter, T.
Feb. 25	Love in the East L	Linley, T.
May 22	Marian L	Shield, W.
July 4	Fourth of July Ph	**
Oct. 25	Doctor and the Apothecary L	Storace, S.
Nov. 6	Highland Reel L	Shield, W.
Dec. 13	Prophet, The L	Shield, W.
?	Match for A Widow L	Dibdin, C.
1789		
May 18	Ut Pictora Poesis! L	Arnold, S.
May 22	British Sailor L	Boyton, W.
Aug. 11	Battle of Hexham L	Arnold, S.
Nov. 13	Island of St. Marguerite L	Shaw, T.
Nov. 24	Darby's Return NY	**
Nov. 24	Haunted Tower L	Storace, S.
*	Better Sort (prem. 1985 Worcester, Mass)	**
1790		
Mar. 8	Czar, The L	Shield, W.
Apr. 16	No Song, No Supper L	Storace, S.
May 7	Crusade, The L	Shield, W.
July 16	New Spain L	Arnold, S.
Sept. 4	Basket Maker L	Arnold, S.
*	Reconciliation, The	**
1791		
Jan. 1	Siege of Belgrade L	Storace, S.
Feb. 12	Distressed Knight D	Giordani, T.
Feb. 26	Woodman, The L	Shield, W.
May 3	Cave of Trophonius L	Storace, S.
July 30	Surrender of Calais L	Arnold, S.
Sept. 22	Poor Old Drury!!! L	Storace, S.
1792		
May 10	Just in Time L	Carter, T.
May 23	Dido L	Storace, S.
July 25	Enchanted Wood L	Arnold, S.
Oct. 16	Philander and Silvia L	Carr, B.
Oct. 18	Prisoner, The L	Attwood, T.
Nov. 3	Hartford Bridge L	Shield, W.
Nov. 21	Isidore de Merida L	Braham et al.
Nov. 21	Pirates, The L	Storace, S.
?	Critic upon Critic L	**
?	Magician No Conjuror L	Mazzinghi, J.
1793		
Jan. 20	Capocchio and Dorinna Annapolis, Md	Taylor, R.
Feb. 25	Midnight Wanderers L	Shield, W.

Mar. 7	**Ozmyn and Daraxa** L	Attwood, T.
Mar. 11	**Prize, The** L	Storace, S.
Apr. 4	**Armourer, The** L	Warner
May 3	**To Arms** L	Shield, W.
May 11	**Sprigs of Laurel** L	Shield, W.
May 20	**Mariners, The** L	Attwood, T.
Aug. 3	**Mountaineers, The** L	Arnold, S.
Aug. 12	**Caernarvon Castle** L	Attwood, T.
Oct. 1	**Children in the Wood** L	Arnold, S.
Oct. 24	**Ward of the Castle** L	Giordani, T.
Dec. 16	**My Grandmother** L	Storace, S.
1794		
Feb. 8	**Purse, The** L	Reeve, W.
Feb. 22	**Travellers in Switzerland** L	Shield, W.
Mar. 3	**Tammany** NY	Hewitt, J.
Apr. 10	**Netly Abbey** L	Shield, W.
Apr. 29	**British Fortitude** L	Reeve, W.
May 13	**Packet Boat** L	Attwood, T.
May 28	**Sicilian Romance** L	Reeve, W.
June 9	**Lodoiska** L	Storace, S.
July 2	**Glorious First of June** L	Storace, S.
July 29	**Auld Robin Gray** L	Arnold, S.
Aug. 9	**How to Be Happy** L	Arnold, S.
Aug. 18	**Britain's Glory** L	Arnold, S.
Aug. 18	**Rule Britannia** L	Arnold, S.
Sept. 3	**Apparition, The** L	Reeve, W.
Oct. 30	**Arrived at Portsmouth** L	Shield, W.
Dec. 20	**Cherokee, The** L	Storace, S.
1795		
Jan. 31	**Mysteries of the Castle** L	Shield, W.
Apr. 6	**Windsor Castle** L	**
Apr. 23	**Irish Mimic** L	Shield, W.
May 1	**Adopted Child** L	Attwood, T.
May 6	**Death of Captain Faulkner** L	Arnold, S.
May 6	**Jack of Newbury** L	Hook, J.
May 29	**Poor Sailor** L	Attwood, T.
June 20	**Zorinski** L	Arnold, S.
July 16	**Who Pays the Reckoning?** L	Arnold, S.
Aug. 28	**Love and Money** L	Arnold, S.
Sept. 2	**Three and the Deuce** L	Storace, S.
Sept. 21	**Love and Madness** L	Arnold, S.
1796		
Feb. 2	**Lock and Key** L	Shield, W.
Mar. 12	**Iron Chest** L	Storace, S.
Apr. 9	**Lad of the Hills** L	Shield, W.
Apr. 13	**Smugglers, The** L	Attwood, T.
Apr. 18	**Archers, The** NY	Carr, B.
Apr. 30	**Mahmoud** L	Storace, S.
June 11	**Bannian Day** L	Arnold, S.
July 25	**Birds of a Feather** L	Moorehead, J.
Oct. 7	**Wicklow Mountains** L	Shield, W.

Nov. 5	**Charity Boy** L	Reeve, W.
Nov. 19	**Abroad and at Home** L	Shield, W.
Nov. 28	**Cottage Festival** D	Giordani, T.
Dec. 10	**Shipwreck, The** L	Arnold, S.
Dec. 19	**Edwin and Angelina** NY	Pelissier, V.
1797		
Jan. 7	**Honey Moon** L	Linley, W.
Jan. 16	**Bourville Castle** NY	Carr, B.
Jan. 30	**Columbus** Ph	Reinagle
Feb. 2	**Friend in Need** L	Kelly, M.
Feb. 18	**Bantry Bay** L	Reeve, W.
Apr. 25	**Italian Villagers** L	Shield, W.
Apr. 26	**Ariadne Abandoned** NY	Pelissier, V.
May 13	**Fairy Festival** L	Attwood, T.
May 17	**Rival Soldiers** L	Shield, W.
May 23	**Diamond Cut Diamond** L	Hook, J.
May 23	**Hovel, The** L	Arnold, S.
June 26	**Irish Legacy** L	Arnold, S.
July 12	**Savoyard, The** Ph	Reinagle, A.
Aug. 24	**Irish Tar** L	Attwood, T.
Nov. 27	**Fast Asleep** L	Attwood, T.
Dec. 19	**Britain's Brave Tars!!** L	Attwood, T.
1798		
Jan. 16	**Blue-Beard** L	Kelly, M.
Feb. 9	**Americana** Charleston	**
Mar. 17	**Devil of a Lover** L	Attwood, T.
Mar. 28	**American in London** Ph	Carr, B.
Mar. 31	**Raft, The** L	Reeve, W.
May 7	**Hannah Hewitt** L	Dibdin, C.
May 23	**Reform'd in Time** L	Attwood, T.
July 8	**Throw Physic to the Dogs!** L	Arnold, S.
July 21	**Cambro-Britons** L	Arnold, S.
Aug. 11	**False and True** L	Arnold, S.
Oct. 17	**Day at Rome** L	Attwood, T.
Oct 25	**Mouth of the Nile** L	Attwood, T.
Nov. 12	**Ramah Droog** L	Reeve, W.
Nov. 14	**Captive of Spilburg** L	Dussek, J.
Dec. 11	**Albert and Adelaide** L	Attwood, T.
?	**Flash in the Pan** NY	Hewitt, J.
1799		
Jan. 14	**Sterne's Maria** NY	Pelissier, V.
Jan. 19	**Feudal Times** L	Kelly, M.
Apr. 2	**Old Clothesman** L	Attwood, T.
Apr. 29	**Pizzaro** L	Kelly, M.
May 29	**Love in a Blaze** D	Stevenson, J.
July 4	**Fourth of July** NY	Pelissier, V.
July 13	**Castle of Sorrento** L	Attwood, T.
Aug. 21	**Red Cross Knights** L	Attwood, T.
Oct. 3	**Embarkation, The** L	Reeve, W.
Oct. 7	**Naval Pillar** L	Moorehead
Nov. 14	**Turnpike Gate** L	Reeve, W.
Nov. 16	**Pavilion, The** L	Linley, W.
?	**Bird Catcher** L	Cleeve

1800

Date	Title	Composer
Feb. 1	Of Age Tomorrow L	Kelly, M.
Feb. 19	True Friends L	Attwood, T.
Mar. 11	Egyptian Festival L	Florio, C.
Mar. 12	Virgin of the Sun NY	Pelissier, V.
Mar. 25	St. David's Day L	Attwood, T.
Apr. 5	Hermione L	Attwood, T.
Apr. 14	Old Fools L	Moorehead
May 1	Paul and Virginia L	Reeve, W.
Aug. 14	What a Blunder L	Davy, J.
Sept. 1	Review, The L	Arnold, S.
Oct. 1	Wilmore Castle L	Hook, J.
Oct. 30	Virginia L	Arnold, S.
Nov. 15	Bondoncani, Il L	Attwood, T.
Dec. 5	Spanish Castle NY	Hewitt, J.
?	Wild Goose Chase NY	Hewitt, J.
*	Pizzaro	Taylor, R.

1801

Date	Title	Composer
Jan. 29	Veteran Tar L	Arnold, S.
Feb. 3	Merry Gardner NY	Pelissier, V.
Apr. 22	Blind Girl L	Reeve, W.
May 1	Bedouins, The D	Stevenson, J.
May 6	Cottagers, The NY	Hewitt, J.
May 12	Sea-Side Story L	Attwood, T.
July 24	Gipsey Prince L	Kelly, M.
Oct. 14	Escapes, The L	Attwood, T.
Dec. 9	Chains of the Heart L	Reeve, W.
*	Jamie and Anna	Reeve, W.

1802

Date	Title	Composer
Feb. 9	Cabinet, The L	Reeve et al.
Apr. 30	Algonah L	Storace, S.
May 1	Speed the Plough L	Moorehead
June 2	Caffres, The L	Davy, J.
July 18	Sixty-Third Letter L	Arnold, S.
July 31	Voice of Nature L	Pelissier, V.
Aug. 14	Fairies' Revels L	Arnold, S.
Nov. 17	House to Be Sold L	Kelly, M.
Dec. 18	Family Quarrels L	Reeve, W.

1803

Date	Title	Composer
Feb. 19	Hero of the North L	Kelly, M.
July 25	Love Laughs at Locksmiths L	Kelly, M.
Nov. 1	Wife of Two Husbands L	Mazzinghi, J.
Dec. 5	Caravan, The L	Reeve, W.
Dec. 14	English Fleet in 1342 L	Braham, J.

1804

Date	Title	Composer
Mar. 8	Paragraph, The L	Braham, J.
July 4	Hunter of the Alps L	Kelly, M.
Aug. 22	Gay Deceivers L	Hawes, W.
Aug. 30	Angelina L	Bishop, H. R.
Nov. 20	Matrimony L	King, M.
Dec. 10	Thirty Thousand L	Reeve, W.
?	Don Raphael NY	Hewitt, J.

1805

Date	Title	Composer
Jan. 31	Honey Moon L	Hewitt/Kelly
Feb. 12	Too Many Cooks L	King, M.
Feb. 28	Out of Place L	Reeve, W.
Apr. 23	Soldier's Return L	Hook, J.
May 24	Youth, Love L	Kelly, M.
Nov. 18	Weathercock, The L	King, M.

1806

Date	Title	Composer
Jan. 22	Travellers, The L	Corri, D.
Feb. 8	Broken Gold L	Dibdin, C.
Feb. 24	Tars from Tripoli NY	Hewitt, J.
Apr. 8	Forty Thieves L	Kelly, M.
Apr. 10	White Plume L	Reeve, W.
Apr. 28	Invisible Girl L	Hook, J.
May 9	Spanish Dollars! L	Davy, J.
June 12	Catch Him Who Can L	Hook, J.
Nov. 24	Tekeli L	Hook, J.
Dec. 26	Mother Goose L	Ware, W. H.

1807

Date	Title	Composer
Jan. 12	False Alarms L	Addison, J.
Mar. 12	Young Hussar L	Kelly, M.
Apr. 1	Wood Daemon L	Kelly, M.
July 16	Fortress, The L	Hook, J.
Aug. 27	Music Mad L	Hook, J.
Nov. 17	Two Faces under a Hood L	Shield, W.
?	Jonathan Postfree NY	**

1808

Date	Title	Composer
Feb. 11	Kais L	Reeve, W.
Feb. 25	Who Wins L	Condell, H.
Apr. 6	Indian Princess Ph	Bray, J.
Whitsun	Magic Minstrel L	Reeve, W.

1809

Date	Title	Composer
Jan. 4	Spanish Patriots NY	Gilfert, C.
Feb. 23	Circassian Bride L	Bishop, H. R.
June 26	Up All Night L	King, M.
July 22	Russian Imposter L	Addison, J.
Aug. 1	Vintagers, The L	Bishop, H. R.
Aug. 21	Killing No Murder L	Hook, J.
?	Exile, The L	Mazzanghi, J.
?	Foundling of the Forest L	Kelly, M.
?	Safe and Sound L	Hook, J.

1810

Date	Title	Composer
Feb. 8	Free Knights L	Mazzinghi, J.
Mar. 1	Maniac, The L	Bishop, H. R.
June 12	Oh, This Love L	King, M.
July 9	Tricks upon Travellers L	Horn, C. E.
Sept. 3	Plots, The L	King, M.
Oct. 16	Bridal Ring L	Condell/Pelissier

1811

Date	Title	Composer
Jan. 15	Lady of the Lake E	Francis, W.
Jan. 19	Bee-Hive L	Horn, C. E.
Jan. 24	Hamlet Travestie L	Bray, J.
Jan. 25	Alberto Albertini NY	Bray, J.
Feb. 5	Knight of Snowdoun L	Bishop, H. R.

Date	Title	Composer
Apr. 27	Americans, The L	King, M.
June 3	Council of Ten L	Reeve, W.
June 10	Royal Oak L	Kelly, M.
June 21	Round Robin L	Dibdin, C.
Aug. 1	One O'Clock L	King/Kelly
Aug. 26	Boarding House L	Horn, C. E.
Sept. 9	M.P. L	King, M. P.
Nov. 6	Up to Town L	Reeve et al.
?	Peasant Boy L	Kelly, M.
1812		
Jan. 31	Virgin of the Sun L	Bishop, H. R.
Mar. 7	Turn Out! L	King, M. P.
May 6	Devil's Bridge L	Horn, C. E.
July 22	Rich and Poor L	Horn, C. E.
Sept. 22	Spanish Patriots L	Stevenson, J.
Oct. 6	Aethiop, The L	Bishop, H. R.
1813		
Jan. 11	Haroun Alraschid L	Bishop, H. R.
Feb. 3	Poor Vulcan L	Bishop, H. R.
May 29	Brazen Bust L	Bishop, H. R.
July 2	Harry le Roi L	Bishop, H. R.
Aug. 4	Sharp and Flat L	Hook, J.
Oct. 1	Heroes of the Lakes Bal	**
Oct. 21	Miller and His Men L	Bishop, H. R.
Nov. 22	Who's to Have Her? L	Reeve, W.
Dec. 15	For England, Ho! L	Bishop, H. R.
?	Illusion, The L	Kelly, M.
?	Secret Mine L	Bishop, H. R.
1814		
Jan. 11	Narensky L	Horn, C. E.
Feb. 1	Farmer's Wife L	Bishop, H. R.
Feb. 24	Wandering Boys L	Bishop, H. R.
Apr. 12	Woodman's Hut L	Horn, C. E.
Aug. 4	Frederick the Great L	Cooke, T.
Oct. 18	Maid of the Mill L	Bishop, H. R.
Nov. 12	John of Paris	Bishop, H. R.
Nov. 29	Ninth Statue L	Horn, C. E.
?	Aethiop, The Ph	Taylor, R.
1815		
Feb. 1	Brother and Sister L	Reeve, W.
Mar. 29	Unknown Guest L	Kelly, M.
Apr. 7	Noble Outlaw L	Bishop, H. R.
Apr. 28	Comus L	Bishop, H. R.
June 7	Telemachus L	Bishop, H. R.
Aug. 1	My Aunt L	Addison, J.
Aug. 15	King's Proxy L	Cooke, T. S.
Sept. 15	Magpie or the Maid L	Bishop, H. R.
Nov. 20	Cymon L	Bishop, H. R.
1816		
Jan. 17	Midsummer Night's Dream L	Bishop, H. R.
Mar. 12	Guy Mannering L	Attwood, T.
Apr. 16	Who Wants a Wife? L	Bishop, H. R.
May 21	Oberon's Oath L	Parry, J.
Sept. 16	Free and Easy L	Addison, J.
Nov. 12	Slave, The L	Bishop, H. R.
1817		
Jan. 18	Humorous Lieutenant L	Bishop, H. R.
Feb. 27	Heir of Vironi L	Bishop, H. R.
Apr. 17	Elphi Bey L	Attwood, T.
May 20	Libertine, The L	Bishop, H. R.
June 7	Election, The L	Horn, C.
June 23	My Uncle L	Addison, J.
July 26	Wizard, The L	Horn, C. E.
Aug. 13	Persian Hunters L	Horn, C. E.
Sept. 29	Duke of Savoy L	Bishop, H. R.
1818		
Feb. 3	Illustrious Traveller L	**
Feb. 21	Zuma L	Bishop, H. R.
Mar. 12	Rob Roy Macgregor L	Davy, J.
Mar. 13	Barber of Seville L	Bishop, H. R.
Apr. 21	Amoroso L	Cooke, T. S.
May 16	December and May L	Bishop, H. R.
Sept. 23	Burgomaster of Saardam L	Bishop, H. R.
?	Lallah Rookh D	Horn, C. E.
*	Amilie	Rooke, W.
	(prem. 1837 L)	
1819		
Mar. 6	Marriage of Figaro L	Bishop, H. R.
Apr. 17	Heart of Midlothian L	Bishop, H. R.
Apr. 29	Roland for an Oliver L	Bishop, H. R.
Dec. 11	Comedy of Errors ?	Bishop, H. R.
1820		
Jan. 25	Antiquary, The L	Bishop, H. R.
Mar. 2	Ivanhoe L	Parry, J.
Apr. 23	Henri Quatre L	Bishop, H. R.
June 17	David Rizzio L	Braham et al.
July 20	Woman's Will L	Davy, J.
May 3	Lady and the Devil L	Kelly, M.
May 22	Battle of Bothwell Brigg L	Bishop, H. R.
Nov. 28	Justice L	Horne, C.
1821		
Feb. 10	Child of the Mountain Ph	Heinrich, A.
Feb. 20	Don John L	Bishop, H. R.
June 2	Dirce L	Horne, C.
July 5	Love's Dream L	Moss, M.
1822		
Jan. 15	Pirate, The L	Rooke, W.
Feb. 14	Montrose L	Bishop, H. R.
Feb. 23	Veteran Soldier L	Cooke, T. S.
May 11	Law of Java L	Bishop
July 6	Annette D	Horn, C. E.
Aug. 26	Family Jars L	Perry, G.
Aug. 27	Sedain Chair L	Bishop, H. R.
Sept. 9	Morning, Noon L	Perry, G.
Dec. 3	Maid Marian L	Bishop, H. R.
?	Deed of Gift Bos	**

Date	Title	Composer
?	Rose of Aragon NY	Taylor, R.
1823		
May 8	Clari L	Bishop, H. R.
July 7	Sweethearts and Wives L	Nathan, I.
Nov. 5	Cortez L	Bishop, H. R.
?	Actors al fresco L	Cooke et al.
?	Snow Storm Atlanta	Hewitt, J.
?	Virgin of the Sun Ph	Gilfert, C.
1824		
Jan. 13	Philandering L	Horn, C. E.
Feb. 10	Native Land L	Bishop, H. R.
Feb. 20	Merry Wives of Windsor L	Horn et al.
Mar. 1	Waverly L	Rodwell, G.
Aug. 10	Alcaid, The L	Nathan, I.
Nov. 10	Freischütz, Der L	Bishop, H. R.
Nov. 26	Frozen Lake L	Reeve, G.
?	Freischütz, Der	**
?	Saw Mill NY	Hawkins, M.
1825		
Jan. 19	Fall of Algiers L	Bishop, H. R.
Feb. 12	Shepherd of Derwent Vale L	Horn, C. E.
Feb. 17	Masaniello L	Bishop, H. R.
Apr. 4	Abou Hassan L	Cooke, T. S.
Apr. 22	Cavern, The L	Stevenson, J.
Apr. 28	Preciosa L	Weber-Hawes
May 16	Faustus L	Bishop, H. R.
July 6	Broken Promises L	Hawes, W.
Oct. 7	Forest Rose NY	Davies, J.
Oct. 21	Lilla L	**
Oct. 28	Wedding Present L	Horn, C. E.
*	Talisman, The	Bishop, H. R.
1826		
Jan. 28	Malvina L	Lee, G. A.
Mar. 16	Benyowsky L	King, M.
Mar. 27	Oberon L	Cooke, T.
Apr. 12	Oberon L	Weber
Apr. 29	Aladdin L	Bishop, H. R.
May 29	Knights of the Cross L	Bishop, H. R.
July 10	Rake's Progress L	Whitaker, J.
July 25	Dead Fetch L	Horn, C. E.
Aug. 7	Oracle, The L	Winter-Hawes
Aug. 31	Before Breakfast L	Barnett, J.
Oct. 9	White Lady L	Cooke, T. S.
Oct. 21	Peveril of the Peak L	Horn, C. E.
Oct. 31	Two Houses of Grenada L	Wade, J.
1827		
Jan. 1	Flying Dutchman L	Rodwell, G.
Jan. 1	Phantom Ship L	Rodwell, G.
Jan. 27	Englishmen in India L	Bishop, H. R.
Apr. 16	Boy of Santillane L	Cooke, T.
May 1	Turkish Loves L	Lacy, M. R.
July 2	Cornish Miners L	Rodwell, G.
July 9	Pay to My Order L	Horn, C. E.
July 12	Rencontre, The L	Bishop, H. R.
Aug. 20	Freebooters, The L	Hawes, W.
Oct. ?	Illustrious Stranger L	Nathan, I.
1828		
Feb. 28	Invincibles, The L	Lee, G. A.
Mar. 17	Auld Robin Gray Surrey	Blewitt, J.
Apr. 7	Talisman, The Surrey	Blewitt, J.
July 7	Bottle Imp L	Rodwell, G.
July 29	Tit for Tat L	Hawes, W.
Aug. 23	Not for Me L	Hawes, W.
Sept. 2	Sylvana L	Weber-Blewitt
Oct. 1	Mason of Buda L	Rodwell, G.
Dec. 4	Love in Wrinkles L	Lacy, M. R.
Dec. 15	Earthquake, The L	Rodwell, G.
?	New Don Juan! L	Rodwell, G.
?	Sublime and the Beautiful L	Lee, G. A.
?	Taming of the Shrew L	Braham, J.
1829		
Jan. 14	My Old Woman L	Blewitt, J.
Jan. 15	Nymph of the Grotto L	Lee, G. A.
Feb. 5	Yelva L	Bishop, H. R.
Mar. 7	Maid of Judah L	Lacy, M. R.
Mar. 10	Casket, The L	Lacy, M. R.
Mar. 19	Home, Sweet Home L	Bishop, H. R.
Apr. 9	Dido NY	Horn, C. E.
Apr. 20	Devil's Elixir L	Rodwell, G.
Apr. 29	Quartette, The NY	Horn, C. E.
May 4	Masaniello L	Cooke/Livius
June	Nothing Superfluous L	Lee, G. A.
July 15	Robber's Bride L	Hawes, W.
Aug. 18	Spring Lock L	Rodwell, G.
Nov. 17	Night before the Weddding L	Bishop, H. R.
1830		
Feb. 2	Robert the Devil L	Barnett, J.
Feb. 4	Ninetta L	Bishop, H. R.
Feb. 8	Teddy the Tiler L	Rodwell, G.
Apr. 13	Cinderella L	Lacy, M. R.
May 1	Hofer L	Bishop, H. R.
June 25	Under the Oak L	Bishop, H. R.
July 16	Skeleton Lover L	Rodwell, G.
July 23	Adelaide L	Bishop, H. R.
July 29	Honest Frauds L	Horn, C. E.
Oct. 4	Black Vulture L	Rodwell, G.
Nov. 30	Catherine L	Burghersh, J.
1831		
Feb. 1	Devil's Brother L	Lee, G. A.
Feb. 3	Romance of a Day L	Bishop, H. R.
Aug. 4	Sorceress, The L	Ries, F.
Aug. 18	Evil Eye L	Rodwell, G.
Oct. 27	Love Spell L	Horn, C. E.
Nov. 3	Fra Diavolo L	Lacy, M. R.
Nov. 3	Love Charm L	Bishop, H. R.

1832		
Jan. 11	**My Own Lover** L	Rodwell, G.
Feb. 9	**Gran Uile** D	Lover, S.
Feb. 20	**Demon, The** L	Bishop, H. R.
Feb. 21	**Fiend-Father** L	Lacy, M. R.
Mar. 20	**Alchymist, The** L	Bishop, H. R.
May 8	**Tyrolese Peasant** L	Bishop, H. R.
June 18	**Magic Fan** L	Bishop, H. R.
July 27	**Bottle of Champagne** L	Bishop, H. R.
Oct. 29	**Doom-Kiss** L	Bishop, H. R.
Dec. 18	**Win Her** L	Barnett, J.
1833		
Feb. 22	**Israelites in Egypt** L	Lacy, M. R.
Mar. 23	**Coiners, The** L	Lacy, M. R.
Apr. 17	**Magic Flute** NY	Horn, C. E.
May 1	**Sonnambula, La** L	Bishop, H. R.
May 4	**Soldier's Widow** L	Barnett, J.
Sept. 9	**Court Masque** L	Dawes, W.
Nov. 13	**Gustavus III** L	Cooke, T. S.
1834		
Apr. 1	**Challenge, The** L	Cooke, T. S.
June 9	**Rural Felicity** L	Bishop, H. R.
July 21	**Nourjahad** L	Loder, E.
Aug. 4	**Dragon, The** L	Lee, G. A.
Aug. 25	**Mountain Sylph** L	Barnett, J.
Oct. 2	**Hermann** L	Thomson, J.
Nov. 3	**Genevieve** L	Macfarren
Nov. 15	**Red Mask** L	Cooke, T. S.
Nov. 20	**Lord of the Isles** L	Rodwell, G.
Dec. 15	**Last Days of Pompeii** L	Rodwell, G.
*	**Climbing Boy**	Hawes, W.
1835		
Feb. 21	**Lestocq** L	Cooke, T. S.
Apr. 20	**Sadak and Kalasrade** L	Packer, C.
Apr. 20	**Shadow on the Wall** L	Thomson, J.
June 8	**Spirit of the Bell** L	Rodwell, G.
Aug. 10	**Covenanters, The** L	Loder, E. J.
Sept. 14	**Dice of Death** L	Loder, E. J.
Oct. 28	**Paul Clifford** L	Rodwell, G.
Oct. 29	**Siege of Rochelle** L	Balfe, M.
Dec. 14	**Agnes Sorel** L	A' Beckett, M.
Dec. 14	**Bronze Horse** L	Rodwell, G.
?	**Jewess, The** L	Cooke, T.
*	**Belshazzar's Feast**	Griesbach, J.
1836		
Feb. 2	**Quasimodo** L	Rodwell, G.
May 26	**Maid of Artois** L	Balfe, M.
June 13	**Sexton of Cologne** L	Rodwell, G.
Sept. 8	**Pacha's Bridal** L	Romer, F.
Nov. 8	**Siege of Corinth** L	Cooke, T. S.
Dec. 6	**Village Coquettes** L	Hullah, J.
?	**Thalaba** L	Rodwell, G.
1837		
Feb. 28	**Fair Rosamond** L	Barnett, J.
Mar. 13	**Postilion!** L	Stansbury, G

May 27	**Catherine Grey** L	Balfe, M.
Oct. 7	**Child of the Wreck** L	Cooke, T. S.
Oct. 19	**Afrancesado, The** L	Lee, G. A.
Nov. 11	**Barbers of Bassora** L	Hullah, J.
Nov. 30	**Joan of Arc** L	Balfe, M.
1838		
Apr. 19	**Gipsy's Warning** L	Benedict, J.
May 17	**Diadesté** L	Balfe, M.
May 17	**Outpost, The** L	Hullah, J.
July 7	**Rob of the Fens** L	Romer, F.
Aug. 13	**Devil's Opera** L	Macfarren, G.
Oct. 19	**Foresters, The** L	Loder, E.
Nov. 6	**Francis the First** L	Loder, E. J.
Dec. 3	**Guillaume Tell** L	Bishop, H. R.
?	**Windsor Castle** L	Griesbach, J.
1839		
Feb. 8	**Farinelli** L	Barnett, J.
May 2	**Henrique** L	Rooke, W.
Oct. 26	**Fairy Lake** L	Lee, G. A.
Oct. 28	**Jack Sheppard** L	Rodwell, G.
1840		
Jan. 7	**Don Quixote**	Rodwell, G.
Feb. 12	**Fortunate Isles**	Bishop, H. R.
Oct. 12	**Ahmad al Ramel**	Horn, C. E.
Dec. 1	**Fridolin** L	Romer, F.
?	**Triboulet** L	Nathan, I.
1841		
Mar. 9	**Keolanthe** L	Balfe, M.
Apr. 12	**Deer Stalker** L	Loder, E. J.
Apr. 19	**Arcadia** L	Harroway, J.
Apr. 22	**Paddy Whack in Italia** L	Lover, S.
June 14	**Queen of a Day** L	Fitzwilliam, E.
1842		
Feb. 25	**Queen of the Thames** L	Hatton, J. L.
May 4	**Mock Catalani** Syd	Nagel, C.
May 23	**Maid of Saxony** NY	Horn, C. E.
Aug.	**Little Red Riding Hood** L	A'Beckett, M.
1843		
May 29	**Merry Freaks** Syd	Nathan, I.
Aug. 14	**Geraldine** L	Balfe, M.
Nov. 27	**Bohemian Girl** L	Balfe, M.
1844		
Mar. 2	**Pasqual Bruno** Vienna	Hatton, J. L.
Apr. 8	**Drama at Home** L	Reed, T. G.
Apr. 22	**Brides of Venice** L	Benedict, J.
May 27	**Currency Lass** Syd	**
Sept. 30	**Enchanted Horse** NY	Jones, J.
Nov. 20	**Castle of Aymon** L	Balfe, M.
Nov. 27	**Daughter of St. Mark** L	Balfe, M.
1845		
Mar. 24	**Golden Fleece** L	Reed, T. G.
May 14	**Enchantress, The** L	Balfe, M.

June 4	**Leonora** Ph	Fry, W.
Oct. 18	**Fairy Oak** L	Forbes, H.
Oct. 28	**Who's the Composer?** L	Reed, T. G.
Nov. 15	**Maritania** L	Wallace, V.
?	**Graciosa** L	**
1846		
Feb. 3	**Adventure of Don Quixote** L	Macfarren, G.
Feb. 26	**Crusaders, The** L	Benedict, J.
July 15	**Wonderful Water Cure** L	Reed, T. G.
Oct. 28	**Night Dancers** L	Loder, E. J.
Nov. 9	**Loretta** L	Lavenu, L.
Dec. 11	**Bondman, The** L	Balfe, M.
Dec. 19	**Seven Maids of Munich** L	Rodwell, G.
?	**Magic Horn** L	Lee, G. A.
1847		
Jan. 27	**Rival Clans** New	Deval, H.
Feb. 22	**Matilda of Hungary** L	Wallace, V.
May 7	**Don John of Austria** Syd	Nathan, I.
Dec. 20	**Maid of Honour** L	Balfe, M.
1848		
Dec. 6	**Quentin Durward** L	Laurent, H.
Dec. 6	**Robin Goodfellow** L	Loder, E. J.
1849		
Jan. 18	**Marie** L	Loder, E. J.
Apr. 18	**Heart of Midlothian** L	**
Oct. 27	**King Charles II** L	Macfarren, G.
1850		
Nov. 15	**Sleeper Awakened** L	Macfarren, G.
1852		
Mar. 6	**Sicilian Bride** L	Balfe, M.
July 26	**Devil's in It** L	Balfe, M.
Sept. 27	**Uncle Tom's Cabin** Troy, NY	Howard, G.
*	**Wittikind and His Brothers**	**
1853		
Mar. 11	**Flower Queen** NY	Root, G. F.
Nov. 17	**Love's Alarms** L	Fitzwilliam, E.
1854		
May 29	**Berta** L	Smart, H.
*	**Pilgrim Fathers**	Root, G. F.
1855		
Mar. 22	**Minstrel's Return** New	Rolfe, F.
Apr. 14	**Raymond and Agnes** Man	Loder, E. J.
May 16	**Mephistopheles** Surrey	Lutz, M.
Sept. 27	**Rip van Winkle** NY	Bristow, G.
1857		
Oct. 29	**Rose of Castille** L	Balfe, M.
?	**Romance** L	Leslie, H.
1858		
Aug. 23	**Ten Nights in a Bar-Room** NY	Pratt, W. W.

1859		
Feb. 14	**Zaida** Liv	Lutz, M.
Dec. 19	**Victorine** L	Mellon, A.
1860		
Jan. 10	**Haymakers, The**	Root, G. F. Ch
Feb. 23	**Lurline** L	Wallace, V.
Feb. ?	**Out of Sight** L	Clay, F.
Oct. 11	**Robin Hood** L	Macfarren
Dec. 6	**Bianca** L	Balfe, M.
Dec. 6	**Satanella** L	Balfe, M.
?	**Garibaldi** L	Cowen, F.
*	**Belshazzar's Feast**	Root, G. F.
1861		
Feb. 28	**Amber Witch** L	Wallace, V.
Oct. 24	**Ruy Blas** L	Glover, W.
Nov. 19	**Toy-Maker** L	Linley, G.
Nov. 30	**Puritan's Daughter** L	Balfe, M.
1862		
Feb. 8	**Lily of Killarney** L	Benedict, J.
Mar. 22	**Court and Cottage** L	Clay, F.
Apr. 7	**Doctor of Alcantara**	Eichberg, J.
May ?	**Pesceballo, Il** Bos	Child, F. J.
Nov. 3	**Love's Triumph** L	Wallace, V.
Dec. 6	**Law Versus Love** L	Linley, G.
1863		
Feb. 12	**Armourer of Nantes** L	Balfe, M.
Mar. 3	**Vivandiere, La** Augusta, Ga	Hewitt, J. H.
Oct. 12	**Desert Flower** L	Wallace, V.
Nov. 2	**Jessy Lea** L	Macfarren, G.
Nov. 21	**Blanche de Nevers** L	Balfe, M.
1864		
Feb. 11	**She Stoops to Conquer** L	Macfarren, G.
Feb. 11	**Soldier's Legacy** L	Macfarren, G.
May 4	**Notre-Dame of Paris** Ph	Fry, W.
Sept. 8	**Sleeping Queen** L	Balfe, M.
Nov. 3	**Helvellyn** L	Macfarren, G.
Nov. 26	**Rose, The** L	Hatton, J. L.
Dec. 3	**Bride of Song** L	Benedict, J.
1865		
Jan. 23	**Constance** L	Clay, F.
Feb. 9	**River-Sprite** L	Mori, F.
Oct. 23	**Felix** L	Lutz, M.
Nov. 15	**Ida** L	Leslie, H.
?	**Castle Grim** L	Allen, G.
?	**Windsor Castle** L	Musgrave, F.
1866		
June 2	**Bluebeard Repaired** L	Tully, J. H.
Sept. 12	**Black Crook** NY	**
Dec. 29	**Dulcamara** L	**
?	**Minna** L	de Lara, I.
1867		
Apr. 13	**Sapphire Necklace** L	Sullivan, A.

May 11	Cox and Box L	Sullivan, A.
June 15	Viandière, La Liv	Wallterstein, F.
Dec. 18	Contrabandista, The L	Sullivan, A.
Dec. 26	Caliph of Bagdad L	Musgrave, F.
1868		
Mar. 5	Two Cadis Bos	Eichberg, J.
1869		
Mar. 29	No Cards L	"Elliott, L."
Nov. 26	Ages Ago L	Clay, F.
1870		
May 26	Gentleman in Black L	Clay, F.
June 20	Our Island Home L	Reed, T.
?	Follies of a Night L	Gabriel, V.
*	Antonio	Pratt, S.
1871		
June 14	Letty Basket-Maker L	Balfe, M.
June 20	In Possession L	Clay, F.
Dec. 26	Thespis L	Sullivan, A.
Dec. 30	Sensation Novel L	Reed, T. G.
1872		
Feb. 7	Charity Begins at Home L	Cellier, A.
Oct. 28	Happy Arcadia L	Clay, F.
Dec. 23	Black Crook L	Clay, F.
1873		
Feb. 16	Oriana L	Clay, F.
May 5	Mildred's Well L	Reed, T. G.
1874		
May 17	He's Coming L	Reed, T. G.
June 24	One Too Many L	Cowen, F.
July 27	Evangeline NY	Rice, E. E.
Aug. 17	Cattarina Man	Clay, F.
Sept. 11	Africanus Blue Beard Gloucester, Mass	Sedgwick, A.
Oct. 16	Sultan of Mocha Man	Cellier, A.
Dec. 16	Three Tenants L	Reed, T. G.
1875		
Jan. 25	Ancient Britons L	Reed, T. G.
Mar. 25	Trial by Jury L	Sullivan, A. S.
June 5	Zoo, The L	Sullivan, A. S.
July 5	Eyes and No Eyes L	Reed, T. G.
Oct. 4	Tower of London Man	Cellier, A.
Nov. 1	Spanish Bond L	Reed, T. G.
?	Leap Year NY	Sedgwick, A.
?	Queerest Courtship Ch?	Sedgwick, A.
1876		
Feb. 28	Indian Puzzle L	Reed, T. G.
Mar. 20	Out of Bondage Lynn, Mass	**
June 9	Wicked Duke L	Reed, T. G.
June 26	Princess Toto Nottingham	Clay, F.
July 21	Gambrinus Jackson, Mich	Sedgwick, A.

Sept. 25	Don Quixote L	Clay, F.
Nov. 6	Matched and Mated L	Reed, T. G.
Nov. 22	Pauline L	Cowen, F.
?	Circumstances Alter Cases NY?	Sedgwick, A.
?	Estranged NY?	Sedgwick, A.
?	My Walking Photograph Ch?	Sedgwick, A.
?	Sold Again NY?	Sedgwick, A.
?	Twin Sisters NY?	Sedgwick, A.
1877		
Feb. 12	Night's Surprise L	Reed, T. G.
May 7	No. 204 L	Reed, T. G.
Nov. 17	Sorcerer, The L	Sullivan, A. S.
1878		
May 25	H.M.S. Pinafore L	Sullivan, A. S.
June 20	Blodwen Swansea	Parry, J.
Oct. 16	Nell Gwynne Man	Cellier, A.
1879		
Jan. 13	Mulligan Guard NY	Braham, D.
Sept. 25	Sleepy Holllow NY	Maretzek, M.
Nov. 7	Light of the Harem L	Thomas, A. G.
Dec. 8	Peculiar Sam Bos	**
Dec. 31	Pirates of Penzance L	Sullivan, A. S.
1880		
Oct. 11	Deseret NY	Buck, D.
?	Deserted Village L	Glover, J.
1881		
Jan. 10	Masque of Pandora Bos	Cellier, A.
Feb. 6	Veiled Prophet of Khorassan Hanover	Stanford, C.
Apr. 1	Vercingétorix Syd	Kowalski, H.
Apr. 23	Patience L	Sullivan, A. S.
1882		
Jan. 22	Moro L	Balfe, M.
Apr. 1	Widow, The Springfield, Ill	Lavallée, C.
May 27	Wreck of the Pinafore L	Searelle, L.
June 15	Zenobia NY	Pratt, S. G.
July 22	Vicar of Bray L	Solomon, E.
Nov. 25	Iolanthe L	Sullivan, A. S.
?	Wicklow Rose Man	Allen, G. B.
?	Lord Bateman L	Solomon, E.
?	Uncle Tom's Cabin Ph	Florio, C.
1883		
Mar. 6	Victorian L	Edwards, J.
Mar. 21	Cymbia L	Pascal, F.
Mar. 26	Esmerelda L	Thomas, A.
Mar. 26	Fortunio Ph	Darley, F.
Apr. 9	Colomba L	Mackenzie
Apr. 17	Royal Word L	de Lara, I.
Apr. 23	Merry Duchess L	Clay, F.
Dec.	Cinderella Harrow, Engl	Farmer, J.
Dec. 3	Golden Ring L	Clay, F.

?	Moustique Brussels	Kowalski, H.
?	Salem Witch Bos	Stahl, R.
?	Single Married Man NY?	Sedgwick, A.
1884		
Jan. 5	Princess Ida L	Sullivan, A. S.
Apr. 18	Savonarola Hamburg	Stanford, C.
Apr. 28	Pilgrims, The L	Stanford, C.
May 1	Désirée Wa	Sousa, J. P.
1885		
Jan. ?	Little Tycoon Ph	Spenser, W.
Mar. 14	Mikado L	Sullivan, A. S.
Apr. 16	Nadeshda L	Thomas, A.
* (ca.)	Charter Oak	Leavitt, B.
1886		
June 8	Guillem the Troubadour L	Mackenzie, A.
Sept. 25	Dorothy L	Cellier, A.
1887		
Jan. 22	Ruddigore L	Sullivan, A. S.
Jan. 26	Nordisa Liv	Corder, F.
Jan. 27	Conspiracy of Pontiac Det	Mayer, C.
Mar. 14	Lucille Ch	Pratt, S.
Nov. 21	Begum, The NY	De Koven, R.
1888		
Oct. 3	Yeomen of the Guard L	Sullivan, A. S.
1889		
Apr. 20	Doris L	Cellier, A.
June 23	Sea King NY	Stahl, R.
July 11	Leo the Royal Cadet Kingston, Ont	Telgmann, O.
Nov. 18	Don Quixote Bos	De Koven, R.
Nov. 25	Dante and Beatrice L	Philpot, S. R.
Dec. 7	Gondoliers, The L	Sullivan, A. S.
1890		
Apr. 22	Thorgrim L	Cowen, F.
June 9	Joan L	Ford, E.
June 9	Robin Hood Ch	De Koven, R.
Aug. 18	Merry Monarch NY	Sousa, J. P.
*	Irmelin (prem. 1953 O)	Delius, F.
1891		
Jan. 15	Knight of the Leopard Liv	Balfe, M.
Jan. 31	Ivanhoe L	Sullivan, A. S.
June 30	Nautch Girl L	Solomon, E.
Dec. 29	Reilly and the 400 NY	Braham, D.
*	American Volunteer	Vinatieri, F. (prem. 1981, Yankton, SD)
* (ca.)	Frogs of Windham (prem 1983 Windham Conn)	Leavitt, B. E.
1892		
Jan. 4	Mountebanks, The L	Cellier, A.
Apr. 14	Jupiter NY	Edwards, J.

June 6	Puritania Bos	Kelley, E. S.
June 11	Light of Asia L	de Lara, I.
July 12	Caedmar L	Bantock, G.
July 27	Haste to the Wedding L	Grossmith, L.
Sept. 10	Wedding Eve L	Ford, E.
Sept. 24	Haddon Hall L	Sullivan, A. S.
Oct. 12	Triumph of Columbus NY	Pratt, S.
Nov. 14	Fencing Master NY	De Koven, R.
Dec. 8	Irmengarda L	Bach, L. E.
?	Fayette Brisbane?	Allen, G. B.
*	Eugene Aram	Bantock, G.
1893		
Jan. 19	Magic Opal L	Albéniz, I.
Jan. 26	Friend Fritz NY	Edwards, J.
Feb. 7	Landsdown Castle Chel	Holst, G.
Feb. 9	Ephelia Den	Freeman, H.
Feb. 15	Golden Web Liv	Thomas, A.
May 3	Jane Annie L	Ford, E.
May 29	Knickerbockers NY	De Koven, R.
July 20	Amy Robsart L	de Lara, I.
Sept.	Martyr, The Den	Freeman, H.
Oct. 7	Utopia Limited L	Sullivan, A.
Oct. 26	Algerian, The Ph	De Koven, R.
Nov. 12	Signa Milan	Cowen, F.
Nov. 23	King Rene's Daughter NY	Edwards, J.
*	Magic Fountain (prem. 1977 L)	Delius, F.
*	Maid of Plymouth	Thorne, T. P.
*	Quentin Durward (prem. 1920 New)	Maclean, A.
1894		
Jan. 29	Tabasco Bos	Chadwick, G.
July 31	Madeleine NY	Edwards, J.
Oct. 29	Rob Roy NY	De Koven, R.
Nov. 15	Jeanie Deans E	MacCunn, H.
Dec. 12	Chieftain, The L	Sullivan, A. S.
?	His Excellency L	Carr, F. O.
*	Pearl of Iran	Bantock, G.
1895		
Apr. 1	Daphne NY	Bird, A.
May 7	Zaporogues, The Bir	Davis, J.
May 16	Tzigaine NY	De Koven, R.
June 8	Harold L	Cowen, F.
June 13	Woodlanders SL	Paulus, S.
June 29	Petruccio L	Maclean, A.
Aug. 12	Sylvia Car	Parry, J.
Nov. 4	Wizard of the Nile NY	Herbert, V.
*	Gentleman Joe	Slaughter, W.
*	Koanga (prem. 1899 L)	Delius, F.
*	Revoke, The	Holst, G.
1896		
Feb. 10	Scarlet Letter Bos	Damrosch, W.
Feb. 26	Goddess of Truth NY	Edwards, J.
Mar. 2	Shamus O'Brien L	Stanford, C.

Date	Title	Composer
Mar. 7	**Grand Duke** L	Sullivan, A. S.
Apr. 13	**Capitan, El** Bos	Sousa, J. P.
Apr. 20	**Lady of Longeford** L	Bach, L. E.
Apr. 25	**Geisha, The** L	Jones, S.
May 18	**On the March**	Clay, F.
	Sheffield, Engl	
Oct. 19	**Brian Boru** NY	Edwards, J.
Nov. 2	**Mandarin, The** NY	De Koven, R.
?	**French Maid** L	Slaughter, W.
?	**Merry Benedicts** Bklyn	Arnold, M.
?	**Prodigal Son** Liv?	Nicholls, F.
?	**Whipping Boy**	Hill, A.
	Wellington, Austral	
*	**Idea, The**	Holst, G.
*	**Magic Mirror**	Holst, G.
1897		
Feb. 20	**His Majesty** L	Mackenzie, A.
Apr. 8	**Wedding Day** NY	Edwards, J.
May 25	**Rip Van Winkle**	Jordan, J.
	Providence, RI	
Sept. 14	**Paris Doll** Hart	De Koven, R.
Sept. 20	**Idols' Eye** Troy, NY	Herbert, V.
Oct. 23	**Diarmid** L	MacCunn, H.
Dec. 13	**Highwayman, The** NY	De Koven, R.
Dec. 27	**Bride Elect** NH	Sousa, J. P.
?	**'Prentice Pillar** L	Somerville, R.
1898		
May 28	**Beauty Stone** L	Sullivan, A. S.
July 25	**Red Spider**	Drysdale, L.
	Lowenstoft, Scot	
Aug. 29	**Charlatan** Montreal	Sousa, J. P.
Sept. 14	**Fortune Teller** Tor	Herbert, V.
?	**Zuluki** Cl	Freeman, H.
*	**Azara** (prem. 1903 NY)	Paine, J. K.
1899		
Jan. 7	**Lucky Star** L	Caryll, I.
Sept. 11	**Cyrano de**	Herbert, V.
	Bergerac Montreal	
Oct. 9	**Ameer, The** Scranton, Pa	Herbert, V.
Oct. 21	**San Toy** L	Jones, S.
Oct. 27	**Royal Vagrants** L	Warner, H.
Nov. 29	**Rose of Persia** L	Sullivan, A. S.
*	**Sita**	Holst, G.
1900		
Feb. 12	**Viceroy, The** SF	Herbert, V.
Feb. 13	**Masque of War**	MacCunn, H.
	and Peace L	
Mar. 31	**Lady Dolly** Syd	Hill, A.
May 7	**Phyllis** NY	Warren, R.
Nov. 5	**Foxy Quiller** NY	De Koven, R.
?	**Nada** Cl	Freeman, H.
1901		
Apr. 27	**Emerald Isle** L	Sullivan, A. S.
May 30	**Much Ado about**	Stanford, C.
	Nothing L	
Sept. 26	**Judith** Worcester, Mass	Chadwick, G.
Nov. 14	**Ib and Little Christina** L	Leoni, F.
?	**Dolly Varden** L	Edwards, J.
*	**Romeo and Juliet**	Shelley, H.
1902		
Jan. 27	**Maid Marian** NY	De Koven, R.
Apr. 2	**Merrie England** L	German, E.
Apr. 9	**Forest, The** Berlin	Smyth, E.
*	**Youth's Choice**	Holst, G.
1903		
Feb. 16	**Nancy Brown** NY	Hadley, H.
Feb. 16	**Tapu** Wellington, NZ	Hill, A.
Feb. 18	**In Dahomey** NY	Cook, W. M.
Mar. 14	**My Lady Molly** L	Jones, S.
June 30	**African Kraal** Ch	Freeman, H.
Aug. 3	**Sarrona** Bruges, Bel	Howland, W.
Oct. 17	**Duchess of Dantzic** L	Caryll, I.
Nov. 9	**Red Feather** NY	De Koven, R.
Nov. 22	**Cross and the Crescent** L	MacAlpin, C.
Dec. 7	**Muirgheis** D?	Butler, O'B.
?	**Columbus** SL	Moore, H.
?	**Guest of Honor** SL	Joplin, S.
1904		
Apr. 29	**King's Price** L	MacLean, A.
*	**Don Quixote**	Hill, A.
*	**Octoroon, The**	Freeman, H.
1905		
June 26	**Moorish Maid**	Hill, A.
	Auckland, NZ	
Dec.	**Hippolytus** Gla	Drysdale, L.
?	**Free Lance** Ph	Sousa, J. P.
*	**Uncle Remus**	Gilbert, H. F.
1906		
Jan. 31	**Pipe of Desire** Bos	Converse, F.
Feb. 2	**Abyssinia** NY	Cook, W. M.
Mar. 1	**Greysteel** Sheffield, Engl	Gatty, N.
June 20	**See-See** L	Jones, S.
Aug. 31	**White Chrysanthemum** L	Talbot, H.
Nov. 11	**Wreckers, The** Leipzig	Smyth, E.
*	**Alice in Wonderland**	Slaughter, W.
*	**King Hal**	Stewart, H.
1907		
Feb. 21	**Village Romeo and**	Delius, F.
	Juliet Berlin	
Apr. 18	**Tom Jones** L	German, E.
June 4	**Otho Visconti** Ch	Gleason, F.
Nov. 18	**Girls of Holland** NY	De Koven, R.
Sept. 3	**King of Cadonia** L	Lonsdale, F.
Oct. 12	**Golden Butterfly** NY	De Koven, R.
Nov. 23	**Patriot, The** NY	Edwards, J.
*	**Pageant of Darkness**	MacCunn, H.
	and Light	
1909		
Jan. 27	**Angelus, The** L	Naylor, E.
Apr. 4	**Safié** Mainz, Ger	Hadley, H.

Date	Title	Composer
May 21	Hoshi-San Ph	Leps, W.
Nov. 11	Pierrot and Pierrette L	Holbrooke, J.
Dec, 15	Fallen Fairies L	German, E.
Dec. 16	Duke or Devil Man	Gatty, N.
?	Don Quixote L	Hewitt, T. J.
*	Birth of Arthur (prem. 1920 Glast)	Boughton,R.
*	Fionn and Terra	Drysdale, L.
*	Land of the Misty Water	Cadman, C.
1910		
July 23	Summer's Night L	Clutsam, G.
Oct. 24	Naughty Marietta Syr	Herbert, V.
Oct. 27	Love Laughs at Locksmiths Portsmouth, Me	Breil, J. C.
1911		
Feb. 25	Natoma Ph	Herbert, V.
Feb. 26	Old Black Joe NY	Shelley, H
Mar. 3	Sacrifice, The Bos	Converse, F.
Mar. 13	Pink Lady NY	Carlyll, I.
May	Tryst, The NY	Freeman, H.
Dec. 25	Wedding Trip NY	De Koven, R.
*	Treemonisha (prem. 1915 NY)	Joplin, S.
1912		
Jan. 30	Pygmalion Den	Houseley, H.
Mar. 5	Olaf Lin	Kirkpatrick, H.
Mar. 14	Mona NY	Parker, H.
May 4	Stella Syd	Marshall-Hall, G.
Apr. 22	Narcissa Sea	Moore, M.
June 15	Children of Don L	Holbrooke, J.
Aug. 10	Atonement of Pan Ph	Hadley, H.
Oct. 15	Dove of Peace Ph	Damrosch, W.
Dec. 14	Romeo and Juliet Mel	Marshall-Hall, G.
?	Prophecy, The ?	Freeman, H.
*	Leper, The	Moore, M.
*	Padrone, The (prem. 1955 Waterbury, Conn)	Chadwick, G.
1913		
Feb. 20	Sun Dance Vernal, Utah	Hanson, W.
Feb. 27	Cyrano NY	Damrosch, W.
Nov. 1	All in a Garden Fair Sea	Tonning, G.
Nov. 1	Joan of Arc L	Rôze, R.
Dec. 4	Westward Ho! L	Miles, P. N.
?	Professor Tattle NY	Breil, J. C.
?	Seventh Chord Ch	Breil, J. C.
*	Merrymount	Smith, D. S.
1914		
Jan. 24	Madeleine NY	Herbert, V.
June 6	Cricket on the Heart L	Mackenzie, A.
July 4	Dylan L	Holbrooke, J.
Aug.	Chapel in Lyonesse Glast	Boughton, R.
Aug. 3	Giovanni Syd	Hill, A.
Aug. 3	Pierrete Syd	Hart, F.
Aug. 26	Immortal Hour Glast	Boughton, R.
Dec. 29	Guido Ferranti Ch	Etten, J. Van
*	Land of Heart's Desire	Hart, F.
*	Plantation, The	Freeman, H.
*	Immigrants, The	Converse, F.
1915		
July 1	Fairyland LA	Parker, H.
Aug. 11	Oithona Glast	Bainton, E.
Nov. 7	Dawn of the West Port	Enna, E.
Dec. 28	Bethlehem Street, Engl	Boughton, R.
?	Enchanter, The Ch	Holbrooke, J.
?	Pippa's Holiday Paris	Beach, J. P.
*	Riders to the Sea	Hart, F.
*	Vision of Ariel (prem. 1955 Ch)	Saminsky, L.
1916		
Jan. 7	Romeo and Juliet Middlesbrough, Engl	Barkworth, J.
Jan. 14	Critic, The L	Stanford, C.
Jan. 15	Lover's Knot Ch	Bucharoff, S.
Jan. 28	Boatswain's Mate L	Smyth, E.
Aug. 14	Round Table Glast	Boughton, R.
Aug. 15	Sumida River Glast	Raybould, C.
Dec. 5	Sâvitri L	Holst, G.
*	Athalia	Freeman, H.
*	Deirdre of the Sorrows	Hart, F.
*	Tigers, The (prem. 1976 L)	Brian, H.
1917		
Feb. 9	Snow Queen SF	Jones, A. G.
Feb. 16	Louis XIV SL	Moore, H.
Mar. 8	Canterbury Pilgrims NY	De Koven, R.
May 18	Blue Wing Sea	Tonning, G.
July 7	Ruth and Naomi Mel	Hart, F.
Aug. 4	Land of Happiness SF	Redding, J.
Aug. 18	Building of Bamba Halcyon, Calif	Cowell, H.
Dec. 15	Rajah of Shivapore Syd	Hill, A.
Dec. 26	Azora Ch	Hadley, H.
?	Osseo Brookline, Mass	Noyes-Greene, E.
1918		
Jan. 5	Daughter of the Forest Ch	Nevin, A.
Mar. 23	Shanewis NY	Cadman, C.
Apr. 23	Moon Maiden Glast	Boughton, R.
May 2	Rose of Destiny Ph	Heckscher
Oct. 15	Bianca NY	Hadley, H.
*	Fantastics, The	Hart, F.
1919		
Mar. 12	Legend, The NY	Breil, J. C.
Mar. 12	Temple Dancer NY	Hugo, J. A.
Oct. 21	Fennimore and Gerda Frankfurt	Delius, F.
Nov. 27	Prince Ferelon L	Gatty, N.

Date	Title	Composer
Dec. 5	Malvolio Mel	Hart, F.
*	Christmas Rose (prem. 1931 L)	Bridge, F.
*	Crier by Night (prem. 1942 BBC)	Bainton, E.
*	Fantasy in Delft	Gilbert, H.
*	Travelling Companion (prem. 1925 Liv)	Stanford, C.
1920		
Jan. 2	Rip Van Winkle Ch	De Koven, R.
Jan. 31	Cleopatra's Night NY	Hadley, H.
Apr. 17	Tempest, The L	Gatty, N.
May 20	Pied Piper of Hamelin Miami	Clokey, J.
Dec. 9	David Garrick L	Somerville, R.
*	Magnifica, La	Spelman, T.
*	Travelling Man	Hart, F.
1921		
Mar. 12	Rebel Maid L	Phillips, M.
Aug. 29	All Fool's Day Glast	Carey, C.
Sept. 13	Thais and Talmaae Man	Campbell, C.
Sept. 17	Egypt Berk	McCoy, W.
*	Fall of the House of Usher	Claflin, A.
*	King, The	Hart, F.
1922		
Feb. 14	Two Sisters Cam, Engl.	Rootham, C.
Mar. 27	Flaming Arrow SF	Moore, M.
May 23	White Bird NY	Carter, E.
June 20	Scene from Pickwick L	Wood, C.
July 11	Shepherds of the Delectable Mountains L	Vaughan Williams
Aug. 26	Alkestis Glast	Boughton, R.
Aug. 28	Blue Monday NY	Gershwin, G.
Aug. 31	Auster Syd	Hill, A.
Sept. 18	Merchant of Venice Brighton	Beecham, A.
Dec. 5	Sunset Trail Denver	Cadman, C.
*	Dumb Wife	Gruenberg, L.
1923		
Jan. 13	Snowbird Ch	Stearns, T.
Feb. 1	Love's Sacrifice Ch	Chadwick, G.
Feb. 10	Markheim L	Miles, P. N.
May 14	Perfect Fool L	Holst, G.
May 19	Undine Baltimore	Ware, H.
June 4	Fête Galante Bir	Smyth, E.
Nov. 12	Vendetta NY	Freeman, H.
Nov. 23	Ekkehard Mel	Ewart, F.
Nov. 26	Bubbles Bel	Bath, H.
Dec. 11	Blue Peter L	Gibbs, C. A.
?	Ship of Heaven Syd	Hill, A.
*	Esther	Hart, F.
*	Sunken Bell	Ruggles, C.
1924		
Feb. 12	Family Papers L	Wood, C.
Apr. 16	Eve of St. John Liv	Mackenzie, A.
Apr. 24	Hound of Heaven SF	Stewart, H.
Apr. 25	Legend of Wiwaste Ontario, Calif	Blakeslee, S.
July 3	Midsummer Madness L	Gibbs, C. A.
July 4	Hugh the Drover L	Vaughan Williams
Aug. 20	Seraphic Vision Glast	Boughton, R.
Aug. 21	Queen of Cornwall Glast	Boughton, R.
Aug. 26	Agincourt Glast	Boughton, R.
Sept. 2	Rose-Marie NY	Friml/Stothart
Sept. 27	Seal-Woman Birm	Bantock, G.
Dec. 2	Student Prince NY	Romberg, S.
Dec. 14	Night in Old Paris NY	Hadley, H.
*	Fairies' Revelry	Kieserling, R.
*	Woman Who Laughed at Faery	Hart, F.
1925		
Feb. 2	Gagliarda of a Merry Plague NY	Saminsky, L.
Feb. 24	Legend of the Piper South Bend, Ind	Freer, E. E.
Mar. 20	Garden of Mystery NY	Cadman, C.
Apr. 3	At the Boar's Head Man	Holst, G.
May 17	Song of David NY	Arnstein, I.
May 28	Alchemist, The Essen	Scott, C.
July 22	Entente cordiale L	Smyth, E.
Dec. 11	Namiko-San Ch	Franchetti, A.
Dec. 12	Nightingale, The Miami	Clokey, J.
Dec. 26	Light from St. Agnes Ch	Harling, W
*	Fall of the House of Usher	Sessions, R.
*	Gay Musketeers	Baron, M.
1926		
Jan. 19	Massimilliano Lin	Freer, E. E.
Feb. 11	Mr. Pepys L	Shaw, M.
Apr. 10	Policeman's Serenade L	Reynolds, A.
Apr. 29	Castle Agrazant Cin	Lyford, R.
May 10	Monk of Toledo Port	Knowlton, E.
June 9	Echo, The Port	Patterson, F.
July 4	Music Robber Cin	Van Grove, I.
Sept. 22	Deirdre in Exile Mel	Hart, F.
Oct. 4	Deep River NY	Harling, W.
Oct. 15	Leper's Flute Glas	Bryson, E.
Nov. 11	Winona Port	Bimboni, A.
Dec. 8	Witch of Salem Ch	Cadman, C.
Dec. 17	Lord Byron S Bend, Ind	Graham, J.
*	Mountain Blood	Patterson, F.
1927		
Feb. 17	King's Henchman NY	Taylor, D.
Apr. 24	Everyman Ch	Lester, W.
Dec. 27	Show Boat NY	Kern, J.
?	Chilkoot Maiden Skagway, Ala	Freer, E. E.

*	American Romance	Freeman, H.	July 10	St. George and the Dragon Mel	Hart, F.
*	Endymion	Bennett, R.	Nov. 19	Jack and the Beanstalk NY	Gruenberg, L.
	(prem. 1935 Roch)		Sept. 10	Rubios, Los LA	Moore, M.
*	Pearl Tree	Bainton, E.	Sept. 19	Pride of the Regiment Midhurst, Engl	Leigh, W.
	(prem. 1944 Syd)				
1928			Dec. 6	Lady of the Lake Ch	Schmidt, K.
March	Enchanted Garden L	Dunhill, T.	Dec. 8	Blonde Donna Bklyn	Carter, E.
Mar. 23	Teora Syd	Hill, A.	Dec. 11	Devil Take Her L	Benjamin, A.
May	Witches' Well Tacoma, Wash	Appleton, A.	*	Cyrano de Bergerac	Pokrass, S.
May 3	Täm-Män'-Näcŭp' Provo, Utah	Hanson, W.	*	Harpies, The (prem. 1953 NY)	Blitzstein, M.
May 25	Order of Good Cheer Quebec	Willan, H.	*	Nativity	Hart, F.
Sept. 10	Voodoo NY	Freeman, H.	*	Night	Weisgall, H.
Nov. 12	Waterloo Leave Norwich, Engl	Shaw, M.	*	Uzziah	Freeman, H.
*	Forced Marriage	Hart, F.	**1932**		
*	Preciosa	Freer, E. E.	Feb. 12	Rip Van Winkle NY	Manning, E.
1929			Feb. 24	Derby Day L	Reynolds, A.
Feb. 1	Bronwen Huddersfield	Holbrooke, J.	May 26	David Rizzio LA	Moore, M.
Mar. 21	Sir John in Love L	Vaughan Williams	Nov.	Ouanga Ch	White, C. C.
Apr. 3	Pierrot of the Minute Cin	Engel, L.	*	Cabildo (prem. 1945 Athens, Ga)	Beach, A.
Apr. 11	Frithiof Ch	Freer, E. E.	*	Condemned, The	Blitzstein, M.
Apr. 23	Bride of Dionysus E	Tovey, D.	*	Fountain of Youth	Reynolds, A.
May 9	Triple Sec Ph	Blitzstein, M.	*	Isolt of the White Hands	Hart, F.
June 25	Judith L	Goossens, E.	*	Rose and the Ring (prem. 1957 LA)	Leginska, E.
July 18	Bitter-Sweet L	Coward, N.	**1933**		
Sept. 25	Yolanda of Cyprus L, Ont	Loomis, C.	Jan. 7	Emperor Jones NY	Gruenberg, L.
Dec. 3	Joan of Arc Ch	Freer, E. E.	Feb. 13	Jolly Roger Man	Leigh, W.
Dec. 8	Beggar's Love NY	Patterson, F.	May 20	Four Saints in Three Acts AA	Thomson, V.
Dec. 21	Samuel Pepys Munich	Coates, A.	May 20	Merry Mount AA	Hanson, H.
Dec. 27	Christmas Tale Hou	Freer, E. E.	July 3	Tom-Tom Cl	Graham, S.
*	Ever Young (prem. 1935 Bath, Engl)	Boughton, R.	Oct. 3	Willow Tree NBC	Cadman, C.
*	Flapper, The	Freeman, H.	Nov. 1	Happy Families Guildford, Engl	Dunhill, T.
*	Parabola and Circula	Blitzstein, M.	Nov. 23	Masque of Pandora Ch	Freer, E. E.
1930			**1934**		
Feb. 9	Shylock Ch	La Violette	Jan. 31	Wandering Scholar Liv	Holst, G.
April 17	Sun-Bride NBC radio	Skilton, C.	Feb. 28	Helen Retires NY	Antheil, G.
May 25	Transatlantic Frankfurt	Antheil, G.	Apr. 2	Little Women Ch	Freer, E. E.
Dec. 10	Camille Ch	Forrest, H.	Apr. 12	Macbeth L	Collingwood
Dec. 10	King Alfred and the Cakes L	Gatty, N.	May 7	Kykuntor the Witch NY	Horton, A.
*	Leah Kleschna	Freeman, H.	Sept. 10	Lily Maid Stroud, Engl	Boughton, R.
1931			Nov. 6	Iernin Penzance, Engl	Lloyd, G.
Jan. 16	Tantivy Towers L	Dunhill, T.	Dec. 15	Hester Prynne Hart	Claflin, A.
Feb. 7	Peter Ibbetson NY	Taylor, D.	*	Lillith	Weisgall, H.
May	Courtship of Miles Standish Mel	Ewart, F.	*	Robin Hood	Tippett, M.
May 22	Marriage of Aude NY	Rogers, B.	*	Tom and Lily	Carter, E.
June 6	Thorn of Avalon L	Shaw, M.	*	Zululand, tetralogy	Freeman, H.
June 19	Legend of Spain Mil	Freer, E. E.	**1935**		
			Jan. 24	In the Pasha's Garden NY	Seymour, J.

Date	Work	Composer
Apr. 8	**Maria Malibran** NY	Bennett, R.
June 28	**Kingdom for a Cow** L	Weill, K.
Sept. 30	**Belle, Le** NY	Kroll, L.
Sept. 30	**Porgy and Bess** Bos	Gershwin, G.
Nov. 23	**Gale** Ch	Leginska, E.
1936		
Apr. 21	**Elizabeth and Leicester** Chatanooga, Tenn	Lindsey, E.
May 12	**Poisoned Kiss** Cam	Vaughan Williams
June	**Master Valiant** L	Shaw, M.
Nov. 20	**Pickwick** L	Coates, A.
Dec. 3	**Julia** L	Quilter, R.
1937		
Jan. 7	**Eternal Road** NY	Weill, K.
Feb. 4	**Caponsacchi** NY	Hageman, R.
Feb. 24	**Garrick** NY	Stoessel, A.
Mar. 4	**Headless Horseman** Bronxville, NY	Moore, D.
Apr. 1	**Amelia Goes to the Ball** Ph	Menotti, G. C.
Apr. 21	**Second Hurricane** NY	Copland, A.
May 12	**Man without a Country** NY	Damrosch, W.
June 16	**Cradle Will Rock** NY	Blitzstein, M.
June 24	**Don Juan de Mañara** L	Goossens, E.
Oct. 17	**Green Mansions** CBS	Gruenberg, L.
Dec. 1	**Riders to the Sea** L	Vaughan Williams
?	**Denmark Vesey** NY	Bowles, P.
*	**Argonauts, The**	Maganini, Q.
*	**St. Francis of Assisi**	Hart, F.
*	**Two Gentlemen of Verona**	Seymour, J.
1938		
Jan. 19	**Sleeping Beauty** NY	Rubinstein, B.
May 11	**Brownings Go to Italy** Ch	Freer, E. E.
June 2	**Scarlet Letter** Hamburg	Giannini, V.
Sept. 23	**Gettysburg** LA	Ruger, M.
Oct. 20	**Serf, The** L	Lloyd, G.
Nov. 24	**Beauty and the Beast** CBS	Giannini, V.
*	**Helena's Husband**	Gruenberg, L.
*	**Julian, the Apostate Caeser**	Saminsky, L.
*	**Légende Provençale**	Moore, M.
*	**River, The**	Hively, W.
*	**Troubled Island** (prem. 1949 NY)	Still, W. G.
1939		
Feb. 16	**Cynthia Parker** Denton, Tex	Smith, J.
Apr. 7	**Bleeding Heart of Timpanogas** Provo, Utah	Hanson, W.
Apr. 22	**Old Maid and the Thief** NBC radio	Menotti, G. C.
May 18	**Devil and Daniel Webster** NY	Moore, D.
May 23	**Mirror for the Sky** Eugene, Oreg	Kubik, G.
May 25	**Return of Odysseus** L	Gundry, I.
Nov. 22	**Blennerhasset** CBS radio	Giannini, V.
*	**Privilege and Privation** (prem. 1982, Ams)	Becker, J.
1940		
Feb. 26	**Jewel Merchants** Bal	Cheslock, L.
Mar. 17	**Thorwald** NY	Dinsmore, W.
Apr. 12	**Poet's Dilemma** NY	Lee, D.-K.
Apr. 14	**François Villon** NY	Baron, M.
May 25	**Return of Odysseus** L	Gundry, I.
Oct. 25	**Cabin in the Sky** NY	Duke, V.
1941		
Jan. 5	**No for an Answer** NY	Blitzstein, M.
Jan. 11	**Fall of the House of Usher** Indianapolis	Loomis, C.
Feb. 18	**It Began at Breakfast** Ph	Elmore, R.
Apr. 20	**Gainsborough** LA	Coates, A.
May 5	**Paul Bunyan** NY	Britten, B.
May 13	**Tarquin** Poughkeepsie	Krenek, E.
Dec. 30	**Lady in the Dark** Bos	Weill, K.
*	**Bayou Legend** (prem. 1974 PBS)	Still, W. G.
*	**Courtship of Miles Standish**	Spelman, T.
*	**Esther**	Knoller, J.
*	**Feast of Samhain**	Chisholm, E.
1942		
Feb. 7	**Ramuntcho** Ph	Taylor, D.
Feb. 20	**Island God** NY	Menotti, G. C.
Mar. 8	**Transit through Fire** CBC radio	Willan, H.
Mar. 29	**Solomon and Balkis** Cam, Mass	Thompson, R.
Apr. 25	**Nightingale and the Rose** NBC radio	Lessner, G.
May 2	**Tree on the Plains** Spartanburg, SC	Bacon, E.
Aug. 11	**Crier by Night** ABC	Bainton, E.
Nov. 3	**Opera Cloak** NY	Damrosch, W.
Dec. 9	**Mother, The** NY	Wood, J.
1943		
Feb. 4	**Crucible, The** LA	Hageman, R.
Mar. 30	**Wind Remains** NY	Bowles, P.
May 4	**Florence Nightingale** NY	Williams, D.
Dec. 2	**Carmen Jones** NY	Bizet-Bennett
Dec. 20	**Even unto Bethlehem** Honolulu	Hart, F.
*	**Galahad**	Boughton, R.
*	**She Stoops to Conquer**	ApIvor, D.
*	**Wuthering Heights** (prem. 1986 Portland, Ore)	Hermann, B.

1944		
May 23	**Gate, The** NY	Brand, M.
Aug.	**Prodigal Son**	Jacobi, F.
	Palo Alto, Calif	
*	**Avalon**	Boughton, R.
*	**Swineherd and the**	Hart, F.
	Princess	
1945		
May 19	**Scarecrow, The** NY	Lockwood, N.
June 7	**Peter Grimes** L	Britten, B.
Dec. 30	**Enchanted Kiss** NY	Bennett, R.
*	**Deirdre of the Sorrows**	Becker, J.
	(prem. 1956–57 Ch)	
*	**What Price Confidence**	Krenek, E.
	(prem. 1962 Saarbrücken)	
1946		
Apr. 20	**Deirdre** CBC radio	Willan, H.
May 1	**Stranger of Manzano**	Smith, J.
	Denton, Tex	
May 8	**Medium, The** NY	Menotti, G. C.
May 28	**Partisans, The** L	Gundry, I.
July 12	**Rape of Lucretia** Gl	Britten, B.
Dec. 16	**Street Scene** Ph	Weill, K.
*	**Cain and Abel**	Rorem, N.
*	**Maureen O'Mara**	Scott, C.
1947		
Jan. 11	**Warrior, The** NY	Rogers, B.
Feb. 18	**Telephone, The** NY	Menotti, G. C.
Feb. 22	**Gooseherd and the**	Smith, J.
	Goblin NY	
Mar. 7	**Press Gang** Letchworth	Bush, A.
Apr. 11	**Avon** L	Gundry, I.
Apr. 18	**Trial of Lucullus** Berk	Sessions, R.
May 7	**Mother of Us All** NY	Thomson, V.
May 18	**Pit, The** L	Lutyens, E.
June 20	**Albert Herring** Gl	Britten, B.
*	**Allah**	Freeman, H.
*	**Vengeance of Faery**	Hart, F.
1948		
Jan. 7	**King Harald** NY	Emile, A.
Jan. 22	**Far Harbour** NY	Bergersen, B.
Mar. 17	**Lady Rohesia** L	Hopkins, A.
Apr. 1	**Escape from**	Doellner, R.
	Liberty Hart	
May 10	**Evangeline** NY	Luening, O.
May 18	**Princess and the**	Freed, I.
	Vagabond Hart	
July 15	**Down in the Valley** Bl	Weill, K.
Aug. 13	**Life Goes to a Party** Len	Middleton, R.
Oct. 7	**Love Life** NY	Weill, K.
?	**Garden of Artemis**	Pinkham, D.
	Cam, Mass	
*	**Sailing of the Nancy**	Davis, A.
	Belle (prem. 1955	
	Duxbury, Mass)	

*	**Volpone**	Gruenberg, L.
1949		
Jan. 20	**Lyneia** Cin	Byrd, W. C.
Feb. 9	**White Wings** Hart	Moore, D.
Feb. 13	**Fit for a King** NY	Kalmanoff, M.
Feb. 19	**Emperor's New**	Moore, D.
	Clothes NY	
Feb. 23	**Prima Donna** L	Benjamin, A.
Mar. 2	**By Gemini** Galesburg, Ill	Baylor, M.
April 11	**Avon** L	Gundry, I.
May 4	**Drumlin Legend** NY	Bacon, E.
May 2	**Slow Dusk** Syr	Floyd, C.
May 9	**Catherine Parr** NY	Collins, A.
May 9	**Don't We All?** Roch	Burrill, P.
May 9	**In the Name of**	Bimboni, A.
	Culture Roch	
June 14	**Let's Make an Opera!/**	Britten, B.
	Little Sweep Al	
summer	**Ordeal of Osbert**	Davis, A.
	Duxbury, Mass	
Sept. 29	**Olympians, The** L	Bliss, A.
Oct. 30	**Lost in the Stars** NY	Weill, K.
Oct. 31	**Regina** NY	Blitzstein, M.
Dec. 15	**Dreams in Spades** Ph	Hovey, S.
Dec. 29	**Boor, The** NY	Bucci, M.
Dec. 29	**In a Garden** NY	Kupferman, M.
*	**O'Higgins of Chile**	Cowell, H.
1950		
Jan. 18	**Barrier, The** NY	Meyerowitz, J.
Feb. 7	**Enchanted Pear Tree** NY	Overton, H.
Mar. 1	**Consul, The** Ph	Menotti, G. C.
May 4	**Catherine Parr**	Barring, M.
	Hopkinton, NH	
May 18	**Jumping Frog** Bl	Foss, L.
May 18	**Veil, The** Bl	Rogers, B.
May	**Triumph of (Saint)**	Dello Joio, N.
	Joan Bronxville, NY	
June	**Once upon a Moon** D	Victory, G.
July 1	**Unto These Hills**	Kilpatrick, J.
	Cherokee, NC	
Aug. 2	**Simoon** Len	Meyerowitz, J.
Oct. 13	**Mr. Bellamy Comes**	Rivington, H.
	Home L	
Nov. 6	**Sunday Costs Five**	
	Pesos Charlotte, NC	Haubiel, C.
Nov. 21	**Corn King** L	Easdale, B.
Dec. 12	**Asses' Ears** LA	Cole, H.
Dec. 16	**Lion, The** New L, Conn	Franchetti, A.
*	**Captain's Parrot**	Brent-Smith, A.
*	**Jonah**	Beeson, J.
1951		
Feb. 18	**Noah and the**	Kalmanoff, M.
	Stowaway NY	
Feb. 22	**Open the Gates** NY	Lee, D.-K.
Mar. 28	**Giants in the Earth** NY	Moore, D.
Mar. 30	**Caliph's Clock** NY	Kraft, L.

Apr. 17	**Fugitives, The** Tallahassee, Fla	Floyd, C.	
Apr. 24	**Letter to Emily** Sea	Johnson, L.	
Apr. 24	**Mississippi Legend** NY	Wolfe, J.	
Apr. 26	**Pilgrim's Progress** L	Vaughan Williams	
May 2	**Dark Waters** LA	Krenek, E.	
May 3	**David** NY	Skilling, R.	
May 4	**Mighty Casey** Hart	Schuman, W.	
May 5	**Red Rose and the Briar** Hart	Mopper, I.	
May 8	**Well, The** Roch	Mennini, L.	
May 15	**John Socman** Bristol	Lloyd, G.	
May 19	**Aria da Capo** Stockton, Calif	Fore, B.	
May 28	**Judgment Day**	Perl, P.	
June 27	**Duenna, The** Wiesbaden, Ger	Gerhard, R.	
June 2	**Wise and Foolish** NY	List, K.	
July 9	**Sleeping Children** Chel	Easdale, B.	
July 20	**Man from Tuscany** Can	Hopkins, A.	
July 30	**Mayor of Casterbridge** Cam	Tranchell, P.	
Aug. 8	**Boney Quillen** Chichester, NY	Haufrecht, H.	
Sept. 4	**Mermaid, The** Bir	More, M.	
Sept. 11	**Rake's Progress** Venice	Stravinsky, I.	
Oct. 4	**Dybbuk, The** NY	Tamkin, D.	
Nov. 16	**Acres of Sky** Fayetteville, Ark	Kreutz, A.	
Nov. 16	**Eastward in Eden** Det	Meyerowitz, J.	
Dec. 1	**Billy Budd** L	Britten, B.	
Dec. 5	**Incognita** O	Wellesz, E.	
Dec. 24	**Amahl** NY, NBC	Menotti, G. C.	
*	**Deirdre of the Sorrows**	Rankl, K.	
*	**Faust**	Becker, J. J.	
*	**Tod's Gal** (prem. 1971 Nor)	Kelly, R.	
1952			
Jan. 12	**Prankster, The** Bowling Green, Ohio	Wykes, R.	
Jan. 17	**Cowherd and the Sky Maiden** Sea	Verrall, J.	
Feb. 11	**Tenor, The** Bal	Weisgall, H.	
Feb. 21	**Parfait for Irene** Bl	Kaufmann, W.	
Mar. 9	**Boston Baked Beans** NY	Kubik, G.	
Mar. 14	**Oedipus** Oakland, Calif	Partch, H.	
Mar. 16	**Princess, The** Hart	Franchetti, A.	
Mar. 30	**Don Perlimplin** Urb	Rieti, V.	
May 2	**Monkey's Paw** Cin	Hamm, C.	
May 5	**Snow Queen** Lake Charles, La	Gaburo, K.	
May 8	**Lowland Sea** Montclair, NJ	Wilder, A.	
May 12	**All at Sea** L	Shaw, G.	

May 24	**Baby Doe** Den	DiJulio, M.	
June 12	**Trouble in Tahiti** Waltham, Mass	Bernstein, L.	
July 6	**Maypole, The** Westport	Franchetti, A.	
July 17	**Statue for the Mayor** L	Cole, H.	
July 22	**Don Fortunato** Inter	Forrest, H.	
Aug. 9/ Aug. 11	**Stronger, The** Lutherville, Md/Westport, Conn	Weisgall, H.	
Aug. 13	**Farmer and the Nymph** Aspen	Tcherepnin, A.	
Oct. 20	**Dark Sonnet** CT	Chisholm, E.	
?	**Van Hunks and the Devil** CT	Coates, A.	
*	**Cenci, The**	Brian, H.	
*	**Ethan Frome**	Allanbrook, D.	
*	**Phineas and the Nightingale**	Lee, D.-K.	
*	**Selfish Giant** (prem. 1965 Cl)	Wilding-White, R.	
*	**Strolling Clerk from Paradise**	Wilson, C.	
*	**Tragicall History of Christopher Marlowe**	Mellers, M.	
1953			
Jan. 9	**Volpone** LA	Antheil, G.	
Jan. 31	**Taming of the Shrew** Cin	Giannini, V.	
Feb. 15	**Godiva** NY	Kalmanoff, M.	
Feb. 21	**Babar the Elephant** NY	Berezowsky, N.	
Mar. 1	**Cask of Amontillado** Cin	Hamm, C.	
Mar. 1	**Open Window** Cin	Ahlstrom, D.	
Mar. 1	**Three Sisters Who Are Not Sisters** Cin	Ahlstrom, D.	
Mar. 5	**Rapunzel** Colchester	Hammond, T.	
Mar. 20	**Carrion Crow** Bl	Fletcher, G.	
Mar. 28	**Junípero Serra** Palma de Mallorca, Spain	Hively, W.	
Apr. 5	**Doctor Faustus** Bronxville, NY	Kupferman, M.	
Apr. 15	**Fall of the House of Usher** LA	Ruger, M.	
Apr. 17	**Sunday Excursion** NY	Wilder, A.	
May 1	**Scena** L, BBC	Hopkins, A.	
May 13	**Charivari** Cam, Mass	Westergaard, P.	
May 22	**Cumberland Fair** Montclair, NJ	Wilder, A.	
May 22	**Tom Sawyer** SF	Elkus, J.	
May 26	**Barber of New York** NY	Vernon, A.	
May 28	**Brother Joe** Cl	Engel, L.	
June 8	**Gloriana** L	Britten, B.	
June 17	**Brandy Is My True Love's Name** NY	Kalmanoff, M.	
June 28	**Night in the Puszta** Cl	Kondorossy, L.	
July 2	**Circus, The** Inter	Chudacoff, E.	
July 3	**Rab the Rhymer** Aberdeen	Dunlop/ Oppenheim	

Date	Title	Composer	Date	Title	Composer
July 22	**Endymion** Syd	Antill, J. H.	May 27	**Malady of Love** NY	Engel, L.
July 30	**Secret Life of Walter Mitty** Athens, Ohio	Hamm, C.	June 6	**Tin Pan Alley** NY	Raphling, S.
Aug. 1	**Tony Beaver** Idyllwild, Calif	Marais, J.	June 8	**Quiet Game of Cribble** NY	Kalmanoff, M.
Aug. 17	**Bad Boys in School** Len	Meyerowitz, J.	June 11	**Swing, The** NBC	Kastle, L.
Aug. 17	**Kingdom Come** Boone, NC	Mason, W.	June 17	**Dinner Engagement** Al	Berkeley, L.
Aug. 18	**Captain Lovelock** Hudson Falls, NY	Duke, J.	July 6	**Murder in Three Keys** NY	Chisholm, E.
Aug. 28	**African Heartbeat** Idyllwild, Calif	Marais, J.	July 21	**Antigone** L, BBC	Joubert, J.
Aug. 28	**Dr. Jekyll and Mr. Hyde** Berk	Fragale, F.	July 21	**Daelia** Inter	Forrest, H.
Sept. 6	**Wat Tyler** Leipzig	Bush, A.	July 27	**Audition, The** Athens, Ohio	Goodman, A.
Sept. 30	**Tinners of Cornwall** L	Gundry, I.	July 28	**Brothers, The** Den	Antheil, G.
Oct. 8	**Dress, The** NY	Bucci, M.	July 27	**Princess and the Pea** Len	Toch, E.
Oct. 21	**Inland Woman** CT	Chisholm, E.	Aug. 17	**Matinee Idyll** Inter	Forrest, H.
Nov. 9	**Menna** Car	Hughes, A.	Sept. 5	**Scent of Sarsaparilla** SF	Hamm, C.
Nov. 10	**Three's Company** Crewe, Engl	Hopkins, A.	Sept. 14	**Turn of the Screw** Venice	Britten, B.
Dec. 8	**Sweet Betsy from Pike** NY	Bucci, M.	Sept. 22	**Nelson** L	Berkeley, L.
?	**Blood Wedding** Cl	Smith, H.	Oct. 14	**Apollo and Persephone** Ch	Cockshott, G.
?	**Dumb Wife** Lowestoft, Engl	Horovitz, J.	Oct. 18	**Governess, The** L	Mallett, C.
?	**Music Critic** Syd	Antill, J. H.	Nov. 10	**Sun-Up** NY	Kassern, T.
?	**Research, The** (prem. 1953 Tallahassee, Fla)	Kaufmann, W.	Nov. 20	**Cask of Amontillado** NY	Perry, J.
*	**Kumana**	Kanitz, E.	Nov. 23	**Sandhog** NY	Robinson, E.
1954			Nov. 30	**Beckoning Fair One** Sea	Kechley, G.
Jan. 21	**Blind Beggar's Daughter** Farnham, Engl	Bush, G.	Dec. 3	**Troilus and Cressida** L	Walton, W.
Feb.	**Smoky Mountain** Monmouth, Ill	Hunkins, E.	Dec. 4	**Double Trouble** Lou	Mohaupt, R.
Feb. 18	**Darling Corie** Hempstead, NY	Siegmeister, E.	Dec. 5	**Cancelling Dark** L	Whelen, C.
Mar. 3	**Lake, The** Van	Pentland, B.	Dec. 6	**archy and mehitabel** NY	Kleinsinger, G.
Mar. 10	**Threepenny Opera** NY	Weill-Blitzstein	Dec. 23	**Christmas Carol** Strat, Conn	Hermann, B.
Mar. 11	**Golden Apple** NY	Moross, J.	Dec. 27	**Barbara Allen** NY	Broekman
Mar. 15	**University Greys** Clinton, Miss	Kreutz, A.	Dec. 27	**Miss Chicken Little** NY	Wilder, A.
spring	**Sicilian Limes** Bal	Argento, D.	Dec. 27	**Saint of Bleecker Street** NY	Menotti, G. C.
Mar. 29	**Mother, The** Ph	Hollingsworth	*	**Admirable Bashville**	Berry, W.
Apr. 1	**Tender Land** NY	Copland, A.	*	**Commission, The** (prem. 1992 Woodstock, NY)	Cowell, H.
Apr. 4	**Transposed Heads** Lou	Glanville-Hicks, P.	*	**Costaso** (prem. 1989 Flagstaff, Ariz)	Still, W. S.
Apr. 23	**Charlie's Uncle** Columbus, Ohio	Ahlstrom, D.	*	**Miracle of Flanders**	Gruenberg, L.
Apr. 24	**Cockcrow** Austin, Tex	Smith, J.	*	**One Night of Cleopatra**	Gruenberg, L.
May 15	**Pumpkin, The** Cl	Kondorossy, L.	**1955**		
May 15	**Voice, The** Cl	Kondorossy, L.	Jan. 10	**Fisherman's Wife** St. Joseph, Mich	Stein, L.
May 20	**Scandal at Mulford Inn** Cin	Byrd, W. C.	Jan. 17	**Lord Byron's Love Letter** NO	Banfield, R. de
May 27	**Hello Out There** NY	Beeson, J.	Jan. 27	**Midsummer Marriage** L	Tippett, M.
			Feb. 16	**Hopitu** NY	Albright, L.
			Feb. 24	**Susannah** Tallahassee	Floyd, C.
			Mar. 1	**Salesgirl, The** Bristol, Va	Hamm, C.
			Mar. 13	**Pepito's Golden Flower** Pasadena, Calif	Caldwell, M.

Date	Title	Composer
Mar. 20	**Game of Cards** Hart	Franchetti, A.
Mar. 29	**Midnight Duel** Cl	Kondorossy, L.
Apr. 2	**Wish, The** Lou	Antheil, G.
Apr. 10	**Two Imposters** Cl	Kondorossy, L.
Apr. 17	**Aria da Capo** NO	Burnham, C.
Apr. 26	**Delinquents, The** Ph	Kalmanoff, M.
May 8	**String Quartet** Cl	Kondorossy, L.
May 9	**Pot of Fat** Cam, Mass	Chanler, T.
May 10	**Childhood Miracle** NY	Rorem, N.
May 10	**Nightingale** NY	Rogers, B.
May 13	**Peter Homan's Dream** East Lansing, Mich	Reed, H. O.
May 13	**Ruby, The** Bl	Dello Joio, N.
May 22	**Three Blind Mice** Sea	Verrall, J.
May 25	**Fatal Oath** NY	Koutzen, B.
June 1	**Eve of Adam** Interlaken, Mass	Duffy, J.
June 3	**Long Way** Nyack, NY	Wilder, A.
June 12	**Mystic Fortress** Cl	Kondorossy, L.
June 25	**Grand Slam** Stamford, Conn	Vernon, A.
July 14	**Persephone** L	Colege, H.
July 15	**Unmusical Impresario** Duxbury, Mass	Davis, K.
July 29	**Fall of the City** Athens, Ohio	Cohn, J.
Aug. 8	**Rope, The** Len	Mennini, L.
Sept. 2	**Moby Dick** Idylwild, Calif	Low, J.
Nov. 6	**Griffelkin** NY	Foss, L.
Dec. 3	**School for Wives** Lou	Liebermann, R.
Dec. 5	**Santa Claus** Ch	Smith, L.
Dec. 5	**Secret, The** Columbia, Mo	Patacchi, V.
Dec. 5	**Wedding Knell** Sea	Verrall, J.
Dec. 17	**Tree That Was Christmas** NY	Kleinsinger, G.
Dec. 29	**Boor, The** SL	Fink, M. S.
?	**Susanna and the Elders** Vienna	Fink, M.
*	**Antony and Cleopatra**	Gruenberg, L.
*	**Celebration, The**	Maury, L.
*	**Delicate King**	Gruenberg, L.
*	**Ellen**	Wilder, A.
*	**My Heart's in the Highlands**	Ahlstrom, D.
*	**Oracle, The**	Lees, B.
*	**Stormy Interlude**	Brand, M.
1956		
Jan. 7	**Lima Beans** NY	Townsend, D.
Jan. 8	**Crescent Eyebrows** NY	Dvorkin, J.
Jan. 27	**Experiment, The** Gambier, Ohio	Schwartz, P.
Feb. 1	**Mañana** L, BBC	Benjamin, A.

Date	Title	Composer
Feb. 15	**Wife of Martin Guerre** NY	Bergsma, W.
Feb. 18	**Dr. Heidegger's Experiment** NY	Raphling, S.
Feb. 22	**Opera, Opera** NY	Kalmanoff, M.
Mar. 4	**Anachronism** Hart	Franchetti, A.
Mar. 12	**Necklace, The** Redlands, Calif	Bohrnstedt, W.
Mar. 21	**Trevallion** L	Phillips, R.
Apr. 6	**Landara** Ph	Zimbalist, E.
Apr. 8	**Trial at Rouen** NY	Dello Joio, N.
May 1	**Loafer and the Loaf** LA	Clarke, H.
May 3	**Most Happy Fella** NY	Loesser, F.
May 9	**Miranda** Hart	Siegmeister, E.
May 14	**Beyond Belief** Roch	Canning, T.
May 14	**Birthday of the Infanta** Roch	Nelson, R.
May 17	**He Who Gets Slapped** NY	Ward, R.
May 18	**Land between the Rivers** Bl	Buskirk, C. van
June 3	**Ladies Voices** Norman, Okla	Martin, V.
July 7	**Ballad of Baby Doe** CC	Moore, D.
July 10	**If the Cap Fits** Chel	Bush, G.
July 11	**Ten O'Clock Call** Chel	Hopkins, A.
July 26	**Bargain, The** Athens, Ohio	Slates, P.
July 26	**Candle, The** Athens, Ohio	Slates, P. M.
July 27	**Cupid and Psyche** Woodstock, NY	Vernon, A
Aug. 4	**Chanticleer** Aspen	Barab, S.
Aug. 11	**Fat Tuesday** Tamiment, Pa	Berkowitz, S.
Aug. 15	**Logan Rock** Porthcurno, Engl	Gundry, I.
Oct. 2	**Ruth** L	Berkeley, L.
Oct. 20	**In the Drought** Johannesburg	Joubert, J.
Oct. 21	**Unexpected Visitor** Cl	Kondorossy, L.
Oct. 21	**Unicorn and the Manticore** Wa	Menotti, G. C.
Oct. 29	**Candide** NY	Bernstein, L.
Nov. 10	**Hello, World!** NY	Mayer, W.
Nov. 15	**Fool, The** Tor	Somers, H.
Nov. 18	**Men of Blackmoor** Weimar	Bush, A.
Nov. 25	**Soldier, The** NY	Engel, L.
Dec. 2	**Door, The** Newark	Mopper, I.
Dec. 4	**Intruder, The** NY	Starer, R.
Dec. 11	**Chelm** WP	Strassburg, R.
Dec. 11	**Isaac Levi** WP	Piket, F.
Dec. 14	**Open Window** BBC	Arnold, M.
?	**Cinderella** Gainesville, Fla	Jarrett, J.

?	**Greek Kalends**	Ridout, A.
	Tunbridge Wells, Engl	
*	**Dismissed with**	Owen, R.
	Prejudice	
*	**Dowser, The**	Franchetti, A.
*	**Fisherman, The**	Scott, T.
*	**Fortunato**	Gideon, M.
1957		
Jan. 11	**Game of Chance**	Barab, S.
	Rock Island, Ill	
Jan. 13	**Golem, The** WP	Weiner, L.
Feb. 3	**Grande Bretèche** NBC	Claflin, A.
Feb. 8	**Speakeasy** NY	Lee, D.-K.
Feb. 10	**Grande Bretèche** NBC	Hollings-
		worth, S.
Feb. 26	**Armor of Life** NY	Newbern, K.
Mar. 17	**Bell Tower** Urb	Krenek, E.
Mar. 17	**Esther** Urb	Meyerowitz, J.
Apr. 7	**Bandit, The** Columbia,	Patacchi, V.
	Mo	
Apr. 7	**Sotoba Komachi** NY	Levy, M. D
Apr. 18	**Sterlingman** Bos	Roy, K. G.
Apr. 28	**Ile** NY	Laufer, B.
May 1	**Unicorn in the**	Smith, R.
	Garden Hart	
May 2	**Volpone** L	Coombs, J.
May 6	**Boor, The** Roch	Argento, D.
May 8	**Esther and Cousin**	Pittman, E.
	Mordecai Paris	
May 9	**Visitors, The** NY	Chávez, C.
May 18	**Deirdre** Ch	Stein, L.
May 22	**Blind Raferty** BBC	Trimble, J.
May 24	**Moon and Sixpence** L	Gardner, J.
May 24	**Venus in Africa** Den	Antheil, G.
June 5	**Curious Fern** NY	Kupferman, M.
June 5	**Voices for a Mirror** NY	Kupferman, M.
July 23	**Tale of Two Cities** L	Benjamin, A.
July 26	**Jacob and the Indians**	Laderman, E.
	Woodstock, NY	
Aug. 2	**Tower, The** SF	Levy, M. D.
Aug. 4	**Tea Party** Athens, Ohio	Gottlieb, J.
Aug. 5	**Tale for a Deaf Ear** Len	Bucci, M.
Sept. 12	**Elanda and Eclipse** L	Halahan, G.
Sept. 26	**West Side Story** NY	Bernstein, L.
Nov. 16	**Mayerling** Cin	Humphreys
Nov. 22	**Sweet Bye and Bye** NY	Beeson, J.
*	**Agamemnon**	Brian, H.
*	**Ma Barker**	Eaton, J.
*	**Two Knickerbocker Tales**	Lee, D.-K.
1958		
Jan. 15	**Vanessa** NY	Barber, S.
Feb. 6	**Dragon, The** NY	Taylor, D.
Feb. 14	**Dido and Aeneas** Bos	Beveridge, T.
Feb. 26	**Room No. 12** LA	Kanitz, E.
Feb. 26	**Royal Auction** LA	Kanitz, E.
Feb. 27	**Love in Transit** L	Arnell, R.

Mar. 6	**Lizzie Strotter**	Kalmanoff, M.
	Des Moines, Iowa	
Mar. 11	**Lord Bateman** L	Forster, A.
Mar. 15	**Committee, The** NY	Doran, M.
Mar. 19	**Gallantry** NY	Moore, D.
Mar. 20	**Little Beggars** L, BBC	Saunders, M.
Apr. 10	**Bottle Imp** Wilton, Conn	Whiton, P.
Apr. 14	**Pet Shop** NY	Rieti, V.
Apr. 14	**Robbers, The** NY	Rorem, N.
Apr. 18	**Holy Devil** NY	Nabokov, N.
Apr. 23	**Good Soldier**	Kurka, R.
	Schweik Lou	
Apr. 23	**Otherwise Engaged** NY	Davis, A.
Apr. 29	**Rajah's Ruby** NY	Barab, S.
May 4	**Escorial, The** NY	Levy, M. D.
May 8	**Draagenfut Girl**	Kupferman,
	Bronxville, NY	M.
June 18	**Noye's Fludde** Al	Britten, B.
June 20	**Scarf, The** Spoleto, Italy	Hoiby, L.
July 13	**Impossible Forest**	Wilder, A.
	Westport, Conn	
July 16	**Wuthering Heights** S Fe	Floyd, C.
July 20	**Mermaid in Lock**	Siegmeister,
	No. 7 Pitt	E.
July 29	**Yerma** Den	Bowles, P.
Aug. 15	**Sire de Maletroit**	Duke, J.
	Schroon Lake, NY	
Aug. 20	**Maria Golovin** Brussels	Menotti, G. C.
Aug. 28	**Sganarelle** Van	Kaufmann, W.
Sept. 27	**Blues in the Subway** NY	Levister, A.
Oct. 3	**Diary of a Madman** Berlin	Searle, H.
Nov. 14	**Triangle, The** Oberlin	Humel, G.
Nov. 30	**Sarah** NY	Laderman, E.
Dec. 12	**Mistress into Maid**	Duke, V.
	Santa Barbara, Calif	
Dec. 14	**Gentleman's Island** L	Horovitz, J.
?	**Little Red Riding**	Barab, S.
	Hood SF	
?	**Lucky Dollar** LA	Kanitz, E.
?	**Proposal, The**	Humel, G.
	Winfield, Kan	
*	**Earth Mother**	Penberthy, J.
*	**Moment of War** (prem.	Owen, R.
	Buenos Aires 1964)	
*	**Tamar and Judah**	Lavry, M.
	(prem. 1970 NY)	
1959		
Jan. 8	**Sourwood Mountain**	Kreutz, A.
	Clinton, Miss	
Jan. 17	**Thief and the Hangman**	Ellstein, A.
	Athens, Ohio	
Jan. 22	**Dalgerie** Perth, Austral	Penberthy, J.
Feb. 7	**Guide to Life**	Fine, V.
	Expectancy NY	
Feb. 16	**Lady of Ephesus** Bel	Warren, R.

Date	Title	Composer
Mar. 4	**Night Blooming Cereus** Tor	Beckwith, J.
Mar. 23	**Hired Hand** NY	Milano, R.
Mar. 24	**I Am the Way** Orange, NJ	Hines, J.
Apr.	**Cage, The** Wa	Jones, G. T.
Apr	**Decorator, The** Wa	Woollen, R.
Apr. 14	**Hand of Bridge** NY	Barber, S.
Apr. 18	**Blessed Wilderness** Dal	Kilpatrick, J.
Apr. 21	**Prelude and Fugue** Hart	Franchetti, A.
Apr. 26	**Six Characters** NY	Weisgall, H.
Apr. 27	**Hunted, The** Roch	Mailman, M.
Apr. 28	**Golden Lion** Seat	Kechley, G.
May 5	**Petrified Princess** L	Arnell, R.
May 14	**Glittering Gate** NY	Glanville-Hicks, P.
May 14	**Rapunzel** NY	Harrison, L.
June 4	**Borderline, The** L	Mellers, W.
June 17	**Spur of the Moment** BBC	Halahan, G.
July 8	**Hands across the Sky** Chel	Hopkins, A.
July 11	**Clarkstown Witch** Piermont, NY	Novak, L.
July 14	**Other Wise Man** Bentonville, Ark	Van Grove, I.
July 23	**Moon Flowers** Kent, Engl	Arnell, R.
July 28	**Golden Child** Iowa City, Iowa	Bezanson, P.
Aug. 9	**Faun in the Forest** Westport, Conn	Cockshott, G.
Oct.	**Young Lincoln** Galesburg, Ill	Hunkins, E
Oct. 23	**Beatrice** Lou	Hoiby, L.
Nov. 5	**Cenci, The** L	Coke, R.
Dec. 11	**Finn and the Black Hag** Bel	Warren, R.
Dec. 13	**Sofa, The** L	Maconchy, E.
Dec. 15	**Blue Flame** San Antonio	Hovhaness, A.
?	**Golden Crucible** Pitt	Kilpatrick, J.
*	**Gardens of Adonis** (prem. 1992 Omaha)	Weisgall, H.
*	**Sacco and Vanzetti**	Blitzstein, M.
*	**Tale from Chaucer** (prem. 1966 Trenton, NJ)	Gordon, P.

1960

Date	Title	Composer
Jan. 28	**Maletroit Door** NY	Barab, S.
Jan. 24	**Christopher Sly** L	Eastwood, T.
Mar. 12	**Giant's Garden** Nor	Krane, S.
Mar. 20	**Goat in Chelm** NY	Binder, A.
May	**Valdo** Cl	Freeman, H.
May 5	**Introductions and Good-Byes** NY	Foss, L.
May 19	**Tobias and the Angel** BBC	Bliss, A.
May 22	**Cat and the Moon** Hart	Putsché, T.
May 22	**Goodbye to the Clown** NY	Laderman, E.
May 26	**Hunted, The** Greenville, SC	Gustafson, D.
June 2	**Volpone** Stuttgart	Burt, F.
June 11	**Midsummer Night's Dream** Al	Britten, B.
June 29	**Captive, The** Bir	Wishart, P.
July 16	**Lodger, The** L	Tate, P.
July 21	**Two Tickets to Omaha** Moorehead, Minn	Hannay, R.
Aug. 4	**Port Town** Len	Meyerowitz, J.
Nov. 26	**Satan's Trap** NY	Piket, F.
Oct. 24	**Tunnel, The** L	Cole, H.
Dec. 16	**Outcasts of Poker Flat** Stockton, Calif	Beckler, S.
*	**Aria da Capo**	Blank, A.
*	**Clock, The**	Rieti, V.
*	**Nightmare Abbey**	Allanbrook, D.
*	**Rocket, The**	Goldman, E.

1961

Date	Title	Composer
Jan. 1	**Deseret** NY	Kastle, L.
Jan. 24	**Bartleby** NY	Flanagan, W.
Jan. 28	**Fox, The** Cl	Kondorossy, L.
Feb. 4	**Box, The** NO	Hamm, C.
Feb. 8	**Sweetwater Affair** Lin	Beadell, R.
Feb. 12	**Mink Stockings** Columbus, Ohio	Marshall, P.
Feb. 17	**Purgatory** Wa	Weisgall, H.
Feb. 22	**Sisters, The** NY	Flagello, N.
Mar. 18	**Enchanted Canary** Bemidji, Minn.	Stevens, N.
Mar. 23	**Kisses for a Quid** Mel	Werder, F.
Mar. 25	**Hunting of the Snark** NY	Laderman, E.
Apr. 26	**Perpetual** LA	Kanitz, E.
May 6	**Scarlet Letter** Bl	Kaufmann, W.
May 20	**Elegy for Young Lovers** Schwetzingen, Ger	Henze, H. W.
May 20	**Silas Marner** CT	Joubert, J.
June 2	**Godfather Death** NY	Meyerowitz, J.
June 9	**Greek Passion** Zurich	Martinů, B.
July 25	**Amiable Beast** NY	Welner, G.
July 29	**Brute, The** NH	Moss, L.
Aug. 7	**Early Dawn** Den	Lockwood, N.
Aug. 19	**Nausicaa** Athens	Glanville-Hicks, P.
Sept. 12	**Ledge, The** L	Bennett, R.
Sept. 18	**Blood Moon** SF	Dello Joio, N.
Oct. 12	**Wings of the Dove** NY	Moore, D.
Oct. 26	**Crucible, The** NY	Ward, R.
Nov.	**Pardoner's Tale** CT	Chisholm, E.
Nov. 10	**Franklin's Tale** BR	Sokoloff, N.
Nov. 11	**Command Performance** Poughkeepsie, NY	Middleton, R.
Nov. 25	**Harvest, The** Ch	Giannini, V.
Dec. 3	**Fifth for Bridge** SF	Sheldon, R.
Dec. 3	**Gift of Song** Pasadena	Caldwell, M.

Dec. 10	**No Neutral Ground** Pullman, Wash	Brandt, W.	*	**You Never Know**	Koutzen, B.
Dec. 12	**Nativity, The** Cam, Mass	Thompson, R.	**1963**		
Dec. 17	**Long Christmas Dinner** Mannheim, Ger	Hindemith, P.	Feb.	**Darkened City** Bl	Heiden, B.
			Feb. 15	**Bald Prima Donna** NY	Kalmanoff, M.
Dec. 17	**Yerma** BBC	ApIvor, D.	Feb. 15	**Spirit of the Avalanche** Tokyo	Hovhaness, A.
Dec. 24	**Novellis, Novellis** Wa	La Montaine			
*	**Anniversary, The**	Rorem, N.	Mar. 3	**Labyrinth, The** NBC	Menotti, G. C.
*	**Canterbury Tales**	Chisholm, E.	Mar. 11	**Highway 1, U.S.A.** Miami	Still, W. G.
*	**Colonel Jonathan the Saint** (prem. 1971 Den)	Argento, D.	Apr. 25	**Young Goodman Brown** Allentown, Pa	Lenel, L.
*	**Fourth Day**	Ahlstrom, D.	May 15	**Plough and the Stars** SL	Siegmeister, E.
*	**Jest of Hahalabra**	Cotel, M.			
*	**King Kong**	Matshikiza, T.	May 17	**Half Magic** Walding River, NY	Kalmanoff, M.
*	**Macbeth**	Goldman, E.			
*	**Pardoner's Tale**	Sokoloff, N.	May 31	**Christopher Sly** Min	Argento, D.
*	**Promised Valley**	Gates, C. M.	June	**Pietro's Petard** NY	Overton, H.
1962			July 2	**Our Man in Havana** Al	Williamson, M.
Feb. 3	**Juggler of Our Lady** NO	Kay, U.	July 10	**Birthday of the Infanta** L	Stoker, R.
Feb. 15	**Rehearsal Call** NY	Giannini, V.			
Feb. 24	**Earth-Trapped** East Lansing, Mich	Reed, H. O.	Oct. 10	**Gentlemen, Be Seated!** NY	Moross, J.
Feb. 24	**Living Solid Face** East Lansing, Mich	Reed, H. O.	Oct. 22	**Last Savage** Paris	Menotti, G. C.
			Nov. 20	**Graduation Ode** Bel	Warren, R.
Mar. 1	**Alcestiad, The** Frankfurt	Talma, L.	Dec.	**Last Puppet** NY	Strilko, A.
Mar. 1	**Dancing Master** L	Arnold, M.	Dec. 2	**Knife, The** L	Jones, D.
Mar. 22	**Golem, The** NY	Ellstein, A.	Dec. 2	**Sojourner and Mollie Sinclair** Raleigh, NC	Floyd, C.
Mar. 27	**Engaged!** Bristol, Engl	Sullivan-Rowell/Mobbs			
			Dec. 21	**Dynamite Tonite** NY	Bolcom, W.
Apr. 11	**Revelation** Urb	Partch, H.	?	**Marko the Miser** Farnham, Engl	Musgrave, T.
May 25	**Jeremiah** Bin	Fink, M.			
May 29	**King Priam** L	Tippett, M.	?	**Rescue, The**	Ridout, A.
June 8	**Outcasts of Poker Flat** Denton, Tex	Adler, S.	*	**Importance of Being Earnest**	Chisholm, E.
June 14	**Flood, The** CBS	Stravinsky, I.	*	**Magic Barrel**	Blitzstein, M.
July 5	**Dark Pilgrimage** L	Tate, P.	*	**Sappho**	Glanville-Hicks, P.
July 10	**Bird in the Bush** LA	Bielawa, H.			
Aug. 1	**Wizards of Balizar** Den	Lockwood, N.	*	**Scarlet Letter**	Lybbert, D.
Oct. 11	**Passion of Jonathan Wade** NY	Floyd, C.	**1964**		
			Jan. 9	**Masque of Angels** Min	Argento, D.
Nov. 9	**One Christmas Long Ago** Muncie, Ind.	Mayer, W.	Feb. 17	**Athaliah** NY	Weisgall, H.
			Feb. 26	**Visions of Midnight** LA	Kanitz, E.
Nov. 11	**Hamlet** Bal	Kagen, S.	Mar. 6	**Ferryman's Daughter** Letchworth, Engl	Bush, A.
Dec. 6	**Many Moons** Poughkeepsie, NY	Doughterty, C.			
			Mar. 6	**Hanging Judge** Den	Lockwood, N.
Dec. 16	**Departure, The** L	Maconchy, E.	Mar. 8	**Photo of the Colonel** L	Searle, H.
Dec. 16	**Wager, The** L	Orr, B.	Mar. 21	**Fortune of Saint Macabie** Moorhead, Minn	Hanning, R.
Dec. 19	**Abbot of Drimock** L	Musgrave, T.			
Dec. 24	**Christmas Carol** L	Coleman, E.	Mar. 25	**Little Billy** Stroud, Engl	Hurd, M.
?	**Pandora's Box** Boulder, Colo	Effinger, C.	Mar. 28	**Miracle, The** Perth, Austral	Penberthy, J.
*	**Amphitryon 4**	Blumenfeld, H.	Apr. 6	**Sack of Calabasas** Phoenix	Fletcher, G.
*	**Boccaccio's Nightingale**	Trimble, L.			
*	**John Barleycorn**	Montgomery	Apr. 16	**Gift of the Magi** Min	Magney, R.
*	**Pathelin**	Josephs, W.	Apr. 19	**Montezuma** West Berlin	Sessions, R.
*	**Yerma**	Wilding-White			

May 23	**Wind Drum** Gatlinburg, Tenn	Hovhaness, A.
June 3	**Martin's Lie** Bath	Menotti, G. C.
June 11	**English Eccentrics** Al	Williamson, M.
June 13	**Curlew River** Al	Britten, B.
June 14	**Cappemakers, The** Charleston Manor, Sussex	Taverner, J.
July 3	**Lady from Colorado** CC	Ward, R.
July 15	**Morvoren** L	Cannon, P.
July 30	**Shining Chalice** Eureka Springs, Ark	Van Grove, I.
Aug. 24	**Burning House** Gatlinburg, Tenn	Hovhannes, A.
Oct. 8	**Natalia Petrovna** NY	Hoiby, L.
Oct. 24	**Virgin and the Fawn** LA	Zador, E.
Nov.	**Gilded Cage** NY	Lees, B.
Nov. 12	**Bartleby** Oberlin, Ohio	Aschaffenburg
Nov. 12	**One Man Show** L	Maw, N.
Nov. 24	**Requiem for a Rich Young Man** Den	Lockwood, N.
Nov. 30	**Tartuffe** L	Benjamin, A.
Dec. 12	**Brideship, The** Van	Turner, R.
?	**In Memoriam** AA	Ashley, R.
?	**Pot of Broth** NY	Haufrecht, H.
?	**Uncle Tom's Cabin** NY	Claflin, A.
*	**Idiots First** (prem. 1976, Bl)	Blitzstein, M.
*	**Selfish Giant**	Perry, J.
1965		
Jan. 5	**Hunting of the Snark** D	Wilson, J.
Feb. 3	**Prince of Coxcombs** L	Gundry, I.
Feb. 18	**Videomania** Granville, Ohio	Kalmanoff, M.
Feb. 24	**Mines of Sulphur** L	Bennett, R.
Mar. 14	**Fisherman Called Peter** Carmel, NY	Owen, R.
Mar. 17	**Patrick** D	Potter, A. J.
spring	**Pyramus and Thisbe** Tuscaloosa, Ala	Bruce, N.
Mar. 22	**Serenade at Noon** BR	Fuchs, P. P.
Mar. 25	**Lizzie Borden** NY	Beeson, J.
Apr. 2	**Amorous Judge** Syd	Gross, E.
Apr. 4	**Macbeth** NY	Halpern, S.
Apr. 4	**Monkey's Paw** NY	Halpern, S.
Apr. 11	**Final Ingredient** NY	Amram, D.
Apr. 22	**Edgar and Emily** NY	Toch, E.
May 15	**Alissa** Geneva	Banfield, R. de
May 22	**Happy Prince** Farnham	Williamson, M.
May 26	**Quarry, The** Wembley	Joubert, J.
May 27	**Judas Tree** L	Dickinson, P.
May 30	**Arrangement, The** L	Davis, C.
June	**Sweeney Agonistes** L	Dankworth, J.
July	**Ophelia** Tasmania, Austral	Penberthy, J.
Aug.	**Nun's Priest's Tale** Hanover, NH	Finney, R.
Aug. 18	**Fall of the House of Usher** Hobart, Austral	Sitsky, L.
Aug. 19	**Young Kabbarli** Hobart, Austral	Sutherland, M.
Aug. 20	**Women, The** Aspen	Pasatieri, T.
Sept. 24	**Hero, The** NY	Bucci, M.
Nov. 4	**Miss Julie** NY	Rorem, N.
?	**Boy from the Catacombs** Can	Ridout, A.
*	**Mad Hamlet**	Reif, P.
*	**Scarlet Letter**	Kroll, F.
1966		
Jan. 4	**Julius Caesar Jones** L	Williamson, M.
Feb. 3	**Loving/Toi** Tor	Schafer, R.
Mar. 16	**Divina, La** NY	Pasatieri, T.
Mar. 18	**Judgment of St. Francis** NY	Flagello, N.
Mar. 21	**Mr. and Mrs. Discobbolos** NY	Westergaard, P.
Mar. 21	**Without Memorial Banners** Kansas City, Mo	Six, H.
Mar. 31	**Markheim** NO	Floyd, C.
Apr. 3	**Empty Bottle** NY	Kalmanoff, M.
Apr. 28	**Carry Nation** Lawrence, Kan	Moore, D.
May 5	**Parlour, The** Car	Williams, G.
May 14	**Magic Chair** BR	Zador, E.
May 15	**Portrait in Brownstone** NY	Reif, P.
June 9	**Burning Fiery Furnace** Al	Britten, B.
June 26	**Pilate** LA	Hovhaness, A.
July 7	**Purgatory** Chel	Crosse, G.
July 7	**What D'Ye Call It** Chel	Tate, P.
July 30	**Hoosier Tale** Bl	Kaufmann, W.
Aug. 6	**Bassarids, The** Salzburg	Henze, H. W.
Sept. 1	**Antony and Cleopatra** NY	Barber, S.
Oct. 11	**Visitation, The** Hamburg	Schuller, G.
Oct. 20	**Notturno in La** Hart	Franchetti, A.
Nov. 19	**Pardoner's Tale** Den	Lubin, E.
Nov. 29	**Violins of St. Jacques** L	Williamson, M.
Dec. 3	**Mr. Scrooge** NY	Kalmanoff, M.
Dec. 5	**Man from Venus** NY	Cannon, P.
Dec. 11	**Sugar Reapers** Bush, A.
Dec. 28	**Shepherdess and the Chimneysweep** Fort Worth, Tex	Smith, J.
?	**Appointment, The** BBC	Josephs, W.
?	**Flax into Gold**	Cole, H.
*	**General, The**	Werder, F.
*	**Judgment, The**	Kupferman, M.
*	**Pariahs, The** (prem. 1985 Albany, NY)	Kastle, L.

Date	Title	Composer
*	**So How Does Your Garden Grow**	Russell, R.
*	**Ubu Roi**	ApIvor, D.
1967		
Jan. 7	**Three Wise Men**	Gundry, I.
Jan. 12	**John Hooten** L	Russo, W.
Jan. 23	**Some Place of Darkness** BBC	Whelen, C.
Mar. 5	**Arden Must Die** Hamburg	Goehr, A.
Mar. 9	**Servant of Two Masters** NY	Giannini, V.
Mar. 10	**Orpheus** Austin, Tex	Austin, J.
Mar. 11	**Canterville Ghost** NY	Kalmanoff, M.
Mar. 17	**Mourning Becomes Electra** NY	Levy, M. D.
spring	**Eye of Horus** Bos	El-Dabh, E.
Apr.	**Virgil's Dream** Brighton, Engl	Colgrass, M.
Apr. 14	**Arabesque** Vermillion, SD	Marek, R.
Apr. 15	**Chanticleer** NY	Barthelson, J.
Apr. 22	**Moonrakers** Brighton	Williamson, M.
Apr. 22	**Travellers, The** SF	Hovhaness, A.
May 15	**Trilby** NY	Piket, F.
May 19	**Dunstan and the Devil** Cookham, Austral	Williamson, M.
May 22	**Brief Candle** NY	Mayer, W.
May 23	**Pardoner's Tale** Tucson	Davis, J. S.
May 24	**Poorest Suitor** Cl	Kondorossy, L.
May 27	**Last Day** NY	Rorem, N.
May 31	**Grant, Warden of the Plains** Winnipeg	Adaskin, M.
June 1	**Shoemaker's Holiday** Min	Argento, D.
June 3	**Bear, The** Al	Walton, W.
June 3	**Castaway** Al	Berkeley, L.
June 3	**Golden Vanity** Al	Britten, B.
June 5	**Time for Growing** Norwich, Engl	Hopkins, A.
Aug. 13	**Lake of Menteith** BBC	Noble, H.
Sept.	**Luck of Ginger Coffey** Tor	Panneil, R.
Sept. 3	**Ray and the Gospel Singer** Toledo, Ohio	Gould, E.
Sept. 5	**Sam Slick** Halifax	Jones, K.
Sept. 23	**Louis Riel** Tor	Somers, H.
Oct.	**Eleanor of Aquitaine** Syd	Whitehead, G.
Oct. 20	**Music Hath Mischief** D	Victory, G.
Oct. 26	**Mandarin, The** NY	Elkus, J.
Oct. 31	**Penny for a Song** L	Bennett, R.
Nov. 18	**Padrevia** Bklyn	Pasatieri, T.
Nov. 30	**Decision, The** L	Musgrave, T.
Dec. 1	**Shephardes Playe** Wa	La Montaine
Dec. 12	**Brideship, The** Van	Turner, R.
Dec. 20	**Gentlemen in Waiting** NY	Booth, T.
Dec. 27	**Magi, The** Wa	La Montaine
?	**Agamemnon**	Werder, F.
?	**Johnson Preserv'd** L	Stoker, R.
?	**Lysistrata & the War** Det	Fink, R.
?	**Song of the Maypole** Canberra	Dreyfus, G.
*	**Agamemnon**	Hamilton, I.
*	**David**	Goldman, E.
*	**Jonah**	Cole, H.
*	**Numbered, The**	Lutyens, E.
*	**Sacrapant**	Aston, P.
*	**Scarlet Letter**	Lybbert, D.
1968		
Jan. 11	**Equation, The** L	Bush, G.
Jan. 26	**Box, The** NY	Eakin, C. G.
Jan. 26	**Feathertop** NY	Barthelson, J.
Feb. 6	**Aria da Capo** NY	Baksa, R.
Feb. 8	**That Morning Thing** AA	Ashley, R.
Feb. 13	**Big Black Box** NY	Morgenstern
Feb. 20	**Bride Comes to Yellow Sky** Charleston, Ill	Nixon, R.
Mar.	**Lysistrata** NY	Barthelson, J.
Mar. 1	**Rehearsal, The** NY	Benjamin, T.
Mar. 5	**Hamlet** Hamburg	Searle, H.
Mar. 12	**Jericho Road** Ph	Aria, P.
Apr. 3	**Boor, The** Lexington, Ky	Kay, U.
Apr. 9	**Goodman Brown**	Fink, H.
Apr. 10	**Full Circle** Perth, Scot	Orr, R.
Apr. 26	**Cask of Amontillado** Rochester, NY	Provenzano, A.
Apr. 30	**Snow Wolf** Brighton	Williamson, M.
May	**Metamorphosis** Ph	White, M.
May 2	**We're Back** NY	Armour, E.
May 18	**Moralities** Cin	Henze, H. W.
May 19	**Rose Affair** L	Kay, N
June 5	**Birds, The** L	Maconchy, E.
June 5	**Three Strangers** L	Maconchy, E.
June 8	**Punch and Judy** Al	Birtwistle, H.
June 10	**Prodigal Son** Al	Britten, B.
July 16	**Naboth's Vineyard** L	Goehr, A.
July 21	**Cyrano de Bergerac** Boulder, Colo	Effinger, C.
Aug. 1	**Twelfth Night** Glens Falls, NY	Amram, D.
Aug. 7	**Elephant Steps** Len	Silverman, S.
Aug. 13	**Growing Castle** Dynevor Castle, Wales	Williamson, M.
Aug. 13	**Lucky-Peter's Journey** Dynevor Castle, Wales	Williamson, M.
Aug. 21	**Audition, The** Pitt	Kalmanoff, M.
Aug. 29	**Falcon, The** Bath	Cole, H.
Oct. 9	**Nine Rivers from Jordan** NY	Weisgall, H.
Oct. 20	**Tommy** NY	Townshend, P.

Oct. 26	Scarlet Mill Bklyn	Zador, E.
Oct. 28	Politics of Harmony NY	Wuorinen, C.
Nov. 8	Passion of Oedipus LA	Travis, R.
Nov. 10	Victory at Masada Det	Kalmanoff, M.
Nov. 14	Great Stone Face Muncie, Ind	Kalmanoff, M.
Nov. 28	Melita Bel	Camilleri, C.
Dec. 19	Help, Help Hamburg	Menotti, G. C.
?	Children's Crusade Can	Ridout, A.
?	Frustration Wa	Harnick, S.
*	Black Epic	El-Dabh, H.
*	Herod, Do Your Worst	Kelly, B.
*	Noelani (prem. 1971 Aptos, Calif?)	Barati, G.
*	Shadows among Us (prem. 1979 Ph)	Laderman, E.
*	Silent Shepherd	Marek, R.
1969		
Jan. 25	Triumph of Punch Bklyn	Vernon, A.
Feb. 15	Horspfal Min	Stokes, E.
Mar. 16	Charcoal Burner BBC, Scot	Wilson, T.
Mar. 20	Dr. Musikus L	Hopkins, A.
spring	Excitement at the Circus Paterson, NJ	Blank, A.
Mar. 28	All the King's Men Coventry, Engl	Bennett, R.
Apr. 4	Rebel, The BBC	Eastwood, T.
Apr. 13	Man on a Bearskin Rug Aberdeen, SD	Ramsier, P.
Apr. 19	Let's Build a Nut House San Jose	Moran, R.
Apr. 22	Eight Songs for a Mad King L	Davies, P. M.
Apr. 22	Shizuka's Dance Cl	Kondorossy, L.
Apr. 27	Combat Zone Hempstead, NY	Arnell, R.
Apr. 29	Lion, the Witch Man	McCabe, J.
May 2	Haircut NY	Morgenstern
May 8	Down by the Greenwood Side Brighton	Birtwistle, H.
May 12	Twice in a Blue Moon Farnham, Engl	Tate, P.
May 15	Greatshot NH	Bolcom, W.
May 19	Opening, The Bos	Wilder, A.
May 26	Incident at Owl Creek BBC	Whelen, C.
May 29	Under Western Eyes L	Joubert, J.
June 7	Grace of Todd Al	Crosse, G.
July 29	Four-Thousand Dollars Iowa City	Turner, T.
Aug.	Aesop Camp Pemiquewasset, NH	Kalmanoff, M.
Aug. 27	Pharsalia E	Hamilton, I.
Sept. 1	Undertaker, The E	Purser, J.

Oct. 15	David and Bathsheba New	Barlow, D.
Oct. 25	Pied Piper of Hamelin Wexford	Wilson, J.
Oct.	All the Tea in China O	Oliver, S.
Oct. 6	Takeover, The Canberra	Dreyfus, G.
Oct. 18	Rich Man, Poor Man Stroud, Engl	Hopkins, A.
Nov. 1	Twelfth Night Wexford	Wilson, J.
Nov. 11	Legends Three NY	Kalmanoff, M.
Nov. 25	Agamemnon O	Morris, R.
Nov. 30	Barnstable Kassel, Ger	Burt, F.
Dec.	Slippery Soules O	Oliver, S.
Dec. 25	First Christmas Syd	Antill, J. H.
Dec. 25	Selfish Giant BBC, Wales	Burtch, M.
Dec. 31	Erode the Great Wa	La Montaine
?	Leper King Ch	Hovhaness, A.
?	Nathan the Wise Cl	Kondorossy, L.
?	Prometheus Bound Wa	El-Debh, H.
*	King of the Golden River	Hand, C.
*	Libertine, The	Alwyn, W.
*	Primal Void (prem. 1973 Vienna)	Vincent, J.
*	Private	Werder, F.
*	Scarapant the Sorcerer	Aston, P.
*	Three Mimes	Cantrick, R.
1970		
Jan. 22	Of Mice and Men Sea	Floyd, C.
Mar. 17	My Heart's in the Highlands NET	Beeson, J.
Mar.	Johnny and the Mohawks L	Maconchy, E.
Mar.	Wanderer, The Min	Boesing, P./ Boesing, M.
Apr.	Day Return L	Head, M.
Apr.	Key Money L	Head, M.
Apr. 3	Mr. Punch Gothenburg	Hurd, M.
Apr. 8	Martyred, The Seoul	Wade, J.
Apr. 13	Victory L	Bennett, R.
Apr. 15	Don Cristóbal Wellesley, Mass	Crawford, J.
Apr. 18	Pied Piper NY	Flagello, N.
May 9	Fisherman and His Wife Bos	Schuller, G.
May 19	America LA	Kohs, E. B.
June	Phoenix Too Far O	Oliver, S.
June 22	Cimarrón, El Al	Henze, H. W.
July 8	Shadowplay L	Goehr, A.
July 19	Rising of the Moon Gl	Maw, N.
Sept. 12	Seven Deadly Sins Brisbane	Brumby, C.
Sept. 29	Joe Hill East Berlin	Bush, A.
Oct. 7	Jessie Tree Dorchester	Maconchy, E.
Oct. 16	Prisoner Paul L	Gundry, I.
Nov. 13	Medea Mil	Elkus, J.
Nov. 30	Helen in Egypt Mil	Elkus, J.

Date	Title	Composer
Dec. 2	**Knot Garden** L	Tippett, M.
?	**Cabaret Opera** NY	Russo, W.
*	**Feather Cloak**	Barati, G.
* (ca.)	**Fee First**	Doran, M.
*	**Joan of Arc**	Burgon, G.
*	**Naked Carmen**	Corigliano/ Hess
*	**Scarlet Letter**	Mann, R. W.
1971		
Jan. 10	**Medea in Corinth** L	Lees, B.
Jan. 22	**Rapunzel** Bin	Brooks, R.
Jan. 28	**Chatterton** Paris, ORTF	Victory, G.
Jan. 30	**Faust Counter Faust** Min	Gessner, J.
Feb. 18	**White Butterfly** NY	Leichtling, A.
Feb. 28	**Survival of St. Joan** NY	Ruffin, H.
Mar. 12	**Capitoline Venus** Quincy, Ill	Kay, U.
Mar. 12	**Most Important Man** NY	Menotti, G. C.
Mar. 26	**Losers, The** NY	Farberman, H.
Apr. 1	**Pardoner's Tale** Can	Ridout, A.
Apr. 1	**Scene Machine** Kassel	Gilbert, A.
Apr. 7	**Calvary** Sea	Pasatieri, T.
Apr. 10	**And David Wept** CBS	Laderman, E.
Apr. 17	**Pandora's Box** LA	Cave, M.
May 1	**Edward John Eyre** Syd	Conyngham, B.
May 5	**Opera Flies** Wa	El-Dabh, H.
May 5	**Who Stole the Crown Jewels?** NY	Siegel, N.
May 10	**Phrases from Orpheus** Gue	Wilson, C.
May 16	**Owen Wingrave** NET/BBC	Britten, B.
May 20	**Huckleberry Finn** NY	Overton, H.
May 21	**All Cats Turn Gray** NY	Six, H.
May 21	**Fables** Martin, Tenn	Rorem, N.
June 8	**Clandestine Marriage** L	Wishart, P.
June 11	**Inspector General** Torrance, Calif	Zador, E.
June 19	**Summer and Smoke** SP	Hoiby, L.
July 24	**Three Sisters Who Are Not Sisters** Ph	Rorem, N.
July 27	**Photograph—1920** Lake Placid, NY	Kalmanoff, M.
Aug. 21	**Young Caesar** Aptos, Calif	Harrison, L.
Aug. 30	**Fair Traders** Workingham, Engl	Cole, H.
Sept. 1	**Mayakovsky** E	Daiken, M.
Sept. 9	**Hunting of the Snark** NY	Roberts, E.
Sept. 9	**Tamburlaine** Liv	Murdoch, E.
Sept. 12	**Kalamona** Cl	Kondorossy, L.
Sept. 18	**Stone Wall** L	Williamson, M.
Oct.	**Vessel** NY	Monk, M.
Oct. 14	**Postcard from Morocco** Min	Argento, D.
Oct. 21	**Jesus Christ Superstar** NY	Lloyd Webber
Oct. 23	**Widow of Ephesus** Stroud, Engl	Hurd, M.
Oct. 31	**Divertissement No. 3** L	Moran, R.
Nov. 21	**Joan** NY	Carmines, A.
Nov. 23	**Duchess of Malfi** O	Oliver, S.
?	**Angelo** Can	Ridout, A.
?	**Cat, The** Berkshire, NY	Ridout, A.
?	**Gift, The** Can	Ridout, A.
?	**Sonata about Jerusalem** Jerusalem	Goehr, A.
?	**Trials of Psyche** Urb-Champaign, Ill	Bruce, N.
*	**Bouvard and Pecuchet**	ApIvor, D.
*	**Vicious Square**	Werder, F.
*	**Will of Her Own** (prem. 1985 L)	Gundry, I.
1972		
Jan. 28	**Marriage Machine** Syd	Brumby, C.
Feb. 14	**Trial of Mary Lincoln** NET	Pasatieri, T.
Mar.	**Hansel & Gretel & Ted & Alice** Dal	Schickele, P.
Mar. 1	**Time Off?** L	Lutyens, E.
Mar. 2	**Black Widow** Sea	Pasatieri, T.
Mar. 22	**Let My People Go** Liv	Warren, R.
Apr. 6	**Happy End** NH	Weill-Feingold
Apr. 14	**Red Sea** Devon, Engl	Williamson, M.
Apr. 15	**Julian** Winston-Salem	Fussell, C.
Apr. 20	**Lord Byron** NY	Thomson, V.
Apr. 27	**Cyrano de Bergerac** Greensboro, NC	Jarrett, J.
May 6	**Tea Symphony** Banff, Ont	Charpentier, G.
May 15	**Heracles** Bl	Eaton, J.
May 16	**Flower and Hawk** Jacksonville, Fla	Floyd, C.
May 16	**Four Note Opera** NY	Johnson, T.
May 24	**Dybbuk, The** NY	Mandelbaum, J.
May 29	**Blind Man's Bluff** L	Davis, P. M.
June 5	**Wheel of the World** Al	Crosse, G.
June 7	**Visitors, The** Al	Gardner, J.
June 22	**Wrestler, The** Dal	Adler, S.
June 29	**Táin, The** D	Wilson, J.
July	**Orpheus II** Strat, Ont	Charpentier, G.
July 12	**Taverner** L	Davies, P. M.
July 16	**Findings, The** BBC	Whelen, C.
Aug.	**Dissolute Punished** E	Oliver, S.
Aug. 12	**Dr. Selavy's Magic Theatre** Stock	Silverman, S.
Aug. 12	**Garni Sands** Syd	Dreyfus, G.

Date	Title	Composer
Aug. 17	Aesop's Fables NY	Russo, W.
Aug. 23	Patria, no. 2 Strat, Ont	Schafer, R.
Sept. 6	Tamu-Tamu Ch	Menotti, G. C.
Sept. 22	Circe D, RTE	Victory, G.
Nov. 29	Medea San D	Henderson, A.
Dec.	Aton and the Word Wa	El-Dabh, H.
Dec.	Osiris Ritual Wa	El-Dabh, H.
Dec. 5	Lord Arthur L	Bush, G.
Dec. 17	Inner Voices NY	Barnett, D.
Dec. 27	Bell, The BBC	Purser, J.
?	After the Wedding L	Head, M.
?	Magic Land of Opera NY	Kalmanoff, M.
*	Enchanted Garden	Shaughnessy
*	Liar, Liar	Raphling, S.
*	Musicians of Bremen	Balkin, A.
*	Outcasts of Poker Flat	MacSems, W.
*	Rose Garden	Boyd, A.
*	Twelve Hours Trip	El-Dabh, H.

1973

Date	Title	Composer
winter	Education of the Girlchild NY	Monk, M.
Feb. 1	Marriage Proposal NY	Murray, J.
Feb. 7	Love's Labour's Lost Brussels	Nabokov, N.
Feb. 8	Suncatcher, The Hart	Franchetti, A.
Feb. 14	Make Me a Willow Cabin L	Stoker, R.
Mar. 11	Daisy Miami	Smith, J.
Mar. 14	Prisoner, The Barnet, L	Joubert, J.
Mar. 17	Notre Dame des Fleurs L	Davies, P. M.
Apr. 6	King's Breakfast Atlantic City, NJ	Barthelson, J.
Apr. 6	Summoning of Everyman Halifax	Wilson, C.
Apr. 7	Pantagleize Bklyn	Starer, R.
Apr. 17	Infidelio L	Lutyens, E.
Apr. 23	Columbine Boulder, Colo	Davis, M.
Apr. 23	Genesis L	Williamson, M.
Apr. 23	Myshkin BBC	Eaton, J.
May 5	Transformations Min	Susa, C.
May 12	Prisoner's Play Tor	Rea, J.
June 6	Some Pig Min	Larsen, L.
June 16	Death in Venice Venice	Britten, B.
June 23	Solomon and Sheba NY	Rivers, S.
Aug. 2	Scene: Domestic Aspen	Turok, P.
Sept. 3	Heloise and Abelard Tor	Wilson, C.
Sept. 20	Donkey, The Stirling, Scot	Oliver, S.
Oct. 12	Truth about Windmills Rochester, NY	Wilder, A.
Oct. 21	Nightingale and the Rose Chester, Pa	Garwood, M.
Nov. 26	Bertha NY	Rorem, N.

Date	Title	Composer
Dec. 1	Queen Christina Oakland, Calif	Anderson, B.
Dec. 21	Selfish Giant Tor	Wilson, C.
?	Antigonae Stock	Kupferman, M.
?	Creation, The Ely, Engl	Ridout, A.
?	Eloise and Abelard D	Victory, G.
?	Murder of Comrad Sharik Sea	Bergsma, W.
?	Patria, no. 1 Tor	Schafer, R.
?	Soap Opera Hart	Franchetti, A.
?	Three Instant Operas L	Oliver, S.
*	Conversion, The	Werder, F.
*	Death of Cuchulain	Brettingham Smith, J.
*	Will of Her Own (prem. 1985 L)	Gundry, I.

1974

Date	Title	Composer
Jan. 25	Magic Trumpet D, RTE	Victory, G.
Feb. 5	Sganarelle Edmonton	Archer, V.
Feb. 13	Clytemnestra L	Wishart, P.
Mar. 3	To Let the Captive Go NY	Stewart, F.
Mar. 4	Cubana, La NY	Henze, H. W.
Mar. 5	Seagull, The Hou	Pasatieri, T.
Mar. 5	System, The NY	Bach, J.
Mar. 9	Miss Donnithorne's Maggot Adelaide	Davies, P. M.
Mar. 13	Story of Vasco L	Crosse, G.
Mar. 14	Affair, The Syd	Werder, F.
Mar. 14	Lenz Syd	Sitsky, L.
Mar. 16	Catiline Conspiracy Stirling, Scot	Hamilton, I.
Mar. 26	Beach of Falesá Car	Hoddinott, A.
Apr. 28	Ruth and Naomi Cl	Kondorossy, L.
May	Newest Opera in the World Min	Balk, W.
May 1	Lion and Androcles Indianapolis	Eaton, J.
May 8	Beauty and the Beast NY	Murray, J.
May 9	Curse of Mauvais-Air NY	Reif, P.
May 18	Sganarelle NY	Kalmanoff, M.
May 24	Beauty and the Beast Syr	DiGiacomo, F.
June 5	Past Tense Huddersfield	Oliver, S.
June 11	Voice of Ariadne Al	Musgrave, T.
July 12	Magic Laurel Tree Cl	Hunkins, E.
July 12	Peter Marshall Chautauqua, NY	Barab, S.
June 15	Letter for Queen Victoria Spoleto, Italy	Lloyd, A.
June 21	Duel, The Bklyn	Carmines, A.
July 27	Signor Deluso Greenway, Va	Pasatieri, T.
Aug. 1	Hotel for Criminals Len	Silverman, S.
Aug. 3	Karla Ithaca, NY	Lehrman, L.

Aug. 3	Penitentes, The Aspen	Pasatieri, T.
Aug. 8	Child, The Albany	Bernardo, J.
Sept. 11	Isabella's Fortune NY	Russo, W.
Sept. 11	Pedrolino's Revenge NY	Russo, W.
Sept. 27	Rites of Passage Syd	Sculthorpe, P.
Oct. 3	Play of Mother Courage Middlesbrough, Engl	McCabe, J.
Oct. 24	Red Carnations NY	Baksa, R.
Oct. 30	Everyman Memphis	Nelhybel, V.
Nov.	Project 1521 LA	Gross, R.
Dec. 9	Holly from the Bongs Man	Crosse, G.
Dec. 21	Yehu LA	Zador, E.
?	Lady of Light ?, Mont	Hovhaness, A.
?	Phaeton BBC	Ridout, A.
?	Vision, A Man	Ridout, A.
*	Esther	Harvey, E.
*	Ladies Voices	Kievman, C.
*	Metamenagerie	Moran, R.
*	Miracle of Nemirov	Silverman, F.
*	Proposal, The	Walker, J.
1975		
Jan. 2	Give Me Liberty NY	Kalmanoff, M.
Jan. 4	Apache Dance NY	Fennimore, J.
Jan. 9	Potter Thompson L	Crosse, G.
Feb. 5	Fanny Robin E	Harper, E.
Mar. 13	Nightingale, Inc. Urb	Colgrass, M.
Mar. 27	Stanley and the Monkey King L	White, J.
Apr. 24	Departure, The Montevallo, Ala	Davis, A.
May 9	Balcony, The Bos	DiDomenica, F.
June 1	Conjurer, The NY	Sahl, M.
June 15	Waiter's Revenge Nottingham	Oliver, S.
Aug.	Odyssey Glens Falls, NY	Shields, A.
Aug. 2	Last Lover Katonah, NY	Starer, R.
Aug. 26	Fand Kilkenny, Ire	Wilson, J.
Aug. 27	Hermiston E	Orr, R.
Sept. 20	Captain Jinks Kansas City	Beeson, J.
Oct. 1	Don't Call Me by My Right Name NY	Fennimore, J.
Oct. 6	Black River SP	Susa, C.
Oct. 10	Masque of the Clouds NY	Johnson, T.
Oct. 29	King of the Golden River O	Maconchy, E.
Nov.	Stoned Guest Ogden, Utah	Schickele, P.
Nov. 1	Fables Wa	Aitken, H.
Dec. 1	Richest Girl in the World Wa	Sandow, G.
Dec. 15	W. of Babylon NY	Wuorinen, C.
*	American Triptych	Burton, S.

	(prem. 1989 Alexandria, Va)	
*	Bad Times	Oliver, S.
*	Bellyful	Werder, F.
*	Dream Child	Mollicone, H.
*	Freak Show	Taylor, C.
*	Lost Child	Ridout, G.
*	Married Men Go to Hell	Franchetti, A.
*	Pericles	Hovhaness, A.
*	Richard III	Turok, P.
	(prem. 1980, Phil)	
*	Rime of the Ancient Mariner	Bedford, D.
*	Stations	Penberthy, J.
1976		
Jan. 16	Alice in Wonderland Van Nuys, Calif	Chauls, R.
Feb.	Magician, The Welsh radio	Hoddinott, A.
Feb. 6	Be Glad Then America University Park, Pa	La Montaine, J.
Feb. 27	Bilby Doll Hou	Floyd, C.
Mar.	Christopher Columbus NY	Kalmanoff, M
Mar. 13	Letter from an Astrologer NY	Knopf, P.
Mar. 14	Tales of Malamud:	
	Idiots First Bl	Blitzstein, M.
	Karla Bl	Lehrman, L.
Mar. 16	And the Walls NY	Roosevelt, W.
Mar. 23	Fiery Tales Adelaide	Sitsky, L.
Mar. 23	Lamentable Reign of Charles Adelaide	Dreyfus, G.
Mar. 26	Death of King Peter Brookline, Mass	Earls, P.
Mar. 30	Ines de Castro Bal	Pasatieri, T.
Apr. 1	Passion, Poision NY	Taub, B.
Apr. 6	Orpheus: Eurydice L	White, J.
Apr. 6	Tom Jones New	Oliver, S.
Apr. 11	Fête at Coqueville Fresno, Calif	Rea, A.
Apr. 11	Gilt-Edged Kid Mel	Dreyfus, G.
Apr. 22	Jenny NY	Weisgall, H.
Apr. 24	Voyage of Edgar Allan Poe SP	Argento, D.
May 5	Meanwhile, Back at Cinderella's NY	Arlen, D.
May 25	Stauf NY	Sahl/Salzman
June 1	Hero, The Ph	Menotti, G. C.
June 12	Last of the Mohicans Wilmington, Del	Henderson, A.
June 12	Mary Dyer Suffern, NY	Owen, R.
June 15	Confessions of a Justified Sinner York, Engl	Wilson, T.
June 17	Egg, The Wa	Menotti, G. C.
June 21	One and the Same York, Engl	Lutyens, E.

July 12	**We Come to the River** L	Henze, H. W.	
July 19	**Evening for Three** D, RTE	Victory, G.	
June 21	**One and the Same** York, Engl	Lutyens, E.	
July 25	**Einstein on the Beach** Avignon	Glass, P.	
Aug. 6	**Sima** Ithaca, NY	Lehrman, L.	
Aug. 28	**My Kinsman** Pitt	Saylor, B.	
Oct. 1	**Washington Square** Det	Pasatieri, T.	
Oct. 7	**Final Alice** Ch	Del Tredici, D.	
Nov.	**Africa Is Calling Me** NY	Reid, B.	
Nov. 6	**Angle of Repose** SF	Imbrie, A.	
Nov. 14	**Night of the Moonspell** Shreveport, La	Siegmeister, E.	
Nov. 20	**Jubilee** Jackson, Miss	Kay, U.	
Nov. 26	**Isis and Osiris** L	Lutyens, E.	
Dec. 9	**Cat Who Went to Heaven** Croyden	Bush, G.	
Dec. 31	**Grimm Duo** Bos	Earls, P.	
?	**David's Violin** Middletown, Conn	Mogulesco-Slobin	
?	**Magic Beanstalk** Monticello, NY	Kalmanoff, M.	
?	**Music with Roots** Paris	Ashley, R.	
?	**Smart Aleck and the Talking Wire** NY	Kalmanoff, M.	
*	**Bang!**	Rutter, J.	
*	**Bell Tower**	Haskins, R.	
*	**Cinderella in Salerno**	Walker, R.	
*	**Great McPorridge Disaster**	Oliver, S.	
*	**King of Cats**	Oliver, H.	
*	**Legend of Sleepy Hollow**	Haskins, R.	
*	**President Lincoln**	Raphling, S.	
*	**Quarry** (prem. 1985 NY)	Monk, M.	

1977

Feb. 2	**Royal Hunt of the Sun** L	Hamilton, I.	
Feb. 25	**Inner Voices** L	Howard, B.	
Mar. 12	**Marriage Counselor** LA	Doran, M.	
Mar. 14	**Tamburlaine** Liv	Hamilton, I.	
Mar. 15	**Hearing** NY	Rorem, N.	
Apr. 9	**Hipopera** Boise, Idaho	Kalmanoff, M.	
Apr. 14	**Lily** NY	Kirchner, L.	
Apr. 29	**Sun and the Wind** Bin	Borroff, E.	
May	**Sid the Serpent** Adelaide	Fox, M.	
May 7	**Seabird Island** Gue	Healey, D.	
May 13	**Neither** Rome	Feldman, M.	
May 19	**Civilization & Its Discontents** NY	Sahl/Salzman	
May 19	**Water Bird Talk** Bklyn	Argento, D.	
June 6	**Gentle Spirit** Bath	Taverner, J.	
June 18	**Martyrdom of St. Magnus** Kirkwall, Scot	Davies, P.	

June 25	**Ballad of the Bremen Band** Katonah, NY	Arlen, D.	
July 5	**Bow Down** L	Birtwistle, H.	
July 7	**Ice Break** L	Tippett, M.	
July 27	**Garden, The** Batignano, Italy	Oliver, S.	
July 27	**What the Old Man Does** Wales, Fishguard Fest	Hoddinott, A.	
Aug.	**William Derrincourt** Perth	Smalley, R.	
Sept. 6	**Mary, Queen of Scots** E	Musgrave, T.	
Sept. 28	**Toussaint** L	Blake, D.	
Sept. 29	**Dawnpath** L	LeFanu, N.	
Oct.	**Chronicles** Rockville, Md	Muller, G. F.	
Oct. 11	**HAPP** Min	Stokes, E.	
Oct. 25	**Whirligig** Muncie, Ind	Brisman, H.	
Nov. 2	**Thanksgiving** NY	Levi, P.	
Nov. 4	**Devil's Disciple** WP	Barthelson, J.	
Nov. 24	**Like a Window** L, BBC	Lutyens, E.	
Dec. 7	**Death of Enkidu** Tor	Somers, H.	
Dec. 21	**Christmas Carol** Stratford, Conn	Sandow, G.	
?	**Not a Spanish Kiss** NY	Barab, S.	
?	**Selfish Giant** Kent, Engl	Ridout, A.	
?	**Sir Gawain** Leicester, Engl	Wilson-Dickson	
*	**Insect Comedy** (prem. 1993 NY)	Kalmanoff, M.	
*	**Stable Home**	Oliver, S.	
*	**Through the Looking Glass**	Josephs, W.	
*	**Voices in Limbo** (prem. 1981 Austral radio)	Sitsky, L.	

1978

Feb. 4	**Judith and Holofernes** Purchase, NY	Fink, M.	
Feb. 10	**Noah** Bklyn	Sahl/Salzman	
Apr. 1	**Specialist, The** NY	Rodgers, L.	
Apr. 14	**Claudia Legare** Min	Ward, R.	
Apr. 21	**Danton and Robespierre** Bl	Eaton, J.	
May	**Something's Gonna Happen** Tor	Colgrass, M.	
May	**Tristan and Iseult** Auckland, NZ	Whitehead, G.	
May 16	**Psycho Red** Gue	Wilson, C.	
May 18	**I Love My Voice** NY	Arlington, D.	
May 19	**Dybbuk, The** NY	DiGiacomo, F.	
May 24	**Trial of the Gipsy** NY	Menotti, G. C.	
May 25	**Marriage Proposal** Mankato, Minn	Goldstaub, P.	
June 3	**Toy Shop** NY	Barab, S.	
June 16	**Two Fiddlers** Kirkwall, Scot	Davies, P. M.	
June 17	**Daughter of the Double Duke** Katonah, NY	Arlan, D.	

Date	Title	Composer
June 18	Jongleur de Notre Dame Kirkwall, Scot	Davies, P.
June 21	Evita L	Lloyd Webber
Jul. 22	Face on the Barroom Floor CC	Mollicone, H.
Aug. 8	Desire under the Elms New L, Conn	Thomas, E.
Aug. 9	Wake Up Len	Kievman, C.
Aug. 18	Duchess of Malfi O	Oliver, S.
Sept. 1	Apology of Bony Anderson Mel	Conyngham, B.
Nov. 19	Dr. Heidegger's Fountain of Youth NY	Beeson, J.
Nov. 29	Paradise Lost Ch	Penderecki, K.
Dec. 2	Woman in the Garden SF	Fine, V.
Dec. 9	Girl and the Unicorn L	Oliver, S.
Dec. 25	Good Tidings Lincoln, Neb	Locklair, D.
Dec. 26	Rumpelstiltskin Ph	Barber, J.
?	Prometheus NY	Kupferman, M.
?	Shloyme Gorgl Middletown, Conn	arr. Slobin, M.
?	Tale of the Sun Goddess Salinas, Calif	Hovhaness, A.
?	Wenceslas Bournemouth	Ridout, A.
*	Five Shaggy-Dog Operas	Johnson, T.
*	Happy Hypocrite	Masland, W.
*	Little Mermaid	Boyd, A.
*	Love and Psyche	Chlarson, L.
*	Perfect Lives	Ashley, R.
*	Photograph, 1920	Lee, T. O.
*	Shaman	Shields, A.
1979		
Jan. 23	Miss Julie L	Alwyn, W.
Feb. 1	Passion of Simple Simon NY	Sahl/Salzman
Feb. 2	Jealous Cellist Min	Stokes, E.
Feb. 3	Fall of the House of Usher NY	Sandow, G.
Feb. 3	Galileo Galilei Bin	Laderman, E.
Mar. 1	Sweeney Todd NY	Sondheim, S.
spring	Twist of Treason Freehold, NJ	Livingston, J.
Mar. 22	Harmfulness of Tobacco NY	Kalmanoff, M.
Mar. 22	Miss Havisham's Fire NY	Argento, D.
Mar. 31	Faust BBC	Brian, H.
Apr. 11	Diable amoureux Dal	Rodriguez, F.
Apr. 19	Crimson Bird Crawfordsville, Ind	Enebach, F.
Apr. 24	Saga NY	Hamilton, K.
Apr. 30	Full Moon in March Bos	Harbison, J.
May 3	Medea Bos	Luke, R.
May 3	St. Patrick Liv	Warren, R.
May 5	Chip and His Dog Gue	Menotti, G. C.
May 11	Silver Fox SP	Larsen, L.
May 17	Conjur Moon Hou	Lloyd, T. C.
May 17	Starbird, The Hou	Mollicone, H.
May 19	King Harald's Saga Dumfries, Scot	Weir, J.
May 22	Apollonia SP	Starer, R.
June 3	Loca, La San D	Menotti, G. C.
June 9	Village Singer SL	Paulus, S.
June 10	Commedia Kassel, Ger	Cowie, E.
June 14	Little Stories NY	Barab, S.
June 17	Last Leaf Saratoga, Calif	Henderson, A.
July 8	Ralph and the Stalking Bear Monticello, NY	Kalmanoff, M.
July 27	Sumidagawa New L	Scarim, N.
July 29	Picnic, The CC	Cumming, R.
July 29	Soyazhe CC	Anderson, G.
Aug. 4	Houdini Aspen	Schat, P.
Aug. 20	Winter's Tale SF	Harbison, J.
Oct. 1	Thérèse L	Taverner, J.
Oct. 5	Actor's Revenge L	Miki, M.
Oct. 13	Emperor's New Clothes Min	Larsen, L.
Nov. 3	Kamouraska Tor	Wilson, C.
Nov. 11	Linnet, The L, BBC	Lutyens, E.
Nov. 24	Rajah's Diamond L	Hoddinott, A.
Dec.	Shepherds' Christmas Ch	Russo, W.
Dec. 7	Christmas Carol Nor	Musgrave, T.
?	Rock Justice SF	Balin, M.
?	Voyage of St. Brendan Norwich, Engl	Paynter, J.
*	Ballad of Kitty	Lee, D.-K.
*	Diet, The	Olenick, E.
*	Dracula	Franchetti, A.
*	Fritzi	Blumenfeld, H.
*	Pizza del destino	Cohen, S.
1980		
Feb. 7	I Rise in Flame NY	Flanagan, T.
Feb. 20	Old Pipes and the Dryad Fresno, Calif	Rea, A.
Feb. 23	Rocking Stone Bristol, Engl	Selwyn, D.
Feb. 24	Things That Gain L	Barry, G.
Feb. 7	Feathertop NY	Barnes, E.
Mar. 1	Cry of Clytaemnestra Bl	Eaton, J.
Mar. 20	Death of Baldur Elgin, Scot	Bedford, D.
Mar. 20	Silverlake NY	Weill-Symonette
Apr.	Americana Middletown, Conn	Bruce, N.
Apr. 26	Rosina Min	Titus, H.
May 16	Tumbledown Dick Min	Larsen, L.
May 22	Hannah Mannheim, Ger	Lehrman, L.
May 27	Tartuffe SF	Mechem, K.

Date	Work	Composer
June 7	**Director, The** Mel	Werder, F.
June 21	**Cinderella** Kirkwall, Scot	Davies, P. M.
June 25	**Madrigal Opera** Ams	Glass, P.
July 9	**Amarantha** L	Ames, R.
Aug. 7	**Frankenstein** Glens Falls, NY	Sandow, G.
Aug. 7	**Sorry, Wrong Number** Lake George, NY	Moross, J.
Aug. 8	**Way of How** Sea	Dresher, P.
Aug. 22	**Piers Plowman** Gloucester, Engl	Schurmann, G.
Sept.	**Servants, The** Car	Mathias, W.
Sept. 2	**Lighthouse, The** E	Davies, P. M.
Sept. 5	**Satyagraha** Rotterdam	Glass, P.
Sept. 18	**Errors** Leicester, Engl	Warren, R.
Oct. 9	**Before Breakfast** NY	Pasatieri, T.
Oct. 9	**Madame Adare** NY	Silverman, S.
Oct. 9	**Student from Salamanca** NY	Bach, J.
Nov. 17	**Man of Feeling** L	Oliver, S.
Nov. 23	**Rappaccini's Daughter** Ph	Garwood, M.
Nov. 28	**Where the Wild Things Are** Brussels	Knussen, O.
Dec. 4	**Aspern Papers** Bl	Hagemann, P.
Dec. 4	**Orpheus in Pecan Springs** Denton, Tex	Latham, W.
?	**Tell Me on a Sunday** L	Lloyd Webber
*	**Beginning of the Day**	Boyd, A.
*	**Courtship of Camilla**	Schonthal, R.
*	**Dr. Jekyll and Mr. Hyde**	O'Neal, B.
*	**Epilogue**	Dansicker, M.
*	**Golem, The**	Sitsky, L.
*	**Rose and the Ring**	Warren, B.
*	**Sweeney Todd**	Blyton, C.
*	**You'll Never Get It Off the Ground**	Kalmanoff, M.
1981		
Jan.	**Death of the Virgin** NY	Owen, R.
Jan. 6	**America, I Love You** NO	Ahlstrom, D.
Jan. 16	**Jack and Roberta** Riverside, Md	Cain, T.
Jan. 18	**Have You Heard** NY	Talma, L.
Jan. 30	**Bride Stripped Bare** SF	Shere, C.
Feb. 6	**Anna Marguerita's Will** NY	Starer, R.
Feb. 15	**Goose Girl** Fort Worth	Pasatieri, T.
Mar. 1	**Rehearsal, The** NY	Benjamin, T.
Mar. 21	**Passion and Resurrection** Winchester, Engl	Harvey, J.
spring	**Drink of Eternity** Wa	El-Dabh, H.
Mar. 27	**Lysistrata** NY	Barthelson, J.
Apr. 1	**Trumpet Major** Man	Hoddinott, A.
May 1	**Miss Havisham's Wedding Night** Min	Argento, D.
May 1	**Willie Stark** Hou	Floyd, C.
May 2	**We're Back** NY	Armour, E.
May 14	**Emperor Norton** SF	Mollicone, H.
May 24	**Selfish Giant** Charleston, SC	Hollingsworth, S.
May 27	**Harrison Loved His Umbrella** Charleston, SC	Hollingsworth, S.
June 3	**Ruined Maid** NY	Barab, S.
June 8	**Wedding, The** D	Potter, A. J.
June 12	**Journey, The** Car	Metcalf, J.
June 20	**Rainbow, The** Kirkwall, Scot	Davies, P.
June 21	**Medium, The** Kirkwall, Scot	Davies, P.
July 2	**Columbine String Quartet** Stock	Silverman, S.
Aug. 16	**Mistake, The** Den	Sheffer, J. B.
Sept. 18	**Thousand Names to Come** Mil	Kitzke, J.
Sept. 26	**Patria, Prologue** Heart Lake, Ont	Schafer, R.
?	**Boxes, The** NY	Sahl/Salzman
?	**Fridhof's Saga** Elgin	Bedford, D.
?	**Lessons, The** NY	Ashley, R.
*	**Columba**	Leighton, K.
*	**Felipe**	Aitken, H.
*	**Jenny Lind**	Lee, D.-K.
1982		
Jan.	**Chakravaka-Bird** L	Gilbert, A.
Jan. 22	**Tell-Tale Heart** Bos	Adolphe, B.
Feb. 2	**Lady of the Castle** NY	Spektor, M.
Feb. 3	**United States** Bklyn	Anderson, L.
Feb. 5	**Frog-Hopping** Bklyn	Boswell, W.
Feb. 5	**Implications of Melissa** Bklyn	Carlsen, P.
Feb. 14	**De Amore** Oberlin	Barkin, E.
Feb. 19	**Abelard and Heloise** Charlotte, NC	Ward, R.
Mar. 28	**Glory Coach** NY	Barnard, F.
Apr. 3	**Cask of Amontillado** NY	Currie, R.
Apr. 3	**Chipita Rodríguez** Corpus Christi, Tex	Weiner, L.
Apr. 3	**Shivaree** Tor	Beckwith, J.
Apr. 14	**Bride from Pluto** Wa	Menotti, G. C.
Apr. 16	**Nightingale** Vienna, Va	Strouse, C.
Apr. 17	**Monkey Opera** Bklyn	Trefousse, R.
Apr. 30	**Mask of Evil** Min	Mollicone, H.
May 7	**Anna Karenina** L	Hamilton, I.
May 7	**Audience, The** NY	Dembo, R.
May 8	**Mikhoels the Wise** NY	Adolphe, B.
May 17	**Something New for the Zoo** Cheverley, Md	Hoiby, L.
May 30	**Photographer, The** Ams	Glass, P.
June	**Emperor and the Nightingale** NH	Bingham, S.
June 4	**Minutes till Midnight** Miami	Ward, R.

June 11	**Cop and the Anthem** NY	Cohen, S.
June 11	**Montezuma's Death** NY	Chlarson, L.
June 19	**Fortune's Favorites** NY	Barab, S.
June 19	**Postman Always Rings Twice** SL	Paulus, S.
July	**Italian Lesson** Newport, RI	Hoiby, L.
July	**Juniper Tree** Len	Kesselman, W.
July 1	**Quiros** Austral television	Sculthorpe, P.
July 7	**Suor Isabella** Dal	Rodríguez, F.
July 17	**Orpheus** Wells, Engl	Burgon, G.
July 22	**In the Beginning** Bristol, Engl	Warren, R.
Aug.	**Confidence Man** S Fe	Rochberg, G.
Sept. 2	**Icarus** Linz, Aust	Earls, P.
Sept. 4	**Judith** Cin	Smith, D.
Sept. 10	**Ponder Heart** Jackson, Miss	Parker, A.
Sept. 14	**Occurrence at Owl Creek Bridge** BBC	Musgrave, T.
Sept. 24	**Boy Who Grew Too Fast** Wilmington, Del	Menotti, G. C.
Oct. 1	**De Profundis** Canberra	Sitsky, L.
Oct. 10	**Hangman, Hangman!** Barcelona	Balada, L.
Oct. 23	**Soldier Boy, Soldier** Bl	Anderson, T.
Oct. 24	**William Penn** Ph	Cascarino, R.
Oct. 29	**Doctor Faustus** SF	Ahlstrom, D.
Nov.	**Atalanta** Paris	Ashley, R.
Dec. 27	**Little Nightmare Music** NY	Schickele, P.
?	**Marquesa of O** ?	Siegmeister, E.
?	**Pyramus and Thisbe** Waterford, Conn	Convery, R.
?	**Stone Soup** Ph	Dorff, D.
?	**Voss** Adelaide	Meale, R.
*	**Alchemist of Trenton**	Busch, D.
*	**Alice in Wonderland**	Meachem, M.
*	**Simple Decision**	Busch, D.
1983		
Jan. 29	**Frieze of Life** Newport Beach, Calif	Applebaum, E.
Feb. 4	**Mystic Trumpeter** Bklyn	Starer, R.
Mar. 11	**Death in the Family** Min	Mayer, W.
Mar. 24	**Pond in a Bowl** NY	Macbride, D.
Mar. 24	**Statues on a Lawn** NY	Flanagan, T.
Apr. 6	**Maria Elena** Tucson	Pasatieri, T.
Apr. 7	**Sasha** Banff, Ont	Oliver, S.
Apr. 9	**False Messiah** NY	Adolphe, B.
May 4	**Patria, no. 6** Tor	Schafer, R.
June 2	**English Cat** Schwetzingen, Ger	Henze, H. W.
June 6	**Light Opera** NY	Morrow, C.
June 17	**Lady of the Inn** Reading, Engl	Wishart, P.
June 17	**Quiet Place** Hou	Bernstein, L.
summer	**Up from Paradise** NY	Silverman, S.
July	**Mrs. Farmer's Daughter** Purchase, NY	Williams, J.
Aug. 10	**Lament of Kamuela** Hanover, NH	Appleton, J.
Oct. 1	**Metamorphosis** Mel	Howard, B.
Oct. 15	**Rebecca** Leeds	Josephs, W.
Nov. 16	**Eros and Psyche** Oberlin, Ohio	Cummings, C.
Dec. 5	**Blue Star** NY	Dvorkin, J.
?	**Christina's World** Syd	Edwards, R.
*	**Cats' Corner**	Riley, D.
*	**Dracula**	Blyton, C.
*	**Fair Means or Foul**	Barab, S.
*	**Magic Bonbons**	Blank, A.
*	**Secret of the Mirror**	Busch, D.
1984		
Jan. 11	**Family Man** NY	Lehrman, L.
Jan. 26	**Emma** Provo, Utah	Boren, M.
Jan. 27	**Anne Boleyn** NY	Beck, J.
Feb. 3	**Farewell Supper** Bklyn	Hart, F.
Feb. 3	**Poison** Bklyn	Hart, F.
Feb. 10	**Intruder, The** Berea, Ohio	Feldman, J.
Feb. 16	**Pay Off** Ch	Russo, W.
Mar. 20	**No. 11 Bus** L	Davies, P. M.
Mar. 25	**CIVIL warS** Rome	Glass, P.
Apr. 4	**Wayfarers, The** Huntingdon, Engl	Joubert, J.
Apr. 13	**Nightingale's Apprentice** NY	Silsbee, A.
Apr. 24	**Abduction of Figaro** Min	Schickele, P.
Apr. 27	**Knee Plays** Min	Byrne, D.
Apr. 29	**Dream within a Dream** Bronx, NY	Currie, R.
May 19	**Bishop's Horse** SF	Ahlstrom, D.
May 30	**Britannia Preserv'd** L	Oliver, S.
June 3	**Raleigh's Dream** Durham, NC	Hamilton, I.
June 5	**King of the Other Country** Syd	Whitehead, G.
July 26	**Beauty and the Beast** Batignano, Italy	Oliver, S.
Aug.	**Weep Torn Land** Hanover, NH	Finney, R.
Aug. 2	**Love of Don Perlimplin** Purchase, NY	Susa, C.
Aug. 25	**Fly** Mel	Conyngham, B.
Sept. 20	**Crossing, The** Car	Metcalf, J.
Oct. 12	**Akhnaten** Stuttgart	Glass, P.
Oct. 13	**Higglety Pigglety Pop!** Gl	Knussen, O.
Oct. 13	**Kiss, The** L	Nyman, M.
Oct. 14	**Passion of Vincent Van Gogh** Dal	Yavelow, C.
Oct. 20	**Intelligent Systems** Baden-Baden, Ger	Kievman, C.
Oct. 23	**Medea** Lyons	Bryars, G.

Oct. 24	**Minette Fontaine** BR	Still, W. G.
Nov. 5	**Three Sisters Who Are Not Sisters** NY	Hellermann, W.
Nov. 22	**José's Carmen** L	Ashman, M.
Nov. 26	**Letters to Leo** D	Wilson, J.
Nov.	**Woman Who Dared** Roch	Bokser, Z.
Dec. 1	**Gift of the Magi** NH	Bingham, S.
?	**At Last I've Found You** Charlotte, SC	Barab, S.
?	**Birth of the Poet** Rotterdam	Gordon, P.
?	**Freshwater** NY	Valinsky, E.
?	**Rappaccini's Daughter** Ph	Dennison, S.
*	**Emperor's New Clothes**	Sessions, R.
*	**Four-Score**	Blumenfeld, H.
*	**Further Voyages**	Stokes, E.
*	**Golden Bird**	Russo, W.
*	**Obelisk, The**	Eaton, M.
*	**Rappaccini's Daughter**	Riley, D.
*	**Ring, The**	Oliver, S.
*	**Sopranos Only**	Johnson, T.
*	**When Opportunity Knocks**	Ashley, R.
1985		
Jan. 6	**Oath of Bad Brown Bill** Mel	Conyngham. B.
Jan. 17	**Dreyfus** Bklyn	Cotel, M.
Feb.	**Harlot and the Monk** Atlanta	Bohmler, C.
Feb. 8	**Butterfly Girl and Mirage Boy** Bklyn	Reed, H. R.
Feb. 22	**Clair de Lune** Little Rock, Ark	Larsen, L.
Feb. 24	**Sojourner** NY	Capers, V.
Mar. 1	**Harriet, a Woman Called Moses** Nor	Musgrave, T.
Mar. 19	**Alice** Jerusalem	Osborne, W.
Apr. 10	**Marriage between Zones** L	Barker, P.
Apr. 11	**Aesop's Fables** De Kalb, Ill	Smith, G.
Apr. 11	**Blake** Oberlin, Ohio	Adams, L.
Apr. 12	**Casanova's Homecoming** SP	Argento, D.
Apr. 13	**Sibyl, The** Ph	Persichetti, V.
Apr. 19	**Behold the Sun** Duisburg, Ger	Goehr, A.
Apr. 26	**Echoes of the Shining Prince** NY	Cooper, S.
May 1	**Pillow-Song** L	Barker, P.
May 5	**Consolations of Scholarship** Durham, Engl	Weir, J.
May 12	**Out the Window**	Barab, S.
May 12	**Predators** NY	Barab, S.

May 13	**Snow Queen** Adelaide	Dudley, G.
May 23	**Piece of String** Greeley, Colo	Barab, S.
May 30	**Jōruri** St. Louis	Miki, M.
June	**Thief of Love** NY	Silver, S.
June	**Tickets, Please** Hou	Nelson, R.
June 5	**Hedda Gabler** Gla	Harper, E.
June 6	**Chicken Little** Hou	Benjamin, T.
June 28	**Frederick Douglass** NY	Moore, D. R.
June 28	**Song of Pegasus** Forest Meadows, Calif	McFarland, R.
July 28	**Tempest, The** S Fe	Eaton, J.
Aug. 20	**Seduction of a Lady** Glens Falls, NY	Wargo, R.
Aug. 24	**Lancelot** Arundel Castle, Wales	Hamilton, I.
Sept. 17	**Medea** Mel	Werder, F.
Oct.	**Music Shop** SP	Wargo, R.
Oct.	**X** Ph	Davis, A.
Oct. 5	**Angel Levine** NY	Siegmeister, E.
Oct. 5	**Lady of the Lake** NY	Siegmeister, E.
Oct. 7	**Father of the Child** Bayside, NY	Barab, S.
Oct. 19	**Meal, The** Edmonton	Archer, V.
Nov. 7	**Question of Love** L	Gilbert, P.
Dec. 4	**Birth of the Poet** Bklyn	Gordon, P.
Dec. 11	**Juniper Tree** Cam, Mass	Glass, P.
?	**Atalanta Strategy** Montreal	Ashley, R.
?	**Gift of the Magi** NO	Warren, B.
?	**RareArea** Brussels	Ream, M.
?	**Zapata!** Ph	Balada, L.
*	**Alice in Wonderland**	Josephs, W.
*	**Gift of the Magi**	Brown, R.
*	**Golden Crane**	Kay, D. H.
*	**Only a Miracle**	Barab, S.
1986		
Jan. 4	**Hells' Angels** L	Osborne, N.
Jan. 5	**Goldilocks** Chappaqua, NY	Zaimont, J.
Jan. 13	**Sagegrass** NY	Atwell, S. J.
Jan. 14	**Africanus Instructus** NY	Silverman, S.
Jan. 18	**Chinchilla** Bin	Fink, M.
Jan. 29	**Tango** Dal	Rodríguez, F.
Feb.	**Hansel and Gretel** Arcata, Calif	Stoddard, M.
Feb. 20	**Bus to Stockport** NY	Valinsky/Schubert
Mar. 13	**Three Sisters** Columbus, Ohio	Pasatieri, T.
Apr.	**Aesop's Fables** SF	Ahlstrom, D.
Apr.	**Good Life** Wa	Silverman, S.
May 15	**Cathedral, The** NY	Spivack, L.
May 15	**Spanish Lady** L	Elgar, E.
May 21	**Mask of Orpheus** L	Birtwistle, H.
May 30	**Grub Street Opera** NY	Bowles, A.

June	Demon Lover D	Nelson, R.	June 13	Diva, The Ch	Ferris, W.
June 6	Guilt of Lillian Sloan Ch	Neil, W.	June 14	Follies and Fancies NY	Allen, J. S.
June 19	Island of Tomorrow NY	Fink, M.	June 14	Song of Insanity NY	Seletsky, H.
June 21	Tempest, The Indianola, Iowa	Hoiby, L.	July 8	Night at the Chinese Opera Chel	Weir, J.
summer	Wife of Bath's Tale Aspen	Legg, J.	July 30	Haydn's Head Cl	Baker, L.
June 24	Exposition of a Picture L	Oliver, S.	Aug. 6	Patria, no. 3 Petersborough, Ont	Schafer, R.
Aug.	Pirate Moon Auckland, NZ	Whitehead, G.	Aug. 7	Hazel Kirke Glens Falls, NY	Houston, M.
Aug. 5	Yan Tan Tethera L	Birtwistle, H.	Aug. 20	Lucy's Lapses NY	Drobny, C.
Aug. 6	Black Sea Follies Stock	Silverman, S.	Sept. 26	Where's Dick Omaha	Wallace, S.
Aug. 6	Directions, The Iraklion, Crete	Torke, M.	Oct. 5	Electrification of the Soviet Union Gl	Osborne, N.
Sept. 13	Bartolo Bir, Ala	Bugg, G. W.	Oct. 23	Nixon in China Hou	Adams, J.
Sept. 20	Queenie Pie Ph	Ellington, E.	Nov. 2	Jacob's Room SP	Subotnick, M.
autumn	We're Not Robots Min	Stokes, E.	Nov. 7	Going, The Cin	Beall, M.
Oct. 5	Tight-Rope Madison, Wisc	Biscardi, C.	Nov. 21	Patria, no. 1 Tor	Schafer, R.
			Dec.	Dialogues Frostburg, Md	Bauman, J.
Oct. 9	Canterbury Tale Oakham, Engl	Roe, B.	Dec.	Europeras 1 & 2 Frankfurt	Cage, J.
Oct. 9	Phantom of the Opera L	Lloyd Webber	Dec. 2	Christmas Carol SF	Hoiby, L.
Oct. 10	Ransom of Red Chief Mesquite, Tex	Rodríguez, F.	Dec. 4	Nativity Midland, Mich	Dello Joio, N.
Oct.16	On Blue Mountain NY	Eyerly, S.	Dec. 14	Abigail Adams NY	Owen, R.
Oct. 27	Man Who Mistook His Wife L	Nyman, M.	?	Psychles Ch	Thomas, A.
			?	White Doe Ripon, Engl	Ridout, A.
Oct. 29	Lorenzaccio Syd	Brumby, C.	*	Albatross, The (prem. 1997 L)	Burrell, D.
Oct. 30	Ladies Voices Berk	Shere, C.	*	Fisherman and His Wife	Bingham, S.
Nov. 9	Harriet Tubman NY	Edwards, L.	*	Foreign Experiences (prem. 1991 NY)	Ashley, R.
Nov. 28	Goya Wa	Menotti, G. C.			
Dec. 12	I Can't Stand Wagner NY	Barab, S.	*	Frankenstein	Blyton, C.
?	Wild Boy Ph	Epstein, S.	*	Frog Man	Hovhaness, A.
*	Foreign Experiences (prem. 1991 NY)	Ashley, R.	*	Moby Dick	Brooks, R.
*	Idle Rumor	Busch, D.	*	Spark Plugs	Granger, M.
*	Improvement (prem. 1991 NY)	Ashley, R.	**1988**		
			Feb.	Tristan and Iseult NY	Cohen, J.
*	Man Who Corrupted Hadleyville	Nelson, R.	Feb. 10	Mellstock Quire E	Harper, E.
*	Swans, The	Henderson, A.	Feb. 28	Esther NY	Swados, E.
1987			Mar. 13	Rasputin NY	Reise, J.
Feb. 2	Della's Gift Austin, Tex	Welcher, D.	Mar. 15	Oedipus Tex Min	Schickele, P.
Feb. 12	Countdown Bos	Yavelow, C.	Mar. 17	Gulliver Lou	Bond, V.
Feb. 18	Monkey See Dal	Rodríguez, F.	Mar. 20	Dream Beach NY	Sahl, M.
Mar.	Howard NY	Earnest, J.	Mar. 28	Alice Meets the Mock Turtle NY	Bingham, S.
Mar. 28	Tomorrow, Tomorrow NY	Sullivan, T.			
Apr. 4	King Who Saved Himself Chico, Calif	Hagemann, P.	Apr. 21	Bennelong Groningen, Neth	Conyngham, B.
Apr. 5	Ligeia Riverdale, NJ	Currie, R.	Apr. 25	Wild Swans NH	Bingham, S.
Apr. 8	Frankie Adelaide	John, A.	May	Undivine Comedy Paris	Finnissy, M.
Apr. 11	Iron Man Adelaide	Fox, M.	May 3	Lodge of Shadows Ft Worth, Tex	Adler, S.
Apr. 23	Benjamin Lancaster, Pa	Carbon, J.	May 11	Dream Play Tor	Sullivan, T.
May 8	Legend, The Cl	Murray, B.	May 11	Realitillusion Tor	Brégent, M.
June	Waiting Buxton	Oliver, S.	May 13	Christina Romana Min	Larsen, L.
			May 19	St. Carmen of the Main Gue	Hodkinson, S.

Date	Title / Location	Composer
May 22	**Pastoral** Albuquerque, NM	Galloway, J.
May 28	**Old Majestic** San Antonio	Rodríguez, F.
May 29	**Fall of the House of Usher** Lou	Glass, P.
June 1	**Nell** L	Bauld, A.
June 17	**Greek** Munich	Turnage, M.
June 27	**On the Razzle** Gla	Orr, R.
July 2	**Donna, La** Syd	Brumby, C.
July 8	**Making of the Representative** Hou	Glass, P.
July 15	**One Thousand Airplanes** Vienna	Glass, P.
Aug. 3	**Birthday of the Bank** Glens Falls, NY	Lehrman, L.
Aug. 6	**Mario and the Magician** Batignano, Italy	Oliver, S.
Aug. 26	**Cat Cinderella** E	De Simone, R.
Sept. 2	**Whitsunday** Syd	Howard, B.
Sept. 8	**Resurrection** Darmstadt	Davies, P.
Sept. 16	**Wedding, The** Seoul	Menotti, G. C.
Oct.	**Forest, The** West Berlin	Byrne, D.
Oct. 1	**Love, Death** SL	White, C.
Oct. 8	**Magic Fishbone** NY	Chapin, T.
Oct. 20	**Charlotte's Web** St. Petersburg, Fla	Ahlin, L.
Nov	**My Brother Called** Ch	Ashley, R.
Nov. 18	**Doctor Ox's Experiment** L	Bryars, G.
Nov. 19	**Aspern Papers** Dal	Argento, D.
Nov. 26	**West of Washington Square** San Jose	Henderson, A.
Nov. 30	**Breakfast Waltzes** Ch	Blumenfeld, H.
Dec. 13	**Death of a Ghost** NY	Gottlieb, J.
?	**Angel Face** SP	Ames, R.
?	**Death of Lincoln** Cl	London, E.
?	**Dissipation of Purely Sound** Tor	Beecroft, N.
?	**eL/Aficionado** Marseilles	Ashley, R.
?	**Jack Benny Show** NY	Moran, J.
?	**Return of Odysseus** L	Bedford, D.
*	**Ba-Ta-Clan**	Oliver, S.
*	**Birds, The**	El-Dabh, H.
*	**ChaplinOperas** (prem. 1992, Strasbourg)	Mason, B.
*	**Journey of Edith Wharton**	Hannay, R.
*	**Love's Labour's Lost**	Bush, G.
*	**Now Eleanor's Idea**	Ashley, R.

1989

Date	Title / Location	Composer
Jan.	**Pied Piper** Orlando, Fla	Swados, E.
Jan. 4	**Story of Mary O'Neill** L	LeFanu, N.
Jan. 29	**Belisa** SP	Biales, A.
Feb.	**Boor, The** Austin, Tex	Grantham, D.
Feb. 6	**I Like It to Be a Play** SF	Shere, C.
Feb. 17	**Charlotte's Web** Wilmington, Del	Strouse, C.
Feb. 28	**Grinning at the Devil** Copenhagen	Wilson, J.
Mar. 8	**Bon Appétit!** Wa	Hoiby, L.
Mar. 8	**Will You Marry Me?** NY	Weisgall, H.
Mar. 9	**Patria, no. 4** Liège	Schafer, R.
Apr. 8	**Casino Paradise** Ph	Bolcolm, W.
Apr. 9	**Rachel** Knoxville, Tenn	Coe, K.
Apr. 9	**Tom Sawyer** NY	Owen, R.
Apr. 22	**Vagabond Queen** LA	Barnes, E.
Apr. 28	**Jane Heir** NY	Healey, P.
May	**Menaced Assassin** L	Jones, J. P.
May 4	**Power Failure** Iowa City	Dresher, P.
May 11	**Crazy to Kill** Gue	Beckwith, J.
May 17	**Yellow Wallpaper** Northampton, Mass	Perera, R.
May 20	**Friends and Dinosaurs** Needham, Mass	Shadle, C.
May 20	**Princess Maleen** WP	Schonthal, R.
May 25	**Plumber's Gift** L	Blake, D.
June 8	**Empty Places** Charleston, SC	Anderson, L.
June 17	**Fan, The** Ch	Goldstein, L.
June 24	**Question of Taste** Cooperstown, NY	Schuman, W.
June 28	**Golem** L	Casken, J.
July 15	**Under the Double Moon** SL	Davis, A.
Aug.	**Computer Marriage** Hanover, NH	Finney, R. L.
Sept.	**Emperor's New Clothes** NY	Dvorkin, J.
Oct. 5	**Heaven Ablaze in His Breast** Basildon, Essex	Weir, J.
Oct. 10	**Holy Blood and Crescent Moon** Cl	Copeland, S.
Oct. 18	**Rip Van Winkle** SD	Rockwell, J.
Oct. 25	**Telephone Show** Mil	Wadsworth, S.
Oct. 27	**New Year** Hou	Tippett, M.
Oct. 28	**Mary Surratt** Ft Washington, Md	Muller, G.
Nov. 2	**Rendezvous, The** D	Victory, G.
Nov. 6	**Pizza con funghi** NY	Barab, S.
Nov. 16	**Kabballah** Bklyn	Wallace, S.
Nov. 25	**Hotel Eden** San Jose	Mollicone, H.
Dec. 1	**VALIS** Paris	Machover, T.
?	**King's Twelve Moons** NY	Wallach, J.
?	**Muskrat Lullaby** LA	Barnes, E.
?	**Prelude to Einstein on the Fritz** NY	Schickele, P.
?	**Beauty and the Beast** Mel	Easton, M.
*	**Cinderella**	Easton, M.
*	**John Brown**	Mechem, K.
*	**Moby Dick**	Epstein, S.
*	**Reverend Jim**	Eaton, J.

1990

Mar. 31	**Black Rider** Hamburg	Waits, T.
Apr.	**Lifework of Juan Diaz** Ch	Rapchak, L.
May	**Mother of Three Sons** Munich	Jenkins, L.
May 5	**Birds, The** SF	Ahlstrom, D.
May 18	**Clarissa** L	Holloway, R.
May 19	**Tornrak** Car	Metcalf, J.
May 21	**Photo-Op** NY	Cummings, C.
May 23	**Mother and Child** NY	McClure, L.
May 25	**Frankenstein** SP	Larsen, L.
May 26	**Hydrogen Jukebox** Charleston, SC	Glass, P.
June 1	**Bohemians, The** NY	Kirschner, B.
June 10	**Triptych** Al	Goehr, A.
June 14	**Albergo Empedocle** L	Barker, P.
June 17	**Europeras 3 & 4** L	Cage, J.
summer	**Reverend Everyman** Tallahassee	Brotons, S.
July 6	**Intelligence Park** L	Barry, G.
July 17	**Manson Family** NY	Moran, J.
July 28	**Chekhov Trilogy** Chautauqua, NY	Wargo, R.
Sept. 18	**Once in a While** L	Godfrey, P.
Oct. 17	**Vanishing Bridegroom** Gl	Weir, J.
Oct. 20	**Tibetan Dreams** NY	Dickman, S.
Oct. 24	**Chinese Canticle** L	Stoker, R.
Dec. 4	**Monster Bed** NY	de Kenessey, S.
Dec. 7	**Blind Witness News** NY	Yarmolinsky, B.
Dec. 7	**Funeral of Jan Palach** NY	Beckley, C.
?	**Rimshot** NY	Currie, R.
?	**Stone Man** Lou	Dutton, D.
?	**Tables Meet** L	Oliver, S.
?	**Visit to the Country** Chautauqua, NY	Wargo, R.
*	**Creation of the World**	Penberthy, J.

1991

Jan. 6	**Found Objects** NY	Trefousse, R.
Feb. 18	**Bride of Fortune** Perth	Whitehead, G.
Feb. 19	**Jewel Box** Nottingham	Mozart-Griffiths
Feb. 22	**Atlas** NY	Monk, M.
Feb. 22	**Secret Garden** Ph	Pliska, G.
Feb. 23	**Harmoonia** Muscatine, La	Paulus, S.
Feb. 26	**Guacamayo's Old Song** Tor	Oliver, J.
Mar. 1	**Mary Stuart** Cl	Murray, B.
Mar. 19	**Death of Klinghoffer** Brussels	Adams, J.
Apr. 11	**Frida** Ph	Rodríguez, F.
Apr. 14	**Frederick Douglass** Newark, NJ	Kay, U.
Apr. 18	**Europa 5** Buffalo, NY	Cage, J.
May 3	**Rip Van Winkle** Syr	Smith, G.

May 17	**Timon of Athens** L	Oliver, S.
May 30	**Gawain** L	Birtwistle, H.
July	**Van Gogh Video** NY	Gordon, M.
July 24	**Noises, Sounds** Avignon	Nyman, M.
Aug. 10	**Summer Carol** Canberra	Brumby, C.
Sept. 25	**Fire on the Wind** Brisbane	Brumby, C.
Oct.	**Three Scenes** Canberra	Sitsky, L.
Oct. 3	**Mer de Glace** Syd	Meale, R.
Oct. 12	**New World** Commack, NY	Lehrman, L.
Oct. 31	**Diary of an African-American** NY	Peterson, H.
Nov.	**Scipio's Dream** BBC 2	Weir, J.
Nov.	**Snow Leopard** SP	Harper, W.
Nov. 3	**Proscenium** NY	Kupferman, M.
Nov. 10	**Letters, Riddles** BBC	Nyman, M.
Nov. 21	**Caritas** Wakefield, Engl	Saxon, R.
Dec. 23	**Ghosts of Versailles** NY	Corigliano, J.
?	**Heloise and Abelard** ?	Tarhoudin, P.
?	**Little Redinka** Mel	Easton, M.
?	**Panic, The** L	Sawyer, D.
*	**Cinderella**	Oliver, S.
*	**Hard Times**	Burgon, G.
*	**Monkey's Paw**	Alexander, W.
*	**Tailor of Gloucester**	Young, D.
*	**Three Musketeers**	Dvorkin, J.
*	**What Happened**	Shere, C.

1992

Jan.	**Petrov** Mel	Easton, M.
Feb. 8	**Cue 67** Richmond, Va	Ching, M.
Feb. 20	**Desert of Roses** Hou	Moran, R.
Mar. 2	**Place to Call Home** LA	Barnes, E.
Mar. 3	**Patria, no. 5** Tor	Schafer, R.
Mar. 27	**From the Towers of the Moon** SP	Moran, R.
Mar. 27	**White Agony** Greensboro, NC	Fuchs, P. P.
Mar. 27	**Wrinkle in Time** Wilmington, Del	Larsen, L.
Apr. 3	**Scarlet Letter** Berk	Herman, M.
Apr. 4	**Shining Brow** Madison, Wisc	Hagen, D.
Apr. 9	**Song of Majnun** Ch	Sheng, B.
May 5	**Bacchae, The** L	Buller, J.
May 11	**Broken Strings** Ams	Vir, P.
May 11	**Snatched by the Gods** Ams	Vir, P.
May 19	**Mario and the Magician** Tor	Somers, H.
June 10	**Biko** L	Paintal, P.
June 17	**Tania** Ph	Davis, A.
June 24	**Mary of Egypt** Ald	Taverner, J.
July 10	**Terrible Mouth** L	Osborne, N.
Sept. 23	**Ubu** Car	Toovey, A.
Oct. 12	**Voyage, The** NY	Glass, P.

Date	Work	Composer
Oct. 16	Under the Arbor Bir, Ala	Greenleaf, R.
Oct. 26	Blood Wedding L	LeFanu, N.
Oct. 28	Rappaccini's Daughter Bos	Bender, E.
Nov. 3	McTeague Ch	Bolcom, W.
Dec. 19	Alice Hamburg	Waits, T.
?	Love Burns Adelaide	Koehne, G.
?	Nigredo Hotel Stratford, Ont	Gotham, N.
*	Belly Bag	Ball, M.
*	Fahrenheit 451	Broadstock, B.
*	Red-Headed League	Dvorkin, J.

1993

Date	Work	Composer
Jan. 18	King of the Clouds Dayton, Ohio	Ching/Moffat
Feb. 16	Ghosts NY	Ito, G.
Feb. 22	Romulus Hunt NY	Simon, C.
Mar. 18	Bundle Man NY	Cold, M.
Apr. 21	California Mystery Park NY	Kievman, C.
Apr. 21	Cat in the Box NY	Miller, R.
Apr. 21	Embrace the Monster NY	Valitsky, K.
May	Cave, The Vienna	Reich, S.
May 31	Singing Child Charleston, SC	Menotti, G. C.
June 5	Inquest of Love L	Harvey, J.
June 9	Roman Fever Durham, NC	Ward, R.
July	Family Affair L	Grant, J.
July	Mrs. Dalloway Cl	Larsen, L.
July 2	Man with Footsoles L	Volans, K.
July 3	Baa Baa Black Sheep L	Berkeley, M.
July 14	Line of Terror L	McQueen, I.
July 27	Juniper Tree Broomhill, Kent	Toovey, A.
Sept. 24	El Greco NY	Harper, W.
Oct.	Dead, The NY	Boren, M.
Oct. 6	Marilyn NY	Laderman, E.
Oct. 8	Esther NY	Weisgall, H.
Oct. 15	Birth/Day Dal	Wolfe, N.
Nov. 27	Tonkin Wilmington, Del	Cummings, C.
Dec. 8	Nosferatu Tor	Peters, R.
*	Cask of Amontillado	Copeland, S.

1994

Date	Work	Composer
Jan. 13	How to Make Love NY	Widdoes, L.
Jan. 15	Dream of Valentino Wa	Argento, D.
Feb. 20	Ligeia Bal	Thomas, A. G.
Mar. 12	Mario and the Magician Bklyn	Thorne, F.
Mar. 13	Three Mimes NY	Cantrick, R.
Mar. 18	Flowers Car	Hardy, J.
Mar. 18	Dracula Diary Hou	Moran, R.
Apr.	Strange Life of Ivan Osokin NY	Gordon, P.
June 8	Lady Kate Wooster, Ohio	Ward, R.
July 3	Baa Baa Black Sheep Chel	Berkeley, M.
July 8	Nightingale and Rose L	Firsova, E.
July 8	Tempest, The Lawrenceville, NJ	Westergaard, P.
July 15	Siren Song L	Dove, J.
Aug. 14	Blond Eckbert S Fe	Weir, J.
Aug. 23	Sarajevo L	Osborne, N.
Oct. 7	Mathew in the School of Life NY	Moran, R.
Oct. 8	Esther NY	Weisgall, H.
Oct. 16	Thérèse Raquin L	Finnissy, M.
Oct. 17	Dangerous Liaisons SF	Susa, C.
Oct. 24	Second Mrs. Kong Gly	Birtwistle, H.
Nov. 11	This is the Rill Speaking NY	Hoiby, L.
Nov. 12	I Am in Search L	Grant, R.
Nov. 12	Lamentations of Doctor Faustus L	Hewitt, M.
?	Cyrano Hagen, Ger	Beeson, J.
?	Playing Away Munich	Mason, B.
*	Chaos	Gordon, M.
*	Elephant's Child	Hagen, D.
*	Selfish Giant	Easton, M.

1995

Date	Work	Composer
Jan. 20	Simón Bolívar Nor	Musgrave, T.
Jan. 21	Harvey Milk Hou	Wallace, S.
Jan. 27	Amazing Adventure NY	Adolphe, B.
Jan. 27	Marita NY	Adolphe, B.
Feb. 3	Dorian Garden City, NY	Deutsch, H.
Feb. 3	Failing Kansas NY	Rouse, M.
Mar.	Village, The Queens, NY	Mandelbaum
Mar. 5	Triumph of Beauty L	Barry, G.
Mar. 12	Good Friday 1663 L	Westbrook, K./Westbrook, M.
Mar. 24	Ondine NY	Barab, S.
Apr. 26	Outcast, The Bklyn	Ain, N.
Apr. 27	Manhattan Book of the Dead NY	First, D.
Apr. 27	Night Passage Sea	Moran, R.
May 11	Hearts on Fire Min	Ames, R.
May 11	I Was Looking Berk	Adams, J.
May 18	Travels Roanoke, Va	Bond, V.
June 1	City Workers Victoria, BC	Weisensel, N.
June 1	Heavenfields Victoria, BC	Buhr, G.
June 1	Nigredo Hotel Victoria, BC	Gotham, N.
June 2	Wildman, The L	LeFanu, N.
June 8	Lady Kate Wooster, Oh	Ward, R.
June 10	Bok Choy Variations SP	Chen, E.
June 17	Woman at the Otowi Crossing SL	Paulus, S.
June 21	Passionate Man D	Wilson, J.
June 22	Small Jewel Box NY	Mozart-Griffiths
July 5	Powder Her Face S Fe	Adès, T.
July 18	East and West L	McQueen, I.

July 29	Modern Painters S Fe	Lang, D.
Oct. 14	Eighth Wonder Syd	John, A.
1996		
Jan. 13	Dreamkeepers, The Salt Lake City	Carlson, D.
Feb. 7	Different Fields NY	Reid, M.
Feb. 8	Seasons in Hell Cin	Blumenfeld, H.
Feb. 13	Rent NY	Larson, J.
Mar.	Beast and Superbeast Wa	Martín, J.
Mar. 8	Vera of Las Vegas Las Vegas	Hagen, D.
Apr. 10	Terra Incognita NY	Sierra, R.
May 7	Marco Polo Munich	Tan Dun
May 8	Picture of Dorian Gray Monte Carlo	Liebermann, L.
June	Patience and Sarah NY	Kimper, P.
June	Time Rocker Hamburg	Reed, L.
June 13	Three Visitations Min	Sherman, K.
June 28	E. & O. Line Annandale, Va	LeBaron, A.
July	Brain Opera NY	Machover, T.
July 5	Doctor of Myddfai Car	Davies, P. M.
July 6	In the House of Crossed Desires Chel	Woolrich, J.
July 27	Emmeline S Fe	Picker, T.
July 27	King of Hearts Aspen	Torke, M.
Aug.	Dreamers, The Sonoma, Calif	Conte, D.
Aug. 1	Kafka's Chimp Banff, Ont	Metcalf, J.
Aug. 23	Inés de Castro E	MacMillan, J.
Sept. 2	Suppose a Wedding Commack, NY	Lehrman, L.
Oct. 10	Politics of Quiet Copenhagen	Monk, M.
Oct. 19	Summer of the Seventeenth Doll Mel	Mills, R.
Oct. 25	Jocasta NY	Schonthal, R.
Oct. 25	Shala Fears NY	Braxton, A.
Nov.	Dennis Cleveland NY	Rouse, M.
Dec. 13	Nights of Annabel Lee NY	Rodgers, L.
Dec. 13	Other Wise Man NY	de Kenessey, S.
*	Sorry, Wrong Number	Beeson, J.
1997		
Jan. 18	Many Moons Princeton	Kapilow, R.
Jan. 27	Buoso's Ghost Pitts	Ching, M.
Jan. 31	Madness and Sorrow Tacoma, Wash	Hagen, D.
Feb. 28	Misper Gly	Lunn, J.
Mar. 1	Conquistador, The San D	Fink, M.
Mar. 8	Wind in the Willows Wilmington, Del	Rutter, J.
Mar. 14	Jackie O Hou	Daugherty, M.
Mar. 17	Promise, The L	Townsend, J.
Apr.	Juniper Tree Munich	Watkins, R.
Apr. 10	Terra Incognita NY	Sierra, R.

Apr. 19	Warchild L	Taylor, R.
Apr. 24	Hotel L	Gough, O.
Apr. 27	Black Water Ph	Duffy, J.
Apr. 29	Three Hermits SP	Paulus, S.
May 9	Roswell Incident Bury St. Edmunds, Engl	Hardy, J.
May 10	Marriages between Zones Heidelberg	Glass, P.
May 16	Balseros Miami Beach	Ashley, R.
June 13	Country of the Blind Ald	Turnage, M.
June 13	Twice through the Heart Ald	Turnage, M.
June 14	Hopper's Wife Long Beach, Calif	Wallace, S.
June 20	Between Two Worlds Ch	Ran, S.
June 23	Hindenburg Berlin	Reich, S.
July	Intimate Immensity NY	Subotnick, M.
July 26	Ashoka's Dream S Fe	Lieberson, P.
July 27	Silver River S Fe	Sheng, B.
Oct. 4	Venus L	Van Rhijn, J.
Oct. 11	Naked Revolution NY	Soldier, D.
Nov.	Sadie Thompson NY	Owen, R.
Nov. 14	My Love Belfast	O'Donnell, K.
Nov. 18	Ethan Frome Morgantown, W Va	Beall, J.
Nov. 29	Amistad Ch	Davis, A.
*	Lilith (prem. 1998 Cooperstown, NY)	Drattell, D.
1998‡		
Feb. 27	Alley Wellington, NZ	Body, J.
Mar.	Hansel and Gretel Hart	Bruce, N.
Mar. 7	Coyote Tales Kansas City	Mollicone, H.
Mar. 7	Redwall Abbey Wilmington, Del	Swensson, E.
Mar. 12	Down Here on Earth Tor	Wiens, R.
Mar. 13	Little Women Hou	Adamo, M.
Apr. 15	Monsters of Grace LA	Glass, P.
Apr. 23	Elsewhereless Tor	Sharman, R.
May 12	Peony Pavilion L	Tan Dun
June 26	Hey Persephone! Ald	Gribbin, D.
July 21	Angel Magick L	Harle, J.
Sept. 11	Black Swan Swarthmore, Pa	Whitman, T.
Sept. 15	Pied Piper Norfolk, Va	Barab, S.
Sept. 19	Streetcar Named Desire SF	Previn, A.
Oct. 30	Bacchae, The Cam, Mass	Harper, W.
Nov. 11	Eric Hermannson's Soul Omaha	Larsen, L.
Nov. 12	Ravenshead NY	Mackey, S.
Dec. 9	Fantastic Mr. Fox LA	Picker, T.

‡1998 operas (not included in A–Z section or in other appendixes).

Selective Bibliography

ANTHOLOGIES AND CATALOGS

GENERAL

The Ballad Opera: A Collection of 171 Original Texts of Musical Plays. Edited by Walter Rubsamen. New York: Garland, 1974. 29 vols.

British Museum, The. *Catalogue of Manuscript Music in the British Museum*. Vol. 2: *Secular Vocal Music*. Edited by Augustus Hughes-Hughes. London: Trustees of the British Museum, 1908. xxvi, 961 pp. Repr. ed. London: British Museum, 1966.

_____. *Catalogue of Printed Music in the British Museum*. 2 vols. Edited by William Barclay Squire. London: Trustees of the British Museum, 1912.

Catalog of the Opera Collections in the Music Libraries: University of California, Berkeley/University of California, Los Angeles. Boston: G. K. Hall, 1983. viii, 697 pp.

Faber Music. *Opera Catalogue. Operas and Stage Works*. London: Faber Music, Faber-Curwen, 1980.

_____. *Opera Catalogue Supplement*. January 1984.

Fuld, James. *The Book of World-Famous Libretti: The Musical Theater from 1598 to Today*. 4th ed., rev. and enlarged. Foreword by Patrick J. Smith. New York: Pendragon Press, 1994. xxxviii, 363 pp.

G. Schirmer and Associated Music Publishers. *Opera & Ballet Catalogue*. Edited by Margaret Ross Griffel. New York: G. Schirmer and Associated Music Publishers, 1988. viii, 183 pp.

Royal College of Music. *Catalogue of Printed Music in the Library of the Royal College of Music*. Edited by William Barclay Squire. London: Royal College of Music, 1909. 368 pp.

Sonneck, Oscar George Theodore. *Catalogue of Opera Librettos Printed before 1800*. 3 vols. Washington, D.C.: Library of Congress, 1914. Repr. New York: Burt Franklin, 1967. 1,674 pp.

_____. *Dramatic Music: Catalogue of Full Scores in the Collection of the Library of Congress*. Washington, D.C.: Library of Congress, 1908; 2d rev. ed, 1917.

Wolff, Barbara Mahrenholz. *Music Manuscripts at Harvard. A Catalogue of Music Manuscripts from the 14th to the 20th Centuries in the Houghton Library at the Eda Kuhn Loeb Music Library*. Cambridge, Mass.: Harvard University Library, 1992. xx, 245 pp.

Wood, David A. *Music in Harvard Libraries: A Catalogue of Early Printed Music and Books on Music in the Houghton Library and the Eda Kuhn Loeb Music Library*. Cambridge, Mass.: Harvard University Press, 1980. xiv, 306 pp.

BY COUNTRY

England

Bradley, Ian, ed. *The Complete Annotated Gilbert and Sullivan*. New York: Oxford University Press, 1996. 1,197 pp.

A Collection of the Most Esteemed Farces and Entertainments Performed on the British Stage. 6 vols. Edinburgh: C. Elliot, 1786–88.

Hunter, David. *Opera and Song Books Published in England, 1703–1736. A Descriptive Bibliography*. New York: Oxford University Press, 1998. 592 pp.

Inchbald, Elizabeth, comp. *A Collection of Farces and Other Afterpieces*. 7 vols. London: Longman et al., 1809. Repr. ed. Hildesheim and New York: Georg Olms, 1969.

Ledbetter, Steven, and Percy M. Young, eds. *W. S. Gilbert–Arthur Sullivan, The Operas, a Critical Edition*. 13 vols. projected. Williamstown, Mass.: Broude Brothers, 1994–.

The London Stage: 1660–1800. A Calendar of Plays, Entertainments & Afterpieces with Artists, Box Receipts, and Contemporary Comment. 5 volumes in 11. Carbondale, Ill.: Southern Illinois University Press, 1960–61. Vol. 1: 1660–1770, ed. William van Lennap. Vol. 2: 1700–1729, ed. Emmett L. Avery (2 parts). Vol. 3: 1729–1747, ed. Arthur W. Scouten (3 parts). Vol. 4: 1747–1776, ed. G. W. Stone (3 parts). Vol. 5: 1776–1800, ed. Charles Beecher Hogan (3 parts).

MacMillan, Dougald, comp. *Catalogue of the Larpent Plays in the Huntington Library.* San Marino, Calif., 1939. xv, 442 pp.

Modern British Drama. Vol. 4: *Comedies.* Vol. 5: *Operas and Farces.* London: William Miller, 1811.

Rubsamen, Walter, ed. *The Ballad Opera: A Collection of 171 Original Texts of Musical Plays.* Vols. 1–27. New York: Garland, 1974.

Stedman, Jane W. *Gilbert before Sullivan: Six Comic Plays.* Chicago: University of Chicago Press, 1967. xii, 270 pp. Includes *Ages Ago* and *Happy Arcadia.* With music.

United States (including Colonial America)

Dennison, Sam, and Martha Furman Schleifer, eds. *Three Centuries of American Music: A Collection of Sacred and Secular Music.* New York: G. K. Hall & Co., 1990. Vol. 5: *The Volunteers* (Reinagle), *The Ethiop* (Taylor), *The Enterprise* (Clifton), and *Robin Hood* (De Koven); Vol. 6: *Iolan (The Pipe of Desire)* (Converse) and *Naughty Marietta* (Herbert).

Graziano, John, general ed. *Recent Researches in American Music.* Madison, Wisc.: A-R Editions. Vols. 3–4: Andrew Barton's *The Disappointment*, ed. Jerold C. Graue and Judith Layng (1976). Vols. 9–10: George F. Root's *The Haymakers*, ed. Dennis R. Martin (1984). Vols. 13–14: *Pelissier's Columbian Melodies*, ed. Karl Kroeger, with music from Pelissier's operas composed between 1794 and 1813 (1984). Vol. 25: Will Marion Cook's *In Dahomey*, ed. Thomas J. Riis (1996).

Hummel, David. *The Collector's Guide to the American Musical Theatre.* Vol. 1: *The Shows.* Vol. 2: *Index.* 2d printing. Metuchen, N.J.: Scarecrow Press, 1984.

Krasker, Tommy, and Robert Kimball. *Catalog of the American Musical: Musicals of Irving Berlin, George & Ira Gershwin, Cole Porter, Richard Rodgers & Lorenz Hart.* Washington, D.C.: National Institute for Opera and Musical Theater, 1988. xv, 442 pp.

Root, Deane L., ed. *Nineteenth-Century American Musical Theater.* 16 vols. New York: Garland, 1994.

Rubsamen, Walter, ed. *The Ballad Opera: A Collection of 171 Original Texts of Musical Plays.* New York: Garland, 1974. Vol. 28: *American Ballad Operas.*

Vernon, Grenville, comp. *Yankee Doodle-Doo: A Collection of Songs of the Early American Stage.* New York: Payson & Clarke, [1927]. 165 pp.

BIBLIOGRAPHIES

Grout, Donald. *A Short History of Opera.* 2d ed. New York: Columbia University Press, 1965, 585–768. 3d ed., with Hermine Weigel Williams. New York: Columbia University Press, 1988, 731–825 (abridged and updated).

Marco, Guy A. *Opera: A Research and Information Guide.* New York and London: Garland, 1984. xvii, 373 pp.

Sonneck, Oscar G. T. *A Bibliography of Early Secular American Music.* Rev. and enlarged by William Treat Upton. Washington, D.C.: Library of Congress, Music Division, 1945. xvi, 616 pp. Repr. ed. New York: Da Capo, 1964.

Wildbihler, Hubert, and Sonja Völklein. *The Musical: An International Annotated Bibliography/Eine internationale annotierte Bibliographie.* Foreword by Thomas Siedhoff. Munich and New York: Saur, 1986. 320 pp.

Wolfe, Richard J. *Secular Music in America 1801–1825. A Bibliography.* Introduction by Carleton Sprague Smith. Vol. 3. New York: New York Public Library, 1964.

DISCOGRAPHIES

Blyth, Alan. *Opera on CD: The Essential Guide to the Best CD Recordings of 100 Operas.* London: Kyles Cathie, 1992. viii, 183 pp.

―――, ed. *Opera on Record.* 3 vols. Discographies compiled by Malcolm Walker. London: Hutchinson, 1979, 1983, 1984. 663, 399, 375 pp.

Marco, Guy, ed. *Encyclopedia of Recorded Sound in the United States.* With Frank Andrews. New York: Garland, 1993. xlix, 910 pp.

Wechsler, Bert. "A Native Harvest." *ON* LIII (Aug. 1988), 30–32, 46.

DICTIONARIES AND ENCYCLOPEDIAS

Anderson, James. *Bloomsbury Dictionary of Opera and Operetta.* London, 1984. 2d ed. London: Bloomsbury, 1989. New York: Wing Books, 1993. ix, 691 pp.

Ewen, David. *The New Encyclopedia of the Opera.* 3d ed. New York: Hill and Wang, 1971. 759 pp. Includes terms, cities, houses, plots, characters, singers.

Hamilton, David. *The Metropolitan Opera Encyclopedia.* New York: Simon & Schuster, 1987. 416 pp. Listing by title; includes operas, performers, terms; two dozen essays on most famous works; brief plots.

The Mellen Opera Reference Index. Compiled by Charles H. Parsons. Lewiston, N.Y., and Queenston, Ont.: Edwin Mellen Press, 1986–. Vols. 1–4: *Opera Composers and Their Works* (1986). Vols. 5–6: *Opera Librettists and Their Works* (1987). Vols. 7–8: *Opera Premieres* (1989).

The New Grove Dictionary of Opera. Edited by Stanley Sadie. 4 vols. London, New York: Macmillan Press, 1992, 1994 (repr. with corrections). 5,424 pp. Covers 1,800 operas.

The Norton/Grove Dictionary of Women Composers. Edited by Julie Anne Sadie and Rhian Samuel. New York and London: W. W. Norton, 1994, 1995. xliii, 548 pp.

Orrey, Leslie. *The Encyclopedia of Opera.* New York: Scribner's, 1976. 376 pp. Listing by title, with operas, performers, terms; very brief plots.

Osborne, Charles. *The Dictionary of the Opera.* New York: Simon & Schuster, 1983. 382 pp. Listing by title, with operas, performers, terms; brief plots.

Pallay, Steven G., comp. *Cross Index Title Guide to Opera and Operetta.* New York: Greenwood Press, 1989. viii, 214 pp.

Pipers Enzyklopädie des Musiktheaters. Edited by Carl Dahlhaus. Munich: Piper, 1986–97. Vol. 1: *Abbiatini-Donizetti.* Vol. 2: *Donizetti-Henze.* Vol. 3: *Henze-Massine.* Vol. 4, *Massine-Piccinni.* Vol. 5: *Piccinni-Spontini.* Vol. 6: *Spontini-Zumsteeg.* Vol. 7: *Register.* Detailed coverage of operas, operettas, musicals, ballets, with information on the premiere, plot, and stylistic elements.

Rosenthal, Harold, and John Warrack, eds. *The Concise Oxford Dictionary of Opera.* 2d ed. London: Oxford University Press, 1979. 561 pp. On operas, composers, performers, cities.

The Simon & Schuster Book of the Opera. New York: Simon & Schuster, 1978. An English translation of *L'opera: repertorio della lirica dal 1597,* edited by Riccardo Mezzanote. Milan: Arnoldo Monadori Editore, 1977. 511 pp. Listings by year, then by title; brief plots.

Stieger, Franz. *Opernlexikon/Opera Catalogue* . . . . Part I (3 vols.): *Titelkatalog.* Part II (2 vols.): *Komponisten.* Part III (3 vols.): *Librettisten.* Part IV (2 vols.): *Nachträge.* Tutzing: Hans Schneider, 1975–83. Completed in 1934. Lists some 50,000 theater works.

Towers, John. *Dictionary Catalog of Operas and Operettas Which Have Been Performed on the Public Stage.* 2 vols. Morgantown, W. Va.: Acme, 1910. 1,045 pp. Repr. ed. New York: Da Capo, 1967. Lists over 28,000 works, with name of composer, nationality.

Warrack, John, and Ewan West. *The Concise Oxford Dictionary of Opera.* Oxford and New York: Oxford University Press. xiv, 571 pp. Updating and shortening of *The Oxford Dictionary of Opera.*

―――. *The Oxford Dictionary of Opera.* Oxford and New York: Oxford University Press, 1992. xviii, 782 pp. Listing by title, with operas, performers, cities, brief plots.

ICONOGRAPHY

Beauvert, Thierry. *Opera Houses of the World.* Photographs by Jacques Moatti and Florian Kleinefenn. New York: Vendome Press, 1996. 277 pp.

PERFORMANCE INFORMATION

GENERAL

British Broadcasting Corporation. *BBC Music Library. Choral and Opera Catalogue.* Vol. 1: *Composers.* Vol. 2: *Titles.* London: BBC, 1967.

Central Opera Service. *Directory of Contemporary Operas and Music Theater Works and North American Premieres, 1980–1989.* New York: Central Opera Service, 1990. Central Opera Service Directory/Bulletin, vol. 30, nos. 2–4. viii, 325 pp.

Citron, Stephen. *The Musical: From the Inside Out.* London: R. Hodder & Stoughton, 1991. 256 pp.

Eaton, Quaintance. *Opera Production. A Handbook.* Minneapolis: University of Minnesota Press, 1961. ix, 265 pp. Repr. New York: Da Capo, 1974. By title. Includes brief plots, major and minor roles, orchestral forces needed, available performance materials.

———. *Opera Production II. A Handbook.* Minneapolis: University of Minnesota Press, 1974. xx, 347 pp. Same arrangement as vol. 1.

Loewenberg, Alfred. *Annals of Opera 1597–1940.* 3d rev. ed. Totowa, N.J.: Rowman and Littlefield, 1978. xxv pp., 1,756 columns. Organized by year, with title, composer, librettist, city and date of first performance, significant subsequent performances.

Musical Woman, The: An International Perspective. Edited by Judith Lang Zaimont, Catherine Overhauser, and Jane Gottlieb. 3 vols. I: 1983. II: 1984–1985. III: 1986–1990. Westport, Conn.: Greenwood Press, 1984, 1986, 1991. Contains extensive brief listings on first or subsequent performances of the works, including operas, of women composers.

Northouse, Cameron. *Twentieth Century Opera in England and the United States.* Boston: G. K. Hall, 1976. viii, 400 pp. Listings include composers, titles, first performances, literary sources.

"Operatic Premières, 1939–1954." In *Opera Annual* I (1954–55), 168–78. An update of Loewenberg (see above).

Rich, Maria. *Who's Who in Opera: An International Biographical Directory of Singers, Conductors, Directors, Designers, and Administrators.* New York: Arno Press, 1976. xxi, 684 pp.

Summers, W. Franklin. *Operas in One Act. A Production Guide.* Lanham, Md., and London: Scarecrow Press, 1997. xiii, 383 pp. Similar in format to the Eaton volumes (see above), with some overlapping of operas discussed.

Suttcliffe, Tom. *Believing in Opera.* Princeton, N.J.: Princeton University Press, 1996. xv, 464 pp. About opera directors after World War II.

BY COUNTRY

Australia

Holmes, Robyn, ed. *Through the Opera Glass: A Chronological Register of Operas Performed in South Australia, 1836 to 1988.* Adelaide: Friends of the State Opera of South Australia, 1991. 369 pp.

England

Nicoll, Allardyce. *A History of English Drama, 1660–1900.* 6 vols. Cambridge: University Press, 1952–59. Information on plays produced or printed in England.

White, Eric Walter, comp. *A Register of First Performances of English Operas and Semi-Operas: From the 16th Century to 1980.* London: Society for Theatre Research, 1983. vi, 130 pp.

United States

Borroff, Edith. *American Operas: A Checklist.* Edited by J. Bunker Clark. Detroit Studies in Music Bibliography, no. 69. Warren, Mich.: Harmonie Park Press, 1992. xxiv, 334 pp. Listings for operas, operettas, music-theater works, some musicals, radio plays.

Central Opera Service. *Directory of American Contemporary Operas.* New York: Central Opera Service, 1967. 79 pp.

_____. *Directory of Contemporary Operas and Music Theater Works and North American Premieres, 1980–1989.* New York: Central Opera Service, 1990.

Drummond, Andrew H. *American Opera Librettos.* Metuchen, N.J.: Scarecrow Press, 1973. v, 277 pp.

Hipsher, Edward Ellsworth. *American Opera and Its Composers.* Philadelphia: Theodore Presser, [1934]. xi, 13–478 pp. Repr. ed. New York: Da Capo, 1978. Brief plots and descriptions of numerous (and now forgotten) operas from the later nineteenth and early twentieth century. Includes works by Bimboni, Bristow, Cadman, Chadwick, Converse, Damrosch, De Koven, Freeman, Freer, Hadley, Moore, Parker, and Pratt, and the early operas of George Antheil, Louis Gruenberg, Deems Taylor, and Virgil Thomson.

Kornick, Rebecca Hodell. *Recent American Opera: A Production Guide.* New York: Columbia University Press, 1991. xvii, 352 pp. A continuation of Eaton's books (see above), with much the same format and including reviews.

Mattfeld, Julius. *Handbook of American Operatic Premieres, 1731–1962.* Detroit Studies in Music Bibliography, no. 5. Detroit: Information Service, 1963. 142 pp.

PLOTS

Cross, Milton, and Karl Kohrs. *More Stories of the Great Operas.* Garden City, N.Y.: Doubleday, 1971. 752 pp. Rev. and expanded by Karl Kohrs. Garden City, N.Y.: Doubleday, 1980. xi, 802 pp. Listing by title.

Ewen, David. *The Book of European Light Opera.* New York: Holt, Rinehart, and Winston, 1962. xiii, 297 pp. Repr. ed. Westport, Conn.: Greenwood Press, 1977. Listing by title.

Harewood, Earl of, ed. *The New Kobbé's Complete Opera Book.* New York: G. P. Putnam's Sons, 1976. Rev. as *The Definitive Kobbé's Opera Book.* New York: G. P. Putnam's Sons, 1987. xv, 1,404 pp. Detailed plots, some performance information, musical descriptions; listed by nationality and, chronologically, by composer.

_____, and Antony Peattie, eds. *The New Kobbé's Opera Book.* New York: Putnam, 1997. xviii, 1,012 pp. This edition covers almost 500 works and includes operas by composers such as Peter Maxwell Davies, Judith Weir, and Dominick Argento.

Lubbock, Mark Hugh. *The Complete Book of Light Opera.* With an American section by David Ewen. London: Putnam, [1962]. xviii, 953 pp. About 300 works.

The Victor Book of Operas. 13th ed. Rev. by Henry W. Simon. New York: Simon & Schuster, 1968. 475 pp. Includes about 120 works.

VIDEOS

Blyth, Alan. *Opera on Video: The Essential Guide.* London: Kyle Cathie, 1995. x, 246 pp.

Levine, Robert. *Guide to Opera and Dance on Videocassette.* Consumer Reports Books. Mount Vernon, N.Y.: Consumers Union, 1989. vii, 213 pp.

HISTORY

GENERAL

Moss, Harold. "Popular Music and the Ballad Opera." *JAMS* XXVI (1973), 365–82.

Porter, Susan L. "English-American Interaction in American Musical Theater at the Turn of the Nineteenth Century. *AM* IV (Spring 1986), 6–19.

By Country

Australia

Bebbington, Warren, ed. *The Oxford Companion to Australian Music*. Melbourne: Oxford University Press, 1997. xvi, 608 pp.

Callaway, Frank, and David Tunley, eds. *Australian Composition in the Twentieth Century*. Melbourne and New York: Oxford University Press, 1978. x, 248 pp.

Gyger, Alison. *Opera for the Antipodes: Opera in Australia 1881–1939*. Sydney: Currency Press and Pellinor, 1990. viii, 364 pp.

Holmes, Robyn. *Through the Looking Glass: A Chronological Register of Opera Performed in South Australia, 1836 to 1988*. Adelaide: Friends of the State Opera of South Australia, 1991. 369 pp.

Canada

Encyclopedia of Music in Canada. Edited by Helmut Kallmann, Gilles Potvin, and Kenneth Winters. 2d ed. Toronto and Buffalo: University of Toronto Press, 1992. 1,524 pp.

MacMillan, Keith, and John Beckwith, eds. *Contemporary Canadian Composers*. Toronto and New York: Oxford University Press, 1975. xxiv, 248 pp.

England

Altieri, Joanne. *The Theatre of Praise: The Panegyric Tradition in Seventeenth-Century English Drama*. Newark, Del.: University of Delaware Press, 1986. 240 pp.

Biddlecombe, George. *English Opera from 1834 to 1864 with Particular Reference to the Works of Michael Balfe*. New York and London: Garland, 1994. xiii, 351 pp.

Carr, Bruce. "The First All-Sung English 19th-Century Opera." *MT* CXV (1974), 125–26.

Fenner, Theodore. *Opera in London: Views of the Press, 1785–1830*. Carbondale: Southern Illinois University Press, 1994. xvi, 788 pp.

Fiske, Roger. *English Theatre Music in the Eighteenth Century*. Oxford: Oxford University Press, 1973. xv, 684 pp.; 2d ed. Oxford and New York: Oxford University Press, 1986. xvi, 684 pp. Descriptions and analyses of numerous stage works.

Foreman, Lewis. *From Parry to Britten: British Music in Letters 1900–1945*. New York: Amadeus Press, 1988. 232 pp. Musical examples.

Gänzl, Kurt. *The British Musical Theatre*. Vol. 1: 1865–1914. Vol. 2: 1915–1984. Basingstoke, Engl.: Macmillan, 1986.

Gibson, Elizabeth. *The Royal Academy of Music 1719–1728: The Institution and Its Directors*. New York: Garland, 1989. 465 pp.

Schmidgall, Gary. *Shakespeare and Opera*. New York: Oxford University Press, 1990. xii, 394 pp.

Temperley, Nicholas. "The English Romantic Opera." *Victorian Studies* IX (1966), 293–301.

Troost, Linda V. "The Rise of English Comic Opera 1762–1800." Ph.D. diss., University of Pennsylvania, 1985. v, 262 pp.

White, Eric Walter. *A History of English Opera*. London: Faber, 1983. 472 pp.

Ireland

O'Kelly, Eve, ed. *Irish Composers*. Dublin: The Contemporary Music Centre, 1993. 32 pp. 28 composers, including Gerald Barry.

New Zealand

Simpson, Adrienne. *Opera's Farthest Frontier: A History of Professional Opera in New Zealand*. Birkenhead, Auckland, N.Z.: Reed, 1996. 288 pp.

Scotland

Oliver, Cordelia. *It Is a Curious Story: The Tale of Scottish Opera, 1962–1987*. Edinburgh: Mainstream Publishing, 1987. 199 pp.

Wilson, Conrad. *Scottish Opera—The First Ten Years*. London: Collins, 1972. [8], 168 pp.

United States

Block, Adrienne Fried, and Carol Neuls-Bates, comps. and eds. *Women in American Music. A Bibliography of Music and Literature.* Westport, Conn.: Greenwood Press, 1979. xxxvi, 302 pp.

Bordman, Gerald Martin. *American Musical Theatre. A Chronicle.* 2d ed. New York and Oxford: Oxford University Press, 1992. viii, 206 pp.

_____. *American Operetta: from H.M.S. Pinafore to Sweeney Todd.* New York: Oxford University Press, 1981. ix, 821 pp.

Cheatham, Wallace. *Dialogues on Opera and the African-American Experience.* Lanham, Md.: Scarecrow Press, 1997. xvii, 185 pp.

Crawford, John C., and Dorothy L. Crawford. *Expressionism in Twentieth-Century Music.* Bloomington, Ind.: Indiana University Press, 1993. xv, 331 pp.

Davis, Ronald L. *The History of Opera in the American West.* Englewood Cliffs, N.J.: Prentice Hall, 1965. xii, 178 pp.

Dizikes, John. *Opera in America: A Cultural History.* New Haven: Yale University Press, 1993. xi, 611 pp. Through 1977.

Engel, Lehman. *The American Musical Theater.* Rev. ed. New York: Macmillan, 1975. xx, 266 pp.

Ewen, David. *New Complete Book of the American Musical Theater.* New York: Holt, Rinehart, and Winston, [1970]. xxv, 800 pp.

Green, Stanley. *Broadway Musicals, Show by Show.* 3d ed. Milwaukee: H. Leonard, 1990. xi, 372 pp.

Hischak, Thomas S. *Stage It with Music: An Encyclopedic Guide to the American Musical Theatre.* Westport, Conn.: Greenwood Press, 1993. viii, 341 pp.

Hummel, David. *The Collector's Guide to the American Musical Theater.* Metuchen, N.J.: Scarecrow Press, 1985, 2 vols. Repr. with additions and corrections.

Layng, Judith. "Black Images in Opera." *OJ* VII (Winter 1969), 29–32.

Lehrman, Leonard. "What Is Jewish Opera?" *OJ* XXIX (June 1, 1996), 56–61.

Ottenberg, June C. *Opera Odyssey: Toward a History of Opera in Nineteenth-Century America.* Westport, Conn.: Greenwood Press, 1994. xi, 203 pp.

Porter, Susan L. *With an Air Debonair: Musical Theatre in America, 1785–1815.* Washington, D.C.: Smithsonian Institution Press, 1991. xii, 631 pp. Includes invaluable "Checklist of Musical Entertainments, 1785–1815," 425–500.

Preston, Katherine. *Opera on the Road: Traveling Opera Troupes in the United States, 1825–60.* Urbana: University of Illinois Press, 1993. xvii, 479 pp.

Rich, Maria. "Opera USA—Perspective: American Opera after the Bicentennial." *OQ* I (Autumn 1983), 90–113.

Riis, Thomas L., *More Than Just Minstrel Shows: The Rise of Black Musical Theatre at the Turn of the Century.* Institute for Studies in American Music Monographs, no. 33. Brooklyn, N.Y.: Institute for Studies in American Music, 1992. 62 pp.

Root, Deane L. *American Popular Stage Music, 1860–1880.* Ann Arbor, Mich.: UMI Research Press, 1989. x, 284 pp.

Rorem, Ned. "In Search of American Opera." *ON* LVI (July 1991), 8–10, 12, 14–17, 44.

Salzman, Eric. "Wither American Music Theater?" *MQ* (Apr. 1979), repr. *MQ* LXXV (Winter 1991), 235–47.

Salzman, Jack, David Lionel Smith, and Cornel West, eds. *Encyclopedia of African-American Culture and History.* Vol. 4: *Mia–Ryd.* New York: Simon & Schuster/Macmillan, 1996.

Smith, Eric Ledell. *Blacks in Opera: An Encyclopedia of People and Companies, 1873–1993.* Jefferson, N.C.: McFarland, 1995. xi, 236 pp.

Sonneck, Oscar G. T. *Early Concert-Life in America, 1731–1800.* Leipzig: Breitkopf & Härtel, 1907. 338 pp.

_____. "Early American Operas. *SIMG* VI (1904–6), 428–95.

_____. *Early Opera in America.* New York: G. Schirmer; Boston: Boston Music Co., [1915]. viii, 230 pp.

Stempel, Larry. "The Musical Play Expands." *AM* IX (Winter 1992), 136–69.

Tick, Judith. *American Women Composers before 1870.* Ann Arbor, Mich.: UMI Press, 1983. 302 pp.

Virga, Patricia H. *The American Opera to 1790.* Studies in Musicology, no. 61. Ann Arbor, Mich.: UMI Research Press, 1982. xix, 393 pp.

Woll, Allen. *Black Musical Theatre: From Coontown to Dreamgirls.* Baton Rouge: Louisiana State University, 1989. xiv, 301 pp.

Wynne, Peter. "Return of the Native." *ON* LX (Jan. 6, 1996), 28–30. On works about Native Americans.

Zietz, Karyl Lynn. *Opera Companies and Houses of the United States: A Comprehensive, Illustrated Reference.* Jefferson, N.C.: McFarland, 1994. xv, 335 pp.

Wales

Fawkes, Richard. *Welsh National Opera.* London: J. MacRae, 1986. x, 368 pp.

CITIES AND FESTIVALS

Aldeburgh

Blythe, Ronald, ed. *Aldeburgh Anthology.* London: Faber, 1972. xiii, 436 pp.

Boston

Bishop, Cardell. *Boston National Opera Company and Boston Theatre Opera Company.* [Santa Monica, Ca.]: C. Bishop, [1981]. vii, 41 leaves. Includes "Repertoire 1915–1918."

Central City, Colorado

Johnson, Charles A. *Opera in the Rockies: The History of the Central City Opera House Association, 1932–1992.* [Central City, Colo.]: The Association, 1992. ix, 123 pp.

Young, Allen. *Opera in Central City.* Denver: Spectographics, 1993. 117 pp.

Chicago

Cassidy, Claudia. *Lyric Opera of Chicago.* Foreword by Saul Bellow; recollections by Carol Fox; graphic design by R. D. Scudellari. [Chicago]: The Opera, 1979. 233 pp.

Davis, Ronald. *Opera in Chicago.* New York: Appleton-Century, 1966. xi, 393 pp.

Lyric Opera of Chicago. *Twenty Years: A Pictorial Souvenir Album to Celebrate the Twentieth Anniversary of the Founding of Lyric Opera in 1954.* With a specially written foreword by Claudia Cassidy. [Chicago, 1974]. 1 vol. (not paginated) of illus.

Dublin

Walsh, T. J. *Opera in Dublin: 1705–1797: The Social Scene.* Dublin: A. Figgis, 1973. xv, 386 pp.

_____. *Opera in Dublin: 1798–1820. Frederick Jones and the Crow Street Theatre.* Oxford: Oxford University Press, 1993. xiv, 294 pp.

Glyndebourne

Hughes, Spike. *Glyndebourne: A History of the Festival Opera Founded in 1934 by Audrey and John Christie.* Devon: Newton Abbott, 1981; North Pomfret, Vt.: David and Charles, 1981. 388 pp. Revision of 1965 edition (London, Methuen).

London

General

Fenner, Theodore. *Opera in London: Views of the Press, 1785–1830.* Carbondale, Ill.: Southern Illinois University Press, 1994. xvi, 788 pp.

Covent Garden

Chapman, Clive. "'Sir, It Will Not Do!' John Rich and Covent Garden's Early Years." *MT* CXXIII (1982), 831–35.

Donaldson, Frances Lonsdale. *The Royal Opera House in the Twentieth Century.* London: Weidenfeld and Nicolson, 1988. xvii, 238 pp.

Handley, Ellenor, and Martin Kinna. *Royal Opera House Covent Garden: A History*. West Wickham, Engl.: Fourlance Books, 1978. 64 pp.

Hume, Robert D. "Covent Garden Theatre in 1732. *MT* CXXIII (1982), 823–26.

Langley, Leanne. "'Our Thing Called Opera.' Some Covent Garden Productions of the 1820s through Contemporary Eyes." *MT* CXXIII (1982), 836–38.

Rosenthal, Harold. *Opera at Covent Garden. A Short History*. London: Gollancz, 1967. 192 pp.

_____. *Two Centuries of Opera at Covent Garden*. London: Putnam, 1958. xiv, 849 pp.

Saint, Andrew. "The Three Covent Gardens." *MT* CXXIII (1982), 826–31.

Drury Lane Theatre

Girdham, Jane. *English Opera in Late Eighteenth-Century London: Stephen Storace at Drury Lane*. New York: Clarendon Press, 1997. xiv, 272 pp.

New York

General

Alquist, Karen. *Democracy at the Opera: Music, Theater, and Culture in New York City, 1815–60*. Urbana: University of Illinois Press, 1997. 272 pp.

Cerf, Steven R. "Pioneers on Morningside Heights." *ON* LVI (July 1991), 22–24.

Krehbiel, Henry Edward. *Chapters of Opera: Being Historical and Critical Observations and Records Concerning the Lyric Drama in New York from Its Earliest Days Down to the Present Time*. New York: Holt, 1909. xvii, 435 pp. Repr. ed. New York: Da Capo Press, 1980.

Riis, Thomas L. *Just before Jazz: Black Musical Theater in New York, 1890–1915*. Washington, D.C.: Smithsonian Institution Press, 1989. xxiv, 309 pp.

Zucker, Stefan. "New York Underground: Opera on a Shoestring," *ON* LIII (Jan. 7, 1989), 20–23.

Academy of Music

Cone, John Frederick. *First Rival of the Metropolitan Opera*. New York: Columbia University Press, 1983. On the Academy and James Henry Mapleson, 1830–1901. xvi, 257 pp.

Juilliard School

Gottlieb, Jane, Stephen E. Novak, and Taras Pavlovsky, comps. *Guide to the Juilliard School Archives*. New York: The Juilliard School, 1992. 113 pp.

Manhattan Opera Company

Cone, John F. *Oscar Hammerstein's Manhattan Opera Company*. Norman, Okla.: University of Oklahoma Press, 1966. xvi, 399 pp.

Metropolitan Opera

Annals of the Metropolitan Opera: the Complete Chronicle of Performances and Artists. Edited by Gerald Fitzgerald. 2 vols. Vol. 1: *Chronology, 1883–1985*. Vol. 2: *Tables, 1883–1985*. New York: Metropolitan Opera Guild, and Boston: G. K. Hall, 1989. xxviii, 1,000 pp.; xxvi, 313 pp.

Jackson, Paul. *Saturday Afternoons at the Old Met: The Metropolitan Opera Broadcasts, 1931–1950*. Portland, Oreg.: Amadeus Press, 1992. xvi, 569 pp.

_____. *Sign-Off for the Old Met: The Metropolitan Opera Broadcasts, 1950–1966*. Portland, Oreg.: Amadeus Press, 1997. xv, 644 pp.

Kolodin, Irving. *The Metropolitan Opera, 1883–1966: A Candid History*. 4th ed. New York: A. A. Knopf, 1966. xxi, 762, xlvii pp.

Merkling, Frank, et al. *The Golden Horseshoe: The Life and Times of the Metropolitan Opera House*. Prologue by Eleanor R. Belmont. Epilogue by Anthony A. Bliss. New York: Viking Press, [1965]. 319 pp.

New York City Opera

Drummond, Andrew H. "The New York City Opera." In *American Opera Librettos*. Metuchen, N.J.: Scarecrow Press, 1973.

McKenna, Harold J., ed. *New York City Opera Sings: Stories and Productions of the New York City Opera, 1944–79*. New York: Richard Rosen Press, 1981. xvii, 404 pp.

Montreal
Amtmann, Willy. *Music in Canada 1600–1800*. Cambridge, Ont.: Habitex Books, [1975]. 320 pp.; enlarged as *La musique au Québec 1600–1875*. Montreal: Les Editions de l'Homme, 1976. 420 pp.

Philadelphia
Albrecht, Otto E. "Opera in Philadelphia, 1800–1830," *JAMS* XXXII (1979), 499–515.

San Francisco
Bloomfield, Arthur. *Fifty Years of the San Francisco Opera*. San Francisco: San Francisco Book Co., [1972]. xi, 450 pp.

Sydney, Australia
Hubble, Ava. *More than an Opera House*. Sydney and New York: Lansdowne, 1983. 176 pp.

Tanglewood (Lenox, Mass.)
Pincus, Andrew L. *Scenes from Tanglewood*. Boston: Northeastern University Press, 1989. xii, 287 pp.

Toronto
Morey, Carl. "Pre-Confederation Opera in Toronto." *Opera in Canada* X/3 (1969), 13–15.
Remembered Moments of the Canadian Opera Company: 1950–1975. N.p.: A. Dunhill, [1976?]. [124] pp., chiefly illustrations.

COMPOSERS
(see also individual works in A–Z section)

ApIvor, Denis
Wright, David C. F. "Denis ApIvor." *MR* L (1989), 53–63.

Arne, Michael
Parkinson, John A. *An Index to the Vocal Works of Thomas Augustine Arne and Michael Arne*. Detroit: Detroit Information Coordinators, 1972. 82 pp.

Arne, Thomas A.
Adas, Jane. "Arne's Progress: An English Composer in Eighteenth-Century London." Ph.D. diss., Rutgers University, 1993. x, 524 leaves.
Parkinson, John A. *An Index to the Vocal Works of Thomas Augustine Arne and Michael Arne*. Detroit: Detroit Information Coordinators, 1972. 82 pp.

Attwood, Thomas
Oldman, C. B. "Attwood's Dramatic Works." *MT* CVI (1966), 23–27.

Balfe, Michael
Barrett. William Alexander. *Balfe: His Life and Works*. London: Remington, 1882. 313 pp.
Kenney, Charles L. *A Memoir of Michael William Balfe*. London: Tinsley, 1875. x, 309 pp.

Barber, Samuel
Hennessee, Don A. *Samuel Barber: A Bio-Bibliography*. Westport, Conn.: Greenwood Press, 1985. xii, 404 pp.
Heyman, Barbara B. *Samuel Barber: The Composer and His Music*. New York and Oxford: Oxford University Press, 1992. xviii, 586 pp.

Beach, Amy
Block, Adrienne Fried. *Amy Beach, Passionate Victorian*. New York: Oxford University Press, 1998. xiii, 409 pp.

Benjamin, Arthur
Boustead, Alan. "Arthur Benjamin and Opera." *Opera* XV (1964), 709–14.

Bergsma, William
Shulsky, Abraham. "The Music of William Bergsma." *Juilliard Review* III (Spring 1956), 12–26.

Bernstein, Leonard
Burton, Humphrey. *Leonard Bernstein*. New York: Doubleday, 1994. xiv, 594 pp.

Fluegel, Jane, ed. *Bernstein Remembered*. Introduction by Donal Henahan. Preface by Isaac Stern. New York: Carroll & Graf, 1991. 160 pp.

Gottlieb, Jack. *Leonard Bernstein: A Complete Catalogue of His Works:* New York: Jalni Publications/Boosey & Hawkes, 1988. 95 pp.

Secrest, Meryle. *Leonard Bernstein: A Life*. New York: A. A. Knopf, 1994. xv, 471 pp.

Bishop, Henry Rowley
Corder, Frederick. "The Works of Sir Henry Rowley Bishop." *MQ* IV (1918), 78–97.

Blitzstein, Marc
Gordon, Eric A. *Mark the Music. The Life and Work of Marc Blitzstein*. New York: St. Martin's Press, 1989. xviii, 605 pp.

Boughton, Rutland
Hurd, Michael. "Rutland Boughton, 1878–1960." *MT* CXIX (1978), 31–33.

_____. *Rutland Boughton and the Glastonbury Festivals*. Oxford: Clarendon Press, 1994. xiv, 415 pp.

Boyce, William
Taylor, Eric. "William Boyce and the Theatre." *MR* XIV (1953), 275–87.

Brian, Havergal
Schaarwächter, Jürgen, ed. *HB. Aspects of Havergal Brian*. Edited from the Havergal Brian newsletters. Aldershot and Brookfield, Vt., 1997. xii, 424 pp.

Bridge, Frank
Little, Karen R. *Frank Bridge: A Bio-Bibliography*. New York: Greenwood Press, 1991. xii, 263 pp.

Britten, Benjamin
Corse, Sandra. *Opera and the Uses of Language: Mozart, Verdi, and Britten*. Rutherford, N.J.: Fairleigh Dickinson University Press, 1986. 168 pp.

Evans, Peter. *The Music of Benjamin Britten*. London: Clarendon Press; New York: Oxford University Press, 1996. vii, 564 pp.

Herbert, David, ed. *The Operas of Benjamin Britten. The Complete Librettos*. New York: Columbia University Press, 1979. xxxi, 382 pp. Rev. ed. London: Herbert Press, 1989. 384 pp.

Howard, Patricia. *The Operas of Benjamin Britten*. London: Praeger, 1969. 236 pp.

Kendall, Alan. *Benjamin Britten*. London: Macmillan, 1973. 112 pp.

Mitchell, Donald. *Britten and Auden in the Thirties: The Year 1936*. London: Faber, 1981. 176 pp.

_____. "Britten's 'Dramatic' Legacy." *Opera* XXVIII (1977), 127–30.

Mitchell, Donald, and John Evans. *Benjamin Britten 1913–1976: Pictures from a Life*. London: Faber, 1978. viii, 193 pp.

Parsons, Charles H. *A Benjamin Britten Discography*. Lewiston, N.Y.: The Edwin Mellen Press, 1990. 247 pp.

White, Eric Walter. *Benjamin Britten: His Life and Operas*. 2d ed. London: Faber, 1983. 322 pp.

Whittall, Arnold. *The Music of Britten and Tippett. Studies in Themes and Techniques*. Cambridge and New York: Cambridge University Press, 1982. vii, 314 pp.

Cage, John
Fetterman, William. *John Cage's Theatre Pieces*. Amsterdam: Overseas Publishing Association, 1996. xviii, 282 pp.

Carr, Benjamin
Siek, Stephen. "Benjamin Carr's Theatrical Career." *AM* XI (Summer 1993), 158–84.

Chadwick, George W.
Yellin, Victor Fell. *Chadwick: Yankee Composer*. Washington, D.C.: Smithsonian Institution Press, 1990. xvi, 238 pp.

Delius, Frederick
Klein, John W. "Delius as a Musical Dramatist." *MR* XXII (1961), 294–301.

Redwood, Christopher. *A Delius Companion*. London: J. Calder, 1976. 270 pp.

_____. "Delius in the Opera House." *MT* CXXV (June 1984), 319–21.

Dibdin, Charles
Fahrner, Robert. *The Theatre Career of Charles Dibdin the Elder (1745–1814)*. New York: Lang, 1989. 241 pp.

Sear, H. G. "Charles Dibdin: 1745–1814." *ML* XXVI (1945), 61–65.

Elgar, Edward
Anderson, Robert. *Elgar*. London: Dent, 1993. xv, 493 pp.

Kent Christopher. *Edward Elgar: A Guide to Research*. Garland Composer Resource Manuals. New York: Garland, 1993. xvii, 523 pp.

Engel, Lehman
Engel, Lehman. *This Bright Day: An Autobiography*. New York: Macmillan, 1974. xiv, 366 pp.

Finney, Ross Lee
Borroff, Edith. *Three American Composers*. Lanham, Md.: University Press of America, 1986. 289 pp.

Finney, Ross Lee. *Profile of a Lifetime: A Musical Autobiography*. New York: C. F. Peters, 1992. 247 pp.

Gershwin, George
Gilbert, Steven E. *The Music of Gershwin*. Composers of the Twentieth Century. New Haven: Yale University Press, 1995. xi, 255 pp.

Jablonski, Edward. *Gershwin*. New York: Doubleday, 1987. xv, 436 pp.

_____, and Lawrence D. Stewart. *The Gershwin Years*. Garden City, N.Y.: Doubleday, 1973. 416 pp.

Peyser, Joan. *The Memory of All That: The Life of George Gershwin*. New York: Simon & Schuster, 1993. 319 pp.

Schwartz, Charles. *Gershwin: His Life and Music*. Indianapolis: Bobbs-Merrill, 1973. 428 pp.

Giannini, Vittorio
Parris, Robert, "Vittorio Giannini and the Romantic Tradition," *Juilliard Review* IV/2 (1957), 32–46.

Glanville-Hicks, Peggy
Hayes, Deborah. *Peggy Glanville-Hicks: A Bio-Bibliography*. New York: Greenwood, 1990. x, 274 pp.

Glass, Philip
Jones, Robert T., ed. *Music by Philip Glass*. New York: Harper & Row, 1987. 222 pp. Concentrates on *Einstein on the Beach*, *Satyagraha*, and *Akhnaten*.

Kostelanetz, Richard, ed. *Writings on Glass: Essays, Original Writings, Interviews, Criticism*. New York: Schirmer Books, 1997. viii, 368 pp.

Gruenberg, Louis
Nisbett, Robert. "Louis Gruenberg: A Forgotten Figure of American Music." *Current Musicology* XVIII (1974), 90–95.

_____. "Louis Gruenberg: His Life and Works." Ph.D. diss., Ohio State University, 1979.

Handel, George Frideric

Dean, Winton, and J. Merrill Knapp. *Handel's Operas 1704–1726*. Oxford and New York: Clarendon Press, 1987. xx, 751 pp.

Harris, Ellen. *Handel and the Pastoral Tradition*. London and New York: Oxford University Press, 1980. xii. 292 pp.

_____. *The Librettos of Handel's Operas*. Vol. 1, ix–xl. New York: Garland, 1989.

Henze, Hans Werner

Hans Werner Henze: Ein Werkverzeichnis 1946–1996. Mainz and New York: Schott, 1996. 436 pp. In German, with parallel English and Italian translations.

Henze, Hans Werner. *Music and Politics: Collected Writings 1953–1981*. Translated by Peter Labanyi. London: Faber, 1982.

Herbert, Victor

Waters, Edward N. *Victor Herbert: A Life in Music*. New York: Macmillan, 1955. xvi, 653 pp.

Hermann, Bernard

Smith, Steven C. A *Heart at Fire's Center: The Life and Music of Bernard Hermann*. Berkeley, Calif.: University of California Press, 1991. 415 pp.

Hill, Alfred

Thomson, John Mansfield. *A Distant Music: The Life and Times of Alfred Hill, 1870–1960*. Auckland and New York: Oxford University Press, 1980. vii, 239 pp.

Holst, Gustav

Dickinson, A. E. F. *Holst's Music: A Guide*. Edited by Alan Gibbs. London: Thames, 1995. xv, 219 pp.

Johnson, Tom

Johnson, Tom. "At Home Abroad." *ON* LIX (Oct. 1994), 32–35.

Joplin, Scott

Haskins, James, and Kathleen Benson. *Scott Joplin*. Garden City, N.Y.: Doubleday, 1978. xiii, 248 pp.

Kalmanoff, Martin

Renard, Ellis. "The Operas of Martin Kalmanoff." *OJ* VII/3 (1974), 14–22.

Kern, Jerome

Bordman, Gerald. *Jerome Kern: His Life and Music*. New York: Oxford University Press, 1980. viii, 438 pp.

Krenek, Ernst

Bailey, O. J. "The Influence of Ernst Krenek on the Musical Culture of the Twin Cities." Ph.D. diss., University of Minnesota, 1980.

Bowles, Garrett H. *Ernst Krenek: A Bio-Bibliography*. New York: Greenwood, 1989. xiv, 428 pp.

Lampe, John Frederick

Martin, Dennis. *The Operas and Operatic Style of John Frederick Lampe*. Detroit: Information Coordinators, 1985. xx, 190 pp.

Loesser, Frank

Loesser, Susan. *A Most Remarkable Fella: Frank Loesser and the Guys and Dolls in His Life: A Portrait by His Daughter*. New York: D. I. Fine, 1993. xvi, 304 pp.

Moore, Mary Carr

Smith, Catherine Parsons. *Mary Carr Moore, American Composer*. Ann Arbor: University of Michigan Press, 1987. xi, 286 pp.

Musgrave, Thea

Hixon, Donald L. *Thea Musgrave: A Bio-Bibliography*. Westport, Conn.: Greenwood Press, 1984. x, 187 pp.

Parker, Horatio

Kearns, William K. *Horatio Parker, 1863–1919: His Life, Music, and Ideas.* Metuchen, N.J.: Scarecrow Press, 1990. xvii, 356 pp.

Persichetti, Vincent

Patterson, Donald L., and Janet L. Patterson. *Vincent Persichetti: A Bio-Bibliography.* New York: Greenwood, 1988. xiv, 336 pp.

Purcell, Henry

Price, Curtis Alexander. *Henry Purcell and the London Stage.* Cambridge and New York: Cambridge University Press, 1984. xiv, 380 pp.

Zimmermann, Franklin B. *Henry Purcell 1659–1695: His Life and Times.* London and New York: Macmillan, 1967. xvii, 429 pp. 2d rev. ed. Philadelphia: University of Pennsylvania Press, 1983. xxxvi, 473 pp.

Rorem, Ned

McDonald, Arlys L. *Ned Rorem: A Bio-Bibliography.* New York: Greenwood Press, 1989. 284 pp.

O'Connor, Patrick. "Imagination Snared." *ON* LIII (Oct. 1988), 24–26, 70.

Schafer, R. Murray

Adams, Stephen. *R. Murray Schafer.* Canadian Composers 4. Toronto: University of Toronto Press, 1983. x, 240 pp.

Sessions, Roger

Olmstead, Andrea. *Roger Sessions and His Music.* Ann Arbor: UMI Research Press, 1985. xvii, 218 pp.

Smyth, Ethel

Smyth, Ethel. *Memoirs.* Abridged and introduced by Ronald Crichton. New York: Viking, 1987. 392 pp.

Somers, Harry

Cherney, Brian. *Harry Somers.* Toronto and Buffalo: University of Toronto Press, 1975. xii, 185 pp.

Sondheim, Stephen

Banfield, Stephen. *Sondheim's Broadway Musicals.* Ann Arbor: University of Michigan Press, 1993. xvi, 453 pp.

Stanford, Charles

Hauger, George. "Stanford's Early Operas." *Opera* XXXV (1984), 724–29.

Storace, Stephen

Girdham, Jane Catherine. *English Opera in Late Eighteenth-Century London: Stephen Storace at Drury Lane.* New York: Clarendon Press, 1997. xiv, 272 pp.

Sullivan, Arthur S.

Dillard, Philip H. *Sir Arthur Sullivan. A Resource Book.* Lanham, Maryland, and London: Scarecrow Press, 1996. xiii, 428 pp.

Eden, David. *Gilbert and Sullivan: The Creative Conflict.* Rutherford, N.J.: Fairleigh Dickinson University Press, 1986. 224 pp.

Jacobs, Arthur. *Arthur Sullivan: A Victorian Musician.* 2d ed. Aldershot: Scolar Press, 1992. xv, 494 pp.

Smith, Geoffrey. *The Savoy Operas. A New Guide to Gilbert and Sullivan.* London: Robert Hale, 1983. 236 pp.

Thomson, Virgil

Meckna, Michael. *Virgil Thomson: A Bio-Bibliography.* New York: Greenwood Press, 1986. xiv, 203 pp.

Tommasini, Anthony. *Virgil Thomson: Composer on the Aisle*. New York: W. W. Norton, 1997. 605 pp.

Wittke, Paul, ed. *Virgil Thomson: Vignettes of His Life and Times*. [New York]: Virgil Thomson Foundation, 1996. v, 106 pp.

Tippett, Michael

John, Nicholas, ed. *The Operas of Michael Tippett*. English National Opera Guide 29. London: J. Calder; New York: Riverrun Press, 1985. 144 pp. Includes *The Midsummer Marriage, King Priam, The Knot Garden, The Ice Break*.

Kemp, Ian. *Tippett: The Composer and His Music*. London: Eulenburg; New York: Da Capo, 1984. xiii, 516 pp.

Scheppach, Margaret. *Dramatic Parallels in the Operas of Michael Tippett*. Lewiston, N.Y.: Edwin Mellen Press, 1990. viii, 184 pp.

Whittall, Arnold. *The Music of Britten and Tippett. Studies in Themes and Techniques*. 2d ed. Cambridge and New York: Cambridge University Press, 1990. vii, 325 pp.

Walton, William

Smith, Carolyn J. *William Walton: A Bio-Bibliography*. New York: Greenwood Press, 1988. x, 246 pp.

Weber, Carl Maria von

Henderson, Donald G., and Alice H. Henderson. *Carl Maria von Weber: A Guide for Research*. New York: Garland, 1990. xxii, 385 pp.

Jones, Gaynor Grey. "Backgrounds and Themes in the Operas of Carl Maria von Weber." Ph.D. diss., Cornell University, 1972.

Kirby, Percival. "Weber's Operas in London, 1824–6," *MQ* XXXII (1946), 333–53.

Warrack, John. *Carl Maria von Weber*. 2d ed. Cambridge: Cambridge University Press, 1976. 411 pp.

Weill, Kurt

Drew, David. *Kurt Weill—A Handbook*. London and Boston: Faber and Faber, 1987. 480 pp.

Kowalke, Kim H., ed. *A New Orpheus. Essays on Kurt Weill*. New Haven: Yale University Press, 1986. xvi, 374 pp.

Kowalke, Kim H., and Horst Edler, eds. *A Stranger Here Myself: Kurt Weill-Studien*. Wissenschaftlichen Abhandlungen, vol. 8. Hildesheim and New York: Georg Olms, 1993. 384 pp. Preface and abstracts in English and German.

Mercado, Mario R., comp. and ed. *Kurt Weill: A Guide to His Works*. 2d ed. New York: Kurt Weill Foundation for Music, 1994. x, 79 pp.

Sanders, Ronald. *The Days Grow Short*. New York: Holt, Rinehart, and Winston, 1980. 469 pp.

Weir, Judith

Griffiths, Paul. "Framed." *ON* LVI (May 1992), 50–51.

Wilder, Alec

Stone, Desmond. *Alec Wilder in Spite of Himself*. New York: Oxford University Press, 1996. x, 244 pp.

Willan, Healey

Clarke, F. R. C. *Healey Willan: Life and Music*. Toronto: University of Toronto Press, 1983. xii, 300 pp.

Wood, Charles

Copley, I[an] A[lfred]. *The Music of Charles Wood*. London: Thomas, 1978. 215 pp.

LIBRETTISTS, LYRICISTS

General

Hischak, Thomas S. *Word Crazy: Broadway Lyricists from Cohan to Sondheim*. New York: Praeger, 1991. xvii, 241 pp.

Auden, W. H.

Marx, Robert. "Auden in Opera: The Libretto as Poetic Style." *ON* LXII (Jan. 17, 1998), 8–11.

Mendelson, Edward, ed. *W. H. Auden and Chester Kallman: Libretti and Other Dramatic Writings*. Princeton, N.J.: Princeton University Press, 1993. xxxvi, 758 pp.

Fitzball, Edward

Clifton, Larry Stephen. *The Terrible Fitzball: The Melodramatist of the Macabre*. Bowling Green, Ohio: Bowling Green State University Popular Press, 1993. 191 pp.

Gershwin, Ira

Furia, Philip. *Ira Gershwin: The Art of the Lyricist*. New York: Oxford University Press, 1996. vii, 278 pp.

Kimball, Robert, and Alfred Simon. *The Gershwins*. New York: Atheneum, 1973. xlii, 292 pp.

Gilbert, William S.

Longyear, Katherine. "Henry F. Gilbert. His Life and Works." Ph.D. diss., University of Rochester, 1968.

Smith, Geoffrey. *The Savoy Operas. A New Guide to Gilbert and Sullivan*. London: Robert Hale, 1983. 236 pp.

Stedman, Jane W. *Gilbert before Sullivan. Six Comic Plays by W. S. Gilbert*. Chicago: University of Chicago Press, 1967. xii, 270 pp. With analyses.

_____. *W. S. Gilbert. A Classic Victorian and His Theatre*. New York: Oxford University Press, 1996. xviii, 374 pp.

Hammerstein II, Oscar

Citron, Stephen: *The Wordsmiths: Oscar Hammerstein 2nd and Alan Jay Lerner*. New York: Oxford University Press, 1995. xii, 446 pp.

Harwood, Gwen

Trigg, Stephanie. *Gwen Harwood*. Melbourne and New York: Oxford University Press, 1994. viii, 120 pp.

Kallman, Chester

Mendelson, Edward, ed. *W. H. Auden and Chester Kallman: Libretti and Other Dramatic Writings*. Princeton, N.J.: Princeton University Press, 1993. xxxvi, 758 pp.

Lerner, Alan Jay

Citron, Stephen: *The Wordsmiths: Oscar Hammerstein 2nd and Alan Jay Lerner*. New York: Oxford University Press, 1995. xii, 446 pp.

Malouf, David

Patrick, Annie. "David Malouf the Librettist." In *Provisional Maps: Critical Essays on David Malouf*. Edited by Amanda Nettlebeck. Perth, Austral.: University of Western Australia, 1994, 133–48.

DIRECTORS, PRODUCERS, DESIGNERS

Prince, Harold

Ilson, Carol. *Harold Prince: From Pajama Game to Phantom of the Opera*. Foreword by Sheldon Harnick. Ann Arbor, Michigan: UMI Research Press, 1989. xiii, 443 pp.

Robbins, Jerome

Schlundt, Christena L. *Dance in the Musical Theatre. Jerome Robbins and His Peers, 1934–1965. A Guide*. New York: Garland, 1989. xiv, 247 pp.

Wilson, Robert

Holmberg, Arthur. *The Theatre of Robert Wilson*. Cambridge and New York: Cambridge University Press, 1996. xix, 229 pp.

Shyer, Laurence. *Robert Wilson and His Collaborators*. New York: Theatre Communications Group, 1989. xxi, 347 pp.

Index of Characters

Each entry includes the character's name, the vocal range (where known), the short title of the opera(s) in which the character appears, and the last name of the composer(s) (or date of premiere/composition, if anonymous). Characters are listed under the names under which they are best known, e.g., "Billy Budd" under "Billy," "Anne Trulove" under "Anne," but "Trulove" [her father] under "Trulove"; titles follow names, e.g., "Alfred, King"; "Valmont, Vicomte de." Covers proper names, specific titles, and personifications, e.g., "Anne," "Caliph of Bagdad," "Beauty"; but not generic characters, e.g., "the mother." a = alto; b = bass; bar = baritone; ct = countertenor; dr = dancer; m = mezzo; s = soprano; sp = speaking; sr = singer; st = silent; t = ten; tr = treble

Aaron, (t) **Victory at Masada** (Kalmanoff)
Aaron Blunder, (b) **Toy Shop** (Barab)
Abbie Cabot, (s) **Desire under the Elms** (Thomas)
Abbot of Drimock, **Abbot of Drimock** (Musgrave)
Abdala, **Thalaba** (Rodwell)
Abdallah, **Caliph of Bagdad** (Musgrave); Il **Bondocani** (Attwood/Moorehead); **The Seraglio** (Dibdin)
Abdul, (bar) **Last Savage** (Menotti)
Abdullah, **Cady of Bagdad** (Linley Jr.); **Holy Blood** (Copeland); **Wizards of Balizar** (Lockwood)
Abel, Mr., **Green Mansions** (Gruenberg)
Abel Conn, **Idols' Eye** (Herbert)
Abel Gudgeon, **Foxy Quiller** (De Koven)
Abelard, (t) **Abelard and Heloise** (Ward); **Eloise and Abelard** (Victory); **Heloise and Abelard** (Tarhoudin); **Heloise and Abelard** (Wilson)
Abgarus, (b-bar) **Other Wise Man** (Grove)
Abigail, (s) **Lizzie Borden** (Beeson); (a) **Puritania** (Kelley); (s) **The Tower** (Levy)
Abigail Adams, (s) **Abigail Adams** (Owen)
Abigail Williams, (s) **The Crucible** (Ward)
Abimelach Jones, (bar) **Sack of Calabasas** (Fletcher)
Abou Hassan, **Abou Hassan** (Cooke)
Abraham, (bar) **Eternal Road** (Weill)
Abraham Bentley, (b) **The Rope** (Mennini)
Abudah, **Almena** (Arne-Battishill)
Acacis, **Indian Queen** (Purcell)
Acantha, **The Echo** (Patterson)
Accaro, King, **Sarrona** (Howland)
Achilles, **Achilles** (1733); **Achilles in Petticoats** (Arne); (t) **Helen in Egypt** (Elkus); **Helen Retires** (Antheil); (t) **King Priam** (Tippett)
Achior, (t) **Judith** (Chadwick); **Judith** (Goossens)
Achlamah, Princess, (s) **The Tower** (Levy)
Acis, **Acis and Galatea** (Eccles); (t) **Acis and Galatea** (Handel)
Ada Lewin, (m) **Karla** (Lehrman)
Adah, **Naughty Marietta** (Herbert)
Adam, **Amorous Judge** (Gross); **Lilith** (Drattell); **Hotel Eden** (Mollicone); **Paradise Lost** (Penderecki); (t) **So How Does Your Garden** (Russell)

Adams, John, (t) **Abigail Adams** (Owen); (t) **Mother of Us All** (Thomson)
Adams, John Quincy, (bar) **Abigail Adams** (Owen)
Adare, Madame, **Madame Adare** (Silverman)
Adela, **English Fleet** (Braham); **Harold** (Cowen); (s) **Haunted Tower** (Storace)
Adelaide, **Albert and Adelaide** (Attwood, Steibelt); **The Vintagers** (Bishop)
Adeline, **Battle of Hexham** (Arnold)
Adine, **Faustus** (Bishop)
Admetus, **Alceste** (Handel); **Alcestiad** (Talma); **Alkestis** (Boughton)
Admiral of Rhodes, **Siege of Rhodes** (Lawes et al.)
Adolph Savigny, **Love's Triumph** (Wallace)
Adolphe, **Daughter of St. Mark** (Balfe)
Adolphus, **Leap Year** (Sedgwick)
Adolphus Bastable, (t) **Passion, Poison** (Taub)
Adonis, (t) **Gardens of Adonis** (Weisgall); **Venus** (Van Rhijn); **Venus and Adonis** (Blow); (s) **Venus and Adonis** (Pepusch)
Adrian, (b-bar/bar) **Poison** (Har)
Adrian Hodgepodge, (bar) **Bad Boys** (Meyerowitz)
Adriana, (s) **The Magician** (Hoddinott)
Aegidius, **Godfather Death** (Meyerowitz)
Aegisthus, **Agamemnon** (Brian); (t) **Agamemnon** (Hamilton); (ct) **Agamemnon** (Werder)
Aegon, **Damon and Phillida** (1729)
Aelfrida, (s) **King's Henchmen** (Taylor)
Aeneas, **Death of Dido** (Pepusch); **Dido** (Storace); **Dido and Aeneas** (Arne); **Dido and Aeneas** (Beveridge); **Dido and Aeneas** (Hook); (t) **Dido and Aeneas** (Purcell)
Aeneas, Mr., (bar) **Happy Hypocrite** (Masland)
Aeolia, **Mountain Sylph** (Barnett)
Aesop, **Aesop the Fabulist** (Kalmanoff); **Blanche de Nevers** (Balfe); **Lethe** (Arne)
Aethelwold, (t) **King's Henchmen** (Taylor)
Aethon, (bar) **Nausicaa** (Glanville-Hicks)
Affenkoff, Baron von, **Golden Butterfly** (De Koven)
Agamemnon, **Agamemnon** (Brian); **Agamemnon** (Hamilton); **Agamemnon** (Morris); (b) **Agamemnon** (Werder); **Cry of Clytaemnestra** (Eaton)
Agatha Lawson, **Crazy to Kill** (Beckwith)
Agave, (m) **The Bassarids** (Henze); **Revelation** (Partch)

Agebda Akawasir, Mrs., (s) **Most Important Man** (Menotti)

Agenor, **Royal Shepherd** (Rush)

Agneh, (m) **Julian** (Saminsky)

Agnes, (m) **Caritas** (Saxon); (s) **Growing Castle** (Williamson); **Joan of Arc** (Balfe); (s) **School for Wives** (Liebermann)

Agnes, Lady, (s) **Raymond and Agnes** (Loder)

Agnes, Queen, **Sleeping Queen** (Balfe)

Agness, **Free Knights** (Mazzinghi)

Agnes Sorel, **Agnes Sorel** (A'Beckett)

Agravain, (bar) **Gawain** (Birtwistle)

Agrippina, **Hell's Angels** (Osborne)

Aguabone, Dr., **Chaos** (Gordon)

Aguilar, Geronimo de, (b-bar) **Montezuma's Death** (Chlarson)

Ah Chin Honk, (t) **Sack of Calabasas** (Fletcher)

Ahab, King, **Naboth's Vineyard** (Goehr)

Ahasuerus, (t) **Esther** (Harvey); (b-bar) **Esther** (Meyerowitz)

Ahmed, **Safié** (Hadley)

Ainsworth, Lord, **Maid of the Mill** (Arnold)

Ajax, (b) **Transatlantic** (Antheil)

Akhnaten, (ct) **Akhnaten** (Glass)

Akibzi, **Don Saverio** (Arne)

Albina, (s) **Elfrida** (Arne)

Al Donfonso, (bar) **Abduction of Figaro** (Schickele)

Aladdin, **Aladdin** (Bishop)

Alain, (t) **The Door** (Mopper)

Alain de Rouzie, **Merrymount** (Smith)

Alan, (bar) **Yan Tan Tethera** (Birtwistle)

Alan-a-Dale, (a) **Robin Hood** (De Koven); **Robin Hood** (Tippett)

Alan Bane (t) **Lady of the Lake** (Schmidt)

Alasman, **Safié** (Hadley)

Alastair Frontenac (t) **The Opening** (Wilder)

Alaster, **Highland Fair** (1731)

Albanius, **Albion and Abanius** (Grabu)

Alberquerque, Duchess d', **Ruy Blas** (Glover)

Albert, **Albert and Adelaide** (Attwood, Steibelt); **Letty, the Basket-Maker** (Balfe); (t) **The Ruby** (Dello Joio); **Night Dancers** (Loder)

Albert Herring (t) **Albert Herring** (Britten)

Alberto, Count, **Heir of Vironi** (Bishop)

Albertine (b) **W. of Babylon** (Wuorinen)

Alberto (t) **La Cubana** (Henze); **Devil of a Duke** (1732); (bar) **Fortunato** (Gideon)

Albion, **Albion and Abanius** (Grabu)

Alceste, **Alceste** (Handel)

Alcestis, **The Alcestiad** (Talma); **Alcestis** (Marshall-Hall)

Alcibiades, **Timon of Athens** (Oliver)

Alcino (t) **Prima Donna** (Benjamin)

Alcinous, King, (b) **Castaway** (Berkeley)

Alcmena, **Jupiter and Alcmena** (Dibdin)

Alcmene, **Amphitryon 4** (Blumenfeld)

Alden, John, **Courtship of Miles Standish** (Ewart)

Aldiborontiphoscophornia, **Chrononhotontho-logos** (Carey)

Alecto, **Gasconado the Great** (1759)

Alethe, **The Earthquake** (Rodwell)

Alex, (boy s) **Lost in the Stars** (Weill)

Alexander Marshall, **Joe Hill** (Bush)

Alexander, King, **Royal Shepherd** (Rush)

Alexander, Sir, (t/bar) **Simple Decision** (Busch)

Alexander VI, Pope, **Hell's Angels** (Osborne)

Alexander the Great, **Court of Alexander** (Fisher); **Macheath in the Shades** (1735); **Rival Queens** (Finger)

Alexandra, (s) **Rasputin** (Reise); (s) **Regina** (Blitzstein)

Alexandra Daniels, **Atlas** (Monk)

Alexina, **The Exile** (Mazzinghi)

Alexis (t) **The Sorcerer** (Sullivan)

Aleyn, **The Wayfarers** (Joubert)

Alfonso, **Masaniello** ((Auber-Cooke/Barham)

Alfonso, Don (b-bar) **La Cubana** (Henze)

Alfonso, King, **Voice of Nature** (Pelissier)

Alford, **Children in the Wood** (Arnold); **Night before the Wedding** (Bishop)

Alfourite, King, (t) **Fortunio** (Darley)

Alfred, **Alfred** (Arne); (bar) **The Olympians** (Bliss); **Yelva** (Bishop)

Alfred Davidson, Rev., **Sadie Thompson** (Owen)

Alfrerez, **Leonora** (Fry)

Algernon Rockwardine, **Fall of Algiers** (Bishop)

Algiziras, **Spanish Castle** (Hewitt)

Algonah, **Algonah** (Storace)

Alhambra del Bolero, Don (b-bar) **The Gondoliers** (Sullivan)

Ali, **Birth of the Poet** (Gordon); **Selima and Azor** (Linley Sr.)

Ali, Princess, **Inner Voices** (Howard)

Alice, **Alice** (Waits); (s) **Alice in Wonderland** (Chauls); **Alice in Wonderland** (Josephs); **Alice in Wonderland** (Meachem); **Alice in Wonderland** (Slaughter); **Alice Meets the Mock Turtle** (Bingham); **Final Alice** (Del Tredici); **Hansel & Gretel** (Schickele); **Murder in Three Keys** (Chisholm); **Peveril of the Peak** (Horn); (s) **Sunday Excursion** (Wilder); (s) **Through the Looking Glass** (Alice)

Alice B. Toklas, **We're Back** (Armour)

Alice Faversham, (m) **Arden Must Die** (Goehr)

Alice Liddell, **Alice** (Osborne)

Alice Van Winkle, (s) **Rip Van Winkle** (Bristow)

Alida Slade, (s) **Roman Fever** (Ward)

Alidoro, **Cinderella** (Lacy)

Ali Hassan, **Egyptian Festival** (Florio)

Aline, (s) **The Sorcerer** (Sullivan)

Alison, (s) **Wandering Scholar** (Holst)

Alison, Sir, **Maid of Honour** (Balfe)

Alisoun, **Canterbury Pilgrims** (De Koven)

Alkestis, **Alkestis** (Boughton)

Alla Nazimova, **Dream of Valentino** (Argento)

Allan, Mrs., (a) **Voyage of Edgar Allan Poe** (Argento)

Anna Ferris, (s) **The Picnic** (Cumming)
Anna Karenina, (s) **Anna Karenina** (Hamilton)
Anna Maurrant, (s) **Street Scene** (Weill)
Anna Semyonovna, (m) **Natalia Petrovna** (Hoiby)
Anne, **Cue 67** (Ching); (a) **Mother of Us All**
  (Thomson); (s/m) **The Opening** (Wilder)
Anne Boleyn, **Anne Boleyn** (Beck)
Anne Kronenberg, (m) **Harvey Milk** (Wallace)
Anne of Neuberg, **Ruy Blas** (Glover)
Anne Page, (s) **Sir John in Love** (Vaughan Williams)
Anne Rice, (s) **Charcoal Burner** (Wilson)
Anne Sexton, **Transformations** (Susa)
Anne Trulove, (s) **Rake's Progress** (Stravinsky)
Annette, **Annette** (Horn); **Annette and Lubin**
  (Dibdin); **Lord of the Manor** (Jackson)
Annie, (m) **The Rope** (Mennini); (s/m) **Tickets
  Please** (Nelson)
Annina, (s) **Saint of Bleecker Street** (Menotti)
Ann Louisa Brice, (s) **Deseret** (Kastle)
Ann Shute, (s) **Lily of Kilarney** (Benedict)
Anonto, (bar) **Tamu-Tamu** (Menotti)
Anso IV, King, **Merry Monarch** (Sousa)
Antenor, (bar) **Troilus and Cressida** (Walton)
Anthony, (bar) **Night of the Moonspell** (Siegmeister)
Anthony, Susan B., (s) **Mother of Us All**
  (Thomson); **Woman Who Dared** (Bokser)
Anthony Hope, (t) **Sweeney Todd** (Sondheim)
Antibioticus, Dr. (t) **Double Trouble** (Mohaupt)
Antichrist (t, sp) **Taverner** (Davies)
Antigonae, **Antigonae** (Kupferman)
Antigone, **Antigone** (Joubert)
Antinou, **Ulysses** (Smith)
Antinous, (t) **Nausicaa** (Glanville-Hicks)
Antiope, **Ulysses** (Smith)
Antoine, **Follies of a Night** (Gabriel); (t) **King of
  Hearts** (Torke)
Antoine, Father, (t) **Wife of Martin Guerre**
  (Bergsma)
Antoinette, (m) **The Opening** (Wilder)
Antoni, (bar) **Raymond and Agnes** (Loder)
Antonia, **Empty Bottle** (Kalmanoff)
Antonio, **Duchess of Malfi** (Burton); **Duchess of
  Malfi** (Oliver); (t) **The Duenna** (Linley Jr./Linley
  Sr.); **Monkey's Paw** (Hamm); **Sancho at Court**
  (1742); **The Tempest** (Westergaard)
Antonio, Don, (t) **The Duenna** (Gerhard)
Antony, (bar) **Antony and Cleopatra** (Barber);
  Antony and Cleopatra (Gruenberg); **Egypt**
  (McCoy)
Aoife, (a) **Death of Cuchulain** (Brettingham Smith)
Aper, **Dioclesian** (Purcell)
Apollo, **Alceste** (Handel); **Alcestiad** (Talma); **Alkestis**
  (Boughton); **Apollo and Daphne** (Hook); **Apollo
  and Daphne** (Pepusch); **Apollo and Persephone**
  (Cockshott); **Asses' Ears** (Cole); **Choice of Apollo**
  (Yates); (bar) **Garden of Artemis** (Pinkham);
  Momus (1729); **Thespis** (Sullivan)
Apollonia, (s) **Apollonia** (Starer)

Apollyon, (b) **Pilgrim's Progress** (Vaughan
  Williams)
Applejack, Justice, **The Czar** (Shield)
Applejack, Mrs., **The Czar** (Shield)
Aquila, Duke d', **The Enchantress** (Bale)
Arabella, **Honest Yorkshireman** (Carey); (s)
  Smoky Mountain (Hunkins)
Arabella Smithson, (a) **Dove of Peace** (Damrosch)
Aranza, Duke of, **Honey Moon** (Hewitt/Kelly)
Arawn, (t) **Children of Don** (Holbrooke)
Arbace, (s) **Artaxerxes** (Arne)
Arcas, **Damon and Phillida** (1729)
Archie Weir, (bar) **Hermiston** (Orr)
archy, **archy and mehitabel** (Kleinsinger)
Arcos, Duke of, **Masaniello** (Auber-Cooke et al.)
Arcott, Charles, **Entente Cordiale** (Smyth)
Ardelia, **Teraminta** (Smith); (s) **Teraminta**
  (Stanley)
Arden Faversham, (b) **Arden Must Die** (Goehr)
Arden Leslie, **Single Married Man** (Sedgwick)
Ardion, (m) **Cleopatra's Night** (Hadley); (bar)
  Helen in Egypt (Elkus)
Arete, Queen, (a) **Castaway** (Berkeley); (m)
  Nausicaa (Glanville-Hicks)
Argyle, Duke of, **Heart of Midlothian** (Loder)
Argyle, Lady, (m) **David Rizzio** (Moore)
Argyll, Duke of, **Powder Her Face** (Adès)
Ariadne, **Ariadne** (Flecknoe); **Ariadne** (Pelissier)
Ariadne Nabratz, (s) **Meantime** (Arlan)
Ariel, **Cue 67** (Ching); (s) **The Mistake** (Sheffer);
  (m) **The Tempest** (Eaton); (s) **The Tempest**
  (Hoiby); **The Tempest** (Smith); **The Tempest**
  (Westergaard); **Vision of Ariel** (Saminsky)
Ariela Hilbo, (s) **Whirligig** (Brisman)
Ariella, **Girls of Holland** (De Koven)
Arimanes, (b) **Satanella** (Balfe)
Arionelli, Signor, **Son-in-Law** (Arnold)
Aristaeus, (b-bar/mime) **Mask of Orpheus**
  (Birtwistle)
Aristo, **Cave of Trophonius** (Storace)
Arkady Sergeitch Islaev, (t) **Natalia Petrovna**
  (Hoiby)
Arlecchino, (t) **Perpetual** (Kanitz)
Arlequin, (bar) **Eyes and No Eyes** (Reed)
Arline, (s) **Bohemian Girl** (Balfe)
Armand, **Camille** (Forrest)
Armen Xykl, (b-bar) **Primal Void** (Vincent)
Armida, **Rinaldo and Armida** (Eccles)
Arnek, Dr., (t) **Most Important Man** (Menotti)
Arnheim, (bar) **Bohemian Girl** (Balfe)
Arnie, (b-bar) **Thanksgiving** (Levi)
Arnold, (b) **English Cat** (Henze)
Arnold, Benedict, **Twist of Treason** (Livingston)
Arnold, George, (t) **Capitoline Venus** (Kay)
Arnold Talbot, **Witch of Salem** (Cadman)
Arnoldus, **Hero of the North** (Kelly)
Arnolphe, (bar) **School for Wives** (Liebermann)
Arrochkoa, (bar) **Ramuntcho** (Taylor)

Bamboola, (b) **Pantagleize** (Starer)
Bampton, (b-bar) **Wat Tyler** (Bush)
Bang, Captain, **Our Island Home** (Reed)
Bannadonna, **Bell Tower** (Krenek)
Baptista, (b) **Taming of the Shrew** (Giannini)
Baptiste, **The Vintagers** (Bishop); **Yelva** (Bishop)
Barbara, (s) **Casanova's Homecoming** (Argento);
 (s) **The Hero** (Menotti); (s) **Iron Chest** (Storace);
 The Knickerbockers (De Koven); **Question of
 Love** (Gilbert)
Barbara Allen, **Barbara Allen** (Broekman)
Barbara Ansley, (m) **Roman Fever** (Ward)
Barbara de la Guerra, (s) **Natoma** (Herbert)
Barberini, Cardinal, (t) **Galileo Galilei** (Laderman)
Barberino, **Devil of a Duke** (1732)
Bardac, Madame, **Blood Moon** (Dello Joio)
Bardeau, Madame, (m) **The Olympians** (Bliss)
Bardolph, (bar) **At the Boar's Head** (Holst); (b)
 King Hal (Stewart)
Barelli, **Aspern Papers** (Argento)
Barlow, Dr. Stanley, (bar) **Malady of Love** (Engel)
Barlow, Rev. William, **Vicar of Bray** (Solomon)
Barre, Sir Bailey, **Utopia Limited** (Sullivan)
Bartleby, (t) **Bartleby** (Aschaffenburg); **Bartleby**
 (Flanagan)
Bartley, (bar) **Riders to the Sea** (Vaughan Williams)
Bartolo, **Bartolo** (Bugg)
Bartolome, **Terra Incognita** (Serrano)
Basil, **The Servants** (Mathias); **White Bird** (Carter)
Basil Hallward, **Picture of Dorian Gray** (Liebermann)
Basilissa, **The Egg** (Menotti)
Basilius, (t) **Adventure of Don Quixote** (Macfarren)
Bathsheba, **And David Wept** (Laderman)
Baucis, **Baucis and Philemon** (Prelleur)
Bauldy, **Gentle Shepherd** (1729)
Baylis, Bill, **Entente Cordiale** (Smyth)
Bays, **Bays's Opera** (1730)
Bazile, (t) **Bayou Legend** (Still)
Beast, (bar) **Beauty and the Beast** (DiGiacomo);
 Beauty and the Beast (Easton); (t) **Beauty and
 the Beast** (Giannini); **Beauty and the Beast**
 (Glover); **Beauty and the Beast** (Murray); (b)
 Beauty and the Beast (Oliver)
Beata, **Once in a While** (Godfrey); (s) **Rape of
 Lucretia** (Britten); **Rappaccini's Daughter**
 (Bender); **Rappaccini's Daughter** (Dennison)
Beaton, Cardinal, (b-bar) **Mary, Queen of Scots**
 (Musgrave)
Beatrice (Béatrice), **Beatrice** (Hoiby); (s) **Diable
 amoureux** (Nelson); **Garden of Mystery**
 (Cadman); **Guido Ferranti** (Van Etten); (s) **Our
 Man in Havana** (Williamson); (s) **Poison** (Hart);
 Servant of Two Masters (Giannini); **The Viceroy**
 (Victor)
Beatrice Cenci, (s) **The Cenci** (Brian); **The Cenci**
 (Coke); **Beatrice Cenci** (Goldschmidt)
Beatrix, **Rose of Castille** (Balfe)
Beau Brummell, (t) **English Eccentrics** (Williamson)

Beaumarchais, (bar) **Ghosts of Versailles**
 (Corigliano)
Beaumont, Cornet John Stephen, (t) **Rising of
 the Moon** (Maw)
Beausant, (bar) **Pauline** (Cowen)
Beauty, (s) **Beauty and the Beast** (DiGiacomo);
 Beauty and the Beast (Easton); (s) **Beauty
 and the Beast** (Giannini); **Beauty and the
 Beast** (Glover); **Beauty and the Beast**
 (Murray); (m) **Beauty and the Beast** (Oliver)
Beauvais, **Joan of Arc** (Balfe)
Beelzebub, **Paradise Lost** (Penderecki)
Beetle, (b) **Insect Comedy** (Kalmanoff)
Beetle, Mrs., (m) **Insect Comedy** (Kalmanoff)
Bégearss, (t) **Ghosts of Versailles** (Corigliano)
Behrman, Mr., (b/bar) **Last Leaf** (Henderson)
Bekusa, **Don Perlimplin** (Rieti)
Belial, **Paradise Lost** (Penderecki)
Belinda, **Bays's Opera**; (s) **Dido and Aeneas**
 (Purcell); **Good Friday 1663** (Westbrook)
Belinda Cratchit, **Christmas Carol** (Musgrave)
Belisa, **Belisa** (Biales); **Love of Don Perlimplin**
 (Susa)
Bella, (s) **Midsummer Marriage** (Tippett)
Bellamira, **Love and Revenge** (1729)
Bellarmine, Cardinal, (bar) **Galileo Galilei**
 (Laderman)
Bellboys, Dorcas, (s) **Penny for a Song** (Bennett)
Bellcamp, Captain, **Positive Man** (Arnold)
Belle, (s) **Voss** (Meale)
Belle Boyd, **Gentlemen, Be Seated!** (Moross)
Belle Fezziwig, (s) **Christmas Carol** (Musgrave)
Belleville, Capt., **Dolly Varden** (Edwards)
Belmont, **Castle of Sorrento** (Attwood)
Belmont, Captain, **Honey Moon** (Linley)
Belphegor, **Belphegor** (Barthelemon)
Belshazzar, **Belshazzar's Feast** (Griesbach);
 Belshazzar's Feast (Root)
Belton, **The Savoyard** (Reinagle)
Belvil[l]e, **Mistakes of a Day** (Callcott)
Belville, Captain, **Rosina** (Shield)
Belzebub, **Gambrinus** (Sedgwick)
Ben, (t) **Buxom Joan** (Taylor); (b) **Harriet**
 (Musgrave); (t) **Smoky Mountain** (Hunkins);
 (bar) **The Telephone** (Menotti)
Ben Alexander, (t) **My Heart's in the
 Highlands** (Beeson)
Ben Blake, **Cumberland Fair** (Wilder)
Benbow, Justice, (sp) **Flitch of Bacon** (Shield)
Benbow, Major, (b) **Flitch of Bacon** (Shield)
Benjamin Coffin 3d, **Rent** (Larson)
Benjamin Giddens, (bar) **Regina** (Blitzstein)
Benjie, (t) **Harriet** (Musgrave)
Bennelong, **Bennelong** (Conyngham)
Benno, **East and West** (McQueen)
Ben Palmer, (bar) **Old Majestic** (Rodríguez)
Ben Porter, (bar/b) **Sourwood Mountain**
 (Kreutz)

Blood, Dr., (actor) **Down by the Greenwood Side** (Birtwistle)
Blount, Charles, (bar) **Gloriana** (Britten)
Blowhard, Chief, **Where's Dick** (Wallace)
Blue Beard, **Africanus Blue Beard** (Sedgwick); **Blue-Beard** (Kelly)
Bluff, (b) **Buxom Joan** (Taylor)
Blumberg, Henry, (bar) **Lady of the Lake** (Siegmeister)
Blumenthal, (b) **Murder of Comrade Sharik** (Bergsma)
Blushington, Mr., **Utopia Limited** (Sullivan)
Bo, **The Losers** (Farberman)
Boaz, (bar) **Eternal Road** (Weill); **The Outcast** (Ain); (t) **Ruth** (Berkeley)
Bob, (bar) **Highway 1, U.S.A.** (Still); (bar) **Old Maid and the Thief** (Menotti)
Bob Cratchit, **Christmas Carol** (Musgrave)
Bobbie Preston, Captain, **San Toy** (Jones)
Boconnion, **Mines of Sulphur** (Bennett)
Bohemond, **The Crusaders** (Benedict)
Bois-Gilbert, (bar) **Ivanhoe** (Sullivan)
Bokelson, (t) **Behold the Sun** (Goehr)
Bolden, Buddy, **Coming through Slaughter** (Westbrook)
Bold Slasher, (actor) **Down by the Greenwood Side** (Birtwistle)
Bolívar, (t) **Simón Bolívar** (Musgrave)
Boney Quillen, (t) **Boney Quillen** (Haufrecht)
Bonifacio, Padre, (b) **Blonde Donna** (Carter)
Bonner, Edward, (b) **Voss** (Meale)
Bonny Jack, (bar) **Mermaid in Lock No. 7** (Siegmeister)
Bonoro, Doctor, **Zuma** (Bishop)
Bony Anderson, **Apology of Bony Anderson** (Conyngham)
Booth, John, (bar) **Mary Surratt** (Muller)
Booze, **Belphegor** (Barthelemon)
Borden, Andrew, (b-bar) **Lizzie Borden** (Beeson)
Borgia, Cesare, (b-bar) **Hell's Angels** (Osborne)
Boris, Prince, **The Charlatan** (Sousa)
Bosola, **Duchess of Malfi** (Oliver)
Bosola, Daniel de, **Duchess of Malfi** (Burton)
Boswell, **Johnson Preserv'd** (Stoker)
Bothwell, Earl of, (t) **Mary, Queen of Scots** (Musgrave)
Bottom, (b-bar) **Midsummer Night's Dream** (Britten)
Botzenheim, Baroness von, (a) **Good Soldier Schweik** (Kurka)
Bouché, Thomas, (b) **Down in the Valley** (Weill)
Bouncer, (bar) **Cox and Box** (Sullivan)
Bounderby, **Hard Times** (Burgon)
Bouvard, **Bouvard and Pécuchet** (ApIvor)
Bowen, **Different Fields** (Reid)
Bowring, (t) **Grace of Todd** (Crosse)
Bowspirit, **Britons, Strike Home** (1739)
Box, John James, (t) **Cox and Box** (Sullivan)
Brack, Judge, **Hedda Gabler** (Harper)

Brack Weaver, (t) **Down in the Valley** (Weill)
Bradford, Count, (t) **Secret of the Mirror** (Busch)
Braddock, Bashford, (bar) **Ordeal of Osbert** (Davis)
Bragadocia, Emperor of, **Free Lance** (Sousa)
Brainkoff, Dr., (t) **The Hero** (Menotti)
Brainworm, **Love and Revenge** (1729)
Bramble, (t) **Our Man in Havana** (Williamson)
Brandon, (b) **Long Christmas Dinner** (Hindemith)
Brant, Adam, (bar) **Mourning Becomes Electra** (Levy)
Brayer, Mr., (t) **The System** (Bach)
Braxton, **Mines of Sulphur** (Bennett)
Brennan, Captain, (b) **Plough and the Stars** (Siegmeister)
Brettschneider, (t) **Good Soldier Schweik** (Kurka)
Bridgenorth, **Peveril of the Peak** (Horn)
Bridget, **Letty, the Basket-Maker** (Balfe)
Bridget Lochmuller, **Mulligan Guard Ball** (Braham)
Brighella, (bar) **Commedia** (Cowie); **Servant of Two Masters** (Giannini)
Briquet, (b-bar) **He Who Gets Slapped** (Ward)
Brissac, **Follies of a Night** (Gabriel)
Britannia, **Britannia** (Lampe); **Choice of Apollo** (Yates); **Restauration of Charles II** (1732)
British Blunt, Sir, **Guardian Outwitted** (Arne)
Briton, Captain, **Britons, Strike Home** (1739)
Britten, Benjamin, **Once in a While** (Godfrey)
Brixcowicz, Mr., (bar) **Bad Boys in School** (Meyerowitz)
Broichan, **Columba** (Leighton)
Brom Van Brunt, **Headless Horseman** (Moore)
Bronwen, **Bronwen** (Holbrooke)
Brother Shannon, (bar) **Hanging Judge** (Lockwood)
Brother Smiley, (b) **Sweet Bye and Bye** (Beeson)
Brown, **Ages Ago** (Clay)
Brown, Captain, **Guy Mannering** (Attwood)
Brown, David, (t) **The Diva** (Ferris)
Brown, Farmer, (bar) **Boney Quillen** (Haufrecht)
Brown, George, **White Lady** (Cooke)
Brown, Goodman, **Goodman Brown** (Fink); (t/bar) **Young Goodman Brown** (Lenel)
Brown, John, (bar) **The Decision** (Musgrave); **John Brown** (Mechem)
Brunetto, **Devil of a Duke** (1732)
Bruno, (bar) **Where the Wild Things Are** (Knussen)
Bruno Broast, (bar) **Ballad of the Bremen Band** (Moore)
Brusard, **Deep River** (Harling)
Buchanan, Dr., (b-bar) **Summer and Smoke** (Hoiby)

Clorinda, **Cinderella** (Lacy); (s) **Garden of Artemis** (Pinkham)
Clothilde, (s) **Bayou Legend** (Still)
Clotilda, (a) **Koanga** (Delius)
Clovis Sangrail, (narr) **Beast and Superbeast** (Martín)
Clump, **Brazen Bust** (Bishop)
Clymante, **Native Land** (Bishop)
Clytemnestra, **Agamemnon** (Brian); (s) **Agamemnon** (Hamilton); (s) **Agamemnon** (Werder); **Clytemnestra** (Wishart); **Cry of Clytaemnestra** (Eaton)
Clytoneus, (t) **Nausicaa** (Glanville-Hicks)
Cocardasse, **Blanche de Nevers** (Balfe)
Cocoliche, (t) **Don Cristóbal** (Crawford)
Cogan, Mrs., (m) **Plough and the Stars** (Siegmeister)
Cohenberg, Colonel, (sp) **Siege of Belgrade** (Storace)
Colette, **Cunning Man** (Burney)
Colin, (t) **The Cooper** (Arne); **Cunning Man** (Burney); **Happy Arcadia** (Clay); (t) **Juggler of Our Lady** (Kay); **Rose and Colin** (Dibdin); **Secret Garden** (Pliska); **Shepherd's Lottery** (Boyce)
Collatinus, (b) **Rape of Lucretia** (Britten)
Colomba, **Colomba** (Mackenzie)
Colombina, **Jewel Box** (Mozart-Griffiths); (s) **Perpetual** (Kanitz)
Colombine, **The Portrait** (Barthelemon)
Columba, **Columba** (Leighton)
Columbine, (s) **Aria da Capo** (Baksa); (s) **Aria di Capo** (Blank); (s) **Commedia** (Cowie); (m) **Eyes and No Eyes** (Reed); **Fête Galante** (Smyth); **The Touchstone** (Dibdin)
Columbus, **Christopher Columbus** (Kalmanoff); **Columbus** (Moore); **Further Voyages** (Stokes); **Tammany** (Hewitt); (b-bar) **The Voyage** (Glass)
Columbus Hebbelthwaite, **Ages Ago** (Clay)
Comedy, **Theatrical Candidates** (Bates)
Commendatoreador, Il, (b) **Stoned Guest** (Schickele)
Commère, (m) **Four Saints** (Thomson)
Compere (Compère), (b-bar) **Crimson Bird** (Enebach); (b) **Four Saints** (Thomson)
Compson, Capt. Richard, **Midnight Angel** (Carlson)
Compton, **Agreeable Surprise** (Arnold)
Comus, **Comus** (Arne); **Comus** (Bishop)
Conchas, (bar) **Kingdom for a Cow** (Weill)
Concord, **Britannia** (Lampe)
Confession, **Everyman** (Lester)
Conner, William, **Hoosier Tale** (Kaufmann)
Conochar, King, (bar) **Deirdre** (Willan)
Conrad, **The Archers** (Carr); **Sicilian Romance** (Reeve)
Conrade, **The Crusaders** (Benedict)
Conradin, **Beast and Superbeast** (Martín)
Conscience, **Piers Plowman** (Schurmann)
Constance, **The Ameer** (Herbert); (s) **The Sorcerer** (Sullivan)
Constance, Lady, (s) **The Highwayman** (De Koven)
Constance Fletcher, (m) **Mother of Us All** (Thomson)

Constance Neville, Miss, **She Stoops to Conquer** (Macfarren)
Constancy, **Scipio's Dream** (Weir)
Constant, **Happy Lovers** (1736)
Constantia, **The Cabinet** (Reeve et al.); **Don John** (Bishop)
Constantine, (bar) **The Seagull** (Pasatieri)
Constanza, (s) **Fortunato** (Gideon)
Consuelo, (s) **He Who Gets Slapped** (Ward); **I Was Looking** (Adams)
Contarini, **Bianca** (Balfe)
Contessa dei Candini, **Midnight Angel** (Carlson)
Contrast, **Lord of the Manor** (Jackson)
Coppelius, **Heaven Ablaze in His Breast** (Weir)
Coppola, **Heaven Ablaze in His Breast** (Weir)
Cora, (s) **Last of the Mohicans** (Henderson); (s) **Most Important Man** (Menotti); **Pizzaro** (Kelly); (s) **Postman Always Rings Twice** (Paulus); **Virgin of the Sun** (Bishop)
Cora Lewis, **The Barrier** (Meyerowitz)
Coralie, **Maid of Artois** (Balfe)
Corbey, Abbot of, **Free Knights** (Mazzinghi)
Corcoran, Captain, (bar) **H.M.S. Pinafore** (Sullivan)
Corcoran, Sir Edward, **Utopia Limited** (Sullivan)
Cordova, **Loretta** (Lavenu)
Coreb, **Il Bondocani** (Attwood/Moorehead)
Corey, (bar) **The Patriot** (Edwards)
Corin, **Alfred** (Arne)
Corinna, (s) **Tarquin** (Krenek)
Coraly, **Fair Peruvian** (Hook)
Cornelia, **Positive Man** (Arnold)
Cornelia Bayard, **Maria Malibran** (Bennett)
Cornelius, Father, **Martin's Lie** (Menotti)
Corrie Mae, (s) **Tree on the Plains** (Bacon)
Corrigan, (b) **Lily of Kilarney** (Benedict)
Cortes, Fernando, (t) **Montezuma's Death** (Chlarson)
Cortez (Hernán), **Cortez** (Bishop); (bar) **Montezuma** (Sessions)
Corvain, (b) **Fairyland** (Parker)
Corydon, (t) **Aria da Capo** (Baksa); (bar) **Aria di Capo** (Blank); **Damon and Phillida** (1729); (bar) **Fairy Queen** (Purcell); **The Rehearsal** (Boyce)
Cosroe, **Dioclesian** (Purcell)
Cothurnus, (b) **Aria di Capo** (Blank)
Coupee, **Boarding School** (1733)
Cousin Foodle, **Haste to the Wedding** (Grossmith)
Couvanski, Count, **Czar** (Shield)
Cox, James John, (bar) **Cox and Box** (Sullivan)
Coyle, Mrs., (s) **Owen Wingrave** (Britten)
Coyle, Spencer, (b-bar) **Owen Wingrave** (Britten)
Craccio, (t) **Student from Salamanca** (Bach)
Craig, **The Journey** (Metcalf)
Crane, Mrs., (a) **The Audition** (Goodman)

David, Rabbi, **Friend Fritz** (Edwards)
Davide, **The Equation** (Bush)
Davy, **Generous Free-Mason** (1730); **Highland Fair** (1731)
Da Wei, **Bok Choy Variations** (Chen)
Dawn Aurora, (s) **The Audition** (Kalmanoff)
Day, Mr., **Tin Pan Alley** (Raphling)
Death, (bar) **Burning House** (Hovhaness); (sr, dr) **Cupid and Death** (Gibbons/Locke); **Everyman** (Lester); (m) **Gardens of Adonis** (Weisgall); **The Labyrinth** (Menotti); **Midnight Angel** (Carlson); (b-bar) **The Mother** (Hollingsworth); **Paradise Lost** (Penderecki); (st) **Rime of the Ancient Mariner** (Bedford); (b) **Sāvitri** (Holst); (bar) **Taverner** (Davies)
Death of Kong, (b-bar) **Second Mrs. Kong** (Birtwistle)
Deborah, **Fisherman Called Peter** (Owen); **The Reconciliation** (1790)
Deborah Carter, (m) **Jeremiah** (Fink)
De Bracy, (t) **Ivanhoe** (Sullivan)
De Brogni, **The Jewess** (Halévy-Cooke)
De Chateaupers, **Notre-Dame of Paris** (Fry)
Decius, **Decius and Paulina** (Galliard)
Dede, (s) **Quiet Place** (Bernstein)
De Feredia, **Fatal Oath** (Koutzen)
Defilée, (s) **Ouanga** (White)
Degagee, **Dead Alive** (Arnold)
De Guiche, (b) **Cyrano** (Damrosch)
Deianira, (m) **Heracles** (Eaton)
Deidamia, **Achilles** (1733)
Deirdre, (s) **Deirdre** (Willan)
Dejanira, **Hercules** (Handel)
Delamarche, (bar) **America** (Kohs)
Delaval, **May Day** (Arne)
Delaware Tom, (bar) **Narcissa** (Moore)
Delia Ashton, (s) **Chinchilla** (Fink)
Delilah, **The Warrior** (Rogers)
Della, (s) **Have You Heard** (Talma)
Della Young, (s) **Della's Gift** (Welcher); (s) **Gift of the Magi** (Magney)
Delphia, **Dioclesian** (Purcell)
Delphin Mahe, (t) **Fête at Coqueville** (Rea)
Deluso, Signor, **Signor Deluso** (Pasatieri)
Demetrius, **Fairy Queen** (Purcell); (bar) **Midsummer Night's Dream** (Britten); **Pyrrus and Demetrius** (Haym)
Demidoff, **The Charlatan** (Sousa)
Demodocus, (t) **Castaway** (Berkeley)
Demophoon, **Dirce** (Horne)
De Mountfort, **English Fleet** (Braham)
Denis, (bar) **The Door** (Mopper)
Denise, (s) **Knot Garden** (Tippett)
Denmark Vesey, **Denmark Vesey** (Bowles)
Dennis, **Monster Bed** (de Kenessey)
Denys, **Grinning at the Devil** (Wilson)
Derek Dude, (bar) **Civilization** (Sahl/Salzman)
Dermott, **Poor Soldier** (Shield)

DeRopp, Mrs., **Beast and Superbeast** (Martin)
Derrincourt, William, **William Derrincourt** (Smalley)
Desideria, (m) **Saint of Bleecker Street** (Menotti)
De Soto, (t) **Royal Hunt of the Sun** (Hamilton)
Despard Murgatroyd, Sir, (bar) **Ruddigore** (Sullivan)
Dessalines, **Toussaint** (Blake); (bar) **Troubled Island** (Still)
Dessie, (m) **Demon Lover** (Nelson)
Deuces Wild, (b) **Sack of Calabasas** (Fletcher)
Devilshoof, (b) **Bohemian Girl** (Balfe)
Dewain, **I Was Looking** (Adams)
Diaghilev, **Madame Adare** (Silverman)
Diana, **Endymion** (Bennett); **Lionel and Clarissa** (Dibdin); (s) **The Olympians** (Bliss); **Secular Masque** (Boyce); **Thespis** (Sullivan)
Diana Vernon, **Rob Roy Macgregor** (Davy)
Diarmid, **Diarmid** (MacCunn)
Dick, **Flora** (Hippisley)
Dick, Captain, **Naughty Marietta** (Herbert)
Dick Dewy, **Mellstock Quire** (Harper)
Dick Deadeye, (b) **H.M.S. Pinafore** (Sullivan)
Dick Fitzgerald, (t) **Highwayman** (De Koven)
Dickie, (m) **The Clock** (Rieti)
Dickinson, Edward, (b-bar) **Letter to Emily** (Johnson)
Dickinson, Emily, **Eastward in Eden** (Meyerowitz); (s) **Letter to Emily** (Johnson); **Woman in the Garden** (Fine)
Dickson, (t) **King Hal** (Stewart); (t) **The Scarecrow** (Lockwood); **White Lady** (Cooke)
Dicky Doo, (t) **Simple Decision** (Busch)
Dicky Gossip, **My Grandmother** (Storace)
Di Clacket, **The Woodman** (Shield)
Didier, (b) **Madeleine** (Herbert)
Dido, **Dido** (Storace); **Dido and Aeneas** (Arne); **Dido and Aeneas** (Beveridge); **Dido and Aeneas** (Hook); (s) **Dido and Aeneas** (Purcell)
Diego, **Junípero Serra** (Hively); **The Padlock** (Dibdin); **Ruy Blas** (Glover); **Wonders in the Sun** (1706)
Dimitri Petrovsky, (bar) **Music Shop** (Wargo)
Dimmesdale, Arthur, (t) **Scarlet Letter** (Claflin); (t) **Scarlet Letter** (Damrosch); **Scarlet Letter** (Herman)
Dimmly, Prince, (t) **Meantime** (Arlan)
Din, Dame, **Belphegor** (Barthelemon)
Dina, **Honey Moon** (Linley)
Dinah, (m) **Trouble in Tahiti** (Bernstein)
Dingle, Mrs., (m/a) **King of Cats** (Oliver)
Diocles (Dioclesian), **Dioclesian** (Purcell)
Diomede, (bar) **Troilus and Cressida** (Walton)
Diomedes, (bar) **Sappho** (Glanville-Hicks)
Dion, **Revelation in the Courthouse** (Partch)
Dione, **Dione** (Lampe)
Dioneo, **The Visitors** (Chávez)

Bearskin Rug (Ramsier); **Midnight Angel** (Carlson); **The Vintagers** (Bishop)
Henry, Baron, **White Plume** (Reeve)
Henry, Bishop, (b-bar) **Caritas** (Saxon)
Henry, King, (ct) **Rosamond** (Clayton)
Henry, Mrs., (s) **The System** (Bach)
Henry II, **Fair Rosamond** (Barnett)
Henry VIII, (bar) **King's Breakfast** (Barthelson)
Henry Davis, (bar) **Street Scene** (Weill)
Heracles, (bar) **Heracles** (Eaton)
Herakles, **Alkestis** (Boughton)
Hercule, **Deep River** (Harling)
Hercules, **Alceste** (Handel); **Birth of Hercules** (Arne); (b) **CIVIL warS** (Glass); **Hercules** (Handel); **Judgment of Hercules** (Greene)
Herefred, **Ballad of the Bremen Band** (Arlan)
Herman, **Letty, the Basket-Maker** (Balfe); **Most Happy Fella** (Loesser); (bar) **Rip Van Winkle** (Bristow)
Hermann, (bar) **And the Walls** (Roosevelt); **Hermann** (Thomson)
Herman Smeltz, **Reilly and the 400** (Braham)
Herman Van Slaus, (t) **Rip Van Winkle** (Bristow)
Hermes, (t) **King Priam** (Tippett)
Hermia, **Fairy Queen** (Purcell); (m) **Midsummer Night's Dream** (Britten)
Hermione, **Hermione** (Attwood); (s) **Winter's Tale** (Harbison)
Hermiston, Lord, (b) **Hermiston** (Orr)
Hermod, (bar) **Death of Baldur** (Bedford)
Hero, **Hero and Leander** (Reeve); **Much Ado about Nothing** (Stanford)
Herod, (bar) **Erode the Great** (La Montaine); **Herod** (Kelly); (b) **Only a Miracle** (Barab)
Herring, Mrs., (m) **Albert Herring** (Britten)
Hertford, (b) **Catherine Grey** (Balfe)
Hertzog, **Black Crook** (Operti)
Herzlodor, **Dreyfus** (Cotel)
Hesse, (bar) **The Hunted** (Mailman)
Hester, (s) **The Sisters** (Flagello)
Hester Bellboys, (m) **Penny for a Song** (Bennett)
Hester (Prynne), **Hester Prynne** (Claflin); (s) **Scarlet Letter** (Damrosch); **Scarlet Letter** (Giannini); **Scarlet Letter** (Herman)
Hewson, **Covenanters** (Loder)
Heyward, (t) **Last of the Mohicans** (Henderson)
Higginson, Colonel, (bar) **Letter to Emily** (Johnson)
Hilarion, (t) **Princess Ida** (Sullivan)
Hilda Mack, (s) **Elegy for Young Lovers** (Henze)
Hilda Von Draga, **Red Feather** (De Koven)
Hildebrand, King, (b-bar) **Princess Ida** (Sullivan)
Hildebrand, Prince, **Undine** (Ware)
Hildegarde Tyler, (s) **Dove of Peace** (Damrosch)
Hillary, (t) **Sunday Excursion** (Wilder)
Hindley Earnshaw, (bar) **Wuthering Heights** (Floyd); (bar) **Wuthering Heights** (Hermann)
Hinkley, **Birth of the Poet** (Gordon)
Hippolytus, **Hippolytus** (Drysdale)

Hiram McCoy, (b) **The System** (Bach)
Hob, **Flora** (Bates); **Flora** (Hippisley)
Hob, Old, **Flora** (Hippisley)
Hobart, Mr., **All in a Garden Fair** (Tonning)
Hobbs, Sir Hannibal, (b) **Dove of Peace** (Damrosch)
Hobson, (b) **Peter Grimes** (Britten)
Ho Chi Minh, **Tonkin** (Cummings)
Hocus, (b-bar) **Double Trouble** (Mohaupt)
Hodur, (bar) **Death of Baldur** (Bedford)
Hofer, Andreas, **Hofer** (Rossini-Bishop)
Hoffman, Dr., **Madame Adare** (Silverman)
Hollee Beebee, **Nautch Girl** (Solomon)
Holly, (s) **Night of the Moonspell** (Siegmeister)
Holofernes, (bar) **Judith** (Chadwick); **Judith** (Goossens); **Judith and Holofernes** (Fink); **Line of Terror** (McQueen)
Homer Croy, (bar) **Wings of the Dove** (Moore)
Honey, Miss, (s) **Three's Company** (Hopkins)
Honour, **Britannia** (Lampe)
Hooten, John, **John Hooten** (Russo)
Hope, Miss, **Boy Who Grew Too Fast** (Menotti)
Hopewell, Richard, **Judgment Day** (Berl)
Hopkins, (sp) **Critic** (Stanford)
Hopper, Edward, **Hopper's Wife** (Wallace)
Hopper, Hedda, **Hopper's Wife** (Wallace)
Horace, (t) **School for Wives** (Liebermann)
Horace Adams, Rev., (t) **Peter Grimes** (Britten)
Horace Giddens, (b) **Regina** (Blitzstein)
Horace Stringfellow, Sir, (t) **One-Man Show** (Maw)
Horace Tabor, (bar) **Ballad of Baby Doe** (Moore)
Horaste, (bar) **Troilus and Cressida** (Walton)
Horemhab, (bar) **Akhnaten** (Glass)
Horselover Fat, **VALIS** (Machover)
Hortensio, (bar) **Taming of the Shrew** (Giannini)
Hoshi-San, **Hoshi-San** (Leps)
Houdini, **Houdini** (Schat)
Howard, (bar) **Howard** (Earnest)
Howard Douglass, (bar) **Frederick Douglass** (Kay)
Howard Sloan, (b) **Guilt of Lillian Sloan** (Neil)
Howja-Dhu, **The Begum** (De Koven)
Hubert, **Canterbury Pilgrims** (Stanford)
Huck, **Huckleberry Finn** (Overton)
Hudson, Hendrick, (bar) **Rip Van Winkle** (Bristow); (b-bar) **Rip Van Winkle** (De Koven)
Hugh, (t) **Hugh the Drover** (Vaughan Williams)
Hugh Crome, (tr) **Little Sweep** (Britten)
Hugh Evans, Sir, (bar) **Sir John in Love** (Vaughan Williams)
Hugh Lacy, (bar) **Shoemaker's Holiday** (Argento)
Hugo, **Blond Eckbert** (Weir); **Haunted Tower**
Hugo the Dull, (t) **Faun in the Forest** (Cockshott)
Hum, **The Disappointment** (Barton)
Humble Jewett, **Amarantha** (Ames)
Huncamunca, Princess, **Tom Thumb** (Markordt)

Jack Average, **The Cherokee** (Storace)
Jack Burden, **Willie Stark** (Floyd)
Jack Finney, (mime), **Down by the Greenwood Side** (Birtwistle)
Jack Hammer, (t) **Sold Again** (Sedgwick)
Jackie O, **Jackie O** (Daugherty)
Jack Ketch, (bar) **Punch and Judy** (Birtwistle)
Jack Point, (bar) **Yeomen of the Guard** (Sullivan)
Jack Potter, **Bride Comes to Yellow Sky** (Nixon)
Jack Sheppard, **Jack Sheppard** (Rodwell); **Quaker's Opera** (1728)
Jackson, Andrew, **Rachel** (Coe)
Jack Spaniard, (bar) **Lady from Colorado** (Ward); **Lady Kate** (Ward)
Jack Taste, **Don Sancho** (1739)
Jack Turner, (bar) **Woman at the Otowi Crossing** (Paulus)
Jacob, **Jacob and the Indians** (Laderman); (t/bar) **Victory at Masada** (Kalmanoff); **The Wrestler** (Adler)
Jacob, Senator, (b) **America** (Kohs)
Jacob Vredenburgh, **Barber of New York** (Vernon)
Jacqueline, (m/s) **Sterlingman** (Roy)
Jacques, **The Rose** (Hatton); **The Savoyard** (Reinagle)
Jade Emperor, **Silver River** (Sheng)
Jake, (bar) **Porgy and Bess** (Gershwin)
Jakob Lenz, (t) **Lenz** (Sitsky)
Jakobus Rey, **In the Drought** (Joubert)
James, **Female Rake** (1736); **Sasha** (Oliver)
James V, **Knight of Snowdoun** (Bishop); (t) **Lady of the Lake** (Schmidt)
James Bell, **Passion of Jonathan Wade** (Harvey)
James Dee, Captain, (t) **Deseret** (Kastle)
James Dillingham Young, (bar) **Gift of the Magi** (Magney)
James of Douglas, **Knight of Snowdoun** (Bishop); (b) **Lady of the Lake** (Schmidt)
Jamie, **Jamie and Anna** (Reeve)
Jamie McSnuffy, **Idols' Eye** (Herbert)
Jane, **Jane Heir** (Healey)
Jane, Lady, (a) **Patience** (Sullivan)
Jane Annie, **Jane Annie** (Ford)
Jane Lane, Miss, **Restauration of Charles II** (1732)
Jane of Flanders, **English Fleet** (Braham)
Jane Rippin, **Daisy** (Smith)
Janet, **Rob Roy** (De Koven)
Janetta, **Adopted Child** (Attwood)
János, **Scarlett Mill** (Zador)
Jan Palach, **Funeral of Jan Palach** (Beckley)
Jaques, **For England, Ho!** (Bishop); **The Vintagers** (Bishop)
Jaquez, **Honey Moon** (Hewitt/Kelly)
Jasmine Jenkins, **Abyssinia** (Cook/William)
Jason, **Golden Fleece** (Reed); **The Harpies** (Blitzstein); **The Harvest** (Giannini); (bar) **Medea** (Bryars); (t) **Medea** (Henderson); **Medea in Corinth** (Lees); (t) **Transatlantic** (Antheil)

Jasper, Sir, **Mock Doctor** (1732)
Jaspur, (t) **Erode the Great** (La Montaine)
Jay Follett, **Death in the Family** (Mayer)
Jealousy, **Rose of Destiny** (Heckscher)
Jean, (bar) **Miss Julie** (Alwyn); (bar) **The Olympians** (Bliss)
Jean, Baron, (t) **W. of Babylon** (Wuorinen)
Jean Acker, **Dream of Valentino** (Argento)
Jeanie Deans, **Heart of Midlothian** (Bishop); **Heart of Midlothian** (Loder); **Jeanie Deans** (MacCunn)
Jean Mathis, **Dream of Valentino** (Argento)
Jeanne Arcot, **Entente Cordiale** (Smyth)
Jeany, **Highland Fair** (1731)
Jeb, **Early Dawn** (Lockwood)
Jed, (b) **Mourning Becomes Electra** (Levy)
Jeff, (t) **Barber of New York** (Vernon); **Early Dawn** (Lockwood); (s) **Second Hurricane** (Copland)
Jefferson, Thomas, **Americana** (Bruce)
Jeffrey, (bar) **Love, Death** (White)
Jeff Stafford, (bar) **Lady from Colorado** (Ward)
Jekyll, Dr., **Dr. Jekyll and Mr. Hyde** (Fragale); (t) **Dr. Jekyll and Mr. Hyde** (O'Neal)
Jemmy, **Auld Robin Gray** (Arnold)
Jemmy Grove, **Barbara Allen** (Broekman)
Jemmy Jumps, **The Farmer** (Shield)
Jenifer, (s) **Midsummer Marriage** (Tippett)
Jenkins, **Wrinkle in Time** (Larsen)
Jennie, **Higglety Pigglety Pop!** (Knussen)
Jennie Parsons, (s) **Down in the Valley** (Weill)
Jenny, **Auld Robin Gray** (Arnold); **Better Sort** (1789); **The Deserter** (Dibdin); **Gentle Shepherd** (1729); **The Grenadier** (Dibdin); **Highland Reel** (Shield); (s) **Jenny** (Weisgall); **Mines of Sulphur** (Bennett); (m) **Threepenny Opera** (Weill-Blitzstein); (s) **Three Sisters** (Rorem); **Two Cadis** (Dibdin)
Jenny, Miss, **Boarding School** (1733)
Jenny Diver, **Polly** (1729)
Jenny Lind, **Jenny Lind** (Lee)
Jenny Melton, **Cobler's Opera** (1728)
Jenny Mere, (s) **Happy Hypocrite** (Masland)
Jenny Slade, (s) **Roman Fever** (Ward)
Jenny Weeper, **The Borderline** (Mellers)
Jenny Wilkins, **Ferryman's Daughter** (Bush)
Jeremiah, (bar) **Eternal Road** (Weill)
Jeremiah Stephens, (bar) **Jeremiah** (Fink)
Jeremiel, (t) **Masque of Angels** (Argento)
Jeremy, (t) **The Proposal** (Humel); **Singing Child** (Menotti)
Jeremy Jive, (t) **Civilization** (Sahl/Salzman)
Jerome, **For England, Ho!** (Bishop)
Jerome, Don, **The Duenna** (Gerhard); (b) **The Duenna** (Linley Jr./Linley Sr.)
Jerry, **Some Place of Darkness** (Whelen)
Jess, (s) **Julius Caesar Jones** (Williamson); (bar) **Slow Dusk** (Floyd); (s) **Smoky Mountain** (Hunkins)

Mendel, (bar) **Idiots First** (Blitzstein)
Mendez, (t buffo) **Kingdom for a Cow** (Weill)
Mendoza, Isaac, (t) **Duenna** (Linley Jr./Linley Sr.)
Menelaos, **Helen Retires** (Antheil)
Menna, **Menna** (Hughes)
Mephistopheles, **Mephistopheles** (Lutz)
Mercury, (b) **Cupid and Death** (Gibbons/Locke);
   Judgment of Paris (Arne); (dr) **The Olympians**
   (Bliss)
Mercutio, (b) **Romeo and Juliet** (Shelley)
Mercy, (s) **Voss** (Meale)
Merit, **Fashionable Lady** (1730); **The Patron** (1729)
Merlin, (bar) **Cymon** (Arne); (t) **New Year**
   (Tippett); **Tom Thumb** (Markordt)
Merret, Count de, **Fatal Oath** (Koutzen)
Merret, Countess de, **Fatal Oath** (Koutzen)
Merrill, Paul, (t) **Natoma** (Herbert)
Merry, (s) **Mighty Casey** (Schuman)
Merteul, Marquise de, (m) **Dangerous Liaisons**
   (Susa)
Meryll, Leonard, (t) **Yeomen of the Guard**
   (Sullivan)
Meryll, Sergeant, (b-bar) **Yeomen of the Guard**
   (Sullivan)
Mesholem, **Shloyme Gorgl** (Lateiner)
Mesrour, **Il Bondocani** (Attwood/Moorehead);
   Caliph of Bagdad (Musgrave)
Messias, **Paradise Lost** (Penderecki)
Metatron, (bar) **Masque of Angels** (Argento)
Mica, **Romulus Hunt** (Simon)
Micah, (t) **Slow Dusk** (Floyd)
Michael, **Adopted Child** (Attwood); **Berta** (Smart);
   Cue 67 (Ching); **For England, Ho!** (Bishop); (t)
   Opera Cloak (Damrosch); **Paradise Lost**
   (Penderecki); (bar) **Royal Auction** (Kanitz); (b)
   Taverner (Davies)
Michel, (t) **Ouanga** (White)
Michele, **Bianca** (Balfe); (t) **Saint of Bleecker**
   Street (Menotti)
Michel Kerouac, **Light from St. Agnes** (Harling)
Mick, (bar) **Oath of Bad Brown Bill** (Conyngham)
Midas, King, **Asses' Ears** (Cole); **Midas** (1762)
Midir, **Immortal Hour** (Boughton)
Miguel de Denia, (t) **La Loca** (Menotti)
Miguel de Estete, (t) **Royal Hunt of the Sun**
   (Hamilton)
Mihail Mihailovitch, (b-bar) **Natalia Petrovna**
   (Hoiby)
Mike, **I Was Looking** (Adams)
Mildred, **Have You Heard** (Talma); (m)
   Thanksgiving (Levi)
Mildred Murphy, (m) **The Hero** (Menotti)
Miles, (boy s) **Turn of the Screw** (Britten)
Miles Bradford, (t) **The Knickerbockers** (De Koven)
Miles Dunster, (bar) **Wings of the Dove** (Moore)
Millais, John Everett, **Modern Painters** (Lang)
Millichip, (b) **Grace of Todd** (Crosse)
Milly, (s) **Our Man in Havana** (Williamson)
Milly Theale, (s) **Wings of the Dove** (Moore)

Milo, **Three Visitations** (Sherman)
Milton, **Paradise Lost** (Penderecki)
Mimi, **The Bohemians** (Kirschner)
Mimi Marquez, **Rent** (Larson)
Mina, **Yelva** (Bishop)
Minette, (s) **English Cat** (Henze)
Minette Fontaine, (s) **Minette Fontaine** (Still)
Minos, (b-bar) **Sappho** (Glanville-Hicks)
Minto, Lord, (b-bar) **Nelson** (Berkeley)
Minutezza, Princess, **Bride Elect** (Sousa)
Mira, **Better Sort** (1789)
Miranda, (s) **Blake** (Adams); **Dancing Master**
   (Arnold); (s) **Miranda** (Siegmeister); (s) **The**
   Tempest (Eaton); **The Tempest** (Smith); **The**
   Tempest (Westergaard)
Miriam, (s) **Christmas Rose** (Bridge); **Early**
   Dawn (Lockwood); (s) **Eternal Road** (Weill);
   (s) **Golem** (Casken); (s) **The Scarf** (Hoiby)
Mirovich, **Inner Voices** (Howard)
Mirvan, **Zuma** (Bishop)
Misael, (t) **Burning Fiery Furnace** (Britten)
Misfortune, **Rose of Destiny** (Heckscher)
Misha, (t) **Visit to the Country** (Wargo)
Mister Banjo, **Gentlemen, Be Seated!** (Moross)
Mister Bones, **Gentlemen, Be Seated!** (Moross)
Mister Interlocutor, **Gentlemen, Be Seated!**
   (Moross)
Mister Tambo, **Gentlemen, Be Seated!** (Moross)
Mitchell, Dr., **Yellow Wallpaper** (Perera)
Mittenhofer, Gregor, (bar) **Elegy for Young**
   Lovers (Henze)
Mitty, Walter, **Secret Life of Walter Mitty**
   (Hamm)
Mizra, Almena (Arne-Battishill); **Generous**
   Free-Mason (1730)
Mocanna, **Veiled Prophet** (Stanford)
Mocenigo, **Daughter of St. Mark** (Balfe)
Mock, **Flowers** (Hardy)
Mock Turtle, (t) **Alice in Wonderland** (Chauls);
   Alice Meets the Mock Turtle (Bingham)
Modely, Mr., **Fashionable Lady** (1730)
Modesty, (s) **Loving/Toi** (Schafer)
Modish, **Happy Lovers** (1736)
Mohammed, **Almena** (Arne-Battishill)
Moishe, (t) **Where the Wild Things Are**
   (Knussen)
Moksada, (s) **Snatched by the Gods** (Vir)
Mole, Mr., **Wind in the Willows** (Rutter)
Molineux, Major, (bar) **My Kinsman** (Saylor)
Moll, **Brickdust Man** (Dibdin); **Cradle Will**
   Rock (Blitzstein)
Moll Plackett, **The Disappointment** (Barton)
Mollser, (s) **Plough and the Stars** (Siegmeister)
Molly, **Boarding School** (1733); **Welsh Opera**
   (1731)
Molly Maybush, **Farmer** (Shield)
Molly Mistress, (m) **Ballad of the Bremen Band**
   (Arlan)

Naimes, Duke, **Marriage of Aude** (Rogers)
Naisi, (t) **Deirdre** (Willan)
Nakamura, Dr., (bar) **Happy End** (Weill-Feingold)
Namiji, Lady, (s) **Actor's Revenge** (Miki)
Namiko-San, **Namiko-San** (Franchetti)
Nan, (m) **New Year** (Tippett)
Nan Caldwell, **Acres of Sky** (Kreutz)
Nancy, **Bird Catcher** (Cleeve); **Nancy** (Carey); (s) **Prodigal Son** (Jacobi); **Silas Marner** (Joubert); **Tom Jones** (Arnold)
Nancy Brown, **Nancy Brown** (Hadley)
Nanda, (bar) **Transposed Heads** (Glanville-Hicks)
Naninga, **Martin's Lie** (Menotti)
Nanki-Poo, (t) **The Mikado** (Sullivan)
Nanna, (s) **Death of Baldur** (Bedford)
Nannetta, **Berta** (Smart)
Nannette, **Fontainbleau** (Shield); **The Savoyard** (Reinagle)
Nanny, (s) **Miss Havisham's Fire** (Argento); **William and Nanny** (Baumgarten)
Naoia, (m) **Pipe of Desire** (Converse)
Naomi, **Jacob and the Indians** (Laderman); **The Outcast** (Ain); (s) **Ruth** (Berkeley); **Ruth and Naomi** (Hart); **Ruth and Naomi** (Kondorossy)
Narcissa, **Inkle and Yarico** (Arnold)
Narcissa Prentiss, (s) **Narcissa** (Moore)
Narcisso de Medicis, Don, **Spanish Rivals** (Linley)
Narcissus, **Pygmalion** (Houseley)
Nat, **Ferryman's Daughter** (Bush)
Natacha Rambova, **Dream of Valentino** (Argento)
Natalia Petrovna, (s) **Natalia Petrovna** (Hoiby)
Natalyia, **The Proposal** (Walker)
Natasha, (m) **Electrification** (Osborne); (s) **Marriage Proposal** (Goldstaub); (s) **Three Sisters** (Pasatieri)
Nate, (t) **Highway 1, U.S.A.** (Still)
Nathan, **Nathan the Wise** (Kondorossy)
Nathanael, **Heaven Ablaze in His Breast** (Weir)
Nathaniel Hazard, (t) **Lowland Sea** (Wilder)
Natoma, (s) **Natoma** (Herbert)
Natura Magen, (a) **Bird in the Bush** (Bielawa)
Nausicaa, (s) **Castaway** (Berkeley); (s) **Nausicaa** (Glanville-Hicks)
Navailles, **Blanche de Nevers** (Balfe)
Nebuchadnezzar, (t) **Burning Fiery Furnace** (Britten)
Ned, (b) **Treemonisha** (Joplin)
Ned Brag, **Boarding School** (1733)
Ned Reilly, **Reilly and the 400** (Braham)
Ned Royster, **Foxy Quiller** (De Koven)
Ned Winner, **Idol's Eye** (Herbert)
Neengay, **The Legend** (Murray)
Nefertiti, (a) **Akhnaten** (Glass)
Nekaya, Princess, **Utopia Limited** (Sullivan)
Nell, **Adopted Child** (Attwood); (a) **Don't We All?** (Phillips); **Merry Cobler** (1735); **Nell** (Bauld)
Nellie Ewell, (s) **Summer and Smoke** (Hoiby)
Nelly, (m/a) **Twin Sisters** (Sedgwick)

Nelly Dean, (m) **Wuthering Heights** (Floyd); **Wuthering Heights** (Hermann)
Nelson, Lady, (m) **Nelson** (Berkeley)
Nelson, Lord, (t) **Nelson** (Berkeley)
Nelsoni, (b-bar) **Old Majestic** (Rodríguez)
Nemesis, **Pygmalion** (Houseley)
Nemorino, **Dulcamara** (1866)
Nenek, (m) **Tamu-Tamu** (Menotti)
Neptune, **Momus** (1729)
Neralbo, (t) **Love's Triumph** (1708)
Netzahualcoyotl, (b) **Montezuma** (Sessions)
Neville, Colonel, **Colomba** (Mackenzie)
Neville, Lady, **Midnight Angel** (Carlson)
Neville, Major, **The Antiquary** (Bishop)
Newtown, Countess of, **Emerald Isle** (Sullivan)
Nial, (t) **Mona** (Parker)
Nicemis, **Thespis** (Sullivan)
Nicey, (a) **Passion of Jonathan Wade** (Harvey)
Nichette, (s) **Madeleine** (Herbert)
Nicholas, (b) **Vanessa** (Barber)
Nicholas II, (t) **Rasputin** (Reise)
Nicholas Avaro, **Mistakes of a Day** (Callcott)
Nicholas Vedder, (b) **Rip Van Winkle** (Bristow); (b) **Rip Van Winkle** (De Koven)
Nick, (t) **Beggar's Love** (Patterson); **Time Rocker** (Reed)
Nick Ashton, (bar) **Chinchilla** (Fink)
Nick Kyriakos, **No for an Answer** (Blitzstein)
Nick Papadakis, (t) **Postman Always Rings Twice** (Paulus)
Nick Shadow, (bar) **Rake's Progress** (Stravinsky)
Nicky, (bar) **Seduction of a Lady** (Wargo)
Nic Mazette, (b-bar) **Night of the Moonspell** (Siegmeister)
Nicodemus, (bar) **Juggler of Our Lady** (Kay)
Nicola, **The Journey** (Metcalf)
Nicolas, **Man from Venus** (Cannon); (b-bar/bar) **Student from Salamanca** (Bach)
Nicolette, (a/m) **Eyes and No Eyes** (Reed)
Niels, (t) **Miss Julie** (Rorem)
Niels Lyhne, (bar) **Fennimore and Gerda** (Delius)
Night, (s) **Fairy Queen** (Purcell); (m) **The Mother** (Hollingsworth)
Nightingale, **Tom Jones** (Arnold)
Nigra, **Egyptian Festival** (Florio)
Nilla, **Lucky-Peter's Journey** (Williamson)
Nils, (t) **Irmelin** (Delius)
Nina, (m) **The Fan** (Goldstein); **Nina** (Malicki); **Nina** (Shield); **Sasha** (Oliver); (m) **The Seagull** (Pasatieri)
Nina Pape, **Daisy** (Smith)
Nincompoop, Alderman, **Boarding School** (1733)
Ninetta, **Ninetta** (Bishop)
Ninette, **Duke of Savoy** (Bishop); **Young Hussar** (Kelly)
Ninette Lafont, **Blood Moon** (Dello Joio)
Ninka, **Maid of Artois** (Balfe)

Pumpolino, Baron, **Cinderella** (Lacy)
Punch, **Gasconado the Great** (1759); (bar) **Punch and Judy** (Birtwistle)
Punch Mowgli, **Baa Baa Black Sheep** (Berkeley)
Punka, Rajah, **Nautch Girl** (Solomon)
Pyefleet, **Cobler's Opera** (1728)
Pyramus, **Pyramus and Thisbe** (Bruce); **Pyramus and Thisbe** (Lampe); **Pyramus and Thisbe** (Leveridge)
Pyrrus, **Pyrrus and Demetrius** (Haym)

Quadrant, **The Disappointment** (Barton)
Quasimodo, **Esmeralda** (Thomas); **Notre-Dame of Paris** (Fry); **Quasimodo** (Rodwell)
Queenie, **Queenie Pie** (Ellington); (s) **Second Hurricane** (Copland)
Queen of Hearts, (m) **Alice in Wonderland** (Chauls)
Queen of the Mardi Grass, (m) **Night of the Moonspell** (Siegmeister)
Quentin Durward, **Quentin Durward** (Maclean)
Quibble Quibus, Sir, **Female Parson** (Coffey)
Quibus, Lady, **Female Parson** (Coffey)
Quickly, Mrs., (m/a) **Sir John in Love** (Vaughan Williams)
Quince, (b) **Midsummer Night's Dream** (Britten)
Quint, Peter, (t) **Turn of the Screw** (Britten)
Quintus, (t) **Mona** (Parker)
Quiroga, Archbishop, **El Greco** (Harper)
Quiteria, **Adventure of Don Quixote** (Macfarren)
Quixote, Don, **Adventure of Don Quixote** (Macfarren); **Don Quixote** (Arnold); **Don Quixote** (De Koven); **Don Quixote** (Rodwell); **Don Quixote in England** (1734)
Quixotte, Don, **Don Quixotte** (Hewitt)
Quiz, **Love in a Camp** (Shield)
Quorum, Alderman, **Beggar's Wedding** (1729)

Raccoon, **The Disappointment** (Barton)
Rachel, **Circassian Bride** (Bishop); (s) **Eternal Road** (Weill); **The Jewess** (Halévy-Cooke); **Jovial Crew** (Bates); **Jovial Crew** (Broome); (s) **Victory at Masada** (Kalmanoff); (a) **Yehu** (Zador)
Rachel Jackson, **Rachel** (Coe)
Rachel Lockhart, **Dr. Heidegger's Fountain** (Beeson)
Rachel Merton, (s) **The Scarecrow** (Lockwood)
Rachel Palfrey, **Merrymount** (Smith)
Rachel Silberchatz, (m) **Pantagleize** (Starer)
Racina, **Prunella** (Clayton)
Radna, (s) **Tamu-Tamu** (Menotti)
Raguell, (bar) **Masque of Angels** (Argento)
Ragueneau, (t) **Cyrano** (Damrosch)
Rahda, (s) **Pearl Tree** (Bainton)
Rahkal, (tr) **Snatched by the Gods** (Vir)
Rainulf, King, (b) **Azara** (Paine)
Raleigh, **Death in the Family** (Mayer); (bar/b) **Hanging Judge** (Lockwood)
Raleigh, Sir Walter, (bar) **Gloriana** (Britten); (t) **Merrie England** (German); **Raleigh's Dream** (Hamilton)

Ralph, (t) **Don't We All?** (Phillips); **The Grenadier** (Dibdin); (b) **King Hal** (Stewart)
Ralph Lewin, (t) **Karla** (Lehrman)
Ralph Rackstraw, (t) **H.M.S. Pinafore** (Sullivan)
Ralph Reformage, Sir, **The Decoy** (1733)
Ralph Winston, **The Ameer** (Herbert)
Ramatzin, **Azora** (Hadley)
Ramirez, Captain, **Castle of Andalusia** (Arnold)
Ramon Castillan, (t) **Chinchilla** (Fink)
Ramoncita, **Los Rubios** (Moore)
Ramuntcho, (t) **Ramuntcho** (Taylor)
Rance Hilbo, (t) **Whirligig** (Brisman)
Randall Paxton, (bar) **Lady in the Dark** (Weill)
Randall Ware, (bar) **Jubilee** (Kay)
Randy Curtis, (bar) **Lady in the Dark** (Weill)
Raoul, **Armourer of Nantes** (Balfe)
Raoul de Noget, **Perfect Lives** (Ashley)
Raphael, Don, **Don Raphael** (Hewitt)
Rappaccini (Dr.), **Garden of Mystery** (Cadman); **Rappaccini's Daughter** (Bender); **Rappaccini's Daughter** (Dennison); (b-bar) **Rappaccini's Daughter** (Garwood)
Rapunzel, (s) **Rapunzel** (Brooks); **Rapunzel** (Hammond); **Rapunzel** (Harrison)
Raquel, (m/s) **Black Widow** (Pasatieri)
Rareback Pinkerton, **In Dahomey** (Cook)
Rashly, **Lord of the Manor** (Jackson)
Rasputin, **Holy Devil** (Nabokov); (b-bar) **Rasputin** (Reise)
Rastus Johnson, **Abyssinia** (Cook/Williams)
Rat, Mr., **Wind in the Willows** (Rutter)
Ravensbane, Lord, (t) **The Scarecrow** (Lockwood)
Ravensburg, Baron, **Free Knights** (Mazzinghi)
Ravina, **Miller and His Men** (Bishop)
Ray, (t) **Ray and the Gospel Singer** (Gould)
Raymond, (bar) **The Audience** (Dembo); (bar) **Bad Boys in School** (Meyerowitz); **The Crusaders** (Benedict); **Nigredo Hotel** (Gotham)
Raymond, Don, (t) **Raymond and Agnes** (Loder)
Raymond Bardac, **Blood Moon** (Dello Joio)
Razoir, **The Wedding** (Pepusch)
Rebecca, (s) **Ivanhoe** (Sullivan); **Maid of Judah** (Lacy)
Rebecca Ferris, (m) **The Picnic** (Cumming)
Rebecca Nurse, (a) **The Crucible** (Ward)
Rebecca Stephens, (s) **Jeremiah** (Fink)
Record, **Adopted Child** (Attwood)
Rectangula, (t) **Parabola and Circula** (Blitzstein)
Red Death, **Gagliarda of a Merry Plague** (Saminsky)
Red Feather, **Sunset Trail** (Cadman)
Red Peter, (bar) **Kafka's Chimp** (Metcalf)
Red Whiskers, (t) **Billy Budd** (Britten)
Reed, Edward, **Our Island Home** (Reed)
Reed, Priscilla, **Our Island Home** (Reed)

Robson, Richard, **My Walking Photograph**
  (Sedgwick)
Rocca Marina, Count, (t) **The Fan** (Goldstein)
Rockalda, **Flying Dutchman** (Rodwell)
Rockwardine, Admiral, **Fall of Algiers** (Bishop)
Roderic de Froila, **Red Cross Knights** (Attwood)
Roderic Murgatroyd, Sir, (b) **Ruddigore** (Sullivan)
Roderick, (bar) **Long Christmas Dinner**
  (Hindemith)
Roderick Dhu, **Knight of Snowdoun** (Bishop);
  (bar) **Lady of the Lake** (Schmidt)
Roderick Usher, **Dream within a Dream** (Currie);
  Fall of the House of Usher (Glass); (bar) **Fall of
  the House of Usher** (Sitsky)
Rodolfo, **Sicilian Bride** (Balfe)
Rodolpho, **Amelia** (Lampe)
Rodríguez, (bar) **Simón Bolívar** (Musgrave)
Roger, **Gentle Shepherd** (1729); **Patie and Peggy**
  (1730)
Roger Davis, **Rent** (Larson)
Roger Doremus, (t) **Summer and Smoke** (Hoiby)
Rogier, (t) **Diable amoureux** (Nelson)
Rohesia, Lady, (s) **Lady Rohesia** (Hopkins)
Roland, Count, **Free Knights** (Mazzinghi)
Roland, Countess, **Free Knights** (Mazzinghi)
Roland, Lord, **Gasconado the Great** (1759)
Rolando, **Honey Moon** (Hewitt/Kelly)
Rolf, (b-bar) **Irmelin** (Delius)
Rolla, **Virgin of the Sun** (Bishop)
Romanoff, **The Exile** (Mazzinghi)
Romeo, **Romeo and Juliet** (Barkworth); **Romeo
  and Juliet** (Marshall-Hall); (t) **Romeo and Juliet**
  (Shelley)
Romilayu, (t) **Lily** (Kirchner)
Romney, Captain, **My Lady Molly** (Jones)
Romulus, **Romulus Hunt** (Simon)
Ronald, **Lord of the Isles** (Rodwell)
Ronnie, (bar) **The Opening** (Wilder)
Roo, **Summer of the Seventeenth Doll** (Mills)
Rosa, **Ages Ago** (Clay); **Fontainbleau** (Shield);
  Red Cross Knights (Attwood)
Rosabel, **The Alcaid** (Nathan)
Rosabella, **Most Happy Fella** (Loesser)
Rosa Gonzales, (m) **Summer and Smoke** (Hoiby)
Rosalba, Princess, **Rose and the Ring** (Leginska)
Rosalie, **Fatal Oath** (Koutzen)
Rosalie Smith, (s) **Kumana** (Kanitz)
Rosalind, **Mines of Sulphur** (Bennett)
Rosalinda, **Rosalinda** (Smith)
Rosalinda Ross, (s) **The Audition** (Goodman)
Rosa Martini, (s) **Opera Cloak** (Damrosch)
Rosambert, Countess de, **Robert the Devil**
  (Barnett)
Rosamond, **Fair Rosamond** (Barnett); (h s)
  Fairyland (Parker); **Rosamond** (Arne);
  Rosamond (Arnold); (s) **Rosamond** (Clayton)
Rosara, **Spanish Barber** (Arnold)
Roschana, (sp) **Oberon** (Weber)

Röschen, **The Forest** (Smyth)
Rose, **Marilyn** (Laderman); **Night before the
  Wedding** (Bishop); **Rose and Colin** (Dibdin);
  Rose Garden (Boyd); (s) **Shoemaker's
  Holiday** (Argento)
Rosellen, (s) **Philip Marshall** (Barab)
Rose-Marie, **Rose-Marie** (Friml/Stothart)
Rosemary, (m) **The Pumpkin** (Kondorossy)
Rose Maurrant, (s) **Street Scene** (Weill)
Rose Maybud, (s) **Ruddigore** (Sullivan)
Rosemonde, Mme. de, (s) **Dangerous Liaisons**
  (Susa)
Rose Parrowe, (m) **Taverner** (Davies)
Rosenberg, Count, (b) **Siege of Rochelle** (Balfe)
Rosetta, **Love in a Village** (Arne)
Rosey, **Tin Pan Alley** (Raphling)
Rosie, **Bride from Pluto** (Menotti)
Rosina, **Castle of Sorrento** (Attwood); (s)
  Ghosts of Versailles (Corigliano); **Rosina**
  (Shield); **Rosina** (Titus); **Spanish Barber**
  (Arnold)
Rosine, **Signor Deluso** (Pasatieri)
Rosita, (s) **Don Cristóbal and Rosita** (Crawford)
Ross, **The Covenanters** (Loder)
Rossmann, Karl, (t) **America** (Kohs)
Rouvières, Baron des, (b-bar) **Diable amoureux**
  (Nelson)
Rovewell, **The Contrivances** (Carey); **Love and
  Revenge** (1729)
Rowan, (s) **Little Sweep** (Britten)
Rowena, **Ligeia** (Thomas)
Rowena, Lady, (s) **Ivanhoe** (Sullivan)
Rowland, Mrs., **Murder in Three Keys**
  (Chisholm)
Rowland Lacy, (t) **Shoemaker's Holiday**
  (Argento)
Roxalana, **The Sultan** (Dibdin)
Roxana, (s) **Other Wise Man** (Grove); **Rival
  Queens** (Finger)
Roxane, (s) **Cyrano** (Damrosch); **Cyrano de
  Bergerac** (Herbert)
Roy, (bar) **Demon Lover** (Nelson)
Rozanne, **Legende Provençale** (Moore)
Ruby Bates, **Ghosts** (Ito)
Ruby Herter, **Amarantha** (Ames)
Rucello, **Savonarola** (Stanford)
Rudiger, Count, **Amber Witch** (Wallace)
Rudolf, **Black Crook** (Operti)
Rudolph, **The Forest** (Smyth); **Grand Duke**
  (Sullivan); **Sylvana** (Weber-Blewitt)
Rudolph, Count, (t) **Lurline** (Wallace)
Rudy Rolando, **The Bohemians** (Kirschner)
Rufus Follett, **Death in the Family** (Mayer)
Ruggio, (b) **Bianca** (Hadley)
Ruins, (t) **Soyazhe** (Anderson)
Rumpelstiltskin, **Rumpelstiltskin** (Barber)
Rundy, **Farmer** (Shield)
Rupee, **Positive Man** (Arnold)

Wotten, Lord Henry, **Picture of Dorian Gray** (Liebermann)
Wrestling Bradford, (bar) **Merry Mount** (Hanson)
Wright, **Shining Brow** (Hagen)
Wu Tse T'ien, (s) **W. of Babylon** (Wuorinen)
Wycherly, Widow, (s) **The Experiment** (Schwartz)
Wylie, **Edward John Eyre** (Conyngham)
Wyndham, Colonel, **Royal Oak** (Kelly)
Wyndham, Lady Matilda, **Royal Oak** (Kelly)

Xalca, **Azora** (Hadley)
Xarino, **Teraminta** (Smith); (ct) **Teraminta** (Stanley)
Xenadechy, Mr., **The Decoy** (1733)
Xerxes (Ahasuersus), King, **Esther** (Knoller); **Esther** (Weisgall)
Ximenes de Cisneros, (bar) **La Loca** (Menotti)
Xola, (s) **Under the Double Moon** (Davis)

Yakov, (t) **Three Sisters** (Pasatieri)
Yankele, **David's Violin** (Mogulesco)
Yannakos, (t) **Greek Passion** (Martinů)
Yarico, **Inkle and Yarico** (Arnold)
Yarini, (t) **La Cubana** (Henze)
Yashoda, (a) **Pearl Tree** (Bainton)
Yasui, **Namiko-San** (Franchetti)
Yehosheba, **Athaliah** (Weisgall)
Yehoyada, **Athaliah** (Weisgall)
Yehu, (t) **Yehu** (Zador)
Yellow Serpent, (bar) **Narcissa** (Moore)
Yen How, **San Toy** (Jones)
Yerma, **Yerma** (ApIvor); **Yerma** (Bowles); **Yerma** (Wilding-White)
Yfel, **The Echo** (Patterson)
Yiro Danyemon, **Naminko-San** (Franchetti)
Yoga, (bar) **Temple Dancer** (Hugo)
Yolanda, Princess, **Free Lance** (Sousa)
Yorick, **Better Sort** (1789); **Sterne's Maria** (Pelissier)
Young, Brigham, **Deseret** (Buck); (bar/b-bar) **Deseret** (Kastle)
Young Meadows, **Love in a Village** (Arne)
Young Rachel, (s) **La Cubana** (Henze)
Young Ramble, **Turk and No Turk** (Arnold)
Yukinojo, (t) **Actor's Revenge** (Miki)
Yum-Yum, (s) **The Mikado** (Sullivan)
Yuri, (bar) **Ice Break** (Tippett)
Yusuf, **Murder in Three Keys** (Chisholm)
Yvonne, **Venus in Africa** (Antheil)
Ywain, (t) **Gawain** (Birtwistle)

Zabdas, (bar) **Zenobia** (Pratt)
Zachary Brag, **Boarding School** (1733)
Zaida, **The Enchanter** (Smith); **Turkish Lovers** (Lacy); **Zaida** (Lutz)
Zamiel, **Black Crook** (Operti)
Zamora, **Honey Moon** (Hewitt/Kelly)
Zamorin, **Zuma** (Bishop)
Zangler, (b) **On the Razzle** (Orr)
Zanita, **Vendetta** (Freeman)
Zapata, **Zapata!** (Balada)

Zara, **Almena** (Arne-Battishill); **Utopia Limited** (Sullivan); **Witches' Well** (Appleton)
Zayde, **Siege of Gibraltar** (Shield)
Zeelick, (b) **Lurline** (Wallace)
Zeena Frome, **Ethan Frome** (Allanbrook)
Zeffirina, **Bianca** (Balfe)
Zehu, **Safié** (Hadley)
Zelica, **Veiled Prophet** (Stanford)
Zelinda, **The Slave** (Bishop)
Zelipha, **Cherokee** (Storace)
Zelley, Mister, (b-bar) **Bilby's Doll** (Floyd)
Zelmana, Queen, **Generous Free-Mason** (1730)
Zelmira, **Egyptian Festival** (Florio)
Zempoalla, **Indian Queen** (Purcell)
Zenobia, (a) **Zenobia** (Pratt)
Zephyr, (bar) **Eros and Psyche** (Cummings)
Zerbino, **Wedding Ring** (Dibdin)
Zhanguo, **Bok Choy Variations** (Chen)
Zillah, **Blanche de Nevers** (Balfe)
Zinaida, **Strange Life of Ivan Osokin** (Gordon)
Zinida, (s) **He Who Gets Slapped** (Ward)
Zita, **Buoso's Ghost** (Ching)
Zodzetrick, (t) **Treemonisha** (Joplin)
Zoe, **The Aethiop** (Taylor)
Zoë, (s) **Gardens of Adonis** (Weisgall)
Zoogy, **Romulus Hunt** (Simon)
Zorah, (s) **Ruddigore** (Sullivan)
Zoraida, **Zoraida** (Linley)
Zorayde, **The Captive** (Dibdin et al.)
Zoreb, **The Enchanter** (Smith)
Zorinski, **Zorinski** (Arnold)
Zoro, **Zuma** (Bishop)
Zossima, (bar) **Mary of Egypt** (Tavener)
Zubeydeh, Sultana, **Rose of Persia** (Sullivan)
Zuckertanz, Dr., (t) **Maria Golovin** (Menotti)
Zulima, **Nourjahad** (Loder)
Zulla, **Tammany** (Hewitt)
Zuma, **Zuma** (Bishop)

Index of Names

The index includes names of singers, conductors (excluding composers conducting their own work), producers, composers (of other English settings), directors, choreographers, and arrangers listed in the A–Z section of this volume (for premieres, arrangements, and revivals), followed by the short title(s) of the work(s) in which they have appeared; name of composer (or date of premiere) is included where there is more than one setting of the title. First names are given where known.

About the Author

MARGARET ROSS GRIFFEL is a production editor at Columbia University's Office of Publications, as well as an editorial consultant to several publishers. Dr. Griffel is the author of a companion volume, *Operas in German* (Greenwood, 1990), and has served as editor and compiler of the G. Schirmer & Associated Music Publishers orchestral and opera catalogs, consulting editor for the *Schirmer History of Music*, contributor to *The New Oxford History of Music*, and music production editor for Garland Publishing.